Visit classzone and get connected

Online resources for students and parents

ClassZone resources are linked together and provide instruction, practice, and learning support.

eEdition Plus ONLINE

This interactive version of the text encourages students to explore mathematics.

eWorkbook Plus ONLINE

Interactive practice, correlated to the text, provides support for key concepts and skills.

eTutorial Plus ONLINE

This interactive tutorial reinforces key skills and helps students prepare for tests.

Chapter-Based Support

Examples, state test practice, quizzes, vocabulary support, and activities help students succeed.

Now it all clicks!™

CLASSZONE.COM

McDougal Littell

FLORIDA EDITION

McDougal Littell Middle School

COURSE 3 Math

$$V = Bh$$

$$3n + 11 = 7$$

(1, 2)

Larson   Boswell   Kanold   Stiff

McDougal Littell

A HOUGHTON MIFFLIN COMPANY

Evanston, Illinois • Boston • Dallas

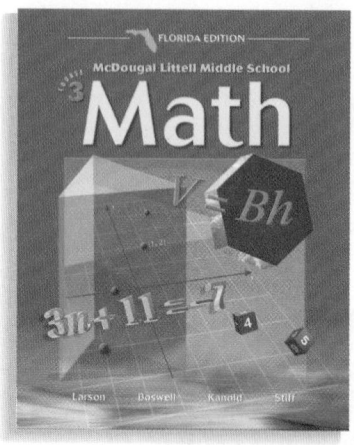

About Middle School Math: Course 3

McDougal Littell Middle School Math, Florida Edition will help you be successful in this course. The clearly written lessons with frequent step-by-step examples make even difficult math concepts and methods easier to understand. The number and variety of problems, ranging from basic to challenging, give you the practice you need to develop your math skills. This book will also help you develop your notetaking and problem-solving skills. Look for notetaking strategies and Help Notes that support problem solving, vocabulary, reading, homework, technology, and review. Enjoy the Brain Games — they will challenge your thinking skills!

In writing this Florida Edition, the authors paid special attention to the Florida curriculum and assessment standards. To help you check your progress in learning this Florida content, there are margin notes indicating the standards you will study. In addition, there are FCAT strategies and practice questions throughout the book.

ISBN: 0-618-29091-5   3456789–DWO–08 07 06 05 04

Internet Web Site: http://www.classzone.com

Ron Larson

Ron Larson is a professor of mathematics at Penn State University at Erie, where he has taught since receiving his Ph.D. in mathematics from the University of Colorado. Dr. Larson is well known as the author of a comprehensive program for mathematics that spans middle school, high school, and college courses. Dr. Larson's numerous professional activities keep him in constant touch with the needs of teachers and supervisors. He closely follows developments in mathematics standards and assessment.

Laurie Boswell

Laurie Boswell is the mathematics department chair at Profile Junior-Senior High School in Bethlehem, New Hampshire. A recipient of the Presidential Award for Excellence in Mathematics Teaching, she has also been a Tandy Technology Scholar. She serves on the National Council of Teachers of Mathematics Board of Directors. She speaks frequently on topics related to instructional strategies and course content.

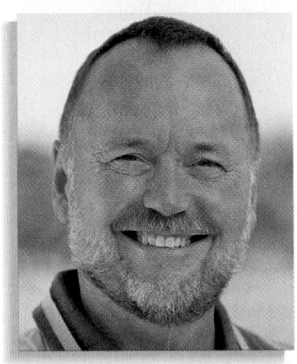

Timothy Kanold

Timothy Kanold is the superintendent of Adlai E. Stevenson High School District 125, where he served as a teacher and the Director of Mathematics for 16 years. He recently received his Ph.D. from Loyola University Chicago. Dr. Kanold is a recipient of the Presidential Award for Excellence in Mathematics and Science Teaching and served on The Academy Services Committee for NCTM. He is a frequent speaker at mathematics meetings where he shares his in-depth knowledge of mathematics teaching and curriculum.

Lee Stiff

Lee Stiff is a professor of mathematics education in the College of Education of North Carolina State University at Raleigh. His extensive experience in mathematics education includes teaching at the middle school and high school levels. He has received the W. W. Rankin Award for Excellence in Mathematics Education, and was Fulbright Scholar to the Department of Mathematics of the University of Ghana. He served as President of the National Council of Teachers of Mathematics (2000–2002).

Advisers and Reviewers

Curriculum Advisers and Reviewers

Donna Foley
Curriculum Specialist for Math
Chelmsford Middle School
Chelmsford, MA

Barbara Nunn
Secondary Mathematics Specialist
Broward County Schools
Fort Lauderdale, FL

Wendy Loeb
Mathematics Teacher
Twin Groves Junior High School
Buffalo Grove, IL

Tom Scott
Resource Teacher
Duval County Public Schools
Jacksonville, FL

Teacher Panels

Florida Panel

Kathy Adams
Mathematics Teacher
Allapattah Middle School
Miami, FL

Micki Hawn
Mathematics Teacher
Pompano Beach Middle School
Pompano Beach, FL

Barbara Schober
Mathematics Department Chair
Okeeheelee Middle School
West Palm Beach, FL

Sue Carrico-Beddow
Mathematics Teacher
Bayonet Point Middle School
New Port Richey, FL

Pat Powell
Mathematics Department Chair
Stewart Middle School
Tampa, FL

Laurie St. Julien
Mathematics Teacher
Oak Grove Middle School
Clearwater, FL

Melissa Grabowski
Mathematics Teacher
Stone Middle School
Melbourne, FL

Kansas and Missouri Panel

Linda Cordes
Department Chair
Paul Robeson Middle School
Kansas City, MO

Rhonda Foote
Mathematics Department Chair
Maple Park Middle School
North Kansas City, MO

Jan Rase
Mathematics Teacher
Moreland Ridge Middle School
Blue Springs, MO

Linda Dodd
Mathematics Department Chair
Argentine Middle School
Kansas City, KS

Cas Kyle
District Math Curriculum Coordinator
Richard A. Warren Middle School
Leavenworth, KS

Dan Schoenemann
Mathematics Teacher
Raytown Middle School
Kansas City, MO

Melanie Dowell
Mathematics Teacher
Raytown South Middle School
Raytown, MO

Texas Panel

Judy Carlin
Mathematics Teacher
Brown Middle School
McAllen, TX

Judith Cody
Mathematics Teacher
Deady Middle School
Houston, TX

Lisa Hiracheta
Mathematics Teacher
Irons Junior High School
Lubbock, TX

Kay Neuse
Mathematics Teacher
Wilson Middle School
Plano, TX

Louise Nutzman
Mathematics Teacher
Sugar Land Middle School
Sugar Land, TX

Clarice Orise
Mathematics Teacher
Tafolla Middle School
San Antonio, TX

Wonda Webb
Mathematics Teacher
William H. Atwell Middle School
and Law Academy
Dallas, TX

Karen Young
Mathematics Teacher
Murchison Elementary School
Pflugerville, TX

Field Test Teachers

Kathryn Chamberlain
McCarthy Middle School
Chelmsford, MA

Sheree Daily
Canal Winchester Middle School
Canal Winchester, OH

Deborah Kebe
Canal Winchester Middle School
Canal Winchester, OH

Jill Leone
Twin Groves Junior High School
Buffalo Grove, IL

Wendy Loeb
Twin Groves Junior High School
Buffalo Grove, IL

Melissa McCarty
Canal Winchester Middle School
Canal Winchester, OH

Deb Mueth
St. Aloysius School
Springfield, IL

Gail Sigmund
Charles A. Mooney Middle School
Cleveland, OH

Teacher Reviewers

Susanne Artiñano
Bryn Mawr School
Baltimore, MD

Lisa Barnes
Bishop Spaugh Academy
Charlotte, NC

Beth Bryan
Sequoyah Middle School
Oklahoma City, OK

Jennifer Clark
Mayfield Middle School
Oklahoma City, OK

Lois Cole
Pickering Middle School
Lynn, MA

Louis Corbosiero
Pollard Middle School
Needham, MA

James Cussen
Candlewood Middle School
Dix Hills, NY

Kristen Dailey
Boardman Center Middle School
Boardman, OH

Shannon Galamore
Clay-Chalkville Middle School
Pinson, AL

Tricia Highland
Moon Area Middle School
Moon Township, PA

Myrna McNaboe
Immaculate Conception
East Aurora, NY

Angela Richardson
Sedgefield Middle School
Charlotte, NC

James Richardson
Booker T. Washington Middle School
Mobile, AL

Dianne Walker
Traverse City Central High School
Traverse City, MI

Stacey Wood
Cochrane Middle School
Charlotte, NC

1

Variables and Equations

	Chapter Warm-Up Games	2
	Getting Ready to Learn	4
1.1	**Interpreting Graphs**	5
1.2	**Order of Operations**	10
	Technology Activity: Using Order of Operations, 14	
1.3	**Variables and Expressions**	15
1.4	**Powers and Exponents**	20
1.5	**Equations and Solutions**	28
	Problem Solving Strategies: Guess, Check, and Revise, 26	
1.6	**Variables in Familiar Formulas**	33
	Hands-On Activity: Modeling Area, 32	
1.7	**A Problem Solving Plan**	38

Assessment
FCAT Practice, 9, 13, 19,
 23, 31, 37, 43
Review Quiz, 25, 45
Chapter Review, 46
Chapter Test, 48
Chapter FCAT Test, 49

**Notetaking and
Student Help**

Notetaking, 4, 10, 21, 24, 33
 34, 39, 44
Reading, 16, 29, 33, 39
Solving, 10
Review, 6
Technology, 14
Vocabulary, 34
Watch Out, 11

Vacation Views, 2
Next Stop, 3
Find the Key, 19
What's Happening?, 43

Internet Resources

· eEdition Plus Online
· eWorkbook Plus Online
· eTutorial Plus Online
· FCAT Practice
· More Examples

**Pre-Course
Assessment**

Pre-Course Test, xxvi
Pre-Course Practice, xxviii

Student Handbook, xx

Exercise 29, p. 31

CHAPTER 2

Integer Operations

	Chapter Warm-Up Game	50
	Getting Ready to Learn	52
2.1	Integers and Absolute Value	53
2.2	Adding Integers	58
	Hands-On Activity: Adding Integers, 57	
2.3	Subtracting Integers	63
2.4	Multiplying Integers	70
	Problem Solving Strategies: Look for a Pattern, 68	
2.5	Dividing Integers	74
2.6	Number Properties	80
2.7	The Distributive Property	85
	Technology Activity: Using Integer Operations, 90	
2.8	The Coordinate Plane	91

Assessment
FCAT Practice, 56, 62, 67, 73, 77, 84, 89, 95
Review Quiz, 79, 97
Chapter Review, 98
Chapter Test, 100
Chapter FCAT Test, 101

Notetaking and Student Help

Notetaking, 52, 59, 63, 70, 71, 74, 78, 80, 81, 85, 86, 96
Reading, 54
Vocabulary, 82
Solving, 56, 71, 81, 87, 92
Review, 81
Watch Out, 74, 90

BRAIN GAME

Four in a Row, 50
Argyle Arithmetic, 67
Spatial Delivery, 95

Internet Resources

- eEdition Plus Online
- eWorkbook Plus Online
- eTutorial Plus Online
- FCAT Practice
- More Examples

EXPLORING MATH IN SCIENCE

Life Science Supercool Squirrels, 102

Exercise 44, p. 89

CHAPTER 3

Solving Equations and Inequalities

| Chapter Warm-Up Games | 104 |

| **Getting Ready to Learn** | **106** |

| 3.1 | **Solving Equations Using Addition or Subtraction** | **109** |
Hands-On Activity: Modeling One-Step Equations, 107

| 3.2 | **Solving Equations Using Multiplication or Division** | **113** |

| 3.3 | **Solving Two-Step Equations** | **119** |
Hands-On Activity: Modeling Two-Step Equations, 117

| 3.4 | **Writing Two-Step Equations** | **124** |
Technology Activity: Searching for Information, 129

| 3.5 | **Applying Geometric Formulas** | **134** |
Problem Solving Strategies: Draw a Diagram, 132

| 3.6 | **Solving Inequalities Using Addition or Subtraction** | **140** |

| 3.7 | **Solving Inequalities Using Multiplication or Division** | **146** |

Assessment
FCAT Practice, 112, 116, 123, 128, 139, 145, 149
Review Quiz, 131, 151
Chapter Review, 152
Chapter Test, 154
Chapter FCAT Test, 155

Notetaking and Student Help

Notetaking, 106, 109, 110, 113, 114, 120, 130, 134, 141, 146, 147, 150
Solving, 113, 120, 125, 141
Review, 120, 135
Watch Out, 110, 114

BrAIN GAME

Name that Planet!, 104
Planet Pinball, 105
Behind the Magic, 128
Prized Positions, 145

 Internet Resources

- eEdition Plus Online
- eWorkbook Plus Online
- eTutorial Plus Online
- FCAT Practice
- More Examples

 Unit 1 Assessment

Building Florida Test Skills:
  Multiple Choice, 156
Practicing Florida Test Skills, 158
Cumulative Practice, 160

Example 3, p. 110

CHAPTER

4

Factors, Fractions, and Exponents

Notetaking and Student Help

Notetaking, 166, 181, 190, 196, 197, 201, 202, 205, 210
Vocabulary, 173
Solving, 180, 192, 195, 205
Review, 169, 193
Technology, 209
Watch Out, 197, 198, 202, 206

Bicycle Math, 164
Marble Mystery, 177
Mix and Match, 200

· eEdition Plus Online
· eWorkbook Plus Online
· eTutorial Plus Online
· FCAT Practice
· More Examples

Chapter Warm-Up Game	164

Getting Ready to Learn	**166**
4.1 **Factors and Prime Factorization**	**168**
Hands-On Activity: Investigating Factors, 167	
4.2 **Greatest Common Factor**	**173**
4.3 **Simplifying Fractions**	**179**
Hands-On Activity: Equivalent Fractions, 178	
4.4 **Least Common Multiple**	**186**
Problem Solving Strategies: Make a List, 184	
4.5 **Comparing Fractions and Mixed Numbers**	**192**
4.6 **Rules of Exponents**	**196**
4.7 **Negative and Zero Exponents**	**201**
4.8 **Scientific Notation**	**205**
Technology Activity: Using Scientific Notation, 209	

Assessment
FCAT Practice, 172, 177, 183, 189,
   195, 200, 204, 208
Review Quiz, 191, 211
Chapter Review, 212
Chapter Test, 214
Chapter FCAT Test, 215

Exercise 10, p. 194

CHAPTER

5

Rational Number Operations

Chapter Warm-Up Games		216
Getting Ready to Learn		218
5.1	Fractions with Common Denominators	219
5.2	Fractions with Different Denominators	224
5.3	Multiplying Fractions	230
	Problem Solving Strategies: Act It Out, 228	
5.4	Dividing Fractions	234
	Technology Activity: Operations with Fractions, 239	
5.5	Fractions and Decimals	242
5.6	Adding and Subtracting Decimals	247
5.7	Multiplying and Dividing Decimals	251
5.8	Mean, Median, and Mode	257
	Hands-On Activity: Collecting and Analyzing Data, 255	

Assessment
FCAT Practice, 223, 227, 233,
 238, 246, 250, 254, 261
Review Quiz, 241, 263
Chapter Review, 264
Chapter Test, 266
Chapter FCAT Test, 267

**Notetaking and
Student Help**

Notetaking, 218, 219, 230,
 234, 240, 244, 251, 252,
 257, 262
Solving, 220, 235
Review, 224, 230
Watch Out, 225, 231, 258

BrAiN GAME

Scale the Cliff, 216
Tangled Fractions, 217
Who's in First?, 238
The Prize is Right!, 261

Internet Resources

- eEdition Plus Online
- eWorkbook Plus Online
- eTutorial Plus Online
- FCAT Practice
- More Examples

Exercise 20, p. 226

6

Multi-Step Equations and Inequalities

Chapter Warm-Up Game		**268**
	Getting Ready to Learn	**270**
6.1	**Solving Multi-Step Equations**	**271**
6.2	**Solving Equations with Variables on Both Sides**	**278**
	Problem Solving Strategies: Work Backward, 276	
6.3	**Solving Equations Involving Fractions and Decimals**	**282**
6.4	**Solving Equations Involving Circumference**	**290**
	Hands-On Activity: Diameter and Circumference, 288	
6.5	**Solving Multi-Step Inequalities**	**295**
	Technology Activity: Solving Inequalities, 300	
6.6	**Problem Solving and Inequalities**	**301**

Assessment
FCAT Practice, 275, 281, 285,
 294, 299, 305
Review Quiz, 287, 307
Chapter Review, 308
Chapter Test, 310
Chapter FCAT Test, 311

Notetaking and Student Help

Notetaking, 270, 282, 286,
 290, 306
Reading, 302
Solving, 283, 291
Review, 272, 292, 295
Technology, 300
Watch Out, 279

BrAiN GAME

Treasure Hunt, 268
Going Bananas, 287
City Solutions, 299

Internet Resources

- eEdition Plus Online
- eWorkbook Plus Online
- eTutorial Plus Online
- FCAT Practice
- More Examples

EXPLORING
MATH IN SCIENCE

Physical Science
The Physics of Basketball, 312

Exercise 23, p. 298

Ratio, Proportion, and Percent

Chapter Warm-Up Games		**314**
Getting Ready to Learn		**316**
7.1	**Ratios and Rates**	**317**
7.2	**Writing and Solving Proportions** Hands-On Activity: Making a Scale Drawing, 321	**322**
7.3	**Solving Percent Problems**	**327**
7.4	**Fractions, Decimals, and Percents**	**331**
7.5	**Percent of Change**	**338**
7.6	**Percent Applications**	**342**
7.7	**Using the Percent Equation** Technology Activity: Compound Interest, 351	**347**
7.8	**Simple Probability** Problem Solving Strategies: Perform an Experiment, 352	**354**

Assessment
FCAT Practice, 320, 326,
  330, 335, 341, 346, 350, 357
Review Quiz, 337, 359
Chapter Review, 360
Chapter Test, 362
Chapter FCAT Test, 363

Notetaking and Student Help

Notetaking, 316, 323, 327,
  328, 336, 338, 347, 348,
  354, 358
Vocabulary, 348, 351
Solving, 322, 332, 343, 355
Review, 318, 338
Watch Out, 339

Video Maze, 314
Find the Path, 315
Balancing Act, 326
Shrink Ray, 346

Internet Resources

- eEdition Plus Online
- eWorkbook Plus Online
- eTutorial Plus Online
- FCAT Practice
- More Examples

Unit 2
Assessment

Building Florida Test Skills:
  Short Response, 364
Practicing Florida Test Skills, 366
Cumulative Practice, 368

Example 1, p. 327

CHAPTER 8

Polygons and Transformations

Notetaking and Student Help

Notetaking, 374, 377, 382, 386, 391, 394, 405, 410, 411, 416, 418, 422
Reading, 383, 390, 398, 410
Vocabulary, 411
Solving, 377, 381
Review, 413, 417
Watch Out, 418, 419

Find the Flags, 372
Buy Oval Car, 389
Deep Reflections, 408

Internet Resources

· eEdition Plus Online
· eWorkbook Plus Online
· eTutorial Plus Online
· FCAT Practice
· More Examples

Chapter Warm-Up Game		372
Getting Ready to Learn		374
8.1	**Angle Pairs**	375
	Special Topic: Constructions, 380	
8.2	**Angles and Triangles**	382
8.3	**Quadrilaterals**	386
8.4	**Polygons and Angles**	390
8.5	**Congruent Polygons**	397
	Hands-On Activity: Copying a Triangle, 396	
8.6	**Reflections and Symmetry**	404
	Problem Solving Strategies: Make a Model, 402	
8.7	**Translations and Rotations**	409
	Special Topic: Tessellations, 414	
8.8	**Similarity and Dilations**	416

Assessment
FCAT Practice, 379, 385, 389, 393, 401, 408, 413, 421
Review Quiz, 395, 423
Chapter Review, 424
Chapter Test, 426
Chapter FCAT Test, 427

Example 1, p. 416

CHAPTER 9

Real Numbers and Right Triangles

Notetaking and Student Help

Notetaking, 430, 443, 454, 456, 457, 463, 470
Reading, 433
Solving, 431, 435, 444, 457, 463
Review, 437, 451
Technology, 464, 469
Watch Out, 438

BrAIN GAME

Spin Your Wheels, 428
Ramp Match, 429
X-cellent Birthday, 436
A Real Winner, 471

Internet Resources

· eEdition Plus Online
· eWorkbook Plus Online
· eTutorial Plus Online
· FCAT Practice
· More Examples

EXPLORING MATH IN SCIENCE

Earth Science
Viewing the Stars, 476

Chapter Warm-Up Games		**428**
Getting Ready to Learn		**430**
9.1	**Square Roots**	**431**
9.2	**Rational and Irrational Numbers**	**437**
9.3	**The Pythagorean Theorem**	**443**
	Hands-On Activity: Modeling the Pythagorean Theorem, 442	
9.4	**Using the Pythagorean Theorem**	**450**
	Problem Solving Strategies: Draw a Diagram, 448	
9.5	**Special Right Triangles**	**456**
9.6	**Using Trigonometric Ratios**	**463**
	Hands-On Activity: Exploring Trigonometric Ratios, 461	
	Technology Activity: Finding an Angle Measure, 469	

Assessment

FCAT Practice, 436, 441, 447, 453, 460, 468
Review Quiz, 455, 471
Chapter Review, 472
Chapter Test, 474
Chapter FCAT Test, 475

Example 5, p. 465

CHAPTER

10

Measurement, Area, and Volume

Notetaking and Student Help

Notetaking, 480, 481, 482, 486, 492, 498, 503, 504, 507, 508, 513, 514, 519, 520, 524
Reading, 482, 515
Vocabulary, 492, 493
Solving, 497, 507, 514
Technology, 504
Watch Out, 513

Measure Match, 478
What's the Score?, 490

· eEdition Plus Online
· eWorkbook Plus Online
· eTutorial Plus Online
· FCAT Practice
· More Examples

Unit 3 Assessment

Building Florida Test Skills:
  Context-Based
  Multiple Choice, 530
Practicing Florida Test Skills, 532
Cumulative Practice, 534

Chapter Warm-Up Game		**478**
Getting Ready to Learn		**480**
10.1	**Areas of Parallelograms and Trapezoids**	**481**
10.2	**Areas of Circles** Technology Activity: Comparing Radii of Circles, 491	**486**
10.3	**Three-Dimensional Figures** Special Topic: Sketching Solids, 496	**492**
10.4	**Surface Areas of Prisms and Cylinders** Problem Solving Strategies: Break into Parts, 500	**502**
10.5	**Surface Areas of Pyramids and Cones**	**507**
10.6	**Volumes of Prisms and Cylinders** Hands-On Activity: Exploring Volume, 512	**513**
10.7	**Volumes of Pyramids and Cones** Hands-On Activity: Comparing Volumes, 518	**519**

Assessment

FCAT Practice, 485, 490, 495, 506, 511, 517, 523
Review Quiz, 499, 525
Chapter Review, 526
Chapter Test, 528
Chapter FCAT Test, 529

Example 1, p. 519

CHAPTER 11

Linear Equations and Graphs

Notetaking and Student Help

Notetaking, 540, 558, 562, 564, 565, 570, 572, 577, 584, 588
Vocabulary, 570, 584
Solving, 542, 550, 557, 582, 583, 584, 585
Review, 571, 577
Watch Out, 541, 558, 571

Sidewalk Scramble, 538
Plot the Picture, 539
Late Night Show, 553

· eEdition Plus Online
· eWorkbook Plus Online
· eTutorial Plus Online
· FCAT Practice
· More Examples

Chapter Warm-Up Games		**538**
Getting Ready to Learn		**540**
11.1	**Relations and Functions**	**541**
11.2	**Scatter Plots**	**545**
11.3	**Equations in Two Variables**	**549**
11.4	**Graphs of Linear Equations**	**556**
	Problem Solving Strategies: Make a Table, 554	
	Technology Activity: Graphing Linear Functions, 561	
11.5	**Using Intercepts**	**564**
11.6	**Slope**	**570**
	Hands-On Activity: Finding the Slope of a Line, 568	
11.7	**Slope-intercept Form**	**577**
	Hands-On Activity: Slope-Intercept Form, 575	
	Special Topic: Systems of Equations, 581	
11.8	**Graphs of Linear Inequalities**	**583**

Assessment

FCAT Practice, 544, 548, 553, 560, 567, 574, 580, 587
Review Quiz, 563, 589
Chapter Review, 590
Chapter Test, 592
Chapter FCAT Test, 593

Exercise 32, p. 586

CHAPTER 12

Data Analysis and Probability

| | Chapter Warm-Up Game | 594 |

Getting Ready to Learn — 596

12.1 Stem-and-Leaf Plots — 597

12.2 Box-and-Whisker Plots — 601

12.3 Using Data Displays — 605
Technology Activity: Making Data Displays, 610
Special Topic: Misleading Graphs, 612

12.4 Counting Methods — 618
Problem Solving Strategies: Solve a Simpler Problem, 616

12.5 Permutations — 623

12.6 Combinations — 627

12.7 Probability and Odds — 632

12.8 Independent and Dependent Events — 639
Hands-On Activity: Probability and Simulations, 637
Special Topic: Samples, 644

Assessment
FCAT Practice, 600, 604, 609, 622, 626, 631, 636, 643
Review Quiz, 615, 647
Chapter Review, 648
Chapter Test, 650
Chapter FCAT Test, 651

Notetaking and Student Help

Notetaking, 596, 606, 614, 619, 624, 628, 629, 640, 646
Reading, 633
Solving, 598, 601, 605, 608, 612, 623, 624, 632
Review, 620

BRAIN GAME

Galapagos Graphs, 594
Safe Cracker, 615
Lucky Numbers, 643

Internet Resources

- eEdition Plus Online
- eWorkbook Plus Online
- eTutorial Plus Online
- FCAT Practice
- More Examples

EXPLORING
MATH IN SCIENCE

Measurement
Investigating Robins, 652

Example 1, p. 627

CHAPTER

13

Polynomials and Functions

Chapter Warm-Up Games   **654**

Getting Ready to Learn   **656**

13.1 Polynomials   **657**

13.2 Adding and Subtracting Polynomials   **661**

13.3 Monomials and Powers   **666**

13.4 Multiplying Binomials   **674**
    Hands-On Activity: Multiplying Binomials, 673

13.5 Non-Linear Functions   **680**
    Problem Solving Strategies: Draw a Graph, 678
    Technology Activity: Graphing Non-Linear Functions, 685

Assessment

FCAT Practice, 660, 665,
   670, 677, 684
Review Quiz, 672, 687
Chapter Review, 688
Chapter Test, 690
Chapter FCAT Test, 691

Notetaking and Student Help

Notetaking, 656, 667, 668,
   671, 674, 686
Reading, 681
Vocabulary, 675
Solving, 662
Review, 658, 665, 666
Watch Out, 657
Technology, 685

BrAIN GAME

Piñata Punch, 654
Unmasking Expressions, 655
Polynomial Potions, 665
Number Crunch, 684

Internet Resources

· eEdition Plus Online
· eWorkbook Plus Online
· eTutorial Plus Online
· FCAT Practice
· More Examples

Unit 4 Assessment

Building Florida Test Skills:
   Extended Response, 692
Practicing Florida Test Skills, 694
Cumulative Practice, 696

End-of-Course Assessment

End-of-Course Test, 699

Example 3, p. 658

Contents of Student Resources

Skills Review Handbook   704

Number Sense
- Place Value, *704*
- Rounding, *705*
- Divisibility Tests, *706*
- Mixed Numbers and Improper Fractions, *707*
- Ratio and Rate, 708

Number Operations
- Adding and Subtracting Decimals, *709*
- Adding and Subtracting Fractions, *710*
- Estimation in Addition and Subtraction, *711*
- Solving Problems Using Addition and Subtraction, *712*
- Multiplying Fractions, *713*
- Multiplication of a Decimal by a Whole Number, *714*
- Dividing Decimals, *715*
- Estimation in Multiplication and Division, *716*
- Solving Problems Using Multiplication and Division, *717*

Measurement and Geometry
- Points, Lines, and Planes, *718*
- Angles, *719*
- Using a Ruler, *720*
- Using a Protractor, *721*
- Using a Compass, *722*

Data Analysis
- Reading and Making Line Plots, *723*
- Reading and Making Bar Graphs, *724*
- Reading and Making Line Graphs, *725*
- Venn Diagrams and Logical Reasoning, *726*

Extra Practice   727
Chapters 1–13

Tables   740
Symbols, Measures, Formulas, Properties, Squares and Square Roots, Equivalent Fractions, Decimals, and Percents

Glossary   747

Index   773

Credits   796

Selected Answers   SA1

Student Handbook

Help with Taking Notes

One of the most important tools for success in mathematics is organizing what you have learned. Writing down important information in a notebook helps you remember key concepts and skills. You can use your notebook as a reference when you do your homework or when you study for a test.

Taking Notes

Your textbook displays important ideas and definitions on a notebook. You'll want to include this information in your notes.

Notetaking Strategies

You'll find a different notetaking strategy at the beginning of each chapter. Within the chapter, you'll find helpful hints about taking notes.

Notebook Review

Your textbook includes frequent notebook reviews. These reviews help you use your notebook to check your understanding of important skills and concepts.

LESSON 2.6 Number Properties

BEFORE You evaluated expressions.
Now You'll use properties to evaluate expressions.
WHY? So you can find your weekly pay, as in Ex. 39.

In the Real World

Word Watch
Review Words
sum, p. 709
product, p. 713

FLORIDA
Standards and Assessment
• Apply number properties. (MA.A.3.3.1)
• Simplify expressions using integers. (MA.A.1.3.4)

Tour Biking You are going on a 400 mile bike trip. You plan to cycle at an average speed of 12 miles per hour for 7 hours a day. Can you complete the trip in 5 days?

The commutative properties of addition and multiplication can be used to make evaluating expressions using mental math easier.

The Commutative Property

	Addition	Multiplication
Words	You can add numbers of a sum in any order.	You can multiply factors of a product in any order.
Numbers	$3 + (-8) = -8 + 3$	$5(-6) = -6(5)$
Algebra	$a + b = b + a$	$ab = ba$

EXAMPLE 1 Using the Commutative Property

To find if you can complete the bike trip in 5 days, find the total distance you plan to cycle. Then compare that distance to the length of the trip.

| = | Average speed | · | Hours per day | · | Number of days |

$= 12 \cdot 7 \cdot 5$ Substitute known values.
$= 12 \cdot 5 \cdot 7$ Commutative property of multiplication
$= 60 \cdot 7$ Multiply.
$= 420$ Multiply.

e result is miles. $\frac{miles}{hour} \cdot \frac{hours}{day} \cdot days = miles$

se 400 miles is less than the 420 miles you can travel in complete the trip in 5 days.

Know How to Take Notes

Including Vocabulary Notes When you write down new vocabulary words, you should also write examples of how they are used. Label the examples with the new words.

Base is 2. — Power 2^3 — Exponent is 3. — Equal to $2 \cdot 2 \cdot 2$

5^2 is read "five squared."
5^3 is read "five cubed."
5^4 is read "five to the fourth power."

rough Chapter 2, label examples of new vocabulary in

LESSONS 3.5 TO 3.7 Notebook Review

Review the vocabulary definitions in your notebook

Check Your Definitions

base, p. 134
height, p. 134
inequality, p. 140
solution of an inequality, p. 140
equivalent inequalities, p. 141

Use Your Vocabulary

Help with Learning Mathematics

Your textbook helps you succeed in mathematics. Keep your eye out for notes that help you with reading mathematics, learning vocabulary terms, solving problems, using technology, and doing your homework. Some examples of the types of notes you'll see are shown below.

Help Notes
These notes help you understand and apply what you've learned.

HELP with Solving
Another way to undo operations is to add the opposite to undo addition or subtraction. Then multiply by the reciprocal to undo multiplication or division.

EXAMPLE 2 Solving with a Variable in the Numerator

$\frac{x}{2} - 14$	$=$	8	Original equation
$+14$		$+14$	Add 14 to each side to undo subtraction.
$\frac{x}{2}$	$=$	22	Simplify.
$\frac{x}{2} \cdot 2$	$=$	$22 \cdot 2$	Multiply each side by 2 to undo division.
x	$=$	44	Simplify.

✓ Check $\frac{44}{2} - 14 \stackrel{?}{=} 8$ Substitute 44 for x in original equation.

$22 - 14 = 8$ ✓

HELP with Review
Remember that you can solve an equation vertically or horizontally. See p. 110.

EXAMPLE 3 Solving with a Negative Coefficient

$8 = 12 - 2x$	Original equation
$8 - 12 = 12 - 2x - 12$	Subtract 12 from each side to undo addition.
$-4 = -2x$	Simplify.
$\frac{-4}{-2} = \frac{-2x}{-2}$	Divide each side by -2 to undo multiplication.
$2 = x$	Simplify.

$6 = 16 - a$

EXAMPLE 2 Simplifying Variable Expressions

Algebra **Simplify the expression.**

a. $\frac{2x}{5} - \frac{x}{6} = \frac{12x}{30} - \frac{5x}{30}$ Rewrite fractions using LCD of 30.

$= \frac{12x - 5x}{30}$ Write difference over LCD.

$= \frac{7x}{30}$ Combine like terms.

b. $\frac{5}{y} + \frac{7}{8} = \left(\frac{5}{y} \cdot \frac{8}{8}\right) + \left(\frac{7}{8} \cdot \frac{y}{y}\right)$ Multiply $\frac{5}{y}$ by $\frac{8}{8}$ and $\frac{7}{8}$ by $\frac{y}{y}$ for LCD of 8y.

$= \frac{40}{8y} + \frac{7y}{8y}$ Multiply inside parentheses.

$= \frac{40 + 7y}{8y}$ Write sum over LCD.

Watch Out!
These notes help you avoid common errors.

Watch Out!
In part (b) of Example 2, notice that
$$\frac{40 + 7y}{8y} \neq \frac{47y}{8y}$$
because 40 and 7y are not like terms. The expression is already in simplest form.

Help with Homework
These notes tell you which textbook examples may help you with homework exercises, and let you know where to find extra help on the Internet.

HELP with Homework

Example	Exercises
1	12–15, 32
2	16–19, 28–31
3	20–27
4	33–34

Online Resources
CLASSZONE.COM
· More Examples
· eTutorial Plus

Practice and Problem Solving

Find the quotient.

12. $\frac{4}{9} \div \frac{4}{7}$ 13. $-\frac{3}{8} \div \frac{7}{12}$ 14. $\frac{9}{14} \div \left(-\frac{3}{26}\right)$ 15. $-\frac{21}{22} \div \frac{-7}{11}$

16. $\frac{8}{11} \div 4$ 17. $\frac{9}{10} \div (-12)$ 18. $-\frac{5}{12} \div 10$ 19. $\frac{63}{8} \div (-9)$

Find the quotient.

20. $5\frac{1}{4} \div 2\frac{1}{3}$ 21. $7\frac{7}{8} \div \left(-2\frac{1}{4}\right)$ 22. $12\frac{1}{7} \div 5\frac{5}{6}$ 23. $-22\frac{2}{3} \div 3\frac{1}{5}$

24. $-9\frac{3}{5} \div (-8)$ 25. $1\frac{5}{7} \div (-6)$ 26. $8\frac{4}{13} \div 6\frac{3}{4}$ 27. $9\frac{9}{14} \div 4\frac{1}{6}$

28. Writing Are the numbers $\frac{1}{9}$ and -9 reciprocals? Explain.

Use mental math to find the quotient.

29. $\frac{1}{2} \div 3$ 30. $4 \div \frac{1}{2}$ 31. $1 \div \frac{4}{7}$ 32. $\frac{2}{3} \div \frac{3}{2}$

Reading Your Textbook

You need special skills to read a math textbook. These skills include *identifying the main idea, learning new vocabulary,* and *focusing on the important concepts* in a lesson. Most important, you need to *be an active reader.* You need to practice and apply the ideas you read about.

Identify the Main Idea

Even before you begin reading a lesson, check to see what the lesson is about. Then you'll know what to focus on in the lesson. You can also assess how well you understand the lesson content when you've finished reading the lesson.

Lesson Opener Look at the lesson opener for information about the main idea of the lesson.

Example Heads Use other clues, such as the heads that appear above examples, to identify the main idea.

Understand the Vocabulary

Reading mathematics involves learning and using new vocabulary terms. Refer to diagrams and worked-out examples to clarify your understanding of new terms. If you forget what a term you've already learned means, look back at previous lessons or use the Glossary, which starts on page 747.

Vocabulary New vocabulary terms are highlighted within a lesson. In addition, the *Word Watch* at the beginning of the lesson lists the important vocabulary terms in the lesson.

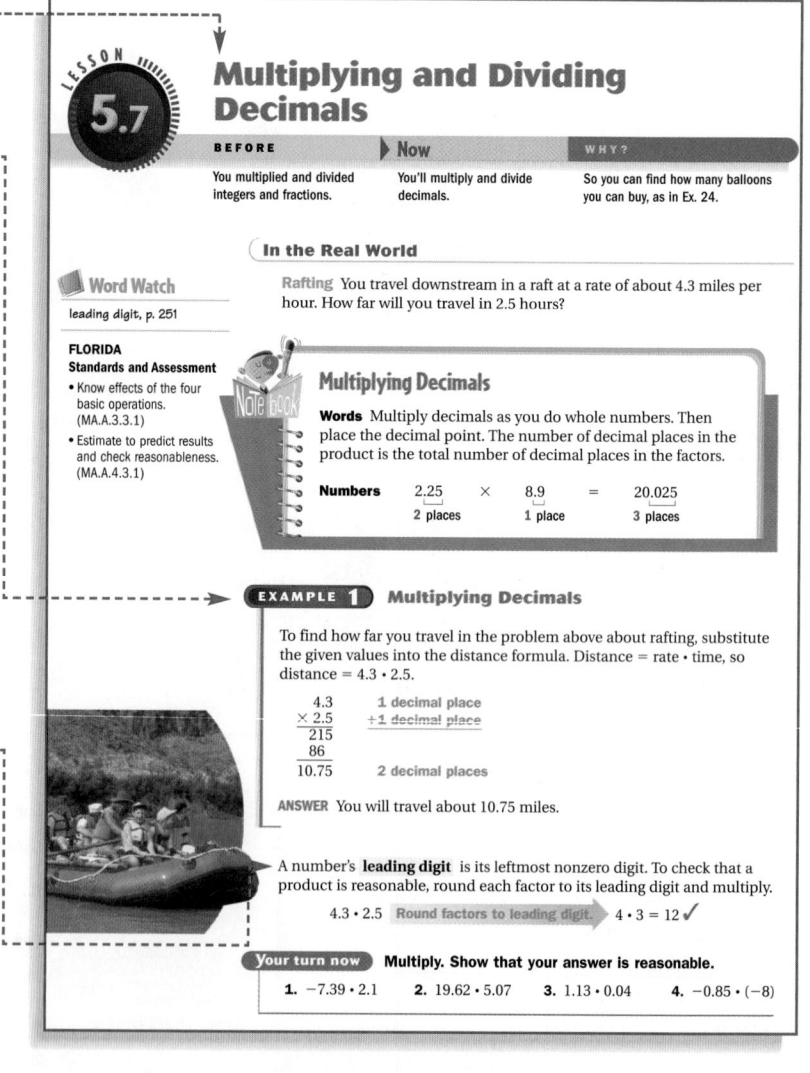

Know What's Important

Focus in on the important information in a lesson. Pay attention to highlighted vocabulary terms and definitions. Be on the lookout for definitions, properties, formulas, and other information displayed on a notebook. Make sure that you understand the worked-out examples.

Notebook Focus in on key ideas that are displayed on a notebook.

Worked-Out Examples Do the worked-out examples to make sure you know how to apply new concepts.

Be an Active Reader

As you read, keep a pencil in your hand and your notebook ready so that you can write down important information, practice new skills, and jot down questions to ask in class.

Your Turn Now Solve the *Your turn now* exercises to check your understanding.

Use Your Notebook As you solve the examples yourself, you may find it helpful to describe the steps you follow. Write down any questions you have so you can ask them in class.

You can also use the addition property of equality to solve an equation.

Addition Property of Equality

Words	Adding the same number to each side of an equation makes an equivalent equation.
Numbers	If $x - 2 = 6$, then $x - 2 + 2 = 6 + 2$.
Algebra	If $a = b$, then $a + c = b + c$.

Watch Out! You can add or subtract horizontally or vertically to solve equations, but remember that when solving, you must perform the same operation on *each* side.

EXAMPLE 2 Solving an Equation Using Addition

$c - 4.5 = 13$	Original equation
$c - 4.5 + 4.5 = 13 + 4.5$	Add 4.5 to each side to undo subtraction.
$c = 17.5$	Simplify. c is by itself.
✓Check $17.5 - 4.5 \stackrel{?}{=} 13$	Substitute 17.5 for c in original equation.
$13 = 13$ ✓	

Your turn now Solve the equation. Check your solution.

1. $x + 9 = 20$ **2.** $-10 = 3 + y$ **3.** $m - 14 = -15$ **4.** $2 = z - 6.4$

EXAMPLE 3 Using a Verbal Model

Rock Climbing A cliff has a height of about 1500 feet. If you have already climbed 675 feet, how much farther do you have to climb to reach the top?

Solution

Write a verbal model. Let x represent the distance left to climb.

Height of cliff	=	Distance left to climb	+	Distance climbed

$1500 = x + 675$	Write an algebraic model.
$1500 - 675 = x + 675 - 675$	Subtract 675 from each side.
$825 = x$	Simplify. x is by itself.

ANSWER You have about 825 feet left to climb.

Reading and Problem Solving

The language in your math textbook is precise. When you do your homework, be sure to read carefully. For example, the direction line below asks you to do three different things for each of the exercises: sketch, measure, and compare.

> **Estimation** **Sketch a line segment of the given length without using a ruler. Then use a ruler to check your estimate. How close was your estimate?**
>
> **21.** 6.5 cm   **22.** 45 mm   **23.** 0.01 m   **24.** 0.15 m

Reading Word Problems

Before you can solve a word problem, you need to read and understand it. You may find it useful to copy a word problem into your notebook. Then you can highlight important information, cross out unnecessary information, and organize your thinking.

> You have a recipe that makes 24 cookies. The ingredients include 2 eggs, 1 cup of sugar, 1.5 cups of flour, 1 teaspoon of vanilla, and 1 teaspoon of baking soda. What is the greatest number of cookies you can make if you have 12 eggs, 4 cups of sugar, and 9 cups of flour?
>
> | | Needed (one batch) | Already have |
> |-----------------|:------------------:|:------------:|
> | Number of eggs | 2 | 12 |
> | Cups of sugar | 1 | 4 |
> | Cups of flour | 1.5 | 9 |

Make sure that you've solved a word problem completely. For example, to solve the word problem at the right, you need to calculate how many more points you need for Levels 5, 6, and 7. But to answer the question, you must determine how many total points you need.

> In a certain video game, when you reach 50 points, you reach Level 2. You need 70 more points to reach Level 3, and then you need 90 more points to reach Level 4. Suppose the pattern continues. How many points do you need to reach Level 7?
>
> Level 5: 110 more, Level 6: 130 more, Level 7: 150 more
>
> Total points:
>
> 50 + 70 + 90 + 110 + 130 + 150 = 600

Additional Resources in Your Textbook

Your textbook contains many resources that you can use for reference when you are studying or doing your homework.

Skills Review Handbook Use the Skills Review Handbook on pages 704–726 to review material learned in previous courses.

Tables Refer to the tables on pages 740–746 if you need information about mathematical symbols, measures, formulas, and properties.

Glossary Use the Glossary on pages 747–772 to look up the meanings of math vocabulary terms. Each glossary entry also tells where in your book a term is covered in more detail.

Index Use the Index on pages 773–795 as a quick guide for finding out where a particular math topic is covered in the book.

Selected Answers Use the Selected Answers starting on page SA1 to check your work or to see whether you are on the right track in solving a problem.

Textbook Scavenger Hunt

Get some practice using your textbook. Use the additional resources described above to answer each question. Give page numbers to show where you found the answer to the question.

1 What is a biased sample?

2 Tell what each of these symbols means: $\stackrel{?}{=}$, $\sim$, $\pm$.

3 How many square inches are there in one square foot?

4 On what page or pages of the book is the distributive property first discussed?

5 What is the normal body temperature in degrees Fahrenheit? in degrees Celsius?

6 What is a variable?

7 On what page can you review the skill of adding and subtracting decimals?

8 On what page of the book can you find selected answers for Lesson 1.1?

9 What formula can you use to find the volume of a cylinder?

Number Sense and Operations

Place Value and Rounding (Skills Review, pp. 704–705)

Write the number in expanded form.

1. 34,777

2. 837.4

3. 5459

4. 1002.003

Round the number to the place value of the red digit.

5. 3465

6. 44,656

7. 66,789

8. 55.677

Operations with Decimals and Fractions (Skills Review, pp. 707–715)

Write the mixed number as an improper fraction or the improper fraction as a mixed number.

9. $4\frac{2}{3}$

10. $12\frac{1}{2}$

11. $\frac{13}{6}$

12. $\frac{24}{5}$

Find the sum, difference, product, or quotient. Simplify if possible.

13. $6.77 + 5.66$

14. $77.555 - 34.55$

15. $\frac{4}{12} - \frac{3}{12}$

16. $\frac{4}{5} + \frac{3}{5}$

17. 3.4×45

18. $10\frac{2}{3} \times 5\frac{1}{4}$

19. $14.49 \div 7$

20. $2.1 \div 84$

21. $\frac{3}{4} \times \frac{1}{4}$

22. 3.89×16

23. $1\frac{2}{3} \times 1\frac{4}{5}$

24. $3 \times 4\frac{1}{2}$

Problem Solving (Skills Review, pp. 712, 717)

25. The computer club has already raised $120.95 for new software. A math program costs $39.50, a game costs $24.75, and a reading program costs $66.29. How much more money does the club need to raise to pay for the software?

26. The soccer team had a car wash to raise money. They charged $3 for each car. If they washed 23 cars, how much money did they earn?

Estimation (Skills Review, pp. 711, 716)

Estimate the sum or difference.

27. $666 + 453 + 123$

28. $45,768 - 23,409$

29. $7666 + 4555 + 994$

Find a low and high estimate for the product or quotient.

30. 54×19

31. $788 \div 9$

32. 560×236

33. $8557 \div 29$

Geometry

Points, Lines, and Planes *(Skills Review, p. 718)*

In Exercises 34–36, use the diagram.

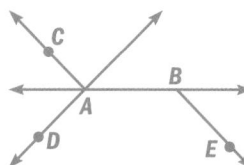

34. Name three points.

35. Name two rays.

36. Name two lines.

Using a Protractor *(Skills Review, p. 721)*

Use a protractor to measure the angle.

37.

38.

Use a protractor to draw an angle that has the given measure.

39. $125°$ **40.** $34°$ **41.** $90°$

Data Analysis

Reading Bar Graphs and Line Graphs *(Skills Review, pp. 724–725)*

In Exercises 42 and 43, use the bar graph.

42. Which sale made the least money?

43. How much more money was made from the bake sale than the yard sale?

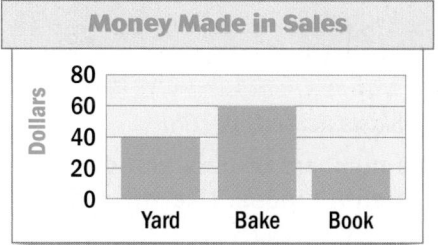

In Exercises 44 and 45, use the line graph.

44. Which month had the greatest concert attendance?

45. What was the difference in concert attendance between June and May?

Number Sense and Operations

Place Value and Rounding *(Skills Review, pp. 704–705)*

Write the number in expanded form.

1. 45,708   **2.** 4.056   **3.** 1003.04   **4.** 405.305

Write the number in standard form.

5. $4 \times 100{,}000 + 7 \times 10 + 8 \times 1 + 8 \times 0.001$ **6.** $5 \times 100 + 8 \times 1 + 3 \times 0.1 + 4 \times 0.01$

Round the number to the place value of the red digit.

7. 2234   **8.** 48,139   **9.** 4.566   **10.** 33.86

11. 13.444   **12.** 556.78   **13.** 73.845   **14.** 546,888

Divisibility *(Skills Review, p. 706)*

Test the number for divisibility by 2, 3, 4, 5, 6, 8, 9, and 10.

15. 44   **16.** 88   **17.** 385   **18.** 870

Mixed Numbers and Improper Fractions *(Skills Review, p. 707)*

Write the mixed number as an improper fraction.

19. $4\frac{1}{2}$ **20.** $2\frac{4}{5}$ **21.** $8\frac{4}{9}$ **22.** $9\frac{4}{7}$

Write the improper fraction as a mixed number.

23. $\frac{12}{7}$ **24.** $\frac{18}{4}$ **25.** $\frac{21}{5}$ **26.** $\frac{33}{7}$

Ratio and Rate *(Skills Review, p. 708)*

The table shows the numbers of cats and dogs owned by the students in the seventh and eighth grades. Use the table to write the ratio.

27. Cats of 8th graders to cats of 7th graders

28. Dogs of 7th graders to dogs of 8th graders

29. Cats of 7th graders to cats of both grades

	Cats	Dogs
8th Grade	12	14
7th Grade	11	15

Write the rate and the unit rate.

30. $3.90 for 30 ounces   **31.** 250 miles in 4 hours

32. $4.50 for 30 minutes long distance   **33.** 329 miles on 14 gallons of gas

Operations with Decimals and Fractions *(Skills Review, pp. 709–714)*

Find the sum or difference.

34. $8.4 - 3.3$ **35.** $23.8 + 84.9$ **36.** $38.6 + 4.7$ **37.** $5.44 - 2.33$

38. $4.67 + 3.85$ **39.** $49.55 - 18.23$ **40.** $66.77 + 3.45$ **41.** $34.56 - 30.89$

42. $5.329 + 8.455$ **43.** $14.86 - 6.656$ **44.** $888.66 - 56.88$ **45.** $475.67 + 89.44$

Find the sum or difference.

46. $\frac{1}{7} + \frac{4}{7}$ **47.** $\frac{14}{17} - \frac{11}{17}$ **48.** $\frac{7}{9} - \frac{5}{9}$ **49.** $\frac{9}{13} + \frac{8}{13}$

50. $\frac{5}{12} + \frac{2}{12}$ **51.** $\frac{3}{9} + \frac{4}{9}$ **52.** $\frac{12}{13} - \frac{4}{13}$ **53.** $\frac{5}{8} - \frac{4}{8}$

54. $\frac{1}{4} + \frac{2}{4}$ **55.** $\frac{12}{14} - \frac{9}{14}$ **56.** $\frac{7}{8} - \frac{4}{8}$ **57.** $\frac{5}{11} + \frac{3}{11}$

Find the product. Simplify if possible.

58. $\frac{2}{9} \times \frac{1}{7}$ **59.** $\frac{1}{5} \times \frac{2}{3}$ **60.** $\frac{3}{4} \times \frac{1}{8}$ **61.** $\frac{1}{4} \times \frac{3}{7}$

62. $\frac{1}{4} \times \frac{3}{4}$ **63.** $\frac{4}{5} \times \frac{7}{8}$ **64.** $\frac{1}{8} \times \frac{4}{5}$ **65.** $3 \times 1\frac{1}{5}$

66. $5\frac{1}{2} \times 6$ **67.** $2 \times 3\frac{1}{7}$ **68.** $4\frac{2}{3} \times 1\frac{3}{4}$ **69.** $1\frac{3}{8} \times 4\frac{2}{3}$

Find the product or quotient.

70. 2.3×67 **71.** $3.42 \div 3$ **72.** $367.5 \div 5$ **73.** 0.55×88

74. 7.54×88 **75.** 8.44×77 **76.** $2.934 \div 9$ **77.** $584.85 \div 7$

78. 555×34.3 **79.** 788×66.4 **80.** $0.48 \div 6$ **81.** 45.905×78

82. $16.68 \div 2$ **83.** $12.32 \div 4$ **84.** 345.88×55 **85.** $401.1 \div 7$

Problem Solving *(Skills Review, pp. 712, 717)*

86. A middle school has three grades and 667 students total. The eighth grade has 216 students. The seventh grade has 229 students. How many students are in the sixth grade?

87. Maria bought a hamburger for $1.59 and juice for $.68. She paid with a $5 bill. How much change should Maria receive?

88. Lee spent $7.89 for a hammer, $2.26 for nails, and $3.55 for a stapler. What was the total cost of Lee's purchase?

89. A sweater costs \$28, and a pair of boots costs \$56. What is the total cost of the sweater and the boots?

90. You bought 98 trading cards and gave 45 to your brother. How many cards do you have left?

91. Sue has 12 CDs, and Kate has 28 CDs. How many CDs do Sue and Kate have all together?

92. The recycling committee collected 2575 newspapers and tied them in bundles. Each bundle contained 25 newspapers. How many bundles of newspapers did they make?

93. Your school cafeteria has enough seats for 540 students. Each table seats 12 students. How many tables are in the cafeteria?

94. A youth organization sold 132 books of carnival ride coupons. Each book contained 18 ride coupons. How many ride coupons were sold?

95. Basketball tickets cost \$35 each. The team sold 12,383 tickets to their first game. How much money did the team make for the first game?

Estimation *(Skills Review, pp. 711, 716)*

Estimate the sum or difference.

96. $6845 + 2687$ **97.** $7356 - 4699$ **98.** $8999 + 3456$ **99.** $4567 - 3499$

100. $1867 + 5409$ **101.** $7865 - 5433$ **102.** $6577 - 3444$ **103.** $6999 + 5987$

Find a low and high estimate for the product or quotient.

104. 44×18 **105.** 555×34 **106.** $333 \div 8$ **107.** $6566 \div 8$

108. 434×56 **109.** $344 \div 23$ **110.** $7656 \div 19$ **111.** 808×66

Geometry

Points, Lines, and Planes *(Skills Review, p. 718)*

In Exercises 112–115, use the diagram.

112. Name three points.

113. Name two rays.

114. Give two different names for the line.

115. Name a segment that has *D* as an endpoint.

Using a Protractor (Skills Review, p. 721)

Use a protractor to measure the angle.

116.

117.

118.

Use a protractor to draw an angle that has the given measure.

119. $56°$ **120.** $125°$ **121.** $140°$ **122.** $15°$

 Data Analysis

Reading Bar Graphs and Line Graphs (Skills Review, pp. 724–725)

In Exercises 123–125, use the line graph. It shows the numbers of books sold on five different days.

123. On what day were the fewest number of books sold?

124. On what day were 8 books sold?

125. How many more books were sold on Wednesday than on Monday?

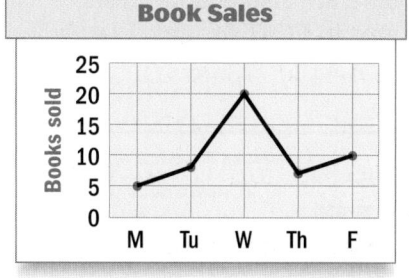

In Exercises 126–128, use the bar graph. It shows the numbers of students that participate in school activities.

126. How many more students participate in the band than in drama?

127. In what activity do the greatest number of students participate?

128. In what activity do 35 students participate?

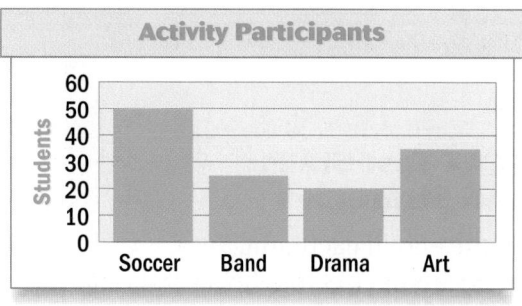

Venn Diagrams and Logical Reasoning (Skills Review, p. 726)

Draw a Venn diagram of the set described.

129. Of the whole numbers less than 14, set *A* consists of numbers that are greater than 9, and set *B* consists of even numbers.

130. Of the whole numbers less than 12, set *C* consists of multiples of 2, and set *D* consists of odd numbers.

Florida Standards and Assessment

Florida Standards

The authors have developed a sequence of lessons that include all the key Florida standards and objectives. The first page of each lesson lists the major Florida standards that you will study in the lesson.

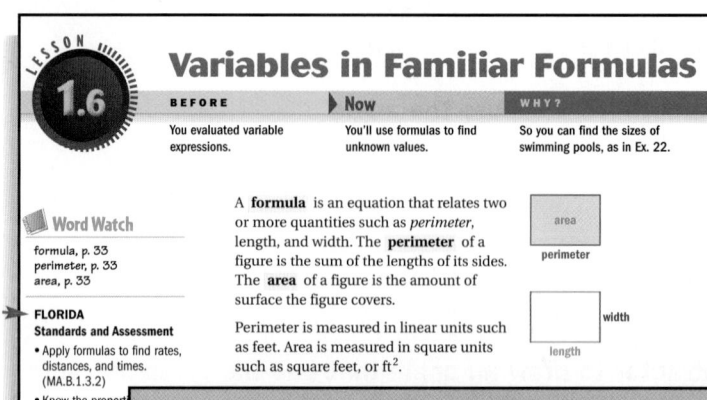

LESSON 1.6

Variables in Familiar Formulas

BEFORE	Now	WHY?
You evaluated variable expressions.	You'll use formulas to find unknown values.	So you can find the sizes of swimming pools, as in Ex. 22.

Word Watch

formula, p. 33
perimeter, p. 33
area, p. 33

FLORIDA
Standards and Assessment
• Apply formulas to find rates, distances, and times. (MA.B.1.3.2)
• Know the properties two-dimensional (MA.C.1.3.1)

A **formula** is an equation that relates two or more quantities such as *perimeter*, length, and width. The **perimeter** of a figure is the sum of the lengths of its sides. The **area** of a figure is the amount of surface the figure covers.

Perimeter is measured in linear units such as feet. Area is measured in square units such as square feet, or ft².

FCAT Practice

Each lesson includes FCAT practice that helps you become comfortable with different formats of FCAT questions. Additional practice is provided on the Internet. There are also chapter tests with questions in FCAT format.

FCAT Practice | FCAT

INTERNET
FCAT PRACTICE
CLASSZONE.COM

48. Multiple Choice What is the correct prime factorization of 120?

A. $2^2 \cdot 3 \cdot 5$ B. $2^3 \cdot 5 \cdot 6$ C. $2^2 \cdot 3^2 \cdot 10$ D. $2^3 \cdot 3 \cdot 5$

49. Short Response You want to buy some soup bowls and some dinner plates. The soup bowls come in boxes of eight, and the dinner plates come in boxes of six. What is the least number of soup bowls and dinner plates that you can buy to get an equal number of each?

Chapter FCAT Practice

FCAT Test-Taking Strategy Avoid spending too much time on one question. Skip questions you have trouble with, and return to them after you have finished.

Multiple Choice

1. Which ratio is *not* equivalent to $\frac{5}{11}$?

A. $\frac{20}{44}$ B. $\frac{2.5}{5.5}$ C. $\frac{1000}{2200}$ D. $\frac{35}{75}$

2. Paul can read at a speed of 228 words per minute. What is his reading speed in words per second?

F. 0.26 words per second

G. 3.8 words per second

_ s per second

_ rds per second

e shows $\frac{12 \text{ meters}}{8 \text{ seconds}}$ correctly

nit rate?

$\frac{6 \text{ m}}{4 \text{ sec}}$ C. $\frac{1.5 \text{ m}}{\text{sec}}$ D. $\frac{4 \text{ m}}{6 \text{ sec}}$

l of a room is 6 inches long and 5 inches wide. The actual room is 10 feet wide. What scale was used?

7. In a class, 80%, or 28, of the students studied for a test. How many students are in the class?

A. 20   B. 22   C. 30   D. 35

8. You deposit $450 in an account that pays a simple interest rate of 3.5% annually? How much interest will you earn in 2 years?

F. $15.75   G. $31.50   H. $157.50   I. $315

9. You draw a sock from a drawer of 6 black, 8 white, and 4 brown socks. What is the probability that the sock is black?

A. $\frac{1}{6}$ B. $\frac{2}{9}$ C. $\frac{1}{3}$ D. $\frac{4}{9}$

Short Response

10. A shirt with a wholesale price of $9.60 is marked up 75%. When it doesn't sell, the item is sold at a 40% discount. Find the retail price of the item. Then find the sale price of the item.

random from a bag
d yellow marbles
ou record its color
he bag of 75 marbles.
in the table below.
lor marble do you
? Explain.

	Green	Yellow
	5	9

FCAT Test Skills and Strategies

At the end of each unit, you'll find pages that help you build and practice Florida test-taking skills and strategies.

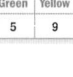

FCAT BUILDING **Florida Test Skills**   **UNIT 2** **Chapters 4–7**

Strategies for Answering
Short Response Questions

Scoring Rubric

Full credit (2 points)
• answer is correct, *and*
• work and reasoning are included

Partial credit (1 point)
• answer is correct, but reasoning is incorrect, *or*
• answer is incorrect, but reasoning is correct

No credit (0 points)
• no answer is given *or*
• answer makes no sense

Problem

You work for your uncle this summer. He pays you $20 on your first day. Each day after that, you will get a raise. You can choose from 2 payment plans. With Plan A, you earn a $5 raise each day. With Plan B, you earn a 20% raise each day. Which plan is a better deal?

Full credit solution

Data is used to justify
the solution.

Plan B is a better deal if you work more than 5 days.

Day	1	2	3	4	5	6
Plan A pay	20.00	25.00	30.00	35.00	40.00	45.00
Plan A total	20.00	45.00	75.00	110.00	150.00	195.00
Plan B pay	20.00	24.00	28.80	34.56	41.47	49.76
Plan B total	20.00	44.00	72.80	107.36	148.83	198.59

The question is
answered clearly
and in complete
sentences.

Plan A is better if you work 5 days or less, but Plan B is better if you work more than 5 days. By day 6, the pay with a 20% increase is more than the pay with a $5 raise, so it will continue to be the better plan.

Partial credit solution

Algebra, Integers, and Equation Solving

CHAPTER

1 Variables and Equations

2 Integer Operations

3 Solving Equations and Inequalities

Meeting the Florida Standards

- **Write and evaluate numerical and algebraic expressions.**
  MA.A.2.3.1, MA.A.3.3.1, MA.A.3.3.2, MA.D.1.3.1, MA.D.2.3.1

- **Use a variety of strategies to predict, find, and check results.**
  MA.A.3.3.2, MA.A.4.3.1

- **Find lengths, perimeters, and areas in real-world situations.**
  MA.B.1.3.2, MA.B.3.3.1, MA.C.1.3.1

- **Use integers in numerical and variable expressions.**
  MA.A.1.3.1, MA.A.1.3.4, MA.A.3.3.1, MA.A.3.3.2, MA.D.2.3.1

- **Use number properties to solve problems.**
  MA.A.1.3.4, MA.A.3.3.1, MA.B.1.3.4, MA.D.2.3.1, MA.E.1.3.2

- **Plot points in a coordinate plane.**
  MA.C.3.3.2, MA.D.2.3.1

- **Write and solve one- and two-step equations.**
  MA.D.1.3.2, MA.D.2.3.1, MA.D.2.3.2

- **Write and solve one-step inequalities.**
  MA.D.1.3.2, MA.D.2.3.1, MA.D.2.3.2

- **Model real-world situations with equations and inequalities.**
  MA.A.3.3.2

From Chapter 3, p. 135

What is the area of the sail?

Variables and Equations

BEFORE

In previous courses you've...

- Compared quantities
- Performed operations on numbers

Now

In Chapter 1 you'll study...

- Using graphs to analyze data
- Evaluating and writing numerical and variable expressions
- Solving equations using mental math
- A four-step problem solving plan

WHY?

So you can solve real-world problems about...

- volcanoes, p. 5
- cliff diving, p. 23
- tiger beetles, p. 35
- parachuting, p. 37

Internet Preview
CLASSZONE.COM

- eEdition Plus Online
- eWorkbook Plus Online
- eTutorial Plus Online
- FCAT Practice
- More Examples

Chapter Warm-Up Games

Review skills you need for this chapter in these quick games.

VACATION VIEWS

Kim	Dave	Ann	Sam
9	4	7.9	8.2
2	8	5.3	4.1
5	6	4.8	6.5
7	3	9.6	9.2
6	7	2.1	1.6

BRAIN GAME

Key Skill:
- Finding the sums of whole numbers and decimals

On a family vacation trip the first stop is a mountain lookout tower. The four ladders lead to the top of the tower. Which child gets to the top first?

- Find the sum of the numbers on the rungs of each ladder.

- The ladder with the least sum is where the fastest person climbs.

NEXT STOP

	415.79		Tens
410 M	420 U	430 E	?
	19.45		Ones
17 D	18 A	19 N	?
	8.178		Hundredths
8.16 A	8.17 T	8.18 H	?
	589.63		Tenths
589.6 C	589.7 R	589.8 S	?
	627.4		Hundreds
600 L	700 E	899 N	?

BrAIN GAME

Key Skills:
- Rounding
- Identifying place value

Help the kids figure out what the next stop is on the family trip by solving the puzzle.

• Each number has been rounded to one of its digits. Select the answer that shows the number rounded correctly.

• On the right, write each letter below the place value it was rounded to.

• Put letters in correct place value order to figure out the next stop.

Stop *and* Think

1. **Critical Thinking** Order the names in *Vacation Views* from who gets to the top first to who gets there last (the least sum to the greatest).

2. **Writing** In *Next Stop*, a student thinks that the result of rounding 8.178 is 8.17 because the last digit is removed. What is wrong with the student's reasoning?

Getting Ready to Learn

Review What You Need to Know

Using Vocabulary **Copy and complete using a review word.**

1. When you add two numbers, the result is called the ? .

2. When you multiply two numbers, the result is called the ? .

Write the place value of the red digit. *(p. 704)*

3. 26.10   4. 45.901   5. 139.07   6. 6.394

Find the sum, difference, product, or quotient. *(p. 709)*

7. 29 + 45   8. 103 + 8   9. 25 − 12   10. 72 − 56

11. 13 × 3   12. 27 × 8   13. 96 ÷ 6   14. 60 ÷ 12

15. 12.7 − 9.4   16. 17.8 + 26.3   17. 9.64 + 6.36   18. 20.24 − 16.5

19. You are shopping for new clothes for school. If you have $75.00 and buy a pair of jeans for $37.75, how much money do you have left? *(p. 709)*

Word Watch

Review Words

whole number, p. 704
sum, p. 709
difference, p. 709
product, p. 713
quotient, p. 715

You should include material that appears on a notebook like this in your own notes.

Know How to Take Notes

Keeping a Notebook Your math notebook is an important tool for learning and reviewing the topics of this course. Here are some tips for organizing your notes. Organize your notes in the same way for each lesson.

> Start with the date and topic.

September 7   Decimals

To add decimals, line up the decimal points.

Example: Adding Decimals

> Copy examples shown in class.

$$
\begin{array}{r}
23.40 \\
+\ 36.15 \\
\hline
59.55
\end{array}
$$

In Lesson 1.4, you should organize your notes by labeling the examples that you copy.

LESSON 1.1

Interpreting Graphs

BEFORE	▶ Now	WHY?
You compared quantities.	You'll use graphs to analyze data.	So you can make conclusions about mall businesses, as in Exs. 6–8.

In the Real World

Word Watch

bar graph, p. 5
data, p. 5
frequency table, p. 6
histogram, p. 6

FLORIDA
Standards and Assessment

• Read and interpret data displays. (MA.E.1.3.1)

• Explain how data displays can affect interpretation of data. (MA.E.1.3.1)

Volcanoes The *bar graph* at the right shows the number of historically active volcanoes in four countries. Which country has the most historically active volcanoes?

A **bar graph** is a type of graph in which the lengths of bars are used to represent and compare *data* in categories. **Data** are information, facts, or numbers that describe something.

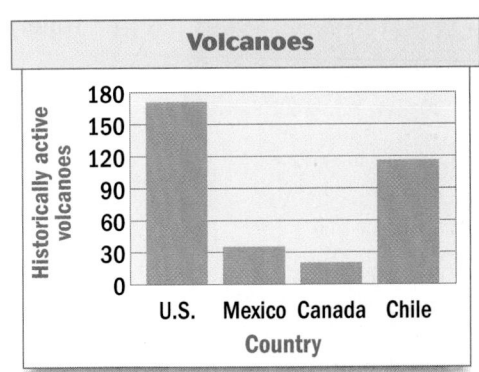

EXAMPLE 1 Interpreting a Bar Graph

Use the bar graph above about volcanoes to answer the question or explain why you can't answer the question using the graph.

a. Which country has the most historically active volcanoes?

b. Which country has the most volcanic eruptions in a given year?

Solution

a. The vertical axis in the bar graph is labeled *Historically active volcanoes*, so the tallest bar represents the country with the most historically active volcanoes. Because the United States has the tallest bar, it has the most historically active volcanoes.

b. Having more historically active volcanoes doesn't necessarily mean having more eruptions, so you can't answer this question from the bar graph.

Your turn now **Use the bar graph about historically active volcanoes.**

1. About how many more historically active volcanoes does Chile have than Mexico?

2. Which country has the least number of historically active volcanoes?

Histograms When you have a large set of data to organize, you may be able to use a **frequency table** to group the data into *intervals*. The frequency of an interval is the number of values in the interval. You can graph data organized into equal intervals in a **histogram**. The height of each bar in a histogram indicates the frequency of an interval.

EXAMPLE 2 **Making a Frequency Table**

Roller Coasters The data show the heights, in meters, of the tallest roller coasters in the world. Make a frequency table of the data.

66.4, 94.5, 68.3, 115, 62.5, 97, 66.4, 126.5, 63.4, 74.7, 63.4, 70.1, 66.4, 64.9, 63.7, 79, 63.4, 63.1, 62.5, 61.9, 71.6

1 Choose intervals of equal size for the data.

2 Tally the data in each interval. Use tally marks to record each occurrence of a height in its interval.

3 Write the frequency for each interval by totaling the tally marks.

Height (m)	Tally	Frequency
60–69.9	JHT JHT III	13
70–79.9	IIII	4
80–89.9		0
90–99.9	II	2
100–109.9		0
110–119.9	I	1
120–129.9	I	1

with Review

For help with data displays, see p. 724.

EXAMPLE 3 **Making a Histogram**

Make a histogram of the data shown in the frequency table in Example 2.

1 Draw and label the horizontal and vertical axes. Start the vertical scale at 0 and end at 15. Use increments of 3.

2 Draw a bar to represent the frequency of each interval. The bars of neighboring intervals should touch.

3 Write a title.

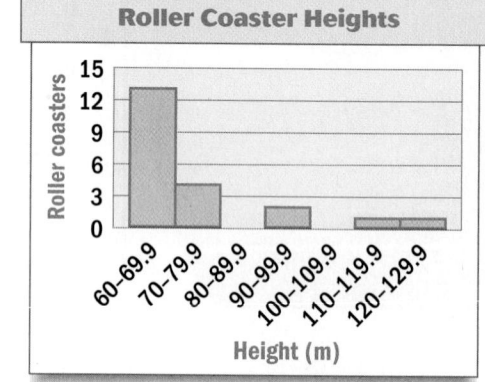

Your turn now

3. Which interval has the greatest number of roller coasters?

4. When the next roller coaster between 60 and 130 meters tall is built, in what interval do you think it will be? Explain.

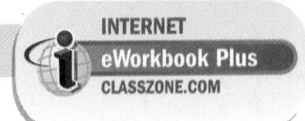
Getting Ready to Practice

1. **Vocabulary** Copy and complete: A histogram is a graph that shows data that are divided equally into ___?___.

In Exercises 2–4, use the graph at the right. It displays the number of times each country has won the World Cup in soccer.

World Cup Winners

[Bar graph showing Wins on vertical axis (0–5) for Uruguay, Italy, W. Germany, Brazil, England, Argentina, France]

2. What type of graph is shown?

3. How many times has Italy won?

4. How many more times has Argentina won than France?

5. **Guided Problem Solving** The frequency table shows when new states were added to the United States. Use the frequency table to make a graph.

   ① Decide what kind of graph to use.

   ② Draw and label horizontal and vertical axes.

   ③ Draw bars. Write a title.

Years	States
1787–1836	25
1837–1886	13
1887–1936	10
1937–1986	2

Practice and Problem Solving

with Homework

Example	Exercises
1	6–10, 15–17
2	12, 18–19
3	12–14, 18–20

Online Resources
CLASSZONE.COM

· More Examples
· eTutorial Plus

Use the bar graph at the right. It shows the number of businesses at a mall in each category.

6. Which category has the greatest number of businesses?

7. Which category has the least number of businesses?

8. About how many more shoe stores are there than jewelry stores?

9. **Writing** Can you tell from the graph which category of businesses uses the most floor space in the mall? Explain.

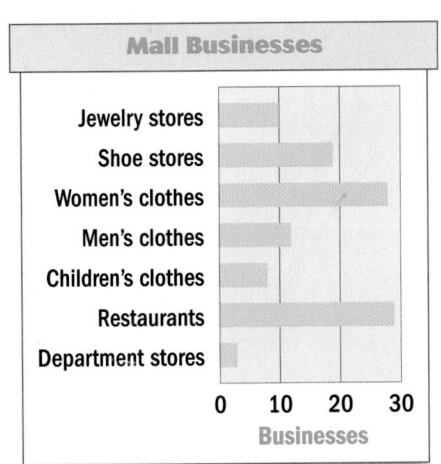

Mall Businesses

[Horizontal bar graph with categories: Jewelry stores, Shoe stores, Women's clothes, Men's clothes, Children's clothes, Restaurants, Department stores; horizontal axis labeled Businesses from 0 to 30]

10. Movies The table shows the numbers of movies released in the United States from 1995 through 2000. Make a bar graph of the data.

Year	1995	1996	1997	1998	1999	2000
Movies	411	471	510	509	461	478

11. Critical Thinking If you need to know an exact amount, is it easier to find this information from a table or a bar graph? Explain.

Meteors **The data show the average numbers of meteors that fall per hour during 39 annual meteor showers. For example, in the first meteor shower, an average of 60 meteors fall each hour.**

60, 4, 1, 5, 5, 1, 40, 4, 5, 20, 2, 15, 8, 6, 21, 15, 20, 30, 3, 15, 10, 62, 25, 26, 50, 12, 20, 12, 15, 30, 10, 10, 20, 12, 12, 60, 10, 12, 20

12. Make a frequency table to organize the data using intervals of 10, starting with 0–9.

13. Make a histogram of the data displayed in the frequency table.

14. Which display would you use to find the number of meteor showers that average 20 to 29 meteors falling per hour? Explain.

Hurricanes **The histogram shows the numbers of hurricanes in the Atlantic Ocean from 1950 through 1999.**

15. About how many hurricanes were there in the Atlantic Ocean from 1980–1989?

16. Can you determine the number of hurricanes there were in the Atlantic Ocean in 1965? Explain.

17. Can you use the histogram to predict the number of hurricanes in 2000–2009? Why or why not?

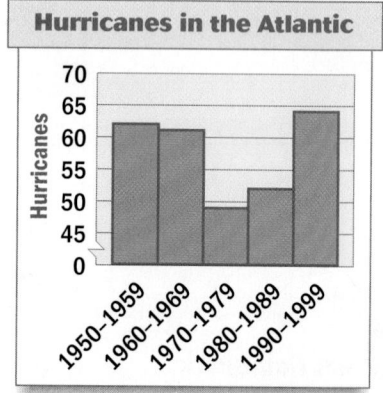

Extended Problem Solving **The data show the numbers of hours 30 students in a class spent on the Internet in a week.**

4, 2.5, 5.7, 1.8, 3.7, 5.4, 5.5, 11.6, 3.7, 6.5, 2, 10, 0.5, 4.5, 5, 9.5, 2.1, 4.5, 7.5, 2.5, 8, 1, 9, 4.2, 8, 7, 3, 7, 5, 6

18. Graph Make a histogram of the data using the intervals 0–1.9, 2–3.9, 4–5.9, 6–7.9, 8–9.9, and 10–11.9.

19. Graph Make a histogram of the data using the intervals 0–2.9, 3–5.9, 6–8.9, and 9–11.9.

20. Compare Does the histogram in Exercise 18 or in Exercise 19 give a clearer representation of the data? Explain your reasoning.

Media In Exercises 21 and 22, use the *double bar graph*. It shows the numbers of U.S. high schools with media activities in 1991 and 1998.

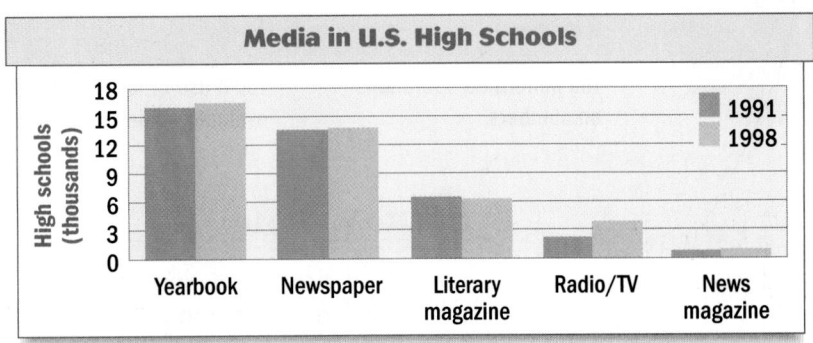

Media in U.S. High Schools

21. About how many of the schools offered radio or TV in 1998?

22. Describe the trends in media at the schools from 1991 to 1998.

23. Challenge What trend do you notice in the number of DVD players sold in the United States shown in the graph at the right? Do you think that this trend continued? Explain your reasoning.

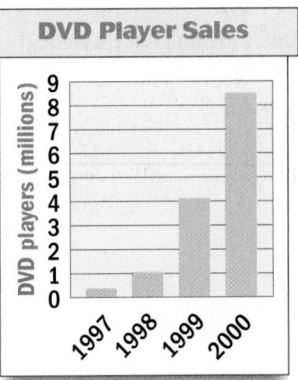

DVD Player Sales

24. Critical Thinking You want to collect data about the pets students in your class have. What data would you collect to make a histogram? What data would you collect to make a bar graph?

Mixed Review

Find the product or quotient. *(p. 713)*

25. 34 × 4   **26.** 6 × 15   **27.** 140 ÷ 20   **28.** 84 ÷ 7

Basic Skills **Find the sum or difference.**

29. 25.8 + 19.64   **30.** 106.58 − 56.33   **31.** 88.7 − 29.92

FCAT Practice

INTERNET

FCAT PRACTICE
CLASSZONE.COM

32. Extended Response The data below are the number of medals the United States has won in each of the Winter Olympic Games since 1924.

4, 7, 12, 4, 9, 11, 7, 10, 6, 7, 8, 10, 12, 8, 6, 11, 13, 13, 34

Create a histogram of the data with intervals of 5 starting with 0–4 and a second histogram with intervals of 10 starting with 0–9. Tell which histogram you would use to predict how many medals the United States will win in the future and why.

Order of Operations

BEFORE	▶ Now	WHY?
You performed operations on numbers.	You'll use order of operations to evaluate numerical expressions.	So you can find how much money to raise for a team, as in Ex. 19.

In the Real World

Word Watch

numerical expression, p. 10
evaluate, p. 10
order of operations, p. 10
verbal model, p. 11

FLORIDA
Standards and Assessment

• Use order of operations.
  (MA.A.3.3.2)

Visiting an Aquarium You and four friends visit an aquarium, but only three of you go to the movie at the aquarium. What is the total cost of the visit? You will find the total cost of the visit in Example 3.

Aquarium Prices	
Admission	$13.50
Sea Lion show	Free
Movie	$8.00

Order of Operations A **numerical expression** consists of numbers and operations. To **evaluate** a numerical expression is to find its value. When a numerical expression has more than one operation, you must use a set of rules called the **order of operations**.

Order of Operations

To evaluate an expression that has more than one operation:

1. Evaluate expressions inside grouping symbols.

2. Multiply and divide from left to right.

3. Add and subtract from left to right.

HELP with Solving

You can express multiplication by using parentheses or the symbols • or ×.
$3(4) = 12$
$3 \cdot 4 = 12$
$3 \times 4 = 12$

EXAMPLE 1 Using the Order of Operations

Evaluate the expression $7 + 16 \cdot 3 \div 6$.

$$7 + 16 \cdot 3 \div 6 = 7 + 48 \div 6 \qquad \text{Multiply 16 by 3.}$$
$$= 7 + 8 \qquad \text{Divide 48 by 6.}$$
$$= 15 \qquad \text{Add 7 and 8.}$$

Grouping Symbols The most common grouping symbols are parentheses ( ), brackets [ ], and fraction bars.

EXAMPLE 2 Using Grouping Symbols

a. $(14 + 6) \cdot 8 = 20 \cdot 8$ Add inside parentheses first.

             $= 160$ Then multiply.

b. $\dfrac{9 \times 8}{4 + 8} = \dfrac{72}{4 + 8}$ Evaluate numerator.

      $= \dfrac{72}{12}$ Evaluate denominator.

      $= 6$ Divide.

c. $45 \div [63 \div (56 \div 8)] = 45 \div [63 \div 7]$ Divide inside the innermost set of grouping symbols.

                  $= 45 \div 9$ Divide inside brackets.

                  $= 5$ Divide.

Your turn now Evaluate the expression.

1. $14 + 6 \div 2$ **2.** $20 - 7 \times 2 + 1$ **3.** $5 \cdot 7 - 2 \cdot 13$

4. $35 \div (9 - 4)$ **5.** $3 \cdot [(11 - 1) \div 5]$ **6.** $\dfrac{45 + 19}{2 \times 8}$

When you solve a problem, it may help to write a **verbal model** using symbols for operations and words to label necessary information.

EXAMPLE 3 Using a Verbal Model

To find the total cost of the visit to the aquarium described on the previous page, you can use a verbal model to write and evaluate an expression.

Total cost of visit	=	Admission price	×	Number of people	+	Movie price	×	Number of people

       $= 13.50 \times 5 + 8 \times 3$ Substitute values.

       $= 67.50 + 24$ Multiply first.

       $= 91.50$ Then add.

ANSWER The total cost of the visit is $91.50.

INTERNET
eWorkbook Plus
CLASSZONE.COM

Getting Ready to Practice

1. **Vocabulary** Use the order of operations to list in order the steps needed to evaluate the following expression: $8 + 2 \times 5 - 4$.

State the first step in evaluating the expression. Then evaluate.

2. $10 \cdot 6 - 20$

3. $5 \times 15 \div 3$

4. $4 + 8 \div 2$

5. $2 \times 5 + (15 - 7)$

6. $6 + 14 - 10 \div 2$

7. $10 \cdot [9 \div (5 - 2)]$

8. **Fundraising Walk** Your friend pledges $10 to you for a fundraising walk and $.25 for each mile you walk. You walk 6 miles. How much money will your friend contribute? Use the expression $10 + 0.25(6)$.

9. **Find the Error** Describe and correct the error in the solution.

$$\begin{aligned} 3 \times 3 + 63 \div 9 &= 9 + 63 \div 9 \\ &= 72 \div 9 \\ &= 8 \end{aligned}$$

Practice and Problem Solving

with Homework

Example	Exercises
1	10–29, 33
2	10–18, 21–29
3	34

Online Resources
CLASSZONE.COM
· More Examples
· eTutorial Plus

Evaluate the expression.

10. $12 + 10 - 4$

11. $7 \cdot 3 + 2 \cdot 4$

12. $\dfrac{16}{7 - 3}$

13. $9 \times 3 + 2 - 5$

14. $16 - 6 + 2 \times 4$

15. $26 - 15 + 8 \div 2$

16. $8 + 2 \times (4 - 3)$

17. $120 \div [(6 + 2) \cdot 3]$

18. $18 \div (8 + 4 - 9)$

19. **Softball Uniforms** Your school softball team has 25 members. The school contributes $30 toward each $40 uniform. To find how much money the team needs to raise, evaluate the expression $40 \cdot 25 - 30 \cdot 25$.

20. **Supplies** You buy 3 notebooks at $2 each and 4 pens at $1.50 each. What is the total cost? Use the expression $3 \times 2 + 4 \times 1.50$.

Evaluate the expression.

21. $\dfrac{7}{4} - \dfrac{5}{4} + \dfrac{1}{4}$

22. $9 \div \left[3 \cdot \left(\dfrac{5}{3} + \dfrac{4}{3} \right) \right]$

23. $3 \cdot \left(\dfrac{7}{2} + \dfrac{1}{2} \right)$

24. $(1.5 - 0.5) \times 2$

25. $9.4 + 4.2 \div 6$

26. $6 \times (2.4 - 0.4 + 3)$

27. $7.8 \times (5 + 2)$

28. $8.4 \div (21 - 14)$

29. $4 + 3.9 \div 1.3$

Critical Thinking Add parentheses to make the statement true.

30. $5 \cdot 2 + 3 - 8 = 17$

31. $12 \div 6 + 4 - 7 = 4$

Extended Problem Solving In Exercises 32–34, suppose Liz and Ty are making cookies for a school bake sale. Liz makes 5 batches of 36 cookies, and Ty makes 4 batches of 48 cookies.

32. Translate Translate *5 batches of 36 cookies plus 4 batches of 48 cookies* into an expression.

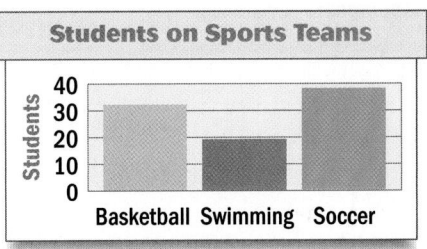

33. Evaluate Evaluate the expression.

34. Extend Liz and Ty decide to make packages of three cookies. Write and evaluate an expression to find the number of packages they can make.

35. Number Sense Complete the statement $12 \underline{\ ?\ } 4 + 2$ using each of the operations $+$, $-$, $\times$, and $\div$. Which operation symbol gives the expression the greatest value? Find the greatest possible value if you add one set of parentheses to the four expressions.

36. Challenge Your cousin is 14 years old. Your brother is 10 years less than twice your cousin's age. Write and evaluate an expression to find your brother's age.

Mixed Review

The bar graph shows the numbers of students on teams. *(Lesson 1.1)*

37. About how many students are on the basketball team?

38. Which team has the most students?

Students on Sports Teams

Basic Skills Find the missing number.

39. $11 - \underline{\ ?\ } = 7$

40. $\underline{\ ?\ } \div 4 = 8$

41. $9 \cdot \underline{\ ?\ } = 54$

FCAT Practice FCAT

42. Multiple Choice In what order should the operations be performed in the expression $3 + (10 \div 2) \times 4 - 5$?

    A. $\div, +, -, \times$ **B.** $\div, \times, +, -$ **C.** $\times, +, \div, -$ **D.** $+, \div, \times, -$

43. Multiple Choice Which operation should be performed first when finding *the sum of three and the product of two and six*?

    F. $2 \cdot 6$ **G.** $3 + 2$ **H.** $3 \cdot 2$ **I.** $2 + 6$

Technology Activity

FLORIDA: Standards and Assessment
Use order of operations. (MA.A.3.3.2)

Using Order of Operations

GOAL Use a calculator to evaluate numerical expressions with decimals.

Example You and three friends are ordering a pizza. The cost of the pizza is $15.90, but you have a coupon for $1.50 off. How much should each of you pay if you want to divide the total cost equally?

Solution

Cost per person $= \dfrac{\text{Price of a pizza} - \text{Coupon}}{\text{Number of friends} + \text{Yourself}}$ **Write a verbal model.**

$= \dfrac{15.90 - 1.50}{3 + 1}$ **Substitute.**

To find the cost per person, use the order of operations.

Keystrokes   **Display**

(15.90 − 1.50) ÷ (3 + 1) =   **3.6**

ANSWER Each person should pay $3.60 for the pizza.

HELP with Technology

The keystrokes shown here may not be the same as on your calculator. See your calculator's instruction manual for the appropriate keystrokes.

Your turn now   Use a calculator to evaluate the expression.

1. $62 + 7 \times 6.4$ **2.** $8.32 - 9 \div 2$

3. $6.8 \div 4 + 15.9 \div 3$ **4.** $36.2 - 4.3 \cdot 5$

5. $\dfrac{14 + 11}{4 + 1}$ **6.** $\dfrac{20 - 3.5}{10.3 - 7}$ **7.** $\dfrac{10}{3.8 + 1.2}$ **8.** $\dfrac{17.7 - 13.7}{0.2 + 4.8}$

9. Snacks You buy 3 bags of snack mix for $1.49 each, 2 boxes of raisins for $1.79 each, and lemonade for $2.39. Find the total cost using the expression $3 \cdot 1.49 + 2 \cdot 1.79 + 2.39$.

10. Clothing You buy 3 T-shirts at $9.99 each, a pair of sneakers for $44.89, a hat for $10.59, and a pair of socks at a cost of 4 pairs for $8.60. Find the total cost.

11. Music You pick out 2 CDs for $12.99 each, 3 CDs for $9.49 each, and a CD for $15.97. At the register you find out that when you buy 5 CDs you get the sixth CD for half off. Find the total cost if you get the most expensive CD for half off. Round to the nearest cent.

LESSON 1.3

Variables and Expressions

You evaluated numerical expressions.

You'll write and evaluate variable expressions.

So you can find how far you travel on a bike, as in Exs. 23–24.

Word Watch

variable, p. 15
variable expression, p. 15

FLORIDA
Standards and Assessment

• Translate and evaluate algebraic expressions. (MA.D.2.3.1)

• Use variables in real-world problems. (MA.D.1.3.1)

In the Real World

Hot Air Balloons You are riding in a hot air balloon. After traveling 5 miles, the balloon speed changes to 6 miles per hour. What is the total distance you travel if the balloon stays at this speed for 1 hour? for 2 hours? You will find the answer in Example 1.

Variable Expressions A **variable** is a symbol, usually a letter, that represents one or more numbers. A **variable expression** consists of numbers, variables, and operations. To evaluate a variable expression, substitute a number for each variable. Then find the value of the numerical expression.

You can write the product of a number and a variable by writing the number next to that variable. For example, you can write $5 \cdot n$ as $5n$.

EXAMPLE 1 **Using a Variable Expression**

To answer the questions above about distance traveled, let t represent the time in hours that the balloon travels at 6 miles per hour. So, the total distance traveled is *original distance + speed · time*, which is $5 + 6t$.

① Write hours traveled t.	② Substitute for t in the expression $5 + 6t$.	③ Evaluate to find total distance.
1	$5 + 6(1)$	11
2	$5 + 6(2)$	17

ANSWER If the balloon travels at 6 miles per hour for 1 hour, you travel a total of 11 miles. After 2 hours you travel a total of 17 miles.

 Use the information above about hot air balloons.

1. If you travel for 3 hours more, what is the total distance?

2. If you travel for $\frac{1}{2}$ hour more, what is the total distance?

EXAMPLE 2 **Evaluating Variable Expressions**

Evaluate the expression when $x = 8$ and $y = 2$.

a. $7x + 15 = 7(8) + 15$ Substitute 8 for x.

$= 56 + 15$ Multiply.

$= 71$ Add.

b. $3x - 5y = 3(8) - 5(2)$ Substitute 8 for x and 2 for y.

$= 24 - 10$ Multiply.

$= 14$ Subtract.

Writing Expressions Many words and phrases suggest mathematical operations. The following common words and phrases indicate addition, subtraction, multiplication, and division.

Addition	Subtraction	Multiplication	Division
plus	minus	times	divided by
the sum of	the difference of	the product of	the quotient of
increased by	decreased by	multiplied by	per
total	fewer than	of	
more than	less than		
added to	subtracted from		

EXAMPLE 3 **Translating Verbal Phrases**

with Reading

Order is important when translating verbal expressions that suggest subtraction and division. *The difference of a number and 6 means $n - 6$, not $6 - n$. The quotient of a number and 10 means $n \div 10$, not $10 \div n$.*

Verbal Phrase	Variable Expression
The sum of a number and 9	$n + 9$
The difference of a number and 21	$n - 21$
The product of 6 and a number	$6n$
The quotient of 48 and a number	$\dfrac{48}{n}$
One third of a number	$\dfrac{1}{3}n$

Your turn now   **Evaluate the expression when $a = 12$ and $b = 3$.**

3. $9a$ **4.** ab **5.** $b(a - 6)$ **6.** $\dfrac{6a}{a - b}$

Write the phrase as a variable expression using x.

7. a number increased by 15   **8.** 8 times a number

What do you think?

Sports

Heart Rate

To find a reasonable target heart rate during exercise, subtract your age from 220, then multiply that number by 0.7. What is your target heart rate?

EXAMPLE 4 **Writing and Evaluating an Expression**

Heart Rate To measure your heart rate in beats per minute, count the number of heartbeats n in 15 seconds. Then multiply by 4 to find your heart rate in beats per minute.

a. Use n to write an expression for heart rate in beats per minute.

b. You count 18 beats in 15 seconds. Find your heart rate.

Solution

a. The phrase *multiply by* suggests multiplication. So, the variable expression for heart rate in beats per minute is $4n$.

b. Substitute 18 for n in the expression $4n$ to find your heart rate.

$$4n = 4(18)$$
$$= 72$$

ANSWER Your heart rate is 72 beats per minute.

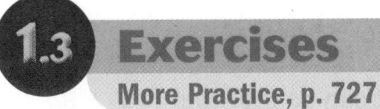

1.3 Exercises

More Practice, p. 727

INTERNET
eWorkbook Plus
CLASSZONE.COM

Getting Ready to Practice

1. **Vocabulary** Copy and complete: $3t - 4$ is a(n) _?_ expression and $5 + 13$ is a(n) _?_ expression.

Match the phrase with the correct variable expression.

2. 8 times a number   **A.** $n + 8$

3. 8 fewer than a number   **B.** $8n$

4. a number increased by 8   **C.** $n - 8$

5. the quotient of 8 and a number   **D.** $8 \div n$

Evaluate the expression when $p = 6$ and $s = 5$.

6. $11p$ 7. $7s + 9$ 8. $6s + 4p$ 9. $\dfrac{50 - s}{p + 3}$

10. **Guided Problem Solving** You buy a hat for $8 and rent 5 videos for $2.50 each. How much do you spend?

   (**1** Write a variable expression for the cost to rent m videos.

   (**2** Add the cost of the hat to this expression.

   (**3** Evaluate the expression for $m = 5$.

Practice and Problem Solving

 with Homework

Example	Exercises
1	23-24
2	11-18, 29-36
3	19-22
4	26-28

 Online Resources
CLASSZONE.COM

· More Examples
· eTutorial Plus

Evaluate the expression for the given value(s) of the variable(s).

11. $4x - 5$, $x = 7$

12. $10n + 115$, $n = 9$

13. $11c + 34$, $c = 0.5$

14. $2s - t$, $s = 8$, $t = 4$

15. $p + 2q$, $p = 3$, $q = 1$

16. $8a - 3b$, $a = 3$, $b = 8$

17. $\frac{3}{4}x + y$, $x = 4$, $y = 3$

18. $\frac{d + 10}{c - d}$, $c = 14$, $d = 8$

Translate Write the phrase as a variable expression. Let x represent the variable.

19. two fifths of a number

20. a number subtracted from 10

21. 12 increased by a number

22. the quotient of a number and 7

Bicycling Evaluate the expression $9t$ to find how many miles you go if you ride your bike for t hours at 9 miles per hour.

23. How far do you go if you ride your bike for 2 hours?

24. How far do you go if you ride your bike for $3\frac{1}{2}$ hours?

25. Writing Write a real world situation that can be modeled by $2 + 8d$.

26. Television You watch x thirty-minute TV shows and y sixty-minute TV shows in one week. Write a variable expression representing the total number of minutes you spend watching television that week.

27. CD Club You are purchasing CDs from a music club. You pay $4 for shipping any number n of CDs, plus $17 for each CD. Write a variable expression for the cost of n CDs. Then find the cost of 6 CDs.

28. Estimation A 17 inch vine grows 3 inches per week. Write a variable expression for the length of the vine after w weeks. Then estimate the vine's length after 19 weeks.

Evaluate the expression when $x = 2.4$ and $y = 8$.

29. $7x + 2y$

30. $y - 2x$

31. $5xy$

32. $\frac{y}{x - 0.4}$

33. $4x - y$

34. $7.2y \div x$

35. $\frac{3y}{x}$

36. $1.6xy$

37. Writing Write a variable expression that requires the use of the order of operations to evaluate correctly. Explain the correct order to use.

38. Nutrition Rice has 13 grams of protein per serving, beans have 15 grams per serving, and an orange has 2 grams per serving. Write a variable expression for the total grams of protein in x servings of rice, y servings of beans, and z oranges.

39. Movies At the movies, popcorn costs $2.75 and drinks cost $1.25. Write an expression to find the total cost of *p* popcorns and *d* drinks. Find the total cost for snacks if 3 people buy popcorn and 4 people buy drinks.

40. Challenge Evaluate the expression $\dfrac{5(3x + 2z + 0.5425)}{x + y + z}$ when $x = 1.05$, $y = 1.3$, and $z = 0.9$.

Mixed Review

Evaluate the expression. *(Lesson 1.2)*

41. $12 \cdot 3 + 14$ **42.** $93 - 74 \div 2$ **43.** $16 + 6 \cdot 3 \div 2 - 7$

Basic Skills **Find the product or quotient.**

44. $17 \cdot 52$ **45.** $91 \cdot 45$ **46.** $123 \div 3$ **47.** $252 \div 6$

FCAT Practice

48. Short Response Admission to a fair costs $19. Games at the fair cost $2. Write an expression to represent the total cost for admission and *g* games. Pat goes to the fair and plays six games. Evaluate your expression to determine the total amount of money Pat spent.

49. Multiple Choice You have one hour forty minutes to finish a test that has 50 questions. You want to divide your time evenly among all of the questions. How many minutes should you spend on each question?

A. 1 minute **B.** 2 minutes **C.** 3 minutes **D.** 4 minutes

Find the Key

A key will unlock a door if the variable expressions on the door have the same value when the number on the key is substituted for the variable.

Which key opens each door?

Powers and Exponents

BEFORE	Now	WHY?
You evaluated numerical and variable expressions.	You'll evaluate expressions with powers.	So you can find the height of a cliff, as in Example 3.

In the Real World

Word Watch

power, p. 20
exponent, p. 20
base, p. 20

FLORIDA
Standards and Assessment
• Evaluate expressions with exponents. (MA.A.2.3.1)
• Use order of operations. (MA.A.3.3.2)

Waterfall A stone falls over the edge of a cliff next to a waterfall. The stone hits the water 5 seconds later. How tall is the cliff?

To find the height of the cliff, you will use an expression with a *power* in Example 3. A **power** is a product with a repeated factor. The **exponent** tells how many times the **base** is used as a factor.

Base   Exponent

$$b^8 = \underbrace{b \cdot b \cdot b \cdot b \cdot b \cdot b \cdot b \cdot b}_{b \text{ is a factor } 8 \text{ times.}}$$

Power

EXAMPLE 1 Reading Powers

Power	Repeated Multiplication	Description in Words
4^2	$4 \cdot 4$	4 to the *second power*, or 4 *squared*
9^3	$9 \cdot 9 \cdot 9$	9 to the *third power*, or 9 *cubed*
y^5	$y \cdot y \cdot y \cdot y \cdot y$	y to the *fifth power*

Taughannock Falls State Park, New York

EXAMPLE 2 Evaluating a Power

Evaluate five cubed.

$$5^3 = 5 \cdot 5 \cdot 5 \qquad \text{Write 5 as a factor 3 times.}$$
$$= 125 \qquad \text{Multiply.}$$

Your turn now Write the product as a power.

1. $7 \times 7 \times 7 \times 7 \times 7 \times 7$ **2.** $10 \cdot 10 \cdot 10 \cdot 10$ **3.** $w \cdot w$

Describe the power in words and then evaluate.

4. 6^3 **5.** 2^5 **6.** 13^2 **7.** 3^1

Order of Operations When you evaluate expressions with powers, evaluate any powers before multiplying or dividing.

Order of Operations

1. Evaluate expressions inside grouping symbols.
2. Evaluate powers.
3. Multiply and divide from left to right.
4. Add and subtract from left to right.

EXAMPLE 3 **Using a Power**

To find the height of the cliff from the previous page, use the expression $16t^2$. This expression gives the distance in feet that an object has fallen t seconds after it begins to fall.

$$16t^2 = 16(5)^2 \qquad \text{Substitute 5 for } t.$$
$$= 16(25) \qquad \text{Evaluate the power.}$$
$$= 400 \qquad \text{Multiply.}$$

ANSWER The height of the cliff is 400 feet.

HELP with Notetaking

In your notes, you may want to label the different examples that you copy.

EXAMPLE 4 **Using the Order of Operations**

Evaluate the expression.

a. $(6-4)^3 + 5 - 3^2 = 2^3 + 5 - 3^2$ Evaluate inside grouping symbols.
$$= 8 + 5 - 9 \qquad \text{Evaluate powers.}$$
$$= 4 \qquad \text{Add and subtract from left to right.}$$

b. $2 \cdot (7+1)^2 \div 4^2 = 2 \cdot 8^2 \div 4^2$ Evaluate inside grouping symbols.
$$= 2 \cdot 64 \div 16 \qquad \text{Evaluate powers.}$$
$$= 8 \qquad \text{Multiply and divide from left to right.}$$

Your turn now Evaluate the expression.

8. $(5-2)^3 - 7 + 4^3$ **9.** $12 + (4+2)^2 - 2^4$ **10.** $7^3 + 24 \div (7-6)^4$

11. Use the expression in Example 3 to find the height of a cliff if a stone hits the water 8 seconds after falling over the edge.

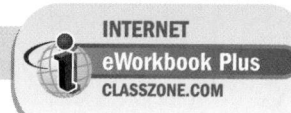

Getting Ready to Practice

1. Vocabulary Write a power and label the base and the exponent.

Evaluate the power.

2. three squared   **3.** eleven cubed   **4.** one to the ninth

5. 2^6 **6.** 5^5 **7.** 0^7

Evaluate the expression.

8. $(2 + 1)^4 \div 9 - 4$ **9.** $48 \div (9 - 7)^3$ **10.** $(5 \times 3)^2 - 4$

11. Find the Error Describe and correct the error in the solution.

$$7^2 = 7 \times 2$$
$$= 14$$

Practice and Problem Solving

Write the product as a power and describe the power in words.

12. $9 \cdot 9 \cdot 9 \cdot 9 \cdot 9$ **13.** $3 \cdot 3 \cdot 3$ **14.** $n \cdot n \cdot n \cdot n \cdot n \cdot n$

Evaluate the power.

15. 6^1 **16.** 11^2 **17.** 2^7

18. 10^3 **19.** 1^8 **20.** 20^2

Evaluate the expression.

21. $(2 \times 5)^2 + 9$ **22.** $500 \div (12 - 7)^1$ **23.** $6 \times 18 \div 3^2$

24. $(9 - 7)^5 + 17$ **25.** $108 \div (5 + 1)^2$ **26.** $9^2 - 3^3$

Evaluate the expression when $g = 4$.

27. $g^4 \div 16$ **28.** $(3 + g)^3$ **29.** $(3g)^2 - 25$

30. Critical Thinking If $x^2 = x^3$, give the two possible values for x.

31. Football The season attendance at your school's football games is 1000 people one year. The attendance doubles each year for the next 3 years. Write an expression with a power that shows the season attendance at the football games after 3 years.

Copy and complete the statement using <, >, or =.

32. $3^2 \ \underline{?} \ 2^3$ **33.** $5^4 \ \underline{?} \ 4^5$ **34.** $10^1 \ \underline{?} \ 1^{10}$

 Evaluate the expression when $x = 4.2$, $y = 5.9$, and $z = 11.8$.

35. $y^2 - x^2$ **36.** $10z^2 \div y$ **37.** $(x + y)^3$

38. Writing Describe how to find the value of 3^9 using the fact that $3^8 = 6561$.

39. Cliff Diving At Kaunolo in Hawaii, divers jump from a platform on top of a cliff 82 feet above the water. At time t seconds, a diver has fallen $16t^2$ feet. Do the divers reach the surface of the water in 2 seconds? Explain your reasoning.

Evaluate the expression when $a = 3$, $b = 7$, and $c = 11$.

40. a^3b^2 **41.** $(c - a)^3 - 210$ **42.** $2 \cdot (b + 2)^2 \div a$

43. Challenge The personal computers of the early 1980s had 64 kilobytes of memory. Computers today often have more than one gigabyte of memory. Use the table to find how much memory personal computers of the early 1980s had in bytes.

Name	Bytes
Kilobyte	2^{10}
Megabyte	2^{20}
Gigabyte	2^{30}

Mixed Review

Evaluate the expression when $x = 3$ and $y = 9$. *(Lesson 1.3)*

44. $5x - 12$ **45.** $6x - y$ **46.** $\dfrac{y}{x} + 20$

Choose a Strategy **Use a strategy from the list to solve the following problem. Explain your choice of strategy.**

> Problem Solving Strategies
> ---
> ■ Look for a Pattern
> ■ Draw a Diagram
> ■ Make a List

47. You have 3 shirts and 2 pairs of pants that you are packing for a trip. You can wear each shirt with each pair of pants. How many different outfits are possible?

FCAT Practice

48. Multiple Choice What is the value of the expression $77 - (9 - 2)^2$?

     A. 0   **B.** 11   **C.** 28   **D.** 70

49. Multiple Choice The *volume* of a cube is s^3, where s is the length of one side of the cube. The length of one side of a cube is 12 centimeters. What is the volume of the cube in cubic centimeters?

     F. 36   **G.** 144   **H.** 1200   **I.** 1728

Notebook Review

Review the vocabulary definitions in your notebook.

Copy the review examples in your notebook. Then complete the exercises.

Check Your Definitions

bar graph, p. 5	numerical expression, p. 10	variable, p. 15
data, p. 5	evaluate, p. 10	variable expression, p. 15
frequency table, p. 6	order of operations, p. 10	power, p. 20
histogram, p. 6	verbal model, p. 11	exponent, base, p. 20

Use Your Vocabulary

1. What is the first step in the order of operations?

1.1 Can you analyze data displays?

EXAMPLE The bar graph shows the average depths of the Great Lakes. Which of the lakes has the greatest average depth?

ANSWER Lake Superior has the longest bar, so it has the greatest average depth.

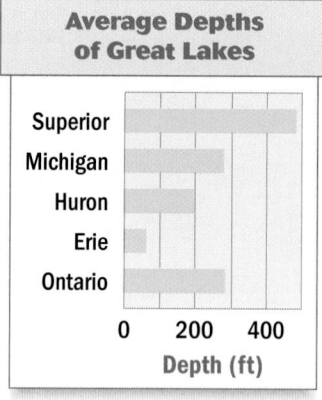

Average Depths of Great Lakes

Superior
Michigan
Huron
Erie
Ontario

0   200   400
Depth (ft)

☑ **Use the bar graph above to answer the question or explain why you can't answer the question using the graph.**

2. Which of the Great Lakes is the largest in area?

3. Which Great Lake is the shallowest on average?

1.2–1.3 Can you evaluate variable expressions?

EXAMPLE Evaluate the expression $4x - y + 12$ when $x = 7$ and $y = 10$.

$$4x - y + 12 = 4(7) - 10 + 12 \qquad \text{Substitute 7 for } x \text{ and 10 for } y.$$
$$= 28 - 10 + 12 \qquad \text{Multiply.}$$
$$= 30 \qquad \text{Add and subtract from left to right.}$$

☑ **Evaluate the expression when $x = 3$ and $y = 6$.**

4. $(x + 3) \cdot x$

5. $\dfrac{3y - 9}{x}$

6. $5 + y \div x$

1.4 Can you evaluate expressions with powers?

Review

EXAMPLE Evaluate the expression $4^3 \div (2 \times 2)^2$.

$$4^3 \div (2 \times 2)^2 = 4^3 \div 4^2 \qquad \text{Multiply inside parentheses.}$$

$$= 64 \div 16 \qquad \text{Evaluate powers.}$$

$$= 4 \qquad \text{Divide.}$$

☑ **Evaluate.**

7. $9 \times 2^3 - 15$ **8.** $(2^5 + 8) \cdot 5^2$ **9.** $(18 \div 6)^3 + (11 - 4)^3$

 Stop *and* **Think** about Lessons 1.1–1.4

10. Critical Thinking The numbers 100 and 1000 can be written as 10^2 and 10^3. How does the number of zeros relate to the exponents of these powers of 10?

Review Quiz 1

1. Home Runs The table shows the record number of home runs hit in a single season by position. Make a bar graph that displays the data.

Position	Home Runs
Catcher	41
1st base	69
Pitcher	9
2nd base	42
Shortstop	52
3rd base	48
Outfield	73

2. How many more home runs is the record for outfield than for pitcher?

Evaluate the expression.

3. $21 - 2 \cdot 7$ **4.** $8 \times 10 - 40 + 25$ **5.** $24 - (9 + 7) \div 4$

6. $(3 + 1)^2 - 1^5$ **7.** $10^4 \div 5^3$ **8.** $3^4 + 7 \cdot 5$

9. Plants A plant is 14 inches tall and grows 4 inches each year. Another plant is 8 inches tall and grows 6 inches each year. Write variable expressions for the plants' heights. Then evaluate the expressions to find the heights in 5 years.

Evaluate the expression for the given value of the variable.

10. $5a - 3 + 7$ when $a = 4$ **11.** $8 + b + 4 \cdot 11$ when $b = 3$

12. $2 \cdot z^4 \div 8$ when $z = 4$ **13.** $(9 - x)^5 \cdot 3 - 16$ when $x = 7$

Problem Solving Strategies

FLORIDA: Standards and Assessment
Solve real-world problems. (MA.A.3.3.2) Estimate to predict results. (MA.A.4.3.1)

Guess, Check, and Revise

- Look for a Pattern
- Draw a Diagram
- Act It Out
- Work Backward
- **Guess, Check, and Revise**
- Make a Table
- Solve a Simpler Problem

Problem Consecutive numbers are numbers that follow one after another. The numbers 1, 2, and 3 are consecutive numbers. The sum of three consecutive numbers is 66. What are these numbers?

❶ Read and Understand

Read the problem carefully.

The problem asks for the three consecutive numbers that add up to 66.

❷ Make a Plan

Decide on a strategy to use.

One way to solve the problem is to use the guess, check, and revise strategy. Guess the answer and check it to see if you are correct. If not, revise your guess and try again.

❸ Solve the Problem

Reread the problem. Then make a guess, check the answer, and revise, if necessary.

Reasoning	Guess	Check
Because 22 is one third of 66, you might choose 22, 23, and 24 for the first guess.	22, 23, 24	$22 + 23 + 24 = 69$ ✗
Because the first guess was too high, revise your guess using smaller numbers.	20, 21, 22	$20 + 21 + 22 = 63$ ✗
Second guess is too low. Try again.	21, 22, 23	$21 + 22 + 23 = 66$ ✓

So, the consecutive numbers that add up to 66 are 21, 22, and 23.

❹ Look Back

Check your answer by adding the numbers again to see if their sum is 66.

$$21 + 22 + 23 \stackrel{?}{=} 66$$
$$66 = 66 \checkmark$$

Use the strategy *guess, check, and revise.*

1. **Consecutive Numbers** The sum of two consecutive numbers divided by 3 is 71. What are the numbers?

2. **Money** There are some nickels, dimes, and quarters in your pocket. You know you have exactly 15 coins, exactly 5 of them are nickels, and the total amount is $2.30. How many dimes do you have? How many quarters?

3. **Game** You are playing a game where you collect blue chips and green chips. For every blue chip you get one point. For every green chip you lose a point. If you have a total of 20 chips and a total of 14 points, how many blue chips do you have? How many green chips do you have?

4. **Video Game** Damon has saved $33 to buy a new video game that costs $52. His mother offers to contribute $5. How much more does he need to save?

5. **Triangle** Copy the triangle below. Fill in the circles using each of the numbers 1, 2, 3, 4, 5, 6, and 7 exactly once so that the sum of each side and the sum of the middle column is 10.

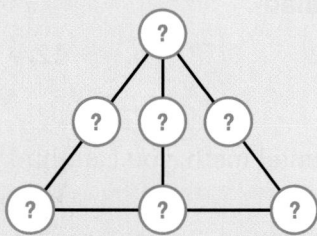

6. **Fundraising** You sell 14 items for a school fundraiser and make a total of $142. A T-shirt costs $11 and a hat costs $9. How many T-shirts did you sell? How many hats did you sell?

Mixed Problem Solving

Use any strategy to solve the problem.

7. **Ice Cream** An ice cream shop offers week-long special deals when you purchase a large ice cream cake. They offer a free small ice cream cake every fifth week, a free pint of ice cream every sixth week, and a free ice cream cone every third week. How many times in one year will they offer all three deals in the same week if they offer all three the first week of the year?

8. **Flowers** Hannah is in charge of buying carnations to give away at a school dance. The flower shop sells carnations at a discount in groups of 12. Hannah needs 170 carnations for the dance. How many groups of 12 carnations should she buy?

9. **Height** Justin, Bob, Kelly, Michelle, and Tim are all different heights. Kelly is taller than Michelle and Justin. Tim is shorter than Justin but taller than Michelle. Bob is the tallest of the group. Put the students in order from tallest to shortest.

10. **Talent Show** Your school talent show allows people to sign up for 3 or 5 minute acts. There is one minute between acts. The talent show has 15 acts and lasts for 79 minutes. How many 3 minute acts are there?

Equations and Solutions

BEFORE	Now	WHY?
You wrote and evaluated variable expressions.	You'll write and solve equations using mental math.	So you can find the weight of a baby elephant, as in Ex. 29.

Word Watch

equation, p. 28
solution, p. 28
solving an equation, p. 28

FLORIDA
Standards and Assessment

• Translate words into algebraic equations. (MA.D.2.3.1)

• Solve and evaluate equations. (MA.D.2.3.1)

Activity **You can use algebra tiles to solve equations.**

In an *equation*, the quantities on each side of the equal sign have the same value. The algebra tile model below represents the equation $x + 2 = 6$.

(1) With how many 1-tiles should you replace the *x*-tile so that the quantities on both sides of the equal sign have the same value? Explain.

(2) What value of *x* makes the equation $x + 2 = 6$ a true statement?

Make a model to represent the equation. Then tell what value of *x* makes the equation a true statement.

   1. $x + 3 = 8$ **2.** $x + 4 = 5$ **3.** $6 + x = 10$

An **equation** is a mathematical sentence formed by placing an equal sign (=) between two expressions.

A **solution** of a variable equation is a number that you can substitute for a variable to make the equation true. Finding all the solutions of an equation is called **solving an equation** .

EXAMPLE 1 **Using Mental Math to Solve Equations**

Solve the equation using mental math.

  a. $15 - n = 4$ **b.** $8x = 32$ **c.** $r \div 12 = 4$

Solution

To solve simple equations using mental math, you can think of the equation as a question.

    a. 15 minus what number equals 4? $15 - 11 = 4$, so $n = 11$.

    b. 8 times what number equals 32? $8(4) = 32$, so $x = 4$.

    c. What number divided by 12 equals 4? $48 \div 12 = 4$, so $r = 48$.

EXAMPLE 2 Checking Solutions of Equations

Tell whether the value of the variable is a solution of $n - 8 = 20$.

a. $n = 12$ **b.** $n = 28$

Solution

Substitute for n and then simplify.

a. $n - 8 = 20$ **b.** $n - 8 = 20$

$12 - 8 \overset{?}{=} 20$ $28 - 8 \overset{?}{=} 20$

$4 \neq 20$ $20 = 20$

ANSWER 12 is not a solution of $n - 8 = 20$, and 28 is a solution.

HELP with Reading

The $\overset{?}{=}$ symbol means *are these values equal?* The $\neq$ symbol means *is not equal to.*

Your turn now Solve the equation using mental math.

1. $5x = 45$ **2.** $16 + n = 21$ **3.** $t \div 6 = 9$

Tell whether the value of the variable is a solution of the equation.

4. $a + 9 = 16$; $a = 7$ **5.** $88 \div y = 8$; $y = 8$ **6.** $7n = 13$; $n = 2$

What do you think?

New Year's

■ **Times Square**

The Times Square New Year's Eve Ball in New York City has a total of 696 lights. Of these, 168 are on the exterior and 432 are on the interior. The remaining lights are strobe lights. How many strobe lights are there?

EXAMPLE 3 Writing an Equation

Times Square The Times Square New Year's Eve Ball drops a total of 77 feet in 60 seconds. After 54 seconds the ball has dropped 69 feet. How many more feet will the ball drop?

Solution

You can use a verbal model to write an equation. Let d represent the distance left to drop.

Total distance ball drops		Distance ball has dropped		Distance left to drop	
77	=	69	+	d	Substitute.
77	=	69	+	**8**	Use mental math.

Write a verbal model.

ANSWER Because $d = 8$, the ball will drop 8 more feet.

✓ **Check** You can check your answer by finding the sum of 8 and 69.

$8 + 69 \overset{?}{=} 77$

$77 = 77$ ✓

Getting Ready to Practice

1. Vocabulary Give an example of an equation with a variable. Explain how to find the solution of the equation.

Solve the equation using mental math.

2. $9 + p = 21$ **3.** $y - 10 = 34$ **4.** $7x = 77$ **5.** $56 \div k = 8$

Tell whether the value of the variable is a solution of the equation.

6. $35 - x = 21; x = 16$ **7.** $75 \div x = 5; x = 15$

8. $x + 29 = 42; x = 13$ **9.** $7x = 84; x = 14$

10. Fireworks Your town's fireworks show cost $1000 per minute. The total cost was $25,000. Use a verbal model to write and solve an equation to find how many minutes the fireworks show lasted.

Practice and Problem Solving

HELP with Homework

Example	Exercises
1	11–14, 19–26
2	15–18
3	27

Online Resources
CLASSZONE.COM
· More Examples
· eTutorial Plus

Match the equation with the corresponding question.

11. $24 \div t = 8$ **A.** What number divided by 24 equals 8?

12. $t + 8 = 24$ **B.** 24 divided by what number equals 8?

13. $24t = 8$ **C.** What number plus 8 equals 24?

14. $\dfrac{t}{24} = 8$ **D.** 24 times what number equals 8?

Tell whether the value of the variable is a solution of the equation.

15. $15 + b = 28; b = 13$ **16.** $37 - d = 14; d = 21$

17. $6w = 72; w = 14$ **18.** $9c = 108; c = 12$

Solve the equation using mental math.

19. $z + 8 = 19$ **20.** $6m = 48$ **21.** $c - 16 = 13$ **22.** $51 \div k = 3$

23. $\dfrac{32}{n} = 16$ **24.** $26 - r = 17$ **25.** $10y = 150$ **26.** $7 + x = 31$

27. Rainfall The highest recorded rainfall in the United States in a 24 hour period is 43 inches. Write an equation to find how much more rain needs to fall in the remaining time to equal the record, if 14 inches has already fallen in less than 24 hours. Then solve the equation.

28. Writing Explain how you would tell whether 5 is a solution of the equation $4x = 20$.

29. Elephants A baby elephant at the Bronx Zoo would get on a scale only with its mother. The zoo weighed the mother as 5033 pounds. They weighed the mother and the baby together as 5396 pounds. Write and solve an equation to find the weight of the baby elephant.

30. Measurement Describe how you could use mental math to find the number of feet in 3600 inches.

31. Invitations You are writing invitations to a party. It takes you four minutes to complete each invitation. Write and solve an equation to find how many invitations you can complete in one hour.

32. Guess, Check, and Revise Find the value of x that makes the equation below true.

$$[(x + 3) \cdot 4 - 7] \div 3 = 3$$

Challenge Tell which of the given values is a solution of the equation.

33. $3x + 6 = x + 12$; $x = 1, 2, 3$ **34.** $2x - 7 = x + 1$; $x = 8, 9, 10$

35. $8 - 4x = 4x$; $x = 0, 1, 2$ **36.** $2x - 4.5 = x \div 2$; $x = 3, 4, 5$

37. Marathon To qualify for the Boston Marathon, Hillary has to run a qualifying time of 3 hours 40 minutes or less. Her best time so far is 4 hours 5 minutes. Write and solve an equation to find by how many minutes Hillary must improve her time to qualify.

Mixed Review

Evaluate the expression when $y = 8$. *(Lesson 1.3)*

38. $7y + 17$ **39.** $(36 - 24) \cdot y$ **40.** $y \cdot 4 + 20 \cdot y$

Basic Skills Estimate the sum or difference.

41. $8748 - 3109$ **42.** $876 + 622$ **43.** $147 + 89 + 791$

FCAT Practice

44. Multiple Choice Which of the following is a solution of $x - 12 = 24$?

   A. 2   **B.** 12   **C.** 36   **D.** 48

45. Short Response Sara and Mary Kate are sisters. Sara is 5 years older than Mary Kate. Sara is 24 years old. Write an equation that could be used to determine Mary Kate's age. Then solve the equation to find Mary Kate's age.

Hands-on Activity

GOAL
Develop formulas for finding the areas of rectangles and squares.

MATERIALS
· square tiles

FLORIDA: Standards and Assessment
Know the properties of two-dimensional figures. (MA.C.1.3.1) Make and test conjectures about geometric relationships. (MA.C.3.3.1)

Modeling Area

You can use square tiles to find the *areas* of rectangles and squares.

Explore **Find the area of a 5 unit by 3 unit rectangle.**

1 Use square tiles to make a rectangle with side lengths of 5 units and 3 units.

1 unit

One square unit

1 unit

2 The area of the rectangle is equal to the number of square unit tiles that cover it. Count the square tiles to find the area of the rectangle.

width = 3 units

length = 5 units

Your turn now

1. Use square tiles to make a rectangle that is the size given in the table. Copy and complete the table.

Dimensions	Length	Width	Number of square tiles	Area of rectangle
3 by 4	?	?	?	?
4 by 4	?	?	?	?
5 by 6	?	?	?	?
3 by 3	?	?	?	?

2. Write a variable equation to find the area of a rectangle and explain what each variable represents.

3. Write a different equation to find the area of a square and explain what each variable represents.

Stop *and* **Think**

4. **Critical Thinking** Area is measured in square units. Perimeter is the distance around a shape. Is perimeter measured in square units? Why or why not?

Variables in Familiar Formulas

LESSON 1.6

BEFORE	▶ Now	WHY?
You evaluated variable expressions.	You'll use formulas to find unknown values.	So you can find the sizes of swimming pools, as in Ex. 22.

Word Watch

formula, p. 33
perimeter, p. 33
area, p. 33

FLORIDA
Standards and Assessment

• Apply formulas to find rates, distances, and times. (MA.B.1.3.2)

• Know the properties of two-dimensional figures. (MA.C.1.3.1)

A **formula** is an equation that relates two or more quantities such as *perimeter*, length, and width. The **perimeter** of a figure is the sum of the lengths of its sides. The **area** of a figure is the amount of surface the figure covers.

Perimeter is measured in linear units such as feet. Area is measured in square units such as square feet, or ft^2.

Perimeter and Area Formulas

	Diagram	Perimeter	Area
Rectangle	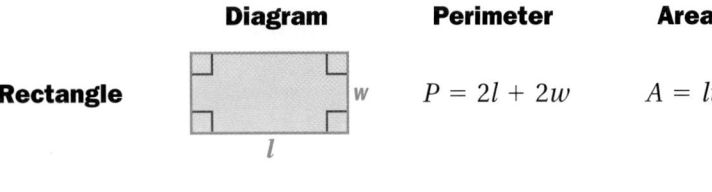	$P = 2l + 2w$	$A = lw$
Square		$P = 4s$	$A = s^2$

HELP with Reading

The mark ⌐ tells you that an angle measures 90°.

EXAMPLE 1 Finding Perimeter and Area

Find the perimeter and area of the rectangle.

Solution

Find the perimeter.

$P = 2l + 2w$	Write formula.
$= 2(8) + 2(5)$	Substitute.
$= 26$	Multiply, then add.

Find the area.

$A = lw$	Write formula.
$= (8)(5)$	Substitute.
$= 40$	Multiply.

ANSWER The perimeter is 26 feet, and the area is 40 square feet.

Lesson 1.6   Variables in Familiar Formulas   **33**

EXAMPLE 2 **Finding Side Length**

Find the side length of a square with an area of 81 square feet.

$A = s^2$ Write formula for area of a square.

$81 = s^2$ Substitute 81 for A.

$9 = s$ Use mental math: $9^2 = 81$.

ANSWER The side length of the square is 9 feet.

$A = 81 \text{ ft}^2$ s
s

Distance Formula Another useful formula is the distance formula. You can use the distance formula to find distance traveled.

HELP with **Vocabulary**

In the formula $d = rt$, rate is the speed of travel.

Distance Formula

Words   The distance traveled d is the product of the rate r and the time t.

Algebra $d = r \cdot t$ or $d = rt$

Numbers $d = 45 \dfrac{\text{miles}}{\text{hour}} \cdot 3 \text{ hours} = 135 \text{ miles}$

EXAMPLE 3 **Using the Distance Formula**

Rabbits A rabbit is running at a rate of 26.4 feet per second. How far does the rabbit travel in 5 seconds?

Solution

$d = r \cdot t$ Write distance formula.

$= 26.4 \cdot 5$ Substitute 26.4 for r and 5 for t.

$= 132$ Multiply.

ANSWER The rabbit travels 132 feet in 5 seconds.

Your turn now Solve.

1. Find the perimeter and area of a square with a 7 inch side length.

2. Find the side length of a square that has an area of 100 square yards.

3. How far does a car travel in 2 hours at a rate of 40 miles per hour?

You can write the distance formula in different forms to find rate or time. Use $t = \dfrac{d}{r}$ to find the time and $r = \dfrac{d}{t}$ to find the rate.

EXAMPLE 4 **Using the Distance Formula to Find Time**

How long will it take a rabbit to travel 264 feet at a rate of 22 feet per second?

Solution

$t = \dfrac{d}{r}$ Write distance formula.

$= \dfrac{264}{22}$ Substitute 264 for *d* and 22 for *r*.

$= 12$ Divide.

ANSWER It will take a rabbit 12 seconds to travel 264 feet.

1.6 **Exercises**
More Practice, p. 727

INTERNET
eWorkbook Plus
CLASSZONE.COM

Getting Ready to Practice

1. Vocabulary Describe the difference between area and perimeter.

Find the perimeter and area of the rectangle or square.

2.
     6 yd
     9 yd

3.
     7 in.
     8 in.

4.   5 m
     5 m

5. Tiger Beetles A tiger beetle runs at a rate of 53 centimeters per second for 3 seconds. How far does the beetle run?

6. Find the Error Describe and correct the error in the solution.

$A = s^2$
$= 4^2$
$= 16$ meters

4 m
4 m

Practice and Problem Solving

with Homework

Example	Exercises
1	7–13, 22
2	14–15, 22
3	17–21, 27
4	17–20, 23

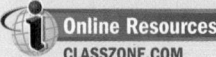

Online Resources
CLASSZONE.COM

· More Examples
· eTutorial Plus

Find the perimeter and area of the rectangle or square.

7.
8 cm

3 cm

8.
5 m

12 m

9.
10 ft

10 ft

In Exercises 10–13, find the perimeter and area of the rectangle or square.

10. length = 17 m, width = 9 m

11. side length = 18 in.

12. length = 11 ft, width = 2 ft

13. length = 14 cm, width = 13 cm

14. Find the side length of a square that has an area of 36 square yards.

15. Find the side length of a square that has a perimeter of 24 meters.

16. Mental Math The area of a rectangle is 88 square inches. The width is 8 inches. Use mental math to find the length of the rectangle.

Use the distance formula to find the unknown value.

17. $d = 36$ km, $r = ?$, $t = 4$ h

18. $d = ?$, $r = 0.5$ mi/min, $t = 10$ min

19. $d = ?$, $r = 7$ mi/h, $t = 1.5$ h

20. $d = 40$ ft, $r = 5$ ft/sec, $t = ?$

21. Arizona The speed limit on rural interstates in Arizona is 75 miles per hour. A car travels at this rate for 3 hours. How far does it travel?

22. Swimming Pools The table shows information about two swimming pools. Copy and complete the table.

	Length	Width	Area	Perimeter
Pool A	60 ft	22 ft	?	?
Pool B	?	30 ft	1800 ft^2	?

23. Train A train travels 226 miles from Washington, D.C., to New York City in about 2 hours 30 minutes. What is the average speed of the train in miles per hour? Round to the nearest mile per hour.

24. Temperature Formula To convert from degrees Celsius to degrees Fahrenheit, you can use the formula $F = \frac{9}{5}C + 32$. Convert 20°C to degrees Fahrenheit.

25. Estimation The driving distance between Houston and Dallas is 224 miles. Suppose a car travels at an average rate of 52 miles per hour. Estimate how long the trip from Houston to Dallas takes.

26. Measurement Write a formula for converting meters to centimeters.

What do you think?

Travel

■ Arizona

U.S. Highway 66, often called Route 66, was commissioned in 1926. It connected Illinois to California traveling through eight states, including Arizona. Route 66 ceased to exist as an official highway in 1984. How many years was it an official highway?

27. Parachutist A parachutist falls for 2 minutes at a speed of 13 feet per second. How far does the parachutist fall during this time?

Yard Fencing In Exercises 28 and 29, your rectangular yard has a length of 50 feet and a width of 45 feet.

28. You want to fence in your yard. How much fencing do you need?

29. You want to fertilize your yard. Each bag of fertilizer covers 2000 square feet. How many bags should you buy?

Challenge Find the perimeter and area of the figure.

30.

31.

32. Critical Thinking Find the perimeter and area of a rectangle with a length of 6 inches and a width of 5 inches. Then find the perimeter and area of a rectangle with a length of 12 inches and a width of 10 inches. How does the perimeter of a rectangle change if length and width are doubled? How does the area of a rectangle change if the length and width are doubled?

Mixed Review

Solve the equation using mental math. *(Lesson 1.5)*

33. $8x = 72$ **34.** $g - 19 = 37$ **35.** $\frac{y}{3} = 10$

Basic Skills **Round the number to the place value of the red digit.**

36. 7.528   **37.** 15.538   **38.** 13.974

FCAT Practice FCAT

39. Multiple Choice You drove 60 miles per hour for 30 minutes. Which expression can be used to find the distance that you traveled?

   A. 60×30 **B.** $60 - 30$ **C.** $60 \div 30$ **D.** 60×0.5

40. Short Response The area of a rectangle is 64 square inches. Explain how you can find the length of the rectangle if its width is 4 inches. What is the length of the rectangle?

LESSON 1.7

A Problem Solving Plan

BEFORE	▶ Now	WHY?
You used problem solving strategies to solve problems.	You'll use a problem solving plan to solve problems.	To find how much cheese you need for lasagna, as in Ex. 9.

 Word Watch

Review Word
formula, p. 33

FLORIDA
Standards and Assessment

• Know strategies to solve problems involving measurement. (MA.B.3.3.1)

• Apply formulas to find rates, distances, and times. (MA.B.1.3.2)

In the Real World

Triathlon You and a friend decide to compete in a triathlon. You both swim 200 meters, bike 10 kilometers, and then run 2 kilometers.

The table shows your speeds for swimming, in meters per minute, and biking, in kilometers per minute. Who has the better total time after these two stages?

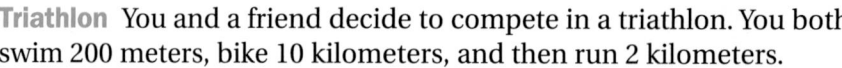

	Swimming (m/min)	Biking (km/min)
You	76.9	0.43
Friend	82.6	0.41

EXAMPLE 1 Understanding and Planning

To solve the triathlon problem, you need to make sure you understand the problem. Then make a plan for solving the problem.

Read and Understand

What do you know?

The table tells you each of your speeds for each stage.

You both swim 200 meters and bike 10 kilometers.

What do you want to find out?

Who has the better total time for swimming and biking

Make a Plan

How can you relate what you know to what you want to find out?

Find each of your swimming and biking times.

Find each of your total times and then compare these times.

You will solve the problem in Example 2.

Your turn now **Use the information at the top of the page.**

1. Which formula would you use to find swimming and running times? Explain your reasoning.

A. $distance = rate \cdot time$ **B.** $time = \dfrac{distance}{rate}$ **C.** $rate = \dfrac{distance}{time}$

EXAMPLE 2 **Solving and Looking Back**

To solve the triathlon problem from the previous page, you need to carry out the plan from Example 1 and then check the answer.

Solve the Problem

To find each of your times, use the formula $time = \dfrac{distance}{rate}$.

	You	Friend
Swimming	$t = \dfrac{d}{r}$ $= \dfrac{200}{76.9}$ ≈ 2.6 min	$t = \dfrac{d}{r}$ $= \dfrac{200}{82.6}$ ≈ 2.4 min
Biking	$t = \dfrac{d}{r}$ $= \dfrac{10}{0.43}$ ≈ 23.26 min	$t = \dfrac{d}{r}$ $= \dfrac{10}{0.41}$ ≈ 24.39 min

HELP with Reading

The $\approx$ symbol means *is approximately equal to.*

Add to find the total time for each of you.

You	$2.6 + 23.26 = 25.86$ min
Friend	$2.4 + 24.39 = 26.79$ min

ANSWER You have the better total time after the two stages.

Look Back

Does your answer make sense?

Notice that you swim at a slower rate than your friend, so it makes sense that your swimming time is greater. You bike at a faster rate than your friend, so it makes sense that your biking time is less. So the calculations appear reasonable.

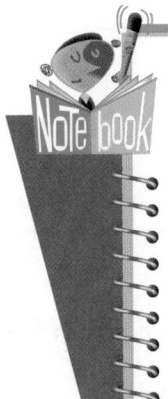

Problem Solving Plan

1. **Read and Understand** Read the problem carefully. Identify the question and any important information.

2. **Make a Plan** Decide on a problem solving strategy.

3. **Solve the Problem** Use the problem solving strategy to answer the question.

4. **Look Back** Check that your answer is reasonable.

Unit Analysis You can use *unit analysis* to evaluate expressions with units of measure and to check that your answer uses the correct units.

For example, when you find the product of rate and time using the units below, the units for distance will be miles.

$$\frac{\text{miles}}{\text{hour}} \cdot \text{hour} = \text{miles}$$

EXAMPLE 3 **Using a Problem Solving Plan**

New York City In parts of New York City, the blocks between avenues are called *long blocks*. There are 4 long blocks per mile. Blocks between streets are called *short blocks*. There are 20 short blocks per mile. You walk 40 short blocks and 6 long blocks. How many miles do you walk?

Solution

Read and Understand You walk 40 short blocks and 6 long blocks. There are 20 short blocks per mile and 4 long blocks per mile. You are asked to find how many miles you walk.

Make a Plan Convert short blocks to miles and long blocks to miles using unit analysis. Then add to find the total miles.

Solve the Problem
Because there are 20 short blocks in one mile, you

can multiply the number of short blocks you walk by $\dfrac{1 \text{ mile}}{20 \text{ short blocks}}$

to convert short blocks to miles.

$$40 \text{ short blocks} \times \frac{1 \text{ mile}}{20 \text{ short blocks}} = 2 \text{ miles}$$

Multiply the number of long blocks you walk by $\dfrac{1 \text{ mile}}{4 \text{ long blocks}}$ to

convert long blocks to miles.

$$6 \text{ long blocks} \times \frac{1 \text{ mile}}{4 \text{ long blocks}} = 1.5 \text{ miles}$$

ANSWER You walk a total of 2 + 1.5 = 3.5 miles.

Look Back Check your answer by drawing a diagram.

From the diagram you can see that 40 short blocks are 2 miles and 6 long blocks are 1.5 miles, which totals 3.5 miles. So, your answer checks. ✓

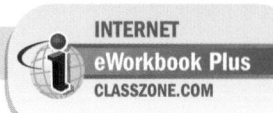
Getting Ready to Practice

1. **Vocabulary** List the four steps of the problem solving plan.

2. **Tickets** You pay $15 a ticket for 4 tickets and a service charge of $2 for every ticket after the second one. You are charged $64 for this order. Describe a way to check that this is the correct price.

3. **Guided Problem Solving** A monorail ride at an amusement park has 5 cars per trainload, and each car can hold 4 passengers. In one hour, 900 people can ride the monorail. How many trainloads run in one hour?

   (1 Write a verbal model of the problem.

   (2 Use the model to find the number of trainloads in one hour.

   (3 Check your answer.

Practice and Problem Solving

HELP with Homework

Example	Exercises
1	4-9
2	4-9
3	4-9

Online Resources
CLASSZONE.COM
· More Examples
· eTutorial Plus

4. **Find the Error** Daniel has enough film to take 96 pictures on a 5 day trip. He takes 45 pictures the first 2 days. He wants to take an equal number of pictures each day for the last 3 days. Describe and correct the error in the solution.

   $$\frac{96}{3} = 32$$

   So, I can take 32 pictures each day.

5. **Saving** Fran is saving money for a color printer that costs $210. She makes $6 an hour baby-sitting, and her parents will contribute $120. Use the problem solving plan to find how many hours she needs to baby-sit to earn enough money for the printer.

6. **Look for a Pattern** Draw the next two shapes in the pattern below.

7. **Music** You practice for 2 hours each weekday and for 3 hours on each weekend day. How many hours per week do you practice?

8. **Bicycle Race** A Tour de France bicycle race covered 3462 kilometers in 21 days. Riders traveled 3152 kilometers during the first 19 racing days and then traveled 160 kilometers the next day. How long was the ride on the last day?

9. Community Service You are making lasagna for 30 people at a homeless shelter. It takes 8 ounces of mozzarella cheese to make enough to serve 10 people. You have 12 ounces of mozzarella cheese. How much more do you need?

Critical Thinking **In Exercises 10–13, complete the pattern.**

10. 2, 7, 12, _?_ , _?_

11. 9, 7, 5, _?_ , _?_

12. 3, 12, 48, _?_

13. 21, 17, 13, _?_ , _?_

14. Writing Is there enough information to answer the following question? Explain how to solve the problem, or tell what information is needed.

Amanda has sold magazine subscriptions worth $330 for a school fundraiser. If she reaches a total of $500, she wins a gift certificate. How many more subscriptions does she need to sell to reach $500?

15. Sales During a 4 week period, a salesperson at a photography studio wants to sell photography packages worth a total of $16,000. Sales for the first 3 weeks are $1240, $3720, and $5980. What does the sales amount need to be in week 4 to reach the $16,000 goal?

16. Number Sense The product of two numbers is 48. Their sum is 16. Find the two numbers.

Critical Thinking **In Exercises 17–20, complete the pattern.**

17. $2x$, $4x$, $6x$, _?_ , _?_

18. $65x$, $52x$, $39x$, _?_ , _?_

19. $7x^2$, $15x^2$, $23x^2$, _?_ , _?_

20. $81x$, $78x^2$, $75x^3$, $72x^4$, _?_ , _?_

21. Garden You have 28 feet of fencing and want to construct a rectangular garden with the largest possible area with whole number dimensions. Find the side lengths of the largest possible garden. What is its area?

Guess, Check, and Revise **In Exercises 22–25, find the solution of the equation.**

22. $4x = 2x + 14$

23. $6x = 9x - 15$

24. $2x + 3 = 5x - 9$

25. $9 - 3x = 2x - 11$

26. Basketball The table shows the numbers of people who attended Women's National Basketball Association (WNBA) games from 1997 through 2001. Describe how you could predict the attendance for WNBA games in 2002. What is your prediction? How can you check your prediction?

Year	1997	1998	1999	2000	2001
Attendance	1,082,093	1,630,315	1,959,733	2,322,429	2,323,164

27. Challenge Bill's house is third in a row of 12 houses. There are 5 houses between Chris's house and Audrey's house, and 2 between Chris's house and Bill's house. How many houses are between Audrey's house and the first house? Explain how you got your answer.

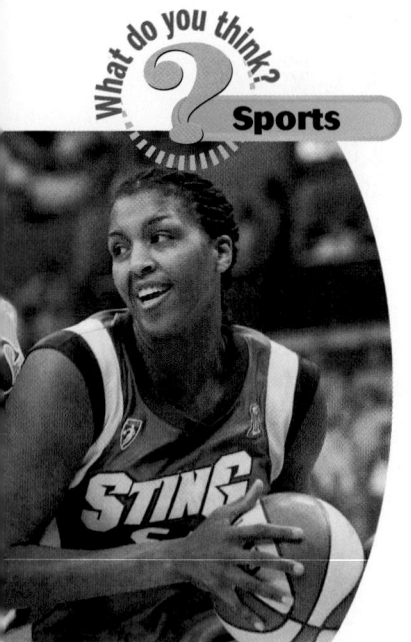

What do you think?

Sports

■ **Basketball**

In 1997, the WNBA had eight teams. Two teams were added in 1998. In 1999, two more teams were added. Four teams were added in 2000. How many teams were in the WNBA in 2000?

Mixed Review

Evaluate the expression. *(Lesson 1.2)*

28. $7 + 4 \times 3 - 6$ **29.** $24 \div (2 \times 4) - 3$ **30.** $70 \div [14 - 2 \times 2]$

Find the perimeter and area of the figure. *(Lesson 1.6)*

31. a 16 in. by 3 in. rectangle   **32.** a square with a 237 ft side

Basic Skills **Complete the statement using < or >.**

33. 23.2 _?_ 23   **34.** 0.5 _?_ 5   **35.** 0.1 _?_ 0.01   **36.** 1.4 _?_ 4.1

FCAT Practice

INTERNET
FCAT PRACTICE
CLASSZONE.COM

37. Multiple Choice Nadia and her father are on an 500 mile car trip. They drove 338 miles, stopped for gas, then went another 75 miles and stopped for lunch. How many more miles must they drive?

A. 50 miles   **B.** 87 miles   **C.** 107 miles   **D.** 142 miles

38. Multiple Choice Which picture represents the next box in the pattern?

F.   **G.**   **H.**   **I.**

BRAIN GAME

What's Happening?

Scott, John, Annie, and Rebecca are each doing a different activity. Who is doing what?

- Scott and John are not at the debate.

- Scott can't go to the student council meeting.

- Annie is not going to student council or to art club.

- Rebecca is not a member of the student council.

- Annie and Rebecca do not tutor.

Notebook Review

Review the vocabulary definitions in your notebook.

Copy the review examples in your notebook. Then complete the exercises.

Check Your Definitions

equation, p. 28   solving an equation, p. 28   perimeter, p. 33

solution, p. 28   formula, p. 33   area, p. 33

Use Your Vocabulary

1. What is the formula for the perimeter of a rectangle?

1.5 Can you solve equations using mental math?

EXAMPLE Solve $32 \div n = 8$.

$$32 \div n = 8 \qquad \text{Write original equation.}$$

$$32 \div 4 = 8, \text{ so } n = 4. \qquad \text{Solve equation using mental math.}$$

☑ **Use mental math to solve the equation.**

2. $5 + m = 18$ **3.** $t - 9 = 3$ **4.** $7h = 21$ **5.** $\dfrac{d}{3} = 6$

1.6 Can you use formulas to find unknown values?

EXAMPLE In 1990, Arie Luyendyk set a record at the Indianapolis 500 race with an average speed of about 186 miles per hour. About how long did it take him to complete the 500 mile race?

Solution

$$t = \dfrac{d}{r} \qquad \text{Write distance formula.}$$

$$= \dfrac{500}{186} \qquad \text{Substitute 500 for } d \text{ and 186 for } r.$$

$$\approx 2.69 \qquad \text{Divide. Round to the nearest hundredth.}$$

ANSWER Arie Luyendyk completed the race in about 2.69 hours.

 6. Find the perimeter and area of a rectangle with a length of 7 meters and a width of 4 meters.

1.7 Can you use a problem solving plan?

EXAMPLE You are filling a 55 gallon aquarium with water using a pitcher from your kitchen. It takes 3 trips with the pitcher to fill a 5 gallon aquarium. How many trips with the pitcher will you need to fill the 55 gallon aquarium?

Read and Understand and Make a Plan Find how many times 5 gallons goes into 55 gallons. Multiply that number by 3, because it takes 3 pitchers to make 5 gallons.

Solve the Problem $\dfrac{55 \text{ gallons}}{5 \text{ gallons}} = 11$

$11 \cdot 3 \text{ trips} = 33 \text{ trips}$

ANSWER It will take 33 trips with the pitcher to fill the aquarium.

 7. If you like 2 teaspoons of sugar in an 8 ounce glass of iced tea, how much sugar should you add to a 36 ounce thermos of iced tea?

Stop *and* **Think** about Lessons 1.5–1.7

8. Critical Thinking Can you tell whether area or perimeter is being measured if you know only the unit of measurement? Explain.

Review Quiz 2

Solve the equation using mental math.

1. $h + 12 = 21$ **2.** $22 - y = 8$ **3.** $54 = 6x$ **4.** $\dfrac{108}{r} = 9$

5. Video Games You have $24 to spend on video game rentals. Each rental costs $3. How many video games can you rent?

6. Geometry Find the perimeter and area of a rectangle with a length of 14 feet and a width of 11 feet.

7. Driving On the highway you drive at a speed of 55 miles per hour for 3 hours. How far do you drive?

8. Exercise You plan to exercise 200 minutes over 5 days. The first four days you exercise 45 minutes, 30 minutes, 20 minutes, and 1 hour. Use the problem solving plan to find the number of minutes you need to exercise on the fifth day to meet your goal.

Chapter Review

 Vocabulary

bar graph, p. 5	verbal model, p. 11	solution, p. 28
data, p. 5	variable, p. 15	solving an equation,
frequency table, p. 6	variable expression, p. 15	p. 28
histogram, p. 6	power, p. 20	formula, p. 33
numerical expression, p. 10	exponent, p. 20	perimeter, p. 33
evaluate, p. 10	base, p. 20	area, p. 33
order of operations, p. 10	equation, p. 28	

Vocabulary Review

Copy and complete the statement.

1. You can graph data organized in a frequency table using a(n) _?_ .

2. _?_ is the amount of surface covered by a figure.

3. To evaluate an expression that has more than one operation, use the _?_ .

4. A(n) _?_ is a symbol, usually a letter, that represents one or more numbers.

5. A power has an exponent and a(n) _?_ .

Tell whether the statement is *true* or *false*.

6. A variable expression is a mathematical sentence that is formed by placing an equal sign between two expressions.

7. A formula is an equation that has only one variable.

8. The perimeter of a figure is the sum of the lengths of its sides.

9. A solution of an equation is a number that, when substituted for a variable, makes the equation true.

Review Questions

In Exercises 10 and 11, use the table at the right. It shows the numbers of volunteers at a local animal shelter. *(Lesson 1.1)*

10. Which age group has the most volunteers? Which age group has the fewest volunteers?

11. Can you determine the number of volunteers who are teenagers? Explain.

Age group	Volunteers
15–24	24
25–34	30
35–44	31
45–54	30
55–64	27
65–74	12
75–84	11

Evaluate the expression. *(Lesson 1.2)*

12. $16 + 5 \times 3 + 8$

13. $40 \div [(14 + 6) \cdot 2)]$

14. $10 + \dfrac{60}{31 - 26}$

15. Clothes You are saving money to buy two sweaters that each cost $28.50. You have already saved $20. To find out how much more money you need to save, translate *2 times 28.5 minus 20* into an expression and then evaluate. *(Lesson 1.2)*

Evaluate the expression when $x = 4$ and $y = 9$. *(Lesson 1.3)*

16. $\dfrac{xy}{3x}$
17. $\dfrac{y + 19}{x + 3}$
18. $5y - 6x$
19. $3xy - xy$

20. Dolphins After swimming 22 miles, a dolphin changes direction and swims at a rate of 18 miles per hour. Use the expression $22 + 18t$ to find the total distance traveled by the dolphin after 2 more hours. *(Lesson 1.3)*

Evaluate the power. *(Lesson 1.4)*

21. 15^2
22. 4^5
23. 10^4
24. 9^3

Evaluate the expression. *(Lesson 1.4)*

25. $(5 + 4)^2 \div 3$
26. $5 \cdot (6 - 3)^5 + 45$
27. $\left[10 + (4 \times 2)^3\right] \div 2$

Solve the equation using mental math. *(Lesson 1.5)*

28. $7b = 56$
29. $\dfrac{84}{x} = 12$
30. $98 - t = 35$

Find the perimeter and area of the rectangle or square. *(Lesson 1.6)*

31.
32.
33.

34. Cars A car travels at an average rate of 50 miles per hour for 3 hours. How far does it travel? *(Lesson 1.6)*

35. Radio You are the disc jockey for a 15 minute radio show at your school. You must leave 3 minutes open for announcements, and you want to play 3 songs. Use the table at the right to determine the 3 songs you can play. *(Lesson 1.7)*

Song	A	B	C	D	E
Length (minutes)	6	4	3	5	6

Chapter Test

Sports In a survey, 3000 people in Japan were asked about their participation in ten sports. The results for four sports are in the table.

Sport	Participants
Gymnastics	1002
Bowling	996
Jogging	807
Swimming	717

1. Make a bar graph of the data.

2. Is it possible to make a histogram of the data? Explain.

Evaluate the expression.

3. $20 + 12 \div 4$

4. $6 \times 5 - 20 \div 2$

5. $(3 + 7) \div 5 + 10$

6. **Plumbing** A plumber charges a flat rate of $25 plus an additional $55 for each hour of work. To find how much money the plumber makes in 5 hours at one location, evaluate the expression $25 + 55 \cdot 5$.

7. **Fruit** You are buying 3 apples and 4 oranges for a fruit salad. The cost of one apple is x dollars. The cost of one orange is y dollars. Write a variable expression to represent the cost of 3 apples and 4 oranges. If one apple costs $.75 and one orange costs $.50, what is the total cost?

Evaluate the expression.

8. $(2 + 3)^4 \div 5$

9. $10^2 - 3^4 + 22$

10. $(11 - 5)^4 - 300 \div 12$

Solve the equation using mental math.

11. $17 - t = 5$

12. $9n = 72$

13. $49 \div b = 7$

14. $21 + a = 27$

Tell whether the value of the variable is a solution of the equation.

15. $z + 2 = 15; z = 13$

16. $65 \div y = 16; y = 4$

17. $11x = 45; x = 4$

18. **Court Area** The lengths and widths of three different types of courts are listed in the table. Find the area of each court. Which court has the largest area? Which court has the smallest area?

Court	Length	Width
Squash	32 feet	21 feet
Tennis	78 feet	27 feet
Racquetball	40 feet	20 feet

19. **Horses** A horse travels at a rate of 60 feet per second. How far does the horse travel in 4 seconds?

20. **Park** A rectangular park that is 90 feet long and 60 feet wide needs to be planted with sod. A roll of sod covers 1 square yard. Use the problem solving plan to find how many rolls of sod are needed to cover the park.

Chapter FCAT Practice

Test-Taking Strategy Most standardized tests are based on concepts and skills taught in school. The best way to prepare is to keep up with your daily studies.

Multiple Choice

1. This histogram shows the scores of 25 students on a math exam. How many students have a score of at least 81?

Test Scores

A. 7   **B.** 9   **C.** 16   **D.** 25

2. In what order should the operations be performed in the expression $8 \times 3 - 4 \div 2 + 6$?

F. $\times, -, \div, +$ **G.** $-, +, \times, \div$

H. $\times, \div, -, +$ **I.** $\div, \times, -, +$

3. Which expression has a value of 4?

A. $36 \div (3 + 6) \times (5 - 4)$

B. $36 \div (3 + 6) \times 5 - 4$

C. $36 \div 3 + 6 \times 5 - 4$

D. $(36 \div 3 + 6) \times 5 - 4$

4. What is the correct value of the expression $(9 - 6)^3 + 5 \times 2$?

F. 19   **G.** 28   **H.** 37   **I.** 64

5. Which statement is true?

A. $6^3 > 3^6$ **B.** $2^4 < 4^2$

C. $7^8 > 8^7$ **D.** $3^2 < 2^3$

6. Which equation represents this statement: *A number divided by four is seven?*

F. $4 \div r = 7$ **G.** $t \div 4 = 7$

H. $p \div 7 = 4$ **I.** $4g = 7$

7. What is the solution of the equation in Exercise 6?

A. $\frac{4}{7}$ **B.** $\frac{7}{4}$ **C.** 3   **D.** 28

8. If $a = 6$ and $b = 8$, which of the following is true?

F. $a - 2 = b$ **G.** $ab = 14$

H. $2a + b = 20$ **I.** $b \div 2 = a$

Short Response

9. The area of the rectangle is 120 square centimeters. Write an equation you can use to find the width w. Then solve the equation for w.

$A = 120$ cm^2 w

15 cm

Extended Response

10. Your car's fuel gauge is broken. The car can go 22 miles on one gallon of gasoline. You start a trip with 13 gallons of gasoline. If you want to always have at least a gallon in the tank, what is the farthest you should drive before stopping for more gasoline? Explain.

2

Integer Operations

Chapter Warm-Up Game

Review skills you need for this chapter in this quick game. Work with a partner.

Key Skill:
Multiplying whole numbers

BEFORE

In previous chapters you've...

- Performed operations on whole numbers
- Evaluated expressions

Now

In Chapter 2 you'll study...

- Operations on integers
- Using properties to evaluate expressions
- Identifying and plotting points in the coordinate plane

WHY?

So you can solve real-world problems about...

- space shuttles, p. 56
- dinosaurs, p. 66
- diving, p. 70
- murals, p. 89

Internet Preview
CLASSZONE.COM

- eEdition Plus Online
- eWorkbook Plus Online
- eTutorial Plus Online
- FCAT Practice
- More Examples

FOUR IN A ROW

MATERIALS

- 2 Answer Cards

- 24 Expression Cards

32
x 26

- 24 Markers

PREPARE Fill in your Answer Card with 16 of the 24 answers given below. Place the Expression Cards face down in a pile. On each turn follow the steps on the next page.

168	196	240	315	338	342
352	361	405	414	418	441
516	522	529	595	720	792
832	851	918	961	975	1020

$$\begin{array}{r} 23 \\ \times\ 23 \\ \hline \end{array}$$

196	342	414	240
529	720	975	918
418	361	352	516
441	832	315	851

1 **FLIP** over an Expression Card. Both players solve the expression.

2 **LOOK** for the answer on your Answer Card. If you find it, place a marker over the answer.

HOW TO WIN Mark 4 answers in a row across, up and down, or diagonally.

Stop *and* Think

1. How many ways can you get 4 answers in a row on your card?

2. Critical Thinking How many squares can you mark without winning?

CHAPTER 2

Getting Ready to Learn

Word Watch

Review Words

variable, p. 15
variable expression, p. 15
perimeter, p. 33
area, p. 33

Review What You Need to Know

Using Vocabulary Copy and complete using a review word.

1. A symbol that represents one or more numbers is called a(n) __?__.

2. The surface covered by a figure is called the __?__.

Round the decimal to the nearest whole number. *(p. 705)*

3. 10.61   **4.** 134.7   **5.** 0.25   **6.** 12.86

Evaluate the expression. *(p. 10)*

7. $32 - 27 + 14$ **8.** $4 \cdot 12 \div 6$ **9.** $6 + 34 \div 2$

Evaluate the expression when $s = 4$ and $t = 16$. *(p. 15)*

10. $(t - 9) + s$ **11.** $s(t - 5)$ **12.** $\frac{1}{4}t - 4$

Solve the equation using mental math. *(p. 28)*

13. $3x = 39$ **14.** $x - 6 = 12$ **15.** $x + 13 = 17$

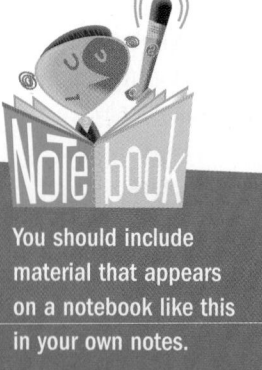

You should include material that appears on a notebook like this in your own notes.

Know How to Take Notes

Including Vocabulary Notes When you write down new vocabulary words, you should also write examples of how they are used. Label the examples with the new words.

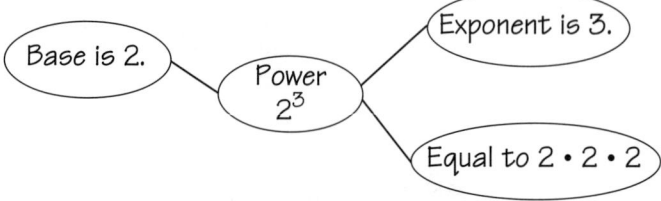

5^2 is read "five squared."

5^3 is read "five cubed."

5^4 is read "five to the fourth power."

As you work through Chapter 2, label examples of new vocabulary in your notes.

LESSON 2.1

Integers and Absolute Value

BEFORE	▶ Now	WHY?
You studied whole numbers.	You'll study integers.	So you can order lake elevations, as in Ex. 24.

In the Real World

Word Watch

integer, p. 53
negative integer, p. 53
positive integer, p. 53
absolute value, p. 54
opposite, p. 54

FLORIDA
Standards and Assessment

• Know the relationship of positive and negative numbers. (MA.A.3.3.1)
• Identify and explain absolute values. (MA.A.1.3.4)
• Know names and numerals for integers. (MA.A.1.3.1)

Geography The Global Positioning System (GPS) can be used to determine elevations. The table shows the minimum elevations of several countries. Which country in the table has the lowest elevation?

Each number in the table is an *integer*. The following numbers are **integers** .

Minimum Elevations	
Country	**Elevation (m)**
United States	−86
Canada	0
China	−154
Bolivia	90
Czech Republic	115

$$\dots, -5, -4, -3, -2, -1, 0, 1, 2, 3, 4, 5, \dots$$

Negative integers are less than 0. They lie *to the left* of 0 on a number line. **Positive integers** are greater than 0. They lie *to the right* of 0 on a number line. Zero is neither positive nor negative. When you use a number line to compare numbers, numbers increase as you move to the right.

EXAMPLE 1 Graphing and Ordering Integers

To find which country in the table above has the lowest elevation, graph each integer on a number line.

ANSWER China has the lowest elevation, at −154 meters.

Global Positioning System (GPS) satellite

Your turn now Order the integers from least to greatest.

1. −7, 2, −1, 0, −2   **2.** 9, −4, 12, −11, −1   **3.** 0, −99, 44, −60, 16

The **absolute value** of a number is the distance between the number and zero on a number line. The absolute value of a number n is written as $|n|$. The absolute value of 0 is 0.

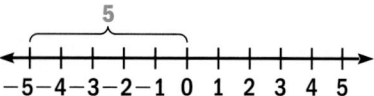

The distance between 4 and 0 is 4. So, $|4| = 4$.

The distance between -5 and 0 is 5. So, $|-5| = 5$.

EXAMPLE 2   **Finding Absolute Value**

Eyeglasses An eyeglass prescription is given as a positive or negative number. A prescription of a person who is farsighted is positive. A prescription of a person who is nearsighted is negative. The greater the absolute value, the stronger the prescription. Which prescription is stronger, -3 or 2?

Solution

$|-3| = 3$ and $|2| = 2$.

ANSWER The prescription of -3 is stronger because $3 > 2$.

HELP with Reading

The integer "-2" can be read "negative 2" or "the opposite of 2."

Two numbers are **opposites** if they have the same absolute value but different signs. Opposites are the same distance from 0 on a number line and are on opposite sides of 0. The opposite of 0 is 0.

-2 and 2 are *opposites*.

EXAMPLE 3   **Finding Opposites**

Write the opposite of the integer.

   a. 5   The opposite of 5 is -5.

   b. -12 The opposite of -12 is 12.

   c. $|-9|$ Because $|-9| = 9$, the opposite of $|-9|$ is -9.

Your turn now   **Write the opposite and the absolute value of the integer.**

   4. -16 **5.** 140   **6.** 1   **7.** $|-55|$

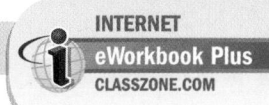

Getting Ready to Practice

1. **Vocabulary** Copy and complete: Two integers are ? if they have the same absolute value but different signs.

Use a number line to order the integers from least to greatest.

2. 5, −10, 15, 27, −20, 13

3. 120, 62, 0, −56, 74, −130

Write the opposite and the absolute value of the integer.

4. 19

5. −8

6. −740

7. 1327

8. **Find the Error** A student was asked to order the integers 3, 1, 0, −9, −2, and 5 from least to greatest. Describe and correct the error in the solution.

$$\times \quad 0, 1, -2, 3, 5, -9$$

Practice and Problem Solving

HELP with Homework

Example	Exercises
1	9–18
2	19–22
3	19–22

Online Resources
CLASSZONE.COM

· More Examples
· eTutorial Plus

Copy and complete the statement with < or >.

9. 4 ? −6

10. −12 ? 1

11. −9 ? −2

12. 0 ? −5

13. 5 ? −5

14. −17 ? 2

15. 34 ? −29

16. −20 ? −14

Use a number line to order the integers from least to greatest.

17. 64, −12, 18, 59, −20, 44

18. 278, 121, −301, 262, −155

Match the integer expression with the verbal expression.

19. −|7|

20. |−7|

21. −|−7|

22. −(−7)

A. the opposite of negative seven

B. the opposite of the absolute value of seven

C. the absolute value of negative seven

D. the opposite of the absolute value of negative seven

In Exercises 23 and 24, use the table showing elevations of lakes.

23. **Compare** Which lake is at a lower elevation, Gieselmann Lake or Silver Lake?

24. Arrange the lake elevations in order from least to greatest.

Name	Elevation (ft)
Jones Lake	−30
Silver Lake	90
Gieselmann Lake	−162
Seneca Lake	445
Craigs Pond	0

HELP with Solving

The opposite of an opposite is the original number. For example, $-(-16) = 16$.

Simplify the expression.

25. $|-32|$ **26.** $-|9|$ **27.** $-|29|$ **28.** $-(-5)$

29. $-(-81)$ **30.** $-|-17|$ **31.** $-|-3|$ **32.** $-(-(-4))$

Copy and complete the statement with <, >, or =.

33. $|4|$ <u>?</u> $|-4|$ **34.** $|-6|$ <u>?</u> $-|6|$ **35.** $-|-9|$ <u>?</u> $-(-9)$

36. Critical Thinking What numbers have opposites that are the same as their absolute values? What numbers have opposites that are different from their absolute values?

37. Launch Countdown Put the following activities for a shuttle launch in the order that they occur. "T−5 minutes" means 5 minutes before liftoff.

T−5 minutes	Pilot starts auxiliary power units.
T+7 seconds	Shuttle clears launch tower, and control switches to the Mission Control Center.
T−2 hours, 55 minutes	Flight crew departs for launch pad.
T−6 seconds	Main engine starts.
T−0	Liftoff.

Challenge **Order the numbers from least to greatest.**

38. $-28, -(-73), |-65|, |95|, -|47|$

39. $|-19|, -74, -|12|, -(-56), -|-58|$

Mixed Review

Evaluate the expression when $a = 8$ and $b = 2$. *(Lesson 1.3)*

40. $5ab$ **41.** $\dfrac{a}{b} + 15$ **42.** $4a - 3b$

43. Patty needs to read a 238 page book in 6 days. By the end of the first day she has read 68 pages. How many pages does she need to read each day to finish the book on time? *(Lesson 1.7)*

FCAT Practice

INTERNET
FCAT PRACTICE
CLASSZONE.COM

44. Multiple Choice Which of the following shows the integers in order from least to greatest?

    A. $-3, -15, -21, -27$ **B.** $-3, -21, -27, -15$

    C. $-27, -21, -15, -3$ **D.** $-27, -15, -21, -3$

45. Multiple Choice The Qattara Depression in Egypt lies 133 meters below sea level. Which number represents this elevation in meters?

    F. -133 **G.** $-(-133)$ **H.** $|-133|$ **I.** $|133|$

Hands-on Activity

GOAL
Model integer addition on a number line.

MATERIALS
· pencil
· paper

FLORIDA: Standards and Assessment
Know effects of the four basic operations
(MA.A.3.3.1)
Interpret and apply scales (MA.B.1.3.4)

Adding Integers

You can model addition of integers by using a number line.

Explore   **Find the sum −15 + 11.**

1 Draw a number line, place a pencil at 0, and move 15 units to the left to show −15.

2 Move 11 units to the right to show the addition of 11.

3 The final position is −4. So, −15 + 11 = −4.

Your turn now   **Write an addition expression to represent the figure. Then evaluate the expression.**

1.

2.

Use a number line to find the sum.

3. −7 + (−14)   **4.** 20 + (−50)   **5.** −10 + 65   **6.** −7 + (−33)

7. 41 + (−25)   **8.** −23 + 52   **9.** −18 + (−34)   **10.** 35 + (−37)

Stop and Think

11. The sum of two positive integers is always positive. What is the sign of the sum of two negative integers? Use a number line to explain.

12. Critical Thinking How can you predict the sign of the sum of a positive and a negative integer before you add the numbers?

13. Writing Write the steps you use to evaluate 25 + (−13) + 5 + (−20). Then evaluate the expression.

LESSON 2.2

Adding Integers

BEFORE	Now	WHY?
You added whole numbers.	You'll add integers.	So you can find a miniature golf score, as in Ex. 43.

Review Words

integer, p. 53
absolute value, p. 54
sum, p. 709

FLORIDA
Standards and Assessment

- Know effects of the four basic operations (MA.A.3.3.1)
- Apply number properties (MA.A.3.3.1)

You can use a number line to add integers.

EXAMPLE 1 Adding Integers Using a Number Line

Use a number line to find the sum.

a. $5 + (-8)$ **b.** $-6 + 10$ **c.** $-4 + (-3)$

Solution

a. Start at 0, move **5** units to the right. Then move **8** units to the left.

ANSWER The final position is -3. So, $5 + (-8) = -3$.

b. Start at 0, move **6** units to the left. Then move **10** units to the right.

ANSWER The final position is 4. So, $-6 + 10 = 4$.

c. Start at 0, move **4** units to the left. Then move **3** units to the left.

ANSWER The final position is -7. So, $-4 + (-3) = -7$.

Your turn now Use a number line to find the sum.

1. $12 + (-5)$ **2.** $-8 + 4$ **3.** $-1 + (-6)$ **4.** $2 + (-2)$

Using a Rule You can add integers without using a number line by following these rules.

Same sign   Add the absolute values and use the common sign.

Different signs   Subtract the lesser absolute value from the greater absolute value. Use the sign of the number with the greater absolute value.

EXAMPLE 2 **Adding Integers**

Find the sum −12 + 4.

$$-12 + 4 = -8$$

Different signs, so subtract $|4|$ from $|-12|$.

Use sign of number with greater absolute value.

✓ **Check** Use a number line to find the sum.

$-13\ -12\ -11\ -10\ -9\ \ -8\ \ -7\ \ -6\ \ -5\ \ -4\ \ -3\ \ -2\ \ -1\ \ \ \ 0$

Additive Identity Property

Words The sum of an integer and zero is the integer.

Numbers $5 + 0 = 5$ **Algebra** $a + 0 = a$
$ -3 + 0 = -3$

EXAMPLE 3 **Adding More Than Two Integers**

a. Use the left to right rule of order of operations to find the sum.

$$-84 + 0 + (-124) = -84 + (-124)$$ Additive identity property

$$= -208$$ Same sign, so sum has common sign.

b. Use the left to right rule of order of operations to find the sum.

$$-46 + (-53) + 63 = -99 + 63$$ Same sign, so sum has common sign.

$$= -36$$ Use sign of number with greater absolute value.

EXAMPLE 4 **Adding More Than Two Integers**

School Fair Your class has a fair to raise money for a field trip. The table shows the incomes and expenses for the fair. How much money was raised?

Games	$750
Display tables	$625
Donations	$36
Advertising	−$16
Decorations	−$60
Game rentals	−$500

Solution

First, add the **positive integers**, and then add the **negative integers**.

$$750 + 625 + 36 + (-16) + (-60) + (-500) = 1411 + (-576)$$
$$= 835$$

ANSWER Your class raised $835.

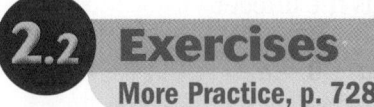 **Find the sum.**

5. $-20 + (-15)$

6. $18 + 0 + (-54)$

7. $300 + 111 + (-44) + (-256)$

8. $-230 + (-512) + 178 + 94$

2.2 Exercises

More Practice, p. 728

Getting Ready to Practice

1. Vocabulary Copy and complete: To add two integers with the same sign, add the _?_ and use the common sign.

Use a number line to find the sum.

2. $-6 + 8$ **3.** $-3 + (-9)$ **4.** $5 + (-7)$ **5.** $-4 + 4$

Find the sum.

6. $42 + (-23)$ **7.** $-32 + 0$ **8.** $-51 + (-67)$

9. $-19 + 19 + (-34)$ **10.** $-12 + 9 + (-5)$ **11.** $20 + (-15) + (-22)$

12. Checking You record withdrawals and deposits in your checkbook. The starting balance is $125. The first withdrawal is $25. The second withdrawal is $13. The first deposit is $35. The second deposit is $50. The third withdrawal is $68. What is the final balance?

HELP with Homework

Example	Exercises
1	13–16
2	17–26
3	18–26, 34–37
4	34–37

Online Resources
CLASSZONE.COM
· More Examples
· eTutorial Plus

Practice and Problem Solving

Use a number line to find the sum.

13. $-2 + (-1)$ **14.** $-10 + (-9)$ **15.** $-3 + 7$ **16.** $7 + (-5)$

17. Find the Error Describe and correct the error in the solution.

Find the sum of -8 and 5.
$-8 + 5 = -13$ $\times$

Find the sum.

18. $-63 + (-49)$ **19.** $-93 + (-16)$ **20.** $0 + (-25)$

21. $-82 + 0$ **22.** $98 + (-128)$ **23.** $-57 + 31 + 27 + 11$

24. $-42 + (-65) + 78$ **25.** $-87 + 48 + 36$ **26.** $-81 + (-75) + (-65)$

Critical Thinking Copy and complete the statement using *always*, *sometimes*, or *never*.

27. The sum of two negative integers is _?_ negative.

28. The sum of two positive integers is _?_ negative.

29. The sum of a positive integer and a negative integer is _?_ negative.

30. The sum of an integer and zero is _?_ zero.

31. Writing Describe a situation where you would need to add positive and negative integers.

In Exercises 32 and 33, use the information to write an expression. Then use a number line to find the sum.

32. Elevator You enter an elevator on the sixth floor. The elevator goes up 3 floors, then down 5 floors, where you exit. What floor is it?

33. Mexico The influential period of the *Olmec* culture in Mexico lasted approximately 800 years. It started about 1200 B.C. About what year did this period end?

Find the sum.

34. $42 + 36 + (-16) + 0 + (-84)$ **35.** $(-17) + (-63) + 91 + 79$

36. $174 + (-196) + 245 + (-210)$ **37.** $-182 + 307 + 163 + (-142)$

Algebra Evaluate $x + (-478)$ for the value of x.

38. $x = 806$ **39.** $x = -729$ **40.** $x = \left|-349\right|$ **41.** $x = -\left|-521\right|$

42. Making Connections The sum of a number and its *additive inverse* is 0. For example, $5 + (-5) = 0$, so 5 and -5 are additive inverses. Give another example of additive inverses. What vocabulary word from this chapter is another name for additive inverses?

Jade sculpture from the Olmec culture in Veracruz, Mexico

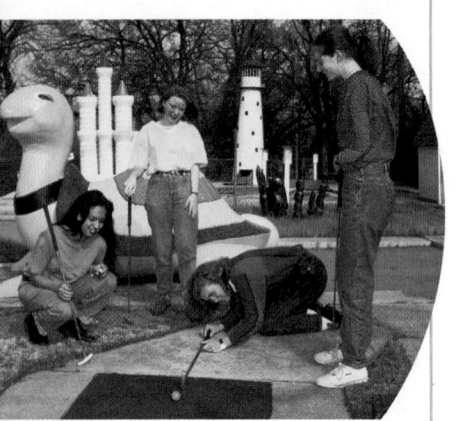

43. Miniature Golf In miniature golf, *par* is the number of strokes considered necessary to get a ball in the hole. The score for each hole is the number of strokes above or below par. Find the total score by adding the scores for each hole. Is Jill's score *above* par, *under* par, or *at* par?

HOLE	1	2	3	4	5	6	7	8	9	OUT
PAR	4	5	3	3	5	4	3	5	3	35
Jill	0	+1	−2	−1	0	+1	+2	0	−1	

Chemistry **In Exercises 44–46, use the information below.**
Find the sum of the charges. Tell whether the atom is an ion.

- A proton has a charge of +1.
- An electron has a charge of −1.
- An atom is an ion if it has a positive or negative charge.

44. Sodium: 11 protons, 10 electrons

45. Chlorine: 17 protons, 17 electrons

46. Oxide: 8 protons, 10 electrons

Mental Math **Solve the equation using mental math.**

47. $-3 + k = 2$ **48.** $-6 = x + (-9)$ **49.** $-7 = 12 + j$

50. Challenge Does $|x + y| = |x| + |y|$ if x and y are both positive? What if x and y are both negative? What if x is positive and y is negative? Explain.

Mixed Review

Evaluate the expression. *(Lesson 1.4)*

51. $5^3 + 21 \div 7 - 6$ **52.** $6^2 \cdot (2 + 4) \div 18$ **53.** $(12 - 4) \cdot (9 - 1)^2$

Order the integers from least to greatest. *(Lesson 2.1)*

54. $-2479, 1802, 2479, -1802$ **55.** $-346, -125, -921, 724, 128$

FCAT Practice   FCAT

66. Multiple Choice Evaluate $-74 + 57$.

     A. -131 **B.** -17 **C.** 49 **D.** 131

67. Multiple Choice Evaluate $-376 + (-623) + 843 + (-758)$.

     F. -2600 **G.** -914 **H.** 914 **I.** 2600

Subtracting Integers

BEFORE	▶ Now	WHY?
You added integers.	You'll subtract integers.	So you can find the length of dinosaur periods, as in Ex. 41.

Word Watch

Review Words

integer, p. 53
opposite, p. 54
difference, p. 709

FLORIDA

Standards and Assessment

• Know effects of the four
  basic operations.
  (MA.A.3.3.1)

• Evaluate algebraic
  expressions. (MA.D.2.3.1)

Activity You can use patterns and mental math to discover a rule for subtracting integers.

① Copy the table. In the second column, write the answer to the subtraction problem. Use a pattern to find the differences involving negative integers.

② In the third column, complete the addition problem so the sum is equal to the number in the difference column.

Subtraction problem	Difference	Addition problem
$3 - 3$	0	$3 + -3$
$3 - 2$	?	$3 + $?
$3 - 1$	?	$3 + $?
$3 - 0$	?	$3 + $?
$3 - (-1)$	?	$3 + $?
$3 - (-2)$	?	$3 + $?
$3 - (-3)$	?	$3 + $?

③ How is the second number in the addition problems related to the second number in the subtraction problems?

④ Describe how to use addition to subtract integers.

In the activity above, you saw that when you subtract integers you can write the expression as an addition expression and then use the rules for adding integers.

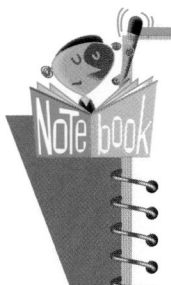

Subtracting Integers

Words   To subtract an integer, add its opposite.

Numbers $3 - 7 = 3 + (-7) = -4$ **Algebra** $a - b = a + (-b)$
$2 - (-6) = 2 + 6 = 8$ $a - (-b) = a + b$

EXAMPLE 1 Subtracting Integers

a. $-56 - (-9) = -56 + 9$ Add the opposite of -9.

$ = -47$ Add.

b. $-14 - 21 = -14 + (-21)$ Add the opposite of 21.

$ = -35$ Add.

Your turn now Find the difference.

1. $15 - 41$ **2.** $-16 - 8$ **3.** $38 - (-27)$ **4.** $-76 - (-109)$

EXAMPLE 2 Evaluating a Variable Expression

Evaluate $15 - a - b$ when $a = 24$ and $b = -36$.

Solution

$15 - a - b = 15 - 24 - (-36)$ Substitute 24 for a and -36 for b.

$ = 15 + (-24) - (-36)$ Add the opposite of 24.

$ = -9 - (-36)$ Add 15 and -24.

$ = -9 + 36$ Add the opposite of -36.

$ = 27$ Add.

Science

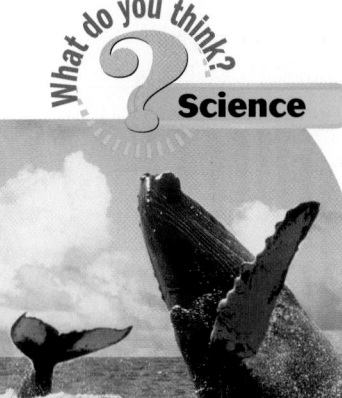

■ SOFAR

Humpback whales use the SOFAR channel to communicate with other whales. The speed of sound in water at 68°F is 1482 meters per second. The speed of sound in air at 68°F is 344 meters per second. How much faster does sound travel in water?

EXAMPLE 3 Using Integer Subtraction

SOFAR The SOFAR (*SO*und *F*ixing *A*nd *R*anging) channel is a layer of water in the oceans that allows sounds to travel extremely long distances. Use the diagram to find the vertical height of the SOFAR channel.

sea level
−500 m

SOFAR channel

−3000 m

Solution

The vertical height is the difference of the upper and lower elevations.

Vertical height $= -500 - (-3000)$ Write subtraction statement.

$ = -500 + 3000$ Add the opposite of -3000.

$ = 2500$ Add.

ANSWER The vertical height of the SOFAR channel is 2500 meters.

Getting Ready to Practice

Vocabulary **Translate the verbal phrase into a numerical expression.**

1. The difference of negative two and six

2. The difference of the opposite of five and the opposite of three

Find the difference.

3. $5 - 12$ **4.** $6 - (-16)$ **5.** $-11 - (-7)$ **6.** $-9 - 10$

Evaluate the expression when $x = 15$ and $y = -8$.

7. $5 - x$ **8.** $-9 - y$ **9.** $y - x$ **10.** $x - y$

11. Guided Problem Solving Use the diagram to find the distances between the bird and the boat, the boat and the reef, and the bird and the reef.

  1 Identify which elevation is greater for each situation.

  2 Subtract the lower elevation from the greater elevation.

  3 Answer the original question by completing each statement.

    The bird is _?_ feet above the boat.
    The boat is _?_ feet above the reef.
    The bird is _?_ feet above the reef.

55 ft

0 ft

−35 ft

Practice and Problem Solving

with Homework

Example	Exercises
1	12–20
2	22–24
3	21, 26–28

Online Resources
CLASSZONE.COM
· More Examples
· eTutorial Plus

Find the difference.

12. $-13 - 12$ **13.** $-14 - (-14)$ **14.** $11 - (-6)$

15. $9 - 17$ **16.** $-18 - (-12)$ **17.** $-20 - 7$

18. $32 - 40$ **19.** $28 - (-16)$ **20.** $-39 - (-13)$

21. Game Show A game show contestant has -400 points. He answers a question incorrectly and loses 600 points. What is his total score?

Evaluate the expression when $c = -5$ and $d = 10$.

22. $c - 6 - d$ **23.** $10 - c - d$ **24.** $c - d - 8 - 4$

25. Critical Thinking Explain how you can find the distance between the points on the number line using subtraction.

Temperatures In Exercises 26–28, use the table. It shows the coldest temperatures ever recorded for four states.

Coldest Recorded Temperatures	
State	**Temperature**
Alaska	−80°F
Colorado	−61°F
Kentucky	−37°F
Mississippi	−19°F

26. How much colder is Alaska's coldest temperature than Kentucky's?

27. How much colder is Colorado's coldest temperature than Mississippi's?

28. Which two states have the greatest difference of coldest temperatures? Which two states have the least difference of coldest temperatures?

Science

Evaluate the expression.

29. $41 - 300$ **30.** $144 - 612$ **31.** $-309 - (-2111)$

32. $-5 - (-5) - (-5)$ **33.** $8 - 2 - 6 - 10$ **34.** $-4 - 7 + (-9) - 1$

35. $-1 + (-8) - 9$ **36.** $6 - (-4) - 10$ **37.** $3 - (-7) - (-2)$

38. $15 + (-29) - (-72)$ **39.** $-52 - (-18) - 37$ **40.** $91 + (-40) - 34$

41. Dinosaurs The table shows the ranges of three dinosaur periods during the Mesozoic Era. Calculate how long each of the periods lasted.

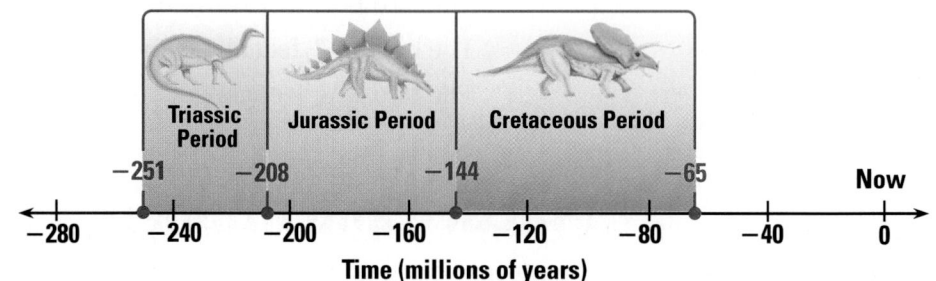

Evaluate the expression when $a = -9$, $b = 18$, and $c = -4$.

42. $a + c - 10$ **43.** $14 - a - b$ **44.** $a - b - c$ **45.** $c + a - b$

Challenge Copy and complete the statement using *always*, *sometimes*, or *never*.

46. A negative number minus a positive number is _?_ negative.

47. A positive number minus a negative number is _?_ negative.

Dinosaurs

Scientists believe that if a Tyrannosaurus Rex was able to run more than 25 miles per hour it would have to have had more than 80% of its body mass in its legs. If a Tyrannosaurus Rex weighed 13,000 pounds, this would mean the legs weighed 10,400 pounds. How much would the rest of its body have weighed?

48. Weather To collect data on winter storms developing in the north Pacific Ocean, a cylinder that measures wind speed, humidity, and temperature at different elevations is dropped from a plane. If the plane is 40,000 feet above sea level and the cylinder drops to the bottom of the Pacific Ocean, 13,000 feet below sea level, how far does the cylinder fall?

Mixed Review

Solve the equation using mental math. *(Lesson 1.5)*

49. $v + 5 = 13$ **50.** $7w = 42$ **51.** $12 - x = 9$

Find the sum. *(Lesson 2.2)*

52. $-8 + 17$ **53.** $11 + (-9)$ **54.** $-22 + (-6)$

Basic Skills Find the difference.

55. $257 - 89$ **56.** $500 - 166$ **57.** $6641 - 992$ **58.** $8250 - 98$

FCAT Practice

59. Multiple Choice What is the value of $-8 - (-3) - (-4) - 12$?

     A. -27 **B.** -13 **C.** 3   **D.** 11

60. Short Response A carpenter cuts 7 feet from a board that is 12 feet long. The carpenter then cuts 24 inches from the board. Is there enough left for a project that requires 4 feet of board? Explain.

BRAIN GAME

Argyle Arithmetic

Each number in a purple diamond is the sum of the two numbers below it. Each number in a green diamond is the difference of the two numbers above it. Copy and complete the argyle arithmetic.

FLORIDA: Standards and Assessment
Know appropriate operations to solve real-world problems. (MA.A.3.3.2)

Look for a Pattern

Guess, Check, and Revise

Draw a Diagram

Act It Out

Work Backward

Look for a Pattern

Make a Table

Solve a Simpler Problem

Problem Greg is setting up for a craft fair and is stacking gift boxes for a display. He knows a pyramid with a height of 2 boxes contains 5 boxes, a pyramid with a height of 3 boxes contains 14 boxes, and a pyramid with a height of 4 boxes contains 30 boxes. How many boxes will he need to make a pyramid with a height of 6 boxes?

❶ Read and Understand

Read the problem carefully.

You need to find how many boxes Greg needs to make a pyramid with a height of 6 boxes.

❷ Make a Plan

Decide on a strategy to use.

Sketch or model a pyramid with 5 boxes and a pyramid with 14 boxes. Look for a pattern. You can follow the pattern to determine how many boxes Greg will need.

❸ Solve the Problem

Reread the problem and look for a pattern.

Sketch or model several rectangular pyramids and count how many boxes are at each level. Make a table that shows the number of boxes in each level.

1 box
4 boxes

1 box
4 boxes
9 boxes

Level n	Boxes in level n	Boxes in n–level pyramid
1	1^2	$1^2 = 1$
2	2^2	$1^2 + 2^2 = 5$
3	3^2	$1^2 + 2^2 + 3^2 = 14$

The number of boxes in each level is the square of the number of the level. The number of boxes in a pyramid is the sum of the squares.

ANSWER To make a rectangular pyramid with a height of 6 boxes, Greg will need $1^2 + 2^2 + 3^2 + 4^2 + 5^2 + 6^2 = 91$ boxes.

❹ Look Back

Sketch a top view of each level to check your answer.

Homemade
Candy
$2.00 a box

Use the strategy *look for a pattern*.

1. Geometry Make a table showing the number of dots in each triangle. Determine the number of dots in the ninth triangle in this sequence.

2. Track Your track coach tells you to do a running drill in which you run 16 feet and run back. Then you run 32 feet and run back. Next you run 48 feet and run back. How far would you expect to run next?

3. Tiling Jason and Emily are laying tiles in the kitchen of a restaurant that measures 36 feet by 24 feet. Each tile measures 1 foot by 1 foot. If they follow the pattern shown below, how many blue tiles will they need to fill the entire kitchen with this pattern?

4. Number Sense Copy and complete the table below. Look for a pattern so you can evaluate 11 · 97 using mental math.

11 · 12	132	12 + 120
11 · 13	143	13 + ?
11 · 14	154	14 + ?
11 · 15	165	15 + ?
11 · 16	176	16 + ?

Use any strategy to solve the problem.

5. Who's Oldest? Scott is two years older than Anne, and Kelly is three years younger than Scott. Ben is nine years less than twice Scott's age, and Anne is 10 years old. Determine the ages of Scott, Ben, and Kelly.

6. Baking You have a recipe that makes 24 cookies. The ingredients include 2 eggs, 1 cup of sugar, 1.5 cups of flour, 1 teaspoon of vanilla, and 1 teaspoon of baking soda. What is the greatest number of cookies you can make if you have 12 eggs, 4 cups of sugar, and 9 cups of flour?

7. Stock Prices A newspaper reports these changes in the price of a stock during a 5-day period: -1, -8, $+2$, -4, and $+6$. The stock price ended at $35 on the fifth day. How much was the price of a stock before the 5-day period started?

8. Cereal You are stacking boxes of cereal for a display. You use a total of 78 boxes, and each row has one fewer box than the row below it. How many rows make up the display if the top row has one box?

9. Basketball In a basketball game, there are 1 point free throws, 2 point field goals and 3 point field goals. How many ways can you score 12 points?

Multiplying Integers

2.4

BEFORE	▶ Now	WHY?
You added and subtracted integers.	You'll multiply integers.	So you can find the worth of a coin in a game, as in Ex. 32.

In the Real World

Review Words
integer, p 53
product, p. 713

FLORIDA
Standards and Assessment
• Know effects of the four basic operations. (MA.A.3.3.1)
• Apply number properties. (MA.A.3.3.1)

Diving A diver is exploring a coral reef. The diver's depth is changing by −6 feet per second. If the diver started at sea level, what is the diver's position after 10 seconds?

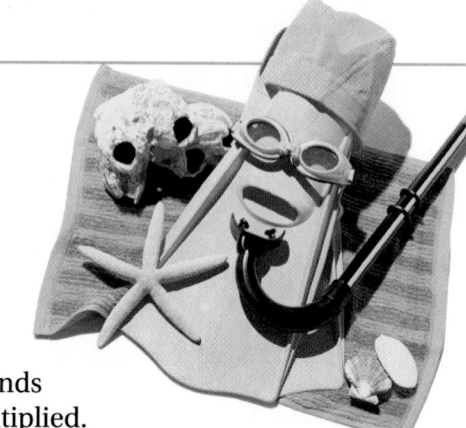

To find the position, you can multiply integers. When you multiply integers, the sign of the product depends on the signs of the integers being multiplied.

Multiplying Integers

Words	Numbers
The product of two integers with the same sign is positive.	$4 \cdot 2 = 8$ $-3 \cdot (-7) = 21$
The product of two integers with different signs is negative.	$4 \cdot (-2) = -8$ $-3 \cdot 7 = -21$

EXAMPLE 1 **Multiplying Integers**

To find the diver's position relative to sea level after 10 seconds, use the distance formula $d = rt$.

$d = rt$	Write the distance formula.
$d = -6(10)$	Substitute −6 for r and 10 for t.
$d = -60$	Different signs, so product is negative.

ANSWER The diver's position relative to sea level is −60 feet.

Your turn now Use the information above.

1. Find the diver's position relative to sea level after 13 seconds.

Multiplication Properties

Multiplication Property of Zero

Words The product of an integer and 0 is 0.

Numbers $-4 \cdot 0 = 0$ **Algebra** For any value of a, $a \cdot 0 = 0$.

Identity Property of Multiplication

Words The product of an integer and 1 is the integer.

Numbers $4(1) = 4$ **Algebra** For any value of a, $a(1) = a$.

When you multiply a number by -1, the product is the *opposite* of the original number.

EXAMPLE 2 **Multiplying Two or More Integers**

HELP with Solving

When you multiply more than two positive or negative integers:

- If there is an *even* number of negative factors then the product is *positive*.

- If there is an *odd* number of negative factors then the product is *negative*.

a. $-1(6) = -6$ Different signs, so product is negative.

b. $-8(-2) = 16$ Same sign, so product is positive.

c. $-15(0) = 0$ Product of an integer and 0 is 0.

d. $4(-10)(-12) = -40(-12)$ Multiply from left to right.

$= 480$ Multiply.

EXAMPLE 3 **Evaluating an Expression with Integers**

Evaluate $a^2 + 3b$ when $a = -5$ and $b = -11$.

$a^2 + 3b = (-5)^2 + 3(-11)$ Substitute -5 for a and -11 for b.

$= 25 + 3(-11)$ Evaluate the power.

$= 25 + (-33)$ Multiply.

$= -8$ Add.

Your turn now **Find the product.**

2. $-1(4)$ **3.** $7(0)$ **4.** $-6(-11)$ **5.** $-1(-12)(-9)$

Evaluate the expression when $a = 3$, $b = -4$ and $c = -8$.

6. $ac - b$ **7.** $ac + b$ **8.** $a^2 + bc$ **9.** $ab - c^2$

Getting Ready to Practice

1. Vocabulary Copy and complete: The product of a positive integer and a negative integer is a ? integer.

Find the product.

2. $-4(-7)$ **3.** $0(-9)$ **4.** $-3(6)$

5. $-1(-2)(-3)$ **6.** $2(-4)(5)$ **7.** $10(-9)(-3)$

8. Banking You have $500 in a savings account. Over a 2 month period, you make 9 withdrawals of $30 each. What is your new balance?

9. Find the Error Describe and correct the error in the solution.

$$\cancel{\quad} \quad -8(-12) = -96$$

Practice and Problem Solving

HELP with Homework

Example	Exercises
1	10–21
2	10–21
3	22–25

Online Resources
CLASSZONE.COM
· More Examples
· eTutorial Plus

Find the product.

10. $-6(7)$ **11.** $-1(-17)$ **12.** $0(-13)$ **13.** $-4(-11)$

14. $9(-2)$ **15.** $3(-5)$ **16.** $-15(-12)$ **17.** $-1(-32)$

18. $-2(5)(-6)$ **19.** $6(-4)(12)$ **20.** $-8(-7)(-5)$ **21.** $12(0)(-45)$

Evaluate the expression when $x = -9$, $y = -7$, and $z = -4$.

22. $xy + z$ **23.** $xy - y$ **24.** $2xyz$ **25.** $-3xy + 2yz$

Find the product.

26. $|-2| \cdot 5$ **27.** $-12 \cdot |11|$ **28.** $-7(-8) \cdot |-4|$

Mental Math Use mental math to solve the equation.

29. $2x = -8$ **30.** $-21y = 63$ **31.** $-5(-4)z = -80$

32. Video Game David is playing a video game. If he falls into a pit, he loses 125 points. If he collects coins, he will gain points. He has 400 points before he falls into 3 pits. After he collects a coin in each pit, his score is 175 points. How many points is each coin worth?

33. Look for a Pattern Evaluate $(-10)^1$, $(-10)^2$, $(-10)^3$, $(-10)^4$, and $(-10)^5$. How is the exponent related to the sign of the power?

34. Critical Thinking Does $(-3)^2$ equal -3^2? Explain your reasoning.

Evaluate the expression when $a = -8$ and $b = -11$.

35. $-a(-a)$ **36.** $a(-b^2)b$ **37.** $[a + (-a)b]^2$

38. Check for Reasonableness A coconut falls 100 feet from a palm tree. The equation $h = -16t^2 + 100$ gives the height h, in feet, of the coconut after falling for t seconds. Evaluate the equation when t equals 2, 2.5, and 3 seconds. When does the coconut hit the ground? What is the actual height of the coconut after 3 seconds?

39. Stock Market Your uncle owns 25 shares of stock A, 45 shares of stock B, and 60 shares of stock C. In one day, the price per share changed by +\$.56 for stock A, −\$1.46 for stock B, and −\$.50 for stock C. Find the total change in value of your uncle's stock.

Evaluate the expression when $w = -31$, $y = 52$, and $z = -63$.

40. wyz **41.** $yz - wyz$ **42.** $3yz - wy$ **43.** $-2wy - 2wz$

44. Challenge The product of a number and its *multiplicative inverse* is 1. For example, $4 \cdot \frac{1}{4} = 1$, so 4 and $\frac{1}{4}$ are multiplicative inverses. Give an example of a negative number and its multiplicative inverse.

Mixed Review

45. Find the side length of a square with a perimeter of 68 feet. *(Lesson 1.6)*

Find the difference. *(Lesson 2.3)*

46. $5 - 7$ **47.** $-9 - 14$ **48.** $-23 - (-12)$

Basic Skills **Find the quotient.**

49. $75 \div 5$ **50.** $0 \div 12$ **51.** $34 \div 17$ **52.** $63 \div 7$

FCAT Practice

53. Multiple Choice What is the value of the expression $-3(-6) \cdot |-4|$?

     A. -72 **B.** -36 **C.** 14   **D.** 72

54. Multiple Choice When you multiply an integer less than -2 and an integer greater than -1, the product is which of the following?

     F. less than zero   **G.** greater than zero

     H. less than or equal to zero   **I.** greater than or equal to zero

Datos

Dividing Integers

BEFORE	▶ **Now**	**WHY?**
You added, subtracted, and multiplied integers.	You'll divide integers.	So you can convert temperatures, as in Ex. 31.

In the Real World

Word Watch

mean, p. 75

FLORIDA

Standards and Assessment
- Know effects of the four basic operations. (MA.A.3.3.1)
- Find the mean of a data set. (MA.E.1.3.2)

Temperatures One of the coldest places on Earth is the Russian town of Verkhoyansk, located near the Arctic Circle. The table shows the average high temperatures in Verkhoyansk. What is the average of these temperatures?

Winter Temperatures	
Month	**Average High**
December	−44°F
January	−48°F
February	−38°F
March	−7°F

You will use the rules for dividing integers to find an average temperature in Example 2. These rules are similar to the rules for multiplying integers.

Dividing Integers

Words	**Numbers**
The quotient of two integers with the same sign is positive.	$\dfrac{12}{6} = 2 \qquad \dfrac{-12}{-6} = 2$
The quotient of two integers with different signs is negative.	$\dfrac{12}{-6} = -2 \qquad \dfrac{-12}{6} = -2$
The quotient of zero and any nonzero integer is 0.	$\dfrac{0}{12} = 0 \qquad \dfrac{0}{-12} = 0$

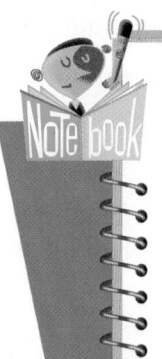
Watch Out!

You cannot divide a number by 0. Any number divided by 0 is *undefined*.

EXAMPLE 1 **Dividing Integers**

a. $\dfrac{-40}{-8} = 5$ Same sign, so quotient is positive.

b. $\dfrac{-14}{2} = -7$ Different signs, so quotient is negative.

c. $\dfrac{36}{-9} = -4$ Different signs, so quotient is negative.

■ **Temperatures**

One of the lowest temperatures on Earth, -90°F, was recorded in Verkhoyansk, Russia, on February 7, 1892. How much colder is this than today's temperature where you live?

The **mean** of a data set is the sum of the values divided by the number of values.

$$\text{mean} = \frac{\text{sum of values}}{\text{number of values}}$$

EXAMPLE 2 **Finding a Mean**

Temperatures To find the mean of the monthly average high temperatures in Verkhoyansk, Russia, given on page 74, first find the sum of the temperatures.

$$-44 + (-48) + (-38) + (-7) = -137$$

Then, divide the sum by the number of temperatures.

$$\frac{-137}{4} = -34.25$$

ANSWER The mean of the temperatures is about -34°F.

Your turn now **Find the quotient.**

1. $\frac{-33}{11}$ **2.** $\frac{-25}{-5}$ **3.** $\frac{0}{-4}$ **4.** $\frac{72}{-9}$

Find the mean of the data.

5. $-16, 17, 8, -23, -31$ **6.** $0, -4, -10, 4, 11 -9, -13$

7. $-9, 26, -78, -40, -34$ **8.** $-7, -2, -12, 15, -8, -25, -17$

EXAMPLE 3 **Evaluating Expressions**

Evaluate the expression when $a = -24$, $b = 8$, and $c = -4$.

a. $\frac{a}{b}$ **b.** $\frac{ab}{c}$

Solution

a. $\frac{a}{b} = \frac{-24}{8}$ Substitute values.

      $= -3$ Different signs, so quotient is negative.

b. $\frac{ab}{c} = \frac{-24 \cdot 8}{-4}$ Substitute values.

      $= \frac{-192}{-4}$ Multiply.

      $= 48$ Same sign, so quotient is positive.

INTERNET
eWorkbook Plus
CLASSZONE.COM

Getting Ready to Practice

1. **Vocabulary** Copy and complete: To find the ? of three numbers, add them and divide the sum by three.

Find the quotient.

2. $\dfrac{-44}{4}$ 3. $\dfrac{0}{-7}$ 4. $\dfrac{-81}{-9}$ 5. $\dfrac{50}{-10}$

Evaluate the expression when $x = 18$, $y = -12$, and $z = -6$.

6. $\dfrac{y}{z}$ 7. $\dfrac{x}{z}$ 8. $\dfrac{xz}{y}$ 9. $\dfrac{z^2}{y}$

10. **Guided Problem Solving** Will opened a used musical instrument shop. The table shows his profits for the first three months. Find his mean profit for these months.

Month	Profit
October	−$172
November	−$203
December	$157

   (1 Add the profits.

   (2 Count the number of months given.

   (3 Divide the sum in Step 1 by the number in Step 2. Should you give an exact or approximate answer?

Practice and Problem Solving

Find the quotient.

11. $\dfrac{-42}{-6}$ 12. $\dfrac{-28}{2}$ 13. $\dfrac{36}{-4}$ 14. $\dfrac{-19}{-1}$

15. $\dfrac{-49}{-7}$ 16. $\dfrac{-66}{-11}$ 17. $\dfrac{0}{-18}$ 18. $\dfrac{-27}{0}$

HELP with Homework

Example	Exercises
1	11–18, 27–30
2	19–20, 26
3	22–25

Online Resources
CLASSZONE.COM

· More Examples
· eTutorial Plus

Find the mean of the data.

19. $-12, 5, -9, 10, 16, -8, -2, 8$ 20. $4, -3, -8, 7, -1, 4, -2, -9, -1$

21. **Writing** Is the mean of a set of negative numbers *always*, *sometimes*, or *never* negative? Give an example to support your reasoning.

Evaluate the expression when $m = 16$, $n = -8$, and $p = -32$.

22. $\dfrac{m}{n}$ 23. $\dfrac{p}{n}$ 24. $\dfrac{n^2}{m}$ 25. $\dfrac{p}{n + m}$

26. Track and Field In five trial runs of a 100 meter dash, a runner has times of 14.01, 15.27, 16.17, 14.42, and 15.01 seconds. The table shows the time differences between the team average, in seconds, and the runner's times. Find the mean of the differences between the team average and the runner's times.

Trial	Difference
1	−1.51
2	−0.25
3	0.65
4	−1.1
5	−0.51

FIN   ISH

Find the quotient.

27. $\dfrac{-9}{6}$ **28.** $\dfrac{15}{-12}$ **29.** $\dfrac{-8}{-10}$ **30.** $\dfrac{-6}{-30}$

31. Reindeer The natural habitat of a reindeer is the Arctic tundra. The average temperature during the winter in the Arctic tundra is $-34°C$. You can convert degrees Celsius C to degrees Fahrenheit F by using the formula $F = \dfrac{9}{5}C + 32$. What is the average winter Arctic tundra temperature in degrees Fahrenheit?

Challenge **Evaluate the expression when $a = -15$, $b = 50$, and $c = 20$.**

32. $\dfrac{b^2 + c}{c^2 a}$ **33.** $\dfrac{-2(a^2 + c^2)}{b}$ **34.** $\dfrac{(b + c)^2}{a}$

Mixed Review

Write the product as a power. *(Lesson 1.4)*

35. $5 \cdot 5 \cdot 5 \cdot 5 \cdot 5$ **36.** $8 \cdot 8 \cdot 8 \cdot 8 \cdot 8 \cdot 8$ **37.** $b \cdot b \cdot b \cdot b$

Find the product. *(Lesson 2.4)*

38. $-11(-8)$ **39.** $12(-6)$ **40.** $6(-8)(-2)$

FCAT Practice

41. Multiple Choice When multiplying the quotient of two negative integers by -1, what is the sign of the result?

   A. Negative   **B.** Positive   **C.** Zero   **D.** Cannot be determined

42. Short Response The table shows golf scores from the last 6 times that you played. Calculate the mean score. Show your work or explain in words how you determined the mean. Should you give an exact or approximate answer?

Day	Score
1	−3
2	1
3	−4
4	−2
5	−2
6	−2

Notebook Review

Review the vocabulary definitions in your notebook.

Copy the review examples in your notebook. Then complete the exercises.

Check Your Definitions

integer, p. 53   positive integer, p. 53   opposite, p. 54

negative integer, p. 53   absolute value, p. 54   mean, p. 75

Use Your Vocabulary

1. Draw a number line. Label three positive integers and three negative integers. Graph the two integers that have an absolute value of 3.

2.1 Can you graph and order integers?

EXAMPLE Order the integers from least to greatest: 24, −6, −45, 0, 12, −20, −32.

In order from least to greatest: −45, −32, −20, −6, 0, 12, 24

☑ **Use a number line to order the integers from least to greatest.**

2. −15, 16, 1, −5, 4, 8   **3.** 40, −60, 98, −85, −6, 42

2.2–2.3 Can you add and subtract integers?

EXAMPLE Find the sum or difference.

    a. $-22 + (-18) = -40$ Same sign, so sum has common sign.

    b. $19 - 34 = 19 + (-34)$ Add the opposite of 34.

                $= -15$ Add.

☑ **Find the sum or difference.**

    4. $-26 + 64$ **5.** $37 + (-92)$ **6.** $-41 + (-78)$

    7. $16 - 82$ **8.** $-51 - 14$ **9.** $-44 - (-29)$

2.4–2.5 Can you multiply and divide integers?

 EXAMPLE Find the product or quotient.

    a. $-7 \cdot 6 = -42$ Different signs, so product is negative.

    b. $\dfrac{-56}{-7} = 8$ Same sign, so quotient is positive.

☑ **Find the product or quotient.**

10. $(-52)(-6)$ **11.** $31(-2)$ **12.** $\dfrac{-90}{15}$ **13.** $\dfrac{-52}{-13}$

Stop *and* **Think**   about Lessons 2.1–2.5

    14. Critical Thinking Is the opposite of the sum of two numbers equal to the sum of the opposites of the numbers? Explain.

Review Quiz 1

Copy and complete the statement with < or >.

    1. $-8 \underline{\ ?\ } 8$ **2.** $0 \underline{\ ?\ } -14$ **3.** $-20 \underline{\ ?\ } -30$ **4.** $-7 \underline{\ ?\ } 5$

Evaluate the expression.

    5. $-6 + 1$ **6.** $-20 + (-10)$ **7.** $-4 - (-3)$

    8. $-6(-8)$ **9.** $-12(4)$ **10.** $\dfrac{-48}{-8}$

Find the mean of the data.

    11. $-9, -15, 16, 4, 2, -10, 8, 20$ **12.** $-10, 6, -11, -6, -7, 3, -4, 1, 1$

    13. $8, -9, -13, 5, -4, -3, -5$ **14.** $5, -6, -10, -15, 7, 9, -1, -3, 4$

Evaluate the expression when $a = -2$, $b = 10$, and $c = -3$.

    15. $b - a$ **16.** $a - c - b$ **17.** abc **18.** $\dfrac{b}{a}$

    19. Gravity You drop a ball out of a window that is 144 feet above the ground. The equation $h = -16t^2 + 144$ gives the height h, in feet, of the ball after falling for t seconds. Find the height of the ball after 1, 2, 3, and 4 seconds. When does the ball hit the ground?

Number Properties

BEFORE	Now	WHY?
You evaluated expressions.	You'll use properties to evaluate expressions.	So you can find your weekly pay, as in Ex. 39.

Word Watch

Review Words

sum, p. 709
product, p. 713

FLORIDA
Standards and Assessment

• Apply number properties.
  (MA.A.3.3.1)
• Simplify expressions using
  integers. (MA.A.1.3.4)

In the Real World

Tour Biking You are going on a 400 mile bike trip. You plan to cycle at an average speed of 12 miles per hour for 7 hours a day. Can you complete the trip in 5 days?

The commutative properties of addition and multiplication can be used to make evaluating expressions using mental math easier.

The Commutative Property

	Addition	**Multiplication**
Words	You can add numbers of a sum in any order.	You can multiply factors of a product in any order.
Numbers	$3 + (-8) = -8 + 3$	$5(-6) = -6(5)$
Algebra	$a + b = b + a$	$ab = ba$

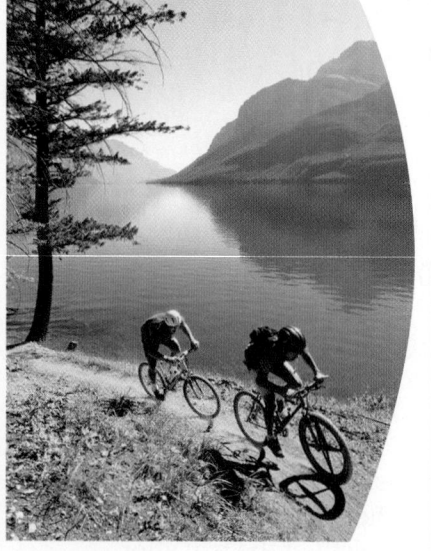

EXAMPLE 1 Using the Commutative Property

To find if you can complete the bike trip in 5 days, find the total distance you plan to cycle. Then compare that distance to the length of the trip.

Total distance	=	Average speed	·	Hours per day	·	Number of days

$= 12 \cdot 7 \cdot 5$ **Substitute known values.**

$= 12 \cdot 5 \cdot 7$ **Commutative property of multiplication**

$= 60 \cdot 7$ **Multiply.**

$= 420$ **Multiply.**

The unit for the result is miles. $\dfrac{\text{miles}}{\text{hour}} \cdot \dfrac{\text{hours}}{\text{day}} \cdot \text{days} = \text{miles}$

ANSWER Because 400 miles is less than the 420 miles you can travel in 5 days, you can complete the trip in 5 days.

HELP with **Solving**

When deciding what numbers to add or multiply first, look for pairs whose sum or product ends in zero, because multiples of 10 are easier to work with.

Subtracting a number is the same as adding the opposite, so you can write expressions to use the commutative property of addition.

EXAMPLE 2 **Using the Commutative Property**

$$-54 + 35 - 16 = -54 + 35 + (-16)$$ Change subtraction to addition

$$= -54 + (-16) + 35$$ Commutative property of addition

$$= -70 + 35$$ Add -54 and -16.

$$= -35$$ Add -70 and -35.

Your turn now **Use the commutative property to evaluate.**

1. $2 \cdot (-9) \cdot 5$ **2.** $47 + (-99) - (-53)$ **3.** $94 - 56 - 44$

The associative properties of addition and multiplication can also be used to make evaluating expressions using mental math easier.

The Associative Property

	Addition	**Multiplication**
Words	Changing the grouping of numbers will not change their sum.	Changing the grouping of factors will not change their product.
Numbers	$(2 + 3) + 4 = 2 + (3 + 4)$	$(7 \cdot 4) \cdot 5 = 7 \cdot (4 \cdot 5)$
Algebra	$(a + b) + c = a + (b + c)$	$(ab)c = a(bc)$

EXAMPLE 3 **Using the Associative Property**

$$\frac{-3}{5} + \left(\frac{-2}{5} + 3\right) = \left(\frac{-3}{5} + \frac{-2}{5}\right) + 3$$ Associative property of addition

$$= \frac{-5}{5} + 3$$ Add fractions.

$$= -1 + 3$$ Write $\frac{-5}{5}$ as -1.

$$= 2$$ Add.

HELP with **Review**

Grouping fractions and adding them makes mental math easier. For help adding fractions with common denominators, see p. 710.

Commute means change locations. You can use the *commutative properties* to change the order of numbers.
Associate means group together. You can use the *associative properties* to group numbers differently.

EXAMPLE 4 **Using the Associative Property**

$$5 \cdot (11 \cdot 2) = 5 \cdot (2 \cdot 11)$$ Commutative property of multiplication

$$= (5 \cdot 2) \cdot 11$$ Associative property of multiplication

$$= 10 \cdot 11$$ Multiply inside grouping symbols.

$$= 110$$ Multiply.

Your turn now **Evaluate the expression using mental math.**

4. $18 + (-34 + 12)$ **5.** $46 + (-63 - 46)$ **6.** $-2(46 \cdot 50)$

7. $4\left(\dfrac{1}{4} \cdot 23\right)$ **8.** $\dfrac{3}{7} + \left(8 + \dfrac{4}{7}\right)$ **9.** $[-21 \cdot (-29)] \cdot 0$

2.6 Exercises

More Practice, p. 728

INTERNET
eWorkbook Plus
CLASSZONE.COM

Getting Ready to Practice

Vocabulary **Match the equation with the property it illustrates.**

1. $(x + 9) + 1 = x + (9 + 1)$ **A.** Identity property of addition

2. $12(1) = 12$ **B.** Commutative property of multiplication

3. $8a = a \cdot 8$ **C.** Commutative property of addition

4. $-16 + 0 = -16$ **D.** Associative property of multiplication

5. $(5 \cdot 7)y = 5(7y)$ **E.** Associative property of addition

6. $-24 + a = a + (-24)$ **F.** Identity property of multiplication

Mental Math **Evaluate the expression using mental math. Name the property or properties you used.**

7. $17 + 15 + 13$ **8.** $43 + (-27) - 13$ **9.** $5 \cdot (-29) \cdot 2$

10. $-2(-9 \cdot 50)$ **11.** $-53 + (-27 + 44)$ **12.** $[-4 \cdot (-7)](-5)$

13. **Juice Box** You have a juice box that is 2.5 inches long, 1.5 inches wide, and 4 inches high. The formula for the *volume* of a box is $V = lwh$. How much juice is in the box, in cubic inches?

2.5 in.

4 in.

1.5 in.

Practice and Problem Solving

 with Homework

Example	Exercises
1	14–29, 32
2	14–26
3	14–26
4	14–26

Online Resources
CLASSZONE.COM
· More Examples
· eTutorial Plus

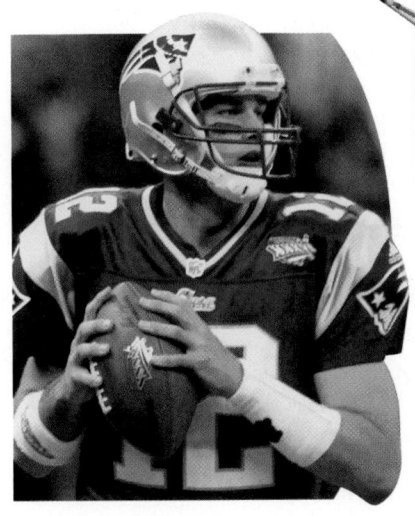

Use the properties of addition and multiplication to find the missing number. Name the property.

14. $28 + \underline{?} = 65 + 28$

15. $54 \cdot 16 = 16 \cdot \underline{?}$

16. $(7 \cdot 3)3 = \underline{?} \, (3 \cdot 3)$

17. $4 + (\underline{?} + 2) = (4 + 9) + 2$

Evaluate the expression. Justify each step.

18. $-86 + 29 + (-34)$

19. $45 - (-68) - 44$

20. $-57 - 38 - (-57)$

21. $12 + (-39 + 48)$

22. $(-26 + 33) + (-4)$

23. $[25 \cdot (-7)]4$

24. $-40\left(\dfrac{1}{2} \cdot 45\right)$

25. $(-20 \cdot 9) \cdot 5$

26. $(3.2 \cdot 4.5)(10)$

Algebra **Simplify the expression.**

27. $7 \cdot x \cdot 10$

28. $-67 + [x + (-13)]$

29. $(52 + x) + 18$

30. **Writing** You need to find the sum of 52, 99, 65, 38, and 11. Explain how the commutative and associative properties of addition can help you find the sum using mental math.

31. **Critical Thinking** Is division commutative? Justify your answer with an example.

32. **Super Bowl** During Super Bowl XXXVI, six New England Patriots rushed the football for 92 yards, 22 yards, 15 yards, 5 yards, 3 yards, and −4 yards. What was the total number of their rushing yards?

Evaluate the expression. Show each step.

33. $3.6 + 5.7 + (-3.6)$

34. $\dfrac{1}{2} \cdot 17 \cdot 20$

35. $5(7 \cdot 4)(0.25)$

36. $\left(-\dfrac{2}{7} + 5\right) + \dfrac{3}{7}$

37. $12 \cdot (7 \cdot 1 \cdot 5)$

38. $\left(\dfrac{2}{3} \cdot 7\right) \cdot 21$

39. **Paycheck** The table shows the hours you worked during one week. Your hourly wage is $6 per hour. Use the commutative property of multiplication to find the amount you earned for the week.

Time Card		
Day	**Time in**	**Time out**
Monday	4 P.M.	6 P.M.
Tuesday	4 P.M.	6 P.M.
Wednesday	—	—
Thursday	3 P.M.	5 P.M.
Friday	3 P.M.	5 P.M.
Saturday	11 A.M.	1 P.M.

40. **Compare** Is the expression $-15 + 34 - 44 - 19 + 51$ equivalent to the expression $34 - 19 + 15 - 44 + 51$? Explain your reasoning.

41. Critical Thinking Explain how the student used the commutative property of addition to go from the first expression to the second expression. Use the same method to find the sum of the numbers from 1 to 19.

$$1 + 2 + 3 + 4 + 5 + 6 + 7 + 8 + 9 = 10 + 10 + 10 + 10 + 5$$
$$= 45$$

42. Sale Price You are buying 8 yards of fabric that costs $5.25 per yard. You have a coupon for half off the original price. What is the price of your purchase after the discount?

43. Challenge Use the commutative properties of addition and multiplication to write three expressions equivalent to $4 \cdot 8 + 5$.

Mixed Review

44. Temperature During the first 10 days of January, 2002, the daily low temperatures in Alaska, in degrees Fahrenheit, were $-29°$, $-24°$, $-18°$, $-42°$, $-42°$, $-42°$, $-40°$, $-44°$, $-26°$ and $-19°$. Find the mean daily low temperature for these 10 days. *(Lesson 2.5)*

Choose a Strategy Use a strategy from the list to solve the following problem. Explain your choice of strategy.

45. You have two stacking bookcases that are 60 inches tall when stacked on top of each other. If you place them side by side, the difference of their heights is 8 inches. How tall is each bookcase?

> **Problem Solving Strategies**
> - Guess, Check, and Revise
> - Look for a Pattern
> - Work Backward

Basic Skills Use a number line to compare the numbers.

46. 1.2 and 0.8 **47.** 1.35 and 1.53 **48.** 0.24 and 0.25

FCAT Practice

49. Multiple Choice Which of the following is equivalent to $2 - 3 + (-5) - 1$?

A. $2 - (-5) + 3 - 1$ **B.** $3 - 2 + (-5) - 1$

C. $2 - 3 + 6$ **D.** $2 + (-3) + (-5) + (-1)$

50. Short Response You need to find the sum of 46, 15, 37, 54, and 85. Explain how the commutative and associative properties of addition can help you find the sum using mental math.

The Distributive Property

BEFORE	▶ Now	WHY?
You used addition and multiplication properties.	You'll use the distributive property.	So you can find the cost of souvenirs, as in Ex. 25.

Word Watch

distributive property, p. 85
terms, p. 86
like terms, p. 86
coefficient, p. 86
constant term, p. 86

FLORIDA

Standards and Assessment

• Apply number properties. (MA.A.3.3.1)

• Simplify algebraic expressions of real-world situations. (MA.D.2.3.1)

In the Real World

Architecture A replica of the Parthenon, an ancient temple in Greece, was built in Nashville, Tennessee, in 1897. The diagram below shows the approximate dimensions of two adjacent rooms inside the replica. How can you find the total area of the two rooms?

EXAMPLE 1 Finding a Combined Area

Two methods can be used to find the total area of the two rooms.

Method 1 Find the area of each room, then find the total area.

Area $= 63(44) + 63(93)$

$= 2772 + 5859$

$= 8631$ square feet

Method 2 Find the total length, then multiply by the common width.

Area $= 63(44 + 93)$

$= 63(137)$

$= 8631$ square feet

63 ft
93 ft
44 ft

ANSWER The total area of the two rooms is 8631 square feet.

Example 1 demonstrates the distributive property.

The Distributive Property

Algebra $a(b + c) = ab + ac$ **Numbers** $6(4 + 3) = 6(4) + 6(3)$

$a(b - c) = ab - ac$ $7(8 - 5) = 7(8) - 7(5)$

The distributive property can be applied to expressions involving a sum or difference of two or more numbers or variable expressions.

EXAMPLE 2 Using the Distributive Property

a. $-5(x + 10) = -5x + (-5)(10)$ Distributive property

$= -5x + (-50)$ Multiply.

b. $3[1 - 20 + (-5)] = 3(1) - 3(20) + 3(-5)$ Distributive property

$= 3 - 60 + (-15)$ Multiply.

$= 3 + (-60) + (-15)$ Add the opposite of 60.

$= -72$ Add.

Your turn now Write two expressions for the total area of the two rectangles. Find the total area.

1.

12 ft   22 ft

10 ft

2. 3 m

14 m

9 m

Use the distributive property to evaluate or simplify the expression.

3. $-2(5 + 12)$ **4.** $-4(-7 - 10)$ **5.** $2(w - 8)$ **6.** $-8(z + 25)$

HELP with Notetaking

When you add new vocabulary words to your notebook be sure to include examples of how they are used.

Combining Like Terms In a sum the parts that are added together are the **terms** of the expression. You can use the distributive property to combine *like terms*. **Like terms** have identical variable parts raised to the same power. In a term the number multiplied by the variable is the **coefficient** of the variable. A term that has no variable is a **constant term**.

Coefficients are 4 and 8.   Constant term is 1.

$4x + 8x + 1$

4x and 8x are like terms.

EXAMPLE 3 Combining Like Terms

a. $3x + 4x = (3 + 4)x$ Distributive property

$= 7x$ Add inside grouping symbols.

b. $-9y + 7y + 5z = (-9 + 7)y + 5z$ Distributive property

$= -2y + 5z$ Add inside grouping symbols.

You may need to use the distributive property before you can combine like terms.

EXAMPLE 4 **Simplifying an Expression**

HELP with Solving

Remember that $x = 1 \cdot x$, so x has a coefficient of 1.

a. $2(4 + x) + x = 8 + 2x + x$ Distributive property

$= 8 + 3x$ Combine like terms.

b. $-5(3x - 6) + 7x = -15x + 30 + 7x$ Distributive property

$= -8x + 30$ Combine like terms.

Your turn now **Simplify the expression by combining like terms.**

7. $4x - 7x$ **8.** $5y + 9z - 7 - 3y$ **9.** $5(x - 6) + 3x + 4$

2.7 **Exercises**
More Practice, p. 728

INTERNET
eWorkbook Plus
CLASSZONE.COM

Getting Ready to Practice

1. **Vocabulary** Identify any *like terms* and *coefficients* in the expression $7x - 3y - 6y + x + 2$.

Use the distributive property to write an equivalent expression.

2. $4(7 + 8)$ **3.** $-7(3 + 2)$ **4.** $3(5 + 6)$

Simplify the expression by combining like terms.

5. $3y + 6y$ **6.** $9a - 4b + a$ **7.** $8m + n - 2m - 4b$

8. **Guided Problem Solving** You are buying three pairs of flip-flops that cost \$12.90 each. Use mental math and the distributive property to find the total cost of the flip-flops.

  (1 Write $3(12.90)$ as $3(13 - 0.10)$.

  (2 Find the products $3(13)$ and $3(0.10)$.

  (3 Find the difference of the products.

Practice and Problem Solving

HELP with Homework

Example	Exercises
1	33, 44
2	9–18, 27–32
3	19–24, 27–32
4	19–24, 27–32

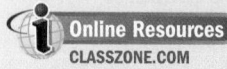

Online Resources
CLASSZONE.COM

· More Examples
· eTutorial Plus

Match the expression with its simplified expression.

9. $3(x + 4)$ **10.** $4(x + 3)$ **11.** $2(2x - 6)$ **12.** $x(4 + 9)$

A. $4x - 12$ **B.** $3x + 12$ **C.** $13x$ **D.** $4x + 12$

Use the distributive property to evaluate or simplify the expression.

13. $9(x - 3)$ **14.** $-12(4 + 5 + y)$ **15.** $8(5 + 2)$

16. $19[7 + w + (-2)]$ **17.** $-34(z - 21 - 5)$ **18.** $-13(-12 + 9)$

Simplify the expression by combining like terms.

19. $r + 2s + 3r$ **20.** $11w + 9z + 3z + 5w$

21. $7a - 2a + 8b - 2b$ **22.** $3x + 2x + y + 2y - 3$

23. $-3x + 2x - 9y - 2x$ **24.** $r + 2s - (-3r) - s$

25. Souvenirs You are on vacation in Massachusetts and want to buy souvenirs for 6 friends at home. You decide to buy a trading pin that costs $2.35 and a pen that costs $.65 for each friend. Explain how to use mental math to find how much money you will need.

26. Find the Error Describe and correct the error in the solution.

$$4x + 2y - 7y - 2x = 4x - 2x + 2y - 7y$$
$$= 2x - 5y$$
$$= -3xy$$

Simplify the expression.

27. $7(y - 2)$ **28.** $9x(4 - 2 + 6)$ **29.** $3x + 2 - 5x + 4x$

30. $5(z + 2z) - 4z$ **31.** $8d - 2(3d - 5d)$ **32.** $4(3c - 4) + 2 - 4c$

33. Area A floor plan of a house is shown. You want to carpet the family room and the living room. The carpeting you want to use in these two rooms sells for $3.12 per square foot. How much will the carpet cost?

Simplify the expression by combining like terms.

34. $3a + 4b - 5 - a + 7b + 3 - b$ **35.** $5(x + 2) - 5(y + 3) - 2x + 5y$

36. $3.2(2z - 3x) + 4(1.1y + x) - 2z$ **37.** $7(y - 1.3) + 2.4 - 5.3y$

38. Writing Explain what you should consider when deciding which expression is easier to evaluate, $8(1000 - 2)$ or $8 \cdot 1000 - 8 \cdot 2$. Give an example of a problem you think is easier to solve using the distributive property and an example you think is not easier to solve using the distributive property.

Mental Math **Use mental math to find the product using a method like the one in Exercise 8 on page 87. Explain your reasoning.**

39. $4(34)$ **40.** $9(19)$ **41.** $24(12)$ **42.** $65(24)$

43. Critical Thinking Are $3xy$ and $4yx$ like terms? Explain your reasoning.

44. Mural Some students have been given permission to paint murals on 5 walls at your school. The walls are all 8 feet tall. The mural widths are 21.5 feet, 35 feet, 27.5 feet, 33.5 feet, and 22.5 feet. Write two expressions to find the total area of the murals. Then find the total area.

45. Challenge You are ordering T-shirts with your school logo. Each T-shirt costs $7.25. There is a $25 setup fee for silk-screening, and a screening charge of $1.85 per shirt. Write an expression to find the total cost for x T-shirts. What is the total cost for 75 T-shirts? for 170 T-shirts?

Mixed Review

Order the integers from least to greatest. *(Lesson 2.1)*

46. $-90, 35, 19, -35, 80$ **47.** $70, -20, -90, 0, -100$

Evaluate the expression. *(Lesson 2.6)*

48. $-5(4 \cdot 17)$ **49.** $(-23 + 14) - 12$

50. $17 + (3 - 12) + 24(0)$ **51.** $(-4 \cdot 7) \cdot 25$

FCAT Practice

52. Extended Response The perimeter of the stage is 200 feet. Find the value of x. Show your work. Then explain one way to find the area of the stage. What is another way to find the area of the stage? Use either method to find the area.

Technology Activity

FLORIDA: Standards and Assessment
Solve multi-step real-world problems. (MA.A.3.3.1)

Using Integer Operations

GOAL Use a calculator to evaluate expressions.

Example **Use a calculator to evaluate the expression.**

a. $-900{,}018 + (-805{,}560)$ **b.** $\dfrac{-278 \cdot (-640)}{-139}$

Solution

Use the following keystrokes to find your answer.

Keystrokes	**Display**
a. (−) 900018 + (−) 805560 =	**−1705578**

ANSWER $-900{,}018 + (-805{,}560) = -1{,}705{,}578$

Keystrokes	**Display**
b. (−) 278 × (−) 640 ÷ (−) 139 =	**−1280**

ANSWER $\dfrac{-278 \cdot (-640)}{-139} = -1280$

Watch Out!

The — button performs subtraction. Use the (−) button to enter a negative number.

Your turn now **Use a calculator to evaluate the expression.**

1. $18{,}432 + (-46{,}978)$ **2.** $-50{,}215 + 1315$ **3.** $7010 - (-3999)$

4. $-14{,}300 - (-500)$ **5.** $-751 \cdot 2804$ **6.** $-1940 \cdot (-689)$

7. $3336(-198 \cdot 398)$ **8.** $\dfrac{-105{,}638}{-221}$ **9.** $\dfrac{-67{,}771}{671}$

10. Moon The distance of the moon's orbit around Earth is about 2,415,000 kilometers. The moon travels at an average speed of 3700 kilometers per hour. How long will it take the moon to complete one orbit?

11. Earth The diameter of Earth is about 4 times the diameter of the moon. The diameter of the moon is 3476 kilometers. What is the diameter of Earth? Find the difference of the diameter of Earth and the diameter of the moon.

moon
diameter
Earth

LESSON 2.8

The Coordinate Plane

BEFORE	Now	WHY?
You used number lines.	You'll identify and plot points in a coordinate plane.	So you can predict the price of a phone call, as in Ex. 29.

Word Watch

coordinate plane, p. 91
x-axis, y-axis, p. 91
origin, p. 91
quadrant, p. 91
ordered pair, p. 91
x-coordinate, p. 91
y-coordinate, p. 91

FLORIDA
Standards and Assessment

• Find ordered-pair solutions given a graph. (MA.C.3.3.1)

• Use graphs to illustrate real-world situations. (MA.D.2.3.1)

A **coordinate plane** is formed by the intersection of a horizontal number line called the **x-axis** and a vertical number line called the **y-axis**. The axes meet at a point called the **origin** and divide the coordinate plane into four **quadrants**.

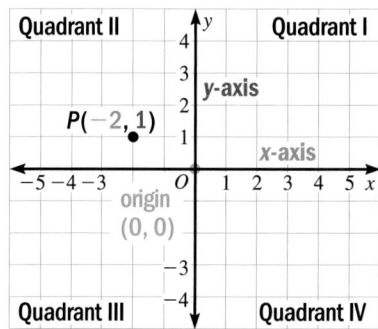

Points in a coordinate plane are represented by **ordered pairs**. The first number is the **x-coordinate**. The second number is the **y-coordinate**. Point P above is represented by the ordered pair $(-2, 1)$.

EXAMPLE 1 **Naming Points in a Coordinate Plane**

Give the coordinates of the point.

   a. A **b.** B **c.** C

Solution

a. Point A is 3 units to the right of the origin and 1 unit up. So, the x-coordinate is 3 and the y-coordinate is 1. The coordinates of A are $(3, 1)$.

b. Point B is 3 units to the left of the origin and 2 units down. So, the x-coordinate is -3 and the y-coordinate is -2. The coordinates of B are $(-3, -2)$.

c. Point C is 2 units up from the origin. So, the x-coordinate is 0 and the y-coordinate is 2. The coordinates of C are $(0, 2)$.

Your turn now Give the coordinates of the point.

  1. D **2.** E **3.** F

EXAMPLE 2 **Graphing Points in a Coordinate Plane**

Plot the point and describe its location.

   a. $A(4, -2)$ **b.** $B(-1, 2)$ **c.** $C(0, -3)$

Solution

   a. Begin at the origin, move 4 units to the right, then 2 units down. Point *A* lies in Quadrant IV.

   b. Begin at the origin, move 1 unit to the left, then 2 units up. Point *B* lies in Quadrant II.

   c. Begin at the origin, move 3 units down. Point *C* lies on the *y*-axis.

HELP with Solving

Points on the *x*-axis or *y*-axis do not lie in any quadrant.

EXAMPLE 3 **Finding Perimeter**

Identify the figure and find its perimeter.

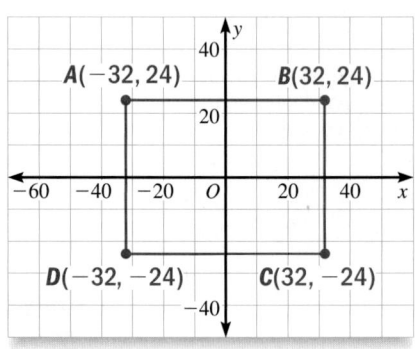

Solution

Points *A*, *B*, *C*, and *D* form a rectangle.

To find the length *l*, find the *horizontal* distance from *A* to *B*.

HELP with Solving

You need to use absolute value signs because length and width are always positive.

$$l = |\text{x-coordinate of } A - \text{x-coordinate of } B|$$
$$= |-32 - 32| = |-64| = 64$$

To find the width *w*, find the *vertical* distance from *A* to *D*.

$$w = |\text{y-coordinate of } A - \text{y-coordinate of } D|$$
$$= |24 - (-24)| = |48| = 48$$

Perimeter $= 2l + 2w = 2(64) + 2(48) = 224$

ANSWER The rectangle has a perimeter of 224 units.

 Plot the point and describe its location.

   4. $R(-3, 4)$ **5.** $S(1, 2)$ **6.** $T(0, 3)$ **7.** $U(-4, 0)$

   8. Plot and connect points $A(-20, 25)$, $B(25, 25)$, $C(25, -20)$, and $D(-20, -20)$. Identify the resulting figure and find its perimeter.

Getting Ready to Practice

1. Vocabulary Draw a coordinate plane and label the *x*-axis, *y*-axis, each quadrant, and the origin.

Give the coordinates of the point.

2. *A*

3. *B*

4. *C*

5. *D*

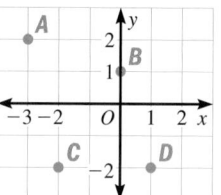

Plot the point in a coordinate plane.

6. $(4, 1)$ **7.** $(2, -3)$ **8.** $(-3, 0)$ **9.** $(-2, -1)$

10. City Park The rectangle with corners *A*, *B*, *C*, and *D* represents a city park. Find the distance around the city park if the length and width of each small square on the coordinate grid represents 100 feet.

Practice and Problem Solving

with Homework

Example	Exercises
1	11–16
2	17–20
3	21–22, 24–26

Online Resources
CLASSZONE.COM

· More Examples
· eTutorial Plus

Give the coordinates of the point.

11. *A*   **12.** *B*

13. *C*   **14.** *D*

15. *E*   **16.** *F*

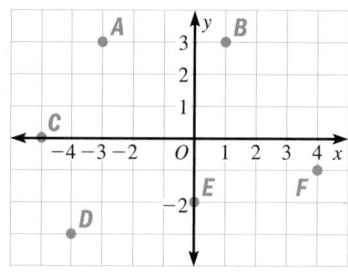

Plot the point in a coordinate plane and describe its location.

17. $(-2, 3)$ **18.** $(3, -1)$ **19.** $(0, -5)$ **20.** $(-3, -4)$

Plot and connect the given points. Then identify the resulting figure and find its perimeter.

21. $A(-2, 6), B(2, 6), C(2, -6), D(-2, -6)$

22. $J(5, 4), K(5, -2), L(-1, -2), M(-1, 4)$

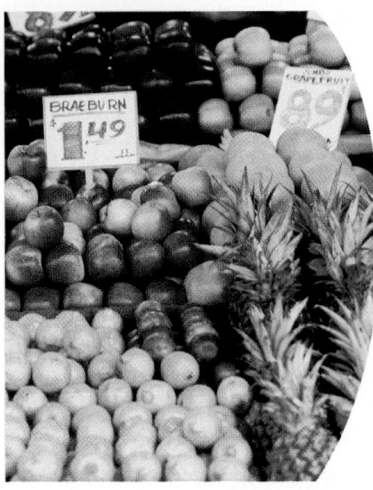

23. Fruit The following ordered pairs represent the cost of buying several weights of pineapple from a fruit stand. The x-coordinate represents the number of pounds and the y-coordinate represents the cost.

(1, $3.50), (2, $7.00), (3, $10.50), (4, $14.00)

Plot the points in a coordinate plane. Identify the pattern.

Use the pattern to estimate the cost of $2\frac{1}{2}$ pounds of pineapple.

Plot and connect the points. Find the perimeter and area of the rectangle formed.

24. $Q(5, 2)$, $R(5, -5)$, $S(-3, -5)$, $T(-3, 2)$

25. $K(0, -5)$, $L(-5, -5)$, $M(-5, 0)$, $N(0, 0)$

26. $W(-1, -7)$, $X(-1, 3)$, $Y(2, 3)$, $Z(2, -7)$

Extended Problem Solving **In Exercises 27–29, suppose your phone card charges 7 cents per minute for a phone call.**

27. Calculate Find the cost of a 10 minute call, a 20 minute call, and a 30 minute call.

28. Graph Plot the costs you found in Exercise 27 in a coordinate plane, where the x-coordinate represents the length (in minutes) of the call and the y-coordinate represents the total cost of the call, in dollars.

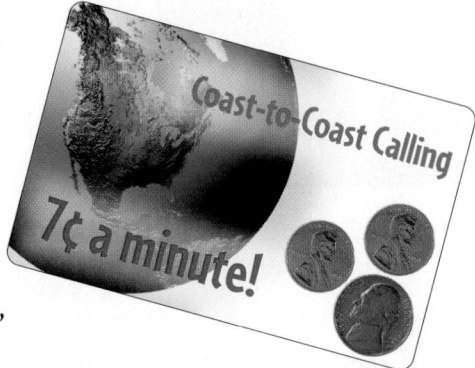

29. Estimate Draw a line through the points. Use the line to estimate the cost of an hour-long call.

30. Challenge Draw a rectangle that has points in all four quadrants. Multiply each coordinate by 2 and draw this rectangle. Compare this rectangle with the original one and compare their perimeters. What do you find?

31. Slide Copy the figure. Move the figure 2 units to the left and 3 units up. Give the new coordinates of A, B, C, D, and E.

Find the sum. (Lesson 2.2)

32. $24 + (-9) + (-12)$ **33.** $-14 + 30 + (-17)$ **34.** $-40 + 8 + 12$

Simplify the expression. (Lesson 2.7)

35. $4(x + 9)$ **36.** $6y(8 - 6)$ **37.** $-9(z - 2)$

38. **Basic Skills** You are selling T-shirts as a fundraiser for your school's soccer team. You need to sell 35 shirts to reach your goal, and you have sold 18 shirts. How many more T-shirts do you need to sell?

FCAT Practice FCAT

INTERNET
FCAT PRACTICE
CLASSZONE.COM

39. **Short Response** On the coordinate plane, plot the points $A(0, 0)$, $B(0, 4)$, $C(6, 4)$, $D(6, 0)$. Connect these points to form a rectangle. Imagine that this rectangle moves 4 units up. Write the new coordinates for points A, B, C, and D.

40. **Multiple Choice** Which labeled points shown have an x-coordinate of -2?

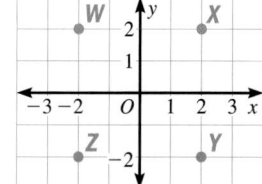

A. Y and Z **B.** W and Y

C. W and Z **D.** W, Y, and Z

BRAIN GAME

Spatial Delivery

Jack delivers balloons in a city. Below is a grid of Jack's city and a list of the deliveries he made today. Copy the diagram on graph paper and plot each stop. How many blocks did Jack travel?

Delivery Stops
Began at Main and State Street
1. E 3rd St. and Main
2. E 3rd St. and N 2nd Ave.
3. E 1st St. and N 2nd Ave.
4. E 1st St. and S 2nd Ave.
5. W 2nd St. and S 3rd Ave.
6. W 3rd St. and S 1st Ave
7. W 3rd St. and N 2nd Ave.
8. W 1st St. and N 2nd Ave.

LESSONS 2.6 TO 2.8

Notebook Review

Review the vocabulary definitions in your notebook.

Copy the review examples in your notebook. Then complete the exercises.

Check Your Definitions

distributive property, p. 85

terms, like terms, p. 86

coefficient, p. 86

constant term, p. 86

coordinate plane, p. 91

x-axis, y-axis, p. 91

origin, p. 91

quadrant, p. 91

ordered pair, p. 91

x-coordinate, p. 91

y-coordinate, p. 91

Use Your Vocabulary

1. What is the *y*-coordinate of the point $(5, -5)$?

2.6 Can you use commutative and associative properties?

 EXAMPLE Evaluate the expression.

$$(-3 + 5) - 7 = (-3 + 5) + (-7)$$ Change subtraction to addition.

$$= [5 + (-3)] + (-7)$$ Commutative property of addition

$$= 5 + [-3 + (-7)]$$ Associative property of addition

$$= 5 + (-10)$$ Add inside grouping symbols.

$$= -5$$ Add.

☑ **Use mental math to evaluate the expression. Justify.**

2. $-5(19 \cdot 2)$ **3.** $-25 \cdot 13 \cdot 4$ **4.** $-42 + (-18 - 23)$

2.7 Can you use the distributive property?

 EXAMPLE Simplify the expression.

$$6(2x + 7) - 9x = 12x + 42 - 9x$$ Distributive property

$$= 12x + 42 + (-9x)$$ Change subtraction to addition.

$$= 12x + (-9x) + 42$$ Commutative property of addition

$$= 3x + 42$$ Combine like terms.

☑ **Use the distributive property to simplify the expression.**

5. $9(3a + 11) - 4$ **6.** $-8b + 12(7b + 3)$ **7.** $2c - 8(9c - 5)$

2.8 Can you identify and plot points?

 EXAMPLE Plot the point and describe its location.

a. $A(-1, 1)$ **b.** $B(4, -3)$

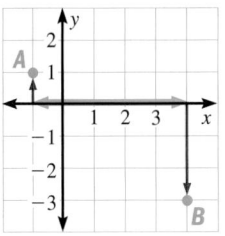

Solution

a. Begin at the origin, move 1 unit to the left and 1 unit up. Point A lies in Quadrant II.

b. Begin at the origin, move 4 units to the right and 3 units down. Point B lies in Quadrant IV.

☑ **Plot the point and describe its location.**

8. $L(3, -5)$ **9.** $M(0, -1)$ **10.** $N(6, 0)$ **11.** $P(-4, 2)$

Stop and Think about Lessons 2.6–2.8

12. Writing Explain how you can use the distributive property and mental math to evaluate the expression $4 \cdot 6.11$.

Review Quiz 2

Evaluate the expression. Justify each step.

1. $(19 + 33) + 11$ **2.** $15(23)(-4)$ **3.** $3(-4 \cdot 9)$

Simplify the expression.

4. $9x + 22x$ **5.** $3a - 2b + 6 - a$ **6.** $8(y + 2) - 4y$

In Exercises 7–9, use the coordinate plane.

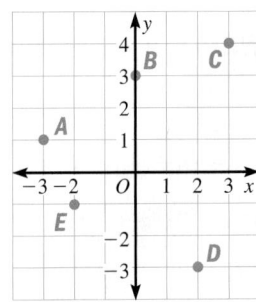

7. Write the coordinates of points A, B, C, D, and E.

8. Which point lies on the y-axis?

9. Which point lies in Quadrant II?

10. Basketball In a basketball game Joe scored 13 points in the first quarter, 6 points in the second quarter, 7 points in the third quarter, and 14 points in the fourth quarter. How many points did Joe score?

Chapter Review

 Vocabulary

integer, p. 53
negative integer, p. 53
positive integer, p. 53
absolute value, p. 54
opposite, p. 54
mean, p. 75

distributive property,
  p. 85
terms, p. 86
like terms, p. 86
coefficient, p. 86
constant term, p. 86
coordinate plane, p. 91

x-axis, p. 91
y-axis, p. 91
origin, p. 91
quadrant, p. 91
ordered pair, p. 91
x-coordinate, p. 91
y-coordinate, p. 91

Vocabulary Review

1. How many numbers have an absolute value of 15? List them.

2. Copy the expression. List any like terms and coefficients.

$$-6y + 8 - 7x + 17x - 21y$$

3. How many quadrants are in a coordinate plane? Draw a coordinate plane and label each quadrant.

Copy and complete the statement.

4. A point in a coordinate plane is represented by a(n) _?_.

5. A(n) _?_ is formed by the intersection of a horizontal number line and a vertical number line.

6. The _?_ is the sum of the values divided by the number of values.

Review Questions

Order the integers from least to greatest. *(Lesson 2.1)*

7. $-42, 53, 8, -31, -5, 11$

8. $-56, -102, 98, -58, 114$

Write the opposite and the absolute value of the integer. *(Lesson 2.1)*

9. 22

10. -13

11. -512

12. 102

Find the sum or difference. *(Lessons 2.2, 2.3)*

13. $-81 + (-91)$

14. $32 + (-79)$

15. $-324 + 500$

16. $-468 + (-196)$

17. $-29 - 57$

18. $62 - (-58)$

19. $-43 - (-122)$

20. $31 - 108$

Find the product. *(Lesson 2.4)*

21. $-6(9)$

22. $31(-4)$

23. $-9(-23)(0)$

24. $-2(-3)(6)(-12)$

Review Questions

Evaluate the expression when $x = -6$, $y = -4$, and $z = -8$. *(Lesson 2.4)*

25. xyz **26.** $9z - 2x$ **27.** $11y - 2xz$ **28.** $2x + 3yz$

29. Hot Air Balloon A hot air balloon at a height of 110 feet rises for 6 minutes at a rate of 18 feet per minute, then drops 22 feet per minute for 3 minutes. What is the height of the balloon? *(Lesson 2.4)*

Find the quotient. *(Lesson 2.5)*

30. $\dfrac{-26}{2}$ **31.** $\dfrac{-98}{-7}$ **32.** $\dfrac{-120}{-15}$ **33.** $\dfrac{63}{-7}$

Find the mean of the data. *(Lesson 2.5)*

34. $5, 7, -9, -2, -6, 8, -9, 6$ **35.** $15, -9, 6, -14, -18, 12, 7, 5, -2, 8$

Evaluate the expression using mental math. Name the property or properties used. *(Lesson 2.6)*

36. $19 - (-58 - 81)$ **37.** $(-45 + 97) - (-45)$ **38.** $(-28 - 95 + 85) + (-62)$

39. $4(19 \cdot 25)$ **40.** $(-15 \cdot 5) \cdot (-20)$ **41.** $[-54 \cdot (-56)] \cdot 0 \cdot (-17)$

Use the distributive property to simplify the expression. *(Lesson 2.7)*

42. $5(12x - 20)$ **43.** $7(9 + 11y)$ **44.** $4(25z - 30)$

Simplify the expression by combining like terms. *(Lesson 2.7)*

45. $14x - 3y - 7x + y$ **46.** $4x - 11y + 2(1 - x)$

47. Baseball Caps Use mental math and the distributive property to find the total price of 3 baseball caps that cost \$12.90 each. *(Lesson 2.7)*

Give the coordinates of the point.
(Lesson 2.8)

48. A **49.** B

50. C **51.** D

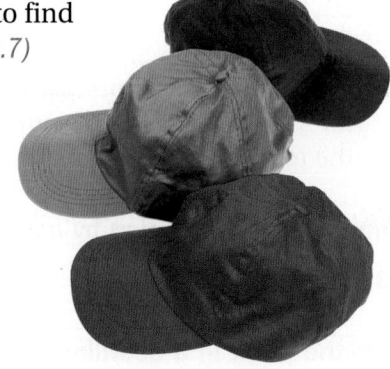

52. Geometry Plot, label, and connect in order the following points in a coordinate plane. Find the perimeter of the figure. *(Lesson 2.8)*

$A(0, 7)$, $B(4, 7)$, $C(4, 4)$, $D(8, 4)$, $E(8, 0)$, $F(0, 0)$

2 Chapter Test

Order the integers from least to greatest.

1. $-9, 8, 14, -11, 0, -1$

2. $123, 87, -59, -12, -111, 22$

Find the number.

3. Find $|x|$ when x is 2 and when x is -4.

4. Find $-(-x)$ when x is -1 and when x is 7.

Find the sum or difference.

5. $17 + (-9)$ **6.** $-8 + (-14)$ **7.** $-2 + (-21)$ **8.** $-33 + 26$

9. $1 - 19$ **10.** $-4 - 17$ **11.** $10 - (-15)$ **12.** $-7 - (-18)$

Find the product or the quotient.

13. $-5(14)$ **14.** $-12(-20)$ **15.** $\dfrac{-152}{-19}$ **16.** $\dfrac{-132}{6}$

17. Temperature The following temperatures were taken during a week in December in Nome, Alaska. What is the mean temperature to the nearest degree?

$-5°F, -8°F, -13°F, -16°F, -8°F, 11°F, 0°F$

Evaluate the expression when $a = 3$, $b = -15$, and $c = 15$.

18. $\dfrac{c}{-a}$ **19.** $\dfrac{6b}{2c}$ **20.** $\dfrac{c}{-5a}$ **21.** $\dfrac{b^2}{a^2}$

22. Groceries You are purchasing a loaf of bread for \$2.16, a box of cereal for \$3.25, and 2 cans of soup for \$.42 each. Write an expression to find the total cost. Then evaluate your expression.

Simplify the expression by combining like terms.

23. $3x + 4 - x + 1$ **24.** $2x - 3y + 5x - (-9y)$ **25.** $2(9x - 22y) + 4x$

Plot the point in a coordinate plane and describe its location.

26. $(-3, 3)$ **27.** $(6, 0)$ **28.** $(-4, -8)$ **29.** $(5, -2)$

30. Critical Thinking Fill in the table for the equation $y = |x|$. Then plot the points on a coordinate plane. Describe the shape of the graph.

x	−3	−2	−1	0	1	2	3
y	?	?	?	?	?	?	?

Chapter FCAT Practice

FCAT **Test-Taking Strategy** If you are unsure of an answer, try to eliminate answers that you know are wrong.

1. Which of the following shows the integers in order from least to greatest?

   A. $-5, 8, 2, -1, 0$ **B.** $0, -5, -1, 2, 8$

   C. $-5, -1, 0, 2, 8$ **D.** $0, -1, 2, -5, 8$

2. Which of the following is equal to -3?

   F. $-|-3|$ **G.** $-(-3)$

   H. $|3|$ **I.** $|-3|$

3. Which numerical expression represents the verbal expression "the opposite of the absolute value of negative 4"?

   A. $-(-|4|)$ **B.** $-(-4)$

   C. $|-4|$ **D.** $-|-4|$

4. Which is equal to $-16 + (-28) - 43$?

   F. -87 **G.** -31

   H. 1 **I.** 55

5. If the temperature is $-4°$ Fahrenheit and it changes by $-9°$ Fahrenheit, what is the new temperature?

   A. $-13°$F   **B.** $-5°$F

   C. $5°$F   **D.** $13°$F

6. What is the value of $14 - x - (-y)$ when $x = 7$ and $y = -4$?

   F. 3 **G.** 11

   H. 17 **I.** 25

7. Which product is *not* equal to -288?

   A. $3(-8)(2)(-3)(-2)$ **B.** $24(-2)(-3)(-2)$

   C. $3(-8)(6)(2)$ **D.** $-3(-8)(-6)(-2)$

8. Evaluate $-3ab + bc - 3b$ when $a = -5$, $b = 4$, and $c = -7$.

   F. -100 **G.** -66

   H. 20 **I.** 44

9. What is the mean of the following set of data? $-9, 8, -3, 11, -15, -13, 2, -5$

   A. -4 **B.** -3

   C. 3 **D.** 4

10. Which ordered pair represents point S in the coordinate plane?

    F. $(1, -2)$

    G. $(-2, 1)$

    H. $(-2, -1)$

    I. $(-1, -2)$

    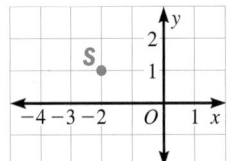

11. **Short Response** Explain how the commutative and associative properties of addition can help you find the sum using mental math.

    $$(61 + 17) + (39 + 3)$$

12. **Extended Response** You are planning a field trip to a museum. The bus ride will cost $250. Admission for each person is $8 and lunch is $5 per person. Write two expressions to find the total cost for x students. What would the cost be if 20 students went on the trip? 25 students? Did you use the distributive property to find your answer? Explain why or why not.

Supercool Squirrels

Hibernating in the Arctic

Animals living in very cold climates may hibernate to survive during winter. Hibernating animals have a decreased heart rate and decreased respiratory rate. The body temperature of a hibernating animal also drops significantly, often to just a few degrees higher than the surrounding temperature.

The arctic ground squirrel's body temperature drops below 0°C during hibernation. The graph below shows the body temperature of an arctic ground squirrel during the last few months of its hibernation.

Arctic Squirrel Body Temperature

The squirrel hibernates from early September until late April.

The peaks in the graph represent short periods of time during which the squirrel wakes up from hibernation and warms itself up.

1. Estimate the difference of the squirrel's highest and lowest body temperatures for the period shown on the graph.

2. Which is the best estimate for the longest period during which the squirrel's body temperature was above zero? below zero?

   A. 1 hour   **B.** 1 day   **C.** 5 days   **D.** 20 days

3. A squirrel's approximate body temperatures for several days in March were –3°C, –1°C, 36°C, 6°C, –2°C, and –3°C. What is the mean of the temperatures?

4. **Critical Thinking** Do you think your answer from Exercise 3 is a good representation of the squirrel's usual body temperature during the period of time shown by the graph? Explain your reasoning.

Soil Temperature

The graph below displays the squirrel body temperature data for March and April. It has a smaller temperature range, so waking periods are not fully displayed in the graph.

It also shows the soil temperature at 1 meter below ground, the depth at which the squirrel usually digs its burrow.

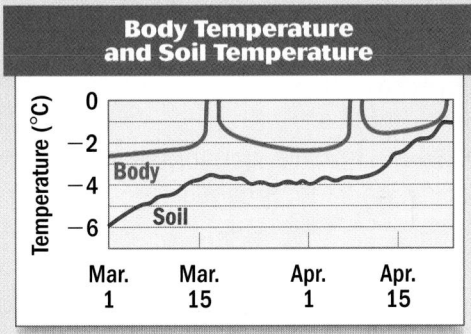

Body Temperature and Soil Temperature

5. What is the difference of body temperature and soil temperature on March 1? What is the difference of these two temperatures on April 15th?

6. **Critical Thinking** A scientist claims that a hibernating animal's body temperature is always within 1 or 2 degrees of the surrounding temperature. Discuss whether this claim seems reasonable for the arctic ground squirrel, based on the data given.

Project IDEAS

- **Report** Find out more about the arctic ground squirrel. In what areas does it live? What foods does it eat? What are its predators? Present your findings to the class.

- **Research** Some reptiles and amphibians, such as the painted turtle and the wood frog, can survive subzero temperatures. Find out more about one of these animals. How low can its body temperature go? What mechanisms does it use to avoid freezing? Present your findings to the class.

- **Career** Find out more about the work that biologists do. What are some topics or areas in which a biologist might specialize? Present your findings to the class.

INTERNET
Project Support
CLASSZONE.COM

3 Solving Equations and Inequalities

BEFORE

In previous chapters you've...

- Evaluated expressions
- Solved word problems

Now

In Chapter 3 you'll study...

- Solving one-step equations
- Solving two-step equations
- Writing equations
- Formulas for area and perimeter
- Writing and solving inequalities
- Real life modeling

WHY?

So you can solve real-world problems about...

- sea lions, p. 112
- cartoonists, p. 121
- biplane rides, p. 143
- DJs, p. 149

Internet Preview
CLASSZONE.COM

- eEdition Plus Online
- eWorkbook Plus Online
- eTutorial Plus Online
- FCAT Practice
- More Examples

Chapter Warm-Up Games

Review Skills you need for this chapter in these quick games. Work with a partner.

Name that Planet!

$$3 \times \boxed{} = 48$$
$$12 \times \boxed{} = 240$$
$$100 - \boxed{} = 79$$
$$3.659 \times \boxed{} = 36.59$$

$$\frac{250}{\boxed{}} = 50 \qquad \frac{\boxed{}}{3} = 6 \qquad \boxed{}^2 = 81$$

BRAIN GAME

Key Skill:
Solving mental math equations

- Use mental math to find the missing number.

- Match each answer with the corresponding letter of the alphabet. (1 = A, 2 = B, etc.)

- Rearrange the letters to find the name of a planet.

Planet Pinball

```
        36
       ↙  ↘
    +12      ×(−1)
   ↙  ↘    ↙  ↘
  ×2     −8     +24
 ↙ ↘   ↙ ↘   ↙ ↘
−30   ×½   ×(−4)   ×2
```

BrAIN GAME

Key Skill:
Operations with integers

Materials:
penny

- Both players start at the top planet with 36 points.

- On your turn, toss a coin. If you get heads, go to the planet on the left. If you get tails, go to the planet on the right.

- Perform the operation written on the planet. The result is your current score.

- Take turns moving until both players reach the bottom row.

- The player with the higher score wins.

Stop *and* Think

1. **Writing** Without tossing the coin, work with your partner to find the route through the planets in the *Planet Pinball* that gives the highest score. Explain how you know you have found the best route.

2. **Extension** Choose another planet name. Write a puzzle like *Name that Planet!* with that name as the solution.

CHAPTER 3
Getting Ready to Learn

Review What You Need to Know

Using Vocabulary **Copy and complete using a review word.**

1. 5 is the _?_ of -5.

2. 6 is the _?_ in the expression $6x$.

3. A(n) _?_ shows that two expressions are equal.

Solve the equation using mental math. *(p. 28)*

4. $x - 1 = 5$ 5. $x - 2 = 9$ 6. $4 + x = 12$ 7. $10 = x + 3$

8. $5 - x = 2$ 9. $x - 3 = 1$ 10. $x + 3 = 4$ 11. $8 + x = 8$

In Exercises 12–15, evaluate the expression. *(pp. 58, 63, 70)*

12. $-3 - 2 + 8$ 13. $3 - 7 + 2 - 1$ 14. $-2(3 + 1) + 2$ 15. $8(1 - 4) - 9$

16. A tsunami wave caused by an underwater earthquake travels across the ocean at 500 miles per hour. Write and solve an equation to find how far it travels in 15 minutes. *(p. 33)*

Know How to Take Notes

Organizing Information Sometimes you can organize complicated information in a table to make it easier to understand.

Multiplying Integers

x	Positive	Negative
Positive	+	−
Negative	−	+

In Lesson 3.7, you may want to make a table to help you organize information about solving inequalities.

GOAL

Solve addition and subtraction equations using algebra tiles.

MATERIALS

· algebra tiles

FLORIDA: Standards and Assessment
Solve linear equations. (MA.D.2.3.1)

Modeling One-Step Equations

You can use algebra tiles to model and solve one-step addition equations and one-step subtraction equations.

Represents the
variable x

$+$

x-tile

Represents a positive
unit, or 1

$+$

1-tile

Represents a negative
unit, or -1

$-$

-1-tile

When you combine a 1-tile and a -1-tile, the result is zero. This pair of tiles is called a *zero pair* and may be removed from the model.

Explore 1   **Model and solve $x + 3 = 8$.**

1 Model $x + 3 = 8$ using algebra tiles.

$+$ $+$ $+$ $+$ $=$ $+$ $+$ $+$ $+$
$+$ $+$ $+$ $+$

2 Remove three 1-tiles from each side so the x-tile is by itself.

$+$ $(+ + +)$ $=$ $+$ $+$ $(+ +)$
$+$ $+$ $+$ $+$

3 The solution of the equation is 5.

$+$ $=$ $+$ $+$
$+$ $+$ $+$

Your turn now

1. Use algebra tiles to model each step below. Draw a picture of each step.

   ① Model the equation $x + 5 = 7$.

   ② Remove five 1-tiles from each side.

   ③ Find the solution.

Use algebra tiles to model and solve the equation.

   2. $x + 4 = 9$ **3.** $5 + x = 7$ **4.** $6 = x + 2$ **5.** $7 + x = 9$

Explore 2 Model and solve $x - 5 = -3$. Write the equation at each step.

Tile Model **Algebra**

1 $x - 5 = -3$

To get the x-tile by itself, you can add
the same number of 1-tiles to each side
to create zero pairs. So, add five 1-tiles
to each side.

2 $x - 5 + 5 = -3 + 5$

You can remove zero pairs from each side.

3 $x = 2$

The solution is 2.

Your turn now Use algebra tiles to model and solve the equation.
Write the equation at each step.

6. $x - 3 = 6$ **7.** $x - 5 = 5$ **8.** $x + 6 = 2$ **9.** $8 + x = 1$

10. $x - 4 = -2$ **11.** $x - 7 = -3$ **12.** $x + 8 = 4$ **13.** $x - 3 = -6$

Stop *and* **Think**

14. Writing Give an example of an equation that requires you
to make zero pairs to solve. How do you know that zero pairs
are required?

15. Critical Thinking Can you model the equation $x + \dfrac{3}{2} = 5$
using x-tiles and 1-tiles? Explain.

Solving Equations Using Addition or Subtraction

BEFORE	▶ Now	WHY?
You solved equations using mental math.	You'll solve equations using addition or subtraction.	So you can find the amount that a sea lion grows, as in Ex. 36.

Word Watch

equivalent equations, p. 109
inverse operation, p. 109

FLORIDA
Standards and Assessment

• Solve and evaluate linear equations. (MA.D.2.3.1)

• Solve linear equations representing real-world situations. (MA.D.2.3.2)

You can model and solve an equation by using a scale as shown.

$x + 3 = 5$ $x = 2$

In the model above, removing three 1-tiles from each side of the scale keeps the scale in balance.

When you perform the same operation on each side of an equation, the result is a new equation that has the same solution. Equations that have the same solution(s) are **equivalent equations** .

You can solve an equation by using *inverse operations* to write equivalent equations. An **inverse operation** is an operation that "undoes" another operation. Addition and subtraction are inverse operations.

Subtraction Property of Equality

Words   Subtracting the same number from each side of an equation makes an equivalent equation.

Numbers   If $x + 5 = 7$, then $x + 5 - 5 = 7 - 5$.

Algebra   If $a = b$, then $a - c = b - c$.

EXAMPLE 1   Solving an Equation Using Subtraction

$$x + 8 = -15 \qquad \text{Original equation}$$
$$\underline{ -8 \quad -8} \qquad \text{Subtract 8 from each side to undo addition.}$$
$$x = -23 \qquad \text{Simplify. } x \text{ is by itself.}$$

ANSWER The solution is -23.

You can also use the addition property of equality to solve an equation.

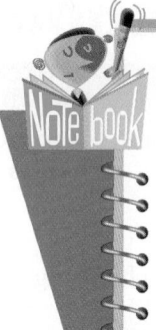

Addition Property of Equality

Words   Adding the same number to each side of an equation makes an equivalent equation.

Numbers   If $x - 2 = 6$, then $x - 2 + 2 = 6 + 2$.

Algebra   If $a = b$, then $a + c = b + c$.

Watch Out!

You can add or subtract horizontally or vertically to solve equations, but remember that when solving, you must perform the same operation on *each* side.

EXAMPLE 2   Solving an Equation Using Addition

$$c - 4.5 = 13$$ Original equation

$$c - 4.5 + 4.5 = 13 + 4.5$$ Add 4.5 to each side to undo subtraction.

$$c = 17.5$$ Simplify. c is by itself.

$\checkmark$ **Check** $17.5 - 4.5 \stackrel{?}{=} 13$ Substitute 17.5 for c in original equation.

$$13 = 13 \checkmark$$

Your turn now   Solve the equation. Check your solution.

1. $x + 9 = 20$ **2.** $-10 = 3 + y$ **3.** $m - 14 = -15$ **4.** $2 = z - 6.4$

EXAMPLE 3   Using a Verbal Model

Rock Climbing A cliff has a height of about 1500 feet. If you have already climbed 675 feet, how much farther do you have to climb to reach the top?

Solution

Write a verbal model. Let x represent the distance left to climb.

Height of cliff	=	Distance left to climb	+	Distance climbed

$$1500 = x + 675$$ Write an algebraic model.

$$1500 - 675 = x + 675 - 675$$ Subtract 675 from each side.

$$825 = x$$ Simplify. x is by itself.

ANSWER You have about 825 feet left to climb.

Getting Ready to Practice

1. Vocabulary Copy and complete: Addition and subtraction are _ ? _ operations.

Solve the equation. Check your solution.

2. $x + 10 = 16$

3. $12 = x - 8$

4. $x + 1.3 = 2.5$

5. Guided Problem Solving You buy new school supplies. The price of the items is $54.99, but after sales tax is added, they cost $58.29. How much is the sales tax?

(1) Copy and complete the verbal model.

Price + _ ? _ = Total cost

(2) Substitute numbers and variables in the verbal model to write an algebraic model.

(3) Solve the algebraic model. Check your solution.

Practice and Problem Solving

HELP with Homework

Example	Exercises
1	9–20
2	9–20
3	21–24

Online Resources
CLASSZONE.COM
· More Examples
· eTutorial Plus

Describe an inverse operation that will undo the given operation.

6. Adding 4

7. Adding 4.5

8. Subtracting 35

Solve the equation.

9. $r + 2 = 7$

10. $t - 5 = 2$

11. $9 = p - 4$

12. $6 + x = 8$

13. $z + 9 = 11$

14. $23 = 6 + s$

15. $y - 15 = 9$

16. $13 = d - 27$

17. $24 = 52 + n$

18. $204 = m - 41$

19. $43 = a - 21$

20. $11 = c + 48$

Tell whether the equation correctly represents the real-life problem. If not, correct the equation.

21. At 62 inches tall, you are 5 inches taller than your sister. How tall is your sister? Equation: $62 = s + 5$.

22. There are 540 freshmen this year. This is 29 more than last year. How many freshmen were there last year? Equation: $f - 29 = 540$.

23. The mean temperature for February 4 in Chicago is 3°F below the mean temperature of 29°F for all of February in Chicago. What is the mean temperature for February 4? Equation: $t - 3 = 29$.

24. An item that usually costs $2.29 will cost $1.79 with a coupon. How much is the coupon worth? Equation: $2.29 - c = 1.79$.

25. Writing Write a word problem that can be represented by the equation $s + 13 = 55$.

26. Critical Thinking What inverse operation undoes adding -5 to a number?

Solve the equation.

27. $x + \dfrac{1}{2} = \dfrac{1}{2}$ **28.** $\dfrac{2}{3} = d + \dfrac{1}{3}$ **29.** $y - \dfrac{3}{4} = \dfrac{1}{4}$

30. $s + 3.4 = 4.4$ **31.** $1.76 = a - 2.94$ **32.** $3.777 + c = 3.977$

33. $m + (-20) = -12$ **34.** $-2 = b + (-4)$ **35.** $r - (-36) = 5$

36. Sea Lions The length of a Steller sea lion at birth is about 45 inches. The average adult female Steller sea lion is 104 inches long. About how many inches do female sea lions grow between birth and adulthood? Write a verbal model. Then write and solve an algebraic model for the problem.

Challenge Solve the equation.

37. $3x - 2x + 8 - 10 = 7$ **38.** $0.2x + 3.4 + 0.8x - 2.1 = 4.2$

39. Cost You spent a total of $11.09 at the store. You bought two bottles of water for $1.29 each, a magazine for $3.50, trail mix for $1.49, and some markers. How much did the markers cost? (Assume there is no sales tax.)

Sea lions

Mixed Review

Plot the point in a coordinate plane and describe its location. *(Lesson 2.8)*

40. $(-2, 5)$ **41.** $(5, -2)$ **42.** $(-2, -5)$ **43.** $(5, 5)$

Basic Skills Find a low and high estimate for the product.

44. 15×19 **45.** 11×13 **46.** 42×7 **47.** 42×71

FCAT Practice

48. Multiple Choice Six less than the total number of teachers is fifteen. Which equation represents this sentence?

    A. $6 - x = 15$ **B.** $15 - 6 = x$ **C.** $x + 15 = 6$ **D.** $x - 6 = 15$

49. Multiple Choice Solve $-7 + x = 20$.

    F. -27 **G.** -13 **H.** 13 **I.** 27

Solving Equations Using Multiplication or Division

BEFORE	▶ Now	WHY?
You solved equations using addition or subtraction.	You'll solve equations using multiplication or division.	So you can find how much a whole pizza costs, as in Ex. 17.

Word Watch

Review Words

equivalent equations, p. 109
inverse operation, p. 109

FLORIDA
Standards and Assessment

• Solve linear equations. (MA.D.2.3.1)

• Solve linear equations representing real-world situations. (MA.D.2.3.2)

Activity **You can use multiplication to solve equations.**

$\dfrac{x}{2} = 5$ ⟶ Multiply each side by 2. $\dfrac{x}{2} \cdot 2 = 5 \cdot 2$ ⟶ Simplify. $x = 10$

Solve the equations.

1. $\dfrac{y}{5} = 4$ **2.** $\dfrac{h}{6} = 9$ **3.** $\dfrac{m}{6} = -3$

4. What operation did you use to solve each division equation? How did you use that operation? Write a rule for solving division equations.

In the activity, you used multiplication to solve equations involving division. Multiplication and division are inverse operations.

Multiplication Property of Equality

Words   Multiplying each side of an equation by the same nonzero number makes an equivalent equation.

Numbers   If $\dfrac{x}{3} = 4$, then $\dfrac{x}{3} \cdot 3 = 4 \cdot 3$.

Algebra   If $a = b$ and $c \neq 0$, then $ac = bc$.

EXAMPLE 1   **Solving an Equation Using Multiplication**

with Solving

Remember to check your answer by substituting it in the original equation.

$\dfrac{y}{3} = 5$ Original equation

$\dfrac{y}{3} \cdot 3 = 5 \cdot 3$ Multiply each side by 3 to undo division.

$y = 15$ Simplify. y is by itself.

✓ Check $\dfrac{15}{3} = 5$ ✓   Substitute 15 for y in original equation.

You can use division to solve equations involving multiplication.

Division Property of Equality

Words　Dividing each side of an equation by the same nonzero number makes an equivalent equation.

Numbers　If $2x = 24$, then $\frac{2x}{2} = \frac{24}{2}$.

Algebra　If $a = b$ and $c \neq 0$, then $\frac{a}{c} = \frac{b}{c}$.

Watch Out!

When solving an equation, remember to perform the same operation on each side.

EXAMPLE 2 Solving an Equation Using Division

$$-2.5x = 20 \qquad \text{Original equation}$$

$$\frac{-2.5x}{-2.5} = \frac{20}{-2.5} \qquad \text{Divide each side by } -2.5 \text{ to undo multiplication.}$$

$$x = -8 \qquad \text{Simplify. } x \text{ is by itself.}$$

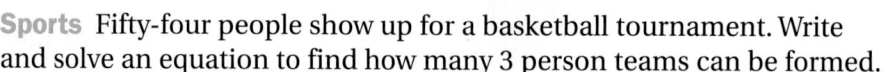 **Your turn now** Solve the equation. Check your solution.

1. $21 = \frac{x}{9}$ **2.** $\frac{x}{3.5} = 14$ **3.** $9x = 54$ **4.** $45 = -9x$

EXAMPLE 3 Writing and Solving an Equation

Sports Fifty-four people show up for a basketball tournament. Write and solve an equation to find how many 3 person teams can be formed.

Solution

Let t be the number of 3 person teams that can be formed.

Total number of people	=	Number per team	·	Number of teams

$$54 = 3t \qquad \text{Write an algebraic model.}$$

$$\frac{54}{3} = \frac{3t}{3} \qquad \text{Divide each side by 3.}$$

$$18 = t \qquad \text{Simplify.}$$

ANSWER Eighteen 3 person teams can be formed.

Getting Ready to Practice

1. Vocabulary Copy and complete: To solve $6x = 36$, _?_ each side of the equation by 6.

Copy and complete the solution. Justify each step.

2. $6x = 72$

$$\frac{6x}{?} = \frac{72}{?}$$

$$x = ?$$

3. $\frac{y}{9} = -3$

$$\frac{y}{9} \cdot ? = -3 \cdot ?$$

$$y = ?$$

4. Concert You are at a sold-out concert. There are 1950 people at the concert, and the arena has 30 seats in each row.

People at concert	=	Seats per row	·	Number of rows

Write and solve an equation to find how many rows of seats there are.

Practice and Problem Solving

HELP with **Homework**

Example	Exercises
1	5–16
2	5–16
3	17–18

Online Resources
CLASSZONE.COM

· More Examples
· eTutorial Plus

Solve the equation. Check your solution.

5. $\frac{p}{2} = 9$

6. $\frac{t}{8} = 6$

7. $14 = \frac{x}{5}$

8. $4x = 32$

9. $18 = 6g$

10. $3b = 39$

11. $7 = \frac{k}{15}$

12. $25 = \frac{h}{14}$

13. $\frac{r}{18} = 12$

14. $17y = 51$

15. $14h = 35$

16. $48 = 96z$

17. Pizza A pizza shop cuts a pizza into 8 slices. One slice costs $1.10. Which equation can you use to find the cost of the whole pizza?

A. $1.10x = 8$ **B.** $8x = 1.10$ **C.** $\frac{x}{8} = 1.10$ **D.** $x = \frac{1.10}{8}$

18. Mowing Lawns You charged your neighbors $56 for mowing their lawn 7 times. How much do you charge for mowing the lawn once?

Describe an inverse operation that will undo the given operation.

19. Multiplying by 5   **20.** Dividing by -9 **21.** Adding -6

Solve the equation. Check your solution.

22. $12 = -2z$ **23.** $\dfrac{h}{6} = -36$ **24.** $-3x = -57$

25. $44 = 4.4p$ **26.** $\dfrac{z}{1.8} = 5$ **27.** $13 = \dfrac{w}{2.3}$

28. $-2.4k = 48$ **29.** $-21 = -0.7p$ **30.** $\dfrac{y}{-1.5} = 21$

31. $1368 = 456x$ **32.** $8 = \dfrac{-b}{5.5}$ **33.** $12m = -25.2$

34. Real Estate A real estate agent receives $6 for every $100 of a house's selling price. The agent receives $10,725 for selling a house. What is the house's selling price?

35. Critical Thinking Write a multiplication equation and a division equation that have the same solution.

36. Challenge Solve the equation.

$$3(6n) + 5(3n) - 2^2 n = 261$$

37. Hens About 240 million laying hens produce about 50 billion eggs each year in the United States. About how many eggs does each hen lay in a month? in a week?

Mixed Review

Copy and complete the statement with < or >. *(Lesson 2.1)*

38. $3 \ \underline{?} \ -6$ **39.** $-21 \ \underline{?} \ -17$ **40.** $-12 \ \underline{?} \ -5$ **41.** $0 \ \underline{?} \ -3$

Basic Skills **Write the number in words.**

42. $12,448$ **43.** 16.02 **44.** 5.107 **45.** $7,540,688$

FCAT Practice   FCAT

46. Multiple Choice Which operation should you perform to solve the equation represented by the verbal sentence?

The product of a number and three is the opposite of nine.

  A. Divide both sides by 3.   **B.** Multiply both sides by 3.

  C. Divide both sides by -3.   **D.** Multiply both sides by -3.

47. Short Response Paula drove for 2.5 hours traveling the same speed throughout her trip. She traveled a total of 150 miles. Write an equation that represents the situation. Let r represent Paula's speed. Solve the equation to find her speed. Show all of your work.

Hands-on Activity

GOAL
Use algebra tiles to solve two-step equations.

MATERIALS
· algebra tiles

FLORIDA: Standards and Assessment
Solve linear equations. (MA.D.2.3.1)

Modeling Two-Step Equations

A *two-step equation* is an equation you solve using two operations. You can use algebra tiles to model and solve two-step equations.

Explore 1 Model and solve $2x + 3 = 7$.

1 Model the equation $2x + 3 = 7$.

2 Remove three 1-tiles from each side.

3 The coefficient of x is 2, so divide the remaining tiles on each side into 2 identical groups.

4 Keep one of these groups. One x-tile is equal to two 1-tiles. So, the solution is 2.

Your turn now Use algebra tiles to model and solve the equation.

1. Model each step described below. Draw a picture of each step.

   (1 Use algebra tiles to model the equation $3x + 1 = 10$.

   (2 Remove one 1-tile from each side.

   (3 Divide the remaining tiles into three identical groups.

   (4 Solve the equation. Then check your solution by substituting in the original equation.

Explore 2 Model and solve $3x - 4 = 5$. Write the equation at each step.

Tile Model	Algebra

1 $3x - 4 = 5$

2 $3x - 4 + 4 = 5 + 4$

Remove zero pairs.

3 $\dfrac{3x}{3} = \dfrac{9}{3}$

4 $x = 3$

Your turn now Use algebra tiles to model and solve the equation. Write the equation at each step.

2. $3x + 1 = 7$ **3.** $2x - 3 = 7$ **4.** $4x + 2 = -10$ **5.** $2x - 5 = -9$

Stop and Think

6. **Writing** Explain what kinds of equations are difficult or impossible to solve using algebra tiles. Give an example.

7. **Work Backward** Use algebra tiles to write a two-step equation whose solution is 1.

Solving Two-Step Equations

LESSON
3.3

BEFORE	▶ Now	WHY?
You solved one-step equations.	You'll solve two-step equations.	So you can make a plan to earn money, as in Ex. 36.

Word Watch

Review Words
equation, p. 28
solution, p. 28

FLORIDA
Standards and Assessment

• Solve linear equations. (MA.D.2.3.1)

• Solve linear equations representing real-world situations. (MA.D.2.3.2)

In the Real World

Music Club You pay $7 to join an Internet music club. You pay $2 for each song that you download. Your cost for joining and downloading some songs is $23. How many songs did you download?

In Example 1, you will answer this question by solving the two-step equation $7 + 2x = 23$. The value of x is the number of songs you downloaded.

JAZZ | CLASSICAL | BLUES | WORLD

ONLINE music

$2

download songs by your favorite artist!

EXAMPLE 1 **Solving a Real-World Problem**

Cost to join	+	Cost per song	•	Number of songs	=	Total Cost

$$7 + 2x = 23 \qquad \text{Write an algebraic model.}$$

$$\underline{-7 \qquad\qquad -7} \qquad \text{Subtract 7 from each side to undo addition.}$$

$$2x = 16 \qquad \text{Simplify.}$$

$$\frac{2x}{2} = \frac{16}{2} \qquad \text{Divide each side by 2 to undo multiplication.}$$

$$x = 8 \qquad \text{Simplify. } x \text{ is by itself.}$$

ANSWER You downloaded 8 songs.

Your turn now **Use the equation in Example 1.**

1. Substitute 8 for x in the original equation in Example 1 to check the solution.

2. What is the cost to join the club and download 5 songs?

3. Suppose the cost to join and download songs is $27. How does this change the equation you solve to find the number of songs?

Solving a Two-Step Equation

Some equations require two inverse operations to solve.

$2x + 1 = 5$	**Original equation**
$2x + 1 - 1 = 5 - 1$	**Undo addition or subtraction.**
$2x = 4$	**Simplify.**
$\dfrac{2x}{2} = \dfrac{4}{2}$	Undo multiplication **or division.**
$x = 2$	**Simplify.**

HELP with Solving

Another way to undo operations is to add the opposite to undo addition or subtraction. Then multiply by the reciprocal to undo multiplication or division.

EXAMPLE 2 Solving with a Variable in the Numerator

$\dfrac{x}{2} - 14$	$=$	8	**Original equation**
$\underline{+14}$		$\underline{+14}$	**Add 14 to each side to undo subtraction.**
$\dfrac{x}{2}$	$=$	22	**Simplify.**
$\dfrac{x}{2} \cdot 2$	$=$	$22 \cdot 2$	**Multiply each side by 2 to undo division.**
x	$=$	44	**Simplify.**

✓ Check $\dfrac{44}{2} - 14 \stackrel{?}{=} 8$ **Substitute 44 for x in original equation.**

$22 - 14 = 8$ ✓

HELP with Review

Remember that you can solve an equation vertically or horizontally. See p. 110.

EXAMPLE 3 Solving with a Negative Coefficient

$8 = 12 - 2x$	**Original equation**
$8 - 12 = 12 - 2x - 12$	**Subtract 12 from each side to undo addition.**
$-4 = -2x$	**Simplify.**
$\dfrac{-4}{-2} = \dfrac{-2x}{-2}$	**Divide each side by −2 to undo multiplication.**
$2 = x$	**Simplify.**

Your turn now Solve the equation. Check your answer.

4. $13 = 11 + \dfrac{y}{3}$ **5.** $\dfrac{z}{5} - 3 = 4$ **6.** $-6x + 5 = 23$ **7.** $6 = 16 - a$

INTERNET
eWorkbook Plus
CLASSZONE.COM

Getting Ready to Practice

1. Write the two operations, in order, that you would use to solve the equation $3w - 2 = 7$. Then solve the equation.

2. **Find the Error** Describe and correct the error in the solution.

$$3x - 9 = 18$$
$$3x = 9$$
$$x = 3$$

Solve the equation. Check your answer.

3. $2x + 1 = 7$ 4. $3y - 4 = 2$ 5. $10 - 7z = 3$

6. $15 = 4p + 7$ 7. $1 = 2k + 9$ 8. $11 = \dfrac{h}{6} + 8$

9. **Guided Problem Solving** You draw illustrations. You charge $50 per illustration and $12 per hour to make changes. You get a check for $198 to pay for 3 illustrations and changes. How many hours did you spend making changes to the illustrations?

   (1 Read the problem. What is the main idea? What do you know and what do you need to find?

   (2 You can use the equation $3(50) + 12n = 198$ to find the number of hours you spent making changes to the illustrations. Why is the value of n the number of hours you spent making changes?

   (3 Solve the equation and check your answer.

Practice and Problem Solving

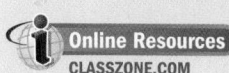
HELP with Homework

Example	Exercises
1	10–23
2	24–35
3	10–21, 24–35

Online Resources
CLASSZONE.COM

· More Examples
· eTutorial Plus

Solve the equation. Check your answer.

10. $4z + 8 = 12$ 11. $18 = 4h + 2$ 12. $29 = 5a + 4$

13. $40 = 8p - 16$ 14. $100 - 7r = 44$ 15. $8q - 9 = -7$

16. $6 + 2c = 15$ 17. $3g + 4 = 13$ 18. $-9 + 2k = -25$

19. $-36 = 18 - 6x$ 20. $7 + 5b = -23$ 21. $10 = 2d + 11$

22. **Measurement** To find the number of inches in 5 feet 4 inches, you can evaluate the expression $5(12) + 4$. The diameter of the largest cookie ever made was 81 feet 8 inches. Write and evaluate an expression that will give the diameter of the cookie in inches.

23. Hiking Trails Students are cleaning up 11 miles of trails in a local park. After an hour, they have cleaned about 3 miles of trails. Solve the two-step equation $3h + 3 = 11$. Explain why the value of h is an estimate of the number of hours it will take to finish.

Solve the equation. Check your answer.

24. $3 = 12 - 3x$

25. $-7 = 7 - 2r$

26. $20 - 6w = 14$

27. $9p + 8 = -7$

28. $\frac{x}{9} - 4 = 5$

29. $-7 + \frac{z}{4} = 3$

30. $8 = 5 + \frac{m}{2}$

31. $3 + \frac{t}{5} = 14$

32. $32 = 17 + \frac{d}{2}$

33. $2 - z = 9$

34. $11 - b = 34$

35. $\frac{c}{3} - 7 = 1$

36. Walking Dogs You earn money by walking dogs in your neighborhood. One neighbor pays you $20 each week, and other neighbors pay you $5 per walk. If your goal is to earn $50 per week, how many walks do you need to do at $5 each? To answer this question, solve the equation $20 + 5w = 50$.

37. Phone Card You have $2.10 remaining on your phone card. You pay 7 cents for each minute of a call and a 75 cent charge for using a pay phone. If you make a call from a pay phone, what is the maximum whole number of minutes that you can talk? (*Hint:* The cost is the sum of the pay phone charge and 7 cents per minute for your call.)

Compare and Contrast In Exercises 38 and 39, a method for solving the equation $2(m + 3) = 18$ is shown. Explain each step of the solution.

38.

$$2(m + 3) = 18$$
$$2m + 6 = 18$$
$$2m + 6 - 6 = 18 - 6$$
$$2m = 12$$
$$\frac{2m}{2} = \frac{12}{2}$$
$$m = 6$$

39.

$$2(m + 3) = 18$$
$$\frac{2(m + 3)}{2} = \frac{18}{2}$$
$$m + 3 = 9$$
$$m + 3 - 3 = 9 - 3$$
$$m = 6$$

Choose a Method In Exercises 40–42, use one of the methods in Exercises 38 and 39 to solve the equation.

40. $3(r + 1) = 9$

41. $4 = -1(z + 11)$

42. $6\left(\frac{1}{3} + h\right) = 20$

Challenge Solve the equation.

43. $2(10 + x) + 4(12 - x) = 34$

44. $-5(3 - z) + 1(z - 9) = 0$

Extended Problem Solving In Exercises 45–47, use the given information about the cost of using the city pool.

45. **Evaluate and Explain** Evaluate the expression $3(40) + 12$. What does the answer tell you about the payment plans?

46. **Interpret** Solve the two-step equation $3x + 12 = 100$. What does the answer tell you about the payment plans?

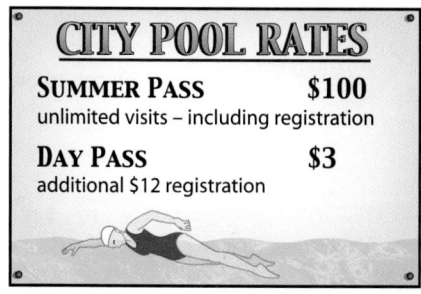

47. **Compare and Contrast** For each payment plan, give one reason why you might choose it.

Mixed Review

Solve the equation. Check your answer. *(Lessons 3.1, 3.2)*

48. $p + 9 = 19$ 49. $13 = n - 6$ 50. $-20 = 4x$ 51. $\frac{1}{2}y = 24$

Choose a Strategy Use a strategy from the list to solve the following problem. Explain your choice of strategy.

52. A running club has six members. The instructor wants each member to race one-on-one against every other member. How many times will each member race? How many races will there be altogether?

> **Problem Solving Strategies**
> ▪ Guess, Check, and Revise
> ▪ Draw a Diagram
> ▪ Look for a Pattern

Basic Skills Write the number as a percent.

53. $\frac{1}{2}$ 54. 0.75   55. $\frac{20}{100}$ 56. 0.35

FCAT Practice

57. **Multiple Choice** Solve the equation $2x - 9 = 21$.

    A. -15 **B.** -6 **C.** 6   **D.** 15

58. **Short Response** Kim is a lifeguard at a beach. She had to take a training course first that cost $25. Now she earns $10 an hour. Which equation would you use to find how long it will take her to make a profit of $45? Solve the equation.

    A. $10h - 25 = 45$ **B.** $10h + 25 = 45$

Writing Two-Step Equations

BEFORE	▶ Now	WHY?
You solved two-step equations.	You'll solve problems by writing two-step equations.	So you can calculate sandwich sales, as in Ex. 9.

Word Watch

Review Words
equation, p. 28
solution, p. 28

FLORIDA
Standards and Assessment

• Write equations to express relationships. (MA.D.1.3.2)

• Translate words into algebraic equations. (MA.D.2.3.1)

In the Real World

American Flamingos This year, a zoo spent $1580 to feed its American flamingos. Next year, its budget for feeding the flamingos is $2370. Next year it will cost $395 to feed each additional flamingo. How many additional flamingos can the zoo buy? You can use a verbal model to help you write a two-step equation.

EXAMPLE 1 Writing and Solving a Two-Step Equation

You can write and solve a two-step equation to find how many additional flamingos the zoo can buy. Write a verbal model. Let n be the number of additional flamingos.

Budget available	=	Cost of each new flamingo	•	Number of new flamingos	+	Cost of existing flamingos

$$2370 = 395n + 1580 \qquad \text{Write an algebraic model.}$$

$$2370 - 1580 = 395n + 1580 - 1580 \qquad \text{Subtract 1580 from each side.}$$

$$790 = 395n \qquad \text{Simplify.}$$

$$\frac{790}{395} = \frac{395n}{395} \qquad \text{Divide each side by 395.}$$

$$2 = n \qquad \text{Simplify.}$$

ANSWER The zoo can buy 2 additional flamingos next year.

✓ **Check** $2370 \stackrel{?}{=} 395(2) + 1580 \qquad$ **Substitute 2 for n in original equation.**

$$2370 \stackrel{?}{=} 790 + 1580$$

$$2370 = 2370 ✓$$

Your turn now Write a two-step equation to solve the problem.

1. It costs a zoo $1150 per year to feed its Aldabra tortoises. Each additional tortoise will cost $575 per year to feed. The zoo's budget for the tortoises' food next year is $2875. Write and solve an equation to find how many new tortoises the zoo can buy next year.

Writing and Solving a Two-Step Equation

The sum of 4 times a number and -6 is 14. What is the number?

Solution

4 times **a number** and -6 is 14.		Write a verbal model.
4 $\cdot$ n $+$ $(-6) = 14$		Translate.
$4n - 6 = 14$		Write equation.
$4n - 6 + 6 = 14 + 6$		Add 6 to each side.
$4n = 20$		Simplify.
$\dfrac{4n}{4} = \dfrac{20}{4}$		Divide each side by 4.
$n = 5$		Simplify.

HELP with **Solving**

Remember that adding
–6 is the same as
subtracting 6.

Your turn now **Write a two-step equation to find the number.**

2. The difference of six times a number and 9 is -3. What is the number?

3. The sum of a number divided by 6 and -5 is -2. What is the number?

Writing and Solving a Two-Step Equation

Reading You have to read several books for a class. You want to find how many pages you need to read per week in order to finish by the time the term is over. There are a total of 1244 pages. You have already read 500 pages. If there are six weeks left in the term, how many pages do you have to read per week?

Solution

Let p be the number of pages to read per week.

Total pages	=	Weeks left	$\cdot$	Pages per week	+	Pages I've read

$1244 = 6p + 500$	Write an algebraic model.
$1244 - 500 = 6p + 500 - 500$	Subtract 500 from each side.
$744 = 6p$	Simplify.
$\dfrac{744}{6} = \dfrac{6p}{6}$	Divide each side by 6.
$124 = p$	Simplify.

ANSWER You have to read 124 pages per week.

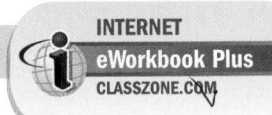

3.4 Exercises

More Practice, p. 729

Getting Ready to Practice

Match the statement with the correct equation.

1. The sum of 3 and a number is 16.
2. The product of 3 and a number is 16.
3. The difference of three times a number and 2 is 16.
4. The product of 3 and twice a number is 16.

A. $3n - 2 = 16$
B. $3(2n) = 16$
C. $3n = 16$
D. $3 + n = 16$

5. **Bicycle Rental** A bicycle rental shop charges $5 per hour plus a fee of $10 each time you rent a bicycle. Which equation can you use to find the number of hours you can rent a bicycle if you have $45?

   A. $5h + 10 = 45$ **B.** $10h + 5 = 45$ **C.** $5 + h + 10 = 45$

6. **Guided Problem Solving** You and your friends decide to have a car wash as a fundraiser. You spend $15 on supplies and charge $6 per car. At the end of the day your profit is $93. How many cars did you and your friends wash?

   (1 Write a verbal model.

   (2 Translate your verbal model into an algebraic model.

   (3 Solve the equation.

   (4 Check that your answer is reasonable.

Practice and Problem Solving

with Homework

Example	Exercises
1	9–13
2	7–8
3	9–13

Online Resources
CLASSZONE.COM
· More Examples
· eTutorial Plus

In Exercises 7 and 8, translate the statement into an equation. Then solve the equation.

7. The sum of 5 times a number and 4 is 9.

8. Seven subtracted from the quotient of a number and 2 is −6.

9. **Restaurant** At a restaurant one day, 60 sandwiches are sold in total, some on rye bread and some on white bread. The number of sandwiches sold on rye bread is twice the number sold the day before. The number of sandwiches on white bread is 28. How many sandwiches on rye bread were sold yesterday?

10. **Hourly Wage** You had $20 at the beginning of the week. You worked 10 hours during the week and ended the week having $70. How much do you earn each hour?

11. Writing Write a word problem that can be modeled by the equation $5x - 6 = 9$.

12. Party Supplies You need 124 plastic forks for a party. At one store you buy 5 boxes that contain 8 forks each. At another store you find boxes that contain 12 forks each. How many of these boxes do you need to buy?

13. Magazine Subscription You subscribe to a magazine that costs $26 yearly. You make an initial payment of $5 and then make three equal payments. How much is each payment?

14. Critical Thinking Write a one-step equation and a two-step equation that both have 8 as a solution.

In Exercises 15–18, translate the statement into an equation. Then solve the equation.

15. The sum of 2 times a number and 5 is 12.

16. The difference of the product of 3 and a number and $-\frac{1}{2}$ is $-\frac{5}{2}$.

17. The sum of -2 times a number and 3.5 is 7.5.

18. Three less than the quotient of a number and 2 is 8.

19. School Fair The senior class at your school made a $300 profit at the school fair by having a dunk tank. The dunk tank cost $125 to rent, and the senior class charged $5 for each person to play. How many people played?

20. Taxicab A taxicab charges a $2 fee plus an additional $1.50 for every mile driven. Your cab ride cost $17. How many miles did you travel?

Critical Thinking Exercises 21 and 22 are missing information. Tell what information is needed in order to solve the problem.

21. You have a job in which you make $6 per hour plus tips. You made a total of $34 yesterday. How much did you make in tips?

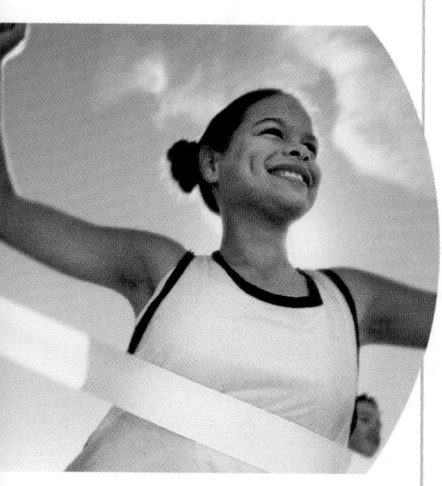

22. To train for a race, you jog for 5 minutes and then you run for 20 minutes. For each week after, you jog for 5 minutes, but increase the time that you run. After how many weeks will you be training for a total of 85 minutes?

Challenge Translate the statement into an equation. Then solve the equation.

23. The product of a number divided by 5 and 2 is 1.

24. The sum of 2 and 3, plus 3 times a number, is -4.

25. The quotient of -36 and 9, subtracted from 4 times a number, is -8.

26. The product of 8 squared divided by 16 and a number is 24.

Mixed Review

Find the perimeter and area of the rectangle or square.
(Lesson 1.6)

27.

3 ft

12 ft

28.

15 in.

15 in.

29.

24 m

18 m

Solve the equation. *(Lessons 2.7, 3.3)*

30. $2(x + 5) = 30$

31. $2x + 8(-2) = 54$

32. $3(t - 6) = 9$

FCAT Practice FCAT

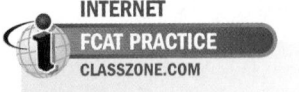

INTERNET
FCAT PRACTICE
CLASSZONE.COM

33. Extended Response Your digital camera can take both high and low quality photos. Each high quality photo uses as much storage space as 3.8 low quality photos. You have enough memory to take 27 low quality photos. If you take 9 low quality photos, how many additional high quality photos can you take? Explain why you need to give an approximate answer. Should you round up or down? Explain.

BRAIN GAME

Behind the Magic

◆ Choose any number.
◆ Multiply the number by 2.
◆ Add 14. Divide by 2.
◆ Subtract the number you started with.
◆ Multiply by 3. Your answer is 21.

To figure out why the answer is always 21, let x be the number you choose and write an algebraic expression that shows all of the steps. Then simplify the expression. What is your answer?

INTERNET

Technology Activity

FLORIDA: Standards and Assessment
Solve linear equations representing real-world situations. (MA.D.2.3.2)

Searching for Information

GOAL Use the Internet to search for information necessary to write an equation.

Example A class is planning a trip to the Naismith Memorial Basketball Hall of Fame in Springfield, Massachusetts. The class has $190 to spend on admission. There are 35 students in the class. How many adults can they afford to bring?

Solution

Follow these steps to perform a search on the Internet:

1 Pick a search engine.

2 Type keywords that cover the topic you would like to search. Then select Search.

3 Of the results the search engine finds, pick a site that is likely to have the information you need.

Use the steps described above to find the prices for students and adults. (*Hint:* There are over 35 people going, so the group rates would apply.)

| Amount to spend | = | Number of students | · | Price per student | + | Number of adults | · | Price per adult |

Your turn now **Use the results of your search.**

1. Write and solve an equation to solve the problem in the example.

2. Your class is planning a trip to a museum. Use the Internet to research prices for student and adult tickets at a nearby museum. If your class has $200 to spend on admission, how many adults can you afford to bring?

LESSONS 3.1 TO 3.4

Notebook Review

Review the vocabulary definitions in your notebook.

Copy the review examples in your notebook. Then complete the exercises.

Check Your Definitions

equivalent equations, p. 109   inverse operation, p. 109

Use Your Vocabulary

1. Name two pairs of inverse operations.

3.1 Can you solve addition and subtraction equations?

 EXAMPLE Solve the equation.

$x - 23 = 9$ **Original equation**	$y + 17.3 = 68.8$ **Original equation**
$\underline{+ 23 + 23}$ **Add 23 to each side.**	$\underline{- 17.3 -17.3}$ **Subtract 17.3 from each side.**
$x = 32$ **Simplify.**	$y = 51.5$ **Simplify.**

✓ **Solve the equation.**

2. $c + 14 = 3$ **3.** $y - 31 = 11$ **4.** $7.7 = s - 4.3$

5. $2 = r - 45$ **6.** $29 = 40 + p$ **7.** $b + 3.09 = -5.91$

3.2 Can you solve multiplication and division equations?

 EXAMPLE Solve the equation.

$\dfrac{y}{4} = -8$ **Original equation**	$-7x = -56$ **Original equation**
$\dfrac{y}{4} \cdot 4 = -8 \cdot 4$ **Multiply each side by 4.**	$\dfrac{-7x}{-7} = \dfrac{-56}{-7}$ **Divide each side by -7.**
$y = -32$ **Simplify.**	$x = 8$ **Simplify.**

✓ **Solve the equation.**

8. $\dfrac{m}{3} = 9$ **9.** $\dfrac{h}{5} = -8$ **10.** $-5 = \dfrac{w}{-11}$

11. $-15n = 60$ **12.** $-25x = 0$ **13.** $7 = 3.5\,t$

3.3–3.4 Can you write and solve two-step equations?

EXAMPLE A catering company charges $100 for setup plus $15 per guest. How many guests can be served within a $1000 budget?

Solution

| Setup | + | Cost per guest | · | Number of guests | = | Budget |

$100 + 15n = 1000$ Write an algebraic model.

$15n = 900$ Subtract 100 from each side.

$n = 60$ Divide each side by 15.

ANSWER Sixty guests can be served within a $1000 budget.

☑ **14.** You are stuffing 560 envelopes for a school event. By 1:00 P.M., you have stuffed 140 envelopes. How many envelopes an hour do you need to stuff to finish by 5:00 P.M.?

Stop *and* **Think**   about Lessons 3.1–3.4

15. Critical Thinking How is the order of the steps you use to solve a two-step equation related to the order of operations for evaluating expressions?

Review Quiz 1

Solve the equation.

1. $x - 16 = 8$ **2.** $-330 = -10x$ **3.** $42 = \frac{1}{6}x$ **4.** $5x - 12 = 23$

5. Field Trip Your class is going to a museum. Your teacher buys 32 tickets that are all the same price. The total charge for all the tickets is $256. Write and solve an equation to find the price of one museum ticket.

Translate the statement into an equation. Then solve.

6. The sum of 10 times a number and 5 is -15.

7. The difference of 4 times a number and -7 is 39.

8. Bicycle Mary wants to buy a bicycle that costs $280. Her parents agree to pay half. Mary will save $20 a week. Write and solve an equation to find how long it will take her to save enough money.

Guess, Check, and Revise
Look for a Pattern
Act It Out
Work Backward
Draw a Diagram
Solve a Simpler Problem
Draw a Graph

FLORIDA: Standards and Assessment
Solve real-world problems. (MA.A.3.3.2)

Draw a Diagram

Problem Your class is hosting a science fair. Your classroom is 30 feet by 20 feet. You need to keep a 10 foot by 10 foot space empty for a demonstration. How much space do you have left for exhibits?

❶ Read and Understand

Read the problem carefully.

• You need to find the area of the room after the demonstration space is identified.

❷ Make a Plan

Decide on a strategy to use.

One way to see the situation is to draw a diagram. To solve this problem, you can draw a diagram of the classroom.

❸ Solve the Problem

Reread the problem and draw a diagram.

First, draw and label a diagram of the classroom.

Next, draw a space to save for the demonstration. The problem doesn't specify where the space needs to be, so you might choose to put it in one corner.

The space available for exhibits is the total area of the classroom minus the area kept for the demonstration.

Total Area = 30 × 20   Demonstration Area = 10 × 10

Area for Exhibits = Total Area − Demonstration Area

$$= 30 \times 20 - 10 \times 10 \qquad \textbf{Write an algebraic model.}$$

$$= 600 - 100 \qquad \textbf{Multiply.}$$

$$= 500 \qquad \textbf{Subtract.}$$

Area is measured in square units, so the area for exhibits is 500 square feet.

❹ Look Back

When the question involves measurements, check to be sure your answer includes the appropriate units.

Practice the Strategy

Use the strategy *draw a diagram.*

1. **Restaurant Space** Your favorite pizza place has a new addition. The original building was 30 feet by 16 feet. The addition is 12 feet by 16 feet. What is the total area of the building with the addition?

2. **Cafeteria** Mark, Kristine, Todd, and Alia are in line for lunch at the cafeteria in that order. Kristine lets Alia cut in front of her. Mark lets Todd cut in back of him. Todd then lets Kristine cut in front of him. In what order are they now?

3. **Mall Stores** Stores rent space in a mall. If the cost to rent Store 58 is $35 per square foot, what is the total rent for the store?

4. **School Gym** A gym is 100 feet by 70 feet. Bleachers are along both 100 foot sides of the gym. The bleachers are 4 feet deep when closed. When open, they are 9 feet deep. Compare the available area in the gym when the bleachers are closed to when they are open.

5. **Classrooms** Two classrooms are the same size. Each has seating for 28 students. In one room, each student has a desk and chair that take up 9 square feet. In the other room, each group of 4 students shares a table and chairs that take up 35 square feet. Each room also has one large table that takes up 15 square feet. Which room has more walking space?

Mixed Problem Solving

Use any strategy to solve the problem.

6. **Internet Sales** In May 2001, spending on online auctions was $556 million, about $\frac{2}{3}$ of which was through one auction site. What was the total spending on auctions at that site in May 2001?

7. **Survey** A group of 1238 students in grades 7–12 were asked to name the reasons for community involvement. How do you know that some students gave more than one answer? Graph the data.

Reason	Number
Makes me feel good	842
Fun to do	829
Right thing to do	805

8. **Video Games** In a video game, when you reach 50 points, you reach Level 2. You need 70 more points to reach Level 3, and then you need 90 more points to reach Level 4. How many points do you need to reach Level 7 without skipping any levels?

9. **Creating a Maze** You are painting a 10 foot by 10 foot maze at your school. Inside the maze will be a 2 foot by 2 foot area that is the goal. What is the longest path you can create if the path, including lines, is one foot wide? Draw one solution. Explain how you know you have found the longest path.

3.5

Applying Geometric Formulas

BEFORE ▶ **Now** **WHY?**

You measured rectangles.

You'll use formulas for perimeter and area.

So you can evaluate advertising claims, as in Ex. 26.

Word Watch

base, p. 134
height, p. 134

FLORIDA
Standards and Assessment

• Evaluate algebraic equations. (MA.D.2.3.1)
• Solve linear equations. (MA.D.2.3.1)

Activity You can use a model to find the area of a triangle.

1. Copy the diagram on graph paper.

2. Cut out the three pieces.

3. Arrange the pieces to make two equal-sized triangles.

4. Compare the height of triangle 2 to the height of the original rectangle. What is the area of the rectangle? of triangle 2?

5. Draw your own triangle on graph paper so that its longest side is a side of the rectangle and the vertex touches the opposite side. Find its area by following the steps above.

6. Write a formula for the area of a triangle.

To find the area of a triangle, you need to know the *base* and the *height*. Any side of a triangle can be labeled as the triangle's **base**. The perpendicular distance from a base to its opposite vertex is the **height** of a triangle.

Area and Perimeter of a Triangle

Words The *area* of a triangle is one half the product of its base b and height h.

The *perimeter* of a triangle is the sum of the lengths of all three sides a, b, and c.

Algebra $A = \frac{1}{2}bh$

$P = a + b + c$

Diagram

134 Chapter 3 Solving Equations and Inequalities

EXAMPLE 1 **Finding Area and Perimeter of a Triangle**

Find the area and perimeter of the triangle.

$A = \frac{1}{2}bh$

$\quad = \frac{1}{2}(14)(12)$

$\quad = 84 \text{ in.}^2$

$P = a + b + c$

$\quad = 13 + 14 + 15$

$\quad = 42 \text{ in.}$

12 in.

15 in.   13 in.

14 in.

EXAMPLE 2 **Finding the Area of a Triangle**

Sailboats Find the area of the sail.

Solution

$A = \frac{1}{2}bh$ **Write area formula.**

$\quad = \frac{1}{2}(171)(134)$ **Substitute values.**

$\quad = 11,457$ **Multiply.**

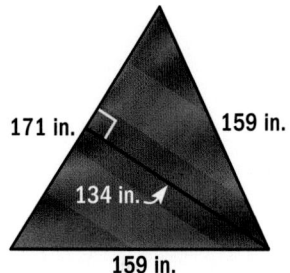

171 in.   159 in.

134 in.

159 in.

ANSWER The area of the sail is 11,457 square inches.

Your turn now **Use the given information about the triangle.**

1. Its height is 9 inches and its base is 10 inches. Find its area.

2. Its side lengths are 4 feet, 6 feet, and 2.5 feet. Find its perimeter.

Now that you can solve equations, you can use area and perimeter formulas to find missing dimensions of geometric shapes.

EXAMPLE 3 **Finding a Missing Width**

Find the width of the rectangle shown if the area is 63 square feet.

$A = lw$ **Write area formula.**

$63 = 9w$ **Substitute values.**

$\dfrac{63}{9} = \dfrac{9w}{9}$ **Divide each side by 9.**

$7 = w$ **Simplify.**

w

9 ft

ANSWER The width of the rectangle is 7 feet.

 with Review

If you need help with area and perimeter of squares and rectangles, see p. 33.

Lesson 3.5   Applying Geometric Formulas   **135**

EXAMPLE 4 Finding a Missing Length

**The rectangle has a perimeter of 20 inches.
Find the length of the rectangle.**

4 in.

l

$P = 2l + 2w$	Write perimeter formula.
$20 = 2l + 2(4)$	Substitute 20 for P and 4 for w.
$20 = 2l + 8$	Multiply.
$20 - 8 = 2l + 8 - 8$	Subtract 8 from each side.
$12 = 2l$	Simplify.
$\dfrac{12}{2} = \dfrac{2l}{2}$	Divide each side by 2.
$6 = l$	Simplify.

ANSWER The length of the rectangle is 6 inches.

Your turn now **Find the unknown dimension.**

3. Perimeter = 36 ft

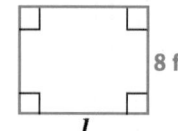

8 ft

l

4. Area = 32 mm^2

h

8 mm

5. Area = 6 in.^{2}

4 in.

b

EXAMPLE 5 Using an Area Formula

Zoo A polar bear exhibit includes a pool
and a region with rocks for climbing. Find
the area of the region with rocks.

pool   20 ft

32 ft   40 ft

rocks

56 ft

Solution

Let r be the area of the region with rocks.

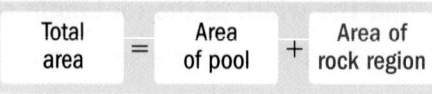

Total area	=	Area of pool	+	Area of rock region

$40 \cdot 56 = 20 \cdot 32 + r$	
$2240 = 640 + r$	Write an algebraic model.
$2240 - 640 = 640 - 640 + r$	Subtract 640 from each side.
$1600 = r$	Simplify.

ANSWER The area of the region with rocks is 1600 square feet.

What do you think?

Biology

■ **Polar Bears**

Polar bears can swim up
to 6.2 mi/h. About how far
can a polar bear swim in
6 minutes?

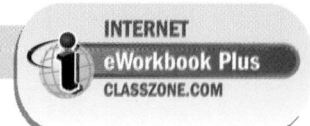

Getting Ready to Practice

1. Vocabulary Copy and complete: In order to find the area of a triangle, you need to know the length of a(n) ? and the ? .

Find the area and perimeter of the figure.

2.

4 in.
6 in.

3.

2 cm
2 cm

4.

9 m   15 m
12 m

5. Guided Problem Solving Find the area of the patio shown at the right.

  ① Find the area of the rectangle.

  ② Find the area of the square.

  ③ Add the two areas.

7 yd
6 yd   3 yd
3 yd
10 yd

Practice and Problem Solving

Find the area and perimeter of the triangle.

6.

5 cm   4 cm   5 cm
6 cm

7.

15 in.   13 in.
12 in.
4 in.

8.

12 ft
13 ft   5 ft

Find the unknown dimension.

9. $A = 18 \text{ ft}^2$

x
6 ft

10. $A = 49 \text{ in.}^2$
s
s

11. $A = 12 \text{ cm}^2$

y   6 cm

Find the unknown dimension.

12. $P = 44 \text{ in.}$

y
9 in.

13. $P = 60 \text{ m}$

23 m   c
17 m

14. $P = 24 \text{ ft}$

4 ft
n

15. Find the Error Describe and correct the error in the solution.

$$A = \frac{1}{2}(5 \text{ in.})(4 \text{ in.})$$

$$A = \frac{1}{2}(20 \text{ in.})$$

$$A = 10 \text{ in.}$$

16. Critical Thinking Explain how the formulas for the perimeter and area of a rectangle can be used to find the perimeter and area of a square.

Find the dimension.

17. A rectangle has a perimeter of 146 inches and a length of 49 inches. What is the width of the rectangle?

18. A triangle has an area of 36 square meters and a height of 8 meters. What is the length of its base?

19. A triangle has an area of 5 square meters and a base of $2x$. What is the height of the triangle in terms of x?

20. A rectangle has an area of 70 square inches and a width of $3.5w$. What is the length of the rectangle in terms of w?

Find the area of the shaded region in the figure.

21.

4 m
6 m
2 m
4 m

22.

6 m
10 m
8 m
10 m

23.

15 ft
24 ft

Extended Problem Solving In Exercises 24–26, use the tent advertisement shown.

24. Calculate Find the area of the tent floor.

25. Estimate Estimate the dimensions of a rectangular sleeping bag and find its area.

26. Critical Thinking Do you think this tent will comfortably fit four sleeping bags? Draw a diagram and explain your answer.

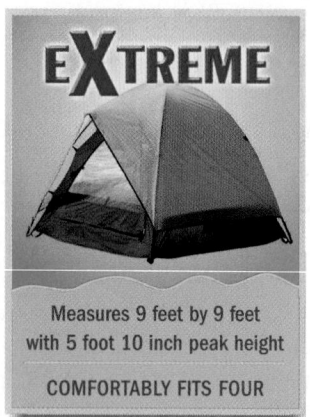

EXTREME

Measures 9 feet by 9 feet
with 5 foot 10 inch peak height

COMFORTABLY FITS FOUR

Critical Thinking Explain how the area of a triangle changes if you change the triangle as described.

27. Double the height.

28. Double the base.

29. Double both the height and the base.

30. Change its shape, but not its base or height.

31. Sharing Space Michelle and her sister Kate share a bedroom that is 18 feet by 14 feet. They want to divide the room so that each sister has half the area. Kate marks out her space. It is a square with sides 11 feet long in the center of the room. Does Kate have half the area of the room? Explain.

Find the area of the figure.

32.

12 in. 18 in.
12 in.
12 in. 12 in.
12 in.

33.

5 m   5 m
3 m
5 m   5 m   5 m

34. Challenge A roll of weather stripping for windows is about 6 feet long. How many rolls are needed to go around three square windows that measure 3 feet on each side, and one rectangular window that measures 3 feet by 5 feet?

Mixed Review

Find the sum or difference. *(Lessons 2.2, 2.3)*

35. $-18 - 42$ **36.** $-21 - (-14)$ **37.** $8 - (-10) - (-3)$

38. $15 + (-10)$ **39.** $-20 + (-12)$ **40.** $11 + (-5) + (-8)$

In Exercises 41–43, evaluate the expression when $a = 2$, $b = -5$, and $c = -7$. *(Lessons 2.3, 2.4)*

41. $a - b$ **42.** $c + b^2$ **43.** $abc - bc$

44. You have $80 today. If you save $40 a week, how many weeks will it take to save enough to buy a camera that costs $320? How many weeks will it take if you save $35 a week? *(Lesson 3.4)*

Basic Skills Copy and complete the statement with <, >, or =.

45. $3 \underline{\ ?\ } -3$ **46.** $-5 \underline{\ ?\ } -6$ **47.** $-17 \underline{\ ?\ } -13$ **48.** $13 \underline{\ ?\ } |13|$

FCAT Practice

49. Multiple Choice Your local park's basketball court has an area of 216 square feet. One side is 24 feet long. Which equation would you use to find the width?

A. $216 - x = 24$ **B.** $2x + 48 = 216$ **C.** $216x = 24$ **D.** $24x = 216$

50. Multiple Choice What is the length of a rectangular room that is 28 feet wide and has a perimeter of 158 feet?

F. 107 feet   **G.** 23 feet   **H.** 51 feet   **I.** 65 feet

3.6

Solving Inequalities Using Addition or Subtraction

BEFORE	▶ Now	WHY?
You solved equations using addition or subtraction.	You'll solve inequalities using addition or subtraction.	So you can find how much to improve your distance, as in Ex. 40.

In the Real World

Word Watch

inequality, p. 140
solution of an inequality,
  p. 140
equivalent inequalities, p. 141

FLORIDA
Standards and Assessment

• Solve linear inequalities.
  (MA.D.2.3.1)

• Solve linear inequalities representing real-world situations. (MA.D.2.3.2)

Disc Golf In a game of disc golf, the target is beyond a pond the far end of which is 300 feet away. Your first throw travels 134 feet. How far does your second throw have to go in order to clear the pond? You will use an inequality to answer this question in Example 3.

Inequalities An **inequality** is a statement formed by placing an inequality symbol between two expressions, such as $x \le 6$.
The **solution of an inequality** is the set of numbers that you can substitute for the variable to make the inequality true.

You can graph the solution of an inequality using a number line. When graphing inequalities with > or <, use an open circle. When graphing inequalities with ≥ or ≤, use a closed circle.

EXAMPLE 1 Graphing Inequalities

Inequality	Graph	Verbal Phrase
a. $y < 7$	2 3 4 5 6 7 8	All numbers less than 7
b. $q \le 3$	−2 −1 0 1 2 3 4	All numbers less than or equal to 3
c. $x > -5$	−6 −4 −2 0	All numbers greater than −5
d. $h \ge 2\frac{1}{2}$	0 1 2 3	All numbers greater than or equal to $2\frac{1}{2}$

Your turn now Graph the inequality.

1. $z \ge -1$ **2.** $4 > p$ **3.** $k \le -3.5$ **4.** $m > \frac{1}{2}$

When you solve an inequality, you find all solutions of the inequality. Inequalities that have the same solutions are **equivalent inequalities** .

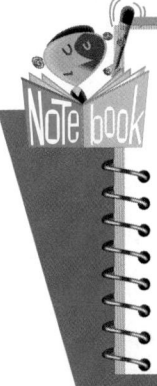

Addition and Subtraction Properties of Inequality

Words   Adding or subtracting the same number on each side of an inequality produces an equivalent inequality.

Algebra   If $a > b$, then $a + c > b + c$.

If $a > b$, then $a - c > b - c$.

 with Solving

Remember that the inequality symbols can be read as follows.
> "greater than"
< "less than"
≥ "greater than or equal to"
≤ "less than or equal to"

EXAMPLE **2**   **Solving Inequalities**

Solve the inequality. Then graph its solution.

a. $x - 5 < 8$ Original inequality

$x - 5 + 5 < 8 + 5$ Add 5 to each side.

$x < 13$ Simplify.

9 10 11 12 13 14 15

b. $y - 7 \geq -10$ Original inequality

$y - 7 + 7 \geq -10 + 7$ Add 7 to each side.

$y \geq -3$ Simplify.

−5 −4 −3 −2 −1 0 1

c. $8 + m > 15$ Original inequality

$8 - 8 + m > 15 - 8$ Subtract 8 from each side.

$m > 7$ Simplify.

4 5 6 7 8 9 10

Your turn now   **Solve the inequality. Then graph its solution.**

5. $x - 3 > -2$ **6.** $6 > t - 1$ **7.** $12 \geq p + 14$

EXAMPLE 3 **Writing and Solving an Inequality**

Disc Golf Using an inequality, you can find the distance needed to clear the pond described on page 140.

Let d be the distance needed to clear the pond on your second throw.

Distance of 2nd throw	+	Distance of 1st throw	>	Distance to far end of pond

$$d + 134 > 300 \qquad \text{Write an algebraic model.}$$
$$d + 134 - 134 > 300 - 134 \qquad \text{Subtract 134 from each side.}$$
$$d > 166 \qquad \text{Simplify.}$$

ANSWER Your second throw needs to travel more than 166 feet.

3.6 Exercises

More Practice, p. 729

INTERNET
eWorkbook Plus
CLASSZONE.COM

Getting Ready to Practice

1. **Vocabulary** Copy and complete: $-4 + x < -6$ and $x < -2$ are ___?___ .

Matching **Match the inequality with its graph.**

2. $x < -1$

3. $x \leq 1$

4. $x \geq 1$

5. $x > -1$

A. ![number line with closed dot at 1, shaded left, marks −2 −1 0 1 2]

B. ![number line with closed dot at 1, shaded right, marks −2 −1 0 1 2]

C. ![number line with open dot at −1, shaded right, marks −2 −1 0 1 2]

D. ![number line with open dot at −1, shaded right, marks −2 −1 0 1 2]

Solve the inequality. Then graph its solution.

6. $x - 5 < 5$

7. $8 > t + 10$

8. $12 + p > 7$

9. **Guided Problem Solving** On four tests you scored 90, 85, 98, and 87. To earn a B in math class, you need at least 425 points on 5 tests. Write and solve an inequality that represents the possible test scores you could get on your fifth test and still get at least a B in the class.

   (1) Add your current scores.

   (2) Let x represent the fifth score. Write and solve the inequality.

   (3) Graph the possible test scores.

Practice and Problem Solving

with Homework

Example	Exercises
1	10–21
2	22–30
3	31, 33

Online Resources
CLASSZONE.COM

· More Examples
· eTutorial Plus

Write the inequality represented by the graph.

10.

11.

12.

13.

In Exercises 14–17, tell whether the number is a solution of the inequality graphed below.

14. -4.5

15. -4

16. $2\frac{1}{2}$

17. 0

Write a verbal phrase to describe the inequality.

18. $z \le 8$

19. $j > -4$

20. $w \ge -15$

21. $n < 0$

Solve the inequality. Then graph its solution.

22. $k + 4 \le 11$

23. $5 < 8 + t$

24. $n - 6 > 3$

25. $17 + r \ge 25$

26. $m + 6 \ge -10$

27. $p - 12 > -5$

28. $-9 < d - 21$

29. $-8 \ge m - 19$

30. $-42 + x > -59$

31. **Banking** You have $33.96 in a savings account. At your bank, you must have a minimum balance of $50 in your account to avoid a fee. Write and solve an inequality to represent the amount of money you must deposit in order to reach or exceed the minimum balance.

32. **Critical Thinking** Write an equivalent inequality that you would use addition to solve and whose solution is $p < 6$.

33. **Biplane Ride** Your family bought your grandmother a biplane ride for her 80th birthday. The flight can last up to one hour and 15 minutes. If she does 10 minutes of corkscrew rolls, 15 minutes of hammerheads, and 30 minutes of over-water flying, how much time can she use for scenic low-altitude flying without going over the time limit?

Solve the inequality. Then graph its solution.

34. $5.45 + b < -3.55$

35. $r - 3.1 < 4.4$

36. $-3.5 < w - 9$

37. $\frac{2}{3} \le p - 2\frac{1}{3}$

38. $-\frac{1}{2} \le k + 2$

39. $t + \frac{1}{4} > 5$

40. Ski Jumping In a ski jumping competition, the top four jumpers perform as shown. How much farther does the fourth place jumper need to jump in order to place first? Write and solve an inequality that describes the situation.

Name	Distance
Cara	238.2 m
Jason	233.6 m
Marisa	250.2 m
Mitchell	236.3 m

41. Writing Explain why $x - 3 \geq 10$ and $x \geq 13$ are equivalent inequalities.

Tell whether −6 is a solution of the inequality.

42. $8 + x \geq -2$ **43.** $x - 15 > -20$ **44.** $-10 - x \leq -4$

45. Vocal Range The frequency range of the human singing voice is between about 81 hertz and about 1100 hertz. Write two inequalities that describe this range.

46. Careers You are investigating a job that pays a maximum of $34,000 and a minimum of $25,000. Write two inequalities that describe this range.

■ **Vocal Range**

In an octave, the frequency doubles from the lowest to the highest note. Aretha Franklin's voice can range over about 3 octaves, but she is an exception. A typical person's singing voice can range over about 2 octaves. If your vocal range is 2 octaves and begins at 220 hertz, predict your full vocal range.

EXAMPLE

Write a compound inequality that represents the set of all numbers greater than or equal to 0 and less than 4.

The set can be represented by two inequalities.

$0 \leq x$ and $x < 4$

The two inequalities can then be combined in a single inequality:

$0 \leq x < 4$

The compound inequality may be read in these two ways:

x is greater than or equal to 0 and x is less than 4.

x is greater than or equal to 0 and less than 4.

In Exercises 47–49, refer to the above example. Write a verbal sentence that describes the *compound inequality*.

47. $-2 < y < 1$ **48.** $7 \leq t < 9$ **49.** $4 \leq m \leq 11$

50. Tigers Until 1900, the tiger population in India was approximately 40,000. Beginning in 1960, the population dropped dramatically until 1972, when the population fell below 2000. Now the tiger population is rising again. The current population can be described by the inequality $2000 \leq x \leq 4556$. Explain what this says about the current population.

51. Challenge Find the values of x that will make the following statement true: $4x - 10 < 8x + 4 - 3x$.

52. Advertising During the first Super Bowl in 1967, a 30 second television commercial cost about $42,000. In 2001, advertisers paid about $2.4 million for a 30 second commercial. Assuming those were the least and greatest costs during that period, write an inequality that describes the cost *c* of 30 seconds of commercial time during the Super Bowl from 1967 through 2001.

Mixed Review

Evaluate the expression. (Lessons 2.2–2.5)

53. $(-24) \div 3 + 5 \times (-9)$

54. $(-12) \div (-33 + 45) - 19$

55. $(-13 - 44) + 100 \div 2$

56. $(-3) \times (15 - 7) \div 2 + 4$

Basic Skills **Write the number in standard form.**

57. Nine and fifty-three thousandths **58.** Sixty-four and seven tenths

FCAT Practice

59. Multiple Choice What value of *x* makes $x - 6 \geq 23$ true?

A. 17   **B.** 30   **C.** 28   **D.** 23

60. Multiple Choice Three people get off the bus at Washington Street. There are more than twenty people remaining on the bus. Based on the inequality $x - 3 > 20$ where *x* represents the number of people on the bus before Washington Street, which of the following could be the number of people on the bus before that stop?

F. 10   **G.** 21   **H.** 22   **I.** 24

BRAIN GAME

Prized Positions

The student council is holding a raffle to raise money. The officers must decide how many prizes to award, but each officer has a different opinion.

◆ The president thinks there should be more than 1 prize.

◆ The vice president wants to give no more than 10 prizes.

◆ The treasurer believes at least 4 prizes should be awarded.

◆ The secretary says there should be fewer than 5.

How many prizes should the student council award? Find a number that will make everyone happy.

Solving Inequalities Using Multiplication or Division

BEFORE	Now	WHY?
You solved equations using multiplication or division.	You'll solve inequalities using multiplication or division.	So you can find how many students must attend a dance, as in Ex. 26.

In the Real World

 Word Watch

Review Words

inequality, p. 140
solution of an inequality, p. 140
equivalent inequalities, p. 141

FLORIDA
Standards and Assessment

• Solve linear inequalities representing real-world situations. (MA.D.2.3.2)

• Write inequalities to express relationships. (MA.D.1.3.2)

Bats About 15,000 fruit-eating bats live on Panama's Barro Colorado Island. Every year they consume up to 61,440,000 grams of fruit. About how many grams of fruit does each bat consume in a year? You will use an inequality to solve this in Example 3.

There is one important difference between solving inequalities and solving equations. When multiplying or dividing each side of an inequality by a negative number, you must *reverse the direction of the inequality symbol.*

HELP with Notetaking

You might want to use a table to organize this information about reversing the inequality symbol.

Multiplication Property of Inequality

Words

Multiplying each side of an inequality by a *positive* number makes an equivalent inequality.

Algebra

If $4x < 10$, then
$$\left(\frac{1}{4}\right)(4x) < \left(\frac{1}{4}\right)(10).$$

Multiplying each side of an inequality by a *negative* number and *reversing the direction of the inequality symbol* makes an equivalent inequality.

If $-5x < 10$, then
$$\left(-\frac{1}{5}\right)(-5x) > \left(-\frac{1}{5}\right)(10).$$

EXAMPLE 1 Solving an Inequality Using Multiplication

$$-\frac{1}{8}n \geq 2 \qquad \text{Original inequality}$$

$$-8 \cdot \left(-\frac{1}{8}\right)n \leq -8 \cdot 2 \qquad \begin{array}{l}\text{Multiply each side by } -8.\\ \text{Reverse inequality symbol.}\end{array}$$

$$n \leq -16 \qquad \text{Simplify.}$$

Division Property of Inequality

Words

Dividing each side of an inequality by a *positive* number makes an equivalent inequality.

Dividing each side of an inequality by a *negative* number and *reversing the direction of the inequality symbol* makes an equivalent inequality.

Algebra

If $2x < 10$, then $\dfrac{2x}{2} < \dfrac{10}{2}$.

If $-5x < 15$, then $\dfrac{-5x}{-5} > \dfrac{15}{-5}$.

What do you think?

Bats

Fruit Bats

Fruit bats help forests regrow by spreading the seeds from the figs that they eat each night. One kind of fruit bat is about 25 grams and can eat 2.5 times its body mass in figs in one night. How many grams of figs can one of these bats eat?

EXAMPLE 2 **Solving an Inequality Using Division**

$15 > -3m$	Original inequality
$\dfrac{15}{-3} < \dfrac{-3m}{-3}$	Divide each side by -3. Reverse inequality symbol.
$-5 < m$	Simplify.

Your turn now Solve the inequality.

1. $\dfrac{t}{6} > 4$ **2.** $-\dfrac{1}{2}x \le 10$ **3.** $27 > -3t$ **4.** $9n < 63$

EXAMPLE 3 **Using the Division Property of Inequality**

Bats You can find how much each fruit-eating bat eats annually as described on the previous page as follows.

Solution

Write a verbal model. Let g represent the number of grams one bat eats in a year.

Number of bats	•	Grams each bat eats	$\le$	Maximum amount eaten annually

$15{,}000g \le 61{,}440{,}000$	Write an algebraic model.
$\dfrac{15{,}000g}{15{,}000} \le \dfrac{61{,}440{,}000}{15{,}000}$	Divide each side by 15,000.
$g \le 4096$	Simplify.

ANSWER Each bat eats as much as 4096 grams of fruit in a year.

Getting Ready to Practice

1. **Vocabulary** Copy and complete: When you multiply both sides of an inequality by a negative number, you need to ? the inequality symbol.

Decide whether the solution strategy will require reversing the inequality symbol.

2. $\frac{1}{3}x < 18$ Multiply each side by 3.

3. $-6x \geq 24$ Divide each side by -6.

Solve the inequality. Then graph its solution.

4. $\frac{1}{2}x < 4$ 5. $\frac{m}{-7} \geq 6$ 6. $9 \leq -3z$ 7. $30 > -6p$

8. **Fundraising** The diving club is selling lessons to raise money. The profit is $15 per lesson. The diving club wants to raise at least $300. How many lessons must be sold?

Practice and Problem Solving

Solve the inequality. Match the inequality with the graph of its solution.

9. $\frac{1}{4}x \leq 8$ 10. $-4x \geq 8$ 11. $4x \geq -8$ 12. $-\frac{1}{4}x \leq 8$

A.
```
←——+——+——+——●——+——+——→
  -8  -6  -4  -2   0   2
```

B.
```
←——+——+——●——+——+——→
 -40 -32 -24 -16  -8   0
```

C.
```
←——+——+——●——+——+——+——→
  -8  -6  -4  -2   0   2
```

D.
```
←——+——+——+——+——●——+——→
   0   8  16  24  32  40
```

Solve the inequality. Then graph its solution.

13. $\frac{1}{4}x > 1$ 14. $-\frac{1}{7}t \geq 3$ 15. $-\frac{1}{5}b \geq 72$ 16. $\frac{1}{3}d < -33$

17. $4g < 24$ 18. $12 \geq -3s$ 19. $-9c \leq 54$ 20. $5z < -15$

21. $7 > -\frac{1}{8}r$ 22. $-6t \geq 36$ 23. $-39 \leq -13k$ 24. $-\frac{1}{7}a < 54$

25. **Critical Thinking** Is it possible to list every number in the solution set of an inequality? Explain your answer.

HELP with Homework

Example	Exercises
1	9-24
2	9-24
3	26

Online Resources
CLASSZONE.COM
· More Examples
· eTutorial Plus

26. Dance The student council must pay a DJ $275 to work at a dance. A ticket to the dance costs $5.50. The amount of money received from ticket sales must at least cover the cost of the DJ. Write and solve an inequality that gives the number of students that must attend the dance in order to pay the $275 for the DJ.

Solve the inequality. Then graph its solution.

27. $12 > 6 - 2x$ **28.** $3y - 4 < 2y + 5$ **29.** $4p - 9 \geq -1$

30. $5(1 - t) \leq 4(3 - t)$ **31.** $4d < -2(33 + d)$ **32.** $7z + 3 \leq 5z - 1$

33. Writing How is solving an inequality like solving an equation? How is solving an inequality different from solving an equation?

34. Borrowing Money You borrow $200 from your aunt to buy a new surfboard. If you pay her back at a rate of $12 per week, when will you owe her less than $60?

Solve the inequality.

35. $5(x - 20) \geq 3x + 60$ **36.** $4(12 - 5x) \geq -4$ **37.** $2(3 - x) \leq 10x$

Challenge Solve the compound inequality.

38. $-6 < 2x < 10$ **39.** $-35 \leq 7x \leq -14$ **40.** $10 < 5x < 100$

41. Monitor The height of a rectangular computer screen is 20 centimeters less than twice the width. The perimeter is at least 53 centimeters. Find the minimum dimensions of the screen if each dimension is an integer.

Mixed Review

Use mental math to solve the equation. *(Lessons 2.2, 2.4)*

42. $-4x = 0$ **43.** $11a = 11$ **44.** $z + (-12) = -12$

Solve the inequality. Then graph its solution. *(Lesson 3.6)*

45. $c + 7 \leq 11$ **46.** $3 < 12 + s$ **47.** $x - 12 > 17$

Basic Skills Find the missing number.

48. 7 hours = _?_ minutes   **49.** 3 days = _?_ hours

FCAT Practice   FCAT

50. Short Response Your class is going on a field trip to the science museum. Your school gives you a budget of $120, to buy the tickets for your class and as many chaperones as they can afford. Your class has 35 students. The student tickets cost $3 and the adult tickets cost $5. Write and solve an inequality that describes how many chaperones can go.

LESSONS 3.5 TO 3.7

Notebook Review

Review the vocabulary definitions in your notebook.

Copy the review examples in your notebook. Then complete the exercises.

Check Your Definitions

base, p. 134
height, p. 134
inequality, p. 140

solution of an inequality, p. 140
equivalent inequalities, p. 141

Use Your Vocabulary

1. Draw a triangle. Label the base and the height.

3.5 Can you use formulas for perimeter and area?

 EXAMPLE Find the height of the triangle. Its area is 21 square inches.

$A = \frac{1}{2}bh$ Write area formula.

$21 = \frac{1}{2}(6)(h)$ Substitute known values.

$21 = 3h$ Multiply.

$7 = h$ Divide each side by 3.

h

6 in.

ANSWER The height of the triangle is 7 inches.

 Find the unknown dimension of the triangle.

2. $A = 50$ cm², $b = 10$ cm, $h = \underline{\ ?\ }$ **3.** $A = 45$ ft², $h = 10$ ft, $b = \underline{\ ?\ }$

3.6 Can you solve addition or subtraction inequalities?

 EXAMPLE Solve $x - 9 < -4$.

$x - 9 < -4$ Write original inequality.

$x - 9 + 9 < -4 + 9$ Add 9 to each side.

$x < 5$ Simplify.

 Solve the inequality. Then graph its solution.

4. $h - 12 > 12$ **5.** $-4 + k \leq 6$ **6.** $7 < 15 + p$ **7.** $d + 11 \geq 5$

3.7 Can you solve multiplication or division inequalities?

 EXAMPLE

$\dfrac{t}{7} > 2$ Original inequality $-12k \le 60$ Original inequality

$7 \cdot \dfrac{t}{7} > 7 \cdot 2$ Multiply each side by 7. $\dfrac{-12k}{-12} \ge \dfrac{60}{-12}$ Divide each side by -12. Reverse inequality symbol.

$t > 14$ Simplify. $k \ge -5$ Simplify.

☑ **Solve the inequality.**

8. $\dfrac{d}{6} \le 34$ **9.** $-\dfrac{1}{5}x \ge 20$ **10.** $5c > 25$ **11.** $-15b < 60$

Stop *and* **Think**   about Lessons 3.5–3.7

12. Writing Mary claims that she has at least 50 CDs at home and she just got 4 more for her birthday. Write an inequality for the number of CDs she has now.

13. Critical Thinking What is the greatest integer solution of $-7x > -56$? Justify your answer.

Review Quiz 2

Find the length of each side.

1. A rectangle has a perimeter of 30 millimeters and a width of 6 millimeters. Find the length.

2. A triangle has an area of 26 square yards and a height of 4 yards. Find the base.

Solve the inequality. Then graph its solution.

3. $a + 9 \ge -1$ **4.** $-16 > y - 12$ **5.** $\dfrac{x}{3} < -3$ **6.** $-x > 5$

7. Apples An empty basket weighs 2 pounds. When filled with apples, the basket weighs more than 13 pounds. Write and solve an inequality that represents this situation. What does the variable stand for?

8. Calling Card You have $9.50 with which to recharge your phone card. Write and solve an inequality to find how many minutes you can add to your phone card if each minute costs $.10.

3

Chapter Review

 Vocabulary

equivalent equations, p. 109
inverse operations, p. 109
base, height, p. 134

inequality, p. 140
solution of an inequality, p. 140
equivalent inequalities, p. 141

Vocabulary Review

1. List 2 pairs of inverse operations. Explain why these are called inverse operations.

2. How can two inequalities be equivalent? Give an example of equivalent inequalities.

Copy and complete the statement.

3. Two equations that have the same solution are _?_.

4. A(n) _?_ is a statement formed by placing an inequality symbol between two expressions.

Review Questions

Solve the equation. *(Lessons 3.1, 3.2)*

5. $r - 11 = 21$

6. $v + 13 = 29$

7. $34 = g + 19$

8. $12p = 108$

9. $\dfrac{h}{5} = 8$

10. $\dfrac{z}{-7} = 23$

11. $-46 = \dfrac{w}{-28}$

12. $t - \dfrac{3}{7} = \dfrac{1}{7}$

13. $x + (-5) = -8$

14. $3.9 + y = 10.9$

15. $-9.5m = -22.8$

16. $-72 = -6n$

17. **ATVs** You rent an all-terrain vehicle that has $\dfrac{5}{8}$ of a tank of fuel. When you are done riding, there is $\dfrac{3}{8}$ of a tank left. Write a verbal model to represent the fraction of a tank of fuel you used. Then write and solve an algebraic model. *(Lesson 3.1)*

18. **Intramurals** A college brochure states that 215 students participate in intramural sports. This is one third of the students. How many students attend the college? *(Lesson 3.2)*

Solve the equation. *(Lesson 3.3)*

19. $2p - 5 = 13$

20. $19 + 8v = 43$

21. $9g + 16 = -29$

22. $-10c + 6 = 46$

23. $-82 = 53 - 5t$

24. $-33 = -15t - 12$

Review Questions

Solve the equation. *(Lesson 3.3)*

25. $\dfrac{d}{5} + 13 = -10$ **26.** $17 = \dfrac{x}{12} - 31$ **27.** $-21 - \dfrac{t}{3} = -6$ **28.** $-57 = -9 + \dfrac{w}{-7}$

29. Fruit Baskets Your class is making fruit baskets and selling them to raise money for a charity. The supplies cost $26 and the baskets sell for $7 each. Your class makes a profit of $100. How many baskets did your class sell? *(Lesson 3.4)*

Find the unknown dimension. *(Lesson 3.5)*

30. Perimeter = 11 in.   **31.** Perimeter = 28 m   **32.** Perimeter = 26 cm

Find the area of the triangle. *(Lesson 3.5)*

33.

34.

35.

36. Ticket Line You are standing in line for concert tickets. The ticket window is at street level at the middle of one side of a building that is 30 feet long and 20 feet wide. The line extends from the ticket window, around the corner of the building, and all the way to the next corner of the building. How long is the line? Explain why there are two possible answers. *(Lesson 3.5)*

Solve and graph the inequality. *(Lessons 3.6, 3.7)*

37. $96 \geq -12 + c$ **38.** $-\dfrac{1}{3}x > 4$ **39.** $-96 < 24h$ **40.** $78 - k \leq 21$

Find the Error **Describe and correct the error in the solution.**
(Lessons 3.6, 3.7)

41.

$$
\begin{aligned}
x + 7 &< 17 \\
\underline{-7} \quad &\phantom{<} \underline{-7} \\
x &> 10
\end{aligned}
$$

42.

$$
\begin{aligned}
-6c &< 18 \\
\frac{-6c}{-6} &< \frac{18}{-6} \\
c &< -3
\end{aligned}
$$

3 Chapter Test

Solve the equation.

1. $s - 6 = 39$

2. $x + 12 = -2$

3. $14.6 = \dfrac{k}{2.5}$

4. $24v = 288$

5. $\dfrac{1}{9} = t + \dfrac{1}{9}$

6. $-9.8 = \dfrac{y}{-4.7}$

7. $5b - 7 = 120$

8. $-236 = 29 - 5g$

9. Hiking You go on a 20 mile hike. In the morning you hike 8.2 miles, and by 2:00 P.M., you have covered 7.5 more miles. Write and solve an equation to find how many miles you have left to go.

In Exercises 10 and 11, write and solve an equation.

10. A bookstore offers three books in a set for $21.75. Each book costs the same amount. How much does each book cost?

11. A calf weighs 90 pounds. The calf gains 65 pounds a month. In how many months will the calf weigh 1000 pounds?

Translate the verbal phrase into an equation. Then solve the equation.

12. A number times 3 subtracted from 20 is -4.

13. The sum of 5 times a number and 14 is 9.

In Exercises 14 and 15, use the formula $P = 2l + 2w$. Solve the equation to find the unknown measure of the rectangle.

14. $P = 28$ in., $l = 13$ in. Find the width.

15. $P = 62$ cm, $w = 10$ cm. Find the length.

16. Find the height of a triangle with a base of 25 centimeters and an area of 200 square centimeters.

Solve the inequality.

17. $y + 78 < -124$

18. $-8.56 + k \geq 5.32$

19. $-8x < 64$

20. Lunch You and a friend are having lunch together. You can spend no more than $30 on both meals. The total cost of your friend's meal is $14.78. Write and solve an inequality to determine how much you can spend on your meal.

21. Figure Skating You are taking figure skating lessons. You can rent skates for $5 per lesson. You can buy skates for $75. What inequality expresses the number of lessons for which it is cheaper to buy skates?

Chapter FCAT Practice

Test-Taking Strategy **Start to work as soon as the testing time begins. Keep working and stay focused on the test.**

Multiple Choice

1. Which is an inverse operation for the operation of adding -5?

   A. Subtracting -5 **B.** Adding -5

   C. Subtracting 5 **D.** Dividing by 5

2. Which expression does *not* have a solution of $x = 11$?

   F. $x - 5 = 6$ **G.** $5 + x = 17$

   H. $x + 4.4 = 15.4$ **I.** $x - 9.2 = 1.8$

3. Which equations are equivalent?

   I. $\frac{4}{5}x = 4$ II. $\frac{x}{5} = 4$

   III. $4x = 20$ IV. $-x = -5$

   A. I and II

   B. II and IV

   C. I, II, and IV

   D. I, III, and IV

4. You are playing a video game. You receive 125 points for every level that you complete, and you received a 30-point bonus at the start of the game. You have 780 total points. How many levels have you completed?

   F. 6   **G.** 7   **H.** 8   **I.** 9

5. Which expression means "the sum of 7 times a number and -8 is 6"?

   A. $7 + (-8)n = 6$ **B.** $7 + n + (-8) = 6$

   C. $7(n + (-8)) = 6$ **D.** $7n + (-8) = 6$

6. A triangle has an area of 18 square feet. Which measurements *cannot* be the base length (b) and height (h) of the triangle?

   F. $h = 3$ ft, $b = 12$ ft   **G.** $h = 6$ ft, $b = 6$ ft

   H. $h = 2$ ft, $b = 9$ ft   **I.** $h = 4$ ft, $b = 9$ ft

7. A square has a perimeter of 28 inches. What is the area of the square?

   A. 14 square inches

   B. 14 inches

   C. 49 square inches

   D. 49 inches

8. Which statement about the inequality $x - 6 < -8$ is true?

   F. The arrow on the graph points to the right.

   G. 3 is not a solution.

   H. -5 is not a solution.

   I. The dot on its graph is solid.

Short Response

9. Write and solve an equation for the sentence: The quotient of a number and -15 is 30.

Extended Response

10. What is the greatest area that a rectangle, with a perimeter of 26 cm and side lengths that are all integers, can have? Explain how you got to your answer.

Strategies for Answering
Multiple Choice Questions

You can use the problem solving plan on page 39 to solve any problem. The strategies below can help you answer a multiple choice question. You can also use these strategies to check whether your answer to a multiple choice question is reasonable.

Strategy: Estimate the Answer

Problem 1

You will use powers and exponents to solve this problem.

The table shows how many pennies you save each day. If the pattern continues, what is the first day you will save more than ten dollars worth of pennies?

Day	1	2	3
Pennies	$2^1 = 2$	$2^2 = 4$	$2^3 = 8$

A. Day 8

B. Day 9

C. Day 10

D. Day 11

Estimate: 2^8 is a little more than 250, so $2^9 > 500$ and $2^{10} > 1000$. The correct answer is C.

Strategy: Use Visual Clues

Problem 2

The garden's area is 900 square feet. Use the Guess, Check, and Revise strategy to find the length of one side of the garden. Each side of the garden is 30 feet long.

How many feet of fencing do you need to enclose the square garden shown?

900 ft²

F. 30 ft

G. 60 ft

H. 90 ft

I. 120 ft

Multiply the side length by 4 to find the total amount of fencing needed. To enclose the garden, you need 120 feet of fencing. The correct answer is I.

Strategy: Use Number Sense

Problem 3

The problem involves integers, not fractions or decimals.

When multiplying a positive integer by a negative integer, the product is __?__.

A. greater than the positive integer

B. greater than the negative integer

C. less than or equal to the negative integer

D. less than the negative integer

The sign is negative and the absolute value of the product is greater than or equal to either factor. C is the correct answer.

Eliminating Unreasonable Choices The strategies used to find the correct answers for Problems 1–3 are the same strategies you can use to eliminate answer choices that are unreasonable or obviously incorrect.

Problem 4

Read the problem carefully. Degrees Fahrenheit are 32° more than almost twice the temperature in degrees Celsius.

The average body temperature of a polar bear is 37°C. Use the formula $F = 1.8C + 32$ to find the temperature in degrees Fahrenheit.

F. 34°F — Not correct. A temperature of about 1°C is 34°F.

G. 69°F

H. 74.95°F

I. 98.6°F — $1.8(37) + 32 = 98.6$, so the correct answer is I.

Watch Out!

Some answers that appear correct at first glance may be incorrect. Be aware of common errors.

Your turn now

Explain why the selected answer choice is unreasonable.

1. Two times a number plus 7 is −21. What is the number?

   A. −14   B. −7   ✗ C. 7   D. 14

2. Your school earns $1.50 for every T-shirt sold. Find the minimum number of T-shirts you must sell in order to raise $500.

   F. 333   G. 334   H. 500   ✗ I. 750

GO ON

Multiple Choice

1. Lou ran $2\frac{1}{2}$ miles in 30 minutes. What is his average speed in miles per hour?

    A. 1.2   **B.** 5   **C.** 6.3   **D.** 12

2. Tom has 30 tickets to redeem for carnival prizes. He wants one yo-yo that costs 20 tickets. Tom will buy erasers with the rest of his tickets. One eraser costs 2 tickets. How many erasers can Tom buy?

    F. 5   **G.** 10   **H.** 15   **I.** 25

3. The graph shows the inches of rainfall in Jacksonville, Florida. What is the best estimate of rainfall in April?

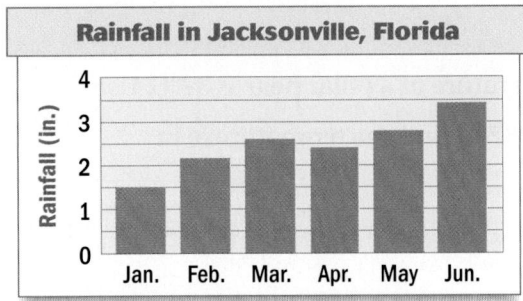

    A. 2 in.   **B.** 2.4 in.   **C.** 2.5 in.   **D.** 2.6 in.

4. What is the area of the triangle?

    F. 88 in.   **G.** 88 in.^{2} **H.** 176 in.   **I.** 176 in.^{2}

5. The student council raised $410 selling raffle tickets. One ticket cost $5. How many tickets were sold?

    A. 80   **B.** 82   **C.** 90   **D.** 410

6. What is the sum of the transactions in the bank statement shown here?

March 5	+$20
March 6	−$22
March 15	+$5

    F. −$7   **G.** −$3

    H. $7   **I.** $3

7. Rosa is scuba diving in Key West. She ascends to the surface at a rate of 25 feet per minute. After 3 minutes, her elevation is −5 feet. What was Rosa's elevation when she began her ascent?

    A. −80 ft   **B.** −70 ft   **C.** 70 ft   **D.** 80 ft

8. A volleyball court is 18 meters long and 9 meters wide. Which of the following is true about a volleyball court?

    F. Its perimeter is 162 meters.

    G. Its perimeter is 27 meters.

    H. Its area is 162 square meters.

    I. Its length is more than twice its width.

9. Jane drove 60 miles at an average speed of 40 miles per hour. How many hours did Jane spend driving?

    A. 0.3   **B.** 0.5   **C.** 1.5   **D.** 2

10. Each day Elizabeth earns $10 tutoring. She spends $1.50 on bus fare and $4.50 on lunch each day. Elizabeth saves the rest of her money. Which expression can be used to find how much money Elizabeth has after 5 days?

    F. $(10 - 4.50 + 1.50) \cdot 5$

    G. $10 - 5 \cdot (4.50 + 1.50)$

    H. $10 - 5 \cdot (4.50 - 1.50)$

    I. $(10 - 1.50 - 4.50) \cdot 5$

Short Response

11. Michael traveled 30 miles in 45 minutes. What is his average speed in miles per hour? Explain how you found your answer.

12. After 17 holes of mini-golf, Bill's total score is −8. Before this game, −6 is the lowest total score Bill ever had after 18 holes. Bill wants to beat this record. What is the highest score Bill can get on the next hole? Write an inequality that expresses the score. Graph the solution of the inequality on a number line. Explain your inequality and your graph.

13. The perimeter of a room is 52 feet. The room is 11 feet wide. Find the length of the room. Write and solve an equation to find your answer. Explain your steps.

14. Sandra needs 72 ounces of oatmeal to make cookies for a bake sale. A 42 ounce can costs $3.29, and an 18 ounce can costs $2.19. How many of each size should Sandra buy in order to pay the least amount of money? Explain your answer.

15. Laura and Natalie have $35. It costs $15 to rent a canoe plus $10 for each hour of use. How many hours can Laura and Natalie use the canoe? Explain.

16. Jack is responsible for half of the houses on a paper route, and he has delivered to 9 houses so far. There are 11 houses remaining on Jack's part of the paper route. How many houses are on the entire paper route? Explain how you found your answer.

Extended Response

17. Sheila bought carpet for two rooms in her house. The floor plan of the rooms is shown here. Find the area of the room with red carpet and the area of the room with blue carpet.

Sheila spent $1170 total on carpet. The red carpet cost $16 per square yard. Find the cost of the blue carpet per square yard.

How much would it cost for Sheila to carpet both rooms in blue? Explain how you found your answer.

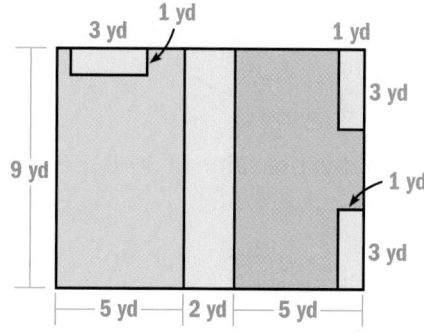

18. The results of a poll are shown at the right. Use the data to make a frequency table using the following 4 intervals: *0–3 hours*, *4–7 hours*, *8–11 hours*, and *12–15 hours*.

Use your frequency table to create a histogram of the data.

How many students polled participate in after school activities more than 3 hours per week? Which data display is more helpful when answering that question? Explain.

How many hours a week do you participate in after school activities?

10	5	1	0	8	3
12	3	0	5	9	6
10	9	2	4	7	0
2	3	5	1	5	

Cumulative Practice for Chapters 1–3

Chapter 1

Multiple Choice   In Exercises 1–8, choose the letter of the correct answer.

1. How many more oranges than limes were sold? Refer to the graph. *(Lesson 1.1)*

   A. 10   **B.** 20   **C.** 30   **D.** 40

Fruit Sales

2. Which operation is performed first when evaluating the expression $8 + 6(5 - 3) \cdot 18 \div 6$? *(Lesson 1.2)*

   F. +   **G.** −   **H.** ·   **I.** ÷

3. What is the value of $3 \cdot 6 - 8 \div 2$? *(Lesson 1.2)*

   A. 2   **B.** 5   **C.** 6   **D.** 14

4. What is the value of the expression $8x - 5y$ when $x = 5$ and $y = 2$? *(Lesson 1.3)*

   F. 6   **G.** 15   **H.** 30   **I.** 33

5. What is the value of the expression $(5 - 3)^4 - 6 + 4^2$? *(Lesson 1.4)*

   A. 10   **B.** 16   **C.** 18   **D.** 26

6. What is the value of t in the equation $t + 17 = 34$? *(Lesson 1.5)*

   F. 2   **G.** 17   **H.** 27   **I.** 51

7. Barbara is driving on the Florida Turnpike at a rate of 54 miles per hour. How many hours will it take her to travel 351 miles? *(Lesson 1.6)*

   A. 5.5   **B.** 6   **C.** 6.5   **D.** 7

8. A package of 12 oranges costs $3.96, and a package of 18 oranges costs $5.04. How much money will you save per orange if you buy a package of 18 instead of a package of 12? *(Lesson 1.7)*

   F. $.05   **G.** $.28   **H.** $.33   **I.** $.61

9. **Short Response** The lunch menu at a restaurant offers 5 salads. There are twice as many sandwiches as salads. There are 2 more salads than soups. What is the total number of salads, sandwiches, and soups on the menu? *(Lesson 1.7)*

10. **Extended Response** There are 28 games at a children's carnival, each at its own table. The tables are arranged so that they form the perimeter of a rectangle. Children play games on the inside of the rectangle. *(Lesson 1.6)*

   a. List all the possible dimensions (length and width) of the rectangular arrangement of tables.

   b. Find the area of each of the rectangles in your list.

   c. Which of the dimensions in your list result in the rectangle with the largest possible area?

   d. Describe the difference in appearance between the rectangles with the largest area and the smallest area.

Chapter 2

Multiple Choice In Exercises 11–20, choose the letter of the correct answer.

11. Which set of integers is listed in order from least to greatest? *(Lesson 2.1)*

A. $0, -11, -6, -4, -2$

B. $0, -2, -4, -6, -11$

C. $-2, -4, -6, -11, 0$

D. $-11, -6, -4, -2, 0$

12. What is the value of the expression $-28 + (-44) + 94 + (-28)$? *(Lesson 2.2)*

F. -194 **G.** -6 **H.** 6 **I.** 50

13. A dolphin dives to an elevation of -540 meters. After a while, the dolphin ascends 165 meters. What is the dolphin's elevation? *(Lesson 2.2)*

A. -695 m **B.** -375 m

C. 375 m **D.** 695 m

14. Find the value of the expression $3c + 3a - b$ when $a = -4$, $b = 8$, and $c = -6$. *(Lesson 2.4)*

F. -38 **G.** -22 **H.** 6 **I.** 18

15. What is the value of $\dfrac{-285}{15}$? *(Lesson 2.5)*

A. -270 **B.** -19 **C.** 19 **D.** 270

16. Which expression is equivalent to $-2 + 7 - (-4) - 5$? *(Lesson 2.6)*

F. $-2 - 5 - 4 + 7$

G. $-2 + (-4) - 5 + 7$

H. $-2 + 7 + (-4) - 5$

I. $-2 - 5 - (-4) + 7$

17. Which expression is equivalent to $7 - 2x + 3 - y - 3x$? *(Lesson 2.7)*

A. $10 - x - y$ **B.** $7 - 6x$

C. $10 - 5x - y$ **D.** $10 - 6xy$

18. Which expression is equivalent to $5(3x - 2)$? *(Lesson 2.7)*

F. $5x - 10$ **G.** $15x - 10$

H. $5x + 20$ **I.** $-15x - 10$

19. Which points have an x-coordinate of 2 in the coordinate plane? *(Lesson 2.8)*

A. A and B

B. B and C

C. C and D

D. D and A

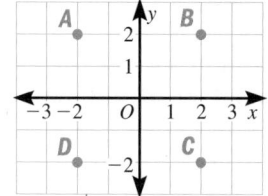

20. The point $(4, -1)$ is in which quadrant? *(Lesson 2.8)*

F. I **G.** II **H.** III **I.** IV

21. **Short Response** Find the mean elevation of the sightseeing and diving attractions in the Florida Keys.

Attraction	Elevation
Sand Key Lighthouse (top)	120 ft
The Thunderbolt	−115 ft
Joe's Tug	−65 ft
Alligator Reef Lighthouse (top)	150 ft
The Grotto, Islamorada	−26 ft
Crocker Wall	−50 ft
Sombrero Lighthouse (top)	160 ft

Which locations have an elevation below the mean? *(Lesson 2.5)*

Cumulative Practice continued

22. **Extended Response** In a coordinate plane, plot the points $A(-3, 2)$, $B(3, 2)$, $C(3, -2)$, and $D(-3, -2)$. Connect the points to form a rectangle. *(Lesson 2.8)*

   a. Find the length, width, and area of the rectangle.

   b. Draw a new rectangle that has half the length and half the width of the original rectangle. Find the area of the new rectangle.

   c. Does the new rectangle have half the area of the original rectangle? Explain.

Chapter 3

Multiple Choice In Exercises 23–29, choose the letter of the correct answer.

23. What is the value of y in the equation $y - 32 = -23$? *(Lesson 3.1)*

   A. -55 **B.** -9 **C.** 9 **D.** 55

24. A rectangular picture is 7 inches long with an area of 35 square inches. Which equation could you use to find the picture's width? *(Lesson 3.2)*

   F. $35x = 7$ **G.** $35 + x = 7$

   H. $7x = 35$ **I.** $7 + x = 35$

25. What is the value of x in the equation $30 = 4x + 6$? *(Lesson 3.3)*

   A. 6 **B.** 9 **C.** 20 **D.** 32

26. James sold snacks at a basketball game. He sold 25 cookies for $.50 each. He also sold 30 bottles of water. James made $42.50 total. What was the price of one bottle of water? *(Lesson 3.4)*

   F. $.75   **G.** $1.00   **H.** $1.50   **I.** $1.75

27. What is the area of the triangle? *(Lesson 3.5)*

   A. 42 m^2 **B.** 70 m^2 **C.** 84 m^2 **D.** 140 m^2

28. Which inequality is represented by the graph? *(Lesson 3.6)*

   F. $x \le -4$ **G.** $x > -4$

   H. $x < -4$ **I.** $x \ge -4$

29. Solve the inequality $x + 6 \ge 14$. *(Lesson 3.6)*

   A. $x \le 8$ **B.** $x \le 20$

   C. $x \ge 8$ **D.** $x \ge 20$

30. **Short Response** You have $5 to spend on aquarium fish. Guppies cost $.40 each, and mollies cost $.50 each. You buy 5 guppies. How many mollies can you buy? Write and solve an equation to answer the question. *(Lesson 3.4)*

31. **Extended Response** Susan, Fae, and Margaret have tickets for carnival games. Susan has four more than twice as many tickets as Fae. Fae has three less than half as many tickets as Margaret. Margaret has 60 tickets. *(Lesson 3.4, 3.6)*

   a. Write equations that you can use to find how many tickets each person has.

   b. Who has the most tickets? Who has the fewest tickets?

   c. Write and solve an inequality to show how many more tickets Fae needs in order to have the most tickets.

UNIT 2

Algebra and Rational Numbers

CHAPTER

4 Factors, Fractions, and Exponents

5 Rational Number Operations

6 Multi-Step Equations and Inequalities

7 Ratio, Proportion, and Percent

Meeting the Florida Standards

- **Find greatest common factors and least common multiples.**
  MA.A.3.3.2, MA.A.5.3.1

- **Identify equivalent fractions and write fractions in simplest form.**
  MA.A.1.3.2, MA.A.1.3.3, MA.A.5.3.1

- **Use rules of exponents and scientific notation for large and small numbers.** MA.A.1.3.4, MA.A.2.3.1, MA.A.3.3.2, MA.A.5.3.1

- **Perform operations with fractions, mixed numbers, and decimals.**
  MA.A.3.3.1, MA.A.3.3.2, MA.A.3.3.3, MA.A.4.3.1, MA.D.2.3.2

- **Compare and convert between fractions, mixed numbers, and decimals.** MA.A.1.3.2, MA.A.1.3.3, MA.A.1.3.4, MA.A.3.3.2

- **Find the mean, median, and mode(s) of a data set.**
  MA.A.3.3.3, MA.E.1.3.2, MA.E.1.3.3

- **Write and solve multi-step equations and inequalities.**
  MA.A.3.3.1, MA.D.1.3.2, MA.D.2.3.1, MA.D.2.3.2

- **Find circumferences of circles.**
  MA.B.1.3.3

- **Use ratios, rates, and proportions to solve problems.**
  MA.A.1.3.1, MA.B.1.3.3, MA.B.1.3.4

- **Use proportions and the percent equation to solve percent problems.**
  MA.A.3.3.2

- **Find the probability of simple events.**
  MA.E.2.3.1, MA.E.3.3.1

From Chapter 4, p. 182

How many known species of birds are in Peru?

CHAPTER 4

Factors, Fractions, and Exponents

BEFORE

In previous chapters you've...

- Multiplied and divided numbers
- Compared and ordered integers

Now

In Chapter 4 you'll study...

- Factoring numbers
- Simplifying fractions
- Multiplying and dividing expressions with exponents
- Reading and writing numbers using scientific notation

WHY?

So you can solve real-world problems about...

- geography, p. 182
- orangutans, p. 193
- computer memory, p. 199
- bubbles, p. 205

Internet Preview
CLASSZONE.COM

- eEdition Plus Online
- eWorkbook Plus Online
- eTutorial Plus Online
- FCAT Practice
- More Examples

Chapter Warm-Up Game

Review skills you need for this chapter in this quick game.

Key Skill:
Whole number division

BICYCLE MATH

HOW TO PLAY

1 **PICK** the number with each letter that divides evenly into the bold number in the matching fact.

    A. 4, 8, 42
    B. 7, 13, 23
    C. 15, 17, 21

2 **USE** the answer for each letter to evaluate the expression below. The value of the expression is the world record bicycle speed in miles per hour, set by Fred Rompelberg in 1995.

    A (B + C) + 30.9

A. In **1884**, the "safety bicycle," a bicycle resembling the ones we use today, was invented.

B. In 2001, **39,000,000** people in the United States rode a bicycle more than once.

C. In 2002, **189** cyclists competed in the Tour de France.

Stop *and* Think

1. **Writing** A student thinks that 42 divides evenly into 1884 because 42 divides evenly into 84. Explain what is wrong with the student's reasoning.

2. **Critical Thinking** What number will divide evenly into any even number? Explain.

Getting Ready to Learn

Word Watch

Review Words

power, p. 20
base, p. 20
exponent, p. 20
fraction, p. 707

Review What You Need to Know

Using Vocabulary Copy and complete using a review word.

1. In the expression 2^6, 2 is called the ?.

2. The expression 3^7 is a(n) ? of 3.

3. In the expression 5^4, 4 is called the ?.

Evaluate the expression. (p. 20)

4. $3^2 \cdot 3$ 5. $(2+3)^2$ 6. $4^2 \div 4^2$ 7. $(6-5)^7$

8. $3^2 + 4 \cdot 5$ 9. $12 - 8 \div 2^2$ 10. $7^2 - 3^3$ 11. $6^2 \div 2^2$

Simplify the expression by combining like terms. (p. 85)

12. $7x + 4 - 3x$ 13. $-2x + 5x - x$ 14. $x + 4 - 12x$ 15. $6x - 5 + x$

Solve the equation. Check your answer. (p. 119)

16. $2a + 6 = 14$ 17. $8 - 4m = 20$ 18. $-7 + 5c = -32$

You should include material that appears on a notebook like this in your own notes.

Know How to Take Notes

Preview the Chapter Skim the content of the chapter you are about to study. If you already know something about the topic, outline what you know in your notes.

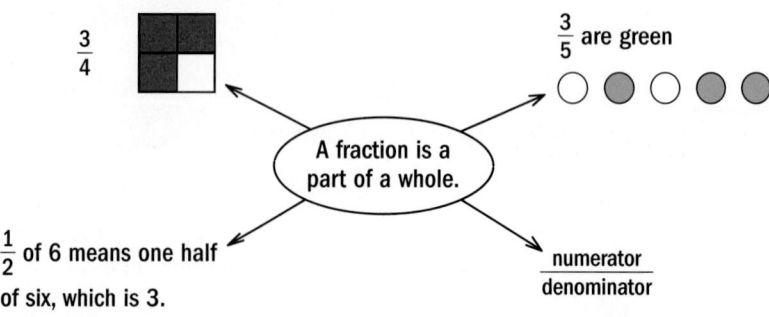

$\frac{3}{4}$

$\frac{3}{5}$ are green

A fraction is a part of a whole.

$\frac{1}{2}$ of 6 means one half of six, which is 3.

$\dfrac{numerator}{denominator}$

In Chapter 4, you will learn more things about fractions that you can add to your outline.

GOAL
Introduce prime and composite numbers.

MATERIALS
- paper
- colored pencils

FLORIDA: Standards and Assessment
Apply number theory to solve problems.
(MA.A.5.3.1)

Investigating Factors

A *prime* number is a whole number that has exactly two factors: 1 and itself. A *composite* number has more than two factors. In this activity, you will look at a number pattern attributed to Eratosthenes, a mathematician who lived in Alexandria, Egypt, around 230 B.C.

Explore   Create the Sieve of Eratosthenes with the integers 1 to 60.

1 Write the whole numbers 1 to 60 in a rectangular array as shown at the right.

```
 1  2  3  4  5  6  7  8  9 10
11 12 13 14 15 16 17 18 19 20
21 22 23 24 25 26 27 28 29 30
31 32 33 34 35 36 37 38 39 40
41 42 43 44 45 46 47 48 49 50
51 52 53 54 55 56 57 58 59 60
```

2 Start with the number 2. Circle it and cross out every multiple of 2 after 2.

3 Move to the next number that is not crossed out, 3. Circle it and cross out every multiple of 3 after 3.

4 Move to the next number that is not crossed out. Circle it and cross out all other multiples of that number.

5 Repeat Step 4 until every number except 1 is either crossed out or circled.

Skip the numbers that have already been crossed out.

Your turn now

1. What type of numbers are circled in your array?

2. What type of numbers are crossed out in your array?

Stop and Think

3. **Writing** If you continued this process with the numbers 61 to 100, what type of numbers would you expect to be circled? Why?

Factors and Prime Factorization

BEFORE	Now	WHY?
You multiplied and divided numbers.	You'll write the prime factorization of numbers.	So you can design a quilt with square patches, as in Ex. 10.

In the Real World

Word Watch

prime number, p. 169
composite number, p. 169
prime factorization, p. 169
factor tree, p. 169
monomial, p. 170

FLORIDA
Standards and Assessment

• Apply number theory to solve problems. (MA.A.5.3.1)

Lettering Members of the art club are designing their own lettering style, as part of their school arts program. Their first project is to make posters to display their new lettering style. Each poster will display the alphabet and the digits 0 through 9.

They want each row on the poster to have the same number of letters or digits. How many ways can they arrange the rectangular display?

You can use factors to determine how many arrangements are possible.

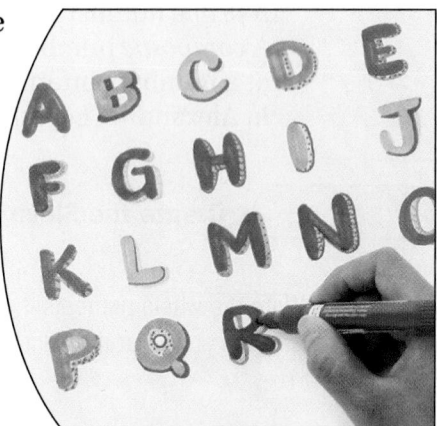

EXAMPLE 1 Writing Factors

Each arrangement will contain a total of 36 letters and digits (26 letters and the digits 0 through 9). To find the number of possible rectangular arrangements, first find the factors of 36.

① Write 36 as a product of two numbers in all possible ways.

1×36 $\qquad$ 2×18 $\qquad$ 3×12 $\qquad$ 4×9 $\qquad$ 6×6

The factors of 36 are 1, 2, 3, 4, 6, 9, 12, 18, and 36.

② Using these factors, find all the possible rectangular arrangements.

1×36 $\qquad$ 2×18 $\qquad$ 3×12 $\qquad$ 4×9 $\qquad$ 6×6

36×1 $\qquad$ 18×2 $\qquad$ 12×3 $\qquad$ 9×4

ANSWER There are nine possible rectangular arrangements.

Your turn now **Write all the factors of the number.**

1. 20 $\qquad$ **2.** 29 $\qquad$ **3.** 42 $\qquad$ **4.** 57

A **prime number** is a whole number greater than 1 whose only positive factors are 1 and itself. A **composite number** is a whole number greater than 1 that has positive factors other than 1 and itself.

HELP with **Review**

You can use divisibility tests to help find all the factors of a composite number. For help with divisibility tests, see p. 706.

EXAMPLE 2 **Identifying Prime and Composite Numbers**

Write all the factors of the number and tell whether it is *prime* or *composite*.

Number	Factors	Prime or Composite?
a. 32	1, 2, 4, 8, 16, 32	Composite
b. 39	1, 3, 13, 39	Composite
c. 43	1, 43	Prime
d. 76	1, 2, 4, 19, 38, 76	Composite
e. 149	1, 149	Prime
f. 189	1, 3, 7, 9, 21, 27, 63, 189	Composite

Prime Factorization When you write a number as the product of prime numbers, you are writing its **prime factorization**. One way to write the prime factorization of a number is to use a **factor tree**.

EXAMPLE 3 **Writing Prime Factorization**

Write the prime factorization of 450.

Three factor trees are shown. Notice that each factor tree produces the same prime factorization, differing only in the order of the factors.

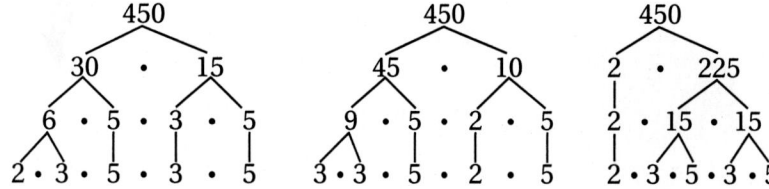

So, $450 = 2 \cdot 3 \cdot 3 \cdot 5 \cdot 5$.

ANSWER Using exponents, the prime factorization of 450 is $2 \cdot 3^2 \cdot 5^2$.

Your turn now Tell whether the number is *prime* or *composite*. If it is composite, write its prime factorization using exponents.

5. 24   **6.** 51   **7.** 73   **8.** 560

Factoring Monomials A **monomial** is a number, a variable, or a product of a number and one or more variables. To factor a monomial means to write the monomial as a product of its factors.

EXAMPLE 4 **Factoring a Monomial**

Factor the monomial $12x^2y$.

Solution

$$12x^2y = 2 \cdot 2 \cdot 3 \cdot x^2 \cdot y \qquad \text{Factor 12.}$$
$$= 2 \cdot 2 \cdot 3 \cdot x \cdot x \cdot y \qquad \text{Write } x^2 \text{ as } x \cdot x.$$

Your turn now Factor the monomial.

9. $3mn$ **10.** $18t^2$ **11.** $14x^2y^3$ **12.** $54w^3z^4$

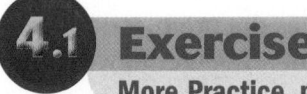 **4.1 Exercises**
More Practice, p. 730

Getting Ready to Practice

1. Vocabulary Copy and complete: The only positive factors of a <u>?</u> number are the number itself and one.

Write all the factors of the number.

2. 18   **3.** 27   **4.** 41   **5.** 66

Write the prime factorization of the number.

6. 28   **7.** 55   **8.** 82   **9.** 96

10. Guided Problem Solving You are making a quilt out of 120 square patches. What are the two most reasonable rectangular arrangements of the patches for the quilt?

   (1 List all of the factors of 120.

   (2 List all the pairs of factors from Step 1 that have a product of 120. These are the possible arrangements of the patches.

   (3 List the two most reasonable arrangements of the patches. Then explain why the other arrangements are not reasonable.

Practice and Problem Solving

with Homework

Example	Exercises
1	11–14, 31–38
2	15–18
3	19–25
4	27–30

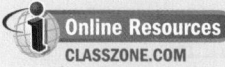
Online Resources
CLASSZONE.COM

· More Examples
· eTutorial Plus

Write all the factors of the number.

11. 34   **12.** 64   **13.** 108   **14.** 175

Tell whether the number is *prime* or *composite*.

15. 21   **16.** 45   **17.** 59   **18.** 91

Write the prime factorization of the number.

19. 56   **20.** 97   **21.** 102   **22.** 135

Copy and complete the factor tree. Then write the prime factorization of the number.

23.

24.

25.
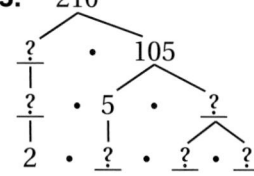

26. Writing Explain how you can create two different factor trees for 540. Do both factor trees result in the same prime factorization?

Algebra Factor the monomial.

27. $15cd$ **28.** $40pq$ **29.** $9a^2b^4$ **30.** $48n^3m^3$

Flags of the United States Each star on the U.S. flag represents a state. Some U.S. flags had a number of stars that could have been arranged in rows and columns evenly. Describe how to do this for the number of stars indicated.

31. 15   **32.** 28   **33.** 30   **34.** 49

Write all the factors of the number.

35. 299   **36.** 336   **37.** 400   **38.** 512

Write the prime factorization of the number using exponents.

39. 280   **40.** 396   **41.** 1125   **42.** 2000

Critical Thinking Many even numbers can be expressed as the sum of two primes. For example, 8 can be expressed as 3 + 5. Write the number as the sum of two primes.

43. 10   **44.** 16   **45.** 28   **46.** 30

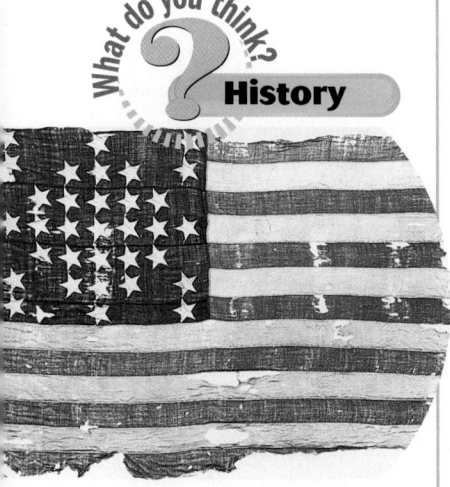

History

■ Flags of the United States

The flag shown above was displayed over Fort Sumter in 1861. The flag has 33 stars. What rectangular arrangement could have been used to display the stars?

47. Ring Toss Game You are in charge of a ring toss game at a school fair. In this game, players try to throw a small ring over a bottle that is in a rectangular display. You have 140 bottles, and you want to arrange them in equal rows. Can you have 40 equal rows? Explain.

48. Field Day There are 180 students participating in field day activities. The students must be divided into teams of equal size. How many students will be on each team? List all the possibilities.

49. Critical Thinking Name two prime numbers that have a difference of 1.

50. Challenge Twin primes are prime numbers that have a difference of 2. For example, 5 and 7 are twin primes. List five pairs of twin primes other than 5 and 7.

51. Volume The volume of a box can be found by using the formula *Volume = length × width × height.* A box has a volume of 200 cubic inches. Find all possible whole number dimensions of the box.

Mixed Review

Simplify the expression by combining like terms. *(Lesson 2.7)*

52. $4x - 5y + 3x - 4 + y$

53. $a - 2b - 5a + 2 + 6b$

Solve the inequality. *(Lesson 3.7)*

54. $5x \le -20$

55. $\frac{1}{8}y \ge 5$

56. $-9z > 108$

Choose a Strategy Use a strategy from the list to solve the following problem. Explain your choice of strategy.

Problem Solving Strategies
▪ Guess, Check, and Revise
▪ Look for a Pattern
▪ Draw a Diagram

57. The bookstore at your favorite mall is expanding to include the space adjacent to it. The original store was 20 feet by 25 feet. The space adjacent to it is 14 feet by 25 feet. What is the total area of the store with the additional space?

Basic Skills **Find low and high estimates for the product or quotient.**

58. 37×21

59. 143×58

60. $700 \div 14$

61. $1330 \div 87$

FCAT Practice

62. Extended Response The area of a rectangular picture is 48 square inches. Its length and width are measured only in whole inches. Find all possible dimensions of the picture. Show your work and explain how you found all of the possibilities.

Greatest Common Factor

BEFORE	▶ Now	WHY?
You found the factors of a number.	You'll find the greatest common factor of two or more numbers.	So you can decide how many food baskets you can make, as in Ex. 21.

Word Watch

common factor, p. 173
greatest common factor (GCF), p. 173
relatively prime, p. 174

FLORIDA
Standards and Assessment

• Know if numbers are relatively prime. (MA.A.5.3.1)
• Apply number theory to solve problems. (MA.A.5.3.1)

Activity The lists below show the factors of the given numbers.

Number	Factors
36	1, 2, 3, 4, 6, 9, 12, 18, 36
24	1, 2, 3, 4, 6, 8, 12, 24
20	1, 2, 4, 5, 10, 20

1. Which number(s) are factors of 20 and 36?

2. Which number(s) are factors of 24 and 36?

3. Which number(s) are factors of 20, 24, and 36?

4. What is the greatest factor that is in all three lists?

with Vocabulary

The GCF is sometimes called the greatest common divisor (GCD) because it is the largest common factor that can be divided evenly into the given numbers.

A **common factor** is a whole number that is a factor of two or more nonzero whole numbers. The greatest of the common factors is the **greatest common factor (GCF)**.

One method for finding the GCF of two or more numbers is to use the prime factorization of each number. The GCF is the product of all the factors that the numbers have in common.

EXAMPLE 1 Finding the Greatest Common Factor

Find the greatest common factor of 42 and 70.

Begin by writing the prime factorization of each number. Find the product of the common prime factors.

$42 = 2 \times 3 \times 7$ $70 = 2 \times 5 \times 7$

The common prime factors are 2 and 7. The GCF of 42 and 70 is the product of these factors.

ANSWER The GCF of 42 and 70 is 2 • 7, or 14.

Two numbers are **relatively prime** if their greatest common factor is 1. For example, 8 and 15 are relatively prime.

EXAMPLE 2 **Identifying Relatively Prime Numbers**

Decide whether the numbers 112 and 45 are relatively prime. If they are not relatively prime, find the greatest common factor.

Begin by writing the prime factorization of each number. Then find the product of the common prime factors.

$$112 = 2^4 \cdot 7 \qquad 45 = 3^2 \cdot 5$$

There are no common prime factors. However, two numbers always have 1 as a common factor. So, the GCF is 1.

ANSWER The numbers 112 and 45 are relatively prime.

Your turn now **Find the greatest common factor of the numbers.**

1. 12, 18   **2.** 24, 60   **3.** 36, 90   **4.** 96, 120

Decide whether the numbers are relatively prime. If they are not relatively prime, find the GCF.

5. 48, 72   **6.** 124, 128   **7.** 39, 44   **8.** 200, 63

You can find the greatest common factor of two monomials by factoring the monomials.

EXAMPLE 3 **Finding the GCF of Monomials**

Find the greatest common factor of $12a^3$ and $9a^2$.

First factor each expression.

$$12a^3 = 2 \cdot 2 \cdot 3 \cdot a \cdot a \cdot a \qquad 9a^2 = 3 \cdot 3 \cdot a \cdot a$$

The common factors are 3 and a^2. The GCF is the product of the common factors.

ANSWER The GCF is $3a^2$.

Your turn now **Find the greatest common factor of the monomials.**

9. $6x, 18x$ **10.** $6xy, 4xy^2$ **11.** $15y, 9x^2y^2$ **12.** $5xy^3, 10x^2y^2$

EXAMPLE **4** **Using the Greatest Common Factor**

Pep Rally Packs Students at your school are planning to hand out pep rally packs to support your school's athletic program. The students have 240 bumper stickers, 360 pennants, and 720 pencils. Every pack must have the same contents, and there should be no leftover items. What is the greatest number of pep rally packs that can be made?

Solution

You can find the greatest number of pep rally packs by finding the GCF.

$$240 = 2^4 \cdot 3 \cdot 5 \qquad 360 = 2^3 \cdot 3^2 \cdot 5 \qquad 720 = 2^4 \cdot 3^2 \cdot 5$$

The common prime factors are 2^3, 3, and 5. The GCF is $2^3 \cdot 3 \cdot 5$, or 120.

ANSWER The greatest number of pep rally packs is 120. Each pack will contain 2 bumper stickers, 3 pennants, and 6 pencils.

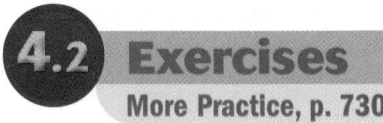

4.2 **Exercises**
More Practice, p. 730

INTERNET
eWorkbook Plus
CLASSZONE.COM

Getting Ready to Practice

1. Vocabulary Copy and complete: Six is the ? of 12 and 18.

Matching **Match the pair of numbers with its GCF.**

2. 6, 9   **3.** 4, 10   **4.** 5, 15   **5.** 14, 21

A. 5   **B.** 3   **C.** 7   **D.** 2

6. Find the Error Describe and correct the error in the solution.

$$210 = 2 \cdot 3 \cdot 5 \cdot 7$$
$$495 = 3 \cdot 3 \cdot 5 \cdot 11$$
The GCF is 5.

7. Guided Problem Solving There are 56 girls and 68 boys in a youth sports league. Each student will be placed on a team. Each team will have an equal number of players and will have the same number of girls. What is the greatest number of teams that can be formed?

    1 Write the prime factorizations of the numbers 56 and 68.

    2 What are the common prime factors of the two numbers?

    3 Multiply the common prime factors to get the GCF. What meaning does the GCF have in the situation?

Practice and Problem Solving

HELP with **Homework**

Example	Exercises
1	8–11
2	12–20
3	22–27
4	21, 33

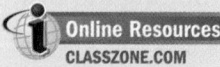

Online Resources
CLASSZONE.COM

· More Examples
· eTutorial Plus

Find the greatest common factor of the numbers.

8. 3, 9, 27 **9.** 21, 28, 56 **10.** 17, 18, 20 **11.** 24, 36, 180

Decide whether the numbers are relatively prime. If not, find the greatest common factor.

12. 5, 18 **13.** 10, 25 **14.** 28, 42 **15.** 55, 72

16. 21, 66 **17.** 18, 216 **18.** 212, 312 **19.** 268, 515

20. Writing Can two even numbers be relatively prime? Explain why or why not.

21. Food Baskets Your class is making Thanksgiving baskets to be distributed by a food bank. You have collected 60 cans of cranberry sauce, 120 cans of canned fruit, 90 cans of corn, and 60 boxes of muffin mixes. You want every basket to be the same with no leftover items. What is the greatest number of baskets you can assemble? What will each basket contain?

Algebra Find the GCF of the monomials.

22. $3x^2, 9x$ **23.** $4z^3, 2z^2$ **24.** $5t^4, 15t^5$

25. $12x^2y^2, 16xy^3$ **26.** $18rs^2, 30st^2$ **27.** $15bc^3, 75b^3c$

Critical Thinking Copy and complete the statement using *always*, *sometimes*, or *never*.

28. The greatest common factor of two numbers is ? equal to one of the two numbers.

29. The number 1 is ? the greatest common factor of relatively prime numbers.

30. The greatest common factor of two numbers is ? greater than both of the numbers.

31. Critical Thinking Name two composite numbers that are relatively prime.

32. Carpentry You must cut four pieces of wood that measure 36 inches, 45 inches, 108 inches, and 81 inches, into smaller, equally sized pieces. What is the longest each piece can be so that each piece is the same length?

33. Bouquets A florist must make a batch of identical bouquets. The florist has 360 tulips, 270 roses, and 180 lilies. There cannot be any flowers left over. What is the greatest number of bouquets that the florist can make?

Jacob sheep can have two, four, and occasionally six horns.

34. Challenge Explain why any two prime numbers are always relatively prime. Give examples to justify your reasoning.

35. Sheep A farmer needs to build two adjacent rectangular pens for his sheep. He wants one pen to have an area of 204 square feet, and the other to have an area of 144 square feet. Fence lengths are available in one-foot increments. What is the greatest length the farmer can make the fence that is shared by the two pens?

A = 144 ft²

x

A = 204 ft²

Mixed Review

In Exercises 36–38, solve the equation. *(Lesson 3.1)*

36. $-6 + n = 4$ 　　　　**37.** $n + 13 = 5$ 　　　　**38.** $n + 2.7 = 5.7$

39. Write the prime factorization of 84. *(Lesson 4.1)*

Basic Skills **Use a metric ruler to draw a segment with the given length.**

40. 7 cm 　　　　**41.** 15 cm 　　　　**42.** 145 mm 　　　　**43.** 84 mm

FCAT Practice

 FCAT

44. Multiple Choice What is the greatest common factor of $6a^3$ and $12a^2$?

　A. $2a$ 　　　　**B.** $3a$ 　　　　**C.** $2a^2$ 　　　　**D.** $6a^2$

45. Multiple Choice What is the greatest common factor of 160, 208, and 240?

　F. 4 　　　　**G.** 8 　　　　**H.** 16 　　　　**I.** 24

Marble Mystery

You have a bucket full of marbles. If the marbles in the bucket are counted by twos, threes, fives, and sevens, there is exactly one left over each time. What is the fewest number of marbles that could be in the bucket?

FLORIDA: Standards and Assessment
Construct models to represent rational
numbers. (MA.A.1.3.3)

GOAL
Use area models
to find equivalent
fractions.

MATERIALS
· graph paper
· colored pencils

Equivalent Fractions

You can use area models to find equivalent fractions.

Explore Find two fractions equivalent to $\frac{6}{8}$.

1 Draw a rectangle on a piece of graph paper. Divide the rectangle into 8 equal parts and shade 6 of the parts.

2 Look for other ways of dividing the rectangle into equal parts.

There are 4 parts
and 3 are shaded.

There are 16 parts
and 12 are shaded.

3 Write the equivalent fractions.

The fractions $\frac{3}{4}$ and $\frac{12}{16}$ are equivalent to $\frac{6}{8}$.

Your turn now Draw a model of the given fraction. Then find two equivalent fractions.

1. $\frac{4}{6}$　　2. $\frac{10}{12}$　　3. $\frac{4}{16}$　　4. $\frac{10}{16}$

Stop *and* **Think**

5. **Writing** How can factoring both the numerator and denominator of a fraction help to write an equivalent fraction?

LESSON

4.3

Simplifying Fractions

BEFORE	▶ Now	WHY?
You evaluated numerical expressions.	You'll simplify fractions.	So you can find the fractions of threatened species, as in Ex. 39.

 Word Watch

simplest form, p. 179
equivalent fractions, p. 179

FLORIDA
Standards and Assessment

• Evaluate expressions with exponents. (MA.A.2.3.1)

• Know examples of rational numbers in real-world situations. (MA.A.1.3.3)

In the Real World

History One of the Czech Republic's royal coronation jewels is the St. Wenceslas crown. It was made around 1345 and is decorated with 44 spinels, 30 emeralds, 22 pearls, 19 sapphires, and 1 ruby. What fraction of jewels in the crown are emeralds? You will see how to solve this problem in Example 1.

Fractions A *fraction* is a number of the form $\frac{a}{b}$ $(b \neq 0)$ where a is called the numerator and b is called the denominator. A fraction is in **simplest form** if its numerator and denominator have 1 as their GCF. **Equivalent fractions** represent the same number. They have the same simplest form.

EXAMPLE 1 **Writing a Fraction in Simplest Form**

Write the fraction of jewels in the crown that are emeralds. Then simplify.

$$\frac{\text{Number of emeralds}}{\text{Total number of jewels in the crown}} = \frac{30}{116}$$

Method 1: Write the prime factorization of each number.

$$30 = 2 \cdot 3 \cdot 5 \qquad 116 = 2^2 \cdot 29$$

The GCF of 30 and 116 is 2.

$$\frac{30}{116} = \frac{30 \div 2}{116 \div 2} \qquad \text{Divide numerator and denominator by GCF.}$$

$$= \frac{15}{58} \qquad \text{Simplify.}$$

Method 2:

$$\frac{30}{116} = \frac{2 \cdot 3 \cdot 5}{2 \cdot 2 \cdot 29} \qquad \text{Write prime factorizations.}$$

$$= \frac{\cancel{2}^1 \cdot 3 \cdot 5}{\cancel{2}_1 \cdot 2 \cdot 29} \qquad \text{Divide out common factor.}$$

$$= \frac{15}{58} \qquad \text{Simplify.}$$

ANSWER The fraction of jewels that are emeralds is $\frac{15}{58}$.

Emerald

Ruby

Sapphire

Pearl

EXAMPLE 2 Identifying Equivalent Fractions

Tell whether the fractions $\frac{3}{8}$ and $\frac{18}{48}$ are equivalent.

Write each fraction in simplest form.

$\frac{3}{8}$ is in simplest form. $\frac{18}{48} = \frac{18 \div 6}{48 \div 6} = \frac{3}{8}$

ANSWER The fractions are equivalent.

EXAMPLE 3 Writing Equivalent Fractions

HELP with Solving

A fraction has many equivalent fractions. There are other correct answers to Example 3.

Write two fractions that are equivalent to $\frac{4}{10}$.

Multiply or divide the numerator and denominator by the same nonzero number.

$\frac{4}{10} = \frac{4 \times 3}{10 \times 3} = \frac{12}{30}$ Multiply numerator and denominator by 3.

$\frac{4}{10} = \frac{4 \div 2}{10 \div 2} = \frac{2}{5}$ Divide numerator and denominator by 2, a common factor of 4 and 10.

ANSWER The fractions $\frac{12}{30}$ and $\frac{2}{5}$ are equivalent to $\frac{4}{10}$.

Spinel

Sapphire

Your turn now   Use the information on page 179. Write the fraction of jewels in the crown that are the given jewel. Simplify if possible.

1. pearls   **2.** sapphires   **3.** spinels

Write two fractions that are equivalent to the given fraction.

4. $\frac{8}{16}$ **5.** $\frac{9}{15}$ **6.** $\frac{10}{12}$ **7.** $\frac{21}{24}$

You can use Method 2 of Example 1 to simplify fractions that contain variable expressions.

EXAMPLE 4 Simplifying a Variable Expression

$\frac{14x}{7xy} = \frac{2 \cdot 7 \cdot x}{7 \cdot x \cdot y}$ Factor numerator and denominator.

$= \frac{2 \cdot \overset{1}{\cancel{7}} \cdot \overset{1}{\cancel{x}}}{\underset{1}{\cancel{7}} \cdot \underset{1}{\cancel{x}} \cdot y}$ Divide out common factors.

$= \frac{2}{y}$ Simplify.

HELP with Notetaking

You may want to add information on simplifying fractions with variable expressions to the outline that you started on p. 166.

EXAMPLE 5 Evaluating a Variable Expression

Evaluate the expression $\dfrac{-4x^3}{2x}$ when $x = 5$.

$$\dfrac{-4x^3}{2x} = \dfrac{-1 \cdot 2 \cdot 2 \cdot x \cdot x \cdot x}{2 \cdot x}$$ Factor numerator and denominator.

$$= \dfrac{-1 \cdot 2 \cdot \overset{1}{2} \cdot \overset{1}{x} \cdot x \cdot x}{\underset{1}{2} \cdot \underset{1}{x}}$$ Divide out common factors.

$$= -2x^2$$ Simplify.

$$= -2(5)^2$$ Substitute 5 for x.

$$= -50$$ Evaluate powers and simplify.

Your turn now Simplify the variable expression.

8. $\dfrac{4xy}{6x}$ **9.** $\dfrac{32a}{8ab}$ **10.** $\dfrac{2m^3}{6m}$ **11.** $\dfrac{5r^2s}{10rs}$

12. Evaluate the expression $\dfrac{35a^4}{-5a^2}$ when $a = 3$.

4.3 Exercises

More Practice, p. 730

 INTERNET
eWorkbook Plus
CLASSZONE.COM

Getting Ready to Practice

Vocabulary **Tell whether the fractions are equivalent.**

1. $\dfrac{2}{3}, \dfrac{4}{6}$ **2.** $\dfrac{15}{25}, \dfrac{3}{4}$ **3.** $\dfrac{15}{18}, \dfrac{5}{6}$ **4.** $\dfrac{21}{49}, \dfrac{3}{7}$

Write the fraction in simplest form.

5. $\dfrac{10}{15}$ **6.** $\dfrac{16}{20}$ **7.** $\dfrac{25}{40}$ **8.** $\dfrac{36}{72}$

9. Write two fractions that are equivalent to $\dfrac{1}{5}$.

10. Write two fractions that are equivalent to $\dfrac{12}{15}$.

11. Evaluate the expression $\dfrac{8x^3}{2x}$ when $x = 4$.

12. Eggs In a carton of one dozen eggs, 2 eggs are broken. What fraction of the eggs are broken? What fraction of the eggs are unbroken? Write your answers in simplest form.

Practice and Problem Solving

with Homework

Example	Exercises
1	13–16, 33–39
2	21–24
3	25–28
4	17–20
5	29–32

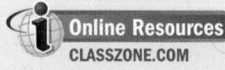
Online Resources
CLASSZONE.COM

· More Examples
· eTutorial Plus

Write the fraction in simplest form.

13. $\dfrac{39}{52}$

14. $\dfrac{18}{27}$

15. $\dfrac{-9}{72}$

16. $\dfrac{-49}{56}$

17. $\dfrac{4ab}{8a}$

18. $\dfrac{6c}{18cd}$

19. $\dfrac{-9rst}{30rs}$

20. $\dfrac{25xy}{35xyz}$

Tell whether the fractions are equivalent.

21. $\dfrac{4}{5}, \dfrac{20}{25}$

22. $\dfrac{21}{28}, \dfrac{1}{3}$

23. $\dfrac{7}{35}, \dfrac{2}{10}$

24. $\dfrac{32}{72}, \dfrac{4}{9}$

Write two fractions that are equivalent to the given fraction.

25. $\dfrac{45}{90}$

26. $\dfrac{36}{81}$

27. $\dfrac{24}{60}$

28. $\dfrac{48}{140}$

Evaluate the expression when $x = 3$ and $y = 5$.

29. $\dfrac{3x}{x^3}$

30. $\dfrac{2y^2}{-5y}$

31. $\dfrac{5y}{y^2}$

32. $\dfrac{4x^4}{24x^3}$

Geography Write the number of states in the region as a fraction of all of the states. Write your answer in simplest form.

33. Northeast: 9

34. Midwest: 12

35. South: 16

36. West: 13

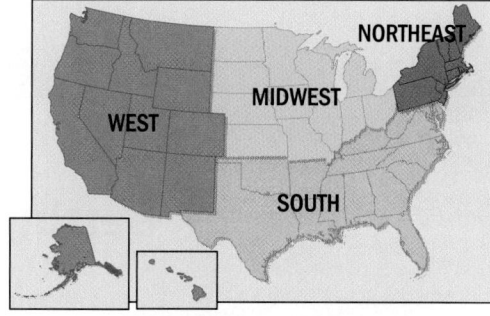

The U.S. Census Bureau divides the 50 states into 4 regions.

Extended Problem Solving In Exercises 37–39, use the table. It gives information about animals in Peru. Write your answer in simplest form.

37. What fraction of mammal species are threatened?

38. What fraction of reptile species are threatened?

39. **Number Sense** Use rounding to compare the fractions of threatened mammal and bird species. Then write the fractions of threatened species in each group (mammals, birds, and reptiles) in order from least to greatest.

Peruvian Animal Species		
	Known	**Threatened**
Mammals	460	46
Birds	1541	64
Reptiles	360	9

Yellow-faced Parrot

Write the fractions in simplest form. Tell whether they are equivalent.

40. $\dfrac{30}{60}, \dfrac{27}{54}$

41. $\dfrac{24}{40}, \dfrac{30}{50}$

42. $\dfrac{15}{18}, \dfrac{36}{48}$

43. $\dfrac{24}{32}, \dfrac{15}{24}$

44. $\dfrac{30}{75}, \dfrac{75}{105}$

45. $\dfrac{45}{54}, \dfrac{90}{108}$

46. $\dfrac{54}{96}, \dfrac{144}{256}$

47. $\dfrac{84}{112}, \dfrac{168}{192}$

Write the fraction in simplest form.

48. $\dfrac{-2x^3y}{xy}$

49. $\dfrac{5xy^2z}{5xz}$

50. $\dfrac{2x^3y}{-3xyz}$

51. $\dfrac{-8^2z^2}{16x^2yz}$

52. Critical Thinking If you divide the numerator and denominator of a fraction by a common factor, will the resulting fraction always be in simplest form? Give an example to justify your answer.

Tell whether the fractions are equivalent.

53. $\dfrac{4abc}{5ab}, \dfrac{4c}{5a}$

54. $\dfrac{3a}{5}, \dfrac{6a^2}{10a}$

55. $\dfrac{2a}{3b}, \dfrac{10a^2b}{15ab^2}$

56. Challenge Jason believes that if the numerator or the denominator of a fraction is prime, then the fraction is in simplest form. Explain why this is not always true.

Mixed Review

In Exercises 57–59, evaluate the expression. Justify each step. *(Lesson 2.6)*

57. $-12 + 46 - 18$

58. $10 \cdot (-25) \cdot 0$

59. $\dfrac{1}{3} \cdot (20 \cdot 15)$

60. Find the greatest common factor of $3x^3y$ and $6x^2y^2$. *(Lesson 4.2)*

Basic Skills Use a protractor to draw an angle with the given measure.

61. $53°$

62. $97°$

63. $145°$

FCAT Practice

64. Multiple Choice Ken has attended 6 of the Miami Dolphins 8 regular season home games. What fraction of the games has he attended?

A. $\dfrac{3}{8}$

B. $\dfrac{2}{3}$

C. $\dfrac{3}{4}$

D. $\dfrac{4}{3}$

65. Multiple Choice Which pair of fractions are equivalent?

F. $\dfrac{5}{7}, \dfrac{15}{49}$

G. $\dfrac{8}{10}, \dfrac{25}{50}$

H. $\dfrac{9}{15}, \dfrac{63}{105}$

I. $\dfrac{1}{4}, \dfrac{12}{16}$

FLORIDA: Standards and Assessment
Solve real-world problems. (MA.A.3.3.2)

Make a List

Guess, Check, and Revise

Look for a Pattern

Draw a Diagram

Act It Out

Make a List

Work Backward

Solve a Simpler Problem

Problem Mia is trying to remember Jasmine's phone number. She knows the first three digits are 889, but she is confused about the last four numbers. Mia knows the last four digits are a 3, 4, 5, and 6, but she cannot recall their correct order. How many possibilities are there for Jasmine's phone number?

❶ Read and Understand

Read the problem carefully.

You know the last four digits of a phone number, but not their order. You need to find how many ways these numbers can be arranged.

❷ Make a Plan

Decide on a strategy to use.

One way to solve the problem is to make a list of all the possible four-digit numbers. Then you can use the list to count the number of possibilities for a phone number.

❸ Solve the Problem

Reread the problem and make a list.

First, list all of the four-digit numbers that begin with the number **3**.

3456   **3**465   **3**546   **3**564   **3**645   **3**654

Similarly, list all of the four-digit numbers that begin with the numbers **4, 5,** and **6**.

4356   **4**365   **4**536   **4**563   **4**635   **4**653

5346   **5**364   **5**436   **5**463   **5**634   **5**643

6345   **6**354   **6**435   **6**453   **6**534   **6**543

Now count all of the four-digit numbers in the list.

ANSWER There are 24 possibilities for Jasmine's phone number.

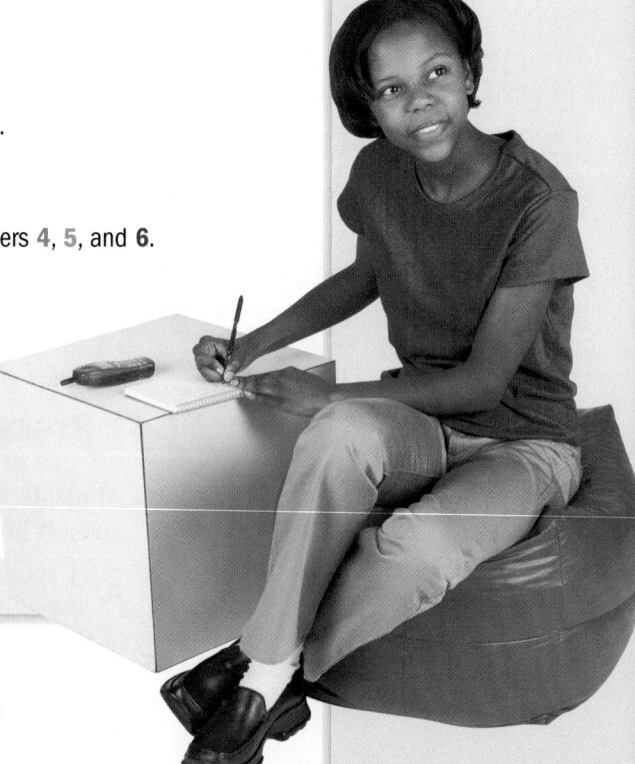

❹ Look Back

Double-check your list to make sure you didn't repeat any numbers or forget a number.

Practice the Strategy

Use the strategy *make a list*.

1. **Baseball** The first team to win 3 out of 5 possible games will be the winner of a baseball tournament. In how many ways can a team win 3 out of 5 games?

2. **Telephone Prefixes** A certain town can use the digits 0, 1, 2, 6, 7, and 8 for its telephone prefixes. How many three-digit telephone prefixes are possible for this town if each digit can be used only once in a prefix and the first digit cannot be a 1 or a 0?

3. **Number Cube** Derek rolled 2 number cubes and added the two numbers on the top of each cube. List all the possible sums. In how many different ways can he roll a sum of 7?

4. **Tennis** Three boys and three girls sign up for a mixed doubles tennis tournament. In mixed doubles a team consists of one boy and one girl. How many mixed doubles teams can be made?

5. **Checkbook Covers** A bank has checkbook covers that are either pocket or desk size. The covers can be white, black, red, or tan. The customer's name will be stamped on the cover in gold or silver. How many different choices are available for checkbook covers?

6. **Summer Job** A student was hired by a city's maintenance department to paint parking space numbers in a city parking lot. Each digit had to be painted separately, and the student earned 20 cents per digit. The student painted parking space numbers from 1 to 225. How much did the student earn?

Mixed Problem Solving

Use any strategy to solve the problem.

7. **Car Show** The manager of a mall is asked to rope off a rectangular section of the parking lot for a car show. The area roped off is 250 feet by 300 feet. Posts are to be placed every 25 feet around the lot. How many posts are needed?

8. **Consultant Fees** Two consultants were hired by a company. The total consultant fees were $12,500. If one consultant had earned $500 less, each consultant would have been paid the same. How much did each consultant earn?

9. **Gardening** Joyce has planted a kudzu vine in her yard. The kudzu vine is a fast growing Japanese plant that was brought to the United States in 1876. Use the information in the table below to predict how long Joyce's vine will be after 2 weeks.

Days	1	2	3	4
Length of kudzu vine (inches)	12	24	36	48

10. **Video Games** Chris buys a video game and two T-shirts for $44 at the mall. One week later he buys two more video games and a T-shirt for $52. Each video game has the same price, and each T-shirt has the same price. How much does one video game cost?

Least Common Multiple

BEFORE	▶ Now	WHY?
You found the greatest common factor of two numbers.	You'll find the least common multiple of two numbers.	So you can plan your weekly schedule, as in Ex. 26.

(In the Real World

Word Watch

multiple, p. 186
common multiple, p. 186
least common multiple
  (LCM), p. 186

FLORIDA
Standards and Assessment

• Apply number theory to solve
  problems. (MA.A.5.3.1)

Animal Clinic A veterinarian at an animal clinic is on call every four days. Today is Saturday, and the vet is on call. In how many more days will the vet be on call on a Saturday again? You will see how to solve this problem in Example 1.

A **multiple** of a number is the product of the number and any nonzero whole number. A multiple that is shared by two or more numbers is a **common multiple**. The least of the common multiples of two or more whole numbers is the **least common multiple (LCM)**.

JUNE

S	M	T	W	T	F	S
						①
2	3	4	⑤	6	7	8
⑨	10	11	12	⑬	14	15
16	⑰	18	19	20	㉑	22
23	24	㉕	26	27	28	㉙
30						

EXAMPLE 1 **Finding the Least Common Multiple**

The veterinarian described above is on call every 4 days. A Saturday occurs every 7 days. To determine the next Saturday the vet will be on call, find the least common multiple of 4 and 7.

Method 1: Make a list.

List the multiples of each number.

Multiples of 4: 4, 8, 12, 16, 20, 24, **28**, 32, 36, 40, 44, …

Multiples of 7: 7, 14, 21, **28**, 35, 42, 49, 56, …

The LCM of 4 and 7 is 28.

Method 2: Use prime factorization.

Write the prime factorization of each number.

$$4 = 2^2 \qquad 7 = 7$$

Write the product of the highest power of each prime number in the prime factorizations.

$$2^2 \cdot 7 = 28$$

The LCM of 4 and 7 is 28.

ANSWER In 28 days, the veterinarian will be on call on a Saturday.

EXAMPLE 2 **Finding the Least Common Multiple**

Find the LCM of 32, 96, and 120 using prime factorization.

Solution

Write the prime factorization of each number.

$$32 = 2^5 \qquad 96 = 2^5 \cdot 3 \qquad 120 = 2^3 \cdot 3 \cdot 5$$

Write the product of the highest power of each prime number in the prime factorizations.

$$2^5 \cdot 3 \cdot 5 = 480$$

ANSWER The LCM of 32, 96, and 120 is 480.

Your turn now **Find the least common multiple of the numbers.**

1. 6, 15   **2.** 4, 20   **3.** 12, 28   **4.** 24, 36, and 72

Method 2 of Example 1 is also useful for finding the least common multiples of monomials.

EXAMPLE 3 **Finding the LCM of Monomials**

Find the LCM of $6x^2y$ and $9x^4z$.

Solution

Factor each expression using exponents.

$$6x^2y = 2 \cdot 3 \cdot x^2 \cdot y$$
$$9x^4z = 3^2 \cdot x^4 \cdot z$$

Find the product of the highest power of each factor, including the variables.

$$2 \cdot 3^2 \cdot x^4 \cdot y \cdot z = 18x^4yz$$

ANSWER The LCM of $6x^2y$ and $9x^4z$ is $18x^4yz$.

Your turn now **Find the least common multiple of the monomials.**

5. $8x^3, 20x^7$ **6.** $12y^4, 36y^8$

7. $4ab^2, 10a^2b$ **8.** $6m^3np^2, 8mp^3$

Getting Ready to Practice

Vocabulary **Copy and complete the statement.**

1. A(n) ? of 6 and 9 is 54.

2. The ? of 6 and 9 is 18.

Matching **Match the pair of numbers with its LCM.**

3. 36, 18

4. 45, 75

5. 6, 18

6. 42, 105

A. 18

B. 36

C. 210

D. 225

7. Find the Error Describe and correct the error in the solution.

> Find the LCM of 12 and 24.
>
> $12 = 2 \cdot 2 \cdot 3$ $24 = 2 \cdot 2 \cdot 2 \cdot 3$
>
> The LCM is $2 \cdot 2$, or 4.

Practice and Problem Solving

with Homework

Example	Exercises
1	8–11, 25, 26
2	12–19
3	20–23

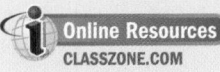
Online Resources
CLASSZONE.COM

· More Examples
· eTutorial Plus

List the first few multiples of each number. Then use the lists to find the LCM of the numbers.

8. 4, 6

9. 6, 21

10. 8, 10

11. 10, 15

Write the prime factorization of the numbers. Then find their LCM.

12. 36, 90

13. 17, 57

14. 90, 108

15. 125, 500

16. 6, 8, 12

17. 8, 16, 32

18. 6, 15, 45

19. 20, 24, 60

Find the LCM of the monomials.

20. $5ab, 7ab^2$

21. $7s^3t, 49st^2$

22. $4x^3y^3, 18xy^5$

23. $24c^2d^3, 60c^2d^6$

24. Writing Could you find the *greatest* common multiple of two numbers? Explain your reasoning.

25. Traffic Lights One traffic light turns red every 45 seconds. Another traffic light turns red every 60 seconds. Both traffic lights just turned red. In how many seconds will they turn red at the same time again?

26. Schedule Your class schedule changes on a three-day rotation. Every three days you have math class during the last class period of the day. This week, you have math class the last period on Friday. In how many more school days will you have math class the last period on Friday?

Find the LCM of the numbers using prime factorization.

27. 160, 432
28. 144, 576
29. 21, 36, 57
30. 18, 54, 84

31. 30, 75, 100
32. 36, 54, 72
33. 10, 12, 30, 60
34. 21, 42, 63, 105

Find the LCM of the monomials.

35. $24x^4y, 30y^7$
36. $17m^3n^3, 9m^2n^6$
37. $45gh^5k^3, 33g^4hk^3$

38. **Lasagna** Zoe is making lasagna for a family reunion. Her recipe calls for twelve noodles for each batch of lasagna. One box of lasagna noodles contains 14 noodles. What is the least number of batches of lasagna that Zoe can make without having any noodles left over?

39. **Swimming** Will swims one lap in 160 seconds, while Martin swims one lap in 180 seconds. The boys start their laps at the same time from the same side of the pool and maintain their pace. When will they both be at their starting place at the same time again? Write your answer in minutes and seconds.

40. **Writing** You are asked to find the LCM of two numbers. One of the numbers is a factor of the other number. Is there a shortcut to finding their LCM? Explain.

41. **Challenge** Could the GCF of two different numbers also be the LCM of those numbers? Explain.

Mixed Review

42. Rebecca ran on her treadmill at 5.6 miles per hour for one half hour. How many miles did Rebecca run? *(Lesson 1.6)*

43. Simplify the expression $7x + 9 + 12x + 11 + 2y$ by combining like terms. *(Lesson 2.7)*

44. Find the greatest common factor of 121 and 187. *(Lesson 4.2)*

Basic Skills **Find the sum.**

45. 24.63 + 49.07
46. 14.125 + 16.8
47. 33.87 + 100.9

FCAT Practice

48. **Multiple Choice** What is the correct prime factorization of 120?

A. $2^2 \cdot 3 \cdot 5$
B. $2^3 \cdot 5 \cdot 6$
C. $2^2 \cdot 3^2 \cdot 10$
D. $2^3 \cdot 3 \cdot 5$

49. **Short Response** You want to buy some soup bowls and some dinner plates. The soup bowls come in boxes of eight, and the dinner plates come in boxes of six. What is the least number of soup bowls and dinner plates that you can buy to get an equal number of each?

Notebook Review

Review the vocabulary definitions in your notebook.

Copy the review examples in your notebook. Then complete the exercises.

Check Your Definitions

prime number, p. 169	monomial, p. 170	equivalent fractions, p. 179
composite number, p. 169	common factor, p. 173	multiple, p. 186
prime factorization, p. 169	greatest common factor (GCF), p. 173	common multiple, p. 186
factor tree, p. 169	relatively prime, p. 174	least common multiple (LCM), p. 186
	simplest form, p. 179	

Use Your Vocabulary

1. Copy and complete: A factor tree can be used to find the __?__ of a number.

4.1 Can you write a prime factorization?

 EXAMPLE Write the prime factorization of 504.

$$504 = 2 \cdot 2 \cdot 2 \cdot 3 \cdot 3 \cdot 7, \text{ or } 2^3 \cdot 3^2 \cdot 7$$

ANSWER The prime factorization of 504 is $2^3 \cdot 3^2 \cdot 7$.

 Write the prime factorization of the number.

2. 40   **3.** 7   **4.** 85   **5.** 120

4.2 Can you find the GCF of two numbers?

 EXAMPLE Find the GCF of 36 and 60.

$$36 = 2^2 \cdot 3^2 \qquad\qquad 60 = 2^2 \cdot 3 \cdot 5$$

The common factors are 2^2 and 3. So, the GCF is $2^2 \cdot 3$, or 12.

ANSWER The GCF of 36 and 60 is 12.

 Find the GCF of the numbers or monomials.

6. 48, 80   **7.** 60, 100   **8.** $14a^3, 21a$ **9.** $20y^4, 60y^5$

4.3 Can you write a fraction in simplest form?

 EXAMPLE Write $\frac{48}{72}$ in simplest form.

$$\frac{48}{72} = \frac{48 \div 24}{72 \div 24} = \frac{2}{3}$$

☑ **Write the fraction in simplest form.**

10. $\frac{15}{45}$ **11.** $\frac{12}{80}$ **12.** $\frac{9ab}{27a}$ **13.** $\frac{18n^3}{54n}$

4.4 Can you find the LCM of two numbers?

 EXAMPLE Find the LCM of 20 and 48.

$20 = 2^2 \cdot 5$ $\qquad\qquad$ $48 = 2^4 \cdot 3$

ANSWER The LCM of 20 and 48 is $2^4 \cdot 3 \cdot 5$, or 240.

☑ **Find the LCM of the numbers or monomials.**

14. 28, 42   **15.** 54, 90   **16.** $10cd, 25c^2$ **17.** $9n^3, 12n^2$

Stop *and* **Think** about Lessons 4.1–4.4

18. Writing Explain the difference between listing the factors of a number and finding the prime factorization of a number.

Review Quiz 1

Find the GCF of the numbers or monomials.

1. 24, 90   **2.** 36, 72, 108   **3.** $20c^3, 48c^2$ **4.** $64m^2, 80m^5$

Find the LCM of the numbers or monomials.

5. 88, 99   **6.** 36, 96   **7.** $7xy, 21y^3$ **8.** $6ab^2, 30ab$

Tell whether the fractions are equivalent.

9. $\frac{9}{27}, \frac{60}{180}$ **10.** $\frac{39}{91}, \frac{42}{56}$ **11.** $\frac{40}{48}, \frac{70}{84}$ **12.** $\frac{108}{120}, \frac{189}{210}$

13. Supermarket A supermarket gives every tenth customer a coupon and every twenty-fifth customer a gift. Which of the first 200 customers receive both a coupon and a gift?

Comparing Fractions and Mixed Numbers

BEFORE	▶ Now	WHY?
You compared and ordered integers.	You'll compare and order fractions and mixed numbers.	So you can determine the greater fraction of games won, as in Ex. 28.

Word Watch

least common denominator (LCD), p. 192

FLORIDA
Standards and Assessment
• Compare and order fractions. (MA.A.1.3.2)
• Compare and order fractions using graphic models. (MA.A.1.3.2)

You can use models to compare the fractions $\frac{2}{3}$ and $\frac{3}{4}$.

$$\frac{2}{3} = \frac{2 \cdot 4}{3 \cdot 4} = \frac{8}{12} \qquad\qquad \frac{3}{4} = \frac{3 \cdot 3}{4 \cdot 3} = \frac{9}{12}$$

In the diagram above, $\frac{8}{12} < \frac{9}{12}$, so $\frac{2}{3} < \frac{3}{4}$.

The **least common denominator (LCD)** of two or more fractions is the least common multiple of the denominators. You can compare fractions by using the least common denominator to write equivalent fractions.

EXAMPLE 1 **Comparing Fractions Using the LCD**

Compare $\frac{3}{8}$ and $\frac{5}{12}$.

1. Find the least common denominator of the fractions.
   The LCM of 8 and 12 is 24, so the least common denominator is 24.

2. Use the least common denominator to write equivalent fractions.

   $$\frac{3}{8} = \frac{3 \cdot 3}{8 \cdot 3} = \frac{9}{24} \qquad\qquad \frac{5}{12} = \frac{5 \cdot 2}{12 \cdot 2} = \frac{10}{24}$$

3. Compare the numerators: $9 < 10$, so $\frac{9}{24} < \frac{10}{24}$.

ANSWER Because $\frac{9}{24} < \frac{10}{24}$, you can write $\frac{3}{8} < \frac{5}{12}$.

HELP with Solving

You can write equivalent fractions by multiplying or dividing the numerator and denominator by the same nonzero number.

Your turn now **Copy and complete the statement with <, >, or =.**

1. $\frac{2}{3} \underline{\ ?\ } \frac{5}{8}$

2. $\frac{2}{4} \underline{\ ?\ } \frac{15}{20}$

3. $\frac{3}{10} \underline{\ ?\ } \frac{2}{4}$

4. $\frac{9}{16} \underline{\ ?\ } \frac{11}{18}$

To compare or order improper fractions and mixed numbers, first write any mixed numbers as improper fractions.

 with Review

For help with writing mixed numbers as improper fractions, see p.707.

EXAMPLE 2 **Ordering Fractions and Mixed Numbers**

Order the numbers $4\frac{7}{16}$, $\frac{19}{4}$, and $\frac{35}{8}$ from least to greatest.

(1 Find the least common denominator of the fractions.

The LCM of 16, 4, and 8 is 16, so the LCD is 16.

(2 Use the least common denominator to write equivalent fractions.

$$4\frac{7}{16} = \frac{4 \cdot 16 + 7}{16} = \frac{71}{16} \qquad \frac{19}{4} = \frac{19 \cdot 4}{4 \cdot 4} = \frac{76}{16} \qquad \frac{35}{8} = \frac{35 \cdot 2}{8 \cdot 2} = \frac{70}{16}$$

(3 Compare the numerators: $70 < 71$, and $71 < 76$, so $\frac{70}{16} < \frac{71}{16}$ and $\frac{71}{16} < \frac{76}{16}$.

ANSWER From least to greatest, the numbers are $\frac{35}{8}$, $4\frac{7}{16}$, and $\frac{19}{4}$.

EXAMPLE 3 **Comparing Mixed Numbers**

Orangutans A female orangutan is about $3\frac{1}{2}$ feet tall. A male orangutan is about $3\frac{2}{5}$ feet tall. Which of the two orangutans is taller?

Solution

The LCM of 2 and 5 is 10, so the least common denominator is 10.

Use the least common denominator to write equivalent fractions.

$$3\frac{1}{2} = \frac{3 \cdot 2 + 1}{2} = \frac{7}{2} \qquad\qquad 3\frac{2}{5} = \frac{3 \cdot 5 + 2}{5} = \frac{17}{5}$$

$$\frac{7}{2} = \frac{7 \cdot 5}{2 \cdot 5} = \frac{35}{10} \qquad\qquad \frac{17}{5} = \frac{17 \cdot 2}{5 \cdot 2} = \frac{34}{10}$$

Because $35 > 34$, you can write $\frac{35}{10} > \frac{34}{10}$.

ANSWER The female orangutan is taller.

What do you think?
Zoology

■ **Orangutans**

An orangutan's arms are about two thirds as long as its height. How long would the arms of a 3 foot orangutan be?

Your turn now Copy and complete the statement with $<$, $>$, or $=$.

5. $\frac{16}{5}$ _?_ $3\frac{1}{3}$ **6.** $1\frac{4}{5}$ _?_ $\frac{21}{12}$ **7.** $-2\frac{2}{3}$ _?_ $-4\frac{5}{6}$

8. Order the numbers $2\frac{7}{9}$, $2\frac{5}{12}$, and $\frac{11}{4}$ from least to greatest.

4.5 Exercises

More Practice, p. 730

Getting Ready to Practice

1. **Vocabulary** Copy and complete: The least common denominator of two fractions is the _?_ of their denominators.

Find the least common denominator of the fractions.

2. $\frac{1}{2}, \frac{2}{3}$ 3. $\frac{3}{4}, \frac{7}{20}$ 4. $\frac{11}{24}, \frac{5}{6}$ 5. $\frac{5}{12}, \frac{7}{18}$

Copy and complete the statement with <, >, or =.

6. $\frac{3}{5} \,?\, \frac{7}{10}$ 7. $\frac{7}{18} \,?\, \frac{5}{9}$ 8. $\frac{24}{32} \,?\, \frac{3}{4}$ 9. $\frac{5}{8} \,?\, \frac{7}{12}$

10. **Guided Problem Solving** Sarah walks two thirds of a mile to school every day. Amy walks five eighths of a mile to school. Whose walk to school is longer?

    (1 Find the least common denominator.

    (2 Rewrite both fractions using the LCD.

    (3 Use your answer to find whose walk is longer.

Practice and Problem Solving

Copy and complete the statement with <, >, or =.

11. $3\frac{1}{4} \,?\, \frac{13}{12}$ 12. $\frac{31}{6} \,?\, 5\frac{1}{6}$ 13. $\frac{5}{11} \,?\, \frac{42}{55}$

14. $2\frac{4}{5} \,?\, \frac{7}{3}$ 15. $\frac{165}{36} \,?\, 4\frac{5}{12}$ 16. $\frac{11}{18} \,?\, \frac{9}{14}$

Order the numbers from least to greatest.

17. $\frac{1}{2}, \frac{1}{8}, \frac{3}{4}, \frac{5}{16}$ 18. $1\frac{1}{2}, \frac{5}{4}, \frac{11}{6}$ 19. $\frac{5}{3}, \frac{35}{15}, 2\frac{2}{5}, \frac{15}{16}$

20. **Commercials** During a 30 minute TV show, there are 8 minutes of commercials. During a 2 hour movie, there are 31 minutes of commercials. Write each commercial time as a fraction of the total time. Which TV program has a greater fraction of commercial time?

21. **Writing** Explain how comparing fractions with like denominators differs from comparing fractions with unlike denominators.

HELP with Homework

Example	Exercises
1	11–16
2	17–19, 22, 23
3	11–16, 20

Online Resources
CLASSZONE.COM
· More Examples
· eTutorial Plus

A negative fraction can be written in various ways. For example,

$$-\frac{a}{b} = \frac{a}{-b} = \frac{-a}{b}.$$

Write the numbers in order from least to greatest.

22. $7\frac{1}{4}, \frac{31}{4}, \frac{63}{8}, \frac{47}{6}, 7\frac{19}{24}$

23. $\frac{-34}{3}, -11\frac{7}{12}, -11\frac{17}{48}, \frac{-23}{2}, \frac{-47}{4}$

Copy and complete the statement with <, >, or = by first comparing each fraction to $\frac{1}{2}$.

24. $\frac{25}{50} \underset{?}{\underline{\quad}} \frac{37}{74}$

25. $\frac{17}{30} \underset{?}{\underline{\quad}} \frac{10}{33}$

26. $\frac{23}{100} \underset{?}{\underline{\quad}} \frac{19}{36}$

27. **Critical Thinking** In Exercises 24–26, does it help to compare each number to $\frac{1}{2}$ first? Will this step always work? If not, could you use another fraction to help make comparisons?

28. **Little League** Teams from California have played in the Little League World Series 19 times and won the championship 5 times. Texas teams have appeared in 7 Little League World Series and won twice. Which state has won a greater fraction of their World Series games?

29. **Challenge** Consider the fractions $\frac{1}{2x}$ and $\frac{1}{x}$. What is their LCD? Write each fraction using the LCD.

Mixed Review

30. Find the area of the figure at the right. *(Lesson 3.5)*

8 ft

4 ft

8 ft

31. Write the prime factorization of 336. *(Lesson 4.1)*

32. **Basic Skills** Find the quotient of 1998 and 42. Round your answer to the nearest thousandth.

FCAT Practice

33. **Multiple Choice** Which list of fractions is written correctly in order from least to greatest?

A. $\frac{7}{10}, \frac{5}{6}, \frac{7}{15}$

B. $\frac{3}{18}, \frac{10}{12}, \frac{18}{21}$

C. $\frac{8}{15}, \frac{5}{12}, \frac{3}{10}$

D. $\frac{5}{8}, \frac{6}{7}, \frac{1}{2}$

34. **Multiple Choice** Leon played in 72 out of 162 baseball games, or $\frac{72}{162}$ of the games. What is another way to express this number?

F. $\frac{1}{2}$

G. $\frac{4}{9}$

H. $\frac{18}{54}$

I. $\frac{26}{81}$

Rules of Exponents

LESSON 4.6

BEFORE	▶ Now	WHY?
You multiplied and divided numerical expressions.	You'll multiply and divide expressions with exponents.	So you can compare the memory in two computers, as in Exs. 49–50.

Word Watch

Review Words

exponent, p. 20
power, p. 20

FLORIDA
Standards and Assessment

- Simplify expressions using exponents. (MA.A.1.3.4)
- Apply number properties. (MA.A.3.3.1)

Activity   **Using patterns to discover rules for multiplying powers.**

1   Copy and complete the table.

Expression	Expanded Expression	Number of Factors	Product as a Power
$2^2 \cdot 2^4$	$(2 \cdot 2) \cdot (2 \cdot 2 \cdot 2 \cdot 2)$	6	2^6
$3^3 \cdot 3^1$	$(3 \cdot 3 \cdot 3) \cdot 3$	?	$3^?$
$7^2 \cdot 7^3$	?	?	?

2   How are the exponents in the first and last columns related?

3   Write the product $6^5 \cdot 6^{11}$ as a single power.

As you saw in the activity, you can expand expressions to find their product. The following equation suggests a rule for multiplying powers with the same base when the exponents are integers.

$$a^4 \cdot a^2 = \overbrace{(a \cdot a \cdot a \cdot a)}^{\text{4 factors}} \cdot \overbrace{(a \cdot a)}^{\text{2 factors}} = a^{4+2} = a^6$$

$$\underbrace{}_{\text{6 factors}}$$

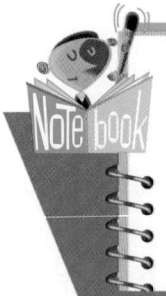

Product of Powers Property

Words   To multiply powers with the same base, add their exponents.

Algebra $a^m \cdot a^n = a^{m+n}$ **Numbers** $5^6 \cdot 5^3 = 5^{6+3} = 5^9$

EXAMPLE 1   **Using the Product of Powers Property**

$$x^4 \cdot x^7 = x^{4+7} \qquad \text{Product of powers property}$$
$$= x^{11} \qquad \text{Add exponents.}$$

Remember that numbers raised to the first power are usually written without an exponent. For example, $3 = 3^1$.

EXAMPLE 2 **Using the Product of Powers Property**

$$3^2 x^2 \cdot 3x^3 = (3^2 \cdot 3) \cdot (x^2 \cdot x^3) \qquad \text{Commutative property of multiplication}$$

$$= 3^{2+1} \cdot x^{2+3} \qquad \text{Product of powers property}$$

$$= 3^3 x^5 \qquad \text{Add exponents.}$$

$$= 27x^5 \qquad \text{Evaluate the power.}$$

The following equation suggests a rule for dividing powers with the same base when the exponents are integers.

$$\frac{a^5}{a^3} = \frac{\overbrace{a \cdot a \cdot a \cdot a \cdot a}^{5 \text{ factors}}}{\underbrace{a \cdot a \cdot a}_{3 \text{ factors}}} = \frac{a \cdot a \cdot \overset{1}{\cancel{a}} \cdot \overset{1}{\cancel{a}} \cdot \overset{1}{\cancel{a}}}{\underset{1}{\cancel{a}} \cdot \underset{1}{\cancel{a}} \cdot \underset{1}{\cancel{a}}} = \overbrace{a \cdot a}^{2 \text{ factors}} = a^{5-3} = a^2$$

Quotient of Powers Property

Words To divide two powers with the same nonzero base, subtract the exponent of the denominator from the exponent of the numerator.

Algebra $\dfrac{a^m}{a^n} = a^{m-n}$ **Numbers** $\dfrac{4^7}{4^4} = 4^{7-4} = 4^3$

EXAMPLE 3 **Using the Quotient of Powers Property**

Simplify the expression. Write your answer as a power.

a. $\dfrac{x^{12}}{x^7} = x^{12-7}$ Quotient of powers property

$\qquad = x^5$ Subtract exponents.

b. $\dfrac{9^7}{9^3} = 9^{7-3}$ Quotient of powers property

$\qquad = 9^4$ Subtract exponents.

Your turn now Simplify the expression. Write your answer as a power.

1. $a^6 \cdot a^4$ **2.** $2^3 \cdot 2^4$ **3.** $\dfrac{a^6}{a^4}$ **4.** $\dfrac{10^9}{10^6}$

The bases of the powers must be the same to use the product or quotient property. In part (b) of Example 4, you cannot simplify the numerator any further because the bases, x and y, are different.

EXAMPLE 4 **Simplifying Fractions with Powers**

a. $\dfrac{y^4 \cdot y}{y^3} = \dfrac{y^5}{y^3}$ Simplify numerator using product of powers property.

$= y^{5-3}$ Quotient of powers property

$= y^2$ Subtract exponents.

b. $\dfrac{xy^4}{y^3} = xy^{4-3}$ Quotient of powers property

$= xy$ Subtract exponents.

Your turn now Simplify the expression. Write your answer as a power.

5. $\dfrac{q^3 \cdot q^5}{q^4}$ 6. $\dfrac{4^3 \cdot 4^{12}}{4^5}$ 7. $\dfrac{a^2 b^8}{b^2}$ 8. $\dfrac{x^5 y^{11}}{y^5}$

4.6 Exercises

More Practice, p. 730

INTERNET
eWorkbook Plus
CLASSZONE.COM

Getting Ready to Practice

Vocabulary Copy and complete the statement.

1. Three is the ? of the expression 3^4.

2. Seven is the ? of the expression 4^7.

Tell whether the product of powers property can be used to simplify the expression.

3. $9^3 \cdot 9^4$ 4. $7^2 \cdot 2^7$ 5. $r^6 \cdot s^6$ 6. $n^5 \cdot n^8$

Simplify the expression. Write your answer as a power.

7. $4^2 \cdot 4^4$ 8. $8 \cdot 8^3$ 9. $a^5 \cdot a^7$ 10. $b^9 \cdot b^9$

11. $\dfrac{c^6}{c^5}$ 12. $\dfrac{5^8}{5^4}$ 13. $\dfrac{8^7}{8^2}$ 14. $\dfrac{d^8}{d}$

15. **Find the Error** Describe and correct the error in the solution.

$2^2 \cdot 2^4 = (2 \cdot 2)^{2+4}$
$= 4^6$

Practice and Problem Solving

Simplify the expression.

16. $u^7 \cdot u^8$ **17.** $v^2 \cdot v^{10}$ **18.** $b^9 \cdot b^6$ **19.** $m^{11} \cdot m^8$

20. $\dfrac{a^4}{a}$ **21.** $\dfrac{x^{10}}{x^6}$ **22.** $\dfrac{w^{15}}{w^9}$ **23.** $\dfrac{y^{20}}{y^{18}}$

Simplify the expression. Write your answer as a power.

24. $3^2 \cdot 3^4$ **25.** $(-4)^2 \cdot (-4)^3$ **26.** $5^4 \cdot 5$ **27.** $7^2 \cdot 7^2$

28. $\dfrac{(-7)^7}{(-7)^4}$ **29.** $\dfrac{2^{13}}{2^3}$ **30.** $\dfrac{6^{11}}{6^8}$ **31.** $\dfrac{9^8}{9^4}$

Determine the number that correctly completes the equation.

32. $2^3 \cdot 2^? = 2^{11}$ **33.** $5^4 \cdot ?^5 = 5^9$ **34.** $\dfrac{8^7}{8^?} = 8^3$ **35.** $\dfrac{12^?}{12^5} = 12^4$

Simplify the expression.

36. $3a^3 \cdot 3a^2$ **37.** $2y^3 \cdot 2y^2$ **38.** $3^2 x^5 \cdot 3^3 x^4$ **39.** $4a^3 b^4 \cdot 4^2 a^4 b^6$

40. $\dfrac{p^5 q^9}{p q^5}$ **41.** $\dfrac{z^6 \cdot z^3}{z^4}$ **42.** $\dfrac{3^3 m^9}{3^2 m^5}$ **43.** $\dfrac{5^5 n^{15}}{5^3 n^{12}}$

44. Critical Thinking Write a quotient that simplifies to $x^4 y^4$.

Measurement **In Exercises 45–48, use the table. It shows the number of meters in some metric measures written as powers of ten.**

Metric Units	
Unit	**Meters**
Yottameter	10^{24}
Zettameter	10^{21}
Exameter	10^{18}
Petameter	10^{15}
Terameter	10^{12}
Gigameter	10^9
Megameter	10^6
Kilometer	10^3
Decameter	10^1

45. How many kilometers are in a petameter?

46. How many gigameters are in a zettameter?

47. How many terameters are in a yottameter?

48. How many megameters are in an exameter?

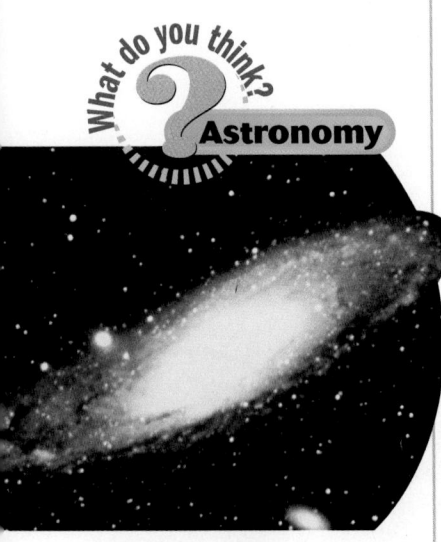
Computers **In the 1970s and early 1980s, computer random access memory was measured in kilobytes (KB) and could be added only in quantities equal to a power of 2. In Exercises 49 and 50, how many times more memory did the newer computer have?**

49. 1979: 2^3 KB; 1980: 2^5 KB   **50.** 1982: 2^6 KB; 1987: 2^9 KB

Evaluate the expression.

51. $(3^2 \cdot 3)^2$ **52.** $(2^0 \cdot 2^2)^3$ **53.** $\left(\dfrac{4^7}{4^5}\right)^2$ **54.** $\left(\dfrac{5^8}{5^7}\right)^4$

Mixed Review

Evaluate the expression. *(Lesson 1.4)*

55. $(4 \times 3)^2 + 13$ **56.** $405 \div (14 - 11)^4$ **57.** $96 \div 2^5 \times 6$

Copy and complete the statement with <, >, or =. *(Lesson 4.5)*

58. $\dfrac{5}{2}$? $\dfrac{15}{6}$ **59.** $\dfrac{9}{24}$? $\dfrac{5}{16}$ **60.** $\dfrac{5}{8}$? $\dfrac{7}{11}$

FCAT Practice FCAT

61. Multiple Choice What is the value of $2^3 \cdot 2^2 - 5^2$?

    A. -57 **B.** -7 **C.** 7 **D.** 57

62. Multiple Choice What is another expression for $\dfrac{4^7 m^{11} \cdot m^4}{4^5 m^7}$?

    F. $4m^7$ **G.** $4m^8$ **H.** $8m^8$ **I.** $16m^8$

BRAIN GAME

Mix and Match

Materials: cards marked from 1 to 6

Number of Players: 2 or 3 players

Winning Strategy: Make the largest number possible in each round.

Mix the cards and place them face down on a flat surface. Each player takes two cards. Then using only the two cards, make the largest number possible. For example, if you picked the cards 2 and 6, you could make the following numbers:

   26   62 2^6 6^2

The largest number you can make is 2^6, or 64. So, you would score 64 points for that round. After each round, reshuffle the cards to play another round.

The player with the highest score after three rounds wins.

Negative and Zero Exponents

BEFORE	▶ Now	WHY?
You simplified expressions with positive exponents.	You'll simplify expressions with negative exponents.	So you can describe very small objects, as in Ex. 31.

In the Real World

Review Words
exponent, p. 20
common factor, p. 173

FLORIDA
Standards and Assessment

• Express numbers in exponential notation. (MA.A.2.3.1)

• Evaluate expressions with exponents. (MA.A.2.3.1)

Strobes The picture at the right was taken using a strobe light. The flash of the strobe light lasted about 1 microsecond. How can you write this time in seconds as a power of ten? You will see how to solve this problem in Example 1.

You have seen two methods for evaluating expressions involving division of powers.

Divide out common factors. **Quotient of powers property**

$$\frac{x^5}{x^7} = \frac{x^1 \cdot x^1 \cdot x^1 \cdot x^1 \cdot x^1}{x_1 \cdot x_1 \cdot x_1 \cdot x_1 \cdot x_1 \cdot x \cdot x} = \frac{1}{x^2} \qquad \frac{x^5}{x^7} = x^{5-7} = x^{-2}$$

So $\frac{1}{x^2} = x^{-2}$, which suggests the definition for negative exponents.

> ## Negative Exponents
>
> **Words** For any integer n and any number $a \neq 0$,
>
> a^{-n} is equal to $\frac{1}{a^n}$.
>
> **Algebra** $a^{-n} = \frac{1}{a^n}$ **Numbers** $2^{-3} = \frac{1}{2^3}$

EXAMPLE 1 Using a Negative Exponent

The flash above lasts 1 microsecond, or $\frac{1}{1,000,000}$ second.

$$\frac{1}{1,000,000} = \frac{1}{10^6} \qquad \text{Write 1,000,000 as } 10^6.$$

$$= 10^{-6} \qquad \text{Definition of negative exponent}$$

ANSWER One flash of a strobe light lasts about 10^{-6} second.

EXAMPLE 2 **Evaluating a Numerical Expression**

$$5^2 \cdot 5^{-5} = 5^{2 + (-5)}$$ Product of powers property

$$= 5^{-3}$$ Simplify.

$$= \frac{1}{5^3} = \frac{1}{125}$$ Use definition of negative exponent and evaluate power.

Zero Exponents

Algebra If a is a nonzero number, then $a^0 = 1$.

Numbers $2^0 = 1$

EXAMPLE 3 **Simplifying Variable Expressions**

Simplify. Write the expression using only positive exponents.

a. $-2n^0 = -2 \cdot n^0$ Zero exponent applies only to n.

$$= -2 \cdot 1$$ Definition of zero exponent

$$= -2$$ Multiply.

b. $4n^{-5} = 4 \cdot n^{-5}$ Exponent applies only to n.

$$= 4 \cdot \frac{1}{n^5}$$ Definition of negative exponent

$$= \frac{4}{n^5}$$ Multiply.

c. $\dfrac{8x^{-3}}{x} = \dfrac{8 \cdot x^{-3}}{x^1}$ Exponent applies only to x.

$$= 8 \cdot x^{-3 - 1}$$ Quotient of powers property

$$= 8 \cdot x^{-4}$$ Simplify.

$$= \frac{8}{x^4}$$ Definition of negative exponent

Your turn now **Evaluate the expression.**

1. 7^{-2} **2.** $(-2)^{-5}$ **3.** $6 \cdot 6^{-3}$ **4.** $10^{-5} \cdot 10^7$

Simplify. Write the expression using only positive exponents.

5. $-6m^{-1}$ **6.** $b^2 \cdot b^{-2}$ **7.** $\dfrac{5x^4}{x^7}$ **8.** $\dfrac{10a^{-3}}{a^4}$

4.7 Exercises

More Practice, p. 730

Getting Ready to Practice

Vocabulary Determine whether the statement is *true* or *false*.

1. The base of the expression 2^{-5} is 2.

2. The exponent of the expression 2^{-5} is 5.

Evaluate the expression.

3. 3^{-4} 4. $(-4)^{-3}$ 5. $2^{-10} \cdot 2^6$ 6. 12^0

7. **Find the Error** Describe and correct the error in the solution.

$$5^{-3} = (-5)(-5)(-5)$$
$$= -125$$

8. **Biology** Plankton is made up of tiny plants (called phytoplankton) and tiny animals (called zooplankton). One type of phytoplankton may be as small as 0.2 micrometer. A micrometer is 10^{-6} meter. What part of a meter is this phytoplankton? Use a positive exponent to write your answer.

Single-celled alga

Practice and Problem Solving

HELP with Homework

Example	Exercises
1	21, 31
2	9–12
3	13–20

Online Resources
CLASSZONE.COM
· More Examples
· eTutorial Plus

Evaluate the expression.

9. $(-6)^{-2}$ 10. $2 \cdot 2^{-6}$ 11. $5^4 \cdot 5^{-8}$ 12. 9^0

Simplify. Write the expression using only positive exponents.

13. $m^{-9} \cdot m^5$ 14. $x^5 \cdot x^{-5}$ 15. $9n^{-3}$ 16. $c^{-1} \cdot c^{-2} \cdot c^{-4}$

17. $b^3 \cdot b^{-4} \cdot b^{-5}$ 18. $\dfrac{4z^{-2}}{z^4}$ 19. $\dfrac{a^{-5}}{a^8}$ 20. $\dfrac{18r^{-6}}{3r^3}$

21. **Physics** Pressure is measured in units called *pascals*. This unit can be expressed as $kg \cdot m^{-1} \cdot s^{-2}$. Write the unit without negative exponents.

Find the missing exponent.

22. $(4x^5)^? = 1$ 23. $15a^? = \dfrac{15}{a^8}$ 24. $y^? \cdot y^4 = \dfrac{1}{y}$ 25. $\dfrac{x^{-3}}{x^?} = \dfrac{1}{x^{13}}$

26. **Writing** Your friend missed today's class. Write a note to show your friend how to simplify the expression $\dfrac{6a^{-3}}{a^3}$.

Lesson 4.7   Negative and Zero Exponents   **203**

Measurement In Exercises 27–30, use the table. It shows the number of meters in some metric measures written as powers of ten.

27. How many picometers are in a decimeter?

28. How many yoctometers are in a micrometer?

29. How many nanometers are in a decimeter?

30. How many attometers are in a centimeter?

31. **Teddy Bear** In 1997, German teddy bear specialist Hanne Schramm made the smallest teddy bear in the world. It measures 0.47 inch or about 10 millimeters. How many nanometers are in 10 millimeters?

Metric Units	
Unit	Meter
Decimeter	10^{-1}
Centimeter	10^{-2}
Millimeter	10^{-3}
Micrometer	10^{-6}
Nanometer	10^{-9}
Picometer	10^{-12}
Attometer	10^{-18}
Yoctometer	10^{-24}

Critical Thinking In Exercises 32–33, copy and complete the statement using *always*, *sometimes*, or *never*.

32. A power with a negative exponent can ? be written as a fraction.

33. A power with a positive base and a negative exponent is ? negative.

34. **Challenge** Use the product of powers property to explain why $a^0 = 1$, where a is a nonzero number, makes sense.

Mixed Review

Simplify the expression. *(Lessons 2.2–2.5)*

35. $-18 + (-7)$ 36. $-46 + 0$ 37. $34 - (-18)$ 38. $16 - 30$

39. $-6 \cdot (-15)$ 40. $0(-8)$ 41. $51 \div (-3)$ 42. $-18 \div (-9)$

Basic Skills **Find the unknown number.**

43. $\underline{?} + 8 = 7$ 44. $9 \times \underline{?} = 108$ 45. $\underline{?} \div 12 = 6$

FCAT Practice

46. **Multiple Choice** Simplify the expression $\left(\dfrac{3^{-4}}{3}\right)^0$.

   A. $\dfrac{1}{243}$ B. $\dfrac{1}{23}$ C. 1   D. 27

47. **Multiple Choice** Simplify the expression $\dfrac{-12c^{-8}}{c^3}$.

   F. $\dfrac{-12}{c^{11}}$ G. $-12c^{11}$ H. $\dfrac{-12}{c^5}$ I. $-12c^5$

LESSON 4.8

Scientific Notation

In the Real World

Word Watch

scientific notation, p. 205

FLORIDA
Standards and Assessment
• Evaluate expressions with exponents. (MA.A.2.3.1)
• Know equivalent forms in scientific and standard notation. (MA.A.1.3.4)

Bubbles The brilliant colors observed in soap bubbles occur as a result of light reflecting from the inner and outer surfaces of the bubble. The thickness of a soap bubble is about 0.000004 meter. How can you use the powers of 10 to write 0.000004? You will see how to solve this problem in Example 1, part (a).

One way to write very small or very large numbers is to use *scientific notation*.

Using Scientific Notation

A number is written in **scientific notation** if it has the form $c \times 10^n$ where $1 \le c < 10$ and n is an integer.

Standard form	Product form	Scientific notation
325,000	$3.25 \times 100{,}000$	3.25×10^5
0.0005	5×0.0001	5×10^{-4}

EXAMPLE 1 Writing Numbers in Scientific Notation

a. The thickness of a soap bubble is about 0.0000004 meter.

Standard form	Product form	Scientific notation
0.000004	4×0.000001	4×10^{-6}
Move decimal point 6 places to the right.		Exponent is −6.

b. There are over 300,000,000,000 stars in the Andromeda Galaxy.

Standard form	Product form	Scientific notation
300,000,000,000	$3 \times 100{,}000{,}000{,}000$	3×10^{11}
Move decimal point 11 places to the left.		Exponent is 11.

EXAMPLE **2** **Writing Numbers in Standard Form**

Scientific notation	Product form	Standard form
a. 7.2×10^5	$7.2 \times 100{,}000$	$720{,}000$
Exponent is 5.		Move decimal point 5 places to the right.
b. 4.65×10^{-7}	4.65×0.0000001	0.000000465
Exponent is −7.		Move decimal point 7 places to the left.

Your turn now   Write the number in scientific notation.

1. 4000 **2.** 7,300,000 **3.** 63,000,000,000

4. 0.00475 **5.** 0.00000526 **6.** 0.0000000082

Write the number in standard form.

7. 3.5×10^3 **8.** 2.48×10^6 **9.** 6×10^{11}

10. 5.1×10^{-4} **11.** 9.16×10^{-2} **12.** 1.02×10^{-8}

You can use the product of powers property to multiply two numbers written in scientific notation.

Watch Out!

When a number is in scientific notation, the factor c must be greater than or equal to 1 and less than 10. The number 28.35×10^{10} is not written in scientific notation because $28.35 > 10$.

EXAMPLE **3**   **Multiplying Numbers in Scientific Notation**

Find the product $(4.5 \times 10^3) \times (6.3 \times 10^7)$.

Solution

$(4.5 \times 10^3) \times (6.3 \times 10^7)$

$\quad = 4.5 \times 6.3 \times 10^3 \times 10^7$ Commutative property of multiplication

$\quad = (4.5 \times 6.3) \times (10^3 \times 10^7)$ Associative property of multiplication

$\quad = 28.35 \times 10^{10}$ Product of powers property

$\quad = 2.835 \times 10^1 \times 10^{10}$ Write 28.35 in scientific notation.

$\quad = 2.835 \times 10^{11}$ Product of powers property

Your turn now   Write the product in scientific notation.

13. $(1.25 \times 10^6) \times (7.6 \times 10^{12})$ **14.** $(8 \times 10^5) \times (5.65 \times 10^4)$

INTERNET
eWorkbook Plus
CLASSZONE.COM

Getting Ready to Practice

Vocabulary Tell whether the number is expressed in scientific notation.

1. 9.32×10^5 **2.** 56.8×10^2 **3.** 7×10^{-4}

Write the number in scientific notation.

4. 89,200,000,000   **5.** 0.468   **6.** 0.0000671

Write the number in standard form.

7. 4.35×10^6 **8.** 5.72×10^{-3} **9.** 9.62×10^7

10. Guided Problem Solving The mass of Earth is about 1.3×10^{25} pounds. The mass of Jupiter is about 4.2×10^{27} pounds. About how many times greater is Jupiter's mass than Earth's mass?

    (1 Write the quotient of 4.2 and 1.3 as a decimal.

    (2 Write the quotient of the powers of 10.

    (3 Write the product of the quotients in scientific notation.

Practice and Problem Solving

with Homework

Example	Exercises
1	11–16, 27
2	17–22, 28
3	23–26

Online Resources
CLASSZONE.COM

· More Examples
· eTutorial Plus

Write the number in scientific notation.

11. 7900   **12.** 8,100,000,000   **13.** 2,130,000

14. 0.0312   **15.** 0.000000415   **16.** 0.0000000342

Write the number in standard form.

17. 8.71×10^{-2} **18.** 6.35×10^{-6} **19.** 1.76×10^{-9}

20. 4.13×10^9 **21.** 2.83×10^{12} **22.** 3.61×10^7

Write the product in scientific notation.

23. $(3 \times 10^3) \times (2 \times 10^5)$ **24.** $(8 \times 10^6) \times (7 \times 10^4)$

25. $(7.8 \times 10^6) \times (8.4 \times 10^7)$ **26.** $(3.6 \times 10^8) \times (5.2 \times 10^5)$

27. Well Water In the United States, 15,000,000 households use private wells for their water supply. Write this number in scientific notation.

28. State Parks The United States has a total of 1.2916×10^7 acres of land reserved for state parks. Write this number in standard form.

29. Number Sense Explain how you can tell whether a number is very small or very large when the number is written in scientific notation.

Copy and complete the statement with <, >, or =.

30. 6.92×10^{11} ? 6.92×10^{12} **31.** 3.67×10^{-3} ? 3.76×10^{-4}

Find the product or quotient. Write your answer in scientific notation.

32. $(6.8 \times 10^{-2}) \times (3.9 \times 10^{-5})$ **33.** $(2.6 \times 10^{7}) \times (4.1 \times 10^{-3})$

34. $(7.6 \times 10^{-8}) \times (4.8 \times 10^{-6})$ **35.** $(5.4 \times 10^{-5}) \times (3.6 \times 10^{-9})$

36. $\dfrac{4.08 \times 10^{6}}{3.4 \times 10^{2}}$ **37.** $\dfrac{2.765 \times 10^{21}}{7.9 \times 10^{9}}$ **38.** $\dfrac{5.46 \times 10^{28}}{6.5 \times 10^{24}}$

39. U.S. Currency The United States Bureau of Engraving and Printing prints about 17 million new $1 bills each day. About how many bills are printed in one week? in one year? Write your answers in scientific notation.

40. Critical Thinking Order the numbers from least to greatest.

3.75×10^{8} $37{,}500{,}000$ 3.57×10^{9} 5.37×10^{7}

41. Science The radius of a proton is about 1.2 Fermis. One Fermi is equal to 10^{-15} meter. How many centimeters is the radius of a proton? Write your answer in scientific notation.

42. Challenge Light travels 1.86×10^{5} miles in 1 second. How far does light travel in one year?

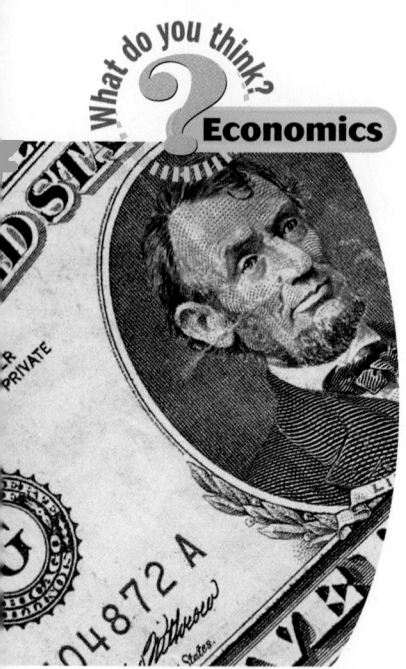

■ **U.S. Currency**

The United States Bureau of Engraving and Printing prints about 4,440,000 new $5 bills each day. What is the dollar value of these bills?

Mixed Review

In Exercises 43–44, evaluate the expression. *(Lessons 2.2, 2.3)*

43. $-8 + 12 + (-16) + 18$ **44.** $34 - (-43) - (3 - 6)$

45. Simplify $\dfrac{6n}{9mn}$. *(Lesson 4.3)*

46. Basic Skills Find the amount of time that has elapsed from 10:46 A.M. to 3:13 P.M.

FCAT Practice FCAT

47. Multiple Choice In 2001, the population of Florida was about 16,400,000 people. Which of the following is *not* another way of expressing the number 16,400,000?

   A. 1.64 million   **B.** 16.4 million   **C.** 1.64×10^{7} **D.** 16.4×10^{6}

48. Short Response A space probe travels about 1.5×10^{6} miles per day to its destination 18 million miles away. It has already traveled 9 million miles. About how many days does it have left to travel?

FLORIDA: Standards and Assessment
Express numbers in scientific or standard notation. (MA.A.2.3.1)

Using Scientific Notation

GOAL Use a calculator to perform operations on numbers written in scientific notation.

Example The Sun is about 1.5×10^8 kilometers from Earth, and Proxima Centauri is about 2.5×10^5 times farther from Earth than the Sun. How far is Proxima Centauri from Earth?

Solution

To find how far Proxima Centauri is from Earth, multiply the distance between the Sun and Earth by 2.5×10^5.

HELP with Technology

The EE key on a calculator means "times 10 raised to the power of."

Keystrokes

1.5 EE 8 × 2.5 EE 5 =

Display

3.75 x10¹³

ANSWER Proxima Centauri is approximately 3.75×10^{13} kilometers from Earth.

Your turn now Use a calculator to evaluate the expression. Write your answer in scientific notation.

1. $(3.19 \times 10^7) \times (8.5 \times 10^6)$ 2. $(6.7 \times 10^{-3}) \times (1.12 \times 10^{15})$

3. $(3.3 \times 10^{-3}) \times (4.8 \times 10^{-9})$ 4. $(7.1 \times 10^{-9}) \times (2.05 \times 10^6)$

5. $\dfrac{8.1 \times 10^{10}}{3.02 \times 10^3}$ 6. $\dfrac{1.44 \times 10^{-15}}{1.6 \times 10}$ 7. $\dfrac{2.8 \times 10^{-11}}{2.05 \times 10^{-4}}$

8. **Water** About 110 billion gallons of water flow through Lake Erie each day. How many gallons of water flow through Lake Erie in a week? in a year?

9. **Biology** The nucleus of a human cell is about 7×10^{-6} meter in diameter. A ribosome, another part of a cell, is about 3×10^{-8} meter in diameter. How many times larger is a nucleus than a ribosome?

Notebook Review

LESSONS 4.5 TO 4.8

Review the vocabulary definitions in your notebook.

Copy the review examples in your notebook. Then complete the exercises.

Check Your Definitions

least common denominator (LCD), p. 192   scientific notation, p. 205

Use Your Vocabulary

1. Copy and complete: A number is written in ? if it has the form $c \times 10^n$ where $1 \le c < 10$ and n is an integer.

4.5 Can you compare and order fractions?

 EXAMPLE Compare $\frac{11}{18}$ and $\frac{3}{4}$.

The LCM of 18 and 4 is 36, so the least common denominator is 36.

$$\frac{11}{18} = \frac{11 \cdot 2}{18 \cdot 2} = \frac{22}{36} \qquad\qquad \frac{3}{4} = \frac{3 \cdot 9}{4 \cdot 9} = \frac{27}{36}$$

ANSWER Because $\frac{22}{36} < \frac{27}{36}$, you can write $\frac{11}{18} < \frac{3}{4}$.

✓ **Copy and complete the statement with <, >, or =.**

2. $\frac{2}{3}$? $\frac{5}{9}$ **3.** $\frac{5}{12}$? $\frac{1}{3}$ **4.** $\frac{4}{5}$? $\frac{6}{7}$ **5.** $\frac{16}{24}$? $\frac{20}{30}$

4.6 Can you use the rules of exponents?

 EXAMPLE Multiply or divide. Write your answer as a power.

a. $x^7 \cdot x^8 = x^{7+8}$

$= x^{15}$

b. $\dfrac{a^6}{a^3} = a^{6-3}$

$= a^3$

✓ **Simplify. Write your answer as a power.**

6. $n^4 \cdot n^9$ **7.** $y^6 \cdot y^{10}$ **8.** $\dfrac{x^7}{x^5}$ **9.** $\dfrac{c^{12}}{c^8}$

4.7 Can you use negative exponents?

 EXAMPLE Write $x^{-4} \cdot x^{-3}$ using only positive exponents.

$$x^{-4} \cdot x^{-3} = x^{-4 + (-3)} = x^{-7} = \frac{1}{x^7}$$

☑ **Simplify. Write the expression using only positive exponents.**

10. $12a^{-5}$　　**11.** $n^7 \cdot n^{-10}$　　**12.** $\dfrac{m^{-6}}{m^5}$　　**13.** $\dfrac{c^{-9}}{c^4}$

4.8 Can you write a number in scientific notation?

 EXAMPLE Write the number in scientific notation.

a. $980{,}000{,}000 = 9.8 \times 10^8$　　**b.** $0.000012 = 1.2 \times 10^{-5}$

☑ **Write the number in scientific notation.**

14. 34,600,000,000　　**15.** 0.0000009　　**16.** 0.000000000502

Stop *and* **Think** about Lessons 4.5–4.8

17. Writing Explain how to find the product $(5 \times 10^9) \times (4 \times 10^{15})$ without using a calculator.

Review Quiz 2

Copy and complete the statement with <, >, or =.

1. $\dfrac{2}{5} \underline{\ ?\ } \dfrac{6}{15}$　　**2.** $\dfrac{5}{6} \underline{\ ?\ } \dfrac{4}{9}$　　**3.** $\dfrac{9}{15} \underline{\ ?\ } \dfrac{5}{9}$　　**4.** $\dfrac{35}{40} \underline{\ ?\ } \dfrac{21}{24}$

Order the numbers from least to greatest.

5. $\dfrac{2}{3}, \dfrac{5}{6}, \dfrac{1}{2}, \dfrac{5}{12}$　　　　**6.** $1\dfrac{4}{7}, 1\dfrac{5}{14}, \dfrac{5}{4}, 1\dfrac{5}{8}$

Multiple or divide. Write your answer as a power using only positive exponents.

7. $b^2 \cdot b^4$　　**8.** $c^5 \cdot c^{-2}$　　**9.** $\dfrac{a^7}{a^2}$　　**10.** $\dfrac{n^{-2}}{n^3}$

11. Popcorn People in the United States eat 1,120,000,000 pounds of popcorn a year. Write this number in scientific notation.

Chapter Review

 Vocabulary

prime number, p. 169
composite number, p. 169
prime factorization, p. 169
factor tree, p. 169
monomial, p. 170
common factor, p. 173
greatest common factor (GCF), p. 173
relatively prime, p. 174

simplest form, p. 179
equivalent fractions, p. 179
multiple, p. 186
common multiple, p. 186
least common multiple (LCM), p. 186
least common denominator (LCD),
  p. 192
scientific notation, p. 205

Vocabulary Review

1. Describe the difference between the *greatest common factor* and the *least common multiple* of two numbers.

2. Give three examples of prime numbers greater than 20.

3. Give three examples of monomials.

4. Describe what it means for two numbers to be relatively prime.

Copy and complete the statement.

5. A fraction is in ? if its numerator and denominator have 1 as their GCF.

6. A(n) ? is a whole number that has positive factors other than 1 and itself.

7. When you write a number as the product of prime numbers, you are writing its ? .

8. Two fractions are ? if they represent the same number.

Review Questions

Write the prime factorization of the number. *(Lesson 4.1)*

9. 54

10. 70

11. 150

12. 184

Factor the monomial. *(Lesson 4.1)*

13. $19a^2b$

14. $28xy^3$

15. $56u^2v^2$

16. $80p^4q^3$

Find the greatest common factor of the numbers or monomials.
(Lesson 4.2)

17. 20, 40, 90

18. 56, 84, 196

19. 48, 60, 165

20. $2x, x^2, x^3$

21. $18xy^2, 81xy$

22. $54s^4t^4, 164st^3$

Write the fraction in simplest form. *(Lesson 4.3)*

23. $\dfrac{16}{48}$ **24.** $-\dfrac{38}{95}$ **25.** $-\dfrac{32}{102}$ **26.** $\dfrac{104}{39}$

27. $\dfrac{3bc}{9b}$ **28.** $-\dfrac{9abc}{12a}$ **29.** $\dfrac{20m}{5mn}$ **30.** $\dfrac{21bcd}{7bc}$

Find the least common multiple of the numbers or monomials.
(Lesson 4.4)

31. $15, 35$ **32.** $180, 240$ **33.** $5m^2n^4, 25mn^3$ **34.** $6p^2q^3r^4, 14pq^2r^3$

35. Fountain A fountain in an amusement park has special-effect devices called *shooters*. They shoot columns of water at different time intervals. One shooter goes off every 8 seconds while another goes off every 12 seconds. How long after the fountain is turned on will both shooters go off at the same time? *(Lesson 4.4)*

Copy and complete the statement with <, >, or =. *(Lesson 4.5)*

36. $\dfrac{79}{16} \,\underline{?}\, \dfrac{35}{8}$ **37.** $6\dfrac{2}{3} \,\underline{?}\, \dfrac{81}{12}$ **38.** $\dfrac{161}{9} \,\underline{?}\, 17\dfrac{8}{9}$ **39.** $\dfrac{223}{15} \,\underline{?}\, 14\dfrac{4}{5}$

40. Calories One serving of rice pilaf has 220 calories, including 35 calories from fat. One serving of soup has 70 calories, including 15 calories from fat. Write the calories from fat as a fraction of the total calories for each food. Which food has a greater fraction of calories from fat? *(Lesson 4.5)*

Simplify the expression. Write your answer as a power. *(Lesson 4.6)*

41. $8 \cdot 8^3$ **42.** $2^2 \cdot 2^5$ **43.** $7^9 \div 7^7$ **44.** $\dfrac{5^{10}}{5^7}$

Simplify. Write the expression using only positive exponents. *(Lesson 4.7)*

45. $7x^{-4}$ **46.** $a^{-6} \cdot a^4$ **47.** $\dfrac{8w^{-6}}{24w^2}$ **48.** $\dfrac{16r^{-2}}{4r^3}$

49. Write 6.58×10^{-4} in standard form. *(Lesson 4.8)*

50. Write $78,900,000,000$ in scientific notation. *(Lesson 4.8)*

51. Niagara Falls In tourist season, the water at Niagara Falls flows at 100,000 cubic feet per second during the day. How fast does it flow per minute? per hour? Write your answers in scientific notation. *(Lesson 4.8)*

4 Chapter Test

Write the prime factorization of the number.

1. 49 **2.** 68 **3.** 95 **4.** 112

Find the greatest common factor of the monomials.

5. $3pq, 12pq$ **6.** $12a^2, 18ab$ **7.** $2z^3, 3z^2$ **8.** $14r^2, 42r$

Find the least common multiple of the numbers or monomials.

9. 4, 16, 32 **10.** 18, 24, 36 **11.** $5x^2y, 21xy^3$ **12.** $54pq^2, 63p^3q^3$

Copy and complete the statement with <, >, or =.

13. $\frac{11}{12} \; ? \; \frac{41}{48}$ **14.** $4\frac{3}{6} \; ? \; \frac{9}{2}$ **15.** $8\frac{7}{16} \; ? \; \frac{17}{2}$

16. Cake Three equal-sized round layer cakes were served at a party. Each cake was cut into a different number of equal-sized slices. After the guests left, $\frac{1}{8}$ of the yellow cake, $\frac{3}{16}$ of the chocolate cake, and $\frac{1}{6}$ of the carrot cake remained. Which type of cake had the least amount left over? Which had the most? Explain your reasoning.

Simplify the expression. Write your answer as a power.

17. $m^8 \cdot m^3$ **18.** $6^2 \cdot 6^6$ **19.** $\frac{n^{16}}{n^{10}}$

Simplify. Write the expression using only positive exponents.

20. $5x^{-3}$ **21.** $c^{-1} \cdot c^{-7}$ **22.** $\frac{-4u^{-9}}{u^3}$ **23.** $\frac{16a^2b^5}{8a^4b}$

24. Science Scientists have created a microfabric using molded plastic. Its narrowest links are $\frac{1}{1,000,000}$ meter. Write this fraction as a power of ten.

Write the product in scientific notation.

25. $(6 \times 10^5) \times (5 \times 10^7)$ **26.** $(8.1 \times 10^4) \times (9.2 \times 10^8)$ **27.** $(4.2 \times 10^{-5}) \times (6 \times 10^{-2})$

Chapter FCAT Practice

FCAT **Test-Taking Strategy** Be careful about choosing an answer that seems obvious. Carefully read the problem and all the choices before answering.

Multiple Choice

1. Which number is a prime number?

   A. 57   **B.** 83   **C.** 93   **D.** 105

2. A rectangle has an area of 144 square meters. Which dimensions are *not* possible for this rectangle?

   F. 24 meters by 6 meters

   G. 12 meters by 12 meters

   H. 14 meters by 10 meters

   I. 16 meters by 9 meters

3. What is the greatest common factor of 360 and 540?

   A. 10   **B.** 90   **C.** 180   **D.** 1080

4. Which fraction is written in simplest form?

   F. $\dfrac{9}{26}$ **G.** $\dfrac{5}{45}$ **H.** $\dfrac{18}{42}$ **I.** $\dfrac{28}{63}$

5. Which fraction is *not* equivalent to $\dfrac{3}{4}$?

   A. $\dfrac{6}{8}$ **B.** $\dfrac{9}{16}$ **C.** $\dfrac{21}{28}$ **D.** $\dfrac{36}{48}$

6. Which list *is* in order from least to greatest?

   F. $\dfrac{4}{10}, \dfrac{8}{15}, \dfrac{1}{5}, \dfrac{49}{100}$ **G.** $\dfrac{1}{3}, \dfrac{5}{6}, \dfrac{13}{18}, \dfrac{7}{12}$

   H. $1\dfrac{7}{16}, \dfrac{6}{4}, \dfrac{4}{2}, 1\dfrac{3}{8}$ **I.** $2\dfrac{3}{14}, 2\dfrac{2}{7}, \dfrac{5}{2}, \dfrac{11}{4}$

7. Which expression is *not* equal to 7^5?

   A. $7^3 \cdot 7^2$ **B.** $7 \cdot 7^4$ **C.** $\dfrac{7^{11}}{7^6}$ **D.** $\dfrac{7^{11}}{7^9}$

8. Which number is equal to $\dfrac{3^{10}}{3^6}$?

   F. 9   **G.** 81   **H.** 243   **I.** 729

9. Write $\dfrac{-8b^{-8}}{b^4}$ using only positive exponents.

   A. $\dfrac{-8}{b^{12}}$ **B.** $\dfrac{1}{8b^{12}}$ **C.** $-8b^4$ **D.** $8b^4$

10. Simplify $(4.2 \times 10^{-9}) \times (5 \times 10^3)$.

    F. 2.1×10^{-9} **G.** 2.1×10^{-3}

    H. 2.1×10^{-6} **I.** 21×10^{-6}

Short Response

11. **Cereal Boxes** A cereal company puts a 25 cent coupon in every 15th box and a 75 cent coupon in every 21st box. In which box of cereal will there be both coupons?

Extended Response

12. **Marbles** A bag contains 3 green marbles, 5 red marbles, 6 yellow marbles, and 10 blue marbles. What is the total number of marbles? What fraction of marbles are green? What fraction are yellow? Write each fraction in simplest form. Jane estimates that about half of the marbles are blue. Do you agree with this estimate? Explain.

CHAPTER 5

Rational Number Operations

BEFORE

In previous chapters you've...

- Added, subtracted, multiplied, and divided integers
- Interpreted tables and graphs

Now

In Chapter 5 you'll study...

- Performing operations on fractions, mixed numbers, and decimals
- Rewriting fractions and decimals
- Describing data sets using mean, median, mode, and range

WHY?

So you can solve real-world problems about...

- snakes, p. 220
- sledding, p. 226
- rafting, p. 251
- deep sea jellies, p. 257

Internet Preview
CLASSZONE.COM

- eEdition Plus Online
- eWorkbook Plus Online
- eTutorial Plus Online
- FCAT Practice
- More Examples

Chapter Warm-Up Games

Review skills you need for this chapter in these quick games.

$\frac{7}{32}$	$\frac{1}{3}$	$\frac{2}{7}$	$\frac{3}{11}$
$\frac{7}{17}$	$\frac{4}{9}$	$\frac{4}{15}$	$\frac{11}{25}$
$\frac{6}{11}$	$\frac{13}{21}$	$\frac{4}{7}$	$\frac{3}{8}$
$\frac{1}{2}$	$\frac{5}{8}$	$\frac{7}{11}$	$\frac{9}{14}$
$\frac{3}{4}$	$\frac{5}{6}$	$\frac{3}{5}$	$\frac{5}{7}$
	$\frac{2}{3}$		

Scale the Cliff

Key Skill:
Comparing fractions

Find the handholds you can use to scale the cliff.

- Start at $\frac{2}{3}$ and move up, selecting a handhold in each row.

- The value of each handhold must be less than the value of the handhold below it.

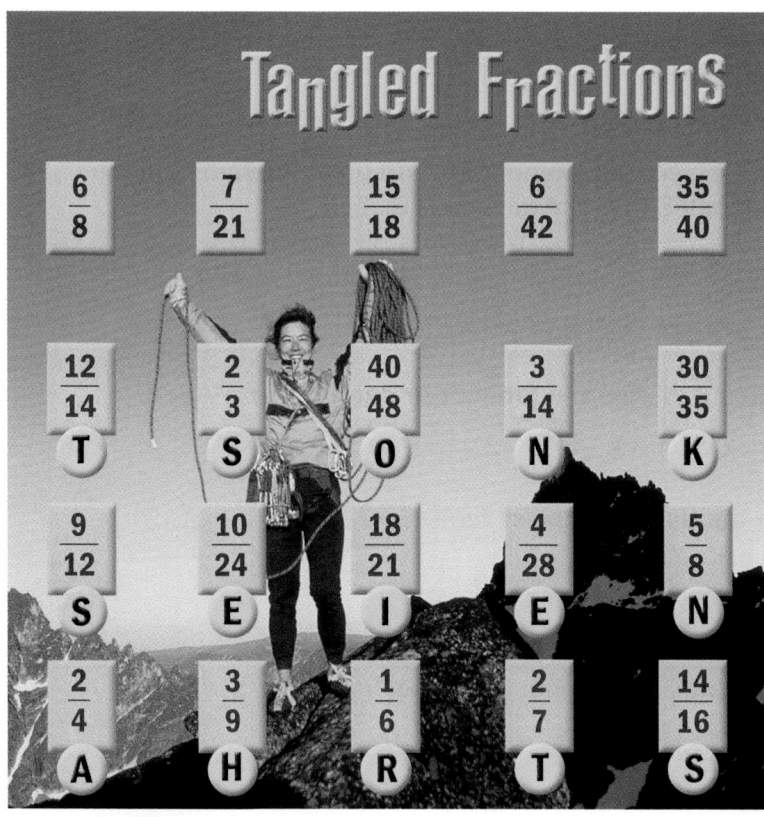

Tangled Fractions

$\frac{6}{8}$	$\frac{7}{21}$	$\frac{15}{18}$	$\frac{6}{42}$	$\frac{35}{40}$
$\frac{12}{14}$ **T**	$\frac{2}{3}$ **S**	$\frac{40}{48}$ **O**	$\frac{3}{14}$ **N**	$\frac{30}{35}$ **K**
$\frac{9}{12}$ **S**	$\frac{10}{24}$ **E**	$\frac{18}{21}$ **I**	$\frac{4}{28}$ **E**	$\frac{5}{8}$ **N**
$\frac{2}{4}$ **A**	$\frac{3}{9}$ **H**	$\frac{1}{6}$ **R**	$\frac{2}{7}$ **T**	$\frac{14}{16}$ **S**

Key Skill:
Identifying equivalent fractions

Susan is going rock climbing. Help her figure out what equipment she is missing.

- In each column, find a fraction equivalent to the top one to decode the name of the equipment Susan is missing.

Stop *and* Think

1. **Critical Thinking** A student thinks that a fraction cannot be smaller than another fraction if the first fraction's denominator is greater than the second fraction's denominator. Explain why the student is wrong.

2. **Writing** Explain how to tell whether fractions with different denominators are equivalent.

Getting Ready to Learn

Review What You Need to Know

Using Vocabulary Copy and complete using a review word.

1. If 1 is the greatest common factor of the numerator and the denominator, then the fraction is in ? .

2. A number like $3\frac{4}{7}$, whose value is the sum of a whole number part and a fraction part, is called a(n) ? .

In Exercises 3–6, find the product or quotient. *(pp. 70, 74)*

3. $-125 \cdot 2$ **4.** $-4 \cdot (-23)$ **5.** $-39 \div 3$ **6.** $-136 \div (-17)$

Write the fraction in simplest form. *(p. 179)*

7. $\frac{4}{12}$ **8.** $\frac{35}{50}$ **9.** $\frac{12}{32}$ **10.** $\frac{24}{52}$ **11.** $\frac{14}{49}$

12. You bought a sweater for $15.65 and a pair of jeans for $23.95. What was the total cost of your purchase? *(p. 709)*

Word Watch

Review Words

simplest form, p. 179
least common
 denominator (LCD),
 p. 192
improper fraction, p. 707
mixed number, p. 707

You should include material that appears on a notebook like this in your own notes.

Know How to Take Notes

Writing Helpful Hints In your notebook, write down any helpful hints your teacher or your textbook gives you for solving problems.

Equivalent Fractions

Write equivalent fractions by multiplying by a fraction that is equal to one.

$$\frac{3}{5} \times \frac{4}{4} = \frac{12}{20} \qquad \frac{3}{5} \times \frac{9}{9} = \frac{27}{45} \qquad \frac{3}{5} \times \frac{100}{100} = \frac{300}{500}$$

← A fraction has many equivalent forms.

You can rename a mixed number as an equivalent improper fraction.

$$3\frac{5}{6} = \frac{6 \cdot 3 + 5}{6} = \frac{23}{6}$$

In Lesson 5.1, you should write down helpful hints about subtracting with mixed numbers.

LESSON 5.1

Fractions with Common Denominators

BEFORE	▶ Now	WHY?
You added and subtracted whole numbers and integers.	You'll add and subtract fractions with common denominators.	So you can compare coin sizes, as in Ex. 28.

Word Watch

Review words

order of operations, p. 10
numerator, p. 707
denominator, p. 707

FLORIDA
Standards and Assessment

• Know effects of the four basic operations. (MA.A.3.3.1)

• Write equations to express relationships. (MA.D.1.3.2)

One way to add or subtract fractions with common denominators is to use a model.

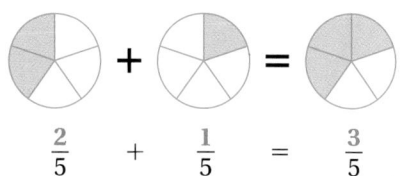

$$\frac{2}{5} \quad + \quad \frac{1}{5} \quad = \quad \frac{3}{5}$$

The model suggests the following rule.

Adding and Subtracting Fractions

Words To add fractions or subtract fractions with a common denominator, write the sum or difference of the numerators over the denominator.

Numbers $\dfrac{3}{9} + \dfrac{5}{9} = \dfrac{8}{9}$ **Algebra** $\dfrac{a}{c} + \dfrac{b}{c} = \dfrac{a+b}{c}$ $(c \neq 0)$

$\dfrac{3}{5} - \dfrac{2}{5} = \dfrac{1}{5}$ $\dfrac{a}{c} - \dfrac{b}{c} = \dfrac{a-b}{c}$ $(c \neq 0)$

To add or subtract mixed numbers, find the sum or difference of the whole numbers and the sum or difference of the fractions. Then combine these quantities.

with Notetaking

Part (b) of Example 1 shows how to operate with negative mixed numbers. You may wish to copy this into your notebook.

EXAMPLE 1   Fractions and Mixed Numbers

a. $-\dfrac{11}{13} + \dfrac{8}{13} = \dfrac{-11+8}{13}$

$= -\dfrac{3}{13}$

b. $-5\dfrac{6}{7} + 3\dfrac{2}{7} = -5 - \dfrac{6}{7} + 3 + \dfrac{2}{7}$

$= -5 + 3 - \dfrac{6}{7} + \dfrac{2}{7}$

$= -2\dfrac{4}{7}$

EXAMPLE 2 Simplifying Fractions with Variables

a. $-\dfrac{a}{9} + \dfrac{7a}{9} = \dfrac{-a + 7a}{9}$ Write sum over common denominator.

$= \dfrac{6a}{9}$ Combine like terms.

$= \dfrac{\overset{2}{\cancel{6}}a}{\underset{3}{\cancel{9}}}$ Divide out common factor.

$= \dfrac{2a}{3}$ Simplify.

b. $\dfrac{6x}{11y} - \dfrac{10x}{11y} = \dfrac{6x - 10x}{11y}$ Write difference over common denominator.

$= \dfrac{-4x}{11y}, \text{ or } -\dfrac{4x}{11y}$ Combine like terms.

HELP with **Solving**

Remember that the following fractions are equivalent.

$\dfrac{-a}{b} = \dfrac{a}{-b} = -\dfrac{a}{b}$

Your turn now Find the sum or difference. Then simplify if possible.

1. $\dfrac{1}{12} + \dfrac{5}{12}$ 2. $\dfrac{3}{8} - 2\dfrac{1}{8}$ 3. $-\dfrac{t}{3} - \dfrac{2t}{3}$ 4. $\dfrac{y}{8a} + \dfrac{-5y}{8a}$

EXAMPLE 3 Solving an Equation with Mixed Numbers

Biology A corn snake that is $14\dfrac{3}{4}$ inches long grows g inches to a length of $27\dfrac{1}{4}$ inches. To find the amount of growth, subtract the original length from the current length.

$g = 27\dfrac{1}{4} - 14\dfrac{3}{4}$ $\dfrac{1}{4} < \dfrac{3}{4}$, so rename $27\dfrac{1}{4}$ so its fraction part is greater than $\dfrac{3}{4}$.

$= 26\dfrac{5}{4} - 14\dfrac{3}{4}$

$= \left(26 + \dfrac{5}{4}\right) - \left(14 + \dfrac{3}{4}\right)$

$= 26 + \dfrac{5}{4} - 14 - \dfrac{3}{4}$ ← Remember to distribute the subtraction.

$= (26 - 14) + \left(\dfrac{5}{4} - \dfrac{3}{4}\right)$

$= 12 + \dfrac{2}{4}$

$= 12\dfrac{1}{2}$ ← $\dfrac{2}{4} = \dfrac{1}{2}$

ANSWER The snake grows $12\dfrac{1}{2}$ inches.

Order of Operations The rules for adding and subtracting fractions can be applied to longer expressions. Remember to use the order of operations.

EXAMPLE 4 **Evaluating Longer Expressions**

a. $\dfrac{2}{11} - \dfrac{5}{11} + \dfrac{9}{11} = \dfrac{2 - 5 + 9}{11}$ Write $2 - 5 + 9$ over common denominator.

$= \dfrac{6}{11}$ Evaluate numerator from left to right.

b. $3\dfrac{6}{7} - 2\dfrac{3}{7} + 4\dfrac{5}{7} = (3 - 2 + 4) + \left(\dfrac{6}{7} - \dfrac{3}{7} + \dfrac{5}{7}\right)$ Group whole numbers and fractions.

$= 5\dfrac{8}{7}$ Evaluate inside parentheses.

$= 6\dfrac{1}{7}$ Rename.

Your turn now **Evaluate. Then simplify if possible.**

5. $\dfrac{3}{4} + \dfrac{7}{4} + \dfrac{5}{4}$ **6.** $\dfrac{15}{8} - \dfrac{7}{8} + \dfrac{3}{8}$ **7.** $2\dfrac{1}{3} - \dfrac{2}{3} + 3\dfrac{2}{3}$

5.1 **Exercises**
More Practice, p. 731

Getting Ready to Practice

1. Vocabulary Copy and complete: In the fraction $\dfrac{4}{9}$, 9 is the $\underline{\ ?\ }$ and 4 is the $\underline{\ ?\ }$.

2. Find the Error Describe and correct the error.

$$\cancel{}\ \dfrac{3}{4} + \dfrac{3}{4} = \dfrac{3 + 3}{4 + 4} = \dfrac{6}{8}$$

Find the sum or difference. Then simplify if possible.

3. $\dfrac{5}{18} + \dfrac{7}{18}$ **4.** $\dfrac{3}{10} - \dfrac{7}{10}$ **5.** $\dfrac{4}{15} - \dfrac{1}{15}$ **6.** $1\dfrac{5}{9} + \dfrac{2}{9}$

7. $3\dfrac{1}{7} - 1\dfrac{5}{7}$ **8.** $2\dfrac{7}{9} + \dfrac{8}{9}$ **9.** $\dfrac{c}{6} + \dfrac{5c}{6}$ **10.** $\dfrac{3d}{5} - \dfrac{2d}{5}$

11. Knitting When the scarf you are knitting is $21\dfrac{3}{8}$ inches long, you find a mistake and have to pull out $2\dfrac{5}{8}$ inches. How much scarf is left?

Practice and Problem Solving

with Homework

Example	Exercises
1	12–23
2	24–27
3	28–30, 40
4	31–39

Online Resources
CLASSZONE.COM

· More Examples
· eTutorial Plus

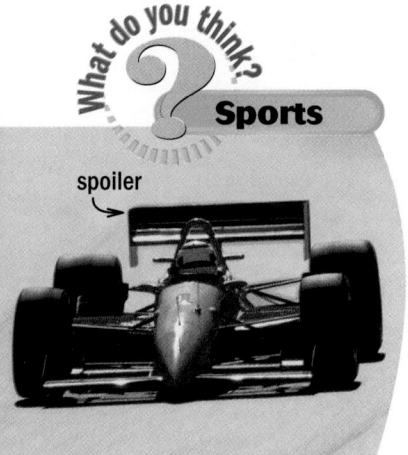

Sports

spoiler

Auto Racing

Decreasing the height of a race car's spoiler reduces *drag*, increasing speed. What do you think happens when the spoiler's height is increased?

Find the sum or difference.

12. $\frac{4}{17} + \frac{8}{17}$ **13.** $\frac{7}{18} - \frac{5}{18}$ **14.** $\frac{9}{14} - \frac{5}{14}$ **15.** $\frac{-13}{24} + \frac{-9}{24}$

16. $\frac{5}{21} + \frac{2}{21}$ **17.** $\frac{12}{25} + \frac{-7}{25}$ **18.** $\frac{1}{6} - \frac{11}{6}$ **19.** $-\frac{3}{4} - \left(-\frac{1}{4}\right)$

20. $-2\frac{5}{12} + 1\frac{11}{12}$ **21.** $1\frac{4}{15} + \left(-\frac{11}{15}\right)$ **22.** $-4\frac{2}{7} - 4\frac{2}{7}$ **23.** $-7\frac{3}{5} - \frac{4}{5}$

Algebra **Simplify the expression.**

24. $\frac{h}{13} + \frac{6h}{13}$ **25.** $-\frac{8n}{21} + \frac{5n}{21}$ **26.** $\frac{9a}{20b} - \frac{7a}{20b}$ **27.** $-\frac{5q}{18p} - \frac{13q}{18p}$

28. **Euros** A 2-euro coin is $25\frac{3}{4}$ millimeters at its widest. A 1-euro coin is $23\frac{1}{4}$ millimeters at its widest. How much wider is a 2-euro coin?

29. **Volunteering** You did volunteer work for $6\frac{1}{6}$ hours last week and $8\frac{5}{6}$ hours this week. For how many total hours have you volunteered? How many more hours did you volunteer this week than last week?

30. **Auto Racing** Some cars in a recent race were allowed to reduce the height of their rear spoilers by one fourth inch. After the change, one car's spoiler was $6\frac{1}{4}$ inches tall. How tall was the spoiler before the change in height?

Evaluate.

31. $\frac{13}{18} + \frac{5}{18} + \frac{11}{18}$ **32.** $-\frac{4}{5} - \frac{1}{5} - \frac{2}{5}$ **33.** $-\frac{4}{25} + \frac{3}{25} + \frac{9}{25}$

34. $\frac{5}{7} - 1\frac{3}{7} + \frac{4}{7}$ **35.** $-\frac{3}{16} + 2\frac{1}{16} - \frac{15}{16}$ **36.** $1\frac{3}{8} + \frac{5}{8} - 1\frac{7}{8}$

37. $-5\frac{4}{15} - 3\frac{7}{15} + \frac{8}{15}$ **38.** $-\frac{9}{20} + \frac{19}{20} - 1\frac{1}{20}$ **39.** $4\frac{5}{12} - \left(1\frac{11}{12} - \frac{7}{12}\right)$

40. **Long Jump** You want to match your school's long jump record of 17 feet $8\frac{1}{4}$ inches. Your best long jump so far is 15 feet $11\frac{3}{4}$ inches. How much farther do you need to jump to match the school record?

Algebra **Solve the equation.**

41. $x + \frac{5}{8} = \frac{7}{8}$ **42.** $\frac{10}{11} - y = \frac{2}{11}$ **43.** $z - \frac{9}{15} = \frac{11}{15}$

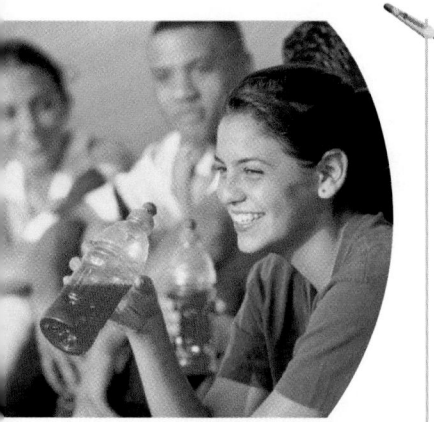

44. Writing One hundred students try three new fruit juice blends, and each picks a favorite, as shown at the right.

Your friend says that if you make each number the numerator in a fraction with a denominator of 100, the sum of these fractions must be 1. Is your friend right? Explain.

Favorite Juice Blend

Juice A 42
Juice B 37
Juice C 21

Challenge **Find the value that makes the equation true.**

45. $\dfrac{5}{11} + \dfrac{9}{11} - \dfrac{?}{} = -\dfrac{2}{11}$

46. $\dfrac{7}{16} + \dfrac{9}{16} - \dfrac{?}{} = \dfrac{5}{16}$

Mixed Review

Find the sum or difference. *(Lessons 2.2, 2.3)*

47. $22 + (-17)$ **48.** $-14 - 9$ **49.** $-7 + (-35)$ **50.** $16 - (-13)$

Find the least common multiple of the numbers. *(Lesson 4.4)*

51. $15, 35$ **52.** $19, 76$ **53.** $37, 50$ **54.** $27, 81$

Find the least common denominator of the fractions. *(Lesson 4.5)*

55. $\dfrac{2}{3}, \dfrac{4}{9}$ **56.** $\dfrac{1}{5}, \dfrac{9}{20}$ **57.** $\dfrac{3}{8}, \dfrac{7}{12}$ **58.** $\dfrac{1}{6}, \dfrac{4}{15}$

Basic Skills **Find the quotient.**

59. $32 \div 2$ **60.** $60 \div 5$ **61.** $10 \div 8$ **62.** $50 \div 4$

FCAT Practice

63. Multiple Choice You have $\dfrac{11}{12}$ of a bag of apples. If you eat $\dfrac{5}{12}$ of the bag during a week, how much of the bag of apples do you have left?

A. $\dfrac{1}{6}$ **B.** $\dfrac{1}{4}$ **C.** $\dfrac{5}{12}$ **D.** $\dfrac{1}{2}$

64. Multiple Choice A work crew is putting guard rail around a triangular traffic island. What is the perimeter, in feet, of the island?

$18\dfrac{5}{8}$ ft $18\dfrac{5}{8}$ ft

$8\dfrac{3}{8}$ ft

F. $44\dfrac{5}{8}$ feet   **G.** $44\dfrac{7}{8}$ feet

H. $45\dfrac{5}{8}$ feet   **I.** $47\dfrac{5}{8}$ feet

LESSON 5.2

Fractions with Different Denominators

BEFORE	▶ Now	WHY?
You added and subtracted with common denominators.	You'll add and subtract with different denominators.	So you can find a sled length, as in Ex. 20.

Word Watch

Review Words

least common denominator
(LCD), p. 192

FLORIDA
Standards and Assessment

• Solve real-world problems
involving fractions.
(MA.A.3.3.2)

• Write equations to express
relationships. (MA.D.1.3.2)

HELP with **Review**

For help with rewriting
fractions with common
denominators, see p. 192.

In the Real World

Carpentry A board is $36\frac{5}{8}$ inches long. You cut
off a piece $12\frac{3}{4}$ inches long. The saw blade
destroys an additional $\frac{1}{16}$ inch of wood.

You will find the length of the remaining
piece of wood in Example 3 on page 225.

Rewriting Fractions To add or subtract
fractions with different denominators, first
rewrite the fractions so the denominators
are the same.

EXAMPLE 1 **Adding and Subtracting Fractions**

a. $\dfrac{7}{8} + \dfrac{-2}{5} = \dfrac{35}{40} + \dfrac{-16}{40}$ Rewrite fractions using LCD of 40.

$= \dfrac{35 + (-16)}{40}$ Write sum over LCD.

$= \dfrac{19}{40}$ Evaluate numerator.

b. $\dfrac{3}{10} - \dfrac{5}{6} = \dfrac{9}{30} - \dfrac{25}{30}$ Rewrite fractions using LCD of 30.

$= \dfrac{9 - 25}{30}$ Write difference over LCD.

$= \dfrac{-16}{30}$ Evaluate numerator.

$= -\dfrac{8}{15}$ Simplify.

Your turn now **Find the sum or difference. Then simplify if possible.**

1. $\dfrac{1}{3} + \dfrac{3}{8}$ **2.** $\dfrac{3}{4} - \dfrac{9}{10}$ **3.** $\dfrac{5}{12} + \dfrac{-7}{9}$ **4.** $\dfrac{1}{6} - \dfrac{11}{15}$

EXAMPLE 2
Simplifying Variable Expressions

Algebra **Simplify the expression.**

a. $\dfrac{2x}{5} - \dfrac{x}{6} = \dfrac{12x}{30} - \dfrac{5x}{30}$ Rewrite fractions using LCD of 30.

$= \dfrac{12x - 5x}{30}$ Write difference over LCD.

$= \dfrac{7x}{30}$ Combine like terms.

b. $\dfrac{5}{y} + \dfrac{7}{8} = \left(\dfrac{5}{y} \cdot \dfrac{8}{8}\right) + \left(\dfrac{7}{8} \cdot \dfrac{y}{y}\right)$ Multiply $\dfrac{5}{y}$ by $\dfrac{8}{8}$ and $\dfrac{7}{8}$ by $\dfrac{y}{y}$ for LCD of 8y.

$= \dfrac{40}{8y} + \dfrac{7y}{8y}$ Multiply inside parentheses.

$= \dfrac{40 + 7y}{8y}$ Write sum over LCD.

Watch Out!

In part (b) of Example 2, notice that

$\dfrac{40 + 7y}{8y} \neq \dfrac{47y}{8y}$

because 40 and 7y are not like terms. The expression is already in simplest form.

EXAMPLE 3   **Modeling with Mixed Numbers**

Carpentry To find the length of the remaining piece of wood from the problem at the top of page 224, write a verbal model.

| Remaining length L | = | Original length | − | (Length cut off | + | Blade width) |

$L = 36\dfrac{5}{8} - \left(12\dfrac{3}{4} + \dfrac{1}{16}\right)$ Write an algebraic model.

$= 36\dfrac{10}{16} - \left(12\dfrac{12}{16} + \dfrac{1}{16}\right)$ Rewrite fractions using LCD of 16.

$= 36\dfrac{10}{16} - 12\dfrac{13}{16}$ Add inside parentheses.

$= 35\dfrac{26}{16} - 12\dfrac{13}{16}$ Rename $36\dfrac{10}{16}$ as $35\dfrac{26}{16}$.

$= (35 - 12) + \left(\dfrac{26}{16} - \dfrac{13}{16}\right)$ Group whole numbers and fractions.

$= 23\dfrac{13}{16}$ Subtract whole numbers and fractions.

ANSWER The remaining piece of wood is $23\dfrac{13}{16}$ inches long.

Your turn now **Find the sum or difference. Then simplify if possible.**

5. $\dfrac{w}{3} + \dfrac{w}{12}$ 6. $\dfrac{2}{5} - \dfrac{2}{z}$ 7. $5\dfrac{3}{4} + 2\dfrac{3}{5}$ 8. $7\dfrac{5}{6} - 3\dfrac{8}{9}$

Getting Ready to Practice

1. **Vocabulary** Copy and complete: To add two fractions with different denominators, rewrite the fractions using the _?_ of the fractions.

Find the sum or difference. Then simplify if possible.

2. $\dfrac{1}{2} + \dfrac{1}{3}$ 3. $4\dfrac{5}{8} - 2\dfrac{2}{3}$ 4. $\dfrac{2x}{7} - \dfrac{x}{2}$ 5. $\dfrac{4}{x} + \dfrac{1}{9}$

6. **Guided Problem Solving** You are building a stone wall 13 feet long. You build $4\dfrac{1}{3}$ feet of wall on Monday and $5\dfrac{3}{4}$ feet on Tuesday. How much wall do you have left to build?

   ① Write a verbal model to describe the problem.

   ② Substitute the given values into the model.

   ③ Solve the equation to find the length left to build.

Practice and Problem Solving

 with Homework

Example	Exercises
1	7–13, 21–22
2	24–27
3	14–20, 23

Online Resources
CLASSZONE.COM

· More Examples
· eTutorial Plus

Find the sum or difference.

7. $\dfrac{7}{8} - \dfrac{1}{4}$ 8. $\dfrac{3}{7} + \dfrac{9}{14}$ 9. $\dfrac{5}{9} + \dfrac{1}{6}$ 10. $\dfrac{2}{3} - \dfrac{3}{10}$

11. $\dfrac{1}{8} - \dfrac{5}{32}$ 12. $-\dfrac{7}{12} + \dfrac{4}{15}$ 13. $\dfrac{-3}{8} + \dfrac{-9}{20}$ 14. $5\dfrac{1}{2} - \dfrac{7}{10}$

15. $12\dfrac{5}{18} - \dfrac{3}{4}$ 16. $-7\dfrac{3}{11} - (-8)$ 17. $7\dfrac{4}{5} + 5\dfrac{3}{7}$ 18. $12\dfrac{2}{9} - 16\dfrac{3}{7}$

19. **Tree Removal** A dead tree $25\dfrac{1}{2}$ feet tall is being cut down. On the first cut, $9\dfrac{1}{3}$ feet are cut off. On the next cut, $7\dfrac{5}{6}$ feet are cut off. How much of the tree remains to be cut down?

20. **Olympic Sledding** Olympic skeleton sleds range from $31\dfrac{1}{2}$ inches to $47\dfrac{1}{4}$ inches long. What is the difference in length of the longest and shortest sleds?

Tell whether the statement is *true* or *false*.

21. $\dfrac{1}{4} - \dfrac{6}{7} + \dfrac{3}{14} = -\dfrac{11}{28}$ 22. $\dfrac{4}{5} + \dfrac{5}{8} - \dfrac{7}{10} = \dfrac{57}{80}$ 23. $1\dfrac{1}{3} - \dfrac{2}{9} - \dfrac{5}{6} = \dfrac{7}{18}$

Algebra Simplify the expression.

24. $\frac{6t}{13} - \frac{6t}{7}$ **25.** $\frac{9s}{4} - \frac{7s}{5}$ **26.** $\frac{18}{7a} + \frac{11}{21}$ **27.** $\frac{16}{25n} + \frac{9}{10n}$

Equator In Exercises 28 and 29, use the following information.

Traveling east from the Galapagos Islands to Nairobi, Kenya, you go about $\frac{9}{25}$ of the way around Earth's equator. It is then about $\frac{9}{50}$ of the way around the equator from Nairobi traveling east to Singapore.

28. What fraction of the equator do you cover if you travel east from the Galapagos Islands to Singapore?

29. Writing Is traveling from the Galapagos Islands to Singapore a shorter trip if you travel *east* or *west*? Explain.

Algebra Solve the equation.

30. $6\frac{3}{8} + 2\frac{5}{12} - x = 4\frac{3}{4}$ **31.** $7\frac{7}{8} - 6\frac{5}{9} - y = \frac{1}{6}$ **32.** $z + 3\frac{4}{7} - 5\frac{2}{5} = 1\frac{1}{2}$

33. Challenge To evaluate $3\frac{1}{4} + 5\frac{3}{8}$, Cal groups the whole numbers and the fractions, and then rewrites the fractions with a common denominator. May rewrites the fractions with a common denominator first, and then groups the whole numbers and the fractions. Do Cal and May get the same sum? Explain.

Mixed Review

Find the product. *(Lesson 2.4)*

34. $-9(7)$ **35.** $0(-5)$ **36.** $7(-3)(13)$ **37.** $-9(-7)(-2)$

Copy and complete the statement with <, >, or =. *(Lesson 4.5)*

38. $\frac{1}{7} \ \underline{?} \ \frac{1}{8}$ **39.** $\frac{3}{8} \ \underline{?} \ \frac{4}{9}$ **40.** $\frac{5}{12} \ \underline{?} \ \frac{7}{16}$ **41.** $\frac{7}{10} \ \underline{?} \ \frac{18}{25}$

FCAT Practice

42. Multiple Choice What is the value of $\frac{3}{4} - \frac{7}{8} + \frac{1}{2}$?

A. $\frac{3}{8}$ B. $\frac{5}{8}$ C. $\frac{3}{4}$ D. $2\frac{1}{8}$

43. Short Response You load into a wagon a rock that weighs $12\frac{7}{8}$ pounds and a shovel that weighs $3\frac{1}{2}$ pounds. The wagon weighs $8\frac{1}{3}$ pounds. When you pull the wagon, what is the total weight you pull?

Problem Solving Strategies

FLORIDA: Standards and Assessment
Construct models to represent rational numbers. (MA.A.1.3.3)

Act It Out

Guess, Check, and Revise
Look for a Pattern
Draw a Diagram
Make a Model
Act It Out
Make a Table
Solve a Simpler Problem

Problem You are hiking a trail that is $7\frac{1}{2}$ miles long. Before your first break, you hike $2\frac{3}{4}$ miles. Then you hike $2\frac{1}{2}$ miles and take another break. How many miles do you have left to hike?

❶ Read and Understand

Read the problem carefully.

- You know that you are hiking a total distance of $7\frac{1}{2}$ miles, and that you have already hiked $2\frac{3}{4}$ miles and $2\frac{1}{2}$ miles.

- You want to find the remaining distance that you have left to hike.

❷ Make a Plan

Decide on a strategy to use.

One way to solve this problem is to use the act it out strategy. You can act out the hike by using a common item like floor tiles to represent distance traveled.

❸ Solve the Problem

Reread the problem and act it out.

The fractions have an LCD of 4, so let each floor tile represent $\frac{1}{4}$ of a mile. Use masking tape to mark off 30 tiles for $7\frac{1}{2}$ miles. Walk across 11 tiles to represent $2\frac{3}{4}$ miles hiked and 10 more tiles to represent $2\frac{1}{2}$ miles hiked. Notice that 9 tiles remain, which represent $2\frac{1}{4}$ miles left to hike.

ANSWER You have $2\frac{1}{4}$ miles left to hike.

❹ Look Back

Add your answer to the first two distances.
$2\frac{3}{4} + 2\frac{1}{2} + 2\frac{1}{4} = 7\frac{1}{2}$ ✓

Use the strategy *act it out*. Tell how you acted out the problem to get your answer.

1. **Pets** There are 18 students in your class. Eight students have a cat and five students have a dog. Two students in your class have both a cat and a dog. How many students have neither a cat nor a dog?

2. **Money** You have 8 quarters, 10 dimes, and 7 nickels. You give half of your dimes and 2 nickels to a friend. Then you spend one fourth of your quarters and one nickel. How much money do you have left?

3. **Gifts** You buy a roll of ribbon 20 yards long. The amounts of ribbon you use to decorate a gift and to make a bow are shown below.

 $2\frac{1}{6}$ yards $2\frac{1}{2}$ yards

You decorate 5 gifts. How many bows can you make with the ribbon you have left?

4. **Beads** There are 24 beads in a bowl. Anna takes $\frac{1}{6}$ of the beads. Then John takes two beads. Lena takes $\frac{1}{9}$ of what Anna and John left. Dawn takes $\frac{1}{4}$ of what Lena left, and then Jamal takes five beads. How many beads are left in the bowl?

5. **Lunch Line** You are in a lunch line with 4 students in front of you and 6 students behind you. You let a friend into the line in front of you, who then lets 2 students get in line behind her. Finally, 2 students join the end of the lunch line. How many students are in the lunch line? What is your new position in the lunch line?

Mixed Problem Solving

Use any strategy to solve the problem.

6. **Vacation** On each day of your three day vacation, you can choose one activity. The table below shows your choices. How many different groups of activities can you choose?

Day	Activities
Friday	museum, picnic, bus tour
Saturday	baseball game, bicycling
Sunday	hike, shopping, water park

7. **Fundraising** To raise money for a class trip, you are selling sweatshirts for $19 and T-shirts for $11. You have sold 17 items worth a total of $227. How many of each item have you sold?

8. **Floors** You are choosing a floor covering for the room shown below. It costs $3 per square foot for carpeting. It costs $8 per square foot for a wood floor.

What is the cost to cover the floor with each type of flooring?

Multiplying Fractions

LESSON 5.3

BEFORE	Now	WHY?
You added and subtracted fractions and mixed numbers.	You'll multiply fractions and mixed numbers.	So you can find a moon crater's depth, as in Ex. 19.

Word Watch

Review Words
numerator, p. 707
denominator, p. 707

FLORIDA
Standards and Assessment
- Construct models to represent rational numbers. (MA.A.1.3.3)
- Solve multi-step real-world problems. (MA.A.3.3.3)

In the Real World

Postcards A postcard is $5\frac{1}{2}$ inches long and $3\frac{3}{4}$ inches wide. What is the area of this postcard? In Example 2 on page 231, you will multiply mixed numbers to find the postcard's area.

Multiplication To multiply fractions, you can use the rule below.

Multiplying Fractions

Words The product of two or more fractions is equal to the product of the numerators divided by the product of the denominators.

Numbers $\frac{3}{4} \cdot \frac{5}{8} = \frac{3 \cdot 5}{4 \cdot 8} = \frac{15}{32}$

Algebra $\frac{a}{b} \cdot \frac{c}{d} = \frac{a \cdot c}{b \cdot d}$ $(b, d \neq 0)$

EXAMPLE 1 Multiplying Fractions

 with Review

Remember that the product of two numbers with the same sign is positive. The product of two numbers with different signs is negative.

a. $-\frac{2}{5} \cdot \left(-\frac{2}{3}\right) = \frac{-2 \cdot (-2)}{5 \cdot 3}$ Use rule for multiplying fractions.

$= \frac{4}{15}$ Evaluate numerator and denominator.

b. $-\frac{3}{10} \cdot \frac{5}{6} = \frac{-3 \cdot 5}{10 \cdot 6}$ Use rule for multiplying fractions.

$= \frac{\overset{-1}{-3} \cdot \overset{1}{5}}{\underset{2}{10} \cdot \underset{2}{6}}$ Divide out common factors.

$= -\frac{1}{4}$ Multiply.

Mixed Numbers To multiply mixed numbers, first write them as improper fractions.

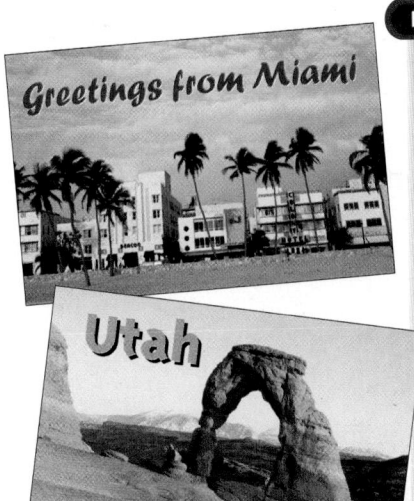
Greetings from Miami

Utah

EXAMPLE 2 Multiplying Mixed Numbers

To find the area of the postcard on page 230, use an area formula.

Area = length • width	Write formula for area of a rectangle.
$= 5\frac{1}{2} \cdot 3\frac{3}{4}$	Substitute values.
$= \frac{11}{2} \cdot \frac{15}{4}$	Write as improper fractions.
$= \frac{11 \cdot 15}{2 \cdot 4}$	Use rule for multiplying fractions.
$= \frac{165}{8}$, or $20\frac{5}{8}$	Multiply.

ANSWER The area of the postcard is $20\frac{5}{8}$ square inches.

Your turn now Find the product. Simplify if possible.

1. $\frac{5}{12} \cdot 15$ 2. $-\frac{5}{12} \cdot \frac{9}{10}$ 3. $1\frac{2}{5} \cdot 3\frac{1}{2}$ 4. $-2\frac{1}{3} \cdot \left(-\frac{3}{4}\right)$

Watch Out!

Be careful when you write a negative mixed number as an improper fraction.

$-4\frac{5}{6} = \frac{-4 \cdot 6 + (-5)}{6}$

$-4\frac{5}{6} \neq \frac{-4 \cdot 6 + 5}{6}$

EXAMPLE 3 Evaluating a Variable Expression

Algebra Evaluate x^2y when $x = -\frac{4}{5}$ and $y = \frac{2}{3}$.

$x^2y = \left(-\frac{4}{5}\right)^2 \cdot \frac{2}{3}$	Substitute $-\frac{4}{5}$ for x and $\frac{2}{3}$ for y.
$= \left(-\frac{4}{5}\right) \cdot \left(-\frac{4}{5}\right) \cdot \frac{2}{3}$	Write $-\frac{4}{5}$ as a factor 2 times.
$= \frac{-4 \cdot (-4) \cdot 2}{5 \cdot 5 \cdot 3}$	Use rule for multiplying fractions.
$= \frac{32}{75}$	Multiply.

Your turn now Evaluate the expression when $x = -\frac{3}{4}$ and $y = \frac{5}{6}$. Simplify if possible.

5. $\frac{1}{2}x$ 6. $2y$ 7. xy 8. xy^2

Getting Ready to Practice

1. **Vocabulary** Copy and complete: The product of two or more fractions is equal to the product of the fractions' ? divided by the product of the fractions' ? .

Find the product. Simplify if possible.

2. $\dfrac{5}{8} \cdot \dfrac{7}{16}$　　　3. $-\dfrac{9}{4} \cdot \dfrac{5}{6}$　　　4. $-4 \cdot \dfrac{3}{5}$　　　5. $5\dfrac{3}{4} \cdot \dfrac{1}{8}$

6. **Snack Mix** A serving of a snack mix is $\dfrac{7}{8}$ cup. You need to take
   15 servings to your friend's party. How many cups of snack mix should you bring? Explain how you can use estimation to check your answer.

Practice and Problem Solving

 with Homework

Example	Exercises
1	7–13, 19
2	14–18
3	20–23

Online Resources
CLASSZONE.COM

· More Examples
· eTutorial Plus

Find the product.

7. $\dfrac{7}{11} \cdot \dfrac{1}{6}$　　　8. $\dfrac{4}{5} \cdot \dfrac{3}{10}$　　　9. $-\dfrac{3}{4} \cdot \left(-\dfrac{2}{9}\right)$　　10. $-\dfrac{5}{6} \cdot \dfrac{5}{12}$

11. $12 \cdot \dfrac{3}{8}$　　　12. $-9 \cdot \dfrac{1}{9}$　　　13. $-5 \cdot \left(-\dfrac{7}{4}\right)$　　14. $-4 \cdot 2\dfrac{9}{16}$

15. $6\dfrac{2}{3} \cdot 4\dfrac{1}{12}$　　16. $-3\dfrac{3}{8} \cdot 7\dfrac{1}{5}$　　17. $-8 \cdot \left(-1\dfrac{4}{5}\right)$　　18. $6\dfrac{3}{16} \cdot \left(-3\dfrac{1}{5}\right)$

19. **Moon Craters** Simple impact craters on the moon are about $\dfrac{1}{5}$ as deep as they are wide. Moltke Crater is a simple impact crater on the moon that is 7 kilometers wide. About how deep is Moltke Crater?

Algebra **Evaluate the expression when $a = \dfrac{5}{8}$ and $b = -\dfrac{7}{6}$.**

20. $-\dfrac{1}{4}a$　　　21. $1\dfrac{1}{2} \cdot b$　　　22. $-8a$　　　23. ab

24. **Critical Thinking** A banana bread recipe uses 3 bananas and $\dfrac{1}{4}$ cup of butter. You need to make a smaller recipe because you have only 2 bananas. How much butter will you need? Explain.

25. **Act It Out** A section of the town beach is shrinking by $1\dfrac{3}{4}$ feet per year. Use the *act it out* strategy to find how much the beach will erode in 20 years. Explain how you used the strategy.

Find the area of the figure.

26.
$\frac{15}{16}$ in.
2 in.

27.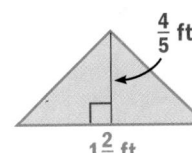
$\frac{4}{5}$ ft
$1\frac{2}{3}$ ft

28.
$3\frac{5}{11}$ m
$3\frac{5}{11}$ m

Find the product.

29. $\frac{1}{4} \cdot \left(-\frac{2}{5}\right) \cdot \frac{9}{10}$

30. $\frac{2}{5} \cdot 1\frac{1}{5} \cdot \left(-4\frac{7}{12}\right)$

31. $-9\frac{2}{7} \cdot 1\frac{2}{5} \cdot \frac{3}{4}$

32. Computers One of the first computers, the ENIAC, performed one operation in $\frac{1}{5000}$ second. How long would it take the ENIAC to perform 11,000 operations?

Evaluate the expression.

33. $-\frac{7}{8} + 5\frac{1}{2} \cdot \frac{11}{15}$

34. $\frac{5}{2} \cdot \left(\frac{8}{9} - \frac{5}{12}\right)$

35. $5 - \left(\frac{1}{3} + \frac{1}{6}\right)^2$

36. Challenge Mosaic tiles sometimes measure $\frac{2}{5}$ inch by $\frac{2}{5}$ inch. What area would 500 tiles cover?

Mosaic tiling

Mixed Review

Multiply or divide. Write your answer as a power. *(Lesson 4.6)*

37. $7^3 \cdot 7^2$

38. $3^5 \cdot 3$

39. $\frac{8^6}{8^4}$

40. $\frac{5^{10}}{5^5}$

Find the sum or difference. *(Lesson 5.2)*

41. $\frac{4}{5} + \frac{7}{10}$

42. $-2\frac{4}{9} + \frac{5}{21}$

43. $\frac{13}{20} - \frac{1}{6}$

44. $-\frac{15}{22} - \frac{9}{16}$

FCAT Practice

45. Multiple Choice You have a photograph that measures $4\frac{3}{4}$ inches by 8 inches. You want to reduce it to $\frac{3}{4}$ of its original area. What is the area of the new photograph?

A. $16\frac{1}{4}$ in.^{2}
B. $28\frac{1}{4}$ in.^{2}
C. $28\frac{1}{2}$ in.^{2}
D. 57 in.^{2}

46. Short Response An ant walks 14 yards in 4 minutes at a constant speed. How far does it walk in 1 minute? Write an equation to represent how far the ant walks in m minutes. How far does it walk in 7 minutes?

Dividing Fractions

LESSON 5.4

BEFORE
You added, subtracted, and multiplied fractions.

▶ Now
You'll divide fractions.

WHY?
So you can find how long your batteries will last, as in Ex. 34.

Word Watch

reciprocal, p. 234
multiplicative inverse, p. 234

FLORIDA
Standards and Assessment

- Know effects of the four basic operations. (MA.A.3.3.1)
- Estimate to predict results and check reasonableness. (MA.A.4.3.1)

Activity You can use models to divide fractions.

1. The model shows that $\frac{3}{4}$ is a part of 6 eight times, so $6 \div \frac{3}{4} = 8$.

$$\frac{3}{4} \quad \frac{3}{4} \quad \frac{3}{4} \quad \frac{3}{4} \quad \frac{3}{4} \quad \frac{3}{4} \quad \frac{3}{4} \quad \frac{3}{4}$$

2. Calculate $6 \cdot \frac{4}{3}$. Compare the values of $6 \div \frac{3}{4}$ and $6 \cdot \frac{4}{3}$.

3. Use the model below to evaluate $4 \div \frac{2}{5}$.

4. Calculate $4 \cdot \frac{5}{2}$. Compare the values of $4 \div \frac{2}{5}$ and $4 \cdot \frac{5}{2}$.

5. What fraction can you multiply by 5 to find the value of $5 \div \frac{2}{3}$?

Reciprocals As the activity suggests, dividing a number by a fraction and multiplying the number by the fraction's *reciprocal* give the same result. Two nonzero numbers are **reciprocals** if their product is 1.

Reciprocals, like $\frac{3}{7}$ and $\frac{7}{3}$, are also called **multiplicative inverses**.

Dividing Fractions

Words To divide by a fraction, multiply by its reciprocal.

Numbers $\frac{3}{10} \div \frac{4}{7} = \frac{3}{10} \cdot \frac{7}{4} = \frac{21}{40}$

Algebra $\frac{a}{b} \div \frac{c}{d} = \frac{a}{b} \cdot \frac{d}{c} \quad (b, c, d \neq 0)$

HELP with Solving

Notice in part (b) of Example 1 that the reciprocal of a negative number is also a negative number.

EXAMPLE 1 Dividing a Fraction by a Fraction

a. $\dfrac{5}{6} \div \dfrac{10}{21} = \dfrac{5}{6} \cdot \dfrac{21}{10}$

$\quad = \dfrac{\cancel{5} \cdot \cancel{21}^{7}}{\cancel{6} \cdot \cancel{10}_{2}}$

$\quad = \dfrac{7}{4}$, or $1\dfrac{3}{4}$

b. $\dfrac{9}{14} \div \dfrac{-2}{7} = \dfrac{9}{14} \cdot \dfrac{7}{-2}$

$\quad = \dfrac{9 \cdot \cancel{7}^{1}}{\cancel{14}_{2} \cdot (-2)}$

$\quad = \dfrac{9}{-4}$, or $-2\dfrac{1}{4}$

EXAMPLE 2 Dividing a Fraction by a Whole Number

$\dfrac{6}{13} \div 3 = \dfrac{6}{13} \cdot \dfrac{1}{3}$ $3 \cdot \dfrac{1}{3} = 1$, so the reciprocal of 3 is $\dfrac{1}{3}$.

$\quad = \dfrac{\cancel{6}^{2} \cdot 1}{13 \cdot \cancel{3}_{1}}$ Multiply fractions. Divide out common factor.

$\quad = \dfrac{2}{13}$ Multiply.

Your turn now   Find the quotient. Simplify if possible.

1. $\dfrac{5}{8} \div \left(-\dfrac{7}{10}\right)$ **2.** $\dfrac{2}{15} \div \dfrac{8}{9}$ **3.** $-\dfrac{3}{4} \div \dfrac{-7}{12}$ **4.** $\dfrac{6}{7} \div 2$

EXAMPLE 3 Dividing Mixed Numbers

$6\dfrac{1}{3} \div \left(-2\dfrac{5}{6}\right) = \dfrac{19}{3} \div \left(-\dfrac{17}{6}\right)$ Write $6\dfrac{1}{3}$ and $-2\dfrac{5}{6}$ as improper fractions.

$\quad = \dfrac{19}{3} \cdot \left(-\dfrac{6}{17}\right)$ Multiply by $-\dfrac{6}{17}$, the reciprocal of $-\dfrac{17}{6}$.

$\quad = \dfrac{19 \cdot (\cancel{-6})^{-2}}{\cancel{3}_{1} \cdot 17}$ Multiply. Divide out common factor.

$\quad = -\dfrac{38}{17}$, or $-2\dfrac{4}{17}$ Multiply.

✓**Check** Use estimation to check your answer. Because $6 \div (-3)$ is equal to -2, you know that $-2\dfrac{4}{17}$ is a reasonable answer.

Your turn now   Find the quotient. Simplify if possible.

5. $6\dfrac{2}{7} \div 4$ **6.** $-12\dfrac{1}{4} \div 7$ **7.** $7\dfrac{1}{3} \div 1\dfrac{4}{7}$ **8.** $15\dfrac{3}{4} \div \left(-2\dfrac{5}{8}\right)$

EXAMPLE 4 **Solving an Equation with a Fraction**

Photography You use 16 of the 24 pictures of a roll of film on your first day of vacation. At this rate, how long will 4 rolls of film last?

Solution

Write a verbal model to describe the problem. Let d = the number of days.

Number of rolls of film	=	Fraction of roll of film used each day	·	Number of days

$$4 = \frac{16}{24}d \qquad \text{Write an algebraic model.}$$

$$4 \cdot \frac{24}{16} = \frac{24}{16} \cdot \frac{16}{24}d \qquad \text{The multiplicative inverse of } \frac{16}{24} \text{ is } \frac{24}{16}.$$

$$\frac{\overset{1}{\cancel{4}}}{1} \cdot \frac{24}{\underset{4}{\cancel{16}}} = d \qquad \text{Divide out common factor.}$$

$$6 = d \qquad \text{Divide.}$$

ANSWER Four rolls will last six days.

5.4 Exercises

More Practice, p. 731

INTERNET
eWorkbook Plus
CLASSZONE.COM

Getting Ready to Practice

1. **Vocabulary** What is the multiplicative inverse of a number?

2. Write the reciprocal of each of the numbers: $\frac{1}{2}, \frac{4}{7}, -8, 1\frac{1}{2}$.

Find the quotient. Simplify if possible.

3. $\frac{3}{4} \div \frac{1}{8}$

4. $\frac{5}{6} \div \left(-\frac{1}{3}\right)$

5. $\frac{11}{12} \div \frac{11}{16}$

6. $-\frac{5}{6} \div (-2)$

7. $\frac{2}{3} \div 3$

8. $2\frac{1}{2} \div \frac{-9}{14}$

9. $2\frac{2}{3} \div \left(-1\frac{3}{5}\right)$

10. $4\frac{1}{8} \div 1\frac{5}{6}$

11. **Guided Problem Solving** How many hamburgers can you make from 5 pounds of hamburger if you use $\frac{1}{4}$ pound of meat per hamburger?

   ① Write a verbal model.

   ② Substitute the given values into the model.

   ③ Solve the equation.

Practice and Problem Solving

HELP with **Homework**

Example	Exercises
1	12–15, 32
2	16–19, 28–31
3	20–27
4	33–34

Online Resources
CLASSZONE.COM

· More Examples
· eTutorial Plus

Find the quotient.

12. $\frac{4}{9} \div \frac{4}{7}$ **13.** $-\frac{3}{8} \div \frac{7}{12}$ **14.** $\frac{9}{14} \div \left(-\frac{3}{26}\right)$ **15.** $-\frac{21}{22} \div \frac{-7}{11}$

16. $\frac{8}{11} \div 4$ **17.** $\frac{9}{10} \div (-12)$ **18.** $-\frac{5}{12} \div 10$ **19.** $\frac{63}{8} \div (-9)$

Find the quotient.

20. $5\frac{1}{4} \div 2\frac{1}{3}$ **21.** $7\frac{7}{8} \div \left(-2\frac{1}{4}\right)$ **22.** $12\frac{1}{7} \div 5\frac{5}{6}$ **23.** $-22\frac{2}{3} \div 3\frac{1}{5}$

24. $-9\frac{3}{5} \div (-8)$ **25.** $1\frac{5}{7} \div (-6)$ **26.** $8\frac{4}{13} \div 6\frac{3}{4}$ **27.** $9\frac{9}{14} \div 4\frac{1}{6}$

28. Writing Are the numbers $\frac{1}{9}$ and -9 reciprocals? Explain.

Use mental math to find the quotient.

29. $\frac{1}{2} \div 3$ **30.** $4 \div \frac{1}{2}$ **31.** $1 \div \frac{4}{7}$ **32.** $\frac{2}{3} \div \frac{3}{2}$

33. Dog Food Your dog Bodie eats about $\frac{3}{5}$ of a pound of dog food per day. How long will a five pound bag of dog food last?

34. CD Player Your CD player runs for about $6\frac{1}{2}$ hours on new batteries. If the average length of the CDs in your collection is about $\frac{5}{6}$ hour, how many CDs can you expect to listen to using one new set of batteries?

35. Critical Thinking Juan says, "To divide a fraction by another fraction, rewrite the fractions with common denominators. Then use the formula $\frac{a}{c} \div \frac{b}{c} = \frac{a}{b}$." Does Juan's method work? Explain.

Algebra **Solve the equation.**

36. $\frac{3}{4}a = 15$ **37.** $\frac{7}{10}b = 28$ **38.** $-\frac{9}{17}r = 3$ **39.** $-11 = -9\frac{1}{6}h$

40. Wages Haley earns \$180 working three days a week. On each of those days she works $7\frac{1}{2}$ hours. How much does Haley earn per hour?

41. Survey Two of every five people surveyed, or 350 people, said they prefer spring to fall. How many people were surveyed? Explain how you got your answer.

Algebra **Evaluate the expression when $a = 4$ and $b = 9$.**

42. $\frac{a}{5} \div \frac{8}{150}$ **43.** $\frac{3}{4}a \div \frac{5b}{6}$ **44.** $-\frac{18}{a} \div \frac{b}{16}$ **45.** $\frac{-4}{21} \div \frac{2a}{-b}$

46. Challenge You are creating a board game. You want to cut square game pieces that measure $1\frac{1}{4}$ inches on each side from a piece of paper that measures $8\frac{1}{2}$ inches by 11 inches. How many game pieces can you cut from the paper? Explain.

Mixed Review

Simplify the variable expression. *(Lesson 4.3)*

47. $\dfrac{9x^2}{27x}$ **48.** $\dfrac{24y^4}{15y^2}$ **49.** $\dfrac{14x^3y}{18xy^3}$ **50.** $\dfrac{54yz^2}{81xz^2}$

Basic Skills **Write the improper fraction as a mixed number.**

51. $\dfrac{17}{9}$ **52.** $\dfrac{16}{5}$ **53.** $\dfrac{28}{3}$ **54.** $\dfrac{120}{7}$

FCAT Practice

55. Multiple Choice When $x = -\dfrac{2}{5}$ and $y = \dfrac{3}{10}$, $y \div x = \underline{\ ?\ }$

A. $-1\dfrac{1}{3}$ **B.** $-\dfrac{3}{4}$ **C.** $\dfrac{3}{4}$ **D.** $\dfrac{4}{3}$

56. Multiple Choice An inch is about $\dfrac{5}{2}$ of a centimeter. About how many inches long is $4\dfrac{1}{10}$ centimeters?

F. $1\dfrac{16}{25}$ in.   **G.** $1\dfrac{4}{5}$ in.   **H.** $4\dfrac{1}{5}$ in.   **I.** $8\dfrac{1}{5}$ in.

Who's in First?

The number that makes each equation true represents the place in which the runner finished the race. Find the order in which the runners finished.

Martin $\quad 1\dfrac{2}{?} \div \dfrac{1}{6} = 10$ Harriet $\quad \dfrac{?}{} \div \dfrac{2}{11} = 22$

Maya $\quad \dfrac{5}{7} \div \dfrac{?}{3} = \dfrac{15}{14}$ Cornell $\quad \dfrac{?}{5} \div \dfrac{7}{9} = \dfrac{9}{35}$

FLORIDA: Standards and Assessment
Know effects of the four basic operations. (MA.A.3.3.1)

Operations with Fractions

GOAL Use a fraction calculator to evaluate expressions with fractions.

You can use a calculator to evaluate expressions with fractions. First, set your calculator to display the answers as fractions or mixed numbers in simplest form.

Press `2nd` [FracMode]. Select $A \sqcup b/c$ and press `=`
to set the calculator to mixed number mode.

Press `2nd` [FracMode]. Select *Auto* and press `=`
to set the calculator to automatically simplify fractions.

Example **Use a calculator to evaluate the expression.**

		Keystrokes	Display	Answer
a.	$\frac{2}{3} - 4\frac{6}{7}$	`2` `/` `3` `-` `4` `UNIT` `6` `/` `7` `=`	$-4\sqcup4/21$	$-4\frac{4}{21}$
b.	$-\frac{5}{17} \cdot \left(-\frac{8}{35}\right)$	`(-)` `5` `/` `17` `×` `(-)` `8` `/` `35` `=`	$8/119$	$\frac{8}{119}$
c.	$\frac{3}{10} \div \left(-1\frac{4}{5}\right)$	`3` `/` `10` `÷` `(-)` `1` `UNIT` `4` `/` `5` `=`	$-1/6$	$-\frac{1}{6}$

Your turn now **Use a calculator to evaluate the expression.**

1. $\frac{5}{11} + \frac{2}{5}$

2. $3\frac{1}{4} + \left(-\frac{6}{7}\right)$

3. $7\frac{1}{2} - 6\frac{5}{6}$

4. $\frac{2}{5} - \frac{2}{3}$

5. $\frac{7}{9} \cdot 1\frac{1}{3}$

6. $\frac{2}{5} \cdot \left(-\frac{3}{4}\right)$

7. $9\frac{4}{5} \div \frac{7}{8}$

8. $-10\frac{2}{13} \div \left(-3\frac{1}{3}\right)$

9. Car Care Rosa's car needs $4\frac{1}{4}$ quarts of oil to run properly.
She notices her car has only three fourths of the amount of oil that it needs. How much oil should she add for her car to run properly?

LESSONS 5.1 TO 5.4

Notebook Review

Review the vocabulary definitions in your notebook.

Copy the review examples in your notebook. Then complete the exercises.

Check Your Definitions

reciprocal, p. 234   multiplicative inverse, p. 234

Use Your Vocabulary

1. What is the product of a number and its reciprocal?

5.1–5.2 Can you add and subtract fractions?

 EXAMPLES

a. $\frac{2}{9} + 3\frac{4}{9} = 3 + \left(\frac{2}{9} + \frac{4}{9}\right)$

$= 3\frac{6}{9}$

$= 3\frac{2}{3}$

b. $\frac{9}{14} - \frac{6}{7} = \frac{9}{14} - \frac{12}{14}$

$= \frac{9-12}{14}$

$= -\frac{3}{14}$

☑ **Find the sum or difference.**

2. $-\frac{5}{12} + \frac{11}{12}$ **3.** $\frac{15}{16} - 2\frac{1}{16}$ **4.** $6\frac{1}{4} - 4\frac{3}{8}$ **5.** $\frac{2x}{3} + \frac{4x}{5}$

5.3 Can you multiply fractions and mixed numbers?

 EXAMPLES

a. $-\frac{5}{8} \cdot \frac{3}{10} = -\frac{5 \cdot 3}{8 \cdot 10}$

$= -\frac{\overset{1}{\cancel{5}} \cdot 3}{8 \cdot \cancel{10}}{}_{2}$

$= -\frac{3}{16}$

b. $3\frac{2}{3} \cdot \frac{4}{9} = \frac{11}{3} \cdot \frac{4}{9}$

$= \frac{11 \cdot 4}{3 \cdot 9}$

$= \frac{44}{27}$, or $1\frac{17}{27}$

☑ **Find the product.**

6. $-\frac{6}{7} \cdot \left(-\frac{5}{12}\right)$ **7.** $2\frac{1}{2} \cdot \frac{4}{5}$ **8.** $-3 \cdot 2\frac{5}{6}$ **9.** $-3\frac{1}{3} \cdot \left(-3\frac{1}{4}\right)$

5.4 Can you divide fractions and mixed numbers?

 EXAMPLES

a. $\dfrac{1}{3} \div \dfrac{5}{6} = \dfrac{1}{3} \cdot \dfrac{6}{5}$

$= \dfrac{1 \cdot \overset{2}{\cancel{6}}}{\underset{1}{\cancel{3}} \cdot 5}$

$= \dfrac{2}{5}$

b. $2\dfrac{1}{5} \div 2\dfrac{3}{4} = \dfrac{11}{5} \div \dfrac{11}{4}$

$= \dfrac{11}{5} \cdot \dfrac{4}{11}$

$= \dfrac{\overset{1}{\cancel{11}} \cdot 4}{5 \cdot \underset{1}{\cancel{11}}} = \dfrac{4}{5}$

☑ **Divide.**   **10.** $\dfrac{3}{4} \div \dfrac{1}{12}$ **11.** $-\dfrac{5}{9} \div \dfrac{7}{18}$ **12.** $-2\dfrac{1}{4} \div \left(-1\dfrac{2}{7}\right)$

Stop *and* **Think**   about Lessons 5.1–5.4

13. Writing How can you check your answer to a division problem involving fractions? Use an example to explain.

14. Critical Thinking You divide a positive number by a fraction greater than 0 and less than 1. Will the result be *less than*, *equal to*, or *greater than* the original number? Explain.

Review Quiz 1

Find the sum or difference.

1. $1\dfrac{5}{8} - \dfrac{7}{8}$ **2.** $\dfrac{4}{9} + 3\dfrac{5}{9}$ **3.** $\dfrac{x}{12} + \dfrac{5x}{12}$ **4.** $\dfrac{4}{9} - \dfrac{8}{9} + \dfrac{5}{9}$

5. $\dfrac{2}{3} + \dfrac{9}{6}$ **6.** $5\dfrac{3}{4} - 2\dfrac{1}{3}$ **7.** $\dfrac{5}{6} + 2\dfrac{1}{8}$ **8.** $\dfrac{3}{10} + 4\dfrac{2}{5} - 1\dfrac{1}{2}$

9. Recipe A recipe uses $4\dfrac{2}{3}$ cups of flour. Another recipe uses $4\dfrac{1}{4}$ cups. If you have 9 cups of flour, can you make both recipes? Explain.

Find the product or quotient.

10. $\dfrac{7}{12} \cdot \dfrac{8}{21}$ **11.** $-\dfrac{11}{12} \cdot \left(-\dfrac{3}{10}\right)$ **12.** $-\dfrac{14}{5} \cdot 2\dfrac{6}{7}$ **13.** $1\dfrac{1}{8} \cdot (-3)$

14. $\dfrac{1}{2} \div \dfrac{5}{6}$ **15.** $\dfrac{4}{9} \div 8$ **16.** $-\dfrac{4}{5} \div \dfrac{3}{2}$ **17.** $-1\dfrac{3}{4} \div \left(-\dfrac{7}{12}\right)$

18. Hair Growth An average human hair grows about $\dfrac{1}{2}$ inch per month. How much does a human hair grow in $3\dfrac{1}{2}$ months?

Fractions and Decimals

BEFORE	▶ Now	WHY?
You divided whole numbers.	You'll write fractions as decimals and decimals as fractions.	So you can analyze breakfast food popularity, as in Exs. 46–48.

 Word Watch

rational number, p. 242
terminating decimal, p. 242
repeating decimal, p. 242

FLORIDA
Standards and Assessment

• Know relationships among fractions and decimals given a real-world context. (MA.A.1.3.4)

• Compare and order fractions and decimals. (MA.A.1.3.2)

A **rational number** is a number that can be written as a quotient $\frac{a}{b}$, where a and b are integers and $b \neq 0$. The diagram shows how rational numbers, integers, and whole numbers are related.

Integers include whole numbers. Rational numbers include integers.

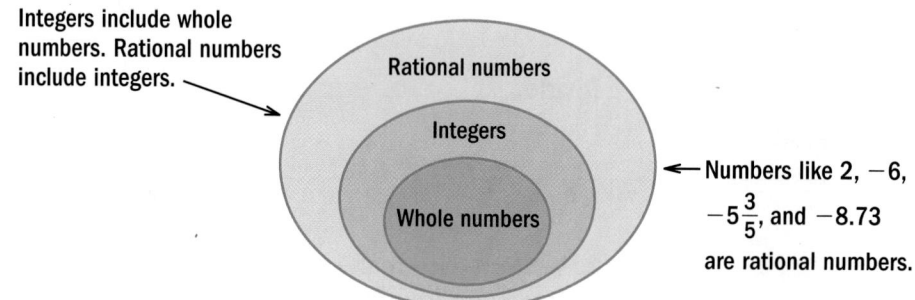

Rational numbers
Integers
Whole numbers

◀— Numbers like 2, −6, $-5\frac{3}{5}$, and −8.73 are rational numbers.

To write any rational number $\frac{a}{b}$ as a decimal, divide a by b. If the quotient has a remainder of zero, the result is a **terminating decimal**. If the quotient has a digit or group of digits that repeats without end, the result is a **repeating decimal**.

EXAMPLE 1 **Writing Fractions as Decimals**

To write a fraction as a decimal, divide the numerator by the denominator.

a.
$$\frac{5}{11} = 11\overline{)\begin{array}{l} 0.4545\ldots \\ 5.0000\ldots \end{array}}$$

$$\begin{array}{r} 44 \\ \hline 60 \\ 55 \\ \hline 50 \\ 44 \\ \hline 60 \\ 55 \\ \hline \end{array}$$

b.
$$\frac{7}{20} = 20\overline{)\begin{array}{l} 0.35 \\ 7.00 \end{array}}$$

$$\begin{array}{r} 60 \\ \hline 100 \\ 100 \\ \hline 0 \end{array}$$

ANSWER The quotient 0.4545... is a repeating decimal. To indicate this, place a bar over the repeating digits: $\frac{5}{11} = 0.\overline{45}$.

ANSWER The remainder is zero, so $\frac{7}{20} = 0.35$, a terminating decimal.

Indigo bunting

EXAMPLE **2** **Ordering Rational Numbers**

Biology The table lists the lengths of five finches. Order the finches from shortest to longest.

Finch Species	Length (inches)
House finch	$5\frac{5}{8}$
Painted bunting	5.25
Lazuli bunting	$5\frac{7}{16}$
Purple finch	$5\frac{3}{4}$
Indigo bunting	5.5

Solution

Write mixed numbers as decimals.

$$5\frac{5}{8} = 5.625 \qquad 5\frac{7}{16} = 5.4375$$

$$5\frac{3}{4} = 5.75$$

Then graph all the finches' lengths on a number line.

ANSWER From shortest to longest: painted bunting, lazuli bunting, indigo bunting, house finch, purple finch.

Your turn now **Order the numbers from least to greatest.**

1. $0.51, \frac{3}{5}, \frac{11}{20}, \frac{2}{3}, 0.62$

2. $-1\frac{1}{8}, -1\frac{3}{7}, -1.1, -1.43, -1\frac{4}{15}$

Terminating Decimals To write a terminating decimal as a fraction or mixed number, use the place value of the decimal's last digit to determine the denominator. For example, you can write 0.37 as $\frac{37}{100}$, or thirty-seven hundredths, because 7 is in the hundredths' place.

EXAMPLE **3** **Writing Terminating Decimals as Fractions**

Write the decimal as a fraction or mixed number.

a. 0.4

b. -1.905

Solution

a. $0.4 = \frac{4}{10}$ 4 is in the tenths' place.

$\quad = \frac{2}{5}$

b. $-1.905 = -1\frac{905}{1000}$ 5 is in the thousandths' place.

$\quad = -1\frac{\cancel{905}^{181}}{\cancel{1000}_{200}}$

$\quad = -1\frac{181}{200}$

Repeating Decimals To write a repeating decimal as a fraction or mixed number, form two equivalent equations by multiplying by a power of 10. Then subtract the equations.

HELP with Notetaking

You may wish to copy examples into your notebook that show writing repeating decimals as fractions. Include examples with one, two, and three repeating digits.

EXAMPLE 4 Writing Repeating Decimals as Fractions

To write $0.\overline{48}$ as a fraction, let $x = 0.\overline{48}$, or 0.484848 . . . .

(1) The number has 2 repeating digits, so multiply by 100.
Let $100x = 48.\overline{48}$, or 48.484848 . . . .

(2) Then subtract x from $100x$.

$$\begin{array}{r} 100x = 48.484848\ldots \\ -\quad x = 0.484848\ldots \\ \hline 99x = 48.000000\ldots \end{array}$$

(3) Solve for x. Simplify.

$$x = \frac{48}{99}, \text{ or } \frac{16}{33}$$

ANSWER The decimal $0.\overline{48}$ is equivalent to the fraction $\frac{16}{33}$.

Your turn now Write the decimal as a fraction or mixed number.

3. 0.3   **4.** 0.62   **5.** −2.45   **6.** −1.24

7. $-0.\overline{7}$ **8.** $-10.\overline{1}$ **9.** $0.\overline{24}$ **10.** $0.8\overline{3}$

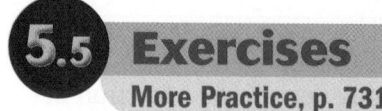

5.5 Exercises

More Practice, p. 731

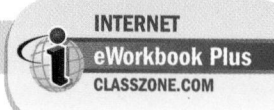

INTERNET
eWorkbook Plus
CLASSZONE.COM

Getting Ready to Practice

Vocabulary Tell whether the number is included in each of the following number groups: *rational number, integer, whole number.*

1. 0   **2.** 0.55   **3.** −14   **4.** $0.\overline{3}$

Write the fraction or mixed number as a decimal.

5. $\frac{4}{5}$ **6.** $2\frac{1}{4}$ **7.** $\frac{1}{3}$ **8.** $1\frac{5}{8}$

Write the decimal as a fraction or mixed number.

9. 0.6   **10.** −1.02   **11.** $0.\overline{8}$ **12.** $0.\overline{53}$

13. Caterpillars Write the following lengths of caterpillars in order from least to greatest: $1\frac{7}{8}$ inches, 1.8 inches, $2\frac{1}{9}$ inches, 2.1 inches.

Practice and Problem Solving

HELP with Homework

Example	Exercises
1	14–25, 44–45
2	42, 43, 46
3	26–33
4	34–41

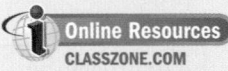

Online Resources
CLASSZONE.COM

· More Examples
· eTutorial Plus

Write the fraction or mixed number as a decimal.

14. $\frac{3}{4}$ **15.** $-\frac{1}{9}$ **16.** $-\frac{12}{25}$ **17.** $\frac{7}{12}$

18. $-\frac{4}{25}$ **19.** $\frac{27}{50}$ **20.** $3\frac{11}{16}$ **21.** $-\frac{33}{80}$

22. $\frac{8}{15}$ **23.** $-14\frac{7}{11}$ **24.** $-\frac{14}{33}$ **25.** $\frac{27}{44}$

Write the decimal as a fraction or mixed number.

26. -0.48 **27.** -0.56 **28.** 1.31 **29.** 2.79

30. 0.365 **31.** 7.253 **32.** -0.0012 **33.** -5.0032

34. $0.\overline{2}$ **35.** $0.\overline{8}$ **36.** $-0.1\overline{5}$ **37.** $0.\overline{15}$

38. $0.6\overline{3}$ **39.** $0.0\overline{42}$ **40.** $-0.\overline{243}$ **41.** $20.2\overline{07}$

Order the numbers from least to greatest.

42. $-\frac{4}{5}, -\frac{3}{10}, -\frac{3}{8}, -0.2, -0.4$ **43.** $9\frac{3}{4}, 9.74, 9\frac{5}{7}, 9.72, 9\frac{9}{13}$

44. Stock Listings The New York Stock Exchange once used fractions to list the values of its stocks. It switched to decimals in 2001. Write the following stock prices as decimals rounded to the nearest cent.

$$\$5\frac{1}{4}, \ \$44\frac{1}{2}, \ \$53\frac{3}{8}, \ \$17\frac{7}{16}$$

45. Look for a Pattern Write the fractions $\frac{1}{11}, \frac{2}{11}$, and $\frac{3}{11}$ as decimals.

Use your results to predict the decimal forms of $\frac{4}{11}$ and $\frac{5}{11}$.

Extended Problem Solving **In Exercises 46–48, use the table below. It tells the fraction of students in a survey that named each breakfast food as their favorite.**

Breakfast food	Bagels	Bacon	Eggs	Cereal	Pancakes
Fraction of students	$\frac{1}{8}$	$\frac{1}{12}$	$\frac{3}{16}$	$\frac{1}{4}$	$\frac{3}{25}$

46. Order Write each fraction as a decimal and order the foods from most popular to least popular.

47. Compare How many more students picked the most popular food than the least popular food if 1200 students responded to the survey?

48. Analyze How many of the 1200 students did not choose any of the foods shown?

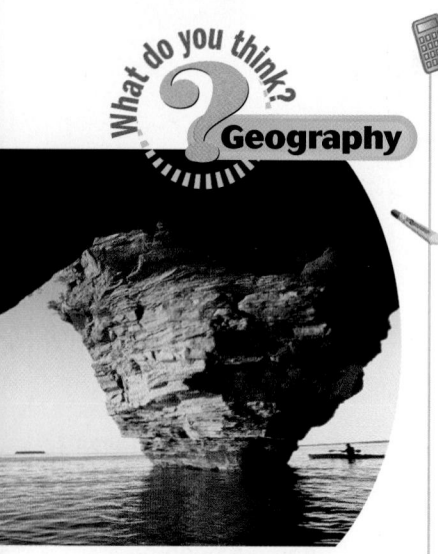
49. Area The total area of the United States is about 3,718,000 square miles. The portion of this area that is covered by water is $\frac{182,000}{3,718,000}$. Express this fraction as a decimal rounded to three places. About what fraction of the area of the United States is covered by water?

50. Writing Jim says, "Write a mixed number as a decimal by writing it as an improper fraction, and then dividing." Estela says, "Just convert the fraction part of a mixed number to a decimal, and then you can add that to the whole number part." Do both methods work? Explain why or why not.

51. Challenge In the following expressions, $x > 0$. Order the expressions from least to greatest: $x, \frac{x}{5}, \frac{x}{3}, \frac{x}{7}, \frac{x}{8}, \frac{x}{6}, \frac{x}{2}, \frac{x}{4}$.

52. Critical Thinking Find a rational number between $\frac{1}{6}$ and $\frac{2}{9}$. Explain your reasoning.

■ **Lake Superior**

Lake Superior has a surface area of about 32,000 square miles. About what fraction of the 182,000 square miles of U.S. water surface area is this? Write this fraction as a decimal.

Mixed Review

Solve the equation using mental math. *(Lesson 1.5)*

53. $s - 7 = 10$ **54.** $4d = 24$ **55.** $5 + t = 18$

Choose a Strategy **Use a strategy from the list to solve the following problem. Explain your choice of strategy.**

56. You are racing with Al, Sue, and Kim. In how many orders can you and your friends finish the race?

> Problem Solving Strategies
> ▪ Guess, Check, and Revise
> ▪ Make a List
> ▪ Draw a Diagram

Basic Skills **Estimate the sum or difference.**

57. $129 + 42$ **58.** $457 + 301$ **59.** $91 - 28$ **60.** $217 - 188$

FCAT Practice (FCAT)

61. Multiple Choice Which list is in order from least to greatest?

A. $\frac{2}{9}, 0.22, -0.23, \frac{3}{13}$ **B.** $-0.23, \frac{2}{9}, \frac{3}{13}, 0.22$

C. $-0.23, 0.22, \frac{2}{9}, \frac{3}{13}$ **D.** $0.22, \frac{2}{9}, -0.23, \frac{3}{13}$

62. Multiple Choice In a survey, $\frac{12}{20}$ of the people asked prefer coffee to tea. What is another way to express this fraction?

F. 0.12 **G.** 0.24 **H.** 0.48 **I.** 0.6

Adding and Subtracting Decimals

BEFORE	▶ Now	WHY?
You added and subtracted fractions.	You'll add and subtract decimals.	So you can compare snowfall amounts, as in Ex. 34.

In the Real World

Word Watch

front-end estimation, p. 248

FLORIDA
Standards and Assessment

• Know effects of the four basic operations. (MA.A.3.3.1)

• Choose an appropriate estimation technique. (MA.A.4.3.1)

Dancing The table shows the amounts of money (in billions of dollars) that people in the United States spent on dance studios, schools, and halls. How much was spent in 1995 and 1996? How much more was spent in 1998 than in 1997?

Money Spent on Dancing	
Year	Dollars (billions)
1994	0.906
1995	0.947
1996	1.046
1997	1.08
1998	1.138

You can use a vertical format to add or subtract decimals. Begin by lining up the decimal points. Then add or subtract as with whole numbers. Be sure to include the decimal point in your answer.

EXAMPLE 1 Adding and Subtracting Decimals

a. To find how many billions of dollars were spent in 1995 and 1996, add the values from the table for 1995 and 1996.

$$\begin{array}{r} 0.947 \\ +\ 1.046 \\ \hline 1.993 \end{array}$$

ANSWER In 1995 and 1996, 1.993 billion dollars was spent.

b. To find how much more was spent in 1998 than in 1997, subtract the value for 1997 from the value for 1998.

$$\begin{array}{r} 1.138 \\ -\ 1.080 \\ \hline 0.058 \end{array}$$

Use a zero as a placeholder.

ANSWER In 1998, 0.058 billion dollars more was spent than in 1997.

Your turn now **Find the sum or difference.**

1. $-12.5 + (-4.55)$ **2.** $8.93 + 0.367$ **3.** $7.624 + (-0.05)$

4. $8.91 - 2.745$ **5.** $-5.3 - 11.49$ **6.** $5.376 - (-0.8)$

EXAMPLE 2 Solving Equations with Decimals

a.

$$y - 1.537 = 6.48$$ Original equation

$$y - 1.537 + \mathbf{1.537} = 6.48 + \mathbf{1.537}$$ Add 1.537 to each side.

$$y = 8.017$$ Simplify.

b.

$$x + (-0.34) = 4.27$$ Original equation

$$x + (-0.34) + \mathbf{0.34} = 4.27 + \mathbf{0.34}$$ Add 0.34 to each side to undo adding −0.34.

$$x = 4.61$$ Simplify.

Estimating You can estimate sums using **front-end estimation** . Add the front-end digits to get a low estimate. Then use the remaining digits to adjust the sum to a closer estimate.

EXAMPLE 3 Using Front-End Estimation

Theater You want to estimate the cost of supplies for a play. Is the cost of the items shown (excluding tax) more or less than your $50 budget?

Theater Supplies	
cowboy hat	$18.97
cotton fabric	$9.49
rope	$3.49
safety pins	$2.19
picnic basket	$16.77

Solution

Use front-end estimation.

(1 Add the **front-end digits**: the dollars.

$18.97
$9.49
$3.49
$2.19
$16.77
$48

(2 Estimate the sum of the **remaining digits**: the cents.

$18.97 —— $1
$9.49
$3.49 —— $1
$2.19
$16.77 —— $1
$3

(3 Add your results.

$48
+ $3
$51

ANSWER The cost of the items is more than your $50 budget.

Your turn now Solve the equation.

7. $x + 1.38 = 2.55$ **8.** $z - 5.3 = 16.29$ **9.** $y - (-0.83) = 0.48$

10. Use front-end estimation to estimate the sum $1.95 + $7.49 + $3.50.

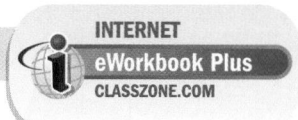

Getting Ready to Practice

1. **Vocabulary** Copy and complete: You can get a low estimate of $13.56 + 11.42 + 25.94$ by adding the front-end digits _?_, _?_, and _?_.

2. **Find the Error** Describe and correct the error in the solution.

$$
\begin{array}{r}
\times\ \ 10.43 \\
+\ 7.521 \\
\hline
8.564
\end{array}
$$

Find the sum or difference.

3. $1.35 + 6.02$ 4. $14.1 - 3.662$

Solve the equation.

5. $x + 2.9 = 5.3$ 6. $y - 4.15 = -4.26$ 7. $z - (-7.7) = 13.31$

Use front-end estimation to estimate the sum.

8. $2.32 + 6.69 + 8.50 + 4.46$ 9. $10.23 + 6.98 + 9.05 + 5.80$

10. **Sales Tax** Your purchase costs $9.87 plus sales tax of $.49. What is the total amount you pay?

Practice and Problem Solving

HELP with Homework

Example	Exercises
1	11-25, 34, 36
2	26-31
3	32-33, 35

Online Resources
CLASSZONE.COM

· More Examples
· eTutorial Plus

Find the sum or difference.

11. $30.193 + 7.91$ 12. $2.507 + 0.586$ 13. $-6.08 + 2.661$

14. $-0.37 + (-1.8)$ 15. $6.8 + (-1.812)$ 16. $-12.09 + 1.20$

17. $3.28 + (-4.91)$ 18. $1.46 + (-1.564)$ 19. $1.57 - 9.28$

20. $68.79 - 9.18$ 21. $15.7 - (-6.4)$ 22. $-0.99 - 0.304$

23. $25.885 - 6.9$ 24. $29.1 - (-3.05)$ 25. $-4.22 - 0.807$

Algebra Solve the equation.

26. $y + 1.5 = 37$ 27. $-2.8 + x = 4.51$ 28. $10.4 = 12.46 + z$

29. $7.81 = 7.98 + y$ 30. $z + (-3.19) = 5.83$ 31. $x - 0.013 = -6.36$

Use front-end estimation to estimate the sum.

32. $5.62 + 4.89 + 3.44 + 9.98$ 33. $23.70 + 16.12 + 5.96 + 14.18$

34. **Snowfall** Chicago's average snowfall in December is 11.2 inches. In 2001, only 1.6 inches fell in December. In inches, how much below average was this?

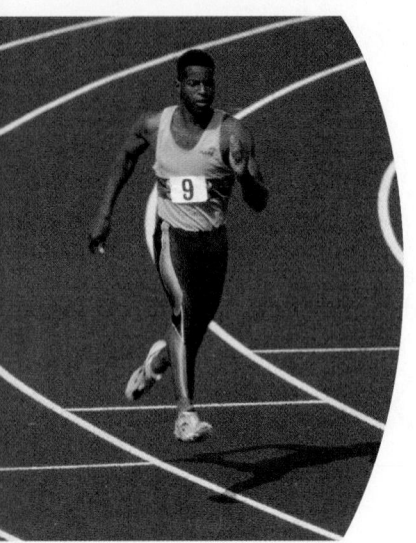

35. Critical Thinking The number 29.32 can be written as the sum $20 + 9 + 0.3 + 0.02$. Write 345.692 as a sum in this form.

36. Track You run 400 meters in 58.01 seconds. What is the difference of your time and the school record of 55.49 seconds?

Geometry **Find the perimeter of the figure.**

37.

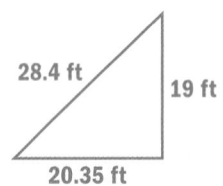

28.4 ft
19 ft
20.35 ft

38.

3.05 cm
5.8 cm   5.8 cm
6.25 cm

39.

3.2 m   7.41 m
3.2 m   3.2 m
9.41 m

40. Banking Use the bank record for the month of January. The beginning balance was $83.47. Estimate the balance at the end of the month. Then find the exact balance.

Date	Transaction	Deposit	Withdrawal
1/02	deposit	$50	
1/10	groceries		$75.35
1/16	bookstore		$12.95
1/22	deposit	$112.81	
1/29	video rentals		$13.08
1/31	computer game		$21.98

Challenge **Find the sum or difference. Write your answer in decimal form.**

41. $6.28 + \dfrac{5}{2}$ **42.** $\dfrac{3}{8} + 4.6$ **43.** $12.853 - \dfrac{3}{4}$ **44.** $\dfrac{9}{20} - 0.35$

Mixed Review

Simplify the expression using only positive exponents. *(Lesson 4.7)*

45. -12^0 **46.** $3^{-2} \cdot 3^5$ **47.** $\dfrac{b^{-4}}{b^{10}}$ **48.** $\dfrac{32m^{-8}}{8m^2}$

Find the product or quotient. Simplify if possible. *(Lessons 5.3, 5.4)*

49. $-\dfrac{8}{9} \cdot \left(\dfrac{-5}{7}\right)$ **50.** $5\dfrac{3}{7} \cdot \dfrac{21}{22}$ **51.** $-5 \div \left(\dfrac{-2}{3}\right)$ **52.** $6\dfrac{5}{12} \div 2\dfrac{3}{4}$

FCAT Practice   FCAT

53. Multiple Choice When adding two negative decimals that are between 0 and –1, the sum is always ___?___ .

   A. less than -1 **B.** negative   **C.** positive   **D.** more than -1

54. Short Response Plot the following points in the coordinate plane. Then connect the points to form a rectangle and find its perimeter.

$A(-2.4, -3)$, $B(5.2, -3)$, $C(5.2, 2.4)$, $D(-2.4, 2.4)$

LESSON 5.7

Multiplying and Dividing Decimals

BEFORE	▶ Now	WHY?
You multiplied and divided integers and fractions.	You'll multiply and divide decimals.	So you can find how many balloons you can buy, as in Ex. 24.

In the Real World

Word Watch

leading digit, p. 251

FLORIDA
Standards and Assessment
• Know effects of the four basic operations. (MA.A.3.3.1)
• Estimate to predict results and check reasonableness. (MA.A.4.3.1)

Rafting You travel downstream in a raft at a rate of about 4.3 miles per hour. How far will you travel in 2.5 hours?

Multiplying Decimals

Words Multiply decimals as you do whole numbers. Then place the decimal point. The number of decimal places in the product is the total number of decimal places in the factors.

Numbers

$$2.25 \quad \times \quad 8.9 \quad = \quad 20.025$$

2 places   1 place   3 places

EXAMPLE 1 Multiplying Decimals

To find how far you travel in the problem above about rafting, substitute the given values into the distance formula. Distance = rate • time, so distance = 4.3 • 2.5.

$$
\begin{array}{r}
4.3 \\
\times\, 2.5 \\
\hline
215 \\
86 \\
\hline
10.75
\end{array}
$$

1 decimal place
+1 decimal place

2 decimal places

ANSWER You will travel about 10.75 miles.

A number's **leading digit** is its leftmost nonzero digit. To check that a product is reasonable, round each factor to its leading digit and multiply.

$4.3 • 2.5$ Round factors to leading digit. ▶ $4 • 3 = 12$ ✓

Your turn now Multiply. Show that your answer is reasonable.

1. $-7.39 • 2.1$ **2.** $19.62 • 5.07$ **3.** $1.13 • 0.04$ **4.** $-0.85 • (-8)$

Dividing Decimals

Words When you divide by a decimal, multiply both the divisor and the dividend by the power of ten that will make the divisor an integer. Then divide.

Numbers $2.75\overline{)15.125}$ ▸ **Multiply by 100.** ▸ $275\overline{)1512.5}$ = 5.5

EXAMPLE 2 **Dividing Decimals**

To find the quotient $60.102 \div 6.3$, multiply the divisor and dividend by 10. Move the decimal points 1 place to the right.

$6.3\overline{)60.102}$ **Move decimal points.** ▸ $63\overline{)601.02}$

Then divide. ——— $63\overline{)601.02}$ = 9.54

✓ **Check** To check that the quotient is reasonable, round the quotient and the divisor to the leading digit. Then multiply. The result should be close in value to the dividend.

$9.54 \cdot 6.3$ **Round.** ▸ $10 \cdot 6 = 60$ ✓

EXAMPLE 3 **Using Zeros as Placeholders**

To find some quotients, you may need to use zeros as placeholders.

Placeholder in Dividend

$6 \div 1.2$

↓

$1.2\overline{)6.0}$ ◂ **Zero as placeholder**

↓

$12\overline{)60}$ = 5
$\underline{60}$
0

Placeholder in Quotient

$0.0126 \div 1.8$

↓

$1.8\overline{)0.0126}$

↓

$18\overline{)0.126}$ = 0.007 ◂ **Zeros as placeholders**
$\underline{126}$
0

Your turn now   **Find the quotient.**

5. $1.6 \div 0.04$ **6.** $0.632 \div 0.79$ **7.** $-13 \div (-0.65)$

8. $-4.365 \div (-4.5)$ **9.** $0.3744 \div 1.56$ **10.** $-0.0108 \div 2.7$

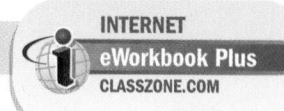

Getting Ready to Practice

1. **Vocabulary** Copy the division problem. Use the words *quotient*, *dividend*, and *divisor* to label each number.

$$0.8 \longleftarrow \underline{?}$$
$$\underline{?} \longrightarrow 9)\overline{7.2} \longleftarrow \underline{?}$$
$$\longleftarrow \underline{?}$$

Multiply or divide. Show that your answer is reasonable.

2. $7.8 \cdot 2.6$ 3. $3.75 \cdot 0.4$ 4. $13.2 \div 1.1$ 5. $0.5 \div 1.25$

6. **Guided Problem Solving** A mother rhinoceros weighs 3600 pounds. Her baby weighs 0.38 of her weight. How much does the baby weigh? Explain why your answer is reasonable.

   (1 Write a verbal model to describe the problem.

   (2 Substitute the given values and solve.

   (3 Check to see that your answer is reasonable.

Practice and Problem Solving

Find the product or quotient.

7. $25 \cdot 0.2$ 8. $2.4 \cdot 0.3$ 9. $-8.2 \cdot 0.7$ 10. $13.65 \cdot 1.1$

11. $4.8 \div 1.2$ 12. $4.9 \div 0.07$ 13. $5 \div (-0.1)$ 14. $-8 \div (-3.2)$

15. $5.41 \cdot 0.35$ 16. $-0.57 \div 0.38$ 17. $4.844 \div 0.56$ 18. $-2.687 \cdot (-9)$

19. $37.41 \div 4.3$ 20. $0.098 \cdot 0.55$ 21. $6.025 \cdot 48.2$ 22. $1.11 \div 0.925$

23. **Find the Error** Describe and correct the error in the solution.

$$
\begin{array}{r}
9.78 \\
\times\ 3.4 \\
\hline
3912 \\
2934 \\
\hline
332.52
\end{array}
$$

24. **Balloons** You are buying balloons that cost $.89 per package to decorate for a school dance. You have $14.75 to spend. How many packages of balloons can you buy?

25. **Look for a Pattern** Copy and complete the table by multiplying each number in the leftmost column by the number at the top of each other column. Describe the pattern.

×	1	0.1	0.01	0.001	0.0001
87	87	8.7	?	?	?
356	356	?	?	?	?
1200	?	?	?	?	?

Kilauea Volcano, Hawaii

26. Lava Flows A lava flow is a stream of molten rock that pours from an erupting vent. A lava flow travels 15.5 miles down a steep slope in 2.5 hours. Find the average rate at which the flow travels. Write your answer in miles per hour. Explain why your answer is reasonable.

Algebra **Solve the equation.**

27. $9 = \dfrac{a}{-0.9}$ **28.** $\dfrac{c}{4.5} = 0.16$ **29.** $1.2x = 0.321$ **30.** $-8.25y = -3.3$

Evaluate the expression.

31. $3.4^3 + 5.1 \div 1.7 - 4.89$ **32.** $6.2 \cdot (18.77 - 6.27) + 9.1^2$

 33. Writing Explain how 4.6 divided by 0.23 is related to 460 divided by 23. Are the quotients the same? Why?

34. Postal Rates The table shows rates to mail a first class letter. How much does it cost to mail a first class letter that weighs 3.5 ounces?

First ounce or fraction of ounce	$.37
Each additional ounce or fraction	$.23

35. Critical Thinking How many decimal places does 1.3^1 have? 1.3^2? 1.3^3? 1.3^7? Explain your reasoning.

36. Challenge One micron is equal to 0.001 millimeter. If a bacteria is 4 microns wide, how many times would you have to magnify it for the bacteria to appear 1 millimeter wide?

Mixed Review

Write the number in standard form. *(Lesson 4.8)*

37. 6.89×10^9 **38.** 1.3×10^{-12} **39.** 7.405×10^{-6}

Order the numbers from least to greatest. *(Lesson 5.5)*

40. $2.32, \dfrac{9}{4}, 2.5, 2\dfrac{3}{10}, 2, \dfrac{11}{5}$ **41.** $-\dfrac{9}{20}, -0.46, -\dfrac{3}{8}, -\dfrac{5}{12}, -0.4$

Basic Skills **Find the quotient.**

42. $55 \div 6$ **43.** $127 \div 5$ **44.** $307 \div 29$ **45.** $8607 \div 42$

FCAT Practice FCAT

46. Multiple Choice The quotient $-0.82 \div -0.83$ is _?_ .

    A. negative   **B.** less than -1 **C.** more than 1   **D.** positive

47. Short Response You need 2 gallons of milk. The store has run out of gallons but has half-gallons. A gallon costs $2.99 and a half-gallon costs $1.79. How much more do you pay? Explain. Show your work.

FLORIDA: Standards and Assessment
Find the mean, median, and mode of a data set.
(MA.E.1.3.2)

GOAL
Collect and analyze data.

MATERIALS
· number cubes

Collecting and Analyzing Data

You can collect data and find a number that represents the data. The *median* is the middle value when the values are written in order. The *mode* is the value that occurs most often.

Explore 1 Collect data by rolling two number cubes to explore how often each sum occurs.

1 Roll a pair of number cubes eleven times and record the results.

3 + 2 = 5   4 + 4 = 8   6 + 6 = 12   1 + 2 = 3   1 + 6 = 7   2 + 1 = 3

5 + 3 = 8   4 + 1 = 5   1 + 5 = 6   2 + 6 = 8   2 + 2 = 4

2 Add the sums together. Divide by the number of rolls to find the mean.

$$\frac{5 + 8 + 12 + 3 + 7 + 3 + 8 + 5 + 6 + 8 + 4}{11} = \frac{69}{11} \approx 6.3$$

3 Order the sums. Find the median and the mode.

3, 3, 4, 5, 5, 6, 7, 8, 8, 8, 12

middle number   most frequent number

4 Which sum do you think occurs most often? Compare your results with other groups.

Your turn now **Find the mean, median, and mode of the data set.**

   1. 4.2, 6.1, 3.8, 4.1, 10.2, 9.6, 6.1, 7.3, 2.1, 2.4, 9.8

   2. 105, 121, 42, 78, 77, 63, 108, 32, 33, 121, 64

   3. $2\frac{1}{2}, 7\frac{3}{4}, 9\frac{1}{4}, 7\frac{1}{2}, 4\frac{3}{8}, 7\frac{3}{4}, 3\frac{7}{8}$

Explore 2 Collect data about the number of letters in the last name of each student in your class.

1 Find the shortest and longest names so you can make a frequency table.

2 Count the number of letters in each name. Make a tally mark for each name.

3 Find the most frequent name length. This is the mode.

4 Find the mean number of letters in the last names.

5 Can you use the mean to describe the average length of a last name in your class? Can you use the mode? Explain.

Cho = 3
Fitzpatrick = 11

Number of Letters

3	4	5	6	7	8	9	10	11
II	III	₩	₩	₩ I	II	I		I

The mode is 7.

Number of Letters

3	4	5	6	7	8	9	10	11
II	III	₩	₩	₩ I	II	I		I

$$\begin{array}{cccccc} 3 & 4 & 5 & 6 & 7 & 8 \\ \times 2 & \times 3 & \times 5 & \times 5 & \times 6 & \times 2 \end{array}$$

$6 + 12 + 25 + 30 + 42 + 16 + 9 + 0 + 11 = 151$

You can multiply to count the number of letters for each column. Then add the column totals.

Divide by the number of students. The mean is $151 \div 25 \approx 6$.

Your turn now

4. A new student whose last name has 16 letters joins your class. If you add "16" to your data, how does this affect the mean and the mode? Explain.

Stop *and* **Think**

5. Writing You are designing a form to collect data. Students will write their last names in a row of small boxes, one letter per box. How many boxes do you think the form should provide? Explain.

Mean, Median, and Mode

BEFORE	▶ Now	WHY?
You used tables and graphs to analyze data sets.	You'll describe data sets using mean, median, mode, and range.	So you can describe World Series attendance, as in Ex. 14.

In the Real World

Word Watch

mean, p. 257
median, p. 257
mode, p. 257
range, p. 258

FLORIDA
Standards and Assessment

• Find the mean, median, and mode of a data set. (MA.E.1.3.2)

• Choose appropriate measures of central tendency. (MA.E.1.3.2)

Biology A marine biologist records the locations of deep sea jellies in relation to the ocean surface. Jellies are found at −2278 feet, −1875 feet, −3210 feet, −2755 feet, −2407 feet, and −2901 feet. What is the average location of a deep sea jelly?

Three types of averages can be used to describe a data set.

Averages

The **mean** of a data set is the sum of the values divided by the number of values.

The **median** of a data set is the middle value when the values are written in numerical order. If a data set has an even number of values, the median is the mean of the two middle values.

The **mode** of a data set is the value that occurs most often. A data set can have no mode, one mode, or more than one mode.

EXAMPLE 1 **Finding a Mean**

To find the mean of the 6 locations of the deep sea jellies in the problem above, divide the sum of the locations by 6.

$$\text{Mean} = \frac{-2278 + (-1875) + (-3210) + (-2755) + (-2407) + (-2901)}{6}$$

$$= \frac{-15,426}{6}$$

$$= -2571$$

ANSWER The mean location in relation to the ocean surface is −2571 ft.

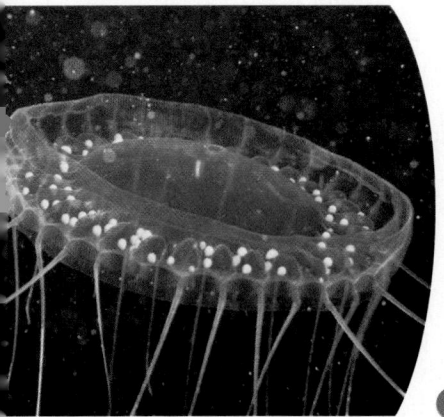

Deep sea jelly

Your turn now Find the mean of the data.

1. −3°C, 44°C, −11°C, 9°C, −21°C   **2.** $12\frac{1}{2}$ in., $14\frac{3}{4}$ in., $20\frac{1}{2}$ in., $16\frac{3}{4}$ in.

Range The **range** of a data set is the difference of the greatest value and the least value.

EXAMPLE 2 **Finding Median, Mode, and Range**

Movies **Find the median, mode(s), and range of the movie prices below.**

$7.20, $13.25, $14.94, $16.56, $18.74, $19.99, $19.99, $29.49

Median: The data set has an even number of prices, so the median is the mean of the two middle values, $16.56 and $18.74.

$$\text{Median} = \frac{\$16.56 + \$18.74}{2} = \frac{\$35.30}{2} = \$17.65$$

Mode: The price that occurs most often is $19.99. This is the mode.

Range: Find the difference of the greatest and the least values.

$$\text{Range} = \$29.49 - \$7.20 = \$22.29$$

Watch Out!

If the data are not ordered, you need to order the data so you can find the median.

Your turn now **Find the median, mode(s), and range of the data.**

3. 14, 13, 20, 24, 15, 10, 22, 17, 18   **4.** 9, 7, 4, 9, 4, 10, 5, 14, 9, 4

EXAMPLE 3 **Choosing a Representative Average**

Ice Cream Groups A and B try a new ice cream flavor and rate it on a scale of 1 to 10 as shown. Which average best represents each group?

Group A Ratings	**Group B Ratings**
1, 2, 3, 3, 5, 5, 5, 7, 8, 10	1, 1, 1, 2, 3, 4, 4, 9, 10, 10

Solution

Group A

$$\text{Mean} = \frac{49}{10} = 4.9$$

$$\text{Median} = \frac{5 + 5}{2} = \frac{10}{2} = 5$$

Mode: 5

ANSWER The mean, median, and mode are very close. So each average is a fair representation of the ratings as a group.

Group B

$$\text{Mean} = \frac{45}{10} = 4.5$$

$$\text{Median} = \frac{3 + 4}{2} = \frac{7}{2} = 3.5$$

Mode: 1

ANSWER The mean is higher than all but 3 ratings. The mode is equal to the lowest rating. So, mean and mode are not good choices. The median best represents the ratings.

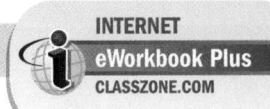

Getting Ready to Practice

Vocabulary In Exercises 1–3, use the data set 6, 12, 4, 15, 10, 6, 2, 9. Complete the statement using *mean*, *median*, *mode*, or *range*.

1. The _?_ is 8.　　　**2.** The _?_ is 6.　　　**3.** The _?_ is 13.

Find the mean, median, mode(s), and range of the data.

4. 8.98, 3.67, 11.13, 8.98, 11.24　　　**5.** −71, −56, −62, −44, −56, −47

6. Find the Error Describe and correct the error in the solution.

3, 6, 5, 2, 8, 9, 5, 8, 1, 5, 10, 8
The mode of the data set is 5.

7. Guided Problem Solving Gwen is training to run in a 5K race. Her practice times (in minutes and seconds) are 22:45, 21:56, 21:03, 20:33, and 20:28. Find her mean time to complete the race.

　(**1** Change Gwen's practice times to seconds.

　(**2** Find the sum of the practice times. Divide by the number of times.

　(**3** Convert your answer to minutes and seconds.

Practice and Problem Solving

Find the mean, median, mode(s), and range of the data.

8. Distances: 16 km, 23 km, 11 km, 6 km, 15 km, 23 km, 17 km, 16 km

9. Weekly hits at a Web site: 115, 157, 289, 185, 164, 225, 185, 208

10. Golf scores: −2, 0, 3, 1, 0, −1, 2, −2, −3, 0, 4, 1

11. Elevations: 127 ft, −8 ft, 436 ft, 508 ft, −23 ft, 47 ft

12. Daily calories: 2000, 1872, 2112, 2255, 2080, 1795, 1977

13. Shoe lengths: $10\frac{3}{4}$ in., $9\frac{1}{2}$ in., $8\frac{7}{8}$ in., $10\frac{1}{2}$ in., $8\frac{3}{8}$ in., $10\frac{1}{2}$ in.

14. Baseball The attendance for the 2001 World Series is shown in the table. Find the mean, median, and mode(s) of the data. Which average do you think best represents the attendance data? Explain.

Game	1	2	3	4	5	6	7
Attendance	49,646	49,646	55,820	55,863	56,018	49,707	49,589

15. Gymnastics A gymnast's performance is rated by six judges. The highest and lowest scores are dropped, and the mean of the remaining four scores is the final score awarded. Find the final score of each gymnast based on the judge's ratings given. Whose final score is the highest?

	Judge 1	Judge 2	Judge 3	Judge 4	Judge 5	Judge 6
Isaac	9.5	9.1	9.3	9.3	9.6	9.4
Carl	9.8	9.7	9.3	9.7	9.6	9.4
Kurt	9.4	9.3	9.3	9.5	9.5	9.6

16. Writing Why does it make sense to find the median of a data set with an even number of values by finding the mean of the middle values?

17. Salary You are researching the average salaries for several different careers. Would you rather know the mean, median, or mode(s) of the salaries for each career? Explain your reasoning.

18. Lakes The average depth of a local lake is reported to be 2 feet. You want to know if you can wade across the lake. What information might be concealed when depth is reported as an average?

19. Algebra Find the mean of $3b$, $5b$, b, $6b$, $-6b$, and $-2b$.

20. Bowling You are bowling three games. In the first two games, you score 125 and 113 points. How many points do you need in the third game to have a mean score of 126 points?

21. Compare and Contrast Jerry and Roberta find the mean of $-2a$, a, $3a$, $6a$, and $9a$ when $a = 2.5$, as shown below. Do both methods work? If so, which method do you prefer? Explain.

Jerry

$-2a = -5 \quad a = 2.5 \quad 3a = 7.5$

$6a = 15 \quad 9a = 22.5$

$$\frac{-5 + 2.5 + 7.5 + 15 + 22.5}{5} = \frac{42.5}{5}$$

$$= 8.5$$

Roberta

$$\frac{-2a + a + 3a + 6a + 9a}{5} = \frac{17a}{5}$$

$$= \frac{17 \cdot 2.5}{5}$$

$$= 8.5$$

22. Number Sense Make two different lists of numbers that have a mean of 8 and a median and mode of 10.

23. Challenge The table shows the numbers of points you scored during your first 14 basketball games of the 15-game season. By halftime of your final game, you have scored 7 points. How many points do you need to score in the second half to have a mean of 10 points per game?

Game	1	2	3	4	5	6	7	8	9	10	11	12	13	14
Points	15	8	7	10	12	4	20	13	7	7	5	3	10	14

Mixed Review

Find the quotient. *(Lesson 2.5)*

24. $\dfrac{-39}{13}$ **25.** $\dfrac{200}{-40}$ **26.** $\dfrac{-44}{-11}$ **27.** $\dfrac{0}{-197}$

Solve the equation. *(Lessons 3.1–3.3)*

28. $x - 15 = -10$ **29.** $-8 + x = -24$ **30.** $-7x = 84$

31. $-\dfrac{1}{6}x = -11$ **32.** $3x - 28 = -37$ **33.** $-\dfrac{x}{4} + 12 = 16$

FCAT Practice

INTERNET
FCAT PRACTICE
CLASSZONE.COM

34. Extended Response The table shows attendance at school dances for a year. Make a bar graph of the data. Find the mean and median attendance. The student council wants to find the total amount of money collected from students for admission to the dances. Would they find the bar graph, the mean, or the median most useful? Explain. What other information is also needed to find how much money was made?

Dance	Number of students
Fall	97
Winter Ball	88
Valentine's Day	133
Spring Fling	210
End of Year	198

The Prize is Right!

You are a contestant on a television game show. To win a trip you must find the prices of the five items in a shopping cart.

The game show host gives you four hints about the prices.

- The mean of the prices is $1.68.
- The mode of the prices is $1.50.
- The median of the prices is $1.65.
- One item costs $.10 more than the median.

List the prices of the items in the cart in order from least to greatest.

Notebook Review

LESSONS 5.5 TO 5.8

Review the vocabulary definitions in your notebook.

Copy the review examples in your notebook. Then complete the exercises.

Check Your Definitions

rational number, p. 242	front-end estimation, p. 248	median, p. 257
terminating decimal, p. 242	leading digit, p. 251	mode, p. 257
repeating decimal, p. 242	mean, p. 257	range, p. 258

Use Your Vocabulary

☑ **1.** Name three averages you can use to represent a data set.

5.5 Can you order rational numbers?

 EXAMPLE Order the numbers 3.7, $3\frac{5}{8}$, 3.6, and $3\frac{2}{3}$ from least to greatest.

$3\frac{5}{8} = 3.625$ $\qquad$ $3\frac{2}{3} = 3.\overline{6}$ $\qquad$ So, the order is 3.6, $3\frac{5}{8}$, $3\frac{2}{3}$, 3.7.

☑ **2.** Order the numbers 6.4, $6\frac{4}{9}$, $6\frac{3}{8}$, and $6\frac{5}{12}$ from least to greatest.

5.6–5.7 Can you perform operations with decimals?

a.
$$\begin{array}{r} 14.02 \\ +\ \ 9.80 \\ \hline 23.82 \end{array}$$

b.
$$\begin{array}{r} 20.500 \\ -\ \ 3.764 \\ \hline 16.736 \end{array}$$

c.
$$\begin{array}{r} 14.75 \\ \times\ \ 1.3 \\ \hline 4425 \\ 1475 \\ \hline 19.175 \end{array}$$
2 decimal places
+1 decimal place

3 decimal places

d.
$$4.26\overline{)21.726} \rightarrow 426\overline{)2172.6}$$
$$5.1$$

☑ **Find the sum, difference, product, or quotient.**

3. $1.2 + 0.67$ $\quad$ **4.** $33.2 + 9.398$ $\quad$ **5.** $3.16 - 1.845$ $\quad$ **6.** $90.3 - (-7.81)$

7. $6.24 \cdot 0.375$ $\quad$ **8.** $3.348 \cdot 0.9$ $\quad$ **9.** $66.96 \div (-2.7)$ $\quad$ **10.** $18.91 \div 9.455$

5.8 Can you find mean, median, mode, and range?

 EXAMPLE Find the mean, median, mode(s), and range of the data set: 4, 5, 6, 6, 7, 9, 11, and 12.

$$\text{Mean} = \frac{4 + 5 + 6 + 6 + 7 + 9 + 11 + 12}{8} = \frac{60}{8} = 7.5$$

$$\text{Median} = \frac{6 + 7}{2} = \frac{13}{2} = 6.5$$

$$\text{Mode} = 6 \qquad\qquad \text{Range} = 12 - 4 = 8$$

☑ **Find the mean, median, mode(s), and range of the data set.**

11. 25, 20, 30, 22, 24, 23, 24

12. 7.2, 7.3, 7.5, 7.7, 7.9, 7.2, 7.7, 7.1

Stop *and* **Think** about Lessons 5.5–5.8

13. Critical Thinking Write an example of a data set whose mode is greater than its mean.

14. Writing Explain why terminating decimals and repeating decimals are rational numbers. Use examples.

Review Quiz 2

Write the fraction as a decimal or the decimal as a fraction.

1. $\frac{1}{25}$ **2.** $\frac{4}{9}$ **3.** 0.58   **4.** $0.\overline{2}$

Find the sum or difference.

5. $-2.301 + 8.4$ **6.** $15.25 + 9.636$ **7.** $14.65 - 3.608$ **8.** $3.2 - (-0.225)$

Find the product or quotient.

9. $-15.3 \cdot 0.48$ **10.** $3.88 \cdot 0.9$ **11.** $0.162 \div 2.7$ **12.** $2.07 \div 0.225$

13. Racing Camel A racing camel can travel at a speed of 11.75 miles per hour. How far does it travel in 0.02 hour at this speed?

14. Tornadoes The table shows the numbers of tornadoes in the United States from 1995–2001. Find the mean, median, mode(s), and range.

Year	1995	1996	1997	1998	1999	2000	2001
Tornadoes	1234	1173	1148	1424	1342	1071	805

5

Chapter Review

 Vocabulary

reciprocal, p. 234	terminating decimal,	leading digit, p. 251
multiplicative inverse,	p. 242	mean, p. 257
p. 234	repeating decimal,	median, p. 257
rational number,	p. 242	mode, p. 257
p. 242	front-end estimation,	range, p. 258
	p. 248	

Vocabulary Review

Copy and complete the statement.

1. The fractions $\frac{3}{5}$ and $\frac{5}{3}$ are _?_ because their product is 1.

2. If the remainder of the quotient $\frac{a}{b}$ is 0, then the decimal form of $\frac{a}{b}$ is a _?_ decimal.

3. You can use _?_ when you do not need to find an exact sum of a set of numbers.

4. A value that occurs most often in a data set is a _?_ .

5. For a data set, the sum of the values divided by the number of values is the _?_ .

6. The difference of the greatest value and the least value of a data set is the _?_ .

Review Questions

Find the sum or difference. *(Lessons 5.1, 5.2)*

7. $\frac{8}{9} + \frac{4}{9}$

8. $-3\frac{5}{8} + \frac{7}{8}$

9. $-\frac{19}{25} - \frac{11}{25}$

10. $\frac{3}{10} - \frac{7}{10} - \frac{9}{10}$

11. $\frac{3}{5} + \frac{1}{4}$

12. $\frac{3}{5} - \frac{2}{3}$

13. $6\frac{2}{7} + \left(-7\frac{1}{8}\right)$

14. $-9\frac{3}{4} - 4\frac{2}{3}$

15. $-\frac{7n}{9} - \frac{5n}{9}$

16. $-\frac{m}{4} + \left(-\frac{m}{4}\right)$

17. $\frac{3}{c} - \frac{7}{2c}$

18. $\frac{5v}{3} + \frac{4v}{5}$

19. **Coins** A quarter's width is about $\frac{15}{16}$ inch. A dime's width is about $\frac{11}{16}$ inch. How much wider is a quarter? *(Lesson 5.1)*

20. **Robots** It took Central High's robot team $107\frac{1}{3}$ hours of labor to build their robot. East High built their robot in $111\frac{5}{6}$ hours. How much longer did East High School take to build their robot? *(Lesson 5.2)*

Review Questions

Find the product or quotient. *(Lessons 5.3, 5.4)*

21. $-\dfrac{5}{8} \cdot \dfrac{2}{5}$

22. $-\dfrac{9}{5} \cdot \left(-\dfrac{11}{15}\right)$

23. $-6\dfrac{3}{7} \cdot 2\dfrac{1}{2}$

24. $4 \cdot \left(-3\dfrac{5}{12}\right)$

25. $\dfrac{9}{21} \div 5$

26. $\dfrac{13}{18} \div \dfrac{5}{6}$

27. $5\dfrac{8}{11} \div \left(-\dfrac{3}{4}\right)$

28. $12\dfrac{1}{2} \div 4\dfrac{1}{6}$

Solve the equation. *(Lesson 5.4)*

29. $\dfrac{5}{6}x = 25$

30. $\dfrac{2}{3}b = \dfrac{8}{9}$

31. $-\dfrac{9}{10}y = 6\dfrac{3}{7}$

32. $\dfrac{4}{9}a + 4\dfrac{1}{3} = 5\dfrac{2}{3}$

Order the numbers from least to greatest. *(Lesson 5.5)*

33. $2\dfrac{3}{10}, \dfrac{11}{5}, 2.32, \dfrac{5}{2}, 2.25, 2$

34. $-0.45, -\dfrac{3}{8}, -\dfrac{5}{12}, -0.4, -0.46$

Find the sum, difference, product, or quotient. *(Lessons 5.6, 5.7)*

35. $5.2 + 20.68$

36. $0.103 + 0.7$

37. $9.6 - 3.555$

38. $-4.23 - 8.093$

39. $16.7 \cdot (-3.2)$

40. $43.4 \cdot 0.13$

41. $3.434 \div 8.08$

42. $-13 \div (-0.52)$

Newborn Animals **In Exercises 43 and 44, use the table. It shows approximate weights, in pounds, of several newborn animals.** *(Lesson 5.6)*

43. How much more does the hippopotamus weigh than the gentoo penguin?

44. How much more does the polar bear weigh than the giant panda?

Newborn Animal	Birth Weight (lb)
Hippopotamus	93
Grizzly bear	1
Giant panda	0.29
Giraffe	150
Polar bear	2.09
Gentoo penguin	0.21

45. **Icebergs** When an iceberg broke free from Antarctica in May of 2002, it was about 34.5 miles long and 6.9 miles wide. About how much area did the iceberg cover? *(Lesson 5.7)*

46. **Cats** A tiger at a zoo has a mass of 144.9 kilograms. This is 40.25 times the mass of a house cat. What is the mass of the house cat? *(Lesson 5.7)*

Find the mean, median, mode(s), and range of the data set. *(Lesson 5.8)*

47. Temperatures (°C): $-7, -1, 0, 8, 4, 2, -7, 2$

48. Jumps (meters): 14.6, 19.2, 11, 16.5, 12, 11, 10.9

49. Hand widths (in.): $3\dfrac{1}{2}, 2\dfrac{7}{8}, 3\dfrac{1}{8}, 3\dfrac{1}{4}, 2\dfrac{3}{4}$

50. Bike trails (km): 7, 8.3, 17.1, 4.8, 3.9, 7, 4.8, 13.1

Chapter Test

Find the sum or difference.

1. $4\frac{5}{11} - 2\frac{6}{11}$

2. $\frac{9}{16} - \left(-\frac{11}{16}\right)$

3. $-\frac{5}{6} + \frac{1}{8}$

4. $\frac{3}{7} + \left(-\frac{8}{21}\right) + \frac{2}{3}$

5. **Roller Coaster** Yesterday you had to wait in line for $1\frac{3}{4}$ hours to ride a roller coaster. Today you waited $1\frac{1}{4}$ hours. How much longer did you wait yesterday?

Find the product or quotient.

6. $\frac{2}{9} \cdot (-4)$

7. $\frac{5}{2} \cdot \frac{4}{15}$

8. $3\frac{1}{2} \div 2$

9. $7\frac{3}{4} \div 2\frac{7}{12}$

10. **Balloons** You are inflating balloons for a party. If you can inflate one balloon in $\frac{5}{6}$ minute, how many balloons can you inflate in $\frac{1}{2}$ hour?

Write the fraction as a decimal or the decimal as a fraction.

11. $\frac{7}{20}$

12. $\frac{3}{40}$

13. 0.0082

14. $0.\overline{4}$

Find the sum, difference, product, or quotient.

15. $6.2 - 5.984$

16. $2.608 + 12.93$

17. $0.7992 \div 0.333$

18. $-34.69 \cdot 12.7$

Bagels In Exercises 19 and 20, use the table. It shows the approximate supermarket sales of three types of bagels (in billions of dollars) in the year 2000 in the United States.

Bagel	Sales (billions)
Frozen	$.145
Refrigerated	$.072
Fresh	$.42

19. How much greater were the sales for frozen bagels than the sales for refrigerated bagels?

20. What is the total amount of supermarket sales of all three types of bagels?

21. **Algebra** Evaluate $0.2x$ and $\frac{x}{0.2}$ when $x = -4.1$, 0.06, and 1.8.

22. **Energy Bill** A gas supplier charges 64.5 cents per therm of gas used. How much does it cost for 116 therms of gas?

23. **Studying** Twelve students spent 2, 5, 3, 7, 10, 9, 8, 7, 6, 7, 6, and 2 hours studying. Find the mean, median, mode(s), and range of the data.

Chapter FCAT Practice

Test-Taking Strategy Mark unanswered questions in your test booklet so you can find them quickly when you go back.

Multiple Choice

1. What is the difference $23\frac{1}{8} - 25\frac{9}{24}$?

   A. $-2\frac{8}{16}$ **B.** $-2\frac{1}{4}$ **C.** $-2\frac{5}{24}$ **D.** $-1\frac{1}{4}$

2. You have biked $5\frac{3}{4}$ miles of a $9\frac{1}{4}$ mile trail. How much farther must you bike?

   F. $2\frac{1}{2}$ miles   **G.** $2\frac{3}{4}$ miles

   H. $3\frac{1}{2}$ miles   **I.** $4\frac{1}{2}$ miles

3. What is the product of $-\frac{2}{9}$ and $-\frac{3}{8}$?

   A. $-\frac{43}{72}$ **B.** $-\frac{1}{12}$ **C.** $\frac{1}{24}$ **D.** $\frac{1}{12}$

4. You need $2\frac{3}{4}$ feet of nylon string to make a set of wind chimes. How much string do you need to make 9 sets of chimes?

   F. $23\frac{1}{2}$ feet   **G.** $24\frac{1}{4}$ feet

   H. $24\frac{3}{4}$ feet   **I.** $25\frac{1}{4}$ feet

5. By what number can you multiply $\frac{7}{8}$ to get the product $\frac{7}{9}$?

   A. $\frac{0}{1}$ **B.** $\frac{49}{72}$ **C.** $\frac{8}{9}$ **D.** $\frac{9}{8}$

6. What is the value of x when $\frac{2}{5}x = \frac{3}{40}$?

   F. $\frac{1}{35}$ **G.** $\frac{3}{100}$ **H.** $\frac{3}{16}$ **I.** $5\frac{1}{3}$

7. You order a CD for $16.99, a book for $9.49, and a movie for $18.39. You pay $3.95 for shipping. What is your total cost?

   A. $47.82   **B.** $48.82

   C. $48.86   **D.** $58.86

8. What is the difference $21.6 - 4.312$?

   F. $5.48   **G.** $14.56

   H. $17.288   **I.** 18.4688

9. Your jogging route is 2.75 miles long. How many times must you run the route to jog 11 miles?

   A. 0.4   **B.** 4   **C.** 5   **D.** 40

10. Which fraction is greater than 0.67?

    F. $\frac{8}{23}$ **G.** $\frac{5}{8}$ **H.** $\frac{29}{44}$ **I.** $\frac{16}{23}$

11. What is the median of the data set -3.5, 2.7, 3.1, -4.8, 0.4, 6.0, 3.1?

    A. 1   **B.** 2.7   **C.** 3.1   **D.** 10.8

Short Response

12. A red rectangular blanket is 6.5 feet by 5.9 feet. A blue square blanket has sides of 6.2 feet. Which blanket is bigger?

Extended Response

13. Your most recent phone calls lasted 1, 2, 5, 46, 2, 8, 5, 3, 7, and 2 minutes. Find the mean, median, and mode(s) of the phone call lengths. Use your understanding of mean, median, and mode to explain which of these averages is most representative of the phone calls.

Multi-Step Equations and Inequalities

Chapter Warm-Up Game

Review skills you need for this chapter in this quick game. Work with a partner.

Key Skill:
Solving one- and two-step equations

BEFORE

In previous chapters you've...

- Solved equations that required using one or two steps
- Solved one-step inequalities

Now

In Chapter 6 you'll study...

- Solving multi-step equations
- Solving equations that have variables on both sides
- Using multi-step inequalities to solve real-world problems

WHY?

So you can solve real-world problems about...

- Venus flytraps, p. 271
- fundraising, p. 274
- drumming, p. 278
- bowling, p. 296

Internet Preview
CLASSZONE.COM

- eEdition Plus Online
- eWorkbook Plus Online
- eTutorial Plus Online
- FCAT Practice
- More Examples

TREASURE HUNT

MATERIALS

- 1 number cube
- 1 Treasure Hunt board
- 20 red markers
- 20 yellow markers

PREPARE Each player gets 20 markers of the same color. On your turn, follow the steps on the next page. You can challenge the other player when you believe they have covered an incorrect space.

The equations on the board:

$$= 14$$
$$8$$
$$5x + 1 = 21$$
$$-9x =$$
$$7x + 8 = 50$$
$$\frac{5x}{2} = 15$$
$$x - 9 = -8$$
$$-12x = -72$$
$$\frac{9x}{-3} = -6$$
$$-7 - x = -9$$
$$29 + x = 33$$
$$\frac{15x}{3} = 5$$

1 **ROLL** a number cube. This is your solution.

2 **COVER** an equation that has your solution with a marker. If there are no equations that have your solution, you cannot place a marker and it is the next player's turn. Each space you cover is a piece of treasure.

3 **CHECK** that you cover a correct space for your roll. If you cover an incorrect space, then you must remove your marker and it is the next player's turn.

HOW TO WIN Be the player with the most spaces covered (the most treasure collected) when all spaces on the board are covered.

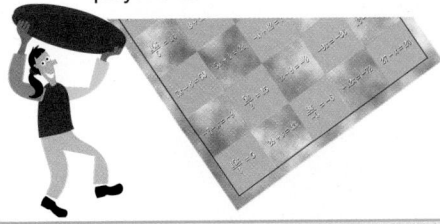

Stop *and* **Think**

1. **Writing** If the only spaces left on the board are $5x + 1 = 21$, $-7 - x = -9$, and $11 - 2x = 3$, what is the best number to roll? What is the second best number to roll? Explain.

2. **Critical Thinking** How many spaces on the board have a solution of 5? Explain how you found your answer.

Getting Ready to Learn

Word Watch

Review Words

perimeter, p. 33
distributive property,
 p. 85
like terms, p. 86
inequality, p. 140
reciprocal, p. 234

Review What You Need to Know

Using Vocabulary **Copy and complete using a review word.**

1. The ? of a figure is the sum of its side lengths.

2. The four ? symbols are $<$, $>$, $\leq$, and $\geq$.

3. To divide by a fraction, you multiply by its ? .

Simplify the expression by combining like terms. *(p. 85)*

4. $3 - 2x + 4$ 5. $4x + 5 + x - 1$ 6. $-2(3x + 1)$ 7. $5(x - 4) - x$

Solve the equation. Check your answer. *(p. 119)*

8. $2x - 1 = 3$ 9. $-3x - 2 = 7$ 10. $4 - x = 12$ 11. $13 = 2x + 3$

Solve the inequality. Then graph its solution. *(pp. 140, 146)*

12. $x + 5 < 18$ 13. $x - 4 \geq -6$ 14. $-6x \leq 54$ 15. $\frac{4}{5}x > 20$

You should include
material that appears
on a notebook like this
in your own notes.

Know How to Take Notes

Recording the Process Copy examples your teacher explains during
class. Be sure to record each step of the solution to help you remember
the process.

Solving Two-Step Equations

$-2x - 3 = 11$	Original equation
$-2x - 3 + 3 = 11 + 3$	Add 3 to each side.
$-2x = 14$	Simplify.
$\dfrac{-2x}{-2} = \dfrac{14}{-2}$	Divide each side by -2.
$x = -7$	Simplify.

Call attention to
important steps
in examples.

In Lesson 6.3, recording each step of the solution may help you remember
the process for solving equations involving fractions and decimals.

LESSON 6.1
Solving Multi-Step Equations

BEFORE	▶ Now	WHY?
You solved equations that required using one or two steps.	You'll solve equations that require using two or more steps.	So you know how long to save to buy a mountain bike, as in Ex. 26.

Word Watch

Review Words

distributive property, p. 85
like terms, p. 86

FLORIDA
Standards and Assessment

• Solve linear equations. (MA.D.2.3.1)

• Solve linear equations representing real-world situations. (MA.D.2.3.2)

• Simplify algebraic expressions of real-world situations. (MA.D.2.3.1)

In the Real World

Science For a science fair, you perform an experiment to see how the number of Venus flytrap seeds planted in a cup affects plant growth. In each cup, you plant either 5 seeds or 10 seeds. You want to use an equal number of cups for each seed amount. You have 75 seeds. How many cups do you need?

Before using inverse operations to solve an equation, check to see if you can simplify one or both sides of the equation by combining like terms.

EXAMPLE 1 **Writing and Solving a Multi-Step Equation**

To find the number of cups for each seed amount, first write a verbal model. Let c = the number of cups for each seed amount.

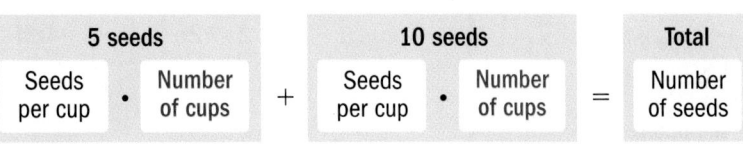

5 seeds			10 seeds			Total
Seeds per cup	•	Number of cups	Seeds per cup	•	Number of cups	Number of seeds

$$5c + 10c = 75 \qquad \text{Write algebraic model.}$$
$$15c = 75 \qquad \text{Combine like terms.}$$
$$\frac{15c}{15} = \frac{75}{15} \qquad \text{Divide each side by 15.}$$
$$c = 5 \qquad \text{Simplify.}$$

ANSWER You can plant five cups with 5 seeds and five cups with 10 seeds.

 Check Substitute 5 for c in original equation.

$$5(5) + 10(5) \stackrel{?}{=} 75$$
$$25 + 50 \stackrel{?}{=} 75$$
$$75 = 75 \checkmark$$

EXAMPLE 2 **Combining Like Terms**

$$3x + 12 - 4x = 20$$ Original equation

$$-x + 12 = 20$$ Combine like terms: $3x - 4x = -x$.

$$-x + 12 - 12 = 20 - 12$$ Subtract 12 from each side.

$$-x = 8$$ Simplify.

$$\frac{-x}{-1} = \frac{8}{-1}$$ Divide each side by -1.

$$x = -8$$ Simplify.

Your turn now Solve the equation. Then check the solution.

1. $-6 = 11w - 5w$ **2.** $4p + 10 + p = 25$ **3.** $-8r - 2 + 7r = -9$

Before you combine like terms in an equation, you may have to use the distributive property.

EXAMPLE 3 **Using the Distributive Property**

with Review

When distributing a negative number, remember to distribute the negative sign to *each* term inside the parentheses. For help with the distributive property, see p. 85.

$$6n - 2(n + 1) = 26$$ Original equation

$$6n - 2n - 2 = 26$$ Distributive property

$$4n - 2 = 26$$ Combine like terms.

$$4n - 2 + 2 = 26 + 2$$ Add 2 to each side.

$$4n = 28$$ Simplify.

$$\frac{4n}{4} = \frac{28}{4}$$ Divide each side by 4.

$$n = 7$$ Simplify.

✓ **Check** Substitute 7 for n in the original equation.

$$6(7) - 2(7 + 1) \stackrel{?}{=} 26$$

$$6(7) - 2(8) \stackrel{?}{=} 26$$

$$42 - 16 \stackrel{?}{=} 26$$

$$26 = 26 ✓$$

Your turn now Solve the equation. Then check the solution.

4. $3(x - 9) = -39$ **5.** $z + 4(6 - z) = 21$ **6.** $8 = -7(y + 1) + 2y$

Clearing Fractions In equations involving a fraction, you may want to multiply each side by a number to change the equation into an equivalent equation that does not have fractions.

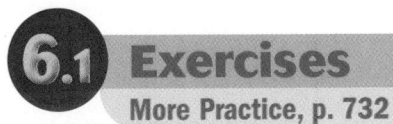 **EXAMPLE 4** **Solving an Equation with a Fraction**

$\dfrac{3x + 10}{4} = 7$	Original equation
$\dfrac{3x + 10}{4} \cdot 4 = 7 \cdot 4$	Multiply each side by 4.
$3x + 10 = 28$	Simplify.
$3x + 10 - 10 = 28 - 10$	Subtract 10 from each side.
$3x = 18$	Simplify.
$\dfrac{3x}{3} = \dfrac{18}{3}$	Divide each side by 3.
$x = 6$	Simplify.

6.1 Exercises
More Practice, p. 732

INTERNET
eWorkbook Plus
CLASSZONE.COM

Getting Ready to Practice

Vocabulary Identify the like terms in the expression.

1. $5x + 6 - 2 - 9x$ **2.** $8y + 3x - 1 + 6y$ **3.** $-t - 15 + 1 - 20$

Solve the equation. Then check the solution.

4. $8b + 2b - 4 = 6$ **5.** $-n - 9 + 8n = 26$ **6.** $5(w - 7) = -15$

7. $m + 3(m - 4) = 16$ **8.** $\dfrac{k - 6}{2} = -10$ **9.** $\dfrac{z + 2}{7} = 12$

10. Guided Problem Solving Tickets to the county fair cost $8 each. Seventy people purchased their tickets in advance and the rest bought them at the gate. The revenue from ticket sales is $2560. How many people bought their tickets at the gate?

(**1** Use the verbal model to write an equation to find the number of tickets sold at the gate.

$$\boxed{\begin{array}{c} \text{Price per} \\ \text{ticket} \end{array}} \cdot \left(\boxed{\begin{array}{c} \text{Tickets sold in} \\ \text{advance} \end{array}} + \boxed{\begin{array}{c} \text{Tickets sold} \\ \text{at gate} \end{array}} \right) = \boxed{\begin{array}{c} \text{Total} \\ \text{revenue} \end{array}}$$

(**2** Solve the equation. Then check the solution.

Practice and Problem Solving

with Homework

Example	Exercises
1	24, 26
2	11–23
3	11–23
4	11–23

Online Resources
CLASSZONE.COM
· More Examples
· eTutorial Plus

Decide whether the given value is a solution of the equation. If not, find the solution.

11. $7x - 3x - 8 = -32; x = 6$

12. $2y - 5(y + 1) = 25; y = -10$

13. $\dfrac{4m - 3}{3} = 3; m = 2$

14. $2 - 8a + 3a = 17; a = -3$

Solve the equation. Then check the solution.

15. $4x - 7 - 7x = -1$

16. $-2z + 6z - 9 = 15$

17. $-22 + 3k + 6 = -28$

18. $-2(m + 7) = -22$

19. $5(3 - 2n) = 65$

20. $-4 = -1 - 3(2p + 3)$

21. $\dfrac{5a - 2}{3} = -9$

22. $\dfrac{2b + 8}{5} = -12$

23. $\dfrac{c - 5}{8} = 4$

24. Fundraiser You are collecting money during a student council T-shirt sale. Today you collected money from Maria for 13 shirts, money from Kevin for 9 shirts, and money from Emma for 10 shirts. You collected a total of $352. How much did each T-shirt cost?

25. Measurement The perimeter of the rectangle is $3(x - 8)$ millimeters. Use a ruler to measure the rectangle and find the perimeter. Then find the value of x.

26. After-school Job You are saving to buy a mountain bike that costs $225. You already have $25. Each week, you make $15 babysitting and $25 working at a grocery store. Write a verbal model for the money you have using *Money already saved, Weeks, Babysitting money per week, Grocery store money per week,* and *Price of mountain bike*. Use the verbal model to write an equation. In how many weeks will you have enough money?

Solve the equation. Then check the solution.

27. $5y - 2y + 9y = -16$

28. $8k - 4 - 3k - 17 = -21$

29. $7t - 3(1 + t) = -19$

30. $2z - 4(9 - 3z) = 62$

31. $-10 = 6n - (3n + 12)$

32. $\dfrac{m - 14}{9} = -27$

33. $-11 = \dfrac{24 - b}{13}$

34. $-34 = \dfrac{3d + 8}{3}$

Geometry **Write an equation for the area of the triangle. Then solve for x.**

35. The lengths are in inches. The area is 228 square inches.

19

$x + 11$

36. The lengths are in meters. The area is 918 square meters.

$x - 9$

51

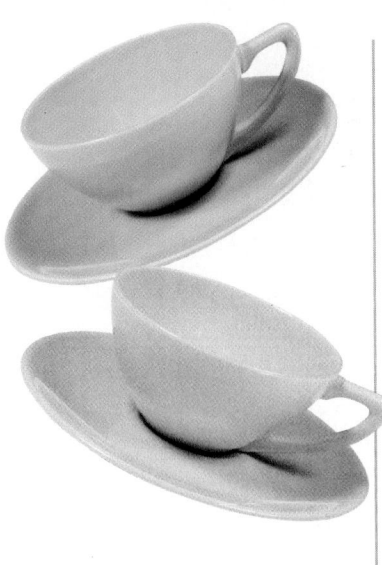

37. Critical Thinking Suppose you want to solve an equation that involves parentheses, such as $3(x + 2) = 9$. You might use the distributive property to rewrite the left side. Would the result be the same if instead you first divide each side by 3? Explain.

38. Number Sense Sara has $20 to spend at a yard sale. She decides to buy a teapot and as many sets of teacups and saucers as she can afford. The teacups are $2 each and the saucers are $1 each. She figures that she can buy 8 teacups and 8 saucers. How can you tell that she's made an error without knowing the cost of the teapot?

39. Geometry Find the values of x and y so that the rectangle and the triangle have the same perimeter. What is the perimeter?

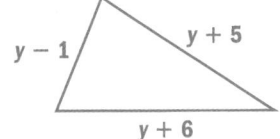

40. Challenge You have $12 to spend on earrings. You can calculate the sales tax by multiplying the price by 0.05. What is the most that the earrings can cost before the sales tax is added on?

Mixed Review

Copy and complete the statement with <, >, or =. *(Lesson 4.8)*

41. 1.54×10^{-5} ? 1.54×10^{-6} **42.** 0.57×10^{4} ? 5.7×10^{4}

Find the mean, median, mode(s), and range of the data. *(Lesson 5.8)*

43. 35, 32, 31, 32, 35, 32, 37, 38, 34 **44.** 101, 100, 101, 105, 112, 105

Basic Skills **Find the unknown number.**

45. 8 hours = ? seconds **46.** 3 days = ? minutes

FCAT Practice FCAT

47. Multiple Choice What is the value of t in the equation $-4t - 9 + 2t = 9$?

A. -9 **B.** 0 **C.** 3 **D.** 9

48. Short Response Mr. Roberts is buying a CD player and several CDs. Each CD costs x dollars and each double CD costs $(x + 8)$ dollars. The CD player costs $45 dollars. He buys 8 CDs and 3 double CDs. His total before tax comes to $234. How much did each CD and double CD cost? Write a verbal model and an algebraic equation. Then solve the algebraic equation.

6.2 Problem Solving Strategies

FLORIDA: Standards and Assessment
Solve multi-step real-world problems. (M.A.A.3.3.3)

Work Backward

- Guess, Check, and Revise
- Look for a Pattern
- Draw a Diagram
- Write an Equation
- **Work Backward**
- Act It Out
- Solve a Simpler Problem

Problem At the beginning of the year your class divides into seven equal study groups. Then your group joins another group, and two students leave your group when they change classes. Now there are four students in your group. How many students were in your class at the beginning of the year?

1 Read and Understand

Read the problem carefully.

- You know how the class divided and how your group changed.
- You need to find the number of students in the class at the beginning of the year.

2 Make a Plan

Decide on a strategy to use.

One way to solve the problem is to work backward. Start with the final number of students in your group and undo each change that your group went through.

3 Solve the Problem

Reread the problem. Work backward from the final number of students.

Size of group now	Size before 2 students left	Size before joining group	Size at beginning

$$4 + 2 = 6$$
$$6 \div 2 = 3$$
$$3 \cdot 7 = 21$$

ANSWER There were 21 students at the beginning of the year.

4 Look Back

Check your answer. Start with your solution and reread the problem, calculating as you read.

At the beginning of the year your class   **21**
divides into seven equal study groups. $21 \div 7 = 3$
Then **your group joins another** group, $3 \cdot 2 = 6$
and **two students leave** your group. $6 - 2 = 4$
Now there are **four students** in your group.   4 ✓

Use the strategy *work backward*.

1. **Road Trip** In the last 3 days you've driven 720 miles, 650 miles, and 800 miles. Your car's odometer reads 20,490 miles. What did the odometer read three days ago?

2. **Money** You put half of your money in the bank. The next day you receive your $10 allowance and buy jeans for $25. You have $17 left. Copy and complete the diagram to find out how much money you started with.

Put money in bank		Received allowance		Bought jeans		
?	? →	?	? →	?	? →	$17
	?		?		?	

3. **Phone Card** Jill uses three fifths of the minutes on her phone card to call her brother, 15 minutes to call a friend, and 5 minutes to order a pizza. If she has 4 minutes left, how many minutes were on the card before she called her brother?

4. **Studying** You spend one hour on math homework and 45 minutes studying for each of your 3 tests. If you finish studying at 6:30 P.M., what time did you start?

5. **Notebook** You use half of your notebook for your research paper and two thirds of the remaining paper for class notes. You have ten pages left for homework. How many pages are in your notebook?

6. **CD Burning** Some friends are recording songs on a CD. The first fifth of the CD has songs from Alex's favorite band. The next 12 minutes are songs Henrique chose. One third of the time remaining is filled with Brian's favorite songs. Sally chose songs for the next 32 minutes. How many minutes of music did they record?

Use any strategy to solve the problem.

7. **Consecutive Odd Numbers** The sum of three consecutive odd numbers is 501. What is the value of each number?

8. **Traveling** The following directions describe the path Denzel takes to his friend's house from school.

   - First he travels 5 miles north and then 8 miles west.

   - Next he travels 2 miles north and then 3 miles east.

   - Finally he travels 1 mile south.

   Draw a map showing Denzel's path from school to his friend's house.

9. **Population** The table shows the population of a small town over 15 years. If the population continues to grow in this manner, in what year will the population reach 160,000?

Year	Population
1987	5,000
1992	10,000
1997	20,000
2002	40,000

10. **Getting Ready** Each morning, Angie needs half an hour to shower and dress, 15 minutes to eat, and 5 minutes to brush her teeth. It takes her 15 minutes to walk to school. What is the latest Angie can get up and still arrive at school by 8:10 A.M.?

LESSON 6.2

Solving Equations with Variables on Both Sides

BEFORE	▶ Now	WHY?
You solved equations that had variables on one side.	You'll solve equations that have variables on both sides.	So you can determine the cost of party supplies, as in Ex. 27.

Word Watch

Review Words

perimeter, p. 33
distributive property, p. 85
like terms, p. 86

FLORIDA
Standards and Assessment

• Write equations to express relationships. (MA.D.1.3.2)
• Apply number properties. (MA.A.3.3.1)

Activity Use algebra tiles to model and solve an equation.

(1) Represent the equation $2x + 3 = x + 5$ using algebra tiles.

(2) Remove one x-tile and three 1-tiles from each side.

(3) The solution is 2.

Use algebra tiles to solve the equation.

1. $2x + 7 = 3x + 2$ **2.** $5x - 2 = 3x + 6$ **3.** $4x - 1 = x - 7$

To solve equations with variables on both sides, collect like terms on the same side.

EXAMPLE 1   Collecting Like Terms

Drum lessons at the youth center cost $8 for members and $12 for nonmembers. Membership is $24. For what number of lessons is the cost the same for a member and a nonmember?

Solution

Cost for member				Cost for nonmember	
Member fee	+	Price for members · Number of lessons	=	Price for nonmembers ·	Number of lessons

$$24 + 8n = 12n \qquad \text{Let } n = \text{the number of lessons.}$$

$$24 = 4n \qquad \text{Subtract } 8n \text{ from each side.}$$

$$6 = n \qquad \text{Divide each side by 4.}$$

ANSWER Six lessons cost the same for members and nonmembers.

EXAMPLE 2 **Finding the Perimeter of a Triangle**

Each side of the triangle has the same length. What is the perimeter of the triangle?

$5x + 9$ $7x + 5$

Solution

$5x + 9 = 7x + 5$	Write an equation.
$5x + 9 - 5x = 7x + 5 - 5x$	Subtract $5x$ from each side.
$9 = 2x + 5$	Simplify.
$9 - 5 = 2x + 5 - 5$	Subtract 5 from each side.
$4 = 2x$	Simplify.
$\dfrac{4}{2} = \dfrac{2x}{2}$	Divide each side by 2.
$2 = x$	Simplify.

Because $5x + 9 = 5(2) + 9 = 19$, each side of the triangle is 19 units long.

The three sides of the triangle are the same length, so the perimeter is $3 \cdot 19$, or 57, units.

ANSWER The perimeter of the triangle is 57 units.

Watch Out!

In Example 2, don't think that because $x = 2$, each side of the triangle has length 2 units. You must substitute 2 into the expressions for side length.

Sometimes you can use the distributive property to simplify one or both sides of an equation before you solve.

EXAMPLE 3 **Using the Distributive Property**

$21x = 3(2x + 30)$	Original equation
$21x = 6x + 90$	Distributive property
$21x - 6x = 6x + 90 - 6x$	Subtract $6x$ from each side.
$15x = 90$	Simplify.
$\dfrac{15x}{15} = \dfrac{90}{15}$	Divide each side by 15.
$x = 6$	Simplify.

Your turn now **Solve the equation.**

1. $4a + 5 = a + 11$ **2.** $3n + 7 = 2n - 1$ **3.** $-6c + 1 = -9c + 7$

4. $28 - 3s = 5s - 12$ **5.** $4(w - 9) = 7w + 18$ **6.** $2(y + 4) = -3y - 7$

Getting Ready to Practice

1. Vocabulary What is the perimeter of a rectangle?

2. Is 5 a solution of the equation $4x - 2 = 3x + 12$?

Solve the equation. Then check the solution.

3. $3x = 2x + 5$ **4.** $5x = 2(x + 5)$ **5.** $x = 5(2x + 3)$

6. Geometry Each side of the triangle has the same length. What is the perimeter of the triangle?

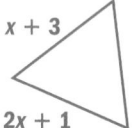

$x + 3$

$2x + 1$

Practice and Problem Solving

Solve the equation.

7. $7x = x + 18$ **8.** $7m = 4m + 21$ **9.** $30 - 2s = 4s$

10. $81 + 2k = 5k$ **11.** $13q - 48 = -3q$ **12.** $-11r = -4r + 56$

13. $5z - 43 = 2z + 80$ **14.** $16y - 43 = 4y + 65$ **15.** $8f + 11 = -7f - 19$

Geometry Find the perimeter of the triangle or rectangle. The sides of each triangle are equal in length.

16.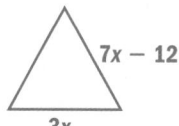

$7x - 12$

$3x$

17.

$2(x + 5)$

$3x - 7$

18.

$2x - 3$

7 7

$3x - 10$

19. Saving David has \$32 and is saving \$8 each week. Emily has \$56 and is saving \$6 each week. When will David and Emily have the same amount of money?

Solve the equation.

20. $-1 + 11a = 6 - 3a$ **21.** $9b - 10 = -b - 18$ **22.** $3(t - 7) = 6t$

23. $-3h = 9(2 - 3h)$ **24.** $-n = 2(n - 33)$ **25.** $3d = 9(d - 1)$

26. Working Backward Mark had \$20 before he began earning the same amount each week at his new job. He used half of his first week's pay to pay back a loan. He spent \$15 at the movies and \$12 on a book, and got \$25 for his birthday. After his second paycheck he had \$20 less than two weeks' pay combined. How much is his paycheck?

27. Party Supplies You are decorating for a school picnic. Balloons cost $8 for a dozen but cost more if bought individually. With the money you have, you can buy 7 dozen and 5 single balloons, or 75 single balloons. How much is one balloon? How much money do you have?

Solve the equation.

28. $5p + 4 = 11p - 2 - p$

29. $-5g + 3 = -3g + 6g$

30. $3(j + 4) = -2j + j$

31. $5(t + 7) = 2(2t + 7)$

32. $2(c + 6) = 5(c + 12)$

33. $6(s - 4) = 3(s + 9)$

34. Critical Thinking How many different values of x will make the equation $2(x + 3) = 2x + 6$ true? Explain your answer.

35. Challenge In 1999, there were 3940 museums and some number of historical sites in the United States. The total number of these attractions was 376 more than five times the number of historical sites. How many historical sites were there in the United States in 1999?

Mixed Review

Find the least common denominator of the fractions. *(Lesson 4.5)*

36. $\dfrac{1}{2}, \dfrac{2}{3}, \dfrac{5}{6}$

37. $\dfrac{2}{9}, \dfrac{3}{4}, \dfrac{11}{12}$

38. $\dfrac{4}{5}, \dfrac{1}{2}, \dfrac{3}{70}$

Find the sum or difference. *(Lesson 5.6)*

39. $7.31 + 2.248$

40. $10.26 - 3.72$

41. $16.508 + 4.53$

Solve the equation. *(Lesson 6.1)*

42. $5c + 24 - 3c = 2$

43. $3(2z - 3) = 75$

44. $7x - 2(x - 11) = -23$

45. $3b - 5b = -14$

46. $4(x - 7) = 4$

47. $\dfrac{y + 3}{5} = 10$

FCAT Practice

48. Multiple Choice A reusable camera costs $24 and a roll of film costs $5.50. Each disposable camera that takes as many pictures as a roll of film costs $10.99. Which equation could be used to find the number of disposable cameras that would cost the same as the same number of rolls of film plus the cost of the reusable camera?

A. $5.5x = 10.99x + 24$

B. $5.5x - 10.99x = 24$

C. $5.5x = 10.99x$

D. $5.5x + 24 = 10.99x$

49. Multiple Choice What is the value of y in the equation $6y - 10 = 4(2y + 3)$?

F. -11 **G.** -1 **H.** 1 **I.** 11

Solving Equations Involving Fractions and Decimals

BEFORE	▶ Now	WHY?
You solved equations involving whole numbers.	You'll solve equations with fractions and decimals.	So you can determine the size of a lawn, as in Ex. 18.

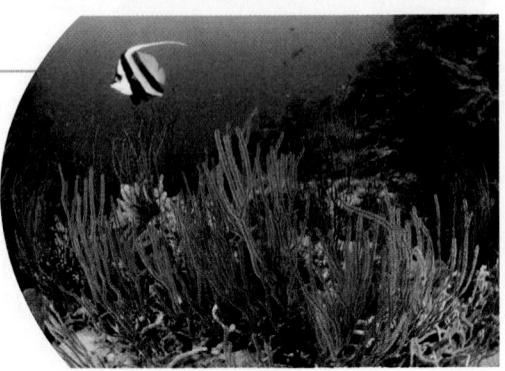

In the Real World

📓 **Word Watch**

Review Words

least common denominator (LCD), p. 192

FLORIDA
Standards and Assessment

• Solve real-world problems. (MA.A.3.3.2)

• Solve linear equations. (MA.D.2.3.1)

Environment A colony of coral is 0.17 meter high and is growing at a rate of 0.025 meter per year. Another colony is 0.11 meter high. It is growing at a rate of 0.041 meter per year. In how many years will the colonies be the same height?

EXAMPLE 1 **Solving an Equation Involving Decimals**

To solve the coral problem, you need to solve an equation involving decimals. First write a verbal model. Let n = the number of years.

Colony 1					Colony 2			
Height	+	Growth rate	•	Years	=	Height	+	Growth rate	•	Years

HELP **with Notetaking**

In Example 1, some of the steps are not shown. You may want to identify these steps and include them in your notes.

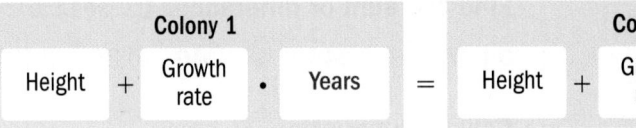

$$0.17 + 0.025n = 0.11 + 0.041n \qquad \text{Write algebraic model.}$$

$$0.17 = 0.11 + 0.016n \qquad \text{Subtract } 0.025n \text{ from each side.}$$

$$0.06 = 0.016n \qquad \text{Subtract } 0.11 \text{ from each side.}$$

$$\frac{0.06}{0.016} = \frac{0.016n}{0.016} \qquad \text{Divide each side by } 0.016.$$

$$3.75 = n \qquad \text{Simplify.}$$

ANSWER The colonies will be the same height in a little less than 4 years.

Your turn now **Write a verbal model. Then solve.**

1. You and a friend are buying snowboarding gear. You buy a pair of goggles that costs $39.95 and 4 tubes of wax. Your friend buys a helmet that costs $54.95 and 2 tubes of wax. If you each spend the same amount, how much does each tube of wax cost?

Clearing Decimals The multiplication property of equality allows you to multiply each side of an equation by the same number, so you can clear decimals from an equation if you wish.

HELP with Solving

To clear decimals, multiply each side of the equation by a power of ten that will make all the coefficients integers. In Example 2, multiply by 100.

EXAMPLE 2 **Solving an Equation Involving Decimals**

$1.4x - 1.8 + 2.35x = 0.21$	Original equation
$(1.4x - 1.8 + 2.35x)\mathbf{100} = (0.21)\mathbf{100}$	Multiply each side by 100 to clear decimals.
$140x - 180 + 235x = 21$	Simplify.
$375x - 180 = 21$	Combine like terms.
$375x = 201$	Add 180 to each side.
$\dfrac{375x}{375} = \dfrac{201}{375}$	Divide each side by 375.
$x = 0.536$	Simplify.

Clearing Fractions When solving an equation with fractions, you can multiply each side by the LCD to clear the fractions.

EXAMPLE 3 **Solving an Equation Involving Fractions**

$\dfrac{3}{10}x = -\dfrac{1}{6}x + \dfrac{7}{10}$	Original equation
$\left(\dfrac{3}{10}x\right)\mathbf{30} = \left(-\dfrac{1}{6}x + \dfrac{7}{10}\right)\mathbf{30}$	Multiply each side by the LCD, 30.
$\left(\dfrac{3}{10}x\right)\mathbf{30} = \left(-\dfrac{1}{6}x\right)\mathbf{30} + \left(\dfrac{7}{10}\right)\mathbf{30}$	Distributive property
$\dfrac{3 \cdot \overset{3}{\cancel{30}}}{\underset{1}{\cancel{10}}}x = -\dfrac{1 \cdot \overset{5}{\cancel{30}}}{\underset{1}{\cancel{6}}}x + \dfrac{7 \cdot \overset{3}{\cancel{30}}}{\underset{1}{\cancel{10}}}$	Divide out common factors.
$9x = -5x + 21$	Simplify.
$14x = 21$	Add 5x to each side.
$x = \dfrac{21}{14} = \dfrac{3}{2}, \text{ or } 1\dfrac{1}{2}$	Divide each side by 14. Simplify.

Your turn now Solve the equation. Then check the solution.

2. $-1.7k + 6.7k = 13.1$ **3.** $1.2n - 0.24 = 0.7n$ **4.** $8.3 - 8y = 1.2y + 6$

5. $\dfrac{4}{5}x + 3 = -\dfrac{7}{10}$ **6.** $2s - 1\dfrac{1}{4}s = \dfrac{1}{3}$ **7.** $\dfrac{5}{6}v + \dfrac{5}{8} = \dfrac{3}{8}v$

Lesson 6.3 Solving Equations Involving Fractions and Decimals **283**

Getting Ready to Practice

1. Vocabulary Copy and complete: 24 is the _?_ of $\frac{1}{4}$, $\frac{5}{6}$, and $\frac{3}{8}$.

Tell what number you would multiply each side of the equation by to eliminate the decimals or fractions. Then solve the equation.

2. $1.5a - 1.2 = 1.8a$ **3.** $5.85b = 8.68 + 3.68b$ **4.** $0.5c + 3.49 - 2c = 4$

5. $\frac{3}{8}m + \frac{7}{8} = 2m$ **6.** $-\frac{4}{15}n + \frac{2}{3} = \frac{2}{5}n$ **7.** $-\frac{1}{5}p + \frac{3}{4}p = 11$

8. Find the Error Describe and correct the error in the solution.

$$1.5x + 0.25 = 1.6x$$
$$15x + 25 = 16x$$
$$25 = x$$

Practice and Problem Solving

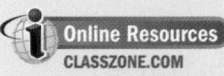
with **Homework**

Example	Exercises
1	23-24
2	9-16, 19-22
3	9-16, 18-23

Online Resources
CLASSZONE.COM

· More Examples
· eTutorial Plus

Solve the equation. Then check the solution.

9. $r + 8.2 + 0.4r = -8.6$ **10.** $1.5s - 1.2 - s = 0.5$

11. $5.3 + u = 3.2u - 2.7$ **12.** $4.93 - 9.20v = 0.66v$

13. $p - \frac{4}{9}p = -\frac{7}{9}$ **14.** $\frac{3}{10} - w = \frac{4}{5} - \frac{3}{5}w$

15. $\frac{1}{6}x + \frac{2}{3}x = 1$ **16.** $\frac{7}{4}z - \frac{1}{6} = \frac{17}{6} + \frac{3}{4}z$

17. Estimation Round each coefficient and constant in the equation $6.95x - 2.13 = 1.8x + 3.07$ to the nearest integer. Solve the new equation. What does your answer tell you about the answer to the original equation? Solve the original equation. Compare your answers.

18. Mowing the Lawn You mow $\frac{1}{5}$ of the lawn and your sister mows $\frac{2}{5}$ of the lawn. The two of you mow a total of 2400 square feet. What is the area of the lawn? How much area is left to mow?

Solve the equation. Then check the solution.

19. $-2.67g - 8.4 = 6.072 + 0.03g$ **20.** $0.25(66 + 42.4h) = 3.1652$

21. $\frac{3}{8} + \frac{9}{20}m = \frac{23}{20} + \frac{7}{8}m$ **22.** $6\frac{4}{5}n - \frac{8}{9} = \frac{7}{15}n$

23. Fabric At a fabric store you buy a clothes pattern for $7. You also buy $\frac{3}{4}$ yard of red fabric, $2\frac{1}{2}$ yards of purple fabric, and $\frac{7}{8}$ yard of blue fabric. The total cost is $23.50. If all three fabrics are the same price per yard, how much do you spend on each fabric?

24. Art Supplies Joyce buys scissors for $6.20 and 7 packages of paper. Paul buys paints for $9.94 and 5 packages of paper. They each spend the same amount, and each package of paper costs the same amount. How much does each package of paper cost?

25. Critical Thinking If you multiply each side of an equation by a common multiple of the denominators that is not the LCD, should you still get the correct answer? Explain.

26. Challenge Your batting average was 0.245 for your first baseball game and 0.251 for your second. After your third game your *overall* batting average is 0.250. What was your batting average for your third game?

Mixed Review

Evaluate the expression. *(Lessons 5.2, 5.3, 5.6, 5.7)*

27. $6.239 + 12.2$ **28.** $5\frac{1}{2} - 2\frac{3}{8}$ **29.** 4.1×8.235 **30.** $\frac{4}{9} \times \frac{11}{13}$

Solve the equation. *(Lesson 6.2)*

31. $6n + 11 = 2n - 1$ **32.** $16 - 3s = 2s - 14$ **33.** $-3(w - 7) = 5w + 3$

Basic Skills **Write an equivalent expression.**

34. $9(8 + x)$ **35.** $-15(y - 4)$ **36.** $-z(4 + 3 - 5)$

FCAT Practice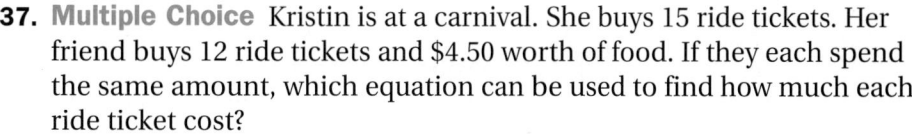

37. Multiple Choice Kristin is at a carnival. She buys 15 ride tickets. Her friend buys 12 ride tickets and $4.50 worth of food. If they each spend the same amount, which equation can be used to find how much each ride ticket cost?

A. $27x = 4.5$ **B.** $4.5 = 12x + 15x$

C. $15x + 4.5 = 12x$ **D.** $15x = 4.5 + 12x$

38. Multiple Choice At the movies, popcorn costs $3.95, a candy bar costs $1.65, and a drink costs $2.25. Joe and his friends buy the same number of each item and spend $39.25 total. How many did they buy of each?

F. 4   **G.** 5   **H.** 6   **I.** 7

LESSONS 6.1 TO 6.3

Notebook Review

Review the vocabulary definitions in your notebook.

Copy the review examples in your notebook. Then complete the exercises.

Check Your Definitions

perimeter, p. 33

distributive property, p. 85

like terms, p. 86

least common denominator (LCD), p. 192

Use Your Vocabulary

1. In your own words, explain how to combine like terms.

6.1–6.2 Can you solve multi-step equations?

EXAMPLE Solve $4(x - 8) = -x + 4 + 7x$.

$4(x - 8) = -x + 4 + 7x$ Original equation

$4x - 32 = 6x + 4$ Use the distributive property and combine like terms.

$-32 = 2x + 4$ Subtract $4x$ from each side.

$-36 = 2x$ Subtract 4 from each side.

$-18 = x$ Divide each side by 2.

☑ **Solve the equation.**

2. $-2x + 8 + x = 12$ **3.** $4z = 8(3 + z)$ **4.** $-6 + 10a = 3 - 2a$

6.3 Can you solve equations involving fractions and decimals?

EXAMPLE Solve $\frac{3}{4}y = \frac{1}{6}y - 4$.

$\frac{3}{4}y = \frac{1}{6}y - 4$ Original equation

$9y = 2y - 48$ Multiply each side by the LCD, 12.

$9y - 2y = 2y - 48 - 2y$ Subtract $2y$ from each side.

$7y = -48$ Simplify.

$y = -\frac{48}{7}$, or $-6\frac{6}{7}$ Divide each side by 7.

☑ **Solve the equation.**

5. $-3.5a - 19.5 + 9.8a = 10.74$

6. $3\frac{1}{4} - 6b = 1\frac{1}{2} + 2\frac{3}{4}b$

Stop *and* **Think** about Lessons 6.1–6.3

7. Writing Explain how you can clear the decimals from the equation $16.2 - 4.32x = 10.8 + 0.023x$ before solving for x.

Review Quiz 1

Solve the equation.

1. $2(x + 16) = 46$

2. $79 = 10x - 23 + 7x$

3. $-108 = -16(x + 5) + 9x$

4. $12n = 17 - 22n$

5. $27.2m + 15.7 = -85.94 + 0.8m$

6. $\frac{1}{2}v + \frac{11}{12} - \frac{5}{4}v = -\frac{5}{12}$

7. Geometry Find the perimeter of the rectangle. The lengths are measured in feet.

$4y - 12$
$2x - 3$
$7x - 18$
$y + 3$

8. Color Printer You have $445 to buy a printer. You find one that costs $235. It uses a black ink cartridge that costs $30 and a color ink cartridge that costs $40. Write and solve an equation to determine how many pairs of ink cartridges you can buy for the printer.

BrAIN GAME

Going Bananas

Solve each equation and use the value to move the monkey that number of spaces in the direction indicated. This will lead the monkey to his favorite set of bananas.

1. $x - 5 = 2x - 8$; right

2. $-4x = 2(x - 6)$; up

3. $\frac{1}{2}x = \frac{1}{3}x - \frac{1}{2} + \frac{4}{3}$; left

4. $5(3x + 6) = 9(6x - 1)$; down

6.4 Hands-on Activity

GOAL
Find the relationship between diameter and circumference.

MATERIALS
· metric tape measure or ruler
· string
· paper and pencil

FLORIDA: Standards and Assessment
Know how a change in dimensions affects circumference. (MA.B.1.3.3)
Write equations to express relationships. (MA.D.1.3.2)

Diameter and Circumference

In this activity, you will investigate the relationship between the diameter and circumference of a circle.

The *diameter* is the distance across a circle through the center.

The *circumference* is the distance around a circle.

diameter

circumference

Explore 1 Find the diameter and circumference of circular objects.

Measure the diameter and circumference of several circular objects. If necessary, wrap a string around the object and measure the length of the string with a ruler. Record the measurements in a table like the one below.

Object	Diameter	Circumference	$\dfrac{\text{Circumference}}{\text{Diameter}}$
Water bottle	65 mm	206 mm	?
Tuna can	84 mm	264 mm	?
Clock	174 mm	549 mm	?
Quarter	24 mm	74 mm	?
Mug	82 mm	261 mm	?

Your turn now

1. Find the quotient of the circumference and the diameter for each object you measured. Round to the nearest hundredth if necessary. Record the quotients in another column of the table.

2. What do you notice about the numbers in the new column of your table?

Chapter 6   Multi-Step Equations and Inequalities

Explore 2 **Write a circumference formula.**

1 Find an average of the quotients $\dfrac{\text{circumference}}{\text{diameter}}$ in your table. How does your average compare to the averages found by the other students in your class?

2 Find an average of the quotients $\dfrac{\text{circumference}}{\text{diameter}}$ collected by your whole class.

3 Use the result in Step 2 to write a formula for the circumference of a circle in terms of the diameter.

Your turn now Use the formula you wrote in Step 3 above to calculate the circumference of the circle given its diameter d.

3. $d = 64$ mm   **4.** $d = 140$ mm   **5.** $d = 36$ cm

6. $d = 20$ cm   **7.** $d = 4$ in.   **8.** $d = 1.25$ in.

Stop *and* **Think**

9. Writing Write a formula for the diameter of a circle in terms of the circumference.

Solving Equations Involving Circumference

BEFORE	▶ Now	WHY?
You solved equations involving fractions and decimals.	You'll solve equations involving the circumference of a circle.	So you can find the diameter of a clock, as in Ex. 28.

Word Watch

circle, p. 290
center, p. 290
radius, p. 290
diameter, p. 290
circumference, p. 290
pi (π), p. 290

FLORIDA
Standards and Assessment

• Know how a change in dimensions affects circumference. (MA.B.1.3.3)

• Estimate to predict results and check reasonableness. (MA.A.4.3.1)

A **circle** is the set of all points in a plane that are the same distance from a fixed point called the **center**. The distance from the center to any point on the circle is the **radius**. The **diameter** is the distance across the circle through the center.

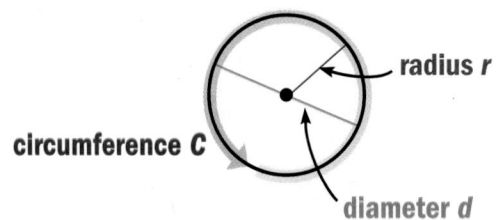

radius *r*

circumference *C*

diameter *d*

The **circumference** of a circle is the distance around the circle. For every circle, the quotient of its circumference and its diameter is the same: about 3.14159. This constant is represented by the Greek letter **pi**, π. You can approximate π using 3.14, $\frac{22}{7}$, or the π key on a calculator.

Circumference of a Circle

Words   The circumference of a circle is the product of π and the diameter.

Algebra $C = \pi d$ or $C = 2\pi r$

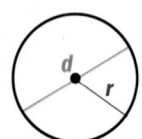

EXAMPLE 1   **Using Radius to Find Circumference**

Find the circumference of a circle with a radius of 11 meters.

Solution

$C = 2\pi r$ Circumference formula

$\approx 2(3.14)(11)$ Substitute 3.14 for π and 11 for *r*.

$= 69.08$ Multiply.

ANSWER The circumference is about 69.08 meters.

EXAMPLE 2   Using Diameter to Find Circumference

Find the circumference of the circle.

21 ft

Solution

The measure shown is a diameter, so use the circumference formula that involves the diameter.

$C = \pi d$ Circumference formula

$\approx \dfrac{22}{\cancel{7}_{1}} \cdot \cancel{21}^{3}$ Substitute. Use $\frac{22}{7}$ for π because 21 is divisible by 7.

$= 66$ Multiply.

ANSWER The circumference is about 66 feet.

Your turn now   **Find the circumference of the circle. Use 3.14 or $\frac{22}{7}$ for π. Explain your choice of value of π.**

1.

28 mi

2.

9.5 m

3.

16 cm

4. diameter = 32 in.   **5.** diameter = 140 ft   **6.** radius = 1.5 km

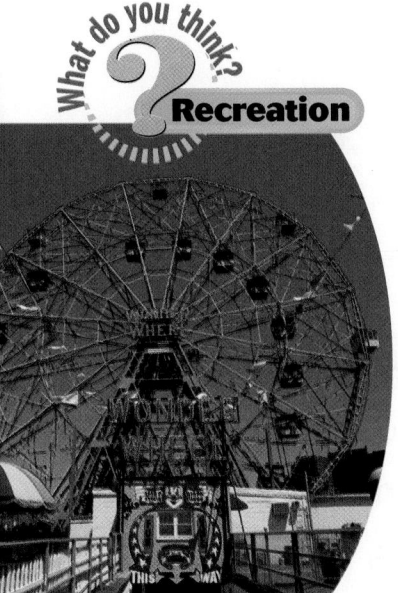

What do you think?

Recreation

■ **Ferris Wheels**

This ride has 16 swinging cars and 8 stationary cars, and it can hold 144 people at a time. How many people can ride in each car?

EXAMPLE 3   Finding Diameter in Real Life

Ferris Wheel A ferris wheel has a circumference of about 423.9 feet. Find its diameter.

Solution

You are asked to find the diameter, so use the circumference formula that involves diameter.

$C = \pi d$ Circumference formula

$423.9 \approx 3.14d$ Substitute 423.9 for C and 3.14 for π.

$\dfrac{423.9}{3.14} \approx \dfrac{3.14d}{3.14}$ Divide each side by 3.14.

$135 \approx d$ Simplify.

ANSWER The diameter is about 135 feet.

with Review

For help with reciprocals, see p. 234.

EXAMPLE 4 **Using Circumference to Find the Radius**

A circle has a circumference of 88 inches. Find the radius.

Solution

$$C = 2\pi r$$ Circumference formula

$$88 \approx 2\left(\frac{22}{7}\right)r$$ Use $\frac{22}{7}$ for π.

$$88 \approx \frac{44}{7}r$$ Simplify.

$$\overset{2}{\cancel{88}} \cdot \frac{7}{\cancel{44}_1} \approx \frac{44}{7}r \cdot \frac{7}{44}$$ Multiply each side by $\frac{7}{44}$, the reciprocal of $\frac{44}{7}$.

$$14 \approx r$$ Simplify.

ANSWER The radius is about 14 inches.

Your turn now Use 3.14 or $\frac{22}{7}$ for π. Explain your choice of value of π.

7. A circle has a circumference of 20.41 inches. Find the diameter.

8. A circle has a circumference of 132 inches. Find the radius.

6.4 **Exercises**

More Practice, p. 732

INTERNET
eWorkbook Plus
CLASSZONE.COM

Getting Ready to Practice

1. Vocabulary Draw and label a circle with a radius and a diameter.

Find the indicated measurement, where r = radius, d = diameter, and C = circumference. Use 3.14 or $\frac{22}{7}$ for π. Explain your choice.

2. $d = 56$ m, $C = \underline{?}$ **3.** $C = 66$ in., $r = \underline{?}$ **4.** $r = 6\frac{1}{4}$ ft, $C = \underline{?}$

5. $d = 11$ cm, $C = \underline{?}$ **6.** $C = 3.14$ m, $r = \underline{?}$ **7.** $C = 330$ yd, $d = \underline{?}$

8. Find the Error Describe and correct the error in the solution.

$$C = 2 \cdot \pi \cdot radius$$
$$\approx 2(3.14)(4.5)$$
$$= 28.26 \text{ inches}$$

Practice and Problem Solving

with Homework

Example	Exercises
1	12–20
2	12–20, 23
3	28–29
4	12–20

Online Resources
CLASSZONE.COM
· More Examples
· eTutorial Plus

Measurement Use a ruler to find the indicated measure. Then use the measure to find the circumference of the circle. Use 3.14 for π.

9.

$d = ?$ cm

10.
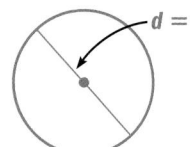
$d = ?$ in.

11.

$r = ?$ mm

In Exercises 12–20, find the indicated measurement, where r = radius, d = diameter, and C = circumference. Use 3.14 or $\frac{22}{7}$ for π.

12. $C = 44$ m

$r = ?$

13. $C = 157$ yd
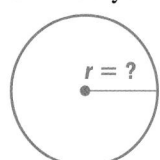
$r = ?$

14. $C = 235.5$ cm
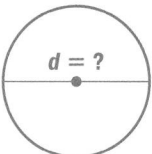
$d = ?$

15. $r = 10$ mm, $C = \underline{?}$ **16.** $r = 21$ ft, $C = \underline{?}$ **17.** $d = 14$ in., $C = \underline{?}$

18. $d = 15$ mi, $C = \underline{?}$ **19.** $C = 33$ km, $d = \underline{?}$ **20.** $C = 628$ cm, $r = \underline{?}$

21. Estimation Use mental math to solve Exercises 9–11 again, using 3 for π. How can these estimates help you to check your answers?

22. Critical Thinking Find the circumferences of circles with the radii 1, 2, 4, 8, and 16 meters. Leave your answers in terms of π. Then compare the circumferences. What happens to the circumference of a circle as its radius doubles?

23. Dome The diameter of the U.S. Capitol Building's dome is 96 feet at its widest point. Find its circumference. Use 3.14 for π.

24. Writing Look up the word *circumnavigate* in the dictionary. How is the definition like the definition of *circumference*?

Extended Problem Solving Adventurer Mike Horn traveled around the world as close to the equator as possible without using any motorized transportation.

25. Calculate The radius of Earth is 3963 miles. Approximate its circumference. Use 3.14 for π.

26. Compare In order to avoid some dangerous areas, Mike Horn actually traveled 29,000 miles. About how much farther did Mike Horn travel than if he had followed the equator?

27. Analyze To the nearest mile, find what the radius of Earth would be if its circumference was 29,000 miles. Use 3.14 for π.

28. Clock Face The Great Clock of Westminster rings the bell known as "Big Ben" in London, England. The circumference of the clock face is about 72 feet 3 inches. What is the diameter of the clock face in feet? Use 3.14 for π. Round your answer to the nearest hundredth.

29. Fashion To measure the leg opening of a pair of flared jeans, you flatten them out and measure the width. The width is 12 inches, which is half the circumference. What is the diameter of the leg opening? Use 3.14 for π. Round your answer to the nearest hundredth.

Challenge Two circles are *concentric* if they share a center, as in the diagrams below. The circumference of the outer circle is given. Find *x*. Use 3.14 for π. (All measures are in meters.)

30. $C = 100.48$ m **31.** $C = 109.9$ m **32.** $C = 94.2$ m

        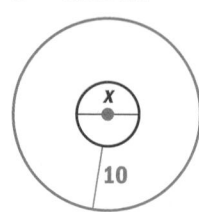

Mixed Review

Plot the point in a coordinate plane. *(Lesson 2.8)*

33. $A(6, -10)$ **34.** $B(-4, 4)$ **35.** $C(-2, -6)$ **36.** $D(-12, 0)$

Solve the inequality. *(Lessons 3.6, 3.7)*

37. $-15 + x \le 8$ **38.** $r + 11 > 6$ **39.** $-4a \ge -8$ **40.** $3m < -63$

Solve the equation. *(Lesson 6.1)*

41. $-4n - 9 + 5n = -6$ **42.** $20 = 8c + 2 + c$ **43.** $6 + 2(5 - z) = 7$

FCAT Practice

INTERNET
FCAT PRACTICE
CLASSZONE.COM

44. Extended Response A basketball hoop has a circumference of about 56.5 inches. A basketball has a circumference of about 28.5 inches. What is the approximate difference between the diameter of the hoop and the diameter of the basketball? Use 3.14 for π. Round your answer to the nearest inch. Show how you found your answer.

$C = 28.5$ in. $C = 56.5$ in.

Solving Multi-Step Inequalities

BEFORE	▶ Now	WHY?
You solved multi-step equations and one-step inequalities.	You'll use two or more steps to solve inequalities.	So you can determine how much a salesperson must sell, as in Ex. 21.

Word Watch

Review Words

distributive property, p. 85
like terms, p. 86
inequality, p. 140

FLORIDA
Standards and Assessment

• Solve linear inequalities representing real-world situations. (MA.D.2.3.2)
• Write inequalities to express relationships. (MA.D.1.3.2)

Activity **Use a table to solve the inequality $x + 4 \geq 3x$.**

① Copy and complete the table.

x	$x + 4$	$3x$	Is $x + 4 \geq 3x$?
-1	3	-3	Yes
0	?	?	?
1	?	?	?
2	?	?	?
3	?	?	?
4	?	?	?

② For what values of x is the inequality true? What do you think is the solution of the inequality? Explain your reasoning.

③ How is the solution of $4x + 3 > 9x - 7$ different from the solution in Part 2?

④ If you substitute a number less than -1 for x in the inequality above, will the inequality be true? Explain.

In Lessons 6.1 through 6.3, you solved multi-step equations algebraically. You can use many of the same steps to solve multi-step inequalities.

HELP with Review

For help with solving inequalities, see pp. 140 and 146.

EXAMPLE 1 **Solving and Graphing a Two-Step Inequality**

$10 + 4y < 18$	Original inequality
$10 + 4y - 10 < 18 - 10$	Subtract 10 from each side.
$4y < 8$	Simplify.
$\dfrac{4y}{4} < \dfrac{8}{4}$	Divide each side by 4.
$y < 2$	Simplify.

Use an open circle and draw the arrow to the left.

(number line: 0 1 2 3 4 5 with open circle at 2, arrow to left)

EXAMPLE **2** **Combining Like Terms**

$3x - 8 < -x + 4$	Original inequality
$3x - 8 - 3x < -x + 4 - 3x$	Subtract $3x$ from each side.
$-8 < -4x + 4$	Combine like terms.
$-8 - 4 < -4x + 4 - 4$	Subtract 4 from each side.
$-12 < -4x$	Simplify.
$\dfrac{-12}{-4} > \dfrac{-4x}{-4}$	Divide each side by -4 and reverse the inequality symbol.
$3 > x$	Simplify.

To check your solution, substitute different values for x in the original inequality. Choose a value less than 3, a value greater than 3, and 3.

Your turn now **Solve the inequality. Then graph the solution.**

1. $-7z + 15 \geq 57$ **2.** $11n + 36 < 3n - 4$ **3.** $9(y - 2) > -16$

EXAMPLE **3** **Writing and Solving a Multi-Step Inequality**

Charity Bowling You are organizing a bowling night for charity. Each ticket costs \$10 and includes shoe rental. Shoes cost you \$5 per pair and door prizes cost you \$50. How many people need to attend for you to raise at least \$200?

Solution

To find the amount you can raise, subtract the total costs from the total ticket sales. Let $x =$ the number of people.

Ticket Sales		Costs				Profit
Ticket price	Number of people	Shoe price	Number of people	Cost of prizes		Amount raised

$$\underbrace{\text{Ticket price} \cdot \text{Number of people}} - \left(\underbrace{\text{Shoe price} \cdot \text{Number of people}} + \underbrace{\text{Cost of prizes}}\right) \geq \underbrace{\text{Amount raised}}$$

$10x - (5x + 50) \geq 200$	Write an inequality.
$10x - 5x - 50 \geq 200$	Distributive property
$5x - 50 \geq 200$	Combine like terms.
$5x \geq 250$	Add 50 to each side.
$x \geq 50$	Divide each side by 5.

ANSWER At least 50 people need to attend the bowling night.

Getting Ready to Practice

1. Vocabulary Write the meanings of the symbols $<$, $>$, $\leq$, and $\geq$.

Solve the inequality. Then graph the solution.

2. $5x - 8 < 2$ **3.** $2x + 1 \geq -7$ **4.** $-3x + 4 \leq -11$

5. $x - 13 - 2x > 2$ **6.** $4x - 8 \geq 7x + 1$ **7.** $1 < 3(x - 1)$

8. Find the Error Describe and correct the error in the solution.

$$9 - 2x \leq 3$$
$$-2x \leq -6$$
$$\frac{-2x}{-2} \leq \frac{-6}{-2}$$
$$\times \qquad x \leq 3$$

Practice and Problem Solving

Example   Exercises
1   9–20
2   15–20
3   21–23

Online Resources
CLASSZONE.COM

· More Examples
· eTutorial Plus

Solve the inequality. Then graph the solution.

9. $4a + 7 \geq 11$ **10.** $16 < 3b + 22$ **11.** $7 - 2p \geq -5$

12. $-3y + 2 < -16$ **13.** $-2w + 6 < 2$ **14.** $23s - 30 \leq 39$

15. $12c + 12 > 48c$ **16.** $5x - 14 \leq 2x + 7$ **17.** $5 - 4z > 17 - z$

18. $10 \geq 5(3 + t)$ **19.** $2(5 + n) \leq 6$ **20.** $-3(d + 2) < -3$

21. Sales A salesperson in a clothing store earns $350 per week plus a 20% commission on the clothes she sells. She wants to know how much she has to sell in one week to earn at least $500 that week. Solve the inequality $350 + 0.2x \geq 500$. What does the solution mean in this situation?

22. Video Games You are approaching the high score of 18,550 on a video game where you have to catch discs for 150 points each. Your current score is 16,000. You want to know how many more discs you need to catch to have a new high score. Use the verbal model to write an inequality. Then solve the inequality. What does the solution mean in this situation?

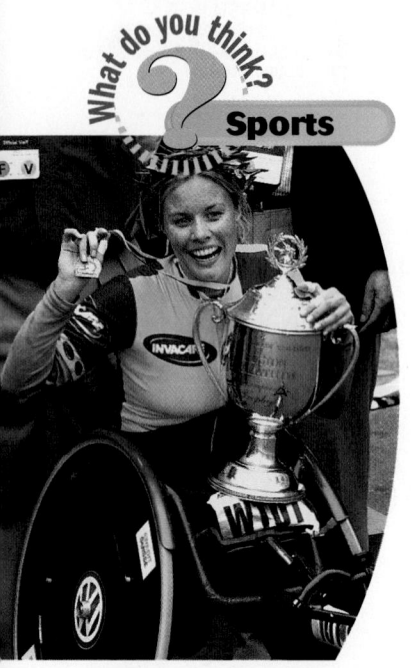

What do you think?

Sports

Boston Marathon

Edith Hunkeler of Switzerland won the women's wheelchair division of the Boston Marathon in 2002. She finished the 26.2 mile race in 1 hour, 45 minutes, and 57 seconds. What was her mean speed?

23. Boston Marathon You are planning to compete in the Boston Marathon. To officially enter, you have to raise at least $1500 for charity. You've already raised $925 by asking people to pledge $25 each. How many more $25 pledges do you need to enter?

Money already raised	+	Amount per pledge	·	Additional pledges	≥	Minimum required

Use the verbal model to write and solve an inequality to find the number p of additional pledges that will satisfy the donation requirements.

24. Writing Describe how solving an inequality is similar to solving an equation and how it is different from solving an equation.

Solve the inequality.

25. $\frac{1}{2}k - 6 \le -\frac{1}{6}k$

26. $\frac{1}{3}m - \frac{1}{2}m > -4$

27. $-\frac{1}{4}d - \frac{2}{5}d \le 13$

28. $4.56h - 7.912 \ge 1.12h$

29. $4.32 - 0.14x < 0.76x$

30. $0.5w > 12.53 - 0.2w$

31. $3.7z \le 33.32 - 3.1z$

32. $-0.6y - 3.79 + 5.2y < 19.67$

33. Magazines It costs a magazine publisher $1.20 to produce each magazine. Overhead costs, such as salaries and office space, are $25,000 per month. The publisher sells the magazine for $3.95. How many magazines does the publisher need to produce and sell each month to make a profit?

Price per magazine	·	Number of magazines	−	Cost per magazine	·	Number of magazines	≥	Overhead costs

Use the verbal model to write and solve an inequality. What does the solution mean in this situation?

Challenge Solve the inequality. Then graph the solution.

34. $\frac{2}{3}x + \frac{4}{3} - \frac{3}{4}x < -\frac{3}{4}$

35. $\frac{2}{3}x + 18 \ge 5 - \frac{4}{7}x$

36. $0.05a + 9.367 - 1.65a \le 5.44$

37. $2.3x - 52.46 \le -0.9(x - 117)$

Number Sense For Exercises 38–40, use the information below. Then tell what the solution represents in this situation and why it cannot be correct.

You and your sisters have $25 to spend at a baseball game. You buy 3 ice creams for $4 each, then use the rest for $3 drinks. You write and solve an inequality to find the number of drinks you can afford.

38. $d < 120$

39. $d \le 0$

40. $d \ge 4$

Choose a Strategy **Use a strategy from the list to solve the following problem. Explain your choice of strategy.**

Problem Solving Strategies
- Guess, Check, and Revise
- Make a List
- Draw a Diagram

41. You are making a sandwich. For bread, you can use either white or wheat. For meat, you can use turkey, ham, or roast beef. Finally, you can have mustard, mayonnaise, or neither. How many different kinds of sandwiches can you make?

Find the mean, median, and mode(s) of the data set. *(Lesson 5.8)*

42. 3.22, 4.45, 6.13, 6.27, 6.34   **43.** 14, 22, 22, 23, 25, 28

Solve the equation. *(Lesson 6.3)*

44. $3.3c - 2.1 = 7.8$ **45.** $4.8 - 2.3x = -3.02$ **46.** $23.06 + 4.3y = 6.72$

FCAT Practice

47. Multiple Choice A school is selling T-shirts as a fundraiser. The shirts cost the school $2500. The school decides to sell each T-shirt for $12. They want to make a profit of at least $1000. Which inequality can be used to find the number of T-shirts the school needs to sell?

A. $12x - 2500 \leq 1000$ **B.** $12x - 2500 \geq 1000$

C. $12x + 2500 \geq 1000$ **D.** $12x + 2500 \leq 1000$

48. Multiple Choice Solve the inequality $-2c - 5 - 7c > -113$.

F. $c < -12$ **G.** $c > -12$ **H.** $c < 12$ **I.** $c > 12$

City Solutions

Fill in the blanks with variables so that each inequality on the right is the solution of an inequality on the left. When you are finished, the letters will spell out the name of a city found in 12 states.

1. $2a + 7 - 3a \geq 12$ $\underline{\ ?\ } < 1$

2. $4p + 1 > 9p - 4$ $\underline{\ ?\ } \leq -5$

3. $s - 2(s + 1) > 3$ $\underline{\ ?\ } \geq 5$

4. $12 \leq -3r - 13 + 8r$ $\underline{\ ?\ } > 1$

5. $-i + 4 + 7i > 10$ $\underline{\ ?\ } < -5$

Technology Activity

FLORIDA
Standards and Assessment
- Solve linear inequalities. (MA.D.2.3.1)
- Solve multi-step real-world problems. (MA.A.3.3.3)

Solving Inequalities

GOAL Use a spreadsheet and truth functions to solve inequalities.

Example Solve the inequality $3x + 2 < 2x - 6$.

Solution

1 Enter the integers -10 to 10 in column A. Column A contains possible solutions of the inequality.

2 Type the formula "$=3*A2 + 2$" in cell B2. Use the fill down feature. Column B contains values of the left side of the inequality.

B2	=3*A2+2			
	A	**B**	**C**	**D**
1	x-values	$3x + 2$		
2	-10	-28		
3	-9	-25		
4	-8	-22		
5	-7	-19		

3 Type the formula "$=2*A2 - 6$" in cell C2. Use the fill down feature. Column C contains values of the right side of the inequality.

C4	=2*A4−6			
	A	**B**	**C**	**D**
1	x-values	$3x + 2$	$2x - 6$	B < C?
2	-10	-28	-26	True
3	-9	-25	-24	True
4	-8	-22	-22	False
5	-7	-19	-20	False

4 Type the truth function "$=B2 < C2$" in cell D2. Use the fill down feature. Column D tells whether the inequality is true or false for the x-value in that row.

HELP with Technology

A *truth function* compares values and returns *True* or *False*.

ANSWER The solution is all numbers less than -8.

Your turn now **Use spreadsheet software to solve the inequality.**

1. $13 - 3y > -2y$ **2.** $7 - 2s < s - 2$ **3.** $2n - 10 \geq 12n$

4. $p + 16 \leq -3p$ **5.** $-2t + 9 > -5t$ **6.** $x - 3 < 5x + 1$

7. **Shopping** Dani has \$10 to buy school supplies. A notebook costs \$1.50, a pencil costs \$.25, and a pen costs \$.95. She needs two notebooks, three pens, and a few pencils. How many pencils can she buy?

Problem Solving and Inequalities

BEFORE	▶ Now	WHY?
You solved multi-step inequalities.	You'll use multi-step inequalities to solve real-world problems.	So you can determine how many CDs you can buy, as in Ex. 16.

In the Real World

Season Tickets Individual tickets for a college hockey game cost $8 each plus a one-time transaction fee of $5. You can buy a season ticket for $99. How many games would you have to attend so that buying a season ticket is a better value than buying individual tickets?

EXAMPLE 1 Writing and Solving an Inequality

To decide how many games you would have to attend so that buying a season ticket is a better value than buying individual game tickets, write and solve an inequality.

Price of single ticket	•	Number of games	+	Transaction fee	>	Price of season ticket

$8x + 5 > 99$	Write an inequality.
$8x > 94$	Subtract 5 from each side.
$x > 11.75$	Divide each side by 8.

ANSWER It doesn't make sense to attend 11.75 games. So you would have to attend 12 or more games to make buying a season ticket a better value than buying individual tickets.

Your turn now Look back at Example 1.

1. Check that the solution in Example 1 is reasonable.

2. Individual tickets for a college basketball game cost $12 each plus a one-time transaction fee of $8. A season ticket costs $125. How many games would you have to attend so that buying a season ticket is a better value than buying individual tickets?

Writing Inequalities The following common sentences indicate the four types of inequalities.

$a < b$	$a > b$
a is less than b.	a is greater than b.
a is fewer than b.	a is more than b.
$a \le b$	$a \ge b$
a is less than or equal to b.	a is greater than or equal to b.
a is at most b.	a is at least b.
a is no more than b.	a is no less than b.

HELP with Reading

The phrase "*a* more than *b*" means $b + a$, while "*a* is more than *b*" means $a > b$.

EXAMPLE 2 Translating Verbal Sentences

Write the sentence as an inequality.

a. Six times the difference of a number and 3 is more than 24.

b. Nine more than 4 times a number is at least 30 plus 11 times the number.

Solution

First decide which inequality symbol to use. Then substitute numbers, variables, and operation symbols.

a. The phrase "is more than" means >.

6 times the difference of a number and 3 **is more than** 24.

$$6 \quad \cdot \quad (x - 3) \quad > \quad 24$$

ANSWER The inequality is $6(x - 3) > 24$.

b. The phrase "is at least" means ≥.

9 more than 4 times a number **is at least** 30 plus 11 times the number.

$$9 \quad + \quad 4x \quad \ge \quad 30 \quad + \quad 11x$$

ANSWER The inequality is $9 + 4x \ge 30 + 11x$.

Your turn now **Write the sentence as an inequality. Let *x* represent the unknown number.**

3. Six times the sum of a number and 8 is no more than 12 less than twice the number.

4. The difference of a number and 4 is less than 10 more than 3 times the number.

EXAMPLE 3 **Writing and Solving an Inequality**

Owning a Business You use the Internet to sell mousepads. You pay a wholesaler $6 for each mousepad. You then sell the mousepads for $10 each. You pay $21 per month for Web page hosting. How many mousepads should you sell each month to earn a profit?

Solution

To earn a profit, your revenue must be greater than your expenses.

| Selling price | · | Number of mousepads | > | Wholesale price | · | Number of mousepads | + | Web page cost |

$10x > 6x + 21$ Write an inequality.

$4x > 21$ Subtract 6x from each side.

$x > 5.25$ Divide each side by 4.

ANSWER You cannot sell part of a mousepad. So, you should sell at least 6 mousepads per month to earn a profit.

6.6 **Exercises**
More Practice, p. 732

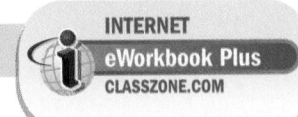

INTERNET
eWorkbook Plus
CLASSZONE.COM

Getting Ready to Practice

Vocabulary **Write the sentence as an inequality. Let *x* represent the unknown number.**

1. A number is at least 5.

2. A number plus 5 is greater than 9.

3. Eight minus a number is at most 6.

4. Four times a number is less than 28.

5. **Guided Problem Solving** You have $200 to spend on a health club membership. The initial fee to join is $50. There is a monthly fee of $32. For how many months can you be a member without spending more than $200?

(1 Write a variable expression for the total cost of a health club membership.

(2 Use the expression from Step 1 to write an inequality.

(3 Solve the inequality and check that the answer makes sense. Explain what the solution means in the situation.

Practice and Problem Solving

HELP with Homework

Example Exercises
  1   16–18
  2   6–13
  3   16–18

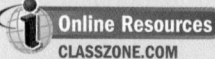
Online Resources
CLASSZONE.COM

· More Examples
· eTutorial Plus

Write the sentence as an inequality. Let _x_ represent the unknown number. Then solve the inequality.

6. A number plus 2 is at most 6.

7. Nine is less than a number plus 1.

8. Seven less than a number is more than 14.

9. Eight times a number is at least 40.

Matching In Exercises 10–13, match the verbal sentence with the inequality.

A. $4(x + 2) \geq 18$ **B.** $4x + 2 < 18$ **C.** $2x - 4 > 18$ **D.** $2(x - 4) \leq 18$

10. Four times the sum of a number and 2 is at least 18.

11. The difference of 2 times a number and 4 is more than 18.

12. Two times the difference of a number and 4 is no more than 18.

13. The sum of 4 times a number and 2 is fewer than 18.

14. Writing Write a real-world problem that can be solved using the inequality $5 + 8x \leq 31$. Solve the inequality and explain what the solution means in the situation.

15. Critical Thinking Explain the difference between _3 less than a number_ and _3 is less than a number_.

16. Buying CDs Each CD you order online costs $12. Shipping and handling charges are $4. You have $50 to spend. Use the verbal model to write and solve an inequality. How many CDs can you buy?

Cost of CD	·	Number of CDs	+	Shipping charges	? ≤	Money you have

17. Teen Club A teen club has weekly dances. You can become a member of the club for $30 a year and pay only $4 to attend each dance. Otherwise, each dance costs $6. How many dances do you have to attend so that becoming a member will cost less than paying the nonmember rate?

18. Signatures To get a question on a state ballot, you need at least 419,260 signatures on a petition. You've collected 209,260 signatures and have 30 days to collect the rest. Find the mean number of signatures you need to collect per day.

19. Snowstorm School will be cancelled if there are at least 6 inches of snow at 6 A.M. There are 2 inches of snow at 7:00 P.M. the night before. The snow is predicted to continue falling at a rate of 0.5 inch per hour. Write an inequality to represent the situation. When will there be at least 6 inches of snow? Will there be school the next day? Explain.

20. Express Mail A package sent via Express Mail must be no more than 108 inches in total length and girth. You want to wrap as many boxes together as possible to send as one package. Each box is the same size. Write and solve an inequality to find how many boxes you could wrap as one package if they are arranged as shown.

girth = 2h + 2w
h = 15 in.
w = 12 in.
l = 6 in.

Extended Problem Solving Town Taxi charges $2.00 plus $.40 for every $\frac{1}{5}$ mile. City Cab charges $2.50 plus $.25 for every $\frac{1}{7}$ mile.

21. Interpret Write expressions for the total cost of a ride with Town Taxi and the total cost of a ride with City Cab.

22. Compare For what distances does City Cab cost less than Town Taxi? Express your answer as an inequality.

23. Analyze Use the expressions from Exercise 21 to express the distances that Town Taxi costs less than City Cab.

Mixed Review

Find the indicated measurement, where *r* = radius, *d* = diameter, and *C* = circumference. Use 3.14 for π. *(Lesson 6.4)*

24. $d = 27$ m, $r = \underline{\ ?\ }$ **25.** $r = 34$ in., $C = \underline{\ ?\ }$ **26.** $C = 62.8$ ft, $d = \underline{\ ?\ }$

Basic Skills Evaluate the expression.

27. $9 + (10 - 8)^4 \times 5$ **28.** $3 + 50 \div 5^2 - 8$ **29.** $275 - 2(3 + 2)^3$

FCAT Practice

30. Multiple Choice Ron wants to buy some souvenirs while on vacation. He decides to buy a magnet for $4.50 and some postcards for $.25 each. Ron has $10 to spend. Solve the inequality $4.5 + 0.25p \leq 10$. How many postcards *p* can Ron buy?

A. less than 22   **B.** no more than 22

C. at most 58   **D.** fewer than 58

31. Short Response Carol earned a 91, 80, and 83 on her last three English tests. What does Carol need to earn on her next test to have an average of at least 86? Write and solve an inequality.

LESSONS 6.4 TO 6.6

Notebook Review

Review the vocabulary definitions in your notebook.

Copy the review examples in your notebook. Then complete the exercises.

Check Your Definitions

circle, p. 290
center, p. 290

radius, p. 290
diameter, p. 290

circumference, p. 290
pi (π), p. 290

Use Your Vocabulary

1. Copy and complete: Pi is the quotient of a circle's ? and its ?.

6.4 Can you solve equations involving circumference?

 EXAMPLE Find the circumference of a circle with diameter 30.5 cm.

$C = \pi d$ **Circumference formula**

$\approx (3.14)(30.5)$ **Substitute 3.14 for π and 30.5 for d.**

$= 95.77$ cm   **Multiply.**

☑ **Find the indicated measurement, where r = radius, d = diameter, and C = circumference. Use 3.14 or $\frac{22}{7}$ for π.**

2. $r = 7$; $C = $?   **3.** $C = 121$; $d = $?   **4.** $C = 314$; $r = $?

6.5 Can you solve multi-step inequalities?

 EXAMPLE Solve $-5(x + 9) \geq 30$.

$-5(x + 9) \geq 30$ **Original inequality**

$-5x - 45 \geq 30$ **Distributive property**

$-5x \geq 75$ **Add 45 to each side.**

$x \leq -15$ **Divide each side by -5 and reverse the inequality symbol.**

☑ **Solve the inequality.**

5. $2b - 32 < 52$ **6.** $5j - 18 > 18 - j$ **7.** $6y \leq 3(9 + y)$

6.6 Can you write and solve an inequality?

EXAMPLE You and 3 friends plan to use a $50 gift certificate to pay for dinner. You order an appetizer that costs $6. What is the most each of you can spend so the total cost of the meal is no more than $50?

Number of people	·	Cost per person	+	Price of appetizer	≤	Amount of gift certificate

$4x + 6 \leq 50$ Write an inequality.

$4x \leq 44$ Subtract 6 from each side.

$x \leq 11$ Divide each side by 4.

ANSWER The most that each of you can spend is $11.

8. You want to work out for at least 45 minutes. You jog for 20 minutes, then divide your time evenly among the stationary bike, stair machine, and rowing machine. How long should you use each machine?

Stop *and* **Think**   about Lessons 6.4–6.6

9. Writing Describe how you know which inequality symbol to use when translating a sentence.

Review Quiz 2

Find the indicated measurement, where *r* = radius, *d* = diameter, and *C* = circumference. Use 3.14 or $\frac{22}{7}$ for π.

1. $d = 28$ in., $C = \underline{?}$ **2.** $C = 150$ cm, $r = \underline{?}$

Solve the inequality.

3. $-8a - 10 > 14$ **4.** $3z \leq 35 - 2z$ **5.** $5b \geq 2(b + 2.25)$

Write the sentence as an inequality. Then solve.

6. Two less than six times a number is at least forty.

7. Five times the sum of four and a number is greater than ten.

8. Video Games Your current score in a video game is 33,600 points. At each level you earn 2500 points for catching objects and 1700 points for overcoming the obstacles. How many more levels must you go through to beat your high score of 54,000?

6

Chapter Review

📓 Vocabulary

circle, p. 290   radius, p. 290   circumference, p. 290
center, p. 290   diameter, p. 290   pi (π), p. 290

Vocabulary Review

Copy and complete the statement.

1. A ___?___ is the set of all points in a plane that are the same distance from a fixed point called the center.

2. You can approximate ___?___ with the decimal 3.14 or the fraction $\frac{22}{7}$.

Matching **Match the word with the correct definition.**

3. diameter   **A.** the distance around a circle

4. circumference   **B.** the distance across a circle through the center

5. radius   **C.** the distance from the center to any point on the circle

Review Questions

Solve the equation. *(Lessons 6.1–6.3)*

6. $6a - 14a = 96$

7. $18 + 4(p - 9) = 6$

8. $4(12 + z) - z = -192$

9. $7c - 10 = c + 44$

10. $6(t - 5) = 2(t + 5)$

11. $-7b + 10 = -11 - 4b$

12. $\frac{11}{16}n - 3 + \frac{1}{4}n = \frac{7}{4}$

13. $5s + 3\frac{1}{8} = \frac{5}{24} - 2s$

14. $5(m - 9) = 13 - 4(10 + m)$

15. **Find the Error** Describe and correct the error made in finding the perimeter of the rectangle. *(Lesson 6.2)*

4x + 2

2y   y + 4

3x + 5

✗ 4x + 2 = 3x + 5
       x = 3
    2y = y + 4
       y = 4
    P = 2(3) + 2(4) = 14

16. **Critical Thinking** What number would you multiply the equation $\frac{5}{9} + \frac{3}{4}x = \frac{2}{3}x - \frac{1}{6}$ by to clear the fractions? *(Lesson 6.3)*

Review Questions

17. **Rowing Teams** Fifty more than twice the number of women's rowing teams is equal to eighty-seven less than three times the number of women's rowing teams. Write and solve an equation to find the number of women's rowing teams. *(Lesson 6.2)*

18. **Recycling Deposit** When you buy a can of soda, you pay for the soda and you pay a $.05 recycling deposit. You pay $4.56 for a 12-pack of soda. How much did each soda cost before the deposit? *(Lesson 6.3)*

19. **Race** You and a friend are running in a race for a charity event. You have completed $\frac{3}{8}$ of the race. Your friend has completed $\frac{1}{4}$ of the race and is $\frac{3}{16}$ mile behind you. How long (in miles) is the race? *(Lesson 6.3)*

Find the indicated measurement, where r = radius, d = diameter, and C = circumference. Use 3.14 or $\frac{22}{7}$ for π. *(Lesson 6.4)*

20. $C = \underline{\ ?\ }$

21. $C = \underline{\ ?\ }$

22. $C = 62.8$ mm

23. $C = 12$ in.

21 ft

8 mm

$d = ?$

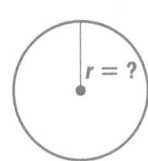
$r = ?$

24. **Dome** The Minnesota State Capitol Building has one of the largest unsupported marble domes in the world, with a diameter of 89 feet at its widest point. Find its circumference using 3.14 for π. *(Lesson 6.4)*

Solve the inequality. Graph the solution. *(Lesson 6.5)*

25. $-5 < 3x + 16$

26. $\frac{2}{3}h - 3 \geq 1$

27. $6 - \frac{2}{5}a > 2$

28. $m + 4(5 - m) > -7$

29. $6 - (g - 7) \leq 6 - 8g$

30. $2(3k + 1) \leq 5(k - 6)$

Write the sentence as an inequality. Then solve the inequality. *(Lesson 6.6)*

31. Fourteen minus three times a number is at most eleven.

32. Nine plus four times a number is less than twenty-one.

33. Seven times the difference of fifteen and a number is at least fifty-six.

34. **School Fundraiser** You are selling magazine subscriptions for a school fundraiser. If you sell at least 75 subscriptions in 2 weeks you win a prize. You sold 26 subscriptions in one week. What is the mean number of subscriptions you have to sell per day to sell at least 75 total? *(Lesson 6.6)*

Chapter Test

Solve the equation.

1. $-3z + 17 + 12z = 11$

2. $m - 6(m + 10) = 50$

3. $7(12 - r) = -84$

4. $3b + 4 = b - 4$

5. $-25 - a = 2a + 20$

6. $3(2x - 11) = 3(x + 10)$

7. $\dfrac{3n - 5}{10} = 7$

8. $\dfrac{-3r + 54}{5} = 2r + 3$

9. $\dfrac{3}{5}w = 5w + \dfrac{22}{25}$

10. Shopping You bought a new shirt for $15.95 and 5 pairs of socks. Your friend bought 10 pairs of socks and spent $4.20 less than you. How much did each pair of socks cost?

11. Newspapers In 1999 there were 1647 daily and 7471 weekly newspapers published in the United States, as well as x other kinds of newspapers. The total number of newspapers was 700 greater than seven times the number x. How many newspapers were published in 1999 that were not daily or weekly?

Find the indicated measurement, where r = radius, d = diameter, and C = circumference. Use 3.14 or $\dfrac{22}{7}$ for π.

12. $d = 12.3$ mm, $C = \underline{\ ?\ }$

13. $C = 22$ in., $r = \underline{\ ?\ }$

14. $C = 9.42$ ft, $d = \underline{\ ?\ }$

15. Tetherball A tetherball pole is 12 feet high. The tetherball is attached to the top of the pole with a string so that the ball hangs 2 feet above the ground. How long is the string attached to the tetherball? What is the circumference of the largest path that the ball could make through the air around the pole? Use 3.14 for π.

Solve the inequality. Then graph the solution.

16. $6n + 19 \leq 7$

17. $10 - 3x > 25$

18. $9c - 8 \geq 3c + 16$

19. $3(k + 3) > k - 1$

20. $8y + 3y + 36 \leq 124$

21. $w - 4(w + 5) < -8$

Write the sentence as an inequality. Then solve the inequality.

22. Nine added to the product of 11 and a number is at most 4.

23. A number times 2 minus 13 is less than the number plus 8.

24. Seven times the difference of 12 and a number is at least 14.

Chapter FCAT Practice

Test-Taking Strategy Work at a pace that is right for you. Do not worry about how fast others are working.

1. What is the radius of a circle whose circumference is 220 feet? Use $\frac{22}{7}$ for π.

   A. 35 inches   **B.** 70 inches

   C. 140 inches   **D.** 691 inches

2. What is the value of x in the equation $\frac{2}{3}x = -2\frac{1}{6} + \frac{5}{6}x$?

   F. $x = -13$ **G.** $x = -3$

   H. $x = 3$ **I.** $x = 13$

3. What is the solution to the inequality $-2x + 5 \geq -13$?

   A. $x \geq -9$ **B.** $x \leq -9$

   C. $x \geq 9$ **D.** $x \leq 9$

4. All three sides of the triangle have equal length. What is the perimeter?

   F. 2 units   **G.** 4 units

   H. 6 units   **I.** 12 units

5. The *Observa*-DOME at the New Orlando Science Center has a diameter of 30 feet at its widest point. What is its circumference? Use 3.14 for π.

   A. 9.55 feet   **B.** 47.1 feet

   C. 94.2 feet   **D.** 188.4 feet

6. What is the value of x in the equation $2(x - 7) = 5x - 11$?

   F. $-8\frac{1}{3}$ **G.** -1 **H.** 1 **I.** $1\frac{1}{3}$

7. The circumference of a clock is 15.7 inches. Which measure is closest to the diameter of the clock?

   A. 2.5 inches   **B.** 5 inches

   C. 10 inches   **D.** 49.3 inches

8. Which inequality represents the sentence *the product of three and a number is less than six more than the number?*

   F. $3n > 6 + n$ **G.** $3n < 6 + n$

   H. $3n - 6 > n$ **I.** $6 - 3n > n$

9. What is the value of x in the equation $8 - 3(x - 5) = -10$?

   A. $x = -1$ **B.** $x = 1$

   C. $x = 4\frac{1}{3}$ **D.** $x = 11$

Short Response

10. One sandwich shop charges $4.50 for each sandwich and $5 for delivery. Another shop charges $6.00 per sandwich but delivers for free. Write and solve an inequality to find out how many sandwiches need to be ordered so that the first shop will be less expensive than the second shop.

Extended Response

11. Jennifer is buying 2.2 pounds of bubble gum that costs $4.50 per pound and lollipops that cost $1.70 per pound. She can't spend more than $15. How many pounds of lollipops can Jennifer buy? Explain your reasoning. Suppose Jennifer buys 3 pounds of bubble gum. Can she buy at least 1 pound of lollipops? Explain.

The Physics of Basketball

Dropping Basketballs

The energy with which a basketball hits the ground affects how high the ball will bounce. When a ball is dribbled, several factors affect this energy, including the energy transmitted to the ball by your hand.

When a ball is dropped, the energy with which it hits the ground depends *only* on the mass of the ball, gravity, and the height from which the ball is dropped. Use the equation below to calculate this energy.

| Energy E (in Joules) | = | mass m (in kilograms) | × | acceleration due to gravity g | × | height h (in meters) |

$$E = mgh$$

For objects on Earth, the acceleration due to gravity g is about 9.8 meters per second squared. You can rewrite the equation above as follows.

$$E = 9.8mh$$

1. Copy and complete the table below. The mass of a typical basketball is 0.6 kilogram. Find the energy with which the ball hits the ground when dropped from each height in the table.

Height (meters)	0.5	1	1.5	2	2.5
Energy (Joules)	?	?	?	?	?

2. You drop a basketball with a mass of 0.6 kilogram. It hits the ground with 12 Joules of energy. From what height did you drop it?

3. You drop a ball from 3 meters and it hits the ground with 15 Joules of energy. What is the mass of the ball?

4. Writing Explain how the energy with which a ball hits the ground changes as you increase the height from which you drop it.

5. Critical Thinking You drop two identical basketballs from two different heights. One height is twice as great as the other. How will the energies of the two balls as they hit the ground compare? Explain.

Bouncing Basketballs

How high a ball bounces is affected by how bouncy the ball is. For example, a fully inflated basketball bounces higher than a partially inflated one, if both balls hit the ground with the same energy. The fully inflated ball is more bouncy.

You can express the bounciness of a ball by finding the ratio of the bounce height to the drop height. Height is measured from the bottom of the ball to the ground. A standard basketball inflated for game play has a bounciness ratio of about 0.6.

$$\frac{\text{Bounce height (in meters)}}{\text{Drop height (in meters)}} \approx 0.6$$

A ball's bounce height is the height of the *first* bounce.

6. You drop a standard basketball 3 meters. About how high will it bounce on its first bounce?

7. You drop a standard basketball. It bounces to a height of 2 meters on its first bounce. From about what height was it dropped?

8. **Critical Thinking** A ball drops 1.5 meters. It bounces 0.6 meters. Is this ball more or less bouncy than a standard basketball? Explain.

9. **Challenge** You drop a standard basketball 6 meters. Explain how to use the bounciness ratio to find how high the ball bounces on its second bounce. Then find the height of the second bounce.

Project IDEAS

- **Experiment** Design and carry out an experiment to compare the bounciness of several types of ball. Describe your experiment and present your results.

- **Report** A given ball may be designed to perform well during the play of the game in which it is commonly used. Choose a sport and find information on the design of the balls and other equipment used in the sport. Present your findings to the class.

- **Research** The unit of energy called the Joule was named after the scientist James Prescott Joule. Find out more about James Prescott Joule and his work. Present your findings to the class.

- **Career** A variety of professionals do scientific research to study how athletes can improve performance and avoid injury. Investigate some of these careers and present your findings to the class.

INTERNET
Project Support
CLASSZONE.COM

CHAPTER 7

Ratio, Proportion, and Percent

BEFORE

In previous chapters you've...

- **Found equivalent fractions**
- **Rewritten fractions and decimals**

Now

In Chapter 7 you'll study...

- **Finding ratios and unit rates**
- **Writing and solving proportions**
- **Solving percent problems**
- **Rewriting fractions, decimals, and percents**
- **Finding probabilities of events**

WHY?

So you can solve real-world problems about...

- lightning, p. 318
- crocodiles, p. 329
- guitars, p. 342
- beaches, p. 347

Internet Preview
CLASSZONE.COM

- eEdition Plus Online
- eWorkbook Plus Online
- eTutorial Plus Online
- FCAT Practice
- More Examples

Chapter Warm-Up Games

Review skills you need for this chapter in these quick games.

Key Skill:
Solving equations

Find a path through the maze from start to finish.

- Then find the sum of all the solutions of the equations to find your total number of points.

- Which path has the least number of points?

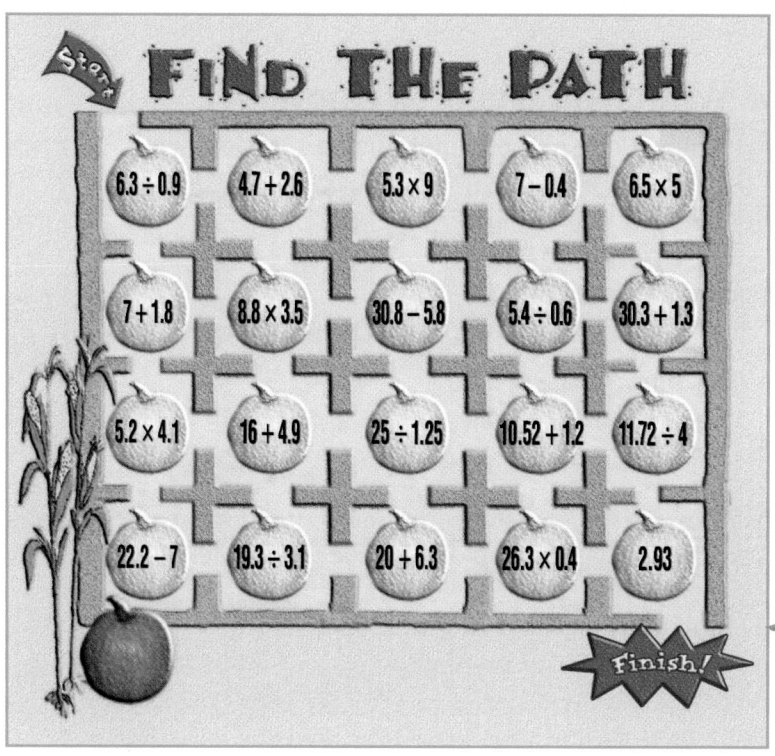

FIND THE PATH

Start

6.3 ÷ 0.9	4.7 + 2.6	5.3 × 9	7 − 0.4	6.5 × 5
7 + 1.8	8.8 × 3.5	30.8 − 5.8	5.4 ÷ 0.6	30.3 + 1.3
5.2 × 4.1	16 + 4.9	25 ÷ 1.25	10.52 + 1.2	11.72 ÷ 4
22.2 − 7	19.3 ÷ 3.1	20 + 6.3	26.3 × 0.4	2.93

Finish!

BRAIN GAME

Key Skill:
Performing operations on decimals

Find your way from start to finish in the maze above.

• Evaluate each expression. Then move to the nearest expression that begins with the number that is the value of the previous expression.

• For example, if you start from 5.3 + 4.2 and your choices are 1.4 + 7.2 and 9.5 − 8, you would move to 9.5 − 8 because 5.3 + 4.2 = 9.5.

Stop and Think

1. **Writing** A student says that a decimal divided by a decimal is never a whole number. Explain the error in the student's reasoning.

2. **Critical Thinking** How many different paths are there through the *Video Maze* that do not cover the same ground more than once?

Getting Ready to Learn

Review What You Need to Know

Using Vocabulary **Copy and complete using a review word.**

Word Watch

Review Words

data, p. 5
equation, p. 28
formula, p. 33
simplest form, p. 179
equivalent fractions, p. 179

1. The fraction $\frac{1}{2}$ is in ? , but $\frac{2}{4}$ is not.

2. The fractions $\frac{2}{3}$ and $\frac{4}{6}$ are ? .

Solve the equation. *(p. 113)*

3. $\frac{x}{7} = 3$ 4. $\frac{x}{-2} = 4$ 5. $-9x = 108$ 6. $8x = 56$

7. You have 15 pairs of socks in your drawer, including exactly 6 pairs of black socks. What fraction of your socks are black? *(p. 179)*

Order the numbers from least to greatest. *(p. 242)*

8. $0, -0.25, \frac{1}{3}, -1.11, \frac{9}{8}, \frac{12}{9}$ 9. $-\frac{7}{8}, 1.28, \frac{1}{12}, -0.02, 0.34, \frac{10}{3}$

You should include material that appears on a notebook like this in your own notes.

Know How to Take Notes

Taking Notes in Class When your teacher answers your question in class, include the answer in your notes.

Writing Decimals as Fractions

$0.007 = \frac{7}{1000}$ 0.007 has **3** decimal places.
1000 has **3** zeros.

Number of decimal places equals number of zeros!

$0.13 = \frac{13}{100}$ 0.13 has **2** decimal places.
100 has **2** zeros.

As you work on solving proportions in Chapter 7, be sure to ask questions about things you don't understand and write the answers in your notes.

LESSON 7.1

Ratios and Rates

BEFORE	▶ Now	WHY?
You found equivalent fractions.	You'll find ratios and unit rates.	So you can tell whether a TV has a wide screen, as in Ex. 22.

Word Watch

ratio, p. 317
equivalent ratios, p. 317
rate, p. 318
unit rate, p. 318

FLORIDA
Standards and Assessment

• Know names and numerals for ratios. (MA.A.1.3.1)

• Know appropriate operations to solve real-world problems. (MA.A.3.3.2)

 You can compare side lengths and perimeters of squares.

(1 Copy and complete the table using the squares shown. Write the relationship between the side length and the perimeter of each square as a fraction in simplest form.

(2 What do you notice about the fractions in the table?

(3 Describe the relationship between the side length and the perimeter of a square with side length *s*.

Side length	2	4	5
Perimeter	?	?	?
Side length / Perimeter	?	?	?

In the activity, you used a *ratio* to reach a conclusion about the relationship between the side length and the perimeter of a square. A **ratio** uses division to compare two numbers. You can write the ratio of *a* to *b* (*b* ≠ 0) in three ways.

$$\frac{a}{b} \qquad a:b \qquad a \text{ to } b$$

Ratios that have the same value are called **equivalent ratios** .

EXAMPLE 1 Writing a Ratio

Skiing A ski resort has 15 easy, 25 intermediate, 7 difficult, and 11 expert-only trails. Write the ratio intermediate trails : easy trails in three ways.

$$\frac{\text{intermediate trails}}{\text{easy trails}} = \frac{25}{15} = \frac{5}{3} \qquad \text{Write as a fraction and simplify.}$$

ANSWER The ratio can be written as $\frac{5}{3}$, 5 : 3 , or 5 to 3.

Your turn now Use the information in Example 1 to write the ratio as a fraction in simplest form and two other ways.

1. easy trails to difficult trails   **2.** expert-only trails to easy trails

Rates A **rate** is a ratio of two quantities that have *different* units. Two rates are equivalent if they have the same value.

EXAMPLE 2 Finding an Equivalent Rate

Weather Lightning strikes about 100 times per second around the world. About how many times does lightning strike per minute around the world?

Solution

Use the fact that 60 sec = 1 min. So, $\frac{60 \text{ sec}}{1 \text{ min}}$ is equivalent to 1.

$$\frac{100 \text{ times}}{1 \text{ sec}} = \frac{100 \text{ times}}{1 \text{ sec}} \cdot \frac{60 \text{ sec}}{1 \text{ min}} \qquad \text{Multiply by a fraction that is equivalent to 1.}$$

$$= \frac{6000 \text{ times}}{1 \text{ min}} \qquad \text{Simplify.}$$

ANSWER Lightning strikes about 6000 times per minute around the world.

Unit Rates A **unit rate** is a rate that has a denominator of 1 unit. To write a unit rate, find an equivalent rate with a denominator of 1 unit.

HELP with Review

For help with equivalent fractions, see p. 179.

EXAMPLE 3 Finding a Unit Rate

Write −24 feet per 5 seconds as a unit rate.

$$\frac{-24 \text{ ft}}{5 \text{ sec}} = \frac{-24 \div 5}{5 \div 5} \qquad \begin{array}{l}\text{Divide numerator and denominator by 5 to} \\ \text{get a denominator of 1 unit.}\end{array}$$

$$= \frac{-4.8}{1} \qquad \text{Simplify.}$$

ANSWER The unit rate is −4.8 feet per second.

✓ **Check** Round −4.8 ft/sec to −5 ft/sec. The product −5 • 5 = −25, which is about −24, so your answer is reasonable.

Your turn now **Write your answer as a rate.**

3. A water pump moves 2 gallons of water per second. How many gallons of water are pumped per minute?

Write the rate as a unit rate.

4. $\frac{114 \text{ points}}{6 \text{ games}}$ 5. $\frac{365 \text{ people}}{5 \text{ months}}$ 6. $\frac{329 \text{ miles}}{10 \text{ gallons}}$ 7. $\frac{-49 \text{ m}}{14 \text{ sec}}$

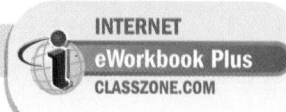

Getting Ready to Practice

with Homework

Example	Exercises
1	10–17, 27–28
2	18–21
3	23–26

Online Resources
CLASSZONE.COM
· More Examples
· eTutorial Plus

1. **Vocabulary** Copy and complete: Three gallons to $4.50 and five gallons to $7.50 are equivalent __?__ .

Write the ratio as a fraction in simplest form and two other ways.

2. $\frac{12}{36}$

3. $\frac{15}{10}$

4. $\frac{6}{4}$

Tell whether the ratios are equivalent.

5. $\frac{5}{2}$ and $\frac{20}{8}$

6. 12 to 3 and 6 to 2

7. $6 : 18$ and $10 : 30$

8. **Wages** You are paid $47.25 for working 7 hours. How much are you paid per hour?

9. **Find the Error** Describe and correct the error in the solution.

Find an equivalent rate of 14 times a day.

$$\times \quad \frac{14 \text{ times}}{\text{day}} \cdot \frac{1 \text{ week}}{7 \text{ days}} = \frac{2 \text{ times}}{\text{week}}$$

Practice and Problem Solving

Write the ratio as a fraction in simplest form and two other ways.

10. $\frac{33}{22}$

11. $\frac{20}{25}$

12. $-8 : 6$

13. 35 to 49

14. 51 to 17

15. $26 : 39$

16. $\frac{27}{42}$

17. $\frac{-12}{4}$

Measurement Write the equivalent rate.

18. $\frac{60 \text{ miles}}{\text{hour}} = \frac{? \text{ miles}}{\text{minute}}$

19. $\frac{32 \text{ ounces}}{\text{serving}} = \frac{? \text{ pounds}}{\text{serving}}$

20. $\frac{105 \text{ min}}{\text{game}} = \frac{? \text{ h}}{\text{game}}$

21. $\frac{\$1.44}{\text{ft}} = \frac{\$?}{\text{yd}}$

22. **Television** The aspect ratio of a TV screen is the ratio of its length to its width. The aspect ratio of a *standard* TV screen is $4 : 3$. The aspect ratio of a *wide screen* TV in the United States is $16 : 9$. Describe how you would tell whether a TV has a standard or wide screen given the length and width of the screen.

Write the rate as a unit rate.

23. $\dfrac{24 \text{ adults}}{6 \text{ cars}}$ **24.** $\dfrac{-34 \text{ meters}}{8 \text{ seconds}}$ **25.** $\dfrac{3 \text{ pounds}}{\$2}$ **26.** $\dfrac{610 \text{ rotations}}{5 \text{ minutes}}$

Write the ratio of shaded to unshaded squares.

27.

28.

Find the value of the variable that makes the ratios equivalent.

29. $\dfrac{x}{8} = \dfrac{4}{16}$ **30.** $\dfrac{9}{c} = \dfrac{27}{30}$ **31.** $\dfrac{6}{10} = \dfrac{15}{n}$ **32.** $\dfrac{2}{12} = \dfrac{z}{18}$

33. Writing About one out of every ten people is left-handed. How many people in your math class would you predict to be left-handed? Explain.

34. Running Speed At top speed, a greyhound can run 330 feet in 5 seconds, a roadrunner can run 75 feet in 3 seconds, and a cheetah can run 198 feet in 2 seconds. Write each speed as a unit rate. Which animal is the fastest? Which animal is the slowest?

35. Population Density New Jersey's population in 2000 was about 8,414,000. New Jersey's area is 7417 square miles. What was the population per square mile, or *population density*, in New Jersey in 2000? Round to the nearest whole number.

36. Challenge You can buy your favorite crackers in a 10 ounce box or a 1 pound box. The 10 ounce box costs $2.69 and the 1 pound box costs $3.28. Which is the better buy? Explain.

Mixed Review

37. Find the radius of a circle with a circumference of 39.25 feet. Use 3.14 for π. *(Lesson 6.4)*

38. Solve the inequality $10y + 4 < 24$ and graph the solution. *(Lesson 6.5)*

Basic Skills Solve the equation.

39. $3c = 18$ **40.** $9x = -81$ **41.** $\dfrac{v}{4} = -2$ **42.** $\dfrac{n}{10} = 8$

FCAT Practice

43. Multiple Choice Which rate is equivalent to $4.62 per 3 liters?

  A. $\dfrac{\$1.54}{3 \text{ L}}$ **B.** $\dfrac{\$3.08}{2 \text{ L}}$ **C.** $\dfrac{\$4.62}{2 \text{ L}}$ **D.** $\dfrac{\$2.31}{1 \text{ L}}$

44. Short Response Ana drives 125 miles in 2 hours 30 minutes, and Rachel drives 150 miles in 3 hours 20 minutes. Who has the faster average speed? Explain your reasoning.

7.2 Hands-on Activity

FLORIDA: Standards and Assessment
Use scale drawings to recreate a situation.
(MA.B.1.3.4)
Interpret and apply scales. (MA.B.1.3.4)

GOAL
Make scale drawings.

MATERIALS
· ruler   · colored pencils
· grid paper   · magazine

Making a Scale Drawing

A *scale drawing* of an object preserves ratios of lengths but is either smaller or larger than the original object.

Explore   **Make an enlarged drawing of the picture.**

1 Draw a grid on the original picture.

2 On your grid paper, draw a rectangle that is the same number of units long and wide as the picture you want to enlarge. These unit squares should be bigger than the grid squares on the original picture.

3 Starting in a corner, copy the image that appears in the corresponding corner of the original onto your grid paper. Continue copying the image one block at a time until you have drawn the entire picture.

4 The *scale* of the drawing is the ratio of corresponding measurements of the copy to the original. Measure the width of the copy and of the original. What is the scale of your drawing?

Your turn now

1. Cut out a picture from a magazine and create an enlarged scale drawing of it. Measure the original picture and the enlarged drawing to determine the scale.

2. Is the ratio of the area of a unit square in the copy to the area of a unit square in the original the same as the ratio of their sides? Explain.

Stop *and* **Think**

3. Critical Thinking What would happen if different scales were used in the same drawing?

LESSON 7.2

Writing and Solving Proportions

BEFORE	Now	WHY?
You wrote ratios.	You'll write and solve proportions.	So you can find the dimensions of a model car, as in Ex. 35.

In the Real World

Word Watch

proportion, p. 322
cross products, p. 323
scale model, p. 324
scale, p. 324

FLORIDA
Standards and Assessment

• Interpret and apply scales. (MA.B.1.3.4)

• Use scale drawings to recreate a situation. (MA.B.1.3.4)

Rhinoceros Beetles An adult rhinoceros beetle weighs only 0.525 ounce but can carry about 446.25 ounces on its back. If a person were as strong as a rhinoceros beetle, how much weight could a 100 pound person carry?

A **proportion** is an equation that states that two ratios are equivalent.

$$\frac{a}{b} = \frac{c}{d}, \ b \neq 0, \ d \neq 0$$

The proportion above is read "a is to b as c is to d."

EXAMPLE 1 Writing and Solving a Proportion

To answer the question about strength above, write and solve a proportion.

HELP with Solving

In Example 1, the ratios in the proportion use the following units:
$\frac{ounces}{ounces}$ and $\frac{pounds}{pounds}$.

	Beetle	Person
Carries	446.25	x
Weighs	0.525	100

Use a table to set up a proportion.

$\frac{446.25}{0.525} = \frac{x}{100}$ Write a proportion.

$\frac{446.25}{0.525} \cdot 100 = \frac{x}{100} \cdot 100$ Multiply each side by 100.

$85,000 = x$ Simplify.

ANSWER If human strength were proportional to that of a rhinoceros beetle, a 100 pound person could carry 85,000 pounds.

Your turn now Solve the proportion.

1. $\frac{n}{12} = \frac{3}{4}$ **2.** $\frac{50}{20} = \frac{z}{16}$ **3.** $\frac{250}{30} = \frac{t}{51}$

Cross Products The proportion $\frac{a}{b} = \frac{c}{d}$ has **cross products** ad and bc.

$$a \cdot d \qquad\qquad b \cdot c$$

You can use cross products to solve a proportion. You can also use cross products to check whether two ratios form a proportion.

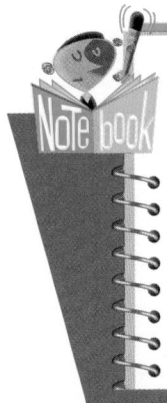

Cross Products Property

Words The cross products of a proportion are equal.

Algebra If $\frac{a}{b} = \frac{c}{d}$, where b and d are nonzero numbers, then $ad = bc$.

Numbers Because $\frac{3}{4} = \frac{9}{12}$, you know that $3 \cdot 12 = 4 \cdot 9$.

EXAMPLE 2 **Using the Cross Products Property**

$$\frac{6.8}{15.4} = \frac{40.8}{m} \qquad \text{Original proportion}$$

$$6.8 \cdot m = 15.4 \cdot 40.8 \qquad \text{Cross products property}$$

$$6.8m = 628.32 \qquad \text{Multiply.}$$

$$\frac{6.8m}{6.8} = \frac{628.32}{6.8} \qquad \text{Divide each side by 6.8.}$$

$$m = 92.4 \qquad \text{Simplify.}$$

✓ **Check** You can check your solution by finding the cross products of the proportion. If the cross products are equal, the solution is correct.

$$\frac{6.8}{15.4} \overset{?}{=} \frac{40.8}{92.4} \qquad \begin{array}{l}\text{Substitute 92.4 for } m \text{ in} \\ \text{original proportion.}\end{array}$$

$$6.8 \cdot 92.4 \overset{?}{=} 15.4 \cdot 40.8$$

$$628.32 = 628.32 \checkmark$$

Your turn now Solve the proportion. Then check your solution.

4. $\frac{6}{c} = \frac{54}{99}$
    5. $\frac{n}{14} = \frac{63}{98}$
    6. $\frac{2.1}{0.9} = \frac{27.3}{y}$

STRAWBERRY POINT

■ **Sculpture**

How many inches tall is the giant strawberry? Write the scale of the strawberry sculpture without units.

Scale The dimensions of a **scale model** are proportional to the dimensions of the actual object. The **scale** gives the relationship between the model's dimensions and the actual object's dimensions. A scale can be written as a ratio with or without units. For example, the scale 1 in. : 3 ft can also be written as 1 : 36.

EXAMPLE 3 **Using a Scale**

Sculpture Strawberry Point, Iowa, has a strawberry sculpture that is 15 feet tall. If the scale of this model is 10 feet to 1 inch, how tall was the original strawberry?

Solution

$$\text{Scale} = \frac{\text{Height of strawberry model}}{\text{Height of original strawberry}} \qquad \text{Write a verbal model.}$$

$$\frac{10 \text{ ft}}{1 \text{ in.}} = \frac{15 \text{ ft}}{h \text{ in.}} \qquad \text{Write a proportion.}$$

$$10h = 15 \qquad \text{Cross products property}$$

$$h = 1.5 \qquad \text{Divide each side by 10.}$$

ANSWER The height of the original strawberry was 1.5 inches.

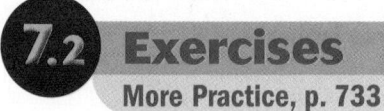

7.2 **Exercises**

More Practice, p. 733

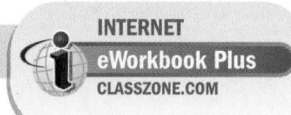

INTERNET
eWorkbook Plus
CLASSZONE.COM

Getting Ready to Practice

1. **Vocabulary** Describe how to use cross products to solve a proportion.

Solve the proportion. Then check your solution.

2. $\dfrac{1}{2} = \dfrac{x}{6}$ 3. $\dfrac{2}{3} = \dfrac{4}{z}$ 4. $\dfrac{6}{a} = \dfrac{3}{1}$ 5. $\dfrac{c}{10} = \dfrac{3}{5}$

6. **Find the Error** Describe and correct the error in solving the proportion.

7. **Cars** A car moving at a constant speed travels 88 feet in 2 seconds. Use a proportion to find how many feet it travels in one minute.

$$\frac{3}{9} = \frac{12}{m} \qquad \times$$

$$9m = 3 \cdot 12$$

$$9m = 36$$

$$m = 4$$

Practice and Problem Solving

with Homework

Example	Exercises
1	12–19
2	8–19, 25–27
3	20–23

Online Resources
CLASSZONE.COM

· More Examples
· eTutorial Plus

Decide Tell whether the ratios form a proportion.

8. $\frac{3}{4} \overset{?}{=} \frac{6}{8}$ **9.** $\frac{1}{2} \overset{?}{=} \frac{2}{5}$ **10.** $\frac{14}{21} \overset{?}{=} \frac{21}{35}$ **11.** $\frac{15}{45} \overset{?}{=} \frac{45}{135}$

Solve the proportion.

12. $\frac{3}{8} = \frac{x}{32}$ **13.** $\frac{4}{c} = \frac{20}{45}$ **14.** $\frac{39}{13} = \frac{9}{d}$ **15.** $\frac{68}{12} = \frac{51}{p}$

16. $\frac{67.2}{g} = \frac{16.8}{3.3}$ **17.** $\frac{t}{29.4} = \frac{5.5}{4.2}$ **18.** $\frac{f}{5.4} = \frac{483}{18.9}$ **19.** $\frac{712}{8.8} = \frac{x}{18.7}$

Scale Models You use a scale of 1 inch to 20 feet to make scale models of buildings. A building's actual height is given. Find the model's height.

20. $h = 100$ ft   **21.** $h = 240$ ft   **22.** $h = 316$ ft   **23.** $h = 545$ ft

24. Mental Math Explain how you can use equivalent fractions and mental math to solve $\frac{5}{x} = \frac{10}{16}$.

25. Earnings You earn $54 mowing 3 lawns. You charge the same amount for each lawn. How much would you earn if you mowed 5 lawns?

Extended Problem Solving To produce one pound of honey, the bees from a hive fly over 55,000 miles and visit about 2 million flowers.

26. About how many flowers are visited to make 10 ounces of honey?

27. About how many miles do the bees fly to make 10 ounces of honey?

28. Explain What is the mean number of flowers visited per mile traveled? Explain your reasoning.

EXAMPLE **Finding the Value of x**

$\dfrac{30}{2 + x} = \dfrac{6}{7}$	Original proportion
$7 \cdot 30 = 6(2 + x)$	Cross products property
$210 = 12 + 6x$	Multiply and use distributive property.
$33 = x$	Solve the two-step equation for x.

In Exercises 29–31, find the value of x.

29. $\frac{2}{x + 2} = \frac{18}{27}$ **30.** $\frac{x - 2}{8} = \frac{30}{40}$ **31.** $\frac{9}{5} = \frac{36}{x - 3}$

Challenge **Find the value of each variable.**

32. $\dfrac{4}{12} = \dfrac{3}{x} = \dfrac{y}{21}$

33. $\dfrac{7}{12} = \dfrac{a}{72} = \dfrac{28}{b}$

34. $\dfrac{8}{5} = \dfrac{n}{7} = \dfrac{21}{p}$

35. Model Car A toy manufacturer plans to make a model version of a car using a scale of 1 inch to 43 inches. The actual vehicle is 215 inches long, 75.25 inches wide, and 53.75 inches high. Find the length, width, and height of the model car.

Mixed Review

36. Write and solve an inequality for the sentence: *Four less than nine times a number is at most 95.* (Lesson 6.6)

Write the rate as a unit rate. (Lesson 7.1)

37. $\dfrac{42 \text{ people}}{14 \text{ taxis}}$

38. $\dfrac{258 \text{ miles}}{6 \text{ hours}}$

39. $\dfrac{36 \text{ dogs}}{18 \text{ households}}$

FCAT Practice

40. Multiple Choice What is the value of x for $\dfrac{15}{18} = \dfrac{x}{30}$?

A. 36   **B.** 27   **C.** 25   **D.** 3

41. Multiple Choice The scalc on a map is $\dfrac{3}{4}$ inch : 25 miles. The distance from Orlando, Florida, to Miami, Florida, is about 6 inches on the map. About how far is it from Orlando to Miami?

F. 75 miles   **G.** 150 miles   **H.** 200 miles   **I.** 300 miles

Balancing Act

The middle person below is holding the same weight on both trays. What shapes do you need to add to the other people's trays to balance the weights they are holding?

LESSON 7.3

Solving Percent Problems

BEFORE	▶ Now	WHY?
You solved proportions.	You'll solve percent problems using proportions.	So you can find the length of a crocodile, as in Ex. 19.

In the Real World

Word Watch

percent, p. 327

FLORIDA
Standards and Assessment
• Know appropriate operations to solve real-world problems. (MA.A.3.3.2)
• Solve problems involving changes in dimensions. (MA.B.1.3.3)

Environment A service club is planting seedlings as part of an erosion prevention project. Out of 240 newly planted seedlings, 15 are laurel sumac. What *percent* of the seedlings are laurel sumac?

The word *percent* means "per hundred." A **percent** is a ratio whose denominator is 100. The symbol for percent is %.

Solving Percent Problems

To represent "*a* is *p* percent of *b*," use the proportion

$$\frac{a}{b} = \frac{p}{100}$$

where *a* is part of the base *b* and *p*%, or $\frac{p}{100}$, is the percent.

EXAMPLE 1 Finding a Percent

To find the percent of seedlings that are laurel sumac as described above, use a percent proportion.

$$\frac{a}{b} = \frac{p}{100}$$ Write a percent proportion.

$$\frac{15}{240} = \frac{p}{100}$$ Substitute 15 for *a* and 240 for *b*.

$$\frac{15}{240} \cdot 100 = \frac{p}{100} \cdot 100$$ Multiply each side by 100.

$$6.25 = p$$ Simplify.

ANSWER Of the seedlings, 6.25% are laurel sumac.

Your turn now Use a percent proportion.

1. 126 is what percent of 150? **2.** 84 is what percent of 70?

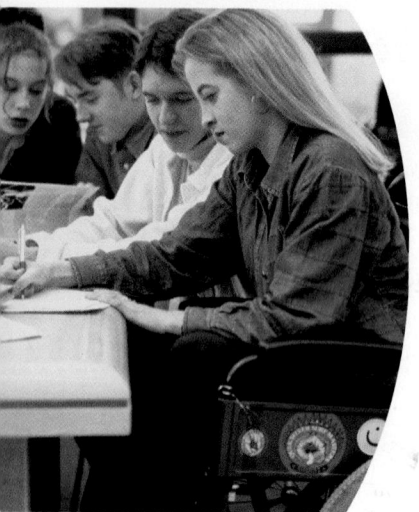

EXAMPLE 2 Finding Part of a Base

School Newspaper Your school newspaper's budget this year is 160% of last year's budget, which was $2125. What is this year's budget?

Solution

$$\frac{a}{b} = \frac{p}{100}$$ Write a percent proportion.

$$\frac{a}{2125} = \frac{160}{100}$$ Substitute 2125 for b and 160 for p.

$$\frac{a}{2125} \cdot 2125 = \frac{160}{100} \cdot 2125$$ Multiply each side by 2125.

$$a = 3400$$ Simplify.

ANSWER This year's budget is $3400.

EXAMPLE 3 Finding a Base

Find the number of which 24 is 0.8%.

$$\frac{a}{b} = \frac{p}{100}$$ Write a percent proportion.

$$\frac{24}{b} = \frac{0.8}{100}$$ Substitute 24 for a and 0.8 for p.

$$24 \cdot 100 = b \cdot 0.8$$ Cross products property

$$3000 = b$$ Divide each side by 0.8 and simplify.

ANSWER The number of which 24 is 0.8% is 3000.

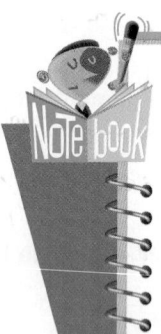

Summary of Percent Problems

Question	Method	Proportion
a is what percent of b?	Solve for p.	$\frac{a}{b} = \frac{p}{100}$
What number is $p\%$ of b?	Solve for a.	$\frac{a}{b} = \frac{p}{100}$
a is $p\%$ of what number?	Solve for b.	$\frac{a}{b} = \frac{p}{100}$

Your turn now Use a percent proportion.

3. What number is 0.5% of 65?   **4.** 260 is 325% of what number?

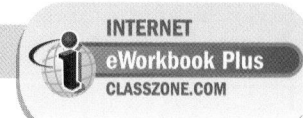

Getting Ready to Practice

1. **Vocabulary** Copy and complete: Another way to say 25 songs of 100 is to say 25 _?_ of the songs.

Use a percent proportion.

2. 6 is what percent of 75?

3. 27 is what percent of 108?

4. What number is 45% of 246?

5. 209 is 38% of what number?

6. **Guided Problem Solving** You ask 356 people if they enjoy drawing. Of these people, 89 say they do like to draw. What percent of the people surveyed like to draw?

   (1) Write a percent proportion.

   (2) Substitute the known values for the variables.

   (3) Solve the proportion.

Practice and Problem Solving

In Exercises 7–18, use a percent proportion.

7. 5 is what percent of 125?

8. 39 is what percent of 50?

9. 756 is what percent of 840?

10. 111 is what percent of 740?

11. What number is 45% of 245?

12. What number is 30% of 120?

13. What number is 76% of 775?

14. What number is 66% of 95?

15. 179.2 is 32% of what number?

16. 16.1 is 35% of what number?

17. 481 is 52% of what number?

18. 351 is 78% of what number?

19. **Reptiles** The largest crocodiles alive today are 24 feet in length. Recently, researchers discovered bones of an ancient crocodile. It was 167% as long as today's crocodiles. How long was the ancient crocodile?

20. **Water** A child's body is approximately 75% water. About how many pounds of a 60 pound child's weight is water?

In Exercises 21–26, use a percent proportion.

21. 567 is what percent of 420?

22. 1.26 is what percent of 42?

23. What number is 520% of 550?

24. What number is 0.36% of 675?

25. 918 is 170% of what number?

26. 79 is 0.01% of what number?

with Homework

Example	Exercises
1	7–18, 21–26
2	7–26
3	7–18, 21–26

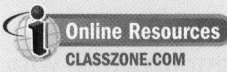

Online Resources
CLASSZONE.COM
· More Examples
· eTutorial Plus

27. Number Sense One day, 32 of 80 people wear a red shirt to school. What percent of the 80 people did *not* wear a red shirt to school?

28. Critical Thinking Explain how to find 10% of 400 without writing a proportion.

Write and solve the percent problem in terms of y.

29. What number is 50% of 8y?   **30.** 3y is 60% of what number?

31. Weekends There are about 52 weeks in a year and two weekend days each week. About what percent of the year falls on a weekend? Round your answer to the nearest tenth of a percent.

32. Dilophosaurus You buy your little brother a scale model of a Dilophosaurus. The scale of the model is 1 inch to 3 feet 4 inches. Use the scale to find what percent the model's height is of the actual height.

33. Challenge You use a photocopier to reduce an 8 inch by 10 inch photograph. When you press the reduction button, it reduces the length and width by the same percent. What is the new area if you reduce the photograph to 64% of its original size and then reduce the result to 78% of its size? What is the new area if you reduce to 78% first and then to 64%? Compare the two values.

34. Marathon Of the 23,513 people who entered the Honolulu Marathon one year, 19,236 finished. What percent of the runners finished? Round your answer to the nearest tenth of a percent.

Mixed Review

Write the decimal as a fraction or mixed number. *(Lesson 5.5)*

35. 1.86   **36.** 8.714   **37.** 0.624

Find the product or quotient. *(Lesson 5.7)*

38. 0.023×8.45 **39.** 47.1×0.96 **40.** $11.48 \div 8.2$

FCAT Practice

41. Multiple Choice The drama club makes surprise gift bags to sell at the school fair. Of the 70 bags, 30% have a music store gift certificate. How many bags have a music store gift certificate?

   A. 21   **B.** 25   **C.** 30   **D.** 40

42. Short Response In a survey of 350 people, 238 said they had at least one pet at home. Write a proportion to find the percent of people who said they had a pet at home. Solve the proportion.

Fractions, Decimals, and Percents

LESSON 7.4

BEFORE	▶ Now	WHY?
You wrote fractions as decimals and decimals as fractions.	You'll rewrite fractions, decimals, and percents.	So you can express circle graph sectors as percents, as in Ex. 46.

In the Real World

Word Watch

circle graph, p. 331

FLORIDA
Standards and Assessment

• Know relationships among fractions, decimals, and percents given a real-world context. (MA.A.1.3.4)

• Compare and order percents, fractions, and decimals. (MA.A.1.3.2)

Survey The *circle graph* below shows the results of a survey of how 500 students prefer to spend time. What percent of students prefer to spend time with friends?

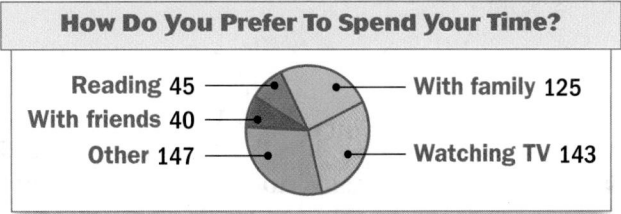

How Do You Prefer To Spend Your Time?

Reading 45 — With family 125
With friends 40 —
Other 147 — Watching TV 143

A **circle graph** represents data as parts of a circle. Each part is a percent of the data. The sum of the percents must equal 100% because the circle graph represents all of the data. Each part is also a fraction of the data. The sum of the fractions must equal 1.

EXAMPLE 1 **Writing a Fraction as a Percent**

The fraction of students who prefer to spend time with friends is $\frac{40}{500}$.

To write this fraction as a percent, write a percent proportion and solve for p.

$$\frac{40}{500} = \frac{p}{100} \qquad \text{Write a percent proportion.}$$

$$\frac{40}{500} \cdot 100 = \frac{p}{100} \cdot 100 \qquad \text{Multiply each side by 100.}$$

$$8 = p \qquad \text{Simplify.}$$

ANSWER 8% of the students prefer to spend time with friends.

Your turn now Write the fraction as a percent.

1. $\frac{4}{5}$ **2.** $\frac{27}{50}$ **3.** $\frac{1}{20}$ **4.** $\frac{3}{8}$

To write a decimal as a percent, write the decimal as a fraction with a denominator of 100. The numerator is the percent. For example:

$$0.89 = \frac{89}{100} = 89\%$$

So, 0.89 = 89%. Notice that 0.89 can be written as a percent by moving the decimal point two places to the right and adding a percent sign.

HELP with Solving

Make sure you move the decimal point two places to the right. Add a zero on the right if necessary, as in part (b) of Example 2.

EXAMPLE 2 **Writing Decimals as Percents**

Write the decimal as a percent.

a. $0.63 = 0.63$
  $= 63\%$

b. $2.7 = 2.70$
  $= 270\%$

c. $0.007 = 0.007$
  $= 0.7\%$

To write a percent as a decimal, remove the % sign and move the decimal point two places to the left. To write a percent as a fraction, write $n\%$ as $\frac{n}{100}$ and simplify.

EXAMPLE 3 **Writing Percents as Decimals and Fractions**

Write the percent as a decimal and as a fraction.

As a decimal	As a fraction
a. $0.32\% = 00.32\%$ $= 0.0032$	$0.32\% = \frac{0.32}{100}$ $= \frac{32}{10,000} = \frac{2}{625}$
b. $120\% = 120\%$ $= 1.2$	$120\% = \frac{120}{100}$ $= \frac{6}{5} = 1\frac{1}{5}$
c. $2.5\% = 02.5\%$ $= 0.025$	$2.5\% = \frac{2.5}{100}$ $= \frac{25}{1000} = \frac{1}{40}$

Your turn now **Write the decimal as a percent.**

5. 0.62   **6.** 0.9   **7.** 0.248   **8.** 5.09

Write the percent as a decimal and as a fraction in simplest form.

9. 45%   **10.** 214%   **11.** 77.5%   **12.** 0.5%

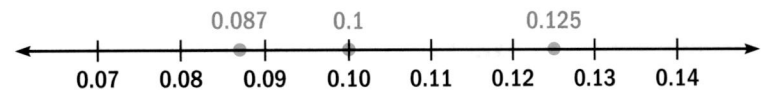

EXAMPLE 4 Ordering Fractions, Decimals, and Percents

Order the numbers from least to greatest: 8.7%, $\frac{1}{8}$, and 0.1.

Write 8.7% as a decimal: $8.7\% = 08.7\% = 0.087$

Write $\frac{1}{8}$ as a decimal: $\frac{1}{8} = 0.125$

Use a number line to order the decimals.

```
          0.087    0.1              0.125
  ←———|——————•———|———♦———|———|———|———•———|———|——→
    0.07  0.08  0.09  0.10  0.11  0.12  0.13  0.14
```

ANSWER The numbers ordered from least to greatest are 8.7%, 0.1, and $\frac{1}{8}$.

Your turn now Order the numbers from least to greatest.

13. $41\%, \frac{9}{20}, 0.389$ **14.** $\frac{9}{10}, 0.099, 95\%$ **15.** $1.5, 145\%, \frac{7}{5}$

7.4 Exercises
More Practice, p. 733

INTERNET
eWorkbook Plus
CLASSZONE.COM

Getting Ready to Practice

1. Vocabulary In a circle graph, what is the sum of the percents? What is the sum of the fractions?

Write the decimal or fraction as a percent.

2. 0.1 **3.** 0.09 **4.** $\frac{5}{8}$ **5.** $\frac{3}{2}$

Write the percent as a decimal and as a fraction in simplest form.

6. 80% **7.** 12.5% **8.** 7.5% **9.** 110%

10. Sleeping You survey 48 people and find that 18 of them sleep eight hours a night. What percent sleep eight hours a night?

11. Find the Error Describe and correct the error in writing 0.001 as a percent.

 $0.001 = \frac{1}{100} = 1\%$

Practice and Problem Solving

with Homework

Example	Exercises
1	12–27, 45–48
2	12–27
3	28–39
4	40–43

Online Resources
CLASSZONE.COM

· More Examples
· eTutorial Plus

Write the decimal or fraction as a percent.

12. 1.27   **13.** 0.057   **14.** 0.039   **15.** 0.004

16. $\dfrac{1}{80}$ **17.** $\dfrac{3}{20}$ **18.** $\dfrac{31}{10}$ **19.** $\dfrac{4}{800}$

20. 47.3   **21.** 1.056   **22.** $\dfrac{1}{125}$ **23.** $\dfrac{105}{200}$

24. $\dfrac{5}{9}$ **25.** $\dfrac{128}{150}$ **26.** 0.0028   **27.** 0.7

Write the percent as a decimal and as a fraction.

28. 40%   **29.** 87%   **30.** 32.5%   **31.** 101%

32. 1%   **33.** 4.2%   **34.** 200.2%   **35.** 124%

36. 187.09%   **37.** 0.4%   **38.** 0.78%   **39.** 44.55%

Order the numbers from least to greatest.

40. $0.022, \dfrac{9}{40}, 22\%, 0.228, \dfrac{28}{125}$ **41.** $6.6\%, \dfrac{3}{50}, 0.0606, 0.6\%, 0.606$

42. $\dfrac{4}{7}, 0.058, 58, 58\%, 0.58\%$ **43.** $212\%, 21.2, \dfrac{21}{100}, 0.212, \dfrac{21}{10}$

44. Critical Thinking If a fraction is greater than 1, what do you know about the equivalent percent?

Languages The circle graph shows the world languages that U.S. high school students studied in a recent year. Each fraction in the graph represents part of the total number of U.S. high school students who studied a world language.

45. Which language was the most popular?

46. What percent of the students studied German?

47. What percent of the students studied French or German?

48. What percent of the students did *not* study Spanish?

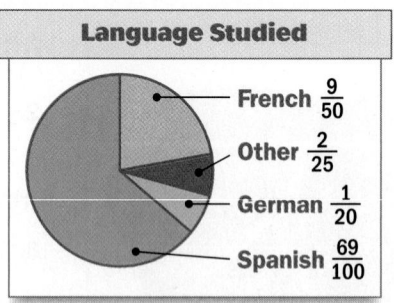

Language Studied

French $\dfrac{9}{50}$

Other $\dfrac{2}{25}$

German $\dfrac{1}{20}$

Spanish $\dfrac{69}{100}$

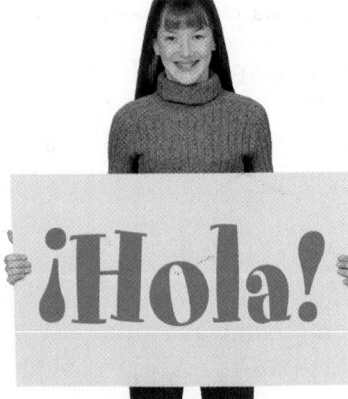

Copy and complete the statement using <, >, or =.

49. $\dfrac{1}{4}$ _?_ 26%   **50.** 450% _?_ $\dfrac{9}{2}$ **51.** $\dfrac{13}{25}$ _?_ 0.5

52. 0.0825 _?_ $\dfrac{17}{200}$ **53.** 4.5% _?_ 0.045   **54.** 101% _?_ 0.101

55. Critical Thinking Sometimes a percent is greater than 100, such as a store selling 125% of the number of sweaters it sold last year. Give an example when a percent should *not* be greater than 100.

56. Measurement A football field is 100 yards long excluding the end zones. What percent of a mile is a football field's length?

57. Challenge Use graph paper to illustrate 45% and 4.5%.

58. Explain The table shows the percents of people who buy various types of music. Explain why the data should not be represented in a circle graph. Then find an appropriate way to display the data.

Music	Percent
Rock	24.4%
Pop	12.1%
Rap	11.4%
R&B	10.6%
Country	10.5%

Mixed Review

Write the sentence as an inequality. Then solve. *(Lesson 6.6)*

59. The sum of 13 and 4 times a number is at most 9.

60. Eight less than the quotient of a number and 6 is greater than −7.

Choose a Strategy Use a strategy from the list to solve the following problem. Explain your choice of strategy.

61. You work for 4 hours. You spend $5.75 of the money you earn on a movie ticket and $2 on popcorn. Then your sister gives you $3 she owes you. You now have $19.25. How much were you paid per hour?

> **Problem Solving Strategies**
> - Guess, Check, and Revise
> - Draw a Diagram
> - Work Backward
> - Solve a Simpler Problem

Basic Skills Find the product or quotient.

62. 9.2×13.4 **63.** $41.3 \div 11.8$ **64.** $9.9 \div 4.5$ **65.** 1.98×6

FCAT Practice FCAT

66. Multiple Choice Which numbers are in order from least to greatest?

A. $0.7, 7.7\%, \frac{7}{9}$ **B.** $7.7\%, 0.7, \frac{7}{9}$ **C.** $0.7, \frac{7}{9}, 7.7\%$ **D.** $7.7\%, \frac{7}{9}, 0.7$

67. Multiple Choice Which choice shows 37.84% written as a decimal?

F. 378.4   **G.** 37.84   **H.** 3.784   **I.** 0.3784

LESSONS 7.1 TO 7.4

Notebook Review

Review the vocabulary definitions in your notebook.

Copy the review examples in your notebook. Then complete the exercises.

Check Your Definitions

ratio, p. 317	proportion, p. 322	scale, p. 324
equivalent ratios, p. 317	cross products, p. 323	percent, p. 327
rate, unit rate, p. 318	scale model, p. 324	circle graph, p. 331

Use Your Vocabulary

1. Copy and complete: In a(n) _?_, the cross products are equal.

7.1 Can you write a unit rate?

EXAMPLE Write 282 miles per 6 hours as a unit rate.

$$\frac{282 \text{ miles}}{6 \text{ hours}} = \frac{282 \div 6}{6 \div 6}$$ Divide numerator and denominator by 6.

$$= \frac{47}{1}$$ Simplify.

ANSWER The unit rate is 47 miles per hour.

☑ **Write the rate as a unit rate.**

2. 30 feet per 4 seconds   **3.** $3.36 per 2 gallons

7.2–7.3 Can you solve percent problems?

EXAMPLE 36 is 15% of what number?

$$\frac{a}{b} = \frac{p}{100}$$ Write a percent proportion.

$$\frac{36}{b} = \frac{15}{100}$$ Substitute 36 for *a* and 15 for *p*.

$$36 \cdot 100 = 15b$$ Cross products property

$$240 = b$$ Divide each side by 15.

☑ **Use a percent proportion.**

4. 72 is what percent of 1200?   **5.** What number is 95% of 26?

7.4 Can you rewrite percents, decimals, and fractions?

EXAMPLE Write 28% as a decimal and as a fraction.

$28\% = 28\% = 0.28$ Remove % sign and move decimal point two places to the left.

$28\% = \dfrac{28}{100} = \dfrac{7}{25}$ Write as a fraction and simplify.

ANSWER 28% can be written as 0.28 or $\dfrac{7}{25}$.

✓ **Write the percent as a decimal and as a fraction.**

6. 74%   **7.** 3.8%   **8.** 16.8%   **9.** 130%

Stop *and* **Think**   about Lessons 7.1–7.4

10. *Writing* Explain how to use the cross products property to check if two ratios form a proportion.

Review Quiz 1

A box of animal crackers contains 6 gorillas, 5 bears, 4 camels, 2 monkeys, 2 sheep, and 1 lion. Write the ratio in simplest form.

1. gorillas to sheep   **2.** monkeys to camels   **3.** bears to lions

Find the value of the variable.

4. $\dfrac{a}{72} = \dfrac{5}{6}$ **5.** $\dfrac{2}{3} = \dfrac{7}{x}$ **6.** $\dfrac{18}{27} = \dfrac{y}{3}$

7. $\dfrac{6}{8} = \dfrac{b}{28}$ **8.** $\dfrac{12}{c} = \dfrac{23}{92}$ **9.** $\dfrac{z+1}{8} = \dfrac{95}{19}$

10. *Clothing* You save 40% when buying a shirt that originally cost $29. How much do you save?

Gardening **The circle graph shows the numbers of flowers that you planted in a flowerbed.**

11. How many flowers did you plant?

12. What percent of the flowerbed is roses?

13. What two types of flowers combine to equal 70%?

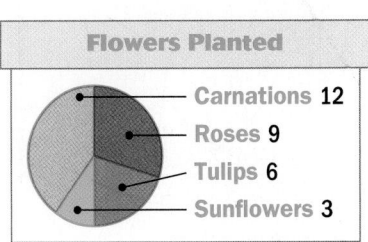

Flowers Planted
- Carnations 12
- Roses 9
- Tulips 6
- Sunflowers 3

Percent of Change

BEFORE	▶ Now	WHY?
You solved problems with percents.	You'll solve problems with percent of increase or decrease.	So you can find tons of hazelnuts produced, as in Ex. 19.

In the Real World

Word Watch

percent of change, p. 338
percent of increase, p. 338
percent of decrease, p. 338

FLORIDA
Standards and Assessment

• Solve real-world percent problems. (MA.A.3.3.2)
• Solve multi-step real-world problems. (MA.A.3.3.2)

Bears During the summer, a bear's heart rate is about 60 beats per minute, but it can drop to as low as 8 beats per minute during winter. What is the *percent of change* in a bear's heart rate from the summer rate to the winter low rate?

A **percent of change** shows how much a quantity has increased or decreased in relation to the original amount. When the new amount is greater than the original amount, the percent of change is called a **percent of increase** . When the new amount is less than the original amount, it is called a **percent of decrease** .

Percent of Change

Use the following equation to find the percent of change.

$$\text{Percent of change, } p\% = \frac{\text{Amount of increase or decrease}}{\text{Original amount}}$$

EXAMPLE 1 **Finding a Percent of Decrease**

HELP with Review

For help with repeating decimals, see p. 242.

To find the percent of decrease in a bear's heart rate as described above, use the percent of change equation.

$$p\% = \frac{60 - 8}{60}$$ Write amount of decrease and divide by original amount.

$$= \frac{52}{60}$$ Subtract.

$$= 0.86\overline{6}$$ Write fraction as a decimal.

ANSWER The percent of decrease is about 86.7%.

EXAMPLE 2 **Finding a Percent of Increase**

School A school had 825 students enrolled last year. This year, 870 students are enrolled. Find the percent of increase.

Solution

$$p\% = \frac{870 - 825}{825}$$ Write amount of increase and divide by original amount.

$$= \frac{45}{825}$$ Subtract.

$$= 0.05\overline{45}$$ Write fraction as a decimal.

ANSWER The percent of increase is about 5.5%.

Watch Out!

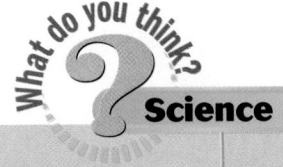

Make sure you use the original amount, not the new amount, in the denominator when finding a percent of change.

Your turn now Tell whether the change is an *increase* or *decrease*. Then find the percent of change.

1. Original amount: 50
New amount: 36

2. Original amount: 10
New amount: 29.5

3. Original amount: 90
New amount: 110

Decimal Method A shortcut to finding a percent of a number is to write the percent as a decimal and then find the product of the decimal and the number. For example, 10% of 60 = 0.10(60) = 6.

What do you think?
Science

EXAMPLE 3 **Using Percent of Increase**

Everglades From October to November one year, there was about a 27.4% increase in attendance at Everglades National Park. There were 59,084 visitors in October. About how many people visited in November?

Solution

① Find the increase.

Increase = **27.4%** of 59,084

= **0.274**(59,084)   Write 27.4% as a decimal.

≈ 16,189   Multiply.

② Add the increase to the original amount.

New Amount ≈ 59,084 + 16,189

= 75,273

ANSWER About 75,273 people visited the park in November.

■ **Everglades**

During the wet season, water flows south through the Everglades at a rate of 100 feet per day. How many days does it take water to flow one mile?

Lesson 7.5   Percent of Change   **339**

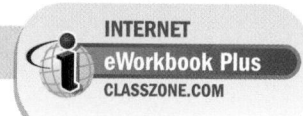

Getting Ready to Practice

1. Vocabulary Copy and complete: When the original amount is less than the new amount, the percent of change is called a(n) ? .

Tell whether the change is an *increase* or *decrease*. Then find the percent of change.

2. Original amount: 10
New amount: 14

3. Original amount: 20
New amount: 16

Find the new amount.

4. 78 is decreased by 22%.

5. 105 is decreased by 78%.

6. Tennis In 1975, there were 130,000 tennis courts in the United States. This number increased by 69% from 1975 to 1985. The number then increased by 9% from 1985 to 1995. How many tennis courts were there in the United States in 1985 and in 1995?

(1 Find the number of tennis courts in 1985.

(2 Find the amount of the second increase.

(3 Find the number of tennis courts in 1995.

Practice and Problem Solving

Decide Tell whether the change is an *increase* or *decrease*. Then find the percent of change.

7. 10 rabbits to 16 rabbits

8. 360 pounds to 352 pounds

9. $33,300 to $31,080

10. 12,200 voters to 13,908 voters

11. 50 minutes to 45 minutes

12. 350 meters to 420 meters

Find the new amount.

13. 1100 is increased by 4%.

14. 24,700 is decreased by 13%.

15. 8 is increased by 60%.

16. 65 is decreased by 30%.

17. 88,450 is decreased by 12.5%.

18. 26,856 is increased by 14.6%.

19. Hazelnuts Oregon produces 98% of the hazelnuts grown in the United States. One year, Oregon produced 46,650 tons of hazelnuts. The crop decreased by 67% the following year. How many tons of hazelnuts were produced in Oregon the second year?

Find the percent of increase or decrease.

20. x to $4x$ **21.** $6b$ to $9b$ **22.** y to $\frac{3}{8}y$ **23.** $4.5a$ to $2.25a$

In Exercises 24–27, tell whether the statement is *true* or *false*. Explain your reasoning.

24. An increase from 1 to 3 is a 200% increase.

25. Multiplying a number by 5 is a 500% increase.

26. Multiplying a number by $\frac{1}{4}$ is a 25% decrease.

27. Dividing a number by 5 is an 80% decrease.

28. Coins In 1996, a 1943 copper penny was sold for $82,500. What was the percent of increase in the penny's value in 1943 to the value it was sold for in 1996?

29. Population The population of the United States in 1992 was about 255,374,000. In 2002, it was about 280,562,000. Find the approximate percent of increase to the nearest tenth.

30. Challenge A number increases by 50%, then decreases by 50%. What is the percent of change from the original number to the final number?

31. Enlargements You have a photograph that is 6 inches by 4 inches. You want to enlarge it so that these dimensions are increased by 50%. What will the new dimensions be? What will be the percent of increase in the area of the new photograph?

Mixed Review

Find the product or quotient. *(Lesson 5.7)*

32. $4.412 \cdot 0.36$ **33.** $-6.7 \cdot 0.8$ **34.** $-0.91 \div 0.35$

Solve the equation. *(Lesson 6.3)*

35. $14.2 + 1.4x = -5.4$ **36.** $0.2s - 1.3 = 0.3$ **37.** $1.14y - 2 = y + 1.64$

Basic Skills **Solve the equation.**

38. $7x = 63$ **39.** $1.5c = 18$ **40.** $2.5n = 80$

FCAT Practice

41. Extended Response The average person in the United States was projected to spend 114 hours playing video games in 2002. The projection of the average time spent on video games increased by about 19.3% from 2002 to 2003. Estimate the projected hours for 2003. Explain your method. Find the actual projection for 2003 using the given information. Compare your estimate to the actual projection.

Percent Applications

BEFORE	▶ Now	WHY?
You solved problems with percent of increase or decrease.	You'll solve percent application problems.	So you can find the sale price of a pair of jeans, as in Ex. 18.

Word Watch

markup, p. 342
discount, p. 342

FLORIDA
Standards and Assessment

• Solve real-world percent problems. (MA.A.3.3.2)

In the Real World

Guitars You are shopping for a guitar and find one with an original price of $160. The store is offering a 30% *discount* on all guitars. What is the sale price of the guitar?

Markup and Discount A retail store buys items from manufacturers at *wholesale prices*. The store then sells the items to customers at *retail prices*. The increase in the wholesale price of an item is a **markup**. A decrease in the price of an item is a **discount**. You can find the retail price or sale price of an item using the equations below.

$$\text{Retail price} = \text{Wholesale price} + \text{Markup}$$

$$\text{Sale price} = \text{Original price} - \text{Discount}$$

EXAMPLE 1 **Finding a Sale Price**

To find the sale price of the guitar above, use the sale price equation.

Solution

① Find the amount of the discount.

Discount = 30% of $160

= 0.3(160)   **Write 30% as a decimal.**

= 48   **Multiply.**

② Subtract the discount from the original price.

$160 - 48 = 112$

ANSWER The sale price of the guitar is $112.

Your turn now **Find the sale price.**

1. Original price: $25
   Percent discount: 10%

2. Original price: $85.50
   Percent discount: 30%

EXAMPLE **2** **Finding a Retail Price**

Clothing A shirt has a wholesale price of $16. The percent markup is 120%. What is the retail price?

Solution

(**1** Find the amount of the markup.

Markup = 120% of $16

$= 1.2(16)$ **Write 120% as a decimal.**

$= 19.2$ **Multiply.**

(**2** Add the markup to the wholesale price.

$16 + 19.2 = 35.2$

ANSWER The retail price of the shirt is $35.20.

Sales Tax and Tips Sales tax and tips are amounts that are added to the price of some purchases. Sales tax and tips are usually calculated using a percent of the purchase price.

EXAMPLE **3**   **Finding Sales Tax**

Compact Disc Player A portable CD player costs $48 before tax. The sales tax is 4.5%. What is the total cost?

Solution

(**1** Find the amount of the sales tax.

4.5% of $48 = 0.045(48)$

$= 2.16$

(**2** Add the sales tax to the price of the portable CD player.

$48 + 2.16 = 50.16$

ANSWER The total cost of the CD player is $50.16.

Your turn now   **Find the retail price.**

3. Wholesale price: $64
Percent markup: 85%

4. Wholesale price: $35
Percent markup: 110%

Find the total cost.

5. Price: $8.90
Sales tax: 5%

6. Price: $54.07
Sales tax: 7%

EXAMPLE 4 **Finding Sales Tax and Tip**

Restaurants Your food bill at a restaurant is $24. You leave a 20% tip. The sales tax is 6%. What is the total cost of the meal?

Solution

(1 Find the amount of the tip.

$$20\% \text{ of } \$24 = 0.20(24)$$
$$= 4.8$$

(2 Find the amount of the sales tax.

$$6\% \text{ of } \$24 = 0.06(24)$$
$$= 1.44$$

(3 Add the food bill, tip, and sales tax.

$$24 + 4.8 + 1.44 = 30.24$$

ANSWER The total cost of the meal is $30.24.

Your turn now **Find the total cost.**

7. Your food bill at a restaurant is $35. The sales tax is 5%. You leave a 15% tip. What is the total cost of the meal?

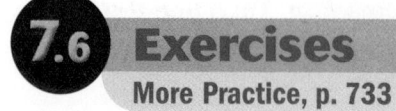

7.6 Exercises

More Practice, p. 733

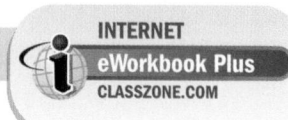

INTERNET
eWorkbook Plus
CLASSZONE.COM

Getting Ready to Practice

1. Vocabulary Copy and complete: To find the retail price, add the ? to the wholesale price.

Find the sale price or retail price.

2. Original price: $60
Percent discount: 15%

3. Original price: $28.50
Percent discount: 60%

4. Wholesale price: $25
Percent markup: 65%

5. Wholesale price: $14.50
Percent markup: 140%

6. Lamps A lamp costs $25.75. The sales tax is 4%. What is the total cost?

7. Restaurants Your food bill at a restaurant is $30. You leave a 20% tip. The sales tax is 6%. What is the total cost of the meal?

Practice and Problem Solving

HELP with Homework

Example	Exercises
1	8–13, 20–25
2	8–13, 20–25
3	14–17
4	14–17

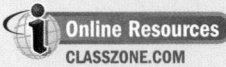

Online Resources
CLASSZONE.COM

· More Examples
· eTutorial Plus

Find the sale price or retail price. Round to the nearest cent.

8. Original price: $42
Percent discount: 30%

9. Wholesale price: $19
Percent markup: 110%

10. Wholesale price: $16.49
Percent markup: 130%

11. Original price: $22.40
Percent discount: 25%

12. Original price: $54.75
Percent discount: 20%

13. Wholesale price: $65.40
Percent markup: 55%

Find the total cost. Round to the nearest cent.

14. Original price: $72
Sales tax: 6%

15. Original price: $58.40
Sales tax: 5.5%

16. Food bill: $25.80
Tip: 18%
Sales tax: 4.5%

17. Food bill: $18
Tip: 20%
Sales tax: 5%

18. Jeans The wholesale price of a pair of jeans is $15. A store marks up the price by 75%. When the jeans don't sell, the store offers a 20% discount. What is the sale price of the jeans?

19. Critical Thinking A store is having an end of season sale and offers a discount of 40% on all coats. One week later the store discounts the coats an additional 60%. Is the store giving away the coats for free? Explain your reasoning.

Tell whether the new price is a *discount* or *markup*. Then find the percent of discount or markup.

20. Old price: $32
New price: $24

21. Old price: $45
New price: $40.50

22. Old price: $19
New price: $33.25

23. Old price: $55
New price: $121

24. Old price: $12.50
New price: $22.50

25. Old price: $199.99
New price: $119.99

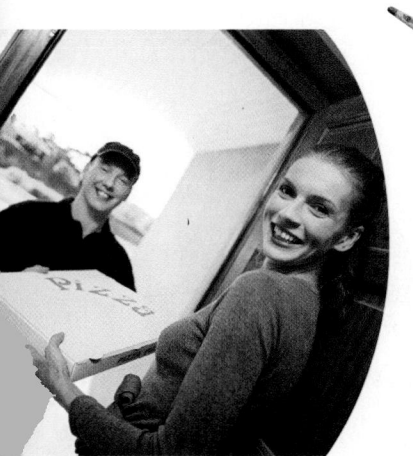

26. Writing People often leave tips between 15% and 20% on restaurant bills. Find both the 15% and 20% tips of a food bill that totals $24.20. Explain why people often leave a tip between 15% and 20% rather than leaving exactly 15% or 20%.

27. Tipping You order a pizza to be delivered. The bill comes to $12.60. You give the delivery person $15 and tell them to keep the change. What percent tip did you give? Round to the nearest percent.

28. DVDs A DVD has a regular price of $26 and is on sale for $16.90. What is the percent discount?

29. Subscription A magazine subscription has a regular price of $24.50. You pay $14.70 for your subscription. What is the percent discount?

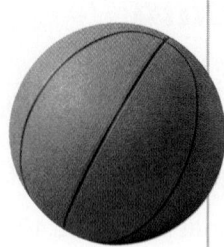

30. Estimation The original price of an item is $42 and the percent of discount is 25%. Explain how to estimate the sale price.

31. Challenge A total restaurant bill including sales tax and tip is $33. The tax is 4% and the tip is 16% of the bill before tax. What was the food bill before tax and tip?

32. Shopping A basketball has a wholesale price of $12 and is marked up 115%. Later it is discounted 15%. The sales tax is 4.5%. Find the final cost of the basketball including tax. Round to the nearest cent.

Mixed Review

Solve the equation. *(Lesson 6.2)*

33. $4a = a + 9$

34. $n - 2 = 2n - 9$

Use a percent proportion. *(Lesson 7.3)*

35. What number is 35% of 80?

36. 308 is what percent of 440?

Basic Skills **Solve the equation.**

37. $2.4b = 108$

38. $8.5y = 51$

39. $3.5x = 140$

40. $1.6d = 38.4$

FCAT Practice

41. Multiple Choice A baseball cap costs $12.50 and is on sale for 30% off. What is the sale price of the cap?

A. $3.75 **B.** $8.75 **C.** $11.20 **D.** $12.20

42. Multiple Choice A backpack has a wholesale price of $15. The price is marked up 80% and there is a 4% sales tax. What is the total cost of the backpack?

F. $12.48 **G.** $18.72 **H.** $27.60 **I.** $28.08

Shrink Ray

Ray invents two zappers that shrink and enlarge things. After shrinking almost everything in the house to 40% of its original size, Ray's mother demands that he return things to normal. What percent setting should he use to zap objects back to their original size?

If Ray had instead used the zapper to enlarge things by 60%, what percent setting would he use on the shrink zapper to get them back to their normal size?

Using the Percent Equation

BEFORE	▶ **Now**	**WHY?**
You solved percent problems using proportions.	You'll solve percent problems using the percent equation.	So you can find the interest paid on a bank loan, as in Ex. 25.

Word Watch

interest, p. 348
principal, p. 348
annual interest rate, p. 348

FLORIDA
Standards and Assessment

• Solve real-world percent problems. (MA.A.3.3.2)
• Solve linear equations. (MA.D.2.3.1)

(**In the Real World**

Beaches In a survey of 2000 people, 26.7% said that they had visited a beach during the past year. Find the number of people who said they had visited a beach.

In Lesson 7.3, you solved percent problems with proportions. You can also use the decimal method from Lesson 7.5 to solve percent problems.

The Percent Equation

To represent the statement "*a* is *p* percent of *b*" use the equation:

$$a = p\% \cdot b \qquad \text{Part of the base} = p \text{ percent} \cdot \text{Base}$$

EXAMPLE 1 **Finding Part of a Base**

To find the number of people who said they had visited a beach in the past year, use the percent equation.

$a = p\% \cdot b$	Write percent equation.
$= 26.7\% \cdot 2000$	Substitute 26.7 for *p* and 2000 for *b*.
$= 0.267 \cdot 2000$	Write percent as a decimal.
$= 534$	Multiply.

ANSWER The number of people who said they had visited a beach during the past year is 534.

 Use the percent equation.

1. Find 45% of 700.   **2.** Find 24.5% of 800.

EXAMPLE 2 Finding a Base

Student Council Marc received 273, or 35%, of the votes in the student council election. How many students voted in the election?

Solution

$a = p\% \cdot b$	Write percent equation.
$273 = 35\% \cdot b$	Substitute 273 for a and 35 for p.
$273 = 0.35 \cdot b$	Write 35% as a decimal.
$780 = b$	Divide each side by 0.35.

ANSWER In the election, 780 students voted.

Your turn now Solve using the percent equation.

3. 6.4 is 62.5% of what number?   **4.** 15 is what percent of 120?

HELP with Vocabulary

When you borrow money from a bank, you pay back interest as well as the amount you borrowed.

Simple Interest **Interest** is an amount paid for the use of money. **Principal** is the amount you borrow or deposit. When interest is paid only on the principal, it is called simple interest. The percent of the principal you pay or earn per year is the **annual interest rate** .

Simple Interest

Words To find simple interest I, find the product of the principal P, the annual interest rate r written as a decimal, and the time t in years.

Algebra $I = Prt$

EXAMPLE 3 Finding Simple Interest

You deposit $500 in a savings account that pays a simple interest rate of 2.5% per year. How much interest will you earn after 18 months?

Solution

$I = Prt$	Write formula for simple interest.
$= (500)(0.025)(1.5)$	Substitute values. 18 months = 1.5 years
$= 18.75$	Multiply.

ANSWER You will earn $18.75 in interest.

Getting Ready to Practice

1. **Vocabulary** Copy and complete: To find simple interest, multiply the annual rate written as a decimal, the time in years, and the ? .

Solve using the percent equation.

2. What number is 46% of 900?

3. 205 is what percent of 250?

4. 132 is 24% of what number?

5. What number is 95% of 420?

6. **Guided Problem Solving** A savings account pays a 3% annual interest rate. How much must you put in the savings account to earn $100 in interest in 6 months?

   ① Write the simple interest formula.

   ② Substitute known values in the formula.

   ③ Solve the equation for *P*. Round to the nearest cent.

Practice and Problem Solving

HELP with Homework

Example	Exercises
1	7–16
2	7–16
3	17–18

Online Resources
CLASSZONE.COM
· More Examples
· eTutorial Plus

Solve using the percent equation.

7. What number is 65% of 320?

8. What number is 6% of 450?

9. What number is 120% of 55?

10. What number is 0.4% of 150?

11. 115 is 46% of what number?

12. 26 is 130% of what number?

13. 62.4 is 80% of what number?

14. 289.25 is 89% of what number?

15. 3 is what percent of 600?

16. 291.04 is what percent of 856?

Find the amount of simple interest earned.

17. Principal: $250
    Annual rate: 2%
    Time: 3 years

18. Principal : $940
    Annual rate: 3.5%
    Time: 30 months

19. **Weather** In Charlotte, North Carolina, an average of 112 days of the year have precipitation of 0.01 inch or more. What percent of days in Charlotte have precipitation of 0.01 inch or more? Round your answer to the nearest percent.

20. **Writing** Are the solutions of $\frac{12}{b} = \frac{3}{100}$ and $12 = 3\% \cdot b$ the same or different? Explain your reasoning.

Copy and complete the statement with <, >, or =.

21. 60% of 75 <u> ? </u> 75% of 60   **22.** 30% of 120 <u> ? </u> 120% of 30

23. *Look for a Pattern* Copy and complete the table by finding the percent of each number. Describe the relationship you see among the three percents in each row.

	5%	10%	15%
22	?	2.2	?
50	?	?	?
76	?	?	?

24. *Savings* How much money must you deposit in a savings account that pays a 4% simple annual interest rate to earn $50 in 2 years?

25. *Loan* You borrow $1200 from the bank. The bank charges an annual simple interest rate of 9.5%. It takes you 15 months to pay back the loan. How much interest do you pay on the loan? What is the total amount that you pay the bank?

26. *Texas* The area of the state of Texas is 171.1 million acres. Of this, 26.9 million acres are cropland. What percent of Texas is cropland? Round your answer to the nearest hundredth of a percent.

27. *Challenge* *Compound interest* on a savings account is earned on both the principal and on any interest that has already been earned. You deposit $500 into an account that earns 4% compounded annually. How much will you have in your account after the third year? after the sixth year? Round your answers to the nearest cent.

Mixed Review

Find the quotient. *(Lesson 5.4)*

28. $\dfrac{8}{3} \div \dfrac{32}{21}$ **29.** $\dfrac{5}{9} \div \dfrac{2}{3}$ **30.** $\dfrac{11}{14} \div \dfrac{1}{2}$

In Exercises 31–33, solve the equation or inequality. *(Lessons 6.3, 6.5)*

31. $5.4 - 4.6x = 19.2$ **32.** $\dfrac{3}{8}u - \dfrac{1}{2} = \dfrac{7}{12}$ **33.** $3n - 27 \le -5n + 64$

34. Solve the proportion $\dfrac{8}{25} = \dfrac{7}{d}$. *(Lesson 7.2)*

FCAT Practice **FCAT**

35. *Short Response* At a local mall, 75%, or 63, of the stores participate in a gift certificate program. Write an equation that could be used to determine the number of stores in the mall. Then solve the equation.

36. *Multiple Choice* What percent of 120 is 72?

    A. 28%   **B.** 48%   **C.** 60%   **D.** 72%

FLORIDA: Standards and Assessment
Solve real-world percent problems. (MA.A.3.3.2)

Compound Interest

GOAL Use a calculator to compute compound interest.

HELP with **Vocabulary**

Compound interest is interest earned on both the principal and on any interest that has already been earned.

> **Example** Mark deposits $2000 into an account that pays an interest rate of 3.5% compounded annually. He doesn't add or remove money from his account for 4 years. How much money will Mark have in 4 years?

Solution

The balance of an account after a year can be found by multiplying the principal balance by the quantity one plus the annual interest rate. Use the keystrokes below to find the amount of money in the account in 4 years.

Keystrokes	Display	
2000 [=] [×] 1.035 [=]	2070	In 1 year
[=]	2142.45	In 2 years
[=]	2217.43575	In 3 years
[=]	2295.046001	In 4 years

ANSWER Mark will have $2295.05 in his account in 4 years.

> **Your turn now** Find the balance of the account earning compound interest.

1. Principal: $7000
Annual rate: 2%
Time: 4 years

2. Principal: $7000
Annual rate: 4%
Time: 2 years

3. Principal: $1995
Annual rate: 6.5%
Time: 10 years

4. You deposit $1500 into an account that pays an interest rate of 4% compounded annually. Your friend deposits $1500 into an account that pays a simple annual interest rate of 4%. Compare the balances of the two accounts after 5 years.

Problem Solving Strategies

FLORIDA: Standards and Assessment
Make inferences and draw conclusions using statistical results. (MA.E.3.3.1)

Perform an Experiment

Guess, Check, and Revise
Look for a Pattern
Draw a Diagram
Act It Out
Perform an Experiment
Work Backward
Make a Table

Problem You are playing a board game that involves rolling 2 cubes numbered from 1 to 6. If your cubes sum to an even number, you may advance your game piece forward. If your cubes sum to an odd number, you may not move your piece. Predict the number of times you will be able to move forward in 100 rolls.

❶ Read and Understand

Read the problem carefully.

The problem asks you to predict the number of times you will roll two number cubes that sum to an even number in 100 rolls.

❷ Make a Plan

Decide on a strategy to use.

Because it might take a while to roll number cubes 100 times, you can make a prediction by performing an experiment. Roll two number cubes 20 times and use the results to make a prediction.

❸ Solve the Problem

Reread the problem and perform an experiment.

First, roll two number cubes 20 times and record the results as shown.

Results

5, 12, 7, 9, 4, 8, 7, 6, 6, 3, 8, 4, 7, 5, 6, 9, 2, 4, 10, 11

> There are 11 even numbers and 9 odd numbers.

Then, use the results of the experiment to set up and solve a proportion.

$$\frac{\text{Number of even numbers in 20 rolls}}{20 \text{ rolls}} = \frac{\text{Number of even numbers in 100 rolls}}{100 \text{ rolls}}$$

$$\frac{11}{20} = \frac{x}{100}$$

$$\frac{11}{20} \cdot 100 = \frac{x}{100} \cdot 100$$

$$55 = x$$

You predict that you will get 55 even numbers in 100 rolls.

❹ Look Back

To test the accuracy of your prediction, perform another experiment and compare the results.

Practice the Strategy

Use the strategy *perform an experiment*.

1. **Marbles** You conduct an experiment by randomly drawing 10 marbles from a bag of 100 red and blue marbles, and recording how many of each color were drawn. The results of 5 of these experiments are shown below. Estimate how many marbles of each color are in the bag. Explain.

	1	2	3	4	5
Red	6	7	5	7	6
Blue	4	3	5	3	4

2. **Spinner** You are playing a board game that uses a spinner like the one below to determine how many spaces to move. The spinner seems to give the result "5" more often than it should. Describe an experiment you could use to test this assumption. What results would support the assumption?

3. **Names** Write each of the letters of your name on a slip of paper. Place all the slips into a bag and then randomly draw one slip. Record what letter it is, replace it, and repeat the process. Design an experiment to help you predict the number of times you would draw a consonant in 60 draws. Describe your experiment.

4. **Socks** A drawer has exactly 20 white socks and 20 black socks. You randomly draw two socks 100 times and replace them after each draw. Describe an experiment you could use to predict how many times out of 100 you would draw matching socks.

Mixed Problem Solving

Use any strategy to solve the problem.

5. **Shopping** You pick out a sweater and a pair of pants. When you get to the cashier, you find that all sweaters are on sale for 40% off the original price and your bill is $40.40. So, you decide to add two more sweaters to your purchase, bringing the bill to $81.20. How much does one pair of pants cost? What is the original price of one sweater?

6. **Groups** A class is divided into groups of four. Betty, Jamal, Fiona, and Juan are in one group. Each person's name is written on a separate slip of paper. The teacher draws a name each week (and then replaces it for the next week) to find the leader of the group for that week. How often do you predict Fiona's name will be picked in 36 weeks?

7. **Triangles** How many triangles are shown in the figure? Be sure to count triangles of different sizes.

Simple Probability

BEFORE	▶ Now	WHY?
You found ratios.	You'll find probabilities of events.	So you can find the probability of a batter getting a hit, as in Ex. 24.

Word Watch

outcome, event, p. 354
favorable outcome, p. 354
probability of an event,
   p. 354
theoretical probability,
   p. 354
experimental probability,
   p. 355

FLORIDA
Standards and Assessment

• Collect, organize, and display data. (MA.E.3.3.1)
• Calculate mathematical probability of independent events. (MA.E.2.3.1)

Activity You can toss a coin to perform a probability experiment.

(1) Copy and complete the table at the right by tossing a coin 20 times.

Number of heads	?
Number of tails	?

(2) Use the data to write each ratio below. Then compare the ratios.

   a. $\dfrac{\text{Number of heads}}{\text{Total number of coin tosses}}$ b. $\dfrac{\text{Number of tails}}{\text{Total number of coin tosses}}$

(3) **Comparing Results** Combine your results with those of the other students in your class. Compare the class ratios with your own ratios.

In the activity, you performed an experiment. The possible results of an experiment are **outcomes**. An **event** is a collection of outcomes. Once you specify an event, the outcomes for that event are called **favorable outcomes**. The **probability of an event** is the likelihood that the event will occur.

Probability of an Event

The **theoretical probability** of an event when all outcomes are equally likely is:

$$P(\text{event}) = \frac{\text{Number of favorable outcomes}}{\text{Number of possible outcomes}}$$

EXAMPLE 1 Using Theoretical Probability

Use theoretical probability to predict the number of times a coin will land heads up in 50 coin tosses. There are two equally likely outcomes when you toss the coin, heads or tails.

$$P(\text{heads}) = \frac{\text{Number of favorable outcomes}}{\text{Number of possible outcomes}} = \frac{1}{2}$$

ANSWER You can predict that $\frac{1}{2}$, or 25, of the tosses will land heads up.

An **experimental probability** is based on the results of a sample or experiment. Experimental probability is the ratio of number of favorable outcomes to total number of times the experiment was performed.

with Solving

A probability can be expressed as a fraction, as a decimal, or as a percent.

EXAMPLE 2 Finding Experimental Probability

You roll a number cube 100 times. Your results are shown. Find the experimental probability of rolling a 6.

Number	Rolls	Number	Rolls
1	17	4	16
2	15	5	14
3	20	6	18

Solution

$$P(\text{rolling a 6}) = \frac{18}{100} \quad \longleftarrow \text{Number of favorable outcomes} \\ \longleftarrow \text{Total number of rolls}$$

$$= 0.18 = 18\%$$

ANSWER The experimental probability of rolling a 6 is 18%.

EXAMPLE 3 Using Experimental Probability

You randomly draw a button from a bag of red, blue, green, and yellow buttons 18 times. Each time you record its color and place it back in the bag. There are 80 buttons in the bag. Predict how many are red.

Color	Tally
Red	JHT JHT
Blue	III
Green	III
Yellow	II

Solution

① Find the experimental probability of drawing a red button.

$$P(\text{red}) = \frac{10}{18} \quad \longleftarrow \text{Number of favorable outcomes} \\ \longleftarrow \text{Total number of draws}$$

$$= \frac{5}{9} \qquad \text{Simplify.}$$

② Multiply the probability by the total number of buttons and round to the nearest whole number.

$$\frac{5}{9} \times 80 \approx 44$$

ANSWER You can predict that there are 44 red buttons in the bag.

Your turn now Use the information in Example 3.

1. There are 18 green buttons in the bag. What is the theoretical probability of drawing a green button at random? What is the experimental probability?

Getting Ready to Practice

1. **Vocabulary** Copy and complete: The favorable outcomes for rolling an even number on a number cube are ? , ? , and ? .

2. **Socks** You have 4 white socks, 2 black socks, and 2 brown socks. What is the probability that you will choose a black sock at random from these socks?

3. **Find the Error** A student spins a two-color spinner 20 times. The pointer lands on red 7 times and on blue 13 times. Describe and correct the error in the solution.

$$\text{Experimental probability}$$
$$\text{of spinning red} = \frac{7}{13}$$ ✗

Practice and Problem Solving

 with Homework

Example	Exercises
1	4–9, 20–22
2	10–14
3	15–18

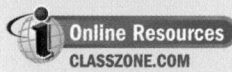 **Online Resources**
CLASSZONE.COM

· More Examples
· eTutorial Plus

You randomly draw a tile from a bag that contains 10 A-tiles, 7 E-tiles, 6 I-tiles, 5 O-tiles, and 2 U-tiles. Find the probability of the event.

4. You draw an A.

5. You draw an I.

6. You draw an I or an O.

7. You draw an E or a U.

8. You draw a Z.

9. You draw a vowel.

You roll a number cube 250 times. Your results are shown in the table. Find the experimental probability of the event.

10. You roll a 4.

11. You roll a 2.

12. You roll a number greater than 3.

Number	Outcomes	Number	Outcomes
1	40	4	50
2	42	5	35
3	48	6	35

13. You roll an odd number.

14. You roll a number divisible by 1.

You randomly draw a marble from a bag of 120 marbles. You record its color and replace it. Use the results to estimate the number of marbles in the bag that are the given color.

15. Yellow

16. Green

17. Red

18. Blue

Red	Yellow	Green
7	3	5

19. Toes In a survey of 896 people, 409 responded that their second toes are longer than their big toes. What is the probability that a randomly chosen person from the survey has a longer second toe?

Find the probability of the event.

20. *Not* rolling a 2 on a number cube

21. *Not* spinning blue on the spinner

22. *Not* spinning blue, red, or yellow on the spinner

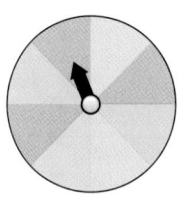

23. Writing Describe the difference between experimental and theoretical probability.

24. Softball Sharon and Erica are both softball players. Out of 20 times at bat, Sharon got 7 hits. Out of 35 times at bat, Erica got 10 hits. Who do you think is more likely to get a hit her next time at bat? Explain.

25. Number Cube Rachel rolled a number cube 24 times and got a 6 once. She thinks that her chances of getting a 6 on her next roll are high. Explain why her chances are no different than on any other roll.

26. Challenge You have 15 coins in your pocket: 4 quarters, 3 pennies, 5 dimes, and 3 nickels. Why wouldn't theoretical probability be a good way to predict which coin you pull out of your pocket?

Mixed Review

27. Find the percent of increase from 140 to 154. *(Lesson 7.5)*

28. You deposit $750 in an account with a simple annual interest rate of 2.75%. Find the interest you will earn after 30 months. Round to the nearest cent. *(Lesson 7.7)*

Basic Skills **Find the sum.**

29. $-47 + 19$ **30.** $20 + (-18)$ **31.** $-7 + (-25)$ **32.** $-32 + (-56)$

FCAT Practice FCAT

33. Multiple Choice What is the probability of getting a number divisible by 2 when rolling a number cube?

A. $\frac{1}{6}$ **B.** $\frac{1}{3}$ **C.** $\frac{1}{2}$ **D.** $\frac{2}{3}$

34. Multiple Choice In a group of 80 people, 44 say their favorite color is blue. One person is selected at random from the larger group. What is the probability that the person's favorite color is blue?

F. 0.36 **G.** 0.44 **H.** 0.55 **I.** 0.8

LESSONS 7.5 TO 7.8

Notebook Review

Review the vocabulary definitions in your notebook.

Copy the review examples in your notebook. Then complete the exercises.

Check Your Definitions

percent of change, p. 338
percent of increase, p. 338
percent of decrease, p. 338
markup, discount, p. 342
interest, annual interest rate, p. 348

principal, p. 348
outcome, favorable outcome, p. 354
event, probability of an event, p. 354
theoretical probability, p. 354
experimental probability, p. 355

Use Your Vocabulary

1. Describe how to find theoretical probability.

7.5–7.6 Can you find a sale price?

 EXAMPLE A pair of shoes has an original price of $40. What is the sale price after a 15% discount?

$40 \times 0.15 = 6$ **Multiply to find discount.**

$40 - 6 = 34$ **Subtract discount from original price.**

ANSWER The sale price of the shoes is $34.

☑ **Find the sale price or retail price.**

2. Wholesale price: $30
Percent markup: 70%

3. Original price: $72
Percent discount: 18%

7.7 Can you use the percent equation?

 EXAMPLE What number is 26% of 300?

$a = p\% \cdot b$ **Write percent equation.**

$a = 26\% \cdot 300$ **Substitute 26 for p and 300 for b.**

$a = 78$ **Multiply.**

 4. 72 is 75% of what number?   **5.** What number is 34% of 856?

7.8 Can you find the probability of an event?

 EXAMPLE   Two scientists spin a Belgian euro coin 250 times and it lands heads up 140 times. Find the experimental probability of the coin landing heads up.

Use the results to find the experimental probability.

$$P(\text{heads}) = \frac{140}{250} \quad \longleftarrow \text{ Number of favorable outcomes}$$
$$\phantom{P(\text{heads})} \longleftarrow \text{ Total number of spins}$$

$$= \frac{14}{25} = 0.56 = 56\%$$

 6. You randomly draw a marble out of a bag that contains 8 red, 5 yellow, and 4 blue marbles. Find the probability of drawing each color.

Stop *and* **Think**   about Lessons 7.5–7.8

7. Critical Thinking You invest $300 at a simple annual interest rate of 3.5% for one year. How much would you need to invest at a 2% simple annual interest rate to earn the same amount of interest that year?

Review Quiz 2

Tell whether the change is an *increase* or *decrease*. Then find the percent of change.

1. Original amount: $120
New amount: $138

2. Original amount: 260 miles
New amount: 169 miles

3. Retail A shirt has a $20 wholesale price and is marked up 50%. The sales tax is 5%. What is the total cost of the shirt?

Solve using the percent equation.

4. 75 is 125% of what number?

5. 552.5 is what percent of 85,000?

6. Koalas Koalas absorb only about 25% of the fiber they eat. How much fiber is absorbed by a koala that eats 10.5 ounces of fiber per day?

You spin the spinner below 40 times. Predict how many times the spinner lands on the specified color.

7. Red

8. Blue

9. Yellow

7

Chapter Review

Vocabulary

ratio, equivalent ratios, p. 317
rate, unit rate, p. 318
proportion, p. 322
cross products, p. 323
scale model, scale, p. 324
percent, p. 327
circle graph, p. 331
percent of change, p. 338
percent of increase, p. 338
percent of decrease, p. 338

markup, discount, p. 342
interest, p. 348
principal, p. 348
annual interest rate, p. 348
outcome, p. 354
event, p. 354
favorable outcome, p. 354
probability of an event, p. 354
theoretical probability, p. 354
experimental probability, p. 355

Vocabulary Review

Copy and complete the statement.

1. If you write $\frac{180 \text{ miles}}{3 \text{ hours}}$ as $\frac{60 \text{ miles}}{1 \text{ hour}}$, you have written the rate as a(n) ? .

2. A(n) ? is a ratio whose denominator is 100.

3. The theoretical probability of an event is the ratio of the number of ? to the number of ? .

Match the word with the correct definition.

4. annual interest rate

5. interest

6. principal

A. the amount of money that you borrow or deposit

B. the amount paid for the use of money

C. the percent of the principal that you pay or earn each year

Review Questions

Write the equivalent rate. *(Lesson 7.1)*

7. $\frac{286.8 \text{ m}}{\text{min}} = \frac{? \text{ m}}{\text{sec}}$

8. $\frac{4.2 \text{ in.}}{\text{month}} = \frac{? \text{ in.}}{\text{year}}$

9. $\frac{6 \text{ times}}{\text{min}} = \frac{? \text{ times}}{\text{hour}}$

Solve the proportion. *(Lesson 7.2)*

10. $\frac{5}{13} = \frac{18}{c}$

11. $\frac{48}{36} = \frac{x}{6}$

12. $\frac{n}{12} = \frac{7}{8}$

13. $\frac{25}{b} = \frac{55}{22}$

Use a percent proportion. *(Lesson 7.3)*

14. What number is 500% of 16?

15. 200.2 is 65% of what number?

16. 44 is what percent of 80?

17. 1.7 is what percent of 340?

Write the decimal or fraction as a percent. *(Lesson 7.4)*

18. 0.43

19. 0.003

20. $\frac{3}{10}$

21. $\frac{29}{20}$

Final Project In Exercises 22–24, use the circle graph. It shows the results of a survey of 300 students who were asked what they would choose for a final project. *(Lesson 7.4)*

22. What percent of students chose an oral report?

23. What fraction of students chose a visual project? Write the fraction in simplest form.

24. Which final project was chosen by 21% of the students?

Final Project

Visual project 105
Writing a paper 96
Taking a test 63
Oral report 36

25. **Moving** A moving van's load changes from 800 to 984 pounds after picking up an appliance. Find the percent of increase. *(Lesson 7.5)*

Find the sale price or retail price. *(Lesson 7.6)*

26. Wholesale price: $22.40
Percent markup: 60%

27. Original price: $21.25
Percent discount: 32%

Find the amount of simple interest earned in 3 years. *(Lesson 7.7)*

28. Principal: $460
Annual rate: 3.5%

29. Principal: $1540
Annual rate: 2.75%

30. **Fundraiser** At a school fundraiser, the science club made 58% of their money selling juice, 27% selling cookies, and 15% selling apples. The club made $87 selling juice. How much did the club make selling cookies? How much did they make selling apples? *(Lesson 7.7)*

Find the probability of the event. *(Lesson 7.8)*

31. A random 5-digit ZIP code ends with a number less than 5.

32. You roll a number cube and get a 7.

33. A number less than 4 is randomly drawn from the numbers 1, 2, 3, and 4.

Chapter Test

Write the ratio of shaded to unshaded squares.

1.

2.

3.

4.

Write the rate as a unit rate.

5. $\dfrac{156 \text{ miles}}{3 \text{ hours}}$

6. $\dfrac{18 \text{ servings}}{6 \text{ people}}$

7. $\dfrac{448 \text{ cycles}}{5 \text{ days}}$

8. $\dfrac{54 \text{ meters}}{21 \text{ seconds}}$

Find the value of the variable

9. $\dfrac{12}{16} = \dfrac{18}{a}$

10. $\dfrac{15}{6} = \dfrac{d}{4}$

11. $\dfrac{9}{n} = \dfrac{21}{14}$

12. $\dfrac{t-3}{12} = \dfrac{11}{6}$

13. Maps The road distance from Miami, Florida, to Columbia, South Carolina, on a map is about 6.7 centimeters. The scale is 1 cm : 150 km. What is the actual distance from Miami to Columbia?

14. Survey In a survey, 34%, or 102 people, said they enjoy in-line skating. How many people were surveyed?

Write the percent as a decimal and as a fraction.

15. 0.7%

16. 419%

17. 8%

18. 7.8%

Find the percent of increase or decrease.

19. Original amount: 40
New amount: 36

20. Original amount: 225
New amount: 324

21. Original amount: 258
New amount: 6.45

22. Food Your food bill at a restaurant totals $26. There is a 6.5% sales tax and you leave a 16% tip. What is the total cost of the meal?

23. Recycling The average person in the United States generates about 4.5 pounds of waste per day. About 30% of this waste is recycled. About how many pounds of waste are recycled per person per day?

A box contains 9 tiles that together spell the word "TENNESSEE." You draw at random one tile from the box. Find the probability of the event.

24. Drawing an E

25. Drawing an S

Chapter FCAT Practice

Test-Taking Strategy Avoid spending too much time on one question. Skip questions you have trouble with, and return to them after you have finished.

Multiple Choice

1. Which ratio is *not* equivalent to $\frac{5}{11}$?

   A. $\frac{20}{44}$ **B.** $\frac{2.5}{5.5}$ **C.** $\frac{1000}{2200}$ **D.** $\frac{35}{75}$

2. Paul can read at a speed of 228 words per minute. What is his reading speed in words per second?

   F. 0.26 words per second

   G. 3.8 words per second

   H. 2280 words per second

   I. 13,680 words per second

3. Which choice shows $\frac{12 \text{ meters}}{8 \text{ seconds}}$ correctly written as a unit rate?

   A. $\frac{3 \text{ m}}{\text{sec}}$ **B.** $\frac{6 \text{ m}}{4 \text{ sec}}$ **C.** $\frac{1.5 \text{ m}}{\text{sec}}$ **D.** $\frac{4 \text{ m}}{6 \text{ sec}}$

4. A scale model of a room is 6 inches long and 5 inches wide. The actual room is 10 feet wide. What scale was used?

   F. 1 in. : 2 ft   **G.** 2 in. : 1 ft

   H. 1 in. : 2 in.   **I.** 2 in. : 1 in.

5. Which choice is equal to 0.62?

   A. 6.2%   **B.** $\frac{3}{5}$ **C.** $\frac{31}{50}$ **D.** 620%

6. A crowd of 420 people shrinks to 357 people. What is the percent of decrease?

   F. 15%   **G.** 17.6%   **H.** 63%   **I.** 85%

7. In a class, 80%, or 28, of the students studied for a test. How many students are in the class?

   A. 20   **B.** 22   **C.** 30   **D.** 35

8. You deposit $450 in an account that pays a simple interest rate of 3.5% annually. How much interest will you earn in 2 years?

   F. $15.75 **G.** $31.50 **H.** $157.50 **I.** $315

9. You draw a sock from a drawer of 6 black, 8 white, and 4 brown socks. What is the probability that the sock is black?

   A. $\frac{1}{6}$ **B.** $\frac{2}{9}$ **C.** $\frac{1}{3}$ **D.** $\frac{4}{9}$

Short Response

10. A shirt with a wholesale price of $9.60 is marked up 75%. When it doesn't sell, the item is sold at a 40% discount. Find the retail price of the item. Then find the sale price of the item.

Extended Response

11. You draw a marble at random from a bag of red, blue, green, and yellow marbles 24 times. Each time you record its color and place it back in the bag of 75 marbles. The results are shown in the table below. How many of each color marble do you predict are in the bag? Explain.

Red	Blue	Green	Yellow
7	3	5	9

Strategies for Answering
Short Response Questions

Problem

You work for your uncle this summer. He pays you $20 on your first day. Each day after that, you will get a raise. You can choose from 2 payment plans. With Plan A, you earn a $5 raise each day. With Plan B, you earn a 20% raise each day. Which plan is a better deal?

Full credit solution

Plan B is a better deal if you work more than 5 days.

Data is used to justify the solution.

Day	1	2	3	4	5	6
Plan A pay	20.00	25.00	30.00	35.00	40.00	45.00
Plan A total	20.00	45.00	75.00	110.00	150.00	195.00
Plan B pay	20.00	24.00	28.80	34.56	41.47	49.76
Plan B total	20.00	44.00	72.80	107.36	148.83	198.59

The question is answered clearly and in complete sentences.

Plan A is better if you work 5 days or less, but Plan B is better if you work more than 5 days. By day 6, the pay with a 20% increase is more than the pay with a $5 raise, so it will continue to be the better plan.

Partial credit solution

I think Plan B is better than Plan A.

The calculations are correct.

Day	1	2	3	4	5	6
Plan A	20.00	25.00	30.00	35.00	40.00	45.00
Plan B	20.00	24.00	28.80	34.56	41.47	49.76

The reasoning is faulty, because the total amount earned was not considered.

The first 4 days, Plan A is better. The next 2 days, Plan B is better. By day 5 Plan B pays you more money, so it is the better plan.

Partial credit solution

The data does not include information past Day 4. So, the answer is incorrect.

Plan A is better. The table shows that over the first four days, Plan A pays out $2.64 more than Plan B.

Day	1	2	3	4
Plan A	20.00	25.00	30.00	35.00
Plan B	20.00	24.00	28.80	34.56
Difference	0	1.00	1.20	0.44

The data is calculated correctly.

No credit solution

The answer is incorrect.

Plan A is better.

Day	1	2	3	4
Plan A	20.00	25.00	30.00	35.00
Plan B	20.00	24.00	26.00	28.00

The data is not calculated correctly.

Watch Out!

Be sure to explain your reasoning clearly.

Your turn now

Score each solution to the short response question below as *full credit*, *partial credit*, or *no credit*. Explain your reasoning.

Problem The Spiff travels 226.8 miles on 14 gallons of gas. The Flyte travels 280 miles on 17.5 gallons of gas. Which car is more fuel efficient?

1. The Spiff is the more fuel efficient car because it gets 16.2 miles per gallon. The Flyte gets 16 miles per gallon.

2. The Flyte gets 16 miles per gallon, because $280 \div 17.5 = 16$. The Spiff gets 16.2 miles per gallon, because $226.8 \div 14 = 16.2$. The more fuel efficient car gets a greater number of miles per gallon. Because 16.2 is greater than 16, the Spiff is more fuel efficient.

Short Response

1. The actual dimensions of Maureen's rectangular yard are shown below. Maureen is building a scale model of her yard. The longer sides of the model are 20 inches in length. What is the length of the model's shorter sides? Explain your answer.

50 ft

30 ft

2. The gauge of a fuel tank indicated that the tank was $\frac{1}{7}$ full. After 24 gallons of fuel are added, the tank is $\frac{4}{7}$ full. What is the greatest number of gallons the fuel tank can hold? Explain your answer.

3. Emily, Diana, and Helen are selling boxes of greeting cards. Emily sells three times as many boxes as Helen. Diana sells three more than twice as many boxes as Helen. Emily and Diana sell the same number of boxes. How many boxes of greeting cards does Helen sell? Explain how you found your answer.

4. Nick is shopping for a new bike. The first bike he finds is on sale for 15% off the original price of $175.50. The second bike he finds is on sale for 20% off the original price of $180.75. There is a 7% sales tax on both bikes. Which bike costs less? Explain how you found your answer.

5. A jar contains 2 purple pens, 3 green pens, 5 blue pens, and 4 red pens. Joe picks a pen from the jar at random. What is the probability that Joe's pen is *not* red? Explain your answer.

6. Pencils are sold in packages of 14. Erasers are sold in packages of 8. Zak wants to buy the same number of pencils and erasers. What is the smallest number of pencils he can buy? Explain how you found your answer.

7. A pair of hiking boots was originally priced at $180. The discounted cost of the boots is $99. By what percent was the price of the boots discounted? Explain your answer.

8. George wants to buy a pizza with toppings. One cheese pizza costs $9.50, and each additional topping costs $.75. George has $12 total. What is the greatest number of additional toppings George can have on his pizza? Write and solve an inequality to answer the question. Explain your inequality.

9. A soccer coach counts the number of goals that each player on the team scores in a season. The table below shows the current totals.

Player	Number of Goals
Katie	3
Madeline	1
Keisha	8
Sarah	0
Angela	4
Jennifer	9
Norma	3
Lisa	5
Kelley	11

What is the mean number of goals scored by the team so far? Which players have scored more goals than this average?

Multiple Choice

10. According to the rules at a summer camp, there must be 2 counselors supervising every 5 campers. There are 65 campers enrolled in the camp. Which proportion can you use to find the number of counselors needed?

A. $\dfrac{2}{5} = \dfrac{x}{65}$ **B.** $\dfrac{2}{5} = \dfrac{65}{x}$

C. $\dfrac{2}{65} = \dfrac{5}{x}$ **D.** $\dfrac{2}{x} = \dfrac{65}{5}$

11. The diameter of a circular rug is 12 feet. What is the best estimate of the rug's circumference?

    F. 24 ft   **G.** 36 ft   **H.** 42 ft   **I.** 72 ft

12. Jane bought windshield wipers and gas for her car. The windshield wipers cost $15, and the gas cost $1.81 per gallon. Jane spent $34.91 total. How many gallons of gas did she buy?

    A. 9   **B.** 10   **C.** 11   **D.** 12

13. Andrea spins the spinner. All of the sections of the spinner are the same size. What is the probability of the arrow landing on blue?

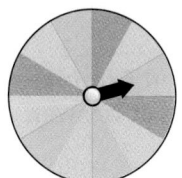

    F. $\dfrac{1}{8}$ **G.** $\dfrac{1}{4}$ **H.** $\dfrac{1}{3}$ **I.** $\dfrac{1}{2}$

14. Luke has $30 in his savings and saves an additional $2 each week. Hector has $50 in his savings and takes $3 from it each week. After how many weeks will Luke and Hector have the same total amount in their savings?

    A. 3   **B.** 4   **C.** 5   **D.** 6

15. Carlos read $\dfrac{5}{12}$ of the pages in a book. Alvaro read $\dfrac{9}{10}$ of the number of pages that Carlos read. The book has 72 pages. How many pages did Alvaro read?

    F. 27   **G.** 30   **H.** 63   **I.** 64

Extended Response

16. Two rectangular tables have the same perimeter. The first table is 15 feet long. The second table is 10 feet long and twice as wide as the first table. What is the width of each table? Explain your answer.

Find the perimeter of each table.

Which table has a greater area? Explain.

17. Jessica buys a pair of jeans on sale for 25% off the original price of $25.97. She uses a coupon for an additional 20% discount. What is the final cost of the jeans? What is the total percent of Jessica's discount with the sale and the coupon?

Jessica finds a second coupon to use when she pays for the jeans. By combining the two coupons and the sale discount, Jessica pays only 50% of the jeans' original price. What percent discount did the second coupon give?

Cumulative Practice for Chapters 4–7

Chapter 4

Multiple Choice In Exercises 1–7, choose the letter of the correct answer.

1. What is the prime factorization of 108? *(Lesson 4.1)*

   A. $2^2 \cdot 3^3$ B. $2^2 \cdot 3^2$

   C. $2^2 \cdot 3 \cdot 9$ D. $2 \cdot 3^3$

2. Which fractions are equivalent? *(Lesson 4.3)*

   F. $\dfrac{5}{8}, \dfrac{8}{20}$ G. $\dfrac{3}{4}, \dfrac{21}{32}$

   H. $\dfrac{4}{9}, \dfrac{32}{72}$ I. $\dfrac{15}{16}, \dfrac{90}{80}$

3. Mark bought notebooks for 15¢ each. Phil bought notebooks for 25¢ each. Mark and Phil spent the same amount of money on notebooks. What is the least amount of money they could have spent? *(Lesson 4.4)*

   A. $.50   B. $.75   C. $1.50   D. $3.75

4. Which set of fractions is ordered from least to greatest? *(Lesson 4.5)*

   F. $\dfrac{1}{6}, \dfrac{5}{24}, \dfrac{1}{3}, \dfrac{5}{12}$ G. $\dfrac{5}{24}, \dfrac{5}{12}, \dfrac{1}{6}, \dfrac{1}{3}$

   H. $\dfrac{1}{3}, \dfrac{1}{6}, \dfrac{5}{12}, \dfrac{5}{24}$ I. $\dfrac{5}{24}, \dfrac{1}{6}, \dfrac{5}{12}, \dfrac{1}{3}$

5. What is the value of the expression $5^2 \cdot 5^3 - 3^2$? *(Lesson 4.6)*

   A. 144   B. 616   C. 619   D. 3116

6. What is the value of the expression $2 \cdot 2^{-4}$? *(Lesson 4.7)*

   F. -8 G. $\dfrac{1}{32}$ H. $\dfrac{1}{8}$ I. 37

7. Which number is *not* written in scientific notation? *(Lesson 4.8)*

   A. 2.2×10^{-9} B. 3.3×10^3

   C. 12×10^5 D. 9.33×10^5

8. **Short Response** A bus to the shopping area departs every 9 minutes. A bus to the business district departs every 8 minutes. A bus to the airport departs every 12 minutes. How often do all three buses depart at the same time? Explain. *(Lesson 4.4)*

9. **Extended Response** Kerry is wrapping cookies in packages for a bake sale. She wants every package to have the same number of cookies. She also wants each package to contain only one kind of cookie. Kerry has 78 oatmeal, 90 peanut butter, and 126 chocolate chip cookies. *(Lesson 4.2)*

   a. What is the greatest number of cookies that Kerry can put into each package?

   b. Use your answer from part (a) to find how many packages of each kind of cookie Kerry will have.

   c. If Kerry makes 30 more oatmeal cookies, what is the greatest number of cookies Kerry can put into each package?

Chapter 5

Multiple Choice In Exercises 10–16, choose the letter of the correct answer.

10. You need $3\dfrac{1}{3}$ yards of fabric for a dress and $1\dfrac{2}{3}$ yards for a jacket. How many yards of fabric should you purchase? *(Lesson 5.1)*

   A. 4   B. $4\dfrac{1}{2}$ C. 5   D. 7

11. Find the difference $\frac{19}{20} - \frac{4}{15}$. *(Lesson 5.2)*

    F. $\frac{41}{60}$ **G.** $\frac{3}{4}$ **H.** $1\frac{13}{60}$ **I.** 3

12. Find the product $-2\frac{1}{2} \cdot 4\frac{2}{3}$. *(Lesson 5.3)*

    A. $-11\frac{2}{3}$ **B.** $-8\frac{1}{3}$ **C.** $-8\frac{1}{6}$ **D.** -7

13. What is the value of b in the equation
$\frac{4}{5}b = -16$? *(Lesson 5.4)*

    F. -20 **G.** $-16\frac{4}{5}$ **H.** $-12\frac{4}{5}$ **I.** 20

14. In your class, $\frac{15}{24}$ of the students are
wearing sneakers. What is another way
to write this number? *(Lesson 5.5)*

    A. 0.6   **B.** 0.625   **C.** 1.6   **D.** 2

15. What is the value of the expression
$-3.448 + (11.2)$? *(Lesson 5.6)*

    F. -14.648 **G.** -7.752

    H. 7.752   **I.** 14.648

16. What is the value of the expression
$-3.44 \cdot -9.9$? *(Lesson 5.7)*

    A. -34.056 **B.** -6.46

    C. 6.46   **D.** 34.056

17. Short Response Four friends carry one
bag of supplies on a hike. Kathy carries the
bag for $\frac{1}{6}$ of the time, and Vicki carries it for
0.25 of the time. Craig carries the bag for
0.5 of the time. Mike carries it for $\frac{1}{12}$ of the
time. Who carries the bag for the most
time? Explain. *(Lesson 5.5)*

18. Extended Response A restaurant offers
hamburger dinners at half the usual price,
if they are ordered before 5:00 P.M. Sue and
Meg each order a hamburger dinner at
4:50 P.M. Tony orders a hamburger dinner at
5:05 P.M. *(Lessons 5.6, 5.7)*

    a. The usual price of a hamburger dinner
is $6.50. What is the total cost of the meal
ordered by the three friends? Explain
how you found your answer.

    b. What fraction of the total cost is the cost
of Tony's hamburger dinner?

    c. Jim joins Sue, Meg, and Tony at 5:15 P.M.
and orders a hamburger dinner. What is
the new total cost of the meal?

Chapter 6

**Multiple Choice In Exercises 19–23, choose
the letter of the correct answer.**

19. What is the value of n in the equation
$2n + 8 + 6n = 8$? *(Lesson 6.1)*

    A. -2 **B.** 0   **C.** 2   **D.** 8

20. What is the value of x in the equation
$5x + 24 = 8x - 66$? *(Lesson 6.2)*

    F. -30 **G.** -14 **H.** 14   **I.** 30

21. What is the circumference
of the circle? Use 3.14
for π. *(Lesson 6.4)*

71 m

    A. 11.31 m   **B.** 22.61 m

    C. 222.94 m   **D.** 445.88 m

22. What is the solution to the inequality
$3y - 6 < 9$? *(Lesson 6.5)*

    F. $y < 1$ **G.** $y > 1$ **H.** $y < 5$ **I.** $y > 5$

Cumulative Practice continued

23. Lana has $30 to spend on tickets that cost $6.75 each. What is the greatest number of tickets that Lana can buy? *(Lesson 6.6)*

    A. 2   **B.** 3   **C.** 4   **D.** 5

24. Short Response Paige ran for $\frac{1}{2}$ of an hour at a speed of 6 miles per hour. Abigail ran the same distance as Paige at a speed of 5 miles per hour. For how many minutes did Abigail run? Explain. *(Lesson 6.3)*

25. Extended Response The seats in a theater are arranged around a circular stage. Each group of seats is a ring with the same width w. The circumference of the outer circle is about 628 feet. *(Lesson 6.4)*

    a. What is the diameter of the outer circle? Use 3.14 for π.

    b. What is the value of w? Explain how you found your answer.

    c. What is the circumference of the stage?

Chapter 7

Multiple Choice In Exercises 26–31, choose the letter of the correct answer.

26. A 25 minute phone call cost $1.25. Which rate is equivalent to this price? *(Lesson 7.1)*

    A. $\frac{\$.05}{1 \text{ min}}$ **B.** $\frac{\$.10}{1 \text{ min}}$

    C. $\frac{\$.50}{1 \text{ min}}$ **D.** $\frac{\$5.00}{1 \text{ min}}$

27. Solve the proportion $\frac{3}{20} = \frac{42}{x}$. *(Lesson 7.2)*

    F. 6.3   **G.** 28   **H.** 60   **I.** 280

28. 26 is what percent of 104? *(Lesson 7.3)*

    A. 2.5%   **B.** 4%   **C.** 40%   **D.** 25%

29. There were 64 players on the first day of soccer practice. On the second day, 25% more players practiced. How many players practiced on the second day? *(Lesson 7.5)*

    F. 16   **G.** 80   **H.** 89   **I.** 160

30. What is the total cost of snorkel gear priced at $87.50 with a 60% discount? *(Lesson 7.6)*

    A. $27.50   **B.** $35.00   **C.** $52.50   **D.** $72.90

31. Kevin invested $130 in an account that pays 5% simple annual interest. What is the account balance after 4 years? *(Lesson 7.7)*

    F. $26   **G.** $150   **H.** $156   **I.** $546

32. Short Response The classrooms in your school are numbered 110 through 150. You choose a room at random. What is the probability that the room you choose has a 4 in its number? Explain. *(Lesson 7.8)*

33. Extended Response The graph shows the results of a poll in which 442 people said that in-line skates are the most fun. *(Lesson 7.4)*

    a. How many people prefer roller skates?

    b. Find the total number of people who participated in the poll.

    c. How many people chose either scooters or skateboards?

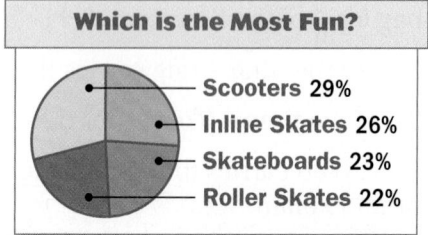

Which is the Most Fun?

Scooters 29%
Inline Skates 26%
Skateboards 23%
Roller Skates 22%

UNIT 3 Geometry and Measurement

CHAPTER

8 Polygons and Transformations

9 Real Numbers and Right Triangles

10 Measurement, Area, and Volume

Meeting the Florida Standards

- **Classify angles, triangles, and other polygons.**
  MA.B.1.3.2, MA.C.1.3.1

- **Use properties of congruent and similar polygons to solve problems.**
  MA.A.3.3.2, MA.B.2.3.1, MA.C.1.3.1, MA.C.2.3.1, MA.C.3.3.1

- **Describe transformations and symmetry of geometric figures.**
  MA.C.2.3.1, MA.C.2.3.2

- **Use square roots and the Pythagorean theorem to solve problems.**
  MA.A.3.3.2, MA.C.1.3.1, MA.C.3.3.1

- **Identify rational and irrational numbers.**
  MA.A.1.3.2, MA.A.1.3.3, MA.A.1.3.4

- **Use special relationships in right triangles to solve problems.**
  MA.C.1.3.1, MA.C.1.3.3

- **Find areas of parallelograms, trapezoids, and circles.**
  MA.A.3.3.2, MA.C.1.3.1, MA.C.3.3.1

- **Find surface areas and volumes of solids.**
  MA.A.1.3.2, MA.A.1.3.3, MA.A.1.3.4

- **Classify and sketch solids.**
  MA.C.1.3.1, MA.C.3.3.1

From Chapter 9, p. 465

What is the height of the water slide?

371

Polygons and Transformations

Chapter Warm-Up Game

Review skills you need for this chapter in this quick game. Work with a partner.

Key Skill:
Plotting points on a coordinate plane

BEFORE

In previous chapters you've...

- Solved equations
- Plotted points in a coordinate plane

Now

In Chapter 8 you'll study...

- Solving equations to find angle measures
- Classifying angles and triangles
- Reflecting, translating, and rotating figures in a coordinate plane

WHY?

So you can solve real-world problems about...

- weaving, p. 378
- referees, p. 384
- geodesic domes, p. 393
- origami, p. 412

Internet Preview
CLASSZONE.COM

- eEdition Plus Online
- eWorkbook Plus Online
- eTutorial Plus Online
- FCAT Practice
- More Examples

MATERIALS

- 2 sheets of grid paper for each player
- Pencils

PREPARE Each player draws a coordinate graph on both sheets of grid paper. Each player draws squares along the grid lines passing through the points $(7, 0)$, $(0, -7)$, $(-7, 0)$, and $(0, 7)$. A player secretly marks 4 flags on one graph. A flag is three consecutive points with integer coordinates, either horizontally or vertically. Flags cannot touch the outside borders. On each turn, a player should follow the steps on the next page.

Find the Flags

```
          6              ·——·
          4
          2       ·
·——·            2  4  6
-6  -4  -2    -2
              -4        ·——·
              -6
```

1 **CALL** out a point. The other player lets you know if you hit or missed one of their flags.

2 **MARK** a hit with an "X" and a miss with an "O" on your second graph where your flags are not marked. If you hit a flag, you get to go again.

HOW TO WIN Be the first player to hit all the points in the other player's flags.

Stop *and* Think

1. **Writing** How did you decide where to put your flags? Did it work? Explain. What strategy did you use when trying to find the other player's flags? Did it work? Explain.

2. **Critical Thinking** How many points are there (not including any on the border) in each graph? Explain how you got your answer.

Getting Ready to Learn

Word Watch

Review Words

point, p. 718
line, p. 718
ray, p. 718
plane, p. 718
angle, p. 719
vertex, p. 719
degree, p. 721

Review What You Need to Know

Using Vocabulary **Identify the object with a review word.** *(p. 718)*

1.   **2.** •   **3.**

4. Copy and complete with a review word: An angle is measured in __?__.

Use a protractor to measure the angle. *(p. 721)*

5.   **6.**   **7.**

8.   **9.**   **10.**

11. You have a giant crayon that is a scale model of a regular crayon.
A regular crayon is about 0.25 inch wide and 3.5 inches long.
The giant crayon is 6 inches wide. How long is it? *(p. 322)*

You should include material that appears on a notebook like this in your own notes.

Know How to Take Notes

Making a Concept Map You will often learn new concepts that are related to each other. It is helpful to organize these concepts in your notes with a map or chart.

A rectangle is a figure with four sides.
Its opposite sides are the same length
and its angles measure 90°.

A square is
a rectangle
with sides that
are the same
length.

In Lesson 8.3, you can use a concept map to organize information about special four-sided shapes.

Angle Pairs

LESSON 8.1

BEFORE | ▶ **Now** | **WHY?**

You solved equations to find the value of a variable. | You'll solve equations to find angle measures. | So you can design stationery, as in Ex. 13.

Word Watch

straight angle,
 right angle, p. 375
supplementary,
 complementary angles,
 p. 375
vertical angles, p. 376
perpendicular lines, p. 376
parallel lines, p. 377

FLORIDA
Standards and Assessment

• Apply formulas to find angle
 measures. (MA.B.1.3.2)

A **straight angle** measures 180°. A **right angle** measures 90°. The mark ⌐ tells you that an angle measures 90°.

Straight angle   **Right angle**

Two angles are **supplementary** if the sum of their measures is 180°.
Two angles are **complementary** if the sum of their measures is 90°.
You can write "the measure of angle 1" as $m\angle 1$.

   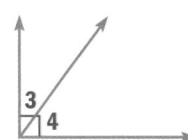

∠1 and ∠2 are supplementary.   ∠3 and ∠4 are complementary.
$m\angle 1 + m\angle 2 = 180°$ $m\angle 3 + m\angle 4 = 90°$

EXAMPLE 1 **Finding an Angle Measure**

∠1 and ∠2 are complementary, and $m\angle 2 = 32°$. Find $m\angle 1$.

Solution

$m\angle 1 + m\angle 2 = 90°$ Definition of complementary angles

$m\angle 1 + 32° = 90°$ Substitute 32° for $m\angle 2$.

$m\angle 1 = 58°$ Subtract 32° from each side.

Your turn now Tell whether ∠1 and ∠2 are *complementary*, *supplementary*, or *neither*.

1. $m\angle 1 = 79°$
 $m\angle 2 = 101°$

2. $m\angle 1 = 64°$
 $m\angle 2 = 36°$

3. $m\angle 1 = 52°$
 $m\angle 2 = 38°$

4. $m\angle 1 = 44°$
 $m\angle 2 = 46°$

5. $m\angle 1 = 53°$
 $m\angle 2 = 47°$

6. $m\angle 1 = 95°$
 $m\angle 2 = 85°$

Vertical Angles When two lines intersect at a point, they form two pairs of angles that do not share a side. These pairs are called **vertical angles**, and they always have the same measure.

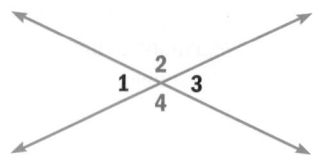

∠1 and ∠3 are vertical angles.
$m\angle 1 = m\angle 3$

∠2 and ∠4 are vertical angles.
$m\angle 2 = m\angle 4$

EXAMPLE 2 **Using Vertical Angles**

Find $m\angle 2$, $m\angle 3$, and $m\angle 4$.

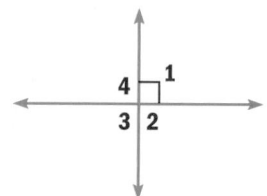

Solution

The diagram shows that $m\angle 1 = 90°$.

∠1 and ∠3 are vertical angles. Their measures are equal, so $m\angle 3 = 90°$.

∠1 and ∠2 are supplementary.

$m\angle 1 + m\angle 2 = 180°$ Definition of supplementary angles

$90° + m\angle 2 = 180°$ Substitute 90° for $m\angle 1$.

$m\angle 2 = 90°$ Subtract 90° from each side.

∠2 and ∠4 are vertical angles. Their measures are equal, so $m\angle 4 = 90°$.

ANSWER $m\angle 2 = m\angle 3 = m\angle 4 = 90°$

Perpendicular Lines You saw in Example 2 that when two lines intersect to form one right angle, they form four right angles. Two lines that intersect at a right angle are called **perpendicular lines**.

Your turn now Find the measures of the numbered angles.

7.

8.

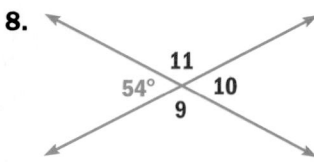

Parallel Lines Two lines in the same plane that do not intersect are called **parallel lines**. When a line intersects two parallel lines, several pairs of angles that are formed have equal measures.

Angles and Parallel Lines

Corresponding Angles

$m\angle1 = m\angle5 \qquad m\angle2 = m\angle6$
$m\angle3 = m\angle7 \qquad m\angle4 = m\angle8$

Alternate Interior Angles

$m\angle3 = m\angle6 \qquad m\angle4 = m\angle5$

Alternate Exterior Angles

$m\angle1 = m\angle8 \qquad m\angle2 = m\angle7$

HELP with Solving

Triangles on lines indicate that lines are parallel.

EXAMPLE 3 Using Parallel Lines

Use the diagram to find $m\angle1$.

Solution

$\angle1$ and $\angle5$ are corresponding angles, so they have equal measures. Find $m\angle5$.

The angle with measure 125° and $\angle5$ are supplementary.

$m\angle5 + 125° = 180°$ Definition of supplementary angles

$m\angle5 = 55°$ Subtract 125° from each side.

$\angle1$ and $\angle5$ have equal measures.

ANSWER $m\angle1 = 55°$

Your turn now Find the angle measure.

9. $m\angle2$ **10.** $m\angle3$

11. $m\angle4$ **12.** $m\angle6$

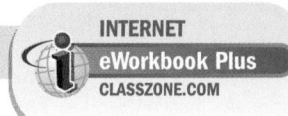
Getting Ready to Practice

Vocabulary Copy and complete the statement.

1. The sum of the measures of two __?__ angles is 180°.

2. Two lines that intersect to form a right angle are called __?__.

Tell whether the angles are *complementary*, *supplementary*, or *neither*.

3. $m\angle 1 = 62°$, $m\angle 2 = 118°$

4. $m\angle 1 = 51°$, $m\angle 2 = 39°$

5. Find the Error Describe and correct the error in the solution.

$$\times \quad m\angle 2 = 68°,$$
because
vertical angles
add up to 180°.

112° / 1
3 / 2

Practice and Problem Solving

Find the angle measure.

6. $\angle 1$ and $\angle 2$ are complementary, and $m\angle 1 = 56°$. Find $m\angle 2$.

7. $\angle 3$ and $\angle 4$ are supplementary, and $m\angle 4 = 71°$. Find $m\angle 3$.

Find the measures of the numbered angles.

8.

2 / 80°
1 / 3

9.

7 / 45°
6 / 5

10. Weaving Find the angle measures in the weaving if $m\angle 1 = 122°$.

11. Intersecting Streets Two streets intersect to form a 75° angle. Sketch the intersection and find the measure of each angle formed.

12. Writing Can parallel lines form vertical angles? Explain.

2 3
1 4

13. Stationery A student designed the stationery border shown here. Explain how to find $m\angle 2$ if $m\angle 1 = 135°$.

14. In the diagram, $m\angle 4 = 44°$. Find the measure of each angle.

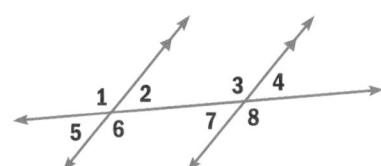

15. Challenge Find the measure of each angle if $m\angle 9 = 106°$.

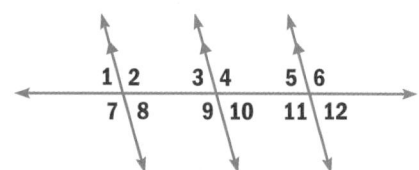

Algebra **Find the value of the variable and the angle measures.**

16. $m\angle 1 = (5x + 15)°$ and $m\angle 2 = 28x°$

17. $m\angle 6 = (100 - 10y)°$ and $m\angle 3 = 45y°$

18. $m\angle 4 = (7n + 39)°$ and $m\angle 5 = (11n - 13)°$

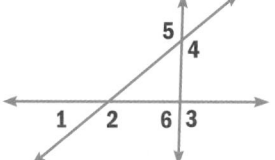

Mixed Review

Write the percent as a fraction in simplest form. *(Lesson 7.4)*

19. 22.6%   **20.** 6.5%   **21.** 0.45%   **22.** 602%

Basic Skills **Find the area of a triangle with the given base and height.**

23. $b = 3$ in., $h = 2$ in.   **24.** $b = 9$ cm, $h = 4$ cm   **25.** $b = 13$ ft, $h = 5$ ft

FCAT Practice

26. Multiple Choice Which angles are supplementary?

    A. $\angle 1$ and $\angle 2$ **B.** $\angle 2$ and $\angle 3$

    C. $\angle 3$ and $\angle 4$ **D.** $\angle 4$ and $\angle 1$

27. Short Response In the diagram, $m\angle 1 = 44°$. Explain how to find $m\angle 2$.

Constructions

GOAL Copy an angle and construct perpendicular lines and parallel lines.

You can *construct* geometric figures using special tools. A *compass* is used to draw parts of circles called *arcs*. A *straightedge* is used to draw a straight line.

EXAMPLE 1 Copying an Angle

1 Draw an angle. Label its vertex *A*. Then draw a ray with endpoint *X*.

2 Draw an arc with center *A*. Label *B* and *C* on ∠*A*. Use the same compass setting to draw an arc with center *X*. Label point *Y*.

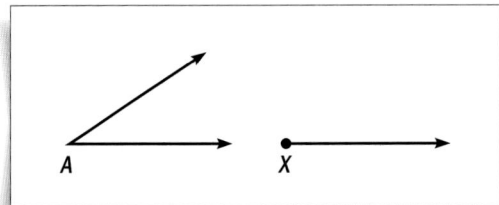

3 Draw an arc with center *B* that passes through *C*. Use the same compass setting to draw an arc with center *Y*. Label point *Z*.

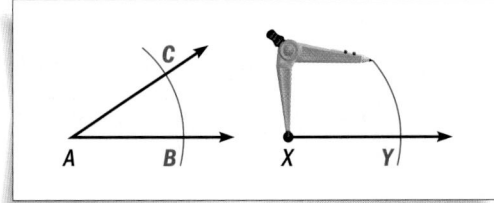

4 Use a straightedge to draw a ray with endpoint *X* through *Z*.

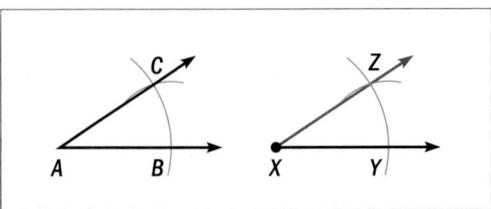

✓ **CHECK** Use a protractor to check that $m\angle A = m\angle X$.

EXAMPLE 2 Constructing a Perpendicular Line

(1) Draw a line and a point *P* not on the line. Draw an arc with center *P* that intersects the line twice. Label *A* and *B*. Using the same compass setting, draw arcs with centers *A* and *B*.

(2) Where the last two arcs intersect label point *Q*. Draw a line through *P* and *Q*. The two lines are perpendicular.

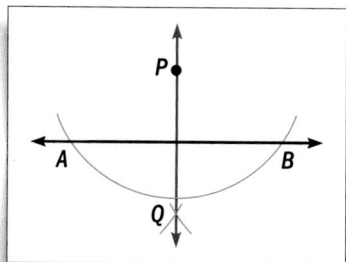

HELP with Solving

The method of construction shown in Example 2 can also work when *P* is on the line through points *A* and *B*. For the last two arcs, use a compass setting greater than half the distance from *A* to *B*.

EXAMPLE 3 Constructing a Parallel Line

(1) Follow the steps in Example 2 to construct perpendicular lines. Label ∠1.

(2) Follow the steps in Example 1 to copy ∠1 at point *P* as shown.

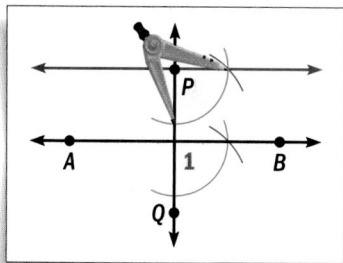

Exercises

Use a protractor to draw an angle with the given measure. Then use a compass and straightedge to copy the angle.

1. 45°   **2.** 120°   **3.** 135°   **4.** 60°

5. Use a compass and a straightedge to construct three parallel lines.

6. Use a compass and straightedge to construct one right triangle.

7. Use a compass and straightedge to construct a rectangle.

Angles and Triangles

LESSON 8.2

BEFORE	Now	WHY?
You identified pairs of angles.	You'll classify angles and triangles.	So you can classify referee signals, as in Exs. 6–8.

Word Watch

acute, right, obtuse angle, p. 382
acute, right, obtuse triangle, p. 382
equilateral, isosceles, scalene triangle, p. 382

FLORIDA
Standards and Assessment

• Know the properties of two-dimensional figures. (MA.C.1.3.1)

• Determine and justify angle measures in figures. (MA.C.1.3.1)

Classifying Angles An angle can be classified by its measure.

Acute angle

Measure is less than 90°.

Right angle

Measure is exactly 90°.

Obtuse angle

Measure is greater than 90° and less than 180°.

Classifying Triangles

By Angles

An **acute triangle** has three acute angles.

A **right triangle** has one right angle.

An **obtuse triangle** has one obtuse angle.

By Sides

An **equilateral triangle** has three sides of equal length.

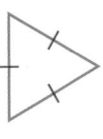

An **isosceles triangle** has at least two sides of equal length.

A **scalene triangle** has no sides of equal length.

EXAMPLE 1 Classifying a Triangle

Classify the triangle by its side lengths.

ANSWER The triangle has no sides of equal length. So, it is a scalene triangle.

8 in.
4 in.
5 in.

HELP with **Reading**

Tick marks in a drawing show that side lengths are equal. Arc marks show that angle measures are equal.

EXAMPLE 2 **Classifying a Triangle**

Classify the triangle by its angles and by its side lengths.

ANSWER The triangle has one right angle and two sides of equal length. So, it is a right isosceles triangle.

Angles in a Triangle From the figures below, you can see that the sum of the angle measures in the triangle is 180°. This is true for all triangles.

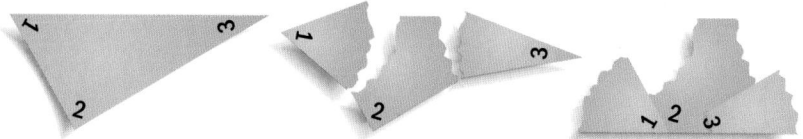

EXAMPLE 3 **Finding an Unknown Angle Measure**

Find the value of x. Then classify the triangle by its angles.

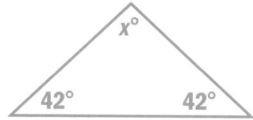

Solution

The sum of the angle measures in a triangle is 180°.

$x° + 42° + 42° = 180°$	Write an equation.
$x + 84 = 180$	Add.
$x + 84 - 84 = 180 - 84$	Subtract 84 from each side.
$x = 96$	Simplify.

ANSWER The triangle has one obtuse angle, so it is an obtuse triangle.

Your turn now **Find the value of x. Then classify the triangle by its angles.**

1.

2.

Getting Ready to Practice

Vocabulary **Copy and complete the statement.**

1. A(n) ? triangle has no sides of equal length.

Classify the triangle by its side lengths.

2.

3.

4.

5. **Find the Error** Describe and correct the error in the solution.

The triangle has an acute angle, so it is an acute triangle.

Practice and Problem Solving

HELP with Homework

Example	Exercises
1	9–11, 15
2	9–11
3	12–14

Online Resources
CLASSZONE.COM

· More Examples
· eTutorial Plus

Estimation **The referee is making calls during a hockey game. Classify the angle made by his arms as *acute*, *obtuse*, or *right*.**

6. Cross Checking

7. Roughing

8. Delayed calling of penalty

Classify the triangle by its side lengths.

9.

10.

11.

Measurement **Find the value of x. Classify the triangle by its angles.**

12.

13.

14.

House of Seven Gables in Salem, Massachusetts

15. House of Seven Gables If the two side edges of this gable are the same length, what kind of triangle is formed? Explain.

Writing Can the angles in a triangle have the measures given? Explain.

16. 43°, 48°, 90°   **17.** 1.5°, 0.5°, 178°   **18.** 21.3°, 56.7°, 102°

Algebra Find the measure of each angle in the triangle.

19.

$(4x - 10)°$
$x°$

20.
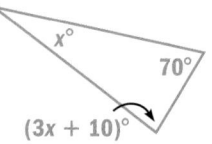
$x°$
70°
$(3x + 10)°$

21.

$(x + 30)°$
$2x°$
$(90 - x)°$

22. Mental Math An *equiangular* triangle has three angles with equal measures. Find the measures of those angles.

23. Measurement Find the measures of the numbered angles

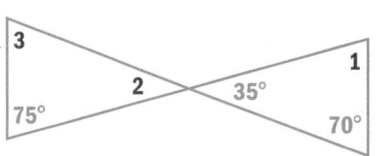
3   1
2   35°
75°   70°

24. Challenge Can two angles of a triangle be supplementary? Explain.

Mixed Review

Find the perimeter and area of the rectangle. *(Lesson 1.6)*

25. $l = 2$ yd, $w = 0.6$ yd   **26.** $l = 13$ m, $w = 12$ m

27. Geography Earth's surface is 29.2% land. The total surface area is 510,072,000 square kilometers. Find the total land area. *(Lesson 7.3)*

28. $\angle 3$ and $\angle 4$ are supplementary and $m\angle 4 = 19°$. Find $m\angle 3$. *(Lesson 8.1)*

FCAT Practice FCAT

INTERNET
FCAT PRACTICE
CLASSZONE.COM

29. Multiple Choice Find the value of x.

A. 2 in.   **B.** 8 in.

C. 10 in.   **D.** 18 in.

x 8 in.
10 in.

30. Multiple Choice The angles in a triangle measure 120°, 25°, and $x°$. Find the value of x.

F. 35   **G.** 40   **H.** 45   **I.** 50

Quadrilaterals

BEFORE	▶ Now	WHY?
You classified angles and triangles.	You'll classify quadrilaterals.	So you can analyze a design, as in Ex. 17.

Word Watch

quadrilateral, p. 386
trapezoid, p. 386
parallelogram, p. 386
rhombus, p. 386

FLORIDA
Standards and Assessment

• Know the properties of two-dimensional figures. (MA.C.1.3.1)

• Determine and justify angle measures in figures. (MA.C.1.3.1)

with Notetaking

You can organize the definitions of quadrilaterals in your notebook using a concept map.

Quadrilaterals A **quadrilateral** is a closed figure with four sides that are line segments. The figures below are special types of quadrilaterals.

Trapezoid A **trapezoid** is a quadrilateral with exactly 1 pair of parallel sides.

Parallelogram A **parallelogram** is a quadrilateral with both pairs of opposite sides parallel.

Rhombus 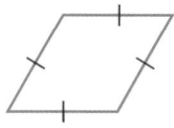 A **rhombus** is a parallelogram with 4 sides of equal length.

Rectangle A rectangle is a parallelogram with 4 right angles.

Square A square is a parallelogram with 4 sides of equal length and 4 right angles.

EXAMPLE 1 **Classifying a Quadrilateral**

Classify the quadrilateral.

Solution

The quadrilateral is a parallelogram with 4 sides of equal length. So, it is a rhombus.

Your turn now **Classify the quadrilateral.**

1.

2.

3.

Angle Measures The figures below show that the sum of the angle measures in a quadrilateral is 360°.

Cut a quadrilateral into 2 triangles.

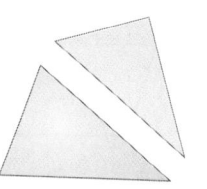

The sum of the angle measures in each triangle is 180°.

The sum of the angle measures in a quadrilateral is 180° + 180° = 360°.

EXAMPLE 2 **Finding an Unknown Angle Measure**

Find the value of x.

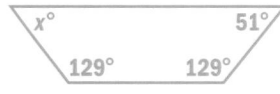

Solution

The sum of the angle measures in a quadrilateral is 360°.

$x° + 51° + 129° + 129° = 360°$ Write an equation.

$x + 309 = 360$ Add.

$x = 51$ Subtract 309 from each side.

8.3 **Exercises**
More Practice, p. 734

Getting Ready to Practice

Vocabulary **Copy and complete the statement.**

1. A ? is a quadrilateral with both pairs of opposite sides parallel.

2. A ? is a quadrilateral with exactly 1 pair of parallel sides.

3. A parallelogram with 4 right angles is a ? .

Classify the quadrilateral.

4.

5.

6.

7. The angles of a quadrilateral measure 85°, 74°, 110°, and x°. Find the value of x.

Practice and Problem Solving

HELP with Homework

Example   Exercises
1   8-10
2   11-16

Online Resources
CLASSZONE.COM
· More Examples
· eTutorial Plus

Measurement **Measure the side lengths. Then classify the quadrilateral.**

8.   9.   10.

Find the value of x.

11.   12.   13.

Find the values of x and y.

14.   15.   16.

17. Classify each of the quadrilaterals in the design shown below.

Tell whether the statement is *always*, *sometimes*, or *never* true.

18. A rhombus is also a parallelogram.

19. A rectangle is also a square.

20. A square is also a parallelogram.

21. A triangle is also a quadrilateral.

22. A quadrilateral is also a rectangle.

Find the value of x and the unknown angle measures.

23.   24.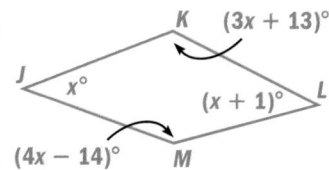

25. **Critical Thinking** What is the greatest number of obtuse angles
that a quadrilateral can have? Explain your answer.

26. Challenge Find the value of x and y in the diagram. Explain your reasoning.

Mixed Review

In Exercises 27–29, solve the equation. *(Lesson 6.2)*

27. $3x + 12 = 7x - 8$ **28.** $5x + 9 = 3x + 19$ **29.** $-6x + 3 = 4x - 7$

30. Two lines intersect to form a 47° angle. Sketch the lines. Find the measure of each angle in the intersection. *(Lesson 8.1)*

Tell whether the statement is *always*, *sometimes*, or *never* true.
(Lessons 8.1, 8.2)

31. The measures of complementary angles have a sum of 180°.

32. An obtuse angle measures more than 90°.

33. An isosceles triangle has three sides of equal length.

FCAT Practice

34. Multiple Choice Which word can describe four sides of a rhombus?

   A. equal   **B.** acute   **C.** parallel   **D.** vertical

35. Multiple Choice Three angles in a quadrilateral are obtuse. Classify the fourth angle.

   F. acute   **G.** right   **H.** obtuse   **I.** straight

Buy Oval Car

Rearrange the letters to make a review word.

1. prizetoad   2. bustoe

3. brushmo   4. tauce

5. allgrapemolar   6. cleanse

7. allearquiet   8. girth

9. catliver   10. includerapper

Polygons and Angles

BEFORE	▶ Now	WHY?
You found angle measures in triangles and quadrilaterals.	You'll find angle measures in polygons.	So you can explore a dome, as in Ex. 24.

Word Watch

polygon, p. 390
regular polygon, p. 390
pentagon, p. 390
hexagon, p. 390
heptagon, p. 390
octagon, p. 390

FLORIDA
Standards and Assessment

• Compare polygons.
(MA.C.1.3.1)

• Make and test conjectures about geometric properties.
(MA.C.3.3.1)

Activity You can use triangles to find the sum of the angle measures in other figures.

① Copy the table. Divide each figure into triangles by drawing as many diagonal lines as you can that begin at the point marked.

② Use your drawings to complete the table.

Shape	Quadrilateral	Pentagon	Hexagon	Octagon
Number of Sides	4	?	?	?
Number of Diagonal Lines	1	?	?	?
Number of Triangles Formed	2	?	?	?
Sum of Angle Measures	360°	?	?	?

③ Use your results to complete a column for a figure with 10 sides.

Polygons A **polygon** is a closed figure whose sides are line segments that intersect only at their endpoints. In a **regular polygon**, all the angles have the same measure and all the sides have the same length.

Polygons   Regular Polygons   Not Polygons

with Reading

You can use *n*-gon, where *n* is the number of sides, to identify a polygon if you haven't learned its name. A 13-gon is a 13-sided polygon.

Polygons can be identified by the number of their sides.

Pentagon	Hexagon	Heptagon	Octagon	12-gon
5 sides	6 sides	7 sides	8 sides	12 sides

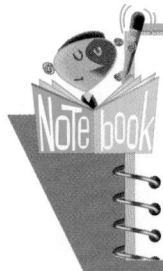

EXAMPLE 1 Identifying Figures

Is the figure a *polygon*, a *regular polygon*, or *not a polygon*? Explain.

a.

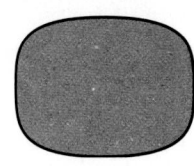

Not a polygon. The figure does not have line segments as sides.

b.

Regular polygon. Its angles have equal measures, and its sides have equal lengths.

Angles In the activity on page 390, you used triangles to find the sum of the angle measures in polygons. In a regular polygon, the measure of one angle is the sum of the angle measures divided by the number of sides.

Angle Measures in a Polygon

Sum of angle measures in an *n*-gon: $(n - 2) \cdot 180°$

Measure of one angle in a *regular n*-gon: $\dfrac{(n - 2) \cdot 180°}{n}$

EXAMPLE 2 Finding an Angle Measure

Find the measure of one angle in a regular octagon.

A regular octagon has 8 sides, so use $n = 8$.

$$\frac{(n - 2) \cdot 180°}{n} = \frac{(8 - 2) \cdot 180°}{8} \qquad \text{Substitute 8 for } n.$$

$$= \frac{1080°}{8} \qquad \text{Simplify numerator.}$$

$$= 135° \qquad \text{Divide.}$$

ANSWER The measure of one angle in a regular octagon is 135°.

Your turn now **Complete the exercise.**

1. Find the sum of the angle measures in a pentagon.

2. Find the measure of one angle in a regular heptagon. Round to the nearest tenth of a degree.

8.4 Exercises

More Practice, p. 734

Getting Ready to Practice

1. Vocabulary Copy and complete: A _?_ is a closed figure with sides that are line segments that intersect only at their endpoints.

Tell whether the figure is a *polygon*, a *regular polygon*, or *not a polygon*.

2.

3.

4.

Find the sum of the angle measures in the polygon.

5. 10-gon   **6.** 9-gon   **7.** 11-gon   **8.** 20-gon

9. Table A table has 7 sides of equal length and 7 equal angles. Find the measure of one angle to the nearest tenth of a degree.

10. Find the Error
Describe and correct the error in the solution.

Sum of Angles = 6 • 180°
X   = 1080°

Practice and Problem Solving

with Homework

Example	Exercises
1	11–13
2	14–17

Online Resources
CLASSZONE.COM
· More Examples
· eTutorial Plus

Tell whether the swimming pool design is a polygon.

11.

12.

13.

Find the measure of one angle in the polygon.

14. regular 10-gon   **15.** regular 14-gon   **16.** regular 15-gon

17. Calculate Find the measure of one angle in a regular 115-gon.

Algebra Find the value of x.

18.

19.

20.

Science

■ **Geodesic Dome**

The Eden Project is an environmental center in England made of connected geodesic domes. Its largest dome is 240 meters long. How many feet is this? (1 meter is equal to 3.281 feet.)

Critical Thinking Find the value of x and the unknown angle measures.

21.

22.

23.

24. Geodesic Dome A geodesic dome has some panels that are hexagons. Sketch a regular hexagon, and find the measure of one angle.

25. Challenge The sum of the angle measures in a polygon is 1980°. How many sides does it have?

Extended Problem Solving In Exercises 26–28, the angles marked with letters are called *exterior angles*.

26. Evaluate Find the measures of the exterior angles of each polygon.

27. Calculate Find the sum of the exterior angle measures for each polygon.

28. Patterns Describe a pattern in the sums you found in Exercise 27.

Mixed Review

Write the percent as a fraction in simplest form. *(Lesson 7.4)*

29. 98%   **30.** 141.3%   **31.** 0.14%   **32.** 82.5%

33. The wholesale price of a pair of shoes is $12.75. The retail price of the shoes is $25.95. Find the percent markup. *(Lesson 7.6)*

34. $m\angle 1 = 56°$ and $m\angle 2 = 34°$. Are the angles supplementary? Explain your answer. *(Lesson 8.1)*

FCAT Practice

35. Multiple Choice Find the measure of one angle in a regular 9-gon.

A. 40°   **B.** 90°   **C.** 140°   **D.** 280°

36. Multiple Choice Angles in a hexagon measure 120°, 95°, 135°, 130°, and 145°. Find the measure of the sixth angle.

F. 85°   **G.** 95°   **H.** 115°   **I.** 120°

LESSONS 8.1 TO 8.4

Notebook Review

Review the vocabulary definitions in your notebook.

Copy the review examples in your notebook. Then complete the exercises.

Check Your Definitions

straight angle, right angle, p. 375

supplementary, complementary angles, p. 375

vertical angles, p. 376

perpendicular lines, p. 376

parallel lines, p. 377

acute, right, obtuse angle, p. 382

acute, right, obtuse triangle, p. 382

equilateral, isosceles, scalene triangle, p. 382

quadrilateral, p. 386

trapezoid, parallelogram, rhombus, p. 386

polygon, regular polygon, p. 390

pentagon, hexagon, heptagon, octagon, p. 390

Use Your Vocabulary

1. Vocabulary How many obtuse angles are in an obtuse triangle?

8.1–8.2 Can you find and use angle measures?

EXAMPLE Refer to the diagram to answer parts (a) and (b).

a. Find $m\angle 2$.

The angle with measure 62° and $\angle 2$ are vertical angles, so their measures are equal.

ANSWER $m\angle 2 = 62°$

b. Find the value of x. Then classify the triangle.

$$x° + 59° + 62° = 180°$$ Sum of angle measures is 180°.

$$x + 121 = 180$$ Add.

$$x = 59$$ Subtract 121 from each side.

ANSWER The triangle is acute and isosceles.

✓ **Find the value of x. Classify the triangle by its angles.**

2.

3.

8.3–8.4 Can you find angle measures in polygons?

EXAMPLE Find the measure of one angle in a regular pentagon.

$$\frac{(n-2) \cdot 180°}{n}$$ Write the formula for measure of one angle in regular polygon.

$$= \frac{(5-2) \cdot 180°}{5}$$ Substitute 5 for *n*.

$$= 108°$$ Simplify.

☑ **Find the angle measure.**

4. Three angles in a quadrilateral measure 203°, 15°, and 90°. Find the measure of the fourth angle.

5. Find the sum of the angle measures in a hexagon.

Stop *and* **Think**   about Lessons 8.1–8.4

6. Writing Can a hexagon have two right angles? Draw a diagram and explain your answer.

7. Illustrate How many pairs of vertical angles do two intersecting lines form? Draw a diagram and explain your answer.

Review Quiz 1

Tell whether the angles are *complementary*, *supplementary*, or *neither*.

1. $m\angle 1 = 32°$, $m\angle 2 = 148°$ **2.** $m\angle 3 = 59°$, $m\angle 4 = 41°$

3. $m\angle 5 = 12°$, $m\angle 6 = 78°$ **4.** $m\angle 7 = 116°$, $m\angle 8 = 64°$

Can the angles in a triangle have the measures given? Explain.

5. 23°, 57°, 95°   **6.** 64.6°, 77.3°, 38.1°   **7.** 155°, 24.9°, 0.1°

Find the value of x.

8.

$3x°$
$x°$

9.

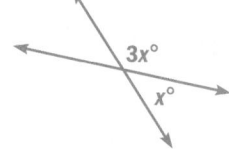

50°   55°
130° $x°$

10.

112°
144°   135°
107°
$x°$

11. Two angles in a triangle measure 75° and 30°. Find the measure of the third angle.

Hands-on Activity

FLORIDA Standards and Assessment
Know the properties of two-dimensional figures.
(MA.C.1.3.1)

GOAL
Copy a triangle.

MATERIALS
· compass
· straightedge
· protractor

Copying a Triangle

You can use a compass and a straightedge to copy a triangle.

Explore | **Use a compass and straightedge to copy a triangle.**

1 Draw a triangle with vertices *A*, *B*, and *C*. Draw a ray with endpoint *P*. Draw an arc with center *A* through point *C*. Use the same compass setting to draw an arc with center *P*. Label point *Q*.

2 Draw an arc with center *C* through point *B*. Use the same compass setting to draw an arc with center *Q*.

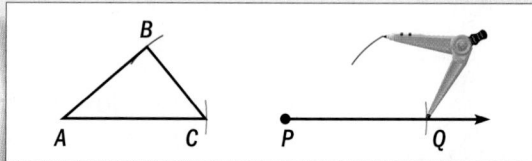

3 Draw an arc with center *A* through point *B*. Use the same compass setting to draw an arc with center *P*. Label point *R*. Connect *P* and *R*. Connect *R* and *Q*.

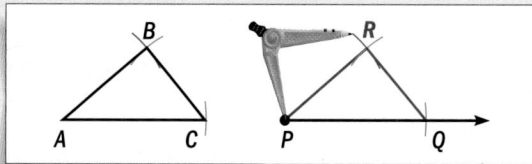

Your turn now **Draw a triangle that fits the description. Then use a compass and straightedge to copy the triangle.**

1. acute   **2.** obtuse   **3.** right

Stop *and* **Think**

4. Critical Thinking Measure the angles of each triangle you copied in Exercises 1–3. What do you notice? Explain.

5. Writing When you use a compass and straightedge to copy a triangle, what measures of the new triangle are identical to the old triangle?

Congruent Polygons

BEFORE	▶ Now	WHY?
You identified polygons.	You'll identify and name congruent polygons.	So you can measure kites, as in Exs. 13 and 14.

Word Watch

congruent sides, p. 397
congruent angles, p. 397
corresponding parts,
p. 397

FLORIDA
Standards and Assessment

• Identify congruent real-world figures and justify reasoning. (MA.C.2.3.1)

• Determine and justify angle measures in figures. (MA.C.1.3.1)

Congruent sides have equal lengths. **Congruent angles** have equal measures. The symbol ≅ means "is congruent to."

Congruent polygons have the same shape and size. Polygons are congruent if their *corresponding* angles and sides are congruent. **Corresponding parts** are in the same position in different figures. To name congruent polygons, list their corresponding vertices in the same order. In the diagram $\triangle KLM \cong \triangle PQR$.

Corresponding angles are congruent.
$$\angle K \cong \angle P \qquad \angle L \cong \angle Q \qquad \angle M \cong \angle R$$

Corresponding sides are congruent.
$$\overline{LM} \cong \overline{QR} \qquad \overline{KL} \cong \overline{PQ} \qquad \overline{KM} \cong \overline{PR}$$

> The side with endpoints *P* and *R*

EXAMPLE 1 **Naming Corresponding Parts**

In the frame below, quadrilateral *ABCD* ≅ quadrilateral *JKLM*. Name all pairs of corresponding angles and sides.

Solution

Corresponding angles are congruent.

$\angle A, \angle J \qquad\qquad \angle B, \angle K$

$\angle C, \angle L \qquad\qquad \angle D, \angle M$

Corresponding sides are congruent.

$\overline{AB}, \overline{JK} \qquad\qquad \overline{BC}, \overline{KL}$

$\overline{CD}, \overline{LM} \qquad\qquad \overline{DA}, \overline{MJ}$

Your turn now In Example 1, quadrilateral *EFGH* ≅ quadrilateral *QRNP*.

1. Name all pairs of corresponding angles and sides.

EXAMPLE 2 **Using Congruent Polygons**

with Reading

△*JKL* is read "triangle *JKL*"
and refers to the triangle
with vertices *J*, *K*, and *L*.

△ *JKL* ≅ △*TSR*
Find *m∠S.*

Solution

∠*K* and ∠*S* are corresponding angles, so they have the same measure.
Find *m∠K.*

$$m\angle J + m\angle K + m\angle L = 180°$$ Sum of angle measures is 180°.

$$31° + m\angle K + 25° = 180°$$ Substitute given values.

$$m\angle K + 56° = 180°$$ Combine like terms.

$$m\angle K = 124°$$ Subtract 56° from each side.

ANSWER Because *m∠K* = *m∠S*, *m∠S* = 124°.

Your turn now   **Find the measure using the triangles in Example 2.**

2. length of $\overline{ST}$ **3.** *m∠T*   **4.** *m∠R*

Congruent Triangles You can use the special rules in the chart to tell
whether triangles are congruent.

with Reading

The angle between two
sides is sometimes called
the *included* angle.
The side between two
angles is sometimes called
the *included* side.

Side-Side-Side (SSS)	If three sides of one triangle are congruent to three sides of another triangle, then the triangles are congruent.	△*ABC* ≅ △*DEF*
Side-Angle-Side (SAS)	If two sides and the angle between them in one triangle are congruent to two sides and the angle between them in another triangle, then the triangles are congruent.	△*JKL* ≅ △*MNP*
Angle-Side-Angle (ASA)	If two angles and the side between them in one triangle are congruent to two angles and the side between them in another triangle, then the triangles are congruent.	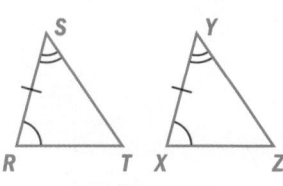 △*RST* ≅ △*XYZ*

EXAMPLE **3** **Identifying Congruent Triangles**

Name the congruent triangles formed by the bridge cables, and explain how you know that they are congruent.

Dames Point Bridge
Jacksonville, Florida

$\overline{CB} \cong \overline{CD}$ Sides are congruent.

$\overline{AC} \cong \overline{AC}$ Side is congruent to itself.

$\angle 1 \cong \angle 2$ Right angles are congruent.

ANSWER $\triangle ACB \cong \triangle ACD$ by Side-Angle-Side.

8.5 Exercises

More Practice, p. 734

INTERNET
eWorkbook Plus
CLASSZONE.COM

Getting Ready to Practice

Vocabulary **Copy and complete the statement.**

1. Two angles with the same measure are ? .

2. ? are in the same position in different figures.

In the diagram, quadrilateral *KLMN* ≅ quadrilateral *SPQR*.

3. Name four pairs of congruent angles.

4. Find $m\angle S$.

5. Find the length of $\overline{NK}$.

6. Find $m\angle R$.

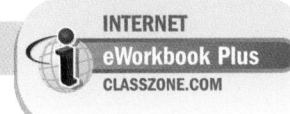

7. **Find the Error** Describe and correct the error in the solution.

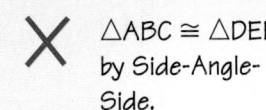

$\triangle ABC \cong \triangle DEF$
by Side-Angle-Side.

Practice and Problem Solving

HELP with **Homework**

Example	Exercises
1	8–11
2	8–11
3	12–14

Online Resources
CLASSZONE.COM

· More Examples
· eTutorial Plus

Measurement Quadrilateral *ABEF* ≅ quadrilateral *DGHC*. Find the unknown measure.

8. length of $\overline{AF}$

9. $m\angle C$

10. length of $\overline{HC}$

11. $m\angle A$

12. Name all the congruent triangles shown. Justify your answer.

Kites Explain how you know the red triangles in the kite are congruent.

13.

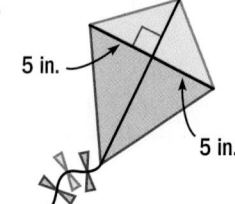

5 in.

5 in.

14.

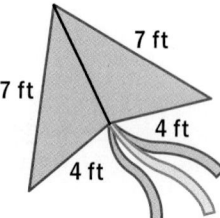

7 ft

7 ft

4 ft

4 ft

Critical Thinking Explain how you know the triangles are congruent. Then write an equation and solve for *x*.

15.

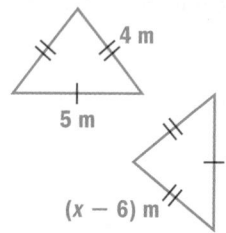

4 m

5 m

$(x - 6)$ m

16.

$(2x + 6)$ cm

32 cm

17.

$x°$

$(2x - 24)°$

18. Soccer Field Some pieces of sod on a field are regular hexagons like the ones shown here. Explain how you know the regular hexagons are congruent.

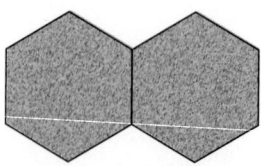

19. Pockets Two back pockets on a pair of jeans are congruent. Find $m\angle 1$.

105°

1

What do you think?

Sports

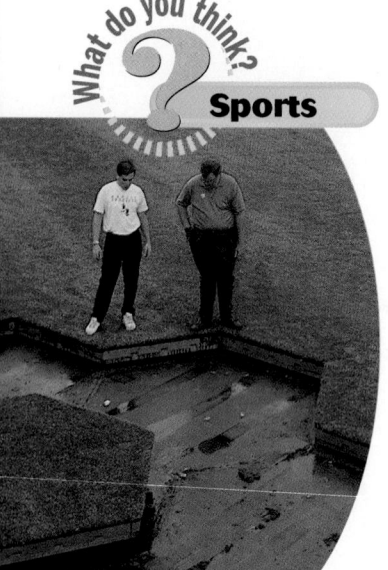

■ **Soccer Field**

In 1994, Michigan State University covered the floor of the Silverdome with natural grass for the World Cup tournament. Why do you think hexagons were used in the design?

20. Pod Shelters The panels of the pod shelter shown are equilateral triangles. The sides of each triangle are 7 feet long. Explain how you know the panels are congruent triangles.

21. Challenge Name the congruent triangles, and explain how you know that they are congruent.

Mixed Review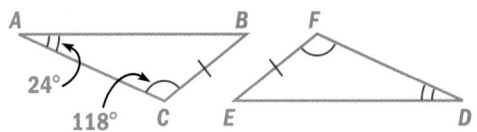

22. Find 1.25% of 400.

23. Find 65% of 91. *(Lesson 7.7)*

24. If you pick a whole number at random from 1 to 100, what is the probability that the number is a multiple of 5? *(Lesson 7.8)*

Find the value of x. *(Lessons 8.3, 8.4)*

25.

26.

Basic Skills **Plot the point in a coordinate plane.**

27. $A(-9, 6)$ **28.** $B(-3, -5)$ **29.** $C(0, -4)$ **30.** $D(4, -1)$

FCAT Practice

31. Multiple Choice Polygon $ABCD \cong$ polygon $EFGH$. Find $m\angle B$.

A. 60°   **B.** 65°   **C.** 105°   **D.** 115°

32. Short Response Name the congruent triangles and explain how you know that they are congruent.

8.6 Problem Solving Strategies

FLORIDA: Standards and Assessment Identify and perform transformations. (MA.C.2.3.1) Solve real-world problems. (MA.A.3.3.2)

Make a Model

Guess, Check, and Revise

Look for a Pattern

Draw a Diagram

Write an Equation

Make a Model

Act It Out

Work Backward

Problem You are looking at a picture of a kaleidoscope image. The image includes six red shapes. Tell which red shapes are mirror images of shape 1.

---

❶ Read and Understand

Read the problem carefully.

You need to decide which red shapes are mirror images of shape 1.

❷ Make a Plan

Decide on a strategy to use.

You can identify the mirror images by making a model. Trace the kaleidoscope image. Then fold your tracing paper to see if two shapes are mirror images.

---

❸ Solve the Problem

Reread the problem and make a model of the kaleidoscope image using tracing paper.

Trace the outline of the kaleidoscope image and the six red shapes. Also trace the lines that divide the image into six equal parts. Cut out the circle.

Fold the paper once so that shape 1 lies on top of shape 2. You can see that shape 1 and shape 2 line up with each other exactly when you fold the paper. So, shape 2 is a mirror image of shape 1.

Unfold the paper. Now fold it once so that shape 1 lies on top of shape 3. You can see that shape 1 and shape 3 do not line up with each other exactly when you fold the paper. So, shape 3 is not a mirror image of shape 1. Continue to test shapes around the circle

---

❹ Look Back

Which shapes are a mirror images of shape 1? Did you do everything asked in the problem?

---

 402   Chapter 8   Polygons and Transformations

Use the strategy *make a model.*

1. **Design** Sketch a kaleidoscope design that includes mirror images of a shape. Divide a circle into six equal parts to make your design. Identify the mirror images.

2. **Bowling Pins** Ten bowling pins are arranged in a triangle, as shown. Explain how you can make the triangle point to the left by moving only three pins.

3. **Seating Arrangements** Alan, David, Mary, Peter, and Scott are sitting on a bench. Alan is between Scott and David. Mary is next to Peter. There is only one person between Mary and Alan, but Mary is not next to Scott. Find two possible seating arrangements.

4. **Boxes** Four boxes of different sizes are stacked on a table, with the largest box on the bottom and the smallest box on the top. You need to move the entire stack of boxes to another table, but you can only move one box at a time. No box can touch the floor, and no box can support a larger box without breaking. You have one extra table to help you. List the moves it takes you to transfer the stack of boxes.

Mixed Problem Solving

Use any strategy to solve the problem.

5. **Hiking** You bring water on a hike. You drink a quarter of the water in the morning and a third of the remaining water at lunch time. In the afternoon, you drink two thirds of the water left in your container. When you get home, there are 16 fluid ounces of water. How much water did you bring on the hike?

6. **Club Planning** The Spanish Club meets every other week. The members decided to have a party during the fifth meeting. The first meeting took place on October 2. Find the date of the party.

7. **Test Scores** John has earned 92, 70, 95, 89, and 90 on his math tests this semester. What score must John receive on his next test to have a mean of 88?

8. **Numbers** You are helping your little sister with her math homework, but you can't read her writing very well. Her sevens and ones look exactly the same. She solved the problem below correctly. Decide which numerals are sevens and which are ones.

Reflections and Symmetry

BEFORE	▶ Now	WHY?
You plotted points in a coordinate plane.	You'll reflect figures and identify lines of symmetry.	So you can find symmetry in starfish, as in Example 4b.

Word Watch

reflection, p. 404
transformation, p. 404
image, p. 404
line symmetry, p. 406

FLORIDA
Standards and Assessment

• Identify and perform transformations. (MA.C.2.3.1)

• Use symmetry to solve real-world problems. (MA.C.2.3.1)

In the Real World

Reflections The photo illustrates a reflection. A **reflection** creates a mirror image of each point of a figure.

A reflection is a **transformation**, an operation that changes a figure into another figure. The new figure created is called the **image**.

EXAMPLE 1 **Identifying a Reflection**

Tell whether the red figure is a reflection of the blue figure.

a.

The figure is a reflection.

b.

The figure is *not* a reflection.

You can describe reflections of figures in a coordinate plane using coordinate notation. The notation $A \rightarrow A'$ is read "A goes to A prime."

EXAMPLE 2 **Reflecting in the y-Axis**

Quadrilateral *ABCD* has been reflected in the *y*-axis. Write the coordinates of each vertex of quadrilateral *ABCD* and its image, quadrilateral *A′B′C′D′*.

Solution

Original		Image
$A(-1, 1)$	$\rightarrow$	$A'(1, 1)$
$B(-3, 1)$	$\rightarrow$	$B'(3, 1)$
$C(-4, 3)$	$\rightarrow$	$C'(4, 3)$
$D(-2, 4)$	$\rightarrow$	$D'(2, 4)$

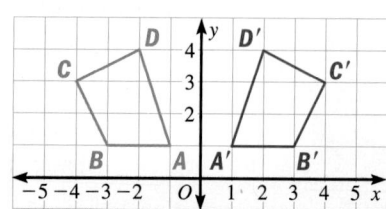

You may have noticed in Example 2 that when a point is reflected in the *y*-axis, its *x*-coordinate is multiplied by −1.

Reflections

Reflection in the *x*-axis

Words   To reflect a point in the *x*-axis, multiply its *y*-coordinate by −1.

	Original	**Image**
Algebra	(x, y)	$\rightarrow$ $(x, -y)$

Reflection in the *y*-axis

Words   To reflect a point in the *y*-axis, multiply its *x*-coordinate by −1.

	Original	**Image**
Algebra	(x, y)	$\rightarrow$ $(-x, y)$

EXAMPLE 3   **Reflecting in the x-Axis**

Reflect $\triangle PQR$ in the *x*-axis.

Solution

Multiply each *y*-coordinate by −1.

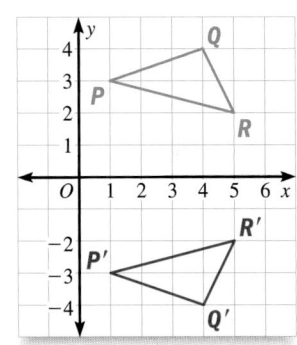

Original		**Image**
(x, y)	$\rightarrow$	$(x, -y)$
$P(1, 3)$	$\rightarrow$	$P'(1, -3)$
$Q(4, 4)$	$\rightarrow$	$Q'(4, -4)$
$R(5, 2)$	$\rightarrow$	$R'(5, -2)$

The graph shows $\triangle PQR$ and its reflection $\triangle P'Q'R'$.

Your turn now   **Graph the polygon and its image.**

1. Graph the triangle with vertices $J(0, 1)$, $K(0, 4)$, and $L(5, 2)$. Reflect the triangle in the *y*-axis.

2. Graph the quadrilateral with vertices $S(-3, 2)$, $T(-1, 4)$, $U(-4, 5)$, and $V(-5, 3)$. Reflect the quadrilateral in the *x*-axis.

Symmetry A figure has **line symmetry** if one half of the figure is a mirror image of the other half. A line of symmetry divides the figure into two congruent parts that are mirror images of each other.

EXAMPLE 4 **Identifying Lines of Symmetry**

How many lines of symmetry does the picture have?

a. one line of symmetry

b. five lines of symmetry

c. no lines of symmetry

8.6 Exercises
More Practice, p. 734

INTERNET
eWorkbook Plus
CLASSZONE.COM

Getting Ready to Practice

Vocabulary Copy and complete the statement.

1. A(n) ? creates a mirror image of the original figure.

2. A(n) ? is an operation that changes a figure into another figure.

Tell whether the red figure is a reflection of the blue figure.

3.

4.

5.

How many lines of symmetry does the design have?

6.

7.

8.

Graph the polygon. Then graph its reflection in the given axis.

9. $K(2, 7)$, $L(3, 3)$, $M(6, 4)$, $N(6, 9)$; x-axis

10. $F(-8, 8)$, $G(-4, 7)$, $H(-3, 3)$, $I(-7, 4)$; y-axis

with Homework

Example	Exercises
1	23
2	13-14
3	11-12
4	15-20

Online Resources
CLASSZONE.COM

· More Examples
· eTutorial Plus

Practice and Problem Solving

Graph the polygon. Then graph its reflection in the given axis.

11. $A(3, 6)$, $B(6, 3)$, $C(5, 0)$, $D(1, 1)$; x-axis

12. $Q(-1, 3)$, $R(-3, 6)$, $S(-6, 4)$, $T(-6, 0)$; x-axis

13. $B(2, -1)$, $C(5, 0)$, $D(7, -2)$, $E(0, -6)$; y-axis

14. $P(0, 0)$, $Q(4, 1)$, $R(7, -3)$, $S(2, -7)$; y-axis

Sports How many lines of symmetry does the diagram have?

15.

16.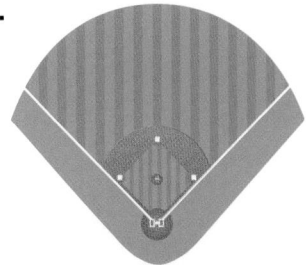

17. Illustrate Draw a quadrilateral with exactly four lines of symmetry. What kind of quadrilateral is this?

Extended Problem Solving For Exercises 18–20, use the table.

Sides	3	4	5	6	8
Regular Polygon		?	?	?	?
Lines of Symmetry	?	?	?	?	?

18. Sketch Copy the table and sketch a regular polygon with the given number of sides in each column. Draw all the lines of symmetry.

19. Evaluate Count the lines of symmetry. Complete the table.

20. Look for a Pattern How is the number of sides related to the number of lines of symmetry?

21. Make a Model Write your name at the top of a piece of tracing paper. Fold the paper and trace your name to create a reflection. Unfold the paper to see your name and its reflection.

22. Challenge Graph the polygon with vertices $S(-6, 0)$, $T(0, 6)$, $V(6, 0)$, $W(2, -4)$, and $X(-2, -4)$. Reflect the polygon in the x-axis and graph its image in the same coordinate plane.

23. Critical Thinking A polygon has vertices $A(1, -2)$, $B(5, -1)$, $C(8, -4)$, $D(7, -7)$, and $E(4, -8)$. Reflect the polygon in the x-axis and find the vertices of its image. Then reflect the image in the y-axis. Graph the new image. Is the third polygon a reflection of the original? Explain.

Mixed Review

In Exercises 24 and 25, find the number. *(Lesson 7.3)*

24. What is 0.8% of 500?   **25.** 756 is what percent of 270?

26. Find the sum of the angle measures in a 9-gon. *(Lesson 8.4)*

27. Find the measure of one angle in a regular 12-gon. *(Lesson 8.4)*

FCAT Practice

28. Multiple Choice Which figure is a reflected image of figure D?

A. Figure A   **B.** Figure B

C. Figure C   **D.** None

29. Short Response Copy figure C and draw all its lines of symmetry. Where do the lines intersect?

Deep Reflections

Use a mirror to read this quotation from William Shakespeare.

Translations and Rotations

BEFORE	▶ Now	WHY?
You reflected figures in a coordinate plane.	You'll translate or rotate figures in a coordinate plane.	So you can describe origami models, as in Exs. 5–6.

Word Watch

translation, p. 409
rotation, p. 410

FLORIDA
Standards and Assessment

• Identify and perform transformations. (MA.C.2.3.1)

Activity **You can see how moving a triangle changes its vertices.**

① Graph an image of A by moving it 7 units to the right and 2 units up. Plot the new vertex and label it A'.

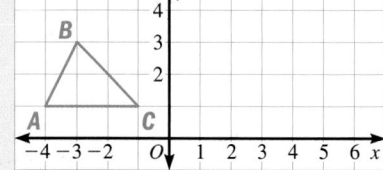

② Repeat Step 1 with B and C. Then connect the vertices to form △A'B'C'.

③ How are the coordinates of A, B, and C related to A', B', and C'?

In the activity, you transformed △ABC by *sliding* it. A **translation** is a transformation that moves each point of a figure the same distance in the same direction. The image is congruent to the original figure.

To translate a figure in a coordinate plane, you change the coordinates of its points. When a and b are positive, you can use the guidelines below.

Slide up b units
$y \rightarrow y + b$

Slide to the left a units
$x \rightarrow x - a$

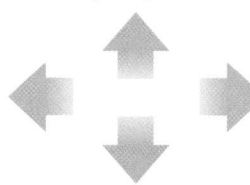

Slide to the right a units
$x \rightarrow x + a$

Slide down b units
$y \rightarrow y - b$

EXAMPLE 1 Using Coordinate Notation

Describe the translation from the blue figure to the red figure.

Solution

Each point moves 6 units to the right and 3 units down. The translation is

$(x, y) \rightarrow (x + 6, y - 3)$.

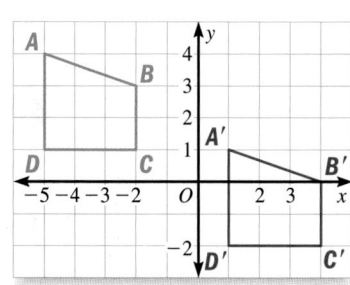

Rotations A **rotation** is a transformation that turns each point of a figure the same number of degrees around a common point. In this lesson, figures will always be turned around the origin.

90° Rotations

90° Clockwise Rotation

Words To rotate a point 90° *clockwise*, switch the coordinates, then multiply the new *y*-coordinate by -1.

Numbers $P(6, 2) \rightarrow P'(2, -6)$ **Algebra** $P(x, y) \rightarrow P'(y, -x)$

90° Counterclockwise Rotation

Words To rotate a point 90° *counterclockwise*, switch the coordinates, then multiply the new *x*-coordinate by -1.

Numbers $P(5, 3) \rightarrow P'(-3, 5)$ **Algebra** $P(x, y) \rightarrow P'(-y, x)$

EXAMPLE 2 **Rotating 90° Clockwise**

with Reading

Clockwise is the direction the hands on a clock turn. Counterclockwise is the opposite direction.

Rotate quadrilateral *FGHJ* 90° clockwise.

Solution

Original		Image
(x, y)	$\rightarrow$	$(y, -x)$
$F(2, 2)$	$\rightarrow$	$F'(2, -2)$
$G(2, 4)$	$\rightarrow$	$G'(4, -2)$
$H(4, 4)$	$\rightarrow$	$H'(4, -4)$
$J(5, 2)$	$\rightarrow$	$J'(2, -5)$

The graph shows *FGHJ* and *F'G'H'J'*.

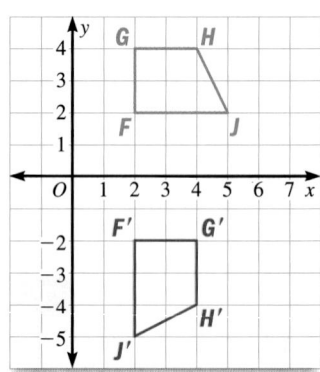

Your turn now Graph the figure with the given vertices and its image after the rotation.

1. $A(1, 1)$, $B(3, 1)$, $C(3, 3)$, and $D(1, 4)$; 90° clockwise

2. $K(-1, 3)$, $L(1, 5)$, and $M(2, 3)$; 90° counterclockwise

180° Rotation

Words To rotate a point 180°, multiply its coordinates by −1.

Numbers $P(4, 1) \rightarrow P'(-4, -1)$ **Algebra** $P(x, y) \rightarrow P'(-x, -y)$

EXAMPLE 3 Rotating 180°

Rotate △**ABC** 180°.

Solution

Original		Image
(x, y)	→	$(-x, -y)$
$A(-6, 0)$	→	$A'(6, 0)$
$B(-5, 2)$	→	$B'(5, -2)$
$C(-1, 3)$	→	$C'(1, -3)$

The graph shows △ABC and △$A'B'C'$.

8.7 Exercises

More Practice, p. 734

INTERNET
eWorkbook Plus
CLASSZONE.COM

Getting Ready to Practice

HELP with **Vocabulary**

Reflection is a **Fl**ip.
Rotation is a **T**urn.
Translation is a **Sl**ide.

Vocabulary **Name the transformation shown in the graph.**

1.

2.

3.
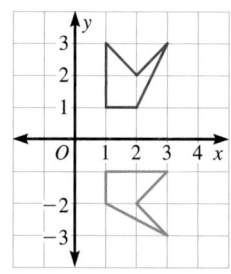

4. **Guided Problem Solving** Rotate △RST 90° counterclockwise.

   ① Graph △RST with vertices $R(-2, -1)$, $S(-5, -2)$, and $T(-4, 2)$.

   ② Find the vertices of the triangle's image.

   ③ Graph △$R'S'T'$, the image of △RST after rotation.

Practice and Problem Solving

with Homework

Example	Exercises
1	15–16
2	20, 23
3	19, 22

Online Resources
CLASSZONE.COM

· More Examples
· eTutorial Plus

Origami **Describe the transformation shown in the origami model.**

5.

6.

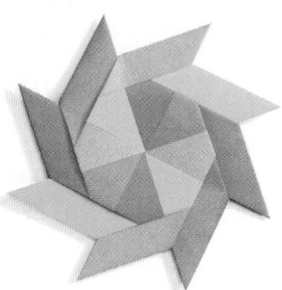

Name the type of transformation modeled by the action.

7. riding down an escalator

8. passing food around a table

9. making a handprint in clay

10. playing checkers

11. opening a combination lock

12. going down a water slide

13. riding a carousel

14. looking in a mirror

Use coordinate notation to describe the translation from the blue figure to the red figure.

15.

16.

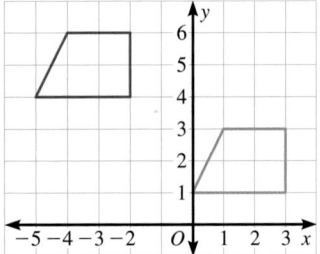

17. $\triangle PQR$ has vertices $P(0, -1)$, $Q(3, -1)$, and $R(5, -3)$. Find the vertices of its image after the translation $(x, y) \rightarrow (x - 5, y + 1)$.

18. $\triangle LMN$ has vertices $L(4, 2)$, $M(0, 3)$, and $N(1, 1)$. Find the vertices of its image after the translation $(x, y) \rightarrow (x + 1, y - 6)$.

Graph $\triangle LMN$ with vertices $L(2, 0)$, $M(2, 3)$, and $N(6, 0)$. Then graph its image after the given transformation.

19. Rotate 180°.

20. Rotate 90° counterclockwise.

21. Translate using $(x, y) \rightarrow (x - 3, y - 4)$.

22. Rotate 180° then translate using $(x, y) \rightarrow (x + 1, y + 1)$.

23. Rotate 90° clockwise three times.

24. Translate using $(x, y) \rightarrow (x + 3, y)$ then rotate 180°.

with Review

For help with quadrants,
see p. 91.

25. Writing Point A in Quadrant II is rotated 180°. Find the quadrant of point A'. Point B in Quadrant IV is rotated 90° clockwise. Find the quadrant of point B'. Explain your reasoning.

26. Challenge The figure is the image of a triangle rotated 90° clockwise and reflected in the y-axis. Graph the original figure.

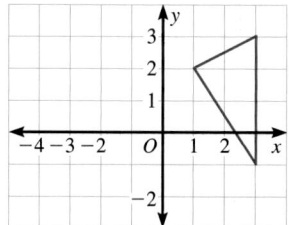

27. Multiple Methods Describe four different transformations of the blue square to the red square. You may include combinations of transformations.

Mixed Review

Solve the proportion. *(Lesson 7.2)*

28. $\dfrac{a}{25} = \dfrac{24}{200}$

29. $\dfrac{32}{9} = \dfrac{c}{108}$

30. $\dfrac{7}{60} = \dfrac{154}{d}$

Find the value of x. Classify the triangle by its angles. *(Lesson 8.2)*

31.

32.

33.

Basic Skills Find the mean, median, and mode(s).

34. 39, 45, 43, 28, 45, 48, 39, 45

35. 110, 108, 118, 110, 105

FCAT Practice

INTERNET
FCAT PRACTICE
CLASSZONE.COM

36. Extended Response Rotate the figure 90° clockwise. Reflect the image in the x-axis. Graph the final image. Complete the rule for the double transformation you performed.

$$(x, y) \rightarrow (\underline{\ ?\ }, \underline{\ ?\ })$$

Explain your reasoning.

Tessellations

GOAL Decide if a shape tessellates. Create tessellations.

Word Watch

tessellation, p. 414

FLORIDA
Standards and Assessment

• Continue a tessellation. (MA.C.2.3.2)

• Create an original tessellation. (MA.C.2.3.2)

Tessellations You can use reflections, rotations, and translations to create a *tessellation*, like the one shown here. A **tessellation** is a repeating pattern of figures that covers a plane with no gaps or overlaps. If a figure can be used to create a tessellation, you say the figure *tessellates*.

EXAMPLE 1 **Identifying Tessellating Polygons**

Tell whether the polygon tessellates.

a.

Yes, you can create a tessellation by translating a rectangle.

b.

No, regular pentagons will not cover the plane without gaps or overlaps.

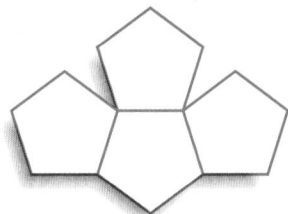

You can create a tessellation by altering a polygon that tessellates.

EXAMPLE 2 **Creating a Tessellation**

Alter a parallelogram to create a tessellation.

Cut a triangle from the parallelogram.

Slide the triangle to the opposite side.

Translate the figure to create a tessellation.

EXAMPLE 3 **Creating a Tessellation**

Create a tessellation by altering an equilateral triangle.

Cut a piece from the triangle.

Slide the piece to another side.

Reflect the figure then translate the pair.

Exercises

Tell whether the figure tessellates.

1.   **2.**   **3.**

4. Explain how you can transform the blue shape to create the tessellation.

5. Copy and continue the pattern.

Copy the polygon and use it to create a tessellation. Describe how the polygon was transformed in your tessellation.

6.   **7.**   **8.**

9. Make a Model Create a tessellation by altering a rectangle.

10. Create a tessellation by altering a parallelogram that is not a rectangle.

11. Create two different tessellations using the shape at the right.

Similarity and Dilations

LESSON 8.8

BEFORE	▶ Now	WHY?
You used congruent polygons to find missing measures.	You'll use similar polygons to find missing measures.	So you can find the height of a sand castle, as in Ex. 14.

📓 Word Watch

similar polygons, p. 416
dilation, p. 418
scale factor, p. 418

FLORIDA
Standards and Assessment

• Identify similar real-world figures. (MA.C.2.3.1)
• Use proportions and similar figures to find measures. (MA.B.2.3.1)

In the Real World

Television Screens The television screens shown here are different sizes, but they have the same shape. How are they related?

Similar polygons have the same shape, but they can be different sizes. The symbol ~ means "is similar to." When you name similar polygons, list their corresponding vertices in the same order.

Similar Polygons

$\triangle ABC \sim \triangle XYZ$

Corresponding angles are congruent.

$\angle A \cong \angle X$ $\angle B \cong \angle Y$ $\angle C \cong \angle Z$

Corresponding side lengths are proportional.

$\dfrac{AB}{XY} = \dfrac{BC}{YZ}$ $\dfrac{BC}{YZ} = \dfrac{AC}{XZ}$ $\dfrac{AC}{XZ} = \dfrac{AB}{XY}$

EXAMPLE 1 Identifying Similar Polygons

Tell whether the television screens are similar.

① Corresponding angles are congruent. Each angle measures 90°.
$\angle A \cong \angle E$ $\angle B \cong \angle F$ $\angle C \cong \angle G$ $\angle D \cong \angle H$

② Corresponding side lengths are proportional.

$\dfrac{30 \text{ inches}}{18 \text{ inches}} = \dfrac{40 \text{ inches}}{24 \text{ inches}}$

$720 = 720$

ANSWER Quadrilateral $ABCD \sim$ quadrilateral $EFGH$

HELP with Review

For help with writing and
solving proportions, see
p. 322.

EXAMPLE 2   Using Similar Triangles

In the diagram, △KLM ~ △NPQ. Find the value of y.

Corresponding side lengths are proportional.

$\dfrac{KL}{NP} = \dfrac{LM}{PQ}$ Write a proportion.

$\dfrac{y}{12} = \dfrac{10}{5}$ Substitute given values.

$y = 24$ Solve the proportion.

ANSWER The value of y is 24 meters.

Your turn now   Find the value of x.

1. Quadrilateral *ABCD* ~ quadrilateral *FGHJ*

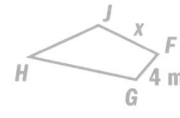

EXAMPLE 3   Using Indirect Measurement

Height Alma is 5 feet tall
and casts a 7 foot shadow.
At the same time, a tree
casts a 14 foot shadow.
The triangles formed are
similar. Find the height
of the tree.

Solution

You can use a proportion to find the height of the tree.

$\dfrac{\text{Tree's height}}{\text{Alma's height}} = \dfrac{\text{Length of tree's shadow}}{\text{Length of Alma's shadow}}$ Write a proportion.

$\dfrac{x \text{ feet}}{5 \text{ feet}} = \dfrac{14 \text{ feet}}{7 \text{ feet}}$ Substitute given values.

$x = 10$ Solve the proportion.

ANSWER The tree is 10 feet tall.

Dilations A **dilation** stretches or shrinks a figure. The image created by a dilation is similar to the original figure. The **scale factor** of a dilation is the ratio of corresponding side lengths. In this course, the center of dilation will always be the origin.

Dilation

Words To dilate a polygon, multiply the coordinates of each vertex by the scale factor k and connect the vertices.

Numbers $P(4, 1) \rightarrow P'(8, 2)$ **Algebra** $P(x, y) \rightarrow P'(kx, ky)$

EXAMPLE 4 **Dilating a Polygon**

Quadrilateral *ABCD* has vertices *A*(−1, −1), *B*(0, 1), *C*(2, 2), and *D*(3, 0). Dilate using a scale factor of 3.

Solution

Graph the quadrilateral. Find the vertices of the image.

Original		Image
(x, y)	$\rightarrow$	$(3x, 3y)$
$A(-1, -1)$	$\rightarrow$	$A'(-3, -3)$
$B(0, 1)$	$\rightarrow$	$B'(0, 3)$
$C(2, 2)$	$\rightarrow$	$C'(6, 6)$
$D(3, 0)$	$\rightarrow$	$D'(9, 0)$

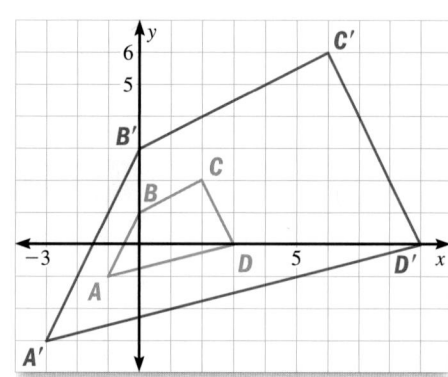

Graph the image of the quadrilateral.

Your turn now **Graph the polygon with the given vertices. Then graph its image after dilation by the scale factor *k*.**

2. Triangle *RST* has vertices $R(1, 1)$, $S(3, 2)$, and $T(2, 3)$; $k = 2$.

3. Quadrilateral *MNPQ* has vertices $M(1, 0)$, $N(0, -1)$, $P(-1, 0)$, and $Q(0, 1)$; $k = 4$.

4. Triangle *JKL* has vertices $J(0, 2)$, $K(6, 4)$, and $L(2, -2)$; $k = \frac{1}{2}$.

5. Quadrilateral *CDGH* has vertices $C(-6, -6)$, $D(-3, -3)$, $G(0, -3)$, and $H(3, -6)$; $k = \frac{1}{3}$.

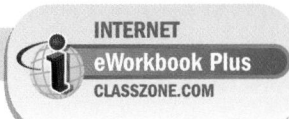
Getting Ready to Practice

Vocabulary **Copy and complete the statement.**

1. The ? of a dilation is the ratio of corresponding side lengths.

2. A figure and its image after dilation are always ?.

Name the similar polygons.

3.

4.

Watch Out!

Remember that corresponding parts are in the same position on different polygons.

5. **Guided Problem Solving** Dilate △ABC using a scale factor of $\frac{1}{3}$.

  ① Graph △ABC with vertices A(3, 6), B(−3, −3), and C(6, 0).

  ② Find the vertices of its image using the scale factor.

  ③ Graph the image.

Practice and Problem Solving

with Homework

Example	Exercises
1	6–7
2	8–13
3	14, 21
4	15–19

Online Resources
CLASSZONE.COM

· More Examples
· eTutorial Plus

In Exercises 6 and 7, name the similar polygons.

6.

7.

Use the similar triangles to find the value of x.

8. △ABC ~ △DEF

9. △GHJ ~ △KHM

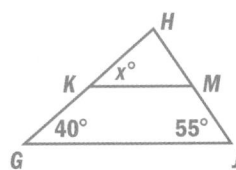

Use the similar polygons to find the value of x.

10. Parallelogram *CDFG* is similar to parallelogram *HJLK*.

11. Trapezoid *MNPQ* is similar to trapezoid *RSTV*.

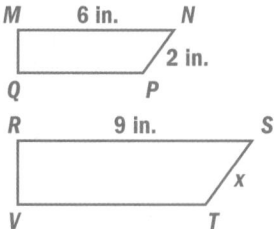

12. △*LMN* is similar to △*PQR*. Find the value of *x*.

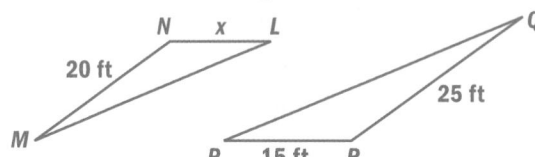

13. Pentagon *ABCDE* ~ pentagon *FGHJK*. Find the values of *x* and *y*.

14. Indirect Measurement A sand castle casts an 18 foot shadow. At the same time, your 5 foot friend casts a 20 foot shadow. How tall is the sand castle?

Graph the polygon with the given vertices. Then graph its image after dilation by the scale factor k.

15. *W*(2, 2), *X*(0, 4), *Y*(4, 6), *Z*(6, 0); *k* = 3

16. *B*(0, −2), *C*(4, 2), *D*(2, 6), *E*(−2, 6), *F*(−4, 2); $k = \frac{1}{2}$

17. *R*(8, 8), *S*(−4, 4), *T*(−4, −4); $k = \frac{3}{4}$

18. *L*(2, −2), *M*(4, 2), *N*(−3, 2), *P*(−1, −2); *k* = 4

19. *G*(−2, −6), *H*(−8, −8), *J*(−6, −2), *K*(0, 0); *k* = 1.5

20. Calculate Pentagon *KLMNP* has vertices *K*(24.1, 5.2), *L*(4.9, 5.3), *M*(6.8, 0.2), *N*(3.3, 4.8), and *P*(25.8, 22.1). Use the scale factor 1.8 to find the vertices of its image after dilation.

21. Photo Reduction You reduce a 12 inch by 24 inch photo to $\frac{1}{3}$ of its original dimensions. What are the new dimensions of the photo?

22. Writing Explain why all squares are similar.

23. Algebra Hexagon *ABCDEF* is similar to hexagon *PQRSTU*. Find the values of *x* and *y*.

24. Analyze If a polygon is dilated by a scale factor of 1, will the image be *larger than*, *smaller than*, or *identical to* the original polygon? Explain.

25. Challenge Name two similar polygons in the diagram. Find their scale factor.

Mixed Review

Choose a Strategy **Use a strategy from the list to solve the following problem. Explain your choice of strategy.**

26. An ice cream stand offers vanilla, chocolate, mint chip, cookie crumble, and strawberry ice cream. Write all the possible 2 scoop cones you can order. How many possibilities are there?

> **Problem Solving Strategies**
> ▪ Look for a Pattern
> ▪ Draw a Diagram
> ▪ Make a List
> ▪ Make a Model

27. You sell your bike for $50 but owe your parents 45% of the selling price. How much money do you have left after you repay your parents? *(Lesson 7.3)*

28. Graph the polygon with vertices *A*(0, 1), *B*(3, 4), *C*(9, 3), and *D*(7, −3). Then graph its image after reflection in the *x*-axis. *(Lesson 8.6)*

FCAT Practice

29. Multiple Choice Rosa is 5 feet tall and casts a 3 foot shadow. At the same time, a flagpole casts a 20 foot shadow. Which property can Rosa use to find the height of the flagpole?

  A. congruence   **B.** similarity   **C.** symmetry   **D.** equality

30. Multiple Choice Find the length of $\overline{AB}$. $\triangle ABD \sim \triangle BCD$.

  F. 22.5 cm   **G.** 14.4 cm

  H. 15 cm   **I.** 12 cm

8.5 TO 8.8

Notebook Review

Review the vocabulary definitions in your notebook.

Copy the review examples in your notebook. Then complete the exercises.

Check Your Definitions

congruent sides, angles, p. 397

corresponding parts, p. 397

reflection, p. 404

transformation, p. 404

image, p. 404

line symmetry, p. 406

translation, p. 409

rotation, p. 410

similar polygons, p. 416

dilation, p. 418

scale factor, p. 418

Use Your Vocabulary

Copy and complete the sentence with a review word.

1. A(n) ? creates a mirror image of a figure.

2. A(n) ? is a transformation that slides a figure.

8.5 Can you name congruent polygons?

EXAMPLE Name the congruent triangles and explain how you know that they are congruent.

ANSWER $\triangle LMN \cong \triangle SRT$ by Angle-Side-Angle

✓ 3. Find the value of x using the triangles above.

8.6–8.7 Can you reflect and rotate figures?

EXAMPLE Graph $\triangle ABC$ with vertices $A(1, 3)$, $B(4, 3)$, and $C(3, 1)$. Then graph its reflection in the x-axis.

Original		Image
(x, y)	$\rightarrow$	$(x, -y)$
$A(1, 3)$	$\rightarrow$	$A'(1, -3)$
$B(4, 3)$	$\rightarrow$	$B'(4, -3)$
$C(3, 1)$	$\rightarrow$	$C'(3, -1)$

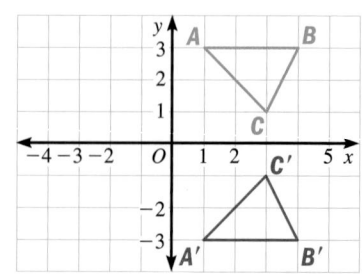

✓ 4. Graph the reflection of $\triangle ABC$ in the y-axis.

 Chapter 8   Polygons and Transformations

EXAMPLE Rotate △*KLM* 90° counterclockwise.

Original		Image
(x, y)	→	$(-y, x)$
$K(3, 1)$	→	$K'(-1, 3)$
$L(1, 4)$	→	$L'(-4, 1)$
$M(3, 3)$	→	$M'(-3, 3)$

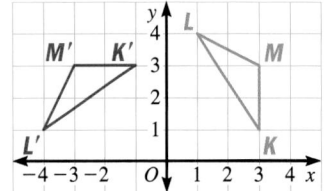

☑ **5.** Rotate △*KLM* 180°.

8.8 Can you use similarity to find measures?

 EXAMPLE Polygons *ABCD* and *FGHJ* are similar. Find the value of *x*.

$\dfrac{AB}{FG} = \dfrac{BC}{GH}$ Write a proportion.

$\dfrac{16}{20} = \dfrac{x}{15}$ Substitute.

$x = 12$ Solve for *x*.

☑ **6.** Use the similar polygons to find the value of *y*.

 Stop *and* **Think**   about Lessons 8.5–8.8

7. Writing Explain how dilation affects the perimeter of a figure.

8. Critical Thinking Give a real world example of a 180° rotation.

Review Quiz 2

1. In the diagram, △*ABC* ≅ △*DEF*. Find *m*∠*D*.

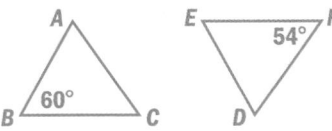

Name the type of transformation modeled by the action.

2. sledding downhill   **3.** leaving fingerprints

4. spinning in place   **5.** opening a drawer

6. Graph △*ABC* with vertices *A*(1, 1), *B*(2, 3), and *C*(3, 0). Dilate the triangle using a scale factor of 4.

Chapter Review

Vocabulary

straight angle, right angle, p. 375	equilateral, isosceles, scalene triangle, p. 382	corresponding parts, p. 397
supplementary, complementary angles, p. 375	quadrilateral, p. 386	reflection, p. 404
	trapezoid, parallelogram, rhombus, p. 386	transformation, p. 404
vertical angles, p. 376		image, p. 404
perpendicular lines, p. 376	polygon, regular polygon, p. 390	line symmetry, p. 406
parallel lines, p. 377	pentagon, hexagon, heptagon, octagon, p. 390	translation, p. 409
acute, right, obtuse angle, p. 382		rotation, p. 410
		similar polygons, p. 416
acute, right, obtuse triangle, p. 382	congruent sides, angles, p. 397	dilation, p. 418
		scale factor, p. 418

Vocabulary Review

Matching **Match each word with the correct definition.**

1. transformation

2. reflection

3. parallel lines

4. complementary angles

5. supplementary angles

6. perpendicular lines

7. translation

8. dilation

A. Two angles whose measures have a sum of 90°

B. A transformation that stretches or shrinks a figure

C. Two angles whose measures have a sum of 180°

D. A transformation that slides a figure

E. A transformation that creates a mirror image of a figure

F. Two lines in the same plane that do not intersect

G. An operation that changes one figure into another figure

H. Two lines that intersect to form a right angle

Review Questions

Find the measure of ∠1. *(Lesson 8.1)*

9.

10.

11.

Review Questions

Classify the polygon. (Lessons 8.2, 8.3)

12.

13.

14.

15. Find the sum of the angle measures in a heptagon. (Lesson 8.4)

16. Find the measure of one angle in a regular pentagon. (Lesson 8.4)

Pentagon *ABCDE* ≅ pentagon *PQRST*. (Lesson 8.5)

17. Name the congruent corresponding angles.

18. Name the congruent corresponding sides.

19. Name the congruent triangles and explain how you know they are congruent. (Lesson 8.5)

Tell whether the red figure is a reflection of the blue figure. (Lesson 8.6)

20. W W   **21.** f ɟ   **22.** p p   **23.** g a

24. △*XYZ* has vertices *X*(−1, 1), *Y*(−3, 1), and *Z*(−2, 5). Reflect △*XYZ* in the *y*-axis. Find the vertices of the image. (Lesson 8.6)

Rotate the polygon 90° clockwise and graph its image. (Lesson 8.7)

25.   **26.**   **27.**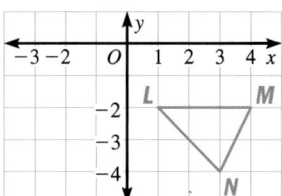

28. Building Height A 20 foot flagpole stands beside a building. The flagpole casts a shadow that is 25 feet long. At the same time, the building casts a shadow that is 60 feet long. How tall is the building? (Lesson 8.8)

29. A polygon has vertices *A*(−2, 0), *B*(−2, 4), *C*(−6, 8), and *D*(−12, 6). Dilate it using a scale factor of 2. Find the vertices of the image. (Lesson 8.8)

8 Chapter Test

Find the measures of the numbered angles.

1.

2.

3.

Classify the triangle by its angles.

4.

5.

6.

Classify the quadrilateral.

7.

8.

9.

Find the measure of one angle in the polygon.

10. square

11. regular octagon

12. regular 9-gon

13. Algebra Write and solve an equation to find the value of x.

Graph the image of the given transformation.

14. Rotate 180°.
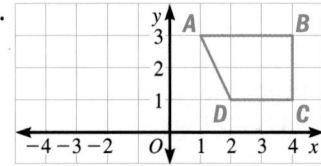

15. Translate using $(x, y) \rightarrow (x - 5, y + 3)$.

16. Shadows Joe is 72 inches tall and has a 108 inch shadow. At the same time, Martha has a 96 inch shadow. How tall is Martha?

Chapter FCAT Practice

Test-Taking Strategy You can make notes, sketches, or graphs in your test booklet to help you solve problems, but you must keep your answer sheet neat.

Multiple Choice

1. $\angle A$ is supplementary to $\angle B$ and $m\angle A = 72°$. What is $m\angle B$?

   A. 18°   **B.** 108°   **C.** 142°   **D.** 288°

2. Which transformation takes the blue figure to the red figure?

   F. Reflection in x-axis

   G. Rotation 180°

   H. $(x, y) \rightarrow (x + 3, y + 2)$

   I. $(x, y) \rightarrow (x - 3, y - 2)$

3. Which is *not* a true statement?

   A. A square has perpendicular sides.

   B. A square has four right angles.

   C. A square has no parallel sides.

   D. A square has four sides of equal length.

4. Find the value of x.

   F. 120   **G.** 720

   H. 180   **I.** 1080

5. Find the sum of the angle measures in a 10-gon.

   A. 1260°   **B.** 1440°   **C.** 1620°   **D.** 1800°

6. How many lines of symmetry does the figure have?

   F. 1   **G.** 2

   H. 4   **I.** 6

7. Which diagram shows a translation?

   A.   **B.**

   C.   **D.**

8. $\triangle ABC \sim \triangle DEF$. Find the value of x.

   F. 5   **G.** 7   **H.** 10   **I.** 14

9. Choose the statement that is *never* true.

   A. Acute angles measure less than 90°.

   B. Right angles measure 90°.

   C. Obtuse angles measure 180°.

   D. Vertical angles have the same measure.

Short Response

10. Find the value of x and explain your steps.

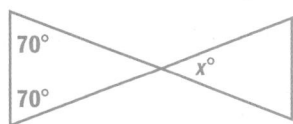

Extended Response

11. Graph $\triangle RST$ with vertices $R(5, -7)$, $S(5, 0)$, and $T(12, 0)$. Dilate the triangle by a scale factor of 3. Find the vertices of the image. Graph the image, and explain why it is similar to the original triangle.

Real Numbers and Right Triangles

BEFORE

In previous chapters you've...

- Found the square of a number
- Investigated rational numbers

Now

In Chapter 9 you'll study...

- Finding square roots
- Classifying real numbers as rational or irrational
- Solving real-world problems using the Pythagorean theorem
- Using trigonometric ratios

WHY?

So you can solve real-world problems about...

- forest rangers, p. 435
- parasailing, p. 444
- softball, p. 456
- totem poles, p. 466

Internet Preview
CLASSZONE.COM

- eEdition Plus Online
- eWorkbook Plus Online
- eTutorial Plus Online
- FCAT Practice
- More Examples

Chapter Warm-Up Games

Review skills you need for this chapter in these quick games.

Spin Your Wheels

Key Skill:
Evaluating powers

Spin the wheels until all three red lines connect equal values.

- You can turn the wheels one click at a time. Each click moves a wheel one space clockwise.

- How many clicks do you need to turn the left wheel?

- How many clicks do you need to turn the right wheel?

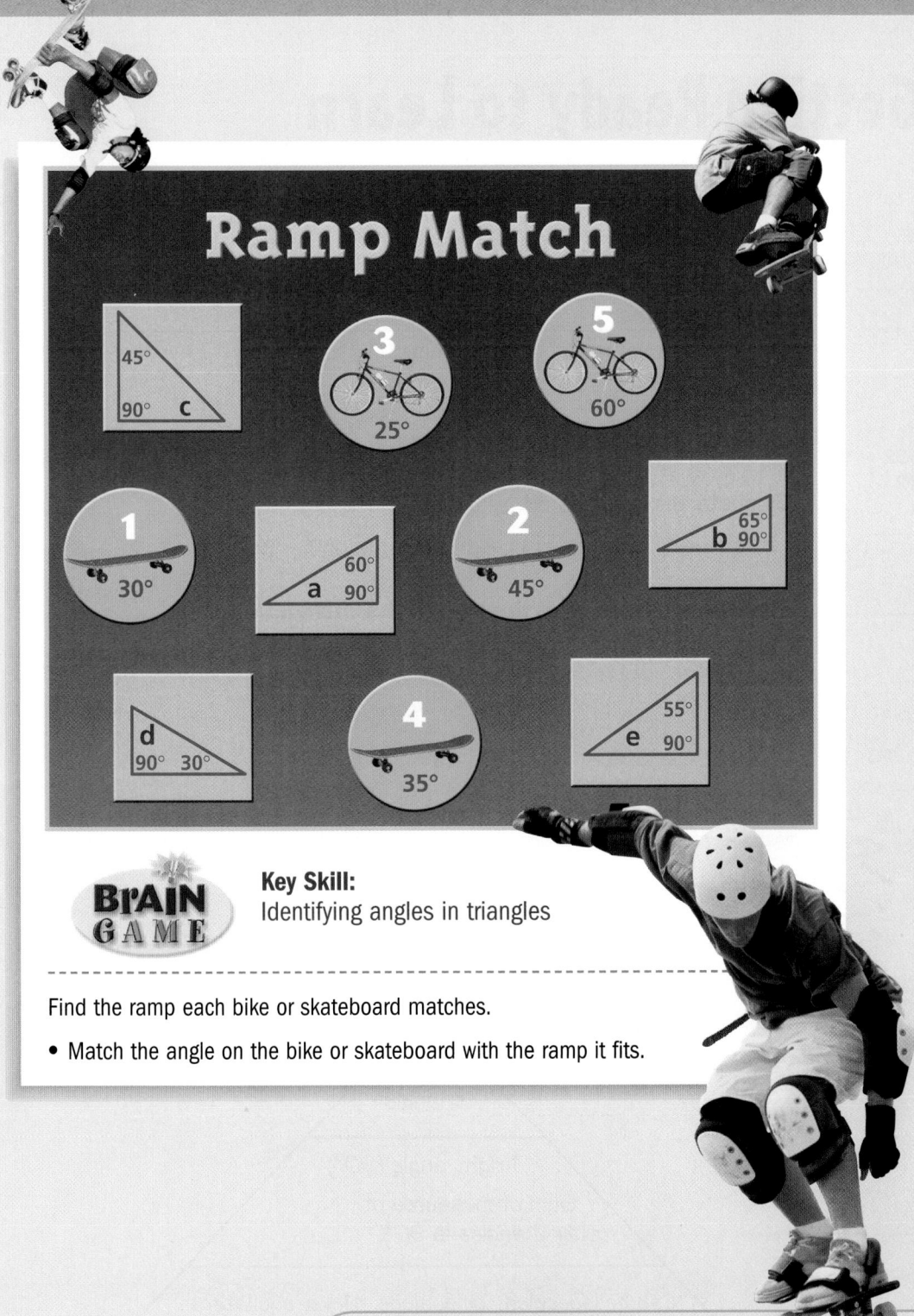

Ramp Match

45°
90° c

3 25°

5 60°

1 30°

60°
a 90°

2 45°

65°
b 90°

d
90° 30°

4 35°

55°
e 90°

BRAIN GAME

Key Skill:
Identifying angles in triangles

Find the ramp each bike or skateboard matches.

• Match the angle on the bike or skateboard with the ramp it fits.

Stop and Think

1. **Critical Thinking** How can you write 4^4 as a power of 2? Explain.

2. **Writing** Explain why a triangular ramp that has angles of 90°, 40°, and 55° cannot exist.

CHAPTER 9 Getting Ready to Learn

Review What You Need to Know

Using Vocabulary Use a review word to classify the triangle by its side lengths.

Word Watch

Review Words

rational number, p. 242
right angle, p. 375
right triangle, p. 382
equilateral triangle, p. 382
isosceles triangle, p. 382
scalene triangle, p. 382

1.   **2.**   **3.**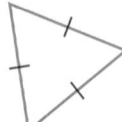

Evaluate the expression. *(p. 20)*

4. $4^2 + 3^2$ **5.** $14^2 - 5^2$ **6.** $27^2 - 3^2$ **7.** $2^2 + 6^2$

Find the measure of each angle in the triangle. *(p. 382)*

8.   **9.**   **10.**

You should include material that appears on a notebook like this in your own notes.

Know How to Take Notes

Illustrating with Examples When you learn a new concept or formula, write it in your notes along with examples and important information.

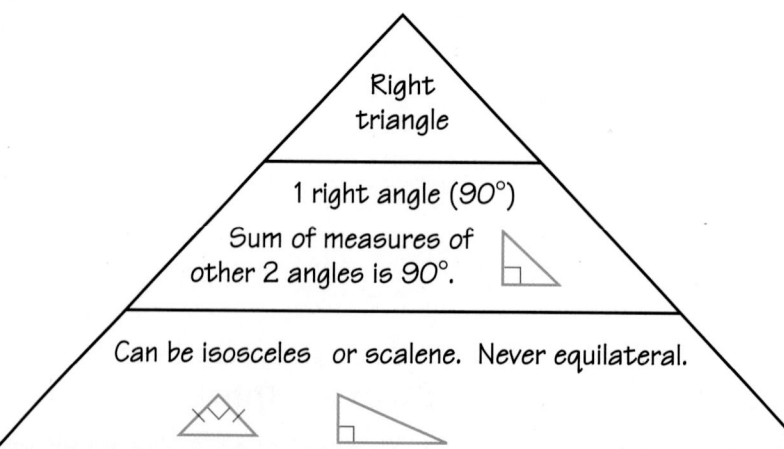

In Lesson 9.3, you will learn a rule about right triangles that you should write in your notebook.

Square Roots

BEFORE ▶ **Now** **WHY?**

You found squares of numbers.

You'll find and approximate square roots of numbers.

So you can find the length of a side of a square pillow, as in Ex. 14.

Word Watch

square root, p. 431
radical expression, p. 431
perfect square, p. 432

FLORIDA
Standards and Assessment

• Simplify expressions using radicals. (MA.A.1.3.4)

• Choose an appropriate estimation technique. (MA.A.4.3.1)

Activity You can find the length of a side of a square if you know its area.

Area = 1   Area = 4   Area = 9

① Copy and complete the table.

Area of square (square units)	1	4	9	16	25	36
Side length (units)	1	2	3	?	?	?

② What is the length of each side of a square with an area of 49 square units? 64 square units? 100 square units? 400 square units?

③ What can you say about the length of a side of a square that has an area between 81 and 100 square units?

The numbers 5 and −5 are the *square roots* of 25 because $5^2 = 25$ and $(-5)^2 = 25$. If $m^2 = n$, then m is a **square root** of n.

Every positive number has a positive square root and a negative square root. The symbol $\sqrt{}$ is called a *radical sign*. It is used to represent the positive square root. A **radical expression** is an expression that involves a $\sqrt{}$.

$$\sqrt{25} = 5 \qquad \text{positive square root}$$

$$-\sqrt{25} = -5 \qquad \text{negative square root}$$

Zero has one square root, which is zero.

EXAMPLE 1 **Evaluating Square Roots**

a. $\sqrt{36} = 6$ because $6^2 = 36$.   **b.** $-\sqrt{64} = -8$ because $(-8)^2 = 64$.

HELP with Solving

You may want to use the Table of Square Roots on p. 745.

Your turn now Find the square root.

1. $\sqrt{4}$ **2.** $\sqrt{0}$ **3.** $-\sqrt{36}$ **4.** $-\sqrt{81}$

Perfect Squares A **perfect square** is any number that has integer square roots. Some examples of perfect squares are 1, 4, 9, and 16. You can approximate the square roots of a number that is not a perfect square using a number line or a calculator.

EXAMPLE 2 **Approximating a Square Root**

You can use a number line to approximate $\sqrt{95}$ to the nearest whole number. You know that 95 is between 81 (or 9^2) and 100 (or 10^2), so $\sqrt{95}$ is between 9 and 10.

To decide whether $\sqrt{95}$ is closer to 9 or to 10, find 9.5^2. You can calculate that $9.5^2 = 90.25$ and $(\sqrt{95})^2 = 95$.

$$\begin{array}{ccccc} \sqrt{81} & & \sqrt{90.25} & \sqrt{95} & \sqrt{100} \\ & & & & \\ 9 & & 9.5 & & 10 \end{array}$$

$$9^2 = 81 \qquad 9.5^2 = 90.25 \qquad 10^2 = 100$$

As shown on the number line, $\sqrt{95}$ is between $\sqrt{90.25}$ and $\sqrt{100}$, so it has a value between 9.5 and 10. Therefore, $\sqrt{95}$ is closer to 10 than it is to 9.

ANSWER To the nearest whole number, $\sqrt{95} \approx 10$.

EXAMPLE 3 **Using a Calculator**

Evaluate the square root. Round to the nearest tenth, if necessary.

   a. $\sqrt{441}$ **b.** $-\sqrt{56.25}$ **c.** $\sqrt{8}$ **d.** $-\sqrt{1256}$

Solution

Keystrokes	Display	Answer
a. 2nd [$\sqrt{\ }$] **441** =	21	21
b. (−) 2nd [$\sqrt{\ }$] **56.25** =	−7.5	−7.5
c. 2nd [$\sqrt{\ }$] **8** =	2.828427125	2.8
d. (−) 2nd [$\sqrt{\ }$] **1256** =	−35.44009029	−35.4

 Your turn now Approximate to the nearest whole number.

   5. $\sqrt{23}$ **6.** $\sqrt{41}$ **7.** $\sqrt{70}$ **8.** $\sqrt{125}$

Use a calculator to evaluate. Round to the nearest tenth.

   9. $\sqrt{236}$ **10.** $\sqrt{11}$ **11.** $-\sqrt{20.96}$ **12.** $-\sqrt{3590}$

EXAMPLE 4 **Using a Square Root Equation**

Amusement Parks On an amusement park ride, riders stand against a circular wall that spins. At a certain speed, the floor drops out and the force of the rotation keeps the riders pinned to the wall.

The model $s = 4.95\sqrt{r}$ gives the speed needed to keep riders pinned to the wall. In the model, s is the speed in meters per second and r is the radius of the ride in meters. Find the speed necessary to keep riders pinned to the wall of a ride that has a radius of 2.61 meters.

Solution

$$\begin{aligned} s &= 4.95\sqrt{r} && \text{Write equation for speed of the ride.} \\ &= 4.95\sqrt{2.61} && \text{Substitute 2.61 for } r. \\ &\approx 4.95(1.62) && \text{Approximate the square root.} \\ &= 8.019 && \text{Multiply.} \end{aligned}$$

ANSWER The speed should be about 8.019 meters per second.

EXAMPLE 5 **Solving Equations Using Square Roots**

a. $\quad x^2 = 64$ Original equation

$\quad\quad x = \pm\sqrt{64}$ Definition of square root

$\quad\quad x = \pm 8$ Evaluate square roots.

ANSWER The solutions are 8 and −8.

with Reading

The symbol $\pm$ is read *plus or minus*. The statement $x = \pm 8$ means that 8 and −8 are the solutions of $x^2 = 64$.

b. $\quad\quad z^2 + 14 = 20$ Original equation

$\quad z^2 + 14 - 14 = 20 - 14$ Subtract 14 from each side.

$\quad\quad\quad\quad z^2 = 6$ Simplify.

$\quad\quad\quad\quad z = \pm\sqrt{6}$ Definition of square root

$\quad\quad\quad\quad z \approx \pm 2.45$ Approximate square roots.

ANSWER The solutions are about 2.45 and about −2.45.

Your turn now **Approximate the square root. Round to the nearest tenth.**

13. $\sqrt{5}$ **14.** $\sqrt{12}$ **15.** $\sqrt{15}$ **16.** $\sqrt{23}$

Solve the equation. Check your solutions.

17. $t^2 = 36$ **18.** $y^2 - 15 = 10$ **19.** $x^2 + 7 = 16$

Getting Ready to Practice

1. Vocabulary Copy and complete: A number b is a square root of c if ___.

Find the two square roots of the number.

2. 9   **3.** 16   **4.** 49   **5.** 121

Use a calculator to approximate the square root. Round to the nearest tenth.

6. $\sqrt{28}$ **7.** $-\sqrt{482}$ **8.** $-\sqrt{34.6}$ **9.** $\sqrt{2440}$

Solve the equation. Check your solutions.

10. $x^2 = 4$ **11.** $b^2 = 49$ **12.** $y^2 + 7 = 56$ **13.** $c^2 - 12 = 69$

14. Guided Problem Solving You want to make a square pillow. You have 729 square inches of material for the front of the pillow. If you use all the material, what is the length of one side of the pillow?

   (1 Write an equation.

   (2 Use definition of square root to solve the equation.

   (3 Evaluate the positive square root.

Practice and Problem Solving

Find the square root.

15. $-\sqrt{1}$ **16.** $\sqrt{100}$ **17.** $\sqrt{144}$ **18.** $-\sqrt{900}$

Approximate the square root to the nearest whole number.

19. $\sqrt{33}$ **20.** $\sqrt{14}$ **21.** $\sqrt{117}$ **22.** $\sqrt{52}$

HELP with Homework

Example	Exercises
1	15–18
2	19–22
3	23–26
4	34
5	27–32

Online Resources
CLASSZONE.COM
· More Examples
· eTutorial Plus

Use a calculator to evaluate the square root. Round to the nearest tenth, if necessary.

23. $\sqrt{22}$ **24.** $\sqrt{43.56}$ **25.** $-\sqrt{1475}$ **26.** $-\sqrt{6204}$

Solve the equation. Check your solution(s).

27. $x^2 = 0$ **28.** $y^2 = 81$ **29.** $z^2 - 169 = 0$

30. $n^2 - 27 = 94$ **31.** $a^2 + 12 = 48$ **32.** $m^2 + 21 = 421$

33. Critical Thinking Can you find $\sqrt{-25}$? Explain your answer.

34. Fire Tower A forest ranger is stationed in a 53 foot tall fire tower. The equation for the distance in miles that the ranger can see is $d = \sqrt{1.5h}$, where h is the height in feet above the ground. Find the distance the ranger can see. Round your answer to the nearest tenth.

with Solving

You can use a calculator or the Table of Square Roots on p. 745 to solve Exercises 35–40.

Solve the equation. Round to the nearest hundredth, if necessary. Check your solutions.

35. $x^2 + 8 = 49$ **36.** $y^2 - 31 = 36$ **37.** $62 + z^2 = 198$

38. $t^2 - 44 = 224$ **39.** $c^2 - 35 = 165$ **40.** $57 + m^2 = 253$

Evaluate the expression $\sqrt{x^2 - y^2}$ for the given values.

41. $x = 5, y = 3$ **42.** $x = 10, y = 8$ **43.** $x = 15, y = 12$

Find the two square roots of the number.

44. 0.81   **45.** 1.44   **46.** 1.21   **47.** 1.96

48. Farming You want to put a fence around a square plot of land that has an area of 6250 square yards. Find the length of a side, to the nearest tenth of a yard, and then use it to approximate the perimeter of the plot of land.

$A = 6250$ yd^2

49. Home Decorating You have a square table with an area of 34.5 square feet. You have a tablecloth that measures 60 inches by 60 inches. Is the tablecloth large enough to cover the table? Explain.

50. Evaluate the expression $\sqrt{\sqrt{16}}$.

EXAMPLE **Finding a Square Root of a Fraction**

$$\sqrt{\frac{9}{16}} = \sqrt{\frac{3}{4} \cdot \frac{3}{4}} = \frac{3}{4} \qquad \text{Definition of square root}$$

In Exercises 51–55, find the square root.

51. $\sqrt{\dfrac{1}{4}}$ **52.** $\sqrt{\dfrac{16}{25}}$ **53.** $\sqrt{\dfrac{49}{64}}$ **54.** $\sqrt{\dfrac{81}{100}}$ **55.** $\sqrt{\dfrac{144}{169}}$

56. Look for a Pattern Find the positive square roots of 0.36, 0.0036, 0.000036, and 0.00000036. What pattern do you notice? Using the pattern, predict the positive square root of 0.0000000036.

57. Challenge In Example 2, you learned how to approximate the value of a square root to the nearest whole number without using a calculator. Explain how to approximate the value of a square root to the nearest tenth if you have a calculator that cannot evaluate square roots.

58. Carnival Nikki is at a carnival and has $6. She would like to buy some cotton candy for $2.25 and use the rest of her money to go on the rides. Each ride costs $.75. How many rides can she go on? *(Lesson 3.4)*

Tell whether the angles are *complementary*, *supplementary*, or *neither*. *(Lesson 8.1)*

59. $m\angle 1 = 89°$
    $m\angle 2 = 31°$

60. $m\angle 1 = 34°$
    $m\angle 2 = 56°$

61. $m\angle 1 = 53°$
    $m\angle 2 = 127°$

62. $m\angle 1 = 78°$
    $m\angle 2 = 102°$

Choose a Strategy **Use a strategy from the list to solve the following problem. Explain your choice of strategy.**

> **Problem Solving Strategies**
> - Look for a Pattern
> - Draw a Diagram
> - Make a Model

63. In how many different ways can three postage stamps be torn from a 3 by 4 sheet of stamps so that the three stamps are still attached to one another?

Basic Skills **Write the decimal as a mixed number.**

64. −1.25   **65.** 5.35   **66.** 2.95   **67.** −9.05

FCAT Practice FCAT

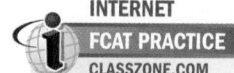
68. Multiple Choice Estimate $\sqrt{235}$ to the nearest whole number.

  A. 12   **B.** 13   **C.** 14   **D.** 15

69. Multiple Choice The area of a square gymnasium is 1024 square feet. Find the perimeter of the base of the gymnasium.

  F. 32 feet   **G.** 64 feet   **H.** 128 feet   **I.** 180 feet

X-cellent Birthday

Augustus De Morgan, a nineteenth century English mathematician, was the first professor of Mathematics at University College, London.

Always interested in strange numerical facts, De Morgan once noted in his writings that he had the distinction of being x years old in the year x^2. If he was born between 1805 and 1815, in what year was he born?

Rational and Irrational Numbers

BEFORE	▶ Now	WHY?
You investigated rational numbers.	You'll work with irrational numbers.	So you can determine how many stencils fill a wall, as in Ex. 24.

Word Watch

irrational number, p. 437
real number, p. 437

FLORIDA
Standards and Assessment

• Describe and know examples of irrational numbers. (MA.A.1.3.3)

• Compare and order decimals and radicals. (MA.A.1.3.2)

Recall that a *rational number* is a number that can be written as a quotient $\frac{a}{b}$, where a and b are integers and $b \neq 0$. An **irrational number** is a number that cannot be written as a quotient of two integers. If n is a positive integer and is not a perfect square, then $\sqrt{n}$ and $-\sqrt{n}$ are irrational numbers.

Together, rational numbers and irrational numbers make up the set of **real numbers** . The Venn diagram shows the relationships among numbers in the real number system.

The decimal form of a rational number is either terminating or repeating. The decimal form of an irrational number neither terminates nor repeats.

HELP with **Review**

For help with writing a rational number as a decimal, see p. 242.

EXAMPLE 1 **Classifying Real Numbers**

	Number	Type	Decimal Form	Type of Decimal
a.	$\frac{3}{4}$	Rational	$\frac{3}{4} = 0.75$	Terminating
b.	$\frac{1}{11}$	Rational	$\frac{1}{11} = 0.0909\ldots = 0.\overline{09}$	Repeating
c.	$\sqrt{3}$	Irrational	$\sqrt{3} = 1.7320508\ldots$	Nonrepeating and nonterminating

Your turn now **Tell whether the number is *rational* or *irrational*. Explain your reasoning.**

1. $\frac{5}{8}$ **2.** $\sqrt{7}$ **3.** $\frac{2}{9}$ **4.** $\sqrt{25}$

EXAMPLE **2** **Comparing Real Numbers**

Graph the pair of numbers on a number line. Then copy and complete the statement with <, >, or =.

a. $\sqrt{2}$? 2

b. $\sqrt{\dfrac{1}{2}}$? $\dfrac{1}{2}$

Solution

Use a calculator to approximate the square root and write any fractions as decimals. Then graph the numbers on a number line and compare.

Watch Out!

You may need to use parentheses when using a calculator to approximate a square root.

a.

$$\sqrt{2} \approx 1.4142 \qquad 2$$

| 1 | 1.1 | 1.2 | 1.3 | 1.4 | 1.5 | 1.6 | 1.7 | 1.8 | 1.9 | 2 | 2.1 |

So, $\sqrt{2} < 2$.

b.

$$\tfrac{1}{2} = 0.5 \qquad \sqrt{\tfrac{1}{2}} \approx 0.7071$$

| 0 | 0.1 | 0.2 | 0.3 | 0.4 | 0.5 | 0.6 | 0.7 | 0.8 | 0.9 | 1 |

So, $\sqrt{\dfrac{1}{2}} > \dfrac{1}{2}$.

Your turn now **Graph the pair of numbers on a number line. Then copy and complete the statement with <, >, or =.**

5. 4 ? $\sqrt{8}$

6. $\sqrt{25}$? 5

7. $\dfrac{1}{4}$? $\sqrt{\dfrac{1}{4}}$

EXAMPLE **3** **Ordering Decimals**

Order the decimals $0.4\overline{7}$, $0.\overline{474}$, $0.\overline{47}$, and 0.477 from least to greatest.

Solution

1 Write each decimal out to six decimal places.

> Notice that the first two digits after the decimal point are the same for each number.

$0.4\overline{7} = 0.477777...$

$0.\overline{474} = 0.474474...$

$0.\overline{47} = 0.474747...$

> Use the second pair of digits to order the decimals.

$0.477 = 0.477000$

2 From least to greatest, the order of the numbers is
$0.474474...$, $0.474747...$, 0.4770, and $0.477777...$.

ANSWER From least to greatest, the order is $0.\overline{474}$, $0.\overline{47}$, 0.477, and $0.4\overline{7}$.

EXAMPLE 4 Using an Irrational Number

Waves For large ocean waves, the wind speed s in knots and the height of the waves h in feet are related by the equation $s = \sqrt{\dfrac{h}{0.019}}$. If the waves are about 9.5 feet tall, what must the wind speed be? (1 knot is equivalent to 1.15 miles per hour.)

Solution

$$s = \sqrt{\dfrac{h}{0.019}} \qquad \text{Write original equation.}$$

$$= \sqrt{\dfrac{9.5}{0.019}} \qquad \text{Substitute 9.5 for } h.$$

$$= \sqrt{500} \qquad \text{Divide.}$$

$$\approx 22.36 \qquad \text{Approximate square root.}$$

ANSWER The wind speed must be about 22.36 knots.

Your turn now Use the equation in Example 4.

8. Find the wind speed required to produce 15 foot waves.

9.2 Exercises

More Practice, p. 735

INTERNET
eWorkbook Plus
CLASSZONE.COM

Getting Ready to Practice

1. Vocabulary Copy and complete: Numbers that cannot be written as a quotient of two integers are called __?__ numbers.

Tell whether the number is *rational* or *irrational*. Explain your reasoning.

2. $\sqrt{36}$ **3.** $\sqrt{5}$ **4.** $\dfrac{\sqrt{3}}{8}$ **5.** $\sqrt{\dfrac{25}{49}}$

Graph the pair of numbers on a number line. Then copy and complete the statement with <, >, or =.

6. $\dfrac{5}{6}$ __?__ $\sqrt{\dfrac{5}{6}}$ **7.** $\dfrac{3}{5}$ __?__ $\sqrt{\dfrac{36}{100}}$ **8.** 5 __?__ $\sqrt{10}$

9. Dimensions The floor of a square room has an area of 90 square feet. What are the dimensions of the room to the nearest tenth of a foot?

Practice and Problem Solving

HELP with **Homework**

Example	Exercises
1	10–13
2	14–17
3	18–19
4	36

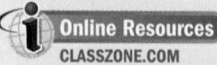

Online Resources
CLASSZONE.COM

· More Examples
· eTutorial Plus

Tell whether the number is *rational* or *irrational*. Explain your reasoning.

10. $\sqrt{144}$　　　**11.** $\dfrac{9}{46}$　　　**12.** 0.30311　　　**13.** $\sqrt{\dfrac{3}{5}}$

Graph the pair of numbers on a number line. Then copy and complete the statement with <, >, or =.

14. $\sqrt{\dfrac{64}{121}} \underline{\ ?\ } \dfrac{8}{11}$　　**15.** $\sqrt{13} \underline{\ ?\ } 3$　　**16.** $\sqrt{21} \underline{\ ?\ } 7$　　**17.** $-5 \underline{\ ?\ } -\sqrt{25}$

Order the decimals from least to greatest.

18. $0.1\bar{3},\ 0.\overline{131},\ 0.\overline{13},\ 0.133$　　　　**19.** $0.2\bar{6},\ 0.266,\ 0.2\bar{6},\ 0.\overline{262}$

Evaluate the expression when $a = 2$, $b = 4$, and $c = 9$. Tell whether the result is *rational* or *irrational*.

20. $\sqrt{a + c}$　　　**21.** $\sqrt{a^2}$　　　**22.** $\sqrt{bc}$　　　**23.** $\sqrt{a^2 + b^2}$

24. Decorating You are decorating your room. You have a square wall stencil that has an area of 20.25 square inches. Find the length of a side of the stencil. The wall you are decorating is $7\dfrac{1}{2}$ feet high. How many stencils can you place in a column from the top to the bottom of your wall?

In Exercises 25–27, graph the pair of numbers on a number line. Then copy and complete the statement with <, >, or =.

25. $\sqrt{0.9} \underline{\ ?\ } 0.9$　　　**26.** $-7 \underline{\ ?\ } -\sqrt{7}$　　　**27.** $\sqrt{2.25} \underline{\ ?\ } \dfrac{3.6}{2.4}$

28. Graph the numbers $-\sqrt{9}$, -8.69, $-\sqrt{45}$, and $-\dfrac{141}{25}$ on a number line.

Order the numbers from least to greatest.

29. $1.5,\ \sqrt{8},\ -4,\ -3.75$　　　　**30.** $\sqrt{81},\ 10.3,\ \sqrt{220},\ -9$

31. $-\sqrt{12},\ -\sqrt{\dfrac{1}{4}},\ -3.5,\ -\dfrac{3}{4}$　　　**32.** $1.02,\ \sqrt{2.5},\ \sqrt{1.25},\ \dfrac{2}{5}$

33. Carpet Your aunt offers you a square piece of carpet that has an area of 110 square feet. You want to use the carpet in a bedroom that measures 10.5 feet by 11.2 feet. Will the carpet fit in the room? Will it be too small? too large? Explain.

34. Critical Thinking Your friend gets a result of 2.645751311 on a calculator and says that it has to be an irrational number. Is your friend right? Explain your reasoning.

35. Challenge Find three rational numbers between $\frac{2}{3}$ and $\frac{3}{4}$. Can you write all of the rational numbers that are between these two numbers? Explain your reasoning.

36. Box Kites To calculate the minimum wind speed required to fly a box kite, you can use the formula $m = \sqrt{\frac{w}{A}}$, where m is the minimum wind speed in miles per hour, w is the weight in ounces, and A is the area in square feet of the surface used to lift the kite. Find the minimum wind speed required to lift a box kite with a weight of 5.6 ounces if the area used to lift the kite is 8.71 square feet.

Mixed Review

Simplify. Write the expression using only positive exponents.
(Lessons 4.6, 4.7)

37. $5a^2 \cdot 6a^9$ **38.** $d^8 \cdot 4d^{-5}$ **39.** $-5m^0$ **40.** $n^{-7} \cdot n^5$

41. $\dfrac{c^5 \cdot c^3}{c^4}$ **42.** $\dfrac{24b^{14}}{8b^9}$ **43.** $\dfrac{-8n^8}{12n^{12}}$ **44.** $\dfrac{24r^{-5}}{r^3}$

Describe the transformation from the blue figure to the red figure using coordinate notation. *(Lessons 8.6, 8.7)*

45.   **46.**   **47.**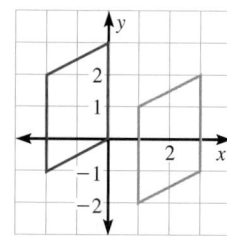

48. You draw a regular hexagon with side lengths of 2 centimeters on an overhead projector transparency. When it is projected, the hexagon is enlarged by a scale factor of 15. Find the perimeter of the image. *(Lesson 8.8)*

FCAT Practice

49. Multiple Choice Which statement is *not* true.

A. $\sqrt{20} > 5$ **B.** $6.8 > \sqrt{42}$ **C.** $\sqrt{1225} = 35$ **D.** $\sqrt{3} < 2.5$

50. Multiple Choice Which of the following shows the numbers in order from least to greatest?

F. $-3, -\sqrt{16}, 7, 8, \sqrt{81}$ **G.** $1, \sqrt{2}, \sqrt{5}, 2, 3$

H. $1, \sqrt{2}, 2, \sqrt{5}, 3$ **I.** $1, \sqrt{2}, 2, 3, \sqrt{5}$

FLORIDA: Standards and Assessment
Make and test conjectures about geometric relationships. (MA.C.3.3.1)

GOAL
Use graph paper to relate the side lengths of a right triangle.

MATERIALS
• graph paper
• pen or pencil

Modeling the Pythagorean Theorem

You can use graph paper to find the length of a right triangle's *hypotenuse*, which is the side opposite the right angle.

Explore **Find the length of the hypotenuse of a right triangle with side lengths of three units and four units.**

1 Draw the right triangle on graph paper. The sides of the triangle that form the right angle are called *legs*. For each leg, draw a square that has a leg as one side. What is the sum of the areas of these two squares?

2 Measure the hypotenuse using graph paper. If you draw a square with the hypotenuse as one side, what is its area?

3 Compare the sum of the areas you found in Step 1 to the area you found in Step 2. What do you notice?

Your turn now **Repeat Steps 1–3 for right triangles with legs of the given lengths.**

1. 5, 12   **2.** 6, 8   **3.** 8, 15

Stop *and* **Think**

4. Let the lengths of the legs of a right triangle be a and b, and the length of the hypotenuse be c. Write a conjecture about the relationship between the lengths of the legs and the length of the hypotenuse.

The Pythagorean Theorem

BEFORE	▶ Now	WHY?
You used formulas to solve problems.	You'll use the Pythagorean theorem to solve problems.	So you can find the length of a volleyball net support, as in Ex. 21.

Word Watch

leg, p. 443
hypotenuse, p. 443
Pythagorean theorem, p. 443
converse, p. 444

FLORIDA
Standards and Assessment

• Apply the Pythagorean theorem in real-world problems. (MA.C.3.3.1)
• Know the properties of two-dimensional figures. (MA.C.1.3.1)

In a right triangle, the sides that form the right angle are called **legs** . The side opposite the right angle is the **hypotenuse** . The lengths of the legs and the hypotenuse are related by the **Pythagorean theorem** .

Pythagorean Theorem

Words For any right triangle, the sum of the squares of the lengths of the legs equals the square of the length of the hypotenuse.

Algebra $a^2 + b^2 = c^2$ **Numbers** $3^2 + 4^2 = 5^2$

EXAMPLE 1 **Finding the Length of a Hypotenuse**

Find the length of the hypotenuse of a right triangle with leg lengths of 15 inches and 20 inches.

$a^2 + b^2 = c^2$	Pythagorean theorem
$15^2 + 20^2 = c^2$	Substitute 15 for a and 20 for b.
$225 + 400 = c^2$	Evaluate powers.
$625 = c^2$	Add.
$\sqrt{625} = c$	Take positive square root of each side.
$25 = c$	Evaluate square root.

ANSWER The length of the hypotenuse is 25 inches.

HELP with Notetaking

Be sure to write the Pythagorean theorem in your notebook.

Your turn now Complete the exercise.

1. Find the length of the hypotenuse of a right triangle with leg lengths of 28 inches and 45 inches.

In application problems, you usually need to take only the positive square root. For example, length, speed, and height are positive, so a negative square root would not give a reasonable answer.

EXAMPLE 2 Finding the Length of a Leg

Parasailing You are parasailing. After getting airborne and reaching cruising speed, you are 200 feet directly behind the boat. How high are you above the water to the nearest foot?

Not drawn to scale

tow line
b
300 ft
boat
200 ft

Solution

$a^2 + b^2 = c^2$	Pythagorean theorem
$200^2 + b^2 = 300^2$	Substitute 200 for a and 300 for c.
$40{,}000 + b^2 = 90{,}000$	Evaluate powers.
$b^2 = 50{,}000$	Subtract 40,000 from each side.
$b = \sqrt{50{,}000}$	Take positive square root of each side.
$b \approx 223.6068$	Approximate square root.

ANSWER You are about 224 feet above the water.

HELP with Solving

If you know the lengths of *any* two sides of a right triangle, you can use the Pythagorean theorem to find the length of the third side.

Your turn now **Find the unknown length. Round to the nearest tenth, if necessary.**

2.

c
$a = 7.5$ in.
$b = 18$ in.

3.
a
$b = 8$ m
$c = 16$ m

4.
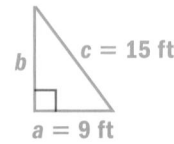
b
$c = 15$ ft
$a = 9$ ft

5. Critical Thinking Does it matter which leg of a right triangle is labeled a or b? Explain.

Converse of the Pythagorean Theorem The Pythagorean theorem can be written as an if-then statement with two parts.

Theorem If a triangle is a right triangle, then $a^2 + b^2 = c^2$.

When you reverse the parts of an if-then statement, the new statement is called the **converse** of the statement.

Converse If $a^2 + b^2 = c^2$, then **the triangle is a right triangle**.

The converse of a statement may or may not be true. The converse of the Pythagorean theorem is true. You can use the converse of the Pythagorean theorem to decide whether a triangle is a right triangle.

EXAMPLE 3 **Identifying Right Triangles**

Use the converse of the Pythagorean theorem to determine whether the triangle with the given side lengths is a right triangle.

a. $a = 6, b = 8, c = 10$

$$a^2 + b^2 \stackrel{?}{=} c^2$$

$$6^2 + 8^2 \stackrel{?}{=} 10^2$$

$$36 + 64 \stackrel{?}{=} 100$$

$$100 = 100 \checkmark$$

ANSWER A right triangle

b. $a = 10, b = 12, c = 16$

$$a^2 + b^2 \stackrel{?}{=} c^2$$

$$10^2 + 12^2 \stackrel{?}{=} 16^2$$

$$100 + 144 \stackrel{?}{=} 256$$

$$244 \neq 256 ✗$$

ANSWER Not a right triangle

9.3 Exercises

More Practice, p. 735

INTERNET
eWorkbook Plus
CLASSZONE.COM

Getting Ready to Practice

1. Vocabulary Copy and complete: In a right triangle, the side opposite the right angle is called the __?__.

Let a and b represent the lengths of the legs of a right triangle, and let c represent the length of the hypotenuse. Find the unknown length.

2. $a = 12, b = ?, c = 20$

3. $a = ?, b = 36, c = 39$

4. $a = 9, b = ?, c = 41$

5. $a = 7, b = 24, c = ?$

Use the converse of the Pythagorean theorem to determine whether the triangle with the given side lengths is a right triangle.

6. $a = 3, b = 7, c = 9$

7. $a = 24, b = 45, c = 51$

8. $a = 20, b = 48, c = 52$

9. $a = 16, b = 18, c = 24$

10. Ladders A 13 foot ladder is leaning against a building. The bottom of the ladder is 5 feet from the building. How high is the top of the ladder?

13 ft   x

5 ft

Practice and Problem Solving

with Homework

Example	Exercises
1	11–16
2	11–16, 21
3	17–19

Online Resources
CLASSZONE.COM
· More Examples
· eTutorial Plus

Find the unknown length. Round to the nearest tenth, if necessary.

11.

12.

13.

14.

15.

16.

Determine whether the triangle with the given side lengths is a right triangle.

17.

18.

19.

20. Find the Error Describe and correct the error in finding the length of the third side of the right triangle. Round to the nearest tenth of a foot.

$$a^2 + b^2 = c^2$$
$$6^2 + 8^2 = c^2$$
$$36 + 64 = c^2$$
$$100 = c^2$$
$$10 = c$$

21. Volleyball Net You are setting up a volleyball net. There are two 8 foot poles that hold up the net. You are going to attach each pole to a stake in the ground using a piece of rope. Each stake should be 4 feet from the pole. Assume that the ropes are taut. How long should each rope be? Round to the nearest tenth of a foot.

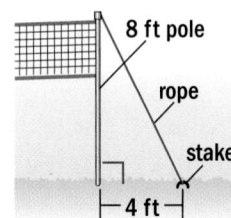

Find the unknown length. Round to the nearest hundredth, if necessary.

22.

23.

24.

25. Critical Thinking An isosceles right triangle has a hypotenuse with a length of 6 feet. Find the length of each leg. Round to the nearest hundredth of a foot.

■ **Utility Poles**

Several states have built nesting platforms on the tops of utility poles to provide safe nesting areas for birds. If a platform is 6 feet wide and the supports meet the pole 6 feet beneath the platform, how long are the supports?

Determine whether the triangle with the given side lengths is a right triangle.

26. $a = 0.65$, $b = 1.56$, $c = 1.69$ **27.** $a = 2.88$, $b = 0.84$, $c = 3.2$

28. $a = 0.12$, $b = 0.16$, $c = 0.2$ **29.** $a = 0.75$, $b = 0.4$, $c = 0.85$

30. Utility Poles A guy wire with a length of 23.8 meters is attached to a utility pole. The wire is anchored to the ground 9 meters from the base of the pole. How high above the ground is the guy wire attached to the utility pole? Round to the nearest tenth of a meter.

Let a and b represent the lengths of the legs of a right triangle, and let c represent the length of the hypotenuse. Find the unknown length.

31. $a = 1.5$, $b = ?$, $c = 2.5$ **32.** $a = ?$, $b = 123$, $c = 139.4$

33. $a = 2.8$, $b = 4.5$, $c = ?$ **34.** $a = 4.5$, $b = ?$, $c = 7.5$

35. $a = \sqrt{8}$, $b = 1$, $c = ?$ **36.** $a = ?$, $b = 2$, $c = \sqrt{13}$

37. Challenge Draw several different obtuse triangles and measure the lengths of the legs. Let a and b represent the lengths of the two shorter sides and let c represent the length of the longest side. Make a conjecture about the relationship between the lengths of the sides of obtuse triangles.

Mixed Review

38. In the figure, $ABCD \sim WXYZ$. Find $m\angle D$. *(Lesson 8.8)*

39. Triangle LMN has vertices $L(1, 5)$, $M(4, 2)$, and $N(0, 0)$. Dilate the triangle using a scale factor of 3. *(Lesson 8.8)*

FCAT Practice

40. Multiple Choice The hypotenuse of a right triangle has a length of 34 inches and one of the legs has a length of 16 inches. What is the length of the other leg?

A. 7 inches   **B.** 18 inches   **C.** 24 inches   **D.** 30 inches

41. Short Response Determine whether a triangle with side lengths of 84 cm, 80 cm, and 116 cm is a right triangle. Explain your reasoning.

Draw a Diagram

FLORIDA: Standards and Assessment
Apply the Pythagorean theorem in real-world problems. (MA.C.3.3.1)

- Guess, Check, and Revise
- Look for a Pattern
- Make a List
- Act It Out
- Draw a Diagram
- Work Backward
- Solve a Simpler Problem

Problem Jeff is flying a kite. He is holding the end of the kite string about 3 feet above the ground. The length of the string is 35 feet. He is standing about 28 feet from the base of a tree when the wind changes and the kite gets stuck in the tree. About how high off the ground is the kite when it is stuck in the tree?

① Read and Understand

Read the problem carefully.

You know the height of Jeff's hands above the ground, the length of the kite string, and the distance to the tree. You need to find the height of the kite after it is in the tree.

② Make a Plan

Decide on a strategy to use.

One way to solve the problem is to draw a diagram of the situation. Then you can use the Pythagorean theorem to find the height of the kite in the tree.

③ Solve the Problem

Reread the problem and draw a diagram.

Show the position of Jeff, the tree, and the kite.

Write known lengths on the diagram. The end of the kite string is about 3 feet above the ground, the string is 35 feet long, and the tree is about 28 feet from Jeff.

Next, use the Pythagorean theorem to find the missing length a.

$$a^2 + b^2 = c^2$$

$$a^2 + 28^2 = 35^2$$

$$a^2 + 784 = 1225$$

$$a^2 = 441$$

$$a = 21$$

> Length is positive. Find positive square root.

$$21 + 3 = 24$$

ANSWER The kite is about 24 feet high.

④ Look Back

Be sure that you used all of the necessary information in the problem.

Practice the Strategy

Use the strategy *draw a diagram*.

1. **Utility Pole** A support wire 10 meters long is attached to the top of a utility pole 7 meters tall and is then stretched taut. How far from the base of the pole will the wire be attached to the ground? Round your answer to the nearest tenth of a meter.

2. **Hiking** Eric is hiking from his campsite to a creek. He walks 3.5 miles directly south, 4 miles directly east, then 1.5 miles directly south. Copy and complete the diagram to find how far he is from the campsite.

3. **Circus** A cable from the top of a circus tent pole is attached to the ground at a point 15 feet from the base of the pole. If the cable is 40 feet long, how high is the pole? Round your answer to the nearest foot.

4. **Distance** You and your friend live on opposite corners of a square park. You usually ride your bike 1280 feet around the outside of the park to reach your friend's house. Today, you walk diagonally across the park to get to your friend's house. How much shorter is the walking distance than the biking distance? Round your answer to the nearest foot.

5. **Moving** You are moving into a new house. The doorway is 78 inches high and 36 inches wide. Can a round table top with a diameter of 82 inches fit through the doorway?

Mixed Problem Solving

Use any strategy to solve the problem.

6. **Pool** To sanitize a swimming pool, you should use 2 parts per million of chlorine, which can also be written as

$$\frac{2 \text{ gallons chlorine}}{1{,}000{,}000 \text{ gallons water}}.$$

How much chlorine should there be in a pool that holds 20,000 gallons of water?

7. **Advertising** A newspaper charges a base fee of $20 for a color ad plus a charge for each line. The table shows the total cost of several color ads. How much would you expect to pay for a 15 line color ad?

Number of lines	2	4	6	8	10
Total Cost	$36	$52	$68	$84	$100

8. **Money** Your grandmother gave you some money for your birthday. You put half of the money in the bank. Then you go to the mall and spend $12.50 on a DVD and give half of what's left to your younger brother. You now have $2.50 left. How much money did your grandmother give you?

9. **Banking** You have an ATM card for your savings account, but you have forgotten your four-digit personal identification number (PIN). You know the first digit is a 4 and the last three digits contain a 4, 2, and 7. How many possibilities are there for your PIN?

Using the Pythagorean Theorem

BEFORE	▶ Now	WHY?
You found the side lengths of right triangles.	You'll solve real-life problems using the Pythagorean theorem.	So you can find the diagonal length of a swimming pool, as in Ex. 5.

Word Watch

Pythagorean triple, p. 451

FLORIDA
Standards and Assessment

• Apply the Pythagorean theorem in real-world problems. (MA.C.3.3.1)

In the Real World

Boating You and your friend live on opposite sides of a lake. To ride your bicycle to your friend's house, you travel 0.5 mile directly east, then 1.2 miles directly south. How far is it to your friend's house by boat?

One way to find the distance from your house to your friend's house by boat is to measure the distance *indirectly*. Because the bicycle and boat paths form a right triangle, you can do this using the Pythagorean theorem.

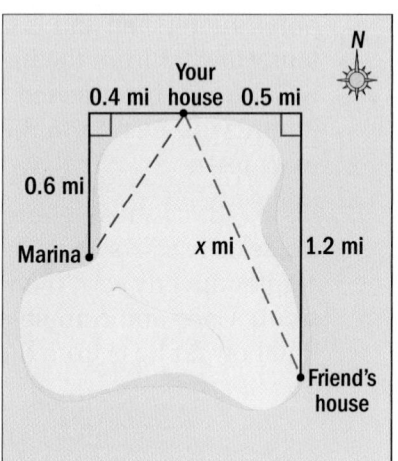

EXAMPLE 1 **Using Indirect Measurement**

Let a and b represent the lengths of the legs (bicycle paths) of the right triangle. Let x represent the length of the hypotenuse (boat path).

$a^2 + b^2 = x^2$	Pythagorean theorem
$0.5^2 + 1.2^2 = x^2$	Substitute 0.5 for a and 1.2 for b.
$0.25 + 1.44 = x^2$	Evaluate powers.
$1.69 = x^2$	Add.
$1.3 = x$	Take positive square root of each side.

ANSWER It is 1.3 miles to your friend's house by boat.

Your turn now Use the information in the map.

1. To get to the marina from your house, you travel 0.4 mile directly west, then 0.6 mile directly south. How far is it to the marina by boat? Round your answer to the nearest hundredth of a mile.

EXAMPLE 2 Finding Perimeter and Area

Find the perimeter and area of the triangle.

Solution

(1 Find the height of the triangle.

$$h^2 + 15^2 = 17^2 \qquad \text{Pythagorean theorem}$$

$$h^2 + 225 = 289 \qquad \text{Evaluate powers.}$$

$$h^2 = 64 \qquad \text{Subtract 225 from each side.}$$

$$h = 8 \qquad \text{Take positive square root of each side.}$$

(2 Use the height to find the perimeter and area.

$$\textbf{Perimeter} = 8 + 15 + 17 = 40 \qquad \textbf{Area} = \frac{1}{2}bh$$

$$= \frac{1}{2}(15)(8)$$

$$= 60$$

ANSWER The perimeter is 40 cm and the area is 60 cm^2.

HELP with **Review**

For help with finding the perimeter and area of a triangle, see p. 134.

Your turn now Complete the exercise.

2. Find the perimeter and area of the triangle.

Pythagorean Triples A **Pythagorean triple** is a set of three positive integers *a*, *b*, and *c* such that $a^2 + b^2 = c^2$. For example, the integers 3, 4, and 5 form a Pythagorean triple because $3^2 + 4^2 = 5^2$.

EXAMPLE 3 Identifying a Pythagorean Triple

Determine whether the side lengths of the triangle form a Pythagorean triple.

Solution

$$a^2 + b^2 = c^2 \qquad \text{Definition of Pythagorean triple}$$

$$12^2 + 35^2 \stackrel{?}{=} 37^2 \qquad \text{Substitute 12 for } a \text{, 35 for } b \text{, and 37 for } c.$$

$$144 + 1225 \stackrel{?}{=} 1369 \qquad \text{Evaluate powers.}$$

$$1369 = 1369 \qquad \text{Add.}$$

ANSWER Because $12^2 + 35^2 = 37^2$, the side lengths form a Pythagorean triple.

Getting Ready to Practice

1. **Vocabulary** Copy and complete: The integers 5, 12, and 13 form a ? because $5^2 + 12^2 = 13^2$.

Find the perimeter of the triangle.

2. 9 in., 40 in.

3. 24 ft, 32 ft

4. 60 cm, 61 cm

5. **Guided Problem Solving** A rectangular swimming pool has a length of 41 feet and a width of 11 feet. Tina swims the diagonal distance across the pool. About how far does she swim?

 (1 Draw a diagram.

 (2 Label the known distances.

 (3 Use the Pythagorean theorem to find the unknown length. Round your answer to the nearest tenth of a foot.

Practice and Problem Solving

with Homework

Example	Exercises
1	17–19
2	6–11
3	12–15

Online Resources
CLASSZONE.COM

· More Examples
· eTutorial Plus

Let a and b represent the lengths of the legs of a right triangle, and let c represent the length of the hypotenuse. Find the unknown length. Then find the area and perimeter.

6. $a = 12$ cm, $b = 5$ cm, $c = ?$

7. $a = 8$ ft, $b = ?$, $c = 17$ ft

8. $a = ?$, $b = 4.2$ km, $c = 5.8$ km

9. $a = 4.8$ in., $b = 3.6$ in., $c = ?$

10. $a = 60$ yd, $b = ?$, $c = 601.5$ yd

11. $a = ?$, $b = 117$ m, $c = 125$ m

Determine whether the numbers form a Pythagorean triple.

12. 9, 36, 41

13. 55, 48, 73

14. 39, 80, 89

15. 45, 96, 104

16. **Critical Thinking** Copy and complete the table. Are the Pythagorean triples still Pythagorean triples after they are multiplied by another positive integer? Explain your reasoning.

Pythagorean Triples	3, 4, 5	5, 12, 13	7, 24, 25
Multiply by 2	6, 8, 10	?	?
Multiply by 3	?	?	?
Multiply by 10	?	?	?

Washington Monument

Find the measure of *x*.

17.

x, 18 in., 24 in.

18.

15 in., x, 15 in.

19. Bookshelf You are making a bookshelf. Find *x*. Round to the nearest inch.

20. Draw a Diagram You are standing 500 feet from the Washington Monument. Using a laser range finder on the ground, you measure the distance to the top of the monument to be 747 feet. Find the height of the Washington Monument to the nearest foot.

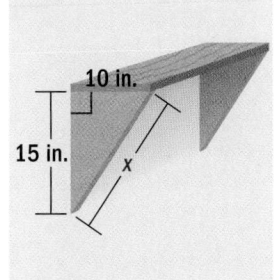

10 in., 15 in., x

Find the perimeter of the right triangle given its area and the length of one leg.

21. $a = 6$ m
Area = 24 m^2

22. $a = 8.8$ mi
Area = 46.2 mi^2

23. $a = 84$ cm
Area = 546 cm^2

24. Challenge Find the area of the shaded region given $\triangle ABC \sim \triangle ADE$, $AB = 10$ ft, $AC = 6$ ft, and $DE = 16$ ft.

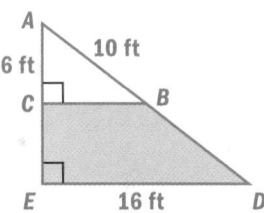

A, 10 ft, 6 ft, C, B, E, 16 ft, D

Mixed Review ⟳

25. Reflect the polygon with the vertices $A(-3, 3)$, $B(-3, 6)$, $C(-5, 3)$, and $D(-6, 1)$ in the *y*-axis. Graph the figure and its image. *(Lesson 8.6)*

Find the square root. *(Lesson 9.1)*

26. $\sqrt{9}$

27. $-\sqrt{144}$

28. $-\sqrt{625}$

29. $\sqrt{72.25}$

FCAT Practice

30. Extended Response Find the area and perimeter of $\triangle ABC$. Explain how you found your answers. Round your answers to the nearest tenth, if necessary.

B, A, C

LESSONS 9.1 TO 9.4

Notebook Review

Review the vocabulary definitions in your notebook.

Copy the review examples in your notebook. Then complete the exercises.

Check Your Definitions

square root, p. 431
radical expression, p. 431
perfect square, p. 432
irrational number, p. 437

real number, p. 437
leg, hypotenuse, p. 443
Pythagorean theorem, p. 443

converse, p. 444
Pythagorean triple, p. 451

Use Your Vocabulary

1. Copy and complete: Together, the rational numbers and the irrational numbers make up the set of _?_.

9.1 Can you solve equations using square roots?

EXAMPLE Solve the equation $x^2 - 18 = 4$.

$x^2 - 18 = 4$	Original equation
$x^2 = 22$	Add 18 to each side.
$x = \pm\sqrt{22}$	Definition of square root
$x \approx \pm 4.69$	Approximate square root.

☑ **Solve the equation.**

2. $a^2 = 169$ **3.** $b^2 - 20 = 101$ **4.** $c^2 + 25 = 89$

9.2 Can you compare two real numbers?

EXAMPLE Graph the numbers $\sqrt{7}$ and 3 on a number line. Then complete the statement $\sqrt{7}$ _?_ 3 with <, >, or =.

$\sqrt{7} \approx 2.6458$ 3

2.5 2.6 2.7 2.8 2.9 3 3.1   So, $\sqrt{7} < 3$.

☑ **Graph the pair of numbers on a number line. Then complete the statement with <, >, or =.**

5. $\sqrt{31}$ _?_ 4   **6.** 7 _?_ $\sqrt{59}$ **7.** -9 _?_ $-\sqrt{81}$ **8.** $\sqrt{48}$ _?_ 6.3

9.3–9.4 Can you use the Pythagorean Theorem?

EXAMPLE Find the unknown length.

$$a^2 + b^2 = c^2 \qquad \text{Pythagorean theorem}$$
$$a^2 + 20^2 = 22^2 \qquad \text{Substitute 20 for } b \text{ and 22 for } c.$$
$$a^2 = 84 \qquad \text{Simplify.}$$
$$a \approx 9.2 \text{ in.} \qquad \text{Take positive square root of each side.}$$

22 in.   a
20 in.

☑ **Let a and b represent the lengths of the legs of a right triangle, and let c represent the length of the hypotenuse. Find the unknown length.**

9. $a = 8, c = 17$ **10.** $b = 24, c = 40$ **11.** $a = 2.4, b = 0.7$

Stop *and* **Think**   about Lessons 9.1–9.4

12. Writing Describe how the decimal forms of rational numbers are different from the decimal form of irrational numbers. Give examples to illustrate your answer.

Review Quiz 1

Use a calculator to approximate the square root. Round to the nearest tenth.

1. $\sqrt{50}$ **2.** $\sqrt{18}$ **3.** $-\sqrt{160}$ **4.** $\sqrt{462}$

Solve the equation. Check your solutions.

5. $x^2 = 400$ **6.** $b^2 - 11 = -2$ **7.** $m^2 + 140 = 284$

8. Order the numbers $2.75, \sqrt{5}, \frac{3}{2}$, and -1 from least to greatest.

9. Find the length of the hypotenuse of a right triangle with leg lengths of 12 meters and 16 meters.

10. Antenna How long must a wire be to connect the top of an 8 foot antenna to a hook 5 feet from the base of the antenna? Round your answer to the nearest tenth of a foot.

?   8 ft
5 ft

Determine whether the numbers form a Pythagorean triple.

11. 5, 12, 15 **12.** 60, 91, 109

Special Right Triangles

BEFORE	▶ Now	WHY?
You solved real-life problems using the Pythagorean theorem.	You'll use special right triangles to solve real-life problems.	So you can find the depth of a subway station, as in Ex. 13.

📖 **Word Watch**

Review Words

equilateral triangle, p. 382
isosceles triangle, p. 382
right triangle, p. 382
scalene triangle, p. 382
leg, p. 443
hypotenuse, p. 443

FLORIDA
Standards and Assessment

• Know the properties of two-dimensional figures. (MA.C.1.3.1)

• Apply the Pythagorean theorem in real-world problems. (MA.C.3.3.1)

In the Real World

Softball The infield of a softball field is a square with a side length of 60 feet. A catcher throws the ball from home plate to second base. How far does the catcher have to throw the ball?

To find missing side lengths of triangles whose angle measures are 45°-45°-90° or 30°-60°-90°, you can use the special relationships among the side lengths.

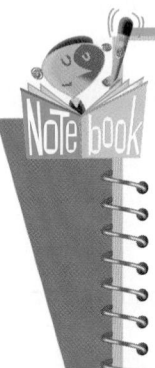

45°-45°-90° Triangle

Words In a 45°-45°-90° triangle, the length of the hypotenuse is the product of the length of a leg and $\sqrt{2}$.

Algebra hypotenuse = leg • $\sqrt{2}$
$$= x\sqrt{2}$$

Diagram

EXAMPLE 1 **Using a 45°-45°-90° Triangle**

To find the distance from home plate to second base, first draw a diagram. Then use the rule for a 45°-45°-90° triangle.

$$\text{hypotenuse} = \textbf{leg} \cdot \sqrt{2}$$
$$= \textbf{60} \cdot \sqrt{2}$$
$$\approx 60(1.414)$$
$$= 84.84$$

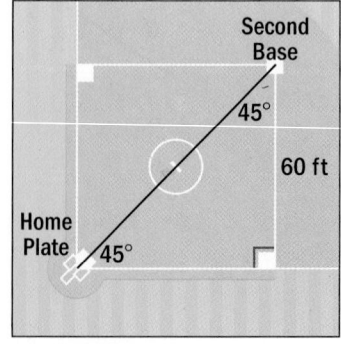

ANSWER A catcher has to throw the ball about 84.84 feet.

30°-60°-90° Triangle

Words In a 30°-60°-90° triangle, the hypotenuse is twice as long as the shorter leg. The length of the longer leg is the product of the length of the shorter leg and $\sqrt{3}$.

Diagram

Algebra hypotenuse = 2 • shorter leg

$$= 2x$$

longer leg = shorter leg • $\sqrt{3}$

$$= x\sqrt{3}$$

HELP with **Solving**

In a 30°-60°-90° triangle, the shorter leg is opposite the 30° angle, and the longer leg is opposite the 60° angle.

To give an *exact answer,* leave your answer as a radical expression.

EXAMPLE 2 **Using a 30°-60°-90° Triangle**

Find the value of each variable in the triangle. Give the exact answer.

You need to find the length of the shorter leg first in order to find the length of the longer leg.

① Find the length of the shorter leg.

hypotenuse = 2 • **shorter leg**	Rule for 30°-60°-90° triangle
$10 = 2 \cdot x$	Substitute.
$5 = x$	Divide each side by 2.

② Find the length of the longer leg.

| longer leg = **shorter leg** • $\sqrt{3}$ | Rule for 30°-60°-90° triangle |
| $y = 5\sqrt{3}$ | Substitute. |

ANSWER The length of the shorter leg is 5 units. The length of the longer leg is $5\sqrt{3}$ units.

HELP with **Solving**

You can use the Pythagorean theorem to check the solutions in Examples 1 and 2.

Your turn now **Find the value of each variable. Give exact answers.**

1.

2.

3.

EXAMPLE 3 **Using a Special Right Triangle**

Water Ski Show The pyramid ski show is a common feature of water parks. Find the horizontal distance from the pyramid to the boat.

⓵ Find the length of the shorter leg.

hypotenuse = 2 • shorter leg

$26 = 2 \cdot x$

$13 = x$

⓶ Find the length of the longer leg.

longer leg = shorter leg • $\sqrt{3}$

$y = 13 \cdot \sqrt{3}$

≈ 22.5166605

ANSWER The horizontal distance is about 23 feet.

9.5 Exercises

More Practice, p. 735

INTERNET
eWorkbook Plus
CLASSZONE.COM

Getting Ready to Practice

1. **Vocabulary** Explain how the length of the hypotenuse in a 45°-45°-90° triangle is related to the length of a leg.

Find the value of the variable. Give the exact answer.

2.

3.

4. **Find the Error** Describe and correct the error in the solution.

5. **Guided Problem Solving** The hypotenuse of a 30°-60°-90° triangle is $5\sqrt{3}$ inches. Find the length of the longer leg.

   ⓵ Find the length of the shorter leg.

   ⓶ Use the shorter leg to find the length of the longer leg.

Practice and Problem Solving

HELP with **Homework**

Example	Exercises
1	6–8
2	9–11
3	13

Online Resources
CLASSZONE.COM
· More Examples
· eTutorial Plus

Find the value of each variable. Give exact answers.

6.

7.

8.

9.

10.

11.

12. Critical Thinking Is it possible to have an equilateral right triangle? Explain your reasoning.

13. Escalator The escalator going down to the main floor of a subway station is 230 feet long and makes a 30° angle with the main floor. How many feet below ground is the subway station?

Find the value of each variable. Give exact answers.

14.

15.

16.

17.

18.

19.

20. Quilting Find the perimeters of the five squares in the diagram of the Snail's Trail quilt pattern at the right. The triangles used in this pattern are 45°-45°-90° triangles. Round your answers to the nearest inch, if necessary.

21. Writing Use the Pythagorean theorem to verify that the 30°-60°-90° rule works. Give an example.

22. Critical Thinking How can you find the area of the triangle shown? (*Hint:* You can fold the triangle in half to create two congruent 30°-60°-90° triangles.)

23. Challenge In the diagram below, △ABC ~ △XYZ. Find all unknown side lengths of the triangles. Give exact answers.

Mixed Review

Find the quotient. (*Lesson 5.4*)

24. $\dfrac{5}{11} \div \dfrac{5}{11}$

25. $\dfrac{3}{10} \div \dfrac{1}{5}$

26. $\dfrac{4}{15} \div \left(-\dfrac{12}{25}\right)$

Write the rate as a unit rate. (*Lesson 7.1*)

27. $\dfrac{28 \text{ people}}{4 \text{ teams}}$

28. $\dfrac{60 \text{ meters}}{20 \text{ seconds}}$

29. $\dfrac{488 \text{ rotations}}{8 \text{ minutes}}$

Basic Skills Solve the equation.

30. $165 = -5z$

31. $77 = 7.7p$

32. $19 = \dfrac{w}{4.2}$

FCAT Practice

33. Multiple Choice The hypotenuse of a 45°-45°-90° triangle has a length of $5\sqrt{2}$ inches. What is the length of a leg?

    A. 5 inches   **B.** $5\sqrt{2}$ inches

    C. 25 inches   **D.** $25\sqrt{2}$ inches

34. Multiple Choice The hypotenuse of a 30°-60°-90° triangle has a length of $20\sqrt{3}$ feet. What is the length of the longer leg?

    F. $10\sqrt{3}$ feet   **G.** 30 feet

    H. 50 feet   **I.** $50\sqrt{3}$ feet

Hands-on Activity

FLORIDA: Standards and Assessment
Make and test conjectures about geometric
relationships. (MA.C.3.3.1)

GOAL
Find the sine and
cosine ratios of right
triangles.

MATERIALS
· metric ruler
· protractor

Exploring Trigonometric Ratios

You can use a protractor and metric ruler to find the ratios of the length of
each leg of a right triangle to the hypotenuse.

Explore   **Find ratios of side lengths of similar right triangles.**

1 Draw a 40° angle. Mark tick marks
every 5 centimeters along one side.

2 Draw perpendicular line segments
from four of the tick marks to intersect
with the other side of the angle.

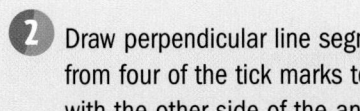

3 There are four similar triangles in your drawing. Measure the legs of each triangle in your
drawing to the nearest tenth. Then copy and complete the table. Round your answers to
the nearest hundredth.

Triangle	Leg 1	Leg 2	Hypotenuse	Leg 1 / Hypotenuse	Leg 2 / Hypotenuse
△ABC	5 cm	?	?	?	?
△ADE	10 cm	?	?	?	?
△AFG	15 cm	?	?	?	?
△AHJ	20 cm	?	?	?	?

Explore **Look for a pattern.**

4 Is there a pattern in the ratios $\dfrac{\text{Leg 1}}{\text{Hypotenuse}}$? If so, what is it?

5 Is there a pattern in the ratios $\dfrac{\text{Leg 2}}{\text{Hypotenuse}}$? If so, what is it?

6 Repeat Steps 1-5 using a 70° angle. Based on your results, do the ratios depend on the lengths of the right triangles' sides or on the measures of their angles?

The ratios $\dfrac{\text{Leg 1}}{\text{Hypotenuse}}$ and $\dfrac{\text{Leg 2}}{\text{Hypotenuse}}$ have special names. They are called the *sine*

and *cosine* ratios and can be defined as follows:

$$\sin A = \dfrac{\text{length of leg opposite } \angle A}{\text{length of hypotenuse}} \qquad \cos A = \dfrac{\text{length of leg adjacent to } \angle A}{\text{length of hypotenuse}}$$

Your turn now **Find the sine and cosine ratios for $\angle A$ and $\angle B$.**

1.

2.

3.

4.

5.

6.

Stop *and* **Think**

7. **Critical Thinking** Measure angle A in each triangle in Exercises 1–6. Write the measures in order from least to greatest. Make a table that shows $m\angle A$, $\sin A$, and $\cos A$. Then copy and complete the following two statements using *increases* or *decreases*.

   a. As $m\angle A$ increases from 0° to 90°, the value of $\sin A$ _?_ .

   b. As $m\angle A$ increases from 0° to 90°, the value of $\cos A$ _?_ .

Using Trigonometric Ratios

BEFORE	▶ Now	WHY?
You found the side lengths of special right triangles.	You'll use trigonometric ratios to find the side lengths.	So you can find the height of a totem pole, as in Ex. 5.

In the Real World

Word Watch

trigonometric ratio, p. 463
sine, p. 463
cosine, p. 463
tangent, p. 463

FLORIDA
Standards and Assessment

• Know the properties of two-dimensional figures. (MA.C.1.3.1)
• Solve real-world problems. (MA.A.3.3.2)

Water Slide A water slide makes an angle of about 18° with the ground. The slide extends horizontally about 64.2 meters. What is the height of the slide? You will see how to solve this problem in Example 5.

You can find the height of the water slide using a *trigonometric ratio*. A **trigonometric ratio** is a ratio of the lengths of two sides of a right triangle. The three basic trigonometric ratios are **sine**, **cosine**, and **tangent**. These are abbreviated as *sin*, *cos*, and *tan*.

Trigonometric Ratios

$$\sin A = \frac{\text{side opposite } \angle A}{\text{hypotenuse}} = \frac{a}{c}$$

$$\cos A = \frac{\text{side adjacent to } \angle A}{\text{hypotenuse}} = \frac{b}{c}$$

$$\tan A = \frac{\text{side opposite } \angle A}{\text{side adjacent to } \angle A} = \frac{a}{b}$$

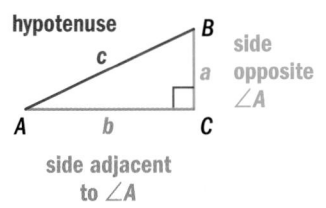

EXAMPLE 1 Finding Trigonometric Ratios

HELP with Solving

Determining the opposite and adjacent sides depends on the angle that is being used. For ∠Q, the length of the opposite side is 12 feet, and the length of the adjacent side is 5 feet.

In △PQR, write the sine, cosine, and tangent ratios for ∠P.

For ∠P, the length of the opposite side is 5 feet, and the length of the adjacent side is 12 feet. The length of the hypotenuse is 13 feet.

$$\sin P = \frac{\text{opposite}}{\text{hypotenuse}} = \frac{5}{13}$$

$$\cos P = \frac{\text{adjacent}}{\text{hypotenuse}} = \frac{12}{13}$$

$$\tan P = \frac{\text{opposite}}{\text{adjacent}} = \frac{5}{12}$$

EXAMPLE 2 Using a Calculator

Use a calculator to find sine, cosine, and tangent of 30°.

	Keystrokes	Display	Answer
a.	[2nd] [TRIG] ☐ 30 ☐	0.5	sin 30° = 0.5
b.	[2nd] [TRIG] ▶ ▶ ☐ 30 ☐	0.8660254	cos 30° ≈ 0.8660
c.	[2nd] [TRIG] ◀ ◀ ☐ 30 ☐	0.5773503	tan 30° ≈ 0.5774

Your turn now Complete the exercise.

1. For $\triangle ABC$, write the sine, cosine, and tangent ratios for $\angle A$ and $\angle C$.

Use a calculator to approximate the given expression. Round your answer to four decimal places.

2. cos 70°   **3.** tan 50°   **4.** sin 25°   **5.** cos 42°   **6.** tan 7°

EXAMPLE 3 Using a Cosine Ratio

Find the value of *x* in the triangle.

The length of the hypotenuse is 8 inches. The unknown side is adjacent to the given angle. Use cosine of $\angle K$.

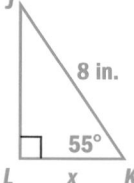

$$\cos K = \frac{\text{adjacent}}{\text{hypotenuse}}$$ **Definition of cosine**

$$\cos 55° = \frac{x}{8}$$ **Substitute.**

$$0.5736 \approx \frac{x}{8}$$ **Use a calculator to approximate cos 55°.**

$$0.5736 \cdot 8 \approx \frac{x}{8} \cdot 8$$ **Multiply each side by 8.**

$$4.5888 \approx x$$ **Simplify.**

ANSWER The value of *x* is about 4.59 inches.

Your turn now Complete the exercise.

7. Find the value of *x* in the triangle. Round your answer to the nearest hundredth of a foot.

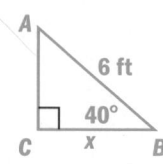

EXAMPLE 4 **Using a Sine Ratio**

Ski Jump A ski jump is 380 feet long and makes a 27.6° angle with the ground. Find the height of the ski jump.

Solution

Use the sine ratio and a calculator to find the value of x.

$$\sin 27.6° = \frac{\text{opposite}}{\text{hypotenuse}} \qquad \textbf{Definition of sine}$$

$$\sin 27.6° = \frac{x}{380} \qquad \textbf{Substitute.}$$

$$0.4633 \approx \frac{x}{380} \qquad \textbf{Use a calculator to approximate sin 27.6°.}$$

$$0.4633 \cdot 380 \approx \frac{x}{380} \cdot 380 \qquad \textbf{Multiply each side by 380.}$$

$$176.054 \approx x \qquad \textbf{Simplify.}$$

ANSWER The ski jump is about 176 feet high.

EXAMPLE 5 **Using a Tangent Ratio**

Water Slide To find the height h of the water slide on page 463, use the tangent ratio.

$$\tan 18° = \frac{\text{opposite}}{\text{adjacent}} \qquad \textbf{Definition of tangent}$$

$$\tan 18° = \frac{h}{64.2} \qquad \textbf{Substitute.}$$

$$0.3249 \approx \frac{h}{64.2} \qquad \textbf{Use a calculator to approximate tan 18°.}$$

$$0.3249 \cdot 64.2 \approx \frac{h}{64.2} \cdot 64.2 \qquad \textbf{Multiply each side by 64.2.}$$

$$20.85858 \approx h \qquad \textbf{Simplify.}$$

ANSWER The height of the water slide is about 21 meters.

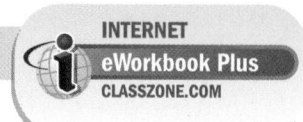

Getting Ready to Practice

Matching **Match the term with the correct ratio.**

1. sine   **2.** cosine   **3.** tangent

A. $\dfrac{\text{adjacent}}{\text{hypotenuse}}$ **B.** $\dfrac{\text{opposite}}{\text{hypotenuse}}$ **C.** $\dfrac{\text{opposite}}{\text{adjacent}}$

4. Write the sine, cosine, and tangent ratios in simplest form, for $\angle A$ and $\angle B$ in $\triangle ABC$.

5. **Guided Problem Solving** You stand 50 feet from a totem pole that is perpendicular to the ground. The angle from the point where you stand to the top of the totem pole is 42°. How tall is the totem pole?

(**1** Draw a diagram and identify the sides of the triangle.

(**2** Write an equation using a trigonometric ratio.

(**3** Solve the equation. Round your answer to the nearest foot.

Practice and Problem Solving

In $\triangle PQR$, write the sine, cosine, and tangent ratios for $\angle P$ and $\angle R$.

6.

7.

8.

Use a calculator to approximate the given expression. Round your answer to four decimal places.

9. tan 51°   **10.** sin 80°   **11.** sin 36°   **12.** cos 76°

Find the value of x. Round your answer to the nearest thousandth.

13.

14.

15.

16. **Writing** Explain how to decide which trigonometric ratio (sine, cosine, or tangent) is best for solving a particular problem.

17. Draw a Diagram Sketch right triangle *ABC* that has the given trigonometric ratios: $\tan A = \frac{15}{8}$ and $\cos B = \frac{15}{17}$. Label each side with its length.

18. Algebra Write the trigonometric ratios for $\angle A$ and $\angle B$ in $\triangle ABC$.

19. Find the Error Describe and correct the error in the solution.

$\tan 25° = \frac{x}{15}$ so $x \approx 7$ cm

20. Cats You are constructing a scratching post and platform for your cat. Find the length *x* of the scratching post. Round your answer to the nearest tenth of a foot.

Find the value of the unknown angle and side. Then write three trigonometric ratios for $\angle A$.

21.

22.

23.

Extended Problem Solving **In Exercises 24–26, use the following information. Round your answer to the nearest whole number.**

Some whales have been known to dive down to a depth of 3000 meters in search of their favorite food.

24. Calculate The whale shown finds food after swimming 2000 m. How deep is the water where the whale found its food?

25. Calculate How far is the whale along the ocean surface from the point where it started to the point directly above the spot where it found its food?

26. Compare Did this whale dive more or less than $\frac{1}{2}$ of the deepest known dive?

Find the perimeter of the triangle. Round your answer to the nearest tenth.

27.

28.

29.

30. **Critical Thinking** Can the values for the sine or cosine of one of the acute angles in a right triangle be greater than or equal to 1? Explain.

31. **Challenge** Find the area of the isosceles triangle. Round your answer to the nearest tenth.

32. **Aviation** An airplane is at an altitude of 33,000 feet when the pilot starts the descent to the airport. The pilot wants the plane to descend at an angle of 3°. How many miles away from the airport must the descent begin? Round your answer to the nearest mile.

Mixed Review

33. Find the sum of 9.87 and $\frac{43}{50}$. Write your answer in decimal form. *(Lessons 5.5, 5.6)*

34. What type of transformation is modeled by a merry-go-round? *(Lesson 8.7)*

Tell whether the number is *rational* or *irrational*. Explain. *(Lesson 9.2)*

35. $\sqrt{484}$

36. $\sqrt{99}$

37. $\sqrt{\frac{17}{29}}$

38. $\sqrt{\frac{144}{225}}$

Basic Skills Use the distance formula to find the rate.

39. $d = 145$ mi, $t = 40$ h

40. $d = 78$ m, $t = 20$ sec

FCAT Practice

41. **Multiple Choice** Find the tangent of $\angle E$.

   A. 13   **B.** $\frac{5}{13}$ **C.** $\frac{12}{13}$ **D.** $\frac{5}{12}$

42. **Multiple Choice** Find the measurement closest to the length of side $\overline{AB}$.

   F. $7\sqrt{2}$ ft   **G.** 10 ft   **H.** 12 ft   **I.** 14 ft

Technology Activity

FLORIDA: Standards and Assessment
Determine and justify angle measures in figures. (MA.C.1.3.1)

Finding an Angle Measure

GOAL Use a calculator to find an angle measure using the inverse of a trigonometric ratio.

In some situations, you need to find a particular angle of a given triangle. You can use the inverse of a trigonometric ratio to find the measure of the angle. For example, you can use the inverse tangent feature of your calculator to solve the following problem. The inverse tangent formula is:

$$\text{If } \tan x° = \frac{a}{b}, \text{ then } x° = \tan^{-1}\left(\frac{a}{b}\right).$$

Example In the 1870s, a cable car system was built in San Francisco. A section of California Street has a vertical height of 76 feet and a horizontal length of 420 feet. Find the angle of the hill, $x°$.

 with Technology

To evaluate an inverse tangent on your calculator, press the 2nd key. Then press the [TRIG] key. Use the right or left arrow to highlight the inverse tangent feature and then press ▭. Enter the ratio and press ▭ again. The result is the angle measure.

Solution

To find the angle, use inverse tangent.

$\tan x° = \dfrac{\text{opposite}}{\text{adjacent}}$ **Definition of tangent**

$\tan x° = \dfrac{76}{420}$ **Substitute.**

$x° = \tan^{-1}\left(\dfrac{76}{420}\right)$ **Definition of inverse tangent**

$x \approx 10.3$ **Use your calculator to approximate.**

ANSWER The angle of the hill is about 10°.

Your turn now Use a calculator to approximate the expression. Round to the nearest tenth of a degree.

1. $\tan^{-1}(0.25)$ **2.** $\tan^{-1}(0.14)$ **3.** $\tan^{-1}(0.92)$

4. $\tan^{-1}(1.05)$ **5.** $\tan^{-1}(24.65)$ **6.** $\tan^{-1}(64.25)$

7. Critical Thinking Given $\tan^{-1}(0.18)$ and $\tan^{-1}(32.46)$, which one would you expect to represent the largest angle? Why?

Notebook Review

Review the vocabulary definitions in your notebook.

Copy the review examples in your notebook. Then complete the exercises.

Check Your Definitions

trigonometric ratio, p. 463

sine, p. 463

cosine, p. 463

tangent, p. 463

Use Your Vocabulary

1. Copy and complete: To write the sine ratio for a given acute angle of a right triangle, you need to know the length of the side _?_ the angle and the length of the _?_.

9.5 Can you find side lengths of special right triangles?

EXAMPLE Find the length of the hypotenuse. Give the exact answer.

hypotenuse = leg · $\sqrt{2}$ Rule for 45°-45°-90° triangle

    = $26\sqrt{2}$ Substitute.

ANSWER The length of the hypotenuse is $26\sqrt{2}$ feet.

☑ **Find the value of each variable. Give the exact answer.**

2.

3.

4.

9.6 Can you use trigonometric ratios?

EXAMPLE In $\triangle ABC$, write the sine, cosine, and tangent ratios for $\angle A$.

$\sin A = \dfrac{\text{opposite}}{\text{hypotenuse}} = \dfrac{12}{37}$

$\cos A = \dfrac{\text{adjacent}}{\text{hypotenuse}} = \dfrac{35}{37}$

$\tan A = \dfrac{\text{opposite}}{\text{adjacent}} = \dfrac{12}{35}$

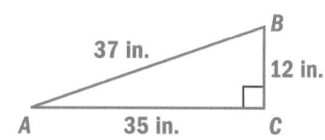

☑ **In △ABC, write the sine, cosine, and tangent ratios for ∠A and ∠B.**

5.

6.

7.

Stop and Think about Lessons 9.5–9.6

8. Writing Describe how to find the cosine ratio for one of the acute angles of a right triangle when you know that its sine ratio is $\frac{3}{5}$.

Review Quiz 2

Find the value of each variable. Give exact answers.

1.

2.

3.

In △ABC, write the sine, cosine, and tangent ratios for ∠A and ∠B.

4.

5.

6.

7. Aviation If a plane flies 1° off course for 2000 miles, how far away will the plane be from the correct path? Round to the nearest tenth of a mile.

A Real Winner

Replace each expression with the letter of its decimal approximation to find the name of a person who won the Nobel Prize in both physics and chemistry.

cos 15° sin 52° cos 85° sin 60° cos 45°

tan 30° tan 12° sin 5° cos 30° sin 45°

A 0.7880
C 0.5774
D 0.6157
E 0.7071
I 0.8660

M 0.9659
R 0.0872
S 0.9962
T 0.5000
U 0.2126

C H A P T E R

9

Chapter Review

 Vocabulary

square root, p. 431
radical expression, p. 431
perfect square, p. 432
irrational number, p. 437
real number, p. 437
leg, p. 443

hypotenuse, p. 443
Pythagorean theorem,
 p. 443
converse, p. 444
Pythagorean triple, p. 451

trigonometric ratio,
 p. 463
sine, p. 463
cosine, p. 463
tangent, p. 463

Vocabulary Review

1. Describe the difference between a *rational number* and an *irrational number*.

2. Give three examples of rational numbers.

3. Give three examples of irrational numbers.

4. Describe how the *lengths of the legs* and *the length of the hypotenuse* of a right triangle are related.

Copy and complete the statement.

5. A(n) _?_ is any number that has integer square roots.

6. In a right triangle, the side opposite the right angle is the _?_.

7. In a 30°-60°-90° triangle, the _?_ leg is opposite the 30° angle.

8. Sine, cosine, and tangent are _?_ ratios.

Review Questions

Use a calculator to approximate the square root. Round to the nearest hundredth, if necessary. *(Lesson 9.1)*

9. $\sqrt{94.09}$ **10.** $-\sqrt{784}$ **11.** $-\sqrt{2118}$ **12.** $\sqrt{941}$

Solve the equation. *(Lesson 9.1)*

13. $m^2 = 196$ **14.** $a^2 - 1296 = 0$ **15.** $c^2 - 28 = 36$ **16.** $x^2 + 15 = 51$

Tell whether the number is *rational* or *irrational*. Explain your reasoning. *(Lesson 9.2)*

17. $\sqrt{100}$ **18.** $0.\overline{6}$ **19.** $\frac{16}{25}$ **20.** $\sqrt{6}$

21. Order the decimals $0.1\overline{8}$, $0.\overline{181}$, $0.\overline{18}$, and 0.188 from least to greatest. *(Lesson 9.2)*

Review Questions

Find the unknown length. *(Lesson 9.3)*

22.
24 ft, c, 32 ft

23.
61 in., 60 in., a

24.
80 m, 48 m, b

Determine whether the numbers form a Pythagorean triple. *(Lesson 9.4)*

25. 9, 40, 45   **26.** 24, 10, 28   **27.** 72, 54, 90   **28.** 133, 156, 205

29. Ski Lift A ski lift has a horizontal length of 662 meters and a vertical height of 152 meters. Find the length of the ski lift. Round to the nearest hundredth of a meter. *(Lesson 9.4)*

Not drawn to scale
Cables
152 m
662 m

Find the value of each variable. Give exact answers. *(Lesson 9.5)*

30.
x, x, 45°, $65\sqrt{2}$ in.

31.
60°, y, 15 m, 30°, x

32.
50 ft, 30°, 60°, y, x

In △*PQR***, write the sine, cosine, and tangent ratios for ∠***P*** and ∠***Q***.** *(Lesson 9.6)*

33.
P, 20 ft, 29 ft, R, 21 ft, Q

34.
P, 36 in., R, 45 in., 27 in., Q

35.
R, 80 cm, 84 cm, P, 116 cm, Q

Use a calculator to approximate the given expression. Round your answer to four decimal places. *(Lesson 9.6)*

36. sin 72°   **37.** tan 18.5°   **38.** cos 49°   **39.** tan 40°

40. Skateboard Ramp You are constructing a skateboard ramp like the one shown in the diagram. Find the lengths of the legs of the triangle that supports the ramp. Round your answers to the nearest tenth of a foot. *(Lesson 9.6)*

x, 8 ft, 20°, y

Chapter Test

Solve the equation.

1. $x^2 = 49$ **2.** $m^2 + 41 = 162$ **3.** $n^2 - 63 = 162$ **4.** $a^2 + 88 = 232$

5. Zoology Dr. R. McNeill Alexander studies the motion of animals. From his studies, he determined that the maximum walking speed s, in feet per second, that an animal can walk is $s = 5.66\sqrt{l}$ where l is the animal's leg length, in feet. What is the maximum walking speed for an ostrich with a leg length of 4 feet?

Graph each pair of numbers on a number line. Then copy and complete the statement with <, >, or =.

6. $\sqrt{9}$ _?_ 3   **7.** -11 _?_ $-\sqrt{11}$ **8.** $\sqrt{12}$ _?_ 4

Find the length of the unknown side of the right triangle. Round to the nearest tenth, if necessary. Then find the area and perimeter.

9.

6.4 m

8 m

10.

11 ft   11 ft

11.

122 mm

120 mm

Determine whether the triangle with the given side lengths is a right triangle.

12. $a = 28, b = 96, c = 100$ **13.** $a = 22.5, b = 30, c = 37.5$ **14.** $a = 3.6, b = 5.8, c = 5.9$

Find the value of each variable. Give exact answers.

15.

y 7 cm

45°

x

16.

x 13 $\sqrt{2}$ ft

45°

x

17.

6 $\sqrt{3}$ in.

30°

x 60° y

18. Incline In the 1870s, a motorized incline was built in Pittsburgh, PA, to climb the steep hill known as Mt. Washington located at the mouth of the Monongahela River. The track of the incline is 793 feet long and makes a 30° angle with the ground. Find the height of the boarding platform at the top of the incline.

793 ft

x

30°

Chapter FCAT Practice

FCAT

Test-Taking Strategy Some questions involve more than one step. Read each question carefully to be sure you are answering the right question.

Multiple Choice

1. What is the negative square root of 144?

    A. -24 **B.** -12 **C.** 12 **D.** 24

2. Which number is not irrational?

    F. π **G.** $\sqrt{7}$ **H.** $\sqrt{97}$ **I.** $\sqrt{324}$

3. Which statement is *not* true?

    A. $\sqrt{24} < 6$ **B.** $-\sqrt{5} < -5$

    C. $-\sqrt{2} < -1$ **D.** $\sqrt{121} = 11$

4. Find the length of the hypotenuse of a right triangle with leg lengths of 1.5 feet and 3.6 feet.

    F. 3.3 feet   **G.** 3.9 feet

    H. 5.4 feet   **I.** 10.71 feet

5. You are flying a kite. You have let out 250 feet of string. The kite's shadow is 150 feet from you, and the sun is directly overhead. How high is the kite?

150 ft

    A. 125 feet   **B.** 175 feet

    C. 200 feet   **D.** 220 feet

6. Which group of numbers *does not* form a Pythagorean triple?

    F. 3, 4, 8   **G.** 5, 12, 13

    H. 12, 16, 20   **I.** 9, 40, 41

7. Find the length of the longer leg.

    A. $\sqrt{3}$ inches   **B.** $12\sqrt{3}$ inches

    C. $24\sqrt{3}$ inches   **D.** 48 inches

8. In $\triangle ABC$, find $\cos A$.

    F. $\dfrac{8}{17}$ **G.** $\dfrac{8}{15}$ **H.** $\dfrac{15}{17}$ **I.** $\dfrac{15}{8}$

Short Response

9. **Gardening** You have a square plot of land with a side length of 15 feet. You want to plant a garden. The packet of flower seeds that you bought says that it will cover 150 square feet. Do you have enough seed? Explain.

Extended Response

10. **Quilting** Jenwa is making a quilt using a design based on the pattern shown below. This pattern is a spiral design using right triangles. It is called the Wheel of Theodorus. Working from left to right, use the Pythagorean theorem in each right triangle to find the values of r, s, t, and u. Then identify the 45°-45°-90° triangle in the figure.

Viewing the STARS

Aiming a Telescope

Earth's atmosphere extends about 1000 kilometers from its surface. As light from stars passes through the atmosphere, some of it is absorbed or scattered by the molecules in the air. Without atmospheric interference, the stars in the night sky would appear much brighter.

An astronomer can minimize this interference by aiming a telescope so that star light passes through as little atmosphere as possible. If you know a star's *angle of elevation*, you can use trigonometry to find how far its light travels through the atmosphere to reach the telescope.

Angle of Elevation In the diagram, light from a star travels a distance of d kilometers through Earth's atmosphere to the telescope. The measure of the star's *angle of elevation* above Earth's surface is $x°$.

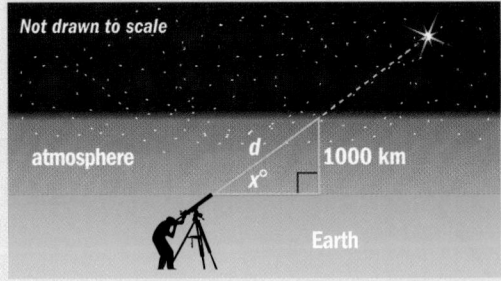

Not drawn to scale

atmosphere d 1000 km

$x°$

Earth

1. Because $\sin x° = \dfrac{1000}{d}$, you can use the equation $d = \dfrac{1000}{\sin x°}$ to find d. Copy and complete the table below.

angle of elevation $x°$	10°	20°	30°	40°	50°	60°	70°	80°
distance d (km)								

2. **Critical Thinking** At what angle should you aim a telescope to look through the least amount of atmosphere? Explain your reasoning.

Comparing Observatories

Observatories, buildings devoted to observing the night sky, are often placed at high elevations. Hanle Observatory in India, the world's highest, is about 4.5 kilometers above sea level.

How does raising a telescope's elevation affect the distance a star's light travels through the atmosphere for a given angle of elevation? Use the formula from the previous page to find out.

Telescope at Sea Level

Telescope at Hanle Observatory

3. Find the distance *d*, in kilometers, that light travels through the atmosphere to reach a telescope at sea level, given an angle of elevation of 45°. Then find the value of *d* for Hanle Observatory.

4. **Critical Thinking** Compare the distances you found in Exercise 3. How does a change in elevation affect *d*? Do you think this difference is significant? Explain.

Project IDEAS

- **Experiment** Measure an object's shadow. Draw a diagram to explain how to use trigonometry to find the object's height if you know the shadow's length and the sun's angle of elevation. Present your findings to the class.

- **Extension** Locate some major astronomical observatories placed at high elevations, and find out why these locations were chosen. Present your findings to the class.

- **Research** The angle of elevation of the moon above Earth's horizon may affect its apparent color. Find out how and why an object's apparent color changes as it moves across the sky. Present your findings to the class.

- **Career** What subjects would you study if you were preparing to be an astronomer? Present your findings to the class.

INTERNET
Project Support
CLASSZONE.COM

10

Measurement, Area, and Volume

BEFORE

In previous chapters you've...

- Found the areas of rectangles
- Identified and sketched polygons

Now

In Chapter 10 you'll study...

- Finding the areas of circles, parallelograms, and trapezoids
- Identifying and sketching three-dimensional figures
- Finding the surface areas and volumes of solids

WHY?

So you can solve real-world problems about...

- architecture, p. 482
- hockey, p. 487
- recycling, p. 515
- swimming pools, p. 517

Internet Preview
CLASSZONE.COM

- eEdition Plus Online
- eWorkbook Plus Online
- eTutorial Plus Online
- FCAT Practice
- More Examples

Chapter Warm-Up Game

Review skills you need for this chapter in this quick game. Work with a partner.

Key Skills:
Finding the perimeter, area, or circumference of squares, rectangles, triangles, and circles

MEASURE MATCH

MATERIALS

- 15 Picture Cards

- 15 Measure Cards

PREPARE Place all cards face down and mix them up. On your turn follow the steps on the next page.

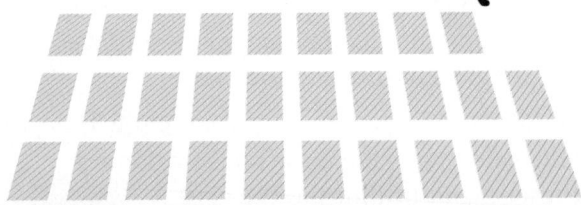

A = 54 in.²

Area

6 in.

9 in.

1 **TURN** over two cards.

2 **DECIDE** whether the two cards match. Cards match when you turn over a Picture Card and a Measure Card that describes the picture. If the cards match, you may keep them. Otherwise, turn them back over.

3 **REMEMBER** where the cards are so you can find matching pairs on future turns.

HOW TO WIN

Be the player with the most cards once all the cards have been matched.

Stop *and* **Think**

1. **Writing** If the Measure Cards did not have A, P, or C on them, would you still be able to tell what was being measured? Explain.

2. **Extension** Design six new cards for *Measure Match*. Three should be Picture Cards and three should be Measure Cards. Make sure each Picture Card matches a Measure Card.

Getting Ready to Learn

Word Watch

Review Words

area, p. 33
base, p. 134
height, p. 134
circle, p. 290
radius, p. 290
pi (π), p. 290
trapezoid, p. 386
parallelogram, p. 386
rhombus, p. 386

Review What You Need to Know

Using Vocabulary **Classify the figure indicated using a review word.**

1. quadrilateral *ABCD*

2. $\overline{PQ}$

3. quadrilateral *JKLM*

Find the area of the shaded region. *(Lessons 1.6, 3.5)*

4.

5.

6.

You should include material that appears on a notebook like this in your own notes.

Know How to Take Notes

Using a Concept Grid You can use a concept grid to organize what you know about a topic.

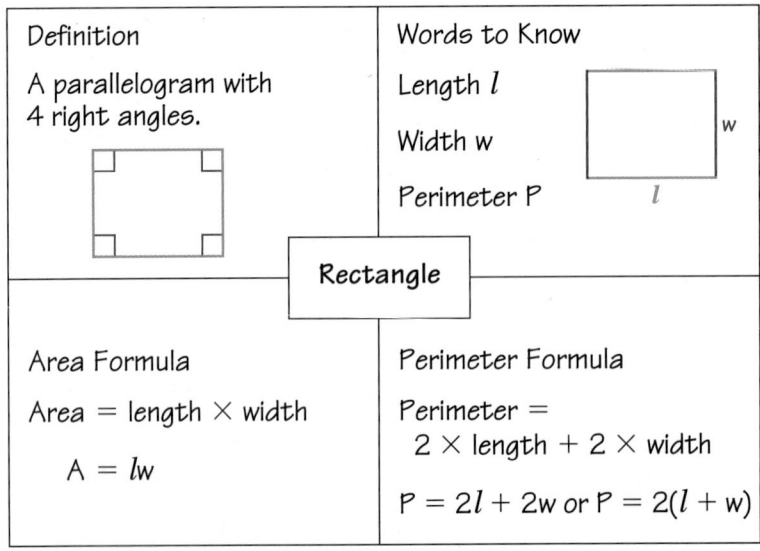

In Lesson 10.2, you will learn the formula for the area of a circle. Then you can make a concept grid for circles.

Areas of Parallelograms and Trapezoids

BEFORE	▶ Now	WHY?
You found the areas of triangles and rectangles.	You'll find the areas of parallelograms and trapezoids.	So you can find the area of one side of a podium, as in Ex. 32.

Word Watch

base of a parallelogram, p. 481
height of a parallelogram, p. 481
bases of a trapezoid, p. 482
height of a trapezoid, p. 482

FLORIDA
Standards and Assessment

• Know the properties of two-dimensional figures. (MA.C.1.3.1)

• Solve problems involving changes in dimensions and area. (MA.B.1.3.3)

The **base of a parallelogram** can be any one of its sides.
The **height of a parallelogram** is the perpendicular distance between the base and the opposite side.

The diagram below shows how to change a parallelogram into a rectangle with the same base, height, and area.

Start with any parallelogram.	**Cut the parallelogram to form a right triangle and a trapezoid.**	**Move the triangle to form a rectangle.**

The area of the rectangle is the product of the base and the height, so the formula for the area of the parallelogram is $A = bh$.

Area of a Parallelogram

Words The area of a parallelogram is the product of the base and the height.

$h = 3$ cm
$b = 5$ cm

Algebra $A = bh$

Numbers $A = 5 \cdot 3 = 15$ cm^2

EXAMPLE 1 Finding the Area of a Parallelogram

Find the area of the parallelogram.

$A = bh$ Write formula for area.

$= 8 \cdot 10$ Substitute 8 for b and 10 for h.

$= 80$ Multiply.

10 in.
8 in.

ANSWER The parallelogram has an area of 80 square inches.

HELP with Reading

The bases of a trapezoid are labeled b_1 and b_2. You read these labels as "b sub one" and "b sub two." For help with trapezoids, see p. 386.

Trapezoids The **bases of a trapezoid** are its parallel sides. The **height of a trapezoid** is the perpendicular distance between the bases. The diagram below shows how two congruent trapezoids with height h and bases b_1 and b_2 can form a parallelogram with height h and base $b_1 + b_2$.

The area of the parallelogram is $(b_1 + b_2)h$, so the area of each trapezoid is $\frac{1}{2}(b_1 + b_2)h$.

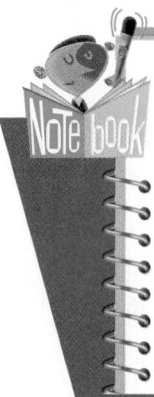

Area of a Trapezoid

Words The area of a trapezoid is one half the product of the sum of the bases and the height.

$b_1 = 4$ m
$h = 3$ m
$b_2 = 8$ m

Algebra $A = \frac{1}{2}(b_1 + b_2)h$ **Numbers** $A = \frac{1}{2}(4 + 8)3 = 18$ m^2

EXAMPLE 2 **Finding the Area of a Trapezoid**

Architecture The Winslow House was designed by Frank Lloyd Wright. The front part of the roof is a trapezoid. What is its area?

31 ft
25 ft
77 ft

Solution

$A = \frac{1}{2}(b_1 + b_2)h$ Write formula for area of a trapezoid.

$= \frac{1}{2}(31 + 77)25$ Substitute values for b_1, b_2, and h.

$= 1350$ Multiply.

ANSWER The front part of the roof has an area of 1350 square feet.

The Winslow House in River Forest, Illinois

Your turn now **Sketch the quadrilateral and find its area.**

1. A parallelogram with base 20 meters and height 9 meters

2. A trapezoid with bases of 17 feet and 14 feet and height 6 feet

---

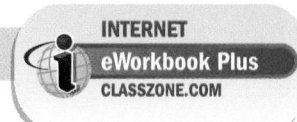

Getting Ready to Practice

Vocabulary Write the area formula for the polygon.

1. parallelogram   **2.** triangle   **3.** trapezoid

Find the area of the parallelogram or trapezoid.

4.   **5.**   **6.**

7. Guided Problem Solving You are designing a putting green for a miniature golf course, as shown. Find the area of the green.

   ① Copy the shape and divide it into a trapezoid and a parallelogram.

   ② Find the area of each quadrilateral.

   ③ Add the two areas to find the total area.

Practice and Problem Solving

HELP with Homework

Example Exercises
1   8–13, 20
2   15–19

Online Resources
CLASSZONE.COM
· More Examples
· eTutorial Plus

Sketch a parallelogram with base *b* and height *h* and find its area.

8. $b = 12$ in., $h = 8$ in.   **9.** $b = 9$ ft, $h = 14$ ft   **10.** $b = 10$ cm, $h = 22$ cm

Find the area of the parallelogram.

11.   **12.**   **13.**

14. Find the Error Describe and correct the error in the solution.

Sketch a trapezoid with bases b_1 and b_2 and height *h* and find its area.

15. $b_1 = 13$ ft, $b_2 = 7$ ft, $h = 6$ ft   **16.** $b_1 = 8$ m, $b_2 = 16$ m, $h = 11$ m

Find the area of the trapezoid.

17.
18 in.
12 in.
9 in.

18.
13 yd
5 yd
10 yd
12 yd

19.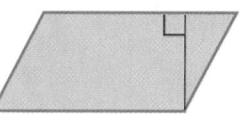
54 m
39 m
15 m
17 m 10 m

20. Measurement Use a metric ruler to measure the dimensions of the parallelogram in millimeters. Then find the area.

Algebra **Sketch the quadrilateral. Then use an area formula to find the unknown dimension.**

21. A parallelogram has an area of 84 square units. Its height is 12 units. Find the base.

22. A trapezoid has an area of 100 square units. Its bases are 10 units and 15 units. Find the height.

Extended Problem Solving **In Exercises 23–26, use the parallelogram and trapezoid shown.**

2 cm
5 cm
4 cm
2 cm
7 cm

23. Calculate Find the areas of the parallelogram and trapezoid.

24. Compare Double each dimension of the quadrilaterals. Find the new areas. How do the new areas compare to the original areas?

25. Compare Triple each dimension of the original quadrilaterals and find the new areas. How do the new areas compare to the original areas?

26. Critical Thinking Suppose you multiply each dimension by a positive number k. What do you think the new areas would be?

Estimation **Use the given scale and the formula for the area of a trapezoid or a parallelogram to estimate the area of the state.**

27. Nevada

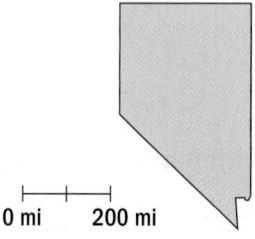

0 mi   200 mi

28. Tennessee

0 mi   200 mi

Find the area of the polygon.

29.

30.

31.

Find the area of the polygon.

32.

33.

34.

Plot the points in a coordinate plane and connect them to form a parallelogram. Then find the area of the parallelogram.

35. $(-3, -1), (0, 4), (6, 4), (3, -1)$ **36.** $(8, 0), (11, -5), (-2, -5), (-5, 0)$

Challenge Find the area of the parallelogram or trapezoid.

37.

38.

39.

Mixed Review

Find the product. *(Lesson 5.3)*

40. $-\dfrac{3}{4} \cdot 1\dfrac{5}{9}$

41. $-7 \cdot \left(-\dfrac{5}{3}\right)$

42. $2\dfrac{3}{8} \cdot \left(-\dfrac{6}{7}\right)$

43. In $\triangle PQR$, write the sine, cosine, and tangent ratios for $\angle P$ and $\angle R$. *(Lesson 9.6)*

FCAT Practice

44. Multiple Choice A trapezoid has bases of 9 feet and 17 feet and a height of 12 feet. What is the area of the trapezoid?

A. 108 ft^2 **B.** 156 ft^2 **C.** 204 ft^2 **D.** 312 ft^2

45. Short Response Sketch a parallelogram and a trapezoid, each with an area of 96 square feet. Label the dimensions needed to find each area.

Areas of Circles

BEFORE	▶ **Now**	**WHY?**
You found the areas of parallelograms and trapezoids.	You'll find the areas of circles.	So you can find the area of a yard watered by a sprinkler, as in Ex. 22.

Word Watch

Review Words

area, p. 33
circle, p. 290
radius, p. 290
diameter, p. 290
circumference, p. 290
pi (π), p. 290

FLORIDA
Standards and Assessment

• Observe and explain geometric properties. (MA.C.3.3.1)

• Know the properties of two-dimensional figures. (MA.C.1.3.1)

Activity **You can use a model to find the area of a circle.**

① Draw a circle and cut it into 8 congruent parts. Arrange the pieces of the circle to resemble a parallelogram, as shown below.

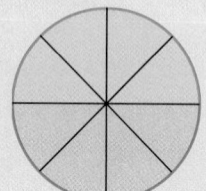

② Copy and complete: The height of the parallelogram is equal to the ? of the circle, and the base of the parallelogram is about equal to one half of the ? of the circle.

③ Use the formula for the area of a parallelogram and your answer from Step 2 to find the formula for the area of the circle in terms of r.

The activity suggests the formula given below.

Area of a Circle

Words The area of a circle is the product of π and the square of the radius.

Algebra $A = \pi r^2$ **Numbers** $A = \pi(6)^2$

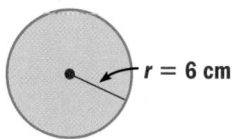

$r = 6$ cm

EXAMPLE 1 Finding the Area of a Circle

HELP with **Notetaking**

To help you organize information about circles, you may want to make a concept grid.

Find the area of a circle with a diameter of 10 inches.

$$A = \pi r^2$$ Write formula for area of a circle.

$$\approx 3.14(5)^2$$ Substitute 3.14 for π and 5 for r.

$$= 78.5$$ Evaluate using a calculator.

10 in.

ANSWER The area is about 78.5 square inches.

EXAMPLE 2 **Finding the Radius of a Circle**

Find the radius of a circle that has an area of 530.66 square feet.

$A = \pi r^2$ Write formula for area of a circle.

$530.66 \approx (3.14)r^2$ Substitute 530.66 for *A* and 3.14 for π.

$169 \approx r^2$ Use a calculator to divide each side by 3.14.

$\sqrt{169} \approx r$ Take positive square root of each side.

$13 \approx r$ Evaluate square root.

ANSWER The radius of the circle is about 13 feet.

Your turn now   **Find the unknown area or radius of the circle. Use 3.14 for π.**

1. $r = 7$ ft, $A = \underline{\ ?\ }$ **2.** $d = 3$ km, $A = \underline{\ ?\ }$ **3.** $A = 628$ cm^2, $r = \underline{\ ?\ }$

EXAMPLE 3 **Using the Area of a Circle**

Hockey Find the combined area of the two face-off circles of an ice hockey rink.

Solution

The distance between the centers is 44 feet and there is 14 feet between the circles. So,

$r + 14 + r = 44$ and $r = 15$.

Now use the formula for the area of a circle.

$A = 2\pi r^2$ Area of two circles

$\approx 2(3.14)(15)^2$ Substitute 3.14 for π and 15 for *r*.

$= 1413$ Evaluate using a calculator.

ANSWER The area of the face-off circles is about 1413 square feet.

Your turn now   **Find the area of the shaded region. Use 3.14 for π.**

4.

5.

Getting Ready to Practice

1. Vocabulary Copy and complete: The area of a circle is the product of π and the square of the _?_.

Find the area of the circle. Use 3.14 for π.

2.

2 ft

3.

10 cm

4.

50 yd

5. Find the radius of a circle that has an area of 154 square meters. Use 3.14 for π.

Practice and Problem Solving

HELP with **Homework**

Example	Exercises
1	6–15
2	16–21
3	22

Online Resources
CLASSZONE.COM
· More Examples
· eTutorial Plus

Find the area of the circle. Use 3.14 for π.

6.

11 yd

7.

13.3 m

8.

17 mm

9.

20.8 cm

Find the area of the circle with the given radius or diameter. Use 3.14 for π.

10. $r = 9$ cm   **11.** $r = 10$ ft   **12.** $r = 30$ m

13. $d = 28$ mm   **14.** $d = 6$ yd   **15.** $d = 40$ in.

Find the radius of the circle with the given area. Use 3.14 for π.

16. $A = 28.26$ ft^2 **17.** $A = 3.14$ m^2 **18.** $A = 200.96$ yd^2

19. $A = 113.04$ in.^{2} **20.** $A = 12.56$ mm^2 **21.** $A = 254.34$ cm^2

22. Sprinklers You are using a rotating sprinkler to water your yard. The sprinkler rotates in a complete circle. It sprays water a distance of 12 feet. Find the area of the yard that is watered. Use 3.14 for π.

23. Measurement Measure the radius of the circle in millimeters. Then find the area of the circle. Use 3.14 for π.

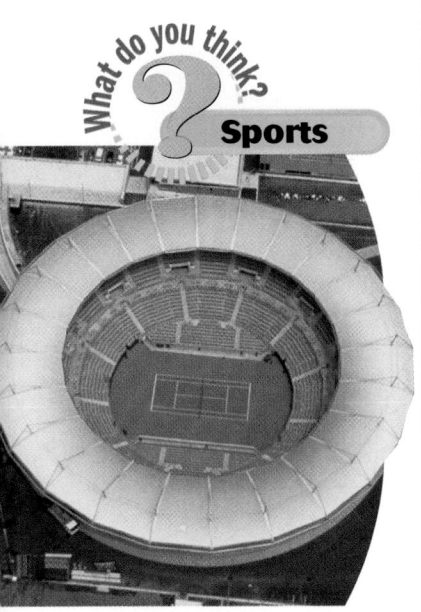
Find the area of the shaded region. Use 3.14 for π.

24.
9 m
4 m

25.
8 in.
20 in.
22 in.

26.
4 km
7 km
10 km

27. Mental Math If the area of a circle is 25π square feet, what is the radius?

28. Tennis Center The roof of the New South Wales Tennis Center in Sydney,
Australia, can be approximated by a circle. A level of seats is covered by
the ring-shaped roof whose outer diameter is about 100 meters and inner
diameter is about 65 meters. What is the area of the roof? Use 3.14 for π.

Algebra Write and solve an equation to find the radius of the circle
given its circumference C. Then use the radius to find the area of the
circle. Use 3.14 for π.

29. $C = 18.84$ ft   **30.** $C = 81.64$ m   **31.** $C = 37.68$ cm

32. Critical Thinking Copy and complete the table. Leave your answers
in terms of π. What happens to the area of a circle when the radius is
multiplied by a number?

Radius r	Area of a circle with radius r	Area of a circle with radius $2r$	Area of a circle with radius $3r$	Area of a circle with radius $4r$
2 in.	4π in.^{2}	?	?	?
3 in.	?	?	?	?
5 in.	?	?	?	?

33. Estimation The diameter of the circle equals
the side length of the larger square and the
diagonal of the smaller square. The diameter
of the circle is 20 millimeters. Find the area of
each square and use the areas to estimate the
area of the circle. Then calculate the area of the
circle and compare it to your estimate. Use 3.14 for π.

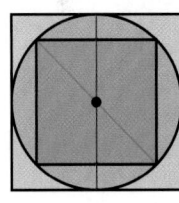

34. Disk Sanders You are using a disk sander to sand a porch that has an
area of 11,520 square inches. One disk for the sander has a diameter
of 7 inches. Another disk has a diameter of 10 inches. You can sand
a surface with the area of five disks in one minute. About how much
time would you save by sanding with the larger disk? Round your
answer to the nearest minute. Use 3.14 for π.

35. Challenge Find the area of the shaded region. Use 3.14 for π.

7 mm

Choose a Strategy Use a strategy from the list to solve the following problem. Explain your choice of strategy.

Problem Solving Strategies
- Make a Table
- Work Backward
- Act It Out

36. For each quarter you put in a parking meter you can park your car for 15 minutes. You know you'll be away from your car for up to an hour and 40 minutes. If you have a $10 roll of quarters, how many quarters will you have after you put the necessary amount in the meter?

Tell whether the side lengths form a right triangle. *(Lesson 9.3)*

37. $a = 0.5, b = 0.9, c = 1.06$

38. $a = 3.6, b = 4.8, c = 6$

FCAT Practice

39. **Multiple Choice** What is the approximate diameter of a circle with an area of 380 square feet? Use 3.14 for π.

A. 120 feet   **B.** 60 feet   **C.** 32 feet   **D.** 22 feet

40. **Short Response** Find the total area of the figure to the right and explain how to find it. Use 3.14 for π.

12 ft   4 ft

BrAIN GAME

What's the Score?

The center circle of the target has a radius of 3 inches and each ring is 3 inches wide. Find the area of each region in terms of π. Then use the formula below to find the score for each region. Round to the nearest whole number.

$$score = \frac{225\pi}{area}$$

For example, the yellow region has an area of $\pi(3)^2$, or 9π square inches. The score in the yellow region is

$$\frac{225\pi}{area} = \frac{225\pi}{9\pi} = 25.$$

Which player, Greg or Jamie, has a higher score?

 Greg   Jamie

FLORIDA: Standards and Assessment
Know how a change in area affects dimensions. (MA.B.1.3.3)
Solve problems involving changes in area. (MA.B.1.3.3)

Comparing Radii of Circles

GOAL Use a spreadsheet to find how the radius of a circle changes when its area changes.

Example How does the radius of a circle change when its area is multiplied by 4?

1 Create a spreadsheet with an original circle area in cell A1 and the multiplier 4 in cell A2. Enter formulas for the Area column that refer to these cells, as shown.

Comparing Radii		
	A	B	C
1	1	Original circle area	
2	4	Multiplier	
3			
4	Area	Radius	Ratio
5	=A1	=SQRT(A5/PI())	
6	=A5*A2	=SQRT(A6/PI())	=B6/B5

2 The radius of a circle with area A is given by $\sqrt{\dfrac{A}{\pi}}$. Enter formulas for the Radius column, as shown.

3 Compare the radii of the two circles by dividing the second radius by the first radius. Enter a formula for this quotient in the Ratio column, as shown.

4 Change the value of the original circle area in cell A1 several times. What do you notice about the ratio of the radii?

	A	B	C
1	1	Original circle area	
2	4	Multiplier	
3			
4	Area	Radius	Ratio
5	1	0.564190	
6	4	1.128379	2

	A	B	C
1	5	Original circle area	
2	4	Multiplier	
3			
4	Area	Radius	Ratio
5	5	1.261566	
6	20	2.523133	2

	A	B	C
1	15	Original circle area	
2	4	Multiplier	
3			
4	Area	Radius	Ratio
5	15	2.185097	
6	60	4.370194	2

ANSWER When the area of a circle is multiplied by 4, the radius is multiplied by 2.

Your turn now Find how the radius of a circle changes when its area is multiplied by the given number.

1. 9   **2.** 16   **3.** 25   **4.** 36

5. Critical Thinking How does the radius of a circle change when its area is doubled? tripled? Explain.

6. Explain why $r = \sqrt{\dfrac{A}{\pi}}$ is the formula for the radius of a circle with area A.

Three-Dimensional Figures

BEFORE	▶ Now	WHY?
You classified and sketched polygons.	You'll classify and sketch solids.	So you can classify solids that form structures, as in Exs. 19–21.

Word Watch

solid, polyhedron, p. 492
face, p. 492
prism, p. 492
pyramid, p. 492
cylinder, p. 492
cone, p. 492
sphere, p. 492
edge, vertex, p. 492

FLORIDA
Standards and Assessment
• Know the properties of three-dimensional figures. (MA.C.1.3.1)
• Draw and build three-dimensional figures. (MA.C.1.3.1)

A **solid** is a three-dimensional figure that encloses a part of space. A **polyhedron** is a solid that is enclosed by polygons. A polyhedron has only flat surfaces. The polygons that form a polyhedron are called **faces**.

Classifying Solids

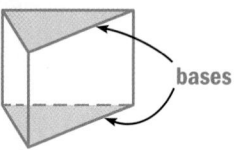

A **prism** is a polyhedron. Prisms have two congruent bases that lie in parallel planes. The other faces are rectangles.

A **pyramid** is a polyhedron. Pyramids have one base. The other faces are triangles.

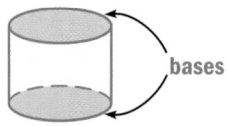

A **cylinder** is a solid with two congruent circular bases that lie in parallel planes.

A **cone** is a solid with one circular base.

A **sphere** is a solid formed by all points in space that are the same distance from a fixed point called the center.

EXAMPLE 1 Classifying Solids

Classify the solid. Then tell whether it is a polyhedron.

The solid has two congruent circular bases that lie in parallel planes, so it is a cylinder. It is not a polyhedron, because circles are not polygons.

HELP with Vocabulary

The plural of vertex is *vertices*.

The segments where faces meet are called **edges**. A **vertex** of a polyhedron is a point where three or more edges meet.

EXAMPLE 2 Counting Faces, Edges, and Vertices

Classify the solid. Then count the number of faces, edges, and vertices.

The solid is a pentagonal pyramid.

6 faces   10 edges   6 vertices

EXAMPLE 3 Sketching a Solid

Show two ways to represent a triangular prism.

Method 1 Sketch the solid.

  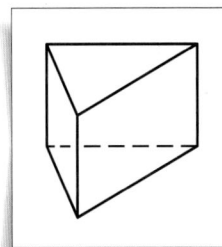

① Sketch two congruent bases.

② Connect the vertices of the bases.

③ Make any hidden lines dashed.

Method 2 Sketch the top, front, and side views of the solid.

top   front   side

Your turn now Classify the solid. Then tell whether it is a polyhedron.

1.

2.

3.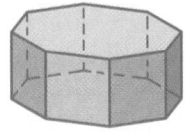

4. Show two ways to represent a rectangular pyramid. Then count the number of faces, edges, and vertices.

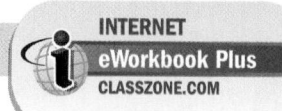
Getting Ready to Practice

Vocabulary Classify the solid. Then tell whether it is a polyhedron.

1.
2.
3.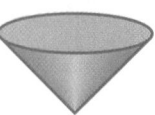

Show two ways to represent the solid. Then count the number of faces, edges, and vertices.

4. triangular pyramid   **5.** pentagonal prism

6. Guided Problem Solving Sketch a square pyramid.

(1) Sketch a parallelogram for the square base.

(2) Draw a dot centered above the parallelogram.

(3) Connect the vertices of the parallelogram to the dot. Make any hidden lines dashed.

Practice and Problem Solving

Classify the solid. Then tell whether it is a polyhedron.

7.
8.
9.

In Exercises 10 and 11, show two ways to represent the solid. Then count the number of faces, edges, and vertices.

10. octagonal prism   **11.** hexagonal prism

12. Writing Give examples of cylinders, cones, and square prisms that you find in your classroom or at home.

Matching Match the description with the solid.

13. one circular base   **A.** triangular prism

14. two rectangular bases   **B.** rectangular pyramid

15. no edges or bases   **C.** rectangular prism

16. three rectangular faces   **D.** cone

17. four triangular faces   **E.** sphere

18. Critical Thinking Copy and complete the table. Use the pattern to write a formula that gives the number of edges in terms of the number of faces and vertices. This is called Euler's Formula.

Figure	Number of faces *F*	Number of vertices *V*	Number of edges *E*	*F + V*
pentagonal pyramid	6	6	10	12
rectangular pyramid	?	?	?	?
triangular prism	?	?	?	?
rectangular prism	?	?	?	?
pentagonal prism	?	?	?	?

Classify the solids that form the structure.

19.

20.

21.

Sketch the solid with the given views.

22.

top   front   side

23.

top   front   side

Mixed Review

24. Find the value of *h*. Then find the perimeter and area of the triangle. *(Lesson 9.4)*

39 cm
h
36 cm

25. Find the area of a circle whose diameter is 21 inches. Use 3.14 for π. *(Lesson 10.2)*

FCAT Practice FCAT

26. Multiple Choice Which of the following solids is *not* a polyhedron?

A. triangular prism   **B.** cylinder

C. rectangular prism   **D.** pyramid

27. Multiple Choice How many faces does a rectangular prism have?

F. 2   **G.** 4   **H.** 6   **I.** 8

Sketching Solids

GOAL Draw views of solids and make isometric drawings.

FLORIDA
Standards and Assessment

• Draw and build three-dimensional figures. (MA.C.1.3.1)

In Lesson 10.3, you drew the top, front, and side views of several common solids. In the following examples, you will see how to draw the top, front, and side views of more complicated solids.

EXAMPLE 1 Drawing Views of a Solid

Draw the top, front, and side views of the solid.

Solution

top   front   side

The interior lines represent edges of faces.

Isometric Drawings An **isometric drawing** is a two-dimensional drawing of a three-dimensional figure. You can create isometric drawings using a grid of dots and a set of three axes that intersect to form 120° angles. Use the dots to guide your drawing.

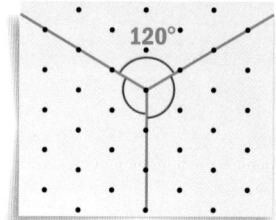

EXAMPLE 2 Creating an Isometric Drawing

Create an isometric drawing of the solid from Example 1.

Solution

The isometric drawing is shown at the right. Each vertical edge of the solid is represented by a vertical line segment.

Add depth to the drawing by shading the top, front, and sides differently.

EXAMPLE **3** **Interpreting an Isometric Drawing**

Draw the top, front, and side views of the solid.

Solution

You can arrange the views this way.

top

front   side

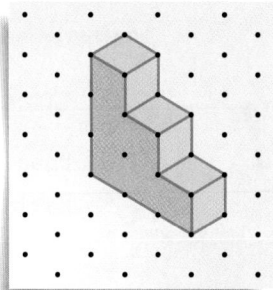

Exercises

Draw the top, front, and side views of the solid.

1.

2.

3.

Create an isometric drawing of the solid.

4.

5.

6.

Draw the top, front, and side views of the solid.

HELP with Solving

For the solids shown here, assume there are no cubes hidden from view except those needed to support the visible ones.

7.

8.

9.

Notebook Review

Review the vocabulary definitions in your notebook.

Copy the review examples in your notebook. Then complete the exercises.

Check Your Definitions

base of a parallelogram, p. 481
height of a parallelogram, p. 481
bases of a trapezoid, p. 482
height of a trapezoid, p. 482
solid, polyhedron, p. 492
face, p. 492

prism, p. 492
pyramid, p. 492
cylinder, p. 492
cone, p. 492
sphere, p. 492
edge, vertex, p. 492

Use Your Vocabulary

1. A(n) <u>?</u> is a solid that is enclosed by polygons.

10.1 Can you find the area of a parallelogram or trapezoid?

EXAMPLE Find the area of the trapezoid.

$$A = \frac{1}{2}(b_1 + b_2)h$$ Write formula for area.

$$= \frac{1}{2}(12 + 18)(5) = 75$$ Substitute values for b_1, b_2, and h.

ANSWER The area of the trapezoid is 75 square inches.

☑ **2.** Find the area of a parallelogram with base 20 feet and height 8 feet.

10.2 Can you find the area of a circle?

EXAMPLE Find the area of the circle. Use 3.14 for π.

$$A = \pi r^2$$ Write formula for area of a circle.

$$\approx 3.14(3)^2$$ Substitute 3.14 for π and 3 for r.

$$= 28.26$$ Evaluate using a calculator.

ANSWER The area of the circle is about 28.26 square centimeters.

☑ **Find the area of the circle with radius r or diameter d. Use 3.14 for π.**

3. $r = 24$ in.   **4.** $r = 4$ mm   **5.** $d = 18$ yd

10.3 Can you classify three-dimensional figures?

 EXAMPLE Count the faces, edges, and vertices of a triangular pyramid.

    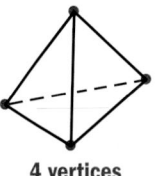

4 faces   6 edges   4 vertices

 6. Show two ways to represent a square prism.

Stop *and* **Think**   about Lessons 10.1–10.3

7. Compare Explain how a cone and a cylinder are alike and how they are different. Then explain how a cylinder and a prism are alike and how they are different.

8. Critical Thinking Can the number of vertices of a prism be odd? Explain.

Review Quiz 1

Find the area of the parallelogram or trapezoid.

1.
8 cm
15 cm

2.
12 ft
6 ft

3. 4.5 cm

6 cm
9 cm

4. A trapezoid has a height of 8 feet. The lengths of the bases are 10 feet and 14 feet. Find the area of the trapezoid.

5. Find the area of a circle with diameter 22 feet. Use 3.14 for π.

Find the radius of the circle with the given area. Use 3.14 for π.

6. $A = 254.34 \text{ ft}^2$ **7.** $A = 452.16 \text{ cm}^2$ **8.** $A = 78.5 \text{ m}^2$

9. Classify the solid. Then tell whether it is a polyhedron.

10. Show two ways to represent a pentagonal pyramid. Then count the number of faces, edges, and vertices.

Problem Solving Strategies

Guess, Check, and Revise

Draw a Diagram

Make a List

Act It Out

Break into Parts

Work Backward

Make a Table

FLORIDA: Standards and Assessment
Know strategies to solve problems involving measurement. (MA.B.3.3.1)

Break into Parts

Problem Each student in your woodworking class has been assigned to make a mailbox. How much wood will you need to make the mailbox?

❶ Read and Understand

Read the problem carefully.

You need to find the amount of wood needed to make the mailbox.

❷ Make a Plan

Decide on a strategy to use.

You can solve this problem by breaking it into parts. Find the area of each side of the mailbox. Then add the areas together.

❸ Solve the Problem

Reread the problem and break the problem into smaller parts.

Area of bottom: $lw = 18(8)$

$= 144$

Area of left and right sides: $2lh = 2(18)(6)$

$= 216$

Area of two roof pieces: $2(5)(18) = 180$

3 in.

5 in.

$h = 6$ in.

$l = 18$ in.

$w = 8$ in.

Area of front door and back door:

Add the area of the two triangles to the area of the two rectangles.

Area of the two triangles: $2\left(\frac{1}{2}\right)(8)(3) = 24$

Area of the two rectangles: $2(8)(6) = 96$

Find the sum of the areas: $A = 144 + 216 + 180 + 24 + 96$

$= 660$ in.^{2}

❹ Look Back

Have you found the area of every side of the mailbox? Did you find the total of these areas?

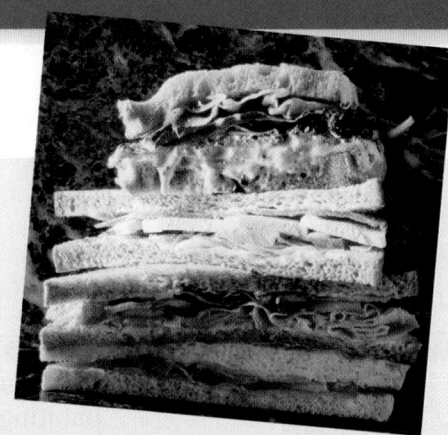

Use the strategy *Break into Parts*.

1. **Mailbox** As an extra credit project, you are making a mailbox with a flat top. The new mailbox is 6 inches wide, 7 inches high, and 12 inches long. How much wood do you need to make this mailbox?

2. **Tiling** You are tiling the L-shaped room shown below. Each tile is 6 inches long by 6 inches wide. How many tiles do you need to tile the room?

3. **Digits** You are making numbers to hang outside the classrooms in your school. The rooms are numbered 1–100. How many of each digit from 0–9 do you need?

4. **Lawn Mowing** You need about 2 hours to mow 3 acres of land. The total land area in the diagram is one acre, or 43,560 square feet. The house and surrounding plants have an area of 1500 square feet. The driveway is 12 feet wide and 50 feet long. How much time would you need to mow the remaining land area? Round your answer to the nearest minute.

Not drawn to scale
1500 ft²
50 ft
12 ft

Mixed Problem Solving

Use any strategy to solve the problem.

5. **Food** Paula is making a sandwich with one type of meat, one type of cheese, and one dressing. How many different kinds of sandwiches can she make using the items in the list?

Meat	Cheese	Dressing
Ham	Swiss	Mayonnaise
Turkey	American	Italian dressing
	Cheddar	

6. **Traveling** Ryan left his house at 7:00 A.M. and traveled in his car. He drove 3 miles north, 2.5 miles east, 1 mile south, 1 mile east, 4 miles south, 1.5 miles west, 2 miles north, and 1.5 miles west. At the end of this trip, how far from home was Ryan?

7. **Numbers** The sum of two numbers is 17. The product of the numbers is 52. Find the two numbers.

8. **Clock** One chime of a clock takes 2.5 seconds to complete. At 1:00 the clock chimes once. At 2:00 the clock chimes twice. If the clock chimes in this way every hour, how many seconds will it spend chiming from 1:00 A.M. to 1:05 P.M.?

LESSON 10.4
Surface Areas of Prisms and Cylinders

BEFORE	▶ Now	WHY?
You classified prisms and cylinders.	You'll find the surface areas of prisms and cylinders.	So you can compare two caramels, as in Ex. 18.

Word Watch

net, p. 502
surface area, p. 503

FLORIDA
Standards and Assessment

• Explore and derive formulas for surface area. (MA.B.1.3.1)

• Draw and build three-dimensional figures. (MA.C.1.3.1)

In the Real World

Storage Chest You are painting a storage chest. Before you begin painting the chest, you need to find the *surface area*. What is the *surface area* of the chest? You'll find the answer in Example 2.

15 in.

30 in.

15 in.

Nets One way to represent a solid is to use a *net*. A **net** is a two-dimensional pattern that forms a solid when it is folded.

  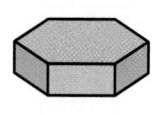

Each polygon of the net represents one face of the solid. There are usually several different possible nets for a given solid.

EXAMPLE 1   Drawing a Net

Draw a net of the triangular prism.

Solution

Method 1 Draw one base with a rectangle adjacent to each side. Draw the other base adjacent to one of the rectangles.

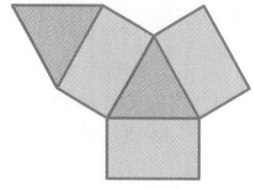

Method 2 For the rectangular faces, draw adjacent rectangles. Draw the bases on opposite sides of one rectangle.

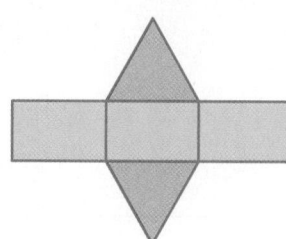

The **surface area** of a polyhedron is the sum of the areas of its faces.

EXAMPLE 2 **Using a Net to Find Surface Area**

Storage Chest Find the surface area of the storage chest shown on page 502. The chest is 30 inches long, 15 inches wide, and 15 inches high.

Solution

Draw a net of the chest.

The area of each square face is 15 in. • 15 in. = **225 in.**^{2}

The area of the rectangular face is 30 in. • 15 in. = **450 in.**^{2}

There are two square faces and four rectangular faces, so the surface area is
2 • **225 in.**^{2} + 4 • **450 in.**^{2} = 2250 in.^{2}

ANSWER The surface area of the storage chest is 2250 square inches.

Notice that in Example 2 the four blue faces form a rectangle that has length equal to the perimeter of the base.

Surface Area of a Prism

Words The surface area of a prism is the sum of twice the area of a base and the product of the base's perimeter and the height.

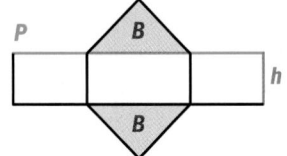

Algebra $S = 2B + Ph$

EXAMPLE 3 **Using a Formula to Find Surface Area**

Find the surface area of the triangular prism.

$$S = 2B + Ph$$

$$= 2\left(\frac{1}{2} \cdot 10 \cdot 12\right) + (13 + 13 + 10)15$$

$$= 660$$

ANSWER The surface area of the prism is 660 square centimeters.

Cylinders The net of a cylinder has two circles for the bases. The curved surface of the cylinder becomes a rectangle in the net. The width of the rectangle is the height of the cylinder, and the length of the rectangle is the circumference of the base.

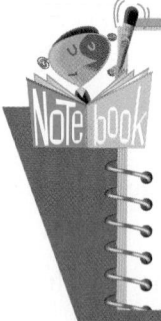

Surface Area of a Cylinder

Words The surface area of a cylinder is the sum of twice the area of a base and the product of the base's circumference and the height.

Algebra $S = 2B + Ch = 2\pi r^2 + 2\pi rh$

EXAMPLE 4 **Finding the Surface Area of a Cylinder**

Sloppy Joe Find the surface area of the can of sloppy joe sauce.

10.7 cm
8 cm

Solution

The radius is one half the diameter, so $r = 4$ cm.

$S = 2\pi r^2 + 2\pi rh$ Write formula for surface area of a cylinder.

$\quad = 2\pi(4)^2 + 2\pi(4)(10.7)$ Substitute 4 for r and 10.7 for h.

$\quad \approx 369.45$ Evaluate using a calculator.

ANSWER The surface area of the can is about 369 square centimeters.

HELP with **Technology**

You can use the ⬚π⬚ key on your calculator instead of 3.14 when evaluating formulas.

Your turn now **Draw a net of the solid. Then find the surface area. Round to the nearest tenth.**

1. 3 ft
    12 ft   5 ft

2. 10 m
    6 m   14 m
    8 m

3. 8 in.
    20 in.

Getting Ready to Practice

1. Vocabulary In your own words, explain what surface area is.

Draw a net. Then find the surface area. Round to the nearest tenth.

2.
2 cm
3 cm
5 cm

3.
5 m
5 m
10 m
6 m   4 m

4.
8 ft
9 ft

Practice and Problem Solving

HELP with **Homework**

Example	Exercises
1	15–17
2	12–17
3	5–8
4	9–17

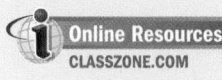
Online Resources
CLASSZONE.COM

· More Examples
· eTutorial Plus

Find the surface area of the prism, where *B* is the area of the base, *P* is the perimeter of the base, and *h* is the height.

5. $B = 4$ in.^{2}, $P = 8$ in., $h = 5$ in.

6. $B = 20$ cm^2, $P = 12$ cm, $h = 3$ cm

7. $B = 45$ yd^2, $P = 30$ yd, $h = 2$ yd

8. $B = 19.3$ m^2, $P = 16$ m, $h = 0.5$ m

Sketch a cylinder with radius *r* and height *h*. Then find its surface area. Round to the nearest tenth.

9. $r = 6$ m, $h = 2$ m

10. $r = 1$ ft, $h = 7$ ft

11. $r = 10$ cm, $h = 20$ cm

Find the surface area of the net. Round to the nearest tenth.

12.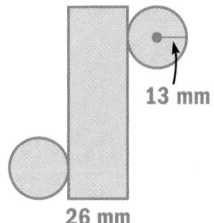
13 mm
26 mm

13.
13 in.
10 in.
12 in.
13 in.
23 in.

14.
7 m
12 m

Draw a net. Then find the surface area. Round to the nearest tenth.

15.
10 in.
10 in.
10 in.

16.
13 mm
2 mm

17.
4 m   5 m
5 m
6 m   4 m

18. Chocolates You are dipping caramels into chocolate. Some of the caramels are 1 inch cubes. Others are cylinders that are 1 inch high and 1 inch in diameter. Which shape will require more chocolate?

Find the surface area of the solid. Round to the nearest tenth.

19.
12 ft
20 ft
13 ft
15 ft
21 ft

20.
14 in.
6 in.

21.
2 cm
$8\frac{1}{2}$ cm
2 cm

22. Crystal Bridge At the Myriad Botanical Gardens in Oklahoma City, there is a tropical conservatory that bridges a small lake. The Crystal Bridge is a cylinder 224 feet long and 70 feet in diameter. Find the surface area of the Crystal Bridge. Round to the nearest tenth.

Breaking into Parts **Draw a net of the solid. Then find the surface area. Round to the nearest tenth.**

23.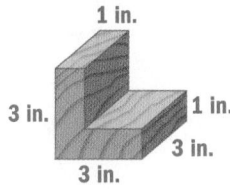
1 in.
3 in.
1 in.
3 in.
3 in.
3 in.

24.
3 in.
8 in.
6 in.
18 in.
US MAIL

25. Challenge Find the surface area of a triangular prism whose edge lengths are all 1 foot. (*Hint*: Each triangular base can be divided into two 30°-60°-90° triangles.)

The Crystal Bridge

Mixed Review

Tell whether the side lengths form a right triangle. (*Lesson 9.3*)

26. $a = 10$, $b = 24$, $c = 26$

27. $a = 28$, $b = 45$, $c = 53$

Use your calculator to approximate the given value. Round your answer to four decimal places. (*Lesson 9.6*)

28. sin 78°   **29.** tan 23°   **30.** cos 14°   **31.** sin 66°

Find the area of a parallelogram with base *b* and height *h*. (*Lesson 10.1*)

32. $b = 16$ ft, $h = 11$ ft

33. $b = 12$ in., $h = 18$ in.

FCAT Practice

34. Short Response Classify the solid. Draw a net of the solid. Then find the surface area.

25 m
15 m
30 m
20 m

35. Multiple Choice What is the approximate surface area of a cylinder with a diameter of 16 feet and a height of 2 feet?

A. 302 ft^2 **B.** 503 ft^2 **C.** 1630 ft^2 **D.** 2440 ft^2

Surface Areas of Pyramids and Cones

BEFORE	▶ Now	WHY?
You found the surface areas of prisms and cylinders.	You'll find the surface areas of pyramids and cones.	So you can find the surface area of icicles, as in Exs. 25–28.

Word Watch

slant height, p. 507

FLORIDA
Standards and Assessment
• Solve real-world surface area problems. (MA.B.1.3.1)
• Know the properties of three-dimensional figures. (MA.C.1.3.1)

The height of a pyramid is the perpendicular distance between the vertex and the base.

The **slant height** l of a regular pyramid is the height of any face that is not the base.

The net for a regular pyramid has a regular polygon as the base and congruent isosceles triangles on each side of the base.

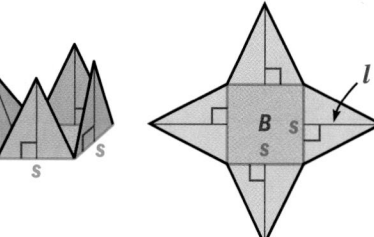

You can use the net of a pyramid to find the surface area of the pyramid.

HELP with Solving

All the pyramids in this lesson have a regular polygon as a base and congruent isosceles triangles as the other faces. The slant height is the same on any face that is not the base.

	Base area	Area of other faces	
Surface area	= Area of base	+ Number of triangles	× Area of each triangle

$$= \quad B \quad + \quad 4 \quad \times \quad \left(\frac{1}{2}sl\right)$$

$$= \quad B + \frac{1}{2}(4s)l$$

$$= \quad B + \frac{1}{2}Pl$$

> The product of the number of triangles and the side length of the base is the perimeter of the base.

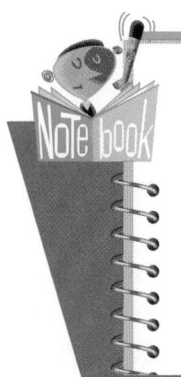

Surface Area of a Pyramid

Words The surface area of a regular pyramid is the sum of the area of the base and one half the product of the base perimeter and the slant height.

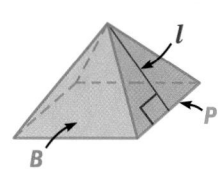

Algebra $S = B + \frac{1}{2}Pl$

EXAMPLE 1 **Finding the Surface Area of a Pyramid**

Find the surface area of the regular pyramid.

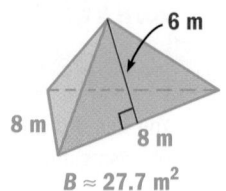

6 m

8 m   8 m

$B \approx 27.7 \text{ m}^2$

① Find the perimeter of the base.

$P = 8 + 8 + 8 = 24$

② Substitute into the formula for surface area.

$S = B + \frac{1}{2}Pl$ Write formula for surface area of a pyramid.

$\approx 27.7 + \frac{1}{2}(24)(6)$ Substitute 27.7 for *B*, 24 for *P*, and 6 for *l*.

$= 99.7$ Simplify.

ANSWER The surface area is about 99.7 square meters.

Cones You can use the net of a cone to find its surface area. The curved surface of a cone is part of a circle with radius *l*, the slant height of the cone. The area of this surface is $A = \pi rl$, where *r* is the radius of the base of the cone.

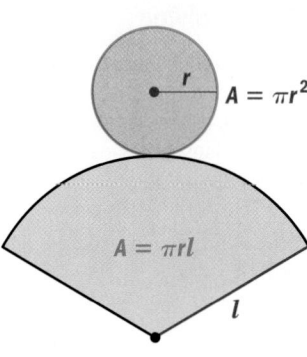

$A = \pi r^2$

$A = \pi rl$

Surface Area of a Cone

Words The surface area of a cone is the sum of the area of the base and the product of pi, the radius of the base, and the slant height.

Algebra $S = \pi r^2 + \pi rl$

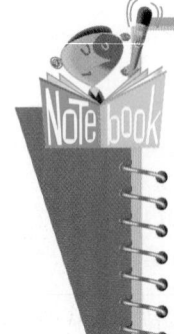

EXAMPLE 2 **Finding the Surface Area of a Cone**

Find the surface area of a cone with radius 4 meters and slant height 9 meters.

$$S = \pi r^2 + \pi r l \qquad \text{Write formula for surface area of a cone.}$$

$$= \pi(4)^2 + \pi(4)(9) \qquad \text{Substitute 4 for } r \text{ and 9 for } l.$$

$$\approx 163.36 \qquad \text{Evaluate using a calculator.}$$

ANSWER The surface area is about 163.36 square meters.

Your turn now **Find the surface area. Round to the nearest tenth.**

1.

12 ft
8 ft
8 ft

2.
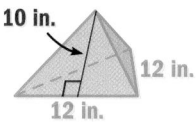
10 in.
12 in.
12 in.
$B \approx 62.4 \text{ in.}^2$

3.

12 cm
6 cm

10.5 Exercises

More Practice, p. 736

Getting Ready to Practice

1. Vocabulary Draw a square pyramid. Label the height h, slant height l, and base B of the pyramid.

Draw a net of the solid. Then find the surface area. Round to the nearest tenth.

2.

11 m
15 m
15 m

3.

5 ft
4 ft
4 ft
$B \approx 6.9 \text{ ft}^2$

4.

13 in.
3 in.

5. Guided Problem Solving Use the figure below to find the surface area of an ice cream cone with an open base.

   ① Write the formula for the surface area of a cone and subtract the area of the base from the formula.

   ② Substitute the values for slant height and radius.

   ③ Evaluate and round to the nearest tenth.

1 in.

$4\frac{1}{4}$ in.

Practice and Problem Solving

HELP with Homework

Example	Exercises
1	6–9, 14–19
2	10–19

Online Resources
CLASSZONE.COM

· More Examples
· eTutorial Plus

Find the surface area of the square pyramid with base side length *s* and slant height *l*.

6. $s = 4$ in.
$l = 11$ in.

7. $s = 6$ m
$l = 9$ m

8. $s = 5$ cm
$l = 4.2$ cm

9. $s = 15$ yd
$l = 10$ yd

Find the surface area of the cone with radius *r* and slant height *l*. Round to the nearest tenth.

10. $r = 3$ ft
$l = 8$ ft

11. $r = 2$ in.
$l = 20$ in.

12. $r = 12$ m
$l = 6.5$ m

13. $r = 4$ mm
$l = 5.5$ mm

Draw a net of the solid. Then find the surface area. Round to the nearest tenth.

14.

10 cm
6 cm

15.

8 in.
14 in.

16.

1.5 mm
1.5 mm
1.5 mm

Find the surface area of the solid. Round to the nearest tenth.

17.

10 in.
9 in.
9 in.

18.

13 ft
10 ft
10 ft
$B \approx 43.3$ ft^2

19.
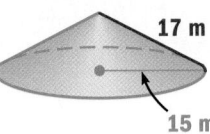
17 m
15 m

Find the surface area of the net. Round to the nearest tenth.

20.
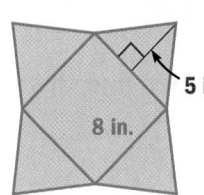
5 in.
8 in.

21.

10 ft
7 ft

22.

$B \approx 43.3$ m^2
10 m
6 m

Sports The formula for the surface area of a sphere is $S = 4\pi r^2$ where *r* is the radius of the sphere. Find the surface area of the sphere. Round to the nearest tenth.

23.

8.8 in.

24.

1.25 in.

Icicles In Exercises 25–28, use the following information. **Find the surface area of the icicle, not including the base, in terms of** π.
Icicles are shaped like cones. As they melt, icicles change size but stay similar in shape.

25. $r = 1$ in., $l = 6$ in. **26.** $r = 2$ in., $l = 12$ in. **27.** $r = 3$ in., $l = 18$ in.

28. Look for a Pattern Describe the pattern developed in Exercises 25–27. Then predict the surface area of an icicle with a radius of 4 inches and a slant height of 24 inches.

29. Critical Thinking Think of a cone as a special type of pyramid. Substitute the formulas for the area and circumference of a circle into the formula for the surface area of a pyramid. Simplify the expression. What do you notice?

30. Number Sense Which has a greater surface area: a square pyramid with a slant height of 12 units and a base side length of 10 units, or a cone with a slant height of 12 units and a diameter of 10 units?

31. Challenge Find the surface area of the regular hexagonal pyramid shown. In the diagram of its base, all the triangles are congruent.

Mixed Review

Tell whether the number is *rational* or *irrational*. *(Lesson 9.2)*

32. $\sqrt{169}$ **33.** $\dfrac{4}{21}$ **34.** $\dfrac{\sqrt{7}}{2}$ **35.** $\sqrt{\dfrac{3}{2}}$

36. Find the surface area of a cylinder with a radius of 3 inches and a height of 8 inches. Round to the nearest tenth. *(Lesson 10.4)*

FCAT Practice

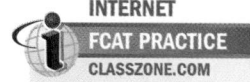
37. Multiple Choice What is the approximate surface area of the cone at the right?

A. 13 cm^2 **B.** 42 cm^2

C. 287 cm^2 **D.** 810 cm^2

38. Short Response Veronica bought a square pyramid shaped gift box. It has a base side length of 6 inches and a slant height of 10 inches. What is the surface area of Veronica's gift box? Susan buys a smaller version of the gift box that has dimensions one half the lengths of those on Veronica's gift box. What is the surface area of Susan's gift box?

FLORIDA: Standards and Assessment
Explore and derive formulas for volume. (MA.B.1.3.1)
Draw and build three-dimensional figures. (MA.C.1.3.1)

Exploring Volume

The *volume* of a solid is a measure of how much space it occupies. Volume is measured in cubic units. One cubic unit is the amount of space occupied by a cube that measures one unit on each side. This cube is called the *unit cube*.

Explore **Find the volume of the rectangular prism.**

To find the volume of the prism shown, first build the prism using sugar cubes to represent unit cubes. Then count the number of cubes you used.

$h = 3$ units
$w = 2$ units
$l = 4$ units

1 It takes 2 rows of 4 cubes, or 8 cubes, to make the bottom of the prism.

4 units   2 units

2 It takes 3 layers of 8 cubes, or 24 cubes, to make the prism the right height.

3 units
4 units   2 units

3 Because each cube is 1 cubic unit, the volume of the prism is 24 cubic units.

Your turn now **Use cubes to model the volume of rectangular prisms.**

1. Copy and complete the table to find the volume of the rectangular prism with the given dimensions.

Dimensions of the prism	Cubes to cover the bottom of the prism	Layers of cubes to make the prism	Volume of the prism
4 × 3 × 3	12	3	36
6 × 1 × 2	?	?	?
7 × 5 × 3	?	?	?
4 × 2 × 8	?	?	?

Stop *and* **Think**

2. Critical Thinking Write a formula for the number of cubes that will make a prism of length l, width w, and height h.

Volumes of Prisms and Cylinders

BEFORE	▶ Now	WHY?
You found the surface areas of prisms and cylinders.	You'll find the volumes of prisms and cylinders.	So you can compare the volumes of pools, as in Ex. 28.

In the Real World

Word Watch

volume, p. 513

FLORIDA
Standards and Assessment
• Know the properties of three-dimensional figures. (MA.C.1.3.1)
• Solve problems involving changes in volume. (MA.B.1.3.3)

Recycling Residents of a community can choose between two recycling bins. Which recycling bin holds more? You will find the answer in Example 3.

The **volume** of a solid is a measure of the amount of space it occupies. Volume is measured in cubic units. One cubic unit is the amount of space occupied by a cube that measures one unit on each side.

Volume of a Prism

Words The volume of a prism is the product of the area of the base and the height.

 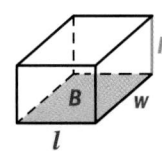

Algebra $V = Bh$

EXAMPLE 1 **Finding Volumes of Prisms**

Find the volume of the prism.

a.

2 in.
8 in.
12 in.

$V = Bh$

$= lwh$

$= 12(8)(2)$

$= 192$

ANSWER The volume is 192 cubic inches.

b.

3 m   10 m
4 m

$V = Bh$

$= \frac{1}{2}(4)(3)(10)$

$= 60$

ANSWER The volume is 60 cubic meters.

Watch Out!

When you find the volume of a triangular prism, be careful not to confuse the height of the prism with the height of the triangular base.

Volumes of Cylinders The formula for the volume of a cylinder is similar to the formula for the volume of a prism.

HELP with **Solving**

Because the base of the cylinder is a circle, its area is πr^2.

 = ×

Volume of a cylinder = Area of base × Height

Volume of a Cylinder

Words The volume of a cylinder is the product of the area of a base and the height.

Algebra $V = Bh$

$\qquad = \pi r^2 h$

height h

base B radius r

EXAMPLE 2 **Finding the Volume of a Cylinder**

Find the volume of the cylinder.

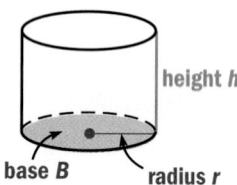

6 cm

9 cm

The radius is one half the diameter, so $r = 3$ cm.

$V = Bh$	Write formula for volume.
$\quad = \pi r^2 h$	Write formula for volume of a cylinder.
$\quad = \pi (3)^2 (9)$	Substitute 3 for r and 9 for h.
$\quad = 81\pi$	Simplify.
$\quad \approx 254.469$	Evaluate using a calculator.

ANSWER The volume is about 254 cubic centimeters.

Your turn now **Find the volume of the solid. Round to the nearest tenth.**

1.

3 ft

11 ft

6 ft

2.

6 mm

8 mm

12 mm

3.

10 in.

$1\frac{1}{2}$ in.

EXAMPLE 3 **Comparing Capacities**

Recycling To decide which recycling bin on page 513 can hold more, find the capacity of each bin.

16 in.

23 in.

14 in.

9 in.

23 in.

Prism

$V = Bh$

$= lwh$

$= 14(23)(16)$

$= 5152 \text{ in.}^3$

Cylinder

$V = Bh$

$= \pi r^2 h$

$= \pi(9)^2(23)$

$\approx 5852.8 \text{ in.}^3$

ANSWER The cylindrical recycling bin holds more.

HELP **with Reading**

When the abbreviation for a unit of measure has an exponent of 3, you read the 3 as "cubic."

ft^3 = cubic feet
cm^3 = cubic centimeters

10.6 Exercises

More Practice, p. 736

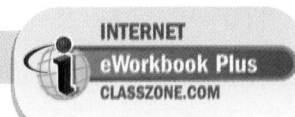

INTERNET
eWorkbook Plus
CLASSZONE.COM

Getting Ready to Practice

1. Vocabulary Explain the difference between area and volume.

Find the volume of the solid. Round to the nearest tenth.

2.

6 cm
3 cm

3.

4 in.
5 in.
10 in.

4.

5 mm
3 mm
6 mm

5. Find the Error
Describe and correct the error in finding the volume of the cylinder.

✗
4 m
5 m

$V = Bh$

$= 2\pi rh$

$= 2\pi(4)(5)$

≈ 125.66

The volume is about 125.66 cubic meters.

Practice and Problem Solving

with Homework

Example	Exercises
1	6-9, 13-18
2	10-18, 23
3	24

Online Resources
CLASSZONE.COM

· More Examples
· eTutorial Plus

Find the volume of the rectangular prism.

6. $l = 6$ m, $w = 2$ m, $h = 11$ m   **7.** $l = 7$ in., $w = 7$ in., $h = 7$ in.

8. $l = 3$ cm, $w = 3.8$ cm, $h = 1.2$ cm   **9.** $l = 16$ ft, $w = 3$ ft, $h = 2\frac{1}{2}$ ft

Find the volume of the cylinder. Round to the nearest tenth.

10. $r = 4$ ft, $h = 11$ ft   **11.** $r = 3$ cm, $h = 9$ cm   **12.** $r = 1.2$ m, $h = 4.5$ m

Find the volume of the solid. If two units of measure are used, give your answer in the smaller units. Round to the nearest tenth.

13.

2 yd
4 yd
8 yd

14.

12 cm   2 cm

15.

7 m
24 m
15 m

16.

8 cm
$B = 60$ cm^2

17.

6 cm
9 mm

18.

15 in.
2 ft
18 in.

Critical Thinking In Exercises 19–22, tell whether you would need to calculate *surface area* or *volume* to find the quantity.

19. The amount of wrapping paper needed to wrap a gift

20. The amount of cereal that will fit in a box

21. The amount of water needed to fill a watering can

22. The amount of frosting needed to decorate a cake

23. **Paint** A paint can is a cylinder 19 centimeters tall and 16 centimeters in diameter. Find the volume of the paint can. Round to the nearest tenth.

24. **Erasers** Find the volume of each eraser in cubic millimeters to the nearest tenth. How many pencil-top erasers would you go through in the time it takes you to go through the larger eraser?

20 mm
10 mm
52 mm
5 mm
3 mm
Not drawn to scale

Find the volume of the solid. Round to the nearest tenth.

25.

2.7 mm
1.5 mm

26.

3 ft
5 ft
9 ft
7 ft

27.

11 m
4 m
17 m
6 m

28. **Swimming Pools** A rectangular in-ground pool is 40 feet long, 16 feet wide, and 4 feet deep. A cylindrical above-ground pool has a radius of 12 feet and is 6 feet deep. How many cubic feet of water does each pool hold? Round to the nearest tenth. Which pool holds more?

29. **Salt Shakers** You buy a cylindrical container of salt that has a diameter of 4 inches and a height of 6 inches. Your salt shaker is a rectangular prism that is $1\frac{1}{2}$ inches by $1\frac{1}{2}$ inches by 3 inches. How many times can the salt in the container fill the salt shaker?

30. **Number Sense** Which would have a greater effect on the volume of a cylinder: *doubling the height* or *doubling the radius*? Explain.

31. **Number Sense** Which would have a greater effect on the volume of a long, thin, short box: *doubling the length* or *doubling the width*? Explain.

32. **Challenge** Find the volume of the solid at the right.

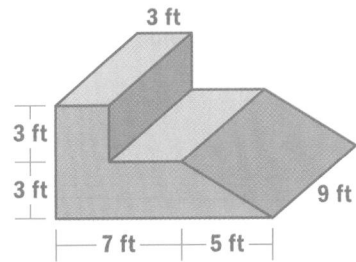

Mixed Review

Let *a* and *b* represent the lengths of the legs of the right triangle, and let *c* represent the length of the hypotenuse. Find the unknown length. *(Lesson 9.3)*

33. $a = 15$, $b = ?$, $c = 39$

34. $a = 16$, $b = 63$, $c = ?$

Find the surface area of the solid to the nearest tenth. *(Lesson 10.5)*

35.

36.

$B \approx 15.6 \text{ mm}^2$

37.

FCAT Practice   FCAT

38. **Extended Response** Find the surface area and volume of the cylinder shown in terms of π. Then triple the radius and height of the cylinder and find the new surface area and volume. Compare the surface area and volume of the new cylinder to the original cylinder. How did the surface area and the volume change?

GOAL
Compare the volumes of a prism and a pyramid.

MATERIALS
- tape
- scissors
- metric ruler
- thin cardboard
- popcorn kernels

FLORIDA: Standards and Assessment
Explore and derive formulas for volume. (MA.B.1.3.1)
Use proportions and similar figures to find measures. (MA.B.2.3.1)

Comparing Volumes

Compare the volume of a pyramid to the volume of a prism.

Explore Compare pyramids and prisms.

1 On cardboard, draw the nets shown. Then cut out the nets and use tape to make an open square prism and an open square pyramid.

2 Compare the height of the prism to the height of the pyramid. Then compare the base of the prism to the base of the pyramid. What do you notice?

3 Fill the pyramid with popcorn kernels and pour the contents into the prism. Repeat until the prism is full. How many times did you have to empty the pyramid into the prism? Use this number to write the ratio of the volume of the pyramid to the volume of the prism.

Your turn now Use the formula for the volume of a rectangular prism and the ratio found in the activity to find the volume of the square pyramid.

1.
4 cm
2 cm 2 cm

2.
5 cm
6 cm
6 cm

3.
8 cm
3 cm 3 cm

Stop and Think

4. **Make a Model** Use the nets shown to make an open cylinder and an open cone. Find the ratio of their volumes.

5 cm
12 cm
31.4 cm
138°
13 cm

Volumes of Pyramids and Cones

BEFORE	▶ Now	WHY?
You found the volumes of prisms and cylinders.	You'll find the volumes of pyramids and cones.	So you can find the amount of space lit by a spotlight, as in Ex. 26.

Word Watch

Review Words
pyramid, p. 492
cone, p. 492
volume, p. 513

FLORIDA
Standards and Assessment
• Solve real-world volume problems. (MA.B.1.3.1)
• Know how a change in dimensions affects volume. (MA.B.1.3.3)

Famous Buildings The Rainforest Pyramid in Galveston Island, Texas, is the home of many plants, butterflies, fish, and reptiles. This square pyramid has a height of 100 feet, and each side of its base measures 200 feet. What is the volume of the Rainforest Pyramid?

The volumes of a pyramid and a prism with the same base area and the same height are related. The volume of the pyramid is exactly one third the volume of the prism.

Volume of a Pyramid

Words The volume of a pyramid is one third the product of the area of the base and the height.

Algebra $V = \frac{1}{3}Bh$

EXAMPLE 1 **Finding the Volume of a Pyramid**

Find the volume of the Rainforest Pyramid described above using the diagram.

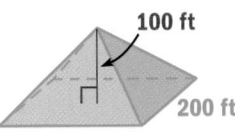

Solution

$$V = \frac{1}{3}Bh \qquad \text{Write formula for volume of a pyramid.}$$

$$= \frac{1}{3}(200^2)(100) \qquad \text{The base is a square, so } B = s^2.$$

$$= 1{,}333{,}333.\overline{3} \qquad \text{Evaluate using a calculator.}$$

ANSWER The Rainforest Pyramid has a volume of about 1,300,000 cubic feet.

EXAMPLE 2 Finding the Volume of a Pyramid

Find the volume of the pyramid.

12 cm
10 cm
24 cm

$$V = \frac{1}{3}Bh \qquad \text{Write formula for volume of a pyramid.}$$

$$= \frac{1}{3}\left(\frac{1}{2} \cdot 24 \cdot 10\right)(12) \qquad \text{The base is a triangle, so } B = \frac{1}{2}bh.$$

$$= 480 \qquad \text{Multiply.}$$

ANSWER The pyramid has a volume of 480 cubic centimeters.

Your turn now Find the volume of the pyramid.

1.

9 in.
8 in.
8 in.

2.

10 ft
12 ft
5 ft

3.

15 m
8 m
20 m

4. Critical Thinking Explain how you found the area of the base of each figure in Exercises 1–3.

Volumes of Cones The volume of a cone is related to the volume of a cylinder in the same way the volume of a pyramid is related to the volume of a prism. That is, the volume of a cone is one third the volume of a cylinder with the same base and height.

Volume of a Cone

Words The volume of a cone is one third the product of the area of the base and the height.

Algebra $V = \frac{1}{3}Bh = \frac{1}{3}\pi r^2 h$

h
B
r

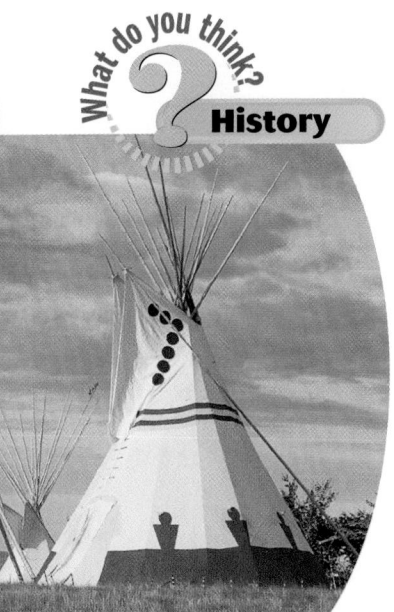

What do you think?

History

■ **Native Americans**

In the United States, 26 of the 50 states have names that originated from Native American languages. What percent is this?

EXAMPLE 3 **Finding the Volume of a Cone**

Native Americans Many Native American tribes built tepees that were cone-shaped. A tepee has a height of 12 feet and a base diameter of 12 feet. Approximate the volume of the tepee.

Solution

The radius is one half the diameter, so $r = \frac{1}{2} \cdot 12 = 6$ ft.

$V = \frac{1}{3}\pi r^2 h$ Write formula for volume of a cone.

$= \frac{1}{3}\pi (6)^2 (12)$ Substitute 6 for *r* and 12 for *h*.

$= 144\pi$ Simplify.

≈ 452.389 Evaluate using a calculator.

ANSWER The tepee has a volume of about 450 cubic feet.

Your turn now Find the volume of the cone with radius *r* and height *h*. Round to the nearest tenth.

5. $r = 24$ m, $h = 18$ m   **6.** $r = 4$ in., $h = 16$ in.   **7.** $r = 15$ ft, $h = 28$ ft

---

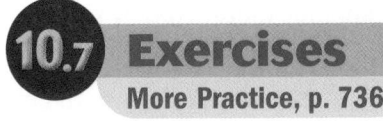

10.7 Exercises

More Practice, p. 736

INTERNET
eWorkbook Plus
CLASSZONE.COM

Getting Ready to Practice

Matching **Match each solid with the *best* formula for its volume.**

1. prism   **2.** cylinder   **3.** pyramid   **4.** cone

A. $V = \frac{1}{3}Bh$ **B.** $V = \pi r^2 h$ **C.** $V = \frac{1}{3}\pi r^2 h$ **D.** $V = Bh$

Find the volume of the solid. Round to the nearest tenth.

5.

8 cm
6 cm
6 cm

6.

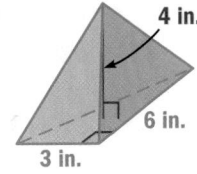

4 in.
6 in.
3 in.

7.

30 ft
10 ft

Practice and Problem Solving

HELP with Homework

Example	Exercises
1	14–16
2	8–16
3	17–25

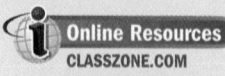

Online Resources
CLASSZONE.COM

· More Examples
· eTutorial Plus

Find the volume of the pyramid with base area *B* and height *h*.

8. $B = 9$ in.^{2}, $h = 4$ in. **9.** $B = 12$ ft^2, $h = 15$ ft **10.** $B = 1.5$ m^2, $h = 0.6$ m

Find the volume of the pyramid.

11.

20 m
24 m
16 m

12.
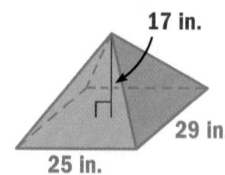
17 in.
29 in.
25 in.

13.

11 ft
15 ft
9 ft

Find the volume of the square pyramid with base side length *s* and height *h*.

14. $s = 5$ m, $h = 4$ m **15.** $s = 12$ yd, $h = 3$ yd **16.** $s = 6$ in., $h = \frac{1}{2}$ in.

Find the volume of the cone. If two units of measure are used, give your answer in the smaller units. Round to the nearest tenth.

17.

27 cm
11 cm

18.

45 ft
15 yd

19.
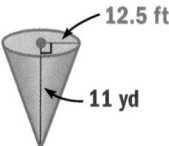
12.5 ft
11 yd

Find the volume of the cone with the given dimensions. If two units of measure are used, give your answer in the smaller units. Round to the nearest tenth.

20. $r = 3$ in., $h = 7$ in. **21.** $r = 11$ ft, $h = 4$ ft **22.** $r = 1.2$ m, $h = 45$ cm

23. $d = 8$ m, $h = 8$ m **24.** $d = 5$ cm, $h = 9$ cm **25.** $d = 3$ ft, $h = 10$ yd

26. Spotlight The light from a spotlight reaches out in a cone shape from the bulb. The light of the beam extends 24 feet before it hits the floor under the spotlight and creates a circle with a radius of 10 feet. What is the volume of the space directly lit by the spotlight? Round to the nearest tenth.

Find the volume of the pyramid with the given height and the base shown. Round to the nearest tenth.

27. $h = 1.8$ cm

1.3 cm
0.5 cm

28. $h = 8$ m
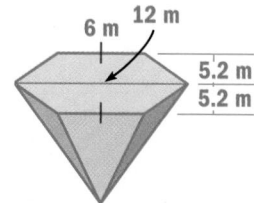
6 m 12 m
5.2 m
5.2 m

29. Critical Thinking Which would affect the volume of a cone more: *doubling the height* or *doubling the radius*? Explain your reasoning.

Writing **Write a sentence describing how to find the volume of the solid. Then write a formula for the volume of the solid.**

30.

31.

32.

33. Construction A rectangular prism-shaped hole 10 feet by 12 feet by 8 feet is dug into the ground. How tall a pyramid can the excavated dirt form if the base is 10 feet by 10 feet? How tall a cone can it form if the base has a radius of 5 feet? Round your answers to the nearest tenth.

34. Challenge A cone-shaped cup has a height of 11 centimeters and a radius of 4 centimeters. You pour water into the cup until it is 2 centimeters from the top. Sketch the cone. How many fluid ounces of water are in the cup? Round to the nearest tenth. (*Hint*: Use similar triangles and the fact that $1 \text{ cm}^3 \approx 0.0338$ fl oz.)

Mixed Review

Show two ways to represent the solid. *(Lesson 10.3)*

35. hexagonal prism

36. square pyramid

37. Find the volume of a cylinder with radius 7 inches and height 18 inches. Round to the nearest tenth. *(Lesson 10.6)*

38. Basic Skills The table shows the average high temperatures in Alexandria, Egypt, during the months April through September. Make a bar graph of the data.

Month	April	May	June	July	August	September
Temperature	75° F	79° F	83° F	84° F	86° F	84° F

FCAT Practice

39. Multiple Choice What is the volume of the pyramid?

A. 62.3 cm³   **B.** 187 cm³

C. 726 cm³   **D.** 2060 cm³

40. Multiple Choice What is the approximate volume of a cone with radius 7 feet and height 4 feet?

F. 58.6 ft³   **G.** 176 ft³   **H.** 205 ft³   **I.** 616 ft³

18 cm

11 cm

11 cm

Notebook Review

Review the vocabulary definitions in your notebook.

Copy the review examples in your notebook. Then complete the exercises.

Check Your Definitions

net, p. 502

surface area, p. 503

slant height, p. 507

volume, p. 513

Use Your Vocabulary

1. In your own words, explain what slant height is.

10.4–10.5 Can you find surface areas?

 EXAMPLE Find the surface area of the cylinder.

$$S = 2\pi r^2 + 2\pi rh$$
$$= 2\pi(9)^2 + 2\pi(9)(26) \approx 509 + 1470 = 1979$$

ANSWER The surface area of the cylinder is about 1979 square centimeters.

 EXAMPLE Find the surface area of the square pyramid.

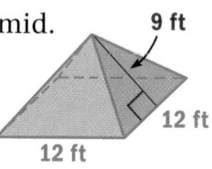

$$S = B + \frac{1}{2}Pl$$
$$= 12^2 + \frac{1}{2}(4 \cdot 12)(9) = 144 + 216 = 360$$

ANSWER The surface area of the pyramid is 360 square feet.

☑ **Find the surface area of the solid. Round to the nearest tenth.**

2. a cylinder with radius 5 meters and height 10 meters

3. a rectangular prism with length 5 inches, width 2 inches, and height 9 inches

4. a square pyramid with base side length 7 meters and slant height 4 meters

5. a cone with diameter 20 feet and slant height 15 feet

10.6–10.7 Can you find volumes?

 EXAMPLE Find the volume of the prism.

$$V = Bh = \frac{1}{2}(7 \cdot 14)(21) = 49 \cdot 21 = 1029$$

ANSWER The volume is 1029 cubic inches.

 EXAMPLE Find the volume of the cone.

$$V = \frac{1}{3}\pi r^2 h = \frac{1}{3}\pi (7)^2 (18) = 294\pi \approx 923.628$$

ANSWER The cone has a volume of about 924 cubic feet.

 6. Find the volume of a pyramid with base area 27 square meters and height 14 meters.

Stop *and* **Think** about Lessons 10.4–10.7

7. Writing What is the difference between area and surface area?

Review Quiz 2

Find the surface area of the solid. Round to the nearest tenth.

1. 6 m / 24 m / 10 m

2. 7 yd / 14 yd

3. 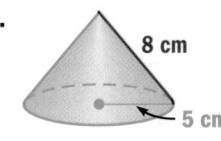 8 cm / 5 cm

Find the volume of the solid. Round to the nearest tenth.

4. 32 yd / 150 yd

5. 3 ft / 3 ft

6. 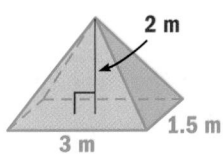 2 m / 1.5 m / 3 m

7. Ramp How much cement is needed to make the ramp shown?

2 ft / 10 ft / 25 ft

Chapter Review

Vocabulary

base of a parallelogram, p. 481
height of a parallelogram, p. 481
bases of a trapezoid, p. 482
height of a trapezoid, p. 482
solid, polyhedron, p. 492

face, p. 492
prism, p. 492
pyramid, p. 492
cylinder, p. 492
cone, p. 492

sphere, p. 492
edge, vertex, p. 492
net, p. 502
surface area, p. 503
slant height, p. 507
volume, p. 513

Vocabulary Review

Match the figure with its area formula.

1.   **2.** ⬤ **3.**   **4.**

A. $A = \pi r^2$ **B.** $A = \frac{1}{2}bh$

C. $A = bh$ **D.** $A = \frac{1}{2}(b_1 + b_2)h$

5. Draw a net of a square prism.

6. How many faces, edges, and vertices does a triangular pyramid have?

Write the formulas for the surface area and the volume of the figure.

7. cylinder   **8.** cone

9. pyramid   **10.** prism

Review Questions

Find the area of the parallelogram with base *b* and height *h*.
(Lesson 10.1)

11. $b = 16$ ft, $h = 7$ ft   **12.** $b = 63$ m, $h = 5.2$ m   **13.** $b = 8\frac{1}{4}$ in., $h = 6\frac{5}{11}$ in.

Find the area of the trapezoid with bases b_1 and b_2 and height *h*.
(Lesson 10.1)

14. $b_1 = 20$ cm, $b_2 = 12$ cm, $h = 8$ cm   **15.** $b_1 = 6$ yd, $b_2 = 9$ yd, $h = 12$ yd

Find the area of the circle with radius *r* or diameter *d*. Use 3.14 for π.
(Lesson 10.2)

16. $r = 3$ ft   **17.** $r = 15$ yd   **18.** $d = 80$ cm   **19.** $d = 1.5$ m

20. Show two ways to represent a hexagonal prism. Then count the number of faces, edges, and vertices. *(Lesson 10.3)*

21. Draw a net for an octagonal pyramid. How many faces, edges, and vertices does the octagonal pyramid have? *(Lessons 10.3, 10.4)*

Find the surface area of the solid. Round to the nearest tenth.
(Lessons 10.4, 10.5)

22.
5 in.
21 in.
7 in.

23.
30 yd
16 yd

24.
25 mm
7 mm
24 mm
4 mm

25.
15 ft
10 ft

26.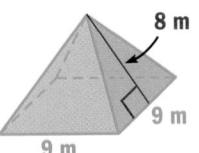
8 m
9 m
9 m

27.
5 in.
8 in.
8 in.

Find the volume of the solid. Round to the nearest tenth.
(Lessons 10.6, 10.7)

28.
10.8 cm
5.4 cm

29.
4.7 mm
9.6 mm
2.3 mm

30.
18.6 m
10.4 m
19.5 m

31.
4 in.
3 in.
5 in.

32.
5 yd
$B \approx 41.5 \text{ yd}^2$

33.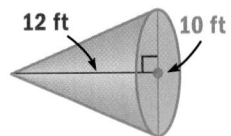
12 ft
10 ft

34. **Containers** A cylinder with a radius of 6 centimeters and a height of 7 centimeters has about the same volume as a rectangular prism with a length of 9 centimeters, a width of 8 centimeters, and a height of 11 centimeters. Which container uses less material to hold the same amount? About how much less material? Round to the nearest tenth. *(Lessons 10.4, 10.6)*

35. **Candles** You have 12 cubic inches of candle wax. You have a mold for a square pyramid candle that has a base side length of 3 inches and a height of 5 inches. Do you have enough wax to make this candle? Explain. *(Lesson 10.7)*

10 Chapter Test

Find the area of the parallelogram or trapezoid.

1.

7 cm
13 cm

2.

26 m
18 m
16 m

3.

21 in.
15 in.
32 in.

Determine the radius of the circle given its area. Use 3.14 for π.

4. $A = 3.7994 \text{ ft}^2$

5. $A = 0.785 \text{ m}^2$

6. $A = 94.985 \text{ yd}^2$

Classify the solid. Then tell whether it is a polyhedron.

7.

8.

9.

10. Painting You plan to paint the 4 walls and ceiling of a rectangular room with dimensions 15 feet by 12 feet by 8 feet. A can of paint covers 400 square feet. How many cans of paint will you need?

Find the surface area of the solid. Round to the nearest tenth.

11.

60 m
8 m

12.

16 in.
15 in.
15 in.

13.

6.5 mm
21 mm

14. Pepperoni A stick of pepperoni is a cylinder, with a radius of 2 centimeters and a length of 12 centimeters. If a slice of pepperoni is 1 cubic centimeter, how many whole slices can be made?

Find the volume of the solid. Round to the nearest tenth.

15.

3 ft
2 ft
4 ft

16.

2 mm
3 mm

17.

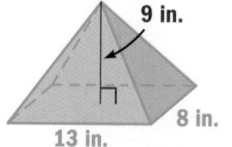

9 in.
13 in.
8 in.

Chapter FCAT Practice

Test-Taking Strategy Go back and check as many of your answers as you can.

Multiple Choice

1. A parallelogram has an area of 24 square inches and a base length of 3 inches. What is the height?

   A. 8 in.   **B.** 21 in.   **C.** 27 in.   **D.** 72 in.

2. The diameter of a dime is 18 millimeters. What is the area of one side of the coin? Use 3.14 for π.

   F. 28.26 mm^2 **G.** 59.66 mm^2

   H. 254.34 mm^2 **I.** 1017.36 mm^2

3. How many edges does the figure have?

   A. 3   **B.** 5   **C.** 6   **D.** 9

4. Which of the following statements is true of the cylinders?

   F. Cylinder A has a greater surface area than Cylinder B.

   G. Cylinder B has a greater surface area than Cylinder A.

   H. Cylinder A and Cylinder B have equal surface areas.

   I. Cylinder A and Cylinder B have equal volumes.

5. What is the surface area of a square pyramid with base side length 2 inches and slant height 8 inches?

   A. 32 in.^{2} **B.** 36 in.^{2} **C.** 40 in.^{2} **D.** 68 in.^{2}

6. What is the diameter of a cylinder with a height of 12 centimeters and a volume of 603 cubic centimeters? Round to the nearest whole number.

   F. 4 cm   **G.** 7 cm   **H.** 8 cm   **I.** 14 cm

7. The base of a triangular prism is a right triangle with legs that measure 8 feet and 11 feet. The height of the prism is 6 feet. What is the volume of the prism?

   A. 88 ft^3 **B.** 176 ft^3 **C.** 264 ft^3 **D.** 528 ft^3

8. Find the volume of a square pyramid that has a height of 12 feet and a base perimeter of 52 feet.

   F. 208 ft^3 **G.** 624 ft^3 **H.** 2028 ft^3 **I.** 676 ft^3

Short Response

9. How does doubling each dimension of a cone affect the surface area of a cone?

Extended Response

10. A company is making two types of aluminum containers. One is a cylinder with a height of 1.25 feet and a diameter of 1 foot. The other is a rectangular prism with a length of 0.75 foot, a width of 0.75 foot, and a height of 1 foot. Aluminum costs $.02 per square foot. How much will it cost to produce each type of container? Round to the nearest cent. Which container holds more?

Strategies for Answering
Context-Based Multiple Choice Questions

Some of the information you need to solve a context-based multiple choice question may appear in a table, a diagram, or a graph.

Problem 1

Ali plants a flower garden in a circle around a tree. The outer edge of the garden has twice the radius of the inner edge. Find the area of the flower garden.

2 ft

flower garden

A. 12.56 ft^2 **B.** 25.12 ft^2 **C.** 37.68 ft^2 **D.** 50.24 ft^2

Solution

Read the problem carefully. Decide how you can use the information you are given to solve the problem.

1) You know that the radius of the inner circle is 2 feet and the radius of the outer circle is double the radius of the inner circle, or 4 feet.

Use the areas of both circles to find the area of the garden.

Find the areas of the two circles.

2) Area of inner circle:
$$\text{radius} = 2 \text{ ft}$$
$$A = \pi r^2$$
$$= \pi \cdot 2^2$$
$$= 4\pi$$

Area of outer circle:
$$\text{radius} = 4 \text{ ft}$$
$$A = \pi r^2$$
$$= \pi \cdot 4^2$$
$$= 16\pi$$

Use the areas of the circles to find the area of the garden.

3) Area of garden = Area of outer circle − Area of inner circle
$$A = 16\pi - 4\pi$$
$$= 12\pi$$
$$\approx 12 \times 3.14$$
$$= 37.68$$

The area of the flower garden is about 37.68 ft^2. The correct answer is C.

Use one of the strategies on pages 156–157.

4) Check to see that the answer is reasonable. Estimate that 16π is about 48 and 4π is about 12. Because $48 - 12 = 36$, C is the most reasonable choice.

Problem 2

Jim walks diagonally across a field. Martha walks along its length and width. The rectangular field is 300 feet wide and 400 feet long. How many feet less does Jim walk than Martha?

F. 1200 feet   **G.** 700 feet   **H.** 500 feet   **I.** 200 feet

Solution

Read the problem carefully. Remember that the field is a rectangle.

Use the Pythagorean theorem to find the length of Jim's path. Add to find the length of Martha's path.

1) Use the information in the problem to make a sketch.

2)
$$a^2 + b^2 = c^2 \quad \text{Pythagorean theorem}$$
$$300^2 + 400^2 = c^2 \quad \text{Substitute for } a \text{ and } b.$$
$$250,000 = c^2 \quad \text{Solve.}$$
$$500 = c \quad \text{Evaluate positive square root.}$$

The length of Jim's path is 500 feet.
The length of Martha's path is $300 + 400 = 700$ feet.

Find the difference of the two distances.

3) Martha's distance − Jim's distance
$$= 700 - 500$$
$$= 200$$

Jim walks 200 feet less than Martha. The correct answer is I.

Jim's path
300 ft
400 ft

Watch Out!

Be sure that you know what question you are asked to answer. Some choices given may be intended to distract you.

Your turn now

1. In Problem 2, Jim and Martha both walk at the rate of 250 ft/min. How many minutes less does Jim walk than Martha?

   A. 0.2 min   **B.** 0.25 min   **C.** 0.8 min   **D.** 1.25 min

In Exercises 2–3, use the diagram.

2. What is the height of the building?

   F. 10 feet   **G.** 16 feet

   H. 20 feet   **I.** 40 feet

3. How long will the person's shadow be when the building's shadow is 14 feet long?

   A. 3 feet   **B.** 3.5 feet

   C. 4 feet   **D.** 7 feet

5 ft
2 ft
8 ft

Multiple Choice

In Exercises 1 and 2, use the diagram below.

1. Which angles are complementary?

A. ∠1 and ∠2

B. ∠2 and ∠3

C. ∠3 and ∠4

D. ∠1 and ∠4

2. Which angles are vertical angles?

F. ∠1 and ∠3 **G.** ∠2 and ∠4

H. ∠3 and ∠2 **I.** ∠4 and ∠1

In Exercises 3 and 4, use the diagram below.

3. What is the value of x?

A. 60 **B.** 120 **C.** 180 **D.** 720

4. How many lines of symmetry does the figure have?

F. 0 **G.** 3 **H.** 6 **I.** 12

5. ∠B and ∠A are supplementary. What is $m\angle B$?

A. 47° **B.** 57° **C.** 137° **D.** 147°

6. The infield of a major league baseball field is a square with a side length of 90 feet. A catcher throws the ball from first base to third base. How far does the ball travel to the nearest foot?

F. 45 ft **G.** 90 ft **H.** 127 ft **I.** 156 ft

7. What is the area of the trapezoid?

A. 20 cm^2

B. 22 cm^2

C. 28 cm^2

D. 36 cm^2

In Exercises 8 and 9, use the gift box below.

8. What is the surface area of the gift box?

F. 1320 cm^2 **G.** 1472 cm^2

H. 1632 cm^2 **I.** 3360 cm^2

9. What is the volume of the gift box?

A. 1472 cm^3 **B.** 2800 cm^3

C. 3360 cm^3 **D.** 4032 cm^3

Short Response

10. A table in a conference room is a regular octagon. What is the measure of one angle in the top of the table?

11. Use coordinate notation to describe the translation from the blue figure to the red figure.

$(x, y) \rightarrow (\underline{\ ?\ }, \underline{\ ?\ })$

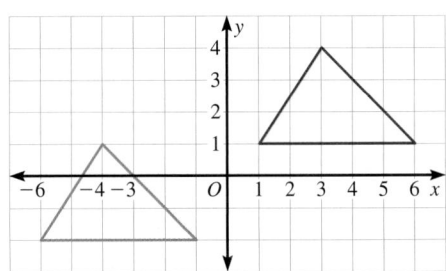

12. A 24 foot pine tree casts a 30 foot shadow. At the same time, a flagpole cast a 10 foot shadow. The triangles formed are similar. What is the height of the flagpole? Explain how you found your answer.

13. A rectangular city park is 100 yards long and 50 yards wide. What is the diagonal distance across the park?

14. An escalator is 15 meters in length with a 35° incline. How high is the escalator? Draw a diagram and explain your steps.

15. A circular swimming pool has a diameter of 24 feet and a height of 6 feet. What is the volume of the pool?

Extended Response

16. Mark wants to have a rectangular deck added to his home.

Find the area of the deck.

Contractor A will charge $800 for every 50 square feet of deck space. Contractor B will charge $18 per square foot of deck space. Which contractor is offering the best price to build the deck? Show how you found your answer.

17. You have an aquarium that is 24 inches long and 12 inches wide. It is filled with water 15 inches deep. Find the volume of water in the tank.

For your fish to live and grow, you should have no more than one fish for every gallon of water (1 gal ≈ 231 in.³). What is the greatest number of fish you should put in your aquarium? Explain how you reached your answer.

Cumulative Practice for Chapters 8–10

Chapter 8

Multiple Choice **In Exercises 1–7, choose the letter of the correct answer.**

1. $\angle 1$ and $\angle 2$ are supplementary, and $m\angle 1 = 76°$. What is $m\angle 2$? *(Lesson 8.1)*

   A. $14°$ **B.** $24°$ **C.** $94°$ **D.** $104°$

2. What is the value of x? *(Lesson 8.2)*

   F. 25   **G.** 52   **H.** 55   **I.** 65

3. What is the perimeter of the rhombus? *(Lesson 8.3)*

   A. 3 in.   **B.** 9 in.   **C.** 12 in.   **D.** 15 in.

4. What is the sum of the angle measures in a pentagon? *(Lesson 8.4)*

   F. $360°$ **G.** $450°$ **H.** $540°$ **I.** $720°$

5. Triangle ABC is congruent to $\triangle DEF$. Which statement is true? *(Lesson 8.5)*

   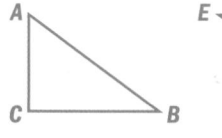

   A. $\overline{AC} \cong \overline{DF}$ **B.** $\overline{CB} \cong \overline{DF}$

   C. $\overline{AB} \cong \overline{EF}$ **D.** $\angle C \cong \angle E$

6. Which transformation is shown? *(Lessons 8.6–8.8)*

   F. reflection
   G. rotation
   H. translation
   I. dilation

7. A tree casts a 21 foot shadow. At the same time your 5 foot tall friend casts a 3 foot shadow. How tall is the tree? *(Lesson 8.8)*

   A. 7 feet   **B.** 12.6 feet

   C. 35 feet   **D.** 105 feet

8. **Short Response** Triangle ABC has vertices $A(-4, -3)$, $B(0, -2)$, and $C(4, -5)$. Reflect $\triangle ABC$ in the x-axis. Find the vertices of the image. *(Lesson 8.6)*

9. **Extended Response** You make a hexagonal coaster with four 135° angles and two other congruent angles. Use the diagram below. *(Lesson 8.4)*

   a. Find the sum of the angle measures of a hexagon.

   b. Write an equation that you can use to find the measure of each of the two other angles.

   c. Solve the equation to find the measure of each of the two angles.

Chapter 9

Multiple Choice **In Exercises 10–17, choose the letter of the correct answer.**

10. What is the approximate value of $\sqrt{1255}$? Round to the nearest hundredth. *(Lesson 9.1)*

A. 12.05 **B.** 18.23 **C.** 35.43 **D.** 52.05

11. What is the value of b in the equation $b^2 - 64 = -36$? *(Lesson 9.1)*

F. $b \approx \pm 5.29$ **G.** $b = \pm 6$

H. $b = \pm 8$ **I.** $b \approx \pm 9.36$

12. Which list shows the numbers in order from least to greatest? *(Lesson 9.2)*

A. $3, \sqrt{5}, 5, 6, \sqrt{8}$ **B.** $\sqrt{5}, \sqrt{8}, 3, 5, 6$

C. $3, 5, \sqrt{5}, \sqrt{8}, 6$ **D.** $\sqrt{5}, 3, 5, \sqrt{8}, 6$

13. One leg of a right triangle is 40 feet long, and the other leg is 42 feet long. What is the length of the hypotenuse? *(Lesson 9.3)*

F. 48 feet **G.** 52 feet

H. 58 feet **I.** 64 feet

14. An 8 foot ladder leans against a building. The bottom of the ladder is 3 feet from the base of the building. About how high is the top of the ladder? *(Lesson 9.4)*

A. 2.2 ft **B.** 5 ft **C.** 7.4 ft **D.** 8.5 ft

15. What is the value of x? *(Lesson 9.5)*

F. 14.14 inches

G. 20 inches

H. 28.28 inches

I. 40 inches

20 √2 in.

x

45°

x

16. Which set of numbers *is not* a Pythagorean triple? *(Lesson 9.4)*

A. 7, 24, 25 **B.** 9, 40, 41

C. 8, 15, 17 **D.** 11, 58, 60

17. In $\triangle ABC$, what is cos A? *(Lesson 9.6)*

25 in. | B | 7 in. | A | 24 in. | C

F. $\dfrac{7}{24}$ **G.** $\dfrac{7}{25}$ **H.** $\dfrac{24}{25}$ **I.** $\dfrac{24}{7}$

18. **Short Response** Carlos is flying a kite. He secures the string to a rock so that it makes a 30° angle with the ground. The string is 80 feet long. How high is the kite? Draw a diagram and explain your steps. *(Lesson 9.6)*

19. **Extended Response** A zip-line is a cable to which people can attach a safety harness and slide down to the ground. The lower end of the zip-line is attached to a 5 foot pole and makes a 15° angle with the horizon. Round your answers to the nearest tenth of a foot. *(Lesson 9.6)*

24 ft

15°

5 ft

a. What is the height of the taller pole?

b. Find the distance between the two poles.

c. Describe how you can change the height of one of the poles so that the angle between the zip-line and the horizon is 20°.

Cumulative Practice continued

Chapter 10

Multiple Choice In Exercises 20–26, choose the letter of the correct answer.

20. What is the area of the parallelogram? *(Lesson 10.1)*

A. 24 ft²   **B.** 48 ft²

C. 150.72 ft²   **D.** 76 ft²

21. What is the approximate radius of a circle with an area of 615.44 square feet? *(Lesson 10.2)*

F. 14 feet   **G.** 24.8 feet

H. 36.24 feet   **I.** 307.72 feet

22. Identify the solid. *(Lesson 10.3)*

A. cone

B. cylinder

C. pyramid

D. triangular prism

23. What is the approximate surface area of the cylinder? *(Lesson 10.4)*

F. 56.52 in.²   **G.** 75.36 in.²

H. 100.48 in.²   **I.** 132 in.²

24. What is the approximate surface area of a cone with radius 3 meters and slant height 10 meters? *(Lesson 10.5)*

A. 28.26 m²   **B.** 94.2 m²

C. 122.52 m²   **D.** 314 m²

25. What is the approximate volume of the cylinder? *(Lesson 10.6)*

F. 16 cm³   **G.** 100.53 cm³

H. 401.92 cm³   **I.** 803.84 cm³

26. What is the approximate volume of the cone? *(Lesson 10.7)*

A. 150.72 cm³

B. 324 cm³

C. 452.39 cm³

D. 1017.36 cm³

27. **Short Response** Identify the solid. Then count the number of faces, edges, and vertices. *(Lesson 10.3)*

28. **Extended Response** The figure below represents a *yurt*, a dwelling used by nomadic tribes in Central Asia. *(Lessons 10.4, 10.5)*

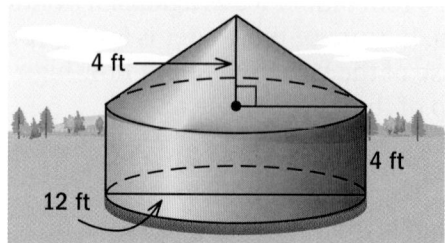

a. What two solids combine to form the figure shown?

b. Sketch a net of the figure.

c. Find the surface area of the figure to the nearest tenth.

Advanced Algebra Topics

CHAPTER

11 Linear Equations and Graphs

12 Data Analysis and Probability

13 Polynomials and Functions

Meeting the Florida Standards

- **Write and use functions to predict outcomes.**
  MA.D.1.3.1, MA.E.1.3.1

- **Write and solve equations and inequalities.**
  MA.C.3.3.2, MA.D.1.3.1, MA.D.1.3.2, MA.D.2.3.1

- **Graph linear equations and inequalities.**
  MA.C.3.3.2, MA.D.1.3.2, MA.D.2.3.1, MA.E.1.3.1

- **Make and interpret data displays. Choose an appropriate display for a data set.**
  MA.E.1.3.1, MA.E.1.3.2, MA.E.1.3.3, MA.E.3.3.2

- **Use tree diagrams, the counting principle, and permutations and combinations to solve problems.**
  MA.A.3.3.2, MA.A.5.3.1

- **Find probabilities of independent and dependent events.**
  MA.E.2.3.1, MA.E.2.3.2, MA.E.3.3.1, MA.E.3.3.2

- **Simplify and evaluate expressions using exponents.**
  MA.A.1.3.4, MA.A.2.3.1, MA.A.3.3.1, MA.D.2.3.1

- **Evaluate and graph non-linear equations.**
  MA.D.1.3.1, MA.D.1.3.2, MA.E.1.3.1, MA.E.1.3.3

From Chapter 11, p. 555

What is the divers' depth?

537

11

Linear Equations and Graphs

BEFORE

In previous chapters you've...

- Translated verbal sentences into mathematical statements
- Solved equations in one variable

Now

In Chapter 11 you'll study...

- Constructing and interpreting scatter plots
- Finding solutions of equations in two variables
- Writing and graphing equations

WHY?

So you can solve real-world problems about...

- gray whales, p. 543
- inline skates, p. 549
- elevators, p. 552
- hiking, p. 577

Internet Preview
CLASSZONE.COM

- eEdition Plus Online
- eWorkbook Plus Online
- eTutorial Plus Online
- FCAT Practice
- More Examples

Chapter Warm-Up Games

Review skills you need for this chapter in these quick games.

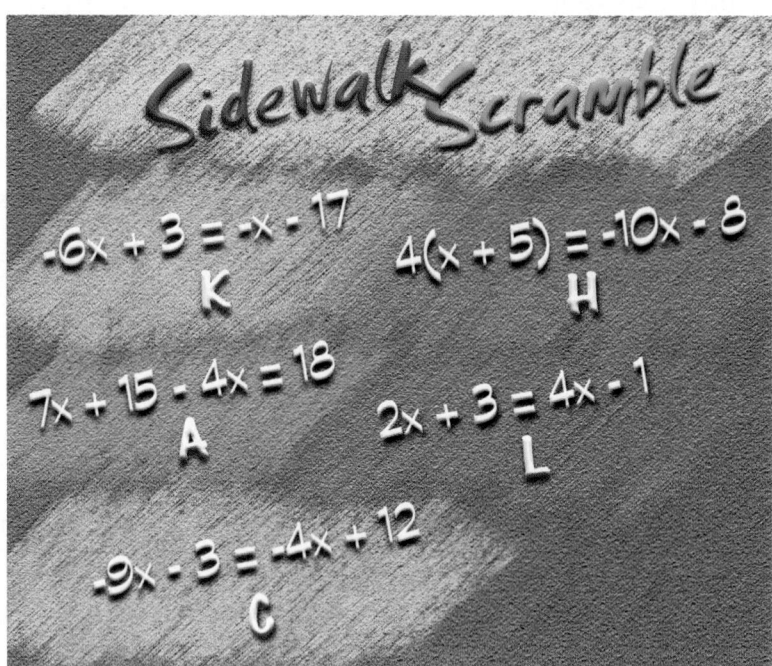

Sidewalk Scramble

$-6x + 3 = -x - 17$ **K** $4(x + 5) = -10x - 8$ **H**

$7x + 15 - 4x = 18$ **A** $2x + 3 = 4x - 1$ **L**

$-9x - 3 = -4x + 12$ **C**

Key Skill:
Solving equations in one variable

Solve the scramble to spell a word associated with sidewalk art.

- Find the solution of each equation.

- Order the equations so that the one with the least solution is first and the one with the greatest solution is last. This will unscramble the letters.

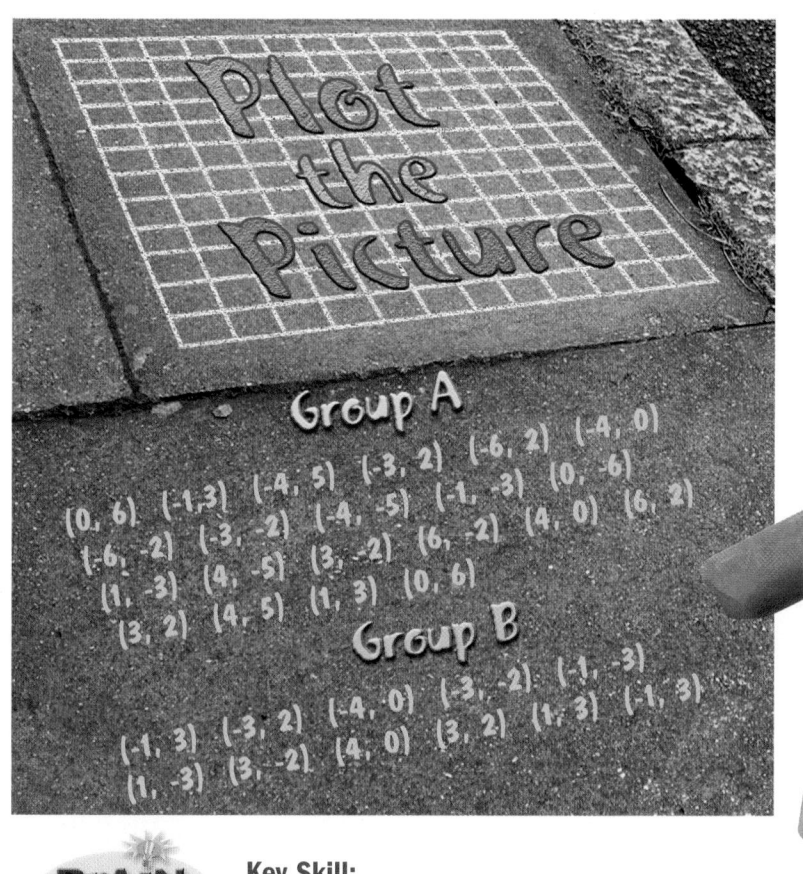

Group A

(0, 6) (-1,3) (-4, 5) (-3, 2) (-6, 2) (-4, 0)
(-6, -2) (-3, -2) (-4, -5) (-1, -3) (0, -6)
(1, -3) (4, -5) (3, -2) (6, -2) (4, 0) (6, 2)
(3, 2) (4, 5) (1, 3) (0, 6)

Group B

(-1, 3) (-3, 2) (-4, 0) (-3, -2) (-1, -3)
(1, -3) (3, -2) (4, 0) (3, 2) (1, 3) (-1, 3)

Key Skill:
Plotting points on a coordinate grid

Create a piece of sidewalk art.

- Plot the points listed in Group A on a coordinate grid. Connect each point with a line to the point that follows it.

- Now find and connect the points in Group B in order.

Stop *and* Think

1. **Writing** A student says that in *Sidewalk Scramble* the first step in solving the equation $-6x + 3 = -x - 17$ is to subtract x from both sides. Explain why the student is wrong.

2. **Extension** Design your own piece of sidewalk art. Write directions for making your sidewalk art using points on a coordinate grid.

Getting Ready to Learn

Review What You Need to Know

1. Using Vocabulary Draw a coordinate plane and label the *x*-axis, *y*-axis, origin, and third quadrant.

2. Write the ordered pair for each labeled point in the coordinate plane.

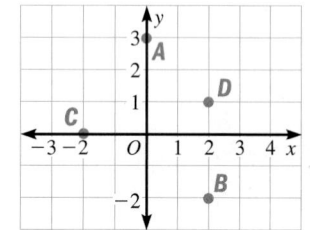

Plot the point in a coordinate plane. *(p. 91)*

3. $(0, 4)$ **4.** $(-2, 3)$ **5.** $(5, -4)$ **6.** $(-2, -3)$

Solve the equation. *(p. 119)*

7. $3 = 9x - 24$ **8.** $7 - 8x = 3$ **9.** $6x + 9 = -45$

Solve the inequality. *(p. 295)*

10. $3x - 4 \leq 5$ **11.** $-4x - 3 \geq 12$ **12.** $6 + 2x < 2$

You should include material that appears on a notebook like this in your own notes.

Know How to Take Notes

Write Questions About Homework If you don't know how to solve a homework problem, make a note in you notebook. Leave room to write the answer to your question.

What is the distance from A to C?

I can't count along the grid from A to C, so how do I solve this?

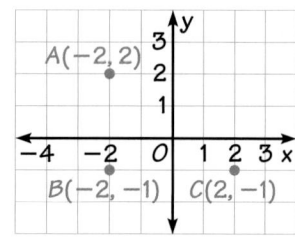

Use the Pythagorean theorem. AB = 3, BC = 4, and △ABC is a right triangle, so AC = 5.

In Chapter 11, you will learn how the coordinate plane is related to equations. Be sure to find answers to any questions you have.

Relations and Functions

LESSON 11.1

BEFORE	Now	WHY?
You translated verbal sentences into algebraic models.	You'll use tables to represent functions.	So you can find the amount of formula consumed, as in Ex. 8.

(**In the Real World**)

Word Watch

relation, p. 541
input, p. 541
output, p. 541
function, p. 541
domain, p. 542
range, p. 542

FLORIDA
Standards and Assessment

• Find a function rule for an input/output table. (MA.D.1.3.1)

• Use functions to predict outcomes. (MA.D.1.3.1)

Fundraisers Your soccer team is selling glow sticks to raise money. The team paid $50 for a case of 48 glow sticks and sells each glow stick for $3. How many glow sticks does the team need to sell to start earning a profit? You will answer this question in Example 2.

A **relation** is a set of ordered pairs that relates an **input** to an **output**. A relation can be written as a set of ordered pairs or by using an *input-output table*.

(**Input,** Output)
(2, 5)
(4, 7)
(−1, 15)
(0, 0)

Input	Output
2	5
4	7
−1	15
0	0

A relation is a **function** if for each input there is exactly one output. In a function, you can say that the output is a *function of* the input.

EXAMPLE 1 Identifying Functions

Tell whether the relation is a function. Explain your answer.

a. (0, 2), (1, 4), (2, 6), (3, 8)

b.

Input	9	9	25	25
Output	3	−3	5	−5

Watch Out!

In a function, two different inputs can have the same output, but each input must have *exactly one* output.

ANSWER The relation is a a function. Each input has exactly one output.

ANSWER The relation is *not* a function. Both 9 and 25 have two outputs.

(**Your turn now**) **Tell whether the relation is a function.**

1. (−2, 4), (2, 4), (4, 2), (−2, −4)

2.

Input	−2	0	2	4
Output	4	0	4	16

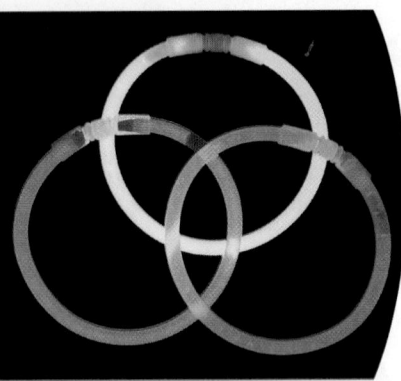

Domain and Range The **domain** of a function is the set of all possible input values. The **range** of a function is the set of all possible output values. A *function rule* assigns each number in the domain to exactly one number in the range.

EXAMPLE **2** **Evaluating a Function**

Fundraising To solve the problem on page 541, use the function rule $P = 3g - 50$, where P is the profit in dollars and g is the number of glow sticks your team sells.

Solution

First, make a table to determine how many glow sticks your soccer team needs to sell to start earning a profit.

 with Solving

In Example 2, a negative output value indicates a loss of money for the team.

Input g	Function	Output P
0	$P = 3(0) - 50$	-50
10	$P = 3(10) - 50$	-20
16	$P = 3(16) - 50$	-2
17	$P = 3(17) - 50$	1

There are 48 glow sticks, so the domain is 0, 1, 2, 3, . . . , 48. The range is $-50, -47, -44, -41, \ldots , 94$.

ANSWER Your soccer team needs to sell at least 17 glow sticks.

EXAMPLE **3** **Writing a Function Rule**

Write a function rule that relates *x* and *y*.

+2 +2 +2 +2

Input x	-4	-2	0	2	4
Output y	1	3	5	7	9

+2 +2 +2 +2

To write a function rule, try to find an equation of the form $y = ax + b$. You can look at differences in the function to find values of a and b.

1. The value of a is $\dfrac{\text{change in output}}{\text{change in input}}$.

$a = \dfrac{2}{2} = 1$ $\qquad\qquad\qquad$ $y = 1x + b$

2. To find b, choose an input-output pair to substitute for x and y.

Let $(x, y) = (0, 5)$ $\qquad\qquad$ $5 = 1(0) + b$, so $b = 5$

ANSWER A function rule that relates x and y is $y = x + 5$.

✓ **Check** $3 = -2 + 5$ $\qquad$ **Substitute (−2, 3) in function rule.**

11.1 Exercises

More Practice, p. 737

Getting Ready to Practice

1. Vocabulary Copy and complete: A relation that has exactly one output value for each input is a(n) ? .

Tell whether the relation is a function.

2. $(3, 0)$, $(0, 6)$, $(1, 5)$, $(3, 7)$
$(-1, 2)$, $(5, 1)$, $(-3, 0)$

3.

Input	−2	3	8	13
Output	0	0	0	0

Copy and complete the table of values for the function rule.

4. $y = x - 3$ **5.** $5x + y = 13$

Input x	−1	0	1	2
Output y	?	?	?	?

Write a function rule that relates x and y.

6.

Input x	−1	0	1	2
Output y	5	6	7	8

7.

Input x	0	1	2	3
Output y	0	−5	−10	−15

8. Whale Calf A gray whale calf was nursed back to health with milk-based formula. The table shows the amounts of formula, in gallons, the whale consumed every 3 to 4 hours. Use the table to write a function rule.

Number of times fed	Total amount consumed (gal)
1	2
2	4
3	6
4	8

Practice and Problem Solving

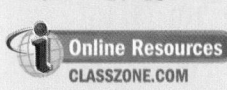

with **Homework**

Example	Exercises
1	9–12
2	13–16
3	17–18

Online Resources
CLASSZONE.COM

· More Examples
· eTutorial Plus

Tell whether the relation is a function. Explain your answer.

9. $(4, 5)$, $(2, -3)$, $(4, 9)$, $(-2, -3)$ **10.** $(-3, 7)$, $(3, 7)$, $(7, 3)$, $(-7, -3)$

11.

Input	−3	−2	0	2
Output	9	4	0	4

12.

Input	4	4	2	5
Output	2	−2	5	−5

Make an input-output table for the function rule. Use a domain of −2, −1, 0, 1, and 2. Identify the range.

13. $y = x - 1$ **14.** $y = -\frac{1}{4}x$ **15.** $y = 5x$ **16.** $y = x^2$

Write a function rule that relates *x* and *y*.

17.

Input *x*	1	2	3	4
Output *y*	5	10	15	20

18.

Input *x*	−3	−2	−1	0
Output *y*	−12	−8	−4	0

19. Recycling Stanley receives $.75 per pound of aluminum cans he recycles. Is the weight of cans he recycles a function of the number of cans? Explain.

20. Tickets Ashley is buying movie tickets that are all the same price. Is the total cost a function of the number of tickets? Explain.

Write a function rule that relates *r* and *t*.

21.

Input *r*	1	2	3	4
Output *t*	1	4	7	10

22.

Input *r*	0	1	2	3
Output *t*	2	1.5	1	0.5

23. Writing Your friend says that the input-output table below represents a function. Is your friend correct? Explain why or why not.

Input *x*	−9	−4.5	0	4.5	9
Output *y*	81	20.25	0	20.25	81

24. Challenge Explain why the distance you travel on your bike is not always a function of the time you spend riding your bike. Describe a situation when it would be a function.

Mixed Review

Find the surface area of the solid. *(Lessons 10.4–10.5)*

25.

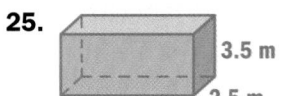

3.5 m
2.5 m
8 m

26.

6 cm
5 cm

27.

60 ft
25 ft

FCAT Practice FCAT

28. Multiple Choice Which set of ordered pairs represents the function rule $y = 5x$?

A. (0, 0), (5, 1), (10, 2), (15, 3) **B.** (0, 0), (1, 5), (2, 10), (3, 15)

C. (0, 5), (1, 6), (2, 7), (3, 8) **D.** (0, −5), (1, −4), (2, −3), (3, −2)

29. Multiple Choice Which of the following relations is *not* a function?

F. (3, 2), (4, 5), (6, 4), (5, 4) **G.** (3, 2), (3, 4), (7, 6), (2, 9)

H. (8, −1), (11, 0), (1, 8), (5, 4) **I.** (5, 3), (4, 3), (6, 4), (9, 6)

Scatter Plots

BEFORE	▶ Now	WHY?
You found a function rule given a table of values.	You'll make and interpret scatter plots.	So you can compare study time to test score, as in Ex. 6.

In the Real World

Word Watch

scatter plot, p. 545

FLORIDA
Standards and Assessment

• Construct and interpret data displays. Contrast data displays. (MA.E.1.3.1)

• Read, analyze, and describe graphs of lines. (MA.D.1.3.1)

NASA NASA's Crawler Transporter is a large vehicle that moves the space shuttle and its launch platform to the launch pad. The crawler uses about 126 gallons of fuel to travel 1 mile.

The table below shows the amount of fuel that is used to travel different numbers of miles. How can you present this information using a graph?

Distance (miles)	1	2	3	4	5	6
Amount of fuel (gallons)	126	252	378	504	630	756

You can represent the information using a *scatter plot*. A **scatter plot** is the graph of a collection of ordered pairs.

EXAMPLE 1 Making and Interpreting a Scatter Plot

You can represent and make conclusions about the information above using a scatter plot.

To make a scatter plot, graph the ordered pairs from the table.

(1, 126), (2, 252), (3, 378),

(4, 504), (5, 630), (6, 756)

Put *Distance* on the horizontal axis and *Fuel used* on the vertical axis.

ANSWER As the distance traveled increases, the amount of fuel used increases. There is exactly one output for each input, so this is a function.

NASA Crawler Transporter

Fuel used (gal) vs Distance (mi)

NASA's Crawler Transporter

Your turn now Make a scatter plot of the data.

1.

c	−2	−1	0	1
d	−5	−4	−3	−2

2.

x	0	3	6	9
y	−2	−4	−6	−8

Interpreting Scatter Plots Scatter plots show what kind of relationship exists between two sets of data.

Positive relationship	Negative relationship	No relationship
		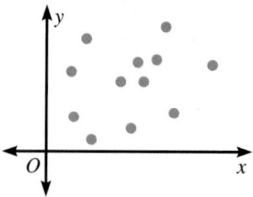
The *y*-coordinates tend to increase as the *x*-coordinates increase.	The *y*-coordinates tend to decrease as the *x*-coordinates increase.	No pattern exists between the coordinates.

EXAMPLE 2 **Interpreting a Scatter Plot**

Shipping and Handling The table shows the cost *y* of shipping and handling per item when you buy *x* items.

Number of items *x*	1	2	3	4	5	6
Cost per item *y*	$6.58	$3.37	$2.37	$1.79	$1.46	$1.24

a. Make a scatter plot of the data. Tell whether *x* and *y* have a *positive relationship*, a *negative relationship*, or *no relationship*.

b. Estimate the cost of shipping and handling per item if you buy eight items.

Solution

a. In the scatter plot, the *y*-coordinates decrease as the *x*-coordinates increase.

> **ANSWER** The quantities have a negative relationship.

b. To estimate the shipping and handling cost per item to buy eight items, draw a curve that shows the overall pattern of the data, as shown. The curve looks like it will pass through the point (8, 1).

> **ANSWER** The shipping and handling cost per item, if you buy eight items, is about $1.

Getting Ready to Practice

1. **Vocabulary** Copy and complete: A(n) _?_ is a graph of a collection of ordered pairs.

2. **Guided Problem Solving** The table shows the number of cookbooks sold at a bookstore in each of the six years it has been open. Predict the number of cookbooks that will be sold in the ninth year.

Year x	1	2	3	4	5	6
Books y	450	650	700	800	1100	1250

(1 Make a scatter plot.

(2 Describe the relationship between the variables.

(3 Estimate the number of cookbooks that will be sold in the ninth year by sketching a curve that follows the trend of the data.

Practice and Problem Solving

Tell whether x and y have a _positive relationship_, a _negative relationship_, or _no relationship_.

3.

4.

5.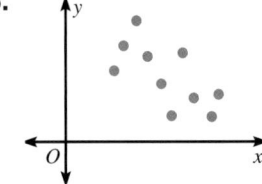

Make a scatter plot of the data. What conclusions can you make?

6.

Hours spent studying	Test score (percent)
1	70
2	80
3	85

7.

Month	Air conditioners sold
1 (Aug.)	1500
2 (Sept.)	1250
3 (Oct.)	975

Make a scatter plot of the data. Describe the relationship between the variables. Use the relationship to find the next ordered pair.

8.

x	1	2	3	4	5
y	5	10	15	20	?

9.

x	3	4	5	6	7
y	3	6	9	12	?

In Exercises 10–12, what type of relationship might you expect for the given data?

10. The height of a student in 8th grade and a test score of the student

11. The size of a pizza and the price of a pizza

12. The amount of money you give back to your friend and the amount you still owe

13. Writing A newspaper claims there is a strong relationship between the weather on the day of an election and voter turnout. What do you think the newspaper means? Could the newspaper use a scatter plot to support its claim? If so, what would the labels on each axis be?

14. Geometry Make a table showing several values of length and width of a rectangle whose perimeter is 12 inches. Make a scatter plot of the data. Draw a curve that shows the overall pattern of the data. Predict the width of a rectangle when the length is 3.5 inches.

Mixed Review

Find the area of a trapezoid with bases b_1 and b_2 and height h.
(Lesson 10.1)

15. $b_1 = 14$ m, $b_2 = 16$ m, $h = 6$ m   **16.** $b_1 = 21$ ft, $b_2 = 32$ ft, $h = 18$ ft

17. Draw the net of a triangular pyramid. *(Lesson 10.3)*

Make a table of values for the function. Use a domain of −2, −1, 0, 1, and 2. Identify the range. *(Lesson 11.1)*

18. $y = 0.7x$ **19.** $y = 3x + 4$ **20.** $y = 0.4x - 1$

Basic Skills Solve the equation.

21. $t - 4 = 15$ **22.** $6 + x = 27$ **23.** $z + 17 = 36$ **24.** $w - 13 = 42$

FCAT Practice

Use the information in the table.

25. Multiple Choice Describe the relationship shown in the data.

    A. positive   **B.** negative

    C. none   **D.** positive and negative

26. Multiple Choice Predict what the average high temperature for July will be in Miami, Florida, according to the data.

    F. 105°F   **G.** 60°F

    H. 89°F   **I.** 85°F

Miami, Florida	
Month	Avg. high temperature
1 (Jan)	75°F
2 (Feb)	76°F
3 (March)	79°F
4 (April)	82°F
5 (May)	85°F
6 (June)	87°F

LESSON 11.3

Equations in Two Variables

BEFORE	▶ Now	WHY?
You found solutions of equations in one variable.	You'll find solutions of equations in two variables.	So you can find how long it takes to pay back a loan, as in Ex. 29.

Word Watch

solution of an equation in two variables, p. 549

FLORIDA
Standards and Assessment
- Find ordered-pair solutions given an equation. (MA.C.3.3.2)
- Solve linear equations. (MA.D.2.3.1)

In the Real World

In-line Skates At a sports store, it costs $7 per hour to rent in-line skates plus $10 for the safety equipment. The total cost can be modeled by the equation $C = 10 + 7h$, where C is the total cost in dollars and h is the number of hours skated. What are some possible costs for renting in-line skates?

A **solution of an equation in two variables** is an ordered pair whose values make the equation true. For example, (2, 3) is a solution of $x + y = 5$ because $2 + 3 = 5$.

EXAMPLE 1 Evaluating an Equation in Two Variables

a. Make a table for $C = 10 + 7h$ to find some possible costs for renting in-line skates.

b. How many hours can you skate if you have $35?

Solution

a. Substitute several values of h into the equation and solve for C.

h-value	Substitute for h.	Solve for C.	Solution
$h = 1$	$C = 10 + 7(1)$	$C = 17$	$(1, 17)$
$h = 2$	$C = 10 + 7(2)$	$C = 24$	$(2, 24)$
$h = 3$	$C = 10 + 7(3)$	$C = 31$	$(3, 31)$
$h = 4$	$C = 10 + 7(4)$	$C = 38$	$(4, 38)$

Use the solutions to make a table.

Hours skated h	1	2	3	4
Total cost C	$17	$24	$31	$38

b. If you have $35, you can rent in-line skates for about $3\frac{1}{2}$ hours.

EXAMPLE 2 Checking Solutions

Tell whether (7, −6) is a solution of $x + 3y = 14$.

$x + 3y = 14$	Write original equation.
$7 + 3(-6) \overset{?}{=} 14$	Substitute 7 for x and −6 for y.
$7 + (-18) \overset{?}{=} 14$	Simplify.
$-11 \neq 14$ ✗	Solution does not check.

ANSWER The ordered pair (7, −6) is *not* a solution of $x + 3y = 14$.

When finding solutions of an equation, it can be helpful to rewrite the equation in *function form*. When an equation is in function form it is solved for y.

Function form	Not function form
$y = -2x + 15$	$2x + y = 15$

HELP with Solving

Generally, an equation involving two variables has an infinite number of solutions.

EXAMPLE 3 Finding Solutions of an Equation

Solve the equation $4x + y = 15$ for y. List four solutions.

① Rewrite the equation in function form.

$4x + y = 15$	Write original equation.
$y = 15 - 4x$	Subtract $4x$ from each side.

② Evaluate the equation for several x-values.

x-value	Substitute for x.	Solve for y.	Solution
$x = -1$	$y = 15 - 4(-1)$	$y = 19$	$(-1, 19)$
$x = 0$	$y = 15 - 4(0)$	$y = 15$	$(0, 15)$
$x = 1$	$y = 15 - 4(1)$	$y = 11$	$(1, 11)$
$x = 2$	$y = 15 - 4(2)$	$y = 7$	$(2, 7)$

ANSWER Four solutions are $(-1, 19)$, $(0, 15)$, $(1, 11)$, and $(2, 7)$.

Your turn now Tell whether the ordered pair is a solution of the equation.

1. $y = 3x - 7$; $(6, 5)$

2. $-2x - 4y = 12$; $(-4, -1)$

List four solutions of the equation.

3. $y = -2x + 6$

4. $15x + 3y = 12$

Getting Ready to Practice

1. **Vocabulary** Copy and complete: A(n) __?__ of an equation in two variables is an ordered pair.

Rewrite the equation in function form.

2. $3x + y = 19$ 3. $-4x + 2y = 8$ 4. $-10x - 5y = -15$

5. **Find the Error** Describe and correct the error made when a student was asked to decide whether $(-5, 4)$ is a solution of $2x + 3y = -7$.

$$2x + 3y = -7$$
$$2(4) + 3(-5) \stackrel{?}{=} -7$$
$$8 + (-15) \stackrel{?}{=} -7$$
$$-7 = -7 \checkmark \quad \text{So, } (-5, 4) \text{ is a solution.}$$

6. **Skateboard Wheels** Your skateboard club decides to replace each club member's wheels for a competition. Sets of four wheels sell for $24 plus a $14 shipping and handling cost added to the total. Use the equation $C = 24n + 14$, where C is the total cost in dollars and n is the number of sets of wheels ordered. If the final cost is $182, how many sets of wheels were bought?

Practice and Problem Solving

HELP with **Homework**

Example	Exercises
1	7-9, 29
2	10-15, 19-22
3	16-18, 23-28

Online Resources
CLASSZONE.COM
· More Examples
· eTutorial Plus

Copy and complete the table for the equation.

x	−5	0	5	10
y	?	?	?	?

7. $y = x + 8$ 8. $y = 4 - 3x$ 9. $y = -20 + x$

Tell whether the ordered pair is a solution of the equation.

10. $y = 4x + 2$; $(2, 10)$ 11. $y = -2x + 5$; $(7, 5)$ 12. $y = 6 - x$; $(-3, 3)$

13. $y = 13 - 5x$; $(4, -7)$ 14. $y = 6x + 7$; $(2, 21)$ 15. $y = 3x - 26$; $(6, -8)$

List four solutions of the equation.

16. $y = -2x + 5$ 17. $y = -10 + (-4x)$ 18. $y = \frac{1}{2}x - 1$

Calculator Tell whether the ordered pair is a solution of the equation.

19. $3x - y = 71.2$; $(-4.6, 8.2)$ **20.** $8x + y = 25$; $(2.25, 1.75)$

21. $x + 4y = 28.75$; $(3.23, 6.38)$ **22.** $x - 2y = -10.42$; $(-5.22, -7.82)$

List four solutions of the equation.

23. $y = 2x - 13$ **24.** $y = 16x + 24$ **25.** $-5x + 3 = y$

26. $y = -x + 17$ **27.** $y = -51 - 6x$ **28.** $y = \frac{1}{3}x - 5$

29. Loan Your friend agrees to lend you $15 to buy a toy rocket. You promise to pay your friend $.75 each week until you have paid back the full $15. Use the equation $P = 15 - 0.75n$, where P is the amount of money in dollars that you have left to pay and n is the number of weeks, to find the number of weeks it takes to pay back your friend.

30. Critical Thinking In Example 3 of the lesson, you solved the equation for y before substituting the x-values. Will you get the same solutions if you substitute the x-values before solving for y?

Solve the equation for y. List four solutions of the equation.

31. $x + y = 8$ **32.** $42 = 4x + y$ **33.** $33 = -3x + y$

34. $4y = 8x + 12$ **35.** $5y + 15x = 10$ **36.** $-32 = 4x - 12y$

Write an equation in two variables for the values in the table.

37.

x	−1	0	1	2
y	2	4	6	8

38.

x	0	2	4	6
y	2	3	4	5

39. Estimation Estimate the values of $9x$ and $8y$ to explain why $\left(\frac{8}{3}, \frac{-7}{10}\right)$ is not a solution of $9x + 8y = 16$.

40. Glass Elevator An elevator is at a height of 800 feet. It is descending at a rate of 150 feet per minute. Use the equation $h = 800 - 150m$, where h is the height of the elevator in feet and m is the time in minutes. What is the height of the elevator after 5 minutes? How long will it take the elevator to reach a height of 0 feet?

41. Challenge Find the ordered pair that is the solution of both of the equations $y = -2x + 3$ and $y = 0.5x - 2$.

42. Carnival You can go to the carnival for 2 hours. You know that each ride takes about 10 minutes (including the wait in line), and you also want to spend time playing games. Write an equation in two variables to model this situation. If you go on 8 rides, how long can you play games?

Mixed Review

43. Plot (2, 3), (−6, 0), (−5, −1), and (8, −4) in a coordinate plane.
(Lesson 2.8)

44. Find the area of a circle whose diameter is 25 inches. Use 3.14 for π.
(Lesson 10.2)

Make a table of values for the function. Use a domain of −2, −1, 0, 1, and 2. Identify the range. *(Lesson 11.1)*

45. $4x + 8y = 16$ **46.** $6x + 3y = 36$ **47.** $14x + 7y = 56$

Basic Skills **Solve the equation.**

48. $6x − 4.25 = 3.55$ **49.** $14.98 + 2.4y = −6.02$

FCAT Practice   FCAT

INTERNET
FCAT PRACTICE
CLASSZONE.COM

50. **Short Response** To join a gym, you pay a $35 initiation fee and then pay $14 per month. This situation can be modeled by the equation $C = 35 + 14m$, where C is the total cost, and m is the number of months for which you join. Copy and complete the table to find some possible costs for joining the gym. If you can spend $80 on membership fees, for how many months can you join the gym?

Number of months m	Total cost C
1	?
2	?
3	?
4	?

51. **Multiple Choice** Which ordered pair is *not* a solution of the equation $y = −4x + 13$?

   A. (−2, 21)   **B.** (0, −13)   **C.** (2, 5)   **D.** (−1, 17)

BRAIN GAME

Late Night Show

Each ordered pair is a solution of exactly one lettered equation. Write the appropriate letters in the blanks to find what kind of show the boy can expect to see.

_?_	_?_	_?_	_?_	_?_	_?_	_?_	_?_	_?_	_?_	_?_
(4, 1)	(9, 12)	(1, 9)	(3, 2)	(2, 5)	(4, 4)	(1, 9)	(17, 9)	(7, 24)	(0, 2)	(8, 15)

L. $y = 2x − 6$ **A.** $x + y = 10$ **T.** $4x + y = 20$ **E.** $y = 2x + 1$

I. $6x − y = 18$ **N.** $2y = 6x − 14$ **R.** $y = x − 8$ **U.** $y = \frac{1}{3}x + 2$

M. $x + 3y = 53$ **P.** $y = \frac{3}{2}x − 5$ **S.** $x + y = 6$ **0.** $y = x + 1$

Problem Solving Strategies

Guess, Check, and Revise
Look for a Pattern
Draw a Diagram
Act It Out
Make a Table
Work Backward
Make a Model

FLORIDA: Standards and Assessment
Read and interpret data displays. (MA.E.1.3.1)

Make a Table

Problem At the beginning of swimming class John can swim 4 laps. Starting after the first week, his swimming teacher wants him to swim 2 laps more than the week before until the end of the 7 week class. At this rate, how many laps will John be able to swim during the last week of class?

❶ Read and Understand

Read the problem carefully.

You need to use the pattern to find the number of laps John can swim after a given number of weeks.

❷ Make a Plan

Decide on a strategy to use.

One way to solve the problem is to make a table of values. Then extend the pattern until you find the answer.

❸ Solve the Problem

Reread the problem and make a table.

First, make a table and enter the information given.

In week 1, John swims 4 laps. In week 2, he swims 4 + 2, or 6 laps. Each week he swims 2 more laps.

You know that the swimming class is 7 weeks long, so extend your table following the pattern to fill it in.

ANSWER John will be swimming 16 laps during the last week of the 7 week class.

W (weeks)	A (laps)
1	4
2	6
3	8
4	10
5	12
6	14
7	?

❹ Look Back

Compare the information in your table to the original problem to be sure you've used the information correctly.

Use the strategy *make a table.*

1. **Diving** Copy and complete the table below representing the depth in feet of a deep-sea diver, currently 160 feet below the surface, ascending at a rate of 20 feet every 4 minutes.

Time (minutes)	4	8	12	16
Depth (feet)	?	?	?	?

2. **Training** Extend the table below using the pattern to find out how many miles you will run in week 10 of training for a race.

Week	1	2	3	4
Distance (miles)	3	3.5	4	4.5

3. **Hot-Air Balloon** A hot-air balloon has just taken off. The balloon is currently 10 feet off the ground and is rising at a rate of 2 feet per second. What is the height of the balloon after 25 seconds?

4. **Reading** You were assigned to read a book over your 2 week spring vacation. The book has 256 pages, so you decide to read 32 pages each day. At this rate when will you finish the book?

5. **DVD Players** Casey and Krystal are each saving money to buy a DVD player that costs $160. Casey already has $55 saved. He will add $7 every week to his fund. Krystal does not have any money saved. She will put $16 in her fund every week until she can afford it. Who will be able to purchase a DVD player first?

Mixed Problem Solving

Use any strategy to solve the problem.

6. **Number Sense** The cube of what number is 3375?

7. **Folding** You are trying to divide a sheet of paper into rectangles by folding it into thirds. You fold the paper 3 times into thirds without opening it. How many of the smallest rectangles do you have as a result? How many of the smallest rectangles will you have if you fold the paper into thirds one more time?

8. **Clothing** The sale price of a rack of sweaters is 80% of the original price. A month later, the sweaters sold for $23.20 each, which is two dollars less than 70% of the sale price. What is the original price of one of the sweaters?

9. **Running** Leslie and Todd each ran in a race. Leslie ran in the girls' 12–16 year old division on a 10 mile track and Todd ran in the boys' 10–12 year old division on an 8 mile track. Leslie came in second place with a time of 1 hour and 20 minutes. Todd came in first place with a time of 1 hour and 8 minutes. Who ran faster?

10. **Surface Area** Find the surface area of the solid shown below.

8 yd
6 yd
5 yd

LESSON 11.4

Graphs of Linear Equations

BEFORE | ▶ **Now** | **WHY?**

You found solutions of equations in two variables.

You'll learn to sketch the graph of a linear equation.

So you can find the amount you pay on a payment plan, as in Ex. 28.

Word Watch

linear equation, p. 556

FLORIDA
Standards and Assessment

- Given an equation, find and graph ordered-pair solutions. (MA.C.3.3.2)
- Read, analyze, and describe graphs of lines. (MA.D.1.3.1)
- Interpret and create graphs. (MA.D.1.3.2)

Activity You can graph a function by plotting ordered pairs from a table of values.

① Copy and complete the table of values using the equation $y = 3x + 2$.

x	−4	−2	0	2	4
y	−10	?	2	?	?

② Graph each ordered pair (x, y) in a coordinate plane.
$(−4, −10), (−2, ?), (0, 2), (2, ?), (4, ?)$

③ Connect the points. What pattern do you notice?

④ Find several more solutions of $y = 3x + 2$. Locate each solution in your coordinate plane. What do you notice?

⑤ Make a conjecture about the graph of all solutions of $y = 3x + 2$.

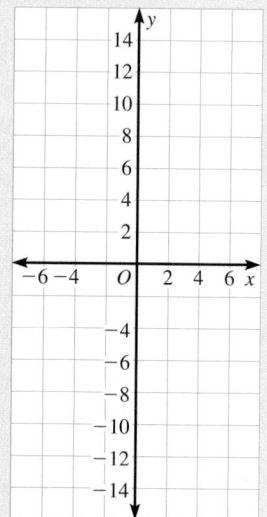

Linear Equations In the activity, you graphed solutions of a *linear equation*. A **linear equation** in two variables is an equation in which the variables appear in separate terms and each variable occurs only to the first power. The graph of a linear equation is a line.

Linear equations	Not linear equations
$y = x − 1$	$24 = rt$
$3p + 5q = 16$	$a^2 + b^2 = c^2$
$s = 0.2t$	

The equation $24 = rt$ is not linear because it has two variables in the same term. The equation $a^2 + b^2 = c^2$ is not linear because the variables are squared.

HELP with **Solving**

The arrowheads on the graph in Example 1 indicate that the line extends forever in both directions.

EXAMPLE 1 **Graphing a Linear Equation**

Graph $y = \frac{1}{2}x + 1$.

Solution

① Choose several x-values and make a table of values.

x	-4	-2	0	2	4
y	-1	0	1	2	3

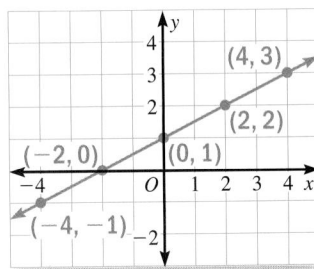

② List the solutions as ordered pairs.

$(-4, -1)$, $(-2, 0)$, $(0, 1)$, $(2, 2)$, $(4, 3)$

③ Graph the ordered pairs. Then draw a line through them.

ANSWER The line is the graph of $y = \frac{1}{2}x + 1$.

Your turn now **Graph the linear equation.**

1. $y = x + 4$ **2.** $y = -2x - 3$ **3.** $y = \frac{1}{2}x - 7$ **4.** $y - x = 6$

What do you think?

Biology

■ **Hair Growth**

If human hair grows at a rate of $\frac{1}{2}$ inch per month, how much does your hair grow in one year? in one and a half years?

EXAMPLE 2 **Using the Graph of a Linear Equation**

Hair Sue's hair is 3 inches long. If her hair grows $\frac{1}{2}$ inch per month, you can model the length l of her hair in inches using the equation $l = \frac{1}{2}m + 3$ where m is the time in months.

a. Graph $l = \frac{1}{2}m + 3$.

b. Estimate how many months it will take Sue to grow her hair to $5\frac{1}{2}$ inches.

Solution

a. Make a table of values.

m	0	1	2	3
l	3	$3\frac{1}{2}$	4	$4\frac{1}{2}$

Then graph each solution and draw a ray through the points.

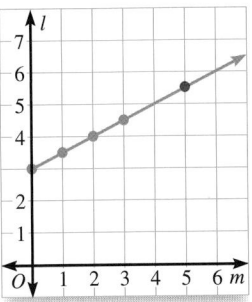

b. The graph shows that it will take about 5 months for Sue to grow her hair to $5\frac{1}{2}$ inches.

Vertical and Horizontal Lines Some linear equations have only one variable. The graphs of these equations are vertical or horizontal lines.

Vertical and Horizontal Lines

The graph of $x = a$ is the vertical line passing through $(a, 0)$.

The graph of $y = b$ is the horizontal line passing through $(0, b)$.

Watch Out!

A vertical line *does not* represent a function, because one input has infinitely many outputs. A horizontal line *does* represent a function.

EXAMPLE 3 **Graphing Vertical and Horizontal Lines**

a. The graph of $x = -2$ is the vertical line through $(-2, 0)$.

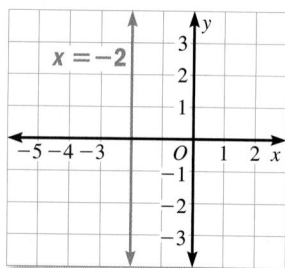

For all values of y, the x-value is -2.

b. The graph of $y = 4$ is the horizontal line through $(0, 4)$.

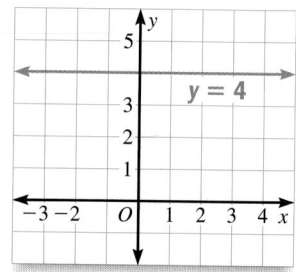

For all values of x, the y-value is 4.

11.4 Exercises

More Practice, p. 737

INTERNET
eWorkbook Plus
CLASSZONE.COM

Getting Ready to Practice

1. Vocabulary Copy and complete: When you graph the solutions of a linear equation, the points form a(n) ? .

Make a table of values for the equation.

2. $3x - y = -2$

3. $y + 4 = 0$

4. $-6x + 2y = 16$

Match the equation with the description of its graph.

5. $y = -16$

6. $x = 20$

7. $y = x + 1$

A. vertical line

B. horizontal line

C. slanted line

Practice and Problem Solving

HELP with Homework

Example	Exercises
1	14-25
2	28
3	14-27, 29

Online Resources
CLASSZONE.COM
· More Examples
· eTutorial Plus

Tell whether the equation is a linear equation.

8. $3x + y = 8$ **9.** $2y - 5x = 10$ **10.** $9x^2 = y + 4$

Find three ordered pairs that are solutions of the given equation.

11. $y = x - 2$ **12.** $y = 3x + 4$ **13.** $y = 6$

Graph the linear equation.

14. $y = x + 9$ **15.** $y = x + 10$ **16.** $y = x - 14$

17. $y = 8x$ **18.** $y = -2x + 1$ **19.** $y = -7x + 8$

20. $y = -5x - 6$ **21.** $y = \frac{1}{2}x + 5$ **22.** $y = -\frac{1}{4}x + 12$

23. $y = 9$ **24.** $x = 8$ **25.** $x = -17$

Critical Thinking **Write the equation of the line.**

26.

27.

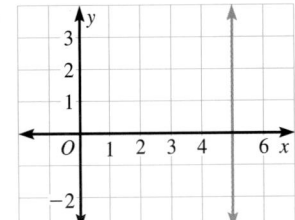

28. Buying a Camera You are taking a photography class and need a digital camera. The payment plan for the camera can be modeled by the equation $C = 10m + 50$, where C is the total amount paid and m is the number of months. Graph the equation and then estimate how much you pay in 12 months.

29. Critical Thinking Graph the equations $x = -3$ and $y = 5$ on the same coordinate grid. Then write the coordinates of the point where the lines intersect. Explain how you can find the coordinates of this point without graphing.

Graph the linear equation.

30. $x - y = 0$ **31.** $10x = -2y$ **32.** $16x - 4y = 8$

33. $9x + 3y = 18$ **34.** $x - 5y = -5$ **35.** $3x - 2y = 6$

36. Savings Account Janet is saving money for a vacation. She has $80 saved and plans to add $15.50 to her savings each month. The equation $y = 15.50x + 80$, where y is the amount of money Janet has saved and x is the number of months, models this situation. Make a table of values and graph the equation. Use your graph to estimate when Janet will have $250.

37. Write the equation of the horizontal line that passes through point A.

38. Write the equation of the vertical line that passes through point B.

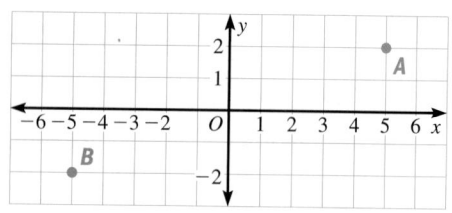

39. **Writing** Explain how to find the equation of a line that is parallel to the x-axis and lies 8.6 units below it.

40. **Challenge** Copy and complete the table for the equation $y = x^2$. Then graph the equation. How can you tell that $y = x^2$ is not a linear equation from looking at the graph? How can you tell from the equation that it is not a linear equation?

x	-2	-1	0	1	2
y	?	?	0	?	?

Mixed Review

Find the area of the parallelogram with height h and base b.
(Lesson 10.1)

41. $h = 10, b = 14$ **42.** $h = 17, b = 23$ **43.** $h = 32, b = 33$

44. Decide whether the relation is a function: $(0, 0)$, $(1, -1)$, $(-1, -1)$, $(2, -2)$. *(Lesson 11.1)*

45. Copy and complete the table for the equation $6x - 2y = 4$. *(Lesson 11.3)*

x	-4	-2	0	1	2	5
y	?	?	-2	?	?	?

Basic Skills **Solve the equation.**

46. $-8n = -240$ **47.** $\dfrac{x}{6} = -42$ **48.** $\dfrac{z}{12} = 4$

FCAT Practice FCAT

49. **Multiple Choice** Which equation is *not* the equation of a line?

A. $y = \dfrac{1}{2}x + 8$ **B.** $2x + 3y = 8$ **C.** $y = x^2 - 8$ **D.** $-2x = -3y + 8$

50. **Short Response** The number of hours Jacob spends on his homework each night can be modeled by the equation $y = 0.5x + 1.5$, where y is the number of hours spent and x is the number of subjects in which he has homework. Make a table of values and graph the equation.

Technology Activity

FLORIDA: Standards and Assessment
Interpret and create graphs. (MA.D.1.3.2)

Graphing Linear Functions

GOAL Use a graphing calculator to graph linear functions.

Example Graph the equation $x - 2y = 6$.

Solution

1 Rewrite the equation so that it is in function form: $y = \frac{1}{2}x - 3$.

2 Use the following keystrokes on a graphing calculator to enter the function:

Keystrokes

  1 2
 3

Display

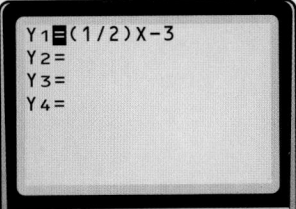

Use the WINDOW feature to set the size of the graph.

```
WINDOW
 Xmin=-5
 Xmax=10
 △X=.1595...
 Xscl=1
 Ymin=-5
 Ymax=5
 Yscl=1
```

View the graph by pressing the GRAPH button.

Your turn now Use a calculator to graph the equation.

1. $y = 2x - 5$ **2.** $y = 5x + 10$ **3.** $x - y = 11$ **4.** $x + y = 6$

Tell whether the viewing window is appropriate for the graph of the equation. If not, give an appropriate window for it.

5. $y = 4x + 5$
```
Xmin=-5
Xmax=5
△X=.1063...
Ymin=-5
Ymax=5
```

6. $y = 2x + 14$
```
Xmin=-5
Xmax=5
△X=.1063...
Ymin=-5
Ymax=5
```

Notebook Review

Review the vocabulary definitions in your notebook.

Copy the review examples in your notebook. Then complete the exercises.

Check Your Definitions

relation, p. 541
input, p. 541
output, p. 541
function, p. 541

domain, p. 542
range, p. 542
scatter plot, p. 545

solution of an equation
  in two variables, p. 549
linear equation, p. 556

Use Your Vocabulary

1. Vocabulary Copy and complete: Two ways to represent a relation are writing the ordered pairs and using a(n) ? .

11.1–11.2 Can you write and plot a function rule?

EXAMPLE Write a function rule that relates x and y. Then make a scatter plot of the data.

Input x	−1	0	1	2
Output y	−6	−5	−4	−3

ANSWER Because each output is 5 less than the corresponding input, a rule for this function is $y = x - 5$. In the scatter plot, the y-coordinates increase as the x-coordinates increase. So the quantities have a positive relationship.

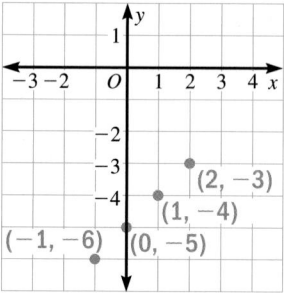

☑ **Write a function rule that relates x and y.**

2.

x	−2	−1	0	1	2
y	8	4	0	−4	−8

3.

x	−6	−3	0	3	6
y	−3	0	3	6	9

4. Make a scatter plot of the data. Describe the relationship.

x	1	1.5	2	2.5	3
y	10	15	20	25	30

EXAMPLE Graph the equation $y = 2x + 1$.

Choose 3 values for x. Substitute each value into the equation and solve for y.

x-value	Substitute for x.	Solve for y.	Solution
$x = -1$	$y = 2(-1) + 1$	$y = -1$	$(-1, -1)$
$x = 0$	$y = 2(0) + 1$	$y = 1$	$(0, 1)$
$x = 1$	$y = 2(1) + 1$	$y = 3$	$(1, 3)$

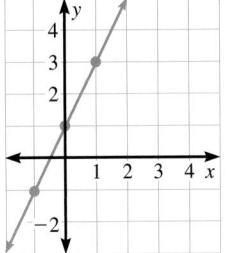

☑ **List three solutions of the equation and then graph it.**

5. $2x + y = 5$ **6.** $-9x + 3y = -18$ **7.** $4y - x = 16$

Stop *and* Think   about Lessons 11.1–11.4

8. Writing The ordered pair $(2, 3)$ is a solution of $8 = 2y + x$. It is also a solution of $4y = -2x + 16$. Explain why every solution of $8 = 2y + x$ is also a solution of $4y = -2x + 16$.

Review Quiz 1

1. Make a table of values for $y = -\frac{1}{3}x$. Use a domain of 0, 1, 2, and 3. Identify the range.

2. Is $(5, -4)$ a solution of the equation $x - 6y = 29$?

List three solutions of the equation and then graph it.

3. $7y + x = 21$ **4.** $-5x - 2y = -20$ **5.** $-3x + 9y = -18$

Write a function rule that relates x and y.

6. $(-2, 0)$, $(-1, 1)$, $(0, 2)$, $(1, 3)$, $(2, 4)$

7. $(-3, -5)$, $(0, 1)$, $(3, 7)$, $(6, 13)$, $(9, 19)$

8. Fundraising An art club raised $120 for supplies by selling pottery made by students. Mugs cost $4 and bowls cost $2. Make an input-output table and a graph for the equation $4x + 2y = 120$, where x is the number of mugs sold and y is the number of bowls sold. Suppose the art club sold 20 mugs. How many bowls did it sell?

LESSON 11.5

Using Intercepts

BEFORE You graphed linear equations.

▶ **Now** You'll find *x*- and *y*-intercepts of a line.

WHY? So you can find the number of CDs you can buy, as in Ex. 4.

Word Watch

x-intercept, p. 564
y-intercept, p. 564

FLORIDA
Standards and Assessment

• Find ordered-pair solutions given an equation or a graph. (MA.C.3.3.2)
• Use graphs to illustrate real-world situations. (MA.D.1.3.2)

Intercepts The **x-intercept** of a graph is the *x*-coordinate of the point where the graph crosses the *x*-axis. The graph of $2x + 3y = 12$ crosses the *x*-axis at $(6, 0)$, so its *x*-intercept is 6.

The **y-intercept** is the *y*-coordinate of the point where the graph intersects the *y*-axis. The graph of $2x + 3y = 12$ crosses the *y*-axis at $(0, 4)$, so its *y*-intercept is 4.

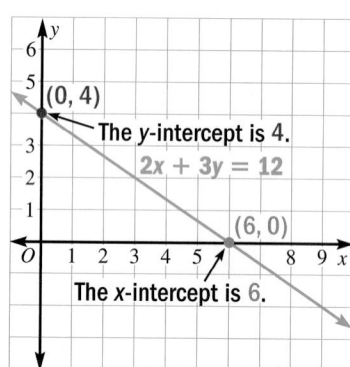

The *y*-intercept is 4.
$2x + 3y = 12$
(6, 0)
(0, 4)
The *x*-intercept is 6.

Finding Intercepts

To find the *x*-intercept of a line, substitute 0 for *y* into the equation and solve for *x*.

To find the *y*-intercept of a line, substitute 0 for *x* into the equation and solve for *y*.

EXAMPLE 1 **Finding Intercepts**

Find the intercepts of the graph of $y = \frac{1}{2}x - 5$.

To find the *x*-intercept, let $y = 0$ and solve for *x*.

$$y = \frac{1}{2}x - 5$$

$$0 = \frac{1}{2}x - 5$$

$$5 = \frac{1}{2}x$$

$$10 = x$$

To find the *y*-intercept, let $x = 0$ and solve for *y*.

$$y = \frac{1}{2}x - 5$$

$$y = \frac{1}{2}(0) - 5$$

$$y = 0 - 5$$

$$y = -5$$

ANSWER The *x*-intercept is 10 and the *y*-intercept is -5. The graph of the equation contains the points $(10, 0)$ and $(0, -5)$.

Graphing The intercepts tell you the points where a line intersects the x-axis and the y-axis. You can use these points to graph a line.

EXAMPLE 2 **Using Intercepts to Graph a Line**

HELP with Notetaking

Be sure to write down in your notebook that the intercepts of a line are numbers, not points.

Graph the line with an x-intercept of −3 and a y-intercept of 2.

The x-intercept is −3, so plot the point (−3, 0). The y-intercept is 2, so plot the point (0, 2).

Draw a line through the two points.

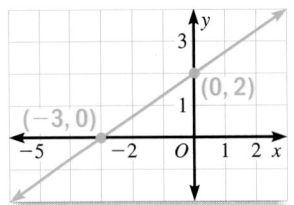

Your turn now Find the intercepts of the graph of the equation. Then graph the line using the intercepts.

1. $5x + 3y = 18$ **2.** $-2x + y = -10$ **3.** $3x + y = -1$

EXAMPLE 3 **Using and Interpreting Intercepts**

Fitness Pamela runs and walks with her dog on a trail that is 8 miles long. She can run 4 miles per hour and walk 2 miles per hour. Graph the equation $4x + 2y = 8$, where x is the number of hours running and y is the number of hours walking. What do the intercepts represent?

Solution

① Find the x-intercept.

To find the x-intercept, let $y = 0$ and solve for x.

$$4x + 2y = 8$$
$$4x + 2(0) = 8$$
$$4x = 8$$
$$x = 2$$

② Find the y-intercept.

To find the y-intercept, let $x = 0$ and solve for y.

$$4x + 2y = 8$$
$$4(0) + 2y = 8$$
$$2y = 8$$
$$y = 4$$

③ The x-intercept is 2 and the y-intercept is 4. So the points (2, 0) and (0, 4) are on the graph. Plot these points and draw a line through them.

ANSWER The x-intercept represents how many hours it would take if Pamela runs the entire time. The y-intercept represents how many hours it would take if Pamela walks the entire time.

Getting Ready to Practice

1. Vocabulary Copy and complete: A line passes through the points (3, 0) and (0, 5). So, the _?_ is 5 and the _?_ is 3.

Identify the *x*-intercept and the *y*-intercept.

2.

3.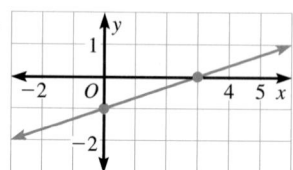

4. Guided Problem Solving You have $60 to spend. CDs are $12 each and videos are $10 each. The number of each item you can buy is modeled by the equation $12x + 10y = 60$. Graph the equation and explain what the intercepts represent.

   ① Find the intercepts.

   ② Graph the equation.

   ③ Decide what x and y represent in the equation. Explain what the intercepts represent.

Practice and Problem Solving

 with Homework

Example	Exercises
1	5–10
2	11–13
3	14

 Online Resources
CLASSZONE.COM

· More Examples
· eTutorial Plus

Find the intercepts of the graph of the equation.

5. $y = 6x - 3$ **6.** $y = 2x + 4$ **7.** $y = 5x + 10$

8. $x + 9y = 18$ **9.** $4x + 5y = 20$ **10.** $7x - 9y = -63$

Graph the line that has the given intercepts.

11. *x*-intercept: 9   **12.** *x*-intercept: −3   **13.** *x*-intercept: 6
   y-intercept: 4   *y*-intercept: 1   *y*-intercept: −10

14. Riding the Bus You are riding the bus home from school. After x minutes, the number of miles from home y is given by $2x + 3y = 18$. Find the intercepts. Then graph the equation. What do the intercepts represent?

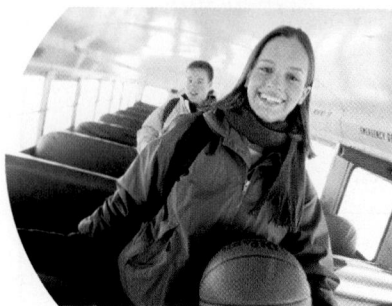

15. Critical Thinking If the x-intercept of a line is positive and the y-intercept is negative, does the line slant up or down from left to right? Explain your reasoning.

Find the intercepts of the graph of the equation.

16. $y = 9$

17. $y = 14$

18. $x = 21$

Graph the equation using intercepts.

19. $y = 5x - 15$

20. $y = -2.5x + 6.5$

21. $8x + 10y = 30$

22. $y = \frac{1}{2}x + 1$

23. $y = -\frac{2}{3}x + 2$

24. $y = \frac{3}{4}x - \frac{1}{2}$

 Find the intercepts of the graph of the equation. Round to the nearest hundredth.

25. $y = -2.14x + 3.65$

26. $y = 1.95x - 12.05$

27. $y = -4.12x - 15.01$

28. Critical Thinking What kind of line has no y-intercept?

29. Investing A bank offers a savings account at a 2% simple annual interest rate and a certificate of deposit at a 5% simple annual interest rate. You want to earn $100 in interest the first year. The equation $0.02s + 0.05c = 100$ models the situation. Find the intercepts of the graph of the equation. What do they represent in terms of the situation?

Mixed Review

30. Evaluate the expression $\dfrac{6a^2b}{2ab^2}$ when $a = 9$ and $b = 4$. *(Lesson 4.3)*

Graph the equation. *(Lesson 11.4)*

31. $y = \frac{3}{4}x + 5$

32. $y = 2x - 6$

33. $y = -7x + 4$

Basic Skills Use the formula $d = rt$ to find the rate.

34. $d = 460$ mi, $t = 8$ h

35. $d = 720$ km, $t = 12$ h

FCAT Practice

36. Multiple Choice What is the y-intercept of the graph of the equation $6x - 3y = 12$?

A. 4   **B.** 2   **C.** -4 **D.** -2

37. Short Response Solve the equation $5x - y = 2$ for y. Graph the equation. What is the x-intercept? What is the y-intercept?

Hands-on Activity

GOAL

Understand slope as a measure of steepness.

MATERIALS

- pencil
- graph paper

FLORIDA: Standards and Assessment

Find ordered-pair solutions given an equation or a graph. (MA.C.3.3.2)

Identify slope from the graph of a line. (MA.C.3.3.2)

Finding the Slope of a Line

You can describe the steepness of a line using its *slope*, or ratio of vertical change (rise) to horizontal change (run) in any two points on a line. You can find slope using the formula: $slope = \dfrac{rise}{run}$.

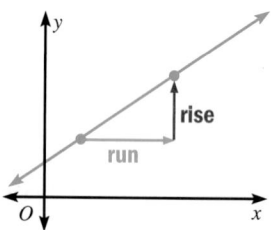

Explore 1 Find the slope of the line passing through the points (2, 3) and (6, 5).

1 Plot the points (2, 3) and (6, 5) on a coordinate grid. Using a straightedge draw a line through the points.

2 Find the rise. Then find the run. Substitute for rise and run in the formula for slope.

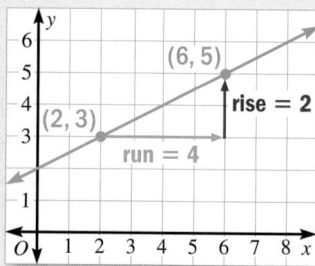

$$slope = \frac{rise}{run} = \frac{2}{4} = \frac{1}{2}$$

The slope of the line passing through the points (2, 3) and (6, 5) is $\dfrac{1}{2}$.

Your turn now Use the formula for slope.

1. Find the slope of the line passing through the points $(-1, 1)$ and $(-3, 5)$.

    (1 Plot the points $(-1, 1)$ and $(-3, 5)$ on a coordinate plane using graph paper. Then draw a line through the points.

    (2 Find the rise. Then find the run. Substitute for rise and run in the formula for slope.

2. Using the points (5, 6) and $(-2, 3)$, what operation can you perform on the *y*-coordinates to find the rise? What operation can you perform on the *x*-coordinates to find the run?

Explore 2 Use two points to find the slope of a line.

1 Copy the graph.

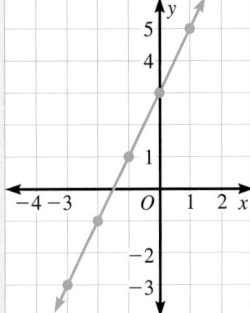

2 Choose two points on the line. Find the rise and run. Calculate the slope.

3 Choose a different pair of points on the line. Find the rise and run. Calculate the slope.

4 What pattern do you notice in your answers to Steps 2 and 3? Make a conjecture about the slope of a line.

Your turn now Find the slope of the line passing through the points.

3. $(1, 4)$, $(4, 2)$ **4.** $(1, -3)$, $(5, -2)$ **5.** $(-3, 4)$, $(0, 6)$

6. $(7, 8)$, $(-1, -5)$ **7.** $(-2, 6)$, $(0, -3)$ **8.** $(-9, 3)$, $(3, -9)$

9. If a line falls from left to right, what can you say about the rise and run?

10. If a line rises from left to right, what can you say about the rise and run?

11. Compare a line with slope greater than 1 to a line with slope between 0 and 1.

Find the slope of the line.

12.   **13.**   **14.**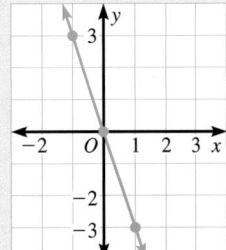

Stop *and* **Think**

15. Challenge What is the slope of the line passing through the points (a, b) and (c, d)?

Slope

LESSON 11.6

BEFORE	▶ Now	WHY?
You graphed linear equations.	You'll find and interpret slopes of lines.	So you can find the slope of the roof of a birdhouse, as in Ex. 9.

In the Real World

Word Watch

slope, p. 570
rise, p. 570
run, p. 570

FLORIDA
Standards and Assessment

• Identify slope from the graph of a line. (MA.C.3.3.2)

• Interpret the meaning of slope. (MA.D.1.3.2)

Cogwheel Railways The Mount Pilatus Railway in the Swiss Alps is the steepest cogwheel railway in the world. The track rises about 20 feet vertically for every 50 feet it runs horizontally. What is the steepness of the track?

You can describe steepness using *slope*. The **slope** of a nonvertical line is the ratio of its vertical change, called the **rise**, to its horizontal change, called the **run**.

EXAMPLE 1 **Finding Slope**

The diagram shows the rise and the run of the Mount Pilatus Railway.

$$\text{slope} = \frac{\text{rise}}{\text{run}} = \frac{\overset{2}{\cancel{20\,ft}}}{\underset{5}{\cancel{50\,ft}}} = \frac{2}{5}$$

rise = 20 ft
run = 50 ft

ANSWER The railway has a slope of $\frac{2}{5}$.

Slope of a Line

The slope m of a nonvertical line passing through the points (x_1, y_1) and (x_2, y_2) is

$$m = \frac{\text{rise}}{\text{run}} = \frac{y_2 - y_1}{x_2 - x_1}$$

The slope of a line is the same no matter which two points you choose to use in the formula.

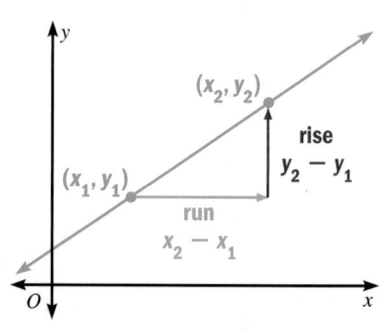

HELP **with Vocabulary**

The rise is the change in y and the run is the change in x.

EXAMPLE 2 **Positive and Negative Slope**

Find the slope of the line.

a.

b.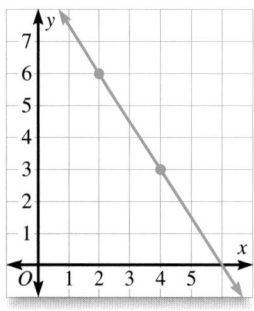

a.
$$m = \frac{\text{rise}}{\text{run}} = \frac{y_2 - y_1}{x_2 - x_1}$$

$$= \frac{7 - 2}{5 - 1}$$

$$= \frac{5}{4}$$

ANSWER The slope is $\frac{5}{4}$.

b.
$$m = \frac{\text{rise}}{\text{run}} = \frac{y_2 - y_1}{x_2 - x_1}$$

$$= \frac{3 - 6}{4 - 2}$$

$$= \frac{-3}{2}, \text{ or } -\frac{3}{2}.$$

ANSWER The slope is $-\frac{3}{2}$.

HELP with **Review**

For help with subtracting integers, see p. 63.

Your turn now **Find the slope of the line passing through the points.**

1. (2, 1), (6, 4)   **2.** (0, 6), (10, 0)   **3.** (−3, −4), (5, 2)

EXAMPLE 3 **Zero and Undefined Slope**

Find the slope of the line.

a.

b.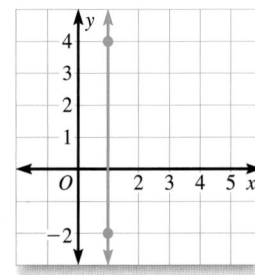

Watch Out!

When finding the slope of a line, make sure that you are using the x- and y-coordinates in the same order.

a.
$$m = \frac{\text{rise}}{\text{run}} = \frac{y_2 - y_1}{x_2 - x_1}$$

$$= \frac{3 - 3}{6 - 2} = \frac{0}{4} = 0$$

ANSWER The slope is 0.

b.
$$m = \frac{\text{rise}}{\text{run}} = \frac{y_2 - y_1}{x_2 - x_1}$$

$$= \frac{4 - (-2)}{1 - 1} = \frac{6}{0}$$

ANSWER The slope is undefined.

Summary of Slope

A line with *positive* slope rises from left to right.

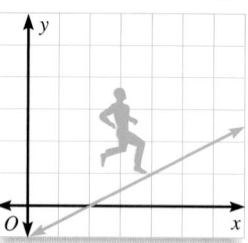

A line with *negative* slope falls from left to right.

A line with *zero* slope is horizontal.

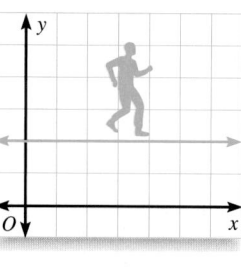

A line with *undefined* slope is vertical.

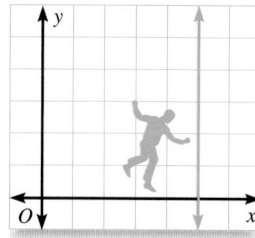

11.6 Exercises

More Practice, p. 737

Getting Ready to Practice

Vocabulary **Copy and complete the statement.**

1. The change in the *y*-coordinates is called the ? .

2. The change in the *x*-coordinates is called the ? .

Sketch a line with the given type of slope.

3. negative   **4.** undefined   **5.** positive   **6.** zero

Birdhouse **Use the red line on the diagram of a birdhouse.**

7. What is the rise of the roof?

8. What is the run of the roof?

9. What is the slope of the roof?

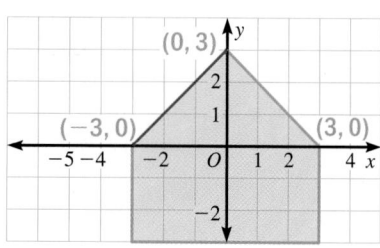

Practice and Problem Solving

with **Homework**

Example	Exercises
1	26
2	10–26
3	10–25

Online Resources
CLASSZONE.COM

· More Examples
· eTutorial Plus

Write the coordinates of the two points on the line. Then find the slope.

10.

11.

12.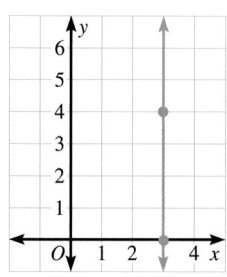

Find the slope of the line passing through the points.

13. $(-4, 8)$, $(6, 6)$ **14.** $(1, 4)$, $(1, -7)$ **15.** $(-2, -4)$, $(4, 2)$

16. $(-5, 4)$, $(3, 4)$ **17.** $(5, 8)$, $(0, 5)$ **18.** $(-3, 1)$, $(-3, -2)$

19. $(-6, -2)$, $(6, -7)$ **20.** $(9, -8)$, $(15, -8)$ **21.** $(12, 22)$, $(-20, 19)$

The three points are vertices of a triangle. Plot and connect the points. Then find the slope of each side of the triangle.

22. $A(0, 0)$, $B(0, 8)$, $C(6, 0)$ **23.** $D(-3, 4)$, $E(4, 1)$, $F(-1, -7)$

24. $G(0, 6)$, $H(4, 0)$, $J(-4, 0)$ **25.** $K(-5, 1)$, $L(-1, -4)$, $M(-2, 4)$

26. Tides The pictures show a floating dock at low and high tide. Find the slopes of the ramp in both pictures. Is the ramp steeper at high tide or at low tide?

27. Writing One line passes through the points $M(1, 1)$ and $N(3, 4)$ and another line passes through the points $P(2, 5)$ and $Q(5, 8)$. Which line has a greater slope? Explain how you can tell by graphing the two lines. Explain how you can tell by calculating the slopes of the lines.

28. Algebra A line contains the points (p, q) and $(p + 2, q + 2)$. Find the slope of the line.

29. Critical Thinking When you have selected two points on a line to find its slope, does it matter which is (x_1, y_1) and which is (x_2, y_2)? Explain. Give examples to justify your reasoning.

30. Ski Jump A ski slope has a starting altitude of 2800 meters and an ending altitude of 1886 meters. The length of the ski slope is about 3299 meters. What is the approximate slope of the ski slope? Round to the nearest hundredth.

start: 2800 m

end: 1886 m

3299 m

Challenge **Find the missing value(s) using the given slope and points.**

31. $m = \frac{7}{4}$ and $(x, -7)$, $(16, 0)$ **32.** $m = 0$ and $(0, 7)$, $(3, y)$

33. $m = \frac{1}{2}$ and $(0, 0)$, $(x, 2)$, $(6, y)$ **34.** $m = -3$ and $(2, -6)$, $(x, 9)$, $(-1, y)$

Mixed Review

35. The table shows the number of runs scored in each inning of a seven-inning softball game. Make a scatter plot of the data. Tell whether the two quantities have a *positive relationship*, a *negative relationship*, or *no relationship*. *(Lesson 11.2)*

Inning	1	2	3	4	5	6	7
Runs	0	0	4	2	1	0	1

Tell whether the ordered pair is a solution of the equation $y = -x + 5$. *(Lesson 11.3)*

36. $(4, 1)$ **37.** $(-9, 14)$ **38.** $(10, 15)$ **39.** $(-31, -26)$

Basic Skills **Solve the equation.**

40. $-7r + 15 = 29$ **41.** $42 = \frac{t}{3} + 21$ **42.** $6s - 5 = 2s$

FCAT Practice   FCAT

43. Multiple Choice What is the slope of the line shown in the graph?

A. $-\frac{2}{3}$ **B.** $-\frac{3}{2}$

C. $\frac{2}{3}$ **D.** $\frac{3}{2}$

44. Multiple Choice A line passes through the points $(4, 6)$ and $(x, 0)$, and has a slope of $\frac{3}{5}$. What is the value of x?

F. 11   **G.** 7   **H.** -6 **I.** 1

GOAL

Find how slope, *y*-intercept, and an equation can relate.

MATERIALS

· pencil
· graph paper

FLORIDA: Standards and Assessment
Identify slope from the graph of a line.
(MA.C.3.3.2)

Apply and explain the properties of lines on a graph.
(MA.C.3.3.2)

Slope-Intercept Form

You can find the slope and *y*-intercept of a line by looking at its equation in *slope-intercept form*.

Explore 1 Find the slope and *y*-intercept of *y* = 4*x* + 3.

1 Make a table of values for the equation *y* = 4*x* + 3.

x	0	1	2
y	3	7	11

2 Plot points and draw a line.

3 Use the graph to find the slope and *y*-intercept of *y* = 4*x* + 3.

slope = $\frac{4}{1}$ = 4   *y*-intercept = 3

Your turn now Use a graph to answer Exercises 1–3.

1. Copy and complete the table of values for *y* = −2*x* − 1.

x	−1	0	1
y	?	?	?

2. Plot the points and draw a line.

3. Use the graph to find the slope and *y*-intercept.

4. Copy and complete the table.

Equation	Slope	*y*-intercept
y = 4*x* + 3	?	?
y = −2*x* − 1	?	?

Explore 2 **Find the slope and *y*-intercept of *y* = 3*x* + 5.**

1 Make a table of values for the equation $y = 3x + 5$.

x	1	2	3
y	8	11	14

2 Calculate the slope of the line from the points.

$$m = \frac{y_2 - y_1}{x_2 - x_1} = \frac{11 - 8}{2 - 1} = 3$$

3 Calculate the *y*-intercept by substitution.

$$y = 3x + 5 = 3(0) + 5 = 5$$

4 Add $y = 3x + 5$ to your table from Exercise 4.

5 Use your table to make a conjecture about using an equation of a line to find the slope and *y*-intercept of the line.

Your turn now **Graph the line using a table of values. Then use the graph to find the slope and *y*-intercept.**

5. $y = 5x - 7$ **6.** $y = -3x + 2$ **7.** $y = -\frac{2}{3}x - 6$ **8.** $y = \frac{5}{4}x + 1$

Solve the equation for *y*. Make a table of values for the equation. Calculate the slope and *y*-intercept.

9. $y + 2 = \frac{1}{2}x$ **10.** $3y = -2x + 9$ **11.** $y + 4x = -5$ **12.** $6x - 2y = 10$

13. Does your conjecture in Step 5 still seem to be true?

Stop *and* **Think**

14. What does *m* stand for in the equation $y = mx + b$? What does *b* stand for in the equation $y = mx + b$?

Slope-Intercept Form

BEFORE	▶ Now	WHY?
You graphed equations using intercepts.	You'll write and graph equations in slope-intercept form.	So you can determine how many bracelets you must sell, as in Ex. 21.

In the Real World

Word Watch

slope-intercept form, p. 577

FLORIDA
Standards and Assessment
• Apply and explain the properties of lines on a graph. (MA.C.3.3.2)
• Write equations to express relationships. (MA.D.1.3.2)

Hiking You are hiking a trail on Mount Rainier in Washington. At the base of the trail, the temperature is 50.9°F. The temperature changes at a rate of -0.005°F per foot as you hike up. What equation can you use to find the temperature after you hike up 1000 feet?

One way to write an equation is to use *slope-intercept form*.

Slope-Intercept Form

Words The linear equation $y = mx + b$ is written in **slope-intercept form** . The slope is m. The y-intercept is b.

Algebra $y = mx + b$ **Numbers** $y = 3x + 2$

HELP with Review

For help with rewriting equations, see p. 549.

EXAMPLE 1 **Identifying Slopes and y-Intercepts**

Find the slope and *y*-intercept of the line.

a. $y = x - 3$ **b.** $-4x + 2y = 16$

Solution

a. The equation $y = x - 3$ can be written as $y = 1x + (-3)$.

   ANSWER The line has a slope of 1 and a y-intercept of -3.

b. Write the equation $-4x + 2y = 16$ in slope-intercept form.

$$-4x + 2y = 16 \qquad \text{Write original equation.}$$
$$2y = 4x + 16 \qquad \text{Add } 4x \text{ to each side.}$$
$$y = 2x + 8 \qquad \text{Divide each side by 2.}$$

   ANSWER The line has a slope of 2 and a y-intercept of 8.

EXAMPLE 2 **Graphing Using Slope-Intercept Form**

Graph the equation $y = \frac{1}{2}x + 3$.

Solution

① The *y*-intercept is 3, so plot the point (0, 3).

② The slope is $\frac{1}{2}$, so plot a second point by moving up 1 unit and right 2 units.

③ Draw a line through the points.

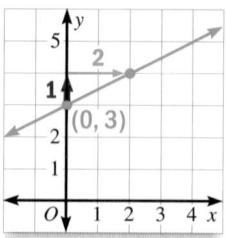

Your turn now **Find the slope and *y*-intercept of the graph of the equation. Then graph the equation.**

1. $y = 2x + 5$ **2.** $-x + y = 6$ **3.** $y = \frac{1}{4}x$

EXAMPLE 3 **Using Slope-Intercept Form**

To answer the question on page 577, you can write an equation in slope-intercept form to find the temperature after hiking up 1000 feet.

Solution

① Write a verbal model.

| Temperature | = | Rate of temperature change | · | Increase in altitude | + | Initial temperature |

② Write an algebraic model in slope-intercept form.

The temperature changes at a rate of $-0.005°F$ per foot, so $m = -0.005$. The initial temperature is $50.9°F$, so $b = 50.9$. Let *y* be the temperature and *x* be the change in altitude.

$y = mx + b$ Write slope-intercept form.

$y = -0.005x + 50.9$ Substitute −0.005 for *m* and 50.9 for *b*.

③ To find the temperature after hiking up 1000 feet, find the value of *y* when $x = 1000$.

$y = -0.005x + 50.9$ Write the equation.

$= -0.005 \cdot (1000) + 50.9$ Substitute 1000 for *x*.

$= 45.9$ Simplify.

ANSWER The temperature after hiking up 1000 feet is $45.9°F$.

Getting Ready to Practice

1. Vocabulary Identify the slope and y-intercept of the graph of the equation $y = -5x + 7$.

Rewrite the equation in slope-intercept form.

2. $x - y = -2$ **3.** $2x = y + 5$ **4.** $8x - 4y = 32$

Find the slope and y-intercept of the graph of the equation.

5. $y = x + 3$ **6.** $y = 6 - x$ **7.** $1 = 2x - y$

8. Find the Error Describe and correct the error made by a student while graphing the equation $y = -2x - 1$.

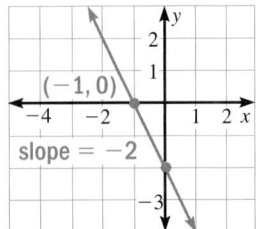

Practice and Problem Solving

HELP with Homework

Example	Exercises
1	9–20
2	9–14
3	21

Online Resources
CLASSZONE.COM
· More Examples
· eTutorial Plus

Find the slope and y-intercept of the graph of the equation. Then graph the equation.

9. $y = x - 8$ **10.** $y = 3$ **11.** $y = -x + 7$

12. $y = x - \dfrac{1}{2}$ **13.** $y = \dfrac{2}{3}x - 4$ **14.** $y = \dfrac{1}{5}x$

Rewrite in slope-intercept form. Then find the slope and y-intercept of the line.

15. $y = 10 - 6x$ **16.** $y - 9 = -\dfrac{3}{4}x$ **17.** $\dfrac{2}{3}x - y = 3$

18. $2y + 2x = 12$ **19.** $y + 12x = 0$ **20.** $13x - 11y = 143$

21. Bracelets You make and sell bracelets. You buy $28 in supplies and sell the bracelets for $3.50 each. Your profit can be modeled by $p = 3.50b - 28$ where p is the profit and b is the number of bracelets sold. Graph the equation. How many bracelets do you need to sell to make a profit?

Write the equation of the graph in slope-intercept form.

22.

23.

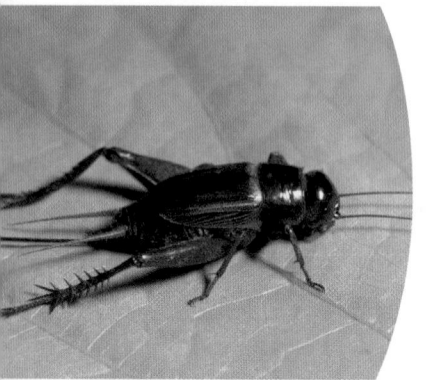

24. Critical Thinking Write the equations of two lines that have the same slope but different *y*-intercepts. Graph the lines. Do the lines appear to be *parallel*, *perpendicular*, or *neither*? Explain.

25. Crickets The number of chirps per minute made by a cricket can be modeled by the equation $c = 4t - 156$, where c is the number of chirps per minute and t is the temperature in degrees Fahrenheit. Graph the equation. What does the x-intercept mean in terms of the temperature and the number of chirps per minute?

26. Critical Thinking When two lines are perpendicular and neither has a slope of zero, the product of their slopes is -1. Write the equation of the line that is perpendicular to and has the same y-intercept as the line $y = 2x + 8$. Then graph both lines to check that they are perpendicular.

27. Challenge Write the equation $ax + by + c = 0$, where b is not equal to 0, in slope-intercept form.

Mixed Review

Write the sentence as an inequality, letting *x* represent the variable. Then solve the inequality. *(Lesson 6.6)*

28. Six is less than a number plus 8.

29. Five times a number is greater than or equal to thirty-five.

Find the volume of the figure. *(Lessons 10.6, 10.7)*

30. A cylinder with radius 3 inches and height 7 inches

31. A pyramid with base area 25 square feet and height 9 feet

Basic Skills Solve the inequality. Then graph its solution.

32. $a + 3 \le -7$ **33.** $8 < 2 + t$ **34.** $n - 4 > 7$

FCAT Practice

35. Extended Response Kyra needs 10 prizes for a contest. Her two choices are T-shirts that come in orders of 4 and gift certificates that come in packs of 2 . The number of prizes Kyra can buy is represented by the equation $4x + 2y = 10$. What is the y-intercept and what is the slope? Graph the equation. What do the intercepts represent?

Systems of Equations

GOAL Solve systems of linear equations.

system of linear equations, p. 581

solution of a linear system, p. 581

FLORIDA
Standards and Assessment

• Find ordered-pair solutions given an equation. (MA.C.3.3.2)

• On a graph, find the intersection point of two lines. (MA.C.3.3.2)

• Use graphs to illustrate real-world situations. (MA.D.2.3.1)

A **system of linear equations** is a set of two or more linear equations with the same variables. A **solution of a linear system** is an ordered pair that is a solution of each equation in the system.

In the system of equations below, (3, 2) is a solution.

System of equations	Check
$2x + 4y = 14$	$2(3) + 4(2) = 6 + 8 = 14$ ✓
$3x - 5y = -1$	$3(3) - 5(2) = 9 - 10 = -1$ ✓

If a system of linear equations has a solution, then the graphs of the equations intersect.

EXAMPLE 1   **Solving a System of Equations by Graphing**

Solve the linear system: $x + y = 5$ **Equation 1**

$y = 2x - 1$ **Equation 2**

Solution

① Write each equation in slope-intercept form.

Equation 1   **Equation 2**

$x + y = 5$ $y = 2x - 1$

$y = -x + 5$

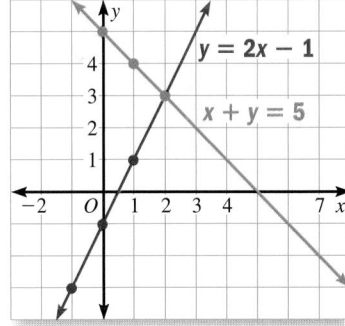

② Graph both equations.

③ Estimate the point of intersection using the graph. It appears that the point of intersection is (2, 3).

④ Check whether (2, 3) is the solution by substituting 2 for x and 3 for y in each of the equations.

Equation 1   **Equation 2**

$x + y = 5$ $y = 2x - 1$

$2 + 3 \stackrel{?}{=} 5$ $3 \stackrel{?}{=} 2(2) - 1$

$5 = 5$ ✓ $3 = 3$ ✓

ANSWER The solution is (2, 3).

HELP with **Solving**

When solving by substitution, solve for the variable that is easier to isolate. You will get the same solution whether you begin by solving for x or for y.

EXAMPLE 2 **Solving Linear Systems by Substitution**

Solve the linear system: $x + 4y = 4$ **Equation 1**

$x - y = -6$ **Equation 2**

Solution

① Choose an equation to solve for one of the variables.

$x - y = -6$ **Write Equation 2.**

$x = y - 6$ **Add y to each side.**

② Substitute $y - 6$ for x in Equation 1. Then solve for y.

$x + 4y = 4$ **Write Equation 1.**

$(y - 6) + 4y = 4$ **Substitute $y - 6$ for x.**

$5y - 6 = 4$ **Combine like terms.**

$5y = 10$ **Add 6 to each side.**

$y = 2$ **Divide each side by 5.**

③ Substitute 2 for y in the original Equation 2 and solve for x.

$x - y = -6$ **Write Equation 2.**

$x - 2 = -6$ **Substitute 2 for y.**

$x = -4$ **Add 2 to each side.**

ANSWER The solution is $(-4, 2)$.

Exercises

Estimate the solution of the linear system using a graph. Then check the solution using algebra.

1. $y = -x + 3$
     $y = x + 1$

2. $x - y = 1$
     $5x - 4y = 0$

3. $y = 2x - 15$
     $x = -2y$

Solve the linear system by substitution.

4. $x = 4$
     $x + y = 2$

5. $a + b = 4$
     $4a + b = 1$

6. $2w - z = -2$
     $4w + z = 20$

7. **Trading Cards** You have 100 trading cards and your friend has 20. Every day you give your friend one card. Use the equations $c = 100 - d$ and $c = 20 + d$ to model this situation. Graph the two equations and find when you both will have the same number of cards.

LESSON 11.8

Graphs of Linear Inequalities

BEFORE	▶ **Now**	**WHY?**
You graphed linear equations.	You'll graph linear inequalities.	So you can find how much water you can bring on a trip, as in Ex. 34.

Word Watch

linear inequality, p. 583
solution of a linear
   inequality, p. 583
half-plane, p. 584

FLORIDA
Standards and Assessment
• Write inequalities to express relationships. (MA.D.1.3.2)
• Evaluate algebraic inequalities. (MA.D.2.3.1)

Activity **You can use a graph to model linear inequalities.**

1. Sketch the graph of $y = x - 1$.

2. Graph and label the following points in your coordinate plane.

   $A(0, 0), B(-3, -2), C(4, -3), D(0, -4)$

   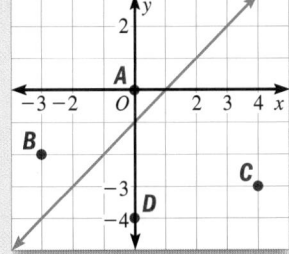

3. Which of the points in Step 2 make the inequality $y < x - 1$ true? Draw a circle around these points.

4. Which of the points in Step 2 make the inequality $y > x - 1$ true? Draw a square around these points.

5. Make a conjecture about the solutions of $y < x - 1$ and the solutions of $y > x - 1$.

In the activity, you investigated solutions of linear inequalities. Some examples of **linear inequalities** in two variables are $y \leq 2x + 5$, $2x + 5y < 7$, and $4x + y \geq -6$.

An ordered pair (x, y) is a **solution of a linear inequality** if the inequality is true when the values of x and y are substituted into the inequality.

HELP with Solving

The symbol $\not\leq$ means *not less than or equal to.* It is equivalent to the symbol $>$, which means *greater than.*

EXAMPLE 1 **Checking Solutions of a Linear Inequality**

Tell whether the point is a solution of $3x - 4y \leq -8$.

(x, y)	$3x - 4y$	$3x - 4y \overset{?}{\leq} -8$	Conclusion
a. $(0, 0)$	$3(0) - 4(0) = 0$	$0 \not\leq -8$	$(0, 0)$ is *not* a solution.
b. $(-1, 4)$	$3(-1) - 4(4) = -19$	$-19 \leq -8$	$(-1, 4)$ is a solution.

Your turn now **Is the ordered pair a solution of $2x + 3y < 5$?**

   1. $(0, 0)$ **2.** $(-4, 2)$ **3.** $(5, -1)$ **4.** $(1, 1)$

HELP with **Vocabulary**

A line divides a coordinate plane into two half-planes.

The graph of a linear inequality in two variables is a **half-plane**. The shaded region includes all the solutions of the inequality.

A solid line indicates that points on the line *are* solutions of an inequality. A dashed line indicates that points on the line are *not* solutions.

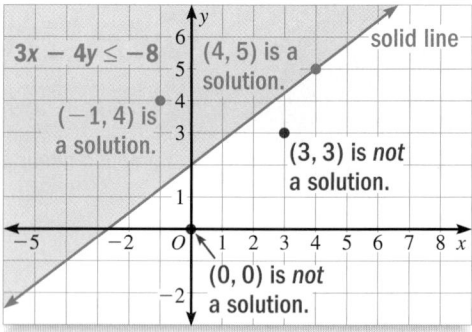

Graphing Linear Inequalities

1. Change the inequality symbol to "=." Graph the equation. Use a dashed line for < or >. Use a solid line for ≤ or ≥.

2. Test a point in one of the half-planes to check whether it is a solution of the inequality.

3. If the test point is a solution, shade its half-plane. If the test point is not a solution, shade the other half-plane.

EXAMPLE 2 **Graphing a Linear Inequality**

Graph $y - 2x > 3$.

(1 Change > to = and write the equation in slope-intercept form.

$$y - 2x = 3 \qquad \text{Replace > with = sign.}$$

$$y = 2x + 3 \qquad \text{Add 2x to each side.}$$

Graph the line that has a slope of 2 and a y-intercept of 3. Because the inequality is >, use a dashed line.

(2 Use (0, 0) as a test point.

$$y > 2x + 3$$

$$0 \overset{?}{>} 2(0) + 3$$

$$0 \not> 3 \qquad \text{(0, 0) is not a solution.}$$

(3 Shade the half-plane that does *not* contain (0, 0).

HELP with **Solving**

You can use any point not on the line as a test point. Using (0, 0) is convenient because 0 is substituted for each variable.

Your turn now **Graph the inequality.**

5. $y < x + 1$ **6.** $3x + y \geq 3$ **7.** $x - 2y \geq -1$ **8.** $y \geq -2$

EXAMPLE 3 **Using the Graph of a Linear Inequality**

Art Supplies You are buying art supplies for your art club. You have $40 to spend. Tubes of paint cost $6 each and brushes cost $4 each. The inequality $6x + 4y \leq 40$, where x represents the number of tubes of paint and y represents the number of brushes, models this situation. How many tubes of paint and how many brushes can you buy with $40?

a. Graph the inequality.

b. Use the graph to find a solution. Then interpret the solution.

Solution

a. Graph the equation $y = -\frac{3}{2}x + 10$.

Use a solid line.

Use $(0, 0)$ as a test point.

$$6(0) + 4(0) \overset{?}{\leq} 40$$

$$0 \leq 40 \checkmark$$

Shade the half-plane that contains $(0, 0)$.

b. One solution is $(4, 4)$. This means that you can buy 4 tubes of paint and 4 brushes.

HELP with Solving

In Example 3, all points in the shaded region and on the line are solutions of the inequality. However, negative and fractional solutions do not make sense. You cannot buy a negative number of items, and you cannot buy part of an item.

11.8 Exercises

More Practice, p. 737

INTERNET
eWorkbook Plus
CLASSZONE.COM

Getting Ready to Practice

1. Vocabulary When graphing the inequality $y < 2x + 1$, the graphed dashed line divides the coordinate plane into two ? .

Tell whether the point is a solution of the inequality $6x + 3y > 24$.

2. $(2, 3)$ **3.** $(4, 5)$ **4.** $(5, 4)$ **5.** $(3, 2)$

Graph the inequality.

6. $y > 14 - 4x$ **7.** $y < x + 5$ **8.** $3x - 4 \geq y$ **9.** $y + 3 \geq 4x$

10. Trail Mix You are making a trail mix of peanuts and raisins. You have $6.00 to spend on trail mix. Peanuts cost $2.00 per pound and raisins cost $1.50 per pound. How much of each item can you buy? Graph the inequality $2x + 1.50y \leq 6$ to find different combinations of pounds of peanuts and raisins that you could buy to use in your trail mix.

Practice and Problem Solving

with Homework

Example	Exercises
1	11–14, 16–19
2	16–31
3	32–34

Online Resources
CLASSZONE.COM

· More Examples
· eTutorial Plus

Tell whether the point is a solution of the inequality.

11. $5x + y \le 17$; $(1, 2)$ **12.** $3x + 7y < 20$; $(-11, 2)$

13. $9x + 12y > 26$; $(3, -4)$ **14.** $11x + 18y \ge 31$; $(-6, -7)$

15. Writing Explain how you can tell when to use a solid line and when to use a dashed line when graphing an inequality.

Matching Match the inequality with its graph.

16. $y \le 2x + 1$ **17.** $y < 2x + 1$ **18.** $y > 2x + 1$ **19.** $y \ge 2x + 1$

A.

B.

C.

D.
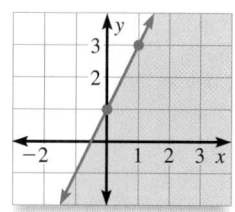

Graph the inequality.

20. $y < x + 6$ **21.** $y > 9 - 2x$ **22.** $y \ge 3x - 7$

23. $y \le 4x - 12$ **24.** $y < 7x + 19$ **25.** $4x - 13 > y$

26. $5x \le 45$ **27.** $22 < 2x$ **28.** $6y > 36$

29. $8y > 64$ **30.** $-96 \le -3x$ **31.** $-2y \ge 74$

Extended Problem Solving In Exercises 32–34, use the information about Catherine's canoe trip.

Catherine is going on a canoe trip. She has to carry a backpack containing the food and water she will need. Catherine can take no more than 10 pounds in her backpack. A bottle of water weighs 16 ounces and a sandwich and fruit weigh 12 ounces.

32. The inequality $16x + 12y \le 160$ models the situation, where x is the number of water bottles and y is the number of meals. How many meals can Catherine take with her if she brings 4 bottles of water?

33. Graph the inequality.

34. Using the graph, find the maximum number of bottles of water Catherine can carry when she packs 2 meals in her backpack.

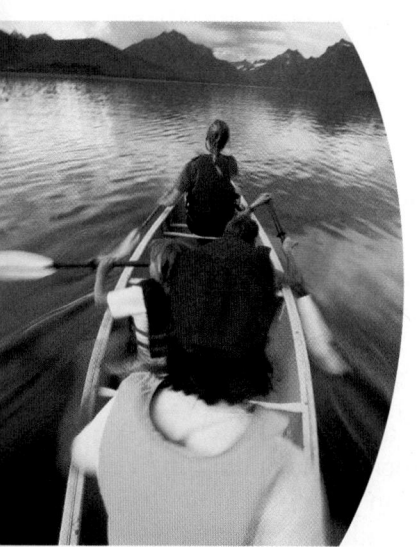

35. Writing Explain how you can write an inequality that represents the half-plane that is *not* the solution of the inequality $5x + y \geq 2$.

36. Critical Thinking If you graph the inequalities $y < x + 3$ and $y > x + 3$, do you cover all of the points in the plane? Explain.

37. Challenge The graph at the right represents all the points that are solutions to four inequalities. The equations used to graph the inequalities are

$y = -\frac{1}{3}x + 5$, $y = \frac{1}{3}x - 5$, $y = \frac{2}{3}x - 6$, and

$y = -\frac{2}{3}x + 6$. What are the four inequalities?

Mixed Review

38. Find the intercepts of $4x + 18y = 36$. *(Lesson 11.5)*

39. Find the slope of the line that passes through $(-3, -4)$ and $(7, 8)$. *(Lesson 11.6)*

Basic Skills Write the decimal as a fraction in simplest form.

40. 1.34   **41.** 3.75   **42.** 8.125   **43.** 7.164

FCAT Practice

44. Multiple Choice The graph shows how many beverages y and how many snacks x need to be sold at the school play to meet the fundraising goal. Which inequality describes the graph?

A. $y \leq \frac{3}{4}x + 300$ **B.** $y \geq \frac{3}{4}x + 300$

C. $y \leq -\frac{3}{4}x + 300$ **D.** $y \geq -\frac{3}{4}x + 300$

45. Multiple Choice Sonya has up to $25 to spend on decorations for a birthday party she is throwing for her friend. A bag of balloons costs $2.50 and a roll of streamers costs $2. Sonya uses $2.50x + 2y \leq 25$ to determine how many bags of balloons and rolls of streamers she can buy, where x is the number of bags of balloons and y is the number of rolls of streamers. Which of the following is a solution?

F. (10, 4)   **G.** (0, 12)   **H.** (4, 10)   **I.** (5, 9)

LESSONS 11.5 TO 11.8

Notebook Review

Review the vocabulary definitions in your notebook.

Copy the review examples in your notebook. Then complete the exercises.

Check Your Definitions

x-intercept, p. 564

y-intercept, p. 564

slope, p. 570

rise, run, p. 570

slope-intercept form, p. 577

linear inequality, solution, p. 583

half-plane, p. 584

Use Your Vocabulary

1. **Vocabulary** Copy and complete: In the equation $y = 4x - 9$, 4 is the ? and -9 is the ? .

11.5–11.7 Can you use slope and y-intercepts?

EXAMPLE Find the slope of the line passing through (0, 3) and (4, 6).

The slope can be found by calculating

$$\frac{y_2 - y_1}{x_2 - x_1} = \frac{6 - 3}{4 - 0} = \frac{3}{4}$$

☑ **Find the slope of the line passing through the two points.**

2. $(-1, 0)$ and $(5, 8)$　　3. $(8, 7)$ and $(-2, 3)$　　4. $(0, 11)$ and $(6, 1)$

EXAMPLE Graph $y = \frac{3}{4}x + 3$.

Since $y = \frac{3}{4}x + 3$ is already in slope-intercept form, you know that $\frac{3}{4}$ is the slope and 3 is the y-intercept of the graph of the equation. To graph the equation, first plot the point (0, 3). Then use the slope to find another point on the line.

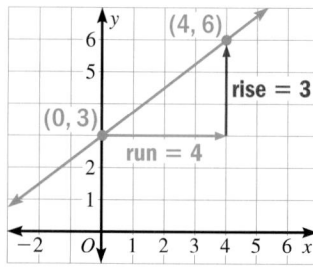

☑ **Find the slope and y-intercept of the graph of the equation. Then graph the equation.**

5. $y = 5x + 20$　　　6. $2x - 3y = -12$　　　7. $x + 4y = 18$

11.8 Can you graph linear inequalities?

 EXAMPLE Graph $y > -2x + 4$.

The graph of $y = -2x + 4$ has a slope of -2 and a y-intercept of 4.

Because the inequality is $>$, use a dashed line.

Use $(0, 0)$ as a test point:

$0 \overset{?}{>} -2(0) + 4$

$0 \not> 4$ **(0, 0) is not a solution.**

Shade the half-plane that does not include $(0, 0)$.

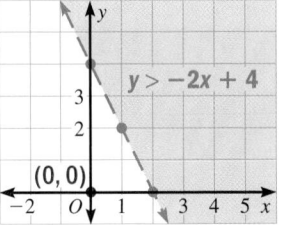

☑ **Graph the inequality.**

8. $y < x - 4$ **9.** $y \geq 2x - 3$ **10.** $x + y > 6$ **11.** $x - y \leq -5$

Stop *and* **Think**   about Lessons 11.5–11.8

12. Critical Thinking Graph $y = 3x + 5$ and $y = 3x - 2$. What do you notice about the lines?

Review Quiz 2

Find the intercepts of the graph of the equation.

  1. $y = 2x + 3$ **2.** $2y + x = 6$ **3.** $x = 3$

Find the slope of the line passing through the points.

  4. $(3, 4), (5, 7)$ **5.** $(-1, -3), (0, 0)$ **6.** $(-5, 3), (4, 3)$

Find the slope and y-intercept of the graph of the equation. Then sketch its graph.

  7. $y = \frac{6}{5}x - 2$ **8.** $-5x - 5y = -20$ **9.** $y = -x$

Graph the inequality. Then list three solutions of the inequality.

  10. $y > x - 3$ **11.** $x - 3y \leq -9$ **12.** $6x + 7y < -21$

13. Car Wash Your club holds a car wash for three hours to raise money for a charity. The equation $10x + 15y = 180$ describes the amount of time it takes to wash small and large vehicles respectively. Find the intercepts of the equation. What do they represent? Graph the equation.

Chapter Review

Vocabulary

relation, p. 541	solution of an equation	slope-intercept form,
input, p. 541	in two variables, p. 549	p. 577
output, p. 541	linear equation, p. 556	linear inequality, solution,
function, p. 541	x-intercept, p. 564	p. 583
domain, p. 542	y-intercept, p. 564	half-plane, p. 584
range, p. 542	slope, p. 570	
scatter plot, p. 545	rise, run, p. 570	

Vocabulary Review

In Exercises 1–3, copy and complete the statement.

1. The graph of a linear inequality in two variables is a(n) _?_ .

2. For a function, the set of all possible input values is called the _?_ , and the set of all possible output values is called the _?_ .

3. The slope of a nonvertical line is the ratio of its _?_ to its _?_ .

4. Explain in your own words how to find the x-intercept and the y-intercept of the graph of an equation.

5. Describe a real-life situation that can be represented by a linear equation. What does the slope of the line tell you about the situation?

6. Write the steps you would take to graph a linear inequality.

Review Questions

Tell whether the relation is a function. Explain your answer.
(Lesson 11.1)

7. (0, 6), (2, 6),

(4, 7), (0, 3),

(2, 3), (4, 8)

8.

Input	Output
0	−8
1	−11
2	−14
3	−17

9.

Input	Output
−4	12
−2	12
0	12
2	12

10. Make a scatter plot of the data. Then describe the relationship. *(Lesson 11.2)*

Number of muffins sold	12	24	36	48
Profit	$6	$12	$18	$24

11. Model Plane You buy a battery operated model plane for $45. It costs you about $8 each month to replace the batteries. The equation $C = 45 + 8m$, where C is the total cost in dollars and m is the number of months, describes this situation. About how much has the plane cost you in the first year? *(Lesson 11.3)*

Matching Match the equation with its graph. *(Lesson 11.4)*

12. $y = -2x$ **13.** $y = -2$ **14.** $x = -2$

A.   **B.**   **C.**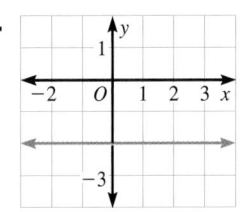

Graph the linear equation. *(Lesson 11.4)*

15. $y = x + 2$ **16.** $y = -\dfrac{3}{2}x - 1$ **17.** $y = 8$

18. Taxes The approximate amount of taxes collected by the Internal Revenue Service from 1980 to 1990 can be modeled by $y = 57.1x + 488$, where y represents taxes, in billions of dollars, and x represents the number of years since 1980. What is the y-intercept of the graph of this equation? What does the y-intercept represent? *(Lesson 11.5)*

Write the coordinates of two points on the line. Then find the slope of the line. *(Lesson 11.6)*

19.   **20.**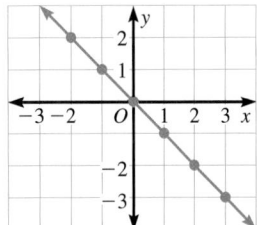

Rewrite the equation in slope-intercept form. Then find the slope and y-intercept of the graph of the equation. *(Lesson 11.7)*

21. $y - 4x = 10$ **22.** $2y + 6 = x$ **23.** $-3x - 7y = 21$

Graph the inequality. *(Lesson 11.8)*

24. $6x + 10y < -30$ **25.** $3x - 7y \geq 21$ **26.** $4x + 8y \leq 32$

11

Chapter Test

In Exercises 1 and 2, write a function rule that relates x and y.

1.

Input x	0	1	2	3
Output y	0	-0.25	-0.5	-0.75

2.

Input x	-2	-1	0	1
Output y	-9	-3	3	9

3. What type of relationship do you expect to find for the number of problems assigned and the time spent doing an assignment?

Tell whether the ordered pair is a solution of the equation $12x + 3y = 21$.

4. $(-1, 11)$ **5.** $(-4, -9)$ **6.** $(2, -15)$ **7.** $(6, -17)$

8. **Temperature** To change a temperature in degrees Celsius C to degrees Fahrenheit F, use the formula $F = \frac{9}{5}C + 32$. Your friend tells you that $45°C$ is equal to $77°F$. Is your friend correct? If not, find the temperature in degrees Fahrenheit.

9. **Gasoline** A scooter uses 1 gallon of gasoline per 60 miles. A linear equation that models the relationship between the number of miles driven n and the amount of gasoline used in gallons g is $n = 60g$. Graph the function and then estimate the number of miles traveled using 12 gallons of gasoline.

Use the diagram of a seesaw.

10. What is the run of the seesaw?

11. What is the rise of the seesaw?

12. What is the slope of the seesaw?

5 ft

12 ft

Find the slope and y-intercept of the graph of the equation. Then graph the equation.

13. $y = 6x - 3$ **14.** $-5x + y = 1$ **15.** $y = -\frac{1}{4}x$

Graph the inequality.

16. $3x + 6y \geq 12$ **17.** $7x - y \leq 49$ **18.** $8x - 15y > 30$

19. **Gift Card** Ken got a $25 movie gift card. Matinee shows cost $4 and evening shows cost $7. Graph the inequality $4x + 7y \leq 25$. Using the graph, find the greatest number of movies Ken can see.

Chapter FCAT Practice

Test-Taking Strategy When you check your answers, try to use a method other than the one you originally used, to avoid repeating the same mistake.

Multiple Choice

1. Which of the following relations is *not* a function?

   A. (3, 4), (4, 3), (−3, 4), (−4, 3)

   B. (−2, 6), (2, 6), (−3, 7), (−3, 4)

   C. (5, 6), (7, 6), (1, 6), (−5, 6)

   D. (3, 2), (−3, −2), (2, 3), (−2, −3)

2. The scatter plot shows the heart rate in beats per minute and the life span in years for several animals. Describe the relationship shown in the data.

   F. positive   **G.** negative

   H. none   **I.** not enough information

3. Which of the ordered pairs is a solution to the equation $y = 3x - 7$?

   A. (3, 17)   **B.** (0, 5)

   C. (−2, −13)   **D.** (7, 3)

4. What is the value for y when x is 7?

x	3	5	7	9
y	16	28	?	52

   F. 30   **G.** 40   **H.** 42   **I.** 48

5. Which of the following is the equation $8x - 4y = 24$ rewritten in slope-intercept form?

   A. $-4y = -8x + 24$ **B.** $y = -2x - 3$

   C. $y = 2x + 6$ **D.** $y = 2x - 6$

6. Which equation is represented by the graph?

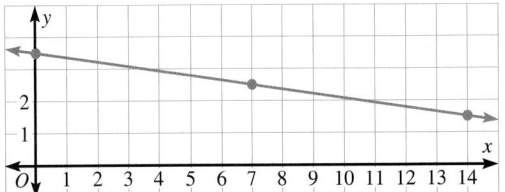

   F. $y = -\frac{1}{7}x + 3.5$ **G.** $y = \frac{1}{7}x + 3.5$

   H. $y = -7x + 3.5$ **I.** $y = 7x + 3.5$

7. What is the slope of the line passing through points (−6, 2) and (8, −5)?

   A. $-\frac{3}{2}$ **B.** $-\frac{1}{2}$ **C.** $\frac{1}{2}$ **D.** -2

Short Response

8. Graph the inequalities $x + y \le 8$, $x \ge 0$, and $y \ge 0$. Find the area of the solution region.

Extended Response

9. Your class needs to raise $120 selling hats and T-shirts. The equation $6x + 5y = 120$, where x is the number of hats sold and y is the number of T-shirts sold, represents the situation. What are the intercepts of the equation? What do they mean in this context?

CHAPTER 12

Data Analysis and Probability

BEFORE

In previous chapters you've...

- Found the median and range of a data set
- Found probabilities of events

Now

In Chapter 12 you'll study...

- Interpreting data displays
- Using permutations and combinations to count possibilities
- Finding the probability of independent and dependent events

WHY?

So you can solve real-world problems about...

- electricity, p. 599
- skateboards, p. 619
- poetry, p. 624
- archery, p. 636

 Internet Preview
CLASSZONE.COM

- eEdition Plus Online
- eWorkbook Plus Online
- eTutorial Plus Online
- FCAT Practice
- More Examples

Chapter Warm-Up Game

Review skills you need for this chapter in this quick game.

Key Skill:
Interpreting bar and circle graphs

GALAPAGOS GRAPHS

HOW TO PLAY

1 **USE** the data displays to answer each question. Record the letter for each correct answer.

About how many times larger is Santa Cruz than San Cristobal?
A. 2   **B.** 3   **C.** 4

What is the area of Isabela?
D. 1680 mi^2 **E.** 1771 mi^2 **F.** 1800 mi^2

What percent of the land vertebrate species in the Galapagos Islands are reptiles?
G. 10%   **H.** 26%   **I.** 30%

2 **WRITE** the letters of the correct answers to the questions in order. Find the number that corresponds to the letter. Put all three numbers together in the order of the answers. This will tell you the age of the oldest Galapagos tortoise on record.

A. 1   **B.** 2   **C.** 0   **D.** 9   **E.** 5
F. 2   **G.** 7   **H.** 2   **I.** 5

594

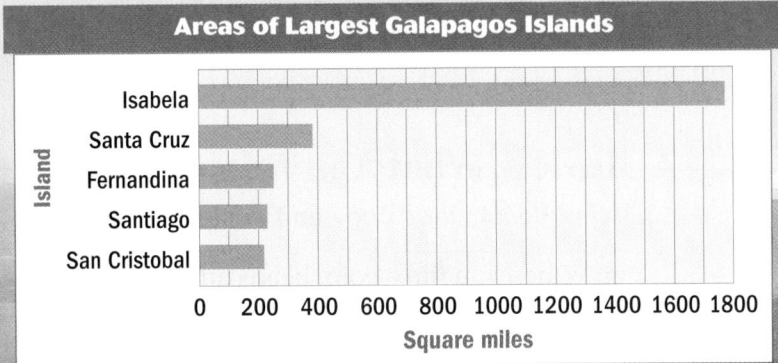

Areas of Largest Galapagos Islands

Island

Isabela
Santa Cruz
Fernandina
Santiago
San Cristobal

0   200   400   600   800 1000 1200 1400 1600 1800

Square miles

Land Vertebrate Species

Birds 57
Reptiles 23
Mammals 9

Great Frigatebird

Giant Galapagos Tortoise

Galapagos Sea Lion

Stop *and* Think

1. **Writing** Describe one way the circle graph would change if you included the ocean life of the Galapagos Islands.

2. **Critical Thinking** Is the area of Isabela greater than the total area of the next four largest islands? Explain.

CHAPTER 12 Getting Ready to Learn

Word Watch

Review Words

data, p. 5
mean, p. 257
median, p. 257
range, p. 258
outcome, p. 354
probability of an event,
   p. 354

Review What You Need to Know

Using Vocabulary **Copy and complete using a review word.**

1. When you flip a coin, heads and tails are the two possible _?_.

2. Find the sum of the values of a set of data and then divide by the number of data values to find the _?_ of the data.

3. The _?_ is a measure of how likely it is that the event will occur.

Find the mean and the median of the data set. *(p. 257)*

4. 23, 27, 13, 24, 19, 21, 25, 25, 12   5. 0.2, 0.35, 1.33, 1.32, 0.05, 0.5

Find the probability of the event. *(p. 354)*

6. You roll a number cube and get a number greater than 4.

7. You randomly choose the letter A from a bag holding the eight lettered tiles that spell ARKANSAS.

NoTebook

You should include material that appears on a notebook like this in your own notes.

Know How to Take Notes

Contrasting Terms When words have similar meanings, you should emphasize their differences in your notes.

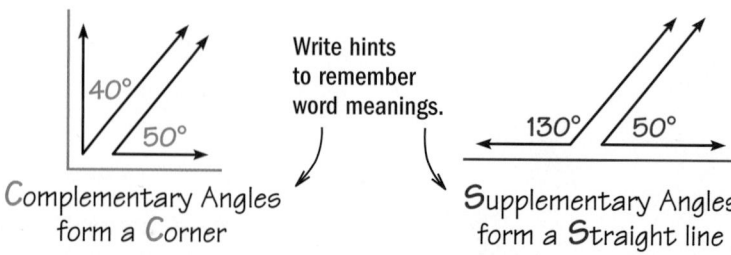

Pairs of Angles

Complementary Angles: The sum of the angle measures is 90°.

Supplementary Angles: The sum of the angle measures is 180°.

Write hints to remember word meanings.

Complementary Angles form a Corner

Supplementary Angles form a Straight line

In Lesson 12.6, you should note the difference between combinations and permutations.

Stem-and-Leaf Plots

LESSON 12.1

BEFORE	▶ Now	WHY?
You organized data using bar graphs and histograms.	You will make and interpret stem-and-leaf plots.	So you can analyze waiting times at a restaurant, as in Ex. 14.

📓 Word Watch

stem-and-leaf plot, p. 597

FLORIDA
Standards and Assessment

• Construct and interpret data displays. (MA.E.1.3.1)

• Interpret range and central tendency. (MA.E.1.3.2)

In the Real World

Track Hurdlers entering the 200 meter hurdles at a track meet were ranked according to their qualifying times, in seconds, shown below.

28.6, 29.2, 28.1, 27.5, 29.8, 28.7, 30.2, 29.3, 28.3, 28.9, 29.9, 28.4

How can the data be displayed to show the distribution of the times?

A **stem-and-leaf plot** is a data display that helps you see how data are distributed. You can use a stem-and-leaf plot to order data.

EXAMPLE 1 **Making a Stem-and-Leaf Plot**

You can display the hurdlers' times given above in a stem-and-leaf plot.

(1 The times range from 27.5 to 30.2. Let the **stems** be the digits in the tens' and ones' places. Let the **leaves** be the tenths' digits.

(2 Write the stems first. Then record each time by writing its tenths' digit on the same line as its corresponding stem. Include a key that shows what the stems and leaves represent.

(3 Make an ordered stem-and-leaf plot.

Unordered Plot	Ordered Plot
27 │ 5	27 │ 5
28 │ 6 1 7 3 9 4	28 │ 1 3 4 6 7 9
29 │ 2 8 3 9	29 │ 2 3 8 9
30 │ 2	30 │ 2
Key: 27│5 = 27.5	Key: 27│5 = 27.5

> The leaves for each stem are listed in order from least to greatest.

Your turn now **Make an ordered stem-and-leaf plot of the data.**

1. Video game prices: $40, $15, $10, $19, $12, $24, $15, $39, $51, $50, $35, $20, $47, $36, $30, $25, $27, $29, $24, $43, $29

HELP with **Solving**

In a stem-and-leaf plot, a stem can be one or more digits. A leaf is usually a single digit.

EXAMPLE 2 Interpreting a Stem-and-Leaf Plot

Biology The stem-and-leaf plot at the right shows the lengths, in millimeters, of young fish in a tank. Use the stem-and-leaf plot to describe the data. What interval includes the most lengths?

```
4 | 9
5 |
6 | 1 2 4 7 8 8
7 | 6 8
8 | 4      Key: 6|8 = 68
```

Solution

The longest fish is 84 mm and the shortest fish is 49 mm, so the range of lengths is 35 mm. Most of the lengths are in the 60–69 interval.

Double Stem-and-Leaf Plots A double stem-and-leaf plot can be used to compare two sets of data. You read to the left of the stems for one set of data and to the right for the other.

EXAMPLE 3 Making a Double Stem-and-Leaf Plot

Test Scores The data below show the test scores for Beth's class and Marisa's class. Overall, which class had the better test scores?

Beth's class: 95, 86, 79, 79, 58, 68, 90, 63, 71, 81, 82, 94, 64, 76, 77, 79, 83, 91, 83, 68, 74, 71

Marisa's class: 95, 73, 76, 84, 84, 89, 67, 82, 88, 86, 93, 97, 96, 84, 60, 75, 91, 87, 89, 86, 76, 93

Solution

You can use a double stem-and-leaf plot to compare the test scores.

```
      Beth's Class      Marisa's Class
                 8 | 5 |
             8 8 4 3 | 6 | 0 7
       9 9 9 7 6 4 1 1 | 7 | 3 5 6 6
           6 3 3 2 1 | 8 | 2 4 4 4 6 6 7 8 9 9
             5 4 1 0 | 9 | 1 3 3 5 6 7      Key: 0|9|1 represents 90 and 91.
```

ANSWER Marisa's class; it had more scores in the eighties and nineties.

Your turn now Complete the following exercises.

2. Make an ordered double stem-and-leaf plot to compare the lengths, in minutes, of the last 10 phone calls made by two friends.

Kenyon: 12, 8, 17, 5, 23, 29, 21, 34, 16, 28
Jason: 31, 28, 7, 5, 11, 5, 13, 16, 11, 24

3. In general, who made longer calls, Kenyon or Jason?

Getting Ready to Practice

1. **Vocabulary** Copy and complete: The key for a stem-and-leaf plot says $7 \mid 4 = 74$. In the plot, 7 is the __?__ and 4 is the __?__ .

Write the number as it would appear in a stem-and-leaf plot. Identify the stem and the leaf.

2. 80   **3.** 117   **4.** 12.9   **5.** 4.6

6. **Guided Problem Solving** The data show the times, in minutes, it takes ten students to get ready for school. Make an ordered stem-and-leaf plot of the data. What interval includes the most time values?

     25, 10, 25, 15, 30, 18, 35, 40, 28, 20

     (1 Identify the range of the data.

     (2 Make the stem-and-leaf plot. Include a key.

     (3 Use the plot to find where most of the times fall.

Practice and Problem Solving

Make an ordered stem-and-leaf plot of the data. Identify the interval that includes the most data values.

7. 45, 48, 65, 50, 67, 82, 74, 63   **8.** 33, 12, 8, 14, 35, 9, 26, 37, 4, 6

9. 108, 95, 89, 112, 109, 94, 103   **10.** 461, 492, 439, 467, 501, 485

11. 20.2, 22.6, 18.3, 18.7, 22.5, 18.1   **12.** 5.1, 4.0, 5.3, 3.2, 5.7, 6.9, 5.3

13. **Writing** Explain how you can use an ordered stem-and-leaf plot to find the median value of a set of data.

14. **Restaurants** The stem-and-leaf plot shows the average waiting times, in minutes, to be seated for fifteen restaurants. What are the shortest and longest waiting times? Which interval has the fewest number of waiting times?

```
0 | 5 6 9
1 | 2 5 5
2 | 0 0 5 8
3 | 2 8
4 | 0 5 5      Key: 2 | 5 = 25
```

15. **Electricity** The data show the amounts, in dollars, of a family's electric bills for twelve months. Make an ordered stem-and-leaf plot. What is the range? Are the bills more often greater or less than $60?

     95, 58, 47, 78, 43, 65, 84, 72, 55, 84, 96, 59

with Homework

Example	Exercises
1	7–12
2	13–15, 18
3	16–17, 19

Online Resources
CLASSZONE.COM

· More Examples
· eTutorial Plus

Make an ordered double stem-and-leaf plot of the two sets of data.

16. Set A: 16, 19, 8, 22, 18, 20, 32, 5

Set B: 12, 8, 25, 42, 31, 15, 16, 9

17. Set C: 102, 98, 111, 70, 118, 92, 77

Set D: 115, 88, 87, 102, 65, 95, 93

18. Critical Thinking Can you make a stem-and-leaf plot from a frequency table? Why or why not?

19. Football The total points that the Cleveland Browns scored in each game of a recent season are given below. Red numbers represent wins and blue numbers represent losses. Make an ordered double stem-and-leaf plot of the data. Describe the relationship between points scored and the outcome of the game.

6, **24**, **23**, **20**, 14, **24**, **21**, 12, **27**, 18, 15, 16, 10, 7, **41**, 7

Extended Problem Solving In Exercises 20–22, use the data below, which show the average monthly temperatures in degrees Fahrenheit (°F) for Los Angeles, California.

56.8, 57.6, 58.0, 60.1, 62.7, 65.7, 69.1, 70.5, 69.9, 66.8, 61.6, 56.9

20. Plot Make an ordered stem-and-leaf plot of the data. What is the range?

21. Convert Convert the data to degrees Celsius (°C) using the formula $C = \frac{5}{9}(F - 32)$. Round to the nearest tenth of a degree.

22. Compare Make an ordered stem-and-leaf plot of the converted data. Compare the two plots. In what ways are they different? Explain.

Mixed Review

23. Find the mean, median, mode(s), and range of the data. *(Lesson 5.8)*

$-22, 14, 12, 6, -10, 14, 20, 16, -7, -5, 6, -2$

24. Find the slope and y-intercept of the line $7x + 4y = 24$. *(Lesson 11.7)*

FCAT Practice FCAT

The stem-and-leaf plot shows the distances between railroad stations, in miles, for a train. Use the plot to answer Exercises 25 and 26.

25. Multiple Choice What is the greatest distance, in miles?

A. 36   **B.** 89   **C.** 257   **D.** 289

26. Multiple Choice What is the median distance?

F. 2   **G.** 5   **H.** 15   **I.** 16

```
0 | 2 2 3
1 | 2 5 6
2 | 8 9
3 | 6
Key: 1|2 = 12
```

Box-and-Whisker Plots

BEFORE	▶ Now	WHY?
You found the median and range of a data set.	You will make and interpret box-and-whisker plots.	So you can analyze camera prices, as in Ex. 12.

Word Watch

box-and-whisker plot, p. 601
lower quartile, p. 601
upper quartile, p. 601
lower extreme, p. 601
upper extreme, p. 601

FLORIDA
Standards and Assessment

• Construct, read, and interpret data displays. Contrast data displays. (MA.E.1.3.1)

• Interpret range and central tendency. (MA.E.1.3.2)

In the Real World

Bridges The lengths, in meters, of the world's ten longest suspension bridges are listed below. How can you display these data to show how the lengths are distributed?

| 1280 | 1118 | 1990 | 1074 | 1298 |
| 1067 | 1624 | 1158 | 1090 | 1410 |

A **box-and-whisker plot** is a data display that organizes data values into four parts. Ordered data are divided into lower and upper halves by the median. The **lower quartile** is the median of the lower half of the data set. The **upper quartile** is the median of the upper half of the data set.

The **lower extreme** is the least data value and the **upper extreme** is the greatest data value.

EXAMPLE 1 **Making a Box-and-Whisker Plot**

HELP with Solving

If a data set has an odd number of values, then the median is not included in either half of the data when determining the quartile values. For help with finding a median, see p. 257.

To display the bridge lengths above in a box-and-whisker plot, first order the data to find the median and the quartiles.

$$\text{Median} = \frac{1158 + 1280}{2} = 1219$$

Lower half					Upper half				
1067	1074	**1090**	1118	1158	1280	1298	**1410**	1624	1990

↑ Lower quartile = 1090   ↑ Upper quartile = 1410

Plot these values below a number line that includes the extremes.

Draw a box with sides at both quartiles. — Draw a vertical line through the median. — Draw "whiskers" from the box to both extremes.

Interpreting a Box-and-Whisker Plot A box-and-whisker plot helps to show how varied, or spread out, the data are. The points divide the data into four parts. Each part represents about one quarter of the data.

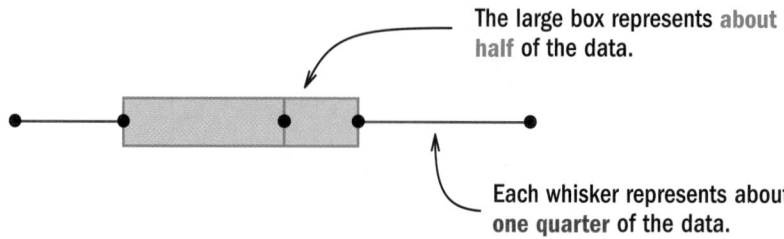

The large box represents about half of the data.

Each whisker represents about one quarter of the data.

You can use box-and-whisker plots to compare two or more data sets.

EXAMPLE 2 **Interpreting Box-and-Whisker Plots**

Food Science You are testing whether a fertilizer helps tomato plants grow. You give fertilizer to the plants in Group 2, but not to Group 1. The box-and-whisker plots show how much the plants grew, in centimeters, for each group of plants after two weeks.

a. About what fraction of the unfertilized plants grew as much as any of the fertilized plants?

b. About what fraction of the fertilized plants grew 4 to 8 centimeters?

Solution

a. Notice that the right whisker for Group 1 overlaps the left whisker for Group 2. So about one quarter of the unfertilized plants grew as much as the any of the fertilized plants.

b. The large box in the plot for Group 2 ranges from 4 to 8, so about one half of the fertilized plants grew 4 to 8 centimeters.

■ **Food Science**

It takes about 24 pounds of tomatoes to make 7 pints of ketchup. At this rate, how many pounds of tomatoes are used to make a 2 pint bottle of ketchup?

Your turn now Use a box-and-whisker plot.

1. Ming worked out for 34, 27, 26, 15, 24, 21, 30, 23, 24, and 35 minutes. Chantelle worked out for 26, 33, 36, 21, 41, 36, 29, 25, 34, and 35 minutes. Make a box-and-whisker plot of the data for each person.

2. Who usually works out longer? Explain.

3. About how often does each person work out for 25–35 minutes?

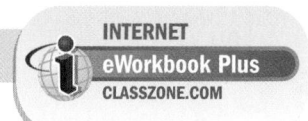
12.2 Exercises
More Practice, p. 738

Getting Ready to Practice

1. **Vocabulary** The median of the lower half of a data set is the ? and the median of the upper half of a data set is the ? .

2. **Guided Problem Solving** You had the following scores while playing a math game: 306, 211, 235, 197, 351, 141, and 227. Make a box-and-whisker plot of your scores. Then predict your next score.

   ① Find the range and draw a number line.

   ② Find the median, quartiles, and extremes.

   ③ Draw the box-and-whisker plot.

   ④ Predict a range for your next score. Explain your reasoning.

Practice and Problem Solving

HELP with Homework

Example	Exercises
1	3–13
2	12–15

Online Resources
CLASSZONE.COM
· More Examples
· eTutorial Plus

In Exercises 3–5, make a box-and-whisker plot of the data.

3. $67, $53, $41, $33, $52, $28, $70, $56

4. 327 ft, 419 ft, 9 ft, 299 ft, 111 ft, 0 ft

5. 26 m, 389 m, 878 m, 144 m, 515 m, 404 m

The box-and-whisker plot shows the lengths, in inches, of the jumps of frogs in a frog-jumping contest. Estimate the following values.

6. range

7. median

8. lower quartile

9. upper quartile

10. lower extreme

11. upper extreme

12. **Camera Prices** The prices of several cameras are $179.99, $329.99, $229.99, $284.99, $399.99, $379.99, $299.99, $259.99, and $259.99. Organize the list of prices from least to greatest. Then make a box-and-whisker plot of the data. What conclusions can you make?

13. **Pumpkins** The weights, in pounds, of 10 giant pumpkins were 853, 811.5, 785, 1020, 826.5, 789, 838, 810, 731, and 822.5. Make a box and-whisker plot of the data. Describe what the plot shows.

14. **Critical Thinking** Explain how making a stem-and-leaf plot can help you to make a box-and-whisker plot.

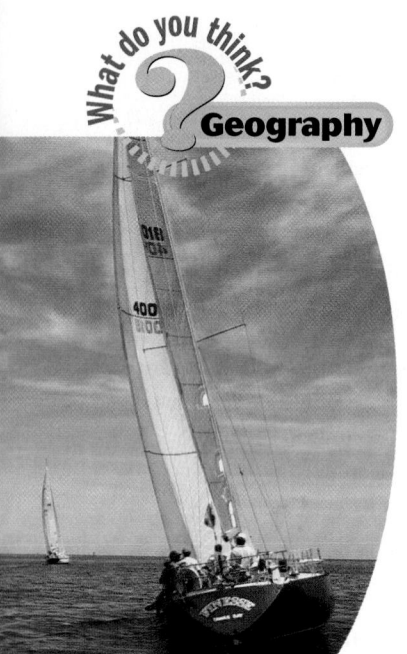
15. Basketball The box-and-whisker plots show the points scored per game for two players. What conclusions can you make about the players' performances? Which player is more consistent? Explain.

Tasha

Karen

Lake Area In Exercises 16 and 17, use the areas, in square kilometers, of the world's ten largest lakes: 371,000, 84,500, 64,500, 63,500, 62,940, 58,020, 32,000, 31,500, 31,400, and 28,400.

An *outlier* is a data value that is much less or much greater than most of the other values in the data set.

16. Make a box-and-whisker plot of the data. Which value is an outlier?

17. Remove the outlier and then make another box-and-whisker plot. Describe how an outlier affects a box-and-whisker plot.

18. Challenge Change one value in the data set 3, 4, 5, 7, 9, 11, 13, 15, 17, 18, 21 so that the median of the set is 13, the lower quartile is 7, and the upper quartile is 17. Explain how you got your answer.

■ **Lake Area**

Three of the world's 10 largest lakes are Great Lakes. The 6 quadrillion gallons in the Great Lakes are 18% of the world's fresh water supply. One quadrillion is equal to one million billions. How much fresh water does the world have?

Mixed Review

19. The table shows the height, in inches, of several players on a soccer team. Make a bar graph of the data. *(Lesson 1.1)*

Name	Ally	Nate	Bob	Inez	Dan	Lisa
Height	68	66	73	66	60	62

Find the *x*-intercept, *y*-intercept, and slope of the graph of the equation. Then graph the line. *(Lessons 11.5, 11.6)*

20. $y = 24$ **21.** $3x - 5y = 30$ **22.** $x = -4$

FCAT Practice

23. Extended Response The masses, in grams, of 10 samples from bolt factories A and B are shown. All bolts should weigh 198.5–202 grams:

Factory A: 199, 201, 200, 198.5, 200.5, 202, 201, 200.8, 200.9, 198.5

Factory B: 201, 200.4, 203, 200.8, 201, 203.4, 200.6, 201, 200.9, 203.1

Make a box-and-whisker plot comparing the samples. Describe how well each factory makes bolts within the desired mass range, based on the samples. Then compare the factories' performances. Use the plot you have made to describe how it supports your answer.

Using Data Displays

BEFORE	▶ Now	WHY?
You organized data using box-and-whisker plots.	You will organize data using circle graphs and line graphs.	So you can represent the areas of boroughs of New York, as in Ex. 13.

Word Watch

circle graph, p. 605
line graph, p. 606

FLORIDA
Standards and Assessment

• Construct and interpret data displays. Contrast data displays. (MA.E.1.3.1)

• Know real-world uses of statistics. (MA.E.3.3.2)

Circle Graphs A survey asked, "How well can you whistle?" The results are shown in the *circle graph* below. It shows that three out of four people can whistle a tune.

A **circle graph** represents data as sections of a circle. Each section can be labeled using a fraction, decimal, or percent. Because the graph represents all the data, the sum of the sections must equal 1, or 100%.

How Well Can You Whistle?

Can whistle a tune 75%
Can whistle a note 12%
Can't whistle 13%

To make a circle graph, find the angle measure to the nearest degree that represents each data value's portion of the whole. The sum of all the angle measures must equal 360°, the number of degrees in a circle.

EXAMPLE 1 Making a Circle Graph

E-mail A survey asked, "How often do you check your e-mail?" Of the 100 people asked, 4 answered *less than weekly*, 23 answered *weekly*, and 73 answered *every day*. You can display the data in a circle graph.

HELP with Solving

In Example 1, you can draw the 14° and 83° angles first. Then the remaining section of the circle will have a measure of 263°.

(1 Use a proportion to find the number of degrees to use to represent each response as a section in a circle graph.

Less than weekly	Weekly	Every day
$\frac{4}{100} = \frac{a}{360°}$	$\frac{23}{100} = \frac{b}{360°}$	$\frac{73}{100} = \frac{c}{360°}$
$a = 14.4° \approx \mathbf{14°}$	$b = 82.8° \approx \mathbf{83°}$	$c = 262.8° \approx \mathbf{263°}$

(2 Draw a circle.

(3 Use a protractor to draw the first angle measure. Then label the section.

(4 Draw and label remaining sections. Include a title.

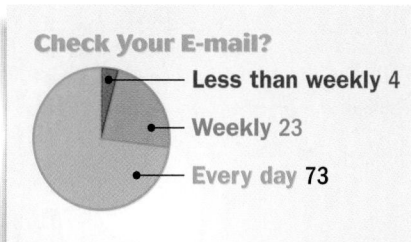

Check Your E-mail?

Less than weekly 4
Weekly 23
Every day 73

ANSWER The graph shows that the majority of people check their e-mail every day.

Line Graphs A **line graph** represents data that change over time.

EXAMPLE 2 **Making a Line Graph**

Environment The table shows the number of insect species on the United States endangered species list. Make a line graph of the data.

Year	1995	1996	1997	1998	1999	2000	2001
Number	20	20	28	28	28	33	35

(**1**) Draw and label the horizontal and vertical scales.

(**2**) Plot a point for each data pair.

(**3**) Draw line segments to connect the points.

(**4**) The graph shows an increase over time.

Karner Blue Butterfly, endangered since 1992

Your turn now **Use the table of polling data.**

1. Make a circle graph of the data for Week 1. What does the graph show?

2. Make a line graph of the data for Ben. What does the graph show?

Who Will You Vote For?			
Week	1	2	3
Ben	55%	50%	40%
Alice	45%	50%	60%

Using appropriate data displays helps you make meaningful conclusions.

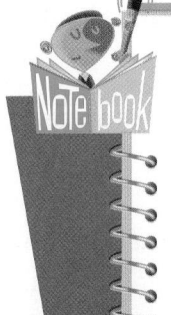

Using Appropriate Data Displays

Use a *circle graph* to represent data as parts of a whole.

Use a *line graph* to display data over time.

Use a *stem-and-leaf plot* to order a data set.

Use a *box-and-whisker plot* to show the data's distribution in quarters, using the median, quartiles, and extremes.

Use a *bar graph* to display data in distinct categories.

Use a *histogram* to compare the frequencies of data that are grouped in equal intervals.

EXAMPLE 3 **Choosing a Data Display**

Choose an appropriate display for the data.

a. The table below shows the results of a survey that asked students if they are going away during summer vacation.

Response	Percent
Yes	48%
No	37%
Don't know	15%

b. The table below shows the results of a survey that asked students about ways they use the Internet.

Purpose	Percent
Research	62%
Shopping	34%
E-mail	45%
News	10%
Browsing	18%

Solution

a. The data add up to 100%, so a circle graph is appropriate.

b. The percents in the categories add up to more than 100%. An appropriate display for the data is a bar graph.

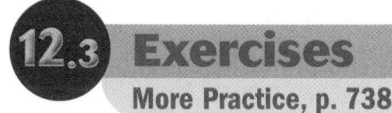

12.3 Exercises
More Practice, p. 738

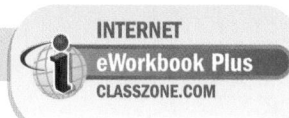

INTERNET
eWorkbook Plus
CLASSZONE.COM

Getting Ready to Practice

Vocabulary **Copy and complete the statement.**

1. You can use a ? to display data as parts of a whole.

2. You can use a ? to display changes in a quantity over time.

Convert the value into an angle measure for display in a circle graph.

3. 31%   **4.** $\frac{3}{8}$ **5.** 14%   **6.** 27 out of 60

Theater **In Exercises 7 and 8, use the table showing attendance at your school play.**

7. Make a circle graph to display each attendance number as a fraction of total attendance at all four performances.

8. Tickets cost $7 each. Make a line graph that shows how much money was collected from each performance.

Play Attendance	
Friday	130
Saturday (2 P.M.)	231
Saturday (8 P.M.)	291
Sunday	185

Practice and Problem Solving

with Homework

Example	Exercises
1	9, 12-17
2	10-11, 15-17
3	15-17

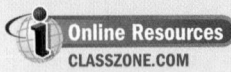
Online Resources
CLASSZONE.COM
· More Examples
· eTutorial Plus

9. Snacking The table shows the results of a survey asking students to describe how often they snack. Represent the data in a circle graph.

How Often Do You Snack?	
Never	10%
Rarely	45%
Sometimes	35%
Often	10%

10. New Houses The table below shows the number, in thousands, of new single-family houses sold in the United States each year from 1997 to 2001. Make a line graph of the data. Describe how the data change over time.

Year	1997	1998	1999	2000	2001
Houses sold (thousands)	804	886	880	877	900

11. Music The table below shows the number of people, in millions, who attended symphony orchestra concerts in the United States each year from 1994 to 1998. Make a line graph of the data. What trend does the graph show?

Year	1994	1995	1996	1997	1998
Attendees (millions)	24.4	30.9	31.1	31.9	32.2

with Solving

The sum of the rounded angle measures in Exercise 13 will not equal 360°. This is the result of *round-off error*. The sum of the unrounded values is 360°.

New York City The map shows the land area, in square miles, of each of the five boroughs of New York City.

12. Find the percent of the total area of New York City that each borough covers.

13. Represent the data using a circle graph.

14. Use the graph to compare the areas of the boroughs.

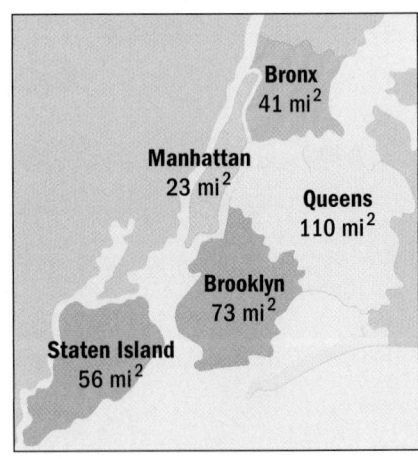

Critical Thinking In Exercises 15–17, tell which type of display you would use for the data described. Explain your reasoning.

15. You record the temperature at noon every day for a month.

16. You record the temperature at five different locations.

17. You record the high temperature every day for a month, and find how often the daily high temperature falls within each 10 degree temperature interval.

Car Color In Exercises 18 and 19, use the table. It shows the percent of people who liked the given color for sports and compact cars.

Color	Silver	Black	Dark blue	White	Dark green	Red	Other
2000	25.4%	14.5%	11.3%	9.8%	6.7%	12.7%	19.6%
2001	22.3%	14.4%	5.0%	11.4%	9.7%	15.8%	21.4%

18. Make a circle graph of the data for 2000 and for 2001.

19. From 2000 to 2001, which color had the largest percent increase? The largest percent decrease?

20. Critical Thinking Is it easier to answer Exercise 19 by comparing the graphs or by using the table? Explain.

21. Camping The data in the circle graph show the percent of people who chose each reason for camping. Can you display the data in a line graph? Why or why not? Can you display the data in a bar graph? Why or why not?

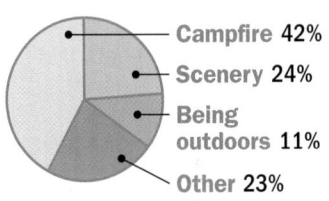

Campfire 42%
Scenery 24%
Being outdoors 11%
Other 23%

22. Challenge Describe a set of data that could be displayed in three different types of data display. Explain how to display it in each.

Mixed Review

Graph the equation using intercepts. *(Lesson 11.5)*

23. $5x + 2y = 10$ **24.** $8x - 3y = 24$ **25.** $9y - 18x = 27$

26. Make an ordered stem-and-leaf plot of the following data: 17, 10, 11, 15, 21, 34, 26, 16, 36, 24, 37, 20, 18, 31, 39, 29, 28. *(Lesson 12.1)*

FCAT Practice

27. Multiple Choice Use the line graph. It shows the population, in millions, in the state of Florida from 1995 to 1999. Between which pair of years is the increase the greatest?

A. 1994–1995   **B.** 1995–1996

C. 1996–1997   **D.** 1998–1999

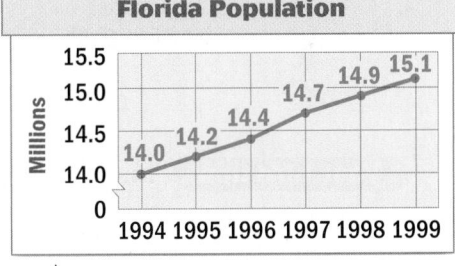

Florida Population

Millions

15.5
15.0
14.5
14.0
0

14.0 14.2 14.4 14.7 14.9 15.1

1994 1995 1996 1997 1998 1999

28. Short Response You poll 100 people about their favorite writing tool. The possible answers are *pen*, *pencil*, and *other*. What types of display would be appropriate for this type of data? Explain.

GRAPHING CALCULATOR

Technology Activity

12.3

FLORIDA: Standards and Assessment
Construct and interpret data displays. Contrast data displays. (MA.E.1.3.1)
Use technology to organize, analyze, and graph data. (MA.E.1.3.3)

Making Data Displays

GOAL Use a graphing calculator to create data displays.

Example 1 The table shows the cost, in dollars, of a phone call, based on the length, in minutes, of the call. Make a scatter plot or a line graph on your calculator.

Minutes	Cost
5	0.5
10	1
15	1.5
20	2
25	2.4
30	2.7

Solution

1 Enter the data into two lists.

2 Choose maximums and minimums for the window.

3 Choose a display from the PLOT menu and set the Xlist and Ylist.

4 Press GRAPH to show the display you have chosen.

Choose ⌊∴ for a scatter plot or ⌐ for a line graph.

Your turn now Make a scatter plot and a line graph of the data.

1.

Year	1997	1998	1999	2000	2001
Rainfall (in.)	21.4	39.8	34.5	26.1	44.9

Example 2 The table shows the number of people out of 200 surveyed who prefer each type of music. You can use a graphing calculator to make a circle graph of the data.

Pop	75
Rock	62
Country	43
Classical	20

Solution

1 Press [LIST]. Then use the TEXT menu to name a list and its categories. Use quotation marks for the first item, so the calculator recognizes that the list is *categorical* (contains words).

Use quotation marks for categorical data.

Enter the numerical data into a second list.

2 Use the PLOT menu to choose the two lists.

You can display the data as numbers or as percents.

3 Press [GRAPH] to display the circle graph.

number display

Your turn now Make a circle graph of the survey data.

2.

Did You Get Enough Sleep?	
Need more	541
Need less	167
Just right	282
Don't know	21

3.

The last movie I saw I watched...	
in a theater.	410
on a television.	483
on a computer.	21

CHAPTER 12 Special Topic

Misleading Graphs

GOAL Identify and analyze misleading graphs.

Word Watch

Review Words

bar graph, p. 5
line graph, p. 606

FLORIDA
Standards and Assessment

• Know real-world uses of statistics. (MA.E.3.3.2)

• Know when statistics are used in misleading ways. (MA.E.3.3.2)

HELP with Solving

Remember that the broken axis symbol ⌇ indicates that some of the values in the axis have been left out.

When you analyze a graph to make conclusions based on the data displayed, it is important to be aware that the display may be misleading.

EXAMPLE 1 Identifying a Misleading Graph

Attendance Which of the bar graphs that show attendance at an annual rock festival from 1998 to 2002 could be misleading?

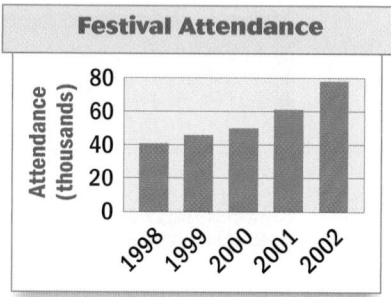

The first graph has a break in the vertical axis, so comparing the bars may lead to incorrect conclusions. It looks as if attendance in 2002 was about three times as great as in 1998, but attendance only doubled during this time. The second graph is less likely to mislead.

EXAMPLE 2 Analyzing Misleading Graphs

Business The line graphs below display a company's profits and sales for each year from 1998 to 2002. What is misleading about each graph?

a.

b.
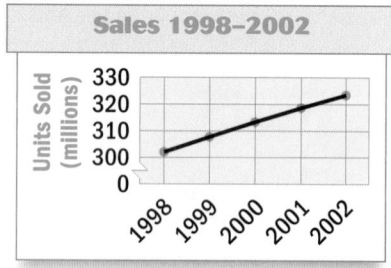

Solution

a. The range of values on the vertical scale is larger than needed. The graph suggests that profits have decreased only slightly, when they have decreased by a third.

b. Because the vertical axis starts at 300, it looks as if sales have risen rapidly. An unbroken axis would show that sales have risen slowly, at less than 2% per year.

EXAMPLE 3 **Misleading Comparisons**

Compare the average monthly temperatures at two resorts.

At a glance, the displays suggest that the temperatures are about the same, but the vertical axes are different. When data for both resorts are graphed together, it becomes clear that Sunny Vista has warmer temperatures.

Exercises

Tell whether the data are represented clearly. If the graph is misleading, explain why. Then redraw the graph so that it is not misleading.

1.

2.

3. Baseball The table below shows a baseball pitcher's wins and losses per season. Make a graph that shows a positive performance. Then make another graph that shows a negative performance.

Year	1998	1999	2000	2001	2002
Wins	6	8	10	12	16
Losses	7	9	9	13	14

Notebook Review

Review the vocabulary definitions in your notebook.

Copy the review examples in your notebook. Then complete the exercises.

Check Your Definitions

stem-and-leaf plot, p. 597

box-and-whisker plot, p. 601

lower quartile, p. 601

upper quartile, p. 601

lower extreme, p. 601

upper extreme, p. 601

circle graph, p. 605

line graph, p. 606

Use Your Vocabulary

1. Copy and complete: The ? is the least value in a data set and the ? is the greatest value in the data set.

12.1–12.2 Can you order and display data?

 EXAMPLE Order the data set 24, 29, 35, 32, 22, 20, 43, 27, 41, 31, 26 in a stem-and-leaf plot. Then make a box-and-whisker plot of the data.

```
2 | 0 2 4 6 7 9
3 | 1 2 5
4 | 1 3
Key: 4 | 1 = 41
```

☑ **2.** Make an ordered stem-and-leaf plot and a box-and-whisker plot of the wind speed data, given in miles per hour: 9, 15, 8, 19, 11, 18, 11, 24, 7, 14.

12.3 Can you use appropriate data displays?

 EXAMPLES

Use a circle graph to represent data as parts of a whole.

Use a line graph to display changes in a quantity over time.

3. Make a circle graph of survey results where 24% of the people surveyed said *no*, 47% said *yes*, and the rest said *not sure*.

4. The hourly temperatures, in degrees Celsius, starting at 1 P.M. were 33°C, 33°C, 34°C, 37°C, 37°C, and 36°C. Make a line graph of the data.

Stop *and* **Think** about Lessons 12.1–12.3

5. Writing Describe some real-world data that a double stem-and-leaf plot would help you analyze.

6. Critical Thinking Could you display the data from Exercise 3 in a line graph? Explain. What other type of display could be useful?

Review Quiz 1

1. Attendance Make an ordered double stem-and-leaf plot comparing the ballpark attendance data below for April and June. Then make a pair of box-and-whisker plots that compare the data. Use the displays to compare April attendance to June attendance.

April: 1025, 1058, 1030, 997, 990, 1116, 1001, 995, 1122, 1099

June: 1056, 1125, 1151, 1048, 1123, 1097, 1042, 1164, 1125, 1131

2. Nuts Consumption of peanuts per person in the United States was as follows: 1995, 5.7 lb; 1996, 5.7 lb; 1997, 5.9 lb; 1998, 5.9 lb; 1999, 6.4 lb. Make a circle graph or a line graph of the data. Explain your choice.

 BrAIN GAME

Safe Cracker

Use the box-and-whisker plot to find the missing leaves in the stem-and-leaf plot of the same group of eight numbers. Take the numbers that the missing leaves represent, and put them in order from least to greatest to find the combination that opens the safe.

11 15   22   29   36

```
1 | 1  4  ?
2 | 0  ?  7
3 | 1  ?
Key: 1 | 4 = 14
```

1?, 2?, 3?

12.4 Problem Solving Strategies

FLORIDA: Standards and Assessment
Solve multi-step real-world problems. (MA.A.3.3.3)

Solve a Simpler Problem

- Guess, Check, and Revise
- Look for a Pattern
- Draw a Diagram
- Act It Out
- Solve a Simpler Problem
- Work Backward
- Make a Table

Problem There are 10 people in a room. They introduce themselves to each other by shaking every other person's hand one time. How many handshakes occur?

1 Read and Understand

Read the problem carefully.

You know that 10 people in a room each shake every other person's hand.

You want to find the total number of handshakes.

2 Make a Plan

Decide on a strategy to use.

By solving a series of simpler problems, you can identify a pattern in the number of handshakes. Then you can extend the pattern to find how many handshakes occur among 10 people.

3 Solve the Problem

Reread the problem and solve a simpler problem.

First, find the number of handshakes between 2 people, 3 people, and so on. You can do this by drawing a diagram. Make a table of your results.

Number of people	2	3	4	5
Number of handshakes	1	3	6	10
Pattern		+2	+3	+4

Extend the pattern to find the number of handshakes among 10 people.

1, 3, 6, 10, 15, 21, 28, 36, 45

+5 +6 +7 +8 +9

ANSWER So, 45 handshakes occur when 10 people shake hands.

4 Look Back

Double-check your calculations to be sure you didn't make any mistakes. You can also use the strategy *act it out* to check your answer.

Practice the Strategy

Use the strategy *solve a simpler problem*.

1. **Restaurants** A restaurant has 28 square tables that seat one person per side. You can join tables together. How many people can fit at two long tables made from all 28 tables? Will it make a difference if the tables are not divided equally?

2. **Triangular Numbers** The dots arranged in a triangle represent triangular numbers.

   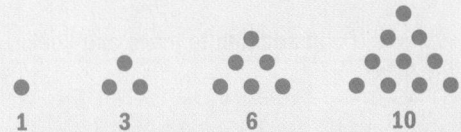

   1   3   6   10

   Predict the number of dots in the eighth triangular number.

3. **Tournament** You are planning a small tournament for a chess club. If each of five members plays one game against each of the other members, how many games must you schedule?

4. **House Numbers** The houses on Stanford Street are numbered consecutively from 10 to 132. How many of each digit do you need to form all the house numbers?

5. **Odd Numbers** Find the sum of the first 50 odd whole numbers.

6. **Marching Band** A marching band is in a triangular formation. There is 1 band member in the front row. Each of the other rows contains 2 more band members than the row in front of it. There are 11 rows in all. How many band members are there?

7. **Palindromes** A palindrome is a number that reads the same backward and forward. For example, the number 1 and the number 414 are both palindromes. How many palindromes are there from 1 to 500?

Mixed Problem Solving

Use any strategy to solve the problem.

8. **Walking** Jay and Paul start walking in opposite directions. Jay walks 0.75 mile every 12 minutes, and Paul walks 2.5 miles every 30 minutes. How far apart are they after 1.5 hours?

9. **Games** What is the total number of squares on the checkerboard? Include squares of all sizes.

10. **Prisms** How does doubling the height of each base of a triangular prism affect its volume? How does halving the height of each base affect the volume?

11. **Calendars** What day of the week is the 3117th day after Thursday?

12. **Checking Account** The list below shows deposits and withdrawals this month. If Rodney has $57.68 in his checking account now, how much money did he have before Week 1?

    Week 1: He bought a shirt for $18 and a pair of pants for $26.

    Week 2: He bought a CD for $14 and lunch for $7.50.

    Week 3: He deposited $20.

Lesson 12.4   Counting Methods   **617**

Counting Methods

LESSON 12.4

BEFORE	▶ Now	WHY?
You found theoretical and experimental probability.	You will use counting methods to count the number of choices.	So you can count the outcomes of an election, as in Ex. 12.

Word Watch

tree diagram, p. 618

FLORIDA
Standards and Assessment

• Know appropriate operations to solve real-world problems. (MA.A.3.3.2)

• Apply number theory to solve problems. (MA.A.5.3.1)

Activity **You can count choices using an organized list.**

You are choosing an outfit. You can choose a T-shirt (T), a button-down shirt (B), or a sweater (S) as a top and jeans (J) or khakis (K) for pants.

 jeans (J) khakis (K) T-shirt (T) button-down (B) sweater (S)

① Use the letters to represent possible outfits. One possible outfit is JT, which means jeans and a T-shirt. Make a list of all possible outfits.

② You decide to consider dress pants (D) in addition to jeans and khakis. How many outfits are possible now?

③ You also decide to include socks as part of the outfit. You can choose between red (R) and green (G). How many outfits are possible now?

In the activity, you made lists to count the number of choices. Another way to count the number of choices is to use a **tree diagram**.

EXAMPLE 1 **Making a Tree Diagram**

You can use a tree diagram to count the number of possible outfits in Step 2 of the activity above.

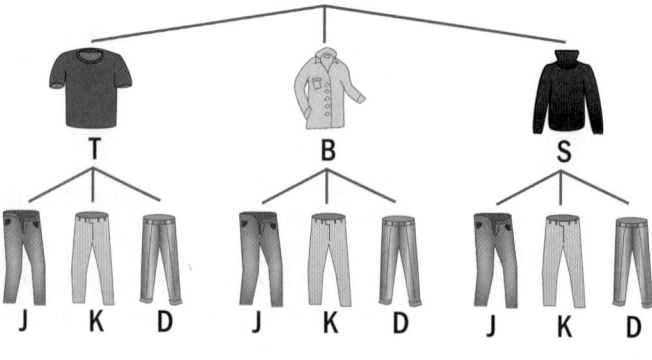

There are 9 different possible outfits.

Another way to count choices is to use the *counting principle*.

The Counting Principle

If one event can occur in *m* ways, and for each of these a second event can occur in *n* ways, then the number of ways that the two events can occur together is $m \cdot n$.

This principle can be extended to three or more events.

EXAMPLE 2 Using the Counting Principle

Skateboards To build a skateboard, you can choose one deck and one type of wheel assembly from those shown. To count the number of different skateboards you can build, use the counting principle.

Decks

$$4 \quad \cdot \quad 3 \quad = \quad 12 \qquad \text{Counting principle}$$

decks   wheel
       assemblies

Wheel Assemblies

ANSWER You can build 12 different skateboards.

EXAMPLE 3 Using the Counting Principle

Passwords You are choosing a password that starts with 3 letters and then has 2 digits. How many different passwords are possible?

Solution

$$\underbrace{26 \cdot 26 \cdot 26}_{\text{letters}} \cdot \underbrace{10 \cdot 10}_{\text{digits}} = 1{,}757{,}600 \qquad \text{Counting principle}$$

ANSWER There are 1,757,600 different possible passwords.

Your turn now Count the choices.

1. Your soccer team's uniform choices include yellow and green shirts, white, black, and green shorts, and four colors of socks. Use a tree diagram to find how many different uniforms are possible.

2. In Example 3, suppose that the passwords may not start with an A or use the digit 0. How many different passwords are possible? Explain.

EXAMPLE 4 **Finding a Probability**

Number Cubes You and three friends each roll a number cube. What is the probability that you each roll the same number?

1 List the *favorable* outcomes. There are 6:

1-1-1-1   2-2-2-2   3-3-3-3   4-4-4-4   5-5-5-5   6-6-6-6

2 Use the counting principle to find the number of *possible* outcomes.

$$\underbrace{6 \cdot 6 \cdot 6 \cdot 6}_{\text{4 number cubes}} = 1296$$

3 Then use the formula for finding probability.

$$\frac{\text{Number of favorable outcomes}}{\text{Number of possible outcomes}} = \frac{6}{1296} = \frac{1}{216}$$

ANSWER The probability that you each roll the same number is $\frac{1}{216}$.

HELP with Review

For help with probability, see p. 354.

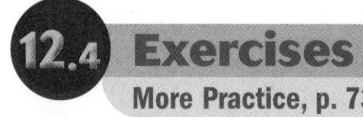

12.4 **Exercises**

More Practice, p. 738

INTERNET
eWorkbook Plus
CLASSZONE.COM

Getting Ready to Practice

1. Vocabulary Copy and complete: If there are *m* ways that one event can occur and for each of those there are *n* ways that a second event can occur, then there are _?_ ways that the two events can occur together.

Make a tree diagram to find the number of choices that are possible. Then check your answer using the counting principle.

2. Choose apple, blueberry, lemon, or cherry pie with juice or tea.

3. Choose a small, medium, or large shirt in red, yellow, or blue.

4. Choose a car or truck with a tape player or a CD player.

5. Choose a hat or scarf in gray, white, or black.

6. Weekend Plans You would like to go to the movies, a play, or the zoo. You can invite your cousin or your best friend. You can go on Friday or Saturday. Make a tree diagram to list all of the possibilities. Then use the counting principle to check your answer.

7. Movies You and three friends all go to the movies on Friday night. You each pick a movie at random from the four choices. What is the probability that you all pick the same movie to see?

Practice and Problem Solving

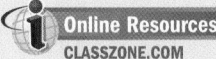
HELP with **Homework**

Example	Exercises
1	8-12, 14, 17
2	8-14, 18
3	8-14, 18
4	15-16

Online Resources
CLASSZONE.COM

· More Examples
· eTutorial Plus

In Exercises 8–11, make a tree diagram to find the number of choices that are possible. Then check your answer using the counting principle.

8. Choose a red, green, blue, or gray ball with a black or silver racquet.

9. Choose one of 6 DVDs and one of 4 CDs.

10. Choose one of 5 essays and one of 3 extra credit questions.

11. Choose a city tour or a park tour with passes to the art or science museum and a trip to the zoo, baseball game, movies, or mall.

12. **Class Election** The lists show the candidates for offices in a class election. Make a tree diagram to find the number of different ways a president, treasurer, and secretary can be chosen. Then use the counting principle to check your answer.

President	Treasurer	Secretary
☐ Amy	☐ Jessica	☐ Scott
☐ Hector	☐ Michael	☐ Nicole
	☐ Carson	☐ Thomas
		☐ Angela
		☐ Isabel

13. **Banking** You open a bank account and need to choose a password with 4 characters that can repeat. The password starts with 3 digits and then has 1 letter. How many different passwords are possible?

14. **Writing** There are 5 CDs and 4 books that you are interested in buying. Describe how to find the number of different pairs of 1 CD and 1 book that you can buy.

15. **Coins** Six people all flip a coin. What is the probability that they all get heads?

16. **States** You and Terry randomly choose the name of a state. What is the probability that you both choose a state whose name starts with a T? (Tennessee and Texas are the two states that start with the letter T.)

Extended Problem Solving **You are at a grocery store buying flavored water. You can choose lime, lemon, cherry, or orange. You can choose a 0.5-liter, 1-liter, or 2-liter bottle.**

17. **Draw** Make a tree diagram that shows all of the different bottles of flavored water that you can choose.

18. **Multiply** How many total different bottles can you choose from if 5 new flavors become available?

19. **Challenge** The sign shows the prices for each bottle size. What are the different total prices that you could be charged for three bottles? What is largest total quantity of water you can buy if you have only $2.60?

Water Sale
0.5 liter — $0.59
1 liter — $0.69
2 liter — $0.99

20. Solve a Simpler Problem If you have 5 cousins, and the probability that a cousin is a boy is 0.5, what is the probability that there is at least one boy and at least one girl among the cousins? Explain how you used a simpler problem to get your answer. (*Hint:* How many of the possible outcomes do *not* include both a boy and a girl?)

21. Critical Thinking A restaurant has 36 possible meal specials that you can choose. A meal has a main course, a vegetable, and a dessert. The restaurant has 6 different main courses and 2 different vegetables. How many different desserts does it have?

Braille In Exercises 22 and 23, use the following information.

Braille uses arrangements of raised dots to form symbols that represent letters, numbers, and punctuation marks. Braille is read by touching the symbols. Each symbol is a cell of 6 dots arranged in 3 rows of 2. In the cell, certain dots are raised to make a particular symbol.

22. How many different Braille symbols are possible? How many symbols are possible with no raised dots? With 6 raised dots?

23. Are the number of symbols possible with one raised dot the same as the number of symbols possible with 5 raised dots? Explain.

Mixed Review

Find the slope of the line passing through the points. (*Lesson 11.6*)

24. (5, 2), (−4, 2) **25.** (−2, 3), (4, 6) **26.** (3, 1), (7, −2)

27. The ages, in years, of youth group members are 12, 9, 8, 16, 12, 13, 8, 10, 11, and 17. Make a box-and-whisker plot of the data. (*Lesson 12.2*)

FCAT Practice FCAT

28. Multiple Choice You try to guess your friend's locker combination, which has 3 numbers, each from 0 to 39. Which of the expressions would you use to find the total number of possible combinations?

A. 39 · 3 **B.** 40 · 3

C. 39 · 39 · 39 **D.** 40 · 40 · 40

29. Short Response You are playing a car racing game. You can choose the red, blue, green, orange, or yellow car, each with an automatic or standard transmission. You can choose from 12 different racetracks. Use the counting principle to count the number of different races you can drive given these choices.

Permutations

BEFORE	▶ Now	WHY?
You used the counting principle to count possibilities.	You will use permutations to count possibilities.	So you can count the ways you can knit a hat, as in Ex. 20.

Word Watch

permutation, p. 623
factorial, p. 623

FLORIDA
Standards and Assessment

• Apply number theory to solve problems. (MA.A.5.3.1)

• Know appropriate operations to solve real-world problems. (MA.A.3.3.2)

In some arrangements of groups, order is important. For example, the diagram shows the different ways that a group of three dogs could finish first, second, and third at a dog show.

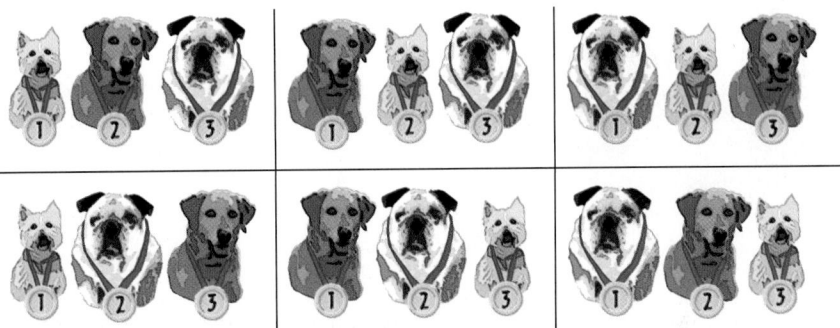

Each arrangement lists the same dogs, but the orders are different. Arrangements such as these are called *permutations*. A **permutation** is an arrangement in which order is important. You can use the counting principle to count permutations.

EXAMPLE 1 **Counting Permutations**

Music You have five CDs. You can use the counting principle to count the number of permutations of 5 CDs. This is the number of different orders in which you can listen to the CDs.

Choices for 1st CD	Choices for 2nd CD	Choices for 3rd CD	Choices for 4th CD	Choices for 5th CD
5 •	4 •	3 •	2 •	1 = 120

ANSWER You can listen to the CDs in 120 different orders.

HELP with Solving

You can use $n!$ to find the number of permutations of n objects.

Factorials In Example 1, you evaluated $5 \cdot 4 \cdot 3 \cdot 2 \cdot 1$. You can write $5 \cdot 4 \cdot 3 \cdot 2 \cdot 1$ as 5!, which is read "5 **factorial**."

$$5! = 5 \cdot 4 \cdot 3 \cdot 2 \cdot 1 \qquad n! = n \cdot (n - 1) \cdot (n - 2) \cdot \ldots \cdot 1$$

The value of 0! is defined to be 1.

Your turn now **Evaluate the factorial.**

1. 3! **2.** 4! **3.** 6! **4.** 1!

Getting Ready to Practice

1. **Vocabulary** Copy and complete: The number of permutations of 15 objects taken 7 at a time can be written as __?__.

Evaluate.

2. $2!$

3. $0!$

4. $7!$

5. $9!$

6. $_4P_2$

7. $_9P_6$

8. $_{10}P_7$

9. $_5P_5$

10. You have three things to do after you wake up tomorrow. You need to take a shower, eat breakfast, and call your friend. Find the number of permutations and list them.

Practice and Problem Solving

HELP with Homework

Example	Exercises
1	11
2	20–22, 24
3	12–22, 24

Online Resources
CLASSZONE.COM
· More Examples
· eTutorial Plus

11. **Movies** You rent four movies. In how many different orders can you watch the movies?

Find the number of permutations.

12. $_3P_1$

13. $_5P_2$

14. $_3P_2$

15. $_9P_3$

16. $_{12}P_6$

17. $_7P_4$

18. $_{15}P_5$

19. $_{20}P_3$

20. **Knitting** You are knitting a hat, and you want it to have 3 different colored stripes. You have 6 different colors of yarn. How many different hats could you knit?

21. **Softball** Your softball team has 15 players. Find the number of different ways that the first, second, third, fourth, and fifth batters can be chosen.

22. **After School** You are given a list of 10 activities you can do after school. You are asked to pick your first, second, third, and fourth choices. How many different permutations are possible?

23. **Critical Thinking** Your friend says that $11! = 11 \cdot 10!$. Is your friend correct? Explain.

24. **Gardening** You are planning a garden with 3 rows. Each row will have one type of flower, and none of the rows will be the same. You can choose from the flowers below. Find the number of permutations.

Day Lily **Poppy** **Gladiolus** **Daffodil** **Rose** **Sunflower** **Tulip**

Extended Problem Solving In Exercises 25 and 26, your team is 1 of 15 in a cheerleading competition.

25. If trophies are awarded for first, second, third, and fourth places, in how many different ways can the trophies be awarded?

26. **Compare and Contrast** Suppose the four teams that perform best are all given *excellence* medals instead of first, second, third, and fourth place trophies. In this case, are there more or fewer ways to give the awards than in Exercise 25? Explain.

27. **Challenge** You choose a 6-letter password for your e-mail. Write an expression to represent the number of different passwords you could choose. Explain how this expression changes if you can use each letter only once.

Mixed Review

28. Find the surface area of a cone that has a slant height of 24 inches and a diameter of 10 inches. Round to the nearest tenth. *(Lesson 10.5)*

29. The table shows the results of a survey that asked students to choose their favorite color. Make a circle graph of the data. *(Lesson 12.3)*

Red	25%
Green	12%
Blue	40%
Other	23%

30. You are making a cake for your younger sister's birthday. You can make vanilla or chocolate cake. You can have white, yellow, or blue frosting. You can make a balloon design or a flower design for the top of the cake. Make a tree diagram to show all of the possible cakes that you could make. *(Lesson 12.4)*

FCAT Practice

31. **Multiple Choice** You go to the movies with six friends. In how many different orders can you and your friends get in the ticket line?

   A. 6   **B.** 7   **C.** 720   **D.** 5040

32. **Short Response** At camp, you are asked to rate your first, second, and third activity choices from archery, canoeing, swimming, and softball. How many different arrangements are possible? Make a list to show all the different arrangements.

Combinations

LESSON 12.6

BEFORE	▶ Now	WHY?
You used permutations to count possibilities.	You will use combinations to count possibilities.	So you can count the ways a team can choose captains, as in Ex. 22.

Word Watch

combination, p. 627

FLORIDA
Standards and Assessment

- Solve multi-step real-world problems. (MA.A.3.3.3)
- Apply number theory to solve problems. (MA.A.5.3.1)

In Lesson 12.5, you studied permutations, which are arrangements in which order is important.

A **combination** is a group of items whose order is *not* important. For example, suppose you go to lunch with a friend. You choose milk, soup, and a salad. Your friend chooses soup, a salad, and milk. The order in which the items are chosen does not matter. You both have same meal.

The two meals are the same.

EXAMPLE 1 **Listing Combinations**

County Fair You have 4 tickets to the county fair and can take 3 of your friends. You can choose from Abby (A), Brian (B), Chloe (C), and David (D). How many different choices of groups of friends do you have?

Solution

List all possible arrangements of three friends. Then cross out any duplicate groupings that represent the same group of friends.

(ABC) A̶C̶B̶ B̶A̶C̶ B̶C̶A̶ C̶A̶B̶ C̶B̶A̶ ← ABC, ACB, BAC, BCA, CAB, and
(ABD) A̶D̶B̶ B̶A̶D̶ B̶D̶A̶ D̶A̶B̶ D̶B̶A̶   CBA all represent
(ACD) A̶D̶C̶ C̶A̶D̶ C̶D̶A̶ D̶A̶C̶ D̶C̶A̶   the same group.
(BCD) B̶D̶C̶ C̶B̶D̶ C̶D̶B̶ D̶B̶C̶ D̶C̶B̶

ANSWER You have 4 different choices of groups to take to the fair.

Your turn now

1. In Example 1, the complete list shows the number of *permutations* of 4 items chosen 3 at a time. How many items would be in the complete list if you had to choose from 8 friends?

Combination Notation In Example 1, after you cross out the duplicate groupings, you are left with the number of combinations of 4 items chosen 3 at a time. Using notation, this is written $_4C_3$.

Combination Notation

Words To find the number of combinations of n objects taken r at a time, divide the number of permutations of n objects taken r at a time by $r!$.

Numbers $_9C_4 = \dfrac{_9P_4}{4!}$ **Algebra** $_nC_r = \dfrac{_nP_r}{r!}$

EXAMPLE 2 **Evaluating Combinations**

Find the number of combinations.

a. $_8C_3$ **b.** $_9C_7$

Solution

a. $_8C_3 = \dfrac{_8P_3}{3!}$ Combination formula

$= \dfrac{8 \cdot 7 \cdot 6}{3!}$ $_8P_3 = \dfrac{8!}{(8-3)!} = 8 \cdot 7 \cdot 6$

$= \dfrac{8 \cdot 7 \cdot \cancel{6}}{\cancel{3} \cdot \cancel{2} \cdot 1}$ Expand. $3! = 3 \cdot 2 \cdot 1$. Divide out common factors.

$= 56$ Simplify.

b. $_9C_7 = \dfrac{_9P_7}{7!}$ Combination formula

$= \dfrac{9 \cdot 8 \cdot 7 \cdot 6 \cdot 5 \cdot 4 \cdot 3}{7!}$ $_9P_7 = \dfrac{9!}{(9-7)!} = 9 \cdot 8 \cdot 7 \cdot 6 \cdot 5 \cdot 4 \cdot 3$

$= \dfrac{9 \cdot \overset{4}{\cancel{8}} \cdot \cancel{7} \cdot \cancel{6} \cdot \cancel{5} \cdot \cancel{4} \cdot \cancel{3}}{\cancel{7} \cdot \cancel{6} \cdot \cancel{5} \cdot \cancel{4} \cdot \cancel{3} \cdot \underset{1}{\cancel{2}} \cdot 1}$ Expand 7!. Divide out common factors.

$= 36$ Simplify.

Your turn now **Find the number of combinations.**

2. $_8C_8$ **3.** $_8C_7$ **4.** $_7C_2$ **5.** $_6C_1$

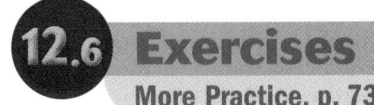

EXAMPLE 3 Permutations and Combinations

Tell whether the possibilities can be counted using a *permutation* or *combination*. Then write an expression for the number of possibilities.

a. Swimming There are 8 swimmers in the 400 meter freestyle race. In how many ways can the swimmers finish first, second, and third?

b. Track Your track team has 6 runners available for the 4-person relay event. How many different 4-person teams can be chosen?

Solution

a. Because the swimmers can finish first, second, or third, order is important. So the possibilities can be counted by evaluating $_8P_3$.

b. Order is not important in choosing the team members, so the possibilities can be counted by evaluating $_6C_4$.

HELP with Notetaking

Mutate means to change. For *permutations*, you count changes in the order of items. For *combinations*, objects *combined* in any order represent the same group. You may wish to copy this hint into your notebook.

12.6 Exercises
More Practice, p. 738

INTERNET
eWorkbook Plus
CLASSZONE.COM

Getting Ready to Practice

1. Vocabulary Copy and complete: The expression $_9C_5$ represents the number of combinations of __?__ objects taken __?__ at a time.

2. Find the Error You choose 3 art projects from the following list: clay, plaster, wood, wire, drawing, painting. Describe and correct the error below in finding the number of possible combinations of 3 projects.

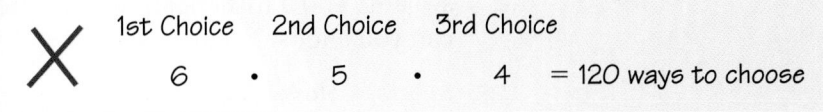

	1st Choice	2nd Choice	3rd Choice	
X	6 •	5 •	4	= 120 ways to choose

Find the number of combinations.

3. $_4C_1$ **4.** $_4C_4$ **5.** $_7C_6$ **6.** $_5C_2$

Tell whether the possibilities should be counted using a *permutation* or *combination*. Then find the answer.

7. Party You are buying balloons for a party. The store has four different colors, and you would like to choose two different colors. How many different pairs of balloon colors can be chosen?

8. Homework You must do homework in math, history, science, and geography. In how many different orders can you do your homework?

Practice and Problem Solving

HELP with Homework

Example	Exercises
1	9
2	10–21, 22–25
3	26–29

Online Resources
CLASSZONE.COM

· More Examples
· eTutorial Plus

9. Essays For a test, you can choose any 2 essay questions to answer from the 5 questions asked. Make a list and cross out the duplicate choices to show how many different pairs of essay questions you could answer.

Find the number of combinations.

10. $_6C_5$ **11.** $_6C_6$ **12.** $_{11}C_9$ **13.** $_8C_4$

14. $_8C_6$ **15.** $_8C_1$ **16.** $_{10}C_8$ **17.** $_9C_5$

18. $_{11}C_3$ **19.** $_{13}C_{11}$ **20.** $_9C_2$ **21.** $_{100}C_{99}$

22. Hockey Your hockey team is choosing 2 team captains from its 18 members. Find the number of combinations that are possible.

23. Debating A debate team has 5 members. Your debating club has 12 students. How many different teams can be chosen?

24. Gardening You want to grow 4 different vegetables. You can choose from 9 types of seed. Find the number of combinations of 4 vegetables.

25. Writing Is it possible to evaluate a combination such as $_3C_4$, $_2C_6$, or $_1C_{10}$? Explain why or why not.

In Exercises 26–29, tell whether the possibilities should be counted using a *permutation* or *combination*. Then find the number of possibilities.

26. Music You want to know the number of ways you can play your four favorite songs.

27. Shopping You are shopping for a trip and want to buy three sweaters from among a red sweater, a blue sweater, a plaid sweater, a striped sweater, and a turtleneck sweater. How many sets of three sweaters can you choose?

28. School Colors Your class is voting for the new school colors. You are asked to choose 2 colors from a list of 8 colors. How many possibilities are there?

29. Geography You are coloring the map shown at the right. You want each state to be a different color, and you have 10 possible colors. In how many ways can you color the map? In how many ways can you choose 8 colors?

30. Look for a Pattern Copy the table. Complete the table by finding the number of combinations. Then describe the pattern.

$_7C_0$	$_7C_1$	$_7C_2$	$_7C_3$	$_7C_4$	$_7C_5$	$_7C_6$	$_7C_7$
?	?	?	?	?	?	?	?

Video Games In Exercises 31 and 32, your friend has a collection of 20 video games.

31. You want to borrow four games from your friend. How many different groups of four games can you choose?

32. If you are already sure about two of the game choices, how many different groups of four games can you choose? Explain.

33. Challenge What is the value of $_nC_r$ when $r = n$? What is the value of $_nC_r$ when $n - r = 1$? Explain.

Mixed Review

Choose a Strategy Use a strategy from the list to solve the following problem. Explain your choice of strategy.

> **Problem Solving Strategies**
> - Act It Out
> - Solve a Simpler Problem
> - Draw a Diagram
> - Make a Table

34. A rectangular room is 20 feet by 12 feet, with walls 7.5 feet high. A decorator charges $.40 per square foot to use paint and $.70 per square foot for wallpaper. Find the cost to decorate the room with each material.

Find the number of permutations. *(Lesson 12.5)*

35. $_{10}P_5$ **36.** $_{11}P_4$ **37.** $_{18}P_3$ **38.** $_{21}P_2$

39. Basic Skills You spin the spinner at the right. What is the probability that the spinner lands on blue?

FCAT Practice

40. Multiple Choice You choose three things to do today, from a list of 12 things that you want to get done. How many different groups of 3 things can you choose to do today?

A. 12   **B.** 36   **C.** 220   **D.** 1320

41. Short Response You have 7 different music CDs, and want to sell some of them. Draw a diagram or write an expression so that you can find the number of ways you can sell 2 CDs. Then find the number of ways you can sell 4 CDs.

Probability and Odds

BEFORE	▶ Now	WHY?
You found the probability of events.	You will find the odds in favor of events.	So you can find the odds of a goalie's save, as in Ex. 18.

Word Watch

complementary events, p. 632
unfavorable outcome, p. 633
odds, p. 633

FLORIDA
Standards and Assessment

• Compare experimental and theoretical probabilities. (MA.E.2.3.1)
• Predict odds. (MA.E.2.3.2)

Activity You can use a spinner to explore probability.

(1) What is the probability of the spinner landing on blue? What is the probability of the spinner landing on red?

(2) Is it more likely that the spinner will land on blue than red?

(3) Find each ratio. Use the ratios to compare the chances of landing on red and on blue.

a. $\dfrac{\text{number of red sections}}{\text{number of blue sections}}$ b. $\dfrac{\text{number of blue sections}}{\text{number of red sections}}$

(4) Explain how to find the probability of the spinner *not* landing on red.

In the activity, the spinner will land on either red or blue. Two events are **complementary** when one event or the other (but not both) must occur. The sum of the probabilities of complementary events is always 1.

When Events A and B are complementary, $P(\text{Event A}) = 1 - P(\text{Event B})$.

HELP with Solving

The probability that Event A occurs and the probability that Event A does *not* occur have a sum of 1 because they are complementary events.

For help with probability, see p. 354.

EXAMPLE 1 Finding Probabilities

Gifts You and seven friends contribute money for a gift. Everyone's name is put in a hat. The person whose name is chosen picks the gift.

a. What is the probability that your name is randomly chosen?

b. What is the probability that your name is randomly *not* chosen?

Solution

a. $P(\text{your name is chosen}) = \dfrac{\text{Number of favorable outcomes}}{\text{Number of possible outcomes}} = \dfrac{1}{8}$

b. $P(\text{your name is not chosen}) = 1 - P(\text{your name is chosen})$

$$= 1 - \frac{1}{8}$$

$$= \frac{7}{8}$$

You are given the probability that an event will occur. Find the probability that the event will not occur.

1. $P(A) = \dfrac{3}{4}$ **2.** $P(A) = 0.45$ **3.** $P(A) = 32\%$ **4.** $P(A) = \dfrac{7}{10}$

5. The 11 letters in the word MISSISSIPPI are each written on pieces of paper and put in a bag. What is the probability of randomly drawing an S from the bag? What is the probability of randomly *not* drawing an S?

Odds Once you specify the event for which you are finding the probability, outcomes for that event are called *favorable outcomes*. The other outcomes are **unfavorable outcomes** .

When all outcomes are equally likely, the **odds** in favor of an event are equal to the ratio of favorable outcomes to unfavorable outcomes.

$$\text{Odds} = \frac{\textbf{Number of favorable outcomes}}{\textbf{Number of unfavorable outcomes}}$$

EXAMPLE 2 **Finding Odds**

You do a survey asking your class to rank three ice cream flavors. Results for vanilla are shown at the right. What are the odds in favor of a randomly chosen student from your class ranking vanilla first?

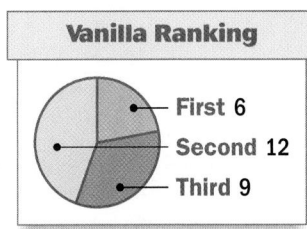

Vanilla Ranking

First 6
Second 12
Third 9

Solution

Vanilla was ranked first by 6 students, so there are 6 favorable outcomes.

It was ranked second by 12 students, and ranked third by 9 students, so there are $12 + 9 = 21$ unfavorable outcomes.

$$\text{Odds} = \frac{\text{Number of favorable outcomes}}{\text{Number of unfavorable outcomes}}$$

$$= \frac{6}{21}$$

$$= \frac{2}{7}$$

ANSWER The odds in favor of a randomly chosen student ranking vanilla first are 2 to 7.

HELP with **Reading**

Odds are always read as a ratio. For example, $\dfrac{5}{2}$ is read "five to two," not "five halves."

You choose a card at random from a set of cards numbered 1 to 24. Find the odds in favor of the event.

6. You choose a 10.   **7.** You choose an odd number greater than 7.

Probability and Odds If you know the probability of an event, you can use the following formula to find the odds in favor of that event.

$$\text{Odds} = \frac{\text{Probability event will occur}}{\text{Probability event will not occur}} = \frac{\text{Probability event will occur}}{1 - \text{Probability event will occur}}$$

EXAMPLE 3 **Finding Odds Using Probability**

Basketball Sean makes 65% of his free throws. What are the odds in favor of Sean making a free throw?

Solution

$$\text{Odds} = \frac{0.65}{1 - 0.65} \qquad \text{Write percents as decimals.}$$

$$= \frac{0.65}{0.35} \qquad \text{Subtract.}$$

$$= \frac{65}{35} \qquad \text{Multiply numerator and denominator by 100.}$$

$$= \frac{13}{7} \qquad \text{Simplify.}$$

ANSWER Sean's odds in favor of making a free throw are 13 to 7.

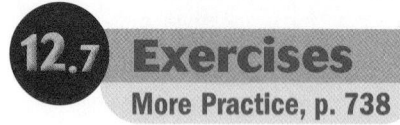

12.7 Exercises
More Practice, p. 738

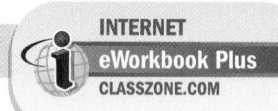

INTERNET
eWorkbook Plus
CLASSZONE.COM

Getting Ready to Practice

1. **Vocabulary** Copy and complete: Find the ratio of the number of favorable outcomes to the number of unfavorable outcomes to find the ? of an event.

You are given the probability that an event will occur. Find the probability that the event will not occur.

2. $P(A) = 84\%$ 3. $P(A) = \frac{2}{5}$ 4. $P(A) = 0.37$ 5. $P(A) = \frac{9}{10}$

You randomly draw a letter tile from a bag. The 8 letters in the word GEOMETRY are in the bag. Find the odds in favor of the event.

6. You choose a G.   7. You choose an E.   8. You choose an S.

9. **Weather** The weather forecast says that there is a 30 percent probability of rain. What are the odds in favor of rain?

Practice and Problem Solving

with Homework

Example	Exercises
1	10-13, 19-20
2	10-20
3	18, 20

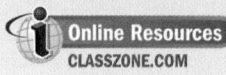

Online Resources
CLASSZONE.COM
· More Examples
· eTutorial Plus

Find the probability of randomly choosing a red marble from the bag of marbles described. Then find the odds in favor of randomly choosing a blue marble.

10. 3 red and 7 blue marbles

11. 4 red and 9 blue marbles

12. 6 red and 5 blue marbles

13. 6 red, 5 blue, and 3 green marbles

Find the odds in favor of the event described when rolling a number cube.

14. Roll a 3.

15. Roll a number less than 6.

16. Roll a number greater than 2.

17. Roll an odd number less than 5.

18. Hockey A hockey goalie has a save percentage of 93%. What are the odds that he makes a save?

19. Compare Sam finds the probability of Event A is 0.2. Jan finds the odds in favor of Event A are 1 to 4. Can they both be right? Explain.

20. Socks In your sock drawer, you have 20 socks. You have 2 pairs of patterned socks, 4 pairs of gym socks, 3 pairs of striped socks, and 1 pair of black socks. What is the probability that you randomly pull a gym sock from the drawer? What are the odds?

Pizza In Exercises 21–23, use the circle graph. It shows the number of people ordering pizza that order each type of crust.

21. What is the probability that a randomly chosen pizza order is for thin crust?

22. What are the odds in favor of a randomly chosen pizza order being for regular crust?

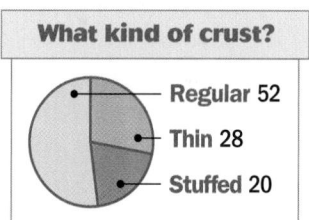

What kind of crust?

Regular 52
Thin 28
Stuffed 20

23. What are the odds in favor of a randomly chosen pizza order *not* being for stuffed crust?

Odds Against In Exercises 24 and 25, use the following information. In this lesson, you learned how to find the *odds in favor* of an event. You can also find the *odds against* an event.

$$\text{Odds against} = \frac{\text{Number of unfavorable outcomes}}{\text{Number of favorable outcomes}}$$

24. You choose a chip from a bag of 6 blue, 3 red, and 5 green chips. Find the odds in favor of choosing a green chip. Then find the odds against choosing a green chip.

25. Challenge You hear a friend claim that "the odds that you get hit by lightning are a million to one." Is your friend talking about *odds in favor* or *odds against*? Explain your reasoning.

Extended Problem Solving **In Exercises 26–28, use the following information.**

You make an archery target like the one shown. Assume that when an arrow is shot and hits the target, the arrow is equally likely to hit any point on the target. The probability that an arrow lands within the red bull's-eye circle is given by the following equation.

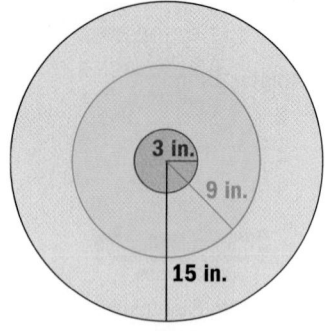

$$P = \frac{\text{Area of bull's-eye}}{\text{Area of target}}$$

26. **Geometry** What is the area of the bull's-eye? What is the total area of the target? Leave your answers in terms of π.

27. **Probability** What is the probability that an arrow that hits the target lands within the bull's-eye?

28. **Odds** What are the odds that an arrow that hits the target lands on the blue region?

Mixed Review

29. Find the length of the hypotenuse of a right triangle with leg lengths of 24 inches and 45 inches. *(Lesson 9.3)*

Find the slope of the line passing through the points. *(Lesson 11.6)*

30. $(-8, 12), (9, 2)$ 31. $(7, 5), (-3, 6)$ 32. $(-1, -5), (-4, -10)$

Basic Skills **Find the product.**

33. $\frac{4}{5} \cdot \frac{7}{12}$ 34. $\frac{5}{9} \cdot \frac{3}{5}$ 35. $\frac{1}{8} \cdot \frac{3}{7}$ 36. $\frac{9}{13} \cdot \frac{5}{6}$

FCAT Practice

37. **Multiple Choice** You roll one number cube. What are the odds in favor of rolling a number less than three?

    A. 6 to 2   **B.** 2 to 1

    C. 1 to 1   **D.** 1 to 2

38. **Multiple Choice** You hear someone say that 1 out of 10 people are left-handed. Based on this, what is the probability that a person chosen at random is left-handed?

    F. 9 to 1   **G.** 1 to 9

    H. 10%   **I.** 90%

GOAL
Use a simulation to explore probability.

MATERIALS
- index cards
- calculator

FLORIDA: Standards and Assessment
Formulate a hypothesis and design an experiment. (MA.E.3.3.1)
Collect, organize, and display data. (MA.E.3.3.1)

Probability and Simulations

You can use a simulation to explore probability. A *simulation* is an experiment done to explore the probability of an event.

Explore 1 **Simulate a real-world situation.**

Do a simulation to find an experimental probability that you and a friend are the 2 students randomly chosen from a group of 8 students.

1 Label eight index cards as shown. Use 1 to represent yourself, 2 to represent your friend, and 3, 4, 5, 6, 7, and 8 to represent the other students.

| 1 | 2 | 3 | 4 |
| 5 | 6 | 7 | 8 |

2 Shuffle the cards. Randomly draw a card, and then another, without replacing the first. Record whether or not the results represent you and your friend being chosen. Replace the cards.

3 Repeat drawing a pair of cards. Draw a total of 10 pairs. For each pair of cards drawn, record the results.

Use the ratio $\dfrac{\text{you and friend are chosen}}{\text{total number of pairs drawn}}$ to find the experimental probability that you and your friend are chosen.

Pair	Times Drawn
5, 8	I
7, 2	II
1, 4	I

Your turn now **Use your results from the simulation above.**

1. Combine all the class results. Based on these results, what is the experimental probability that you and your friend are chosen?

Explore 2 Use technology to simulate a real-world situation.

Use your calculator's random integer function to simulate randomly choosing 1 student from a group of 8. Find the experimental probability that any of the students is randomly chosen twice in a row.

1 Use 1, 2, 3, 4, 5, 6, 7, and 8 to represent the students.

2 Clear your calculator screen. Press MATH and choose the PRB menu. Select *randInt(,* the random integer function.

3 Enter **1** , **8** ENTER) to select an integer at random from 1 to 8. Press ENTER again to simulate choosing a student again. Record whether your results represent a match.

Notice that getting a 4 and a 4 represents choosing the same student twice in a row.

4 Do the simulation a total of 10 times. Record your results. What is the experimental probability that any of the students is randomly chosen twice in a row?

Your turn now Design a simulation of the situation.

2. You randomly choose to go to the library, from the choices mall, library, or bowling lanes.

3. You and your friend Chris are randomly chosen from a group of 10 team members to be co-captains.

Stop and Think

4. Critical Thinking Refer to Exercise 1 on page 637. Which results do you think are more likely to be close to the theoretical probability that you and your friend are chosen, your results or the class results? Explain.

5. Writing Explain how the simulation in Explore 2 above would be different if you wanted to find the probability that you are randomly chosen twice in a row from a group of eight people.

Independent and Dyependent Events

LESSON 12.8

Independent and Dependent Events

BEFORE	▶ Now	WHY?
You found the probability of an event.	You will study independent and dependent events.	So you can find the probability of winning a free snack, as in Ex. 13.

Word Watch

independent events, p. 639
dependent events, p. 639

FLORIDA
Standards and Assessment

• Calculate mathematical probability of independent and dependent events. (MA.E.2.3.1)

• Know relationships among fractions, decimals, and percents given a real-world context. (MA.A.1.3.4)

Two events are **independent events** if the occurrence of one event does *not* affect the probability that the other event will occur. Two events are **dependent events** if the occurrence of one event *does* affect the probability that the other event will occur.

Suppose you randomly choose two gumballs one at a time from the jar below. The probability of choosing two red gumballs with replacement is different than the probability without replacement.

Independent Events		**Dependent Events**	
First Event	Second Event	First Event	Second Event

$$P(\text{red}) = \frac{2}{5} \qquad P(\text{red}) = \frac{2}{5} \qquad\qquad P(\text{red}) = \frac{2}{5} \qquad P(\text{red}) = \frac{1}{4}$$

If you replace the gumball, the probability of choosing a red gumball is the same for each choice.

If you don't replace the gumball after choosing, the probability changes.

EXAMPLE 1 **Independent and Dependent Events**

Tell whether the events are *independent* or *dependent*.

a. You roll a number cube. Then you roll the number cube again.

b. You randomly draw a number from a bag. Then you randomly draw a second number without putting the first number back.

Solution

a. The result of the first roll does not affect the result of the second roll, so the events are independent.

b. There is one fewer number in the bag for the second draw, so the events are dependent.

Multiple Events To find the probability that Event A *and* Event B happen, you multiply probabilities. Because the occurrence of an event may affect the probability of another event, you should determine whether the events are independent or dependent before multiplying.

Probability of Independent Events

For two independent events, the probability that both occur is the product of the probabilities of the events.

$$P(A \text{ and } B) = P(A) \cdot P(B) \qquad \text{Events A and B are independent.}$$

EXAMPLE 2 **Probability of Independent Events**

School Fair Your class is raising money by operating a ball toss game. You estimate that about 1 out of every 25 balls tossed results in a win. What is the probability that someone will win on two tosses in a row?

Solution

The tosses are independent events, because the outcome of a toss does not affect the probability of the next toss resulting in a win.

So the probability of each event is $\frac{1}{25}$.

$$P(\text{win and win}) = P(\text{win}) \cdot P(\text{win}) = \frac{1}{25} \cdot \frac{1}{25} = \frac{1}{625}$$

ANSWER The probability of two winning tosses in a row is $\frac{1}{625}$.

Dependent Events If A and B are dependent events, the probability that B occurs given that A also occurs is not the same as the probability of B. So, you should use $P(B \text{ given } A)$ instead of $P(B)$ to represent the probability that B occurs given that A also occurs.

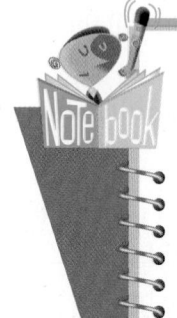

Probability of Dependent Events

For two dependent events, the probability that both events occur is the product of the probability of the first event and the probability of the second event given that the first event also occurs.

$$P(A \text{ and } B) = P(A) \cdot P(B \text{ given } A) \qquad \text{A and B are dependent.}$$

EXAMPLE **3** **Finding Probability of Dependent Events**

Bingo You are playing the bingo card shown. The caller has 50 numbers left to call. What is the probability that you will get bingo on the next 2 numbers called?

BINGO

B	I	N	G	O
12	18	41	51	66
7	26	44	54	70
6	27	FREE SPACE	58	63
5	23	39	52	73
3	30	36	57	75

Solution

You need B7 and N44 for bingo. Find the probability of success when each of the next 2 numbers is drawn. Then multiply.

$P(\text{B7 or N44}) = \dfrac{2}{50} = \dfrac{1}{25}$ There are 50 numbers left to call.

$P(\text{remaining number}) = \dfrac{1}{49}$ There are 49 numbers left to call.

$P(\text{both numbers}) = \dfrac{1}{25} \cdot \dfrac{1}{49} = \dfrac{1}{1225}$ Multiply the probabilities.

ANSWER The probability is $\dfrac{1}{1225}$, or about 0.0008.

Your turn now **Find the probability.**

1. You toss a coin twice. Find the probability of getting two heads.

2. Find the probability for Example 3 if there are 36 numbers left to call.

12.8 **Exercises**

More Practice, p. 738

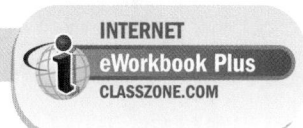

INTERNET
eWorkbook Plus
CLASSZONE.COM

Getting Ready to Practice

1. **Vocabulary** Copy and complete: When the occurrence of an event does not affect the probability of the next event, the events are ? .

Tell whether the events are *independent* or *dependent*. Then find the probability.

2. You randomly choose a green marble from a jar of 8 green and 3 blue marbles. You replace the marble and randomly choose another green marble.

3. Your teacher randomly chooses you to give a report. She then randomly chooses Pam from the 22 remaining students.

Practice and Problem Solving

HELP with Homework

Example	Exercises
1	10-14
2	4-6, 10-14
3	7-14

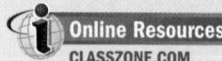
Online Resources
CLASSZONE.COM

· More Examples
· eTutorial Plus

Events A and B are independent. Find the missing probability.

4. $P(A) = 0.4$
$P(B) = 0.6$
$P(A \text{ and } B) = \underline{?}$

5. $P(A) = 0.9$
$P(B) = \underline{?}$
$P(A \text{ and } B) = 0.09$

6. $P(A) = \underline{?}$
$P(B) = 0.6$
$P(A \text{ and } B) = 0.12$

Events A and B are dependent. Find the missing probability.

7. $P(A) = 0.75$
$P(B \text{ given } A) = 0.5$
$P(A \text{ and } B) = \underline{?}$

8. $P(A) = 0.8$
$P(B \text{ given } A) = \underline{?}$
$P(A \text{ and } B) = 0.32$

9. $P(A) = \underline{?}$
$P(B \text{ given } A) = 0.3$
$P(A \text{ and } B) = 0.039$

In Exercises 10–12, tell whether the events are *independent* or *dependent*. Then find the probability.

10. Banquet At a banquet, you can order a main course of a chef's salad, salmon and potatoes, ham and beans, or steak and rice. You can drink water, juice, milk, coffee, or iced tea. If all choices are equally likely, what is the probability that a randomly chosen person orders a chef's salad and juice?

11. Cookies You have a jar filled with 5 oatmeal cookies, 6 sugar cookies, 8 frosted cookies, and 9 chocolate cookies. You randomly choose a cookie, keep it, and then choose another. What is the probability that you pick a frosted cookie and then a chocolate cookie?

12. Buttons You draw a button at random from the jar at the right. Without replacing the first button, you draw another. What is the probability that you draw a red button and then a yellow button?

13. Lucky Plate Each day, the person who gets the lucky plate wins a free snack from the school cafeteria. The cafeteria sells 127 lunches on Wednesday and 134 lunches on Thursday. What is the probability that you win on both days if you buy lunch both days?

14. Critical Thinking What is the probability that when you toss a coin you get heads 7 times in a row? If you have already gotten heads 6 times in a row, what is the probability that you will get heads on the next toss?

15. Challenge A brochure says, "If you invested money with us 5 years ago, that money grew by an average of 20%." The brochure also says, "Past performance is no guarantee of future results." Which statement leads you to think that investing money today is independent of past events? Which statement suggests the opposite? Explain.

16. Elections A town's election for mayor drew 75% of the town's 800 eligible voters. What is the probability that two different randomly selected people both voted in the election?

Mixed Review

17. The table shows the amount of time, in minutes, that Cindy ran on the treadmill each day. Make a line graph of the data. Predict how long Cindy will run on Saturday. Explain your reasoning. *(Lesson 12.3)*

Monday	20
Tuesday	25
Wednesday	25
Thursday	35
Friday	41

Basic Skills **Evaluate the expression.**

18. $5 \cdot (11 - 4)$ **19.** $3 + 9 \cdot 6$ **20.** $35 - 21 \div 3$ **21.** $\dfrac{35}{9 - 2}$

FCAT Practice

22. Multiple Choice You pick a letter at random from the lettered tiles at the right. Without replacing the first tile, you draw another. What is the probability that you draw a "B" and then a "T"?

A. $\dfrac{1}{36}$ **B.** $\dfrac{1}{30}$ **C.** $\dfrac{1}{15}$ **D.** $\dfrac{1}{5}$

23. Short Response You sell one of 150 raffle tickets to your brother, for two prizes chosen by random drawing. The 150 tickets are put into a hat. You draw the first ticket. Then you draw the second ticket without replacing the first one. What is the probability that your brother wins on the first drawing? Does the probability that your brother's ticket is drawn second depend on the first event? Explain why or why not.

Lucky Numbers

Two balls will be randomly chosen without replacement from the globe shown.

Bo wins if the first ball is blue, and the next ball is a 3 or a 4.

Sherry wins if the first ball is an even number and the next ball is green.

Eva wins if both balls are red.

Who has the best chance of winning?

Samples

GOAL Identify biased samples and surveys.

Word Watch

population, p. 644
sample, p. 644
random sample, p. 644
biased sample, p. 644

FLORIDA
Standards and Assessment

• Identify and use different
  sampling techniques.
  (MA.E.3.3.2)

• Know whether a sample is
  biased. (MA.E.3.3.2)

One way to collect data about a group is by doing a survey. A **population** is the entire group of people or objects that you want information about. When it is difficult to survey an entire population, a **sample**, or a part of the entire group, is surveyed.

In a **random sample**, each person or object has an equally likely chance of being selected. A non-random sample can result in a **biased sample** that is not representative of the population.

EXAMPLE 1 **Identifying Potentially Biased Samples**

Costume Dance The student council wants students to help decide on a theme for a costume dance. Students can choose one of the council's three ideas from the options listed at the right.

Which dance theme
do you prefer?

Choose one:
☐ movies
☐ famous historical
   figures
☐ sports and games

Surveying all of the students will take too long, so a sample will be surveyed. Tell whether the survey method could result in a biased sample. Explain.

  a. Survey members of the movie club.

  b. Survey students as they enter the school.

  c. Survey students on the football team.

Solution

  a. This method could result in a biased sample because this group is more likely to favor the movie theme.

  b. This method is not likely to result in a biased sample because a wide range of students will be surveyed.

  c. This method could result in a biased sample because the football players are more likely to favor sports and games.

Survey Questions When you do a survey, you need to phrase the questions so that the responses of the people surveyed accurately reflect their opinions or actions. If not, claims based on the survey results may be biased.

EXAMPLE 2 **Identifying Potentially Biased Questions**

Tell whether the question could produce biased results. Explain.

> **a.** Do you support the unfair policy of requiring students to do a time-consuming community project? YES ☐ NO ☐

> **b.** Do you like our new apple-nut yogurt flavor, now on sale in stores everywhere? YES ☐ NO ☐

Solution

a. This question suggests that the policy is unfair and that the project is time-consuming. It encourages a response of *no*. So, the question could lead to biased results.

b. The question assumes that the person responding has tried the new yogurt flavor. Those who have not tried the new flavor may not give an accurate opinion. So, the question could lead to biased results.

Exercises

Stadiums In Exercises 1–3, a city wants to know whether residents favor using public funds to pay for a new baseball stadium. Tell whether the method could result in a biased sample. Explain.

1. Ask people that call in to a sports radio talk show.

2. Ask every tenth person listed in the phone book.

3. Ask every fifth person who enters the sporting goods store in town.

4. **Food** A restaurant wants to know what kinds of food to add to its menu to attract new customers. Describe a sampling method that the restaurant can use that is not likely to result in a biased sample.

Tell whether the survey question could produce biased results. Explain your reasoning.

5. Would you rather relax at home while reading a book, or go to a noisy, crowded mall?

6. Allowing messy, dangerous dogs into the park will cause safety and health problems. Will you vote to allow dogs into the park?

7. How often do you buy lunch in the school cafeteria?

8. Do you agree with this store's policy for returning purchases?

Notebook Review

Review the vocabulary definitions in your notebook.

Copy the review examples in your notebook. Then complete the exercises.

Check Your Definitions

tree diagram, p. 618

permutation, p. 623

factorial, p. 623

combination, p. 627

complementary events, p. 632

unfavorable outcome, p. 633

odds, p. 633

independent events, p. 639

dependent events, p. 639

Use Your Vocabulary

1. Vocabulary Copy and complete: A(n) _?_ is an arrangement in which order is important.

12.4 Can you use the counting principle?

EXAMPLE You need to choose one of 3 birdhouse designs and one of 6 possible colors. How many different birdhouses can you build?

ANSWER 3 • 6 = 18, so you can build 18 different birdhouses.

2. You have 5 designs of birdhouses and 4 colors from which to choose. How many different birdhouses can you build?

12.5–12.6 Can you find permutations and combinations?

EXAMPLE At a swim meet, 10 swimmers are in an event. In how many ways can first, second, third, and fourth place medals be awarded?

The order is important, so find the number of permutations.

$$_{10}P_4 = \frac{10!}{(10-4)!} = \frac{10!}{6!} = 10 \cdot 9 \cdot 8 \cdot 7 = 5040$$

ANSWER There are 5040 ways to award the medals.

3. You are making a braided rope out of three different colors of yarn. You have seven colors of yarn. In how many ways can you choose the colors so the rope has three different colors?

12.7 Can you find odds?

 EXAMPLE You have a bag of 6 red, 5 blue, and 3 white marbles. What are the odds in favor of randomly drawing a red marble from the bag?

ANSWER $\text{Odds} = \dfrac{\text{Number of favorable outcomes}}{\text{Number of unfavorable outcomes}} = \dfrac{6}{8} = \dfrac{3}{4}$

☑ **4.** What are the odds in favor of randomly drawing a white marble?

12.8 Can you calculate probabilities?

 EXAMPLE Tiles with each of the 11 letters in PROBABILITY are in a bag. You randomly draw a tile, replace it, and then randomly draw a second tile. What is the probability that both tiles are I's?

ANSWER $P(\text{I and I}) = P(\text{I}) \cdot P(\text{I}) = \dfrac{2}{11} \cdot \dfrac{2}{11} = \dfrac{4}{121}$

☑ **5.** What is the probability that the first tile is B and the second is L?

Stop *and* **Think** about Lessons 12.4–12.8

6. *Writing* Give a real-world example of a situation where you use combinations to count possibilities.

Review Quiz 2

1. **Shoes** You can buy sandals or sneakers in black, brown, tan, or white. Make a tree diagram to show the possible choices for shoes.

2. **Camp** You are scheduling swimming, crafts, canoeing, and softball. How many different schedules of four different activities are possible?

3. **Hockey** Find the number of ways two players can be chosen from 20 team members.

4. **Rain** If the probability that it will rain today is 0.4, what are the odds in favor of rain? What is the probability that it will *not* rain?

Find the probability.

5. You roll a 5 on a 6-sided number cube. Then you roll another 5.

6. A bag has 3 red and 5 blue tiles. You randomly draw a red tile, keep it, and then randomly draw a blue tile.

12 Chapter Review

 Vocabulary

stem-and-leaf plot,
  p. 597
box-and-whisker plot,
  p. 601
lower quartile, p. 601
upper quartile, p. 601
lower extreme, p. 601

upper extreme, p. 601
circle graph, p. 605
line graph, p. 606
tree diagram, p. 618
permutation, p. 623
factorial, p. 623
combination, p. 627

complementary events,
  p. 632
unfavorable outcome,
  p. 633
odds, p. 633
independent events,
  p. 639
dependent events, p. 639

Vocabulary Review

Matching **In Exercises 1–6, match the description with the correct word(s).**

1. An arrangement in which order is important

2. An arrangement in which order is not important

3. A graph to display data that fall into distinct categories

4. A graph used to display changes in a quantity over time

5. A plot used to order a data set

6. A plot used to summarize a data set

A. bar graph

B. line graph

C. box-and-whisker plot

D. stem-and-leaf plot

E. combination

F. permutation

7. Copy the box-and-whisker plot at the right. Label the median, upper and lower quartiles, and upper and lower extremes.

5   7   12.5 15   20

Review Questions

Make an ordered stem-and-leaf plot to organize the data. Identify the interval that includes the most data values. *(Lesson 12.1)*

8. 20, 25, 36, 16, 29, 32, 27, 42

9. 11.2, 7.5, 15.1, 15.7, 15.0, 6.7, 11.3

10. **Chess** The prices of several chess sets are $15, $20, $38, $95, $60, $45, $40, $35, and $50. Make a box-and-whisker plot of the data. What conclusions can you make? *(Lesson 12.2)*

11. Summer Treats The table shows the favorite summer treats of students surveyed. Represent the data in a circle graph. *(Lesson 12.3)*

Ice Cream	50%
Frozen fruit	25%
Ices	10%
Other	15%

12. Election Your class is having an election for president, vice president, and secretary. For president there are 4 candidates, for vice president there are 5 candidates, and for secretary there are 3 candidates. No one is running for more than one office. How many groups of winners are possible? *(Lesson 12.4)*

Evaluate the expression. *(Lessons 12.5, 12.6)*

13. $_8P_4$ **14.** $_{10}P_3$ **15.** $_9C_2$ **16.** $_6C_1$

17. Photograph You and six friends are posing for a photograph. In how many ways can you line up for the photograph if you line up in one row? *(Lesson 12.5)*

In Exercises 18 and 19, tell whether the situation describes a *combination* or a *permutation*. Then find the answer. *(Lessons 12.5, 12.6)*

18. Pizza In how many ways can you select 4 different pizza toppings from 12 toppings?

19. Bobblehead Dolls You have six different bobblehead dolls, and you want to choose three to give as gifts to Ali, Lin, and Rhea. How many different ways can you do this?

20. Contest The probability that you will win a contest is 76%. What is the probability that you will lose the contest? What are the odds that you will lose the contest? *(Lesson 12.7)*

21. Softball A softball player has a batting average of 0.350, which means she gets a hit 35% of her times at bat. What are the odds that she will get a hit in her next at bat? *(Lesson 12.7)*

22. Weather The weather forecaster says there is a 60% chance that it will snow on Wednesday and a 25% chance that it will snow on Thursday. Find the probability that it will snow on both Wednesday and Thursday. *(Lesson 12.8)*

23. Cards Two cards are dealt randomly, one after another, from a deck of cards numbered from 1 through 20. The first card is not returned to the deck before the second is dealt. Find the probability that the first card is a 7 and the second card is a 4. *(Lesson 12.8)*

Chapter Test

In Exercises 1 and 2, make a stem-and-leaf plot. Tell which interval includes the most values. Then make a box-and-whisker plot.

1. 46 kg, 70 kg, 21 kg, 136 kg, 55 kg, 60 kg, 72 kg, 104 kg, 52 kg

2. 12.1 in., 13.5 in., 12.8 in., 10 in., 7 in., 11.2 in., 12.9 in., 11.1 in., 12 in., 13.7 in.

3. **Academy Awards** The lengths, in minutes, of the Best Picture Academy Award winning movies for the years 1990–1999 are 99, 118, 122, 131, 142, 160, 177, 183, 194, and 197. Make a box-and-whisker plot of the data.

4. **Temperature** The record low temperatures in Miami, Florida, are given in the table. Display the data in an appropriate graph.

Month	Jan.	Feb.	Mar.	Apr.	May	Jun.	Jul.	Aug.	Sep.	Oct.	Nov.	Dec.
Temp (°F)	30	32	32	46	53	60	69	68	68	51	39	30

5. **Golf** There are five members on a golf team. Make a tree diagram to count the number of ways you can select a captain and an assistant.

6. **Movies** You and four friends are going to a movie. In how many different orders can you pick your friends up? List all the possible orders.

7. **School Dance** You are making a banner for a school dance and have a choice of 8 colors. You want to use 4 different colors. How many different combinations are possible?

In Exercises 8 and 9, use the circle graph. It shows student replies to *Which animal career would you enjoy?*

8. What is the probability that a randomly chosen student replied *veterinarian*?

9. What are the odds in favor of a randomly chosen student replying *zookeeper*?

Animal Careers

Veterinarian 35%
Pet store owner 22%
Zookeeper 21%
Rodeo star 13%
Circus animal trainer 9%

Tell whether the events are *independent* or *dependent*. Then find the probability.

10. You roll a 6 on a number cube. Then you roll again and roll a 2.

11. You have 8 blue marbles and 12 red marbles in a bag. You randomly pick a blue marble on the first draw. Then you randomly pick another blue marble without replacing the first one.

Chapter FCAT Practice

Test-Taking Strategy Learn as much as you can about a test ahead of time, such as the types of questions and the topics the test will cover.

Multiple Choice

1. When the number 57 is plotted on a stem-and-leaf plot, the 5 is which of the following?

   A. key   **B.** stem   **C.** leaf   **D.** median

2. Which number represents the lower quartile on the box-and-whisker plot?

   F. 14   **G.** 19   **H.** 23   **I.** 25

3. Which is an appropriate display for the data in the table below?

Favorite fruit	Percent of students
Apple	30%
Orange	20%
Banana	35%
Pineapple	5%

   A. bar graph   **B.** line graph

   C. circle graph   **D.** histogram

4. Your family's favorite pizza toppings are hamburger, sausage, mushroom, and onion. You choose one meat topping and one vegetable topping. How many choices are possible?

   F. 2   **G.** 4   **H.** 8   **I.** 16

5. There are 7 people hiking together. They walk single file on a narrow trail. How many ways can they be lined up on the trail?

   A. 7   **B.** 49   **C.** 343   **D.** 5040

6. The Fairfield school board has 7 members. How many 3-person committees can be formed from this board?

   F. 3   **G.** 7   **H.** 21   **I.** 35

7. Crystal, Martha, Francesco, and Brad stand in a row to rehearse a song. They are equally likely to stand in any order. What are the odds of them standing in alphabetical order from left to right?

   A. 1 to 4   **B.** 1 to 12

   C. 1 to 23   **D.** 1 to 24

8. At Mill High School, there are 39 players on the football team, 20 players on the hockey team, and 16 players on the soccer team. A player is chosen at random to represent the school at a forum on sports. Find the probability that a football player is chosen.

   F. $\frac{16}{75}$ **G.** $\frac{4}{25}$

   H. $\frac{7}{25}$ **I.** $\frac{13}{25}$

Short Response

9. Sean is choosing 2 photographs for a bulletin board. He has 6 good photographs to choose from. How many different pairs of photographs can he choose?

Extended Response

10. Describe the difference between independent and dependent events. How is the probability of independent events different from the probability of dependent events?

INVESTIGATING
Robins

Geometric Probability

When a robin hunts for worms, does it search randomly, or can it sense a worm's location? Scientists used geometric probability to investigate this. Geometric probability is based on area. For events dependent on area, you can find the *geometric probability* using the following formula:

$$P(\text{event}) = \frac{\textbf{Area representing favorable outcomes}}{\textbf{Area representing possible outcomes}}$$

There are 4 treasure chests buried in a 5 yard by 10 yard field. Each chest has an area of 1 square yard. Use geometric probability to describe the expected results of searching a randomly chosen spot in the field.

1. Find the area of the treasure chests.

    $$4 \text{ chests} \cdot \frac{1 \text{ square yard}}{\text{chest}} = 4 \text{ square yards}$$

2. Find the area of the field.

    $$5 \text{ yards} \cdot 10 \text{ yards} = \textbf{50} \text{ square yards}$$

3. Find the geometric probability of finding a treasure chest by random search.

    $$P(\text{finding a chest}) = \frac{\textbf{Area of treasure chests}}{\textbf{Area of field}}$$

    $$= \frac{4}{50} = 0.08$$

10 yd

5 yd

So, the geometric probability of finding a chest by random search is 8%.

1. Suppose there are 6 treasure chests in the field. What is the geometric probability of finding a chest by random search?

2. Suppose there are 9 treasure chests in the field, and each has an area of 2 square feet. Find the geometric probability of finding a chest by random search. Remember to measure the field in the same units as the chests.

How Robins Find Worms

To investigate how robins find worms, scientists did a series of experiments. They buried four worms in pans of soil that were marked into a 10 by 10 grid and calculated the geometric probability of a robin finding a worm at random.

Then they let robins search the pan and recorded the percent of the time a worm was found. A robin was counted as finding a worm if the square that it searched contained a worm. The experiment was repeated under different conditions.

Condition	Correct Finds
Robins could use all senses.	90%
Robins prevented from using visual clues.	50%
White noise decreased robins' ability to hear worms.	59%

3. Find the geometric probability of finding a worm by searching randomly. Write the probability as a percent.

4. The table above shows the percent of attempts in which the robins found worms under each condition. For each condition, compare the percent of correct finds to the geometric probability of randomly finding a worm.

5. Critical Thinking What can you conclude from the results of the experiment? How do the results suggest that robins don't search randomly for worms but instead use their senses?

Project IDEAS

- **Experiment** Design and perform an experiment or a search involving geometric probability. Compare the theoretical and experimental geometric probabilities. Explain any discrepancies. Present your findings to the class.

- **Investigate** Learn more about how different birds find food. Present your findings.

- **Research** Look up information about search and rescue techniques. What techniques do people use to increase the probability of finding something? Present your findings.

- **Career** Learn about people who study animal behavior. What sorts of careers do they have? Present your findings.

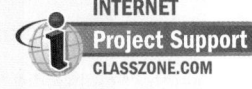

INTERNET
Project Support
CLASSZONE.COM

13 Polynomials and Functions

BEFORE

In previous chapters you've...

- Simplified expressions by combining like terms
- Graphed linear functions

Now

In Chapter 13 you'll study...

- Simplifying polynomials
- Adding and subtracting polynomials
- Multiplying binomials
- Graphing non-linear functions

WHY?

So you can solve real-world problems about...

- treehouses, p. 663
- baseball, p. 676
- stage design, p. 677
- juggling, p. 680

Internet Preview

CLASSZONE.COM

- eEdition Plus Online
- eWorkbook Plus Online
- eTutorial Plus Online
- FCAT Practice
- More Examples

Chapter Warm-Up Games

Review skills you need for this chapter in these quick games.

PIÑATA PUNCH

$(5 - 11)^3 \cdot 2 \cdot (-6)^{-2}$

$\dfrac{4^7}{(9 - 5)^3}$

$3^{-3} \cdot 3^8 + 5$

$2^5 \cdot 7 \cdot 2^{-1}$

$\dfrac{(7 + 1)^6}{8^4}$

18

12

250

112

8

-64

BrAIN GAME

Key Skill:
Using properties of exponents

To break open the piñata on your turn, you need to pick the right stick.

- Evaluate the expression under each stick.
- A stick breaks the piñata if it has the same value as one of the spots.
- Which stick breaks the piñata? Which spot should you hit?

Unmasking Expressions

$x - 4x + 3 + 9x$

$-7x + 8 - 2(3x + 4)$

$5(x - 6) + 10x - 3$

$8x - 3 - 4(2x + 3)$

$4 - (3x - 1) + x$

$17 - 4x - 13 + 2x$

John	Maria	Sam	Carol	Vincent	Sophie
$6x + 3$	$-2x + 4$	$-13x$	-15	$-2x + 5$	$15x - 33$

BRAIN GAME

Key Skill:
Combining like terms

Find who is behind each of the masks.

- Match the expression under the mask with the correct simplified expression below a name.

Stop *and* Think

1. **Writing** Explain the steps for simplifying the expression $-7x + 8 - 2(3x + 4)$.

2. **Critical Thinking** Write $2^5 \cdot 7 \cdot 2^{-1}$ as an expression with only positive exponents.

CHAPTER 13 Getting Ready to Learn

Review What You Need to Know

Using Vocabulary Copy and complete with a review word.

Word Watch

Review Words

power, p. 20
exponent, p. 20
like terms, p. 86
coefficient, p. 86
monomial, p. 170
function, p. 541

1. The <u>?</u> of $2x^3$ is 2.

2. A(n) <u>?</u> is a relation that assigns exactly one output value to each input value.

3. A number, a variable, or a product of a number and one or more variables is a(n) <u>?</u>.

Simplify the expression. *(p. 85)*

4. $6x - 4 + 4x - 3$ 5. $-5(2x + 3) - 4x$ 6. $7(3x - 5) - (-x)$

7. $-2x - (-5x)$ 8. $-2(-4x - 8)$ 9. $-3(3x) + 18x$

Simplify the expression. *(p. 196)*

10. $\dfrac{y^4}{y^6}$ 11. $\dfrac{5^{37}}{5^{35}}$ 12. $x^4 \cdot x^5$

List four solutions of the equation. *(p. 550)*

13. $y = 3x - 5$ 14. $y = -2x + 1$ 15. $y = \dfrac{1}{2}x$

You should include material that appears on a notebook like this in your own notes.

Know How to Take Notes

Summarizing Material Summarize the main ideas from different lessons in your notebook. This will help you to see how key ideas are related.

Exponent Rules

Product of Powers

$x^2 \cdot x^3 = x^{2+3}$

$= x^5$

Quotient of Powers

$\dfrac{x^5}{x^2} = x^{5-2}$

$= x^3$

Zero Exponent

for $x \neq 0$,

$x^0 = 1$

Negative Exponents

for $x \neq 0$,

$x^{-4} = \dfrac{1}{x^4}$

In Lesson 13.4, you can summarize key ideas about algebra in your notebook.

Polynomials

BEFORE	Now	WHY?
You simplified expressions by combining like terms.	You will simplify polynomials by combining like terms.	So you can find the height of a falling pinecone, as in Example 3.

Word Watch

polynomial, p. 657
binomial, p. 657
trinomial, p. 657
standard form, p. 657

FLORIDA
Standards and Assessment
• Simplify expressions using exponents. (MA.A.1.3.4)
• Evaluate expressions with exponents. (MA.A.2.3.1)

A **polynomial** is a monomial or a sum of monomials. Each monomial in a polynomial is called a *term*. Polynomials are classified by the number of their terms. If a polynomial has more than three terms, it is simply called a polynomial.

Monomial (1 term)	Binomial (2 terms)	Trinomial (3 terms)
$-2x$	$3x - 2$	$-2a^2 + 3a + 1$
4	$-s^4 + 6s^3$	$3 + 5r - 7r^2$

A polynomial is written in **standard form** if the exponents of the variable decrease from left to right.

Standard Form	Not Standard Form
$3x^3 - 2x^2 + 4$	$3 + 5y$
$-2m^6 + 5m^3 - m$	$7t^4 - t^7 - 2t^2 + 3t$

Watch Out!

If you do not see an exponent with a variable, then its exponent is 1.

$2x = 2x^1$

EXAMPLE 1 **Writing Polynomials in Standard Form**

Write the polynomial in standard form. Classify the polynomial.

a. $x - 9 + 5x^2$

$\qquad = x + (-9) + 5x^2$ Write subtraction as addition.

$\qquad = 5x^2 + x + (-9)$ Order terms with decreasing exponents.

ANSWER The polynomial $5x^2 + x - 9$ has 3 terms, so it is a trinomial.

b. $2x - 3x^3$

$\qquad = 2x + (-3x^3)$ Write subtraction as addition.

$\qquad = -3x^3 + 2x$ Order terms with decreasing exponents.

ANSWER The polynomial $-3x^3 + 2x$ has 2 terms, so it is a binomial.

Your turn now Write the polynomial in standard form and classify it.

1. $4 + b^2 - 8b$ **2.** $-5 + 3x^2$ **3.** $11 + 2n^4 - 7n + 5n^2$

Lesson 13.1   Polynomials   **657**

Simplifying Polynomials Remember that *like terms* have the same variables raised to the same powers. To simplify a polynomial, combine like terms by adding their coefficients.

EXAMPLE 2 Simplifying Polynomials

Simplify the polynomial and write it in standard form.

a. $3x^2 + 4x^2 - 2x - 3$

$$= (3x^2 + 4x^2) - 2x - 3 \qquad \text{Group like terms.}$$
$$= 7x^2 - 2x - 3 \qquad \text{Simplify.}$$

b. $x^2 + 2 + 4(x^2 - 2x)$

$$= x^2 + 2 + 4x^2 - 8x \qquad \text{Use the distributive property.}$$
$$= (x^2 + 4x^2) + 2 - 8x \qquad \text{Group like terms.}$$
$$= 5x^2 + 2 - 8x \qquad \text{Simplify.}$$
$$= 5x^2 - 8x + 2 \qquad \text{Write in standard form.}$$

HELP with **Review**

Remember that $x^2 = 1x^2$. For help with like terms, see p. 85.

For help with like terms, see p. 85.

Your turn now Simplify the polynomial and write it in standard form.

4. $7p + 5p^2 - 2 - 3p^2$

5. $10s^4 - 3s + s^4 - 1$

6. $2(a^2 + 3a - 1) + 2a^2$

7. $8x + 3(2x^2 - x + 1)$

EXAMPLE 3 Evaluating a Polynomial Expression

Pinecone You drop a pinecone from a 150 foot bridge. The height of the pinecone, in feet, after t seconds of falling, can be found using the polynomial $-16t^2 + 150$. Find the pinecone's height after 2 seconds.

Solution

$$-16t^2 + 150 = -16(2)^2 + 150 \qquad \text{Substitute 2 for } t.$$
$$= -16(4) + 150 \qquad \text{Evaluate the power.}$$
$$= -64 + 150 \qquad \text{Multiply.}$$
$$= 86 \qquad \text{Add.}$$

ANSWER The pinecone's height after 2 seconds is 86 feet.

Your turn now Find the height of the pinecone in Example 3 after it falls for the given number of seconds.

8. 0.5 sec **9.** 1 sec **10.** 1.5 sec **11.** 3 sec

Getting Ready to Practice

Vocabulary Classify the polynomial as a *monomial*, a *binomial*, or a *trinomial*.

1. $x^2 + 3x - 7$ **2.** $y - 5$ **3.** $8s^2t$ **4.** $2a^2 + 9a^3 + a$

Write the polynomial in standard form.

5. $7 + 3m$ **6.** $5n - 1 - n^2$ **7.** $4b - 4 + 6b^3$

Simplify the polynomial and write it in standard form.

8. $3x + x^2 - 2x$ **9.** $4 + 5y - 5$ **10.** $-9 + 7m^3 - 2m^3$

11. Find the Error Describe and correct the error in simplifying the polynomial.

$$\begin{aligned} -3x^2 - 4(5x + 1) \\ = -3x^2 - 20x - 4 \\ = -23x - 4 \end{aligned}$$

Practice and Problem Solving

HELP with Homework

Example	Exercises
1	12–14
2	15–20, 23–26
3	27–30

Online Resources
CLASSZONE.COM
· More Examples
· eTutorial Plus

Write the polynomial in standard form. Classify the polynomial.

12. $2 - 5y + y^2$ **13.** $-13x^3 + 4x^{10}$ **14.** $3 - r^4 + r + 2r^3$

Simplify the polynomial and write it in standard form.

15. $3x - 4 + x$ **16.** $2c^2 - c^2 + 5c$

17. $4q^3 - 7q^5 + 3q - q^3$ **18.** $7 - 4d^2 - 3d^2 + d$

19. $12 + 3b - 6b + 5$ **20.** $g^3 - 10 + 2g^2 - 5g^3$

Measurement Write a polynomial expression for the perimeter. Simplify the polynomial and write it in standard form.

21.

$2x + 3$

22.

$2(x + 1)$

Simplify the polynomial and write it in standard form.

23. $1 + 12m^2 - 5m + 6m - 7$ **24.** $7 - p^3 - 5p^3 + 3p + p - p^3$

25. $3x^2 + 5(x^2 - 3x + 6)$ **26.** $-6(2y^3 - 4y^2 + 1) + 10y^2$

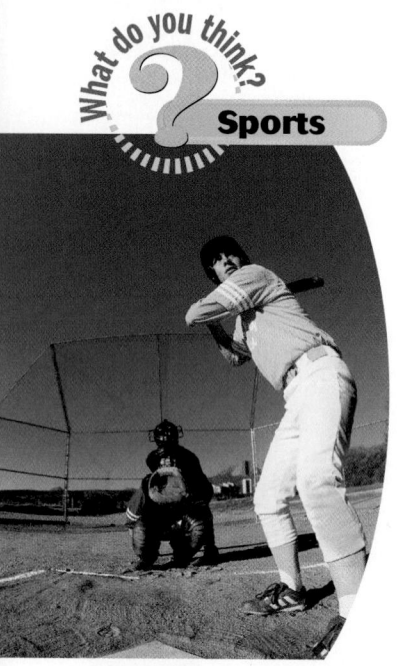

What do you think?

Sports

■ **Baseball**

A player hits a ball 60 mi/h into right field. The ball has the same height after 2 seconds as it has after 3.5 seconds. How is this possible?

Baseball A player hits a ball 60 mi/h, or 88 ft/sec, toward right field. Evaluate the polynomial $-16t^2 + 88t + 2$ to find the ball's height, in feet, after t seconds.

27. $t = 1.5$ **28.** $t = 2$ **29.** $t = 2.5$ **30.** $t = 3$

Simplify the polynomial and write it in standard form.

31. $-4(t - 3t^2 + 8 - 4t) + 6t^2 - 5$ **32.** $-3(-s^4 + 2s - 6 - s) - 8s + s^4$

Critical Thinking Tell whether the statement is *always*, *sometimes*, or *never* true.

33. The terms of a trinomial are monomials.

34. A monomial has one factor.

35. A binomial has more than two terms.

Challenge **Simplify the polynomial.**

36. $3x^2 - 2y + 5x^2 - 4$ **37.** $-16t - 7h + 3t^2 + 4h$

38. $5a - 4(3b + 6) + 4b$ **39.** $-z^2 + 3z - 2(4y - 5z)$

40. **Make a Connection** Find the meaning of the prefix *poly*. Explain what this tells you about the words *polygon* and *polynomial*.

Mixed Review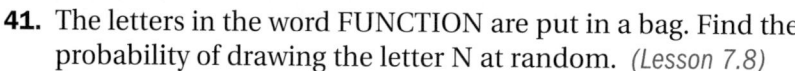

41. The letters in the word FUNCTION are put in a bag. Find the probability of drawing the letter N at random. *(Lesson 7.8)*

42. Find the volume of the cylinder. Round to the nearest hundredth of a cubic meter. *(Lesson 10.6)*

4 m

5 m

43. Make a stem-and-leaf plot of the data. *(Lesson 12.1)*
38.6, 35.8, 36.3, 34.2, 37.6, 37.5, 36.4, 36.2, 38.6, 36.6

Basic Skills **Evaluate the expression.**

44. $8(3 + 9)$ **45.** $-3(11 - 4)$ **46.** $-5(7 + 2)$ **47.** $12(6 - 1)$

FCAT Practice FCAT

48. **Multiple Choice** Simplify the polynomial $7(x^2 + 3x - 1) - 4x^2$.

    A. $-3x^2 + 21x - 7$ **B.** $3x^2 + 21x + 7$

    C. $3x^2 + 14x$ **D.** $3x^2 + 21x - 7$

49. **Multiple Choice** Find the value of $x^2 + 3x - 5$ for $x = -4$.

    F. -33 **G.** -9 **H.** -1 **I.** 23

INTERNET
FCAT PRACTICE
CLASSZONE.COM

LESSON 13.2

Adding and Subtracting Polynomials

BEFORE	▶ Now	WHY?
You simplified polynomials.	You'll add and subtract polynomials.	So you can find the area of clay coasters, as in Ex. 29.

📖 **Word Watch**

Review Words

opposite, p. 54
like terms, p. 86

FLORIDA
Standards and Assessment

• Evaluate expressions with exponents. (MA.A.2.3.1)

• Apply number properties. (MA.A.3.3.1)

 You can model polynomial addition with algebra tiles.

You can model polynomials with algebra tiles.

x^2-tile x-tile   1-tile

① Write the two polynomials represented by the algebra tiles.

② Group the algebra tiles to model the sum of the polynomials. Draw your model. Write the polynomial that your drawing represents.

③ Use algebra tiles to model the sum of the polynomials below. Write the polynomial that your model represents.

a. $(3x^2 + 6x + 1) + (x^2 + x)$ **b.** $(2x^2 + 3x + 1) + (4x^2 + x)$

In the activity, you used algebra tiles to add two polynomials. You add polynomials by combining like terms.

EXAMPLE 1   **Adding Polynomials Vertically**

Find the sum $(-4x^3 + x^2 - 3x - 1) + (4x^2 - 7x + 5)$.

Solution

$$-4x^3 + x^2 - 3x - 1$$ Write the second polynomial under the first.

$$+ \underline{4x^2 - 7x + 5}$$ Arrange like terms in columns.

$$-4x^3 + 5x^2 - 10x + 4$$ Add like terms.

Lesson 13.2   Adding and Subtracting Polynomials   **661**

In Example 1, you combined like terms vertically. You can also add polynomials by combining like terms horizontally.

 with Solving

When you regroup terms, you must move a subtraction or addition sign with the term that follows it.

EXAMPLE 2 **Adding Polynomials Horizontally**

Find the sum $(2y^2 - 4y + 6) + (y^2 + 3y - 2)$.

Solution

$(2y^2 - 4y + 6) + (y^2 + 3y - 2)$

$= 2y^2 + y^2 - 4y + 3y + 6 - 2$ Group like terms.

$= 3y^2 - y + 4$ Combine like terms.

Your turn now **Find the sum.**

1. $(6x^2 - 3x + 1) + (3x^2 + 4x - 5)$ **2.** $(5n^2 + 2n - 9) + (3n^2 - n + 4)$

3. $(y^2 - y + 1) + (-2y^2 + 2y - 1)$ **4.** $(3p^2 - p - 1) + (p^2 + p - 4)$

Subtracting Polynomials You can subtract a polynomial by adding its *opposite*. To find the opposite of a polynomial, multiply each of its terms by -1. You can subtract polynomials vertically or horizontally.

EXAMPLE 3 **Subtracting Polynomials Vertically**

Find the difference $(4x^3 + 5x^2 - 2x - 5) - (3x^3 - 4x + 2)$.

Solution

① Find the opposite of the second polynomial.

$-(3x^3 - 4x + 2) = -3x^3 + 4x - 2$

② Find the sum $(4x^3 + 5x^2 - 2x - 5) + (-3x^3 + 4x - 2)$.

$4x^3 + 5x^2 - 2x - 5$ Write the second polynomial under the first.

$\underline{+\ -3x^3 + 4x - 2}$ Arrange like terms in columns.

$x^3 + 5x^2 + 2x - 7$ Add like terms.

Your turn now **Find the difference.**

5. $(4r^2 - r + 8) - (r^2 + 6r - 1)$ **6.** $(6m^2 + 2m - 3) - (7m^2 + 4)$

7. $(5t^2 + 4t + 1) - (2t^2 + 8t + 11)$ **8.** $(x^2 + 5x + 7) - (3x^2 - 4x - 2)$

EXAMPLE **4** **Finding the Area of a Tree House**

Tree House The design for a tree house calls for a rectangular hole in the floor. Write a polynomial expression for the area of the tree house floor.

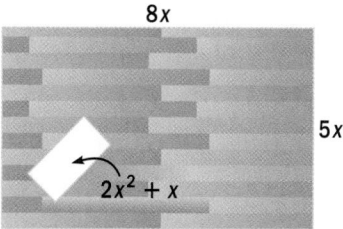

Solution

To find the area of the floor, use the area of the two rectangles.

Area of Large Rectangle

$8x \cdot 5x = 40x^2$

Area of Small Rectangle

$2x^2 + x$

Area of floor	=	Area of large rectangle	−	Area of small rectangle

$$= 40x^2 - (2x^2 + x)$$

$$= 40x^2 - 2x^2 - x \qquad \text{Distributive property}$$

$$= 38x^2 - x \qquad \text{Combine like terms.}$$

ANSWER A polynomial expression for the area of the floor is $38x^2 - x$.

13.2 **Exercises**

More Practice, p. 739

INTERNET
eWorkbook Plus
CLASSZONE.COM

Getting Ready to Practice

1. **Vocabulary** Copy and complete: To add polynomials, you should combine _?_.

Find the sum or difference.

2. $(8y + 5) + (4y - 3)$

3. $(7x + 10) - (x - 2)$

4. $(x - 6) + (2x + 9)$

5. $(4p + 1) - (p - 7)$

6. $(5n^2 + 2n + 1) - (4n^2 - 1)$

7. $(-3a + 10) + (2a - 4)$

8. **Find the Error** Describe and correct the error(s) in the solution.

$$
\begin{array}{r}
-4x^3 + 5x^2 - 7x + 2 \\
+ \quad 2x^3 - 6x + 10 \\
\hline
-2x^3 - x^2 + 3x + 2
\end{array}
$$

Practice and Problem Solving

HELP with Homework

Example	Exercises
1	9–14
2	9–14
3	15–20
4	29

Online Resources
CLASSZONE.COM

· More Examples
· eTutorial Plus

Find the sum.

9. $(4x + 7) + (x - 3)$

10. $(-2a - 9) + (a + 4)$

11. $(3n - 7) + (4n + 5)$

12. $(t^2 + 3t) + (3t^2 + 8t)$

13. $(-g^2 + g + 9) + (7g^2 - 6)$

14. $(3z^2 - 2z + 1) + (4z^3 + 3z)$

Find the difference.

15. $(-5d - 1) - (5d + 6)$

16. $(7y + 1) - (3y - 2)$

17. $(2h^2 + 9h) - (13h^2 - h)$

18. $(4x^2 + 9x) - (x^2 + 7x - 1)$

19. $(6r^2 + 2r - 5) - (3r^2 - 9)$

20. $(-4b^3 - 9b + 2) - (b^3 - b + 3)$

Geometry Write a polynomial expression for the perimeter of the figure. Simplify the polynomial.

21.

22.

Find the sum or difference.

23. $(2k^2 + 5k) + (4k^2 - 5k)$

24. $(5a^2 + 3a + 8) - (2a^2 - 2a - 9)$

25. $(6x^3 - 12x + 1) + (8x^2 - 4)$

26. $(4p^3 + p^2 - 8) - (7p^3 + 2p + 5)$

27. $(4n - 3) + (9n + 5) - (n - 1)$

28. $(-8m + 1) - (2m - 6) + 5m$

29. Coasters To make a set of coasters, you cut identical circles out of a square piece of clay. Write a polynomial expression for the area of clay that remains after you remove the circles. Simplify the polynomial. Is there enough clay left over to make another coaster of the same radius and thickness? Explain your answer.

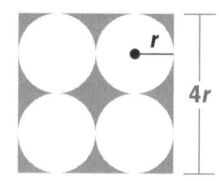

Perform the indicated operations.

30. $-2(5y + 3) - 9(y + 1)$

31. $4(-3s^2 + s - 4) + (5s^2 + s + 7)$

32. $3(q^2 - q) + 2(7q^2 - 2q)$

33. $6(t^3 - t^2 + 3t) - 4(5t^3 + t^2 - t)$

34. $5(4x^3 - 2x^2 + 1) + 3(7x^2 - 5x)$

35. $-7(2v^4 + 3v^2 - 1) - 5(-3v^3 - 6)$

36. Critical Thinking Can the sum of two trinomials be a binomial? Give an example to justify your answer.

37. Challenge Solve the equation $(2x^2 - 3x + 4) - (2x^2 + x - 8) = 0$.

with Review

For help with surface area
of a pyramid, see p. 507.

38. Science Fair You are constructing
two wooden pyramids using the
designs shown. Write a simplified
polynomial expression for the total
surface area of the two pyramids.

Mixed Review

Simplify the expression. *(Lesson 4.6)*

39. $b^3 \cdot b^7$ **40.** $\dfrac{x^{12}}{x^5}$ **41.** $\dfrac{m^4 n^5}{n^2}$ **42.** $\dfrac{a^2 \cdot a^6}{a^3}$

43. How many different passwords can be made using 4 digits from 0 to 9?
(Lesson 12.4)

FCAT Practice FCAT

INTERNET
FCAT PRACTICE
CLASSZONE.COM

44. Multiple Choice Find the sum $(2x^3 + x^2 - 6) + (-4x^3 + 5x - 2)$.

   A. $-2x^3 + x^2 + 5x + 8$ **B.** $-6x^3 + 6x^2 - 4$

   C. $-2x^3 + x^2 + 5x - 8$ **D.** $-6x^3 + 6x^2 + 4$

45. Short Response Explain how to find the difference.

$$(3x^5 - 2x^4 + x^3 - 4x) - (x^3 + 8x^2 - 6)$$

Polynomial Potions

You need to make six potions using the six
ingredients in the laboratory. Each potion is
made by adding two ingredients together. Use
the list of ingredients and the potion labels to
find the secret formulas.

Ingredients

Dog Biscuits
$x^2 - 2x + 2$

Cotton Balls
$-x^2 - 6x - 2$

Green Slime
$2x^2 - 3x + 1$

Muck
$-3x^2 + 2x - 1$

Fish Oil
$3x^2 + 5x - 4$

Nail Polish
$-2x^2 + x - 3$

*Potion labels:*

$-2x - 2$

$5x^2 + 2x - 3$

$x^2 - 9x - 1$

$-8x$

$7x - 5$

$x^2 + 6x - 7$

LESSON 13.3

Monomials and Powers

BEFORE	Now	WHY?
You added and subtracted polynomials.	You will apply properties of exponents to monomials.	So you can find the volume of Saturn, as in Ex. 48.

Word Watch

Review Words

power, p. 20
exponent, p. 20
coefficient, p. 86
monomial, p. 170

FLORIDA

Standards and Assessment

• Simplify expressions using exponents. (MA.A.1.3.4)

• Apply number properties. (MA.A.3.3.1)

Activity You can use the properties of exponents to simplify monomials.

① Copy and complete the table by expanding each expression, regrouping factors, and simplifying.

Expression	Expand	Regroup	Simplify
$(3x)(4x^2)$	$3 \cdot x \cdot 4 \cdot x \cdot x$	$3 \cdot 4 \cdot x \cdot x \cdot x$	$12x^3$
$(-2x)(5x^4)$	?	?	?
$(xy)^3$	$xy \cdot xy \cdot xy$	$x \cdot x \cdot x \cdot y \cdot y \cdot y$	x^3y^3
$(4x)^2$	?	?	?
$(-3x)^3$	?	?	?

② What patterns do you notice in the table?

③ Use your results to simplify the expressions $(5x)(2x^3)$ and $(3pq)^2$.

In the activity, you used properties of exponents that you learned in Lesson 4.6 to multiply monomials. To multiply factors that have the same base, add their exponents. Multiply their coefficients.

HELP with Review

For help with rules of exponents, see p. 196.

EXAMPLE 1 Multiplying Monomials

Simplify the expression $(2x^3)(-3x)$.

$$
\begin{aligned}
(2x^3)(-3x) &= 2 \cdot x^3 \cdot (-3) \cdot x && \text{Expand the expression.} \\
&= 2 \cdot (-3) \cdot x^3 \cdot x && \text{Regroup factors.} \\
&= -6 \cdot x^3 \cdot x && \text{Multiply coefficients.} \\
&= -6x^4 && \text{Product of powers property}
\end{aligned}
$$

Your turn now Simplify the expression.

1. $4a(a^2)$ **2.** $(-2m)(7m^2)$ **3.** $(-x)(8x^2)$ **4.** $(y^5)(5y)$

You can use the distributive property and the properties of exponents to find the product of a monomial and a binomial.

EXAMPLE 2 Using the Distributive Property

Simplify the expression $2n(4n^2 - 5)$.

$$2n(4n^2 - 5) = (2n)(4n^2) - (2n)(5) \quad \text{Distributive property}$$
$$= 8n^3 - 10n \quad \text{Product of powers property}$$

Your turn now Simplify the expression.

5. $p(2p + 3)$ **6.** $-t^2(-2t + 8)$ **7.** $n^2(5n^2 - 3)$ **8.** $2x(3x - 4)$

In the activity on page 666, you found powers of products. You can use the rule below to simplify a power of a product.

Power of a Product Property

Words To simplify a power of a product, find the power of each factor and multiply.

Algebra $(ab)^m = a^m \cdot b^m$ **Numbers** $(5 \cdot 2)^3 = 5^3 \cdot 2^3$

EXAMPLE 3 Simplifying a Power of a Product

Container The radius of a container is twice its height. Write an expression for the volume of the container. Use the formula $V = \pi r^2 h$.

Solution

The radius is twice the height, so $r = 2h$.

$$V = \pi(2h)^2 h \quad \text{Substitute } 2h \text{ for } r.$$
$$= \pi(2^2 \cdot h^2)h \quad \text{Power of a product property}$$
$$= \pi \cdot 4 \cdot h^2 \cdot h \quad \text{Evaluate the power.}$$
$$= 4\pi h^3 \quad \text{Product of powers property.}$$

ANSWER An expression for the volume of the container is $V = 4\pi h^3$.

Power of a Power Property

Words To simplify a power of a power, multiply exponents.

Algebra $(a^m)^n = a^{mn}$ **Numbers** $(5^3)^2 = 5^{3 \cdot 2} = 5^6$

EXAMPLE 4   **Simplifying a Power of a Power**

Simplify the expression $(2y^2)^3$.

$$(2y^2)^3 = 2^3 \cdot (y^2)^3 \qquad \text{Power of a product property}$$
$$= 8 \cdot y^{2 \cdot 3} \qquad \text{Power of a power property}$$
$$= 8y^6 \qquad \text{Simplify.}$$

Your turn now   **Simplify the expression.**

9. $(2^4)^2$ **10.** $(x^6)^2$ **11.** $(5m^3)^2$ **12.** $(a^2b)^2$

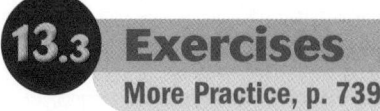

13.3 Exercises

More Practice, p. 739

INTERNET
eWorkbook Plus
CLASSZONE.COM

Getting Ready to Practice

Vocabulary **Match the expression with the rule used to simplify it.**

1. $(2y)^5$ **A.** power of a power property

2. $(x^2)^7$ **B.** power of a product property

3. $3 \cdot x^4 \cdot x^6$ **C.** product of powers property

Simplify the expression.

4. $(5x)(7x^6)$ **5.** $2x(x^2 - 1)$ **6.** $(4y)^3$ **7.** $(z^4)^4$

8. **Guided Problem Solving** Simplify the expression $\left(\dfrac{x}{y}\right)^4$.

   (1 Write the expression in expanded form.

   (2 Simplify by multiplying numerators and multiplying denominators.

   (3 Write a rule you could use to find the power of a quotient.

Practice and Problem Solving

with Homework

Example	Exercises
1	9-14
2	15-20
3	22-29
4	30-37

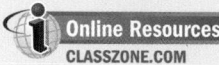
Online Resources
CLASSZONE.COM

· More Examples
· eTutorial Plus

Simplify the expression by multiplying the monomials.

9. $(-4x)(5x^3)$ **10.** $(-16t)(-3t^9)$ **11.** $(-x^2)(-3x)$

12. $(3s)(-2s^3)$ **13.** $(-b^3)(-b^8)$ **14.** $(-y^2)(y^3)$

Simplify the expression by using the distributive property.

15. $m(m + 4)$ **16.** $2w(3w + 1)$ **17.** $-t(t^2 - 4)$

18. $-8x(x^5 + x)$ **19.** $w^2(-2w - 1)$ **20.** $3k^2(12 - k^5)$

21. Seat Cushion You need fabric for a window seat cushion. Use the trapezoid pattern shown to write a polynomial expression for the area of the top of the cushion. Simplify the expression.

Simplify the expression by using the power of a product property.

22. $(5z)^3$ **23.** $(xyz)^5$ **24.** $(2ab)^4$ **25.** $(-6z)^3$

26. $(-dt)^4$ **27.** $(3rs)^2$ **28.** $(-3xy)^3$ **29.** $(10bh)^5$

Simplify the expression by using the power of a power property.

30. $(t^4)^2$ **31.** $(y^2)^2$ **32.** $(c^2)^9$ **33.** $(x^2)^{10}$

34. $(ab^3)^2$ **35.** $(x^2y^2)^3$ **36.** $(3a^2)^2$ **37.** $(2r^3)^3$

38. Compare and Contrast Explain why $(4y)^2$ is different from $4y^2$.

39. Photo Albums You are making photo albums in different sizes. Each page is twice as long as it is wide and needs a 2 inch margin for binding. Write a polynomial expression for the total area of one page.

Simplify the expression.

40. $2(5mn^4)^3$ **41.** $-3a^{10}(a^4b^2c)^4$ **42.** $(-2x^4)^3(x^4yz^8)$

43. Critical Thinking Write a ratio comparing the area of the circle to the area of the square. Simplify the ratio. Leave your answer in terms of π.

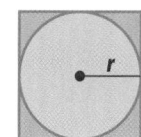

44. Volume Write and simplify a polynomial expression for the volume of the square pyramid.

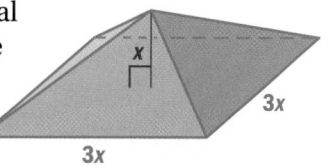

Scientific Notation Simplify the expression and write it in scientific notation.

45. $(3 \times 10^4)^3$ **46.** $(9 \times 10^{10})^3$ **47.** $(5 \times 10^7)^4$

Extended Problem Solving In Exercises 48–50, use the formula $V = \frac{4}{3}\pi r^3$ for the volume of a sphere to find the volumes of spherical objects in our solar system.

48. Saturn The radius of Saturn is about 6.0×10^4 kilometers.

49. Moon of Saturn The radius of Saturn's moon Dione is about 560 kilometers.

50. Estimate Write a ratio comparing the volume of Saturn to the volume of Dione. Use this ratio to estimate how many times larger Saturn is than Dione.

Challenge Simplify the expression.

51. $3[(a^4b^3)^4 \cdot a^8b]^3$ **52.** $\left(\frac{2x^2}{x}\right)^3$ **53.** $\frac{(-2xy)^2}{(x^2)^3}$

Mixed Review

In Exercises 54–57, write the percent as a fraction in simplest form. *(Lesson 7.4)*

54. 55% **55.** 71% **56.** 29% **57.** 18%

58. In one out of every eight holes of mini-golf, you get a hole in one. Find the odds of getting a hole in one on the next hole that you play. *(Lesson 12.7)*

59. Find the probability of rolling first a 2 and then a 4 if you roll a number cube twice. *(Lesson 12.8)*

FCAT Practice

60. Multiple Choice Simplify the expression $2a(8a^2 - 3)$.

   A. $16a^2 - 6a$ **B.** $16a^2 - 6$ **C.** $16a^3 - 6a$ **D.** $16a^3 + 6a$

61. Multiple Choice Simplify the expression $(3b^3)^4$.

   F. $3b^7$ **G.** $3b^{12}$ **H.** $81b^7$ **I.** $81b^{12}$

LESSONS 13.1 TO 13.3

Notebook Review

Review the vocabulary definitions in your notebook.

Copy the review examples in your notebook. Then complete the exercises.

Check Your Definitions

polynomial, p. 657   trinomial, p. 657

binomial, p. 657   standard form, p. 657

Use Your Vocabulary

Copy and complete the statement.

1. A polynomial with one term is called a ? .

2. A ? is a monomial or a sum of monomials.

13.1 Can you simplify polynomials?

EXAMPLE Simplify the polynomial $4x^2 - 5(x^2 - x + 3 - 2x)$.

$4x^2 - 5(x^2 - x + 3 - 2x)$

$= 4x^2 - 5x^2 + 5x - 15 + 10x$ **Distributive property**

$= -x^2 + 15x - 15$ **Combine like terms.**

☑ **Simplify the polynomial and write it in standard form.**

3. $10 - 3a^2 + 4a^2 + 8$ **4.** $6 + z^2 - 3z + z^2 - 5$

13.2 Can you add and subtract polynomials?

EXAMPLE Find the sum $(3x^2 - 2x + 7) + (5x - 9)$.

$3x^2 - 2x + 7$ **Write the second polynomial under the first.**

$+ \qquad 5x - 9$ **Arrange like terms in columns.**

$\overline{3x^2 + 3x - 2}$ **Combine like terms.**

☑ **Find the sum or difference.**

5. $(n^3 + 4n^2 - 9) + (n^3 + n^2 - 2n + 6)$

6. $(2x^2 + 3x - 1) - (7x^2 - x - 5)$

13.3 Can you multiply monomials?

 Review

EXAMPLE Simplify the expression $(x^3)(3x)^2$.

$$(x^3)(3x)^2 = x^3(3^2 \cdot x^2)$$ Power of a product property

$$= x^3 \cdot 9 \cdot x^2$$ Evaluate the power.

$$= 9x^5$$ Product of powers property

☑ **Simplify the expression.**

7. $(8x^8)(6x^2)$ **8.** $(6n^3m)^2$ **9.** $(2ab)^4$ **10.** $(4r^2)(r - 5)$

Stop *and* **Think**   about Lessons 13.1–13.3

11. Writing Simplify the expression $(2x)(x^2y)$ and explain your steps.

12. Critical Thinking The radius of a cylinder is three times its height. Write a polynomial expression for the surface area of the cylinder using only one variable. Use the formula $S = 2\pi r^2 + 2\pi rh$.

Review Quiz 1

Simplify the polynomial and write it in standard form.

1. $5x^2 + 4x - 3x^2 - 11$ **2.** $-9y^2 + 7y - 2y + 10 - y$

3. $-5k^3 + 2(3k^3 + k - 4)$ **4.** $8r^3 - 4r - 5r^3 - 3r + 1$

Find the sum or difference.

5. $(6n^3 - 2n^2) + (n^3 + 7n^2 - 4n)$ **6.** $(4b^2 - 3b + 8) - (2b^2 - 6)$

7. $(x^2 + 6x + 1) - (2x^2 - 8x + 4)$ **8.** $(3m^2 + m - 9) + (7m^2 + 2)$

9. Area Write a polynomial expression for the area of the floor surrounding the rug in the diagram. Simplify the polynomial.

Simplify the expression.

10. $(x^3)(-5x)$ **11.** $(3t^4)(4t^2)$ **12.** $(2c^3)^4$

13. $(-2y)^4$ **14.** $r^3(3r - 4)$ **15.** $-5d(3d^2 + 2)$

Hands-on Activity

FLORIDA: Standards and Assessment
• Evaluate expressions with exponents. (MA.A.2.3.1)
• Apply number properties. (MA.A.3.3.1)

Multiplying Binomials

You can model binomial multiplication with algebra tiles.

Explore   **Model the product $(x + 3)(3x + 2)$ with algebra tiles.**

① Model each binomial with algebra tiles. Arrange the first binomial vertically and the second binomial horizontally, as shown.

② The binomials define a rectangular area with length $(3x + 2)$ units and width $(x + 3)$ units. Fill in the region with the appropriate tiles.

③ The rectangle on the inside of the model represents $3x^2 + 11x + 6$. This is the product of the binomials.

Your turn now   **Find the product with algebra tiles. Draw your model.**

   1. $(x + 1)(x + 2)$ **2.** $(x + 4)(x + 4)$ **3.** $(x + 2)(2x + 2)$

Stop _and_ Think

Model the expression with algebra tiles. Arrange the tiles in a rectangle. Find the two binomials that have this product.

   4. $x^2 + 5x + 6$ **5.** $x^2 + 2x + 1$ **6.** $3x^2 + 8x + 4$

Multiplying Binomials

LESSON 13.4

BEFORE	Now	WHY?
You multiplied monomials and polynomials.	You'll multiply binomials.	So you can find an account balance after 2 years, as in Ex. 22.

Review words

polynomial, p. 657
binomial, p. 657

FLORIDA
Standards and Assessment

- Apply number properties. (MA.A.3.3.1)
- Simplify algebraic expressions of real-world situations. (MA.D.2.3.1)

You can use a visual model to multiply binomials. The model below shows that the product $(x + 2)(3x + 1)$ equals $3x^2 + 7x + 2$.

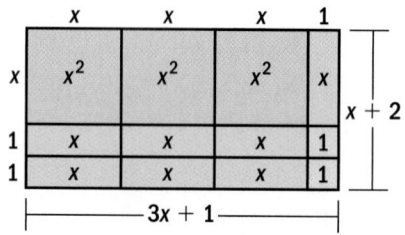

You can multiply two binomials using a table or a vertical method.

HELP with Notetaking

You should summarize key ideas about polynomials in your notebook.

EXAMPLE 1 Multiplying Binomials with a Table

Find the product $(-3x + 2)(8x + 7)$ and simplify.

Write the first polynomial on the left of the table.

	$8x$	7
$-3x$	$-24x^2$	$-21x$
2	$16x$	14

Write the second polynomial above the table.

Multiply to fill in the table.

The product is $-24x^2 - 21x + 16x + 14$. Combine like terms.

ANSWER The product is $-24x^2 - 5x + 14$.

EXAMPLE 2 Multiplying Binomials Vertically

Find the product $(2x - 5)(3x + 4)$ and simplify.

$$
\begin{array}{r}
2x - 5 \\
\times \quad 3x + 4 \\
\hline
8x - 20 \\
6x^2 - 15x \\
\hline
6x^2 - 7x - 20
\end{array}
$$

Write the first binomial.

Write the second binomial.

Multiply $4(2x - 5)$.

Multiply $3x(2x - 5)$. Line up like terms.

Add $8x - 20$ and $6x^2 - 15x$.

HELP with Vocabulary

Compound interest is earned on the original amount of money in an account and on the interest already earned.

EXAMPLE 3 Multiplying Binomials Horizontally

Banking You deposit $1 into a savings account with interest compounded annually. The balance of the account after two years can be found using the expression $(1 + r)^2$, where r represents the interest rate. Expand this expression and simplify.

Solution

To expand the expression, multiply 2 binomials.

$$(1 + r)^2 = (1 + r)(1 + r) \qquad \text{$(1 + r)^2$ means $(1 + r)(1 + r)$.}$$
$$= 1(1 + r) + r(1 + r) \qquad \text{Distributive property}$$
$$= 1 + r + r + r^2 \qquad \text{Distributive property}$$
$$= 1 + 2r + r^2 \qquad \text{Combine like terms.}$$
$$= r^2 + 2r + 1 \qquad \text{Write in standard form.}$$

Your turn now Find the product and simplify.

1. $(x + 1)(x + 3)$ **2.** $(b - 4)(b - 3)$ **3.** $(3t - 4)(t + 2)$

The FOIL Method The letters in the word FOIL can help you remember how to multiply binomials. The letters should remind you of the words **F**irst, **O**uter, **I**nner, and **L**ast.

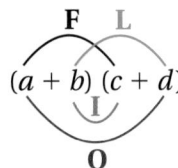

EXAMPLE 4 Multiplying with the FOIL Method

Find the product $(2x + 3)(3x - 1)$ and simplify.

F	**O**	**I**	**L**	
First	+ Outer	+ Inner	+ Last	
$2x \cdot 3x$	$+ 2x \cdot (-1)$	$+ 3 \cdot 3x$	$+ 3 \cdot (-1)$	Group terms.
$6x^2$	$+ (-2x)$	$+ 9x$	$+ (-3)$	Multiply.
		$6x^2 + 7x - 3$		Combine like terms.

Your turn now Find the product and simplify.

4. $(d + 6)(d + 5)$ **5.** $(x - 3)(x - 1)$ **6.** $(5s + 3)(2s - 4)$

Getting Ready to Practice

1. Vocabulary Copy and complete: A polynomial with two terms is called a _?_ .

Find the product and simplify.

2. $3x(x - 4)$ **3.** $2m(3m + 1)$ **4.** $-2y(y + 5)$

5. $(y - 4)(y + 1)$ **6.** $(g + 3)(g + 7)$ **7.** $(z + 4)(z - 2)$

8. Find the Error Describe and correct the error in the solution.

$$(x + 2)(x - 4)$$
$$= x \cdot x + x \cdot 4 + 2 \cdot x + 2 \cdot (-4)$$
$$= x^2 + 4x + 2x - 8$$
$$= x^2 + 6x - 8 \qquad \times$$

Practice and Problem Solving

Find the product and simplify.

9. $(x + 9)(x - 2)$ **10.** $(p + 6)(p + 4)$ **11.** $(a + 10)(a - 4)$

12. $(2m + 3)(m - 7)$ **13.** $(3q - 1)(q - 1)$ **14.** $(b - 3)(9b + 4)$

15. $(6r + 7)(r - 1)$ **16.** $(t - 1)(-3t - 4)$ **17.** $(-x - 5)(11x - 12)$

Critical Thinking Find the product and simplify.

18. $(x + 3)(x - 3)$ **19.** $(x - 4)(x + 4)$ **20.** $(x + 1)(x - 1)$

21. Look for a Pattern Describe the pattern in the binomials and their products in Exercises 18–20.

22. Savings Account You deposit $50 into a savings account with interest compounded annually. The expression $50(1 + r)^2$, where r is the interest rate, gives the account balance after 2 years. Expand this expression and simplify. Find the account balance for $r = 0.03$.

23. Baseball The middle of a baseball is a cork sphere with a radius of 0.6875 inch. Use the formula $S = 4\pi r^2$ to write a polynomial expression for the surface area of the baseball. Expand the expression and simplify.

0.6875 in.

Find the product and simplify.

24. $\left(\frac{1}{2}x + 2\right)(4x - 6)$ **25.** $(9b - 12)\left(\frac{1}{3}b - 6\right)$ **26.** $(n^2 - 2)(n^2 + 1)$

27. Stage Design You are building a
platform on stage for a school talent
show. Write and simplify a polynomial
expression for the area of the platform
using the design shown. Then find the
area when x is 5 feet.

28. Writing Explain why $(x + 3)^2$ does not equal $x^2 + 9$.

29. Challenge Find the product and simplify: $(x + 4)(3x^2 - 2x + 1)$.

30. Savings You put $20 into a savings account with interest compounded
annually. The expression $20(1 + r)^3$, where r is the interest rate, gives
the account balance after 3 years. Expand this expression and simplify.
Find the account balance for $r = 0.05$.

31. Work Backward Find the unknown binomial in the equation
$x^2 + 8x + 7 = (\underline{\quad ? \quad})(x + 7)$.

Mixed Review

Graph the linear equation. *(Lesson 11.4)*

32. $y = 6x - 4$ **33.** $y = x - 3$ **34.** $y = -2x + 7$

Find the product. *(Lesson 13.3)*

35. $-4r(r + 6)$ **36.** $3c(4c^2 + 2c)$ **37.** $-5x(-3x + 2)$

Basic Skills **Plot the point in a coordinate plane.**

38. $(2, -9)$ **39.** $(-7, 6)$ **40.** $(-3, -8)$ **41.** $(0, 4)$

FCAT Practice

42. Multiple Choice Find the product $(x - 3)(x - 5)$.

  A. $x^2 - 2x + 15$ **B.** $x^2 - 2x - 15$

  C. $x^2 - 8x + 15$ **D.** $x^2 - 8x - 15$

43. Multiple Choice Find the product $(3x - 2)(x + 4)$.

  F. $3x^2 + 10x - 8$ **G.** $4x^2 + 12x - 8$

  H. $4x^2 + 10x - 8$ **I.** $3x^2 + 12x - 8$

Problem Solving Strategies

FLORIDA: Standards and Assessment
Construct and interpret data displays. Contrast data displays. (MA.E.1.3.1)
Interpret and create graphs. (MA.D.1.3.2)

Draw a Graph

Look for a Pattern
Draw a Diagram
Act It Out
Work Backward
Draw a Graph
Break into Parts

Daylight The table below shows the total hours of daylight, to the nearest quarter hour, in Anchorage, Alaska, on the 20th day of each month. The table is missing data for the month of July. Estimate the total hours of daylight on July 20.

Month	Jan.	Feb.	March	April	May	June	July	Aug.	Sept.	Oct.	Nov.	Dec.
Hours of Daylight	$6\frac{3}{4}$	$9\frac{1}{2}$	$12\frac{1}{4}$	$15\frac{1}{4}$	$17\frac{3}{4}$	$19\frac{1}{4}$	?	$15\frac{1}{2}$	$12\frac{1}{2}$	$9\frac{3}{4}$	7	$5\frac{1}{2}$

❶ Read and Understand

Read the problem carefully.

You need to estimate the total hours of daylight on July 20.

❷ Make a Plan

Decide on a strategy to use.

You can estimate the hours by drawing a graph. Use the table of values to sketch a curve.

❸ Solve the Problem

Reread the problem and draw a graph.

The data in the table are ordered pairs. Let the x-axis show the date (Jan. 20 = 1, Feb. 20 = 2, etc.). Let the y-axis show the hours of daylight. Plot the points in the coordinate plane.

Connect the points with a curve, and use it to estimate the total hours of daylight on July 20.

ANSWER There are about 18 hours of daylight on July 20.

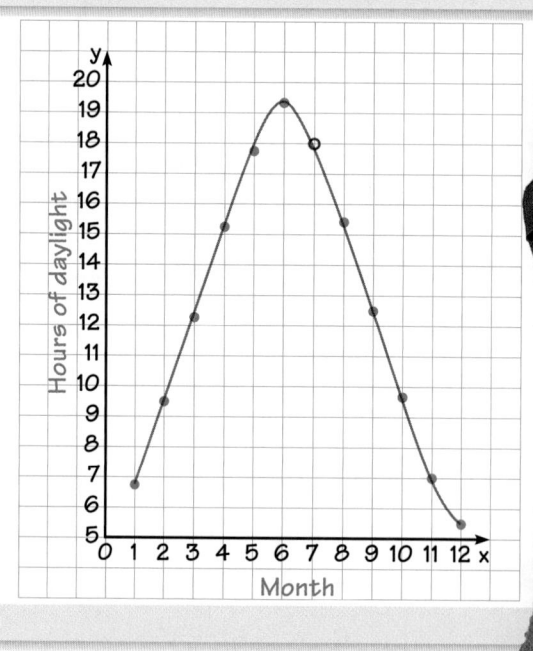

❹ Look Back

Because the graph decreases from June to December it is reasonable to say that there are between $19\frac{1}{4}$ and $15\frac{1}{2}$ hours of daylight on July 20. A reasonable estimate is 18 hours.

Use the strategy *draw a graph.*

1. **E-mail** You e-mail two copies of a joke on January 1. Each recipient e-mails two copies of the joke on the day after receiving it. How many e-mails are sent on January 7?

2. **Square Root** Copy and complete the table.

x	1	4	9	16	25	36
$\sqrt{x}$	?	?	?	?	?	?

   Estimate the square roots below.

   a. $\sqrt{7}$ **b.** $\sqrt{30}$ **c.** $\sqrt{20}$

3. **Cutting** The area of a poster board is 1000 square inches. You repeatedly cut the poster in half, setting aside one half each time. Estimate how many cuts you will make before the area of the remaining piece is less than 1 square inch.

4. **Kiwi Bird** A female kiwi bird weighs from 3 to 9 pounds. A kiwi bird's egg weighs about $\frac{1}{5}$ of the mother's body weight. Estimate the weight of a female bird whose egg weighs less than 0.7 pound.

5. **Tutoring** For each hour you spend tutoring after school, you earn 5 extra-credit points. Make a table that shows how many extra-credit points you can earn for hours you spend tutoring. Estimate how many extra-credit points you would earn after tutoring for 1 hour and 45 minutes.

Mixed Problem Solving

Use any strategy to solve the problem.

6. **Peanut Butter** In a poll, 44% of the people said the best thing to eat with peanut butter is jelly. About 23% chose chocolate. Only 15% preferred marshmallow spread with peanut butter. The rest of the people chose bananas. If 2916 people participated in the poll, about how many people choose bananas with peanut butter?

7. **Draw** Copy the grid. How many squares can you draw by connecting dots?

8. **Encyclopedia** You have a two-volume music encyclopedia. Each volume has 600 pages, and its front and back covers are each 0.4 centimeter thick. If the books sit in the usual order on a shelf, what is the distance, in centimeters, from the first page of Volume 1 to the last page of Volume 2?

9. **Solid** Find the volume of the solid shown. The formula for the volume of a sphere is $V = \frac{4}{3}\pi r^3$.
   Round to the nearest hundredth of a cubic centimeter.

   6 cm

   12 cm

LESSON 13.5

Non-Linear Functions

BEFORE	Now	WHY?
You wrote function rules and graphed linear functions.	You'll use function notation and graph non-linear functions.	So you can find the height of a falling penny, as in Ex. 11.

In the Real World

Word Watch

function notation, p. 680
vertical line test, p. 681

FLORIDA
Standards and Assessment

• Determine if a function is linear. (MA.D.1.3.1)

• Graph equations to show cause and effect. (MA.D.1.3.2)

Juggling You are juggling three balls. The height of one ball, in feet, is found with the equation $h = -16t^2 + 20t + 3$, where t is seconds that pass after you let go of the ball. Write the equation in function notation. Use this function to find the height of one ball 0.5 second after you let go of it.

In Lesson 11.1, you wrote functions as equations in x and y. You used x to name the input and y to name the output. Sometimes it is useful to use **function notation** instead.

equation in *x* and *y*   function notation
$$y = 3x - 4 \qquad\qquad f(x) = 3x - 4$$

The symbol $f(x)$ is read as "the function of f at x" or "f of x."

EXAMPLE 1 Using Function Notation

Write a function that models the height of a ball x seconds after you let go of it. Use function notation. Evaluate for $x = 0.5$.

Solution

Let $f(x) =$ height in feet and $x =$ time in seconds.

$$f(x) = -16x^2 + 20x + 3 \qquad \text{Write the height equation above in function notation.}$$

$$f(0.5) = -16(0.5)^2 + 20(0.5) + 3 \qquad \text{Substitute 0.5 for } x.$$

$$f(0.5) = -16(0.25) + 10 + 3 \qquad \text{Evaluate.}$$

$$f(0.5) = 9$$

ANSWER The function is $f(x) = -16x^2 + 20x + 3$. The height of the ball is 9 feet after 0.5 second.

Your turn now Rewrite using function notation.

1. $y = x^2$ **2.** $y = 3x^2 + 4$ **3.** $y = -\frac{1}{2}x^2$

Graphing Functions The function in Example 1 is non-linear. A non-linear function has a graph that is not a straight line. You can graph non-linear functions by first making a table of values.

HELP with Reading

$f(x)$ does not mean "f times x." It means "the value of the function at x."

EXAMPLE 2 Graphing a Non-Linear Function

Graph the function $f(x) = x^2 - 1$.

① Choose several x-values and make a table of values.

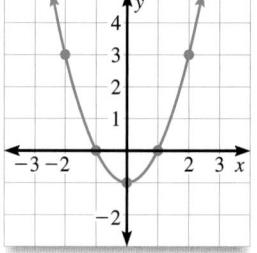

x	-2	-1	0	1	2
$f(x)$	3	0	-1	0	3

② List the solutions as ordered pairs.
$(-2, 3), (-1, 0), (0, -1), (1, 0), (2, 3)$

③ Plot the ordered pairs. Then draw a smooth curve through the points, as shown.

Your turn now Graph the function using a table of values.

4. $f(x) = -x^2 + 4$ **5.** $f(x) = x^2 + 1$ **6.** $f(x) = 2x^2$

Vertical Line Test You can use the **vertical line test** to tell whether a graph represents a function. If a vertical line intersects the graph at more than one point, then the graph does *not* represent a function. Remember, a function has exactly one output value for each input value.

EXAMPLE 3 Using the Vertical Line Test

Tell whether the graph represents a function.

a.

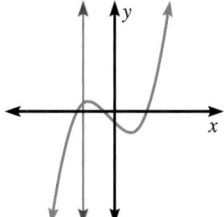

No vertical line intersects the graph at more than one point. So, the graph represents a function.

b.

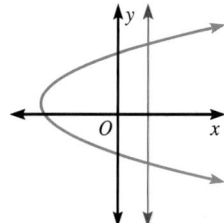

A vertical line intersects the graph at more than one point. So, the graph does *not* represent a function.

Getting Ready to Practice

HELP with **Homework**

Example	Exercises
1	8–11
2	12–17
3	18–20

Online Resources
CLASSZONE.COM

· More Examples
· eTutorial Plus

1. Vocabulary Which is written in function notation?

A. $f = 2x + 4$ **B.** $f(x) = 2x + 4$ **C.** $2(f) + 4$

Evaluate the function for $x = -2, 0,$ and 2.

2. $f(x) = x^2$ **3.** $f(x) = x^2 - 5$ **4.** $f(x) = -3x^2$

Tell whether the graph represents a function.

5.   **6.**   **7.**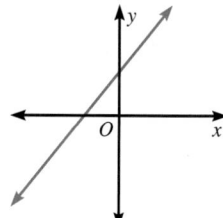

Practice and Problem Solving

Rewrite using function notation.

8. $y = 4x^2$ **9.** $y = 2x^2 - x$ **10.** $y = -x^2 + 10$

11. Penny Drop You drop a penny into a well and hear it hit the water after 3 seconds. The function $d = -16t^2 + 4$ gives the elevation of the penny, in feet, after it falls for t seconds. Write this in function notation, and find how far the penny falls before hitting the water.

Graph the function using a table of values with $x = -3, -2, -1, 0, 1, 2,$ and 3.

12. $f(x) = 4x^2$ **13.** $f(x) = x^2 + 8$ **14.** $f(x) = -x^2 + 5$

15. $f(x) = -x^2$ **16.** $f(x) = 3x^2 - 4$ **17.** $f(x) = -2x^2 - 1$

Tell whether the graph represents a function.

18.   **19.**   **20.**

21. **Reflecting Pool** A rectangular reflecting pool is 50 feet long and 30 feet wide, but you do not know how deep the water is. Write a function that you can use to find the volume of water in the pool for different depths.

22. **Baseball** A ball is hit 75 mi/h, or 110 ft/sec, into center field. The height of the ball, in feet, is found with the function $f(x) = -16x^2 + 110x + 3$, where x is the number of seconds after the ball is hit. Graph this function. Use the graph to estimate how many seconds will pass before the ball lands on the ground.

Graph the function using a table of values.

23. $f(x) = -\frac{1}{2}x^2$ 24. $f(x) = 5 - 5x^2$ 25. $f(x) = 4x^2 + x$

26. $f(x) = x^2 - 3x$ 27. $f(x) = (x - 1)^2$ 28. $f(x) = (x + 2)^2$

29. **Make a Table** Graph the function $f(x) = x^3$ using a table of values. Describe how the graph of this function is different from the graph of the function $f(x) = x^2$. Be sure to include negative and positive x-values in your table.

30. **Draw a Graph** Write a function for the area of the triangle. Graph the function using a table of values. Estimate the value of x if the area of the triangle is 30 square inches.

31. **Interpret** Write a function for the area of the rectangle shown. Graph the function using a table of values, and use it to find the greatest possible area of the rectangle. If the rectangle has the maximum area, what are its length and width?

Work Backward Write a function in function notation for the values in the table.

32.

x	-2	-1	0	1	2
$f(x)$	5	2	1	2	5

33.

x	-4	-2	0	2	4
$f(x)$	-64	-8	0	8	64

34. **Challenge** You deposit $20 into a savings account that earns 2% interest compounded monthly. The expression $20(1.02)^t$ gives the account balance after t months. Write a function for the account balance, and find the balance after 1, 2, and 3 months.

35. **Population** In 2001, the United States population was about 2.8×10^8 people and growing 0.8% each year. You can predict the future population with the expression $(2.8 \times 10^8)(1.008)^t$, where t is the number of years after 2001. Write the expression as a function and use it to predict the population of the United States in 2005.

In Exercises 36–43, solve the equation. *(Lesson 3.3)*

36. $3x + 1 = 7$ **37.** $2x - 3 = 5$ **38.** $-x + 1 = 2$ **39.** $6x - 1 = -11$

40. $2x + 5 = -17$ **41.** $2x + 4 = 10$ **42.** $-3x - 4 = 11$ **43.** $5x + 3 = -12$

44. List four solutions of the equation $2x + 4y = -12$. *(Lesson 11.3)*

Find the product and simplify. *(Lesson 13.4)*

45. $(x + 2)(x + 2)$ **46.** $(3z - 2)(2z - 1)$ **47.** $(5a - 1)(a + 3)$

Choose a Strategy Use a strategy from the list to solve the following problem. Explain your choice of strategy.

> **Problem Solving Strategies**
> ─────────────────
> ▪ Draw a Diagram
> ▪ Break into Parts
> ▪ Solve a Simpler Problem

48. You are saving pennies in a coffee can. On the first day, you put one penny in the can. On the second day, you put two pennies in the can. On the third day, you put three pennies in the can. If you continue this method of saving, how many pennies will be in the can on day 100?

FCAT Practice   FCAT

INTERNET
FCAT PRACTICE
CLASSZONE.COM

49. **Extended Response** Graph the four functions below using tables of values. Describe the differences in the graphs. Explain the effect of a negative coefficient on a graph.

$$f(x) = x^2 \qquad f(x) = -x^2 \qquad f(x) = \tfrac{1}{2}x \qquad f(x) = -\tfrac{1}{2}x$$

BRAIN GAME

Number Crunch

Why was ten afraid of seven?

Use the function $f(x) = 2x^2 - 3x + 7$ to break the code.

?	?	?	?	?	?	?	?	?	?	?	?
-3	5	0	3	-4	1	5	1	5	2	5	6

?	?	?	?	?	?	?	?	?
5	4	-2	-1	-5	6	4	6	5

A	B	C	E	G	H	I	N	S	T	U	V
16	34	7	42	21	12	27	61	6	72	51	9

Technology Activity

FLORIDA: Standards and Assessment
Interpret and create graphs. (MA.D.1.3.2)
Use technology to organize, analyze, and graph data. (MA.E.1.3.3)

Graphing Non-Linear Functions

GOAL Use a graphing calculator to graph non-linear functions.

> **Example** **Use a graphing calculator to compare the functions.**
>
> $$y_1 = x^2 \qquad y_2 = 2x^2 \qquad y_3 = 3x^2 \qquad y_4 = 4x^2$$

HELP with **Technology**

You may need to adjust your viewing window in order to see the graphs.

Solution

Use the following keystrokes to enter the functions into a graphing calculator:

ANSWER The graphs are curves that pass through $(0, 0)$. As the coefficient of x^2 increases, the curve gets narrower.

> **Your turn now** **Graph the functions using a graphing calculator. Describe the pattern in the graphs.**
>
> **1.** $y = x^2 + 5$ **2.** $y = x^2 - 5$ **3.** $y = x^2 + 7$ **4.** $y = x^2 - 7$
>
> **Graph the functions. Describe the pattern in the graphs.**
>
> **5.** $y = -x^2$ **6.** $y = -2x^2$ **7.** $y = -3x^2$ **8.** $y = -4x^2$

Notebook Review

Review the vocabulary definitions in your notebook.

Copy the review examples in your notebook. Then complete the exercises.

Check Your Definitions

function notation, p. 680   vertical line test, p. 681

Use Your Vocabulary

Copy and complete the statement.

1. The equation $f(x) = 7x - 4$ is written using _?_ .

2. The _?_ helps you tell whether a graph represents a function.

Write the function using function notation.

3. $y = 5x - 12$ **4.** $y = 2x^3 + 8$ **5.** $y = x^3 + 3x^2 - 10$

6. Draw a graph that is *not* a function. Use the vertical line test to show why your graph is *not* a function.

13.4 Can you multiply binomials?

 EXAMPLE Find the product and simplify.

a. $(4x - 7)(2x + 3)$

$4x - 7$	Write the first binomial.
$\times 2x + 3$	Write the second binomial.
$12x - 21$	Multiply $3(4x - 7)$.
$8x^2 - 14x$	Multiply $2x(4x - 7)$. Line up like terms.
$8x^2 - 2x - 21$	Add $12x - 21$ and $8x^2 - 14x$.

b. $(x + 3)(x + 2)$

$= x(x + 2) + 3(x + 2)$ Distributive property

$= x^2 + 2x + 3x + 6$ Distributive property

$= x^2 + 5x + 6$ Combine like terms.

☑ **Find the product and simplify.**

7. $(x + 5)(x + 7)$ **8.** $(g + 10)(g - 2)$ **9.** $(y - 4)(3y - 1)$

13.5 Can you graph non-linear functions?

 EXAMPLE Graph $f(x) = -2x^2 + 5$.

Choose several x-values and make a table of values.

x	-2	-1	0	1	2
$f(x)$	-3	3	5	3	-3

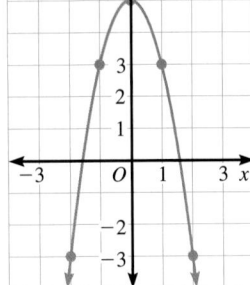

List the solutions as ordered pairs.
$(-2, -3), (-1, 3), (0, 5), (1, 3), (2, -3)$

Graph the ordered pairs. Draw a smooth curve through them, as shown.

☑ **Graph the function using a table of values.**

10. $f(x) = 3x^2$ **11.** $f(x) = -x^2 + 3$ **12.** $f(x) = 2x^2 - 6$

Stop *and* **Think**   about Lessons 13.4–13.5

13. Writing Explain how you can use the vertical line test to tell whether a graph represents a function.

Review Quiz 2

Find the product and simplify.

1. $(x - 1)(x + 9)$ **2.** $(a + 4)(a + 9)$ **3.** $(m - 2)(m - 8)$

4. $(4y + 5)(y - 2)$ **5.** $(b + 3)(4b - 3)$ **6.** $(3z - 2)(2z - 7)$

Rewrite using function notation.

7. $y = 3x + 9$ **8.** $y = -2x^2 - 4$ **9.** $y = 19 - x + x^2$

Evaluate the function for $x = -2, -1, 0, 1,$ and 2.

10. $f(x) = 2 - x^2$ **11.** $f(x) = \frac{1}{2}x^2 - 6$ **12.** $f(x) = x^2 + x$

Graph the function using a table of values.

13. $f(x) = -x^2 + 1$ **14.** $f(x) = \frac{1}{4}x^2$ **15.** $f(x) = -3x^2 - 4$

13 Chapter Review

 Vocabulary

polynomial, p. 657   trinomial, p. 657   function notation, p. 680
binomial, p. 657   standard form, p. 657   vertical line test, p. 681

Vocabulary Review

Copy and complete the statement.

1. The polynomial $x^3 - 2x + 1$ is a ___?___ .

2. A polynomial is written in ___?___ if the exponents of the variable decrease from left to right.

3. You can use the ___?___ to tell whether a graph represents a function.

Classify the polynomial as a *monomial*, a *binomial*, or a *trinomial*.

4. $5x^3 + 2x + 3$ **5.** $5a^3$ **6.** $5y + 3$ **7.** $-r + 3$

Review Questions

Write the polynomial in standard form. *(Lesson 13.1)*

8. $7 - 2a^2 + 10a$ **9.** $5x - 3x^3 - 4 + x^2$ **10.** $4 + 7y^2 - 8y^3 + y$

11. $9t + 8 - t^2 + 6t^3$ **12.** $9 + 2m^5 + m^2 - m^4$ **13.** $25 + n^2 - 3n^4 + 5n$

Simplify the polynomial and write it in standard form. *(Lesson 13.1)*

14. $8k + 1 + 3k + k^2 - 4$ **15.** $5w - 2w + 2w^2 - 8$ **16.** $6p^2 + 9(2p^3 + 3 + p^2)$

17. $3x^2 + 4(7 - x^2 + 4x)$ **18.** $-8(2s - 3s^2 + 7) + 4s^3$ **19.** $4(5y - 2y^2 + 11) - 2y^2$

Find the sum or difference. *(Lesson 13.2)*

20. $(10q^2 - 6) + (q^2 + 1)$ **21.** $(2p^2 + 9p) - (5p^2 + 9p)$

22. $(3x^2 - x + 7) - (6x^2 + 4x - 11)$ **23.** $(7y^2 + y - 4) + (y^2 - y - 1)$

24. $4(m^2 - 3m) + 5(2m^2 - m)$ **25.** $-2(v^3 - v^2 + v) - 3(v^3 + 4v^2)$

Review Questions

Simplify the expression. *(Lesson 13.3)*

26. $(3r^2)^3$

27. $(2xy)^3$

28. $(7z)(-4z)^2$

29. $(-6a^2b^4)^3$

30. $(-c^3)(2c^4)$

31. $(-9n)(-7p^2)^4$

Simplify the expression. *(Lesson 13.3)*

32. $x^2(5x - 7)$

33. $-3a(a^2 - 2a)$

34. $4y(6y^2 - 8y)$

35. $-y^3(-y^2 + 11y)$

36. $7b(14 - 6b^2)$

37. $-6g(3g^2 + 10g)$

Write a polynomial expression for the area of the figure and simplify. *(Lesson 13.3)*

38.

$2x$

$x + 4$

39.
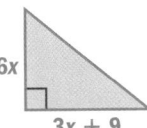
$6x$

$3x + 9$

40.

$x - 5$

$4x$

Find the product and simplify. *(Lesson 13.4)*

41. $(t + 3)(t - 4)$

42. $(2x + 3)(x + 5)$

43. $(q - 7)(q - 9)$

44. $(m - 4)(m - 5)$

45. $(3d + 8)(d - 6)$

46. $(h + 3)(2h - 5)$

47. $(2k - 9)(-4k - 1)$

48. $(2n + 6)(3n - 12)$

49. $(-2b + 1)(-b - 4)$

50. Write a polynomial expression for the area of the swimming pool's walkway and simplify. The walkway is x ft wide. *(Lesson 13.4)*

x

x

25 ft

50 ft

Graph the function using a table of values. *(Lesson 13.5)*

51. $f(x) = x^2 + 3$

52. $f(x) = 7 - x^2$

53. $f(x) = x^2 - 4$

54. $f(x) = 3x^2 + 1$

Tell whether the graph represents a function. *(Lesson 13.5)*

55.

56.

57.

Chapter Test

Simplify the polynomial and write it in standard form.

1. $10x - 7x + 4 + x^2 - 3x + 4$

2. $-y + 6(y^2 - y^3 + 1)$

3. Apple Picking An apple falls from a 28 foot tall tree. The height of the apple, in feet, after t seconds of falling, can be found using the polynomial $-16t^2 + 28$. Find the apple's height after 0.5 second.

Find the sum or difference.

4. $(3r^2 + 4r - 7) + (-r^2 - r + 11)$

5. $(4s^2 - 11s) - (s^2 - 6s + 21)$

6. $(4a^5 - a) + (-3a^5 + 1)$

7. $(-y^2 + 12) + (8y^2 - 10)$

8. $(5x^6 - 3x^2 + x) - (4x^2 + 2x)$

9. $(-7z^3 + z^2 - 5) - (z^3 - 3z^2 + 1)$

10. Perimeter Write a polynomial expression for the perimeter of the triangle. Simplify the polynomial.

Simplify the expression.

11. $(3a^2)(5a^2b)$

12. $(9z)^2$

13. $(3d^2)^4$

14. $(-2w^4)^3$

15. $(-2p^2)^4$

16. $(x^4y)^8$

17. $(4n^2)(-3n)$

18. $(3r)^3(3r)$

Find the product and simplify.

19. $m^2(3m^2 + 8m)$

20. $7n(n^2 - 2n)$

21. $3p(2p^2 + 3p)$

22. $(2x + 7)(3x + 2)$

23. $(4y + 12)(y - 3)$

24. $(z - 9)(5z + 8)$

Graph the function using a table of values.

25. $f(x) = -5x^2$

26. $f(x) = x^2 + 3$

27. $f(x) = x^2 - 1$

Tell whether the graph represents a function.

28.

29.

30.

Chapter FCAT Practice

FCAT

Test-Taking Strategy Think positively during a test. This will help you keep up
your confidence and enable you to focus on each question.

Multiple Choice

1. Simplify the polynomial and write it in standard form.
$$8 - 7x^2 + 3x^3 + 2x^2 - 1$$
A. $7 - 5x^2 + 3x^3$ **B.** $3x^3 + 5x^2 + 7$

C. $3x^3 - 5x^2 + 7$ **D.** $7 + 5x^2 + 3x^3$

2. Find the sum.
$$(5x^2 + 5x - 6) + (3x^2 - x - 10)$$
F. $8x^2 + 4x - 16$ **G.** $8x^2 + 4x - 4$

H. $8x^2 - 4x - 16$ **I.** $8x^2 + 4x + 4$

3. Find the difference.
$$(3x^2 - 4x + 4) - (x^2 + 3x + 4)$$
A. $2x^2 - x$ **B.** $2x^2 - 7x$

C. $2x^2 + x + 8$ **D.** $2x^2 - 7x + 8$

4. Simplify $9x(x^2 - 3x - 7)$.
F. $9x^3 - 27x^2 + 63$

G. $9x^3 - 27x^2 - 63x$

H. $9x^2 + 27x - 63$

I. $9x^2 + 27x + 63x$

5. Simplify the expression $(-4n^3)^2$.
A. $16n^6$ **B.** $16n^5$ **C.** $64n^5$ **D.** $64n^6$

6. Simplify the expression $(3x^3)(x^2y)$.
F. $3x^6y$ **G.** $3xy^5$ **H.** $3x^5y$ **I.** $3x^5y^3$

7. Simplify the expression $(3pq)^2$.
A. $9pq^2$ **B.** $6p^2q$ **C.** $6pq^2$ **D.** $9p^2q^2$

8. Find the product $(x + 5)(x - 3)$ and simplify.
F. $x^2 + 8x - 15$ **G.** $x^2 - 2x - 15$

H. $x^2 + 2x - 15$ **I.** $x^2 - 8x - 8$

9. You deposit $15 into a savings account with interest compounded annually. The account balance after 2 years is given by the expression $15(r + 1)^2$. Expand this expression and simplify.
A. $15r^2 + 2r + 15$ **B.** $15r^2 + 15r + 1$

C. $15r^2 + 30r + 1$ **D.** $15r^2 + 30r + 15$

10. Find the value of the function for $x = -3$.
$$f(x) = -2x^2 + 6$$
F. -12 **G.** -6 **H.** 18 **I.** 24

Short Response

11. Write an expression for the area of the rectangle. Simplify the expression, and write it in standard form.

Extended Response

12. Graph each function using a table of values. Explain how the graphs are different.
$$f(x) = x^2$$
$$f(x) = x^2 + 1$$
$$f(x) = x^2 + 2$$

Describe the graph of the function $f(x) = x^2 + 125$.

Strategies for Answering
Extended Response Questions

Problem

A tank contains 30 gallons of water. You pull out the drain plug, and water begins to flow from the tank at a rate of 4 gallons per minute. Make a table and draw a graph that shows the amount of water in the tank as the water drains. After how much time will the tank contain exactly 16 gallons of water? Give your answer in minutes and seconds. Explain how you found your answer.

Full credit solution

In the graph, the horizontal axis shows minutes after pulling the plug, and the vertical axis shows the gallons of water in the tank.

The table and graph are correct and reflect an understanding of the problem.

minutes	gallons
0	30
1	26
2	22
3	18
4	14
5	10
6	6
7	2

The answer is correct.

After 3 minutes and 30 seconds, the tank will contain 16 gallons of water.

The reasoning behind the answer is explained clearly.

To find my answer, I looked at the graph and saw that the tank will hold 16 gallons at $3\frac{1}{2}$ minutes. Because $\frac{1}{2}$ of a minute equals 30 seconds, I know that the tank will hold 16 gallons of water after 3 minutes and 30 seconds.

Partial credit solution

The table and graph are correct.

minutes	0	1	2	3	4
gallons	30	26	22	18	14

The answer is incorrect.

The tank will hold 16 gallons after 3 minutes and 5 seconds. The graph shows that there are 16 gallons after 3.5 minutes.

No credit solution

The table is correct, but there is no graph.

minutes	0	1	2	3	4
gallons	30	26	22	18	14

The answer is incorrect, and there is no explanation.

The tank will never have exactly 16 gallons in it.

Watch Out!

Scoring is often based on how clearly you explain your reasoning.

Your turn now

1. Score one student's answer to the problem on page 692 as *full credit*, *partial credit*, or *no credit*. Explain your choice. If you choose *partial credit* or *no credit*, explain how to change the answer so that it earns *full credit*.

minutes	0	1	2	3	4
gallons	30	26	22	18	14

The tank will have 16 gallons after 3 minutes and 30 seconds. The table shows that the tank will have 16 gallons between 3 and 4 minutes. 16 is halfway between 14 and 18. So, the tank must have 16 gallons halfway between 3 and 4 minutes. The tank has 16 gallons at 3 minutes and 30 seconds.

Extended Response

1. The scatter plot shows the average science scores and average math scores on a state test at several schools.

   What type of relationship does the scatter plot show?

   Copy the scatter plot and draw a curve that shows the overall pattern of the data.

   Estimate the average math score at a school whose average science score is 530.

2. Five bands have offered to play at a school dance. Only two bands will be selected to play. You will decide which band plays first and which band plays second by randomly picking letters from a bag. The bands are represented by the letters A, B, C, D, and E.

   Make a tree diagram to show all possible ways that two bands can play at the dance.

   How many possibilities are there?

   Find the probability that band C will play first, followed by band B.

3. The table shows the number of residents of the Gulf States who were 5 to 17 years old in 2000.

   Is a bar graph an appropriate display for the data? Explain why or why not.

   Is a line graph an appropriate display for the data? Explain why or why not.

   Make a circle graph to display each state's youth population as a fraction of the total youth population of the Gulf States in 2000.

Gulf State Population in 2000	
State	**Population aged 5 to 17 years (in thousands)**
Texas	4262
Louisiana	902
Alabama	827
Mississippi	1924
Florida	2701

4. A ball of foam is dropped from a building. The height of the ball, in feet, is found using the function $h = -16t^2 + 100$, where t is the number of seconds that pass after the ball is dropped.

   Write the function using function notation.

   Graph the function using a table of values.

   After how many seconds does the ball hit the ground? Use your graph to estimate.

Multiple Choice

5. What is the slope of the graph of the equation $3x - 2y = 4$?

A. -2 **B.** $-\dfrac{3}{2}$ **C.** $\dfrac{3}{2}$ **D.** 3

6. You choose the reading order of students in a poetry contest at random. Each student reads only once. There are 6 girls and 4 boys in the contest. You choose a girl to read first. What is the probability that the second person chosen is a boy?

F. $\dfrac{2}{5}$ **G.** $\dfrac{4}{9}$ **H.** $\dfrac{3}{5}$ **I.** $\dfrac{2}{3}$

7. Simplify the expression $(4m^3n^5)^2$.

A. $8m^5n^7$ **B.** $8m^6n^{10}$

C. $16m^5n^7$ **D.** $16m^6n^{10}$

8. What is the value of $f(x)$ for $x = 5$?

x	1	2	3	4	5
$f(x)$	1	5	9	13	?

F. 8 **G.** 11 **H.** 15 **I.** 17

9. The box-and-whisker plot shows the prices of couches at a furniture store. What does the value $762 represent on the box-and-whisker plot?

A. lower extreme **B.** lower quartile

C. median **D.** upper quartile

Short Response

10. You sell tickets to a school play. You make $120 total. In the equation $8x + 4y = 120$, x is the number of adult tickets you sell, and y is the number of student tickets. Find the x- and y-intercepts of the graph of the equation. Then graph the equation. What do the intercepts represent?

11. The data show the number of games played by each of the basketball players on the Orlando Magic during a recent season.

76, 14, 63, 82, 81, 80, 76, 68, 65, 9, 53, 10, 68, 61, 60, 7, 7

Make a stem-and-leaf plot of the data. What interval includes the most values? Explain.

12. A school has a rotating schedule. Find the number of ways to schedule the classes Math, Science, English, History, and Language. Explain your answer.

13. Plot the points (1, 4) and (3, 0) in a coordinate plane, and draw a line through the points. Find the slope of the line. Use your graph to find the y-intercept of the line. Write an equation of the line.

14. Find the sum of the polynomials. Explain your steps.

$(4x^4 + 5x^3 - 13) + (2x^4 + 5x^2 - 4x + 7)$

15. Draw a graph that represents a function. Then draw a graph that does *not* represent a function. Explain your reasoning.

Cumulative Practice for Chapters 11–13

Chapter 11

Multiple Choice **In Exercises 1–7, choose the letter of the correct answer.**

1. Which of the following relations is *not* a function? *(Lesson 11.1)*

   A. (1, −3), (2, −1), (3, 1), (4, 3)

   B. (5, 5), (1, −1), (3, 6), (−1, −1)

   C. (1, 5), (3, 0), (2, −5), (3, −3)

   D. (−4, 2), (−1, 1), (2, 2), (−3, 3)

2. The scatter plot shows the numbers of minutes students spent on homework and their quiz score. What conclusion can you make? *(Lesson 11.2)*

   F. The more time a student spent on homework, the higher the quiz score.

   G. The less time a student spent on homework, the higher the quiz score.

   H. There is no relationship.

   I. The more time a student spent on homework, the less the student slept.

3. Which ordered pair is a solution of the equation $y = -3x + 4$? *(Lesson 11.3)*

   A. (−2, −2)   **B.** (−2, 10)

   C. (−4, −8)   **D.** (8, 9)

4. Which equation is *not* linear? *(Lesson 11.4)*

   F. $y = -3x + 7$ **G.** $y = x^5 - 5$

   H. $4x + 3y = 9$ **I.** $5x = 7 - 3y$

5. What is the y-intercept of the graph of the equation $9x + 2y = 18$? *(Lesson 11.5)*

   A. −9   **B.** −2   **C.** 2   **D.** 9

6. What is the slope of the line? *(Lesson 11.6)*

   F. −2

   G. $-\dfrac{1}{2}$

   H. $\dfrac{1}{2}$

   I. 2

7. Which ordered pair is a solution of $4x + 3y < 8$? *(Lesson 11.8)*

   A. (1, 3)   **B.** (2, 4)   **C.** (1, 1)   **D.** (−3, 7)

8. **Short Response** Write a function rule that relates x and y. *(Lesson 11.1)*

Input x	−2	0	2	4
Output y	5	15	25	35

9. **Extended Response** Balloons cost $7 per dozen. It costs $5 to have balloons delivered. *(Lesson 11.7)*

   a. Graph the equation $y = 7x + 5$, where x is the number of dozens ordered, to see the possible costs of a balloon delivery order.

   b. You have $40 to spend on a balloon delivery. How many balloons can you buy?

Chapter 12

The stem-and-leaf plot shows the number of home runs for each player on a softball team. Use the plot for Exercises 10–11. *(Lesson 12.1)*

0	3 5 6 7
1	1 3 5 6 8
2	2 3 4 4

Key: 2│3 = 23

10. What is the greatest number of home runs hit by one player?

A. 19   **B.** 24   **C.** 42   **D.** 68

11. What is the median number of home runs?

F. 5   **G.** 15   **H.** 24   **I.** 51

The box-and-whisker plot shows the numbers of cards in baseball card collections. Use the plot for Exercises 12–13. *(Lesson 12.2)*

12. What is the greatest number of cards in a collection?

A. 15   **B.** 20   **C.** 25   **D.** 30

13. What is the median number of cards?

F. 5   **G.** 10   **H.** 15   **I.** 20

14. The line graph shows the numbers of CD sales made. Which year shows the greatest increase in CD sales? *(Lesson 12.3)*

A. 2000

B. 2001

C. 2002

D. 2003

CD sales (thousands) / Year

15. You have 4 kinds of cheese, 5 kinds of meat, 3 kinds of bread, and 2 kinds of pickles. How many different sandwiches can you make using one type each of cheese, meat, bread, and pickle? *(Lesson 12.4)*

F. 4   **G.** 14   **H.** 60   **I.** 120

16. Six speed skaters are racing. Trophies are awarded to the people who come in first, second, and third place. In how many different ways can the trophies be awarded? *(Lesson 12.5)*

A. 3   **B.** 20   **C.** 120   **D.** 720

17. There are 12 apples and 8 oranges in a fruit basket. You randomly choose a piece of fruit. What is the probability that you choose an orange? *(Lesson 12.7)*

F. $\frac{1}{20}$ **G.** $\frac{1}{5}$ **H.** $\frac{2}{5}$ **I.** $\frac{3}{5}$

18. You roll a number cube once. What are the odds in favor of rolling a six? *(Lesson 12.7)*

A. $\frac{1}{6}$ **B.** $\frac{1}{5}$ **C.** $\frac{1}{4}$ **D.** $\frac{1}{3}$

19. A bag contains 24 blue buttons and 16 red buttons. You draw a button at random, replace it, and draw a second button. What is the probability of drawing a red button and then a blue button? *(Lesson 12.8)*

F. $\frac{46}{195}$ **G.** $\frac{6}{25}$ **H.** $\frac{2}{5}$ **I.** $\frac{3}{5}$

20. A bag contains the letters of the word *Tallahassee.* You draw one letter at random, do not replace it, and then draw a second letter. What is the probability that you draw the letter *s* twice? *(Lesson 12.8)*

A. $\frac{2}{121}$ **B.** $\frac{1}{55}$ **C.** $\frac{4}{121}$ **D.** $\frac{2}{55}$

GO ON

Cumulative Practice continued

21. Short Response A group of 12 people have dinner together. They sit at 2 tables of 6. How many different groups can sit at one table? How many ways can the group split into 2 tables? Explain your answers. *(Lesson 12.6)*

22. Extended Response The ten fastest fish in the world are listed below, each with its fastest known speed, in miles per hour.

Sailfish	68	Blue Shark	43
Swordfish	40	Marlin	50
Bluefin Tuna	46	Wahoo	41
Tarpon	35	Bonefish	40
Yellowfin Tuna	44	Tiger Shark	33

a. Use an appropriate display to represent the data.

b. Explain your choice of display.

c. Identify a type of display that is not a good choice for the data. Explain why it is not a good choice.

Chapter 13

Multiple Choice In Exercises 23–29, choose the letter of the correct answer.

23. Simplify the polynomial. *(Lesson 13.1)*
$3(x^2 + 2x + 4) - 2x$

A. $3x^2 + 4x + 12$ **B.** $3x^2 + 6x + 12$

C. $3x^2 - 4x + 12$ **D.** $3x^2 - 6x + 12$

24. What is the value of $-4x^2 - 3x + 7$ for $x = 3$? *(Lesson 13.1)*

F. -38 **G.** -26 **H.** -14 **I.** 34

25. Find the sum $(4x - 5) + (2x + 5)$. *(Lesson 13.2)*

A. $6x$ **B.** $x - 10$ **C.** $2x$ **D.** $6x + 10$

26. Find the difference. *(Lesson 13.2)*
$(x^2 - 2x + 5) - (2x^2 + x - 4)$

F. $3x - x - 1$ **G.** $-x^2 - 3x + 9$

H. $-x^2 + x - 1$ **I.** $3x - x + 1$

27. Simplify the expression $(4a^2)(6a + 2)$. *(Lesson 13.3)*

A. $24a^3 + 8a^2$ **B.** $10a^3 + 6a^2$

C. $24a^2 + 8a$ **D.** $24a^2 + 8$

28. Simplify the expression $(2y^2)^4$. *(Lesson 13.3)*

F. $2y^8$ **G.** $8y^6$ **H.** $16y^6$ **I.** $16y^8$

29. Find the product and simplify. *(Lesson 13.4)*
$(2x - 3)(x - 2)$

A. $2x^2 + 6$ **B.** $2x^2 + 7x - 6$

C. $2x^2 - 6$ **D.** $2x^2 - 7x + 6$

30. Short Response A pecan falls from a tree 100 feet off the ground. The polynomial $-16t^2 + 100$ gives the pecan's height, in feet, after t seconds of falling. Find its height after 1 second and 2 seconds. Estimate how many seconds the pecan falls before hitting the ground. *(Lesson 13.1)*

31. Extended Response Use your graphs to look for a pattern. *(Lesson 13.5)*

a. Graph each function in a coordinate plane.

$$f(x) = 2x^2 - 6$$
$$f(x) = 2x^2 - 8$$
$$f(x) = 2x^2 - 10$$

b. Describe the graph of the function $f(x) = 2x^2 - 50$.

Algebra, Integers, and Equation Solving

1. The table shows the number of visits to your Web site for five days. Make a bar graph of the data.

Days	Mon	Tues	Wed	Thurs	Fri
Visits	12	18	21	25	28

Evaluate the expression.

2. $8 \cdot 4 + 3 \cdot 5$

3. $46 - 25 + 8 \div 2$

4. $(3 + 1)^3 \div 8 - 2$

5. $7a - 4$ when $a = 2$

6. $\dfrac{9}{2y - 5}$ when $y = 4$

7. x^4 when $x = 5$

Use a number line to order the integers from least to greatest.

8. $65, -13, 19, 61, -19, 34$

9. $878, 433, -602, 1074, -1222$

Find the sum, difference, product, or quotient.

10. $-61 + (-44)$

11. $-13 + 8 + (-6)$

12. $-49 - (-16)$

13. $85 - (-18) - 12$

14. $5(-8)$

15. $-9(-6)(-4)$

16. $\dfrac{-64}{8}$

17. $\dfrac{-55}{-11}$

18. In a local school committee election, 250 votes were cast for two candidates. Candidate A won the election by 10 votes. How many votes did Candidate A receive?

19. Plot and connect points $A(-10, 12)$, $B(10, 12)$, $C(10, -12)$, and $D(-10, -12)$. Identify the figure. Then find the perimeter and area of the figure.

Simplify the expression by combining like terms.

20. $6y + 5y$

21. $8a - 6b + a$

22. $6(x - 7) + 4x + 3$

23. $3(2x + y) - (8 + 5x)$

Solve the equation.

24. $49 = d + 12$

25. $b - 18 = 12$

26. $8 = \dfrac{56}{x}$

27. $15 = \dfrac{x}{5}$

28. $4b = -64$

29. $-6x = 72$

30. $5b + 9 = 18$

31. $-21 = 19 - 4x$

Solve the inequality. Then graph the solution.

32. $b + 6 \le 12$

33. $6 > 8 + t$

34. $-\dfrac{1}{6}a < 24$

35. $8 \ge -\dfrac{1}{4}x$

Algebra and Rational Numbers

36. Write the following fractions in simplest form: $\frac{12}{26}, \frac{18}{54}, \frac{16}{82}, \frac{24}{84}$.

Find the GCF and LCM of the numbers.

37. 12, 16, 48   **38.** 16, 32, 64   **39.** 45, 90, 180   **40.** 10, 15, 50

Simplify. Write the expression using only positive exponents.

41. $y^6 \cdot y^4$ **42.** $x^{-7} \cdot x^5$ **43.** $\dfrac{x^{18}}{x^{11}}$ **44.** $y^8 \cdot y^{-5}$

Find the sum, difference, product, or quotient.

45. $\dfrac{13}{24} + \left(-\dfrac{7}{24}\right)$ **46.** $-2\dfrac{2}{5} - 2\dfrac{2}{5}$ **47.** $8\dfrac{1}{2} + 5\dfrac{1}{4}$ **48.** $11\dfrac{2}{9} - 14\dfrac{1}{2}$

49. $5\dfrac{1}{4} \cdot \left(-4\dfrac{1}{5}\right)$ **50.** $-3\dfrac{1}{3} \cdot \left(-8\dfrac{4}{5}\right)$ **51.** $1\dfrac{1}{2} \div \left(-3\dfrac{3}{8}\right)$ **52.** $5\dfrac{1}{9} \div 2\dfrac{4}{7}$

53. $7.9 + (-2.344)$ **54.** $-8.1 - (-4.06)$ **55.** $14.66 \cdot 2.1$ **56.** $4.844 \div (-0.56)$

57. Order the numbers from least to greatest: $8\dfrac{2}{3}$, 8.5, 13.35, $7\dfrac{2}{3}$, $8\dfrac{9}{20}$, $8.\overline{6}$, 7.7. Then find the mean, median, and mode(s) of the numbers.

Solve the equation or inequality.

58. $3(b - 9) = -39$ **59.** $-6 = 11a - 5a$ **60.** $3x = 9(x - 1)$ **61.** $6(y - 4) = 3(y + 9)$

62. $\dfrac{1}{6}n + \dfrac{2}{3}n = 1$ **63.** $5.9 + c = 3c - 2.1$ **64.** $5a + 8 \geq 12$ **65.** $-2(d + 4) < -4$

66. $\dfrac{2}{9} = \dfrac{10}{a}$ **67.** $\dfrac{x}{4} = \dfrac{21}{12}$ **68.** $\dfrac{45}{15} = \dfrac{y}{1}$ **69.** $\dfrac{12}{15} = \dfrac{p}{100}$

Write the number as a percent, as a decimal, and as a fraction.

70. 22.5%   **71.** 0.37   **72.** $\dfrac{13}{20}$ **73.** 0.1%

74. You buy a stereo for $74 plus 8% sales tax. What is your total cost?

75. What is 0.5% of 65? Five is what percent of 125?

76. You draw a tile randomly from a bag that contains 12 B tiles, 6 C tiles, 8 D tiles, and 5 A tiles. What is the probability that you draw a D?

Geometry and Measurement

77. ∠1 and ∠2 are complementary, and $m\angle 1 = 74°$. Find $m\angle 2$.

Find the value of x. Then classify the figure.

78.

79.

80.

81. Draw △ABC in the coordinate plane with vertices $A(2, 5)$, $B(2, 2)$, and $C(6, 2)$. Draw △DEF congruent to △ABC. Then translate △DEF using $(x, y) \longrightarrow (x - 4, y - 7)$. Identify the coordinates of △DEF and △$D'E'F'$.

82. Find the following square roots: $-\sqrt{2}$, $\sqrt{121}$, $\sqrt{81}$, $-\sqrt{400}$

83. Is $\sqrt{\dfrac{4}{81}}$ a rational or irrational number? $\sqrt{18}$? Explain.

A right triangle has leg lengths a and b and a hypotenuse of length c. Find the unknown length. Then find the triangle's area and perimeter.

84. $a = 12$ cm, $b = 5$ cm, $c = ?$

85. $a = 12$ ft, $b = 16$ ft, $c = ?$

Find the value of each variable. Give exact answers.

86.

87.

88.

89. Find the area of a trapezoid with bases of 18 feet and 12 feet and a height of 5 feet.

90. What is the area of a circle with a radius of 5 feet? with a diameter of 12 centimeters? Use 3.14 for π.

Find the surface area and volume of the solid. Use 3.14 for π.

91.

92.

93.

Advanced Algebra Topics

94. Make tables of values for the functions $y = 2x$ and $y = x - 2$. Use a domain of $-2, -1, 0, 1,$ and 2. Identify the range of each function.

95. Make a scatter plot of $(1, 4), (2, 8), (3, 12),$ and $(4, 16)$. Describe the relationship between the variables. Then find the next ordered pair.

Graph the equation. Identify the intercepts of the graph.

96. $y = 2x - 12$ **97.** $y = 4 - 3x$ **98.** $y = -x + 17$ **99.** $y = -5x - 6$

100. $y = -\frac{1}{2}x + 5$ **101.** $y = -6x + 8$ **102.** $x + 9y = 18$ **103.** $y = 2x + 4$

104. Find the slope of the line passing through the points $(5,8)$ and $(0,5)$.

105. Rewrite $y + 12x = 6$ and $13x - 11y = 12$ in slope-intercept form. Then find the slope and the y-intercept of the graph of each equation.

106. Tell whether $(-8, -9)$ is a solution of the inequality $12x - 16y \geq 34$.

Make a stem-and-leaf plot and a box-and-whisker plot of the data.

107. 46, 49, 66, 51, 68, 83, 78, 64   **108.** \$68, \$63, \$51, \$43, \$53, \$38, \$60, \$66

109. In an election poll, 32% preferred Atkins, 47% preferred Liu, and 21% were undecided. Make a circle graph of the data.

110. You can choose from 3 sandwiches, 4 drinks, and 2 snacks. How many different sandwich-drink-snack groupings are possible?

Evaluate.

111. $_{18}P_2$ **112.** $_{14}P_3$ **113.** $_9C_6$ **114.** $_8C_5$

115. You roll a number cube. What are the odds of getting an odd number?

Simplify the polynomial and write it in standard form.

116. $4x^2 - 5x - 2x^2 + 7x$ **117.** $-3x^2 + 3x - x + 7$

Simplify the expression.

118. $(x^2 - 2x + 5) + (x^2 - 4)$ **119.** $(5y^2 - y - 1) - (y^2 + 4y)$ **120.** $(3x^2 - 4x + 2) + (x^2 + 6x - 5)$

121. $(6x)(8x^6)$ **122.** $(8y)^3$ **123.** $(x^6)^3$

124. $(n - 3)(n - 3)$ **125.** $(4x - 2)(8x - 3)$ **126.** $(12b - 4)(8b + 3)$

127. Graph $f(x) = x^2 + 6$. Use a table of values with $x = 2, 1, 0, -1,$ and -2.

Contents of Student Resources

Skills Review Handbook   704

Number Sense
- Place Value, *704*
- Rounding, *705*
- Divisibility Tests, *706*
- Mixed Numbers and Improper Fractions, *707*
- Ratio and Rate, *708*

Number Operations
- Adding and Subtracting Decimals, *709*
- Adding and Subtracting Fractions, *710*
- Estimation in Addition and Subtraction, *711*
- Solving Problems Using Addition and Subtraction, *712*
- Multiplying Fractions, *713*
- Multiplication of a Decimal by a Whole Number, *714*
- Dividing Decimals, *715*
- Estimation in Multiplication and Division, *716*
- Solving Problems Using Multiplication and Division, *717*

Measurement and Geometry
- Points, Lines, and Planes, *718*
- Angles, *719*
- Using a Ruler, *720*
- Using a Protractor, *721*
- Using a Compass, *722*

Data Analysis
- Reading and Making Line Plots, *723*
- Reading and Making Bar Graphs, *724*
- Reading and Making Line Graphs, *725*
- Venn Diagrams and Logical Reasoning, *726*

Extra Practice   727
Chapters 1–13

Tables   740
Symbols, Measures, Formulas, Properties, Squares and Square Roots, Equivalent Fractions, Decimals, and Percents

Glossary   747

Index   773

Credits   796

Selected Answers   SA1

Skills Review Handbook

Place Value

The **whole numbers** are the numbers 0, 1, 2, 3, ... A **digit** is any of the numbers 0, 1, 2, 3, 4, 5, 6, 7, 8, or 9. The decimals are numbers such as 121.32, 25.6, and 3.456. For example, the decimal 4.5 has the digits 4 and 5. The place value of each digit in a whole number or a decimal depends on its position within the number. For example, in the number 491,037.892, the 8 has a value of 0.8 or 8×0.1 because it is in the tenths' place.

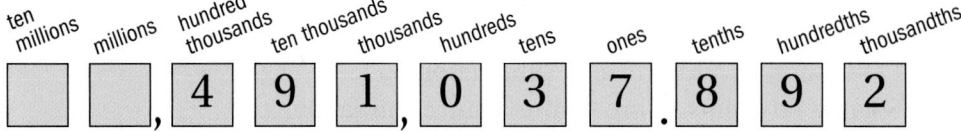

ten millions | millions | hundred thousands | ten thousands | thousands | hundreds | tens | ones | tenths | hundredths | thousandths

, 4 9 1 , 0 3 7 . 8 9 2

EXAMPLE Write the number 27,037.6 in expanded form.

$27{,}037.6 = 20{,}000 + 7000 + 30 + 7 + 0.6$ The zero in the hundreds' position is a placeholder.

$= 2 \times 10{,}000 + 7 \times 1000 + 3 \times 10 + 7 \times 1 + 6 \times 0.1$

EXAMPLE Write the number in standard form.

a. $4 \times 1000 + 5 \times 10 + 6 \times 0.1 + 8 \times 0.01$

b. Four million, sixty thousand, five and two thousandths

Solution

a. $4 \times 1000 + 5 \times 10 + 6 \times 0.1 + 8 \times 0.01 = 4000 + 50 + 0.6 + 0.08$

$= 4050.68$

b. Write 4 in the millions' place, 6 in the ten thousands' place, 5 in the ones' place, and the 2 in the thousandths' place. Use zeros as placeholders for the other places. The answer is 4,060,005.002.

Practice

Write the number in expanded form.

1. 56,809 **2.** 3.075 **3.** 1002.003 **4.** 306.405

Write the number in standard form.

5. $5 \times 100{,}000 + 6 \times 10 + 9 \times 1 + 7 \times 0.001$ **6.** Five million, ten and thirty-six thousandths

Rounding

To **round** a number means to approximate the number to a given place value. When rounding, look at the digit to the right of that place value. If the digit to the right is less than 5 (0, 1, 2, 3, or 4), round down. If the digit to the right is 5 or greater (5, 6, 7, 8, or 9), round up.

EXAMPLE Round the number to the place value of the red digit.

    a. 6932   **b.** 45.674

Solution

   a. Because the 9 is in the hundreds' place, round 6932 to the nearest hundred. Notice that 6932 is between 6900 and 7000, so it will round to one of these two numbers.

                                 Notice that 6932 is closer to 6900 than to 7000.

     The digit to the right of the 9 in the hundreds' place is the 3 in the tens' place. Because 3 is less than 5, round down.

     ANSWER 6932 rounded to the nearest hundred is 6900.

   b. Because 6 is in the tenths' place, round 45.674 to the nearest tenth. Notice that 45.674 is between 45.6 and 45.7, so it will round to one of these two numbers.

                                 Notice that 45.674 is closer to 45.7 than to 45.6.

     The digit to the right of the 6 in the tenths' place is the 7 in the hundredths' place. Because 7 is 5 or greater, round up.

     ANSWER 45.674 rounded to the nearest tenth is 45.7.

● Practice

Round the number to the place value of the red digit.

  1. 1253   **2.** 57,309   **3.** 8.183   **4.** 32.76   **5.** 44,380

  6. 12.535   **7.** 452.84   **8.** 998,543   **9.** 62.847   **10.** 640,796

 11. 164.479   **12.** 1209.4   **13.** 52.961   **14.** 12,742.5   **15.** 3,501,652

Skills Review

Divisibility Tests

When two nonzero whole numbers are multiplied together, each number is a **factor** of the product. A number is **divisible** by another number if the second number is a factor of the first. For example, $2 \times 5 = 10$, so 2 and 5 are factors of 10, and 10 is divisible by both 2 and 5.

You can use the following tests to test a whole number for divisibility by 2, 3, 4, 5, 6, 8, 9, and 10.

Divisible by 2:   The last digit of the number is 0, 2, 4, 6, or 8.
Divisible by 3:   The sum of the digits of the number is divisible by 3.
Divisible by 4:   The last two digits of the number are divisible by 4.
Divisible by 5:   The last digit of the number is 0 or 5.
Divisible by 6:   The number is divisible by both 2 and 3.
Divisible by 8:   The last three digits of the number are divisible by 8.
Divisible by 9:   The sum of the digits of the number is divisible by 9.
Divisible by 10: The last digit of the number is 0.

EXAMPLE Test the number for divisibility by 2, 3, 4, 5, 6, 8, 9, and 10.

   a. 2736   **b.** 74,420

Solution

a. The last digit of 2736 is 6, so it is divisible by 2 but not by 5 or 10. The sum of the digits is $2 + 7 + 3 + 6 = 18$, so it is divisible by 3 and 9. The last two digits, 36, are divisible by 4, so 2736 is divisible by 4. Because 2736 is divisible by both 2 and 3, it is divisible by 6. The last three digits, 736, are divisible by 8, so 2736 is divisible by 8.

   ANSWER 2736 is divisible by 2, 3, 4, 6, 8, and 9.

b. The last digit of 74,420 is 0, so it is divisible by 2, 5, and 10. The sum of the digits is $7 + 4 + 4 + 2 + 0 = 17$, so it is not divisible by 3 or 9. The last two digits, 20, are divisible by 4, so 74,420 is divisible by 4. Because 74,420 is divisible by 2, but not by 3, it is not divisible by 6. The last three digits, 420, are not divisible by 8, so 74,420 is not divisible by 8.

   ANSWER 74,420 is divisible by 2, 4, 5, and 10.

● Practice

Test the number for divisibility by 2, 3, 4, 5, 6, 8, 9, and 10.

1. 34	**2.** 84	**3.** 285	**4.** 560	**5.** 972
6. 4210	**7.** 2815	**8.** 6390	**9.** 88,004	**10.** 75,432

Mixed Numbers and Improper Fractions

A **fraction** is a number of the form $\frac{a}{b}$ ($b \neq 0$) where a is called the **numerator** and b is called the **denominator**. A number $1\frac{3}{5}$, read as "one and three fifths," is a *mixed number*. A **mixed number** is the sum of a whole number part and a fraction part. An **improper fraction**, such as $\frac{21}{8}$, is any fraction in which the numerator is greater than or equal to the denominator.

EXAMPLE Write $3\frac{2}{5}$ as an improper fraction.

$3\frac{2}{5} = \frac{15 + 2}{5}$ 1 whole $= \frac{5}{5}$, so 3 wholes $= \frac{3 \times 5}{5}$, or $\frac{15}{5}$.

$\quad\quad = \frac{17}{5}$ Add.

EXAMPLE Write $\frac{13}{4}$ as a mixed number.

1. Divide 13 by 4.

$$4\overline{)13} \quad \begin{array}{r} 3R1 \\ \hline \end{array}$$
$$\frac{12}{1}$$

2. Write the mixed number. $3 + \frac{1}{4} = 3\frac{1}{4}$

● Practice

Copy and complete the statement.

1. $7\frac{3}{5} = \frac{?}{5}$

2. $3\frac{1}{6} = \frac{?}{6}$

3. $\frac{23}{4} = 5\frac{?}{4}$

4. $\frac{17}{7} = 2\frac{?}{7}$

Write the mixed number as an improper fraction.

5. $3\frac{1}{2}$

6. $1\frac{5}{6}$

7. $4\frac{3}{8}$

8. $8\frac{5}{7}$

9. $10\frac{3}{4}$

Write the improper fraction as a mixed number.

10. $\frac{11}{4}$

11. $\frac{15}{2}$

12. $\frac{25}{6}$

13. $\frac{17}{3}$

14. $\frac{33}{8}$

Ratio and Rate

One way to compare numbers is to use a ratio. The **ratio** uses division to compare two numbers. You can write the ratio of a to b as $\frac{a}{b}$, as $a : b$, or as "a to b."

EXAMPLE There are 15 boys and 17 girls in the band. Write the ratio of the number of boys to girls in the band in three ways.

$$\frac{\text{Number of boys}}{\text{Number of girls}} = \frac{15}{17} = 15 \text{ to } 17 = 15 : 17$$

A **rate** is a ratio of two quantities that have different units, such as $\frac{150 \text{ miles}}{3 \text{ hours}}$. A **unit rate** is a rate with a denominator of 1 unit.

EXAMPLE Write the rate $\frac{150 \text{ miles}}{3 \text{ hours}}$ as a unit rate.

$$\overset{\div 3}{\frac{150 \text{ mi}}{3 \text{ h}} = \frac{50 \text{ mi}}{1 \text{ h}}}_{\div 3}$$

Divide 3 by 3 to get 1, so divide 150 by 3 also.

ANSWER The unit rate is 50 miles per hour.

● Practice

The table shows the numbers of boys and girls in Mr. Smith's class and in Ms. Jung's class. Use the table to write the specified ratio.

1. Boys in Mr. Smith's class to girls in Mr. Smith's class

2. Boys in Mr. Smith's class to boys in Ms. Jung's class

3. Girls in Ms. Jung's class to all girls

	Boys	Girls
Mr. Smith's class	13	12
Ms. Jung's class	17	11

Write the rate and unit rate.

4. 8 feet in 2 seconds

5. $24 for 8 pens

6. 333 miles in 6 hours

7. 280 words in 5 minutes

8. 3 quarts for $2.50

9. 8 inches in 6 days

Adding and Subtracting Decimals

To add and subtract decimals, start with the digits in the place on the right. Moving to the left, add or subtract the digits one place value at a time, regrouping as needed.

EXAMPLE   Find the sum 0.157 + 0.663.

1 Add the thousandths. Regroup 10 thousandths as 1 hundredth and 0 thousandths.

$$\begin{array}{r} \overset{1}{} \\ 0.157 \\ + \, 0.663 \\ \hline 0 \end{array}$$

2 Add the hundredths. Regroup 12 hundredths as 1 tenth and 2 hundredths.

$$\begin{array}{r} \overset{11}{} \\ 0.157 \\ + \, 0.663 \\ \hline 20 \end{array}$$

3 Add the tenths. Place the decimal point in the answer.

$$\begin{array}{r} \overset{11}{} \\ 0.157 \\ + \, 0.663 \\ \hline 0.820 \end{array}$$

EXAMPLE   Find the difference 30.7 – 3.8.

1 Start with the tenths. There are not enough tenths in 30.7 to subtract 8 tenths.

$$\begin{array}{r} 30.7 \\ - \, 3.8 \\ \hline \end{array}$$

2 Move to the ones. There are no ones in 30.7, so regroup 1 ten as 9 ones and 10 tenths.

$$\begin{array}{r} \overset{9}{2\,\cancel{10}17} \\ \cancel{30.7} \\ - \, 3.8 \\ \hline \end{array}$$

3 Subtract. Place the decimal point in the answer.

$$\begin{array}{r} \overset{9}{2\,\cancel{10}17} \\ \cancel{30.7} \\ - \, 3.8 \\ \hline 26.9 \end{array}$$

✓ **Check** Because addition and subtraction are inverse operations, you can check your answer by adding: 26.9 + 3.8 = 30.7.

Practice

Find the sum or difference.

1. 3.56 + 2.74   **2.** 12.7 + 93.8   **3.** 27.5 + 3.6   **4.** 0.923 + 0.179

5. 4.217 + 6.739   **6.** 9.3 − 2.8   **7.** 4.56 − 1.65   **8.** 13.64 − 5.85

9. 38.45 − 19.57   **10.** 741.52 − 48.66   **11.** 56.98 + 0.82   **12.** 100.476 − 4.989

13. 365.57 − 79.38   **14.** 49.86 + 2.65   **15.** 97.156 − 9.092   **16.** 232.543 − 209.692

Skills Review

Skills Review

Adding and Subtracting Fractions

To add two fractions with a common denominator, write the sum of the numerators over the denominator.

Numbers $\frac{2}{5} + \frac{1}{5} = \frac{3}{5}$ **Algebra** $\frac{a}{c} + \frac{b}{c} = \frac{a+b}{c}$ $(c \neq 0)$

EXAMPLE Find the sum $\frac{4}{7} + \frac{6}{7}$.

$\frac{4}{7} + \frac{6}{7} = \frac{4+6}{7}$ Write sum of numerators over denominator.

$= \frac{10}{7}$ Add.

$= 1\frac{3}{7}$ Write the improper fraction as a mixed number.

To subtract two fractions with a common denominator, write the difference of the numerators over the denominator.

Numbers $\frac{7}{9} - \frac{2}{9} = \frac{5}{9}$ **Algebra** $\frac{a}{c} - \frac{b}{c} = \frac{a-b}{c}$ $(c \neq 0)$

EXAMPLE Find the difference $\frac{10}{11} - \frac{4}{11}$.

$\frac{10}{11} - \frac{4}{11} = \frac{10-4}{11}$ Write difference of numerators over denominator.

$= \frac{6}{11}$ Subtract.

● Practice

Find the sum or difference.

1. $\frac{1}{3} + \frac{1}{3}$ **2.** $\frac{8}{9} + \frac{5}{9}$ **3.** $\frac{6}{7} - \frac{3}{7}$ **4.** $\frac{11}{12} - \frac{4}{12}$ **5.** $\frac{1}{8} + \frac{7}{8}$

6. $\frac{8}{11} + \frac{7}{11}$ **7.** $\frac{13}{15} - \frac{2}{15}$ **8.** $\frac{5}{6} - \frac{4}{6}$ **9.** $\frac{1}{9} + \frac{1}{9}$ **10.** $\frac{10}{11} - \frac{2}{11}$

11. $\frac{11}{12} + \frac{8}{12}$ **12.** $\frac{9}{10} - \frac{6}{10}$ **13.** $\frac{5}{9} - \frac{4}{9}$ **14.** $\frac{9}{16} + \frac{12}{16}$ **15.** $\frac{11}{14} - \frac{2}{14}$

16. $\frac{8}{15} - \frac{8}{15}$ **17.** $\frac{5}{12} + \frac{2}{12}$ **18.** $\frac{8}{10} + \frac{1}{10}$ **19.** $\frac{6}{7} + \frac{5}{7}$ **20.** $\frac{5}{8} - \frac{2}{8}$

Estimation in Addition and Subtraction

To **estimate** a solution means to find an approximate answer. When numbers being added have about the same value, you can use *clustering* to estimate their sum. Another way to estimate is to add the digits in the greatest place, then round the remaining parts of the numbers and add. Finally, add the sums together.

EXAMPLE **Estimate the sum 3836 + 4235 + 3982.**

3836	4000	
4235	4000	The numbers all cluster
+ 3982	+ 4000	around the value 4000.
	12,000	

ANSWER The sum 3836 + 4235 + 3982 is *about* 12,000.

To estimate a difference, first subtract the digits in the greatest place. Then round the remaining parts of the numbers and subtract the lesser number from the greater number. Finally, combine the two differences using addition or subtraction as shown below.

EXAMPLE **Estimate the difference 68,453 − 32,792.**

1 First subtract the digits in the ten thousands' place.

68,453	60,000
− 32,792	− 30,000
	30,000

2 Then round the remaining digits to the nearest thousand. Subtract the lesser number from the greater number.

8,000
− 3,000
5,000

3 Because the greater remaining number was originally on the *top*, you *add* the differences.

$$30,000 + 5,000 = 35,000$$

Note that if the greater remaining number had originally been on the *bottom*, you would *subtract* the differences.

Practice

Estimate the sum or difference.

1. 935 + 887 + 912
2. 4967 + 4802 + 5218
3. 5971 + 6032 + 7865
4. 8891 − 4932
5. 4373 − 2158
6. 449,739 − 285,921

FLORIDA: STANDARDS AND ASSESSMENT
Know appropriate operations to solve real-world problems. (MA.A.3.3.2)

Solving Problems Using Addition and Subtraction

You can use the following guidelines to tell whether to use addition or subtraction to solve a word problem.

- Use addition when you need to combine, join, or find a total.
- Use subtraction when you need to separate, compare, take away, find how many are left, or find how many more are needed.

EXAMPLE **You have 36 stamps in your stamp collection. You want to collect 18 more stamps. How many stamps will you have in all?**

You need to combine, so you need to add.

$$36 + 18 = 54$$

ANSWER You will have 54 stamps in your stamp collection.

EXAMPLE **Your total bill for lunch is $4.78. You pay with a $5 bill. How much change do you receive?**

You need to take away, so you need to subtract.

$$\$5.00 - \$4.78 = \$.22$$

ANSWER You receive $.22 in change.

● Practice

1. You spend $48 for a coat and $45 for a pair of shoes. How much do you spend in all?

2. You bought a box of 96 pencils. You gave 28 of the pencils to your friend. How many pencils do you have left?

3. You have $18. You buy a video for $15.99. How much money do you have left?

4. You have 24 country CDs and 18 pop CDs. How many country and pop CDs do you have in all?

5. You have 900 minutes a month on your cell phone plan. You have used 652 minutes so far this month. How many minutes do you have left?

6. You have $149. You make $24 babysitting. How much money do you have?

Multiplying Fractions

To multiply a fraction by a whole number, multiply the numerator of the fraction by the whole number and write the product over the denominator of the fraction. Simplify if possible.

EXAMPLE Find the product.

a. $3 \times \frac{2}{7} = \frac{3 \times 2}{7}$ Write the product of the whole number and the numerator over the denominator.

$= \frac{6}{7}$ Multiply.

b. $\frac{3}{8} \times 5 = \frac{3 \times 5}{8}$ Write the product of the whole number and the numerator over the denominator.

$= \frac{15}{8}$, or $1\frac{7}{8}$ Multiply. Then write as a mixed number.

To multiply two fractions, write the product of the numerators over the product of the denominators. Simplify if possible.

$$\text{product of fractions} = \frac{\text{product of numerators}}{\text{product of denominators}}$$

EXAMPLE Find the product.

$\frac{4}{5} \times \frac{2}{3} = \frac{4 \times 2}{5 \times 3}$ Use rule for multiplying fractions.

$= \frac{8}{15}$ Multiply.

Practice

Find the product. Simplify if possible.

1. $6 \times \frac{2}{15}$ **2.** $2 \times \frac{6}{11}$ **3.** $4 \times \frac{5}{9}$ **4.** $8 \times \frac{5}{9}$ **5.** $\frac{3}{4} \times 7$

6. $\frac{4}{7} \times 5$ **7.** $\frac{6}{7} \times 3$ **8.** $\frac{3}{7} \times \frac{6}{11}$ **9.** $\frac{2}{3} \times \frac{4}{5}$ **10.** $\frac{3}{4} \times \frac{1}{7}$

11. $\frac{1}{8} \times \frac{3}{5}$ **12.** $\frac{7}{9} \times \frac{5}{8}$ **13.** $\frac{5}{9} \times \frac{2}{3}$ **14.** $\frac{3}{8} \times \frac{4}{5}$ **15.** $\frac{5}{12} \times \frac{5}{6}$

Skills Review

Multiplication of a Decimal by a Whole Number

To multiply a decimal by a whole number, multiply the entire first number (ignoring the decimal point) by the digit in each place value of the second number to get partial products. Add the partial products. Then place the decimal point in the answer, showing the same number of decimal places as in the decimal.

EXAMPLE Find the product 31.5 × 206.

(1 Multiply 31.5 by the ones' digit in 206. Ignore the decimal point.

$$
\begin{array}{r}
{\scriptstyle 3} \\
31.5 \\
\times\ 206 \\
\hline
1890
\end{array}
$$

(2 Skip the 0 in the tens' place, and multiply by the hundreds' digit. Start the partial product in the hundreds' place.

$$
\begin{array}{r}
{\scriptstyle 1} \\
31.5 \\
\times\ 206 \\
\hline
1890 \\
630
\end{array}
$$

(3 Add the partial products. The decimal has one decimal place, so show one decimal place in the answer.

$$
\begin{array}{r}
31.5 \\
\times\ 206 \\
\hline
1890 \\
630 \\
\hline
6489.0
\end{array}
$$

● Practice

Find the product.

1. $\begin{array}{r}2.3\\ \times\ 98\\ \hline\end{array}$	**2.** $\begin{array}{r}0.62\\ \times\ 46\\ \hline\end{array}$	**3.** $\begin{array}{r}85\\ \times\ 7.9\\ \hline\end{array}$	**4.** $\begin{array}{r}0.56\\ \times\ 63\\ \hline\end{array}$	**5.** $\begin{array}{r}2.08\\ \times\ 14\\ \hline\end{array}$
6. $\begin{array}{r}6.52\\ \times\ 36\\ \hline\end{array}$	**7.** $\begin{array}{r}7.24\\ \times\ 89\\ \hline\end{array}$	**8.** $\begin{array}{r}8.35\\ \times\ 16\\ \hline\end{array}$	**9.** $\begin{array}{r}77.6\\ \times\ 22\\ \hline\end{array}$	**10.** $\begin{array}{r}3.45\\ \times\ 105\\ \hline\end{array}$
11. $\begin{array}{r}453\\ \times\ 41.2\\ \hline\end{array}$	**12.** $\begin{array}{r}614\\ \times\ 6.71\\ \hline\end{array}$	**13.** $\begin{array}{r}32.6\\ \times\ 463\\ \hline\end{array}$	**14.** $\begin{array}{r}71.8\\ \times\ 934\\ \hline\end{array}$	**15.** $\begin{array}{r}90.5\\ \times\ 407\\ \hline\end{array}$
16. $\begin{array}{r}15.36\\ \times\ 123\\ \hline\end{array}$	**17.** $\begin{array}{r}3.442\\ \times\ 276\\ \hline\end{array}$	**18.** $\begin{array}{r}93.08\\ \times\ 306\\ \hline\end{array}$	**19.** $\begin{array}{r}5.436\\ \times\ 682\\ \hline\end{array}$	**20.** $\begin{array}{r}60.97\\ \times\ 708\\ \hline\end{array}$
21. $\begin{array}{r}142.82\\ \times\ 35\\ \hline\end{array}$	**22.** $\begin{array}{r}25.987\\ \times\ 76\\ \hline\end{array}$	**23.** $\begin{array}{r}32.903\\ \times\ 55\\ \hline\end{array}$	**24.** $\begin{array}{r}243.72\\ \times\ 38\\ \hline\end{array}$	**25.** $\begin{array}{r}75.032\\ \times\ 73\\ \hline\end{array}$
26. $\begin{array}{r}380.07\\ \times\ 114\\ \hline\end{array}$	**27.** $\begin{array}{r}508.25\\ \times\ 237\\ \hline\end{array}$	**28.** $\begin{array}{r}15.456\\ \times\ 591\\ \hline\end{array}$	**29.** $\begin{array}{r}36.902\\ \times\ 205\\ \hline\end{array}$	**30.** $\begin{array}{r}8257.6\\ \times\ 459\\ \hline\end{array}$

Dividing Decimals

In a division problem, the number being divided is called the **dividend** and the number it is being divided by is called the **divisor**. The result of the division is called the **quotient**. To **divide** two numbers, you start with the leftmost digit of the dividend and move to the right. Before you start dividing decimals, place the decimal point in the quotient.

EXAMPLE Find the quotient 5.2 ÷ 8.

(1 Place the decimal point in the quotient directly above the decimal point in the dividend. Then divide as with whole numbers. Because 8 is greater than 5, place a zero above the 5.

$$
\begin{array}{r}
0. \\
\text{divisor} \longrightarrow 8\overline{)5.2} \longleftarrow \text{dividend}
\end{array}
$$

(2 Because 8 × 6 = 48, estimate that 8 divides 52 about 6 times. Multiply 6 and 8. Then subtract 48 from 52. Be sure the difference is less than the divisor: 4 < 8.

$$
\begin{array}{r}
0.6 \\
8\overline{)5.2} \\
-48 \\
\hline
4
\end{array}
$$

(3 Add **zero** as a placeholder. Bring down the zero. Divide 40 by 8 to get 5. Multiply 5 and 8. Subtract 40 from 40. The remainder is zero.

$$
\begin{array}{r}
0.65 \\
8\overline{)5.20} \\
-48 \\
\hline
40 \\
-40 \\
\hline
0
\end{array}
$$

EXAMPLE Find the quotient 12 ÷ 2.8.

(1 To multiply the divisor and the dividend by 10, move both decimal points 1 place to the right. Then divide as with whole numbers.

$$
\text{divisor} \longrightarrow 28\overline{)120} \longleftarrow \text{dividend}
$$

(2 Because 28 × 4 = 112, estimate that 28 divides 120 about 4 times. Multiply 4 and 28. Then subtract 112 from 120.

$$
\begin{array}{r}
4 \\
28\overline{)120} \\
-112 \\
\hline
8
\end{array}
$$

(3 Be sure the difference is less than the divisor: 8 < 28. So 12 ÷ 2.8 is equal to $4\frac{8}{28}$, or $4\frac{2}{7}$.

$$
\begin{array}{r}
4R8 \\
28\overline{)120} \\
-112 \\
\hline
8
\end{array}
$$

● Practice

Find the quotient.

1. 2.7 ÷ 6   **2.** 3.8 ÷ 4   **3.** 6.8 ÷ 8   **4.** 46.9 ÷ 7   **5.** 13.71 ÷ 3

6. 15 ÷ 2.5   **7.** 8 ÷ 1.3   **8.** 32 ÷ 5.46   **9.** 63 ÷ 7.12   **10.** 75 ÷ 6.357

Skills Review

Estimation in Multiplication and Division

One way to estimate a product or a quotient is to find a range for the product or quotient by finding a low estimate and a high estimate. A low estimate and a high estimate can be found by using *compatible numbers*, which are numbers that make a calculation easier.

EXAMPLE Find a low and high estimate for the product 56 × 35 using compatible numbers.

For a low estimate, round both factors *down*. $50 \times 30 = 1500$

For a high estimate, round both factors *up*. $60 \times 40 = 2400$

ANSWER The product 56×35 is between 1500 and 2400.

EXAMPLE Find a low and high estimate for the quotient 23,400 ÷ 45 using compatible numbers.

When the divisor has more than one digit, round it .

For a *low* estimate, round the divisor *up* and choose a compatible dividend that is *lower* than the original dividend.

$$\frac{400}{50)\overline{20,000}}$$

For a *high* estimate, round the divisor *down* and choose a compatible dividend that is *higher* than the original dividend.

$$\frac{600}{40)\overline{24,000}}$$

ANSWER The quotient $23,400 \div 45$ is between 400 and 600.

● Practice

Find a low and high estimate for the product or quotient using compatible numbers.

1. 43×16 **2.** 359×28 **3.** 852×53 **4.** 734×76

5. $225 \div 6$ **6.** $2795 \div 7$ **7.** $17,934 \div 77$ **8.** $41,042 \div 92$

9. 326×48 **10.** 612×273 **11.** 745×158 **12.** 905×657

13. 625×28 **14.** 809×97 **15.** $742 \div 8$ **16.** $231 \div 38$

17. $5421 \div 7$ **18.** $4972 \div 18$ **19.** $1583 \div 82$ **20.** $43,789 \div 64$

Solving Problems Using Multiplication and Division

You can use the following guidelines to tell whether to use multiplication or division to solve a word problem.

- Use multiplication when you need to find the total number of objects that are in groups of equal size or to find a fractional part of another number.

- Use division when you need to find the number of equal groups or the number in each equal group.

EXAMPLE You baked 48 muffins. You give $\frac{1}{3}$ of them to your friend. How many muffins did you give to your friend?

You need to find the fractional part of another number, so you need to multiply.

$$48 \cdot \frac{1}{3} = 16$$

ANSWER You gave 16 muffins to your friend.

EXAMPLE You bought 4 cans of soup for a total of $3.56. How much did you pay for each can of soup?

You need to find the amount in each equal group, so you need to divide.

$$3.56 \div 4 = 0.89$$

ANSWER You paid $.89 for each can of soup.

Practice

1. You bought 6 notebooks. Each notebook cost $1.58. How much did you pay for all of the notebooks?

2. You have 92 baseball cards. You give $\frac{1}{4}$ of your cards to your friend. How many cards did you give your friend?

3. You have 12 flats of flowers. If each flat contains 48 flowers, how many flowers do you have?

4. You paid $22.95 for the plates for your party. If you bought 9 packages of plates, how much did you pay for each package?

Points, Lines, and Planes

In geometry, a **point** is usually labeled with an uppercase letter, such as *A* or *B*. Points are used to name *lines, rays,* and *segments*. A **plane** is a flat surface that extends without end in all directions. You can represent a plane by a figure that looks like a floor or a wall.

Words	Diagram	Symbols
A **line** extends without end in two *opposite* directions.	X Y	$\overleftrightarrow{XY}$ or $\overleftrightarrow{YX}$
A **ray** has one **endpoint** and extends without end in *one* direction.	X Y	$\overrightarrow{XY}$
A **segment** has two endpoints.	X Y	$\overline{XY}$ or $\overline{YX}$

EXAMPLE Identify and name the *line, ray,* or *segment.*

a.
b.
c.

Solution

a. The figure is a segment that can be named $\overline{AB}$.

b. The figure is a line that can be named $\overleftrightarrow{MN}$.

c. The figure is a ray that can be named $\overrightarrow{PQ}$.

Practice

Match the name with the correct figure.

1. $\overline{CD}$

2. $\overleftrightarrow{CD}$

3. $\overrightarrow{CD}$

A.

B.

C.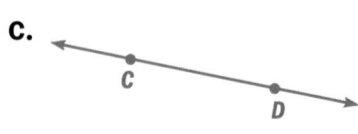

In Exercises 4–7, use the diagram.

4. Name three points.

5. Name two rays.

6. Name two lines.

7. Name a segment that has *S* as an endpoint.

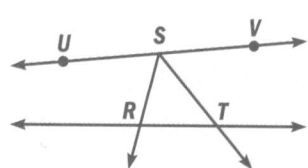

Angles

An **angle** is formed by two rays with the
same endpoint. The endpoint is called
the **vertex**. The symbol $\angle$ is used to
represent an angle.

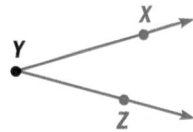

EXAMPLE **Name the angle above in three ways.**

Name the angle by its vertex alone: $\angle Y$

Name the angle by its vertex and two points, with the vertex as the
middle point: $\angle XYZ$

Name the angle by its vertex and two points, but reverse the order
of the points: $\angle ZYX$

● Practice

Match the name with the correct angle.

1. $\angle ABC$

2. $\angle RST$

3. $\angle MNP$

A.

B.

C.

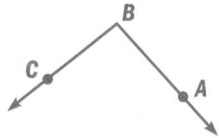

Name the angle in three ways.

4.

5.

6.

7.

8.

9.

10. Draw a triangle with vertices P, Q, and R. Name each angle of the triangle
in three ways.

Skills Review

FLORIDA: STANDARDS AND ASSESSMENT
Know precision of instruments. (MA.B.4.3.1)

Using a Ruler

An **inch ruler** has markings for inches, halves of an inch, fourths of an inch, eighths of an inch, and sixteenths of an inch. As the lengths get shorter, so do the markings.

A **centimeter ruler** has markings for centimeters, halves of a centimeter, and tenths of a centimeter (also called *millimeters*). Like an inch ruler, as the lengths get shorter, so do the markings.

EXAMPLE Use a ruler to draw a segment with the given length.

a. $2\frac{1}{8}$ inches   **b.** 3.8 centimeters

Solution

a. Start at the leftmost mark on the ruler.

Draw a segment so that the other end is at the first $\frac{1}{8}$ in. mark after 2.

b. Start at the leftmost mark on the ruler.

Draw a segment so that the other end is at the 3.8 cm mark.

● Practice

Use a ruler to draw a segment with the given length.

1. $\frac{7}{16}$ inch   **2.** $4\frac{5}{8}$ inches   **3.** 4.3 centimeters   **4.** 2.7 centimeters

5. $2\frac{5}{16}$ inches   **6.** 6.5 centimeters   **7.** 2.9 centimeters   **8.** $1\frac{1}{4}$ inches

Using a Protractor

A **protractor** is a tool you can use to draw and measure angles. A unit of measure for angles the **degree** (°). To measure an angle, place the center of the protractor on the vertex of the angle and line up one ray with the 0° line. Then read the measure where the other ray crosses the protractor.

The measure of ∠XYZ is 135°. You can write this as m∠XYZ = 135°.

EXAMPLE Use a protractor to draw an angle that has a measure of 48°.

1. Draw and label a ray.

2. Place the center of the protractor at the endpoint of the ray. Line up the ray with the 0° line. Then draw and label a point at the 48° mark on the inner scale.

3. Remove the protractor and draw $\overrightarrow{KL}$ to complete the angle.

● Practice

Use a protractor to measure the angle.

1.

2.

3.

4. Use a protractor to draw angles measuring 46°, 125°, and 73°.

Skills Review

Using a Compass

A **compass** is an instrument used to draw circles. A **straightedge** is any object that can be used to draw a segment.

EXAMPLE Use a compass to draw a circle with radius 3 cm.

Recall that the *radius* of a circle is the distance between the center of the circle and any point on the circle.

Use a metric ruler to open the compass so that the distance between the point and the pencil is 3 cm.

Place the point on a piece of paper and rotate the pencil around the point to draw the circle.

EXAMPLE Use a straightedge and a compass to draw a segment whose length is the sum of $\overline{MN}$ and $\overline{PQ}$.

$$\overline{}\quad\overline{}$$
$$M\qquad\qquad N\ P\qquad\qquad\qquad Q$$

Solution

Use a straightedge to draw a segment longer than both given segments.

Open your compass to measure $\overline{MN}$. Using this compass setting, place the point at the left end of your segment and make a mark that crosses your segment.

Then open your compass to measure $\overline{PQ}$. Using this compass setting, place the point at the first mark you made on your segment and make another mark that crosses your segment.

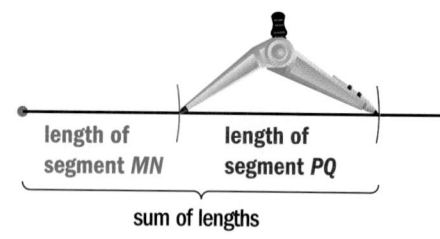

Practice

1. Use a compass to draw a circle with radius 4 cm.

2. Use a straightedge and a compass to draw a segment whose length is the *sum* of the lengths of the two given segments.

3. Use a straightedge and a compass to draw a segment whose length is the *difference* of the lengths of the two given segments in Exercise 2.

Reading and Making Line Plots

A **line plot** uses a number line to show how often data values occur.

EXAMPLE You surveyed 20 of your friends and asked them how many pets they have. Their responses were:
6, 2, 3, 1, 5, 0, 2, 4, 1, 1, 6, 2, 0, 3, 1, 4, 3, 2, 1, 1.

a. Make a line plot of the data.   **b.** What was the most frequent response?

Solution

a.

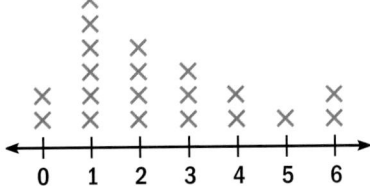

b. The greatest number of ✕s is above 1, so 1 was the most frequent response.

Practice

Make a line plot of the data.

1. In a survey, 15 people were asked how many TVs they own. Their responses were: 1, 2, 1, 4, 3, 2, 1, 5, 1, 2, 3, 1, 2, 1, 2.

2. In a survey, 18 people were asked how many times they eat out each week. Their responses were: 2, 4, 1, 3, 5, 6, 3, 7, 2, 1, 4, 8, 5, 4, 3, 4, 1, 2.

Use the line plot below. It shows the results of a questionnaire asking people how many hours they exercise each week.

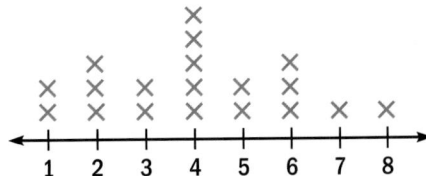

3. How many people completed the questionnaire?

4. How many more people exercise 4 hours each week than exercise 6 hours each week?

5. How many people exercise less than 3 hours each week?

Skills Review

FLORIDA: STANDARDS AND ASSESSMENT
Interpret and analyze data displays. (MA.E.1.3.1)

Reading and Making Bar Graphs

Data are numbers or facts. A **bar graph** is one way to display data. A bar graph uses bars to show how quantities in categories compare.

EXAMPLE **The bar graph shows the results of a survey on favorite flavors of ice cream. Which flavor was chosen the most? Which flavor was chosen the least?**

The longest bar on the graph represents the 11 people who chose chocolate. So, chocolate was chosen the most.

The shortest bar represents the 2 students who chose strawberry. So, strawberry was chosen the least.

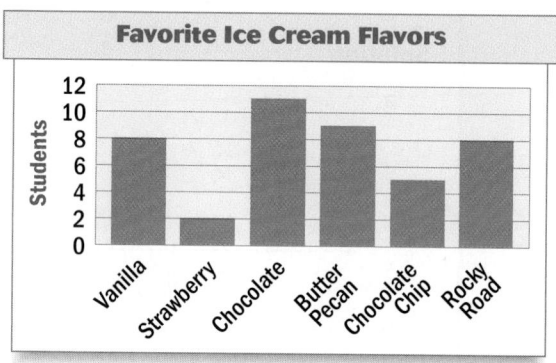

To make a bar graph, choose a title and a scale. Draw and label the axes. Then draw bars to represent the data given.

EXAMPLE **Draw a bar graph for the data given.**

Subject	Number of Students
Math	8
English	15
History	20
Science	16

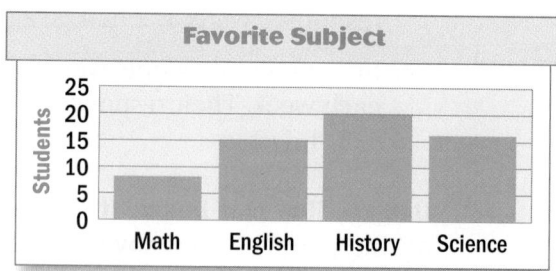

● Practice

In Exercises 1–3, use the bar graph of ice cream flavors above.

1. How many students chose butter pecan as a favorite ice cream flavor?

2. How many students chose vanilla as a favorite ice cream flavor?

3. Which two flavors were chosen by the same number of students?

4. Suppose 8 more students took the survey shown in the second example. Draw a new bar graph if 3 of the students chose math, 4 chose history, and 1 chose science.

Reading and Making Line Graphs

Another way to display data is to use a *line graph*. A **line graph** uses line segments to show how a quantity changes over time.

EXAMPLE The line graph shows plant growth data collected by students every day for 7 days. The greatest increase in growth occurred between what two days? What was the amount of the increase?

The steepest segment in the line graph is from Monday to Tuesday. The students recorded a height of 1 inch on Monday and a height of 3.5 inches on Tuesday, for an increase of 2.5 inches.

To make a line graph, choose a title and scales. Draw and label the axes. Then plot and connect points to represent the data given.

EXAMPLE Draw a line graph for the data given.

Month	Weight of Puppy (pounds)
1	3
2	5.5
3	7
4	11

● Practice

In Exercises 1 and 2, use the plant growth line graph above.

1. Between which two days was the growth 1 inch?

2. Between which two days did the height remain the same?

3. Suppose in month 5 the puppy in the second example weighed 15 pounds. Copy the graph and add this data to it.

Skills Review

Venn Diagrams and Logical Reasoning

A **Venn diagram** uses shapes to show how sets are related.

EXAMPLE Draw and use a Venn diagram.

    a. Draw a Venn diagram of the whole numbers from 6 through 19 where set *A* consists of even numbers and set *B* consists of multiples of 5.

    b. Is the following statement *true* or *false*? Explain. *No even whole number from 6 through 19 is a multiple of 5.*

    c. Is the following statement *always, sometimes,* or *never* true? Explain. *A multiple of 5 from 6 through 19 is even.*

Solution

    a.

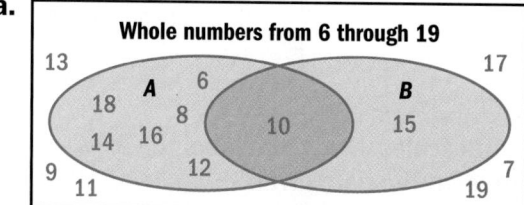

    b. False. 10 is an even whole number that is a multiple of 5.

    c. Sometimes. It is true that 10 is a multiple of 5 that is even, but 15 is a multiple of 5 that is odd.

Practice

Draw a Venn diagram of the sets described.

    1. Of the whole numbers less than 12, set *A* consists of numbers that are greater than 8 and set *B* consists of odd numbers.

    2. Of the whole numbers less than 10, set *C* consists of multiples of 3 and set *D* consists of even numbers.

Use the Venn diagrams you drew in Exercises 1 and 2 to answer the question. Explain your reasoning.

    3. Is the following statement *true* or *false*?
There is only one odd number greater than 8 and less than 12.

    4. Is the following statement *always, sometimes,* or *never* true?
A whole number less than 10 is both a multiple of 3 and even.

Extra Practice

Chapter 1

1.1 The frequency table shows the heights of 30 students.

Height (inches)	54-55.9	56-57.9	58-59.9	60-61.9	62-63.9	64-65.9	66-67.9	68-69.9
Frequency	1	2	4	5	7	6	3	2

1. Make a histogram of the data shown in the frequency table.

2. Which height interval has the greatest number of students?

3. Can you use the histogram to determine the number of students who are between 60 and 69.9 inches tall? Explain.

1.2 Evaluate the expression.

4. $15 - 3 \cdot 2 + 4$

5. $42 \div [(5 - 2) \cdot (1 + 1)]$

6. $2 + \dfrac{100 - 36}{7 + 9}$

7. $4 \cdot 7 - 8 \cdot 3$

8. $3 + 10 \cdot 5 \div 2$

9. $(11 - 56 \div 8) \cdot 9$

1.3 Evaluate the expression when $r = 1.5$ and $s = 2.4$.

10. $10r + s$

11. $\dfrac{7s}{r + 0.5}$

12. $8rs$

13. $3(r + s)$

1.4 Evaluate the expression.

14. $24 - (2^3 + 1) \cdot 2$

15. $6^3 \div (2 + 1)^2 + 3$

16. $(8 - 5)^4 + 7 \cdot 5^2$

1.5 In Exercises 17–24, solve the equation using mental math.

17. $5n = 35$

18. $\dfrac{60}{t} = 4$

19. $12 + w = 75$

20. $41 - a = 23$

21. $9 + b = 17$

22. $63 - c = 10$

23. $6x = 54$

24. $\dfrac{m}{12} = 9$

1.6 25. Find the perimeter and area of a rectangular garden with a length of 13 feet and a width of 8 feet.

1.6 26. Ramon jogs at a rate of 5 miles per hour. How far does he jog in 1.5 hours?

1.6 27. Find the side length of a square that has a perimeter of 32 centimeters.

1.7 28. You do 5 hours of yard work each day for 4 days and earn $6 per hour. Then you buy 2 concert tickets for $12 each. Use the problem solving plan to find how much money you have left.

Chapter 2

2.1 **Use a number line to order the integers from least to greatest.**

1. $33, -24, -43, 7, 19, -2$

2. $-230, 157, -68, -146, 5, 94$

2.1 **Write the opposite and the absolute value of the integer.**

3. -25 **4.** 467 **5.** 0 **6.** $|-2|$

2.2 **Find the sum.**

7. $342 + (-751)$ **8.** $-147 + 71$ **9.** $-89 + 268$

10. $-29 + (-51) + 36$ **11.** $-78 + 65 + 13$ **12.** $93 + (-57) + (-102)$

2.3 **Find the difference.**

13. $-12 - 4$ **14.** $10 - 13$ **15.** $34 - (-17)$ **16.** $-18 - (-17)$

17. $23 - 38$ **18.** $81 - (-16)$ **19.** $-9 - (-77)$ **20.** $-63 - 19$

2.4 **Find the product.**

21. $(-7)(-50)$ **22.** $25(-7)$ **23.** $-4(16)$ **24.** $(-12)(-21)$

25. $-95(0)(-58)$ **26.** $54(-1)(5)$ **27.** $8(-2)(-3)(5)$ **28.** $(-14)(4)(6)(9)$

2.5 **In Exercises 29–32, find the quotient.**

29. $\dfrac{96}{-8}$ **30.** $\dfrac{-48}{-12}$ **31.** $\dfrac{0}{4}$ **32.** $\dfrac{-80}{5}$

2.5 **33.** Find the mean of the data: $-8, 6, 3, -20, -9, 4$.

2.6 **Evaluate the expression. Justify each step.**

34. $-28 + (74 - 32)$ **35.** $7\left(2 \cdot \dfrac{3}{7}\right)$ **36.** $(-7.2 + 3.5) + (-3.5)$

2.7 **Use the distributive property to evaluate or simplify the expression.**

37. $-5(-3 + 8)$ **38.** $3(m - 4)$ **39.** $-1(4 + 9r)$ **40.** $8(-4j - 3)$

2.7 **Simplify the expression by combining like terms.**

41. $-x + 3y - 5y + 6x$ **42.** $2(3k - 6) + 4 + 5k$ **43.** $5a - 3(2a + b) - 7b$

2.8 **Plot the point in a coordinate plane and describe its location.**

44. $A(3, -2)$ **45.** $B(5, 1)$ **46.** $C(0, -4)$ **47.** $D(-1, -3)$

Chapter 3

3.1 **Solve the equation. Check your solution.**

1. $n - 3 = 5$ **2.** $36 = p + 20$ **3.** $-4 = h - 9$ **4.** $27 + z = 51$

3.2 **Solve the equation. Check your solution.**

5. $32 = \dfrac{x}{2}$ **6.** $11k = -55$ **7.** $76 = 19r$ **8.** $\dfrac{y}{-1.4} = -5$

3.3 **Solve the equation. Check your solution.**

9. $5a - 2 = 33$ **10.** $\dfrac{d}{3} + 8 = -6$ **11.** $-1 = 14 - 2h$ **12.** $84 - z = 96$

13. $\dfrac{c}{4} + 7 = 12$ **14.** $47 = -6y + 5$ **15.** $73 = 15 - b$ **16.** $55 = 7t - 8$

3.4 **In Exercises 17 and 18, translate the statement into an equation. Then solve the equation.**

17. Five less than the product of 6 and a number is 13.

18. The sum of 5 and the quotient of a number and 3 is -1.

3.4 **19.** An auto repair shop charges $48 per hour for labor plus the cost of parts. Your car needs new parts that cost $129, and the total cost is $201. How much time is required to repair the car?

3.5 **Find the area and perimeter of the triangle.**

20.

21.

22.

3.5 **23.** A rectangle has an area of 60 square meters and a length of 12 meters. What is the width of the rectangle? What is the perimeter?

3.5 **24.** A square has an area of 81 square feet. What is the length of each side?

3.6 **Solve the inequality. Then graph its solution.**

25. $4 + j \geq -1$ **26.** $0 < m - 6$ **27.** $z + 4.5 \leq 2$ **28.** $-38 > t - 46$

3.7 **Solve the inequality. Then graph its solution.**

29. $5x < -25$ **30.** $3 \leq -\dfrac{1}{3}y$ **31.** $2 \geq \dfrac{s}{4}$ **32.** $-13k > -65$

Chapter 4

4.1 **Write the prime factorization of the number.**

1. 72   **2.** 65   **3.** 153   **4.** 196

4.1 **Factor the monomial.**

5. $25pq$ **6.** $7a^3$ **7.** $22xy^2$ **8.** $54s^2t$

4.2 **Find the greatest common factor of the numbers or monomials.**

9. $45, 75$ **10.** $108, 162$ **11.** $6bc, 35abc^2$ **12.** $4p^2, 18qr$

13. $21mn, 9km^2$ **14.** $14x^2y^3, 28xy^2$ **15.** $34w^2z^2, 51w^5z^4$ **16.** $abcdf, a^2d^3gh$

4.3 **Write the fraction in simplest form.**

17. $\dfrac{32}{64}$ **18.** $\dfrac{-15}{39}$ **19.** $\dfrac{-22}{77}$ **20.** $\dfrac{17}{51}$

21. $\dfrac{10x}{45xy}$ **22.** $\dfrac{-16mn}{40mn}$ **23.** $\dfrac{-6ab}{4bc}$ **24.** $\dfrac{28rs}{7rst}$

4.4 **Find the least common multiple of the numbers or monomials.**

25. $30, 60$ **26.** $4x, 18xy^2$ **27.** $5ab^2, 3bc^2$ **28.** $12x^3y, 8x^2y^4$

4.5 **Copy and complete the statement with <, >, or =.**

29. $\dfrac{7}{8} \; \underline{?} \; \dfrac{9}{11}$ **30.** $3\dfrac{3}{5} \; \underline{?} \; \dfrac{11}{3}$ **31.** $\dfrac{17}{6} \; \underline{?} \; 2\dfrac{13}{18}$ **32.** $1\dfrac{10}{15} \; \underline{?} \; \dfrac{35}{21}$

33. $\dfrac{11}{10} \; \underline{?} \; 1\dfrac{1}{8}$ **34.** $\dfrac{4}{5} \; \underline{?} \; \dfrac{6}{11}$ **35.** $\dfrac{50}{9} \; \underline{?} \; 5\dfrac{2}{7}$ **36.** $\dfrac{63}{15} \; \underline{?} \; 4\dfrac{5}{12}$

4.6 **Simplify the expression. Write your answer as a power.**

37. $z^5 \cdot z$ **38.** $5^8 \cdot 5^4$ **39.** $(-7)^6 \cdot (-7)^3$ **40.** $a^2 \cdot a^4$

41. $\dfrac{6^9}{6^5}$ **42.** $\dfrac{(-8)^{12}}{(-8)^2}$ **43.** $\dfrac{(-v)^7}{(-v)^4}$ **44.** $\dfrac{c^9}{c}$

4.7 **Simplify. Write the expression using only positive exponents.**

45. $6k^{-1}$ **46.** $a^3 \cdot a^{-3}$ **47.** $\dfrac{s^{-3}}{s^4}$ **48.** $n^{-4} \cdot n^{-2}$

4.8 **Write the number in scientific notation.**

49. $124{,}000{,}000$ **50.** 0.0000005 **51.** 0.0000791 **52.** $32{,}100$

4.8 **Write the number in standard form.**

53. 2.7×10^{-3} **54.** 9.09×10^2 **55.** 5.88×10^{11} **56.** 6.2×10^{-8}

Chapter 5

Find the sum or difference.

5.1
1. $\frac{7}{8} + \frac{5}{8}$ **2.** $5\frac{1}{5} - 3\frac{4}{5}$ **3.** $-\frac{11m}{15} + \frac{m}{15}$ **4.** $-\frac{5a}{9b} - \frac{4a}{9b}$

5.2
5. $\frac{9}{10} - \frac{5}{6}$ **6.** $\frac{2}{5} - \frac{3}{7}$ **7.** $4\frac{1}{4} + 3\frac{7}{8}$ **8.** $-\frac{5}{12} + \frac{11}{16}$

5.3 Find the product.

9. $\frac{7}{8} \cdot \frac{3}{14}$ **10.** $5 \cdot \left(-3\frac{1}{4}\right)$ **11.** $-\frac{5}{18} \cdot 1\frac{1}{3}$ **12.** $-1\frac{3}{5} \cdot \left(-2\frac{1}{4}\right)$

5.4 Find the quotient.

13. $\frac{5}{9} \div 2$ **14.** $-\frac{7}{12} \div \frac{2}{3}$ **15.** $4\frac{1}{8} \div \left(-1\frac{1}{3}\right)$ **16.** $-2\frac{1}{2} \div (-10)$

5.5 Write the fraction or mixed number as a decimal. Write the decimal as a fraction or mixed number.

17. $-\frac{48}{125}$ **18.** $4\frac{11}{12}$ **19.** -0.28 **20.** $0.\overline{72}$

21. 0.006 **22.** -8.34 **23.** $3\frac{7}{8}$ **24.** $-\frac{16}{250}$

5.5 Order the numbers from least to greatest.

25. $-\frac{7}{3}, -2\frac{5}{12}, -2.43, -2.5, -2\frac{2}{5}$ **26.** $\frac{18}{5}, 3\frac{1}{3}, 3.8, 3.55, 3\frac{7}{12}$

27. $\frac{26}{5}, 5.3, 5\frac{2}{9}, 5.21, 5\frac{3}{8}$ **28.** $-4.2, -4\frac{1}{6}, -\frac{59}{14}, -4\frac{3}{7}, -4.04$

5.6 Find the sum or difference.

29. $7.21 + (-3.4)$ **30.** $-9.8 + (-3.7)$ **31.** $0.8 - (-12.3)$ **32.** $8.217 - 9.68$

33. $-10.2 + (-6.35)$ **34.** $-8.78 + 3.9$ **35.** $3.28 - 11.395$ **36.** $-0.04 - 5.789$

5.7 Find the product or quotient.

37. $-8.32 \cdot (-0.47)$ **38.** $-20.51 \cdot 3.14$ **39.** $0.435 \div 0.29$ **40.** $2.072 \div (-0.74)$

41. $4.7 \cdot (-6.78)$ **42.** $-0.14 \cdot (-9.43)$ **43.** $-19.27 \div 2.35$ **44.** $0.224 \div 5.6$

5.8 Find the mean, median, mode(s), and range of the data.

45. Finishing times for a race in minutes: 24, 37, 57, 81, 31, 25, 43, 39, 33, 40, 34, 65, 50

46. Daily low temperatures: $-6°F$, $-7°F$, $-6°F$, $5°F$, $3°F$, $0°F$, $-3°F$

47. Grades on quizzes: 93, 84, 100, 95, 89, 78, 78, 85, 83, 95

Chapter 6

Solve the equation. Then check the solution.

6.1
1. $6k - 8 - 4k = 6$

2. $16 = 2(s + 9) - 4$

3. $5(n + 7) + 1 = -9$

4. $-8 = -3m + 2 + 5m$

5. $\dfrac{7a - 2}{3} = 4$

6. $2 = \dfrac{3 - 4t}{5}$

6.2
7. $3a + 2 = 7a + 10$

8. $9y - 8 = 6y + 7$

9. $5x + 7 = 8(x - 1)$

10. $13v = 7(9 - v)$

11. $5(w + 3) = -10w$

12. $2(z + 5) = 3z + 14$

6.3
13. $2.8y + 8.6 = 9.12 - 1.2y$

14. $7.25p - 3 + p = 14.325$

15. $7 - 2.65z = -4.4z$

16. $x - \dfrac{2}{3}x = \dfrac{3}{4}$

17. $\dfrac{9}{10}n + \dfrac{1}{5} = \dfrac{7}{10}n - \dfrac{3}{5}$

18. $\dfrac{6}{4}r - \dfrac{21}{8} = \dfrac{3}{4}r$

6.4 **Find the indicated measurement, where r = radius, d = diameter, and C = circumference. Use 3.14 or $\dfrac{22}{7}$ for π. Explain your choice of value for π.**

19. $r = \underline{\ ?\ }$

20. $C = \underline{\ ?\ }$

21. $r = \underline{\ ?\ }$

22. $d = \underline{\ ?\ }$

$d = 9$ cm

$r = 14$ ft

$C = 44$ yd
r

$C = 15.7$ in.
d

6.5 **Solve the inequality. Then graph the solution.**

23. $19 - 8c > 3$

24. $2(7 + n) \le -10$

25. $5s + 3 \ge -7 - 5s$

26. $20 - 11x \ge -2$

27. $4(b - 3) > 20$

28. $-6y - 13 < 11 + 2y$

6.6 **In Exercises 29–32, write the sentence as an inequality. Let n represent the unknown number. Then solve the inequality.**

29. Twelve more than half a number is at most 8.

30. The difference of 3 times a number and 2 is greater than 7.

31. Four times a number is no less than 16.

32. The quotient of 18 and 6 times a number is less than 3.

6.6 **33.** You want to ride your bike for at least 28 miles. You have already biked for 10 miles. If you bike at a speed of 12 miles per hour, how much longer do you need to bike?

6.6 **34.** Nathan has $20 to spend at a carnival. The carnival has a $10 entrance fee. Ride tickets cost $.75 each. What number of tickets can Nathan buy?

Extra Practice

Chapter 7

7.1 **A baseball team had 12 wins, 4 losses, and 2 ties in one season. Write the ratio as a fraction in simplest form and two other ways.**

   1. wins to losses   **2.** losses to games played   **3.** wins to games played

7.1 **Write the equivalent rate.**

   4. $\dfrac{9000 \text{ tickets}}{6 \text{ hours}} = \dfrac{? \text{ tickets}}{\text{hour}}$ **5.** $\dfrac{240 \text{ tickets}}{\text{hour}} = \dfrac{? \text{ tickets}}{\text{minute}}$ **6.** $\dfrac{7 \text{ meters}}{\text{second}} = \dfrac{? \text{ meters}}{\text{minute}}$

7.2 **Solve the proportion. Then check your solution.**

   7. $\dfrac{x}{18} = \dfrac{25}{2}$ **8.** $\dfrac{4}{9} = \dfrac{5}{y}$ **9.** $\dfrac{3.6}{n} = \dfrac{4.8}{12.4}$ **10.** $\dfrac{m}{6} = \dfrac{35}{42}$

7.3 **Use a percent proportion.**

   11. 9 is what percent of 75?   **12.** 42 is 25% of what number?

   13. What number is 7% of 128?   **14.** 7 is what percent of 56?

7.4 **Write the decimal or fraction as a percent.**

   15. 0.125   **16.** 1.42   **17.** $\dfrac{18}{25}$ **18.** $\dfrac{197}{200}$

7.4 **Write the percent as a decimal and as a fraction.**

   19. 31%   **20.** 55%   **21.** 175%   **22.** 1.28%

7.5 **In Exercises 23–25, tell whether the change is an *increase* or *decrease*. Then find the percent of change.**

   23. Original amount: 25   **24.** Original amount: 144   **25.** Original amount: 5000
       New amount: 28   New amount: 126   New amount: 4950

7.6 **26.** A pair of shoes has a wholesale price of $28. The percent markup is 110%. What is the retail price?

7.6 **27.** Your food bill at a restaurant is $18.40. You leave a 15% tip. The sales tax is 5%. Find the total cost of the meal.

7.7 **Solve using the percent equation.**

   28. What number is 121% of 412?   **29.** 13 is 15.6% of what number?

   30. 57 is what percent of 76?   **31.** What number is 0.3% of 28?

7.8 **A bag contains 12 slips of paper numbered from 1 through 12. A slip of paper is chosen at random. Find the probability of the event.**

   32. Drawing a number greater than 4   **33.** Drawing a number that is divisible by 5

Chapter 8

8.1 Find the measure(s) of the numbered angle(s).

1.

2.

3.

8.2 Find the value of *x*. Classify the triangle by its angles.

4.

5.

6.

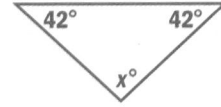

8.3 In Exercises 7–9, classify the quadrilateral.

7.

8.

9.

8.4   **10.** Find the sum of the angle measures in an 11-gon.

8.4   **11.** Find the measure of one angle in a regular 18-gon.

8.5   **In Exercises 12–14, use the diagrams.**

     12. Name all pairs of congruent sides.

     13. Name all pairs of congruent angles.

     14. Explain how you know that $\triangle ABC \cong \triangle PQR$.

Graph $\triangle ABC$ with vertices $A(-2, 4)$, $B(0, 2)$, and $C(-2, -6)$. Then graph its image after the given transformation.

8.6   **15.** Reflect $\triangle ABC$ in the *x*-axis.

8.6   **16.** Reflect $\triangle ABC$ in the *y*-axis.

8.7   **17.** Translate $\triangle ABC$ using $(x, y) \rightarrow (x - 1, y + 4)$.

8.7   **18.** Translate $\triangle ABC$ using $(x, y) \rightarrow (x + 2, y - 3)$.

8.7   **19.** Rotate $\triangle ABC$ 90° clockwise.

8.8   **20.** Dilate $\triangle ABC$ by a scale factor of 2.

8.8   **21.** Dilate $\triangle ABC$ by a scale factor of $\frac{1}{2}$.

Chapter 9

9.1 Use a calculator to approximate the square root. Round to the nearest tenth.

1. $\sqrt{52}$ **2.** $\sqrt{9.6}$ **3.** $-\sqrt{738}$ **4.** $-\sqrt{2037}$

9.1 Solve the equation. Check your solutions.

5. $k^2 = 900$ **6.** $h^2 - 5 = 44$ **7.** $153 + z^2 = 378$ **8.** $168 = v^2 - 1$

9. $a^2 + 7 = 88$ **10.** $m^2 = 3600$ **11.** $x^2 - 11 = 53$ **12.** $w^2 + 78 = 478$

9.2 In Exercises 13–16, graph the pair of numbers on a number line. Then copy and complete the statement with $<$, $>$, or $=$.

13. $\sqrt{18}$? 4   **14.** $\sqrt{\dfrac{9}{16}}$? $\dfrac{3}{4}$ **15.** -8 ? $-\sqrt{70}$ **16.** $\dfrac{2}{3}$? $\sqrt{\dfrac{1}{9}}$

9.2 **17.** Order the decimals 0.12, $0.\overline{1}$, $0.\overline{12}$, 0.123, and $0.\overline{123}$.

9.2 **18.** Order the decimals 0.34, $0.\overline{3}$, $.\overline{34}$, and 0.334 from least to greatest.

9.3 Let a and b represent the lengths of the legs of a right triangle, and let c represent the length of the hypotenuse. Find the unknown length.

19. $a = 21$, $b = 28$, $c = \underline{\ ?\ }$ **20.** $a = \underline{\ ?\ }$, $b = 63$, $c = 65$ **21.** $a = 56$, $b = \underline{\ ?\ }$, $c = 65$

22. $a = 1.5$, $b = 3.6$, $c = \underline{\ ?\ }$ **23.** $a = \underline{\ ?\ }$, $b = 100$, $c = 125$ **24.** $a = 32$, $b = \underline{\ ?\ }$, $c = 68$

9.4 Determine whether the numbers form a Pythagorean triple.

25. 40, 42, 58   **26.** 37, 39, 54   **27.** 15, 112, 113   **28.** 12, 35, 38

9.5 Find the values of the variables. Give exact answers.

29.   **30.**   **31.**

9.6 In $\triangle ABC$, write the sine, cosine, and tangent ratios for $\angle A$ and $\angle B$.

32.   **33.**   **34.**

9.6 **35.** Use a calculator to approximate the sine, cosine, and tangent of $62°$. Round your answers to four decimal places.

Chapter 10

10.1 **Sketch a parallelogram with base *b* and height *h* and find its area.**

    1. $b = 15$ in., $h = 13$ in.   **2.** $b = 9.4$ ft, $h = 4.8$ ft   **3.** $b = 8\frac{1}{3}$ cm, $h = 1\frac{1}{5}$ cm

10.1 **Sketch a trapezoid with bases b_1 and b_2 and height *h* and find its area.**

    4. $b_1 = 9$ m, $b_2 = 16$ m, $h = 18$ m   **5.** $b_1 = 40$ yd, $b_2 = 28$ yd, $h = 10.5$ yd

10.2 **In Exercises 6–13, find the area of the circle given its radius *r* or diameter *d*. Use 3.14 for π.**

    6. $r = 18$ mi   **7.** $d = 80$ in.   **8.** $d = 11$ mm   **9.** $r = 2.9$ ft

    10. $d = 7.8$ in.   **11.** $r = 0.3$ cm   **12.** $r = 11$ ft   **13.** $d = 16$ mi

10.3 **14.** How many faces, edges, and vertices does a hexagonal pyramid have?

10.3 **15.** Show two ways to represent a cylinder. Tell whether it is a polyhedron.

10.4 **Draw a net for the solid. Then find the surface area. Round to the nearest tenth.**

    16.   **17.**   **18.**

10.5 **Find the surface area of the solid. Round to the nearest tenth.**

    19. A square pyramid with base side length 12 m and slant height 9 m

    20. A cone with radius 8 cm and slant height 9 cm

    21. A cone with diameter 15 m and slant height 8.2 m

10.6 **Find the volume of the solid. Round to the nearest tenth.**

    22. The prism in Exercise 16

    23. The prism in Exercise 17

    24. The cylinder in Exercise 18

10.7 **Find the volume of the solid. Round to the nearest tenth.**

    25. A square pyramid with base side length 10 ft and height 8 ft

    26. A cone with radius 18 m and height 6 m

    27. The triangular pyramid shown at the right

Chapter 11

11.1 **1.** Decide whether the relation $(-3, 3)$, $(-2, 2)$, $(-1, 1)$, $(0, 0)$, $(1, 1)$ is a function. Explain your answer.

11.1 **2.** Make an input-output table for the function $y = 0.5x$. Use a domain of -4, -2, 0, 2, and 4. Identify the range.

11.1 **3.** Write a function rule that relates x and y.

Input x	-5	-3	-1	1
Output y	-6	-4	-2	0

11.2 **4.** Make a scatter plot of the data in Exercise 3. Describe the relationship between x and y.

11.3 **Tell whether the ordered pair is a solution of the equation.**

  5. $y = 3x - 7$; $(1, 4)$ **6.** $4x + y = 5$; $(2, -1)$ **7.** $y = \frac{1}{2}x + \frac{1}{2}$; $(-3, -1)$

11.3 **List four solutions of the equation.**

  8. $y = -x - 3$ **9.** $y = 7 + 2x$ **10.** $y = -\frac{2}{3}x$ **11.** $y = -x$

  12. $-x + y = 1$ **13.** $3x + y = -2$ **14.** $x + 2y = 8$ **15.** $-3y + 4x = 7$

11.4 **Graph the linear equation.**

  16. $y = -3$ **17.** $y = \frac{1}{4}x - 2$ **18.** $x = 4$ **19.** $3x + y = 4$

11.5 **In Exercises 20–23, find the intercepts of the graph of the equation.**

  20. $y = -2x + 4$ **21.** $y = 5x - 1$ **22.** $x + 5y = -5$ **23.** $2x - 3y = 12$

11.5 **24.** Graph the line with an x-intercept of 4 and a y-intercept of -1.

11.5 **25.** Graph the line with an x-intercept of -2 and a y-intercept of 10.

11.6 **Find the slope of the line passing through the points.**

  26. $(-2, 3)$, $(6, 1)$ **27.** $(5, 0)$, $(5, -9)$ **28.** $(6, -4)$, $(2, -4)$ **29.** $(7, -5)$, $(-2, -14)$

  30. $(-7, 8)$, $(-9, 5)$ **31.** $(-3, -2)$, $(-7, 2)$ **32.** $(4, 9)$, $(3, 13)$ **33.** $(0, 7)$, $(-3, -10)$

11.7 **Find the slope and y-intercept of the graph of the equation.**

  34. $y = 3x - 5$ **35.** $y = 2$ **36.** $y = -\frac{1}{3}x + 1$ **37.** $2x - y = 8$

11.8 **Graph the inequality.**

  38. $y > -x - 3$ **39.** $6 \le 3y$ **40.** $5 + 2x > y$ **41.** $4x + 3y \le -12$

Chapter 12

In Exercises 1–3, use the following lengths, in inches, of alligators at an alligator farm: 140, 127, 103, 140, 118, 100, 117, 101, 116, 129, 130, 105, 99, 143.

12.1 **1.** Make an ordered stem-and-leaf plot of the data. Identify the interval that includes the most data values.

12.1 **2.** Find the median and range of the data.

12.2 **3.** Make a box-and-whisker plot of the data. What conclusions can you make?

12.3 **4.** In a survey about favorite kinds of movies, 20 people chose dramas, 4 chose horror movies, 8 chose science fiction, and 18 chose comedies. Represent the data in a circle graph.

12.3 **5.** You want to display the average monthly price of a stock for each month in 2001. What type of display would you use? Explain.

12.4 **6.** You can take one of three different classes in the morning or the afternoon. Make a tree diagram to find the number of choices that are possible.

12.4 **7.** A license plate has 3 digits followed by 3 letters. How many different license plates are possible?

12.5 **In Exercises 8–11, find the number of permutations.**

    8. $_7P_2$ **9.** $_{11}P_1$ **10.** $_8P_5$ **11.** $_{10}P_3$

12.5 **12.** There are 8 students in the school play. How many different ways can the cast be arranged in a row?

12.6 **In Exercises 13–16, find the number of combinations.**

    13. $_5C_4$ **14.** $_{20}C_2$ **15.** $_6C_3$ **16.** $_{12}C_9$

12.6 **17.** A CD case holds 30 CDs. How many ways can you select 3 CDs from the case?

12.7 **18.** A telephone number is chosen at random. Find the odds that the last digit is greater than 3.

12.8 **19.** You flip two coins. Find the probability that you do *not* get two heads.

12.8 **20.** You and two friends each roll a number cube. What is the probability that all of you roll a 3?

12.8 **21.** Ten slips of paper numbered 1 through 10 are placed in a bag. You draw a slip at random and draw another without replacing the first. Find the probability that both numbers are odd.

Chapter 13

13.1 **In Exercises 1–3, simplify the polynomial and write it in standard form.**

    1. $3 + 5x - x^2 - 7x + 4$ **2.** $2t^4 + t^3 - 6 - 3t^3 + t^2$ **3.** $4(5 - k) + 4k - k^2 + 1$

13.1   **4.** The height, in feet, of a falling pebble after t seconds of falling from a height of 45 feet can be found using the polynomial $-16t^2 + 45$. Find the pebble's height after 1.5 seconds.

13.2 **Find the sum or difference.**

    5. $(3x^2 + 5x - 4) + (-2x^3 + x^2 + 9x)$ **6.** $(-8x^2 - x + 1) - (7x^2 - 5x + 1)$

    7. $(4x^3 - 8x^2 + 2) - (x^3 + x^2 - 6x + 5)$ **8.** $(-x^2 - 3x + 7) + (x^2 + 4x - 9)$

    9. $(2x^3 - 2x^2 + 1) + (-x^3 + 9x + 5)$ **10.** $(3x^2 - 5x - 10) - (5x^3 + x - 2)$

13.3 **Simplify the expression.**

    11. $(4z)(-7z^5)$ **12.** $(-r^2)(-3r^2)$ **13.** $-3n(2n - 5)$ **14.** $q^3(-q + 2)$

    15. $(5ab)^3$ **16.** $(-rst)^4$ **17.** $(p^6)^4$ **18.** $(3y^5)^2$

13.4 **Find the product and simplify.**

    19. $(2x + 1)(x - 5)$ **20.** $(m - 3)(-m + 4)$ **21.** $(d + 6)(d + 4)$

    22. $(4y - 3)(4y + 3)$ **23.** $(a - 8)(a - 7)$ **24.** $(5x + 2)(2x - 1)$

13.5 **Rewrite using function notation.**

    25. $y = 2x - 5$ **26.** $y = 3x^2$ **27.** $y = 5x^2 + 1$

13.5 **Evaluate the function for $x = -2, -1, 0, 1,$ and 2.**

    28. $f(x) = 2x^2 + x$ **29.** $f(x) = \frac{1}{4}x^2$ **30.** $f(x) = \frac{1}{2}x^2 - x$

    31. $f(x) = -3x^2 + 2x$ **32.** $f(x) = x^2 + 4x$ **33.** $f(x) = -x^2 - 3$

13.5 **Graph the function using a table of values.**

    34. $f(x) = 3x^2$ **35.** $f(x) = -x^2 + 2$ **36.** $f(x) = 2x^2 - 4$

13.5 **Tell whether the graph represents a function.**

37.   **38.**   **39.**

Table of Symbols

Symbol	Meaning	Page
28.6	decimal point	4
$=$	equals, is equal to	10, 28
$3 \cdot x$ $3(x)$ $3x$	3 times x	10, 15
$\dfrac{14}{2}$	14 divided by 2	11
( )	parentheses—a grouping symbol	11
[ ]	brackets—a grouping symbol	11
4^3	$4 \cdot 4 \cdot 4$	20
$\stackrel{?}{=}$	is equal to?	26, 29
$\neq$	is not equal to	29
⌐	right angle	33, 375
$\approx$	is approximately equal to	39
$\ldots$	continues on	53
-3	negative 3	53
-3	the opposite of 3	54
$\lvert a \rvert$	the absolute value of a number a	54
(x, y)	ordered pair	91
$<$	is less than	141, 302
$>$	is greater than	141, 302
$\leq$	is less than or equal to	141, 302
$\geq$	is greater than or equal to	141, 302

Symbol	Meaning	Page
$1.1\overline{6}$	repeating decimal 1.16666. . .	242
π	pi—a number approximately equal to 3.14	290
$a : b, \dfrac{a}{b}$	ratio of a to b	317
%	percent	327
$\circ$	degree(s)	375, 721
$\angle A$	angle with vertex point A	375, 719
$m\angle B$	the measure of angle B	375
$\perp$	is perpendicular to	376
$\parallel$	is parallel to	377
$\rightleftarrows$	parallel lines	377
$\cong$	is congruent to	397
$\overline{AB}$	line segment AB	397
$\triangle ABC$	triangle with vertices A, B, and C	398
A'	the image of point A	404
$\sim$	is similar to	416
$\sqrt{a}$	the positive square root of a number a where $a \geq 0$	431
$\pm$	plus or minus	433
$\nleq$	is not less than or equal to	583
3!	3 factorial, or $3 \cdot 2 \cdot 1$	623
$f(x)$	the function of f at x	680
$\overleftrightarrow{AB}$	line AB	718
$\overrightarrow{AB}$	ray AB	718

Table of Measures

Time

60 seconds (sec) = 1 minute (min)
60 minutes = 1 hour (h)
24 hours = 1 day (d)
7 days = 1 week (wk)
4 weeks (approx.) = 1 month

$$\left.\begin{array}{l}\text{365 days}\\\text{52 weeks (approx.)}\\\text{12 months}\end{array}\right\} = \text{1 year}$$

10 years = 1 decade
100 years = 1 century

METRIC

Length

10 millimeters (mm) = 1 centimeter (cm)

$$\left.\begin{array}{l}\text{100 cm}\\\text{1000 mm}\end{array}\right\} = \text{1 meter (m)}$$

1000 m = 1 kilometer (km)

Area

100 square millimeters = 1 square centimeter
(mm^2) (cm^2)
$10,000\ cm^2 = 1$ square meter (m^2)
$10,000\ m^2 = 1$ hectare (ha)

Volume

1000 cubic millimeters = 1 cubic centimeter
(mm^3) (cm^3)
$1,000,000\ cm^3 = 1$ cubic meter (m^3)

Liquid Capacity

$$\left.\begin{array}{l}\text{1000 milliliters (mL)}\\\text{1000 cubic centimeters }(cm^3)\end{array}\right\} = \text{1 liter (L)}$$

1000 L = 1 kiloliter (kL)

Mass

1000 milligrams (mg) = 1 gram (g)
1000 g = 1 kilogram (kg)
1000 kg = 1 metric ton (t)

Temperature   Degrees Celsius (°C)

0°C = freezing point of water
37°C = normal body temperature
100°C = boiling point of water

UNITED STATES CUSTOMARY

Length

12 inches (in.) = 1 foot (ft)

$$\left.\begin{array}{l}\text{36 in.}\\\text{3 ft}\end{array}\right\} = \text{1 yard (yd)}$$

$$\left.\begin{array}{l}\text{5280 ft}\\\text{1760 yd}\end{array}\right\} = \text{1 mile (mi)}$$

Area

144 square inches $(in.^2) = 1$ square foot (ft^2)
$9\ ft^2 = 1$ square yard (yd^2)

$$\left.\begin{array}{l}43{,}560\ ft^2\\4840\ yd^2\end{array}\right\} = \text{1 acre (A)}$$

Volume

1728 cubic inches $(in.^3) = 1$ cubic foot (ft^3)
$27\ ft^3 = 1$ cubic yard (yd^3)

Liquid Capacity

8 fluid ounces (fl oz) = 1 cup (c)
2 c = 1 pint (pt)
2 pt = 1 quart (qt)
4 qt = 1 gallon (gal)

Weight

16 ounces (oz) = 1 pound (lb)
2000 lb = 1 ton

Temperature   Degrees Fahrenheit (°F)

32°F = freezing point of water
98.6°F = normal body temperature
212°F = boiling point of water

Table of Formulas

Geometric Formulas

Rectangle (p. 33)

Area
$A = lw$

Perimeter
$P = 2l + 2w$

Square (p. 33)

Area
$A = s^2$

Perimeter
$P = 4s$

Triangle (p. 134)

Area
$A = \frac{1}{2}bh$

Parallelogram (p. 481)

Area
$A = bh$

Trapezoid (p. 482)

Area
$A = \frac{1}{2}(b_1 + b_2)h$

Circle (pp. 290, 486)

Area
$A = \pi r^2$

Circumference
$C = \pi d$ or
$C = 2\pi r$

Prism (pp. 503, 513)

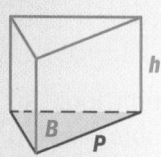

Surface Area
$S = 2B + Ph$

Volume
$V = Bh$

Cylinder (pp. 504, 514)

Surface Area
$S = 2\pi r^2 + 2\pi rh$

Volume
$V = \pi r^2 h$

Pyramid (pp. 507, 519)

Surface Area
$S = B + \frac{1}{2}Pl$

Volume
$V = \frac{1}{3}Bh$

Cone (pp. 508, 520)

Surface Area
$S = \pi r^2 + \pi rl$

Volume
$V = \frac{1}{3}Bh = \frac{1}{3}\pi r^2 h$

Other Formulas

Distance traveled (p. 34)	$d = rt$ where d = distance, r = rate, and t = time
Simple interest (p. 348)	$I = Prt$ where I = simple interest, P = principal, r = annual interest rate, and t = time in years
Pythagorean theorem (p. 443)	In a right triangle, $a^2 + b^2 = c^2$ where a and b are the lengths of the legs, and c is the length of the hypotenuse.

Table of Properties

Identity Properties (pp. 59, 71)

Addition The sum of a number and the additive identity, 0, is the number.

Numbers $7 + 0 = 7$

Algebra $a + 0 = a$

Multiplication The product of a number and the multiplicative identity, 1, is the number.

Numbers $3 \cdot 1 = 3$

Algebra $a \cdot 1 = a$

Inverse Properties (pp. 61, 73, 234)

Addition The sum of a number and its additive inverse, or opposite, is 0.

Numbers $4 + (-4) = 0$

Algebra $a + (-a) = 0$

Multiplication The product of a nonzero number and its multiplicative inverse, or reciprocal, is 1.

Numbers $\frac{2}{3} \cdot \frac{3}{2} = 1$

Algebra $\frac{a}{b} \cdot \frac{b}{a} = 1 \ (a, b \neq 0)$

Commutative Property (p. 80)

Addition In a sum, you can add terms in any order.

Numbers $-2 + 5 = 5 + (-2)$

Algebra $a + b = b + a$

Multiplication In a product, you can multiply factors in any order.

Numbers $3(-6) = -6(3)$

Algebra $ab = ba$

Associative Property (p. 81)

Addition Changing the grouping of terms in a sum will not change the sum.

Numbers $(2 + 4) + 6 = 2 + (4 + 6)$

Algebra $(a + b) + c = a + (b + c)$

Multiplication Changing the grouping of factors in a product will not change the product.

Numbers $(6 \times 2.5) \times 4 = 6 \times (2.5 \times 4)$

Algebra $(ab)c = a(bc)$

Distributive Property (p. 85)

You can multiply a number and a sum by multiplying each term of the sum by the number and then adding these products. The same property applies to subtraction.

Numbers $3(4 + 6) = 3(4) + 3(6)$ $2(8 - 5) = 2(8) - 2(5)$

Algebra $a(b + c) = a(b) + a(c)$ $a(b - c) = a(b) - a(c)$

Properties of Exponents (pp. 196, 197)

To find the *product of powers* with the same base, add their exponents.

Numbers $5^2 \cdot 5^3 = 5^{2+3} = 5^5$

Algebra $a^b \cdot a^c = a^{b+c}$

To find the *quotient of powers* with the same nonzero base, subtract the denominator's exponent from the numerator's exponent.

Numbers $\frac{7^4}{7^2} = 7^{4-2} = 7^2$ **Algebra** $\frac{a^b}{a^c} = a^{b-c}$

Cross Products Property (p. 323)

The cross products of a proportion are equal.

Numbers Because $\frac{3}{4} = \frac{6}{8}$, $3 \cdot 8 = 4 \cdot 6$.   **Algebra** If $\frac{a}{b} = \frac{c}{d}$, then $ad = bc$, $b, d \neq 0$.

Finding Squares and Square Roots

EXAMPLE 1 **Finding a Square**

Find 54^2.

Find 54 in the column labeled *No.* (an abbreviation for *Number*).
Read across to the column labeled *Square*.

No.	Square	Sq. Root
51	2601	7.141
52	2704	7.211
53	2809	7.280
54	2916	7.348
55	3025	7.416

ANSWER So, $54^2 = 2916$.

EXAMPLE 2 **Finding a Square Root**

Find a decimal approximation of $\sqrt{54}$.

Find 54 in the column labeled *No.* Read across to the column labeled *Sq. Root*.

No.	Square	Sq. Root
51	2601	7.141
52	2704	7.211
53	2809	7.280
54	2916	7.348
55	3025	7.416

ANSWER So, to the nearest thousandth, $\sqrt{54} \approx 7.348$.

EXAMPLE 3 **Finding a Square Root**

Find a decimal approximation of $\sqrt{3000}$.

Find the two numbers in the *Square* column that 3000 is between. Read across to the column labeled *No.*; $\sqrt{3000}$ is between 54 and 55, but closer to 55.

No.	Square	Sq. Root
51	2601	7.141
52	2704	7.211
53	2809	7.280
54	2916	7.348
55	3025	7.416

ANSWER So, $\sqrt{3000} \approx 55$. A more accurate approximation can be found using a calculator: 54.772256.

Table of Squares and Square Roots

No.	Square	Sq. Root	No.	Square	Sq. Root	No.	Square	Sq. Root
1	1	1.000	51	2601	7.141	101	10,201	10.050
2	4	1.414	52	2704	7.211	102	10,404	10.100
3	9	1.732	53	2809	7.280	103	10,609	10.149
4	16	2.000	54	2916	7.348	104	10,816	10.198
5	25	2.236	55	3025	7.416	105	11,025	10.247
6	36	2.449	56	3136	7.483	106	11,236	10.296
7	49	2.646	57	3249	7.550	107	11,449	10.344
8	64	2.828	58	3364	7.616	108	11,664	10.392
9	81	3.000	59	3481	7.681	109	11,881	10.440
10	100	3.162	60	3600	7.746	110	12,100	10.488
11	121	3.317	61	3721	7.810	111	12,321	10.536
12	144	3.464	62	3844	7.874	112	12,544	10.583
13	169	3.606	63	3969	7.937	113	12,769	10.630
14	196	3.742	64	4096	8.000	114	12,996	10.677
15	225	3.873	65	4225	8.062	115	13,225	10.724
16	256	4.000	66	4356	8.124	116	13,456	10.770
17	289	4.123	67	4489	8.185	117	13,689	10.817
18	324	4.243	68	4624	8.246	118	13,924	10.863
19	361	4.359	69	4761	8.307	119	14,161	10.909
20	400	4.472	70	4900	8.367	120	14,400	10.954
21	441	4.583	71	5041	8.426	121	14,641	11.000
22	484	4.690	72	5184	8.485	122	14,884	11.045
23	529	4.796	73	5329	8.544	123	15,129	11.091
24	576	4.899	74	5476	8.602	124	15,376	11.136
25	625	5.000	75	5625	8.660	125	15,625	11.180
26	676	5.099	76	5776	8.718	126	15,876	11.225
27	729	5.196	77	5929	8.775	127	16,129	11.269
28	784	5.292	78	6084	8.832	128	16,384	11.314
29	841	5.385	79	6241	8.888	129	16,641	11.358
30	900	5.477	80	6400	8.944	130	16,900	11.402
31	961	5.568	81	6561	9.000	131	17,161	11.446
32	1024	5.657	82	6724	9.055	132	17,424	11.489
33	1089	5.745	83	6889	9.110	133	17,689	11.533
34	1156	5.831	84	7056	9.165	134	17,956	11.576
35	1225	5.916	85	7225	9.220	135	18,225	11.619
36	1296	6.000	86	7396	9.274	136	18,496	11.662
37	1369	6.083	87	7569	9.327	137	18,769	11.705
38	1444	6.164	88	7744	9.381	138	19,044	11.747
39	1521	6.245	89	7921	9.434	139	19,321	11.790
40	1600	6.325	90	8100	9.487	140	19,600	11.832
41	1681	6.403	91	8281	9.539	141	19,881	11.874
42	1764	6.481	92	8464	9.592	142	20,164	11.916
43	1849	6.557	93	8649	9.644	143	20,449	11.958
44	1936	6.633	94	8836	9.695	144	20,736	12.000
45	2025	6.708	95	9025	9.747	145	21,025	12.042
46	2116	6.782	96	9216	9.798	146	21,316	12.083
47	2209	6.856	97	9409	9.849	147	21,609	12.124
48	2304	6.928	98	9604	9.899	148	21,904	12.166
49	2401	7.000	99	9801	9.950	149	22,201	12.207
50	2500	7.071	100	10,000	10.000	150	22,500	12.247

Squares and Square Roots

Equivalent Fractions, Decimals, and Percents

Fraction	Decimal	Percent
$\frac{1}{10}$	0.1	10%
$\frac{1}{8}$	0.125	$12\frac{1}{2}\%$
$\frac{1}{5}$	0.2	20%
$\frac{1}{4}$	0.25	25%
$\frac{3}{10}$	0.3	30%
$\frac{1}{3}$	$0.\overline{3}$	$33\frac{1}{3}\%$
$\frac{3}{8}$	0.375	$37\frac{1}{2}\%$
$\frac{2}{5}$	0.4	40%
$\frac{1}{2}$	0.5	50%
$\frac{3}{5}$	0.6	60%
$\frac{5}{8}$	0.625	$62\frac{1}{2}\%$
$\frac{2}{3}$	$0.\overline{6}$	$66\frac{2}{3}\%$
$\frac{7}{10}$	0.7	70%
$\frac{3}{4}$	0.75	75%
$\frac{4}{5}$	0.8	80%
$\frac{7}{8}$	0.875	$87\frac{1}{2}\%$
$\frac{9}{10}$	0.9	90%
1	1	100%

Glossary

	Example
a	
absolute value (p. 54) The absolute value of a number a is the distance between a and 0 on a number line. The absolute value of a is written $\lvert a \rvert$.	$\lvert 4 \rvert = 4 \quad \lvert -7 \rvert = 7 \quad \lvert 0 \rvert = 0$
acute angle (p. 382) An angle whose measure is less than 90°.	
acute triangle (p. 382) A triangle with three acute angles.	
addition property of equality (p. 110) Adding the same number to each side of an equation produces an equivalent equation.	If $x - 5 = 2$, then $x - 5 + 5 = 2 + 5$, so $x = 7$. If $x - a = b$, then $x - a + a = b + a$.
additive identity (p. 59) The number 0 is the additive identity because the sum of any number and 0 is the original number.	$-7 + 0 = -7$ $a + 0 = a$
additive inverse (p. 61) The additive inverse of a number a is the opposite of the number, or $-a$. The sum of a number and its additive inverse is 0.	The additive inverse of 6 is -6, so $6 + (-6) = 0$.
angle (p. 719) A figure formed by two rays that begin at a common point, called the vertex.	
angle of rotation (p. 410) In a rotation, the angle formed by two rays drawn from the center of rotation through corresponding points on the original figure and its image.	*See* rotation.
annual interest rate (p. 348) In simple interest, the percent of the principal earned or paid per year.	*See* simple interest.
area (p. 33) The number of square units covered by a figure.	 *Area* = 14 square units
associative property of addition (p. 81) Changing the grouping of terms in a sum does not change the sum.	$(9 + 4) + 6 = 9 + (4 + 6)$ $(a + b) + c = a + (b + c)$
associative property of multiplication (p. 81) Changing the grouping of factors in a product does not change the product.	$(2 \cdot 5) \cdot 3 = 2 \cdot (5 \cdot 3)$ $(ab)c = a(bc)$

b	Example

bar graph (p. 5) A type of graph in which the lengths of bars are used to represent and compare data in categories.

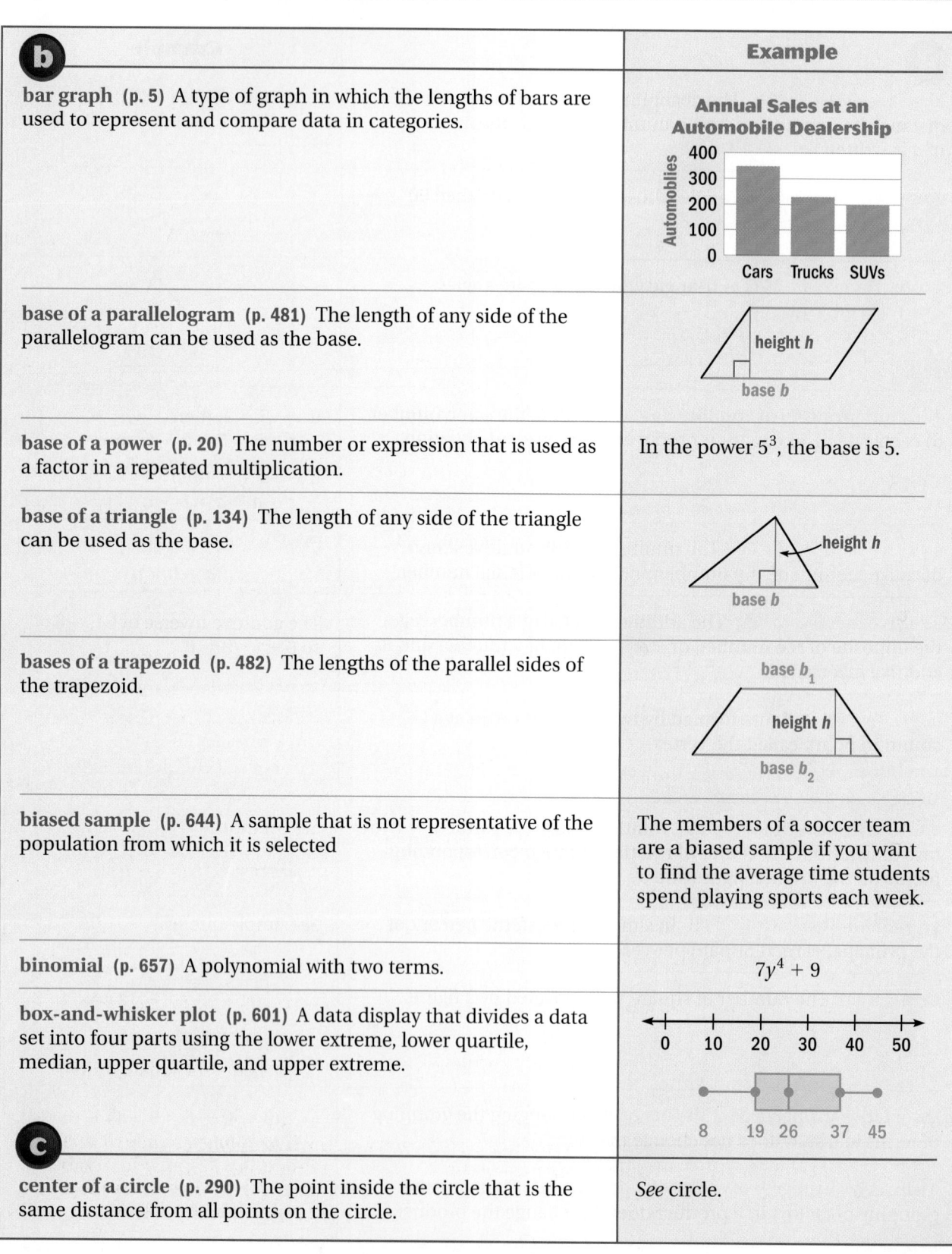

Annual Sales at an Automobile Dealership

base of a parallelogram (p. 481) The length of any side of the parallelogram can be used as the base.

height *h*
base *b*

base of a power (p. 20) The number or expression that is used as a factor in a repeated multiplication.

In the power 5^3, the base is 5.

base of a triangle (p. 134) The length of any side of the triangle can be used as the base.

height *h*
base *b*

bases of a trapezoid (p. 482) The lengths of the parallel sides of the trapezoid.

base b_1
height *h*
base b_2

biased sample (p. 644) A sample that is not representative of the population from which it is selected

The members of a soccer team are a biased sample if you want to find the average time students spend playing sports each week.

binomial (p. 657) A polynomial with two terms.

$7y^4 + 9$

box-and-whisker plot (p. 601) A data display that divides a data set into four parts using the lower extreme, lower quartile, median, upper quartile, and upper extreme.

0   10   20   30   40   50

8   19   26   37   45

c	

center of a circle (p. 290) The point inside the circle that is the same distance from all points on the circle.

See circle.

Glossary

	Example
center of rotation (p. 410) The point about which a figure is turned when the figure undergoes a rotation.	*See* rotation.
circle (p. 290) The set of all points in a plane that are the same distance, called the radius, from a fixed point, called the center.	
circle graph (p. 331, 605) A circle graph displays data as sections of a circle. The entire circle represents all the data. Each section is labeled using the actual data or using data expressed as fractions, decimals, or percents of the sum of the data.	
circumference (p. 290) The distance around a circle.	*See* circle.
coefficient (p. 86) The number part of a term that includes a variable.	The coefficient of $7x$ is 7.
combination (p. 627) A grouping of objects in which the order is not important.	There are 6 combinations of 2 letters chosen from VASE: VA VS VE AS AE SE
common factor (p. 173) A whole number that is a factor of two or more nonzero whole numbers.	The common factors of 8 and 12 are 1, 2, and 4.
common multiple (p. 186) A multiple that is shared by two or more numbers.	The common multiples of 4 and 6 are 12, 24, 36, ...
commutative property of addition (p. 80) In a sum, you can add terms in any order.	$4 + 7 = 7 + 4$ $a + b = b + a$
commutative property of multiplication (p. 80) In a product, you can multiply factors in any order.	$5(-8) = -8(5)$ $ab = ba$
complementary angles (p. 375) Two angles whose measures have a sum of 90°.	
complementary events (p. 632) Two events are complementary when one event or the other (but not both) must occur.	When rolling a number cube, the events "getting an odd number" and "getting an even number" are complementary events.

	Example
composite number (p. 169) A whole number greater than 1 that has positive factors other than 1 and itself.	6 is a composite number because its factors are 1, 2, 3, and 6.
cone (p. 492) A solid with one circular base.	base
congruent angles (p. 397) Angles that have the same measure.	*See* congruent polygons.
congruent polygons (p. 397) Similar polygons that have the same size. For congruent polygons, corresponding angles are congruent and corresponding sides are congruent. The symbol $\cong$ indicates congruence and is read "is congruent to."	$\triangle ABC \cong \triangle DEF$
congruent sides (p. 397) Sides that have the same length.	*See* congruent polygons.
constant term (p. 86) A term that has a number but no variable.	In the expression $5y + 9$, the term 9 is a constant term.
converse (p. 444) An if-then statement where the hypothesis and conclusion of the original statement have been reversed.	Original: If you clean your room, then it will be neat. Converse: If your room is neat, then you cleaned it.
coordinate plane (p. 91) A coordinate system formed by the intersection of a horizontal number line, called the *x*-axis, and a vertical number line, called the *y*-axis.	

Glossary

	Example
corresponding angles (p. 377) Angles that occupy corresponding positions when a line intersects two other lines.	\n\n$\angle 1$ and $\angle 2$ are corresponding angles.
corresponding parts (p. 397) Pairs of sides and angles of polygons that are in the same relative position.	\n\n$\angle A$ and $\angle E$ are corresponding angles. $\overline{AB}$ and $\overline{ED}$ are corresponding sides.
cosine (p. 463) The cosine of any acute angle A of a right triangle is the ratio of the adjacent leg to the hypotenuse.	\n\n$\cos A = \dfrac{b}{c}$
counting principle (p. 619) If one event can occur in m ways, and for each of these a second event can occur in n ways, then the number of ways that the two events can occur together is $m \cdot n$. The counting principle can be extended to three or more events.	If a T-shirt is made in 5 sizes and in 7 colors, then the number of different T-shirts that are possible is $5 \cdot 7 = 35$.
cross products (p. 323) In a proportion $\dfrac{a}{b} = \dfrac{c}{d}$ where $b \neq 0$ and $d \neq 0$, the cross products are ad and bc.	The cross products of the proportion $\dfrac{2}{3} = \dfrac{4}{6}$ are $2 \cdot 6$ and $3 \cdot 4$.
cylinder (p. 492) A solid with two congruent circular bases that lie in parallel planes.	

d

data (p. 5) Information, facts, or numbers that describe something.	Numbers of cars sold annually at a dealership:\n340, 350, 345, 347, 352, 360, 365
degrees (p. 721) Unit of measure for angles. The symbol for degrees is °. There are 360° in a circle.	

	Example
dependent events (p. 639) Two events such that the occurrence of one affects the likelihood that the other will occur.	A bag contains 5 red and 8 blue marbles. You randomly choose a marble, do not replace it, then randomly choose another marble. The events "first marble is red" and "second marble is red" are dependent events.
diameter of a circle (p. 290) The distance across the circle through the center.	*See* circle.
dilation (p. 418) A transformation that stretches or shrinks a figure.	The scale factor is $\frac{1}{2}$.
discount (p. 342) A decrease in the price of an item.	The original price of a pair of jeans is \$42 but the store sells it for \$29.99. The discount is \$12.01.
distributive property (p. 85) For all numbers a, b, and c, $a(b + c) = ab + ac$ and $a(b - c) = ab - ac$.	$8(10 + 4) = 8(10) + 8(4)$ $3(4 - 2) = 3(4) - 3(2)$
division property of equality (p. 114) Dividing each side of an equation by the same nonzero number produces an equivalent equation.	If $6x = 54$, then $\frac{6x}{6} = \frac{54}{6}$, so $x = 9$. If $ax = b$ and $a \neq 0$, then $\frac{ax}{a} = \frac{b}{a}$.
domain of a function (p. 542) The set of all possible input values for the function.	*See* function.

e

edge of a polyhedron (p. 492) A line segment where two faces of the polyhedron meet.	

	Example
equation (p. 28) A mathematical sentence formed by setting two expressions equal.	$3 \cdot 6 = 18$ and $x + 7 = 12$ are equations.
equilateral triangle (p. 382) A triangle with three congruent sides.	
equivalent equations (p. 109) Equations that have the same solution(s).	$2x - 6 = 0$ and $2x = 6$ are equivalent equations because the solution of both equations is 3.
equivalent fractions (p. 179) Fractions that represent the same part-to-whole relationship. Equivalent fractions have the same simplest form.	$\frac{6}{8}$ and $\frac{9}{12}$ are equivalent fractions that both represent $\frac{3}{4}$.
equivalent inequalities (p. 141) Inequalities that have the same solution.	$3x \leq 12$ and $x \leq 4$ are equivalent inequalities because the solution of both inequalities is all numbers less than or equal to 4.
equivalent ratios (p. 317) Ratios that have the same value.	$\frac{15}{12}$ and $\frac{25}{20}$ are equivalent ratios because $\frac{15}{12} = 1.25$ and $\frac{25}{20} = 1.25$.
evaluate (p. 10) To find the value of an expression with one or more operations.	$4(3) + 6 \div 2 = 15$
event (p. 354) A collection of outcomes of an experiment.	An event for rolling a number cube is "getting a number divisible by 3."
experimental probability (p. 355) A probability based on a sample or repeated trials of an experiment. The experimental probability of an event is given by: $P(\text{event}) = \dfrac{\text{Number of favorable outcomes}}{\text{Number of trials or items in sample}}$	During one month, your school bus is on time 17 out of 22 school days. The experimental probability that the bus is on time is: $P(\text{bus is on time}) = \dfrac{17}{22} \approx 0.773$
exponent (p. 20) A number or expression that represents how many times a base is used as a factor in a repeated multiplication.	In the power 5^3, the exponent is 3.

	Example
face of a polyhedron (p. 492) A polygon that is a side of the polyhedron.	*See* edge of a polyhedron.
factor tree (p. 169) A diagram that can be used to write the prime factorization of a number.	$$\begin{array}{c} 54 \\ 6 \times 9 \\ 2 \times 3 \times 3 \times 3 \end{array}$$
factorial (p. 623) The expression $n!$ is read "n factorial" and represents the product of all integers from 1 to n.	$4! = 4 \cdot 3 \cdot 2 \cdot 1 = 24$
favorable outcomes (p. 354) Outcomes corresponding to a specified event.	When rolling a number cube, the favorable outcomes for the event "getting a number greater than 4" are 5 and 6.
formula (p. 33) An equation that relates two or more quantities such as perimeter, length, and width.	$P = 2l + 2w$
fraction (p. 179) A number of the form $\frac{a}{b}$ ($b \neq 0$) where a is called the numerator and b is called the denominator.	$\frac{5}{7}$ and $\frac{18}{10}$ are fractions.
frequency (p. 6) The number of data values that lie in an interval of a frequency table or histogram.	*See* frequency table *and* histogram.

frequency table (p. 6) A table used to group data values into intervals.

Interval	Tally	Frequency
0–9	II	2
10–19	IIII	4
20–29	IIII	5

front-end estimation (p. 248) A method for estimating the sum of two or more numbers. In this method, you add the front-end digits, estimate the sum of the remaining digits, and then add the results.

To estimate $3.81 + 1.32 + 5.74$, first add the front-end digits: $3 + 1 + 5 = 9$. Then estimate the sum of the remaining digits: $0.81 + (0.32 + 0.74) \approx 1 + 1 = 2$. The sum is about $9 + 2 = 11$.

function (p. 541) A pairing of each number in a given set with exactly one number in another set. Starting with a number called an input, the function associates with it exactly one number called an output.

Input x	1	2	3	4
Output y	2	4	6	8

The input-output table above represents a function.

Glossary

	Example
function notation (p. 680) An equation that uses $f(x)$ to represent the output of the function f for an input of x.	$f(x) = 5x + 13$ is written using function notation.

g

graph of an inequality (p. 140) On a number line, the set of points that represents the solution of the inequality. (*See* half-plane.)	The graph of the inequality $x < 2$ is shown below. -3 -2 -1 0 1 2 3
greatest common factor (GCF) (p. 173) The greatest whole number that is a factor of two or more nonzero whole numbers.	The GCF of 18 and 27 is 9. The GCF of 48, 24, and 36 is 12.

h

half-plane (p. 584) The graph of a linear inequality in two variables.	
height of a parallelogram (p. 481) The perpendicular distance between a side whose length is the base and the opposite side.	*See* base of a parallelogram.
height of a trapezoid (p. 482) The perpendicular distance between the bases of the trapezoid.	*See* bases of a trapezoid.
height of a triangle (p. 134) The perpendicular distance between a side whose length is the base and the vertex opposite that side.	*See* base of a triangle.
heptagon (p. 390) A polygon with seven sides.	
hexagon (p. 390) A polygon with six sides.	

	Example
histogram (p. 6) A graph that displays data from a frequency table. A histogram has one bar for each interval of the frequency table. The height of the bar indicates the frequency for the interval.	**Library Visitors on a Saturday** A bar graph with Frequency on the vertical axis (0 to 6) and Age (years) on the horizontal axis with intervals 0-9, 10-19, 20-29, 30-39, 40-49. Bar heights: 0-9 is 2, 10-19 is 4, 20-29 is 5, 30-39 is 3, 40-49 is 4.
hypotenuse (p. 443) The side of a right triangle that is opposite the right angle.	A right triangle with the hypotenuse labeled and two legs labeled "leg".
identity property of addition (p. 59) The sum of a number and the additive identity, 0, is the number.	$8 + 0 = 8$ $a + 0 = a$
identity property of multiplication (p. 71) The product of a number and the multiplicative identity, 1, is the number.	$4 \cdot 1 = 4$ $a \cdot 1 = a$
image (p. 404) The new figure formed by a transformation.	*See* reflection, rotation, *and* translation.
improper fraction (p. 707) A fraction whose numerator is greater than or equal to its denominator.	$\frac{8}{7}$ is an improper fraction.
independent events (p. 639) Two events such that the occurrence of one does not affect the likelihood that the other will occur.	You toss a coin and roll a number cube. The events "getting heads" and "getting a 6" are independent events.
inequality (p. 140) A mathematical sentence formed by placing an inequality symbol between two expressions.	$3 < 5$ and $x + 2 \geq -4$ are inequalities.
input (p. 541) A number on which a function operates. An input value is in the domain of the function.	*See* function.
integers (p. 53) The numbers . . . , $-4, -3, -2, -1, 0, 1, 2, 3, 4, \ldots$ consisting of the negative integers, zero, and the positive integers.	-8 and 14 are integers. $-8\frac{1}{3}$ and 14.5 are *not* integers.

	Example
interest (p. 348) The amount earned or paid for the use of money.	*See* simple interest.
inverse operations (p. 109) Operations that "undo" each other.	Addition and subtraction are inverse operations. Multiplication and division are also inverse operations.
inverse property of addition (p. 61) The sum of a number and its additive inverse, or opposite, is 0.	$5 + (-5) = 0$ $a + (-a) = 0$
inverse property of multiplication (pp. 73, 234) The product of a nonzero number and its multiplicative inverse, or reciprocal, is 1.	$\frac{3}{4} \cdot \frac{4}{3} = 1$ $\frac{a}{b} \cdot \frac{b}{a} = 1 \quad (a, b \neq 0)$
irrational number (p. 437) A real number that cannot be written as a quotient of two integers. The decimal form of an irrational number neither terminates nor repeats.	$\sqrt{2}$ and $0.313113111\ldots$ are irrational numbers.
isosceles triangle (p. 382) A triangle with at least two congruent sides.	

l

leading digit (p. 251) The first nonzero digit in a number.	The leading digit of 725 is 7. The leading digit of 0.002638 is 2.
least common denominator (LCD) (p. 192) The least common multiple of the denominators of two or more fractions.	The LCD of $\frac{7}{10}$ and $\frac{3}{4}$ is 20, the least common multiple of 10 and 4.
least common multiple (LCM) (p. 186) The least number that is a common multiple of two or more whole numbers.	The LCM of 4 and 6 is 12. The LCM of 3, 5, and 10 is 30.
legs of a right triangle (p. 443) The two sides of a right triangle that form the right angle.	*See* hypotenuse.
like terms (p. 86) Terms that have identical variable parts raised to the same power. (Two or more constant terms are considered like terms.)	In the expression $x + 4 - 2x + 1$, x and $-2x$ are like terms, and 4 and 1 are like terms.
linear equation (p. 556) An equation in which the variables appear in separate terms and each variable occurs only to the first power.	$7y = 14x + 21$ is a linear equation.

	Example
linear function (pp. 556, 681) A function whose graph is a line or part of a line.	
linear inequality (p. 583) An inequality in which the variables appear in separate terms and each variable occurs only to the first power.	$y \le 2x + 5$ is a linear inequality
line graph (pp. 606, 725) A type of graph in which points representing data pairs are connected by line segments. A line graph is used to show how a quantity changes over time.	
line of reflection (p. 404) The line over which a figure is flipped when the figure undergoes a reflection.	*See* reflection.
line of symmetry (p. 406) A line that divides a figure into two parts that are mirror images of each other.	*See* line symmetry.
line symmetry (p. 406) A figure has line symmetry if it can be divided by a line, called a line of symmetry, into two parts that are mirror images of each other.	A square has 4 lines of symmetry.
lower extreme (p. 601) The least value in a data set.	*See* box-and-whisker plot.
lower quartile (p. 601) The median of the lower half of a data set.	*See* box-and-whisker plot.

m

markup (p. 342) The increase in the wholesale price of an item.	The wholesale price of a loaf of bread is $1 but the store sells it for $1.59. The markup is $.59.

	Example
mean (pp. 75, 257) The sum of the values in a data set divided by the number of values.	The mean of the data set 85, 59, 97, 71 is $\dfrac{85 + 59 + 97 + 71}{4} = \dfrac{312}{4} = 78$.
median (p. 257) The middle value in a data set when the values are written in numerical order. If the data set has an even number of values, the median is the mean of the two middle values.	The median of the data set 8, 17, 21, 23, 26, 29, 34, 40, 45 is the middle value, 26.
mixed number (p. 707) A number that has a whole number part and a fraction part.	$3\dfrac{2}{5}$ is a mixed number.
mode (p. 257) The value in a data set that occurs most often. A data set can have no mode, one mode, or more than one mode.	The mode of the data set 73, 42, 55, 77, 61, 55, 68 is 55 because it occurs most often.
monomial (p. 170, 657) A number, a variable, or a product of a number and one or more variables.	$3xy$, $8x^2$, x, and 14 are monomials.
multiple (p. 186) A multiple of a number is the product of the number and any nonzero whole number.	The multiples of 3 are 3, 6, 9, ...
multiplication property of equality (p. 113) Multiplying each side of an equation by the same nonzero number produces an equivalent equation.	If $\dfrac{x}{3} = 7$, then $3 \cdot \dfrac{x}{3} = 3 \cdot 7$, $\quad$ so $x = 21$. If $\dfrac{x}{a} = b$ and $a \neq 0$, $\quad$ then $a \cdot \dfrac{x}{a} = a \cdot b$.
multiplication property of zero (p. 71) The product of a number and 0 is 0.	$-4 \cdot 0 = 0$ $a \cdot 0 = 0$
multiplicative identity (p. 71) The number 1 is the multiplicative identity because the product of any number and 1 is the original number.	$9 \cdot 1 = 9$ $a \cdot 1 = a$
multiplicative inverse (p. 73, 234) The multiplicative inverse of a number $\dfrac{a}{b}$ ($a, b \neq 0$) is the reciprocal of the number, or $\dfrac{b}{a}$. The product of a number and its multiplicative inverse is 1.	The multiplicative inverse of $\dfrac{3}{2}$ is $\dfrac{2}{3}$, so $\dfrac{3}{2} \cdot \dfrac{2}{3} = 1$.

n	**Example**
negative integers (p. 53) The integers that are less than zero.	The negative integers are -1, -2, -3, -4, ...
net (p. 502) A two-dimensional representation of a solid. This pattern forms a solid when it is folded.	
numerical expression (p. 10) An expression consisting of numbers and operations.	$4(3) + 24 \div 2$

o

obtuse angle (p. 382) An angle whose measure is greater than 90° and less than 180°.	
obtuse triangle (p. 382) A triangle with one obtuse angle.	$120°$ $35°$ $25°$
octagon (p. 390) A polygon with eight sides.	
odds in favor of an event (p. 633) The ratio of favorable outcomes to unfavorable outcomes.	The odds of rolling an even number on a six sided number cube is $\frac{3}{3}$, or 1.
opposites (p. 54) Two numbers that are the same distance from 0 on a number line but are on opposite sides of 0.	-3 and 3 are opposites.
order of operations (p. 10) A set of rules for evaluating an expression involving more than one operation.	To evaluate $3 + 2 \cdot 4$, you perform the multiplication before the addition: $3 + 2 \cdot 4 = 3 + 8 = 11$
ordered pair (p. 91) A pair of numbers (x, y) that can be used to represent a point in a coordinate plane. The first number is the x-coordinate, and the second number is the y-coordinate.	$(-2, 1)$

Glossary

	Example
origin (p. 91) The point (0, 0) where the *x*-axis and the *y*-axis meet in a coordinate plane.	*See* coordinate plane.
outcomes (p. 354) The possible results when an experiment is performed.	When tossing a coin, the outcomes are heads and tails.
output (p. 541) A number produced by evaluating a function using a given input. An output value is in the range of the function.	*See* function.

p

	Example
parallel lines (p. 377) Two lines in the same plane that do not intersect. The symbol ‖ is used to indicate parallel lines.	$a \parallel b$
parallelogram (p. 386) A quadrilateral with both pairs of opposite sides parallel.	
pentagon (p. 390) A polygon with five sides.	
percent (p. 327) A ratio whose denominator is 100. The symbol for percent is %.	$\dfrac{17}{20} = \dfrac{17 \cdot 5}{20 \cdot 5} = \dfrac{85}{100} = 85\%$
percent of change (p. 338) A percent that shows how much a quantity has increased or decreased in comparison with the original amount: Percent of change $p = \dfrac{\text{Amount of increase or decrease}}{\text{Original amount}}$	The percent of change p from 15 to 19 is: $p = \dfrac{19 - 15}{15} = \dfrac{4}{15} \approx 0.267 = 26.7\%$
percent of decrease (p. 338) The percent of change in a quantity when the new amount of the quantity is less than the original amount.	*See* percent of change.
percent of increase (p. 338) The percent of change in a quantity when the new amount of the quantity is greater than the original amount.	*See* percent of change.
perfect square (p. 432) A number that is the square of an integer.	49 is a perfect square because $49 = (\pm 7)^2$.

Glossary

	Example
perimeter (p. 33) The distance around a figure. For a figure with straight sides, the perimeter is the sum of the lengths of the sides.	7 ft 4 ft 4 ft 7 ft *Perimeter* = 22 ft
permutation (p. 623) An arrangement of a group of objects in a particular order.	There are 6 permutations of the 3 letters in the word CAT: CAT ACT TCA CTA ATC TAC
perpendicular lines (p. 376) Two lines that intersect to form a right angle. The symbol ⊥ is used to indicate perpendicular lines.	$a \perp b$
pi (π) (p. 290) The ratio of the circumference of a circle to its diameter.	You can use 3.14 or $\frac{22}{7}$ to approximate π.
plane (p. 718) A plane can be thought of as a flat surface that extends without end.	
polygon (p. 390) A closed geometric figure made up of three or more line segments that intersect only at their endpoints.	**Polygon** **Not a polygon**
polyhedron (p. 492) A solid that is enclosed by polygons.	
polynomial (p. 657) A monomial or a sum of monomials.	*See* binomial, trinomial, monomial.
population (p. 644) In statistics, the entire group of people or objects about which you want information.	If a biologist wants to determine the average age of the elephants in a wildlife refuge, the population consists of every elephant in the refuge.
positive integers (p. 53) The integers that are greater than zero.	The positive integers are 1, 2, 3, 4, ...

Glossary

	Example
power (p. 20) A product formed from repeated multiplication by the same number or expression. A power consists of a base and an exponent.	2^4 is a power with base 2 and exponent 4. $2^4 = 2 \cdot 2 \cdot 2 \cdot 2 = 16$
prime factorization (p. 169) Expressing a whole number as a product of prime numbers.	The prime factorization of 54 is $2 \times 3 \times 3 \times 3 = 2 \times 3^3$.
prime number (p. 169) A whole number greater than 1 whose only positive factors are 1 and itself.	5 is a prime number because its only positive factors are 1 and 5.
principal (p. 348) An amount of money that is deposited or borrowed.	*See* simple interest.
prism (p. 492) A solid, formed by polygons, that has two congruent bases lying in parallel planes.	bases Rectangular prism Triangular prism
probability of an event (p. 354) A number from 0 to 1 that measures the likelihood that the event will occur.	*See* experimental probability *and* theoretical probability.
proportion (p. 322) An equation stating that two ratios are equivalent.	$\frac{3}{5} = \frac{6}{10}$ and $\frac{x}{12} = \frac{25}{30}$ are proportions.
pyramid (p. 492) A solid, formed by polygons, that has one base. The base can be any polygon, and the other faces are triangles.	base
Pythagorean theorem (p. 443) For any right triangle, the sum of the squares of the lengths a and b of the legs equals the square of the length c of the hypotenuse: $a^2 + b^2 = c^2$.	25 15 20 $15^2 + 20^2 = 25^2$
Pythagorean triple (p. 451) A set of three positive integers a, b, and c such that $a^2 + b^2 = c^2$.	5, 12, and 13 is a Pythagorean triple.

	Example
quadrant (p. 91) One of the four regions that a coordinate plane is divided into by the x-axis and the y-axis.	*See* coordinate plane.
quadrilateral (p. 386) A closed geometric figure made up of four line segments, called sides, that intersect only at their endpoints; a polygon with four sides.	

radical expression (p. 431) An expression involving a radical sign, $\sqrt{\ }$.	$\sqrt{3}(22 + 5)$ is a radical expression.
radius of a circle (p. 290) The distance between the center and any point on the circle.	*See* circle.
random sample (p. 644) A sample selected in such a way that each member of the population has an equally likely chance to be part of the sample.	A random sample of 5 eighth graders can be selected by putting the names of all eighth graders in a hat and drawing 5 names without looking.
range of a data set (p. 258) The difference of the greatest and least values in the data set.	The range of the data set 60, 35, 22, 46, 81, 39 is $81 - 22 = 59$.
range of a function (p. 542) The set of all possible output values for the function.	*See* function.
rate (p. 318) A ratio of two quantities measured in different units.	An airplane climbs 18,000 feet in 12 minutes. The airplane's rate of climb is $\frac{18{,}000 \text{ ft}}{12 \text{ min}} = 1500 \text{ ft/min}$.
ratio (p. 317) A comparison of two numbers using division. The ratio of a to b (where $b \neq 0$) can be written as a to b, as $\frac{a}{b}$, or as $a:b$.	The ratio of 17 to 12 can be written as 17 to 12, as $\frac{17}{12}$, or as $17:12$.
rational number (p. 242) A number that can be written as $\frac{a}{b}$ where a and b are integers and $b \neq 0$.	$6 = \frac{6}{1}$, $-\frac{3}{5} = \frac{-3}{5}$, $0.75 = \frac{3}{4}$, and $2\frac{1}{3} = \frac{7}{3}$ are all rational numbers.
real numbers (p. 437) The set of all rational numbers and irrational numbers.	0, $-\frac{5}{9}$, 2.75, and $\sqrt{3}$ are all real numbers.

Glossary

	Example
reciprocals (p. 234) Two nonzero numbers whose product is 1.	$\frac{2}{3}$ and $\frac{3}{2}$ are reciprocals.
reflection (p. 404) A transformation that creates a mirror image of each point of a figure; also known as a *flip*.	 flip Reflection in the *y*-axis.
regular polygon (p. 390) A polygon with all sides equal in length and all angles equal in measure.	 **Regular pentagon**
relation (p. 541) A set of ordered pairs.	(5, 7), (6, 5), (0, 5), (6, 0) is a relation
relatively prime numbers (p. 174) Two or more nonzero whole numbers whose greatest common factor is 1.	9 and 16 are relatively prime because their GCF is 1.
repeating decimal (p. 242) A decimal that has one or more digits that repeat without end.	0.7777. . . and $1.\overline{29}$ are repeating decimals.
rhombus (p. 386) A parallelogram with four congruent sides.	
right angle (p. 375) An angle whose measure is exactly 90°.	
right triangle (p. 382) A triangle with one right angle.	 50° 40°
rise (p. 570) The vertical change between two points on a line.	*See* slope.

	Example
rotation (p. 410) A transformation that rotates a figure through a given angle, called the angle of rotation, and in a given direction about a fixed point, called the center of rotation; also known as a *turn*.	
rotational symmetry (p. 410) A figure has rotational symmetry if a turn of 180° or less produces an image that fits exactly on the original figure.	 A square has rotational symmetry.
run (p. 570) The horizontal change between two points on a line.	*See* slope.

S

sample (p. 644) A part of a population.	To predict the results of an election, a survey is given to a sample of voters.
scale (p. 324) In a scale drawing, the scale gives the relationship between the drawing's dimensions and the actual dimensions.	The scale "1 in. : 10 ft" means that 1 inch in the scale drawing represents an actual distance of 10 feet.
scale drawing (p. 321) A diagram of an object in which the dimensions are in proportion to the actual dimensions of the object.	 1 cm : 12 m
scale factor (p. 418) The ratio of corresponding side lengths of a figure and its image after dilation.	*See* dilation.

Glossary

	Example
scale model (p. 324) A model of an object in which the dimensions are in proportion to the actual dimensions of the object.	A scale model of the White House appears in Tobu World Square in Japan. The scale used is 1 : 25.
scalene triangle (p. 382) A triangle with no congruent sides.	
scatter plot (p. 545) The graph of a set of data pairs (x, y), which is a collection of points in a coordinate plane.	
scientific notation (p. 205) A number is written in scientific notation if it has the form $c \times 10^n$ where c is greater than or equal to 1 and less than 10, and n is an integer.	In scientific notation, 328,000 is written as 3.28×10^5, and 0.00061 is written as 6.1×10^{-4}.
similar polygons (p. 416) Polygons that have the same shape but not necessarily the same size. Corresponding angles of similar polygons are congruent, and the ratios of the lengths of corresponding sides are equal. The symbol $\sim$ is used to indicate that two polygons are similar.	 $\triangle LMN \sim \triangle PQR$
simple interest (p. 348) Interest that is earned or paid only on the principal. The simple interest I is the product of the principal P, the annual interest rate r written as a decimal, and the time t in years: $I = Prt$.	You deposit $700 in a savings account that pays a 3% simple annual interest rate. After 5 years, the interest is $I = Prt = (700)(0.03)(5) = \$105$, and your account balance is $\$700 + \$105 = \$805$.
simplest form of a fraction (p. 179) A fraction is in simplest form if its numerator and denominator have a greatest common factor of 1.	The simplest form of the fraction $\frac{6}{8}$ is $\frac{3}{4}$.

Glossary

	Example
sine (p. 463) The sine of any acute angle A of a right triangle is the ratio of the opposite leg to the hypotenuse.	$\sin A = \dfrac{a}{c}$
slant height (p. 507) The height of any face that is not the base of a regular pyramid.	slant height
slope (p. 570) The slope of a nonvertical line is the ratio of the rise (vertical change) to the run (horizontal change) between any two points on the line.	The slope of the line above is: $\text{slope} = \dfrac{\text{rise}}{\text{run}} = \dfrac{-2}{5} = -\dfrac{2}{5}.$
slope-intercept form (p. 577) The form of a linear equation $y = mx + b$ where m is the slope and b is the y-intercept.	$y = 6x + 8$ is in slope-intercept form.
solid (p. 492) A three-dimensional figure that encloses a part of space.	*See* cone, cylinder, prism, pyramid, *and* sphere.
solution of an equation (p. 28) A number that makes the equation true when substituted for the variable in the equation.	The solution of the equation $n - 3 = 4$ is 7.
solution of an equation in two variables (p. 549) An ordered pair (x, y) that makes the equation true when the values of x and y are substituted into the equation.	$(3, 8)$ is a solution of $y = 3x - 1$.
solution of an inequality (p. 140) The set of all numbers that make the inequality true when substituted for the variable in the inequality.	The solution of the inequality $y + 2 > 5$ is $y > 3$.
solution of a linear inequality (p. 583) An ordered pair (x, y) that makes the inequality true when the values of x and y are substituted into the inequality.	A solution of $y \geq 2x - 9$ is $(5, 1)$.

Glossary

	Example
solving an equation (p. 28) Finding all solutions of the equation by using mental math or the properties of equality.	To solve the equation $4x = 20$, find the number that can be multiplied by 4 to equal 20; $4(5) = 20$, so the solution is 5.
sphere (p. 492) A solid formed by all points in space that are the same distance from a fixed point called the center.	 center
square root (p. 431) A square root of a number n is a number m which, when multiplied by itself, equals n.	The square roots of 81 are 9 and -9 because $9^2 = 81$ and $(-9)^2 = 81$.
standard form (p. 657) A polynomial written with the exponents of the variable decreasing from left to right.	$3x^5 - 8x^3 + 5x^2 + x - 2$ is in standard form.
stem-and-leaf plot (p. 597) A data display that helps you see how data values are distributed. Each data value is separated into a leaf (the last digit) and a stem (the remaining digits). In an ordered stem-and-leaf plot, the leaves for each stem are listed in order from least to greatest.	stems leaves 10 | 8 11 | 2 2 5 12 | 1 3 Key: 10|8 = 108
straight angle (p. 375) An angle whose measure is exactly 180°.	
subtraction property of equality (p. 109) Subtracting the same number from each side of an equation produces an equivalent equation.	If $x + 7 = 9$, then $x + 7 - 7 = 9 - 7$, so $x = 2$. If $x + a = b$, then $x + a - a = b - a$.
supplementary angles (p. 375) Two angles whose measures have a sum of 180°.	79° \101°
surface area of a polyhedron (p. 503) The sum of the areas of the faces of the polyhedron.	3 in. 4 in. 6 in. *Surface area* $= 2(6)(4) + 2(6)(3) + 2(4)(3)$ $= 108$ in.^{2}

t	**Example**
tangent (p. 463) The tangent of any acute angle A of a right triangle is the ratio of the opposite leg to the adjacent leg.	$\tan A = \dfrac{a}{b}$ side adjacent to $\angle A$
terminating decimal (p. 242) A decimal that has a final digit.	0.4 and 3.6125 are terminating decimals.
terms of an expression (p. 86) The parts of an expression that are added together.	The terms of $2x + 3$ are $2x$ and 3.
tessellation (p. 414) A covering of a plane with congruent copies of the same pattern so that there are no gaps or overlaps.	
theoretical probability (p. 354) When all outcomes are equally likely, the theoretical probability of an event is the ratio of the number of favorable outcomes to the number of possible outcomes.	A bag of 20 marbles contains 7 red marbles. The theoretical probability of randomly choosing a red marble is: $$P(\text{red}) = \frac{7}{20} = 0.35.$$
transformation (p. 404) An operation that changes a figure into another figure, called the image.	*See* translation, reflection, *and* rotation.
translation (p. 409) A transformation that moves each point of a figure the same distance in the same direction; also known as a *slide*.	
trapezoid (p. 386) A quadrilateral with exactly one pair of parallel sides.	

	Example
tree diagram (p. 618) A branching diagram that shows all the possible choices or outcomes of a process carried out in several stages.	Outcomes: HH, HT, TH, TT
trigonometric ratio (p. 463) A ratio of the lengths of two sides of a right triangle.	*See* sine, cosine, and tangent.
trinomial (p. 657) A polynomial with three terms.	$3x^2 + 2x - 4$

u

unfavorable outcome (p. 633) An outcome that is not a favorable outcome.	*See* favorable outcome.
unit rate (p. 318) A rate that has a denominator of 1 unit.	$9 per hour is a unit rate.
upper extreme (p. 601) The greatest value in a data set.	*See* box-and-whisker plot.
upper quartile (p. 601) The median of the upper half of a data set.	*See* box-and-whisker plot.

v

variable (p. 15) A symbol, usually a letter, that is used to represent one or more numbers.	In the expression $m + 5$, the letter m is the variable.
variable expression (p. 15) An expression that consists of numbers, variables, and operations.	$n - 3$, $\frac{2s}{t}$, and $x + 4yz + 1$ are variable expressions.
verbal model (p. 11) A word equation that represents a real-world situation.	$\text{Distance traveled} = \text{Speed of car} \cdot \text{Time traveled}$
vertex of a polyhedron (p. 492) A point where three or more edges of the polyhedron meet.	*See* edge of a polyhedron.
vertical angles (p. 376) A pair of opposite angles formed when two lines meet at a point.	$\angle 1$ and $\angle 3$ are vertical angles. $\angle 2$ and $\angle 4$ are also vertical angles.

	Example

vertical line test (p. 681) If a vertical line intersects a graph at more than one point, then the graph does not represent a function.

Function   Not a function

volume of a solid (p. 513) The amount of space the solid occupies.

$$Volume = \pi r^2 h$$
$$\approx (3.14)(2)^2(3)$$
$$\approx 37.7 \text{ m}^3$$

X

x-axis (p. 91) The horizontal number line in a coordinate plane.

See coordinate plane.

x-coordinate (p. 91) The first number in an ordered pair representing a point in a coordinate plane.

The *x*-coordinate of the ordered pair $(-2, 1)$ is -2.

x-intercept (p. 564) The *x*-coordinate of the point where the graph intersects the *x*-axis.

The x-intercept is 4.

y

y-axis (p. 91) The vertical number line in a coordinate plane.

See coordinate plane.

y-coordinate (p. 91) The second number in an ordered pair representing a point in a coordinate plane.

The *y*-coordinate of the ordered pair $(-2, 1)$ is 1.

y-intercept (p. 564) The *y*-coordinate of the point where the graph intersects the *y*-axis.

The y-intercept is 2.

Glossary

Index

a

Absolute value, 54–56
  length on the coordinate plane
    and, 92–95
  modeling on a number line, 54
  opposites and, 54–56
Accuracy of a measurement
  angle, 721
  length
    customary, 720
    metric, 720
Act it out, problem solving strategy,
  228–229, 232
Activities, *See also* Games
  algebra
    adding polynomials, 661
    binomial multiplication, 673
    division equations, 113
    graphs of linear inequalities,
      583
    monomials and powers, 666
    multi-step inequalities, 295
    one-step equations, 107–108
    slope-intercept form, 575–576
    solving equations, 28
    solving equations with variables
      on both sides, 278
    two-step equations, 117–118
  data
    collecting and analyzing,
      255–256
    counting choices, 618
  fractions
    dividing, 234
    equivalent, 178
  geometry
    copying a triangle, 396
    modeling the Pythagorean
      theorem, 442
  graphing
    a linear function, 556
    line slope, 568–569
  integer
    addition, 57
    subtraction, 63
  measurement
    angle sums for polygons, 390
    area of a circle, 486
    area of a rectangle, 32
    area of a triangle, 134
    comparing volumes, 518
    diameter and circumference,
      288–289

    side length to perimeter ratios
      for squares, 317
    volume of a rectangular prism,
      512
  number
    investigating factors, 167
    using patterns to multiply
      powers, 196
    square root, 431
  probability
    complementary events, 632
    perform an experiment, 354
    simulations, 637–638
  ratio, making a scale drawing, 321
  trigonometry, exploring
    trigonometric ratios, 461–462
Acute angle, 375, 382
Acute triangle, 382
Addition
  to check subtraction, 709
  decimal, 247–250, 709
    estimating sums, 248, 711
  equations, 107–112
    modeling, 107–108, 109
  of exponents to multiply powers,
    196–200
  of fractions
    with common denominators,
      219–223, 710
    with different denominators,
      224–227
  integer, 57–62
    modeling, 57–59
    multiple addends, 59–62
    rules for, 59
  as inverse of subtraction, 109
  of mixed numbers
    with common denominators,
      219–223
    with different denominators,
      225–227
  order of operations and, 10–14
  polynomial, 661–665
    game, 665
  properties
    associative, 81
    commutative, 80
    equality, 110
    identity, 59
    inequality, 141
  to solve inequalities, 140–145
  words indicating, 16
Addition property of equality, 110
Addition property of inequality, 141

Additive identity property, 59
Additive inverse, 61
Adjacent side, of a right triangle, 463
Algebra
  equations
    addition, 107–112, 219
    checking solutions, 29
    decimal, 282–285
    division, 113–116, 234
    with fractions, 219, 230, 234,
      282–285
    graphing, 556–561
    integer, 57–67
    linear, 556–561, 564–580
    using mental math to solve,
      28–31
    multiplication, 113–116, 230
    multi-step, 271–275
    percent, 327, 327–330, 347–350
    percent of change, 338
    probability of an event, 354
    square root, 433–435
    subtraction, 107–112, 219
    two-step, 117–128
    in two variables, 549–553
    variables on both sides, 278–281
  exercises, 83, 171, 176, 222, 227,
    232, 237, 249, 254, 260, 266,
    379, 385, 392, 421, 426, 467,
    484, 489, 573
  expressions
    evaluating, 221–222, 239
    numerical, 10–14
    polynomial, 658–660
    simplifying, 225–227
    variable, 15–19, 64–67, 180–183,
      225–227
    writing, 16–19
  formulas
    area of a circle, 486
    area of a parallelogram, 481
    area of a rectangle, 33
    area of a square, 33
    area of a trapezoid, 482
    area of a triangle, 134
    circumference, 289, 290–294
    for combinations, 628
    energy, 312
    percent of change, 338
    perimeter of a triangle, 134
    for permutations, 624
    probability, 354
    Pythagorean theorem, 443
    simple interest, 348

slope of a line, 568, 570
surface area of a cone, 508
surface area of a cylinder, 504
surface area of a prism, 503
surface area of a pyramid, 507
surface area of a sphere, 510
volume of a cone, 520
volume of a cylinder, 514
volume of a prism, 513
volume of a pyramid, 519
functions
  evaluating, 542–544
  graphing, 556–561
  non-linear, 680–685
games, 19, 104, 238, 268–269, 287,
  299, 314, 326, 538, 553, 654,
  665, 684
inequalities, 140–149
  multi-step, 295–300
monomials
  multiplying, 666–670
  powers and, 666–670
negative exponents, 201
order of operations, 10–14, 21,
  221
polynomials
  adding, 661–665
  evaluating, 658–660
  simplifying, 658–660
  subtracting, 662–665
powers and exponents, 20–23
properties
  addition property of equality,
    110
  addition property of inequality,
    141
  additive identity, 59
  associative, 81
  commutative, 80
  cross product, 323
  distributive, 85
  division property of equality,
    114
  division property of inequality,
    147
  multiplication property of
    equality, 113
  multiplication property of
    inequality, 146
  multiplicative identity, 71
  power of a power, 668
  power of a product, 667
  product of powers, 196
  quotient of powers, 197

subtraction property of equality,
  109
subtraction property of
  inequality, 141
proportion, 322–326
variable, definition of, 15
Algebra tiles, 28, 107–108, 117–118,
  278, 661, 673
Alternate exterior angles, 377
Alternate interior angles, 377
Alternative assessment, *See*
    Activities; Extended response
    questions; Games; Projects;
    Short response questions;
    Test-taking skills
Analyze, exercises, 245, 293, 305,
  421
Angle(s)
acute, 382
alternate exterior, 377
alternate interior, 377
in circle graphs, 605–609
classifying, 382–385
classifying triangles by, 382–385
complementary, 375
congruent, 397–401
constructions
  copying, 380
  copying a triangle, 396
corresponding, 377, 397–401
definition of, 719
of elevation, 476
included, 398
inverse trigonometric ratios and,
  469
measures
  of a polygon, 391
  of quadrilaterals, 387
  of a triangle, 383
measuring with a protractor,
  382–383, 461–462, 605–609,
  721
naming, 719
obtuse, 382
pairs of, 375–379
polygons and, 390–393
right, 375, 382
  symbol for, 33
of rotation, 410–411
straight, 375
sums
  for polygons, 390–393
  for a quadrilateral, 387, 390–393
  for a triangle, 383

supplementary, 375
trigonometric ratios and, 461–469
vertex of, 719
vertical, 376
Angle-side-angle congruence,
  398–401
Annual interest rate, 348
Applications
advertising, 145, 449
agriculture, 340, 350, 435
airplanes, 143, 468, 471
amusement parks, 6, 213, 266, 291,
  433, 463, 465, 552
animals, 34, 35, 47, 48, 64, 66, 77,
  102–103, 112, 116, 124, 136,
  144, 146, 147, 157, 161, 162,
  177, 186, 193, 229, 237, 244,
  253, 263, 265, 320, 322, 329,
  359, 474, 543, 580, 593, 594–
  595, 603, 623, 650, 652–653,
  679, 698, 723, 725, 738
apparel, 14, 23, 47, 54, 99, 160, 259,
  325, 337, 345, 353, 356, 400,
  555, 579, 618, 620, 630, 635,
  647, 712, 733
aquarium, 10, 11, 533
architecture, 85, 385, 482, 519
art, 61, 89, 168, 285, 324, 412, 585,
  664
astronomy, 8, 90, 199, 207, 232,
  476–477, 670
banking, 143, 158, 250, 363, 370,
  449, 567, 621, 675, 676, 677,
  683, 691
baseball, 12, 25, 185, 195, 259, 357,
  407, 456, 532, 574, 613, 625,
  645, 649, 660, 676, 683, 717,
  733
basketball, 42, 69, 97, 114, 129, 139,
  260, 294, 312–313, 634, 695
bicycling, 18, 41, 80, 126, 131, 164–
  165, 265, 267, 450, 697, 732
biology, 102–103, 209, 220, 243,
  257, 598
bowling, 296, 403
boxes, 82, 403
Braille, 622
business, 7, 42, 116, 126, 191, 298,
  303, 604, 612, 631
chemistry, 62
climbing, 110
clubs, 304, 403, 617, 630, 651
community service, 42, 46, 176,
  222

computers, 23, 133, 149, 199, 233, 679

construction, 67, 69, 176, 223, 224, 225, 453, 467, 489, 500, 501

consumer, 12, 14, 17, 27, 41, 84, 88, 100, 111, 122, 127, 151, 154, 159, 160, 185, 189, 253, 254, 258, 266, 267, 275, 281, 287, 298, 300, 303, 304, 305, 307, 310, 311, 320, 344, 345, 346, 353, 358, 359, 361, 363, 366, 367, 368, 370, 546, 551, 553, 559, 566, 580, 585, 591, 599, 603, 613, 695, 696, 700, 712, 717, 729

containers, 504, 511, 513, 516, 517, 523, 527, 529

culture, 61, 294, 334, 521, 654

currency, 208, 222, 264, 341, 529

dance, 149, 247, 261, 304, 644, 650, 694

decorating, 440

design, 379, 403

distance, 15, 160, 324, 362, 435, 449, 600, 682

diving, 23, 70, 158, 555

earth science, 5, 8, 20, 106, 213, 254, 265, 439, 594–595

employment, 83, 115, 121, 122, 123, 126, 144, 159, 162, 185, 237, 260, 274, 284, 297, 319, 335, 364, 727

entertainment, 612, 620, 680, 732

environment, 282, 327, 606

exercise, 45

fabric arts, 84, 170, 221, 285, 368, 378, 434, 459, 625, 646, 669

fairs, 19, 60, 68, 127, 132, 158, 160, 162, 273, 627, 640, 665

fashion, 294

fireworks, 30

flags, 171

food, 13, 27, 48, 69, 94, 115, 151, 153, 160, 181, 189, 211, 213, 214, 223, 232, 241, 258, 266, 344, 362, 366, 368, 369, 421, 501, 505, 528, 585, 602, 615, 620, 622, 626, 633, 635, 642, 645, 649, 651, 679, 697, 702, 717, 724, 733

football, 22, 83, 183, 335, 600

fund raising, 12, 27, 126, 148, 229, 274, 299, 309, 361, 541, 542, 563, 640

games, 27, 45, 65, 72, 133, 162, 172, 185, 297, 307, 352, 353, 603, 617, 631, 636, 641, 648, 649

gardening, 156, 160, 185, 337, 475, 488, 530, 603, 625, 630, 690, 717, 727

geography, 182, 227, 385, 630

geometry, 45, 69, 99, 172, 274, 275, 280, 287, 353, 421, 436, 548, 636, 664, 679

gifts, 229, 592, 632

Global Positioning System (GPS), 53

golf, 62, 77, 140, 142, 159, 201, 259, 650

gymnastics, 260

hiking, 154, 228, 369, 403, 449, 577, 651

history, 179

hockey, 301, 487, 630, 635, 647

home improvement, 37, 159, 229, 502, 528

hot air balloon, 15, 99, 555

kites, 400, 441, 448, 475, 535

maps, 277, 362, 608, 630

measurement, 31, 88, 94, 121, 133, 151, 172, 199, 204, 260, 274, 293, 305, 319, 335, 388, 439, 440, 445, 447, 449, 455, 459, 484, 488, 501, 516, 529, 533, 659

models, 325, 326, 330, 363, 366, 591

money, 27, 41, 48, 69, 72, 139, 149, 156, 158, 159, 229, 277, 280, 348, 349, 350, 351, 361, 367, 370, 421, 449, 552, 559, 567, 617, 712

movies, 8, 19, 285, 544, 620, 625, 626, 650, 738

music, 14, 18, 41, 76, 119, 144, 151, 237, 277, 335, 342, 343, 345, 608, 623, 630, 651, 708, 712

newspapers, 310, 328

nutrition, 18

parks, 207

parties, 281, 587, 629, 717

passwords, 619, 622, 626

photography, 128, 201, 233, 236, 341, 420, 649, 651, 669

physics, 79, 203, 208

physiology, 17, 27, 241, 265, 329, 333, 357

plants, 25, 73, 176, 271, 725

poetry, 624, 695

population, 208, 277, 320, 341, 609, 683, 694

postcards, 230, 231

recreation, 122, 133, 159, 216, 217, 251, 282, 285, 310, 475, 586, 626, 647

recycling, 309, 362, 515, 544

robots, 264

running, 31, 123, 158, 189, 259, 267, 309, 320, 330, 370, 555, 565, 727

schedule, 186, 188, 277, 307, 631

school, 9, 19, 60, 101, 125, 133, 149, 175, 229, 266, 276, 277, 305, 328, 348, 353, 363, 366, 367, 370, 403, 560, 614, 629, 630, 649, 679, 694, 695, 696, 708, 724

skateboarding, 428–429, 619

skating, 154, 549, 697

soccer, 7, 175, 366, 370, 400, 510, 619

space exploration, 56, 208, 545

sports, 9, 13, 17, 38, 48, 152, 158, 222, 226, 260, 298, 309, 317, 400, 444, 446, 465, 574, 651

stock market, 69, 73, 245, 738

structures, 61, 293, 309, 311, 393, 401, 425, 449, 453, 473, 474, 489, 506, 517, 519, 525, 533, 535, 536, 552, 572, 573, 646, 663, 683, 689, 692

survey, 133, 159, 237, 246, 330, 347, 361, 370, 605, 607, 608, 609, 611, 615, 633, 644, 645, 679, 723, 724, 738

swimming, 36, 123, 189, 449, 554, 629

tax, 249, 591

telephone, 267, 277, 370, 560, 712, 738

television, 18, 65, 194, 319

temperature, 36, 66, 74, 75, 77, 84, 100, 101, 157, 265, 523, 548, 592, 613, 615, 650

tennis, 185, 340, 489, 510

theater, 27, 89, 115, 153, 248, 370, 607, 677, 695

time, 259, 330, 368, 501, 566, 589, 599, 643

toys, 204, 215, 592, 643, 649

track, 69, 77, 222, 250, 265, 597, 629
trains, 36, 570
travel, 36, 37, 43, 45, 47, 116, 158, 159, 277, 320, 501
vacation, 229, 607
vehicles, 49, 135, 152, 185, 222, 239, 365, 366, 545, 592, 609, 620, 622
walking, 194, 531, 617
water, 207, 209
weather, 30, 67, 75, 158, 249, 263, 304, 318, 349, 634, 647, 649
Approximately equal to, 39
Approximation, *See also* Estimation
of angle measures, 469
of square root, 432–436
with a calculator, 432, 434, 435
Arc, 380
Arc notation, to show equal angle measures, 383
Area(s), *See also* Surface area
of a circle, 486–491
comparing, 37, 138, 330, 341, 484, 489, 491, 511, 669
of a composite figure, 37, 85, 86, 89, 132, 133, 136, 138, 139, 485, 489, 500, 501
definition of, 33
geometric probability and, 652–653
of a parallelogram, 481, 483–485
modeling, 481
of a rectangle, 32–37, 136–139
modeling, 32
of a right triangle, 451–453
of a square, 33–37
of a trapezoid, 482–485
modeling, 482
of a triangle, 134–139
modeling, 134
Area models
to compare fractions, 192
geometric probability and, 652–653
to show addition of fractions, 219
to show area
of a circle, 486
of a parallelogram, 481
of a rectangle, 32
of a trapezoid, 482
of a triangle, 134
to show division by fractions, 234
to show equivalent fractions, 178

to show fractions, 166
to show percent, 331, 334
to show square root, 431
to show surface area, 503–505, 507–508, 510, 511
Arrangement(s)
combinations, 627–631
permutations, 623–626, 629–631
Assessment, *See also* FCAT Practice; Internet; Review
Chapter FCAT Practice, 49, 101, 155, 215, 267, 311, 363, 427, 475, 529, 593, 651, 691
Chapter Test, 48, 100, 154, 214, 266, 310, 362, 426, 474, 528, 592, 650, 690
Cumulative Practice (FCAT), 160–162, 368–370, 534–536, 696–698
End-of-Course Test, 699–702
Pre-Course Practice, xxviii–xxxi
Pre-Course Test, xxvi–xxvii
Review Quiz, 25, 45, 79, 97, 131, 151, 191, 211, 241, 263, 287, 307, 337, 359, 395, 423, 455, 471, 499, 525, 563, 589, 615, 647, 672, 687
Florida Skills (FCAT)
building, 156–157, 364–365, 530–531, 692–693
practicing, 158–162, 366–370, 532–536, 694–698
Test-Taking Strategies, 49, 101, 155, 215, 267, 311, 363, 427, 475, 529, 593, 651, 691
Associative property
for addition, 81
for multiplication, 81
Average, 257, *See also* Mean; Median; Mode
game, 261
representative, 258–261
Axis (axes), coordinate, 91

b

Bar graph, *See also* Histogram
choosing a data display, 606, 608–609
definition of, 5, 724
double, 9
interpreting, 5–9, 24, 724
game, 594–595

making, 8, 724
misleading, 612
Bar notation, for repeating decimals, 242
Base(s)
of a cone, 492
of a cylinder, 492
of a parallelogram, 481
in a percent equation, 327, 328, 347, 348
of a power, 20
of a prism, 492
of a pyramid, 492
of a trapezoid, 482
of a triangle, 134
Biased question, 645
Biased sample, 644–645
Binomial(s), 657
multiplying, 673–677
FOIL method, 675
using models, 673, 674
Box-and-whisker plot, 601–604
choosing a data display, 606, 608–609
comparing data on, 602
extremes, 601
interpreting, 602–604
making, 601–604
outliers and, 604
quartiles, 601
Brain Games, *See* Games
Break into parts, problem solving strategy, 500–501, 502

c

Calculator, *See also* Technology activities
2nd key, 239, 432, 464, 469
approximating square root with, 432–435
EE key, 209
exercises, 23, 73, 77, 116, 246, 259, 298, 330, 341, 392, 420, 434, 435, 466, 489, 552, 567, 670, 683
FracMode, 239
inverse tangent feature, 469
order of operations and, 14
pi key, 290, 504
random integer function, 638
sign key, 90
square root key, 432

TRIG key, 464, 469
trigonometric ratios of angles, 464, 466
Unit key, 239
Careers
in animal behavior, 653
astronomer, 477
biologist, 103
carpenter, 224
salesperson, 297
in scientific research, 313
veterinarian, 186
Cartesian plane, *See* Coordinate plane
Center
of a circle, 290
of rotation, 410
of a sphere, 492
Centimeter ruler, measuring with, 720
Challenge, exercises, 9, 13, 19, 23, 31, 37, 42, 56, 62, 66, 73, 77, 84, 89, 94, 112, 116, 122, 127, 139, 144, 149, 172, 177, 183, 189, 195, 200, 204, 208, 223, 227, 233, 238, 246, 250, 260, 275, 281, 285, 294, 298, 313, 320, 326, 330, 335, 341, 346, 350, 357, 385, 389, 393, 401, 408, 413, 421, 435, 441, 447, 453, 460, 468, 485, 489, 506, 511, 517, 523, 544, 552, 560, 569, 574, 580, 587, 604, 609, 621, 626, 631, 635, 642, 660, 664, 670, 677, 683
Change, percent of, 338–341
Chapter Test, *See* Assessment
Checking
using the counting principle, 621
equations using substitution, 29, 113, 114, 119, 120, 124, 276, 296, 323, 542, 550, 581
using estimation, 156, 235, 251
inequalities using substitution, 583–587
integer addition, 59, 60
by measuring, 380
problem solving and, 39–42
using rounding, 318
subtraction by adding, 709
whether two ratios form a proportion, 323–326
Choose a strategy, 23, 27, 69, 84, 123, 133, 172, 185, 229, 246, 277, 299, 335, 353, 403, 421, 436,

449, 490, 501, 555, 617, 631, 679, 684, *See also* Test-taking skills
Circle
area of, 486–491
game, 490
center of, 290
circumference of, 288, 290
equations involving, 290–294
comparing circumference and diameter, 288–289
definition of, 290
diameter of, 288, 290
radius of, 290
Circle graph
choosing a data display, 606–609
examples, 223, 331, 337, 361
on a graphing calculator, 611
interpreting, 331, 334, 605, 607–609, 611
game, 594–595
making, 605–609, 611
percent and, 331, 334
Circumference
comparing with diameter, 288–289
definition of, 288, 290
equations involving, 290–294
Classifying
angles, 382–385
polynomials, 657, 659
quadrilaterals, 386-389, 426, 492–494
real numbers, 437, 439, 440
solids, 492, 494
triangles, 382–385, 426
Clustering, 711
Coefficient
of a variable, 86
negative, 120
Combination notation, 628
Combinations, 627–631
permutations and, 629–631
Combining like terms, 86–89, 272–275
inequalities and, 296–300
Common denominator(s)
adding fractions with, 219–223
adding mixed numbers with, 219–223
subtracting fractions with, 219–223
subtracting mixed numbers with, 219–223
Common factor, 173
Common multiple, 186

Communication, *See* Error analysis; Reading mathematics; Writing mathematics
Commutative property
of addition, 80
of multiplication, 80
Comparing
areas, 37, 138, 330, 341, 484, 489, 491, 511, 669
data
using box-and-whisker plots, 602
using double stem-and-leaf plots, 598
diameter and circumference, 288–289
exercises, 8, 55, 83, 122, 123, 245, 260, 293, 305, 467, 484, 499, 600, 626, 635, 669
fractions, 192–195, 216
misleading comparisons, 613–615
radii of circles, 491
using ratio, 708
real numbers, 438–441
volumes, 517, 518, 523
Compass, 380–381, 396, 722
Compatible numbers, estimation and, 716
Complementary angles, 375
Complementary events, 632–636
Composite figure
area of, 37, 85, 86, 89, 132, 133, 136, 138, 139, 485, 489
perimeter of, 37
Composite number, 167, 169
Composite solid, 495, 496–497
surface area of, 506, 555
volume of, 516, 517
Compound interest, 350, 351, 675
Computer, *See also* Internet; Technology activities
spreadsheet, 300, 491
truth function, 300
Concept grid, 480
Concept map, 374, 386
Conclusions
drawing
choosing a representative average, 258–261
from an experiment, 352–353, 653
from graphs, 334, 546, 547, 548, 612–613

from plots, 598–600, 602–604
supporting, 83, 151, 183
Cone, 492
  base of, 492
  height of, 520
  slant height of, 508
  surface area of, 508–511
    formula, 508
  volume of, 520–523
    formula, 520
Congruence
  angle-side-angle, 398–401
  side-angle-side, 398–401
  side-side-side, 398–401
Congruent angles, 397–401
Congruent figures
  symmetry and, 406
  tessellation and, 414–415
Congruent polygons, 397–401
  naming, 397, 399
Congruent sides, 397–401
Congruent triangles, 398–401
Conjecture, *See also* Critical
    thinking; Prediction
  examples, 583
Connections to other disciplines
  art, 324
  astronomy, 199
  biology, 136, 147, 193, 203, 557
  geography, 246, 350, 604
  history, 171, 521
  science, 64, 66, 102–103, 214, 291,
    312–313, 339, 393, 476–477,
    602, 652–653, 670
Connections to real world,
  See Applications
Consecutive numbers, 26, 27
Constant term, 86
Constructions
  combining segments, 722
  copying an angle, 380
  copying a line segment, 722
  copying a triangle, 396
  parallel lines, 381
  perpendicular lines, 381
Converse, of a statement, 444
**Converse of the Pythagorean
    theorem,** 444–447
Converting
  decimals, fractions, and percents,
    331–335
  fractions and decimals, 242–246
  improper fractions and mixed
    numbers, 193–195, 707

Coordinate notation
  to describe reflection, 404–408
  to describe rotation, 410–411
  to describe translation, 409
Coordinate plane
  definition of, 91
  dilation in, 418, 420
  distance on, 92–95
  graphing functions on, 556–561
  graphing linear equations on,
    556–561
    using intercepts, 564–567
    using slope-intercept form,
      578–580
  graphing linear inequalities,
    583–587
  graphing non-linear functions,
    681–685
  half plane, 584
  parts of, 91
  plotting points on, 91–95
    game, 95, 372–373, 539
  reflection in, 404–408
  rotation in, 410–413
  scatter plots, 545–548
  translation in, 409, 411–413
Copying
  an angle, 380
  a line segment, 722
  a triangle, 396
Corresponding angles, 377, 397–401
Corresponding sides, 377, 397–401
Cosine ratio, 462–468
Counting methods, 618–622
Counting principle, 619–622
  definition of, 619
  permutations and, 623–626
Critical thinking
  describe, 100
  exercises, 3, 9, 13, 22, 32, 37, 42,
    51, 56, 57, 61, 83, 103, 112,
    116, 127, 131, 138, 143, 151,
    171, 172, 176, 183, 195, 199,
    204, 208, 237, 241, 246, 250,
    254, 263, 275, 281, 285, 293,
    308, 315, 321, 334, 335, 359,
    393, 423, 444, 446, 460, 462,
    469, 484, 489, 495, 511, 512,
    516, 552, 559, 567, 580, 589,
    600, 622, 642, 653, 655, 660,
    664, 669, 672, 676
  explain, 8, 45, 66, 73, 79, 84, 89,
    102, 108, 138, 148, 165, 217,
    232, 237, 241, 254, 256, 269,

    275, 285, 304, 312, 313, 330,
    345, 373, 388, 396, 400, 429,
    434, 440, 452, 459, 468, 476,
    477, 491, 499, 520, 523, 559,
    567, 573, 587, 595, 603, 608,
    609, 615, 625, 638
Cross products
  distributive property and, 325
  proportions and, 323–326
Cross products property, 323
Cubic units, 512, 513, 515
Cylinder, 492
  bases of, 492
  height of, 504
  radius of, 504
  surface area of, 504–506
    formula, 504
  volume of, 514–518
    formula, 514

d

Data
  analyzing, 255–256
  biased question, 645
  biased sample, 644–645
  choosing a display, 606–609
  choosing a representative average,
    258–261
  collecting, 255–256
  definition of, 5, 724
  displays, 606
    bar graph, 5–9, 24, 724
    circle graph, 605–609, 611
    line graph, 606–609, 725
    misleading, 612–613
  grouping into intervals, 6–9
  lower extreme, 601
  lower quartile, 601
  mean, 255–261
  median, 255–261
  mode, 255–261
  organizing
    box-and-whisker plot, 601–604
    frequency table, 6–9
    line plot, 723
    stem-and-leaf plot, 597–600
    tree diagram, 618–622
  outlier, 604
  prediction from, 352, 353, 355,
    356
  random sample, 644
  range of, 258–261

samples, 644–645
survey
    biased questions, 645
    results, 331
    samples and, 644–645
upper extreme, 601
upper quartile, 601

Decimal(s)
adding, 247–250, 709
clearing to solve equations,
    283–285
dividing, 251–254, 715
    zero as placeholder, 252
equivalent fractions, percents,
    and, 746
estimating sums, 248
fractions and, 242–246, 331–335
mixed numbers and, 243–246
multiplying, 251–254
    by a whole number, 714
ordering, 438–441
ordering fractions, percents, and,
    333–334
percent and, 331–335
repeating, 242–246
rounding, 705
subtracting, 247–250, 709
terminating, 242–246

Decimal form, of a real number, 437
Decision making, *See also* Choose a
    strategy
choosing a representative average,
    258–261
identifying biased samples,
    644–645
supporting conclusions, 83, 151,
    183

Decrease, percent of, 338–341
Deductive reasoning, *See* Activities;
    Critical thinking
Denominator, 707
least common, 192
Dependent event(s), 639–643
definition of, 639
game, 643
Diagram(s)
to check answers, 40
concept grid, 480
concept map, 374, 386
tree, 618–622
Venn, 242, 437, 726
Diameter
of a circle
    circumference and, 288–294

comparing with circumference,
    288–289
definition of, 288, 290
Digit, 704
Dilation, 418–421
in the coordinate plane, 418, 420
Discount, 342–346
Discrete mathematics
combinations, 501
counting faces, edges, and
    vertices, 493, 495
counting principle, 619–622
divisibility tests, 706
Euler's formula, 495
factorials, 623–626
functions, 541–544
networks, 493, 495
outlier, 604
perfect squares, 432
permutations, 623–626
Pythagorean triples, 451–452
Sieve of Eratosthenes, 167
tree diagrams, 169, 171, 618–622
triangular numbers, 617
Venn diagrams, 242, 437, 726
Distance
on the coordinate plane, 92–95
formula, 34
    forms of, 35
    using, 34–37, 70
Distributive property, 85–89
cross products and, 325
equations with variables on both
    sides and, 279–281
to multiply a monomial and
    binomial, 667–670
multi-step equations and,
    272–275
Dividend, 715
Divisibility tests, 706
Division
checking, using estimation, 252
decimal, 251–254, 715
    zero as placeholder, 252
divisibility tests, 706
equations, 113–116
estimating quotients, 716
to find equivalent fractions, 192
to find mean, 255–261
with fractions, 234–238
    multiplicative inverse and, 234
integer, 74–77
as inverse of multiplication, 113
with mixed numbers, 235–238

order of operations and, 10–14
properties
    equality, 114
    inequality, 147
    quotient of power, 197–200
to solve inequalities, 146–151
words indicating, 16
to write a fraction as a decimal,
    242–246
by zero, 74
Division property of equality, 114
Division property of inequality, 147
Divisor, 715
Domain, of a function, 542
Double bar graph, 9
Double stem-and-leaf plot, 598–600
Draw a diagram, problem solving
    strategy, 132–133, 134,
    448–449, 453, 467
Draw a graph, problem solving
    strategy, 678–679, 681
Drawing, *See also* Constructions;
    Graphs
to add fractions, 219
to enlarge a picture, 321
to find patterns, 68, 69
isometric, 496–497
to model fractions, 192
nets, 502–506
to show division by a fraction, 234
to show equivalent fractions, 178
solids, 493–497

e

Edge(s), of a polyhedron, 492–493
Elevation, angle of, 476
Eliminate possibilities, 157, *See also*
    Problem Solving
Endpoint, definition of, 718
Enlargement, drawing, 321
Equality
addition property of, 110
division property of, 114
multiplication property of, 113
subtraction property of, 109
Equation(s), *See also* Linear
    equation
addition, 107–112
checking solutions, 29, 113, 114,
    119, 120, 124, 276, 296, 323,
    542, 550, 581
circumference, 290–294

decimal, 248–250, 282–285
definition of, 28
division, 113–116
equivalent, 109
formulas as, 33–37
with fractions, 220–223, 236–237,
    273–275, 282–285
in function form, 550
game, 314
mental math, 28–31
with mixed numbers, 220–223
modeling
    addition and subtraction, 28,
        107–108, 109
    two step, 117–118
    variables on both sides, 278
multiplication, 113–116
multi-step, 271–275
    game, 287
percent, 327–330, 347–350
percent of change, 338–341
proportion, 322–326
simple interest, 348
slope of a line, 570
solution of, 28
square root, 433–435
subtraction, 107–112
two step
    solving, 117–123
    writing, 124–128
in two variables, 549–553
    game, 553
variable, 248–250
    game, 538
with variables on both sides,
    278–281
    distributive property and,
        279–281
writing, 114
    two-step, 124–128
Equiangular triangle, 385
Equilateral triangle, 382
Equivalent equations, 109
Equivalent fractions, 179–183
decimals, percents, and, 746
modeling, 178
negative, 220
Equivalent inequalities, 141
Equivalent ratios, 317–320
Erathosthenes, sieve of, 167
Error analysis, 12, 22, 35, 41, 55, 61,
    72, 88, 121, 138, 153, 175, 188,
    198, 203, 221, 249, 253, 259,
    284, 292, 297, 308, 319, 324,

333, 356, 378, 384, 392, 446,
458, 467, 483, 515, 551, 579,
629, 659, 663, 676
Estimation
angle measures, 469
to answer multiple choice
    questions, 156
to check answers are reasonable,
    235, 251, 252
using clustering, 711
using compatible numbers, 716
definition of, 711
differences, 711
exercises, 18, 36, 94, 138, 284, 293,
    346, 484, 489, 552, 582, 670
front-end, 248–250, 711
using graphs, 546, 581–582
high and low estimates, 716
using leading digits, 251
products, 716
quotients, 716
using rounding, 711, 716
square root, 432–436
sums, 248, 711
value of pi, 288–289, 290
Euler's formula, 495
Event(s), 354, *See also* Outcome
complementary, 632–636
dependent, 639–643
independent, 639–643
multiple, 640
odds of, 633–636
probability of, 354–357
Expanded form
expression, 196
number, 704
Experiment
conducting, 352–353, 354
designing, 313
Experimental probability, 352–357,
    652–653, *See also* Probability
    simulation, 637–638
Exponent(s)
adding to multiply powers,
    196–200
game, 200, 654
negative, 201–204
patterns for multiply powers, 196
powers and, 20–23
prime factorization and, 169–172
rules of, 196–200
scientific notation and, 205–209
standard form of a polynomial
    and, 657

subtracting to divide powers,
    197–200
zero, 202
Expression(s)
combining like terms, 86–89
distributive property and, 85–89
monomial, 666–670
numerical, 10–14
    evaluating, 10–14, 81, 82, 83, 90,
        202–204, 221–222, 239
order of operations and, 10–14
polynomial, 658–660
terms of, 86
variable, 15–19
    evaluating, 16–19, 64–67, 71–73,
        75–77, 86–89, 90, 181–183
    simplifying, 87–89, 180–183
    writing, 16–19
Extended problem solving, *See*
    Problem solving
Extended response questions, *See*
    Problem solving

f

Face(s), of a polyhedron, 492–493
Factor(s), 167–172
common, 173
definition of, 706
divisibility tests and, 706
factor tree, 169, 171
greatest common, 173–177
powers and, 196–200
prime factorization, 169–172
relatively prime numbers and,
    174
Sieve of Eratosthenes, 167
writing, 168–172
Factor tree, 169, 171
Factorial notation, 623
Factorial(s), 623–626
Factoring
a monomial, 170–172
a number, 167–172
Favorable outcome, 354, 633
FCAT Practice
    9, 13, 19, 23, 31, 37, 43, 49, 56,
    62, 67, 73, 77, 84, 89, 95, 101,
    112, 116, 123, 128, 139, 145,
    149, 155, 156–162, 172, 177,
    189, 195, 200, 204, 208, 215,
    223, 227, 233, 238, 246, 250,
    254, 261, 267, 275, 281, 285,

294, 299, 305, 311, 320, 326,
330, 335, 341, 346, 350, 357,
363, 364–370, 379, 385, 389,
393, 401, 408, 413, 421, 427,
436, 441, 447, 453, 460, 468,
475, 485, 490, 495, 506, 511,
517, 529, 530–536, 544, 548,
553, 560, 567, 574, 587, 593,
600, 604, 609, 622, 626, 631,
636, 643, 651, 660, 665, 670,
677, 684, 691, 692–698

Florida
See also FCAT Practice; Internet
applications, 158, 160, 161, 183,
208, 311, 326, 339, 362, 399,
545, 548, 609, 630, 650, 694,
695, 697
Cumulative Practice (FCAT),
160–162, 368–370, 534–536,
696–698
Florida Test Skills (FCAT)
building,156–157, 364–365,
530–531, 692–693
practicing, 158–162, 366–370,
532–536, 694–698
Florida standards,
Throughout the book. See first
pages of lessons and special
features. For example:
1, 5, 10, 14, 15, 20, 26, 28, 32,
33, 38, 53, 57, 58, 63, 68, 70,
74, 80, 85, 90, 91, 107, 109,
113, 117, 119, 124, 129, 132,
134, 140, 146, 163, 167, 168,
173, 178, 179, 184, 186, 192,
196, 201, 205, 209, 219, 224,
228, 230, 234, 239, 242, 247,
251, 255, 257, 271, 276, 278,
282, 288, 290, 295, 300, 301,
317, 321, 320, 327, 331, 338,
342, 347, 351, 352, 354, 371,
375, 382, 386, 390, 396, 397,
402, 404, 409, 414, 416, 431,
437, 442, 443, 448, 450, 456,
461, 463, 481, 486, 491, 492,
496, 500, 502, 507, 512, 513,
518, 519, 537, 541, 545, 549,
554, 556, 564, 568, 570, 575,
577, 583, 597, 601, 605, 616,
618, 623, 627, 632, 637, 639,
644, 657, 661, 666, 673, 674,
678, 680, 685
FOIL method, for multiplying
binomials, 675

Formula(s)
applying, 134–139
area
of a circle, 486
of a parallelogram, 481
of a rectangle, 33
of a square, 33
of a trapezoid, 482
of a triangle, 134
circumference, 289, 290
combination, 628
definition of, 33
distance, 34
energy, 312
inverse tangent, 469
mean, 75
odds, 633, 634
percent of change, 338
perimeter
of a rectangle, 33
of a square, 33
permutation, 624
probability, 354
Pythagorean theorem, 443
simple interest, 348
slope, 568
spreadsheet, 300
surface area
of a cone, 508
of a cylinder, 504
of a prism, 503
of a pyramid, 507
of a sphere, 510
table of, 742
volume
of a cone, 520
of a cylinder, 514
of a prism, 513
of a pyramid, 519
45°-45°-90° right triangle, 456,
458–460
Fraction(s), See also Mixed numbers;
Proportion; Rate; Ratio
adding
common denominators,
219–223, 710
different denominators,
224–227
clearing to solve equations,
273–275
comparing, 192–195
game, 216
decimals and, 242–246, 331–335,
746

definition of, 179, 707
denominator, 707
dividing, 234–238
game, 238
equivalent, 179–183
game, 217
modeling, 178
improper, 193–195
modeling, 192
multiplying, 230–233
by a whole number, 713
negative, 195
numerator, 707
ordering decimals, percents, and,
333–334
percent and, 331–335, 746
repeating decimals and, 242–246
simplest form, 179
simplifying, 179–183
by combining like terms,
220–223
using powers properties, 198
slope and, 568–574
square root of, 435
subtracting
common denominators,
219–223, 710
different denominators,
224–227
Fraction bar, evaluating expressions
containing, 11
Frequency table
definition of, 6
intervals for, 6
making, 6–9, 256
scale, 6
Front-end estimation, 248–250,
711
Front view
of a solid, 493, 496–497
drawing, 496–497
Function(s)
definition of, 541
domain, 542
evaluating, 542–544
graphing, 556–561
identifying, 541, 543
input-output tables and, 541–544
non-linear, 680–685
game, 684
graphing, 681–685
range, 542
relations and, 541, 543
truth, 300

vertical lines and, 558
vertical line test and, 681
writing rules for, 542–544
Function form, 550
Function notation, 680–684
Function rule, 542
writing, 542–544

g

Games
algebra
combining like terms, 655
dividing fractions, 238
equations in one variable, 538
equations in two variables, 553
mental math equations, 104
multi-step equations, 287
multi-step inequalities, 299
non-linear functions, 684
one- and two-step equations, 268–269
polynomial addition, 665
proportions, 326
solving equations, 314
variable expressions, 19
writing expressions, 128
coordinate, plotting points, 95, 372–373, 539
data, interpreting plots, 615
fractions
comparing, 216
equivalent, 217
geometry
identifying angles in triangles, 429
reflections, 408
vocabulary, 389
graphing
interpret bar graphs, 594–595
interpret circle graphs, 594–595
integer, sums and differences of, 67
measurement
area of a circle, 490
perimeter, area, circumference, 478–479
number
evaluating powers, 428
exponents, 200
greatest common factor, 177
place value, 3
properties of exponents, 654

rounding, 3
square root, 436
operations
decimal operations, 315
integer operations, 105
multiplying whole numbers, 50–51
whole number and decimal sums, 2
whole number division, 164–165
percent, enlarging and reducing, 346
probability, dependent events, 643
reasoning, logic, 43, 145
statistics, averages, 261
trigonometry, trigonometric ratios, 471
Geometric probability, 652–653
Geometry, *See also* Applications; Area; Connections to math strands; Coordinate plane; Geometry; Measurement; Perimeter; Surface area; Volume
angles
acute, 382
alternate exterior, 377
alternate interior, 377
classifying, 382–385
complementary, 375
congruent, 397–401
corresponding, 377
obtuse, 382
right, 33, 375, 382
straight, 375
supplementary, 375
arc, 380
circle, 290–294, 486–491
circumference, 288–289, 290–294
classification
angle, 382–385
quadrilateral, 386–389
solids, 492, 494
triangle, 382–385
compass use, 380–381, 396, 722
constructions, 380–381, 396, 722
corresponding parts, 397–401
endpoint, 718
half plane, 584
intersecting lines, 376
line, 718
parallel lines, 377

parallelogram, 386, 481, 483–485
perpendicular lines, 376
plane, 718
point, 718
polygon, 382–385, 386–389, 390–393, 416–421
protractor use, 396, 461–462
Pythagorean theorem, 442–447, 450–453
quadrilateral, 386–389
ray, 718
rhombus, 386
segment, 718
sides
adjacent, 463
congruent, 397–401
corresponding, 377, 397–401
hypotenuse, 463
opposite, 463
similarity, 416–421
solids
classifying, 492, 494
cone, 492, 508–511, 520–523
cylinder, 492, 504–506, 514–518
drawing, 493–497
prism, 492, 502–506, 512–518
pyramid, 492, 507–511, 519–523
sphere, 492, 510, 679
square, 33–37, 386
symmetry, 406–408
tessellation, 414–415
three-dimensional figure, 492–495
transformations
reflection, 404–408
rotation, 410–413
translation, 409, 411–413
trapezoid, 386, 482–485
triangles
acute, 382
classifying, 382–385
equilateral, 382
isosceles, 382
obtuse, 382
right, 382
scalene, 382
sum of angle measures, 383
trigonometric ratios, 461–468
Graphing
functions, 556–561
non-linear, 681–685
inequalities, 140–145, 295, 297, 298
linear, 583–587

integers on a number line, 53
linear equations, 556–561
   using the slope-intercept form,
     578–580
   systems of, 581–582
reflections on the coordinate
   plane, 404–408

Graphing calculator, *See also*
   Calculator; Technology
   activities
graphing linear functions, 561
graphing non-linear functions,
   685
making data displays, 610–611

Graphs, *See also* Plots
bar, 5–9, 724
choosing a data display, 606–609
circle, 331, 334, 605, 607–609, 611
coordinate
   non-linear functions, 681–685
   plotting points, 91–95
   transformations, 404–415,
     418, 420
double bar, 9
histogram, 6–9
line, 606–609
linear, 556–561
   of horizontal lines, 558–560
   using intercepts, 564–567
   line slope, 568–574
   using the slope-intercept form,
     578–580
   systems of equations, 581–582
   of vertical lines, 558–560
misleading, 612–613

Greatest common divisor (GCD),
   173
Greatest common factor (GCF),
   173–177
game, 177
of monomials, 174–177
Grouping symbols, 11
order of operations and, 11–14
Guess, check, and revise,
   problem solving strategy,
   26–27, 31
Guided problem solving, *See*
   Problem solving

h

Half plane, 584
Hands-on activities, *See* Activities;
Games; Math in Science;
Technology activities

Height
of a cone, 520
of a cylinder, 504
of a parallelogram, 481
of a prism, 503
of a pyramid, 507
of a trapezoid, 482
of a triangle, 134
Heptagon, 390
Hexagon, 390
Histogram
choosing a data display, 606,
   608–609
interpreting, 6–9
making, 6–9
scale, 6
Homework, *See* Student help
Horizontal line, graph of, 558–560
Hypotenuse, 442, 443, 463
Hypothesis, *See* Critical thinking;
Prediction

i

Identity property
of addition, 59
of multiplication, 71
Image, 404
Improper fraction(s)
mixed numbers and, 193–195, 707
ordering, 193–195
Inch ruler, measuring with, 720
Included angle, 398
Included side, 398
Increase, percent of, 338–341
Independent events, 639–643
definition of, 639
Indirect measurement, 417, 420,
   421
Pythagorean theorem and, 450,
   452–453
Inductive reasoning, *See* Activities;
Critical thinking; Reasoning
Inequality (inequalities)
combining like terms in, 296–300
definition of, 140
equivalent, 141
graphing, 140–145, 295, 297, 298
   linear, 583–587
multi-step, 295–300
   game, 299

problem solving and, 301–305
solution of, definition, 140
solving
   using addition or subtraction,
     140–145
   using multiplication or division,
     146–149
symbols, 141
writing, 296–300, 301–305
Input, 541
Input-output table, 541–544
Integer(s)
absolute value and, 54–56
adding, 57–62
   game, 67
     multiple addends, 59–62
     on a number line, 57–59
     rules for, 59
additive identity, 59
definition of, 53
dividing, 74–77
mean, 257, 259, 260
modeling on a number line, 53–54
multiplying, 70–73
negative, 53
opposite, 54–56
ordering, 53, 55–56
   on a number line, 53
positive, 53
subtracting, 63–67
   game, 67
   using patterns, 63
zero, 53
Intercept(s)
definition of, 564
finding, 564–567
using to graph a line, 565–567
Interdisciplinary, *See* Applications;
Connections to other
disciplines; Math in science
Interest
compound, 350, 351
simple, 348
Internet, *See also* Student help
eTutorial Plus, 7, 12, 22, 30, 36, 41,
   55, 61, 65, 72, 76, 83, 88, 93,
   111, 115, 121, 126, 137, 143,
   148, 171, 176, 182, 188, 194,
   199, 203, 207, 222, 226, 232,
   237, 245, 249, 253, 259, 274,
   280, 284, 293, 297, 304, 319,
   325, 329, 334, 340, 345, 349,
   356, 378, 384, 388, 392, 400,
   407, 412, 419, 434, 440, 446,

452, 459, 466, 483, 488, 494, 505, 510, 516, 522, 543, 547, 551, 559, 566, 573, 579, 586, 599, 603, 608, 621, 625, 630, 635, 642, 659, 664, 669, 676, 682

eWorkbook Plus, 7, 12, 17, 22, 30, 35, 41, 55, 60, 65, 72, 76, 82, 93, 111, 115, 121, 126, 137, 142, 148, 170, 175, 181, 188, 194, 198, 203, 207, 221, 226, 232, 236, 244, 249, 253, 259, 273, 280, 284, 292, 297, 303, 319, 324, 329, 333, 340, 344, 349, 356, 378, 384, 387, 392, 399, 406, 411, 419, 434, 439, 445, 452, 458, 466, 483, 488, 494, 505, 509, 515, 521, 543, 547, 551, 558, 566, 572, 579, 585, 599, 603, 607, 620, 625, 629, 634, 641, 659, 663, 668, 676, 682

FCAT practice, 9, 13, 19, 23, 31, 37, 43, 56, 62, 67, 73, 77, 84, 89, 95, 112, 116, 123, 128, 139, 145, 149, 172, 177, 183, 189, 195, 200, 204, 208, 223, 227, 233, 238, 246, 250, 254, 261, 275, 281, 285, 294, 299, 305, 320, 326, 330, 335, 341, 346, 350, 357, 379, 385, 389, 393, 401, 408, 413, 421, 436, 441, 447, 453, 468, 485, 495, 506, 511, 517, 523, 544, 548, 553, 560, 567, 574, 580, 587, 600, 604, 609, 622, 626, 631, 636, 643, 660, 665, 670, 677, 684

project support, 103, 313, 477, 653
searching for information, 129
Intersecting lines, 376
Interval, 6
Inverse
additive, 61
multiplicative, 234
Inverse operations
addition and subtraction, 109–112
definition of, 109
multiplication and division, 113–116
Inverse tangent, 469
Investigations, *See* Activities; Math in Science; Technology activities

Irrational number, 437, 439–441
definition of, 437
Isometric drawing, 496–497
Isosceles triangle, 382

j

Journal, *See* Notebook; Notebook review; Note taking; Writing in mathematics

l

Labs, *See* Activities; Technology Activities
Leading digit(s), estimation and, 251
Leaf, in a stem-and-leaf plot, 597
Least common denominator (LCD), 192
adding fractions, 224–227
comparing fractions, 192–195
subtracting fractions, 224–227
Least common multiple (LCM), 186–189
of monomials, 187–189
Legs, of a right triangle, 442, 443–444
Length, on the coordinate plane, 92–95
Like terms, 86
collecting on one side of an equation, 278–281
combining, 86–89
to add polynomials, 661–665
game, 655
to simplify fractions, 220–222
to solve equations, 272–275
Linear equation(s)
graphing, 556–561
using a graphing calculator, 561
horizontal lines, 558–560
using intercepts, 564–567
using slope-intercept form, 578–580
vertical lines, 558–560
slope of graph, 568–574
slope-intercept form, 575–580
systems of, 581–582
Linear function, *See* Linear equation
Linear graph, 556–561
using intercepts, 564–567

using slope-intercept form, 578–580
slope of a line, 568–574
Linear inequality (inequalities),
graph of, 583–587
Line graph
choosing a data display, 606, 608–609
interpreting, 606–609, 725
making, 606–609, 725
misleading, 612–613
Line plot
making, 723
reading, 723
Line(s)
definition of, 718
intersecting, 376
parallel, 377
perpendicular, 376
Line of symmetry, 406–408
List, make a, problem solving strategy, 184–185, 186, 618, 627
Logical reasoning, *See also* Classification; Critical thinking; Error analysis; Games, Number sense; Problem solving
concept grid, 48
concept map, 374, 386
converse of a statement, 444
tree diagram, 169, 171, 618–622
truth function, 300
unit analysis, 40
Venn diagrams, 242, 437, 726
Look for a pattern, problem solving strategy, 68–69
Lower extreme, 601
Lower quartile, 601

m

Make a list, problem solving strategy, 184–185, 186, 618, 627
Make a model, problem solving strategy, 402–403, 407
Make a table, problem solving strategy, 554–555, 556, 683
Manipulatives, *See also* Calculator; Mathematical tools; Modeling; Technology activities

Index

algebra tiles, 28, 107–108, 117–118, 278, 661, 673
cards, 50, 200, 478, 637
compass, 380–381, 396, 722
markers, 50, 268
number cube, 255–256, 268, 352
real world objects, 518
ruler, 321, 461–462, 518, 720
square tiles, 32
straightedge, 380–381, 396, 722
unit cubes, 512

Mathematical reasoning, *See*
Reasoning
Mathematical techniques, *See*
Estimation; Mental math;
Number sense; Problem
solving
Mathematical tools, *See also*
Calculator; Estimation;
Manipulatives; Mental math
balance scale, 109
compass, 380–381, 396, 722
protractor, 396, 461–462, 721
ruler, 321, 461–462, 518, 720
straightedge, 380–381, 396, 722

Math in Science
aiming a telescope, 476–477
geometric probability, 652–653
hibernating in the Arctic, 102–103
the physics of basketball, 312–313

Mean, 75, 255–261
choosing a representative average,
258–261
definition of, 75, 257

Measurement, *See also* Area;
Measurement tools;
Perimeter; Surface area;
Volume
accuracy of measurement, 720,
721
angle, 382–383, 461–462, 605–609,
721
of a polygon, 391
of a quadrilateral, 387
of a triangle, 383
circumference of a circle, 288–294
comparing diameter and
circumference, 288–289
exercises, 36, 384, 385, 388, 400,
484
indirect, 417, 420, 421, 450,
452–453
using a ruler, 321, 461–462, 518,
720

scale drawing, 321
similar figures and, 416–421

Measurement tools
balance scale, 109
compass, 380–381, 396, 605–609
how to use, 722
protractor, 382–383, 461–462,
605–609
how to use, 721
ruler, 321, 461–462, 518, 720
how to use, 720

Measures, table of, 741
Measures of dispersion, *See* Range
Median, 255–261
box-and-whisker plots and, 601
choosing a representative average,
258–261
definition of, 257

Mental math
exercises, 36, 62, 72, 82, 89, 99,
149, 237, 325, 385, 489
integer subtraction and, 63
to solve equations, 28–31

Misleading graph, 612–613

Mixed number(s)
adding
common denominators,
219–223
different denominators,
224–227
decimals and, 243–246
definition of, 707
dividing, 235–238
improper fractions and, 193–195,
707
multiplying, 231–233
ordering, 193–195
subtracting
common denominators,
219–223
different denominators,
224–227

Mode, 255–261
choosing a representative average,
258–261
definition of, 257

Model
make a, problem solving strategy,
402–403, 407
scale, 324, 325

Modeling
addition
of fractions, 219
integer, 57–59

area
of a circle, 486
of a parallelogram, 481
of a rectangle, 32
of a trapezoid, 482
of a triangle, 134
binomial multiplication, 673, 674
equations
using algebra tiles, 28, 107–108,
117–118, 278
using a balance scale, 109
two-step, 117–118
fractions, 192
division, 234
equivalent, 178
integers, 53–54
linear inequalities, 583–587
patterns, 68
percent on a circle graph, 331, 334
polynomial addition, 661
the Pythagorean theorem, 442
rational numbers, 242
real numbers, 438
rounding, 705
square root, 432
surface area
of a cone, 508, 510
of a cylinder, 504, 505
of a prism, 502, 503, 505
of a pyramid, 507, 510
volume, 512, 518

Monomial(s), 657
definition of, 170
factoring, 170–172
greatest common factor of,
174–177
least common multiple of,
187–189
multiplying, 666–670
powers and, 666–670

Multiple(s), 186
common, 186
least common, 186–189

Multiple choice questions, *See*
Problem solving
Multiple events, 640
Multiple representations, *See*
Representation
Multiplication
binomial, 673–677
checking, using estimation, 251
cross products, 323–326
decimal, 251–254
by a whole number, 714

equations, 113–116
equivalent fractions and, 179–183, 192
estimating products, 716
exponents and, 20–23
of fractions, 230–233, 713
  by a whole number, 713
integer, 70–73
as inverse of division, 113
mixed number, 231–233
monomial, 666–670
order of operations and, 10–14
percent equation and, 347–350
properties
  associative, 81
  commutative, 80
  equality, 113
  identity, 71
  inequality, 146
  product of powers, 196–200
  zero, 71
in scientific notation, 206–209
to solve inequalities, 146–149
words indicating, 16
Multiplication property of equality, 113
for clearing decimals, 283–285
for clearing fractions, 273–275, 283–285
Multiplication property of inequality, 146
Multiplicative identity, 71
Multiplicative inverse, 234
Multi-step equation, 271–275
Multi-step inequality (inequalities)
problem-solving and, 301–305
solving, 295–300
writing, 296–300, 301–305
Multi-step problem, *See* Problem solving; Test-taking skills

n

Negative exponent, 201–204
Negative integer, 53
Negative slope, 571, 572
Negative square root, 431
Net, 502–505, 507, 508, 510, 518
Nonexamples, 215, 325, 335, 375, 390, 391, 392, 404, 681
Non-linear function(s), 680–685
game, 684

graphing, 681–685
  using a graphing calculator, 685
Non-routine problem *See* Problem solving strategies; Test-taking skills
Non standard form, of a polynomial, 657
Notation
arc, to show equal angle measures, 383
combination, 628
factorial, 623
fraction bar, 11
function, 680–684
permutation, 624
rotation in the coordinate plane, 410–411
Notebook
entries
  adding and subtracting fractions, 219
  addition property of equality, 110
  addition and subtraction properties of inequality, 141
  additive identity property, 59
  angle measures in a polygon, 391
  angles and parallel lines, 377
  using appropriate data displays, 606
  area of a circle, 486
  area of a parallelogram, 481
  area and perimeter of a triangle, 134
  area of a trapezoid, 482
  the associative property, 81
  average, 257
  circumference of a circle, 290
  classifying triangles, 382
  combination notation, 628
  the commutative property, 80
  counting principle, 619
  cross products property, 323
  dilation, 418
  distance formula, 34
  dividing decimals, 252
  dividing fractions, 234
  dividing integers, 74
  division property of equality, 114
  division property of inequality, 147

  finding intercepts, 564
  45°-45°-90° triangle, 456
  graphing linear inequalities, 584
  multiplication property of equality, 113
  multiplication property of inequality, 146
  multiplying decimals, 251
  multiplying fractions, 230
  multiplying integers, 70
  negative exponents, 201
  90° rotation, 410
  180° rotation, 411
  order of operations, 10, 21
  percent of change, 338
  the percent equation, 347
  perimeter and area formulas, 33
  permutation, 624
  power of a power property, 668
  power of a product property, 667
  probability of an event, 354
  probability of dependent events, 640
  probability of independent events, 640
  problem-solving plan, 39
  product of powers property, 196
  Pythagorean theorem, 443
  quotient of powers property, 197
  reflection, 405
  using scientific notation, 205
  similar polygons, 416
  simple interest, 348
  slope-intercept form, 577
  slope of a line, 570
  solving a percent problem, 327
  solving a two-step equation, 120
  subtracting integers, 63
  subtraction property of equality, 109
  summary of percent problems, 328
  summary of slope, 572
  surface area of a cone, 508
  surface area of a cylinder, 504
  surface area of a prism, 503
  surface area of a pyramid, 507
  30°-60°-90° triangle, 457
  trigonometric ratios, 463

Index

volume of a cone, 520
volume of a cylinder, 514
volume of a prism, 513
volume of a pyramid, 519
zero exponents, 202
how to take notes
using a concept grid, 480
contrasting terms, 596
illustrating with examples, 430
keeping a notebook, 4
making a concept map, 374
noting vocabulary, 52
organizing information, 106
preview the chapter, 166
recording the process, 270
summarizing material, 656
taking notes in class, 316
write questions about
homework, 540
writing helpful hints, 218
Notebook review, 24–25, 44–45,
78–79, 96–97, 130–131,
150–151, 190–191, 210–211,
240–241, 262–263, 286–287,
306–307, 336–337, 358–359,
394–395, 422–423, 454–455,
470–471, 498–499, 524–525,
562–563, 588–589, 614–615,
646–647, 671–672, 686–687
Notetaking, student help with, 21,
86, 146, 219, 244, 282, 328,
386, 443, 486, 565, 629, 674
Number line
to approximate square root,
432
for comparing real numbers,
438
for graphing, inequalities,
140–145
integer addition on, 57–59
for line plots, 723
for modeling absolute value, 54
for modeling opposites, 54
for ordering
fractions, decimals, and
percents, 333
integers, 53, 78
rational numbers, 243
for rounding
decimals, 705
whole numbers, 705
time line, 66
Number sense, *See also* Comparing;
Estimation; Ordering;

Properties
absolute value, 54–56
circumference, diameter, and pi,
288–289, 290
common factor, 173
common multiple, 186
comparing radii of circles, 491
composite number, 167, 169
consecutive numbers, 26, 27
digits, 704
divisibility tests, 706
exercises, 13, 42, 182, 208, 260,
275, 277, 298, 330, 511, 517
expanded form, 704
factorials, 623–626
factors, 167–172
front-end estimation, 248–250
greatest common divisor (GCD),
173
greatest common factor (GCF),
173–177
irrational numbers, 437, 439–441
leading digit, 251
least common denominator
(LCD), 192
least common multiple (LCM),
186–189
multiple choice questions and,
157
multiplicative inverse, 234
negative exponents, 201–204
number relationships, 242
opposite integers, 54–56
percent
discount, 342, 344–346
increase and decrease, 338–341
markup, 342–346
sale price, 342, 344–346
perfect square, 432
prediction from experiments, 352,
353, 355, 356
prime factorization, 169–172
prime number, 167, 169
product form, 205–206
Pythagorean triple, 451, 452
rational numbers, 242, 437–441
real numbers, 437
reciprocals, 234
relatively prime numbers, 174
repeating decimal, 242–246
rules of exponents, 196–200
scientific notation, 205–209
selecting a representative average,
258–261

Sieve of Eratosthenes, 167
square root, 431–436
standard form, 205–207, 704
terminating decimal, 242–246
triangular number, 617
whole number, 704
Numerator, 707

Obtuse angle, 382
Obtuse triangle, 382
Octagon, 390
Odds, 632–636
Opposite(s), 54–56
of a polynomial, 662
Opposite side, of a right triangle,
463
Ordered pair
definition of, 91
plotting, 91–95
relations and, 541, 543
as solution to an equation in two
variables, 549
as solution to a linear inequality,
583
Ordering
data
in a box-and-whisker plot,
601–604
to find median, 255–261
in a stem-and-leaf plot,
597–600
decimals, 438–441
exercises, 55, 245, 265
fractions, decimals, and percents,
333–334
improper fractions, 193–195
integers, 53, 55–56
mixed numbers, 193–195
rational numbers, 242–246
Order of operations, 10–14
for evaluating expressions,
221–222
Origin, coordinate plane, 91
Outcome(s), 354, *See also* Event
using counting methods to find,
618–622
favorable, 354, 633
odds of, 633–636
unfavorable, 633
Outlier, 604
Output, 541

p

Palindrome(s), 617
Parallel lines, 377
  constructing, 381
Parallelogram, 386
  area of, 481, 483–485
  base of, 481
  height of, 481
Patterns
  exercises, 41, 72, 245, 253, 350,
    393, 407, 435, 631, 676,
    685
  exponent, 156, 666
  geometric, 68, 69, 495
  integer, 63
  number, 68, 69, 616, 617
  tessellation, 414–415
  in trigonometric ratios, 461–462
  writing function rules from,
    542–544
Pentagon, 390
Percent
  applications, 342–346
    discount, 342, 344–346
    interest, 348–351
    markup, 342–346
    sale price, 342, 344–346
    sales tax, 343–346
    tip, 344–346
  of change, 338–341
  circle graphs and, 331, 334
  decimals and, 331–335
  decrease, 338–341
  definition of, 327
  equation, 347–350
  equivalent fractions, decimals
    and, 746
  fractions and, 331–335
  game, 346
  greater than 100%, 332–335
  increase, 338–341
  proportion and, 327–330
  summary of types of percent
    problems, 328
Perfect square, 432
Perform an experiment, problem
    solving strategy, 352–353,
    354
Perimeter
  of a composite figure, 37
  in the coordinate plane, 92–95
  of a rectangle, 33–37, 136–139
  of a right triangle, 451–453

  of a square, 33–37
    ratio of side length to, 317
  of a triangle, 134, 136–139, 279
Permutation notation, 624
Permutations, 623–626
  combinations and, 629–631
  definition of, 623
Perpendicular lines, 376
  constructing, 381
Pi
  circumference, diameter and,
    288–289
  definition of, 290
  estimating the value of, 288–289
Place value, 704
  game, 3
  rounding to, 705
Plane figures, *See* Geometry
Plane, *See* Coordinate plane
Plot(s)
  box-and-whisker, 601–604
  choosing a data display, 606–609
  line, 723
  scatter plot, 545–548
  stem-and-leaf, 597–600
    double, 598–600
Point(s)
  in the coordinate plane, 91–95
  definition of, 718
Polygon(s), 390–393
  angle sums for, 390–393
  congruent, 397–401
  dilating, 418–421
  quadrilaterals, 386–389
  regular, 390–391
  similar, 416–421
  tessellation and, 414–415
  triangles, 382–385
Polyhedron, *See also* Solids, 492
  edges of, 492–493, 495
  faces of, 492–493, 495
  vertices of, 492–493, 495
Polynomial(s)
  adding, 661–665
    game, 665
  binomial, 657
  classifying, 657, 659
  definition of, 657
  evaluating, 658–660
  monomial, 657
  monomials and powers, 666–670
  multiplying
    binomials, 673–677
    monomials, 666–670

  non standard form, 657
  opposite of, 662
  simplifying, 658–660
  standard form, 657–660
  subtracting, 662–665
  trinomial, 657
Population, 644
Positive integer, 53
Positive slope, 571, 572
Positive square root, 431
Power of a power property, 668
Power of a product property, 667
Powers
  base, 20
  dividing, 197–200
  evaluating, 20–23
    game, 428
  exponents and, 20–23
  monomials and, 666–670
  multiplying, 196–200
  negative, 201–209
  order of operations and, 21
  of powers, 668–670
  of products, 667–670
  reading, 20
  scientific notation and, 205–209
  of ten, 205–209
  writing products as, 20–23
  zero, 202
Precision, *See also* Error analysis
  front-end estimation and, 248–250
Precision measurement tools, *See*
    Measurement tools
Prediction
  exercises, 8, 103, 359, 363, 617,
    683
  from an experiment, 352, 353, 355,
    356
  from a graph, 103
  from a table, 42
  using geometric probability,
    652–653
  using a pattern, 616, 617
Prime factorization, 169–172
  factor tree, 169, 171
  greatest common factor and,
    173–177
Prime factor(s), 169
Prime number, 167, 169
  relatively prime, 174
Principal, interest and, 348
Prism, 492
  bases of, 492
  height of, 503

Index

sketching, 493
surface area of, 502–506
   formula, 503
volume of, 512–518
   formula, 513
Probability
of an event, 354–357
complementary events, 632–636
counting methods and, 618–622
dependent events, 639–643
experimental, 352–357, 652–653
formula, 354
geometric, 652–653
independent events, 639–643
multiple events, 640
odds and, 633–636
outcome, 354
   favorable, 354, 633
   unfavorable, 633
prediction from an experiment, 352, 353, 355, 356
simulations, 637–638
theoretical, 354, 355–357
tree diagrams and, 618–622
Problem solving, *See also* Error analysis
choose a method, exercises, 122
choose a strategy, 23, 27, 69, 84, 123, 133, 172, 185, 229, 246, 277, 299, 335, 353, 403, 421, 436, 449, 490, 501, 555, 617, 631, 679, 684
eliminate possibilities, 157
extended problem solving, 8, 13, 94, 123, 138, 182, 245, 293, 305, 325, 393, 407, 467, 484, 586, 600, 621, 626, 636, 670
extended response questions, 9, 49, 89, 101, 128, 155, 159, 160, 162, 172, 215, 261, 267, 294, 311, 341, 363, 367, 368, 369, 370, 413, 427, 453, 475, 529, 533, 534, 535, 536, 580, 593, 604, 651, 684, 691, 694, 696–698
guided problem solving, 7, 17, 41, 65, 76, 87, 111, 121, 126, 137, 142, 170, 175, 194, 207, 226, 236, 253, 259, 273, 303, 329, 349, 411, 419, 434, 452, 458, 466, 483, 494, 509, 547, 566, 599, 603, 668
inequalities and, 301–305

multiple choice questions, 13, 19, 23, 31, 37, 43, 56, 62, 67, 77, 84, 95, 112, 116, 123, 128, 139, 145, 155, 156–157, 158–162, 172, 177, 189, 195, 200, 204, 208, 223, 227, 233, 238, 246, 250, 254, 275, 281, 285, 299, 305, 311, 320, 326, 330, 335, 346, 350, 357, 363, 366–370, 379, 385, 389, 393, 401, 408, 421, 436, 441, 447, 460, 468, 485, 490, 495, 506, 511, 523, 530–531, 532–536, 544, 548, 553, 560, 567, 574, 587, 593, 600, 604, 609, 622, 626, 631, 636, 643, 660, 665, 670, 677, 695–698
short response questions, 19, 31, 37, 49, 77, 84, 95, 101, 116, 123, 145, 149, 155, 159, 160, 161, 162, 189, 208, 215, 227, 233, 250, 254, 267, 275, 305, 311, 320, 330, 350, 363, 364–365, 366, 368, 369, 370, 379, 401, 408, 427, 447, 475, 485, 490, 506, 511, 517, 529, 533, 534, 535, 536, 553, 560, 567, 593, 609, 622, 626, 631, 643, 651, 691, 695–698
Problem-solving plan, 38–42
Problem-solving strategies, *See also* Test-taking skills; Test-taking strategies
act it out, 228–229
   exercises, 232
break into parts, 500–501, 502
   exercises, 506
draw a diagram, 132–133, 134, 448–449
   exercises, 453, 467
draw a graph, 678–679, 681
   exercises, 683
guess, check, and revise, 26–27
   exercises, 31
look for a pattern, 68–69
make a list, 184–185, 186, 618, 627
make a model, 402–403
   exercises, 407
make a table, 554–555, 556
   exercises, 683
perform an experiment, 352–353, 354
solve a simpler problem, 616–617
   exercises, 622

work backward, 276–277,
   exercises, 280, 677, 683
Product form, 205–206
Product of powers property, 196
Project ideas, 103, 313, 477, 653, *See also* Math in Science
Properties
associative
   addition, 81
   multiplication, 81
commutative
   addition, 80
   multiplication, 80
cross product, 323–326
distributive, 85–89
   equations with variables on both sides and, 279–281
   multi-step equations and, 272–275
of equality
   addition, 110
   division, 114
   multiplication, 113
   subtraction, 109
identity
   additive, 59
   multiplicative, 71
of inequality
   addition, 141
   division, 147
   multiplication, 146
   subtraction, 141
power of a power, 668
power of a product, 667
product of powers, 196
quotient of powers, 197
table of, 743
zero, multiplication, 71
Proportion
cross products and, 323–326
definition of, 322
dilation and, 418–421
for finding angles in circle graphs, 605, 607–609, 611
game, 326
indirect measurement and, 417, 420, 421
percent and, 327–330
prediction and, 352, 353, 355, 356
scale and, 324–326
similarity and, 416–421
writing and solving, 322–326

Proportional reasoning
  comparing radii of circles, 491
  cross products and, 323–326
  diameter and circumference,
    288–289
  equivalent fractions, 179–183
  making a circle graph, 605,
    607–609, 611
  percent and, 327–330
  rates and, 318–320
  ratios and, 317–320
  scale and, 324–326
  scale drawing, 321
  similarity and, 416–421
  unit rate and, 318–320
Protractor, 382–383, 396, 461–462,
    605, 607–609, 721
  how to use, 721
Pyramid, 492
  base of, 492
  height of, 507
  slant height of, 507
  surface area of, 507–511
    formula, 507
  volume of, 519–521
    formula, 519
Pythagorean theorem, 442–447,
    450–453
  converse of, 444–447
  formula for, 443
  indirect measurement and, 450,
    452–453
  modeling, 442
Pythagorean triple, 451, 452

q

Quadrant(s), coordinate, 91
Quadrilateral(s), 386–389
  classifying, 386–389
  congruent, 397–401
  definition of, 386
  dilating, 418, 420
  parallelogram, 386
  rectangle, 386
  rhombus, 386
  square, 386
  sum of the angle measures of,
    390–391
  trapezoid, 386
Quotient, 715
Quotient of powers property,
    197

r

Radical sign, 431
Radius
  of a circle, 290
    circumference and, 290–294
  of a cylinder, 504
Random sample, 644
Range
  of data, 258–261
  of a function, 542
Rate(s), 318–320, 708
  definition of, 318, 708
  equivalent, 318–320
  unit, 318–320, 708
Ratio(s), *See also* Proportion; Rate;
    Scale
  circumference and diameter,
    288–289
  comparison and, 708
  cosine, 462–468
  definition of, 317, 708
  equivalent, 317–320
  percent and, 327–330
  probability and, 352–357, 632–636
  proportion and, 322–326
  rates and, 317–320, 708
  scale factor and, 418–421
  sine, 462–468
  slope, 568–574
  tangent, 462–468
    inverse, 469
  trigonometric, 461–468
Rational number(s), 437–441, *See
    also* Fractions
  definition of, 242, 437
  ordering, 243–246
Ray, definition of, 718
Reading mathematics
  identifying points, lines, and
    planes, 718
  naming angles, 719
  reading angle markings, 383
  reading bar graphs, 5–9, 24, 724
  reading box-and-whisker plots,
    601–604
  reading circle graphs, 605,
    607–609
  reading coordinate notation,
    404–405, 409–411
  reading double bar graphs, 9
  reading histograms, 6–9
  reading integer values, 54
  reading line graphs, 606–609, 725

  reading misleading graphs,
    612–614
  reading powers, 20
  reading scatter plots, 545–548
  reading stem-and-leaf plots,
    598–600
  scientific notation, 205–209
  student help with, 16, 29, 33, 39,
    54, 302, 351, 383, 390, 398,
    410, 433, 482, 515, 633, 681
  translating verbal phrases, 16
  translating verbal sentences,
    302–305
Real number(s)
  classifying, 437, 439, 440
  comparing, 438–441
  definition of, 437
  Venn diagram of, 437
Reasoning, *See also* Critical thinking;
    Decision making; Error
    analysis; Extended response
    questions; Patterns;
    Proportional reasoning; Short
    response questions; Thinking
    skills
  concept grid, 480
  concept map, 374, 386
  converse of a statement, 444
  games, 43
  problem-solving plan, 38–42
  Pythagorean theorem, 444
  tree diagram, 169, 171, 618–622
  truth function, 300
  unit analysis, 40
  Venn diagram, 242, 437, 726
Reciprocal(s), 234
Rectangle, 386
  area of, 32–37, 136–139
    modeling, 32
  perimeter of, 33–37, 136–139
Rectangular prism, *See* Prism
Reflection, 404–408
  in the *x*-axis, 405
  in the *y*-axis, 405
  tessellation and, 414–415
Regular polygon, 390–391
Relation(s)
  definition of, 541
  functions and, 541, 543
Relatively prime numbers, 174
Repeating decimal(s), 242–246
  fractions and, 242–246
  irrational numbers and, 437
  rational numbers and, 437

Report, project, 313
Representation, *See also* Graphs;
　　　Modeling; Number line; Plots
　of the additive identity property,
　　　59
　of area, 32–33
　area of a circle as area of a
　　　parallelogram, 486
　area of a parallelogram as area of a
　　　rectangle, 481
　of data, averages, 255–261
　of equations using algebra tiles, 28
　expressions in expanded form, 196
　forms of a fraction, 166
　fractions as percents, 331–335
　functions in tables, 541–544
　improper fractions as mixed
　　　numbers, 193–195, 707
　mixed numbers as improper
　　　fractions, 193–195, 707
　of number sets in a Venn diagram,
　　　242, 437, 726
　numbers in expanded form, 704
　numbers in standard form, 704
　percents as decimals, 332–335
　percents as fractions, 332–335
　of perimeter, 33
　of points, lines, and planes, 718
　of polynomials with algebra tiles,
　　　661
　of the Pythagorean Theorem, 442
　of real numbers with a Venn
　　　diagram, 437
　verbal model, 11
　verbal phrases as expressions,
　　　16–19
Research, project, 103, 313, 477, 653
Review, *See also* Assessment;
　　　Internet; Notebook Review;
　　　Skills Review Handbook
　basic skills, 9, 13, 19, 31, 37, 43, 67,
　　　73, 84, 95, 112, 116, 123, 139,
　　　145, 149, 172, 177, 183, 189,
　　　195, 204, 208, 223, 238, 246,
　　　254, 275, 285, 305, 320, 335,
　　　341, 346, 357, 379, 401, 413,
　　　436, 460, 468, 523, 548, 553,
　　　560, 567, 574, 580, 587, 631,
　　　636, 643, 660, 677
　Chapter Review, 46–47, 98–99,
　　　152–153, 212–213, 264–265,
　　　308–309, 360–361, 424–425,
　　　472–473, 526–527, 590–591,
　　　648–649, 688–689

　extra practice, 727–739
　mixed review, 9, 13, 19, 23, 31, 37,
　　　43, 56, 62, 67, 73, 77, 84, 89,
　　　95, 112, 116, 123, 128, 139,
　　　145, 149, 172, 177, 183, 189,
　　　195, 200, 204, 208, 223, 227,
　　　233, 238, 246, 250, 254, 261,
　　　275, 281, 285, 294, 299, 305,
　　　320, 326, 330, 335, 341, 346,
　　　350, 357, 379, 385, 389, 393,
　　　401, 408, 413, 421, 436, 441,
　　　447, 453, 460, 468, 485, 490,
　　　495, 506, 511, 517, 523, 544,
　　　548, 553, 560, 567, 574, 580,
　　　587, 600, 604, 609, 622, 626,
　　　631, 636, 643, 660, 665, 670,
　　　677, 684
　student help with, 6, 81, 120,
　　　135, 169, 193, 224, 230, 272,
　　　292, 295, 318, 338, 413, 417,
　　　437, 451, 571, 577, 620, 658,
　　　665
Rhombus, 386
Right angle, 375, 382
　symbol for, 33, 375
Right triangle, 382
　area of, 451–453
　converse of the Pythagorean
　　　theorem and, 444–447
　45°-45°-90°, 456–460
　hypotenuse of, 442, 443
　indirect measurement and, 450,
　　　452–453
　legs of, 442, 443
　perimeter of, 451–453
　Pythagorean theorem and,
　　　442–447, 450–453
　Pythagorean triple and, 451, 452
　30°-60°-90°, 457–460
　trigonometric ratios and, 461–469
Rise, vertical change, 568, 570
Rotation, 410–413
　coordinate notation for, 410–411
　in the coordinate plane, 410–413
　tessellation and, 414–415
Rounding
　to approximate square root,
　　　432–436
　to check answers are reasonable,
　　　251, 252
　definition of, 705
　to estimate, 711, 716
　game, 3
　to a place value, 705

Rule(s)
　for adding integers, 59
　of exponents, 196–200
Ruler, using, 720
Run, horizontal change, 568, 570

S

Sales tax, 343–346
Sample(s), 644–645
　biased, 644–645
　random, 644
Scaffolding, *See* Problem solving
Scale
　definition of, 324
　for a drawing, 321
　misleading graphs and, 612–613
　for a model, 324, 325
　proportion and, 324–326
Scale drawing, making, 321
Scale factor, 418–421
Scale model, 324, 325
Scalene triangle, 382
Scatter plot
　on a graphing calculator, 610
　interpreting, 545–548
　making, 545–548
Scientific notation, 205–209
　multiplying numbers in,
　　　206–209
　standard form numbers and,
　　　205–209
Segment
　definition of, 718
　drawing with a compass, 722
　length on the coordinate plane,
　　　92–95
Sequences, *See* Patterns
Short response questions, *See*
　　　Problem solving
Side(s)
　congruent, 397–401
　corresponding, 377, 397–401
　included, 398
　of a polygon, 390
　of a right triangle
　　　adjacent, 463
　　　hypotenuse, 442, 443, 463
　　　opposite, 463
　of a triangle, classifying by,
　　　382–383
Side-angle-side congruence,
　　　398–401

Side-side-side congruence, 398–401
Side view
  of a solid, 493, 496–497
    drawing, 496–497
Sieve of Eratosthenes, 167
Similarity, 416–421
Similar polygons, 416–421
Simple interest, 348–350
Simplifying fractions, 179–183, 198,
  220–222
Simulation, 637–638
Sine ratio, 462–468
Skills Review Handbook, 704–726
  data displays
    bar graphs, 724
    line graphs, 725
    line plots, 723
  decimals
    adding, 709
    dividing, 715
    multiplication by a whole
      number, 714
    rounding, 705
    subtracting, 709
  estimation
    differences, 711
    products, 716
    quotients, 716
    sums, 711
  fractions
    adding, 710
    multiplying, 713
    subtracting, 710
  geometry
    angles, 719
    lines, 718
    planes, 718
    points, 718
  improper fractions, mixed
    numbers and, 707
  logical reasoning, 726
  measurement
    using a compass, 722
    using a protractor, 721
    using a ruler, 720
  mixed numbers, improper
    fractions and, 707
  number sense
    divisibility tests, 706
    place value, 704
    rounding, 705
  problem solving
    using addition and subtraction,
      712

    using multiplication and
      division, 717
  rate, 708
  ratio, 708
  Venn diagrams, 726
Slant height
  of a cone, 508
  of a pyramid, 507
Slope
  line, 568–574
    definition of, 570
    negative, 571, 572
    positive, 571, 572
  undefined, 571, 572
  zero, 571, 572
Slope-intercept form, 575–580
Solid(s), *See also* specific solids;
    Surface area; Volume
  bases of, 492
  classifying, 492, 494
  composite, 495, 496–497, 506
  definition of, 492
  drawing, 493–497
  edges of, 492–493
  faces of, 492–493
  vertices of, 492–493
  views of, 493, 496–497
Solution
  of an equation, 28
    in two variables, 549
  of a linear inequality, 583
  of a system of linear equations, 581
Solve a related/simpler problem,
    problem solving strategy,
    616–617, 622
Solving equations, *See* Equations
Spatial reasoning, *See also* Drawing;
    Graphs; Modeling
  algebra tiles, 28, 107–108, 117–118,
    278, 661, 673
  area of a circle, 486
  area of a parallelogram, 481
  area of a trapezoid, 482
  classifying angles, 382–385
  classifying triangles, 382–385
  diameter and circumference,
    288–289
  drawing, solids, 493–497
  geometric probability, 652–653
  nets, 502–505, 507, 508, 510, 518
  reflection, 404–408
  similarity, 416–421
  stem-and-leaf plots, 597–600
  surface area, 502–511

  tessellation, 414–415
  translation, 409, 411–413
  tree diagram, 618–622
  Venn diagram, 242, 437, 726
  vertical line test, 681
  volume
    of a cone, 520
    of a cylinder, 514
    of a pyramid, 519
    of a rectangular prism, 513
Sphere, 492
  center of, 492
  surface area of, 510
  volume of, 679
Spreadsheet
  for comparing radii of circles, 491
  for solving inequalities, 300
Square, 386
  area of, 33–37
  perimeter of, 33–37
  ratio of side length to perimeter,
    317
  square root and side length, 431
Square root, 431–436
  approximating, 432–436
  definition of, 431
  equation, 433–435
  finding, 744
  of a fraction, 435
  game, 436
  negative, 431
  perfect square and, 432
  positive, 431
  radical sign, 431
  table of, 745
Squares
  finding, 744
  table of, 745
Standard form
  of a number, 205–207, 704
  of a polynomial, 657–660
Standardized test practice, *See*
    Assessment; FCAT Practice;
    Test-taking skills; Test-taking
    strategies
Statistics, *See also* Graphs; Plots
  analyzing data, 255–256
  choosing a representative average,
    258–261
  game, 261
  collecting data, 255–256
  lower extreme, 601
  lower quartile, 601
  mean, 75, 255–261

median, 255–261
mode, 255–261
outliers, 604
range, 258–261
upper extreme, 601
upper quartile, 601
Stem(s), in a stem-and-leaf plot, 597
Stem-and-leaf plot, 597–600
choosing a data display, 606,
608–609
double, 598–600
interpreting, 598–600
making, 597–600
Stop and Think exercises, *See*
Thinking skills
Straight angle, 375
Straightedge, 380–381, 396, 722
Strategies, *See* Problem-solving
strategies; Test-taking
strategies
Student help
with homework, 7, 12, 18, 22, 30,
36, 41, 55, 61, 65, 72, 76, 83,
88, 93, 111, 115, 121, 126, 137,
143, 148, 171, 176, 182, 188,
199, 203, 207, 222, 226, 232,
237, 245, 249, 253, 259, 274,
280, 284, 293, 297, 304, 319,
325, 329, 334, 340, 345, 349,
356, 378, 384, 388, 392, 400,
407, 412, 419, 434, 440, 446,
452, 459, 466, 483, 488, 494,
505, 510, 516, 522, 543, 547,
551, 559, 566, 573, 579, 599,
603, 608, 621, 625, 630, 635,
642, 659, 664, 669, 676, 682
with notetaking, 21, 86, 146, 219,
244, 282, 328, 386, 443, 486,
565, 629, 674
with reading, 16, 29, 33, 39, 54,
302, 351, 383, 390, 398, 410,
433, 482, 515, 633, 681
with review, 6, 81, 120, 135, 169,
193, 224, 230, 272, 292, 295,
318, 338, 413, 417, 437, 451,
571, 577, 620, 658, 665
with solving problems, 10, 56, 71,
81, 87, 92, 113, 120, 125, 141,
180, 192, 195, 205, 220, 235,
283, 291, 292, 322, 332, 343,
355, 377, 381, 431, 444, 457,
463, 497, 507, 514, 542, 550,
557, 582, 583, 584, 585, 598,
601, 605, 612, 623, 624, 632

with technology, 14, 209, 300, 464,
469, 504, 685
with vocabulary, 34, 82, 173, 348,
411, 492, 493, 570, 675
Substitution
to check equations, 29, 113, 114,
119, 120, 124, 276, 296, 323,
542, 550, 581
to solve linear systems, 582
Subtraction
checking with addition, 709
decimal, 247–250, 709
equations, 108–112
modeling, 108
estimating differences, 711
of exponents to divide powers,
197–200
of fractions
common denominators,
219–223, 710
different denominators,
224–227
integer, 63–67
as inverse of addition, 109
of mixed numbers
common denominators,
219–223
different denominators,
225–227
order of operations and, 10–14
polynomial, 662–665
properties
equality, 109
inequality, 141
to solve inequalities, 141–145
words indicating, 16
Subtraction property of equality,
109
Subtraction property of inequality,
141
Supplementary angles, 375
Surface area
of a cone, 508–511
of a cylinder, 504–506
of a prism, 502–506
of a pyramid, 507–511
of a sphere, 510
Survey
questions, 644–645
biased, 645
samples and, 644–645
Symbols, table of, 740
Symmetry, 406–408
line of, 406

System of linear equations, 581–582
solution of, 581

t

Table(s)
data, 32, 199, 243, 260, 288, 390,
545–548
frequency, 6–9, 256
for graphing linear equations,
556–561
input-output, 541–544
patterns and, 68, 69
representing functions, 541–544
Table of formulas, 742
Table of measures, 741
Table of properties, 743
Table of squares and square roots,
745
Table of symbols, 740
Tally chart, *See* Frequency table
Tally mark, 6
Tangent ratio, 462–468
inverse, 469
Technology, *See also* Calculator;
Graphing calculator;
Technology activities
student help with, 14, 209, 300,
464, 469, 504, 685
Technology activities
calculator
compound interest, 351
finding an angle measure,
469
integer operations, 90
operations with fractions, 239
using order of operations, 14
using scientific notation, 209
simulation using the random
function, 638
computer
comparing radii of circles, 491
solving inequalities, 300
graphing calculator
graphing linear functions, 561
graphing non-linear functions,
685
making data displays, 610, 611
internet, searching for
information, 129
Terminating decimal(s), 242–246
irrational numbers and, 437
rational numbers and, 437

Term(s)
of an expression, 86
constant, 86
like, 86
Tessellation, 414–415
Test practice, *See* Assessment;
Review; Test-taking strategies
Test-taking skills
building, 156–157, 364–365,
530–531, 692–693
practicing, 158–162, 366–370,
532–536, 694–698
strategies for extended response
questions, 692–693
strategies for multiple choice
questions, 156–157
context based, 530–531
strategies for short response
questions, 364–365
Test-taking strategies, 49, 101, 155,
215, 267, 311, 363, 427, 475,
529, 593, 651, 691
Theoretical probability, 354,
355–357, *See also* Probability
Thinking skills, *See also* Critical
thinking; Error analysis
Stop and Think, 3, 25, 32, 45, 51,
79, 97, 105, 108, 118, 131, 151,
165, 167, 178, 191, 211, 217,
241, 256, 263, 269, 287, 289,
307, 315, 321, 337, 359, 373,
395, 396, 423, 429, 442, 455,
462, 471, 479, 499, 512, 518,
525, 539, 563, 569, 576, 589,
595, 615, 638, 647, 655, 672,
673, 687
30°-60°-90° right triangle, 457–460
Three-dimensional figure, 492–495,
See also Solids
Tiling patterns, *See* Tessellation
Tip, percent, 344–346
Top view
of a solid, 493, 496–497
drawing, 496–497
Transformations
reflection, 404–408
rotation, 410–413
tessellation and, 414–415
translation, 409, 411–413
Translating
verbal phrases, 16
verbal sentences, 302–305
Translation, 409, 411–413
coordinate notation for, 409

in the coordinate plane, 94, 409,
411–413
tessellation and, 414–415
Trapezoid, 386
area of, 482–485
bases of, 482
height of, 482
Tree diagram
as a counting method, 618–622
factor tree, 169, 171
Triangle(s), *See also* Right triangle
acute, 382
angle-side-angle congruence,
398–401
area of, 134–139
base of, 134
classifying, 382–385
congruent, 397–401
copying, 396
equiangular, 385
equilateral, 382
height of, 134
isosceles, 382
obtuse, 382
perimeter of, 134, 136–139, 279
right, 382
scalene, 382
side-angle-side congruence,
398–401
side-side-side congruence,
398–401
sum of angle measures, 383
game, 429
Triangular numbers, 617
Trigonometric ratio, 461–469
cosine, 462–468
game, 471
inverse of, 469
sine, 462–468
tangent, 462–468
Trinomial, 657
Truth function, 300
Two-dimensional figures, *See*
Geometry
Two-step equations
modeling, 117–118
solving, 117–123
writing, 124–128

u

Undefined slope, 571, 572
Unfavorable outcome, 633

Unit analysis, 40, 80
Unit rate, 318–320
definition of, 318
Upper extreme, 601
Upper quartile, 601

v

Variable(s)
on both sides of an equation,
278–281
coefficient of, 86
definition of, 15
equations in two, 549–553
in formulas, 33–37
Variable equation, *See also*
Equations
solution of, 28
Variable expression(s), 15–19
definition of, 15
evaluating, 16–19, 64–67, 71–73,
75–77, 86–89, 181–183,
231–233
integer, 64–67
game, 19
simplifying, 180–183, 202–204,
225–227
writing, 16–19
Venn diagram
definition of, 726
drawing, 726
real number, 437
to show number relationships,
242, 726
Verbal model
definition of, 11
examples, 14, 38, 39, 75, 92, 111,
112, 126, 132, 179, 236, 253,
274, 275, 276, 304
writing to solve problems, 11, 29,
80, 110, 114, 115, 119, 124,
125, 129, 131, 136, 142, 147,
225, 236, 271, 273, 278, 282,
296, 297, 301, 303, 307, 324,
342, 507, 578, 663
Verbal phrases
indicating inequality, 302
translating, 16, 28
Verbal sentences, translating,
302–305
Vertex (vertices)
of an angle, 719
of a polyhedron, 492–495

Index

Vertical angles, 376
Vertical line, graph of, 558–560
Vertical line test, 681
Views of a solid, 493, 496–497
Volume(s)
    comparing, 517, 518, 523
    of a cone, 520–523
        formula, 520
    of a cylinder, 514–517
        formula, 514
    of a prism, 512–518
        formula, 513
    of a pyramid, 519–523
        formula, 519
    of a sphere, 679
        formula, 679

What do you think?, 17, 29, 36, 42,
      64, 66, 75, 123, 136, 147, 171,
      193, 222, 246, 291, 298, 324,
      339, 350, 393, 400, 447, 489,
      521, 557, 602, 604, 660, 670
Whole number
    definition of, 704
    place value, 704
    rounding, 705
Work backward
    problem solving strategy, 276–277
    exercises, 116, 280, 677, 683
Writing
    using coordinate notation,
        404–405
    decimals
        as fractions, 243–246
        as percents, 332–335
    equations, 114, 124–128, 578–580
    equivalent fractions, 180–183
    equivalent ratios, 317–320
    formula for circumference, 289
    fractions
        as decimals, 242–246
        with different denominators,
          224–227
        as percents, 331
    a function rule, 542–544
    improper fractions as mixed
        numbers, 193–195, 707
    inequalities, 296–300, 301–305
    mixed numbers as improper
        fractions, 193–195, 707
    multi-step equations, 271–275

    multi-step inequalities, 296–300,
        301–305
    a number
        in expanded form, 704
        in scientific notation, 205–209
        in standard form, 704
    percents
        as decimals, 332–335
        as fractions, 332–335
    products as powers, 20–23
    proportions, 322–326
    rates, 318–320, 708
    ratios, 317–320, 708
    repeating decimals as fractions,
        224
    scientific notation in standard
        form, 206–209
    two-step equations, 124–128
    unbiased survey questions, 645
    variable expressions, 16–19
Writing in Mathematics, exercises, 3,
      7, 18, 23, 31, 42, 57, 61, 76, 83,
      89, 97, 105, 108, 112, 118, 127,
      144, 149, 151, 165, 167, 171,
      176, 178, 188, 189, 194, 203,
      211, 217, 223, 227, 237, 241,
      246, 254, 256, 260, 263, 287,
      289, 293, 304, 307, 312, 315,
      320, 337, 345, 349, 357, 373,
      378, 385, 395, 396, 413, 420,
      423, 429, 455, 460, 466, 471,
      479, 494, 523, 525, 539, 544,
      548, 560, 563, 573, 586, 587,
      595, 599, 615, 621, 630, 638,
      647, 655, 672, 677, 687

x-axis, 91
    reflection in, 405
x-coordinate, 91
x-intercept, 564

y-axis, 91
    reflection in, 405
y-coordinate, 91
y-intercept, 564

Zero
    as an exponent, 202
    as an integer, 53
    division by, 74
    multiplication property of, 71
    as a place holder, 247, 252
    slope, 571, 572
    square root for, 431

Credits

Photography

iii *top to bottom* Meridian Creative Group, RMIP/Richard Haynes, Michael Girard, Jerry Head Jr.; **vi** Copyright © AFP/Corbis; **vii** Jim Schwabel/Index Stock; **viii** Bobby Model/National Geographic/Getty Images; **ix** Copyright © Tom Stewart/ Corbis; **x** Copyright © Reuters NewMedia/Corbis; **xi** Charles Krupa/AP Wide World Photos; **xii** *left* PhotoDisc; *right* Lee Celano/AP Wide World Photos; **xiii** Frank Siteman; **xiv** Paul Sancya/AP Wide World Photos; **xv** Kevin Bartram/The Galveston County Daily News/AP Wide World Photos; **xvi** Scott Spiker/ImageState; **xvii** West Rock/Stone/Getty Images; **xviii** Matthias Clamer/Stone/Getty Images; **1** Copyright © Cosmo Condina; **2** Copyright © Corbis; **3** *left* Copyright © Joseph Sohm; Chromosohm, Inc./Corbis; *right* Royalty-Free/Corbis; **5** Diaphor Agency/ Index Stock; **6** Copyright © Alan Schein/CorbisStockMarket; **7** Copyright © Corbis; **8** Silvia Flores,The Press-Enterprise/AP Wide World Photos; **9** PhotoDisc; **10** Copyright © Mark Richards/PhotoEdit/PictureQuest; **11** Copyright © Galen Rowell/Corbis; **12** Jerry Trafford; **13** *left* Julie Blum/Columbus Telegram/AP Wide World Photos; *right* Copyright © Becky Luigart-Stayner/Corbis; **15** *top* Copyright © PunchStock; *bottom* Zefa Visual Media-Germany/Index Stock; **17** *top* Greer & Associates, Inc/SuperStock; *bottom left* Stockbyte; *bottom right* PhotoDisc; **18** *left* James Meyer/The Image Bank/Getty Images; *right* Copyright © Comstock; **20** Copyright © Ron Watts/Corbis; **22** PhotoDisc; **23** Eric Wessman/ Photonica; **26** Frank Siteman; **27** Syracuse Newspapers/The Image Works; **29** *both* Copyright © Reuters NewMedia, Inc./Corbis; **31** Copyright © AFP/Corbis; **34** Barbara Strnadova/Photo Researchers, Inc.; **35** Larry West/Photo Researchers, Inc.; **36** Ken Osburn/Index Stock; **37** Johner/ Photonica; **38** Ted S. Warren/AP Wide World Photos; **42** Kevork Djansezian/AP Wide World Photos; **47** Copyright © Stephen Frink/Corbis; **48** PhotoDisc; **53** Artville; **54** *top left* Copyright © Comstock; *bottom left* Photo by Jerry Trafford, Courtesy of Vintage IWear; *right* Artville; **56** *left* NASA; *right* Ken O'Donoghue; **61** *both* The Picture Desk; **62** Copyright © Bob Daemmrich/PictureQuest; **64** Jeff Hunter/The Image Bank/Getty Images; **66** Tim Haske/Index Stock; **68** Frank Siteman; **69** Copyright © Kwame Zikomo/SuperStock; **70** *top* Teisuke Shinoda/Photonica; *bottom* Copyright © Stephen Frink/Corbis; **73** *left* Copyright © Corbis; *right, both* PhotoDisc; **75** Copyright © Dean Conger/Corbis; **76** PhotoDisc; **77** Copyright © Paul A. Souders/Corbis; **80** *top* School Division, Houghton Mifflin Company; *bottom* Steve Casimiro/Getty Images; **83** Steven Senne/AP Wide World Photos; **84** *left* Ken O'Donoghue, *right* PhotoDisc; **85** SuperStock; **87, 88** *all* Ken O'Donoghue; **89** Jim Schwabel/Index Stock; **93** Copyright © Bill Ross/Corbis; **94** *top left* Copyright © PhotoDisc/Getty Images; *top right* EyeWire Collection/Getty Images; **99** School Division, Houghton Mifflin Company; **102** *top* Copyright © Galen Rowell/Corbis; *bottom* Copyright © Darrell Gulin/Corbis; **103** *top* Copyright ©Bjorn Backe; Papilio/Corbis; *bottom* Copyright © Richard Hamilton Smith/ Corbis; **104** *all* NASA; **105** *left* NASA; *right* Copyright © NASA/Corbis; **110** Bobby Model/National Geographic/Getty Images; **111** Ken O'Donoghue; **112** Darryl Torckler/Getty Images; **114** Steve Hix/Getty Images; **115** G.D.T./Getty Images; **119** *top* Stockbyte; *bottom* Frank Siteman; **121** Ken O'Donoghue; **123** Dennis O'Clair/Getty Images; **124** Mitchell Funk/Getty Images; **127** *left* Copyright © Image 100/Royalty-Free/Corbis; *right* Ken O'Donoghue; **132** Frank Siteman; **133** Antonio Mo/Getty Images; **135** Copyright © Cosmo Condina; **136** John Warden/ Getty Images; **138** Brand X Pictures; **139** RubberBall Productions/CorbisStockMarket; **140** *left* Ken O'Donoghue; *right* Copyright © Kurt Wittman/Corbis; **143** Adrian Weinbrecht/Getty Images; **144** Copyright © Reuters NewMedia Inc./ Corbis; **147** Art Wolfe/Getty Images; **148** Brand X Pictures; **149** Dale Durfee/Stone/Getty Images; **154** Ryan McVay/PhotoDisc/Getty Images; **163** Claus Meyer/Minden Pictures; **164** Alistair Cowin/Index Stock; **165** *background* Benelux Press/Index Stock; *top left* Stephen Simpson/Taxi/Getty Images; *top right* Copyright © Tom Stewart/Corbis; *bottom left* Benelux Press/Index Stock; **168** *both* Ken O'Donoghue; **170** School Division, Houghton Mifflin Company; **171** National Park Service Historic Photograph Collection; **172** Ken O'Donoghue; **175** *top* School Division, Houghton Mifflin Company; *bottom* Bob Torrez/Stone/Getty

Images; **176** *both* PhotoDisc; **177** Courtesy of Jonathan Wheeler; **179** *top* Copyright © Erich Lessing/Art Resource, NY; *center three images* Christie's Images; *bottom image* Eric Kamp/Index Stock; **180** *both* Christie's Images; **181** both PhotoDisc; **182** Claus Meyer/Minden Pictures; **184** Frank Siteman; **185** David Davis/Index Stock; **186** *left* Copyright © Guy Cali/Picturequest; *right* Copyright © Comstock; **188** Copyright © Corbis; **193** Konrad Wothe/Minden Pictures; **194** Copyright © Tom Stewart/Corbis; **195** Steve Miller/AP Wide World Photos; **199** Copyright © NASA/Corbis; **201** *top* Copyright © Roger Holden/Index Stock/PictureQuest; *bottom* Copyright © M. Hans/Vandystadt/Photo Researchers, Inc.; **203** Copyright © MICROFIELD SCIENTIFIC LTD/Photo Researchers, Inc.; **204** *left* Artville; *right* Pho/AP Wide World Photos; **205** *top* Courtesy of Fan Yang; The Science of Bubbles; *center* International Stock/ImageState; **207** NASA; **208** Artville; **213** Robb Helfrick/Index Stock; **214** G.K. & Vikki Hart/The Image Bank/Getty Images; **216** © David Brooks/Corbis; **217** *left* Don Mason/Corbis; *right* School Division, Houghton Mifflin Company; **220** Photo by Shawn Lockhart, courtesy of Southwest Wisconsin Reptiles; **222** David Madison/Stone/Getty Images; **223** David Young-Wolff/Stone/Getty Images; **224** Ryan McVay/PhotoDisc/ PictureQuest; **225** Ken O'Donoghue; **226** Copyright © Reuters NewMedia Inc./Corbis; **228** Frank Siteman; **229** Donna Day/Stone/Getty Images; **230** EyeWire Collection/Getty Images; **231** *top* F. Schussler/Photolink/Getty Images; *bottom* PunchStock; **232** Ken O'Donoghue; **233** Gianni Cigolini/Image Bank/Getty Images; **236** Copyright © Image 100/Royalty-Free/Corbis; **243** Steve Maslowski/Photo Researchers, Inc.; **244** G.K. & Vikki Hart/The Image Bank/Getty Images; **245** Frank Siteman; **246** Tom Bean/Stone/Getty Images; **247** Frank Siteman; **248** Ken O'Donoghue; **250** Copyright © Peter Adams/Index Stock/PictureQuest; **251** Bruce Leighty/Index Stock; **253** Michael K. Nichols/National Geographic/Getty Images; **254** Brad Lewis/Adventure Photography/ImageState; **257** Copyright © Ralph White/Corbis; **258** Copyright © Tom Stewart/Corbis; **259** PhotoDisc; **260** Copyright © Jon Feingersh/Corbis; **265** Kevin Schafer/The Image Bank/Getty Images; **266** Copyright © Comstock; **269** Ken O'Donoghue; **271** *both* Ken O'Donoghue; **273** Neo Vision/Photonica; **274** Copyright © Chuck Savage/ CorbisStockMarket; **275** Ken O'Donoghue; **276** Copyright © Rob Lewine/CorbisStockMarket; **277** Volo Pictures/ Photonica; **278** Stockbyte; **281** Tony Anderson/Taxi/Getty Images; **282** *top* Gary Bell/Taxi/Getty Images; *bottom* Georgette Douwma/Taxi/Getty Images; **285, 288** Ken O'Donoghue; **289** *top row: left, center* Ken O'Donoghue; *right* PhotoDisc; *bottom row: left, right* Ken O'Donoghue; *center* Comstock; **291** Copyright © Alan Schein Photography/Corbis; **294** Frank Siteman; Copyright © Anthony Nex/Corbis; **296** *left* Antonio Mo/Getty Images; *right* Copyright © Comstock; **298** Charles Krupa/AP Wide World Photos; **301** *top* Copyright © Duomo/Corbis; *bottom* Frank Siteman; **303** Ken O'Donoghue; **304** Josef Peter Fankhauser/Getty Images; **312** *left* Copyright © Tony Freeman/Photo Edit; *type background* Copyright © Corbis; **313** Zefa Visual Media Germany/Index Stock; **315** Ken O'Donoghue; **317** Copyright © Marc Muench/Corbis; **318** Copyright © J Silver/SuperStock Images; **319** Frank Siteman; **321** PhotoDisc; **322** Copyright © Wolfgang Kaehler/Corbis; **324** Courtesy of the city of Strawberry Point, Iowa; **325** Copyright © Paul A. Souders/ Corbis; **326** School Division, Houghton Mifflin Company; **327** *top* PhotoDisc; *bottom* Lee Celano/AP Wide World Photos; **328** *left* Ian Shaw/ Stone/Getty Images; *right: inset top* Stockbyte; *inset bottom* Photospin; **329** Stuart Cohen/The Image Works; **330** Ken O'Donoghue; **331** Philip Lee Harvey/Getty Images; **334** C Squared Studios/PhotoDisc/Getty Images; **335** Ken O'Donoghue; **338** PhotoDisc; **339** Copyright © Nik Wheeler/ Corbis; **340** *left* Copyright © Patrik Giardino/Corbis; *right* Corbis; **341** Getty Images; **342** *top* Darrell Gulin/Stone/Getty Images; *bottom* Nick Daly/Stone/Getty Images; **344** Ken O'Donoghue; **345** Copyright © Stockbyte/PunchStock; **346** PhotoDisc; **347** *top* PhotoDisc; *bottom* Copyright © Ariel Skelley/Corbis; **348** PhotoDisc; **349** James L. Stanfield/ National Geographic Image Collection; **350** Inga Spence/Index Stock; **352** Frank Siteman; **353** Daniel Allan/Taxi/Getty Images; **355** Ken O'Donoghue; **357** Don Smetzer/Stone/Getty Images; **361, 362** PhotoDisc; **371** Paul Sancya/AP Wide World Photos; **373** Ken O'Donoghue; **376** Copyright © Mike Chew/Corbis; **379, 380** Ken O'Donoghue; **385** Copyright © Lee

Snider/Corbis; **391** *top* Ken O'Donoghue; *bottom* PhotoDisc; PhotoDisc; **393** Lionel Glyn Coates/www.bciusa.com; **397** *top* David Young-Wolff/Stone/Getty Images; *bottom* Stockbyte/PunchStock; *frames*: Ken O'Donoghue; **399** Copyright © Richard Cummins/Corbis; **400** Courtesy of Michigan State University, Department of Crop and Soil Sciences; **401** *both* Sanford Ponder www.thepod.net; **402** Frank Siteman; **403** Copyright © Tim Pannell/Corbis; **404** Frank Siteman; **406** *all* PhotoDisc; **412** *top left, right* Ken O'Donoghue; *center left* Copyright © SuperStock Images; **414, 415** Ken O'Donoghue; **416** Frank Siteman; *televisions*: PhotoDisc; **428** *background* PhotoDisc; *top left* ImageState; *center, both* Ken O'Donoghue; **429** *top left* Joe McBride/Stone/Getty Images; *top right* PhotoDisc/Getty Images; *bottom right* Copyright © Royalty-Free/Corbis; *background insets* PhotoDisc; **432** Ian Shaw/Getty Images; **433** Eunice Harris/Photo Researchers, Inc.; **434** Frank Siteman; **435** Ed Elberfeld/Index Stock; **436** Benelux Press/Index Stock; **439** *left* Rex Ziak/Stone/Getty Images; *right* AP Photo/Goran Stenberg; **440** Ken O'Donoghue; **441** Frank Siteman; **444** Copyright © Royalty-Free/Corbis; **446** Arthur Tilley/Stone/Getty Images; **447** *top* Alan Carey/Photo Researchers, Inc.; *left* Copyright © George Lepp/Corbis; **448** *background* Ken O'Donoghue; *center* Frank Siteman; **449** Sentinel-Tribune, J.D. Pooley/AP Wide World Photos; **450** *left* Copyright © Tony Freeman/PhotoEdit, Inc.; *right* School Division, Houghton Mifflin Company; **453** *left* Copyright © Royalty-Free/Corbis; *center* Jeffrey Sylvester/Taxi/Getty Images; *center left* Ken O'Donoghue; *right* PhotoDisc; **456** *top* Ken O'Donoghue; *bottom* Copyright © Cleve Bryant/PhotoEdit, Inc.; **458** Telegraph Herald, David Raoyal/AP Wide World Photos; **459** Copyright © SuperStock Images; **463** Copyright © Jeff Greenberg/eStock Photography/PictureQuest; **465** Paul Sancya/AP Wide World Photos; **466** Harvey Lloyd/Taxi/Getty Images; **468** Greg Kiger/Index Stock; **473** Copyright © Tony Freeman/PhotoEdit, Inc.; **474** Christophe Ratier/Photo Researchers, Inc.; **476** *top left* courtesy of The Planetarium, Armagh, Northern Ireland; *bottom left* Ken Wardius/Index Stock; *type background* Digital Vision Getty Images; **477** *top right* courtesy of The Planetarium, Armagh, Northern Ireland; *top inset* Copyright © Corbis; *bottom* Copyright © Roger Ressmeyer/Corbis; **482** Copyright © Thomas A. Heinz/Corbis; **485** Stockbyte; **487** Mike Powell/Allsport Concepts/Getty Images; **488** David Lees/Taxi/Getty Images; **489** Copyright © Australian Picture Library/ Corbis; **494** *all* Ken O'Donoghue; **495** Copyright © Philip Gould/Corbis; **500** Frank Siteman; **501** Moggy/Stone/Getty Images; **502** courtesy of Kerry Cashman, photo by Ken O'Donoghue; **505** Ken O'Donoghue; **506** Copyright © Dave G. Houser/Corbis; **509** Copyright © Greer & Associates, Inc./SuperStock Images; **510** *left* PhotoDisc; *right, both* Copyright © Corbis; **511** Copyright © Royalty-Free/Corbis; **513** Copyright © Mark Gibson/Corbis; **516** PhotoDisc; **517** David Hanover/Stone/Getty Images; **519** Kevin Bartram/The Galveston County Daily News/AP Wide World Photos; **521** EyeWire Collection/Getty Images; **537** Copyright © Royalty-Free/Corbis; **539** *left* Jason Hindley/Stone/Getty Images; *right* Ken O'Donoghue; **541, 542** Frank Siteman; **543** Sea World/AP Wide World Photos; **544** Copyright © Peter Beck/Corbis; **545** NASA/AP Wide World Photos; **548** Copyright © Royalty-Free/Corbis; **549** *top* Copyright © Brooklyn Productions/Royalty-Free/Corbis; *bottom* Copyright © Merritt Vincent/PhotoEdit, Inc.; **551** Ken O'Donoghue; **552** Copyright © Mark Garten/Corbis; **554** Frank Siteman; **555** Copyright © Corbis; **557** Donna Day/Stone/Getty Images; **559** Antonio Mo/Taxi/Getty Images; **565** Copyright © Kevin Radford/SuperStock; **566** Copyright © Tom Stewart/ Corbis; **570** Jim Schwabel/Index Stock; **572** Nancy R. Cohen/PhotoDisc/ Getty Images; **574** Glyn Kirk/Stone/Getty Images; **577** RO-MA Stock/Index Stock; **578** Copyright © Larry Prosor/SuperStock; **579** Ken O'Donoghue; **580** Copyright © J. H. Robinson/Photo Researchers, Inc.; **585** Ken O'Donoghue; **586** Scott Spiker/ImageState; **591** WEST ROCK/Taxi/Getty Images; **592** Stewart Cohen/Index Stock; **594–595** *background* Tui De Roy/Minden Pictures; **595** *left* Tui De Roy/Minden Pictures; *center* Michio Hoshino/Minden Pictures; *right* Franz Lanting/Minden Pictures; **597** *top* David Young-Wolff/PhotoEdit, Inc.; *bottom* Rubberball/PunchStock; **600** Ron Schwane/AP Wide World Photos; **601** Paul Nicklen/National Geographic/Getty Images; **602** Jason

Homa/The Image Bank/Getty Images; **604** The Time Herald, Tony Pitts/AP Wide World Photos; **606** A. H. Rider/Photo Researchers, Inc.; **607** *top* Stuart Hughs/Stone/Getty Images; *bottom* School Division, Houghton Mifflin Company; **609** Antonio Mo/ Taxi/Getty Images; **616** Frank Siteman; **617** Copyright © Lisette Le Bon/SuperStock; **618** Frank Siteman; **619** Copyright © Roger Allyn Lee/SuperStock Images; **622** Billy Hustace/Stone/Getty Images; **624** Myrleen Cate/Index Stock; **625** *all* PhotoDisc *except 4th from right*: Photospin; **626** Rubberball/PunchStock; **627** *top, both* Ken O'Donoghue; *center left* West Rock/Stone/Getty Images; **629** Ken O'Donoghue; **631** Marc Romanelli/The Image Bank/Getty Images; **634** Photo by David Gray, Copyright © Reuters 1998; **635** Ken O'Donoghue; **636** Stephen Simpson/ Taxi/Getty Images; **639** School Division, Houghton Mifflin Company; **644** Ken O'Donoghue; **645** Marvin E. Newman/The Image Bank/Getty Images; **648** Dorling Kindersley; **649** Zbigniew Bzdak/The Times of Northwest Indiana/AP Wide World Photos; **652** *left* Copyright © Eric and David Hosking/Corbis; *right* Copyright © Gary W. Carter/Corbis; **653** *top right* PhotoDisc; *bottom right* Copyright © Arthur Morris/Corbis; **654, 655** *all* Ken O'Donoghue, *except* **655** *bottom row, far right*: Comstock; **658** Matthias Clamer/Stone/ Getty Images; **660** Copyright © Royalty-Free/ Corbis; **663** PhotoDisc/ Getty Images; **664** Ken O'Donoghue; **667** Ken O'Donoghue; **669** Ken O'Donoghue; *inset* Stockbyte; **670** Copyright © NASA/Corbis; **676** PhotoDisc; **677** PhotoDisc/Getty Images; **678** Frank Siteman; **679** Copyright © Royalty-Free/Corbis; **680** Frank Siteman; **683** Copyright © M.Dillon/Corbis

Illustration

Brian White
19, 30, 43, 60, 67, 72, 95, 116, 128, 145, 177, 189, 200, 221, 237, 238, 261, 280, 287, 299, 320, 326, 333, 346, 389, 408, 420, 436, 445, 467, 471, 522, 546, 553, 582, 599, 615, 620, 642, 643, 665, 682, 684

Rob Dunlavey
268, 269 372, 373, 478, 479

Sam Ward
122

Selected Answers

Chapter 1

1.1 Getting Ready to Practice (p. 7) **1.** intervals
3. 3 times **5.** Step 1: histogram;
Steps 2–3:

States Admitted to U.S. Statehood

1.1 Practice and Problem Solving (pp. 7–9)
7. department stores **9.** No. *Sample answer:* The category with the most stores might not have the most floor space if each store is small, while a category with fewer stores might have the most floor space if each store is large. **11.** Table; exact amounts are given in a table but may be difficult to read from a bar graph.

13.

Meteors Falling per Hour

15. 52 hurricanes
17. No; there does not appear to be a pattern in the data.

19.
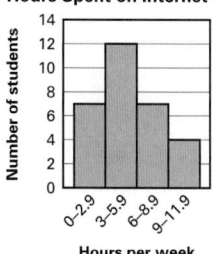
Hours Spent on Internet

21. about 4000 schools
25. 136 **27.** 7
29. 45.44 **31.** 58.78

1.2 Getting Ready to Practice (p. 12) **1.** Multiply 2 by 5. Add the result (10) to 8. Subtract 4 from this sum (18) to obtain the final result (14).
3. Multiply 5 by 15; 25. **5.** Subtract 7 from 15; 18.
7. Subtract 2 from 5; 30. **9.** In the second step, 63 must be divided by 9 before being added to 9: $3 \times 3 + 63 \div 9 = 9 + 63 \div 9 = 9 + 7 = 16$.

1.2 Practice and Problem Solving (pp. 12–13)
11. 29 **13.** 24 **15.** 15 **17.** 5 **19.** $250 **21.** $\frac{3}{4}$ **23.** 12
25. 10.1 **27.** 54.6 **29.** 7 **31.** $12 \div (6 + 4 - 7) = 4$
33. 372 cookies **35.** $\times$; $12 \times (4 + 2) = 72$
37. 32 students **39.** 4 **41.** 6

1.2 Technology Activity (p. 14) **1.** 106.8 **3.** 7
5. 5 **7.** 2 **9.** $10.44

1.3 Getting Ready to Practice (p. 17) **1.** variable; numerical **7.** 44 **9.** 5

1.3 Practice and Problem Solving (pp. 18–19)
11. 23 **13.** 39.5 **15.** 5 **17.** 6 **19.** $\frac{2}{5}x$ **21.** $12 + x$
23. 18 mi **25.** *Sample answer:* Serena is saving to buy a gift for her sister. She starts with $2 and saves an additional $8 per week. **27.** $4 + 17n$; $106
29. 32.8 **31.** 96 **33.** 1.6 **35.** 10 **37.** A good answer will include an expression that can only be evaluated correctly by using the order of operations. The explanation of the correct order to use will follow the rules for the order of operations. **39.** $2.75p + 1.25d$; $13.25 **41.** 50
43. 18 **45.** 4095 **47.** 42

1.4 Getting Ready to Practice (p. 22) **1.** *Sample answer:* base $\rightarrow 3^2 \leftarrow$ exponent **3.** 1331 **5.** 64 **7.** 0
9. 6 **11.** 7^2 means 7×7; $7^2 = 7 \times 7 = 49$.

1.4 Practice and Problem Solving (pp. 22–23)
13. 3^3; 3 to the third power, or 3 cubed **15.** 6
17. 128 **19.** 1 **21.** 109 **23.** 12 **25.** 3 **27.** 16
29. 119 **31.** $1000 \cdot 2^3$ **33.** < **35.** 17.17
37. 1030.301 **39.** No; $16 \cdot 2^2 = 64$, so the divers have fallen 64 feet after 2 seconds. **41.** 302 **45.** 9
47. 6 outfits. *Sample answer:* I used Draw a Diagram because a tree diagram allowed me to find the total number of outfits in an organized way.

1.1–1.4 Notebook Review (pp. 24–25) **1.** Evaluate expressions inside grouping symbols. **2.** The question cannot be answered using the bar graph because the depth does not determine the area of the lake. **3.** Erie **4.** 18 **5.** 3 **6.** 7 **7.** 57 **8.** 1000
9. 370 **10.** The number of zeros is the same as the exponent.

1.5 Problem Solving Strategies (p. 27) **1.** 106, 107
3. 17 blue chips; 3 green chips
5. *Sample:*   **7.** twice   **9.** Bob, Kelly, Justin, Tim, Michelle

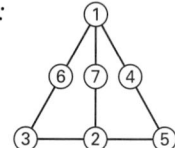

1.5 Getting Ready to Practice (p. 30) **1.** *Sample answer:* $4 + x = 7$; use mental math and ask "4 plus what number is 7?" The answer is 3.   **3.** 44
5. 7   **7.** yes   **9.** no

1.5 Practice and Problem Solving (pp. 30–31)
15. yes   **17.** no   **19.** 11   **21.** 29   **23.** 2   **25.** 15
27. $14 + r = 43$; 29 in.   **29.** $5033 + b = 5396$; 363 lb
31. $4p = 60$; 15 invitations   **37.** $x + 220 = 245$;
25 min   **39.** 96   **41.** 6000   **43.** 1000

1.6 Getting Ready to Practice (p. 35) **1.** Area is the surface a figure covers, while perimeter is the distance around the figure.   **3.** $P = 30$ in., $A = 56$ in.^{2} **5.** 159 cm

1.6 Practice and Problem Solving (pp. 36–37)
7. $P = 22$ cm, $A = 24$ cm^2 **9.** $P = 40$ ft, $A = 100$ ft^2
11. $P = 72$ in., $A = 324$ in.^{2} **13.** $P = 54$ cm,
$A = 182$ cm^2 **15.** 6 m   **17.** 9 km/h   **19.** 10.5 mi
21. 225 mi   **23.** 90 mi/h   **25.** about 4 h   **27.** 1560 ft
29. 2 bags   **33.** 9   **35.** 30   **37.** 15.54

1.7 Getting Ready to Practice (p. 41) **1.** Step 1.
Read and Understand, Step 2. Make a Plan, Step 3.
Solve the Problem, Step 4. Look Back   **3.** Step 1:
Trains in one hour = people in one hour ÷ people
per train, so trains in one hour = people in one
hour ÷ (cars per train • passengers per car);
Step 2: 45 trains; Step 3: 45 • 20 = 900

1.7 Practice and Problem Solving (pp. 41–43)
5. 15 h   **7.** 16 h   **9.** 12 oz   **11.** 3, 1   **13.** 9, 5
15. $5060   **17.** $8x$, $10x$ **19.** $31x^2$, $39x^2$ **21.** 7 ft; 49 ft^2
23. 5   **25.** 4   **29.** 0   **31.** $P = 38$ in., $A = 48$ in.^{2}
33. >   **35.** >

1.5–1.7 Notebook Review (pp. 44–45) **1.** $P = 2l + 2w$ **2.** 13   **3.** 12   **4.** 3   **5.** 18   **6.** $P = 22$ m, $A = 28$ m^2 **7.** 9 teaspoons

8. Yes; perimeter is measured in linear units and area is measured in square units.

Chapter Review (pp. 46–47) **1.** histogram
3. order of operations   **5.** base   **7.** false   **9.** true
11. No; the age group that includes teenagers also includes other ages.   **13.** 1   **15.** 2 • 28.5 − 20; $37
17. 4   **19.** 72   **21.** 225   **23.** 10,000   **25.** 27   **27.** 261
29. 7   **31.** $P = 32$ m, $A = 60$ m^2 **33.** $P = 32$ in., $A = 64$ in.^{2} **35.** B, C, and D

Chapter 2

2.1 Getting Ready to Practice (p. 55) **1.** opposites
3. −130, −56, 0, 62, 74, 120   **5.** 8, 8   **7.** −1327, 1327

2.1 Practice and Problem Solving (pp. 55–56)
9. >   **11.** <   **13.** >   **15.** >   **17.** −20, −12, 18, 44, 59,
64   **23.** Gieselmann Lake   **25.** 32   **27.** −29   **29.** 81
31. −3   **33.** =   **35.** <   **37.** Flight crew departs for
launch pad. Pilot starts auxiliary power units.
Main engine starts. Liftoff. Shuttle clears launch
tower, and control switches to the Mission
Control Center.   **41.** 19   **43.** 34 pages

2.2 Getting Ready to Practice (p. 60) **1.** absolute
values   **3.** −12   **5.** 0   **7.** −32   **9.** −34   **11.** −17

2.2 Practice and Problem Solving (pp. 61–62)
13. −3   **15.** 4   **17.** Since the signs are different, the
lesser absolute value should be subtracted from
the greater absolute value and the sign of the
number with the greater absolute value should be
used; $−8 + 5 = −3$.   **19.** −109   **21.** −82   **23.** 12
25. −3   **27.** always   **29.** sometimes   **31.** *Sample
answer:* when you are balancing your checkbook
33. $−1200 + 800 = −400$; 400 B.C.   **35.** 90   **37.** 146
39. −1207   **41.** −999   **43.** 0; at   **45.** 0; no   **47.** 5
49. −19   **51.** 122   **53.** 512   **55.** −921, −346, −125,
128, 724

2.3 Getting Ready to Practice (p. 65) **1.** $−2 − 6$
3. −7   **5.** −4   **7.** −10   **9.** −23   **11.** Step 1: 55 ft,
0 ft, 55 ft; Step 2: $55 − 0 = 55$ ft, $0 − (−35) = 35$ ft, $55 − (−35) = 90$ ft; Step 3: 55, 35, 90

2.3 Practice and Problem Solving (pp. 65–67)
13. 0   **15.** −8   **17.** −27   **19.** 44   **21.** −1000 points
23. 5   **25.** Subtract −137 from 123.   **27.** 42°F

29. -259 **31.** 1802 **33.** -10 **35.** -18 **37.** 12 **39.** -71 **41.** Triassic Period: 37 million yr; Jurassic Period: 64 million yr; Cretaceous Period: 79 million yr **43.** 5 **45.** -31 **49.** 8 **51.** 3 **53.** 2 **55.** 168 **57.** 5649

2.4 Problem Solving Strategies (p. 69) **1.** 55 dots
3. 144 blue tiles **5.** Scott: 12 yr old, Ben: 15 yr old, Kelly: 9 yr old **7.** $40 **9.** 19 ways

2.4 Getting Ready to Practice (p. 72) **1.** negative
3. 0 **5.** -6 **7.** 270 **9.** The product of two negative integers is positive; $-8(-12) = 96$.

2.4 Practice and Problem Solving (pp. 72–73)
11. 17 **13.** 44 **15.** -15 **17.** 32 **19.** -288 **21.** 0
23. 70 **25.** -133 **27.** -132 **29.** -4 **31.** -4
33. The power is positive when the exponent is even and negative when the exponent is odd.
35. 64 **37.** 9216 **39.** $-\$81.70$ **41.** $-104{,}832$
43. -682 **45.** 17 ft **47.** -23 **49.** 15 **51.** 2

2.5 Getting Ready to Practice (p. 76) **1.** mean
3. 0 **5.** -5 **7.** -3 **9.** -3

2.5 Practice and Problem Solving (pp. 76–77)
11. 7 **13.** -9 **15.** 7 **17.** 0 **19.** 1 **21.** Always. *Sample answer:* The mean of -3, -5, and -1 is $\frac{-9}{3} = -3$. **23.** 4 **25.** -4 **27.** -1.5 **29.** 0.8
31. $-29.2°$F **35.** 5^5 **37.** b^4 **39.** -72

2.1–2.5 Notebook Review (pp. 78–79)
1. ◄—●——+——+——+——+——+——●—► **2.** $-15, -5, 1, 4, 8, 16$
   $\quad -3\ -2\ -1\ \ 0\ \ 1\ \ 2\ \ 3$
3. $-85, -60, -6, 40, 42, 98$ **4.** 38 **5.** -55 **6.** -119
7. -66 **8.** -65 **9.** -15 **10.** 312 **11.** -62 **12.** -6
13. 4 **14.** Yes. *Sample answer:* The opposite of the sum can be written as $-1(a + b)$. Using the distributive property you get $-a + (-b)$ which is the sum of the opposites.

2.6 Getting Ready to Practice (p. 82) **7.** 45; commutative and associative properties of addition **9.** -290; commutative and associative properties of multiplication **11.** -36; associative property of addition **13.** 15 in.^{3}

2.6 Practice and Problem Solving (pp. 83–84)
15. 54; commutative property of multiplication
17. 9; associative property of addition **19.** 69
21. 21 **23.** -700 **25.** -900 **27.** $70x$ **29.** $70 + x$
31. No. *Sample answer:* $20 \div 4 = 5$, but $4 \div 20 = 0.2$.
33. 5.7 **35.** 35 **37.** 420 **39.** $60 **41.** The student grouped the first and last numbers, the second and next to last numbers, and so on, to make 10, and then all of the 10s and the 5 were added to find the sum; 190. **45.** 26 in. and 34 in. *Sample answer:* I used Guess, Check, and Revise because I decided to choose two numbers whose sum was 60 and then check to see if the difference was 8. I revised my guess until it was correct.
47. $1.35 < 1.53$

2.7 Getting Ready to Practice (p. 87) **1.** like terms: $7x$ and x, $-3y$ and $-6y$; coefficients: 7, -3, -6, 1 **3.** $-7(3) + (-7)(2)$ **5.** $9y$ **7.** $6m + n - 4b$

2.7 Practice and Problem Solving (pp. 88–89)
13. $9x - 27$ **15.** 56 **17.** $-34z + 884$ **19.** $4r + 2s$
21. $5a + 6b$ **23.** $-3x - 9y$ **25.** Add $2.35 and $.65 to get $3.00. Multiply $3.00 by 6 to find the total, $18. **27.** $7y - 14$ **29.** $2x + 2$ **31.** $12d$ **33.** $786.24
35. $3x - 5$ **37.** $1.7y - 6.7$ **39.** *Sample answer:* $4(30 + 4) = 120 + 16 = 136$; mental math can be used to multiply and then add. **41.** *Sample answer:* $24(10 + 2) = 240 + 48 = 288$; mental math can be used to multiply and then add. **43.** Yes; by the commutative property of multiplication, $xy = yx$.
47. $-100, -90, -20, 0, 70$ **49.** -21 **51.** -700

2.7 Technology Activity (p. 90) **1.** $-28{,}546$
3. 11,009 **5.** $-2{,}105{,}804$ **7.** $-262{,}890{,}144$
9. -101 **11.** about 13,904 km; about 10,428 km

2.8 Getting Ready to Practice (p. 93)
1. 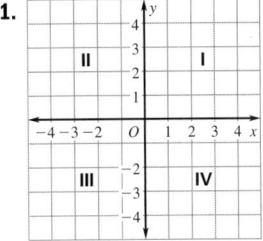   **3.** $(0, 1)$ **5.** $(1, -2)$

6-9.

6. (4, 1)
8. (−3, 0)
9. (−2, −1)
7. (2, −3)

2.8 Practice and Problem Solving (pp. 93–95)

11. (−3, 3)   **13.** (−5, 0)   **15.** (0, −2)

17-20.

17. (−2, 3)
18. (3, −1)
20. (−3, −4)
19. (0, −5)

17. Quadrant II
19. *y*-axis

21.

rectangle; 32 units

23.

The points lie along a line; $8.75.

25.

20 units; 25 square units

M   N
L   K

27. $.70, $1.40, $2.10   **29.** $4.20

31.

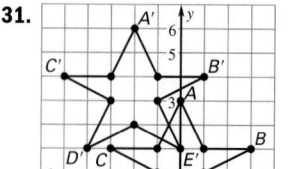

$A(-2, 6), B(1, 4), C(-5, 4),$
$D(-4, 1), E(0, 1)$

33. −1   **35.** $4x + 36$ **37.** $-9z + 18$

2.6–2.8 Notebook Review (pp. 96–97)

1. −5
2. −190   **3.** −1300   **4.** −83   **5.** $27a + 95$
6. $76b + 36$ **7.** $-70c + 40$

8-11.

P
N
M
L

8. Quadrant IV
9. *y*-axis
10. *x*-axis
11. Quadrant II

12. Use $4(6 + 0.11) = 4(6) + 4(0.11) = 24 + 0.44 =$ 24.44.

Chapter Review (pp. 98–99)
1. 2; 15, −15

3. 4;

II   I
III   IV

5. coordinate plane   **7.** −42, −31, −5, 8, 11, 53
9. −22, 22   **11.** 512, 512   **13.** −172   **15.** 176
17. −86   **19.** 79   **21.** −54   **23.** 0   **25.** −192
27. −140   **29.** 152 ft   **31.** 14   **33.** −9   **35.** 1
37. 97; commutative and associative properties of addition   **39.** 1900; commutative and associative properties of multiplication   **41.** 0; multiplication property of zero   **43.** $63 + 77y$ **45.** $7x − 2y$
47. $38.70   **49.** (−4, 3)   **51.** (−2, −3)

Chapter 3

3.1 Getting Ready to Practice (p. 111)   **1.** inverse
3. 20   **5.** Step 1: Sales tax; Step 2: $54.99 + x = 58.29$; Step 3: $3.30

3.1 Practice and Problem Solving (pp. 111–112)
7. subtracting 4.5 **9.** 5 **11.** 13 **13.** 2 **15.** 24
17. -28 **19.** 64 **21.** yes **23.** no; $t = 29 - 3$
25. *Sample answer:* There are 55 cats at the shelter.
There are 13 more cats than dogs. How many dogs
are at the shelter? **27.** 0 **29.** 1 **31.** 4.7 **33.** 8
35. -31 **39.** $3.52
40–43.

41. Quadrant IV
43. Quadrant I

45. *Sample answer:* 130, 220 **47.** *Sample answer:*
2800, 4000

3.2 Getting Ready to Practice (p. 115) **1.** divide
3. $\frac{y}{9} = -3$ [original equation]; $\frac{y}{9} \cdot 9 = (-3) \cdot 9$
[Multiply each side by 9.]; $y = -27$ [Simplify.]

3.2 Practice and Problem Solving (pp. 115–116)
5. 18 **7.** 70 **9.** 3 **11.** 105 **13.** 216 **15.** 2.5
19. dividing by 5 **21.** subtracting -6, or adding 6
23. -216 **25.** 10 **27.** 29.9 **29.** 30 **31.** 3 **33.** -2.1
35. *Sample answer:* $3x = 18$, $\frac{x}{2} = 3$ **37.** about
17 eggs; about 4 eggs **39.** < **41.** > **43.** sixteen
and two hundredths **45.** seven million, five
hundred forty thousand, six hundred eighty-eight

3.3 Getting Ready to Practice (p. 121)
1. addition, division; 3 **3.** 3 **5.** 1 **7.** -4

3.3 Practice and Problem Solving (pp. 121–123)
11. 4 **13.** 7 **15.** $\frac{1}{4}$, or 0.25 **17.** 3 **19.** 9 **21.** $-\frac{1}{2}$, or
-0.5 **23.** $2\frac{2}{3}$; because 3 miles is an estimate,
$3h$ is an estimate for the number of miles of trail
cleaned per hour, so the number of hours will also
be an estimate. **25.** 7 **27.** $-1\frac{2}{3}$ **29.** 40 **31.** 55
33. -7 **35.** 24 **37.** 19 min **39.** Divide each side
by 2; simplify; subtract 3 from each side; simplify.
41. -15 **45.** 132; the summer pass would be
cheaper than paying for 40 day passes.

47. *Sample answer:* Choose the summer pass if
you go to the pool more than 29 days because it
is cheaper. Choose the day pass if you go to the
pool 29 days or less because it is cheaper. **49.** 19
51. 48 **53.** 50% **55.** 20%

3.4 Practice and Problem Solving (pp. 126–128)
7. $4 + 5n = 9$; 1 **9.** 16 sandwiches on rye bread
11. *Sample answer:* You buy 5 boxes of your favorite
cereal at the store. With the store's double-coupon
policy, you save $6 with your coupons. You pay $9
for the cereal. What was the original price of each
box? **13.** $7 **15.** $2x + 5 = 12$; 3.5 **17.** $-2n + 3.5 =$
7.5; -2 **19.** 85 people **21.** the number of hours
worked **27.** $P = 30$ ft; $A = 36$ ft^2 **29.** $P = 84$ m;
$A = 432$ m^2 **31.** 35

3.4 Technology Activity (p. 129) **1.** *Sample*
answer: $35(4) + 10x = 190$; 5 adults

3.1–3.4 Notebook Review (pp. 130–131)
1. addition and subtraction; multiplication and
division **2.** -11 **3.** 42 **4.** 12 **5.** 47 **6.** -11
7. -9 **8.** 27 **9.** -40 **10.** 55 **11.** -4 **12.** 0 **13.** 2
14. 105 envelopes per hour **15.** It uses inverse
operations in reverse order to their corresponding
operations.

3.5 Problem Solving Strategies (p. 133) **1.** 672 ft^2
3. $118,125 **5.** the room where students share
tables **7.** The total number of students is greater
than 1238.

9. 96 ft;

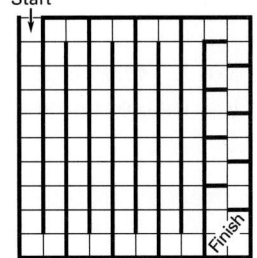

Sample answer:
I tried drawing
other mazes.

3.5 Getting Ready to Practice (p. 137) **1.** base, height **3.** $A = 4$ cm^2; $P = 8$ cm **5.** Step 1: 42 yd^2; Step 2: 9 yd^2; Step 3: 51 yd^2

3.5 Practice and Problem Solving (pp. 137–139)
7. $A = 24$ in.^{2}; $P = 32$ in. **9.** 3 ft **11.** 4 cm **13.** 20 m **15.** Area is given in square units; $A = 10$ in.^{2}
17. 24 in. **19.** $\dfrac{5}{x}$ m **21.** 16 m^2 **23.** 180 ft^2
25. *Sample answer:* about 3 ft by 6 ft; 18 ft^2
27. Doubles the area. **29.** Quadruples the area.
31. No; Kate has 121 square feet and the room has an area of 252 square feet, so Kate has less than half the area of the room. **33.** 37.5 m^2 **35.** -60
37. 21 **39.** -32 **41.** 7 **43.** 35 **45.** > **47.** <

3.6 Getting Ready to Practice (p. 142)
1. equivalent inequalities
7. $t < -2$;
9. Step 1: 360; Step 2: $360 + x \geq 425$, $x \geq 65$; Step 3:

3.6 Practice and Problem Solving (pp. 143–145)
11. $x \geq -5$ **13.** $x < 6$ **15.** no **17.** yes **19.** j is greater than -4. **21.** n is less than 0.
23. $t > -3$;
25. $r \geq 8$;
27. $p > 7$;
29. $m \leq 11$;
31. $33.96 + x \geq 50$; $x \geq \$16.04$ **33.** 20 min
35. $r < 7.5$;
37. $p \geq 3$;
39. $t > 4\dfrac{3}{4}$;
41. $x \geq 13$ is the solution to $x - 3 \geq 10$. **43.** no
45. $x > 81$ hertz and $x < 1100$ hertz **47.** y is greater than -2 and y is less than 1. **49.** m is greater than or equal to 4 and m is less than or equal to 11.
53. -53 **55.** -7 **57.** 9.053

3.7 Getting Ready to Practice (p. 148) **1.** reverse
3. yes **5.** $m \leq -42$;

7. $p > -5$;

3.7 Practice and Problem Solving (pp. 148–149)
13. $x > 4$;
15. $b \leq -360$;
17. $g < 6$;
19. $c \geq -6$;
25. No; there are infinitely many solutions.
33. You undo the operations in the same way. If you multiply or divide by a negative number in an inequality, you must reverse the direction of the inequality. **35.** $x \geq 80$ **37.** $x \geq \dfrac{1}{2}$ **41.** 12 cm by 16 cm **43.** 1 **45.** $c \leq 4$;
47. $x > 29$;
49. 72

3.5–3.7 Notebook Review (pp. 150–151)
1. *Sample:* **2.** 10 cm **3.** 9 ft
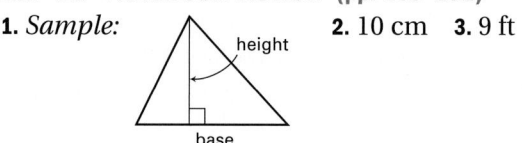
4. $h > 24$;
5. $k \leq 10$;
6. $p > -8$;
7. $d \geq -6$;
8. $d \leq 204$ **9.** $x \leq -100$ **10.** $c > 5$ **11.** $b > -4$
12. $c \geq 54$ **13.** 7; the solution to the inequality is $x < 8$ and the greatest integer that is less than 8 is 7.

Chapter Review (pp. 152–153) **1.** Addition and subtraction, multiplication and division; one operation undoes the other. **3.** equivalent equations **5.** 32 **7.** 15 **9.** 40 **11.** 1288 **13.** -3
15. 2.4 **17.** Fuel in tank $-$ Fuel used = Fuel left; $\dfrac{5}{8} - x = \dfrac{3}{8}$; $x = \dfrac{2}{8} = \dfrac{1}{4}$ **19.** 9 **21.** -5 **23.** 27
25. -115 **27.** -45 **29.** 18 baskets **31.** 8 m
33. 20 in.^{2} **35.** 60 yd^2
37. $c \leq 108$;
39. $h > -4$;
41. The inequality sign should not be reversed when subtracting; $x < 10$.

Chapter 4

4.1 Getting Ready to Practice (p. 170) **1.** prime
3. 1, 3, 9, 27   **5.** 1, 2, 3, 6, 11, 22, 33, 66   **7.** $5 \cdot 11$
9. $2^5 \cdot 3$

4.1 Practice and Problem Solving (pp. 171–172)
11. 1, 2, 17, 34   **13.** 1, 2, 3, 4, 6, 9, 12, 18, 27, 35, 54,
108   **15.** composite   **17.** prime   **19.** $2^3 \cdot 7$
21. $2 \cdot 3 \cdot 17$ **23.** second row: 8; fourth row: 2, 2, 2,
11; $2^3 \cdot 11$ **25.** second row: 2; third row: 2, 21;
fourth row: 5, 3, 7; $2 \cdot 3 \cdot 5 \cdot 7$ **27.** $3 \cdot 5 \cdot c \cdot d$
29. $3 \cdot 3 \cdot a \cdot a \cdot b \cdot b \cdot b \cdot b$ **31.** 3 stars by 5 stars
33. 5 stars by 6 stars (or 3 stars by 10 stars, or 2 stars
by 15 stars)   **35.** 1, 13, 23, 299   **37.** 1, 2, 4, 5, 8, 10,
16, 20, 25, 40, 50, 80, 100, 200, 400   **39.** $2^3 \cdot 5 \cdot 7$
41. $3^2 \cdot 5^3$ **43.** *Sample answer:* $3 + 7$ **45.** *Sample
answer:* $11 + 17$ **47.** No; 40 is not a factor of 140.
49. 2 and 3   **53.** $-4a + 4b + 2$ **55.** $y \geq 40$
57. 850 ft^2. *Sample answer:* I used Draw a Diagram
to draw the spaces and find the area.   **59.** *Sample
answer:* 7000; 9000   **61.** *Sample answer:* 13; 20

4.2 Getting Ready to Practice (p. 175)
1. greatest common factor, or GCF   **7.** Step 1:
$56 = 2 \cdot 2 \cdot 2 \cdot 7$, $68 = 2 \cdot 2 \cdot 17$; Step 2: 2 and 2;
Step 3: 4; the greatest number of teams that can be
formed is 4, where each has 14 girls and 17 boys.

4.2 Practice and Problem Solving (pp. 176–177)
9. 7   **11.** 12   **13.** no; 5   **15.** yes   **17.** no; 18   **19.** yes
21. 30 baskets; 2 cans of cranberry sauce, 4 cans of
fruit, 3 cans of corn, 2 boxes of muffin mix   **23.** $2z^2$
25. $4xy^2$ **27.** $15bc$ **29.** always   **31.** *Sample answer:*
6 and 25   **33.** 90 bouquets   **35.** 12 ft   **37.** -8
39. $2^2 \cdot 3 \cdot 7$

4.3 Getting Ready to Practice (p. 181) **1.** yes
3. yes   **5.** $\frac{2}{3}$ **7.** $\frac{5}{8}$ **9.** *Sample answer:* $\frac{2}{10}, \frac{3}{15}$ **11.** 64

4.3 Practice and Problem Solving (pp. 182–183)
13. $\frac{3}{4}$ **15.** $\frac{-1}{8}$, or $-\frac{1}{8}$ **17.** $\frac{b}{2}$ **19.** $\frac{-3t}{10}$, or $-\frac{3t}{10}$
21. yes   **23.** yes   **25.** *Sample answer:* $\frac{1}{2}, \frac{2}{4}$
27. *Sample answer:* $\frac{2}{5}, \frac{4}{10}$ **29.** $\frac{1}{3}$ **31.** 1   **33.** $\frac{9}{50}$

35. $\frac{8}{25}$ **37.** $\frac{1}{10}$ **39.** For birds, about $\frac{60}{1500} = \frac{1}{25}$ are
threatened; a greater fraction of mammals is
threatened than birds; $\frac{1}{40}$ (reptiles), $\frac{64}{1541}$ (birds),
$\frac{1}{10}$ (mammals).   **41.** $\frac{3}{5}, \frac{3}{5}$; yes   **43.** $\frac{3}{4}, \frac{5}{8}$; no
45. $\frac{5}{6}, \frac{5}{6}$; yes   **47.** $\frac{3}{4}, \frac{7}{8}$; no   **49.** y^2 **51.** $\frac{-4z}{x^2 y}$, or $-\frac{4z}{x^2 y}$
53. no   **55.** yes
61.   **63.**

4.4 Problem Solving Strategies (p. 185)
1. 10 ways   **5.** 16 choices   **7.** 44 posts   **9.** 168 in., or
14 ft

4.4 Getting Ready to Practice (p. 188)
1. common multiple   **7.** 4 is the GCF of 12 and 24.
The LCM is $2 \cdot 2 \cdot 2 \cdot 3$, or 24.

4.4 Practice and Problem Solving (pp. 188–189)
9. multiples of 6: 6, 12, 18, 24, 30, 36, 42; multiples
of 21: 21, 42; LCM: 42   **11.** multiples of 10: 10, 20,
30; multiples of 15: 15, 30; LCM: 30   **13.** $17 = 17$,
$57 = 3 \cdot 19$; 969   **15.** $125 = 5^3$, $500 = 2^2 \cdot 5^3$; 500
17. $8 = 2^3$, $16 = 2^4$, $32 = 2^5$; 32   **19.** $20 = 2^2 \cdot 5$,
$24 = 2^3 \cdot 3$, $60 = 2^2 \cdot 3 \cdot 5$; 120   **21.** $49s^3 t^2$
23. $120c^2 d^6$ **25.** 180 sec   **27.** 4320   **29.** 4788
31. 300   **33.** 60   **35.** $120x^4 y^7$ **37.** $495g^4 h^5 k^3$
39. 24 min; 1440 sec   **43.** $19x + 20 + 2y$ **45.** 73.7
47. 134.77

4.1–4.4 Notebook Review (pp. 190–191) **1.** prime
factorization   **2.** $2^3 \cdot 5$ **3.** 7   **4.** $5 \cdot 17$ **5.** $2^3 \cdot 3 \cdot 5$
6. 16   **7.** 20   **8.** $7a$ **9.** $20y^4$ **10.** $\frac{1}{3}$ **11.** $\frac{3}{20}$ **12.** $\frac{b}{3}$
13. $\frac{n^2}{3}$ **14.** 84   **15.** 270   **16.** $50c^2 d$ **17.** $36n^3$
18. *Sample answer:* When you list the factors of a
number, you list all numbers by which the
number is divisible, including 1, composite
numbers, and the number itself. When you find
the prime factorization of a number, you write the
number as a product only of its prime factors.

4.5 Getting Ready to Practice (p. 194) **1.** least
common multiple or LCM   **3.** 20   **5.** 36   **7.** <   **9.** >

4.5 Practice and Problem Solving (pp. 194–195)

11. > **13.** < **15.** > **17.** $\frac{1}{8}, \frac{5}{16}, \frac{1}{2}, \frac{3}{4}$ **19.** $\frac{15}{16}, \frac{5}{3}, \frac{35}{15}, 2\frac{2}{5}$

23. $\frac{-47}{4}, -11\frac{7}{12}, \frac{-23}{2}, -11\frac{17}{48}, \frac{-34}{3}$ **25.** >

31. $2^4 \cdot 3 \cdot 7$

4.6 Getting Ready to Practice (p. 198) **1.** base
3. yes **5.** no **7.** 4^6 **9.** a^{12} **11.** c **13.** 8^5 **15.** The
bases should not be multiplied;. $2^2 \cdot 2^4 = 2^{2+4} = 2^6$.

4.6 Practice and Problem Solving (pp. 199–200)
17. v^{12} **19.** m^{19} **21.** x^4 **23.** y^2 **25.** $(-4)^5$ **27.** 7^4
29. 2^{10} **31.** 9^4 **33.** 5 **35.** 9 **37.** $4y^5$ **39.** $64a^7b^{10}$
41. z^5 **43.** $25n^3$ **45.** 10^{12} **47.** 10^{12} **49.** 2^2 **55.** 157
57. 18 **59.** >

4.7 Getting Ready to Practice (p. 203) **1.** true
3. $\frac{1}{81}$ **5.** $\frac{1}{16}$ **7.** 5^{-3} means $\frac{1}{5^3}$; $5^{-3} = \frac{1}{5^3} = \frac{1}{5 \cdot 5 \cdot 5} = \frac{1}{125}$.

4.7 Practice and Problem Solving (pp. 203–204)
9. $\frac{1}{36}$ **11.** $\frac{1}{625}$ **13.** $\frac{1}{m^4}$ **15.** $\frac{9}{n^3}$ **17.** $\frac{1}{b^6}$ **19.** $\frac{1}{d^{13}}$
21. $\frac{kg}{m \cdot s^2}$ **23.** -8 **25.** 10 **27.** 10^{11} **29.** 10^8 **31.** 10^7
33. never **35.** -25 **37.** 52 **39.** 90 **41.** -17

4.8 Getting Ready to Practice (p. 207) **1.** yes
3. yes **5.** 4.68×10^{-1} **7.** 4,350,000 **9.** 96,200,000

4.8 Practice and Problem Solving (pp. 207–208)
11. 7.9×10^3 **13.** 2.13×10^6 **15.** 4.15×10^{-7}
17. 0.0871 **19.** 0.00000000176
21. 2,830,000,000,000 **23.** 6×10^8 **25.** 6.552×10^{14}
27. 1.5×10^7 **31.** > **33.** 1.066×10^5 **35.** 1.944×10^{-13} **37.** 3.5×10^{11} **39.** 1.19×10^8; 6.205×10^9
41. 1.2×10^{-13} cm **43.** 6 **45.** $\frac{2}{3m}$

4.8 Technology Activity (p. 209) **1.** 2.7115×10^{14}
3. 1.584×10^{-11} **5.** 2.682119205×10^7
7. $1.365853659 \times 10^{-7}$ **9.** about 2.3×10^2

4.5–4.8 Notebook Review (pp. 210–211)
1. scientific notation **2.** > **3.** < **4.** < **5.** = **6.** n^{13}
7. y^{16} **8.** x^2 **9.** c^4 **10.** $\frac{12}{a^5}$ **11.** $\frac{1}{n^3}$ **12.** $\frac{1}{m^{11}}$ **13.** $\frac{1}{c^{13}}$
14. 3.46×10^{10} **15.** 9×10^{-7} **16.** 5.02×10^{-10}

17. *Sample answer:* Use the commutative and
associative properties to rewrite the product as
$(5 \times 4) \times (10^9 \times 10^{15})$. Use multiplication and the
product of powers property to simplify this to
20×10^{24}. Move the decimal point to write the
product in scientific notation as 2.0×10^{25}.

Chapter Review (pp. 212–213) **1.** The greatest
common factor is the greatest number that is a
factor of both numbers. The least common
multiple is the smallest number that is a multiple
of both numbers. **3.** *Sample answer:* $3x, 4s^2, 7ab^3$
5. simplest form **7.** prime factorization **9.** $2 \cdot 3^3$
11. $2 \cdot 3 \cdot 5^2$ **13.** $19 \cdot a \cdot a \cdot b$ **15.** $2 \cdot 2 \cdot 2 \cdot 7 \cdot u \cdot u \cdot v \cdot v$ **17.** 10 **19.** 3 **21.** $9xy$ **23.** $\frac{1}{3}$ **25.** $-\frac{16}{51}$
27. $\frac{c}{3}$ **29.** $\frac{4}{n}$ **31.** 105 **33.** $25m^2n^4$ **35.** 24 sec
37. < **39.** > **41.** 8^4 **43.** 7^2 **45.** $\frac{7}{x^4}$ **47.** $\frac{1}{3w^8}$
49. 0.000658 **51.** 6×10^6 ft^3/min; 3.6×10^8 ft^3/h

Chapter 5

5.1 Getting Ready to Practice (p. 221)
1. denominator, numerator **3.** $\frac{2}{3}$ **5.** $\frac{1}{5}$ **7.** $1\frac{3}{7}$
9. c **11.** $18\frac{3}{4}$ in.

5.1 Practice and Problem Solving (pp. 222–223)
13. $\frac{1}{9}$ **15.** $-\frac{11}{12}$ **17.** $\frac{1}{5}$ **19.** $-\frac{1}{2}$ **21.** $\frac{8}{15}$ **23.** $-8\frac{2}{5}$
25. $-\frac{n}{7}$ **27.** $-\frac{q}{p}$ **29.** 15 h; $2\frac{2}{3}$ h **31.** $1\frac{11}{18}$ **33.** $\frac{8}{25}$
35. $\frac{15}{16}$ **37.** $-8\frac{1}{5}$ **39.** $3\frac{1}{12}$ **41.** $\frac{1}{4}$ **43.** $1\frac{1}{3}$ **47.** 5
49. -42 **51.** 105 **53.** 1850 **55.** 9 **57.** 24 **59.** 16
61. 1.25

5.2 Getting Ready to Practice (p. 226) **1.** least
common denominator or LCD **3.** $1\frac{23}{24}$ **5.** $\frac{36 + x}{9x}$

5.2 Practice and Problem Solving (pp. 226–227)
7. $\frac{5}{8}$ **9.** $\frac{13}{18}$ **11.** $-\frac{1}{32}$ **13.** $-\frac{33}{40}$ **15.** $11\frac{19}{36}$ **17.** $13\frac{8}{35}$
19. $8\frac{1}{3}$ ft **21.** true **23.** false **25.** $\frac{17s}{20}$ **27.** $\frac{77}{50n}$

29. West; traveling east is $\frac{27}{50}$ of the way around the equator, while traveling west is $1 - \frac{27}{50} = \frac{23}{50}$ of the way. Since $\frac{23}{50} < \frac{27}{50}$, traveling west is shorter.

31. $1\frac{11}{72}$ **35.** 0 **37.** -126 **39.** $<$ **41.** $<$

5.3 Problem Solving Strategies (p. 229)

1. 7 students. *Sample answer:* Choose 18 classmates. Let 2 classmates represent the students that have both a dog and a cat. Six more classmates are needed to represent the students that have a dog and 3 more to represent those that have a cat. There are 7 classmates left over. **3.** 3 bows. *Sample answer:* Let one floor tile represent $\frac{1}{6}$ of a yard. Mark off $13 \cdot 5 = 65$ tiles to represent the amount of ribbon needed to decorate 5 gifts. Mark off 120 tiles to represent the amount of ribbon you have. The difference, 55 tiles, represents the length of ribbon left from which to make bows. Since 15 tiles represent the amount of ribbon needed to make a bow and $55 \div 15 = 3\frac{2}{3}$, 3 bows can be made with the remaining ribbon. **5.** 16 students; eighth. *Sample answer:* I had 4 classmates stand in front of me and 6 stand behind me. Then I had another classmate stand in front of me, and then two more classmates stood behind her but in front of me. Then I had 2 more classmates join the end of the line. Counting showed 16 classmates in line, of which I was eighth. **7.** 5 sweatshirts and 12 T-shirts

5.3 Getting Ready to Practice (p. 232)

1. numerators, denominators **3.** $-1\frac{7}{8}$ **5.** $\frac{23}{32}$

5.3 Practice and Problem Solving (pp. 232–233)

7. $\frac{7}{66}$ **9.** $\frac{1}{6}$ **11.** $4\frac{1}{2}$ **13.** $8\frac{3}{4}$ **15.** $27\frac{2}{9}$ **17.** $14\frac{2}{5}$ **19.** $1\frac{2}{5}$ km **21.** $-1\frac{3}{4}$ **23.** $-\frac{35}{48}$ **25.** 35 ft. *Sample answer:* Let one floor tile represent $\frac{1}{4}$ foot. Mark off 7 tiles to represent $1\frac{3}{4}$ feet. Mark off 7 tiles 19 more times to get 140 total tiles. Since 140 tiles times $\frac{1}{4}$ foot per tile equals 35, the answer is 35 feet.

27. $\frac{2}{3}$ ft^2 **29.** $-\frac{9}{100}$ **31.** $-9\frac{3}{4}$ **33.** $3\frac{19}{120}$ **35.** $4\frac{3}{4}$ **37.** 7^5 **39.** 8^2 **41.** $1\frac{1}{2}$ **43.** $\frac{29}{60}$

5.4 Getting Ready to Practice (p. 236)

1. The multiplicative inverse, or reciprocal, of a number is the number that when multiplied by the original number equals 1. **3.** 6 **5.** $1\frac{1}{3}$ **7.** $\frac{2}{9}$ **9.** $-1\frac{2}{3}$ **11.** Step 1: Number of pounds of hamburger = Pounds per hamburger · Number of hamburgers; Step 2: $5 = \frac{1}{4}h$; Step 3: 20 hamburgers

5.4 Practice and Problem Solving (pp. 237–238)

13. $-\frac{9}{14}$ **15.** $1\frac{1}{2}$ **17.** $-\frac{3}{40}$ **19.** $-\frac{7}{8}$ **21.** $-3\frac{1}{2}$ **23.** $-7\frac{1}{12}$ **25.** $-\frac{2}{7}$ **27.** $2\frac{11}{35}$ **29.** $\frac{1}{6}$ **31.** $1\frac{3}{4}$ **33.** about $8\frac{1}{3}$ days **35.** Yes. *Sample answer:* When the two fractions are written with the same denominator c, then they can be represented as $\frac{a}{c}$ and $\frac{b}{c}$. Then $\frac{a}{c} \div \frac{b}{c} = \frac{a}{c} \cdot \frac{c}{b} = \frac{a}{b}$, so Juan's method works. **37.** 40 **39.** $1\frac{1}{5}$ **41.** 875 people. *Sample answer:* I solved the equation $\frac{2}{5}p = 350$. **43.** $\frac{2}{5}$ **45.** $\frac{3}{14}$ **47.** $\frac{x}{3}$ **49.** $\frac{7x^2}{9y^2}$ **51.** $1\frac{8}{9}$ **53.** $9\frac{1}{3}$

5.4 Technology Activity (p. 239)

1. $\frac{47}{55}$ **3.** $\frac{2}{3}$ **5.** $1\frac{1}{27}$ **7.** $11\frac{1}{5}$ **9.** $1\frac{1}{16}$ qt

5.1–5.4 Notebook Review (pp. 240–241)

1. 1 **2.** $\frac{1}{2}$ **3.** $-1\frac{1}{8}$ **4.** $1\frac{7}{8}$ **5.** $\frac{22x}{15}$ **6.** $\frac{5}{14}$ **7.** 2 **8.** $-8\frac{1}{2}$ **9.** $10\frac{5}{6}$ **10.** 9 **11.** $-1\frac{3}{7}$ **12.** $1\frac{3}{4}$ **13.** Multiply the answer by the divisor. The answer should be the dividend. *Sample answer:* $\frac{2}{5} \div \frac{5}{6} = \frac{12}{25}$ and $\frac{12}{25} \cdot \frac{5}{6} = \frac{2}{5}$ **14.** Greater than. *Sample answer:* Since dividing by a number is the same as multiplying by its reciprocal, and the reciprocal of a fraction between 0 and 1 will be greater than 1, the quotient will be greater than the original number.

5.5 Getting Ready to Practice (p. 244)

1. rational number, integer, whole number

3. rational number, integer **5.** 0.8 **7.** $0.\overline{3}$ **9.** $\frac{3}{5}$

11. $\frac{8}{9}$ **13.** 1.8 in., $1\frac{7}{8}$ in., 2.1 in., $2\frac{1}{9}$ in.

5.5 Practice and Problem Solving (pp. 245–246)

15. $-0.\overline{1}$ **17.** $0.58\overline{3}$ **19.** 0.54 **21.** -0.4125

23. $-14.\overline{63}$ **25.** $0.6\overline{136}$ **27.** $-\frac{14}{25}$ **29.** $2\frac{79}{100}$

31. $7\frac{253}{1000}$ **33.** $-5\frac{2}{625}$ **35.** $\frac{8}{9}$ **37.** $\frac{5}{33}$ **39.** $\frac{14}{333}$

41. $20\frac{41}{198}$ **43.** $9\frac{9}{13}$, $9\frac{5}{7}$, 9.72, 9.74, $9\frac{3}{4}$ **45.** $0.\overline{09}$,

$0.\overline{18}$, $0.\overline{27}$; $0.\overline{36}$, $0.\overline{45}$ **47.** 200 students **49.** 0.049;

$\frac{1}{20}$ **53.** 17 **55.** 13 **57.** *Sample answer:* 170

59. *Sample answer:* 60

5.6 Getting Ready to Practice (p. 249) **1.** 13, 11,

25 **3.** 7.37 **5.** 2.4 **7.** 5.61 **9.** 32

5.6 Practice and Problem Solving (pp. 249–250)

11. 38.103 **13.** -3.419 **15.** 4.988 **17.** -1.63

19. -7.71 **21.** 22.1 **23.** 18.985 **25.** -5.027

27. 7.31 **29.** -0.17 **31.** -6.347 **33.** 60

35. $300 + 40 + 5 + 0.6 + 0.09 + 0.002$ **37.** 67.75 ft

39. 26.42 m **45.** -1 **47.** $\frac{1}{b^{14}}$ **49.** $\frac{40}{63}$ **51.** $7\frac{1}{2}$

5.7 Getting Ready to Practice (p. 253)

1. divisor → $9\overline{)7.2}$ ← dividend $\overset{0.8 \,\leftarrow\, \text{quotient}}{}$ **3.** 1.5; $4 \cdot 0.4 = 1.6$

5. 0.4; $0.5 \div 1 = 0.5$

5.7 Practice and Problem Solving (pp. 253–254)

7. 5 **9.** -5.74 **11.** 4 **13.** -50 **15.** 1.8935 **17.** 8.65

19. 8.7 **21.** 290.405 **23.** The answer should have

$2 + 1 = 3$ decimal places; 33.252. **27.** -8.1

29. 0.2675 **31.** 37.414 **33.** If you multiply both 4.6

and 0.23 by 100, you get 460 and 23; yes; because

you have multiplied $\frac{4.6}{0.23}$ by $\frac{100}{100} = 1$ to get $\frac{460}{23}$.

37. 6,890,000,000 **39.** 0.000007405 **41.** -0.46, $-\frac{9}{20}$,

$-\frac{5}{12}$, -0.4, $-\frac{3}{8}$ **43.** 25 R2 **45.** 204 R39

5.8 Getting Ready to Practice (p. 259) **1.** mean

3. range **5.** -56; -56; -56; 27 **7.** Step 1: 1365 sec,

1316 sec, 1263 sec, 1233 sec, 1228 sec; Step 2:

6405 sec; 1281 sec; Step 3: 21:21

5.8 Practice and Problem Solving (pp. 259–261)

9. 191; 185; 185; 174 **11.** $181.1\overline{6}$ ft; 87 ft; none; 531 ft

13. $9\frac{3}{4}$ in.; 10 in.; $10\frac{1}{2}$ in.; $2\frac{3}{8}$ in. **15.** Isaac: 9.375,

Carl: 9.6, Kurt, 9.425; Carl's **17.** *Sample answer:*

The median; there are equally many salaries

above and below it, so it should reflect the most

likely salary for me in each career. **19.** $\frac{7b}{6}$

21. Yes. *Sample answer:* I prefer Roberta's method

because it is shorter and can be used for any value

of a. **25.** -5 **27.** 0 **29.** -16 **31.** 66 **33.** -16

5.5–5.8 Notebook Review (pp. 262–263)

1. mean, median, mode **2.** $6\frac{3}{8}$, 6.4, $6\frac{5}{12}$, $6\frac{4}{9}$

3. 1.87 **4.** 42.598 **5.** 1.315 **6.** 98.11 **7.** 2.34

8. 3.0132 **9.** -24.8 **10.** 2 **11.** 24; 24; 24; 10

12. 7.45; 7.4; 7.2 and 7.7; 0.8 **13.** *Sample answer:*

3, 4, 12, 12 **14.** They both can be written as ratios.

Sample answer: $0.2 = \frac{1}{5}$ and $0.\overline{2} = \frac{2}{9}$.

Chapter Review (pp. 264–265) **1.** reciprocals

3. front-end estimation **5.** mean **7.** $1\frac{1}{3}$ **9.** $-1\frac{1}{5}$

11. $\frac{17}{20}$ **13.** $-\frac{47}{56}$ **15.** $-\frac{4n}{3}$ **17.** $-\frac{1}{2c}$ **19.** $\frac{1}{4}$ in.

21. $-\frac{1}{4}$ **23.** $-16\frac{1}{14}$ **25.** $\frac{3}{35}$ **27.** $-7\frac{7}{11}$ **29.** 30

31. $-7\frac{1}{7}$ **33.** 2, $\frac{11}{5}$, 2.25, $2\frac{3}{10}$, 2.32, $\frac{5}{2}$ **35.** 25.88

37. 6.045 **39.** -53.44 **41.** 0.425 **43.** 92.79 lb

45. 238.05 mi^2 **47.** 0.125°C; 1°C; -7°C and 2°C;

15°C **49.** $3\frac{1}{10}$ in.; $3\frac{1}{8}$ in.; no mode; $\frac{3}{4}$ in.

Chapter 6

6.1 Getting Ready to Practice (p. 273) **1.** $5x$ and

$-9x$, 6 and -2 **3.** -15, 1, and -20 **5.** 5 **7.** 7

9. 82

6.1 Practice and Problem Solving (pp. 274–275)

11. no; -6 **13.** no; 3 **15.** -2 **17.** -4 **19.** -5

21. -5 **23.** 37 **25.** length: 40 mm, width: 17 mm,

perimeter: 114 mm; 46 **27.** $-1\frac{1}{3}$ **29.** -4 **31.** $\frac{2}{3}$

33. 167 **35.** $\frac{19(x + 11)}{2} = 228$; 13

37. Yes. *Sample answer:* If you divide each side by 3, you get $x + 2 = 3$, so $x = 1$. This is the same answer you get using the distributive property.
39. $x = 5$, $y = 8$; 34   **41.** >   **43.** 34, 34, 32, 7
45. 28,800

6.2 Problem Solving Strategies (p. 277)
1. 18,320 mi   **3.** 60 min   **5.** 60 pages   **7.** 165, 167, 169   **9.** 2012

6.2 Getting Ready to Practice (p. 280) **1.** the sum of the lengths of the sides, or twice the length plus twice the width   **3.** 5   **5.** $-1\frac{2}{3}$

6.2 Practice and Problem Solving (pp. 280–281)
7. 3   **9.** 5   **11.** 3   **13.** 41   **15.** -2 **17.** 132   **19.** 12 wk
21. $-\frac{4}{5}$ **23.** $\frac{3}{4}$ **25.** $1\frac{1}{2}$ **27.** $.80; \$60   **29.** $\frac{3}{8}$
31. -21 **33.** 17   **37.** 36   **39.** 9.558   **41.** 21.038
43. 14   **45.** 7   **47.** 47

6.3 Getting Ready to Practice (p. 284) **1.** least common denominator or LCD   **3.** 100; 4   **5.** 8; $\frac{7}{13}$
7. 20; 20

6.3 Practice and Problem Solving (pp. 284–285)
9. -12 **11.** $3.\overline{63}$ **13.** $-1\frac{2}{5}$ **15.** $1\frac{1}{5}$ **17.** $7x - 2 = 2x + 3$; 1; it is about 1; about 1.0097; the answers are very close.   **19.** -5.36 **21.** $-1\frac{14}{17}$ **23.** \$3 on red, \$10 on purple, and \$3.50 on blue   **25.** Yes. *Sample answer:* The extra factor(s) will divide out, so the simplified result will be the same.   **27.** 18.439
29. 33.7635   **31.** -3 **33.** 2.25   **35.** $-15y + 60$

6.1–6.3 Notebook Review (pp. 286–287)
1. *Sample answer:* To combine like terms, find the terms with the same variable part, including exponents, and add or subtract the coefficients. The result is the coefficient of the term with that same variable part. Constants are like terms.
2. -4 **3.** -6 **4.** $\frac{3}{4}$ **5.** 4.8   **6.** $\frac{1}{5}$ **7.** Multiply each side by 1000.

6.4 Getting Ready to Practice (p. 292)
1.
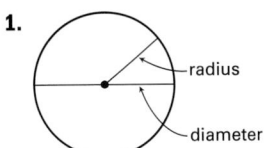
3. 10.5 in.; I used $\frac{22}{7}$ because 66 is divisible by 22.   **5.** 34.5 cm; I used 3.14 because 11 is not divisible by 7.
7. 105 yd; I used $\frac{22}{7}$ because 330 is divisible by 22.

6.4 Practice and Problem Solving (pp. 293–294)
9. 2; 6.28 cm   **11.** 7; 44.0 mm   **13.** 25 yd
15. 62.8 mm   **17.** 44 in.   **19.** 10.5 km   **21.** Ex. 9: 6 cm; Ex. 10: 2.25 in.; Ex. 11: 42 mm; the actual answers should be close to these estimates.
23. about 301 ft   **25.** about 24,900 mi   **27.** about 4620 mi   **29.** 7.64 in.   **37.** $x \le 23$ **39.** $a \le 2$ **41.** 3
43. $4\frac{1}{2}$

6.5 Getting Ready to Practice (p. 297) **1.** less than; greater than; less than or equal to; greater than or equal to
3. $x \ge -4$;
5. $x < -15$;
7. $x > 1\frac{1}{3}$;

6.5 Practice and Problem Solving (pp. 297–299)
9. $a \ge 1$;
11. $p \le 6$;
13. $w > 2$;
15. $c < \frac{1}{3}$;
17. $z < -4$;
19. $n \le -2$;
21. $x \ge 750$; the salesperson must sell at least \$750 in clothes in that week to make at least \$500 for the week.   **23.** at least 23 pledges; $925 + 25p \ge 1500$; $p \ge 23$ **25.** $k \le 9$ **27.** $d \ge -20$ **29.** $x > 4.8$
31. $z \le 4.9$ **33.** $3.95m - 1.2m \ge 25{,}000$; $m \ge 9090.\overline{90}$; the publisher must sell at least 9091 magazines each month to make a profit.
39. *Sample answer:* You cannot buy a negative number of soft drinks.

41. 18 sandwiches. *Sample answer:* I used Make a List to list all of the possibilities. **43.** $22\frac{1}{3}$, 22.5, 22 **45.** 3.4

6.5 Technology Activity (p. 300) **1.** $y < 13$ **3.** $n \le -1$ **5.** $t > -3$ **7.** 16 pencils

6.6 Getting Ready to Practice (p. 303) **1.** $x \ge 5$ **3.** $8 - x \le 6$ **5.** Step 1: $32m + 50$; Step 2: $32m + 50 \le 200$; Step 3: $m \le 4.6875$; you can be a member up to 4 months without spending more than $200.

6.6 Practice and Problem Solving (pp. 304–305) **7.** $9 < x + 1$; $x > 8$ **9.** $8x \ge 40$; $x \ge 5$ **15.** "3 less than a number" is equivalent to the expression $n - 3$, while "3 is less than a number" is equivalent to the inequality $3 < n$. **17.** more than 15 dances **19.** $2 + 0.5n \ge 6$; 3 A.M.; no. *Sample answer:* If there are 6 inches of snow at 3 A.M., and it keeps snowing at the same rate, then there will be 7.5 inches of snow at 6 A.M. **21.** $2 + 0.4 \cdot 5 \cdot m$; $2.50 + 0.25 \cdot 7 \cdot m$ **23.** $m < 2$ mi **25.** 213.52 in. **27.** 89 **29.** 25

6.4–6.6 Notebook Review (pp. 306–307) **1.** circumference; diameter **2.** 44 **3.** 38.5 **4.** 50 **5.** $b < 42$ **6.** $j > 6$ **7.** $y \le 9$ **8.** $8\frac{1}{3}$ min **9.** *Sample answer:* Use < if the expressions "is less than" or "is fewer than" are used. Use > if "is greater than" or "is more than" are used. Use ≤ if "is less than or equal to," "is at most," or "is not more than" are used. Use ≥ if "is greater than or equal to," "is at least," or "is not less than" are used.

Chapter Review (pp. 308–309) **1.** circle **7.** 6 **9.** 9 **11.** 7 **13.** $-\frac{5}{12}$ **15.** In the last step, the values of x and y were substituted for the length and the width to find the perimeter. Instead, the values of x and y must first be substituted into the expressions for the length and width of the rectangle. The length is $4x + 2 = 4(3) + 2 = 14$. The width is $2y = 2(4) = 8$. So, $P = 2(14) + 2(8) = 44$. **17.** $2w + 50 = 3w - 87$; 137 teams **19.** $1\frac{1}{2}$ mi **21.** 25.1 mm **23.** 1.91 in. **25.** $x > -7$;

27. $a < 10$;

29. $g \le -1$;

31. $14 - 3x \le 11$; $x \ge 1$ **33.** $7(15 - x) \ge 56$; $x \le 7$

Chapter 7

7.1 Getting Ready to Practice (p. 319) **1.** rates **3.** $\frac{3}{2}$, 3 to 2, 3 : 2 **5.** yes **7.** yes **9.** Multiply by $\dfrac{7 \text{ days}}{1 \text{ week}} \cdot \dfrac{14 \text{ times}}{1 \text{ day}} \cdot \dfrac{7 \text{ days}}{1 \text{ week}} = \dfrac{98 \text{ times}}{1 \text{ week}}$.

7.1 Practice and Problem Solving (pp. 319–320) **11.** $\frac{4}{5}$, 4 to 5, 4 : 5 **13.** $\frac{5}{7}$, 5 to 7, 5 : 7 **15.** $\frac{2}{3}$, 2 to 3, 2 : 3 **17.** $\frac{-3}{1}$, −3 to 1, −3 : 1 **19.** 2 **21.** 4.32 **23.** $\dfrac{4 \text{ adults}}{1 \text{ car}}$ **25.** $\dfrac{1.5 \text{ lb}}{1 \text{ dollar}}$ **27.** $\frac{5}{5} = \frac{1}{1}$ **29.** 2 **31.** 25 **33.** Check work; $\frac{1}{10}$ of the people in the class are left-handed, so divide the number of people by 10. **35.** 1134 people/mi^2 **37.** 6.25 ft **39.** 6 **41.** −8

7.2 Getting Ready to Practice (p. 324) **1.** Find the cross products and solve the resulting equation to solve the proportion. **3.** 6 **5.** 6 **7.** 2640 ft

7.2 Practice and Problem Solving (pp. 325–326) **9.** no **11.** yes **13.** 9 **15.** 9 **17.** 38.5 **19.** 1513 **21.** 12 in. **23.** 27.25 in. **25.** $90 **27.** 34,375 mi **29.** 1 **31.** 23 **35.** length: 5 in.; width: 1.75 in.; height: 1.25 in. **37.** $\dfrac{3 \text{ people}}{1 \text{ taxi}}$ **39.** $\dfrac{2 \text{ dogs}}{1 \text{ household}}$

7.3 Getting Ready to Practice (p. 329) **1.** percent **3.** 25% **5.** 550

7.3 Practice and Problem Solving (pp. 329–330) **7.** 4% **9.** 90% **11.** 110.25 **13.** 589 **15.** 560 **17.** 925 **19.** 40.08 ft **21.** 135% **23.** 2860 **25.** 540 **27.** 60% **29.** $4y$ **31.** 28.5% **35.** $1\frac{43}{50}$ **37.** $\frac{78}{125}$ **39.** 45.216

7.4 Getting Ready to Practice (p. 333) **1.** 100%; 1 **3.** 9% **5.** 150% **7.** 0.125, $\frac{1}{8}$ **9.** 1.1, $1\frac{1}{10}$ **11.** The numerator of the fraction should be 0.1; $0.001 = \dfrac{0.1}{100} = 0.1\%$.

7.4 Practice and Problem Solving (pp. 334–335)

13. 5.7% **15.** 0.4% **17.** 15% **19.** 0.5% **21.** 105.6%

23. 52.5% **25.** $85\frac{1}{3}$% **27.** 70% **29.** 0.87, $\frac{87}{100}$

31. 1.01, $1\frac{1}{100}$ **33.** 0.042, $\frac{21}{500}$ **35.** 1.24, $1\frac{6}{25}$

37. 0.004, $\frac{1}{250}$ **39.** 0.4455, $\frac{891}{2000}$ **41.** 0.6%, $\frac{3}{50}$,

0.0606, 6.6%, 0.606 **43.** $\frac{21}{100}$, 0.212, $\frac{21}{20}$, 212%, 21.2

45. Spanish **47.** 23% **49.** < **51.** > **53.** =

55. *Sample answer:* when referring to part or all of a group of people **59.** $13 + 4x \le 9$; $x \le -1$ **61.** $6. *Sample answer:* I used Work Backward because it allowed me to start with the known final amount and then "undo" each of the steps one at a time.
63. 3.5 **65.** 11.88

7.1–7.4 Notebook Review (pp. 336–337)

1. proportion **2.** $\frac{7.5 \text{ ft}}{1 \text{ sec}}$ **3.** $\frac{\$1.68}{1 \text{ gal}}$ **4.** 6% **5.** 24.7

6. 0.74, $\frac{37}{50}$ **7.** 0.038, $\frac{19}{500}$ **8.** 0.168, $\frac{21}{125}$ **9.** 1.3, $1\frac{3}{10}$

10. If the cross products are equal, then the ratios form a proportion.

7.5 Getting Ready to Practice (p. 340)

1. increase **3.** decrease; 20% **5.** 23.1

7.5 Practice and Problem Solving (pp. 340–341)

7. increase; 60% **9.** decrease; 6.$\overline{6}$% **11.** decrease; 10% **13.** 1144 **15.** 12.8 **17.** 77,393.75 **19.** about 15,390 tons **21.** 50% increase **23.** 50% decrease **25.** False; multiplying by 5 gives a 400% increase.
27. True; to find an 80% decrease, multiply by 80% and subtract. The final result is 20% of the original number, and finding 20% of a number is the same as dividing by 5. **29.** 9.9% **31.** 9 in. by 6 in.; 125%
33. −5.36 **35.** −14 **37.** 26 **39.** 12

7.6 Getting Ready to Practice (p. 344) **1.** markup
3. $11.40 **5.** $34.80 **7.** $37.80

7.6 Practice and Problem Solving (pp. 345–346)

9. $39.90 **11.** $16.80 **13.** $101.37 **15.** $61.61
17. $22.50 **21.** discount; 10% **23.** markup; 120%
25. discount; about 40% **27.** 19% **29.** 40% **33.** 3
35. 28 **37.** 45 **39.** 40

7.7 Getting Ready to Practice (p. 349)

1. principal **3.** 82% **5.** 399

7.7 Practice and Problem Solving (pp. 349–350)

7. 208 **9.** 66 **11.** 250 **13.** 78 **15.** 0.5% **17.** $15
19. 31% **21.** = **23.** Row 1: 1.1, 3.3; Row 2: 2.5, 5, 7.5; Row 3: 3.8, 7.6, 11.4; for 22, the number increased by 1.1 each time; for 50, the number increased by 2.5 each time; for 76, the number increased by 3.8 each time. **25.** $142.50; $1342.50 **29.** $\frac{5}{6}$ **31.** −3
33. $n \le 11\frac{3}{8}$

7.7 Technology Activity (p. 351) **1.** $7577.03
3. $3744.89

7.8 Problem Solving Strategies (p. 353) **1.** 62 red, 38 blue. *Sample answer:* In the 5 trials, 31 red marbles were chosen and 19 blue marbles were chosen. So $\frac{31}{50} = \frac{x}{100}$, or $x = 62$, and $\frac{19}{50} = \frac{y}{100}$, or $y = 38$. **3.** *Sample answer:* Draw and then replace a letter 20 times and record the results. Write a proportion comparing the ratio of the number of consonants drawn in the experiment to the ratio that would be drawn in 60 trials. Solve the proportion to find the predicted number of consonants drawn. **5.** $20; $34 **7.** 27 triangles

7.8 Getting Ready to Practice (p. 356) **1.** 2, 4, 6
3. The experimental probability is the ratio of favorable outcomes to total outcomes, not to unfavorable outcomes as shown. The number of total outcomes is 20, so the experimental probability of spinning red is $\frac{7}{20}$.

7.8 Practice and Problem Solving (pp. 356–357)

5. $\frac{1}{5}$ **7.** $\frac{3}{10}$ **9.** 1 **11.** 16.8% **13.** 49.2% **15.** 24
17. 56 **19.** about 46% **21.** $\frac{3}{4}$ **25.** *Sample answer:* Each time she rolls the number cube has no effect on any other time she rolls the number cube.
27. 10% **29.** −28 **31.** −32

7.5–7.8 Notebook Review (pp. 358–359) **1.** Find the ratio of the number of favorable outcomes to the number of possible outcomes. **2.** $51
3. $59.04 **4.** 96 **5.** 291.04 **6.** red: $\frac{8}{17}$; yellow: $\frac{5}{17}$; blue: $\frac{4}{17}$ **7.** $525

Chapter Review (pp. 360–361) **1.** unit rate
3. favorable outcomes; possible outcomes **7.** 4.78
9. 360 **11.** 8 **13.** 10 **15.** 308 **17.** 0.5% **19.** 0.3%
21. 145% **23.** $\frac{7}{20}$ **25.** 23% **27.** $14.45 **29.** $127.05
31. $\frac{1}{2}$ **33.** $\frac{3}{4}$

Chapter 8

8.1 Getting Ready to Practice (p. 378)
1. supplementary **3.** supplementary **5.** Vertical angles have the same measure, so $m\angle 2 = 112°$.

8.1 Practice and Problem Solving (pp. 378–379)
7. 109° **9.** $m\angle 6 = 45°$, $m\angle 5 = m\angle 7 = 135°$
11.

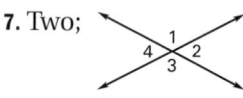

13. *Sample answer:* Together, the angles form a straight angle, so the sum of their measures is 180°. So, $135° + m\angle 2 = 180°$, and $m\angle 2 = 180° - 135° = 45°$. **17.** $y = 2$; $m\angle 6 = 90°$, $m\angle 3 = 90°$
19. $\frac{113}{500}$ **21.** $\frac{9}{2000}$ **23.** 3 in.² **25.** 32.5 ft²

Special Topic Exercises (p. 381) **1–7.** Sample answers are given.

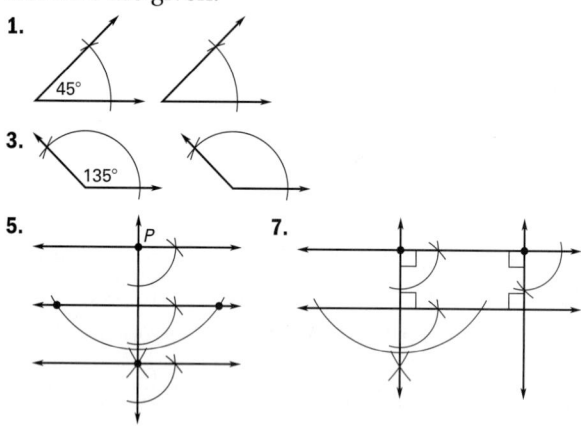

8.2 Getting Ready to Practice (p. 384) **1.** scalene
3. equilateral **5.** The triangle has one right angle, so it is a right triangle.

8.2 Practice and Problem Solving (pp. 384–385)
7. right **9.** scalene **11.** isosceles **13.** 24; right

15. Isosceles; an isosceles triangle has two sides of equal length. **17.** Yes; the sum of the measures of the angles is 180°. **19.** 20°, 70°, 90° **21.** 60°, 60°, 60° **23.** $m\angle 1 = 75°$, $m\angle 2 = 35°$, $m\angle 3 = 70°$
25. 5.2 yd, 1.2 yd² **27.** 148,941,024 km²

8.3 Getting Ready to Practice (p. 387)
1. parallelogram **3.** rectangle **5.** parallelogram, rectangle **7.** 91

8.3 Practice and Problem Solving (pp. 388–389)
9. 1.6 cm; parallelogram, rhombus **11.** 109
13. 65 **15.** $x = 65$, $y = 115$ **17.** dark blue rectangle, red square, green trapezoid, light blue parallelogram, purple parallelogram, yellow trapezoid **19.** sometimes **21.** never **23.** 5; $m\angle E = 121°$, $m\angle H = 119°$ **27.** 5 **29.** 1 **31.** never
33. sometimes

8.4 Getting Ready to Practice (p. 392)
1. polygon **3.** not a polygon **5.** 1440° **7.** 1620°
9. 128.6°

8.4 Practice and Problem Solving (pp. 392–393)
11. yes **13.** yes **15.** about 154° **17.** about 176.9°
19. 78 **21.** $x = 72$; $m\angle R = m\angle N = 72°$; $m\angle L = m\angle M = m\angle P = m\angle Q = 144°$ **23.** $x = 45$; $m\angle B = m\angle E = 135°$ **27.** 360°; 360°; 360°
29. $\frac{49}{50}$ **31.** $\frac{7}{5000}$ **33.** about 103.5%

8.1–8.4 Notebook Review (pp. 394-395) **1.** one
2. 122; obtuse **3.** 26; right **4.** 52° **5.** 720°
6. Yes; *Sample answer:* The sum of the other four angles just needs to be 540°.

7. Two; *Sample answer:* There are two pairs of angles that do not share a side: $\angle 1$ and $\angle 3$, and $\angle 2$ and $\angle 4$.

8.5 Getting Ready to Practice (p. 399)
1. congruent **3.** $\angle K$ and $\angle S$, $\angle L$ and $\angle P$, $\angle M$ and $\angle Q$, $\angle N$ and $\angle R$ **5.** 12 in. **7.** The corresponding vertices are not listed in the correct order; $\triangle ABC \cong \triangle DFE$ by Side-Angle-Side.

8.5 Practice and Problem Solving (pp. 400–401)

9. 80° **11.** 100° **13.** Side-Angle-Side **15.** Side-Side-Side; $x - 6 = 4$; 10 **17.** Angle-Side-Angle; $2x - 24 = x$; 24 **19.** 127.5° **23.** 59.15 **25.** 103

27–30.

8.6 Problem Solving Strategies (p. 403)

1. *Sample:*

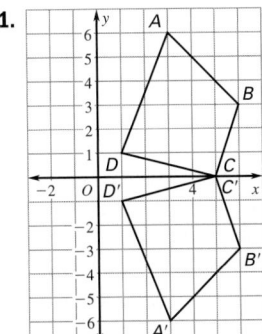

mirror images: 1 and 2, 3 and 4, 5 and 6, 1 and 6, 2 and 3, 4 and 5, 1 and 4, 2 and 5, 3 and 6

3. Scott, Alan, David, Mary, Peter; Scott, Alan, Peter, Mary, David **5.** 96 oz **7.** 92

8.6 Getting Ready to Practice (p. 406)

1. reflection **3.** no **5.** no **7.** none

8.6 Practice and Problem Solving (pp. 407–408)

11.

13.

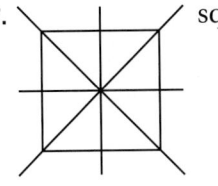

15. two

17. square

19. Lines of Symmetry entries in table: 3, 4, 5, 6, 8
21. A good answer will include a clearly drawn reflection. **25.** 280% **27.** 150°

8.7 Getting Ready to Practice (p. 411)

1. reflection **3.** rotation

8.7 Practice and Problem Solving (pp. 412–413)

5. reflection **7.** translation **9.** reflection
11. rotation **13.** rotation **15.** $(x + 5, y + 4)$
17. $P'(-5, 0)$, $Q'(-2, 0)$, $R'(0, -2)$

19.

21.

23.

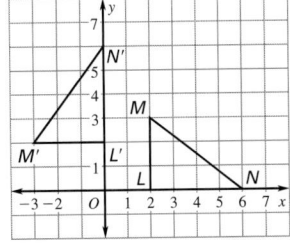

27. *Sample answer:* Reflect in the *y*-axis and then the *x*-axis; make two 90° clockwise rotations; make two 90° counterclockwise rotations; reflect in the *x*-axis and then the *y*-axis. **29.** 384
31. 49.5; right **33.** 74.8; acute **35.** 110.2, 110, 110

Special Topic Exercises (p. 415) **1.** no **3.** no
5. Check work.
7. *Sample:*

translation

9. A good answer will include a rectangle with a piece cut from one side and slid to another side. The translation of that figure forms a tessellation.
11. *Sample:*

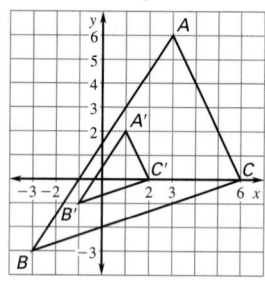

8.8 Getting Ready to Practice (p. 418) **1.** scale factor **3.** $\triangle MNL \sim \triangle PQR$
5. Steps 1, 3:

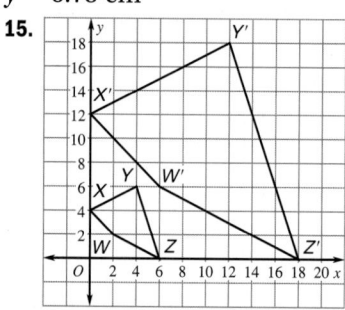

Step 2: $A'(1, 2)$, $B'(-1, -1)$, $C'(2, 0)$

8.8 Practice and Problem Solving (pp. 419–421)
7. $ABCD \sim EDGF$ **9.** 40 **11.** 3 in. **13.** $x = 90$, $y = 6.75$ cm
15.

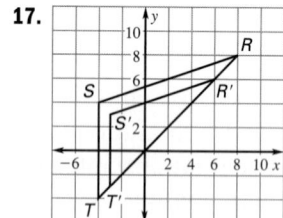

17. **19.**

21. 4 in. by 8 in. **23.** $x = 44$, $y = 136$ **27.** $27.50

8.5–8.8 Notebook Review (pp. 422–423)
1. reflection **2.** translation **3.** 3 cm
4.

5.

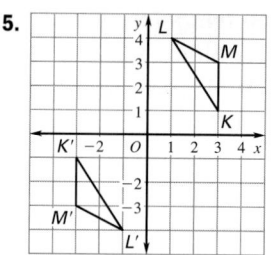

6. 25 m **7.** *Sample answer:* The perimeter of the image is the product of the scale factor and the perimeter of the original figure. **8.** *Sample answer:* A person turning around to face the opposite way

Chapter Review (pp. 424–425) **9.** 109° **11.** 25°
13. rectangle **15.** 900° **17.** $\angle A \cong \angle P$, $\angle B \cong \angle Q$, $\angle C \cong \angle R$, $\angle D \cong \angle S$, $\angle E \cong \angle T$ **19.** $\triangle ABC \cong \triangle GFH$; two sides and the included angle of one triangle are congruent to two sides and the included angle of the other triangle, so the triangles are congruent by Side-Angle-Side. **21.** no **23.** no
25. **27.**

 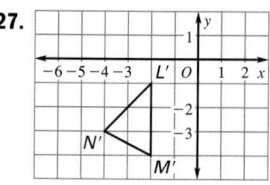

29. $A'(-4, 0)$, $B'(-4, 8)$, $C'(-12, 16)$, $D'(-24, 12)$

Chapter 9

9.1 Getting Ready to Practice (p. 434) **1.** $b^2 = c$
3. ± 4 **5.** ± 11 **7.** -22.0 **9.** 49.4 **11.** ± 7 **13.** ± 9

9.1 Practice and Problem Solving (pp. 434–436)
15. -1 **17.** 12 **19.** 6 **21.** 11 **23.** 4.7 **25.** -38.4
27. 0 **29.** ± 13 **31.** ± 6 **33.** No. *Sample answer:* There is no real number whose square is a negative number. **35.** ± 6.40 **37.** ± 11.66
39. ± 14.14 **41.** 4 **43.** 9 **45.** ± 1.2 **47.** ± 1.4
49. No. *Sample answer:* The table measures $\sqrt{34.5} \approx 5.9$ feet on a side. Since 5.9 feet is over 70 inches, the tablecloth is not big enough. **51.** $\frac{1}{2}$
53. $\frac{7}{8}$ **55.** $\frac{12}{13}$ **59.** neither **61.** supplementary
63. 34 ways. *Sample answer:* I used the strategy Draw a Diagram so that I could draw all the ways that 3 stamps can be arranged and still be attached. **65.** $5\frac{7}{20}$ **67.** $-9\frac{1}{20}$

9.2 Getting Ready to Practice (p. 439)

1. irrational **3.** Irrational. *Sample answer:* 5 is not a perfect square. **5.** Rational. *Sample answer:*
$\sqrt{\dfrac{25}{49}} = \dfrac{5}{7}$ which is a quotient of two integers.

7.

$\dfrac{3}{5} = \sqrt{\dfrac{36}{100}} = 0.6$ = **9.** 9.5 ft by 9.5 ft

9.3 Practice and Problem Solving (pp. 440–441)

11. Rational. *Sample answer:* $\dfrac{9}{46}$ is a quotient of two integers. **13.** Irrational. *Sample answer:* neither 3 nor 5 is a perfect square.

15.

$\sqrt{13} \approx 3.6056$ >

17.

$-5 = -\sqrt{25}$ =

19. $0.\overline{262}, 0.\overline{26}, 0.266, 0.2\overline{6}$ **21.** $\sqrt{4} = 2$; rational
23. $\sqrt{20}$; irrational

25.

$\sqrt{0.9} \approx 0.9487$ >
0.9

27.

$\sqrt{2.25} = \dfrac{3.6}{2.4} = 1.5$ =

29. $-4, -3.75, 1.5, \sqrt{8}$ **31.** $-3.5, -\sqrt{12}, -\dfrac{3}{4}, -\sqrt{\dfrac{1}{4}}$
33. Yes; too small. *Sample answer:* Because $\sqrt{110} \approx$ 10.5, the piece of carpet should about fit the 10.5 foot dimension, but will be about 0.7 foot too short in the other dimension. **37.** $30a^{11}$ **39.** -5
41. c^4 **43.** $-\dfrac{2}{3n^4}$ **45.** rotation; $(x, y) \to (y, -x)$
47. translation; $(x, y) \to (x - 3, y + 1)$

9.3 Getting Ready to Practice (p. 445)
1. hypotenuse **3.** 15 **5.** 25 **7.** yes **9.** no

9.3 Practice and Problem Solving (pp. 446–447)
11. 34 ft **13.** 19.6 ft **15.** 24.5 in. **17.** no **19.** yes
21. 8.9 ft **23.** 9 m **25.** 4.24 ft **27.** no **29.** yes
31. 2 **33.** 5.3 **35.** 3

39.

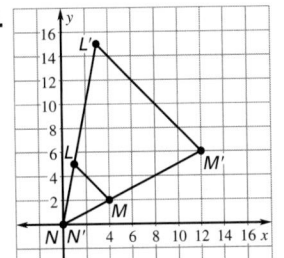

9.4 Problem Solving Strategies (p. 449) **1.** 7.1 m
3. 37 ft **5.** yes **7.** $140 **9.** 6 possibilities

9.4 Getting Ready to Practice (p. 452)
1. Pythagorean triple **3.** 96 ft
5. Steps 1–2:

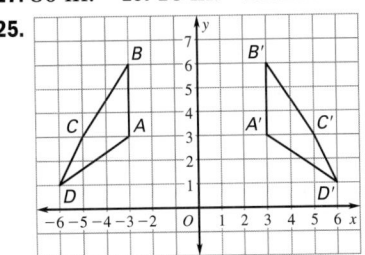

Step 3:
42.4 ft

9.4 Practice and Problem Solving (pp. 452–453)
7. 15 ft; 60 ft², 40 ft **9.** 6 in.; 8.64 in.², 14.4 in.
11. 44 m; 2574 m², 286 m **13.** yes **15.** no
17. 30 in. **19.** 18 in. **21.** 24 m **23.** 182 cm
27. -12 **29.** 8.5

25.

9.1–9.4 Notebook Review (pp. 454–455) **1.** real
numbers **2.** ± 13 **3.** ± 11 **4.** ± 8

5.

$\sqrt{31} \approx 5.5678$ >

6.

$\sqrt{59} \approx 7.6811$ <

7.

$-9 = -\sqrt{81}$ =

8.

$\sqrt{48} \approx 6.9282$ >
6.3

9. 15 **10.** 32 **11.** 2.5

12. *Sample answer:* The decimal form of a rational number terminates or repeats, while the decimal form of an irrational number does neither. For example, $\frac{3}{4}$ and $\frac{1}{3}$ are rational because $\frac{3}{4} =$ 0.75 (terminates) and $\frac{1}{3} = 0.\overline{3}$ (repeats), but $\pi \approx$ 3.1415926535..., which never terminates or repeats.

9.5 Getting Ready to Practice (p. 458)
1. The length of the hypotenuse is $\sqrt{2}$ times the length of a leg. **3.** 50 ft **5.** Step 1: $\frac{5\sqrt{3}}{2}$ in.; Step 2: 7.5 in.

9.5 Practice and Problem Solving (pp. 459–460)
7. 28 cm **9.** $x = 11$ in., $y = 11\sqrt{3}$ in.
11. $y = 36\sqrt{3}$ m, $z = 72$ m **13.** 115 ft **15.** 10 in.
17. $x = 8$ m, $y = 8\sqrt{3}$ m **19.** $x = 32\frac{1}{2}$ cm, $y = \frac{65\sqrt{3}}{2}$ cm **21.** $x^2 + (x\sqrt{3})^2 \stackrel{?}{=} (2x)^2$, $x^2 + 3x^2 \stackrel{?}{=} 4x^2$, $4x^2 = 4x^2$. *Sample answer:* $3^2 + (3\sqrt{3})^2 \stackrel{?}{=} 6^2$, $9 + 27 \stackrel{?}{=} 36$, $36 = 36$. **25.** $1\frac{1}{2}$ **27.** $\frac{7 \text{ people}}{1 \text{ team}}$
29. $\frac{61 \text{ rotations}}{1 \text{ min}}$ **31.** 10

9.6 Getting Ready to Practice (p. 466)
5. Step 1:

42°; totem pole; 50 ft

Step 2: $\tan 42° = \frac{x}{50}$; Step 3: 45 ft

9.6 Practice and Problem Solving (pp. 466–468)
7. $\sin P = \frac{11}{61}$, $\cos P = \frac{60}{61}$, $\tan P = \frac{11}{60}$, $\sin R = \frac{60}{61}$, $\cos R = \frac{11}{61}$, $\tan R = \frac{60}{11}$ **9.** 1.2349 **11.** 0.5878
13. 3.440 in. **15.** 20.796 m **19.** The tangent ratio is the length of the opposite side over the length of the adjacent side, not over the length of the hypotenuse. So $\tan 25° = \frac{x}{13}$, and $x \approx 6$ cm.
21. $m\angle C = 60°$, $AC = 10$ in.; $\sin A = \frac{1}{2}$, $\cos A = \frac{8.7}{10}$, $\tan A = \frac{5}{8.7}$ **23.** $m\angle A = 19.7°$, $BC \approx 17.2$ cm; $\sin A = \frac{17.2}{51}$, $\cos A = \frac{48}{51}$, $\tan A = \frac{17.2}{48}$
25. about 1813 m **27.** 84.4 in. **29.** 119 ft

33. 10.73 **35.** Rational. *Sample answer:* 484 is a perfect square, $22^2 = 484$. **37.** Irrational. *Sample answer:* Neither 17 nor 29 is a perfect square. **39.** 3.625 mi/h

9.6 Technology Activity (p. 469) **1.** 14.0° **3.** 42.6°
5. 87.7° **7.** $\tan^{-1}(32.46)$. *Sample answer:* The greater the tangent of an angle, the larger the angle.

9.5–9.6 Notebook Review (pp. 470–471)
1. opposite; hypotenuse **2.** $8\sqrt{2}$ in. **3.** 20 cm
4. $x = 6$ m, $y = 6\sqrt{3}$ m **5.** $\sin A = \frac{3}{5}$, $\cos A = \frac{4}{5}$, $\tan A = \frac{3}{4}$, $\sin B = \frac{4}{5}$, $\cos B = \frac{3}{5}$, $\tan B = \frac{4}{3}$
6. $\sin A = \frac{48}{73}$, $\cos A = \frac{55}{73}$, $\tan A = \frac{48}{55}$, $\sin B = \frac{55}{73}$, $\cos B = \frac{48}{73}$, $\tan B = \frac{55}{48}$ **7.** $\sin A = \frac{36}{85}$, $\cos A = \frac{77}{85}$, $\tan A = \frac{36}{77}$, $\sin B = \frac{77}{85}$, $\cos B = \frac{36}{85}$, $\tan B = \frac{77}{36}$
8. *Sample answer:* Use the Pythagorean theorem to find that the length of the other leg is 4. Use this fact to find the cosine ratio, $\frac{4}{5}$.

Chapter Review (pp. 472–473) **1.** *Sample answer:*
A rational number can be written as a quotient of two integers, while an irrational number cannot. A rational number has a decimal representation that either terminates or repeats, while an irrational number does not. **3.** *Sample answer:* $\sqrt{2}$, π, $\sqrt{7}$ **5.** perfect square **7.** shorter **9.** 9.7
11. -46.02 **13.** ± 14 **15.** ± 8 **17.** Rational. *Sample answer:* 100 is a perfect square, since $10^2 = 100$.
19. Rational. *Sample answer:* $\frac{16}{25}$ is the quotient of two integers. **21.** $0.\overline{181}$, $0.\overline{18}$, 0.188, $0.1\overline{8}$ **23.** 11 in.
25. no **27.** yes **29.** 679.23 m **31.** $x = 15\sqrt{3}$ m, $y = 30$ m **33.** $\sin P = \frac{21}{29}$, $\cos P = \frac{20}{29}$, $\tan P = \frac{21}{20}$, $\sin Q = \frac{20}{29}$, $\cos Q = \frac{21}{29}$, $\tan Q = \frac{20}{21}$ **35.** $\sin P = \frac{21}{29}$, $\cos P = \frac{20}{29}$, $\tan P = \frac{21}{20}$, $\sin Q = \frac{20}{29}$, $\cos Q = \frac{21}{29}$, $\tan Q = \frac{20}{21}$ **37.** 0.3346 **39.** 0.8391

Chapter 10

10.1 Getting Ready to Practice (p. 483) **1.** $A = bh$
3. $A = \frac{1}{2}(b_1 + b_2)h$ **5.** 56 in.²

7. Step 1:

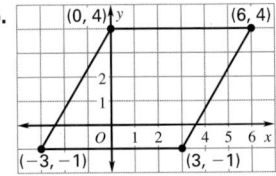

Step 2: trapezoid: $49\frac{1}{2}$ ft^2; parallelogram: 72 ft^2;

Step 3: $121\frac{1}{2}$ ft^2

10.1 Practice and Problem Solving (pp. 483–485)

9. 126 ft^2 **11.** 35 ft^2 **13.** 70 in.^{2}

15. 60 ft^2 **17.** 162 in.^{2}
19. 480 m^2

21. 7 units   **23.** 10 cm^2, 11 cm^2

25. 90 cm^2, 99 cm^2; the new areas are nine times the original areas.   **27.** *Sample answer:* about 112,500 mi^2 **29.** 79.85 in.^{2} **31.** 162 m^2 **33.** 360 ft^2

35. 30 units^2

41. $11\frac{2}{3}$ **43.** $\sin P = \frac{8}{17}$, $\cos P = \frac{15}{17}$, $\tan P = \frac{8}{15}$, $\sin R = \frac{15}{17}$, $\cos R = \frac{8}{17}$, $\tan R = \frac{15}{8}$

10.2 Getting Ready to Practice (p. 488)   **1.** radius
3. 314 cm^2 **5.** about 7 m

10.2 Practice and Problem Solving (pp. 488–490)

7. 555 m^2 **9.** 340 cm^2 **11.** 314 ft^2 **13.** 615 mm^2
15. 1256 in.^{2} **17.** 1 m   **19.** 6 in.   **21.** 9 cm
23. 10 mm; 314 mm^2 **25.** 239 in.^{2} **27.** 5 ft
29. $18.84 = 2(3.14)r$; 3 ft; 28.3 ft^2 **31.** $37.68 = 2(3.14)r$; 6 cm; 113 cm^2

33. Larger square: 400 mm^2, smaller square: 200 mm^2, estimate: 300 mm^2; actual: 314 mm^2. *Sample answer:* The estimate is close to the actual area of the circle.   **37.** no

10.2 Technology Activity (p. 491)   **1.** multiplied by 3   **3.** multiplied by 5   **5.** Multiplied by $\sqrt{2}$; multiplied by $\sqrt{3}$. *Sample answer:* If the area of a circle is multiplied by n, then the radius is multiplied by $\sqrt{n}$.

10.3 Getting Ready to Practice (p. 494)
1. cylinder; no   **3.** sphere; no

5.

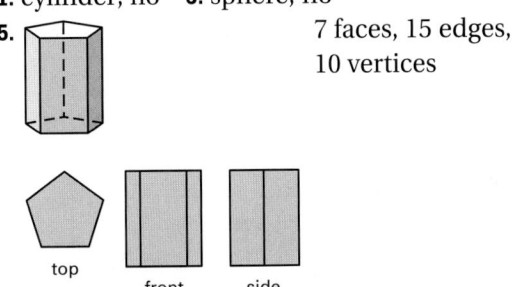

7 faces, 15 edges, 10 vertices

10.3 Practice and Problem Solving (pp. 494–495)
7. sphere; no   **9.** cylinder; no

11.

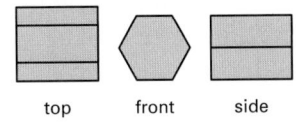

4 faces, 6 edges, 4 vertices

19. pentagonal prisms   **21.** cylinder and cone
23.   **25.** 346 in.^{2}

Special Topic Exercises (p. 497)

1.   **3.**

5.

7.

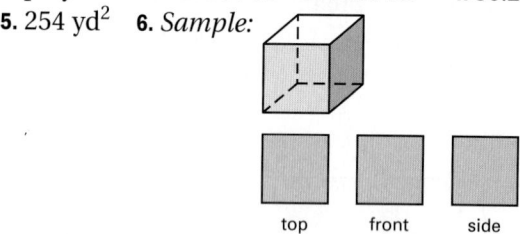

top   front   side

9.

top   front   side

10.1–10.3 Notebook Review (pp. 498–499)
1. polyhedron   **2.** 160 ft^2 **3.** 1810 in.^{2} **4.** 50.2 mm^2
5. 254 yd^2 **6.** *Sample:*

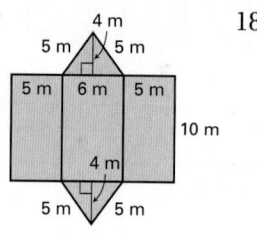

top   front   side

7. *Sample answer:* A cone and a cylinder both have circular bases, but a cone has only one circular base while a cylinder has two. A cross-section of either solid parallel to a base is a circle, but for the cone these circles get smaller toward the vertex, while for the cylinder they are all the same size. A cylinder and a prism both have two parallel bases, but the bases of a cylinder are circles, while the bases of a prism are polygons.
8. No. *Sample answer:* The only vertices of a prism are on its bases. Because the bases are two congruent polygons, the total number of vertices is twice the number on one base, so it is an even number.

10.4 Problem Solving Strategies (p. 501)
1. 396 in.^{2} **3.** 11 0's, 21 1's, 20 of each of the digits 2–9   **5.** 12 sandwiches   **7.** 4 and 13

10.4 Getting Ready to Practice (p. 505)
1. *Sample answer:* Surface area is the sum of the areas of all the faces and lateral surfaces of a solid.
3. *Sample:*   184 m^2

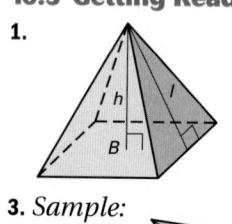

10.4 Practice and Problem Solving (pp. 505–506)
5. 48 in.^{2} **7.** 150 yd^2
9.   301.6 m^2

11.   1885.0 cm^2

13. triangular prism; 680 in.^{2}
15. *Sample:*   600 in.^{2}

17. *Sample:*   88 m^2

19. 1062 ft^2 **21.** 76 cm^2
23. *Sample:*   46 in.^{2}

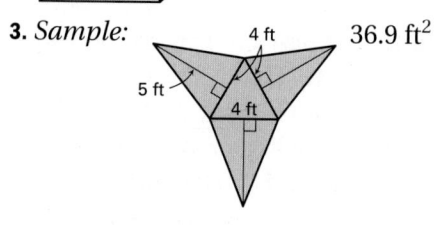

27. yes   **29.** 0.4245   **31.** 0.9135   **33.** 216 in.^{2}

10.5 Getting Ready to Practice (p. 509)
1.

3. *Sample:*   36.9 ft^2

5. Step 1: $(\pi r^2 + \pi rl) - \pi r^2 = \pi rl$; Step 2: $\pi(1)\left(4\frac{1}{4}\right)$;

Step 3: 13.4 in.^{2}

10.5 Practice and Problem Solving (pp. 510–511)
7. 144 m^2 **9.** 525 yd^2 **11.** 138.2 in.^{2} **13.** 119.4 mm^2
15. *Sample:*

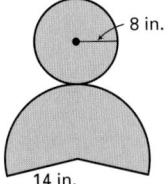
8 in.
14 in.
552.9 in.^{2}

17. 261 in.^{2} **19.** 1508.0 m^2 **21.** 373.8 ft^2
23. 243.3 in.^{2} **25.** 6π in.^{2} **27.** 54π in.^{2}
29. $S = B + \frac{1}{2}Pl = \pi r^2 + \frac{1}{2}(2\pi r)l = \pi r^2 + \pi rl$; the
simplified expression is the same as the formula
for the surface area of a cone.   **33.** rational
35. irrational

10.6 Getting Ready to Practice (p. 515)
1. *Sample answer:* Area is the measure of the
region inside a two-dimensional shape, while
volume is the measure of the space inside a solid.
3. 200 in.^{3} **5.** The area of the base is πr^2, not $2\pi r$;
$V = Bh = \pi r^2 h = \pi(4^2)5 \approx 251.3$ m^3.

10.6 Practice and Problem Solving (pp. 516–517)
7. 343 in.^{3} **9.** 120 ft^3 **11.** 254.5 cm^3 **13.** 64 yd^3
15. 1260 m^3 **17.** 25,446.9 mm^3 **19.** surface area
21. volume   **23.** 3820.2 cm^3 **25.** 8.6 mm^3
27. 336 m^3 **29.** 11 times   **31.** They would have the
same effect. *Sample answer:* Since $V = lwh$, if any
dimension is doubled, the volume is doubled.
33. 36   **35.** 192 in.^{2} **37.** 75.4 ft^2

10.7 Getting Ready to Practice (p. 521)
5. 96 cm^3 **7.** 3141.6 ft^3

10.7 Practice and Problem Solving (pp. 522–523)
9. 60 ft^3 **11.** 2560 m^3 **13.** 247.5 ft^3 **15.** 144 yd^3
17. 3421.2 cm^3 **19.** 5399.6 ft^3 **21.** 506.8 ft^3
23. 134.0 m^3 **25.** 70.7 ft^3 **27.** 0.2 cm^3 **29.** Doubling
the radius. *Sample answer:* The radius is squared in
the volume formula, but the height is not.   **31.** Find
the volume of the rectangular pyramid and the
volume of the rectangular prism and add; $V =$
$\frac{1}{3}lwh_1 + lwh_2$.   **33.** 28.8 ft; 36.7 ft   **37.** 2770.9 in.^{3}

10.4–10.7 Notebook Review (pp. 524–525) **1.** For
a regular pyramid, it is the height of a face that is
not a base; for a cone, it is the length of any
segment joining the edge of the base to the top
point of the cone.   **2.** 471.24 m^2 **3.** 146 in.^{2}
4. 105 m^2 **5.** 785.40 ft^2 **6.** 126 m^3 **7.** *Sample
answer:* Area is the measure of the region inside a
two-dimensional figure, while surface area is the
sum of the areas of all faces or surfaces of a solid.

Chapter Review (pp. 526–527)
5. *Sample:*

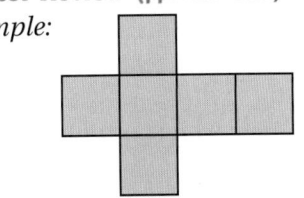

7. $S = 2\pi r^2 + 2\pi rh$; $V = \pi r^2 h$ **9.** $S = B + \frac{1}{2}Pl$;
$V = \frac{1}{3}Bh$ **11.** 112 ft^2 **13.** $53\frac{1}{4}$ in.^{2} **15.** 90 yd^2
17. 707 yd^2 **19.** 1.77 m^2
21. *Sample:*

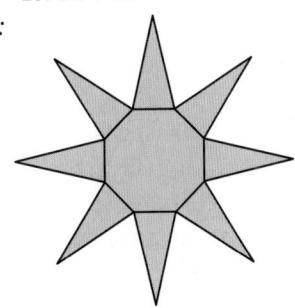

9 faces,
16 edges,
9 vertices

23. 2921.7 yd^2 **25.** 785.4 ft^2 **27.** 144 in.^{2}
29. 103.8 mm^3 **31.** 20 in.^{3} **33.** 314.2 ft^3 **35.** No.
Sample answer: The volume of the pyramid is
15 cubic inches, which is greater than the 12 cubic
inches of candle wax.

Chapter 11

11.1 Getting Ready to Practice (p. 543)
1. function   **3.** yes   **5.** 18, 13, 8, 3   **7.** $y = -5x$

11.1 Practice and Problem Solving (pp. 543–544)
9. No; one input, 4, has two output values.
11. Yes; each input has exactly one output value.
13.

Input *x*	-2	-1	0	1	2
Output *y*	-3	-2	-1	0	1

range: $-3, -2, -1, 0, 1$

15.

Input x	-2	-1	0	1	2
Output y	-10	-5	0	5	10

range: $-10, -5, 0, 5, 10$
17. $y = 5x$ **19.** No; the weight of the cans that Stanley recycles is a function of the amount of money.   **21.** $t = 3r - 2$ **23.** Yes; each input has exactly one output value.   **25.** 113.5 m^2 **27.** 6670 ft^2

11.2 Getting Ready to Practice (p. 547)
1. scatter plot

11.2 Practice and Problem Solving (pp. 547–548)
3. no relationship   **5.** negative relationship
7.

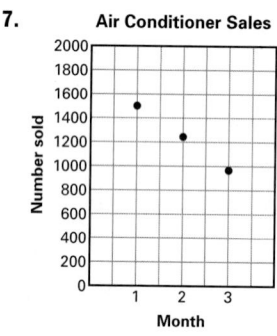

Air Conditioner Sales

There is a negative relationship. As the summer turns to fall, sales of air conditioners decrease.

9.

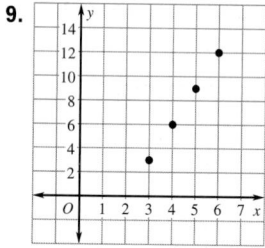

There is a positive relationship, with each increase of 1 in x corresponding to an increase of 3 in y; (7, 15).

11. positive relationship   **13.** *Sample answer:* When the weather is nicer, more people will vote; no, because it would be hard to find a single measure that would accurately indicate how "nice" the weather is.   **15.** 90 m^2
17.

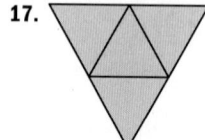

21. 19   **23.** 19

11.3 Getting Ready to Practice (p. 551)
1. solution   **3.** $y = 2x + 4$ **5.** The x value was substituted for y and the y value was substituted for x. The second step should be $2(-5) + 3(4) \overset{?}{=} -7$, followed by $-10 + 12 \overset{?}{=} -7$ and $2 \neq -7$. So,

$(-5, 4)$ is not a solution.

11.3 Practice and Problem Solving (pp. 551–553)
7. y values in the table: 3, 8, 13, 18   **9.** y values in the table: $-25, -20, -15, -10$ **11.** no   **13.** yes
15. yes   **17.** *Sample answer:* $(-1, -6), (0, -10),$ $(1, -14), (2, -18)$ **19.** no   **21.** yes   **23-27.** Sample answers are given.   **23.** $(-1, -15), (0, -13),$ $(1, -11), (2, -9)$ **25.** $(-1, 8), (0, 3), (1, -2), (2, -7)$
27. $(-1, -45), (0, -51), (1, -57), (2, -63)$
29. 20 wk   **31.** $y = -x + 8$. *Sample answer:* $(-1, 9),$ $(0, 8), (1, 7), (2, 6)$ **33.** $y = 3x + 33$. *Sample answer:* $(-1, 30), (0, 33), (1, 36), (2, 39)$ **35.** $y = 2 - 3x$. *Sample answer:* $(-1, 5), (0, 2), (1, -1), (2, -4)$
37. $y = 2x + 4$ **39.** *Sample answer:* $9x = 24$ and $8y \approx -6$, so $9x + 8y \approx 18$, which is greater than 16.
41. $(2, -1)$ **43.**

45.

Input x	-2	-1	0	1	2
Output y	3	2.5	2	1.5	1

range: 1, 1.5, 2, 2.5, 3
47.

Input x	-2	-1	0	1	2
Output y	12	10	8	6	4

range: 4, 6, 8, 10, 12   **49.** -8.75

11.4 Problem Solving Strategies (p. 555)
1. 2nd row: 140, 120, 100, 80   **3.** 60 ft   **5.** Krystal
7. 27 rectangles; 81 rectangles   **9.** Leslie

11.4 Getting Ready to Practice (p. 558) **1.** line
3. *Sample:*

Input x	-2	-1	0	1	2
Output y	-4	-4	-4	-4	-4

11.4 Practice and Problem Solving (pp. 559–560)
9. yes   **11.** *Sample answer:* $(-1, -3), (0, -2), (1, -1)$
13. *Sample answer:* $(-1, 6), (0, 6), (1, 6)$
15.

17.

19.

23.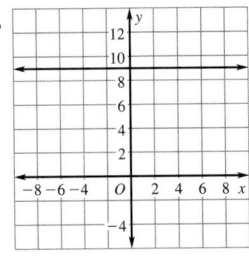

27. $x = 5$

29. $(-3, 5)$. *Sample answer:* Since $x = -3$ and $y = 5$, $(-3, 5)$ will be the coordinates of the point of intersection.

37. $y = 2$ **39.** *Sample answer:* The line must be horizontal and contain all points with a y-coordinate of -8.6, so the equation of the line is $y = -8.6$. **41.** 140 square units **43.** 1056 square units **45.** y values in table: $-14, -8, 1, 4, 13$ **47.** -252

11.4 Technology Activity (p. 561)

1. **3.**

5. yes

11.1–11.4 Notebook Review (pp. 562–563)

1. input-output table **2.** $y = -4x$ **3.** $y = x + 3$

4. The data have a positive relationship, with every increase of 0.5 in x there is a corresponding increase of 5 in y.

5–7. Sample solutions are given.

5. $(0, 5), (1, 3), (2, 1)$

6. $(0, -6), (1, -3) (2, 0)$

7. $(0, 4), (4, 5), (8, 6)$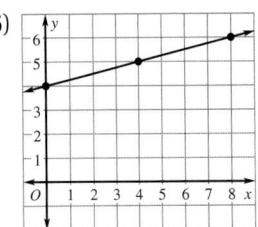

8. *Sample answer:* $4y = -2x + 16$ can be rewritten as $16 = 2x + 4y$, or $8 = x + 2y$, so the equations are equivalent and have the same solutions.

11.5 Getting Ready to Practice (p. 566)

1. y-intercept, x-intercept **3.** x-intercept: 3, y-intercept: -1

11.5 Practice and Problem Solving (pp. 566–567)

5. x-intercept: $\frac{1}{2}$, y-intercept: -3 **7.** x-intercept: -2, y-intercept: 10 **9.** x-intercept: 5, y-intercept: 4

11. **13.**

15. Up. *Sample answer:* The x-intercept will be on the positive side of the x-axis and the y-intercept will be on the negative side of the y-axis, so the line will slant up from left to right. **17.** x-intercept: none, y-intercept: 14

19. **21.**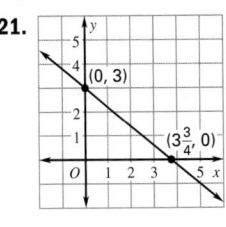

25. x-intercept: 1.71, y-intercept: 3.65
27. x-intercept: -3.64, y-intercept: -15.01

31.

33.

35. 60 km/h

11.6 Getting Ready to Practice (p. 572) **1.** rise

3, 5. Sample answers are given.

3. **5.**

7. 3 **9.** 1

11.6 Practice and Problem Solving (pp. 573–574)

11. $(1, 0)$, $(-2, 6)$; -2 **13.** $-\dfrac{1}{5}$ **15.** 1 **17.** $\dfrac{3}{5}$

19. $-\dfrac{5}{12}$ **21.** $\dfrac{3}{32}$

23. slope of $\overline{DE} = -\dfrac{3}{7}$,
slope of $\overline{EF} = \dfrac{8}{5}$,
slope of $\overline{FD} = -\dfrac{11}{2}$

25. slope of $\overline{KL} = -\dfrac{5}{4}$,
slope of $\overline{LM} = -8$,
slope of $\overline{MK} = 1$

27. The line through $(1, 1)$ and $(3, 4)$; the line with the greater slope is steeper; the line with the greater slope has a greater number for the slope.
31. $x = 12$ **33.** $x = 4, y = 3$ **37.** yes **39.** no **41.** 63

11.7 Getting Ready to Practice (p. 579) **1.** $-5, 7$
3. $y = 2x - 5$ **5.** $1, 3$ **7.** $2, -1$

11.7 Practice and Problem Solving (pp. 579–580)

9. $1, -8$;

11. $-1, 7$;

13. $\dfrac{2}{3}, -4$;

15. $y = -6x + 10$; $-6, 10$ **17.** $y = \dfrac{2}{3}x - 3$; $\dfrac{2}{3}, -3$

19. $y = -12x$; $-12, 0$

21. 9 bracelets **23.** $y = -\dfrac{3}{2}x - 3$

25.

At 39°F, the number of chirps per minute is 0.

27. $y = -\dfrac{a}{b}x - \dfrac{c}{b}$ **29.** $5x \geq 35; x \geq 7$ **31.** 75 ft^3

33. $t > 6$;

Special Topic Exercises (p. 582)

1. $(1, 2)$

3. 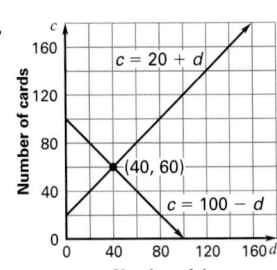 $(6, -3)$ **5.** $(-1, 5)$

7. 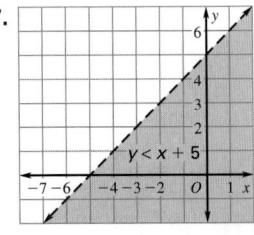 in 40 days

11.8 Getting Ready to Practice (p. 585)

1. half-planes   **3.** yes   **5.** no

7.   **9.**

11.8 Practice and Problem Solving (pp. 586–587)

11. yes   **13.** no   **15.** Use a dashed line when the inequality symbol is < or >. Use a solid line when the inequality symbol is ≤ or ≥.

21.   **23.**

27.   **29.**

31.   **33.**

37. $y < -\frac{1}{3}x + 5; \ y > \frac{1}{3}x - 5; \ y > \frac{2}{3}x - 6; \ y < -\frac{2}{3}x + 6$

39. $\frac{6}{5}$ **41.** $3\frac{3}{4}$ **43.** $7\frac{41}{250}$

11.5–11.8 Notebook Review (pp. 588–589)

1. slope; y-intercept   **2.** $\frac{4}{3}$ **3.** $\frac{2}{5}$ **4.** $-\frac{5}{3}$

5. 5, 20;

6. $\frac{2}{3}$, 4;

7. $-\frac{1}{4}, 4\frac{1}{2}$;

8.   **9.**

10.

11.

12. 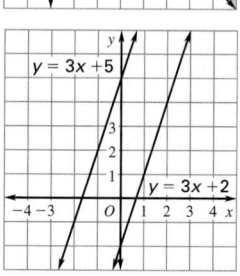 They are parallel.

Chapter Review (pp. 590–591) **1.** half-plane
3. rise, run **5.** A good answer will include a situation that changes over time, such as time and distance traveled, and an explanation that the slope tells you how quickly something changes.
7. No; each input has more than one output.
9. Yes; each input has exactly one output. **11.** $141

15. **17.**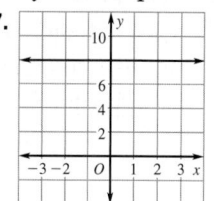

19. *Sample answer:* $(-2, 3)$, $(2, 3)$; 0 **21.** $y = 4x + 10$; 4, 10 **23.** $y = -\frac{3}{7}x - 3$; $-\frac{3}{7}$, -3

25.

Chapter 12

12.1 Getting Ready to Practice (p. 599) **1.** stem, leaf **3.** 11 | 7; stem: 11, leaf: 7 **5.** 4 | 6; stem: 4, leaf: 6

12.1 Practice and Problem Solving (pp. 599–600)
7.
4	5 8
5	0
6	3 5 7
7	4
8	2

60–69

Key: 5 | 0 = 50

9.
8	9
9	4 5
10	3 8 9
11	2

100–109

Key: 10 | 3 = 103

11.
18	1 3 7
19	
20	2
21	
22	5 6

18.0–18.9

Key: 18 | 1 = 18.1

13. Count the total number of values in the data set. Then count from the first leaf to half the total number of values to find the median value.

15.
4	3 7
5	5 8 9
6	5
7	2 8
8	4 4
9	5 6

53; greater than

Key: 4 | 3 = 43

17.
Set C		Set D
	6	5
7 0	7	
	8	7 8
8 2	9	3 5
2	10	2
8 1	11	5

Key: 2 | 9 | 3 = 92 and 93

19.
Wins		Losses
	0	6 7 7
8	1	0 2 4 5 6
7 4 4 3 0	2	1
	3	
1	4	

Key: 0 | 2 | 1 = 20 and 21

Sample answer: When the Browns scored less than 20 points, they usually lost. When they scored more than 20 points, they usually won.
21. 13.8, 14.2, 14.4, 15.6, 17.1, 18.7, 20.6, 21.4, 21.1, 19.3, 16.4, 13.8 **23.** 3.5, 6, 6 and 14, 42

12.2 Getting Ready to Practice (p. 603)
1. lower quartile; upper quartile

12.2 Practice and Problem Solving (pp. 603–604)

3.

5.   **7.** 15 in.   **9.** 22 in.
11. 28 in.

13.   *Sample answer:*
The middle half of the pumpkin weights clustered within about a 50 pound range, from 789 pounds to 838 pounds, but the range was much wider, nearly 300 pounds.

17. 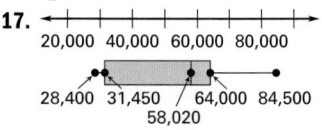   *Sample answer:* The outlier does not have much of an effect on the quartiles, but it makes a whisker very long and thus greatly increases the range.

19.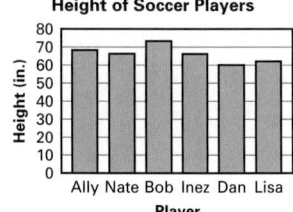

21. x-intercept: 10, y-intercept: -6, slope: $\frac{3}{5}$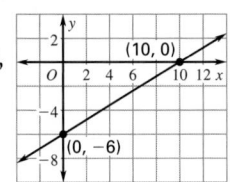

12.3 Getting Ready to Practice (p. 607)   **1.** circle graph   **3.** $112°$ **5.** $50°$ **7.**

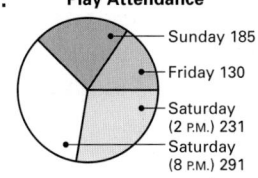

12.3 Practice and Problem Solving (pp. 608–609)

9.

11.   *Sample answer:* The number of people who attend symphony orchestra concerts increased rapidly from 1994 to 1995, and then at a slower rate from 1995 to 1998.

13.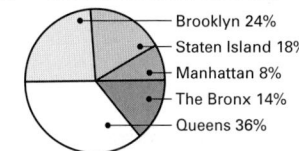

15. *Sample answer:* Line graph; the data is collected over time.   **17.** *Sample answer:* Histogram; the data is the frequency of occurrence in equal intervals for a certain range.   **19.** red; dark blue   **21.** No; it does not show a change in data over time; yes; it shows data in distinct categories.

23.   **25.**

12.3 Technology Activity (pp. 610–611)

1.

3.

Special Topic Exercises (p. 613)

1. No. *Sample answer:* There is a break in the vertical scale, so the relative change is smaller than it appears.

3.

12.1–12.3 Notebook Review (pp. 614–615)

1. lower extreme, upper extreme

2.
```
0 | 7 8 9
1 | 1 1 4 5 8 9
2 | 4
```
Key: 1 | 4 = 14

3.

4. Hourly Temperatures

5. *Sample answer:* movie attendance each night for two weeks   **6.** No. *Sample answer:* It does not show data that vary over time; bar graph.

12.4 Problem Solving Strategies (p. 617)

1. 60 people; no   **3.** 10 games   **5.** 2500
7. 58 palindromes   **9.** 55 squares   **11.** Saturday

12.4 Getting Ready to Practice (p. 620) **1.** $m \cdot n$

3. 9 choices   **5.** 6 choices   **7.** $\frac{1}{64}$

12.4 Practice and Problem Solving (pp. 621–622)

9. 24 choices   **11.** 16 choices   **13.** 26,000 PINs
15. $\frac{1}{64}$ **21.** 3 desserts   **25.** $\frac{1}{2}$

27.

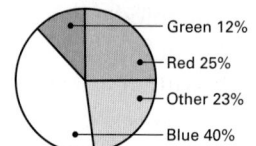

12.5 Getting Ready to Practice (p. 625) **1.** $_{15}P_7$

3. 1   **5.** 362,880   **7.** 60,480   **9.** 120

12.5 Practice and Problem Solving (pp. 625–626)

11. 24 orders   **13.** 20   **15.** 504   **17.** 840   **19.** 6840
21. 360,360 ways   **23.** yes; 11! = 11 • 10 • 9 • 8 • 7 • 6 • 5 • 4 • 3 • 2 • 1 = 11 • 10!   **25.** 32,760 ways

29. Favorite Color
- Green 12%
- Red 25%
- Other 23%
- Blue 40%

12.6 Getting Ready to Practice (p. 629) **1.** 9; 5

3. 4   **5.** 7   **7.** combination; 6 pairs

12.6 Practice and Problem Solving (pp. 630–631)

11. 1   **13.** 70   **15.** 8   **17.** 126   **19.** 78   **21.** 100
23. 792 teams   **25.** No. *Sample answer:* You cannot choose more items than you have to start with, that is, r must be less than or equal to n.
27. combination; 10 sets   **29.** permutation; 1,814,400 ways; combination, 45 ways   **31.** 4845
35. 30,240   **37.** 4896   **39.** $\frac{2}{3}$

12.7 Getting Ready to Practice (p. 634) **1.** odds
in favor   **3.** $\frac{3}{5}$ **5.** $\frac{1}{10}$ **7.** $\frac{1}{3}$ **9.** $\frac{3}{7}$

12.7 Practice and Problem Solving (pp. 635–636)

11. $\frac{4}{13}$; $\frac{9}{4}$ **13.** $\frac{3}{7}$; $\frac{5}{9}$ **15.** $\frac{5}{1}$ **17.** $\frac{1}{2}$ **21.** $\frac{7}{25}$ **23.** $\frac{4}{1}$
27. 0.04   **29.** 51 in.   **31.** $-\frac{1}{10}$ **33.** $\frac{7}{15}$ **35.** $\frac{3}{56}$

12.8 Getting Ready to Practice (p. 641)

1. independent   **3.** dependent; $\frac{1}{506}$

12.8 Practice and Problem Solving (pp. 642–643)

5. 0.1   **7.** 0.375   **9.** 0.13   **11.** dependent; $\frac{2}{21}$
13. $\frac{1}{17,018}$

17.

Sample answer: About 46 min; if you extend the graph, it passes through 46 on Saturday.

19. 57 **21.** 5

Special Topic Exercises (p. 645) **1.** Yes; people who call in to a sports talk show are likely to favor sports. **3.** Yes; people who enter a sporting goods store are likely to favor sports. **5.** *Sample answer:* Yes; this question suggests the mall is noisy and crowded. It encourages respondents to favor staying at home. So, the question could lead to biased results. **7.** *Sample answer:* No; this question is straight forward with no suggestions. It is not likely to lead to biased results.

12.4–12.8 Notebook Review (pp. 646–647)
1. permutation **2.** 20 birdhouses **3.** 35 ways
4. $\frac{3}{11}$ **5.** $\frac{2}{121}$ **6.** *Sample answer:* Ordering toppings on a pizza

Chapter Review (pp. 648–649)
7.

9.   15.0–15.9

Key: 7 | 5 = 7.5

11.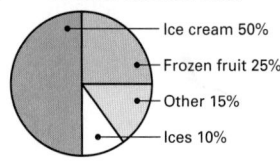

Favorite Summer Treat
— Ice cream 50%
— Frozen fruit 25%
— Other 15%
— Ices 10%

13. 1680 **15.** 36
17. 5040 ways
19. permutation; 120 ways
21. $\frac{7}{13}$ **23.** $\frac{1}{380}$

Chapter 13

13.1 Getting Ready to Practice (p. 659)
1. trinomial **3.** monomial **5.** $3m + 7$
7. $6b^3 + 4b - 4$ **9.** $5y - 1$ **11.** $-3x^2$ and $-20x$ are not like terms and cannot be combined. The expression $-3x^2 - 20x - 4$ cannot be simplified.

13.1 Practice and Problem Solving (pp. 659–660)
13. $4x^{10} - 13x^3$; binomial **15.** $4x - 4$ **17.** $-7q^5 + 3q^3 + 3q$ **19.** $-3b + 17$ **21.** $2(2x + 3) + 4x$; $8x + 6$
23. $12m^2 + m - 6$ **25.** $8x^2 - 15x + 30$ **27.** 98 ft
29. 122 ft **31.** $18t^2 + 12t - 37$ **33.** always **35.** never
41. $\frac{1}{4}$ **43.**
34	2
35	8
36	2 3 4 6
37	5 6
38	6 6

Key: 35 | 8 = 35.8

45. -21 **47.** 60

13.2 Getting Ready to Practice (p. 663) **1.** like terms **3.** $6x + 12$ **5.** $3p + 8$ **7.** $-a + 6$

13.2 Practice and Problem Solving (pp. 664–665)
9. $5x + 4$ **11.** $7n - 2$ **13.** $6g^2 + g + 3$
15. $-10d - 7$ **17.** $-11h^2 + 10h$ **19.** $3r^2 + 2r + 4$
21. $(x + 7) + (3x - 2) + (4x - 1)$; $8x + 4$ **23.** $6k^2$
25. $6x^3 + 8x^2 - 12x - 3$ **27.** $12n + 3$
29. $16r^2 - 4(\pi r^2)$; $3.44r^2$; yes; one coaster needs $3.14r^2$ of clay, which is less than what is left over.
31. $-7s^2 + 5s - 9$ **33.** $-14t^3 - 10t^2 + 22t$
35. $-14v^4 + 15v^3 - 21v^2 + 37$ **39.** b^{10}
41. m^4n^3 **43.** 10,000 passwords

13.3 Getting Ready to Practice (p. 668)
5. $2x^3 - 2x$ **7.** z^{16}

13.3 Practice and Problem Solving (pp. 669–670)
9. $-20x^4$ **11.** $3x^3$ **13.** b^{11} **15.** $m^2 + 4m$
17. $-t^3 + 4t$ **19.** $-2w^3 - w^2$ **21.** $\frac{1}{2}(b - 6)(3b + b)$; $2b^2 - 12b$ **23.** $x^5y^5z^5$ **25.** $-216z^3$ **27.** $9r^2s^2$
29. $100,000b^5h^5$ **31.** y^4 **33.** x^{20} **35.** x^6y^6 **37.** $8r^9$
39. $(2w^2 + 4w)$ in.^{2} **41.** $-3a^{26}b^8c^4$ **43.** $\frac{\pi r^2}{(2r)^2}$; $\frac{\pi}{4}$
45. 2.7×10^{13} **47.** 6.25×10^{30} **49.** about 7.36×10^8 km^3 **55.** $\frac{71}{100}$ **57.** $\frac{9}{50}$ **59.** $\frac{1}{36}$

13.1–13.3 Notebook Review (pp. 671–672)

1. monomial   **2.** polynomial   **3.** $a^2 + 18$ **4.** $2z^2 -$
$3z + 1$ **5.** $2n^3 + 5n^2 - 2n - 3$ **6.** $-5x^2 + 4x + 4$
7. $48x^{10}$ **8.** $36n^6m^2$ **9.** $16a^4b^4$ **10.** $4r^3 - 20r^2$
11. *Sample answer:* By the associative property
of multiplication, $(2x)(x^2y) = 2(x \cdot x^2)y$. By the
product of powers property, $2(x \cdot x^2)y = 2x^3y$.
So $(2x)(x^2y) = 2x^3y$.   **12.** $24\pi h^2$ or $\dfrac{8\pi r^2}{3}$

13.4 Getting Ready to Practice (p. 676)

1. binomial   **3.** $6m^2 + 2m$ **5.** $y^2 - 3y - 4$
7. $z^2 + 2z - 8$

13.4 Practice and Problem Solving (pp. 676–677)

9. $x^2 + 7x - 18$ **11.** $a^2 + 6a - 40$ **13.** $3q^2 - 4q + 1$
15. $6r^2 + r - 7$ **17.** $-11x^2 - 43x + 60$ **19.** $x^2 - 16$
23. $4\pi(0.6875 + x)^2 = 4\pi(0.4727 + 1.375x + x^2) =$
$1.8908\pi + 5.5\pi x + 4\pi x^2$ **25.** $3b^2 - 58b + 72$
27. $(30 - 2x)(20 - x) = 600 - 70x + 2x^2$; 300 ft^2
31. $x + 1$
33.
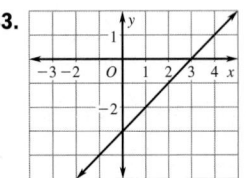

35. $-4r^2 - 24r$ **37.** $15x^2 - 10x$
38–41.

13.5 Problem Solving Strategies (p. 679)

1. 128 e-mails   **3.** 10 cuts

5.

Hours	0.5	1	1.5	2
Points	2.5	5	7.5	10

about 9 points

7. 50 squares   **9.** 1809.56 cm^3

13.5 Getting Ready to Practice (p. 682)   **3.** -1,
-5, -1 **5.** yes   **7.** yes

13.5 Practice and Problem Solving (pp. 682–684)

9. $f(x) = 2x^2 - x$ **11.** $f(t) = -16t^2 + 4$; -140 ft

13.

x	-3	-2	-1	0	1	2	3
$f(x)$	17	12	9	8	9	12	17

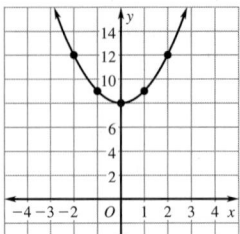

15.

x	-3	-2	-1	0	1	2	3
$f(x)$	-9	-4	-1	0	-1	-4	-9

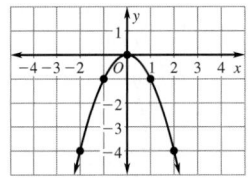

19. yes   **21.** $f(x) = 1500x$

23.

27.

33. $f(x) = x^3$ **35.** $f(t) = (2.8 \times 10^8)(1.008)^t$; about
2.9×10^8 **37.** 4   **39.** $-1\dfrac{2}{3}$ **41.** 3   **43.** -3
45. $x^2 + 4x + 4$ **47.** $5a^2 + 14a - 3$

13.5 Technology Activity (p. 685)   **1–4.** *Sample
answer:* The graphs are all parabolas with the
same shape and with vertices on the y-axis, but
the graph moves up or down compared to the
graph of $y = x^2$ by the number of units that are
added to or subtracted from x^2. The graph moves
up if this number is positive and down if this
number is negative.   **5–8.** *Sample answer:* The
graphs are all downward-opening parabolas with
vertices at the origin, but opening to different
widths. As the absolute value of the coefficient of
x^2 gets larger, the parabola becomes narrower
(rises more steeply).

13.4–3.5 Notebook Review (pp. 686–687)
1. function notation   **2.** vertical line test   **3.** $f(x) = 5x - 12$ **4.** $f(x) = 2x^3 + 8$ **5.** $f(x) = x^3 + 3x^2 - 10$
6.

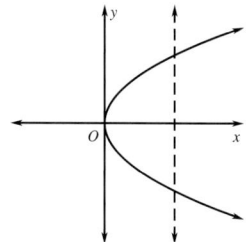

Sample answer: The graph is not that of a function because there are vertical lines that pass through more than one point of the graph.

7. $x^2 + 12x + 35$ **8.** $g^2 + 8g - 20$ **9.** $3y^2 - 13y + 4$
10.

11.

12.

13. *Sample answer:* If there is any vertical line that intersects a graph at more than one point, then the graph does not represent a function. If every vertical line intersects a graph in at most one point, then the graph does represent a function.

Chapter Review (pp. 688–689)   **1.** trinomial
3. vertical line test   **5.** monomial   **7.** binomial
9. $-3x^3 + x^2 + 5x - 4$ **11.** $6t^3 - t^2 + 9t + 8$
13. $-3n^4 + n^2 + 5n + 25$ **15.** $2w^2 + 3w - 8$
17. $-x^2 + 16x + 28$ **19.** $-10y^2 + 20y + 44$
21. $-3p^2$ **23.** $8y^2 - 5$ **25.** $-5v^3 - 10v^2 - 2v$
27. $8x^3y^3$ **29.** $-216a^6b^{12}$ **31.** $-21,609p^8n$
33. $-3a^3 + 6a^2$ **35.** $y^5 - 11y^4$ **37.** $-18g^3 - 60g^2$
39. $9x^2 + 27x$ **41.** $t^2 - t - 12$ **43.** $q^2 - 16q + 63$
45. $3d^2 - 10d - 48$ **47.** $-8k^2 + 34k + 9$
49. $2b^2 + 7b - 4$

51.

53.

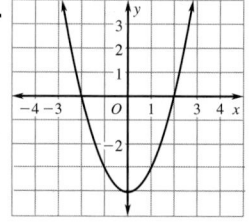

55. yes   **57.** yes

Skills Review Handbook

Place Value (p. 704)   **1.** $5 \times 10,000 + 6 \times 1000 + 8 \times 100 + 9$ **3.** $1 \times 1000 + 2 \times 1 + 3 \times 0.001$
5. 500,069.007

Rounding (p. 705)   **1.** 1300   **3.** 8.2   **5.** 40,000
7. 450   **9.** 62.8   **11.** 164.5   **13.** 52.96   **15.** 3,501,700

Divisibility Tests (p. 706)   **1.** 2   **3.** 3, 5   **5.** 2, 3, 4, 6, 9
7. 5   **9.** 2, 4

Mixed Numbers and Improper Fractions (p. 707)
1. 38   **3.** 3   **5.** $\frac{7}{2}$ **7.** $\frac{35}{8}$ **9.** $\frac{43}{4}$ **11.** $7\frac{1}{2}$ **13.** $5\frac{2}{3}$

Ratio and Rate (p. 708)   **1.** $\frac{13}{12}$; 13 to 12; 13 : 12
3. $\frac{11}{23}$; 11 to 23; 11 : 23   **5.** $\frac{\$24}{8 \text{ pens}} = \frac{\$3}{1 \text{ pen}}$
7. $\frac{280 \text{ words}}{5 \text{ min}} = \frac{56 \text{ words}}{1 \text{ min}}$ **9.** $\frac{8 \text{ in.}}{6 \text{ days}} = 1\frac{1}{3}$ in. per day

Adding and Subtracting Decimals (p. 709)   **1.** 6.3
3. 31.1   **5.** 10.956   **7.** 2.91   **9.** 18.88   **11.** 57.8
13. 286.19   **15.** 88.064

Adding and Subtracting Fractions (p. 710)   **1.** $\frac{2}{3}$
3. $\frac{3}{7}$ **5.** 1   **7.** $\frac{11}{15}$ **9.** $\frac{2}{9}$ **11.** $1\frac{7}{12}$ **13.** $\frac{1}{9}$ **15.** $\frac{9}{14}$
17. $\frac{7}{12}$ **19.** $1\frac{4}{7}$

Estimation in Addition and Subtraction (p. 711)
1–5. Estimates may vary.   **1.** 2700   **3.** 20,000
5. 2200

Solving Problems Using Addition and Subtraction (p. 712)   **1.** $93   **3.** $2.01   **5.** 248 min

Multiplying Fractions (p. 713) **1.** $\frac{4}{5}$ **3.** $2\frac{2}{9}$ **5.** $5\frac{1}{4}$
7. $2\frac{4}{7}$ **9.** $\frac{8}{15}$ **11.** $\frac{3}{40}$ **13.** $\frac{10}{27}$ **15.** $\frac{25}{72}$

Multiplication of a Decimal by a Whole Number
(p. 714) **1.** 225.4 **3.** 671.5 **5.** 35.28 **7.** 644.36
9. 1707.2 **11.** 18,663.6 **13.** 15,093.8 **15.** 36,833.5
17. 949.992 **19.** 3707.352 **21.** 4998.7 **23.** 1809.665
25. 5477.336 **27.** 120,455.25 **29.** 7564.91

Dividing Decimals (p. 715) **1.** 0.45 **3.** 0.85 **5.** 4.57
7. 6R2 **9.** 8R604

Estimation in Multiplication and Division (p. 716)
1–19. Estimates may vary. **1.** 400 and 1000
3. 40,000 and 54,000 **5.** 30 and 40 **7.** 200 and 300
9. 12,000 and 20,000 **11.** 70,000 and 160,000
13. 12,000 and 21,000 **15.** 90 and 100 **17.** 700 and
800 **19.** 10 and 20

**Solving Problems Using Multiplication and
Division** (p. 717) **1.** $9.48 **3.** 576 flowers

Points, Lines, and Planes (p. 718) **5.** *Sample
answer:* $\overrightarrow{SR}$ and $\overrightarrow{ST}$ **7.** *Sample answer:* $\overline{SR}$

Angles (p. 719) **5.** $\angle HJK$, $\angle J$, $\angle KJH$ **7.** $\angle TUV$, $\angle U$,
$\angle VUT$ **9.** $\angle FGH$, $\angle G$, $\angle HGF$

Using a Ruler (p. 720) **1–7.** Check drawings.

Using a Protractor (p. 721) **1.** 110° **3.** 88°

Using a Compass (p. 722) **1.** A good answer will
show a circle with radius 4 centimeters.
3. ———

Reading and Making Line Plots (p. 723)
1.   **3.** 19 people
5. 5 people

Reading and Making Bar Graphs (p. 724)
1. 9 students **3.** Vanilla and Rocky Road

Reading and Making Line Graphs (p. 725)
1. Thursday and Friday **3.**

Venn Diagrams and Logical Reasoning (p. 726)
1.

3. false; both 9 and
11 are odd numbers
greater than 8 and
less than 12

Extra Practice

Chapter 1 (p. 727)
1. Student Heights **3.** Yes; you can add
the frequencies
for the intervals
60–61.9, 62–63.9,
64–65.9, 66–67.9,
and 68–69.9.
5. 7 **7.** 4 **9.** 36 **11.** 8.4 **13.** 11.7 **15.** 27 **17.** 7
19. 63 **21.** 8 **23.** 9 **25.** 42 ft; 104 ft^2 **27.** 8 cm

Chapter 2 (p. 728) **1.** -43, -24, -2, 7, 19, 33
3. 25; 25 **5.** 0; 0 **7.** -409 **9.** 179 **11.** 0 **13.** -16
15. 51 **17.** -15 **19.** 68 **21.** 350 **23.** -64 **25.** 0
27. 240 **29.** -12 **31.** 0 **33.** -4
35. $7\left(2\cdot\frac{3}{7}\right)$ [original expression]
$=7\left(\frac{3}{7}\cdot2\right)$ [commutative property of
multiplication]
$=\left(7\cdot\frac{3}{7}\right)\cdot2$ [associative property of
multiplication]
$=3\cdot2$ $\left[\text{Multiply 7 and }\frac{3}{7}.\right]$
$=6$ [Multiply 3 and 2.]
37. $(-5)(-3)+(-5)(8)$; -25 **39.** $-4-9r$
41. $5x-2y$ **43.** $-a-10b$

44–47.   **45.** Quadrant I
47. Quadrant III

Chapter 3 (p. 729) 1. 8   **3.** 5   **5.** 64   **7.** 4   **9.** 7
11. 7.5   **13.** 20   **15.** -58 **17.** $6n - 5 = 13;$ 3
19. 1.5 h   **21.** 60 in.^{2}; 36 in.   **23.** 5 m; 34 m
25. $j \geq -5;$
27. $z \leq -2.5;$
29. $x < -5;$
31. $s \leq 8;$

Chapter 4 (p. 730) 1. $2^3 \cdot 3^2$ **3.** $3^2 \cdot 17$ **5.** $5^2 \cdot p \cdot q$
7. $2 \cdot 11 \cdot x \cdot y \cdot y$ **9.** 15   **11.** bc **13.** $3m$ **15.** $17w^2z^2$
17. $\frac{1}{2}$ **19.** $-\frac{2}{7}$ **21.** $\frac{2}{9y}$ **23.** $-\frac{3a}{2c}$ **25.** 60   **27.** $15ab^2c^2$
29. $>$ **31.** $>$ **33.** $<$ **35.** $>$ **37.** z^6 **39.** $(-7)^9$ **41.** 6^4
43. $(-v)^3$ **45.** $\frac{6}{k}$ **47.** $\frac{1}{s^7}$ **49.** 1.24×10^8
51. 7.91×10^{-5} **53.** 0.0027   **55.** 588,000,000,000

Chapter 5 (p. 731) 1. $1\frac{1}{2}$ **3.** $-\frac{2m}{3}$ **5.** $\frac{1}{15}$ **7.** $8\frac{1}{8}$
9. $\frac{3}{16}$ **11.** $-\frac{10}{27}$ **13.** $\frac{5}{18}$ **15.** $-3\frac{3}{32}$ **17.** -0.384
19. $-\frac{7}{25}$ **21.** $\frac{3}{500}$ **23.** 3.875   **25.** -2.5, -2.43,
$-2\frac{5}{12}$, $-2\frac{2}{5}$, $-\frac{7}{3}$ **27.** $\frac{26}{5}$, 5.21, $5\frac{2}{9}$, 5.3, $5\frac{3}{8}$ **29.** 3.81
31. 13.1   **33.** -16.55 **35.** -8.115 **37.** 3.9104
39. 1.5   **41.** -31.866 **43.** -8.2 **45.** 43; 39; no mode;
57   **47.** 88; 87; 78 and 95; 22

Chapter 6 (p. 732) 1. 7   **3.** -9 **5.** 2   **7.** -2 **9.** 5
11. -1 **13.** 0.13   **15.** -4 **17.** -4 **19.** 4.5 cm
21. 7 yd; use $\frac{22}{7}$ for π since 44 is divisible by 22.
23. $c < 2;$
25. $s \geq -1;$
27. $b > 8;$
29. $\frac{1}{2}n + 12 \leq 8; n \leq -8$ **31.** $4n \geq 16; n \geq 4$
33. at least $1\frac{1}{2}$ h

Chapter 7 (p. 733) 1. $\frac{3}{1}$, 3 : 1, 3 to 1   **3.** $\frac{2}{3}$, 2 : 3,
2 to 3   **5.** 4   **7.** 225   **9.** 9.3   **11.** 12%   **13.** 8.96
15. 12.5%   **17.** 72%   **19.** $0.31; \frac{31}{100}$ **21.** $1.75; \frac{7}{4}$
23. increase; 12%   **25.** decrease; 1%   **27.** $22.08
29. $83\frac{1}{3}$ **31.** 0.084   **33.** $\frac{1}{6}$

Chapter 8 (p. 734) 1. $m\angle 1 = 50°$ **3.** $m\angle 5 = 50°$;
$m\angle 6 = 50°; m\angle 7 = 130°$ **5.** $x = 90;$ right
7. rhombus   **9.** trapezoid   **11.** 160°   **13.** $\angle A \cong \angle P$;
$\angle B \cong \angle Q; \angle C \cong \angle R$
15.   **17.**

19.   **21.**

Chapter 9 (p. 735) 1. 7.2   **3.** -27.2 **5.** 30, -30
7. 15, -15 **9.** 9, -9 **11.** 8, -8 **13.** $>$ **15.** $>$ **17.** $0.\overline{1}$,
0.12, $0.\overline{12}$, 0.123, $0.\overline{123}$ **19.** 35   **21.** 33   **23.** 75
25. yes   **27.** yes   **29.** $x = 7\sqrt{2}; y = 7$ **31.** $x = 19\sqrt{3};$
$y = 38$ **33.** $\sin A = \frac{36}{85}; \cos A = \frac{77}{85}; \tan A = \frac{36}{77};$
$\sin B = \frac{77}{85}; \cos B = \frac{36}{85}; \tan B = \frac{77}{36}$ **35.** $\sin 62° \approx$
0.8829; $\cos 62° \approx 0.4695; \tan 62° \approx 1.8807$

Chapter 10 (p. 736) 1. 195 in.^{2}

3. 10 cm²

$1\frac{1}{5}$ cm

$8\frac{1}{3}$ cm

5. 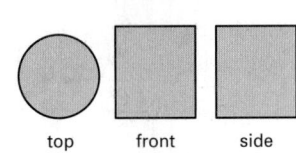 357 yd²

40 yd

10.5 yd

28 yd

7. 5020 in.²   **9.** 26.4 ft²   **11.** 0.283 cm²   **13.** 201 mi²

15.

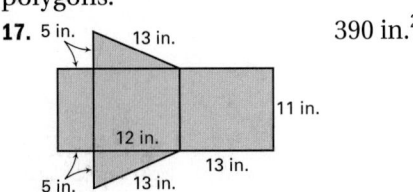

top   front   side

It is not a polyhedron because circles are not polygons.

17. 5 in.   13 in.   390 in.²

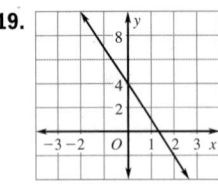

11 in.

12 in.

5 in.   13 in.   13 in.

19. 360 m²   **21.** 369.9 m²   **23.** 330 in.³
25. 266.7 ft³   **27.** 252 cm³

Chapter 11 (p. 737)   **1.** Yes; each input has exactly one output.   **3.** $y = x - 1$ **5.** no   **7.** yes
9. *Sample answer:* $(-2, 3), (-1, 5), (0, 7), (1, 9)$
11. *Sample answer:* $(-2, 2), (-1, 1), (0, 0), (1, -1)$
13. $(-2, 4), (-1, 1), (0, -2), (1, -5)$ **15.** $(-2, -5),$
$(1, -1), (4, 3), (7, 7)$

17.

19.

21. x-intercept, $\frac{1}{5}$; y-intercept, -1 **23.** x-intercept,
6; y-intercept, -4

25.

27. undefined   **29.** 1
31. -1 **33.** $\frac{17}{3}$ **35.** 0; 2
37. 2; -8

39.

41.

Chapter 12 (p. 738)
1.
9	9
10	0 1 3 5
11	6 7 8
12	7 9
13	0
14	0 0 3

100 to 109

Key: 13 | 0 = 130

3.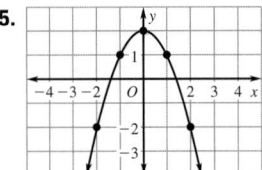

100 110 120 130 140

99 103 117.5 130 143

Sample answer: About 50% of the lengths were between 103 inches and 130 inches.

5. Line graph; a line graph is used to represent data that change over time.   **7.** 17,576,000 license plates
9. 11   **11.** 720   **13.** 5   **15.** 20   **17.** 4060 ways
19. $\frac{3}{4}$ **21.** $\frac{2}{9}$

Chapter 13 (p. 739)   **1.** $-x^2 - 2x + 7$ **3.** $-k^2 + 21$
5. $-2x^3 + 4x^2 + 14x - 4$ **7.** $3x^3 - 9x^2 + 6x - 3$
9. $x^3 - 2x^2 + 9x + 6$ **11.** $-28z^6$ **13.** $-6n^2 + 15n$
15. $125a^3b^3$ **17.** p^{24} **19.** $2x^2 - 9x - 5$
21. $d^2 + 10d + 24$ **23.** $a^2 - 15a + 56$ **25.** $f(x) =$
$2x - 5$ **27.** $f(x) = 5x^2 + 1$ **29.** 1; $\frac{1}{4}$; 0; $\frac{1}{4}$; 1
31. -16; -5; 0; -1; -8 **33.** -7; -4; -3; -4; -7
35.

37. no   **39.** yes